TRAVAUX DE DROIT, D'ÉCONOMIE,
DE SOCIOLOGIE ET DE SCIENCES POLITIQUES

N° 64

Collection dirigée par Giovanni Busino

Krystyna MAREK, licenciée en droit of the Jagellonian University, Cracow (Poland), diplômée of the Polish Foreign Office (London, 1944), docteur ès sciences politiques of the Geneva University, is at present Professor of International Law at the Graduate Institute of International Studies in Geneva.

The problem of the identity and continuity of a State is the problem of its very existence. This is so because it represents another aspect of the problem of State extinction. It arises only in circumstances which may give rise to legitimate doubts as to the continued existence of the State concerned, in other words, when such a State has been the object of some grave interference with its normal and peaceful development. In such a case the question becomes: has the State become extinct or does it continue to exist?

The author investigates both the theoretical foundations of the problem and the relevant State practice. The latter deals with the cases of Italy during the period of the Risorgimento, Austria and Yugoslavia after the First World War, Ethiopia, Czechoslovakia, Albania, Austria, the Baltic States and Poland after the Second World War.

Under traditional customary International Law, State identity and continuity are safeguarded in case of territorial changes, revolutionary upheavals and belligerent occupation. Moreover, the more recent State practice would point to the development of yet another rule of International Law, protecting the identity and continuity of an illegally overpowered State on condition of its effective restoration within a reasonable time. Such practice conforms to the principle "ex iniuria ius non oritur," but finds its limits in the antinomic principle "ex factis ius oritur."

KRYSTYNA MAREK

Professor at the Graduate Institute of International Studies, Geneva

IDENTITY AND CONTINUITY
OF STATES
IN PUBLIC INTERNATIONAL
LAW

GENÈVE
LIBRAIRIE DROZ
11, RUE MASSOT

1968

1re édition : décembre 1954

2e édition : mars 1968

© 1968 by Librairie Droz S.A.
11, rue Massot, Genève (Suisse)

Manibus Patris Mei

On concluding these pages, my thoughts turn to all those without whose help and support this book could neither have been written nor published.

My moral and intellectual debt to Professor Paul Guggenheim cannot be repaid. All I can do is to put on record my lasting gratitude to him for his guidance and support. The shortcomings of this book I claim as my own; but whatever merits it may possess are due to my having been Professor Guggenheim's student. — I also wish to thank Professors Maurice Bourquin and Hans Wehberg for their friendly interest in my work.

I further wish to express my deep gratitude to His Excellency Count Edward Raczynski, Polish Ambassador to the Court of St. James's from 1934 to 1945, and to Dr. Charles Poznanski, Polish Consul-General in London from 1934 to 1945, for their help and support so generously given me at all stages of my work.

I am also anxious to record my indebtedness to Dr. A.C. Breycha-Vauthier, Librarian of the United Nations Library in Geneva, for his unfailing kindness to me during my work in the U.N. Library. My thanks also go to Mr. N. S. Field, Deputy Librarian, to the staff of the U.N. Library, and in particular to Mr. B. Kasme, Reference Librarian, for their untiring helpfulness and courtesy.

I cannot close this list without adding my sincere thanks to Mr. I.C. Jackson, LL.M., Barrister-at-Law, for reading and correcting the manuscript, and to Mme. Jacqueline Belin, Licenciée ès Sciences Politiques, Geneva, for her work in typing it.

Geneva, December 1954.

PART I.

CHAPTER I.

THE PROBLEM DEFINED.

1. STATEMENT OF THE PROBLEM AND THEORETICAL BASIS OF ITS EXAMINATION.

The problem of the identity and continuity of a State is the problem of its very existence. This is so because it merely represents another aspect of the problem of State extinction. To ask whether a State is identical with a State which has preceded it in time and with which it has enough common features for the question to be asked at all, is to enquire whether one State has died and another has been born in its place, or whether the old State continues its unchanged legal personality.

The practical importance of the question is obvious. The rights and duties of a new State will initially be derived exclusively from customary international law. The new State will not be internationally responsible for what has taken place on its territory prior to its birth. Its population and its frontiers will be undefined and doubtful, pending a final delimitation by way of international agreements. On the other hand, an old State will naturally enough continue to bear its international rights and duties both customary and conventional. It will enjoy the same international status, defined by both customary and conventional international law. Its territory and population will remain the same, except in the case of changes which, relating precisely to territory and population, leave the personality of the State unaffected [1]. It will be subject to all legal duties and it will be entitled to claim all legal rights arising out of agreements to which it has been a party. It may be held internationally responsible for what has occurred in its territory. Thus, the question of the identity and continuity of a State raises the whole issue of its international status [2].

The problem is therefore intimately connected with that of the birth and death of States which traditional doctrine considered as

---

1. See below, pp. 15-24.
2. It is therefore incorrect to reduce the practical aspect of the problem chiefly to the question of debts and the survival of treaties in case of revolutions and territorial changes, as is done by Herz, *Beiträge zum Problem der Identität der Staaten*, *Ztscht.f.öff.R.*, XV, 1935, p. 241.

metajuridical bare facts, incapable of legal appraisal [1]. This would indeed be the case if the problem of the birth and death of States were approached from the point of view of municipal law [2]. But it is clear that this problem can be investigated only from " outside " States themselves, since the norms of municipal law are valid only " within " the State and cannot serve as a legal criterion of external happenings. Moreover, the creation of municipal norms does not precede the birth of a State, but coincides with it, — just as the end of their validity coincides with the State's extinction. Hence, the time factor alone prevents the application of municipal norms to the question of the birth and death of States. For those who regard State law as the summit of the legal pyramid, the birth, extinction and transformation of States are thus metajuridical matters, not capable of legal appraisal. Any attempt to solve these problems within the framework of municipal law fully deserves Kelsen's picturesque analogy with Baron Münchhausen's efforts to drag himself out of the mud by his own hair [3]. Nor is any legal explanation possible on a dualist basis which introduces an artificial cleavage between international and municipal law [4].

When, however, the problem is seen in its proper perspective, all such artificial difficulties disappear. Since they break the framework of municipal law, the birth, extinction and transformation of States can be made the subject of a legal enquiry only by reference to a legal order which is both higher than State law and yet belongs to the same system of norms, in other words, on the basis of monism and the primacy of international law.

On this clearly correct assumption, a legal evaluation of the birth, death and transformation of States can easily be undertaken from " without " and from " above ", by means of a higher legal system whose norms have existed before the formation, and continue to exist after the extinction, of the State in question. Moreover, such an evaluation becomes not only possible, but indeed indispensable. A legal system which does not itself determine the character and existence of its subjects is unthinkable [5]. International law does not " create " States, just as State law does not " create " individuals. But it is international law and international law alone which provides the legal evaluation of the process, determines whether an entity is in fact a State, delimits its competences and decides when it ceases to exist [6].

---

1. Jellinek speaks of the " Unhaltbarkeit aller Versuche ... die Entstehung der Staaten juristisch zu konstruieren ". *Allgemeine Staatslehre*, pp. 263-264.
2. " ...das Staatsrecht ist unfähig, den Staatenbildungsprozess zu erklären ". Jellinek, *op. cit.* p. 266.
3. *Das Problem der Souveränität und die Theorie des Völkerrechts*, p. 236.
4. Jellinek, *op. cit.*, p. 266.
5. « De même que tout ordre juridique détermine quels sont ses sujets, de même il détermine aussi le moment où ils commencent à exister ». Anzilotti, *Cours de Droit International*, p. 160. " ...aus jedem Normensystem selbst beantwortet werden muss, welches die Subjekte seiner Pflichten und Rechte sind... " Kelsen, *Souveränität*, p. 230.
6. The following remark of Jellinek thus loses the meaning which he intended to give it : " Das Völkerrecht knüpft ... an das Faktum der staatlichen Existenz an, vermag dieses Faktum aber nicht zu schaffen ". *Op. cit*, p. 266.

The acceptance of international law as the highest and all-embracing legal order leaves no legal vacuum in which " bare facts " could exist and not be subject to legal appraisal [1]. Thus, a legal enquiry into the problem of State identity and continuity presupposes a definite attitude towards fundamental issues of legal theory. A repudiation of what is submitted to be the only correct view of the relations between international and State law, namely : monism based upon the primacy of the former, would necessarily result in the abandonment of this study. It could possibly be undertaken as a historical or sociological, but never as a juridical enquiry [2].

The problem of State identity and continuity can, consequently, arise only within the international legal order and only on the basis of a co-existence within this order of a number of co-ordinated subjects, between which such rights and obligations can exist. However legitimate a purely theoretical and abstract enquiry into the problem of the " internal identity and continuity " of States [3], it is submitted that the problem is an artificial one and that in practice it does not exist.

This submission may be illustrated by an imaginary example of a State, existing like a collective Robinson Crusoe, in complete isolation from the outside world. The question of its continued rights and obligations could simply not arise, failing any party to such rights and obligations and failing a higher legal order which could decide the question. There would be no practical reason or inducement for the State organs to affirm or to deny its continuity. The population of the State would similarly lack any such incentive. The whole problem would be utterly unreal [4].

Therefore, the assertion by certain writers that a given State is " old " internationally and " new " internally is not only the result of a dualist approach but simply the creation of an artificial problem [5].

---

1. Kelsen, *Souveränität*, pp. 235-236 ; *Allg. Staatslehre*, p. 127 ; *La naissance de l'Etat et la formation de sa nationalité*, p. 613 ; Verdross, *Die Verfassung der Völkerrechtsgemeinschaft*, pp. 125-131. Incorrectly, the Report of the Committee of Jurists on the question ot the Aaland Islands : " From the point of view of both domestic and international law, the formation, transformation and dismemberment of States as a result of revolutions and wars create situations of fact which, to a large extent, cannot be met by the application of the normal rules of positive law ". *LNOJ*, Special Supplement, No. 3, p. 6. Similarly Scelle, *Manuel de Droit International Public*, p. 125.

2. The problem thus stands and falls with the acceptance of the primacy of international law. But it is submitted that *no* international legal problem can be correctly solved on any other basis. Thus, correctly, the Swiss Federal Council, in its Memorandum of 1934 to the League of Nations, in the dispute between Switzerland and other States concerning reparation for damage suffered by Swiss citizens as a result of the First World War : " The questions which Switzerland desires to bring before the Permanent Court of International Justice deal with some of the most delicate problems of the law of nations, including the central basic problem of all international law — namely, the origin of rules of international law. There can be no correct solution of these problems which is not based on the postulate of the primacy of international law ". *LNOJ*, 1934, p. 1485.

3. See below, pp. 26-30.

4. An entirely opposite view is put forward by Merkl in his *Das Problem der Rechtskontinuität und die Forderung des einheitlichen Weltbildes*, *Ztschl.f.öff.R.*, V, 1926 ; see below, p. 28, f-n. 2.

5. See below, p. 244. The possibility of a State being " old " internationally and " new " internally is admitted by Kelsen in his *Théorie générale du droit international public*, see below, pp. 11-13.

2. Background of the Problem.

From what has already been said as to the relation between the problems of State continuity and State extinction it is clear that the question of identity and continuity does not in practice arise under normal and settled conditions. On the contrary, it can only arise in circumstances which may give rise to legitimate doubts as to the continued existence of the State concerned. There must be a shock grave enough to cast a doubt on its survival : belligerent occupation, revolution, revolutionary dismemberment and so forth. The question therefore is : has the State become extinct or does it continue to exist ?

Thus, for example, there would be no reason to enquire whether the Austro-Hungarian Monarchy of 1913 was identical with the Austro-Hungarian Monarchy of 1914, since no event took place which would even remotely have endangered the continued legal existence of that State. But whether the Austro-Hungarian Monarchy of 1914 was identical with the Austrian Republic of 1918 is, of course, a legitimate question. For between 1914 and 1918 events occurred which shook the Austro-Hungarian Monarchy to its very foundations and imperilled its very existence.

Two important conclusions follow from the above. First, the problem can only arise as a result of some violent upheaval, and never in a period of stability and with regard to a State whose continued existence has in no way been interefered with. Its historical background will not be one of peace, but of storm. Secondly, the notions of State identity and continuity thus assume a distinctly polemical character. By its very nature the problem is a highly controversial one. The affirmation, as well as the denial, of the identity and continuity of a State in face of a radical and violent change in its structure will be of an essentially defensive character.

3. Initial Definition.

Before a definition of State identity and continuity can be attempted, two observations should be made.

In the first place, since this is a purely juridical enquiry, the question of the physical, or material, identity of States must be excluded at the very outset. This aspect of the matter is of no concern to the lawyer. Moreover, an " identity " in this sense could hardly be determined at all. A State, like Heraclitus' river, is in a constant state of flux [1]. Generations pass away ; territory may undergo even purely physical changes ; while the legal order itself, far from being static, continually develops by reason of its essentially dynamic character [2].

---

1. " In der Wirklichkeit der Erscheinungen ist der Staat ... in steter Bewegung begriffen ". Jellinek, *op. cit.*, p. 15.

2. The need for the complete exclusion of this aspect, which is irrelevant to a legal enquiry, was already clearly seen by Grotius, *De Iure Belli ac Pacis*, II, IX, III. " Sic ergo populus ... idem hoc tempore putatur qui ab hins centum annis fuit, cum ex illis nemo nunc vivat. " Cf. Rivier, *Principes*, I, pp. 63-65. " Das Element Volk ist in der Regel kein konstantes, sondern variables Element, der Wechsel der Generationen rührt nicht an die Identität des Staates ". Kelsen, *Souveränität*, p. 238.

Secondly, any definition of legal identity is, to some extent, relative. It is true that absolute identity, in the logical meaning of the term, implies the complete identity of all the attributes of an object [1]. No such absolute identity is possible with regard to notions which have an ideal, not a material existence and which are, moreover, inherently dynamic, as in the case of law [2]. Hence, the criterion of this relative identity cannot be one of substance, but only one of form [3].

Subject to these two reservations, the following definitions of State identity and State continuity are proposed :

a) *State Identity defined as Identity of International Rights and Obligations.*

The legal identity of a State is the identity of the sum total of its rights and obligations under both customary and conventional international law. It is quite clear that the term " obligations " includes international responsibility [4]. In view of what has been said regarding the conditions in which the problem can arise at all, the following proviso should immediately be added : the identity of rights and obligations in this connection refers to the period immediately before and immediately after the event which has cast doubt upon the State's continued existence. It is clear that when no such event has taken place, then normal dynamic changes in its conventional rights and obligations — due to the expiration of certain conventions and the conclusion of new ones — are of no relevance to its continued existence.

It will be noticed that this definition places the problem squarely within the framework of international law and international law alone [5].

b) *State Continuity defined as the Dynamic Predicate of State Identity.*

Whereas identity is a static notion, continuity is its dynamic predicate. It simply means that one and the same subject of rights and obligations continues to exist, thus supplying the dynamic aspect of the same problem. This takes into consideration the factor of *time* which it is Kelsen's great merit to have introduced into the study of the State. As Kelsen rightly points out, a State possesses not only a material, personal, and territorial but also a temporal sphere of validity [6]. There is a beginning and an end to the State, as to everything else. States

---

1. Herz, *op. cit.*, p. 260.
2. " Der Rechtsordnung als einem Normensystem gegenüber, dessen Wesen in seiner immanenten Entfaltung, Entwicklung, Veränderung in stufenförmiger Rechtssetzung besteht, ist der Begriff absoluter Identität sinnlos ". Herz, *op. cit.*, p. 261. Cf. the cautious note sounded by von Tuhr, according to whom the notion of identity " beruhe, besonders bei Gedankenbilden, wie es die Rechte sind, auf einer mehr oder minder willkürlichen Begrenzung der Identitätsmerkmale ". Quoted by Guggenheim, *Beiträge zur völkerrechtlichen Lehre vom Staatenwechsel*, p. 43.
3. Herz, *op. cit.*, p. 262.
4. State identity is sometimes defined as identity of its conventional obligations only ; see Rousseau, *Principes généraux du droit international public*, p. 65. On the correct assumption that customary international law is automatically binding on new States, this restricted definition is unexceptionable. Rights and obligations of a State under customary law have been retained in the above definition *ex superabundante cautela*, so as to avoid any possible misunderstanding.
5. See above, p. 3.
6. *Théorie générale*, p. 260 ; *General Theory of Law and State*, pp. 218-219 ; *Allg. Staatslehre*, pp. 137 and 147.

are born and die, and the determination of these two facts is precisely the proper function of international law. Whatever the claims and aspirations of existing States, it would be legally unsound and historically untrue to affirm their immortality [1].

Thus, the problem of continuity has nothing whatever to do with a claim to immortality on behalf of States. On the contrary, the two notions are, directly contradictory. It States were indeed immortal, the question of their continuity could not arise at all. It can arise only on the assumption of a possible time-limit to their existence. In other words, the question concerning State continuity reads : has a State become extinct or does it continue to exist? There is no possible formulation of the question on the basis of an immortality of States [2].

c) *Inseparability of the Notions of Identity and Continuity.*

Viewed in this way, the two notions of identity and continuity cannot be separated. There can obviously be no continuity without identity, since this would imply the logical absurdity of a predicate without a subject to which it could apply. It could, however, be asked whether the reverse might not, in certain circumstances, be true, whether there might not be identity of a State without its continuity. Unless the possibility of legal miracles is admitted, the question must be answered emphatically in the negative : there is no legal resurrection in international law. Once a State has become extinct, it cannot resume a continued existence. There may well be a *historical* revival of an extinct State, but not of a pre-existing legal entity. Former rights of the old State entity may be invoked in order to establish what may be just, useful or politically desirable in the particular circumstances ; they are however, of no legal value [3]. Thus the final extinction of a State disposes of any further enquiry into the problem of its identity and continuity.

---

1. No value can be attached to the following : " Dixit Isocrates et post eum Julianus Imperator civitates esse immortales ". Grotius, *op. cit.*, II, IX, III.

2. The above obvious remarks might indeed seem entirely superflous, were it not for the possibility — however unexpected — of an elementary confusion between the two notions discussed, a striking example of which is supplied by Burdeau, *Traité de science politique*, III, Paris : Librairie générale de droit et de jurisprudence, 1950, pp. 573, 575, 579. See also for the correct view, Kelsen, *Allg. Staatslehre*, p. 148. It should be made absolutely clear once again that this study is concerned with the dynamic notion of the continuity of *the State*, and not with the predominantly static notion of a continuity of law, used by Merkl, *op. cit.* This writer is concerned not with the continuity of a given legal entity *in time*, but with a simultaneous organic connection between all existing legal orders. He thus deals with a phenomenon which has been much more aptly described by Verdross as " die Einheit des rechtlichen Weltbildes ". Thus, according to Merkl, there is a relation of legal continuity between all co-existing States from the point of view of international law ; *op. cit.*, p. 511. This is neither the terminology nor the problem of this study. For consequences of Merkl's theory see below, p. 28, *f.-n.* 2.

3. In this sense Jellinek's view of the problem can be accepted : " Auch ein Wiederaufleben eines untergegangenen Staates ist möglich, wofern die Verbandselemente sich von neuem zusammenfügen. Dass der wiederhergestellte Staat mit dem untergegangenen identisch sei, ist wiederum nur durch soziale, *nicht durch formal juristische Betrachtung zu erkennen*. Die Kontinuität und Diskontinuität der durch Absterben und Wiedererstehen eines Staates hervorgerufenen Rechtsverhältnisse kann nur *gemäss einer über dem Rechte stehenden Billigkeit gemessen werden* ." It. mine, *op. cit.*, pp. 278-279. The old and artificial concept of an international *postliminium* has been long ago discredited. See Oppenheim-Lauterpacht, *International* Law, II, pp. 483-484 and, already, Jellinek, *op. cit.*, p. 279, *f.-n.*

4. STATE EXTINCTION.

Are there any such criteria which, by determining the extinction of a State, would automatically solve the problem of its identity and continuity? For if it could be stated with any degree of finality that a given State has ceased to exist, then — automatically — another State which has been created on, or otherwise came to occupy its territory, would not be identical with its territorial predecessor.

Customary international law does not supply any definite criterion for determining when a States ceases to exist. Obviously enough, no conventional solution of the problem has ever been undertaken. Nor are any pronouncements on the subject to be found in international judicial decisions.

While there is a large measure of agreement among writers concerning the birth of a State [1], this is not so with regard to its extinction, which is not even examined at any great length [2]. The results of such examination as exists are most unhelpful [3]. Traditional doctrine generally seeks to simplify the problem by affirming that a State becomes extinct with the disappearance of one of its so-called " elements ", — territory, population, legal order [4]. With regard to the material elements of a State, the argument is so obvious as to be unnecessary. That a State would cease to exist if for instance the whole of its population were to perish or to emigrate, or if its territory were to disappear (e.g. an island which would become submerged) can be taken for granted. But with regard to the real and decisive problem the traditional view leads nowhere. A State — it is said — ceases to exist when its legal order (or " government " as is sometimes said) ceases to exist. But this is precisely the question : *when* does the legal order cease to exist? For there can be no doubt that it is around this question that the whole problem centres, and that it is precisely this question which is juridically relevant [5].

Failing an answer, the traditional doctrine confines itself to enumerating possible examples of State extinction, such as dismemberment, merger with another State, debellatio, and so forth, — while admitting that many concrete cases may be doubtful [6].

Against this background of uniform vagueness, two doctrinal opinions stand out clearly owing to their decisive character.

---

1. See below, pp. 161-162.
2. « La question de la reconnaissance des nouveaux Etats occupe une grande place dans la littérature du droit international. Par contre, les considérations relatives aux conditions dans lesquelles un Etat cesse d'exister d'après le droit des gens n'occupent pas une place importante dans la littérature du droit international ». Raestad, *La cessation des Etats d'après le droit des gens, RDILC*, 1939, pp. 441-442.
3. The following quotations represent a striking example of a reasoning in circle : " A State ceases to be an International person when it ceases to exist ". Oppenheim — Lauterpacht, *op. cit.*, I, p. 150. " Once international personality has been acquired by a State, it is lost only by the extinction of the State ". Fenwick, *International Law*, p. 149.
4. Fauchille, *Traité*, p. 373 ; Liszt, *Das Völkerrecht*, p. 89.
5. « ... le problème est important en ce qui concerne l'élément formel de l'Etat, c'est-à-dire son ordre juridique ». Anzilotti, *op. cit.*, p. 184.
6. Anzilotti, *op. cit.*, p. 124, with regard to Italy and Austria. Similarly Jellinek, *op. cit.*, p. 274 and 279.

Professor Kelsen considers that the criterion of State extinction is to be found exclusively in the absence of effectiveness of its legal order [1]. *Prima facie* the argument is convincing, especially in view of the predominance of the principle of effectiveness in international law. It would, however, be rash to adopt it as a generally valid principle. For there are cases in which customary international law temporarily dispenses with the principle of effectiveness as a condition for the continued existence of a State. The classical example is supplied by belligerent occupation which the occupied State survives even though its legal order may have become totally ineffective in the whole of its territory [2]. There may be other cases of a State retaining only a *nudum ius* in its own territory, in which its legal order has yielded all effectiveness to the legal order of other States [3]. Therefore, the absence of effectiveness does not necessarily mean the extinction of a State.

Another attempt to answer the question has been made by Raestad in an interesting article on the subject of State extinction. Raestad admits the possibility of the continued existence of a State whose legal order is no longer effective, as in the case of debellatio, — but makes such existence depend on the will of third States not to recognize the debellatio and to continue the recognition of the conquered State. Should such attitude of third States change, should they finally recognize the debellatio, this would mean the definite extinction of the State concerned [4].

Since it bears on the problem of recognition, Raestad's view will have to be dealt with at greater length under that heading [5]. It is, however, necessary to state already here that it represents an extreme voluntarist view, transferring, as it does, the vital problem of the legal existence of States from the realm of objective law to the province of politically motivated will of third States. Moreover, it is hardly of any practical value for determining the continued existence or the extinction of a State, for — as recent history has abundantly shown — third States hardly ever adopt a uniform attitude on the issue. On the contrary, a politically controversial case, like the one quoted by Raestad, produces two groups of States, one group recognizing the conquest and the other one refusing to do so. Such mutually exclusive attitudes can provide no criterion for the continuity or extinction of a State.

The two theories discussed above do not provide a solution of the difficulty. State extinction seems to escape all definition. The difficulty was clearly recognized in the course of the relevant discussion of the Institute of International Law at its session of 1936 [6]. In its Resolution

---

1. « De même qu'elle commence en vertu du droit international avec son efficacité, la validité de l'ordre étatique prend fin également, en vertu de ce même droit, avec cette efficacité. » *Théorie générale*, p. 294. Cf. *Allg. Staatslehre*, p. 127, *General Theory*, p. 220.
2. See below, pp. 73-126.
3. The example of the survival of Germany after World War II may be a case in. point, considering that it was not covered by classical rules of belligerent occupation.
4. *Op. cit.*, p. 449.
5. See below, p. 131.
6. See e.g. the intervention of M. Henri Rolin and his conclusion to the effect that it would be desirable « d'établir une autorité chargée de constater la disparition d'un Etat ». *Annuaire de l'Institut de Droit international*, 1936, vol .II, p. 212.

on the recognition of new States and new governments, the Institute adopted the following attitude with regard to the problem of State extinction, embodied in Art. 5 :

« La reconnaissance *de iure* est irrévocable ; elle ne cesse ses effets qu'en cas de disparition *définitive* de l'un des éléments essentiels dont la réunion se trouvait constatée au moment de la reconnaissance [1]. »

On the proposal of M. Fernand De Visscher, the operative word " définitive " was added just before the Resolution was finally adopted

« pour la raison que cette restriction évite que l'Art. 5 ne s'applique à un Etat victime de troubles passagers » [2].

The Institute thus adopted a consciously cautious attitude. Renouncing the formulation of any rigid rules which could not possibly envisage every possible situation, it laid down general outlines leaving ample scope for a searching examination of each particular case. It did, however, take a definite stand against a hasty and premature recognition of extinction, thus safeguarding the continued legal existence of a State against temporary disturbances.

It may thus be taken for granted that there exist no fixed criteria of State extinction. If they did exist, this study would be wholly unnecessary. For — as had been seen [3] — a positive answer to the problem of State extinction would *ipso facto* supply the negative answer to that of its continuity. Failing such criteria, the enquiry into the autonomous notions of identity and continuity of States can, and must, proceed.

5. STATE IDENTITY AND CONTINUITY AND STATE SUCCESSION.

The question may, however, be asked whether State identity and continuity are indeed autonomous notions of international law, which are well-defined and not liable to be confused with any other notion.

a) *Autonomy of the Notions of State Identity and Continuity.*

It is intended in this paragraph to vindicate the complete autonomy of the notions now being discussed, particularly against the ever recurring confusion between identity and continuity on the one hand, and State succession on the other [4]. Why this confusion should have arisen at all is difficult to understand, since even superficial observation reveals not only a complete lack of connection between these two notions but moreover the fact that they are mutually exclusive [5]. It should be

1. *It. mine., ibid.*, p. 301.
2. *Ibid.*, p. 252.
3. See above, p. 7.
4. See in particular the chapter on Austria (I).
5. " The word « succession » has been much misused... Thus it is wrong to say that in 1870 the Third Republic succeeded to the rights and obligations of Napoleon III. The rights and obligations ... were those of France and the personality of France persisted in spite of the changes in her constitutional structure and in her Government ". McNair, *Aspects of State Sovereignty, B. Y.*, 1949, p. 8.

clearly understood that whereas the problem of State identity and continuity bears on the *identity of the subject* (within the meaning of the proposed definition), the problem of succession relates to the identity of *certain* rights and obligations between *different subjects*. In other words : in the case of identity there is *one* subject of international law ; in case of succession there are at least *two* [1].

Consequently, the question of identity will of necessity always precede that of succession, historically as well as logically. There can be no succession at all, unless the enquiry into the problem of identity and continuity has been answered in the negative [2].

b) *Absence of Universal Succession in General International Law.*

This strict separation of the two notions of identity and succession can be upheld only, if it is found that universal succession does not exist in general international law [3].

The existence of universal succession would destroy the independent and sharply delimited notion of State identity. The possibility of one State becoming the bearer of the sum total of the rights and obligations of another State would make it quite impossible to distinguish between the case of universal succession and that of identity for which there would be no criterion whatever.

---

1. This can clearly be seen in all judicial decisions whether international or municipal dealing with matters of succession. Thus, e.g., it is Great Britain who is successor to Turkey in the *Mavromatis* case, *P.C.I.J.*, Ser. A 2 ; Poland to Prussia in the *German settlers in Poland* case, *P.C.I.J.*, Ser. B 6. With regard to municipal decisions, the District Court of Beuthen, in a judgment of February 12, 1920, considered Czechoslovakia a successor to the Austro-Hungarian Monarchy, *A.D.*, 1919-22, p. 69, note ; the Court of Appeal of Milan held Fiume to be the successor of Hungary, *Foro Italiano*, I, p. 228. Examples could be easily multiplied.

2. See Huber, *Die Staatensuccession:* " Diskontinuität der Staatsperson und ... Kontinuität des Rechtszustandes... ", p. 20. Cf. Guggenheim : " Die Staatenwechsellehre... knüpft an das Faktum der Diskontinuität der Staaten an. " *Op. cit.*, p. 26. " Die rechtliche Verknüpfung von Altstaat zu Folgestaat stellt sich aber nicht dar, als eine « Rechtskontinuität », da die Folgestaatsordnung ·· ·ht aus der Altstaatsordnung hergeleitet werden kann. Es besteht lediglich eine vom Völkerrecht ermöglichte « Rechtsbrücke » zwischen zwei diskontinuierlichen Staatsordnungen. " *Ibid.*, p. 28. " Innerhalb der Völkerrechtsordnung besteht solche Sukzession immer dann, wenn ein Recht oder eine Pflicht auf ein anderes Rechtssubjekt kraft Völkerrechts übergeht ". *Ibid.*, p. 44. It is clear that non-identity of the subject is a *conditio sine qua non* of succession in what Prof. Guggenheim rightly considers as a special category of the general case of succession namely the " Staatenwechsel ". The relation of non-identity in cases of an ordinary cession of territory is, of course, obvious. Consequently, in all cases of succession the notion of continuity can apply only to rights and obligations, never to the subject. Huber makes this quite clear, adding to his definition of succession " Substitution + Kontinuation " the immediate proviso " quoad iura, nicht quoad defunctum ", *op. cit.*, pp. 18-19. Similarly Schönborn, *Staatensukzessionen*, p. 7 and in particular, p. 13, where State identity is affirmed in case of constitutional changes : " So fehlt hier zum Begriff der Staatensukzession die Verschiedenheit der Staatspersönlichkeit... " Similarly, Udina, *La succession des Etats:* « La succession juridique, c'est-à-dire la substitution d'un sujet à l'autre dans un rapport juridique donné qui demeure identique ... » *Rec.*, 1933, II, p. 671.

3. By universal or partial succession is meant the succession into all or certain rights and obligations of the predecessor ; to use these expressions in order to denote whether a State has taken over the whole or a part of another State's territory is therefore a misleading use of terminology. It is used by Huber for whom " Teilnachfolge " means " Nachfolge in einen Teil des Staatsgebietes ", whereas " Gesamtnachfolge " means " Nachfolge in das ganze Staatsgebiet ", *op. cit.*, p. 32. Oppenheim-Lauterpacht attach the same meaning to the terms " universal " and " partial succession ", *op. cit.*, I, p. 152. The terms are correctly used by Udina, *op. cit.*, p. 678.

Failing any evidence to the contrary, it may, however, be safely affirmed that general international law admits partial succession only [1].

Even a superficial observation reveals the impossibility of succession to treaties of a clearly " personal " character — in other words, concluded *intuitu personæ* [2] — as well as of succession to delictual responsibility. On the latter problem there exist two important pronouncements of international tribunals, namely the award of the British and American Claims Arbitration Tribunal in the *Claim of Robert E. Brown* of November 23, 1923 [3] and the award of the British and American Claims Arbitrations Tribunal in the case of the *Hawaiian Claims*, of November 10, 1925 [4]. The following passage from the latter decision is worth quoting :

" ... it (the British contention) assumes a general principle of succession to liability for delict... We think there is no such principle... The analogy of universal succession in private law, which is much relied on by those who argue for a large measure of succession to liability for obligations of the extinct State, even if admitted (and the aptness of the analogy it disputed) would make against succession to liability for delicts [5]. "

Thus, a successor State can never be held responsible for the illegal acts of its predecessor, whereas obviously enough, one and the same State continues to be the subject of such responsibility.

It is against this generally accepted background that a surprising view put forward by Kelsen has to be considered [6]. Having admitted at the outset the non-existence of universal succession in positive international law, Kelsen nonetheless advocates the possible practical use of this notion. Namely, it could be used as an emergency notion in those cases where the identity of a State is in doubt [7]. Surprisingly enough, the " doubtful cases " are those of territorial or constitutional changes which a State may undergo, — in other words, precisely those

---

1. " Da bei einem Wechsel der staatlichen Zuständigkeit über einen Gebietsraum die Verpflichtung zum Uebergang sämtlicher sich aus der Vorgängerstaatsordnung ergebenden Rechte und Pflichten nicht nachgewiesen werden kann, kommt nur eine Nachfolge in einzelne Rechte und Pflichten in Frage. Universalsukzession liegt daher auch dann nicht vor, wenn mehrere Staaten einem zergliederten Vorgängerstaat folgen oder der Vorgängerstaat in den Folgestaat einverleibt wird ". Guggenheim, *Lehrbuch des Völkerrechts*, I, pp. 422-423. " Nobody has ever maintained that on the successor devolve *all* the rights and duties of his predecessors ". Oppenheim-Lauterpacht, *op. cit.*, I, p. 152. Similarly, Verdross, *Völkerrecht*, p. 192. Udina uses the notion of universal succession in a " limited sense " after having emphatically excluded « les droits et obligations intransmissibles ». The use or — for that matter — the logic of the conception of a " limited universal succession " is not clear ; however the fact remains that Udina categorically rejects the idea of a true universal succession. « ...on ne peut accepter l'idée d'une succession dans tous les droits et obligations d'un Etat... » *Op. cit.*, p. 684.

2. « ...la transmissibilité des droits et obligations internationaux ne peut être admise, en général, quant aux rapports qui supposent des capacités ou qualités strictement personnelles chez des ayants droit ou obligés, et qu'en effet la succession à de tels droits et obligations n'a pas lieu en droit international, selon une règle coutumière désormais bien établie ». Udina, *op. cit.*, p. 160.

3. *B. Y.*, 1924, V, p. 210.

4. *A. J.*, 1926, pp. 381-382.

5. *Ibid.* See also Sir Cecil J. B. Hurst, *State Succession in Matters of Tort*, *B. Y.*, 1924, pp. 163-178.

6. *Théorie générale*, pp. 333-338.

7. « L'extrême difficulté qu'il y a à déterminer le vrai critère de l'identité fait déjà paraître l'utilité que présenterait l'application de cette notion de succession universelle ». *Ibid.*, p. 334.

changes on which there happens to be no doubt whatever in general international law and for which Kelsen himself provided the criterion of identity in his earlier. writings. However, Kelsen complicates the problem even further by introducing the idea of a State which will consider itself " new " internally, while continuing to bear the same international rights and obligations. According to Kelsen international law cannot " impose " on a State any view concerning its identity. It can only require it to act in a given manner. The problem of identity is in any event a theoretical one which it is not the task of international law to solve [1]. Thus, in order to avoid an utterly illogical conception according to which a State would be identical and non-identical at the same time, it is necessary to adopt the notion of universal succession to international rights and duties which would safeguard these rights and duties while allowing the State to consider itself new. Such a conception would make it possible to avoid the problem of State identity [2].

The whole argument of Kelsen gives rise to serious objections.

1. It artificially produces a non-existing problem. As will be seen [3] the international identity of the State in cases of territorial or revolutionary changes is laid down by most certain rules of positive international law [4].

2. It is submitted that the argument is scientifically unsound : either universal succession does, or does not, exist in positive international law. If the latter is true, which is readily admitted by Kelsen himself, then it is inadmissible that the contrary should be claimed for reasons of expediency.

3. As has been pointed out [5], whether or not the State changes internally, is of no relevance in international law which alone has to consider and decide the question of identity and continuity. The conception of a State " new internally " — whatever that means — and " old internationally " seems particularly unsatisfactory from a monist point of view.

4. It is submitted that such an attitude does not even stand any chance of achieving any practical results. If a State has the will *and* the means to disclaim its international identity in order to evade its responsibilities, it will certainly not allow these same responsibilities to be imposed on it under a different label.

5. Finally, strong exception must be taken to a view professing that it is not the task of international law to solve the problem of State identity. As has been seen, this is precisely the concern of international law [6].

---

1. *Ibid.*, p. 336.
2. « ...notre notion aurait ici l'utilité de permettre de passer outre au problème de l'identité de l'Etat ». *Ibid.*, p. 337.
3. See below, pp. 15-73.
4. For an exception see below, pp. 23-24.
5. See above, p. 3.
6. See above, p. 3.

It is not surprising therefore that Kelsen's view should have met with outspoken criticism [1].

Neither State practice nor international judicial decisions provide the slightest evidence in support of universal succession in general international law, whereas both afford proof to the contrary.

To sum up : since there is no universal succession in general international law, any confusion between the problem of identity and continuity on the one hand, and succession on the other, is plainly inadmissible. State identity and continuity represents an autonomous problem of international law which it is both legitimate and necessary to investigate on its own merits.

c) *Universal Succession on a Conventional Basis.*

However, the non-existence of universal succession in general international law does not necessarily exclude the possibility of such succession on a conventional basis. It is perfectly conceivable that a State, particularly a new State, should be made to succeed to the sum total of the rights and obligations of its predecessor on the basis of a convention.

A striking example of such a possibility is supplied by Art. 12 of the Yugoslav Minorities Treaty, which imposed on Yugoslavia a succession to all rights and obligations arising out of conventions between the Kingdom of Serbia and the Allied and Associated Powers [2]. In spite of its radical character, even this can hardly be regarded as a case of universal succession proper. For the provision only applies to rights and obligations as between the contracting parties, leaving aside all the rights and obligations of old Serbia in relation to other States. But it very nearly approximates to a universal succession and, in any case, shows that such succession is not impossible within the framework of conventional international law. (Its incompleteness in the Yugoslav case arises only out of the limited number of the contracting parties, not out of any intrinsic limitation.) Thus, universal succession, which does not exist in general international law, may nevertheless result from a convention. But clearly, such conventional taking over by one State of all the rights and obligations of another State will always represent a transaction concerning *two* subjects of international law, and will never mean their identity.

---

1. Prof. Guggenheim says : " Kelsen ..... behauptet, der Begriff der Universalsukzession finde im Völkerrecht Anwendung, wenn gemäss Landesrecht die Kontinuität der Rechtsordnung durch revolutionäre Verfassungsänderung aufgehoben werde, ihr räumlicher und personeller Geltungsbereich jedoch der gleiche bleibe. Eine vom Primat des Völkerrechts ausgehende Lehre, die gemäss Völkergewohnheitsrecht die Identität des Staates als Völkerrechtsubjekt annimmt, bedarf dieser Konstruktion nicht ". *Op. cit.*, I, pp. 422-423, *f.-n.* 3. Similar criticism is voiced by Udina, in spite of his relying on dualist premises. « Kelsen nous propose pour la solution d'un problème particulier la même notion d'une succession universelle qu'il critique avec raison». *Op cit.* p. 683. «Notre conclusion sera donc que la notion d'une succession universelle des Etats, au point de vue du droit international, au cas de changement révolutionnaire de leur constitution interne ou de changements essentiels dans leurs éléments matériels, ne peut être substituée au concept de l'identité des mêmes Etats... ». *Ibid.*, p. 688.
2. See below, p. 258.

Consequently, in order to represent the identity and continuity of a State, the identity and continuity of the sum total of its international rights and obligations must not be the result of a convention, but must be assured directly by general international law, in particular, by the customary norm *pacta sunt servanda*.

The above argument has a direct bearing on the definition of the notions discussed, as originally proposed. In view of the provisos introduced, the final definition of State identity should now read :

The identity of a State is the identity of its international rights and obligations, as before and after the event which called such identity in question, and solely on the basis of the customary norm "pacta sunt servanda".

The object of this study is precisely to discover when a State can claim all its rights under the heading of identity and be held responsible for all its obligations ; when there is one and when there are two States ; which are the facts which break its continuity and which are those which, in spite of appearances to the contrary, fail to do so ; which events, interfering with its normal development, mark an end of its legal existence and which are those out of which it emerges perhaps shaken, but whole. To this end both theoretical foundations and the actual practice of States will have to be surveyed.

CHAPTER II.

EXISTING RULES CONCERNING STATE IDENTITY AND CONTINUITY.

General international law contains three undoubted and fully developed rules bearing on the problem under discussion. The first two provide that territorial changes and internal revolutions in no way affect the identity and continuity of States. According to the third rule, which is only rarely mentioned in this connection [1], the same applies in the case of belligerent occupation. The latter is also a customary rule, although it has now been codified in Art. 43 of the Hague Regulations respecting the laws and customs of war on land.

These three rules will now be examined in some detail.

I. THE RULE RELATING TO TERRITORIAL CHANGES.

1. STATEMENT OF THE RULE AND THE SECURITY OF INTERNATIONAL LEGAL RELATIONS ; PRINCIPLE OF VARIABLE TREATY-LIMITS.

According to this customary rule, described by Anzilotti as one of the most certain in international law [2], territorial changes do not affect the identity and continuity of States.

Whatever its actual formulation, it appears that the rule in question did not originate from theoretical considerations concerning the identity of States, but from practical concern for the continued validity of treaty rights and obligations of a State which either loses or acquires territory. It would be subversive of all legal security in international relations if the acquisition or loss of territory could have the effect of undermining the rights and obligations of the State affected by the change as well as those of third States.

Viewed in this way, the rule is identical with the so-called " principle of variable treaty-limits " [3].

---

1. See, however, Verdross, *Die völkerrechtliche Identität von Staaten*, in *Festschrift Heinrich Klang*, p. 20.
2. " ...nessun principio più sicuro di questo nel diritto internazionale ", *Formazione del Regno d'Italia*, p. 9, f.-n. 2.
3. « La doctrine et la pratique sont d'accord pour admettre que les traités internationaux continuent à être en vigueur pour l'Etat qui les a conclus, soit que cet Etat étende son territoire, soit qu'il le réduise ; sauf exceptions déterminées par des raisons particulières, dans le premier cas (accroissements de territoire) les traités s'étendent au nouveau territoire acquis ; dans le second cas (diminution de territoire) les traités cessent d'être applicables au territoire perdu ; c'est ce que l'on appelle la *variabilité des limites territoriales des traités*. » Anzilotti, *Cours*, pp. 183-184. " Blosse Gebietsveränderungen, bei denen die beteiligten Staaten in ihrem Bestande erhalten bleiben, haben grundsätzlich

It is only because it is the identity of rights and obligations which, failing universal succession in international law, makes out the identity of a State, that the original principle of variable treaty-limits could come to be formulated as the principle of State identity.

2. STATE PRACTICE, JUDICIAL DECISIONS AND DOCTRINE.

The rule finds full confirmation in State practice, in judicial decisions and in the views of writers.

State practice seems to have been entirely consistent in this connection already at the beginning of the 19th century.

" Prussia, after the peace of Tilsit in 1807 lost almost a third of its territory. The Kingdom of Saxony by the treaty of Vienna, was reduced to a half of its previous dimensions. France in 1815 and 1871, and Turkey, in 1829 and 1878, both were deprived of territory. Austria lost, in 1859, its richest province, Lombardy, and, in 1866, Venetia. In none of these cases was the continuity or the identity of the State destroyed, nor was the general force of its international obligations held to be impaired [1]. "

In connection with the Anglo-French dispute concerning the applicability of the Anglo-French Convention of 1826 to Algeria, Lord Clarendon wrote on February 19, 1857, to the British Ambassador in Paris :

" Her Majesty's Government would hardly have thought that the argument founded on the fact of Algeria not having been acquired until after the conclusion of the Convention of 1826 could have been seriously advanced, but as Count Walewski has put it forward in his note, I am compelled to say that such a doctrine is wholly inconsistent with the true spirit and intention, as well as with the national and legal construction of the Convention of 1826, or *of any similar Convention. ... The obligations of a Treaty are permanent and indefeasible while the geographical and political boundaries of the dominions of the Contracting Parties are necessarily subject to change.* ... The argument, therefore, that the operation of the Convention was intended by the Contracting Parties to be confined to their actual dominions at that particular moment, and not to extend to any others which they might subsequently acquire, thus creating as it were two classes of dominions, one pre-conventional to be embraced by the Convention, the other post-conventional, to be excluded from it, appears to Her Majesty's Government to be altogether untenable... [2]. "

It was in accordance with this rule that, far from freeing a State whose territory had undergone a change from its treaty obligations, — in other words, far from denying its identity, — the validity of those treaties was actually extended to cover newly acquired territory. The rule seemed so certain that no special conventional provisions to this

---

keinen Einfluss auf die bestehenden völkerrechtlichen Berechtigungen und Verpflichtungen. Die von dem erwerbenden Staate geschlossenen Verträge bleiben trotz des Gebietsverlusts weiter bestehen. Das ist das sogenannte « Prinzip der beweglichen Vertragsgrenzen »..." Liszt, *op. cit.*, p. 276. See also Guggenheim, *op. cit.*, I, p. 425-426.

1. Moore, *A Digest of International Law*, I, p. 248, quoting Martens and Rivier. For further examples, Fenwick, *op. cit.*, p. 148.

2. *It. mine. Fontes Iuris Gentium*, Ser. B, Sectio 1, Tomus 1, Pars 1, pp. 750-751. Cf. on the same subject the Report by the Queen's Advocate dated November 21, 1856, quoted by McNair, *The Law of Treaties*, pp. 438-441.

effect were required [1] and the extension took place automatically. Thus, the Convention of Commerce of 1815 between Great Britain and the United States survived the whole extension of the latter's territory in the course of the 19th century and applied automatically to the newly acquired areas [2]. Similarly Sardinia extended her treaties to the whole of Italy during the period of the Risorgimento and unification [3], Japan to Korea in 1910 [4], England to Cyprus in 1915 [5], Germany to Alsace-Lorraine in 1871, and so forth.

While there is no pronouncement on the subject by an international tribunal, municipal decisions unequivocally confirm the rule. Thus, in a judgment of April 13, 1923 the German Supreme Court held that :

" A State continues to exist as such even though large portions of its territory are taken from it [6]. "

The Court of Appeal of the Canton of Zurich stated on July 5, 1920 :

" ... no importance can be attached to the fact that the Hungarian territory has been diminished as the result of the Peace Treaty. The present Hungarian State is still the same person of international law as that which adhered to the Hague Convention on Civil Procedure [7]. "

In the case *Roselius and Co. v. Dr. Karsten and the Turkish Republic intervening*, before the District Court of Amsterdam, the plaintiff denied the identity of the Turkish Republic with the Ottoman Empire

" on account of the difference in size of the territory which constituted the Ottoman Empire at Constantinople and the territory of the Turkish Republic at Angora ".

The Court, however, held that

" although Turkey was no longer an Empire but a Republic and its size had been considerably curtailed after the Great War by loss of territory, yet it could not be considered that the Republic was not the successor of the Empire. The remaining part, which was the main portion of the country, was the continuation of the State which, under another form of government and larger in size, had formed Turkey, and it had retained all its rights and duties except such as were attached to the lost territories [8] ".

The emphasis of the Court on the rule in question is in no way weakened by the obvious confusion between the notions of continuity and succession. The same principle was upheld by Lord Wright in the case of *Lazard Brothers and Co. v. Midland Bank* [9]. The principle

---

1. For the example of an exception see Liszt, *op. cit.*, p. 276, quoting Art. 12 of the German-Belgian Treaty of Commerce and Customs, of December 6, 1891 : " Der gegenwärtige Vertrag erstreckt sich auf die mit einem der vertragsschliessenden Teile gegenwärtig oder künftig zollgeeinten Länder oder Gebiete. "
2. Mc Nair, *op. cit.*, p. 436.
3. See below, p. 197.
4. Mc. Nair, *op. cit.*, p. 442.
5. *Ibid.*, p. 444.
6. *Fontes*, Ser. A, Sectio II, Tomus 1, p. 29.
7. *In re Ungarische Kriegsprodukten Aktiengesellschaft. A.D.*, 1919/22, case no. 45.
8. *A. D.*, 1925/26, case no. 26.
9. *A. D.*, 1931/32, case no. 69.

of State identity in case of territorial changes has equally been upheld by courts in the case of acquisition as well as loss of territory [1].

Nor is there any hesitation on the part of the writers who affirm the rule with rare unanimity [2].

Finally, the present position under international law is correctly summarized by Art. 26 of the Harvard Draft Convention on the Law of Treaties :

" A change in the territorial domain of a State, whether by addition or loss of territory, does not, in general, deprive the State of rights or relieve it of obligations under a treaty, unless the execution of the treaty becomes impossible as the result of change [3]. "

3. THEORETICAL FOUNDATIONS.

The unquestioned validity of the rule presupposes, and even demands, a correct view of the legal nature of State territory and territorial sovereignty. In the first place the rule presupposes the existence of a State territory. No community of nomadic States could possibly have evolved a rule such as the one under discussion. On the contrary, the rule definitely establishes an unavoidable connection between the notion of the State and the territory [4].

It is impossible within the framework of this study to review all existing theories of territory [5]. Roughly speaking, they fall into three groups : the theory that territory is the property of the State, the theory that territory is an " attribute " of the State [6], and finally the theory that territory represents the spatial sphere of validity of the State's legal order, also called the " competence " theory. The first considers the relation between a State and its territory on the analogy of the *ius in rem* of private law ; the State is the " owner " of its territory as a person is the owner of his house or garden. The second sees territory as an essential quality, an inherent element of the very personality of the State. The third, finally, regards it merely as the space within which the legal order of the State is valid. It may be added that, apart from convinced supporters of the last mentioned theory, there exists a

---

1. See below, p. 198.
2. " Mere territorial changes, whether by increase or by diminution, do not, as long as the identity of the State is preserved, affect the continuity of its existence, or the obligations of its treaties. " Moore, *loc. cit.* Cf. Fauchille, *op. cit.*, I, p. 343. Oppenheim-Lauterpacht, *op. cit.*, I, p. 148. Anzilotti, *op. cit.*, p. 183. Rivier, *op. cit.*, I, pp. 63-64. Liszt, *op. cit.*, p. 276. Jellinek, *op. cit.*, p. 273. Phillimore, *Commentaries upon International Law*, I, pp. 202-203.
3. *A. J.*, vol. 29, Suppl. No. 4.
4. « ...la formation d'Etats au sens actuel est donc liée à la condition préalable de la résidence fixe de l'Etat. » « ...il reste acquis à la conception moderne de l'Etat en général qu'un Etat ne peut exister sans un territoire fixe... » Schönborn, *La nature juridique du territoire*, Rec. 1929, V, pp. 92 and 113. In their earlier writings Kelsen— *Souveränität*, p. 72, *Allg. Staatslehre*, p. 147 — and Guggenheim — *Beiträge*, p. 47 — admitted the possibility of a State without a fixed territory. They seem now to have abandoned this view, — Kelsen, *Théorie générale*, pp. 204-214 ; Guggenheim, I, p. 336.
5. See Schönborn, *op. cit.*, pp. 91-125.
6. " Moment am Staatssubjekt ", Jellinek, *op. cit.*, pp. 382-385.

considerable degree of confusion among writers so that it is sometimes difficult clearly to perceive which of these views they really hold.

The " property " theory proved generally untenable [1]. It was unable to supply a correct view of State territory and could only be upheld in obvious contradiction to positive international law. In particular, as regards the rule under consideration, the logical result of the conception of territory as the " property " of the State would be that even a total and final loss of territory would in no way interfere with the State's continued existence. For property, being something external to the owner, can be lost without the personality of the owner being affected. Such a conclusion would, however, run counter to the obvious principle of international law according to which a total loss of territory means the end of the State [2]. The " property " theory seems now to have been generally abandoned [3].

In the light of positive international law, the " attribute " theory appears equally unworkable. Its ultimate logical conclusion with regard to territorial changes, while exactly opposite to the conclusion of the " property " theory, is just as untrue. If territory did indeed pertain to the very essence of the State, then no territorial changes whatever could leave the identity of the State unaffected [4]. Such a theory could only lead to one logical conclusion which was in fact drawn by its author, Fricker, namely that a change in territory represents a change in the State itself [5]. Yet, as has been seen [6], one of the most certain rules of positive international law lays down the exact opposite and State practice has consistently conformed to this rule.

Fricker is at least consistent in his views which is more than can be said of other writers who uphold the " attribute " theory. Thus Jellinek fully accepts its premise [7] while declining to draw the logical conclusion. On the contrary, he seems to admit that the cession of territory does not give rise to a change of the identity of the State concerned [8]. Moreover, the theory does not seem to prevent Jellinek from admitting a second characteristic of territory, which is also the spatial basis of the

---

1. See the searching criticisms of Schönborn, *op. cit.*, pp. 111-113. Cf. Guggenheim, *op. cit.*, I, p. 335.

2. Cf. Schönborn, *op. cit.*, p. 113.

3. See already Jellinek : " Die Herrschaft über das Gebiet ist ... öffentlich-rechtlich, sie ist nicht Dominium, sondern Imperium. " *Op. cit.*, pp. 385-386.

4. « L'Etat perdrait, au fond, son identité par suite de tout changement du terri- toire. Si le territoire est réellement un élément important de l'essence de la personnalité étatique, on ne peut pas bien se représenter que l'Etat puisse se séparer en principe de parties de son territoire, c'est-à-dire de parties de son essence. " Schönborn, *op. cit.*, p. 116.

5. " ...eine Aenderung des Staatsgebiets ist eine Aenderung des Staates selbst. " Fricker, *Gebiet und Gebietshoheit*, quoted by Guggenheim, *Beiträge*, p. 48, *f.-n.* 103, and : *Vom Staatsgebiet*, quoted by Schönborn, *op. cit.*, p. 116.

6. See above, p. 15.

7. " ...das Sein des Staates selbst, nicht das Haben einer ...Sache erzeugt den Anspruch auf Respektierung des Gebietes. Gebietsverletzung ist daher nicht völkerrecht- liche Besitzstörung, sondern Verletzung der angegriffenen Staatspersönlichkeit selbst. " *Op. cit.*, pp. 384-385.

8. *Ibid.*, pp. 389-390. In *f.-n.* 1 on p. 390, Jellinek speaks emphatically of the result of cession being " Aenderung nicht Untergang und Neuschöpfung, wie Fricker... behauptet ".

dominion over all individuals within the State [1]. In this he comes unexpectedly close to the "competence" theory [2], while involving himself in a contradiction with his first view. For territory cannot possibly be at one and the same time an essential attribute of the State and the mere sphere of the validity of its legal order [3].

Thus, the "attribute" theory is in glaring contradiction to positive international law [4]. It is therefore necessary to find a real scientific explanation which would be both logical and consistent with legal and historical reality.

Such an explanation is supplied by recent doctrine which, abandoning artificial concepts, considers territory as the sphere of validity of the legal order of the State, also called the competence theory. A legal order has to be valid somewhere, and the legal order of the State is — generally — valid within a given space known as State territory [5]. Thus, a loss or an increase of territory cannot possibly mean a change in the "essence" or "personality of the State". It simply means that the norms of the State's legal order are from now on valid throughout a larger or a more restricted space [6]. It is only on the basis of such a theory that the positive rule under consideration becomes comprehensible and clear. And it is only this theory which is in accordance with positive international law [7].

---

1. " ...räumliche Grundlage der Herrschaftsentfaltung über sämtliche im Staate weilenden Menschen. " *Ibid.*, p. 385.

2. See below.

3. The same contradictions are to be found again and again in the traditional doctrine. Thus, Oppenheim-Lauterpacht declare the territory to be " the public property of the State ", — *op. cit.*, I, p. 408 — only in order to declare it on the same page to be " the space within which the State [exercises its supreme authority ". Following in Jellinek's foot-steps, Carré de Malberg first rejects the theory of property in favour of the view of the territory as the « cadre dans lequel est capable de s'exercer la puissance étatique ou imperium ». *Contribution à la Théorie générale de l'Etat*, p. 4. But he then goes on to say that territory is an « élément constitutif de l'Etat, c'est-à-dire un élément de son *être* et non point de son *avoir*, un élément par conséquent de sa personnalité même... », *ibid.*, p. 4, *f.-n.* 4. And like Jellinek, he draws back from the last logical conclusion which had been drawn by Fricker. Similarly Fauchille, who declares : «... la possession exclusive et complète d'un territoire est un des éléments essentiels et constitutifs de la notion même d'Etat. Le droit de propriété sur une certaine partie du globe est donc pour tous les Etats un droit primordial ». *Op. cit.*, I, p. 450. And yet : « Ce démembrement et cette annexion, s'ils produisent une transformation dans la constitution territoriale de l'Etat, ne touchent en rien à son existence. L'Etat est resté la même personne internationale... ». *Ibid.*, p. 343.

4. " Eine solche Ansicht der räumlichen Gebietsbeziehung des Staates stellt eine Konstruktion dar, welche die Norm aus dem Vorstellungsinhalt eines Begriffes und nicht aus dem Inhalt eines Rechtssatzes ableitet (Begriffsjurisprudenz). " Guggenheim, *Lehrbuch*, I, p. 336.

5. " Das Staatsgebiet ist der Raum in welchem die staatliche Rechtsordnung gilt, d.h. in welchem die Organe des Staates zur Vollstreckung von Rechtsnormen gemäss Völkerrecht zuständig erscheinen. " Guggenheim, *op. cit.*, I, p. 336. Cf. Kelsen, *Allg. Staatslehre*, p. 136. Cf. Scelle's « théorie du territoire-limite », *op. cit.*, p. 88.

6. " ...questa potestà si esplica in uno spazio maggiore o minore. " Anzilotti, *Formazione*, p. 9, *f.-n.* 2.

7. «...la théorie de la compétence éclaircit d'une façon naturelle cette difficulté — au fond insoluble pour la théorie de la qualité — et qui consiste en ce que, lorsque le territoire de l'Etat change, l'essence, c'est-à-dire la personnalité de l'Etat lui-même — conformément à l'opinion dominante — ne change pas nécessairement. En effet, une autorité ne subit aucun changement dans sa nature propre et particulière lorsque sa compétence locale est étendue ou restreinte. » Schönborn, *op. cit.*, p. 119.

4. EXCLUSION OF TERRITORY AS A CRITERION OF STATE IDENTITY.

The fact that territorial changes have no effect on the identity of States leads to the important conclusion, that it is *not* territory which determines that identity. On the contrary, it must be completely discarded as a determining factor.

Against this conclusion, resulting necessarily from an analysis of positive international law, two assertions to the contrary stand out in a truly surprising manner.

Burckhardt seeks a criterion for the continued responsibility of States despite constitutional changes and maintains that it lies in the identity of territory. It is therefore territory which, according to him, is decisive for the international identity of States [1].

In his latest work on State and law, Kelsen states :

" That the whole territory of one State becomes the territory of one other State is impossible since, if the territory is identical, the identity of the State is maintained [2]. "

Kelsen thus assumes that territory forms the criterion of State identity. Yet, this assumption is contrary to the clear rule of international law that territorial changes are irrelevant to the problem of State identity [3]. Moreover, it does not take the time factor into account. For it is obvious that one and the same territory can, at different times, carry different State structures [4]. This is fully admitted by Kelsen himself, a few pages earlier in the same work :

" When it is said that not more than one State can exist within a given space, it is obviously meant that *not more than one State can exist within the same space at the same time. It is taken as self-evident that, as history shows, two different States can exist one after the other, at least partly, within the same space* [5]. "

The two statements of Kelsen are wholly contradictory. For, if it is admitted — as it must be admitted — that more than one State can, and has, in fact, existed in one and the same territory at different times, — in other words, that the same territory can supply the geographical basis of two or even more different States, then such territory can no longer serve as criterion of State identity. With the necessary introduction of the time factor, territory disappears as a possible test

---

1. " Darin besteht, durch alle Verfassungsänderungen hindurch, die völkerrechtliche Identität des Staates ; die Verfassung macht also nicht völkerrechtlich, sondern nur staatsrechtlich die Identität des Staates aus. Was völkerrechtlich die Identität, wie die Individualität des Staates ausmacht, ist das Gebiet. " *Die völkerrechtliche Verantwortlichkeit der Staaten*, Bern, 1924, p. 18.

2. *It. mine, General Theory*, p. 231 ; similarly, on p. 220, Kelsen explains the continued existence of a State in spite of revolution by the identity of territory. " According to international law, the State remains the same as long as the territory remains essentially the same. The identity of the State in time is based directly upon the identity of territory and only indirectly upon the identity of the population living in the territory. " — This is hardly consistent with his earlier view, as expressed in *Souveränität* and *Allg. Staatslehre*, see below, p. 46, *f.-n.* 4.

3. For the only exception see below pp. 23-24.

4. " ...dass ein und derselbe Boden den verschiedenartigsten Staaten und Völkern als physikalische Grundlage gedient hat.. " Jellinek, *op. cit.*, p. 75.

5. *It. mine, General Theory*, p. 218.

of State identity. Even if identity of territory *alone* could be admitted as a criterion of State identity in the concrete case of revolution [1], it can certainly not serve as a generally valid criterion in every case [2].

Il may then be safely affirmed that in the light of positive international law, as well as history and logic, territory must be excluded as a factor capable of determining the identity of a State.

5. APPARENT AND REAL EXCEPTIONS TO THE RULE.

The rule safeguarding State identity and continuity in case of territorial changes has, as Anzilotti says, proved one of the most certain in international law. However, certain exceptions have been suggested, and these must now be examined.

According to certain earlier writers territorial changes do not affect a State's identity only so long as the State concerned does not lose its territorial " nucleus " [3]. Theoretically, it would be extremely difficult to determine which part of the territory represents this " nucleus ". Is it the so-called historical " cradle " of the State, or the part including the capital or yet another part possessing a historical, emotional or economic importance? What legal relevance do such criteria possess? Which would be the " nucleus " of a Federal State, particularly if composed of various races, as e.g. Switzerland? None of these possible criteria seems even reasonable and, certainly, none is juridical. If what is meant is that part of the State which may be said to be essential to its existence, then the realistic argument of the Harvard Draft Convention on the Law of Treaties [4] meets the objection by affirming that in practice States either lose the whole of their territory or — if they retain anything, it is precisely the " essential part ".

The " nucleus " theory does not therefore constitute a real exception to the rule.

Another exception seems to be contained in the relevant Article of the Harvard Draft Convention, quoted above [5]. While emphasizing the continued validity of the rights and obligations of a State, undergoing territorial changes, the Article adds :

" ... unless the execution of the treaty becomes impossible as the result of change. "

The comment to the Article gives possible examples:

" Thus, the execution of a treaty provision granting the right of navigation on a river or lake is possible only so long as the river or lake remains within the

---

1. See below, p. 46.
2. This recent view of Kelsen seems hardly in keeping with his own theory of the identity of State and law ; consistently with this theory, Kelsen formerly identified the State with its legal order, in particular, its basic norm. See *Allg. Staatslehre*, p. 249. It is difficult to understand how he now comes to identify an ideal notion with a material element.
3. Hall, W. E. *A Treatise on International Law*, 8th edition, edited by A. P. Higgins, Oxford, Clarendon Press, 1924, p. 22 ; Bluntschli, *Das moderne Völkerrecht der civilisirten Staaten als Rechtsbuch dargestellt*, p. 80.
4. *A. J.* vol. 29, Suppl. No. 4, p. 1068.
5. See above, p. 18.

possession of the State granting the right. So it would be with a treaty granting fishery rights within waters which are subsequently lost by the State granting the right, or a treaty relating to maritime matters, when by reason of territorial losses a State ceases to be a maritime power, or a treaty granting economic concessions or privileges within territory which ceases to belong to a State... " etc. etc. [1].

As regards the survival of certain treaty rights and obligations, the exception is no doubt a real one. It is, however, submitted that it is only apparent with regard to the problem of State identity and continuity. For, the whole body of the State's rights and obligations will survive territorial changes, and only a few special treaties will become extinct *not by reason of the State's discontinuity, but only and exclusively on the strength of the principle " impossibilium nulla obligatio "*, as would be the case with any other treaty, even without a territorial change, if it were to become incapable of execution. To return to the examples in the Harvard Draft Convention : the river or the lake to which certain obligations attach, may not only be ceded to another State ; it may dry up. The State's identity and continuity, in view of the survival of all its other rights and obligations, is as little affected by the extinction of this type of treaty following a territorial change, as it is in the case of a similar extinction without a territorial change[2].

This correct reservation in the Harvard Draft Convention does not therefore constitute an exception to the rule under consideration.

There exists, however, one real exception which has been formulated by Prof. Guggenheim : the identity of a State is no longer safeguarded against territorial loss if such loss is either total or very considerable [3].

This first — and only — real exception to the rule is interesting in more than one respect. In the first place, it represents the phenomenon of the difference in degree becoming a difference in kind. Secondly, it illustrates the constant intrusion of facts into the world of norms ; for it will be precisely the physical nature of this reduced territory which will prevent a State from preserving its old legal order and from being able to bear its previous international rights and obligations [4]. Finally, it points to an interdependence of the so-called elements of the State.

---

1. *Ibid*, p. 1069.
2. In accordance with the Draft Convention, stress should be laid on the " impossibility of execution " and *not* the *Clausula rebus sic stantibus*, which is an entirely different matter, covering precisely cases where there *is* a possibility of execution. For the difference between the two notions see : the same Harvard Draft Convention, dealing separately with the impossibility of execution in Art. 26 and with the Clausula in Art. 28 ; the Habana Convention on Treaties between American States of February 20, 1928, dealing with the former in Art. 14 G, and with the latter in Art. 15 ; the two notions are also treated separately by Anzilotti, *Cours*, p. 456 and pp. 456-465 respectively, Scelle, *Précis de droit des gens*, II, p. 419, Rousseau, *Principes*, pp. 355-366 and pp. 579-617.
3. " Die Identität des gebietserwerbenden bzw. des gebietsverlierenden Staates wird solange durch Gebietsveränderungen nicht berührt, als der gebietsverlierende Staat nicht den räumlichen Geltungsbereich seiner Rechtsordnung völlig oder *in sehr bedeutendem Umfange einbüsst.* ... Die Kontinuität eines Staates steht jedoch zur Diskussion, wenn die Gebietsveränderung *in einem quantitativ bedeutsamen Umfange eintritt* ". *It. mine, op. cit.*, I, p. 406. See also Kelsen, *Souveränität*, p. 238.
4. " Dass z.B. die Grösse des Staatsgebietes die Organisation des Staates mitbestimmt, bedarf kaum näherer Ausführung. " Jellinek, *op. cit.*, p. 73, and examples quoted.

To give a concrete example : no one would maintain that the Free City of Cracow, as created in 1815, could possibly have been identical with the old Polish Republic of the 18th century. Yet there was no doubt whatever about the continued identity of that Republic following both the first (1772) and the second partition (1793), and the very considerable loss of territory involved. In the case of the Free City of Cracow, the loss of territory went far beyond the quantitative limit within which the rule under consideration could still have operated. The tiny territory of the Free City, with its limited population, could not possibly have carried either the State form of the old Republic stretching from west of the Warta to the Dnieper, or its international rights and obligations [1].

To take an imaginary example : it is obvious that a territorial reduction of the United States down to the limits of one state would not leave its State identity unaffected. In the first place, it would not even be *the United States* any longer. Secondly, it would not be able to carry the international rights and obligations of the United States.

The question could be asked : is there any possibility of fixing a limit up to which the rule would be valid and beyond which the identity and continuity of a State would be lost ? The answer is obviously in the negative. Once again, as so often in international law, the solution must depend upon an evaluation of the facts of each particular case.

With this sole exception, the rule of territorial changes not affecting the identity and continuity of States stands out as one of the most certain in positive international law.

II. THE RULE RELATING TO REVOLUTIONARY CHANGES.

1. STATEMENT OF THE RULE AND THE SECURITY OF INTERNATIONAL LEGAL RELATIONS.

The second customary rule, which is equally well established as the first, lays down that the identity and continuity of the State are not affected by changes of government which it may undergo.

Here again, the starting point for the development of the rule was provided not by theoretical considerations, but by practical concern for the maintenance of international rights and obligations, — in other words, for the stability and security of international legal relations [2].

---

1. The writer is fully aware of the two flaws in the argument : first, the Free City was created *after* the extinction of Poland by the third partition (1795); it was, consequently, a new creation and not the result of an uninterrupted process of territorial reduction. Secondly, even the State character of the Free City is doubtful. It is believed however, that its value as an illustration of this particular aspect of the case, stands.

2. " If the Ministers of the Court of Naples mean to affirm positively that " solemn contracts which have long subsisted between one nation and another are solely dependent for their Force on the Persons of Sovereigns or the Possession of a particular Family " I humbly apprehend not only that His Majesty's particular interest is affected, but that the Interest of all Sovereigns are deeply concerned in opposing it. Because it cannot fail to place on the most unstable Foundation the Repose of Europe and to destroy that Confidence among all Orders of Mankind which is so necessary to the Glory of Sovereigns and the Intercourse of Nations. " From the Report of Dr. John Marriott, the Advocate-General, of November 30, 1764. Quoted by McNair, *Aspects of State Sovereignty*, p. 9. " ...no doctrine more fatal than this to the tranquility of the globe can well be maintained. " Phillimore, *op. cit.*, I, p. 206.

For such stability would be non-existent, if treaties were to become void with every internal change within a State and moreover, if a State could at will repudiate its international obligations by the simple device of changing its form of government [1].

2. Scope of the rule and definition of Revolution.

Before analyzing the rule in question it is essential to determine the circumstances to which it applies.

It should be made clear at the outset that the somewhat general expression " changes of government " in fact covers two entirely distinct possibilities : constitutional changes and revolutionary changes [2].

No international rule safeguarding the identity and continuity of the State is necessary in the former case [3]. The problem of such identity and continuity cannot even arise. For a change in the constitutional structure of a State, however fundamental, is of no legal relevance whatever, as long as it is carried out by constitutional means. There is every reason to agree with Sander who considers the revision clause of any constitution as a norm which is in substance superior to all the remaining constitutional norms [4]. As long as the change proceeds according to that superior norm, it is in fact no change at all ; throughout all constitutional changes the State and, contrary to appearances, the constitution itself remain legally the same [5].

It is only in the case of a revolutionary change that the question of State identity and continuity can arise at all.

The definition of revolution is implied in what has just been said with regard to constitutional changes. In contradistinction to the latter, it covers every change in the legal order of the State other than one brought about by constitutional means. Thus, whatever its political, social and economic implications, from the legal point of view the essential feature of the revolution is the formal manner in which the change is brought about. To the lawyer therefore it is exclusively a matter of procedure.

---

1. " If changes in the organisation of a State's form of governement or modification of its constitutional system had the effect of terminating or altering its treaty obligations or of rendering them voidable, a State which desired to avoid or reduce its obligations would need only to introduce a change in the organisation of its government or alter its constitutional system. If such changes produced that effect, States would hesitate to enter into treaties, because in that case one of the foundations of the treaty system, namely the permanence of treaties, would cease to exist and treaty obligations would be terminable or impairable at the will of any party. " *Harvard Draft Convention*, comment on Art. 24, p. 1045.

2. Cf. Kelsen, *Souveränität*, p. 237.

3. The problem of a mere change in the personal composition of the governing group must, of course, be immediately dismissed, as irrelevant, whatever the possible political implications of such a change. It is of no legal significance whatever, either for municipal or — a fortiori — for international law ; international rights and obligations are those of the State and not of the government.

4. *Das Faktum der Revolution und die Kontinuität der Rechtsordnung*, Ztscht. f. öff. R., I, 1919, p. 153.

5. " Die Identität der Verfassung ist keineswegs durch die Unveränderlichkeit und Unverändertheit des Verfassungsinhaltes, sondern nur ... durch die Erfüllung der selbstgesetzten Voraussetzungen der Aenderung bedingt. " Merkl, *op. cit.*, p. 513. Cf. Kelsen, *Allg. Staatslehre*, p. 249.

Accordingly, a revolution does not depend upon the extent of the material changes involved but solely upon the change being brought about in violation of the prescribed procedure of revision [1]. It need hardly be added that it is certainly not determined by acts of violence which may or may not accompany a revolution, while they may equally occur under a constitutional regime [2].

This purely formal criterion of a revolution is the only one which is both reliable and legally correct. Any attempt to substitute for this stable and formal criterion a necessarily unstable and material one is bound to undermine all legal certainly and to lead to all kinds of intellectual vagaries in the field of law [3].

To sum up : the international rule safeguarding the identity and continuity of States undergoing the so-called " changes of government " applies only to revolutionary changes. For constitutional changes no such rule is necessary. It is therefore only with revolution that this chapter is concerned.

3. " INTERNAL " STATE IDENTITY AND CONTINUITY.

It is particularly with regard to revolution that the two distinct notions of State identity and continuity — one international and one internal — are advanced by writers. The practical non-existence of an " internal " identity and continuity has already been pointed out [4], and it has been shown that the problem simply cannot arise in the case of a Robinson Crusoe State. It is now necessary to deal with the purely theoretical aspect of the problem. Can there really be " two sorts " of State identity and continuity ? Can a State be a two-faced Janus, capable of being identical and non-identical at the same time ?

---

1. " Dies ist das entscheidende Kriterium, nicht aber ob die Verfassungsänderung eine mehr oder weniger tiefgreifende ist. " Kelsen, *Souveränität*, p. 237. It is interesting to recall that several undoubted revolutions introduced but little change in the whole body of the country's laws and had little bearing on the legal position of its citizens, whereas some of the greatest upheavals were — at least at the time of their happening — not revolutions at all. Thus a large body of French law, including the Code Napoléon, successfully survived more than a century of revolutions, whereas in Germany the National Socialists seized power in full conformity with the provisions of the Weimar Constitution ; the latter, it may be observed, was as little formally abolished as was the 1848 Statuto Fondamentale by Italian Fascism. After the Second World War, a considerable change of the general structure of Great Britain took place by way of a strictly constitutional procedure. Cf. Lauterpacht, *Recognition*, p. 139, *f.-n.* 1.

2. " It is unnecessary to point out that when a lawyer uses the word « revolution » he is not concerned with the question whether there was a bloody revolution but simply with the question whether there was a break in the chain of legal continuity, however produced. " McNair, *Aspects*, p. 8. It is therefore truly surprising to find the following statement in Lauterpacht's *Recognition:* " So long as international law does not stigmatize revolutions as being in the nature of crimes against the law of nations, it cannot condemn the means *necessarily violent*, by which revolutions are achieved ". *It. mine*, p. 107.

3. E. g., M. Burdeau's conception of an « idée de droit » being the proper criterion of revolutions and, consequently of State identity. « L'Etat étant une institution dans laquelle s'incarne un Pouvoir, lui-même énergie d'une idée de droit, il est clair qu'il doit disparaître lorsque cette idée de droit perd sa valeur. Le remplacement violent d'une idée de droit par une autre entraîne une rupture de la continuité étatique ». *Op. cit.*, p. 577. This quotation is taken from a treatise of political science ; it is, however, difficult to know whether it is advanced as a scientific, a literary, or a political statement.

4. See above, p. 3.

In the first place, it is very doubtful whether the question of internal identity and continuity can logically arise at all. For it is submitted that logically such problem can only exist on the assumption of, and in relation to, a higher legal order, which alone can provide the *tertium comparationis*. The identity and continuity of a given legal order cannot be tested and determined except by the criterion of a higher legal order [1].

For the sake of argument, however, the admissibility of such a question may be accepted, the more so since it has in fact been asked and answered many times and since the results of such investigation should not here be disregarded.

The most famous answer was the one given by Aristotle who categorically denied the continued identity of a State in the case of a constitutional change [2]. Here as elsewhere, Aristotle remained faithful to his conception of pure form. To him the State was represented by its legal order, and not by its material elements [3]. What is more, his attention was, very naturally, concentrated on the Greek City-State. What embryonic international law there may have been among the Greek cities was certainly not sufficient to influence the political horizon of the period. The City-State was conceived as an ultimate entity, whose basic norm stood at the summit of the legal pyramid.

Such a conception is incompatible with the existence of international law. Its rejection forms the very basis on which an international law can be conceived [4]. For over and above the legal order of States there rises the superior hierarchy of norms of the international legal order, culminating in the latter's basic norm. Viewed in this way, the basic norm of the State ceases to be the last and the highest one, and takes its proper place within the complete structure of the system of norms. It is no longer all-embracing even as regards the State itself. It only

---

1. " Ob zwischen dem alten und dem neuen Gesetze Kontinuität herrscht, lässt sich nicht durch Betrachtung dieser Systemstufe, durch Vergleichung des alten oder neuen Gesetzes bestimmen, sondern durch Bestimmung eines Gesetzes höherer Stufe, welches Erzeugungsregel der " Veränderung " war. Dieser Grundsatz gilt selbstverständlich für Rechtsveränderungen auf allen Stufen. Ob zwischen den Rechtserscheinungen einer Stufe Kontinuität herrscht, kann nur durch Rückgang zur nächsthöheren Stufe, durch einen Schritt dem Ursprunge des Systems entgegen ausgemacht werden. Ob also zwischen zwei (empirischen) Verfassungen Kontinuität herrscht, lässt sich nicht durch Vergleichung dieser beiden Verfassungen, sondern nur durch Aufsuchen einer höheren Stufe bestimmen. Ist die Abänderung in den Formen der alten Verfassung erfolgt, dann verbürgt der die Revisionsklausel enthaltende Rechtssatz die Kontinuität, denn er ist im Verhältnisse zu den übrigen Verfassungsgesetzen eine logisch höhere Stufe. Ist die Verfassungsänderung unter Verletzung der Revisionsklausel oder trotz Mangels einer solchen Revisionsklausel erfolgt, dann ist es das Völkerrecht welches die Kontinuität verbürgt. " Sander, *op. cit.*, pp. 153-154.

2. " For, since the State is a partnership, and is a partnership of citizens in a constitution, when the form of the government changes, and becomes different, then it may be supposed that the State is no longer the same... And if this is true, it is evident that the sameness of the State consists chiefly in the sameness of the constitution. " *The Works of Aristotle*, Translated into English under the editorship of W.D. Ross, M.A., Vol. X, *Politica*, by Benjamin Jowett, Oxford, at the Clarendon Press, 1921, 1276 b.

3. " It would be a very superficial view which considered only the place and the inhabitants... It is further asked: When are men, living in the same place, to be regarded as a single city — what is the limit? Certainly not the walls of the city... " *Ibid.*, 1276 a.

4. « Le droit international est basé sur la croyance que cette analyse de la hiérarchie politique est incomplète. » Brierly, *Règles générales*, p. 5.

determines that sphere of the legal order of the State which has been left by international law to its own competence, but it does not cover its temporal or its territorial sphere of validity, which is determined by international law.

It is only if this view is rejected either in favour of a denial of existence of international law, or at least of its superiority in relation to State law, that the existence of an " internal " problem of State identity and continuity can be maintained. It is only then that the theoretical discontinuity of a revolutionary State be upheld [1].

But on the assumption of the correct view of both the existence and the primacy of international law, there is only one correct method of dealing with the question of identity and continuity : namely, by going back to the higher norm as the *tertium comparationis*. The result is that the problem assumes an exclusively international aspect and that the solution thus reached is valid both in the international and internal sphere. To combine both methods of reasoning, to make a halfway stop on the level of the basic norm of the State with the resulting denial of its continuity, and only then to continue the upward course with the resulting confirmation of that same continuity, seems to be a procedure which is just as unnecessary as it is illogical [2].

---

1. Accordingly, the identity and continuity of the State following a revolution is denied by those authors who reject the superior character of international law and consequently consider revolutions, as well as birth of States, meta-juridical " pure facts ". See Rauschenberger, W. *Die staatsrechtliche Bedeutung von Stastsstreich und Revolution, Ztscht. f. öff. R.*, II, 1921, p. 113.

2. Accordingly, the identity and continuity of a revolutionary State is maintained by those writers who profess the view of the primacy of international law. " Within the State the revolution destroys irrevocably the continuity of the legal order ; the former law subsists only in so far as it is adopted by the new, revolutionary order. It is, in fact, international law which preserves the legal continuity of the State. " " Thus as between the old and the finally successful new regime within the State there is not — and cannot conceivably be — any legal continuity so far as that State is concerned. It is international law which bridges the gap by proclaiming the principle of State continuity unaffected by revolutionary changes. " Lauterpacht, *op. cit.*, pp. 92 and 245. " Vom Standpunkte der Rechtsordung des Einzelstaates aus betrachtet ist seine Rechtskontinuität ausgeschlossen, insofern das Staatsgrundgesetz (Verfassung) nicht unter Wahrung der von ihm selbst vorgeschriebenen Formen verändert wird ; denn das Staatsgrundgesetz kann nicht seine eigene, auf revolutionärem Wege vollzogene Aenderung regeln. Dennoch nimmt vielfach die staatsrechtliche Theorie an, es verbleibe der Staat trotz revolutionären Wandels der gleiche, da die dem gesellschaftlichen Verband « Staat » auf abgegrenzten Gebiet angehörenden Menschen nach wie vor die gleichen seien. Solche Auffassung widerspricht indessen jeder möglichen Konstruktion der Rechtsordnung des Einzelstaates : denn die Vielheit der menschlichen Individuen auf abgegrenzten Gebiet wird doch erst zum Staat durch die Ordnung, welche die rechtlichen Beziehungen der ihr unterworfenen Menschen regelt. Wird diese unter Nichtbeobachtung der in ihr vorgeschriebenen Revisionsformen geändert, so verändert sich auch die alte staatliche Ordnung, ohne dass die neuentstandene rechtlich aus jener abgeleitet werden kann. Nur ein aus der überstaatlichen Rechtsordnung hergeleiteter Rechtssatz kann die rechtliche Staatskontinuität trotz revolutionärer Verfassungsänderung gewährleisten. " Guggenheim, *Beiträge*, pp. 16-17. Similarly Kelsen, *Souveränität*, pp. 237-238. It is believed that these quotations are not meant to proclaim the existence of two kinds of identity, internal and international, but that they merely intend to show *what the solution would be*, if the problem were not investigated in the light of a higher legal order. The one important exception in this connection is supplied by Merkl's unusual theory, which, admittedly, follows from his premise, i.e. his notion of the " continuity of law ", see above, p. 6, f.-n.2. Since, according to this theory, all existing legal systems are connected with each other by the " continuity of law ", it is clear that there exists for Merkl only the internal, never the international problem of State continuity. " Das in der Umstürzung im Gefolge des Weltkrieges aktuell gewordene Kontinuitätsproblem... ist einleuchtenderweise ausschliesslich das der staatsrechtlichen Kontinuität. " *Op. cit.*, p. 511.

It therefore seems legitimate to draw the conclusion that there can be no " two aspects " of the problem ; there can be only one of them, according to whether the supremacy of international over internal law is accepted or rejected. In the case of this study, based as it is on monism with primacy of international law, there exists only the international aspect of the problem [1].

Finally, it may be observed that a differentiation between the two " aspects " seems the more artificial since the two systems of law react in a similar way when confronted with the problem of revolution.

i) The fact that international law, disregarding the legal break, considers any *de facto* power in the State as the legal power, is regarded by Kelsen as its weakness, its tendency to capitulate before facts [2]. Yet exactly the same weakness and the same capitulation before the same facts is to be found in internal law. This is revealed by an analysis of any penal code : whereas all other crimes are punishable, both as regards their actual perpetration and the attempt, it is only revolution (and high treason) in respect of which the attempt alone is punishable. The penal code — reasonably enough — renounces in advance any attempt to punish a successful revolution with which it will no longer have the strength to deal. This admission of the municipal law's capitulation in the face of a revolution is outspoken enough. A State can hardly be expected to proclaim its sense of reality any louder.

Thus, a revolution is in some way " legalized " not only by international, but also by municipal law [3]. Similarly, in both systems of law

---

1. This incidentally confirms the correctness of the definition of the notions of identity and continuity as here accepted ; it would be both inadmissible and unworkable for an " internal " problem of State continuity. A striking assimilation of the " two aspects " of the problem is to be found in the award of the Franco-Chilean Arbitral Tribunal of 1901 : after proclaiming the uninterrupted continuity of *external* rights and obligations of the State in case of a revolution, the Tribunal went on to say : « ...Que ce principe n'est pas sans doute d'une application immédiate en l'espèce, puisqu'il s'agit de la validité, non d'un acte passé par le Dictateur Pierola avec une puissance étrangère, et sujet aux règles du droit des gens, mais d'un contrat de droit commun conclu avec un particulier étranger qui avait expressément déclaré se soumettre aux lois du Pérou et à la juridiction des tribunaux péruviens. *Mais qu'il y a lieu de le considérer comme faisant règle également, au point de vue du droit public interne*, pour l'appréciation des rapports contractuels formés entre un Gouvernement de fait et un particulier, à raison de sa conformité avec la notion même de l'Etat... Attendu, en effet, que les raisons de décider sont identiques dans les deux hypothèses ; qu'en dehors des cas d'anarchie pure, la permanence de l'existence de l'Etat suppose nécessairement la présence d'un pouvoir qui agit en son nom et qui le représente... ...Qu'il n'est pas concevable, en effet, que pendant le temps qu'un nouveau Gouvernement subsiste dans des conditions semblables, les affaires intérieures de l'Etat restent en suspens, alors que les actes extérieurs sont, d'après le droit des gens, valablement accomplis; qu'une solution qui dénierait, sous prétexte d'illégitimité, leur effet légal à des contrats passés avec un Gouvernement de fait à un moment où ce Gouvernemnet était le seul organe reconnu de la Nation, impliquerait la négation même de l'idée de l'Etat... » *It. mine*, Descamps-Renault, *Recueil international des traités du XXᵉ siècle*, Année 1901, pp. 395-396. See below, p. 39. The reasoning of the Tribunal is no less interesting in that, in this particular case, the international element was introduced into the case by the fact of one party to the contract being a foreigner, whose claim was subsequently espoused by his State. Thus, more convincingly, the Permanent Court of Arbitration, in the same case, see below, p. 72.

2. *Souveränität*, p. 238.

3. See judgment of the German Reichsgericht of July 8, 1920 : " The illegality of the establishment of a new sovereignty (Staatsgewalt) in a State, does not prevent its recognition under constitutional law, since legality of establishment is not an essential characteristic of State sovereignty (" kein wesentliches Merkmal der Staatsgewalt ")." *Fontes*, Series A, Sectio II, Tomus I, p. 66.

attempts have been made to refuse such legalization. Thus, several South American Constitutions contained provisions to the effect that no revolution would ever be recognized [1]. In international law the refusal of legalization expressed itself in its most striking form in the 19th century in the Holy Alliance, — in the 20th century in the Tobar Doctrine (1907), the Central American Conventions (the Washington Convention of 1907 and the Central American Treaty of 1923) and Wilson's " constitutionalism ". Both attempts necessarily miscarried. The provisions of the South American Constitutions are truly pathetic. For, either a revolution is successfully put down, in which case the provision in question is utterly unnecessary ; or it succeeds, in which case the provision is even more unnecessary [2]. As for the attempt to refuse legalization of revolutions by international law, it may be safely said that all these attempts failed [3].

ii) While it is undoubtedly true that a State continues to be the bearer of its international rights and obligations regardless of a revolution, it is no less true that a State usually takes over at least a part of the legal heritage of its overthrown predecessor on the internal plane. The history of 19th century France abounds in examples of this. The most striking one is perhaps that of the qualified recognition accorded by the French Government even to certain acts of the Paris Commune which was, after all, only a local *de facto* Government [4]. Thus, even the taking over of rights and obligations is not necessarily limited to international law.

---

1. " This Constitution shall not lose its force and vigour even though its observance be interrupted by rebellion. " Art. 136 of the Mexican Constitution of January 31, 1917. " Acts of persons who usurp public functions and posts conferred without the requisites laid down by the constitution and the laws are null and void. " Art. 19 of the Peruvian Constitution of April 9, 1933. Peaslee, A. J., *Constitutions of Nations.* Similarly, the constitutions of Salvador, Honduras, Venezuela, Chile.

2. The absurdity of this conception is emphatically brought out by international judicial decisions. Thus, the Franco-Chilean Arbitral Tribunal of 1901, declared : « Attendu que le Gouvernement du Pérou conteste la validité des actes du Gouvernement dictatorial en se fondant en première ligne sur l'Art. 10 de la Constitution péruvienne de 1860 d'après lequel « sont nuls les actes de ceux qui usurpent les fonctions publiques... » ; mais que cette disposition n'a pu déployer d'effet qu'autant qu'elle était en vigueur à l'époque de la liquidation de la créance Dreyfus ; qu'il n'est pas contesté que le dictateur Pierola a promulgué, lors de son avènement, le 29 décembre 1879, des « Statuts provisoires » qui suspendaient les effets de la Constitution de 1860 ; qu'ainsi la question de l'applicabilité de l'Art. 10 de la Constitution de 1860 se réduit à savoir si la Constitution ancienne doit prévaloir sur la nouvelle ; que cette question se confond avec celle de la validité même du régime dictatorial ; qu'elle ne peut dès lors être résolue que par un principe supérieur à la loi positive, *puisque les révolutions de l'organisme politique auxquelles les pouvoirs publics sont impuissants à résister échappent par leur force propre à l'application de cette loi,* établie en vue d'un ordre de choses différent... " *It. mine,* Descamps-Renault, *op. cit.,* p. 394 ; see below, p. 39. It is submitted that while the problem can indeed be resolved only by reference to a superior principle, that principle need not be superior to *positive* law as such. It is quite sufficient if it is superior to positive municipal law of the State concerned, i.e. if it is a principle of positive *international* law. See above, pp. 27-28. Similarly the Award in the *Britain-Costa Rica* case declared : " The change by revolution upsets the rule of the authorities in power under the then existing fundamental law, and sets aside the fundamental law in so far as the change of rule makes it necessary. To speak of a revolution creating a *de facto* government which conforms to the limitations of the old constitution is to use a contradiction in terms. " *A. J.,* 1924, p. 154. See below, p. 40.

3. See below, pp. 51-56.

4. See Larnaude, *Les gouvernements de fait,* RGDIP, 1921, pp. 472 473. Also Gemma, *Les gouvernements de fait,* p. 407.

4. State Practice, Judicial Decisions and Doctrine.

a) *State Practice.*

The rule that revolution does not affect State identity and continuity has been fully adhered to in State practice for an impressively long period of time. It was applied as far back as the English revolutions of 1649 and 1688, when the successive rulers of England fully respected international obligations incurred by their predecessors. This was equally so in the case of the restoration of the Stuarts in 1660 [1]. When, in 1793, the question arose as to the continued validity of treaties between the United States and revolutionary France, Jefferson declared that the treaties in question were not " between the United States and Louis Capet ", but " between the two nations of America and France ", and that " the nations remaining in existence, though both of them have since changed their forms of government, the treaties are not annulled by these changes " [2].

" The principle of continuity " — says Moore — " has important results. The State is bound by engagements entered into by governments that have ceased to exist ; the restored government is generally liable for the acts of the usurper. The government of Louis XVIII and Louis-Philippe so far as practicable indemnified the citizens of foreign States for losses caused by the government of Napoleon ; and the King of the Two Sicilies made compensation to citizens of the United States for the wrongful acts of Murat [3]. "

On May 28, 1827 Secretary of State Clay, wrote to the American Minister in Paris :

" The King of France, in reascending the throne of his ancestors, assumed the government with all the obligations, rights and duties which appertain to the French nation. He can justly claim absolution from none of those obligations and duties [4]. "

In 1877 Secretary of State Fish stated :

" A successful revolution does not relieve the country revolutionized from liability on its prior engagements to foreign States [5]. "

Such instances could easily be multiplied [6].
Nor was it only a claim on the part of third States. The rule was in general freely acknowledged by the States concerned themselves. Thus, in connection with American claims arising out of the seizure

---

1. Martens, *Traité de droit international*, I, pp. 363-364 ; Anzilotti, *op. cit.*, p. 178 ; Spiropoulos, *Die de facto-Regierung im Völkerrecht*, p. 65 ; Fauchille, *op. cit.*, I, pp. 340-343.
2. Moore, *Digest*, V, p. 336.
3. *Ibid.*, I, p. 249.
4. *Ibid.*, I, p. 250.
5. *Ibid.*, V, p. 337. Cf. the dispatch of the Secretary of State Bayard to the U.S. Minister in Peru, of September 23, 1886, *ibid.*, I, pp. 251-252.
6. See e.g. McNair, *Law of Treaties*, pp. 383-384 ; also comment to Art. 24 of the *Harvard Draft Convention on the Law of Treaties;* Fauchille, *op. cit.*, I, pp. 340-343 : McNair, *Aspects*, I, pp. 9-13 ; Verdross, *Verfassung*, p. 145.

and destruction of American ships by French naval squadrons during the continental blocade, the French Foreign Minister, the Duc de Broglie, declared in the Chamber of Deputies on March 31, 1834 :

« On faisait aussi valoir un autre argument odieux qui a été reproduit à cette tribune. C'était que le gouvernement légitime (Louis XVIII) n'était pas responsable des faits du gouvernement usurpateur (Napoléon 1er) ; qu'il fallait s'adresser à l'usurpateur, à ses ayants droit, que le gouvernement légitime ne devait rien. Messieurs, il faut le dire à l'honneur de la Restauration, jamais cet argument n'a été sérieusement employé... Devions-nous, comme le gouvernement de la Restauration l'avait fait ou plutôt avait tenté timidement de le faire, devions-nous invoquer l'irresponsabilité d'un gouvernement nouveau à l'égard des actes d'un gouvernement ancien ? Nous en aurions rougi. C'était un argument qui n'était pas digne de vous... »

In the course of the same debate, the deputy Sebastiani castigated those

« qui penseraient qu'il fallait dénier les créances anciennes, répudier la solidarité du gouvernement impérial, et le lendemain d'une révolution faite au nom du droit, établir au mépris de la morale des nations qu'un Etat pour se libérer de ses dettes n'a qu'à changer de souverain... [1] ».

Similarly, after the 1889 revolution in Brazil, the following telegram was sent by the new Brazilian Minister of Finance to the U.S. Secretary of State :

" Government is constituted in Republic of the United States of Brazil. Monarchy deposed ; imperial family left the country ; provinces adhere ; tranquility and general satisfaction ; ... Republic respects strictly all engagements and contracts entered upon by the State [2]. "

It was, however, in 1831 that the rule has received its best known formulation. The Powers, assembled in London to discuss the Belgian crisis, declared it to be

« le grand principe de droit public, dont les actes de la conférence de Londres n'ont fait qu'offrir une application salutaire et constante. ... D'après ce principe d'ordre supérieur, les Traités ne perdent pas leur puissance, quels que soient les changements qui interviennent dans l'organisation intérieure des peuples. ... Les Puissances devaient faire prévaloir la salutaire maxime, que les événements qui font naître en Europe un Etat nouveau, ne lui donnent pas plus le droit d'altérer le système général dans lequel il entre, que les changements survenus dans la condition d'un Etat ancien ne l'autorisent à se croire délié de ses engagements antérieurs. Maxime de tous les peuples civilisés ; — maxime qui se rattache au principe même d'après lequel les Etats survivent à leurs gouvernements, et les obligations imprescriptibles des Traités à ceux qui les contractent ; maxime enfin qu'on n'oublierait pas sans faire rétrograder la civilisation dont la morale et la foi publique sont heureusement et les premières conséquences et les premières garanties [3] ».

The principle was carried on into modern times. On May 20, 1919, Clemenceau replied as follows to a Note from the German delegation to the peace negotiations, which sought to evade German responsibility for the war :

1. Quoted by Larnaude, op. cit., p. 467.
2. Moore, op. cit., I, p. 252.
3. Protocole du 19 février 1831, Martens, N. R., X, pp. 197-199.

« Vous prétendez que le peuple allemand ne saurait être tenu pour solidaire des fautes commises par l'ancien gouvernement allemand. L'Allemagne cependant ne l'a jamais admis, et une pareille affirmation eut été contraire à tous les principes du droit international, qu'il pût suffire d'une modification de son régime politique ou d'une transformation de son personnel dirigeant pour dégager un peuple de toute responsabilité née de la guerre. Elle ne l'a reconnu ni en 1871 vis-à-vis de la France, après la proclamation de la République, ni en 1917 au regard de la Russie, lors de la révolution qui abolit le régime tsariste [1]. »

In a joint declaration of March 28, 1918, concerning the famous problem of the Russian debts, Great Britain and France stated that :

« ... aucun principe n'est mieux établi que celui d'après lequel une nation est responsable des actes de son gouvernement, sans qu'un changement d'autorité affecte les obligations encourues ; ces engagements ne peuvent être répudiés par aucune autorité, quelle qu'elle soit, sans quoi la base même du droit international se trouverait ébranlée [2]. »

Thus, it is taken so completely for granted that international obligations survive a change of regime that in the overwhelming majority of cases there are even no special treaty provisions to this effect. Such exceptions as there are merely confirm the rule, being themselves not only an expression of " superabundant caution ", but also of particular political circumstances. Thus, Art. 24 of the Convention between the United States and Panama for the construction of a ship canal, of November 18, 1903, reads :

" No change either in the Government or in the laws and treaties of the Republic of Panama shall, without the consent of the United States, affect any right of the United States under the present convention, or under any treaty stipulation betwenn the two countries that now exists or may hereafter exist touching the subject matter of this convention [3]. "

A contrary provision, again reflecting a particular political background, was included in the 1907 Convention for the Establishment of the Central American Court of Justice [4].

Certain deviations from this otherwise constant practice should, however, be noted. Some of them took place in Central and South America where attempts were made to contest the rule. None of them succeeded ; they were all emphatically rejected by international tribunals [5].

In Europe three historical occurences may be quoted in this connection : the attitude of the French Convention of 1793, that of the French revolutionary government of 1848 and, finally, the much discussed Soviet case. It may safely be stated that in none of these cases was there any outspoken denial of the continuity of the State concerned, — in other words, no denial of the sum total of its rights and obligations under international law. What was attempted was merely the repudiation of certain specific treaties and obligations and even that repudiation was never consistently carried through.

---

1. *La documentation internationale, La Paix de Versailles*, Paris, Les éditions internationales, 1930, vol. 12, p. 14.
2. Quoted by Fauchille, *op. cit.*, I, p. 342, *f.-n.* 2.
3. Martens, *N. R. G.* 2nd series, XXXI, p. 599.
4. Art. 27. Martens, *N. R. G.* 3rd series, III, p. 105.
5. See below, pp. 38-40.

In the first case, the French Convention, unlike the National Assembly of 1790 which considered itself bound by all obligations incurred by Louis XVI and his predecessors, loudly proclaimed its non-liability for the existing treaties [1]. However, it appears that the repudiation was chiefly declamatory in character [2] and that no official steps were taken to give practical effect to this view [3].

The case of the 1848 French Revolution and Lamartine's alleged rejection of the treaties of Vienna was even less dramatic [4]. In the first place, Lamartine's would-be repudiation was never intended to cover the whole of France's conventional obligations, but only the Vienna Treaties of 1815. Lamartine's circular note of March 4, 1848, was by no means a revolutionary step. It is true that it included a statement to the effect that in the view of the French Republic the 1815 treaties were no longer in existence. It would, however, appear that this was so mainly on account of their previous violation by other contracting parties ; in which case Lamartine's note should properly be regarded not as a denial of State continuity, but as a withdrawal from a convention consequent upon its violation by other contracting parties *(inadimplenti non est adimplendum)*. Even so the note contained conciliatory assurances ; it admitted that the Republic considered the existing state of affairs created by the treaties in question as the basis of her relations with other nations, and that certain modifications were to be sought by agreement. The case thus amounts to a mere attempt at revision. In any case, Lamartine's immediate successor as France's Foreign Minister, did not hesitate to invoke these same treaties which has been attacked, without being expressly repudiated, by Lamartine [5].

Finally, the most passionate discussion developed on the morrow of the First World War with regard to the Soviet refusal to recognize the debts of the Tsarist regime. It ought to be remembered, however, that the repudiation did not relate to debts alone, but equally affected other Soviet obligations and, significantly enough, rights. It is submitted that this repudiation, bearing as it did on *certain* Russian rights and obligations, was made under the *clausula rebus sic stantibus* and that, far from denying its identity with Tsarist Russia, Bolshevik Russia actually confirmed it. In view of the great confusion prevailing in the matter, it may be of value to analyze the question in some detail.

As regards debts, it is true that the Soviet decree of January 28, 1918, adopted an extreme attitude :

" All foreign loans are hereby annulled, without reserve or exception of any kind whatsoever [6]. "

---

1. Martens, *Traité*, I, p. 364. *Harvard Draft Convention*, p. 1050. See also the Soviet Note to the Genoa conference of May 11, 1922, in *Doc. dipl.*, p. 130.
2. « La souveraineté des peuples n'est point liée par les traités des tyrans. " Brissot, in the Convention, quoted by Martens, *op. cit.*, I, p. 150, *f.-n.* 1.
3. " ...no repudiation of treaties took place. " *Harvard Draft Convention, loc. cit.*
4. « Les traités de 1815 n'existent plus en droit aux yeux de la République française ; toutefois, les circonscriptions territoriales de ces traités sont un fait qu'elle admet comme base et comme point de départ dans les rapports avec les autres nations. » Quoted by Phillimore, *op. cit.*, I, p. 562.
5. See Bastid, *La révolution de 1848 et le droit international, Rec.* 1948, I, pp. 13-15.
6. Para. 3 ; quoted by Korovin, *Soviet Treaties and International Law, A. J.* 1928. p. 763.

This attitude was, however, soon to be abandoned. As early as 1918, when attempting to open negotiations with the Allies, Soviet statesmen let it be understood that they were prepared to settle the problem of debts in accordance with international law [1]. The Soviet answer of February 4, 1919, to the Allied invitation to the proposed conference to be held at Prinkipo, already contained a clear recognition of Russian indebtedness [2]. Offers of a settlement were repeatedly made [3], and, at one point, Tchitcherin adopted the attitude that the Russian debt towards France should, first of all, be reduced by 30%, which would be equivalent to the amount of territory lost by Russia [4]. Such a view unequivocally implied the conception of State continuity.

As from 1920, two further elements entered into the argument. The first concerned the possibility of making payment and Russia's economic needs, the second concerned Russian counter-claims. With regard to the first, Tchitcherin stated on October 28, 1921 :

« Le Gouvernement russe se déclare prêt à reconnaître les obligations à l'égard des autres Etats et de leurs citoyens découlant des emprunts d'Etat conclus par le Gouvernement tsariste jusqu'en 1914, sous réserve expresse qu'il soit fait des conditions spéciales et des facilités lui rendant possible la réalisation de cet engagement [5]. »

With regard to the second, Russian counter-claims, arising out of the Allied intervention in Russia, were first formulated on January 7, 1920, in Krassin's reply to the British Memorandum which laid down the conditions for agreement. According to that reply, Russian counter-claims fully covered the Russian debt. [6] The two arguments which were to be further and more fully developped at the Genoa Conference, represent a clear recognition by the Soviets of the principle of State continuity.

The formulation of the Soviet attitude at the Genoa Conference is of particular significance. The very first Russian document, Tchitcherin's letter to Lloyd George of April 20, 1922, left no doubt whatever as to the Russian recognition of the principle of the revolutionary regime's continued responsibility for the debts of its predecessor [7]. The Memorandum of the Russian Delegation of the same date, while emphatically affirming Soviet adherence to the principle " pacta sunt servanda ", declared :

« Si le Pouvoir des Soviets s'est refusé à reconnaître les engagements des gouvernements précédents ou à satisfaire les prétentions des personnes qui ont souffert de ses mesures de politique intérieure... ce n'est pas qu'il soit « incapable » ou « indésireux » de faire honneur à ses engagements, mais pour bien des raisons

---

1. Lagarde, La Reconnaissance des Soviets, p. 27.
2. Ibid., p. 36.
3. Ibid., p. 43.
4. Mirkine-Guetzevitch, La doctrine soviétique du droit international, RGDIP, 1925, p. 324.
5. Lagarde, op. cit., p. 114.
6. Ibid., p. 84.
7. « La délégation russe persiste à penser que la situation économique actuelle de la Russie et les circonstances qui l'ont déterminée, devraient justifier amplement, pour la Russie, sa libération totale, par la reconnaissance de ses contre-réclamations, de toutes ses obligations visées dans les propositions susmentionnées. » Doc. dipl., p. 60.

de principe ou pour des motifs de nécessité politique. — La révolution de 1917, par le fait même qu'elle détruisait de fond en comble l'ancien état de choses politique, social et économique, pour mettre à sa place une organisation toute différente de la société, et qu'elle faisait passer le pouvoir entre les mains de couches sociales nouvelles, *interrompait la continuité des engagements civils* faisant partie intég-ante du régime économique de la société disparue, et ces engagements tombèrent en déchéance en même temps que cette société même. ... Cette révolution fut un cataclysme grandiose tel que le monde n'en a connu qu'à des moments exceptionnels de son histoire et son caractère de *force majeure* ne peut être discuté par aucun homme d'Etat objectif [1]. »

There can hardly be any doubt that what is denied here is not the continuity of the Russian State, nor the continuity of the sum total of its rights and obligations, but merely the continuity of civil obligations forming an integral part of the former economic system. Such discontinuity is directly related to the character of " force majeure ", attributed to the Russian Revolution. The argument is merely based on the *Clausula rebus sic stantibus*, and not on a denial of State continuity [2]. On the contrary, a clear claim to State continuity was made by the Russian Memorandum in the following forceful passage :

« La Délégation russe ... est obligée d'écarter de la façon la plus catégorique toute invitation à payer ces dettes, comme une tentative inadmissible pour charger la Russie ruinée d'une portion considérable des dépenses de guerre des Puissances alliées. Ce qu'on appelle les dettes de guerre de la Russie représente en réalité le matériel de guerre fabriqué par les usines alliées et envoyé sur le front russe pour assurer le succès des armées alliées. Le peuple russe a sacrifié à la cause commune des Alliés plus de vies que tous les autres ensemble ; il a subi des pertes matérielles colossales et le résultat de cette guerre a été pour lui la perte de territoires immenses, d'importance primordiale pour son développement. Et c'est alors que les autres Alliés ont obtenu de par les Traités de paix des augmentations énormes de territoire et de grosses contributions, que l'on voudrait faire payer au peuple russe les frais d'une opération qui a été si lucrative pour d'autres [3]. »

The meaning of this passage is unmistakable : the Russian Delegation spoke on behalf of that same Russian State which had gone to war alongside the Allies, of that same Russian people which had shouldered sacrifices for the common Allied cause, of that same State which had lost vast territories and suffered heavy losses, whereas the other Allies had acquired considerable gains. It was this same State which — in the name not of law, but of justice — refused to pay the bill.

Again, the Russian Memorandum, submitted by Rakowski to the Committee of Experts on April 24, 1922, contained the following statements :

« Le Gouvernement de Russie se déclare prêt à payer les obligations financières du ci-devant Gouvernement impérial de Russie, contractées avant le 1er août 1914, envers des Puissances étrangères et leurs ressortissants. ..... Le Gouvernement de Russie reconnaît tous les engagements des entreprises d'utilité publique garantis en son temps par le ci-devant Gouvernement impérial [4]. »

---

1. *It. mine; ibid.*, p. 64.
2. The same view of the Russian repudiation of Tsarist debts is strongly maintained by Taracouzio, *The Soviet Union and International Law*, New York, MacMillan Co. 1935, pp. 249-250.
3. *Doc. dipl.*, p. 67.
4. *Ibid.*, p. 78.

As against these clear and definite formulations of the Russian attitude, undue weight should not be attached to the one and only Russian statement to the contrary [1]. It would rather seem that this statement, entirely inconsistent with the whole trend of the Russian argument, was produced for purely tactical reasons towards the end of the Conference which was to end in failure.

So much for the Russian repudiation of debts. It should, however, be recalled that there were other Russian acts of repudiation, which never gave rise to so much discussion or acquired the same degree of notoriety, probably because they did not affect such widespread economic interests. The best example is the unilateral Russian repudiation of a number of Tsarist treaties providing for the partitions of Poland [2]. It is quite clear that the very acts of expressly repudiating certain treaties presupposes the identity of the repudiating party. It is obviously unthinkable that a State should take the trouble of declaring void treaties to which it never was a party and with which it is in no way concerned.

That there was, however, no all-round repudiation of old Russian treaties, and that such repudiation as there was was made exclusively under the heading of the *Clausula* and not of the non-identity of Bolshevist with Tsarist Russia, is made perfectly clear by additional documents bearing on the question.

Thus, the British Note of February 1, 1924, extending *de iure* recognition to the Soviet Government brought up the question of existing treaties and stated :

" H.M. Government are advised that the recognition of the Soviet Government of Russia will, according to the accepted principles of international law, automatically bring into force all the treaties concluded between the two countries previous to the Russian Revolution, except where these have been denounced or have otherwise juridically lapsed. It is obviously to the advantage of both countries that the position in regard to these treaties should be regularized simultaneously with recognition [3]. "

Without in any way objecting to the thesis of Russian continuity, as expressed in the British Note, the Soviet reply of February 8, 1924, declared :

" ... my Government is prepared to arrive at an understanding with the British Government to replace those former treaties which have either been denounced or have lost their juridical force as a result of events during or after the war [4]. "

---

1. « ...la Délégation russe est obligée de rapporter ce principe de droit que les révolutions, qui sont une rupture violente avec le passé, apportent avec elles de nouveaux rapports juridiques dans les relations extérieures et intérieures des Etats. Les gouvernements et les régimes sortis de la révolution ne sont pas tenus à respecter les obligations des gouvernements déchus. » Soviet reply to Allied proposals of May 11, 1922 ; *ibid.*, p. 130.

2. See below, p. 418. See also the Russo-Persian Treaty of February 26, 1921, particularly Articles 1, 2, 8 and 9 ; Martens, *N. R. G.*, 3rd series, XIII, p. 173 ; also the Russo-Turkish Treaty of March 16, 1921, particularly Articles 6 and 7 ; *ibid.*, XVI, p. 37.

3. *Survey of International Affairs*, 1924, by A. J. Toynbee, Oxford University Press, London : Humphrey Milford. Under the Auspices of the British Institute of International Affairs, 1926, p. 491.

4. *Ibid.*, p. 492.

The following Russian declaration to the Institut Intermédiaire International of April 2, 1924, finally dispels any doubt which may still remain as to the Soviet attitude :

« La rupture extraordinairement prolongée des relations politiques avec tous les Etats du monde, qui suivit la révolution de 1917, et les changements survenus entretemps dans l'ensemble de tous les engagements internationaux ne permettraient certainement pas une reconstitution pure et simple des traités des anciens gouvernements russes. Peu d'entre eux pourraient, en effet, être mis en exécution sans qu'il s'ensuivit une collision avec le règlement ultérieur des mêmes questions qui survint après 1917 sans la participation de l'une des parties engagées dans ces traités... C'est donc une question à résoudre dans chaque cas séparé... *Une abrogation générale de tous les traités conclus par la Russie sous l'ancien régime et sous le gouvernement provisoire n'eût jamais lieu.* Mais il ne s'ensuit pas que tous les traités soient susceptibles d'être reconfirmés, et *il y aurait lieu d'examiner cette question du point de vue de la clause rebus sic stantibus pour chaque Etat et chaque traité séparément* [1]. »

The inescapable conclusion which emerges from the above analysis is that, whatever changes Bolshevik Russia attempted to introduce in her existing rights and obligations, were conceived exclusively under the heading of the *Clausula rebus sic stantibus* and never under the heading of non-identity. On the contrary, the identity and continuity of Bolshevik and Tsarist Russia was clearly asserted and acted upon by the Soviet Government both expressly and impliedly [2]. It need hardly be added that logically the *Clausula* can only be invoked on the assumption of the identity of the subject of the original obligation and the subject which invokes it. A different subject neither needs, nor can, have recourse to it. Consequently, whatever view is taken regarding the Russian repudiation of particular international rights and obligations, a closer examination of the problem leaves no room for the current fallacy, according to which Soviet Russia denied the basic principle of State continuity in the case of revolution.

The above examination has shown that the rule under consideration has been uniformly and consistently applied in State practice.

b) *Judicial Decisions.*

The first important international decision to be mentioned is the Award of July 7, 1901, of the Franco-Chilean Arbitral Tribunal. The relevant facts of this complex case are as follows : a French bank, Dreyfus Frères & Co., had substantial claims against Peru, arising out of prolonged and large-scale business dealings with that country. In 1879, during Peru's war with Chile, the constitutional governement of Peru was replaced by the revolutionary and dictatorial regime of

---

1. *It mine;* quoted by Makarov, *Der Sowjetrussisch-finnische Konflikt, Ztscht.f.a. öff.R.u.V.-r.,* 1940-41, p. 319.
2. It is interesting to compare the Russian attitude with that of the Austrian Republic after the First World War : not once in the Russian case is there the categorical denial of State continuity and the emphatic assertion of the " new character " of the State which is to be found in every Austrian note, speech or declaration. Unlike the Russian Memorandum of April 20, 1922, Austria never spoke of lost territories, but of territories she had never possessed. There was no repudiation of the Polish partition treaties, since — according to the Austrian view — the new Austria was never a party to these treaties, etc., etc. See below, pp. 218-219.

President Pierola. It was to him that the French bank appealed for a settlement of its claims, submitting in advance to his decision. Acting on the basis of exceptional powers, Pierola decided the issue of the French claims on July 30, 1880, leaving a balance in favour of the claimants. However, on Pierola's fall, the restored constitutional government of Peru, had an Act passed by the Peruvian Congress, on October 25, 1886. It consisted of a single Article :

« Sont déclarés nuls tous les actes du gouvernement intérieurs pratiqués par don Nicolas de Pierola et don Miguel Iglesias... »

In the meantime, Chile occupied and subsequently annexed, by the Treaty of Ancon of 1883, certain portions of the Peruvian territory, at the same time undertaking to take over a corresponding part of Peru's public debt [1]. This is how the first *Dreyfus* case came to be arbitrated between France and Chile.

In denying the validity of the French claims, the Peruvian Government took its stand on the nullity of the acts of the revolutionary Government, as proclaimed by the Peruvian Congress, and generally on a repudiation of the obligations of that government. Dismissing the Peruvian contention, the Arbitral Tribunal declared :

« Attendu que d'après un principe du droit des gens, d'abord nié théoriquement dans un intérêt dynastique par la diplomatie des monarchies européennes, appliqué cependant en fait dans une série de cas, aujourd'hui universellement admis, la capacité d'un gouvernement pour représenter l'Etat dans les relations internationales ne dépend à aucun degré de la légitimité de son origine ; en sorte que les Etats étrangers ne se refusent plus à la reconnaissance des gouvernements *de facto*, et que l'usurpateur qui détient le pouvoir avec l'assentiment exprès ou tacite de la nation agit et conclut valablement au nom de l'Etat des traités, que le gouvernement légitime restauré est tenu de respecter [2]. ... Qu'ainsi les principes du droit public général qui consacrent la validité des actes d'un gouvernement, même usurpateur et révolutionnaire, quand ce gouvernement a fait preuve de vitalité, et exercé en fait le pouvoir à l'exclusion de tout autre gouvernement trouvent leur entière application en l'espèce ; d'où il suit que la reconnaissance de dette souscrite le 1er décembre 1880 par le Gouvernement de Nicolas de Pierola doit être considérée comme valablement consentie par le représentant légal de l'Etat péruvien à l'époque, et comme obligatoire pour le Pérou ...[3] »

The remaining claims of the Dreyfus Co. against Peru were later submitted for arbitration to the Permanent Court of Arbitration at The Hague. The Award, rendered on October 11, 1921, allowed the French claim, declaring *inter alia :*

" Whereas Nicolas de Pierola was proclaimed supreme chief of the Republic by popular assemblies and maintained by numerous plebiscitary adhesions ; whereas, he exercised the legislative power, the executive power and, in part, the judicial power ; whereas on June 28, 1881, he voluntarily resigned these functions but was immediately invested with the presidency of the Republic by the National Assembly ; whereas, his government was recognized especially by France, England, Germany and Belgium ; whereas, finally, the High Court of Justice of England (decree of February 23, 1888), the Court of Appeals of Brussels (decree of July 10, 1888),

---

1. Descamps-Renault, *op. cit.*, pp. 190-191.
2. *Ibid.*, p. 394.
3. *Ibid.*, p. 398.

the Franco-Chilean Arbitral Court (award called Award of Lausanne of July 5, 1901), being decrees and an award of which the arbitral court adopts the reasons, have deemed that this government represented and bound the nation [1]... "

A similar situation formed the background of the *Tinoco* case, arbitrated by W.H. Taft on October 18, 1923. In 1917, the Costa-Rican Government was overthrown by the then War Minister, Tinoco. This revolutionary government established a new constitution, maintained itself in power for over two years and in turn fell in 1919, whereupon the former constitution and a constitutional government was restored. On August 22nd, the restored Congress passed the so-called Law of Nullities, declaring null and void the acts of the Tinoco Government. Since the Law affected, *inter alia*, the claims of British corporations, Great Britain and Costa Rica agreed to submit the dispute to arbitration. The arbitrator fully confirmed the principle of the State continuity resulting in the responsibility of the restored government for the acts of the usurper government.

" The issue is not whether the new government assumes power or conducts its administration under constitutional limitations established by the people during the incumbency of the government it has overthrown. The question is, has it really established itself in such a way that all within its influence recognize its control, and that there is no opposing force assuming to be a government in its place [2]."

In the *Ottoman Debt Arbitration*, April 4, 1925, Prof. Borel held, that notwithstanding both the territorial losses and the revolution

" in international law, the Turkish Republic was deemed to continue the international personality of the former Turkish Empire [3] ".

On March 31, 1926, the U.S.-Mexican General Claims Commission decided the claim of an American national, George W. Hopkins, who had purchased postal money orders in Mexico, then under the administration of the revolutionary Huerta Government. The restored constitutional government of Mexico issued decrees of nullity on February 19, 1913 and July 11, 1916 and sought to repudiate its responsibility for the acts of the Huerta administration. In adjudicating the American claim, the Commission said :

" ... how far can an administration which seizes the reins of government by force and is illegal in its inception bind the nation ?... As long as the Huerta regime was in fact the master in the administration of the affairs of the Government of Mexico, its illegal origin did not defeat the binding force of its executive acts [4]. ... the Commission concludes that Hopkins' contracts are unaffected by the legality or illegality of the Huerta administration as such, that they bind the Government of Mexico [5]... "

---

1. Scott, *The Hague Court Reports*, 2nd Ser., p. 36. See on the case : Ruzé, *France et Pérou, RGDIP*, 1922, pp. 256-283. Also comment by Spiropoulos, *op. cit.*, pp. 97-98, *f.-n.* 50. Gemma, *op. cit.*, pp. 357-362. For the view of the U.S. Government, see Moore, *op. cit.*, I, pp. 251-252.
2. *A.J.*, 1924, p. 154.
3. *A.D.*, 1925/26, case no. 57.
4. *A.J.*, 1927, pp. 164-165.
5. *Ibid.*, p. 166.

The principle which is unanimously and categorically affirmed by all international judicial decisions on the subject, is upheld with equal consistency in municipal decisions of all countries. The fact that they correctly express an established rule of international law was confirmed by the Permanent Court of Arbitration which, in the case of the French claims against Peru, did not hesitate to invoke the two decisions to that effect by the English High Court of Justice and the Belgian Court of Appeals [1].

The leading municipal decision on the subject is undoubtedly *The Sapphire*. In December 1867, following a collision between the French vessel Euryale and the American ship Sapphire, action was brought before an American court against the Sapphire in the name of Napoleon III, as owner of the Euryale. The case reached the Supreme Court of the United States as late as February 16, 1871, i.e. after the overthrow of the Second Empire. One of the questions to be decided was whether the suit had not become abated by the deposition of the Emperor. The Supreme Court answered :

" We think it has not. ... Napoleon was the owner of the Euryale, not as an individual, but as sovereign of France. ... On his deposition the sovereignty does not change, but merely the person or persons in whom it resides. ... The reigning Emperor, or National Assembly, or other actual person or party in power, is but the agent and representative of national sovereignty. A change in such representative works no change in the national sovereignty or its rights [2]. "

Ever since the *Sapphire* case there has been practically no deviation from the principle in any municipal decision in any country. Thus, in the *Agency of Canadian Car and Foundry Co. Ltd. v. American Can Co.*, the District Court of New York declared on August 5, 1918 :

" Since the notable precedent of the Sapphire... the principle is firmly established in our courts that the rights and liabilities of a State are unaffected by a change either in the form or personnel of its government, however accomplished, whether by revolution or otherwise. No other doctrine is thinkable, at least among nations which have any conception of international honour. "

On appeal, the Circuit Court of Appeals held on April 21, 1919 :

" The principle of law is well established that the rights and liabilities of a State are not affected by a change in the form of the personnel of a government, no matter how that change may be effected. The obligations of a State, the debts due to and from it, are not affected by any transformation in the internal organization of its government [3]. "

In the *Russian Roubles Case*, the Supreme Court of Japan held in 1919 :

" It is of no consequence that Russia internally has been undergoing a political change. The primary consideration is that she has not thereby ceased to exist internationally, as a State [4]. "

---

1. See above, pp. 39-40.
2. Scott, *Cases on International Law*, p. 77.
3. *A.D.*, 1919/22, case no. 14.
4. *Ibid.*, case no. 15.

In the *Russian Government v. Lehigh Valley Railroad Co.*, the District Court of New York stated on October 2, 1923 :

"The real party in interest is the State of Russia, and that Russia, the State, still lives and is a continuing entity in the contemplation of the law, is true [1]..."

Similarly, the Civil Tribunal of Cairo, in the case *Golovitschiner v. Dori*, affirmed on December 24, 1923, that

"Russia, not having been conquered or annexed by a foreign State, has kept her existence as a distinct State [2]..."

Affirming the continued validity of the Hague Convention on Civil Procedure of July 17, 1905, as between Holland and Russia, the District Court of Amsterdam stated on June 7, 1932, in the case *Lowinsky v. Receiver in Bankruptcy of the Egyptisch-Türkische Handwerkzigaretten-fabrik " Jaka " Ltd.* :

"In conformity with an established principle of public international law, changes in the form of government of a State have no influence on its rights and obligations under the Law of Nations so long as its existence as a State and, therefore, as an international person, remains unimpaired. This is the case with the U.S.S.R., which has to be looked upon as a sovereign federal State embracing by far the greater part of the territory and the population of the former Russian Empire [3]."

An identical attitude was adopted by the Cantonal Court of The Hague on July 6, 1931 in the case *N. and M. Shipoff v. Elte* [4], and again by the Swiss Federal Court *in re Lepeschkin* on February 2, 1923, when it was stated that

"It is a generally recognized principle of international law that changes in the Government and organisation of a State have no effect on its international rights and duties [5]..."

On November 28, 1932, in the case of *Lazard Brothers and Co. v. Midland Bank Ltd.*, the House of Lords spoke of

"... the territorial jurisdiction of what was up to 1917 the Russian Empire but is now the Union of Soviet Republics. This internal change in the system of government, once the new Government is recognized by this country, has no effect on the external status of Russia quoad this country as a personality in International Law. The identity of the State remains the same for international purposes : the change from monarchy to republic does not, in general, abrogate treaties or conventions, any more than loss or increase in territory [6]."

Against this impressive background of unanimity in municipal decisions, no undue weight should be attached to a solitary decision to the contrary by the District Court of Amsterdam of May 27, 1937, in case *C.J.H. v. D.V.P.*, which runs counter not only to international decisions, but also to the uniform trend in municipal decisions, including the earlier decisions of the Dutch courts themselves [7].

1. *A.D..*, 1923/24, case no. 20.
2. *Ibid.*, case no. 24.
3. *A.D.*, 1931/32, case no. 16.
4. *Ibid.*, case no. 17.
5. *A.D.*, 1923/24, case no. 189.
6. *A.D.*, 1931/32, case no. 69.
7. *A.D.*, 1935/37, case no. 16.

c) *Doctrine.*

In view of such consistency of both State practice and judicial decisions, it is not surprising to find the same unanimity among writers.

It is true that the authority of Aristotle could be invoked to the contrary. But in the first place, it may be questioned whether Aristotle can be considered a writer on international law, and secondly, it may be observed that precisely with regard to obligations of a State he did not draw any categorical conclusions from his view of the discontinuity of a State following a change of its constitution. On the contrary, he seems rather to have been in favour of such obligations being honoured [1].

This caution on the part of Aristotle has been rightly emphasized by Grotius [2] who, as it behoves the " father " of modern international law, was the first clearly to formulate the rule in a famous passage :

" Neque refert quomodo gubernatur, regione, an plurium, an multitudinis imperio. Idem est enim populus Romanus sub regibus, consulibus, imperatoribus [3]. "

The formula was taken by Bynkershoek, quoting Grotius :

" Forma regiminis mutata, non mutatur ipse populus ; eadem utique Republica est, quamvis nunc hoc nunc alio modo regatur ; alioquin diceres, Rempublicam in statu, quo nunc est, exsolutam videri pactis et debitis [4]. "

It was upheld by Puffendorf :

" Ex iisdem quoque potest colligi foedera quæ populus aliquis, in quo summa potestas est penes plures uno, init, esse realia uti vocant, seu continuo durare, etiamsi personæ Rempublicam administrantes fuerint mutatæ ; quippe cum, uti iam dictum, quamvis personæ mutantur una semper eademque præsentium et præsentibus succedentium civitas censeatur [5]. »

and by Vattel :

« Puis donc qu'un pareil Traité regarde directement le Corps de l'Etat ; il subsiste quoique la forme de la République vienne à changer, quand même elle se transformeroit en Monarchie. Car l'Etat et la Nation sont toujours les mêmes quelque changement qui se fasse dans la forme du Gouvernement ; et le Traité fait avec la Nation demeure en force, tant que la Nation subsiste [6]. »

Laid down by the founders of international law, the rule has been consistently upheld to this day [7].

---

1. " It is quite another question, whether a State ought or ought not to fulfil engagements when the form of government changes. " *Op. cit.*, 1276 b.
2. *Op. cit.*, II, IX, VIII, 2.
3. *Ibid.*, II, IX, VIII, 1. Cf. II, XVI, XVI, 1.
4. *Quaestionum Iuris Publici Libri Duo*, The Classics of International Law, edited by J. Brown Scott, Oxford, At the Clarendon Press, London : Humphrey Milford, 1930, II, XXV, 1.
5. *Elementorum Iurisprudentiae Universalis Libri Duo*, The Classics of International Law, edited by J. Brown, Scott I, 31. Cf. *ibid.*, p. 32.
6. *Droit des Gens*, 2, chap. XII, pp. 392-393. Cf. pp. 396-397.
7. « Les modifications survenues dans la forme du gouvernement... n'influent en rien sur la situation internationale de l'Etat. Le régime change, la nation ne change pas. » Rivier, *op. cit.*, I, p. 62. « ...les transformations qu'il (l'Etat) subit ne changent en rien sa position juridique, ses droits et ses devoirs envers les autres Etats. » Martens, *op. cit.*, I, p. 362. " Changes in the government or the internal policy of a State do not as a rule affect its position in international law. A monarchy may be transformed into a republic

Against this impressive background of rare consensus among writers, only few discordant voices can be noted. Thus Merkl insists that the rule discussed, far from implying the identity and continuity of a State following a revolution, only implies universal succession [1]. The argument is as artificial as it is unnecessary. For, international law, as has been seen, does not know universal succession [2]. In any case, while taking refuge in the notion of a non-existent universal succession Merkl automatically admits the identity of rights and obligations of a State before and after a revolution, thus confirming the general rule in spite of himself [3].

Finally, it is generally believed that the Soviet doctrine of international law adopted the conception of a revolution breaking the legal continuity of the State. It is submitted that this view is just as erroneous as the one concerning the alleged denial of State continuity by the Soviet State [4]. The truth is that following Soviet practice, Soviet writers

---

or a republic into a monarchy; absolute principles may be substituted for constitutional, or the reverse, but, though the government changes, the nation remains with rights and obligations unimpaired. " Moore, *Digest*, I, p. 249. " France, for instance, has retained her personal identity from the time the Law of Nations came into existence until the present day, although she acquired, lost and regained parts of her territory, changed her dynasty, was a kingdom, a republic, an empire, again a kingdom, again a republic, again an empire, and is now, finally as it seems, a republic. All her international rights and duties as an International Person remained the very same throughout the centuries in spite of these important changes in her condition and appearance. " Oppenheim-Lauterpacht, *op. cit.*, I, pp. 148-149. " Veränderungen in der Regierungsform eines Staates haben keinen Einfluss auf seine völkerrechtlichen Berechtigungen und Verpflichtungen, es sei denn, dass sie den Bestand des Staates an der Wurzel treffen und damit über die blosse innerstaatliche Wirkung hinausgreifen. " Liszt, *op. cit.*, p. 92. Cf. p. 275. « Les changements constitutionnels, qu'ils soient pacifiques ou qu'ils soient révolutionnaires, n'exercent pas d'influence sur les obligations internationales de l'Etat. » Anzilotti, *op. cit.*, p.178. " Es ist ein unbestrittener Völkerrechtssatz, dass die Identität der Staatspersönlichkeit auch durch revolutionäre Verfassungsänderung nicht berührt wird, und dass daher die völkerrechtlichem Verpflichtungen mit der Identität des Pflichtsubjektes grundsätzlich bestehen bleiben... " Kelsen, *Souveränität*, p. 238. Cf. Fauchille, *op. cit.*, I, p. 338, Verdross, *Verfassung*, pp. 17 and 145; Spiropoulos, *op. cit.*, p. 63; Lauterpacht, *op. cit.*, p. 111; Guggenheim, *op. cit.*, I, p. 199.

1. " Jedenfalls ist die Tatsache, dass... das Völkerrecht alle völkerrechtlichen Rechte und Pflichten nach wie vor der Verfassungsänderung « bestehen » lässt, nicht als positivrechtlicher Beweis für die Staatidentität zu werten, denn diese Rechte und Pflichten können ebensowohl auch infolge positivrechtlicher Uebertragung gelten, das Rechtssubjekt also gewechselt haben ". *Op. cit.*, p. 514. " Die Völkerrechtslehre behauptet bekanntlich einen Völkerrechtssatz des ungefähren Inhaltes, dass der Bestand des Staates auch bei revolutionärer Aenderung seiner Verfassung unberührt bleibe. Dieser und mancher ähnlicher Wortlaut ist aber m.E. eine falsche Formulierung eines ähnlichen, aber doch notwendig anders lautenden Volkerrechtssatzes. Der falsch ausgedrückte Völkerrechtssatz besagt in Wirklichkeit, dass gewisse Berechtigungen und Verpflichtungen des revolutionär dethronisierten Kompetenzträgers auf den revolutionär inthronisierten Kompetenzträger übergehen ". *Ibid.*, p. 524. " Inhaltsgleichheit von Berechtigungen und Verpflichtungen bedingt durchaus nicht Identität der dieser Art verknüpften Rechtssubjekte. " *Ibid.*, p. 525.

2. See above, pp. 10-13.

3. The opinion of M. Burdeau who confuses the material extent of the revolution with its legal essence — just as he confuses the continuity of States with their immortality — does not seem to call for a lengthy comment. See above p. 6, *f.-n.* 2 and p. 26 *f.-n.* 3. According to this writer — who even goes to the length of distinguishing between „ major " and „ minor " revolutions — there is discontinuity of a State following a revolution because the latter has introduced a new « idée de droit ». M. Burdeau does not enlighten the reader either as to the contents of this « idée de droit », or how it is to be handled as a useful criterion of the legal status of a State.

4. See above, pp. 34-38.

have insisted upon far-reaching modifications in the rights and obligations of a post-revolutionary State under the heading of the *Clausula rebus sic stantibus* [1].

5. THEORETICAL FOUNDATIONS.

Like the rule relating to territorial changes, the one safeguarding the continuity of States in case of revolutions, requires an adequate theoretical explanation. A number of explanations have been put forward.

a) *Existing Theories : Jellinek, Carré de Malberg, Anzilotti, Kelsen, Verdross, Scelle.*

According to Jellinek, the continued identity of a State in case of both territorial and revolutionary changes can be explained only by the theory of association (Verbandstheorie). The existence of an association does not depend either upon the number of its members or upon the extent of its power. A change in its constitution is reflected in its form, but not in its essence. The association therefore remains identical as long as its elements continue in being and its purposes continue to be generally fulfilled [2].

Carré de Malberg explains the continuity of States despite constitutional changes by the notion of the personality of the State. This personality is superior to, and distinct from, all elements of the State

---

1. See e.g. Korovin, the leading Soviet authority on international law : " The train of argument adopted by the Soviets is somewhat as follows : Every international agreement is the expression of an established social order, with a certain balance of collective interests. So long as this social order endures, such treaties as remain in force, following the principle *pacta sunt servanda*, must be scrupulously observed. But if in the storm of a social cataclysm one class replaces the other at the helm of the State, for the purpose of reorganizing not only economic ties but the governing principles of internal and external politics, the old agreements, in so far as they reflect the preexisting order of things, destroyed by the revolution, become null and void. To demand of a people at last freed of the yoke of centuries the payment of debts contracted by their oppressors for the purpose of holding them in slavery would be contrary to those elementary principles of equity which are due all nations in their relations with each other. *Thus in this sense the Soviet Doctrine appears to be an extension of the principle of rebus sic stantibus, while at the same time limiting its field of application by a single circumstance — the social revolution.* " Soviet Treaties and International Law, under the heading " The Rebus sic stantibus Clause ", *A.J.*, 1928, p. 763. — Korovin is even more outspoken in his earlier work, *Das Völkerrecht der Uebergangszeit*, where he declares : " Die verantwortlichen Politiker Europas vermieden es in der Regel von der Anerkennung Sowjetrusslands als Staat zu sprechen, denn *man braucht nicht qualifizierter Jurist zu sein, um zu begreifen, dass « der russische Staat » nicht erst seit 1917 existiert* und dass er von Niemandem eine neue, faktische oder juristische Anerkennung seiner Existenz braucht ". *It. mine*, p .18.
2. " Die herrschende völkerrechtliche Lehre erklärt, dass weder tiefgreifende Verfassungswechsel und Revolutionen, noch Vergrösserungen und Verkleinerungen des Staatsgebietes und damit des Staatsvolkes die Identität des Staates stören. Dieser allgemein anerkannte Satz ist aber nur möglich vom Standpunkt der Verbandstheorie aus. Eine Verbandseinheit ist unabhängig von der Zahl ihrer Mitglieder und der Ausdehnung ihres Herrschaftsbereiches. Ein Wechsel in seiner Verfassung ändert die Form, aber nicht das Wesen des Verbandes. Eine Verbandseinheit bleibt vielmehr dieselbe, so lange die Verbandselemente in ununterbrochener zeitlicher Kontinuität stehen und die konkreten Verbandszwecke wenigstens zum grössten Teil ununterbrochen besorgt werden ". *Op. cit.*, pp. 273-274.

considered separately. It cannot be identified with any of them. This is why a change in one of the elements is unable to affect the State as such [1].

Anzilotti relies on the unchanging material elements of the State, i.e. territory and population, which, according to him, international law takes as a basis of the identity of a post-revolutionary State [2].

Kelsen equally relies on the material elements of the State to explain the rule [3]. However, unwilling to draw a normative conclusion from mere facts, he no longer regards them as " material elements " but as the content of an international norm. Instead of admitting the law-creating force of facts, he prefers to speak of facts acquiring a normative character [4].

Verdross in turn supplies a totally different explanation of the phenomenon. Starting from his latest identification of State with its population, he affirms the identity of a State following a revolution on the basis of the identity of that population [5].

---

1. « Il résulte de là que le concept de l'être juridique Etat doit se déterminer en dehors de toute considération relative à la forme du gouvernement national ou à la personne des gouvernants. Les formes de gouvernement sont des modalités qui affectent la constitution politique de l'Etat, mais non son essence ; elles peuvent varier sans que les caractères, la capacité ou l'identité de la personne étatique s'en trouvent modifiés. La notion d'Etat est donc supérieure à celle de gouvernement. L'Etat, c'est la collectivité organisée, mais ce n'est point l'organisation de cette collectivité. A plus forte raison, l'observation des faits juridiques relatifs à l'immutabilité de l'Etat implique-t-elle condamnation de la doctrine qui confond l'Etat avec les personnages détenant le pouvoir étatique ; ceux-ci sont les porteurs de la puissance de l'Etat, ils n'incarnent point l'Etat en eux. Enfin, et par les mêmes motifs, l'Etat ne saurait être identifié avec le peuple envisagé comme somme des individus qu'il renferme à un moment donné ». Op. cit., p. 49.

2. « Le principe repose manifestement sur la continuité de fait de l'élément matériel de l'Etat : la population établie sur le territoire dont il s'agit. Sur cette base de fait, le droit international affirme la continuité de la personnalité de l'Etat, nonobstant les interruptions éventuelles qu'un mouvement révolutionnaire peut déterminer dans l'ordre juridique interne... » Op. cit., p. 179.

3. ,, Es ist die faktische Kontinuität der den Inhalt der staatlichen Rechtsordnung bildenden, auf einem und demselben Gebiete ansässigen Menschen, die das Völkerrecht als entscheidendes Kriterium für die Identität der Staatsperson aufgenommen hat. Und dieses Moment der Faktizität wird auch sonst in der Sphäre des Völkerrechts zu einem Rechtsprinzip. " Souveränität, p. 238.

4. ,, ...eine Metamorphose des Faktischen zum Normativen... " op. cit., p. 241. Cf. Allg. Staatslehre, p. 249. In his latest work, General Theory of Law and State, Kelsen seems to have modified his earlier views : he now explains the continuity of the post-revolutionary State simply by the identity of its territory, p. 220. See above, pp. 21-22. Contrary to his earlier views, there is no longer a mention of the material elements being merely the content of an international norm, and the population is taken into account only indirectly. It is believed that his earlier theory as expressed in Souveränität is both more interesting and more representative of Kelsenian thought.

5. " Ein Staat im Sinne des VR ist also nicht der blosse Staatsapparat, sondern das staatlich organisierte Volk. Es ist daher auch unrichtig, den Staat im Sinne des VR als eine wirksame « Rechtsordnung » zu definieren (Kelsen, Guggenheim). Eine solche Identifikation ist schon deshalb abzulehnen, da die Begriffe Rechtsordnung und Rechtsgemeinschaft zwar korrelativ, aber nicht identisch sind. Jene ist eine Ordnung von Normen für eine bestimmte Gruppe von Menschen, diese hingegen eine Gruppe von Menschen, die durch diese Normen verbunden sind. Dazu kommt, dass ein Staat im Sinne des VR auch Staatsstreiche, Revolutionen und Verfassungsbrüche überdauern kann. Daher kann ein Staat im Sinne des VR nicht durch seine Rechtsordnung, sondern einzig und allein durch seine Materie, nämlich das konkrete, ihn bildende Volk bestimmt werden. " Völkerrecht, p. 79. " Wir haben schon früher darauf hingewiessen, dass ein Staat im Sinne des VR nicht bloss aus dem Staatsapparat, sondern aus dem staatlich organisierten Volk besteht. Daher geht ein Staat weder durch eine Revolution noch durch einen Staatsstreich unter ". Ibid., p. 161. Cf. pp. 68 and 92. See also Die Identität der Staaten, p. 19.

Scelle, who rejects the " classical and anthropomorphic " doctrine of State personality, sees the problem rather from the point of view of international law than from that of the State concerned. To him the continuity of a State despite a revolution simply means that local changes of government are powerless to modify the relations of subordination existing between the international and the internal order. What is relevant therefore is not so much the continuity of the State concerned as the permanence of the general contexture of the international legal order [1].

b) *Critical Examination of these Theories.*

Each of these theories gives rise to certain doubts.

Jellinek's views are hardly convincing from the strictly legal point of view. An association, in the legal sense, cannot be conceived separately from a legal order which alone makes a legal association out of a non-descript human agregate. In this sense an association is precisely a notion of form and not of substance. When it is said that the form changes, but not the substance, then the explanation becomes meta-juridical, since there is no way of defining this substance. The same applies to the " purposes " of the association, which, being inevitably vague, are incapable of supplying a criterion of State continuity [2].

Nor does Carré de Malberg's theory seem entirely satisfactory. It is perfectly correct to reject the identification of the State with any one of its elements. What would happen, however, if all these elements were to undergo a simultaneous change? What would then still remain as the " essence " of the State? What seems to be lacking in Carré de Malberg's theory is an explanation of the actual relation of the State to these elements or of these elements to each other.

With regard to Anzilotti, his theory appears *prima facie* to be the most obvious, natural and simple one. However, from a purely theoretical point of view it may be wondered whether the explanation of normative phenomena by way of mere facts is adequate.

It is this logical error which Kelsen attempts to correct, although his conception of facts acquiring a normative character seems an intellectual *tour de force*, performed for the sake of logical perfection. But, moreover, Kelsen's view is difficult to reconcile with his whole system, based as it is on the assumption of a complete identity of State and law. For, if State and law are really identical, how is it to be explained that mere territory and population — even if considered as the content of a superior norm — suddenly become the basis and criterion of State existence, while the legal order which admittedly *was* the State, had crumbled away? Thus, Kelsen's view is contradicted by

---

1. « La technique juridique récente préfère constater que de nouvelles investitures gouvernementales locales *ne peuvent évidemment modifier les rapports de subordination qui existent entre l'ordre jurdique international et l'ordre juridique étatique.* Il s'agit donc bien moins de continuité de l'Etat que de *permanence* de *l'ordonnancement juridique international dans lequel il se trouve englobé* ». *Op. cit.,* p. 130.

2. Cf. Kelsen's criticism of the " Verbandstheorie ", *Souveränität,* pp. 237-238.

Kelsen himself [1], while the opposite view, disclaiming the continuity of the post-revolutionary State on the assumption of identity of State and law is far more consistent [2].

Thus, in the light of no uncertain rule of positive international law a complete and exclusive identity of State and law must be denied in the same way and for the same reason as a complete and exclusive identity between State and territory had to be denied in the light of an equally certain positive rule [3].

Just as Kelsen goes to the extreme in identifying State and law, so does Verdross in identifying State and population. Population is supposed to yield the criterion of the identity of the pre-revolutionary with the post-revolutionary State. It should, however, be observed that the view of Verdross represents a *petitio principii* : for he does not speak simply of the *population* as being identical with the State, but of a State population or a population organized within the State (" Staatsvolk " or " staatlich organisiertes Volk "). Such a formulation, however, presupposes the existence, or the continued existence, of the State whose very existence or continuity are to be proved. For there can obviously be no State population without a State. Secondly, population cannot possibly be regarded as identical with the State and, consequently, cannot supply the criterion of its continuity. Like territory, population also can form the substratum of different States. Moreover, can it be seriously asserted that there would be State identity in case of the population not only effecting a revolution but also settling on an entirely new territory under an entirely new, revolutionary legal order ? The example is perhaps less fantastic than might appear at first sight. After all, the famous " Great Trek " of 1836, resulted in the revolutionary creation by the Boer population of two new States, the Transvaal and the Orange Free State, neither of which could ever be considered identical with the Cape Colony. Admittedly, only a part of the population emigrated. Yet, it seems legitimate to invoke this example in order to show the impossibility of a continued State identity in the case of a

---

1. " Der Verband wird erst konstituiert durch die Ordnung; Volk und Gebiet sind Inhaltselemente, *und bei Verschiedenheit der Ordnung liegt eine Verschiedenheit des Verbandes vor, selbst wenn Volk und Gebiet dasselbe bleiben*, während bei Identität der Ordnung die Identität des Verbandes auch dann gewahrt bleibt, wenn Volk und Gebiet sich ändern ". *It. mine. Souveränität*, p. 238.

2. Thus Merkl, who rightly maintains that if State and law are identical then " ist es selbstverständlich, dass der Staat das Schicksal des Rechtes teilt". *Op. cit.*, p. 521. " Unter der Voraussetzung eines mit dem Rechtsbegriff identischen, aber selbst schon mit dem Rechtsbegriff korrespondierenden Staatsbegriffes bedeutet der Bruch der Rechtsordnung das Heraustreten aus dem einen Staate, die Preisgabe der Staatseinheit. Die revolutionäre Staatsänderung ist eine extreme Staatsänderung ; von einer internen Staatsänderung könnte in diesem Fall nur unter Voraussetzung eines vom Rechtsbegriffe grundsätzlich losgelösten Staatsbegriffes die Rede sein ". *Op. cit.*, p. 525. Thus according to Merkl, a revolution irrevocably destroys the State and several States in the legal sense correspond to one and the same State in the historical sense.

3. See above, pp. 21-22. It may asked whether the following statement by Kelsen was not intended to suggest at least a certain modification of his rigid and absolute views concerning the identity of State and law : « Car la nature de l'Etat fait que, *s'il n'est pas lui-même un ordre juridique*, il ne peut exister sans ordre juridique. Même si l'on distingue entre l'Etat et l'ordre juridique, on doit généralement reconnaître qu'il faut, pour qu'une collectivité puisse être considérée comme un Etat, qu'elle soit dotée d'un ordre juridique ». *It. mine. Naissance de l'Etat*, p. 614.

simultaneous and complete change in both legal order and territory [1]. Finally, it has been abundantly proved [2] that loss of territory and, hence, population, does not affect the identity of the State. This positive rule is another proof of the impossibility of an identification of State and population. Thus, the theory of identity of State and population has proved to be untenable.

Scelle's theory of the permanence of the all-round contexture (" ordonnancement ") of the international legal order seems to overlook the fact that this " ordonnancement " is not at all unable to withstand even fundamental changes within the inferior internal orders, including their very extinction. It thus does not therefore explain State survival in case of revolution, nor why in other cases States do become extinct. It is not made at all clear why the international legal order should accept State extinction in other cases and refuse do so in the case of revolution.

c) *The Foundation proposed.*

It would thus appear that none of the theories put forward is entirely satisfactory. Yet, the phenomenon calls for an explanation, particularly as it has been seen that it is closely connected with the question of the essence of the State and the question of the international legal order itself.

Most of these theories, however, place their reliance on the so-called " material elements " of the State. This approach provides a correct, realistic and indeed, unavoidable basis for maintaining the continuity of a State which has undergone a revolutionary change. It has been seen, however, that these " material elements " can be relied on in widely different ways. It must be accepted with Kelsen that the identity and continuity of the revolutionary State represents a norm of international law, since the birth, extinction and transformation of a legal order can admittedly be pronounced only by a higher legal order. The question remains : why should international law proclaim the identity and continuity of a State which has undergone a revolution ?

The argument, it is submitted, must start from the basic assumption that the international community consists of a number of States, whose legal, personal and territorial sphere of validity are delimited from each other by international law. No State can exist, or continue to exist, without such delimitation ; nor, for that matter, can international law, based as it is on the co-existence of separate States [3].

---

1. Cf. also the speech of William of Orange to the States General of 1672 : « Les Hollandais pourraient survivre à la Hollande si la Hollande était engloutie par la mer ; la liberté et la pure religion, chassées d'Europe par les tyrans... trouveraient un asile dans les îles lointaines de l'Océan Pacifique ; les navires hollandais seraient en état d'y porter 200.000 émigrés ; la république hollandaise y pourrait recommencer une existence nouvelle et plus glorieuse encore, et sous la Croix du Sud, au sein d'une végétation plus belle, créer la Bourse d'un Amsterdam plus riche et les écoles d'un Leyde plus savant. » Quoted by Rivier, *op. cit.*, p. 65, who rightly comments : « Cet Etat magique, grandiose et radieuse vision d'un prince magnanime, politique de premier ordre, n'aurait pas été la Hollande ancienne, mais une Hollande nouvelle, fondée par la population émigrée. »
2. See above, pp. 15-24.
3. See below, pp. 162-163.

There can be no doubt that it is the legal order of a State which is decisive for its separate existence. It will be seen that this priority of the legal order over territory and population is duly taken into account in the process of the final delimitation of a State, that is, in the process of its birth [1]. This principle of the priority of the legal order remains equally valid for the case of a change in the territory and, consequently, the population of a State. It has been seen that in such a case it is precisely the continuing legal order which provides the basis of the State continuity.

If, however, that legal order breaks down in an already existing, i.e. fully delimited State, its territorial and personal delimitation under international law remains. If international law, in spite of such breakdown, yet recognizes the continuity of the State concerned, this is precisely because that delimitation remains unaffected. It is true that the basic norm of the revolutionary State has been replaced by a new basic norm, with no internal legal connection between the two ; but the old basic norm has not been replaced by the basic norm of any other State. The territorial and personal delimitation of the State concerned remaining in principle unchanged, the new basic. norm has been produced from within the same international. delimitation as the old one, and is valid for the same international delimitation. The international order has not been upset ; the status of the international community remains the same.

In this sense indeed the " material elements ", relied on, in one way or another, by most writers, assume the character of supporting elements. The principle of international delimitation of the State has been upheld. It is only the order of priority of such delimitation which has been reversed. The continuing, unchanged delimitation of the two " material " spheres of validity has temporarily taken precedence over the legal order and has upheld and safeguarded both the continuity of the State concerned and the existing international system. The latter continues unchanged and unaffected : the internal change within a State has been confined within its borders. It is thus, in this case at least, not necessarily international law's capitulation before facts which lies at the basis of its recognition of the continuity of the revolutionary State [2], but its acceptance of an event which in no way interferes with its existing organisation. This organisation being in no way affected, international law has no reason to proclaim the discontinuity of the State [3].

Thus in place of theories identifying the State either with its territory, its population, or its legal order, a different conclusion emerges from an examination of positive international law, namely : the organic

---

1. See below, p. 163.
2. See Kelsen, *Souveränität*, p. 241.
3. It is believed that the answer to the question which has been asked in connection with Scelle's thesis is to be found precisely in this view : the « permanence de l'ordonnancement juridique international » is by far not absolute enough to disregard effective changes in the « ordonnancement », such as annexations of States, mergers, etc. But in the case of a revolution precisely no effective changes in the « ordonnancement » have taken place, and this is why international law can disregard them.

interdependence — not a mechanical juxtaposition — of the particular elements forming the complex phenomenon of State [1]. For, while it is undoubtedly true that it is the legal order which endows a human aggregate and a sector of the earth's surface with the qualification of State population and State territory, it is no less true that this same legal order in turn requires a territory and a population for its validity and effectiveness, — that is, for its existence. It is therefore natural and logical that, if an event occurs which could throw doubt on the continued existence of a State by reason of one of these elements being impaired, international law relies on the remaining ones to maintain the continuity of the State concerned.

6. Legality of Revolution under International Law.

a) *Attempts to outlaw Revolution.*

In the light of the foregoing analysis there can be no doubt that international law does not prohibit revolutions [2]. This remains the position in spite of several attemps to the contrary. Of these, the best known was undertaken by the Holy Alliance on behalf of monarchical legitimacy, at a time when the customary rule under consideration had already been fully established since the 17th century. Thus, the doctrine of the Holy Alliance ran counter to both positive international law of the period and historical realities.

i) *Monarchical Legitimacy.*

This doctrine was fully revealed not in the original declaration of September 14 (26), 1815, proclaiming the constitution of the Holy Alliance but in the Protocol of the Troppau Conference of October 1820, which stated unequivocally :

"States which have undergone a change of government due to revolution, the results of which threaten other States, *ipso facto* cease to be members of the European alliance, and remain excluded from it until their situation gives guarantees for legal order and stability. If owing to such alterations, immediate danger threatens other States, *the Powers bind themselves, by peaceful means, or if need be by arms, to bring the guilty State into the bosom of the Great Alliance* [3]."

This first international document on the subject reveals at one stroke the necessary, indeed, automatic connection between any attempt at an international prohibition of revolution on the one hand, and intervention on the other [4], — a problem which will have to be examined more closely [5].

---

1. «...étroite connexité des éléments de l'Etat, collectivité, territoire et organisation gouvernementale ». Scelle, *op. cit.*, p. 91.
2. See Lauterpacht, *op. cit.*, p. 92.
3. *It. mine*, quoted by Sir Charles Petrie, *Diplomatic History*, 1713-1933, London, Hollis and Carter Ltd., 1946, p. 133.
4. " There is good reason for extending the traditional notion of intervention (as meaning dictorial interference, in relation to an existing and unchallenged government, with its external or internal freedom of action) to cover interference with the right of a nation to determine its political regime. " Lauterpacht, *op. cit.*, p. 233, *f.-n.* 4.
5. See below, pp. 54-56.

It was in the following terms that the Powers of the Holy Alliance announced their decision to implement their doctrine in the concrete case of the Napolitan revolution :

« Les puissances ont exercé un droit incontestable en s'occupant de prendre en commun des mesures de sûreté contre des Etats dans lesquels le renversement du gouvernement opéré par la révolte, ne dût-il être considéré que comme un exemple dangereux, devait avoir pour suite une attitude hostile contre toutes les constitutions et les gouvernements légitimes [1]. »

It was left to Castlereagh to formulate the correct position under international law in his circular of January 19, 1821, expressing the fundamental difference of principle between the policy of Great Britain and her war-time Allies :

« Le système des mesures proposé ... seroit, s'il étoit l'objet d'une réciprocité d'action, diamétralement opposé aux lois fondamentales de la Grande Bretagne. Mais lors même que cette objection décisive n'existeroit pas, le gouvernement britannique n'en jugeroit pas moins que les principes qui servent de base à ces mesures, ne peuvent être admis avec quelque sûreté comme système des lois entre les nations. Le gouvernement du Roi pense que l'adoption de ces principes sanctionneroit inévitablement et pourroit amener par la suite de la part de souverains moins bienveillants une intervention dans les affaires intérieures des Etats, beaucoup plus fréquente et plus étendue que celle, dont il est persuadé que les augustes personnages ont l'intention d'user, ou qui puisse se concilier avec l'intérêt général, ou avec l'autorité réelle et la dignité des souverains indépendants. Le gouvernement de Sa Majesté ne croit pas que d'après les traités existants les alliés aient le droit d'assurer aucuns pouvoirs généraux de cette espèce, et il ne croit pas davantage qu'ils puissent s'arroger des pouvoirs aussi extraordinaires en vertu d'aucune nouvelle transaction diplomatique entre les cours alliées, sans s'attribuer une suprématie incompatible avec les droits d'autres Etats ou même, en acquérant ces pouvoirs du consentement spécial des dits Etats, sans introduire en Europe un système fédératif, oppresseur, et qui non seulement seroit inefficace dans son objet, mais encore pourroit avoir les plus graves inconvénients.

... il doit être clairement entendu, qu'aucun gouvernement ne peut être plus disposé que le gouvernement britannique à maintenir le droit de tout Etat ou Etats, à intervenir, lorsque sa sûreté immédiate ou ses intérêts essentiels seront sérieusement compromis par les transactions domestiques d'un autre Etat ; mais comme le gouvernement du Roi pense que l'usage d'un tel droit ne peut être justifié que par la nécessité la plus absolue d'après laquelle il doit être réglé et limité, le dit gouvernement ne peut admettre que ce droit puisse recevoir une application générale et sans distinction à tous les mouvements révolutionnaires, sans avoir égard à leur influence immédiate sur quelque Etat ou Etats particuliers, où l'on puisse en faire en perspective la base d'une alliance. Le gouvernement de S. M. considère ce droit comme une exception de la plus haute importance aux principes généraux, exception qui ne peut résulter que des circonstances du cas spécial ; mais il considère que des exceptions de cette nature ne peuvent jamais sans le plus grand danger, être réduites en règle de manière à être incorporées dans la diplomatie ordinaire des Etats ou dans les instituts de la loi des nations [2]. »

Nothing could be more emphatic or more correct. Castlereagh's circular firmly puts forward and defends the three following propositions : 1) intervention is prohibited by international law ; 2) it is only permissible in exceptional circumstances when the immediate interests of the intervening State are directly affected by domestic changes of the revolutionary State ; 3) the latter being an exception, it may only be resorted to within extremely strict limits.

---

1. Martens, N. R., V, p. 593. Cf. documents published at the occasion of the Laibach Conference, on May 12, 1821, ibid., pp. 638-646.
2. Ibid., pp. 596-598.

The doctrine of the Holy Alliance ended in failure, as it was bound to, notwithstanding the few attempts to implement it. (Spain, Piedmont, Naples.) The striking confession of this failure is to be found in the London Protocol of 1831 [1], bearing the signature of the very same Powers who had only recently constituted the Holy Alliance. For it is abundantly clear that by proclaiming the duty of revolutionary States to continue to fulfil their obligations, the Concert of Europe again reverted to the principle of recognition of revolution by international law. Thus ended the attempt to introduce the notion of monarchical legitimacy into international law, and hardly a more devastating judgment could have been passed on it than that of Bismarck, himself certainly no friend of revolutions [2].

ii) *Democratic Legality.*

Modern times have witnessed the replacement of the old and discarded notion of legitimacy by the new and democratic notion of legality [3]. The development took place chiefly on the American continent, owing to the particular political conditions prevailing in

---

1. See above, p. 32.

2. " Einer der hauptsächlichsten Gründe der Abneigung, auf welche nähere Verbindung mit dem heutigen-Frankreich bei uns stösst, liegt in der Auffassung, dass der Kaiser Napoleon der hauptsächliche Repräsentant der Revolution und mit ihr identisch sei, und dass ein Kompromiss mit der Revolution ebensowenig in der äussern wie in der innern Politik zulässig sei. In den auswärtigen Beziehungen ist es nicht möglich, den letzteren Grundsatz in der Weise durchzuführen, dass die äussersten, davon abgeleiteten Konsequenzen noch immer jede andere Rücksicht durchbrechen sollen, und ausserdem ist es nicht richtig die Revolution gerade in dem gegenwärtigen Kaiser der Franzosen ausschliesslich zu verkörpern. Die nächste Anleitung dazu gibt die ins Auge fallende Illegimität des Ursprunges seiner Herrschaft. Aber wieviel Existenzen gibt es in der heutigen politischen Welt, welche mit voller Kontinuität im Rechte wurzeln. Spanien, Portugal, Brasilien, alle amerikanischen Republiken, Belgien, Holland, die Schweiz, Griechenland, Schweden, das noch heute mit Bewusstsein in der Revolution von 1688 fussende England können ihre dermaligen Rechtszustände auf keinen legitimen Ursprung zurückführen. Selbst für das Terrain, welches die deutschen Fürsten teils Kaiser und Reich, teils ihren Mitständen, den Standesherren, teils ihren Landständen abgewonnen haben, lässt sich kein vollständig legitimer Besitztitel nachweisen...

Die meisten der oben berührten Zustände sind eingealtert, wir haben uns an sie gewohnt und deshalb ihre revolutionäre Geburt vergessen. Aber auch dann, wenn sie noch nicht diesen Grad von Verjährung hatten, stiess man sich früher nicht an ihrer revolutionären Natur. Cromwell wurde von den europäischen Potentaten « Herr Bruder » genannt und seine Freundschaft gesucht, wenn sie nutzlich erschien. Mit den Generalstaaten waren die ehrbarsten Fürsten im Bündniss, bevor sie von Spanien anerkannt wurden. Wilhelm von Oranien und seine Nachfolger in England hatten, auch während die Stuarts noch prätendierten, nichts an sich, was unsere Vorfahren von den intimsten Beziehungen mit ihnen abgehalten hätte ; den Vereinigten Staaten haben wir schon in dem Haager Vertrage von 1785 ihren revolutionären Ursprung verziehen. In neuster Zeit hat unser Hof den Besuch des Königs von Portugal empfangen, und mit dem Hause Bernadotte hätten wir uns verschwägert, wären nicht zufällige Hindernisse eingetreten.

Wann und nach welchen Kennzeichen haben alle diese Mächte aufgehört, revolutionär zu sein ? Es scheint, dass man ihnen die illegitime Geburt verzeiht, sobald wir keine Gefahr von ihnen besorgen, und dass man sich alsdann auch nicht prinzipiell daran stösst, wenn sie fortfahren, ohne Busse, ja mit Rühmen sich zu ihrer Wurzel im Unrecht zu bekennen.

Es scheint nicht, dass vor der französischen Revolution ein Staatsmann auf den Gedanken gekommen ist, die Beziehungen seines Landes zu andern Staaten lediglich dem Bedürfnis unterzuordnen, von Berührungen mit revolutionären Erscheinungen frei zu bleiben..." Bismarck's Denkschrift für M. v. Manteuffel, June 2nd, 1857. *Fontes*, Series B, Sectio I, Tomus I, Pars 1, pp. 160-161. For earlier historical examples, see Gemma, *op. cit.*, pp. 338-339.

3. Larnaude, *op. cit.*, p. 469 ; Spiropoulos, *op. cit.*, pp. 42-43 ; Sharp, *Non-Recognition*, pp. 34-36.

Central and South America, as well as to the interest of the United States in the political stability of the Western Hemisphere [1]. The principle of legality was proclaimed in the famous Tobar Doctrine of 1907 in the following words :

" The American Republics, for their reputation and credit, if not for other considerations of humanity and altruism, should *intervene* indirectly in the internal discussions of the Republics of the continent. The *intervention* should consist at least in the refusal to recognize *de facto* governments, issuing from revolutions against the Constitution [2]. "

It is clear that, whether the interest protected is monarchical legitimacy or democratic legality, any attempt to prohibit revolution under international law automatically becomes synonymous with intervention.

The American continent was the only region where an anti-revolutionary and interventionist doctrine was embodied in conventional obligations. Both the Central American Convention of 1907 and the Central American Treaty of 1923 pronounced an anathema against revolutionary governments and imposed a duty of their non-recognition on the contracting parties. Both were concluded in Washington, under the auspices of the United States, itself not a party. The preponderant influence of the latter on the developments under discussion cannot be overestimated. For, although Tobar was the first to formulate the new doctrine, it was no doubt Wilson's " constitutionalism " [3], proclaimed in 1913 and put into practice over a number of years, which was of decisive influence in this connection. It would appear that Central American Governments came into power or ended in failure, according to whether they met with the support or the opposition of the United States, who, moreover, seems to have reserved a wide measure of freedom with regard to the interpretation and application of the said conventions, which it could always invoke without being bound by them.

It is only natural that a reaction should have set in under the heading of a struggle for the independence of States and against intervention. In 1930 Estrada formulated his doctrine, constituting a challenge to, and a repudiation of, the Tobar doctrine [4]. In 1928, at the Conference of American States in Habana, the prohibition of intervention was officially moved. The matter was temporarily adjourned, but the Montevideo Conference of the American States of 1933 was soon to adopt the Convention on Rights and Duties of States, Art. 8 of which read :

" No State has the right to intervene in the internal or external affairs of another. "

The United States adhered to the Convention, though with reservations. As for the 1923 Treaty, it was denounced by Costa Rica and Salvador,

1. Sharp, *op. cit.*, p. 38.
2. *It. mine*, quoted by Sharp, *op. cit.*, p. 35.
3. See Hackworth, *Digest of International Law*, I, p. 181.
4. See Sharp, *op. cit.*, pp. 61-62.

while remaining in force between Nicaragua, Guatemala and Honduras. The 1934 Conference of Central American States did not change that situation [1].

The doctrine and practice of non-recognition of revolutionary governments, including Wilsonian constitutionalism, has been subjected to outspoken criticism as being incompatible with the principles of international law [2]. It was emphatically repudiated by Chief Justice Taft in the *Tinoco* arbitration :

" Such a treaty could not affect the rights of subjects of a government not a signatory thereto, *or amend or change* the rules of international law in the matter of *de facto* governments [3]. "

It is therefore not surprising that the doctrine in general and Wilson's constitutionalism in particular could prevail against general international law and political realities just as little as the Holy Alliance. In 1930 the United States recognized revolutionary Governments in Argentina, Peru and Bolivia, on the sole basis of their effectiveness. The revolutionary Government of Brazil was recognized on the assurance of free elections which never materialized [4]. In 1931 the abandonment of Wilsonian doctrine by the United States was officially proclaimed by Secretary Stimson [5]. In 1935 there followed the recognition of the revolutionary Government of Ecuador [6]. In 1948 the United States signed the " anti-legitimist " Resolution No. 35 of Bogota, on the basis of which it acted when recognizing the revolutionary government of General Odria in Peru in November of the same year [7].

iii) *Failure of such Attempts ; State Independence ; Intervention.*

As has already been seen [8], any anti-revolutionary doctrine in international law must necessarily founder on the problem of intervention, without which no such doctrine is thinkable. But intervention

1. For a comprehensive survey of the American developments, see Sharp, *op. cit.*, pp. 34-66.
2. « Nous pensons... qu'on ne doit voir dans cette déclaration (Wilson's) qu'un conseil politique, qu'un Etat puissant et qui jouit d'un très grand crédit peut se permettre de donner à d'autres. Quant au traité entre les cinq républiques, il a la valeur d'un droit particulier pour les Etats qui l'ont signé, mais pour eux seulement. » Gemma, *op. cit.*, p. 336. Similarly Spiropulos : " Von der Wissenschaft wird diese Doktrin folgerichtig einhellig abgelehnt ; nur in der Praxis ist es ihr gelungen in zwei Vereinbarungen der zentralamerikanischen Staaten der Jahre 1907 und 1923 einen Niederschlag zu finden. Aber derartige Abmachungen vermögen nur die kontrahierenden Staaten zu binden, darüber hinaus fehlt ihnen jede Berechtigung ". *Op. cit.*, pp. 43-44. Even more violently does Spiropoulos criticize Wilson's constitutionalism which " sich zu den Grundlagen der modernen Völkerrechtswissenschaft in Widerspruch setzt. ...praktisch-politisch stellt sich die Wilsonsche Forderung der Legalität... als reine Erpressung dar ". *Ibid.*, p. 46. Cf. Larnaude, *op. cit.*, pp. 498-499 ; Williams, *La doctrine de la reconnaissance en droit international et ses développements récents*, pp. 248-251 ; Kunz, *op. cit.*, pp. 150-151.
3. *It. mine*, A.J., 1924, p. 155.
4. Lauterpacht, *op. cit.*, pp. 131-133.
5. " The present administration has refused to follow the policy of Mr. Wilson and has followed consistently the former practice of this Government since the days of Jefferson ". Hackworth, *op. cit.*, I, p. 185.
6. Lauterpacht, *loc. cit.*
7. Chen, *International Law of Recognition*, p. 116.
8. See above, pp. 54-55.

being unequivocally prohibited by international law, there is no legal possibility of suppressing revolution by what is unquestionably an unlawful act [1].

This being the position, even a refusal to recognize a government on account of its revolutionary origin might border on illegal intervention and thus be contrary to positive international law [2].

On the contrary, the right of States to select their own form of government by whatever means they choose has again and again been proclaimed [3]. Legality, whether democratic or otherwise, is still not protected by positive international law whereas independence of States is. As things stand to-day, the prohibition of intervention is fully valid and without it, the duty of the revolutionary Government to honour the obligations of the State would be as unjust as it would be illogical.

b) *Right to Revolution.*

If the above is accepted, and if the theory of a legal vacuum ("rechtsleerer Raum") is rejected, then it follows that, by not prohibiting and even by protecting the revolution against outside intervention, international law positively allows it [4], in other words, that revolution is a legal phenomenon under international law [5].

It is this right to revolution, conceived not in a social or political sense, but as the content of an international norm which finds expression in Jefferson's letters to the American Minister in Paris :

" It accords with our principles to acknowledge any Government to be rightful which is formed by the will of the nation, substantially declared [6]. " " We surely can not deny to any nation that right whereon our own Government is founded

---

1. " That intervention is, as a rule, forbidden by the Law of Nations which protects the international personality of the States, there is no doubt. " Oppenheim-Lauterpacht, *op. cit.*, I, p. 272. " ...no intervention, apart from interventions taking place under a treaty giving such a right to the intervening State, can be strictly legal, except one which is directed against a State which, either by commission or omision, is guilty of an international wrong. " Brierly, *The Law of Nations*, p. 268. For a recent authoritative pronouncement see *Corfu Channel Case*, Judgment of April 9th, 1949, *I.C.J.* Reports 1949 : " The Court can only regard the alleged right of intervention as the manifestation of a policy of force, such as has, in the past, given rise to most serious abuses and such as cannot, whatever be the present defects in international organisation, find a place in international law." p. 35.

2. « ...un refus (to recognize a revolutionary government) fondé sur la prétendue illégitimité du changement impliquerait un jugement qu'aucun Etat n'est autorisé à porter et constituerait une intervention illicite dans les affaires intérieures de cet Etat.» Anzilotti, *op. cit.*, p. 179. Cf. Gemma, *op. cit.*, p. 334, and Larnaude, *op. cit.*, p. 497. This is the real meaning of the Estrada doctrine which refuses to pass any judgment of that kind. See comment by Williams, *op. cit.*, p. 245.

3. See e.g. point 1 of the famous conditions of Cannes of January 1922 : « Les nations ne peuvent pas revendiquer le droit de se dicter mutuellement les principes suivant lesquels elles entendent organiser à l'intérieur leur régime de propriété, leur économie et leur gouvernement. Il appartient à chaque pays de choisir pour lui-même le principe qu'il préfère à cet égard. » *Doc. dipl.*, p. 15. The principle proclaimed carries particular weight when it is remembered that it marks the final abandonnent by the Western Powers of the policy of intervention with regard to the Russian Revolution.

4. Scelle, *op. cit.*, p. 128.

5. The rejection of the theory of legal vacuum makes it impossible to admit the formulation by Lauterpacht : " ...so far as international law is concerned, the legality or otherwise of the revolution is a mater of indifference. ". *Op. cit.*, p. 92.

6. Letter of November 7, 1792 ; quoted by Moore, *op. cit.*, I, p. 120.

— that everyone might govern itself according to whatever form it pleases, and change these forms at its own will and *that it may transact business with foreign nations through whatever organ it thinks proper*, whether king, convention, assembly, committee, president or anything else it may choose ...[1] "

In 1923, Secretary Hughes did not hesitate to state expressly :

" We recognize the right of revolution [2]... "

The conception of a right to revolution is confirmed by international judicial decisions. Thus, the arbitrator in the *Tinoco* case declared :

" To hold that a government which establishes itself and maintains a peaceful administration, with the acquiescence of the people for a substantial period of time, does not become a *de facto* government unless it conforms to a previous constitution, would be to hold that within the rules of international law a revolution contrary to the fundamental law of the existing government cannot establish a new government. This cannot be, and is not, true [3]. "

This right to, and respect of, the revolution was fully recognized by the Covenant of the League of Nations, Art. 10 of which expressly guaranteed the territorial integrity and the political independence of the League Members against external aggression only. It is clear that there was no such guarantee against internal revolution [4].

Nor has the right to revolution remained unacknowledged by writers, either implicitly [5] or explicitly [6].

It should also be mentioned that the legality of revolution under international law results indirectly from the recognition of insurgents and belligerents. This is only logical : for if international law recognizes the final result of revolution in the form of revolutionary government and State continuity, it must necessarily recognize the means leading to that result [7].

c) *Prohibition of Intervention and the Principle of Effectiveness.*

The legality of revolution under international law having thus been established, it is necessary to find the explanation of this fact. It is perfectly correct to reject all explanations based on private law analogies,

---

1. *It. mine.* Letter of March 12th, 1793, *ibid.*
2. Hackworth, *op. cit.*, I, p. 177.
3. *A.J.*, 1924, p. 154.
4. Thus Schücking and Wehberg : " Garantiert sind die Unversehrtheit des Gebietes und die politische Unabhängigkeit nicht schlechthin, sondern nur gegen Angriffe « von aussen ». ...Wenn irgendwo eine Revolution ausbricht, oder sich ein Teil des Staates für unabhängig erklärt, so mischt sich der Völkerbund in solche Fragen nicht ein... " *Die Satzung des Völkerbunds*, p. 461. See also the Additional Protocol to the Montevideo Convention, Hudson, *International Legislation*, VI, p. 626.
5. See above, p. 56, *f.-n.* 1.
6. " ...the right of rebellion which, in terms of international law, is the right of every nation to choose its own form of government. " Chen, *op. cit.*, p. 336. As against all this evidence of the international right to revolution, no particular value is to be attached to the decision of the District Court of New York of 1885, in the case of *Ambrose Light:* " International law has no place for rebellion... " Hudson, M.O. *Cases and other Materials on International Law*, St Paul West Publishing Co, 1929, p. 694. This opinion is just as isolated as it is incorrect.
7." ...a certain degree of force and consistency acquired by any mass of population engaged in war entitles that population to be treated as belligerent. " Canning on the Greek war of independence ; quoted by Lauterpacht, *op. cit.*, p. 188.

such as prescription in favour of the revolutionary government, presumption of abdication on the part of the deposed government, *negotiorum gestio*, etc. etc. [1]. As has been submitted, continuity of States is a problem of international law [2], and it is impossible to admit that international law should provide no autonomous explanation of it. Nor is it possible to accept a strongly sociological explanation according to which the State being the organisation of the community, running its public services, simply must continue, in spite of revolution [3]. There is no such necessity. The State can equally well become extinct and the organisation of the community can be wholly or partly taken over by some other State entity or entities.

It is submitted that international law furnishes its own explanation, both negative and positive. With regard to the former : as has already been indicated, the undoubted principle of State independence and the resulting prohibition of intervention definitely exclude any possibility of outlawing an internal revolution. The two propositions are mutually exclusive, and as long as State independence is protected by international law, the right to revolution stands [4].

With regard to the latter : it is the principle of effectiveness which, constitutes an overriding principle of international law. It has been formulated — with all the ruthlessness involved — by Secretary of State Fish in 1877 in the following words :

" The origin and organization of government are questions generally of internal discussion and decision. Foreign powers deal with the existing *de facto* government, when sufficiently established to give reasonable assurance of its permanence, and of the acquiescence of those who constitute the State in its ability to maintain itself, and to discharge its internal duties and its external obligations. If the government which a people have placed in power, or have consented to its exercise of power, misbehave and violate or transcend their limited functions, it is the misfortune of those who have placed it in power or consented to its elevation and to its discharge of public trusts. Its misconduct should not be visited upon individuals who honestly enter into engagements with its official representatives. To admit this would destroy all security in such contracts or engagements and would necessarily destroy the credit of the State, while working grievious injustice to those who may be furnishing the very means for the conduct of the affairs of the government [5]. "

Even more ruthless is the formulation by Spiropoulos :

---

1. Larnaude, *op. cit.*, pp. 486-498 ; Gemma, *op. cit.*, pp. 309-313.
2. See above, p. 3.
3. Larnaude, *op. cit.*, pp. 490-491, starting from the unfortunate idea of a " perennity " of States.
4. " ...the liberty incident to every Independant State of adopting whatever form of government, whatever political and civil institutions and whatever rulers she may please, without the interference or control of any foreign Power. This elementary proposition of international law is so unquestionable that it would be superfluous to cite authorities in support of it. " Phillimore, *op. cit.*, I, p. 318. " It is the essence of the notion of independence of States that changes in the structure or in the composition of their governments are, in international law as at present constituted, an internal question of the States concerned and that foreign States are not, in general, entitled to interfere in the matter by raising the question of recognition or by refusing to grant it. " Lauterpacht, *op. cit.*, p. 91. The connection between State independence and recognition of belligerents and insurgents is particularly emphasized by Lauterpacht, *op. cit.*, pp. 228-230. See also, pp. 87 and 91.
5. Moore, *op. cit.*, I, p. 250.

" The manner in which the *de facto* government maintains itself in power — whether it be through terror or by peaceful means — is irrelevant from the point of view of international law .[1] "

It may also be noted that the principle of effectiveness is forcefully emphasized in all the judicial decisions quoted, as the basis of the legality of revolutionary governments [2]. The principle of effectiveness is not all-powerful in international law, and certainly not in the primitive sense which is sometimes being advocated. In the long run, however, it has everything — including common sense — to commend it. As a rule, negotiations can only be conducted with a real and effective government ; treaties can only be concluded with such a government which alone can give the guarantee of their implementation, and only a real and effective government can successfully be held responsible. In all those real transactions of international law fictitious or merely claimant governments can have no place.

Important exceptions to this principle — to be discussed elsewhere[3] — bear a distinctly provisional character.

In the case of a definitely victorious and established revolution, the principle of effectiveness finds its full application and its flouting can only lead to absurdities [4] and undermine the very foundation of international intercourse. It must be regretfully conceded that it is of no relevance whatever whether the revolution expresses the will of the overwhelming majority of the nation or only of a fraction of terrorists. At the present time, " man's right to governement by consent " [5] is still unprotected by positive international law, however obvious the connection between internal freedom and international peace. Whatever the possibilities of future developments within a fully integrated international society which would have the legal right and the means to intervene through its central organs in the internal affairs of member States in defence of a centrally determined legality, including democratic principles and the rights of man [6], that time has not come yet ; nor must the arbitrary judgment of individual States be mistaken for this vision of a democratic *Civitas Maxima*.

---

1. *Trans. mine, op. cit.*, p. 26. Criticizing the American practice of requiring popular approval of a revolutionary government before recognizing it Spiropoulos declares : " Ob eine Regierung dem Volkswillen entspricht, ist, völkerrechtlich gesprochen, für die Drittstaaten irrelevant. ...wesentlich ist bloss die Tatsache, dass sie Effektivität besitzt". pp. 40-41. See also Anzilotti : « ...au point de vue du droit international, on ne distingue pas entre les gouvernements légitimes et les gouvernements illégitimes, les gouvernements *de iure* et les gouvernements *de facto*. Celui qui détient réellement le pouvoir de commander *(qui actu regit)* a, dans les rapports internationaux, la qualité d'organe de la personnalité internationale dont il s'agit ; celui qui perd en fait ce pouvoir cesse de représenter internationalement l'Etat... » *Op. cit.*, p. 179. " Es ist ein allgemein anerkannter Völkerrechtssatz, dass die siegreiche Revolution, der siegreiche Usurpator zu legitimen Staatsgewalt wird. " Kelsen, *Allg. Staatslehre*, p. 128. See also Larnaude, *op. cit.*, p. 499, and Gemma, *op. cit.*, pp. 337-338.
2. See above, pp. 38-40. Kunz, *op. cit.*, pp. 134-138.
3. See below, pp. 73-126 and 551-587.
4. Cf. American non-recognition of the Soviet Government. See e.g. Hershey, *The Status of Mr. Bakhmeteff, the Russian Ambassador at Washington*, A.J., 1922, p. 426.
5. Lauterpacht, *op. cit.*, p. 171.
6. « En l'absence de cette garantie constitutionnelle superétatique, il paraît difficile d'interdire « l'occupation des compétences » dans l'ordre juridique interne qui correspond à l'occupation des territoires et à celle, consécutive, des compétences, dans l'ordre juridique international. » Scelle, *op. cit.*, pp. 129-130.

7. EXCEPTIONS TO THE RULE.

As in the case of the rule concerning territorial changes, possible exceptions to the rule now discussed must be considered.

a) *Extinction of Particular Treaties.*

The first exception, as formulated by writers, relates to such treaties as may have been concluded between Heads of State not so much in their official but rather in a semi-private capacity, that is, primarily, treaties between dynasties. Such treaties obviously cannot survive a revolutionary change [1]. The objection is valid, but historical developments have robbed it of any immediate relevancy. It can be dealt with together with the more practical exception formulated by Gemma.

Gemma affirms that certain treaties are, by their very nature, linked with the existing regime within the contracting States. He therefore concludes that it would be an exaggeration to say that no change of regime, however radical, can affect the survival of the treaties. It is true that the rule is in favour of their survival and that the contrary should only be affirmed with the utmost caution. Yet the possibility of the extinction of certain treaties following a revolution cannot be categorically excluded [2].

This is indeed true ; with regard to a special kind of treaty the danger may always subsist that it will fall to the ground with the fall of a regime with whose continued existence it is intrinsically bound. But the exception is more apparent than real and it is to be met literally by the same counter-argument as that which has been advanced with regard to certain territorial changes i.e. those, affecting the fate of a particular obligation of the State concerned [3]. The type of treaty Gemma has in mind will fall to the ground not on account on any discontinuity of the State, but solely on the basis of the principle *impossibilium nulla obligatio.* It will become extinguished on the strength of this principle, whether the change of regime was revolutionary or constitutional, just as a treaty providing for navigation on a lake will become extinguished, whether the lake has been ceded to another State or whether it has dried up. All the rest of the State's rights and obligations remaining unaffected, such exceptions, resulting solely from an impossibility of execution, cannot possibly produce a break in the continuity of the

---

1. " Der allgemeine Grundsatz, wonach Staatsverträge von den einzelnen sich ablösenden Regierungen zu halten sind, gilt indessea *nicht* für diejenigen Abkommen, die zwischen Staatshäuptern, nicht in ihrer Eigenschaft als Staatsvertreter, sondern in anderer Stellung — etwa als Häupter von Dynastien — getroffen werden. " Spiropoulos, *op. cit.*, p. 67. Cf. Martens, *op. cit.*, I, pp. 364-365.

2. « Il serait donc excessif d'affirmer qu'un changement de régime, surtout si le changement est radical, n'influe en rien sur l'existence des traités de l'Etat ; on pourra seulement prétendre qu'il faut exercer la plus grande prudence dans l'appréciation des circonstances dont on veut tirer une cause d'extinction ; on pourra rappeler que la règle est pour la continuité des engagements de l'Etat et que toute exception doit être rigoureusement prouvée, mais on ne pourra pas contester que la permanence du régime est quelquefois essentielle pour la subsistance des obligations conventionnelles de l'Etat. » *op. cit.*, p. 347.

3. See above, pp. 22-23.

State in question. This apparent exception concerns the fate of a certain type of treaty which, by its very nature, is exposed to greater risks, quite irrespective of revolution.

The exception, hesitatingly formulated by the comment to the Harvard Draft Convention is of a somewhat different kind and takes up the arguments of Soviet lawyers :

" It can hardly be denied that there is some foundation for the distinction which the Soviet jurists and the writers on international law cited above make between the effect on treaty obligations of ordinary governmental and constitutional changes, on the one hand, which occur normally in the process of the political and constitutional development of a State, and changes, on the other hand, which are the result of violent revolutions which involve not only an alteration of the governmental organization or constitutional regime of the State but also a complete transformation of the political and even the economic and social organisation of the State, and which result in the establishment of a new order of things with which treaties concluded under preceding regimes are wholly or largely incompatible. "

However, the draftsmen admit that the very vagueness of the problem and the impossibility of formulating it in precise terms militate against including it, as an exception, in the text of the proposed Article and they conclude that it is more satisfactory to leave it to the States concerned

" to seek by negotiation a revision or abrogation of the treaties or to invoke the application of the rule *rebus sic stantibus* [1]... "

The obvious answer to this further apparent exception to the rule, is given in the very text quoted. The problem has nothing whatever to do with State continuity, being at the same time entirely different from the impossibility of execution just discussed. It concerns solely and exclusively the problem of " changed circumstances ", the famous Clausula, which, far from constituting a proof of a State's discontinuity, is on the contrary, positive proof of its actual continuity ; for only the same subject of rights and obligations can invoke the Clausula.

A striking confirmation of this view is found in the judgment of the Swiss Federal Court *in re Lepeschkin* already referred to [2] ; the Court, while emphatically affirming Russia's continuity in spite of the revolution, admitted the possibility of invoking the Clausula as a result of changes which may vitally affect the possibility of execution [3].

b) *Territorial Extent of the Revolution ; Secession ; Revolutionary Dismemberment.*

The other exception results from an enquiry into what may be called the territorial extent of the revolution. Here, two possibilities have to be distinguished.

The " normal " case is certainly one in which the revolution extends to the whole territory of the State. In view of the definition

---

1. *Harvard Draft Convention*, p. 1054.
2. See above, p. 42.
3. It is to be observed that the Federal Court does not speak of a complete " impossibility of execution ", but only of the possibility of execution being vitally affected.

of revolution, given above [1], it need hardly be added that it is neither actual fighting nor disturbances of any sort whose territorial extent is meant; what is meant is the territorial scope, aim and, possibly, the success of the revolution. In such a case, the revolution aims at the seizure of power in the entire original State and concerns the whole State in its existing territorial delimitation. This is the classical case, fully covered by the rule under consideration, which clearly considers the revolution as *a State phenomenon*.

There may, however, be a totally different type of revolution which, far from aiming at a seizure of power in the original State, is, on the contrary, bent on separating part of the territory from that State. It does not aim at a change within the State; its aim is not *within*, but *against* it. Starting, necessarily, as an internal State occurence, it later assumes an international character, upsetting the frontiers laid down by international law. Should such an " anti-State " revolution succeed, the result will be either secession or revolutionary dismemberment. Now, it is a well-established rule of international law that a secession — like any other loss of territory — leaves the personality of the original State unaffected, whereas a revolutionary dismemberment brings about its final extinction.

The question arises, how a mere secession is to be distinguished from revolutionary dismemberment. The very notion of " revolutionary dismemberment " undoubtedly presupposes simultaneous revolutions taking place throughout the whole territory of the State, each of them aiming at, and achieving, not a seizure of power in the whole of the original State, but an independent State creation in a part of its territory. On the other hand, it would not be true to say that a secession takes place only in case of a centrifugal " local " revolution, unaccompanied by a similar revolution in the Mother Country. If that were the case, the distinction between secession and revolutionary dismemberment would lie in the absence or presence of a simultaneous revolution in the Mother Country. There is, however, no such simple solution. For, what is definitely considered as secession in the history of international relations, has taken place in both cases. Suffice it to mention on the one hand the secession of the United States from Britain, or of Belgium from Holland, the legal order of the Mother Country remaining intact in both cases, — and, on the other hand, the acknowledged secession of Finland, the Baltic States, etc. from Russia, with simultaneous revolutions going on in all these territories.

Thus, the fact that *one* basic norm, which has hitherto been valid throughout a given territory and for a given human community, has been replaced by *several* new basic norms, is in itself not sufficient to determine whether a secession or a dismemberment has taken place.

The answer is to be found in the juxtaposition of the two customary rules, the one concerning territorial, the other revolutionary changes. The former lays down that a State survives territorial changes because its legal order remains unchanged, its territorial sphere of validity being

---

1. See above, pp. 25-26.

merely extended or restricted. The latter lays down that the State
survives revolutionary changes because its territorial and personal
delimitation under international law remains unchanged. In both cases
it is clear on which elements international law relies in order to resist
the change and to provide the supporting link for the continued identity
of the State concerned. Since these are two separate rules, there is no
one rule providing for State continuity in case of both changes in its
legal order and its territorial and personal delimitation. The identity
of a State could not survive the simultaneous impact of these two
changes. Nor would the general delimitation of the international
community remain unaffected.

However, possible territorial changes accompanying a revolution
can be so small in proportion to the original State that they may safely
be denied any destructive effect on the State's personality. Nor would
in such a case the general delimitation under international law be
disturbed to any considerable extent. It is therefore correct to say
that, in their capacity of supporting elements, territory and population
must remain *essentially*, not absolutely, the same, if revolution is not
to destroy the State [1].

Once again, as in the case of the exception to the rule concerning
territorial changes [2], a legal problem cannot be solved in legal terms
alone. Once again the solution can only be a quantitative one and will
therefore depend upon a searching examination of every particular case.
In the Russian case, only border territories fell away from the Mother
Country ; their territorial extent was insignificant as compared with that
of the original State ; it can safely be said that the new basic norm of
the Russian State remained valid for what was essentially the same
territorial and personal delimitation. No such claim could reasonably
be put forward in the case of Austria, which thus represents a classical
example of State extinction by revolutionary dismemberment [3].

Thus, international law provides for the identity and continuity of
a State in case of a revolution on condition that the validity of the new
revolutionary order corresponds *more or less* to the pre-revolutionary
territorial and personal delimitation of that State. It does *not* provide
either for more or for less. In the case of a revolution accompanied
by a considerable loss of territory there is no identity and continuity
of the State affected ; there is extinction of the State through revolutionary dismemberment. In this sense, revolutionary dismemberment
differs fundamentally from revolution and does not, therefore, constitute
an exception to the customary rule under discussion.

---

1. Asserting revolutionary dismemberment in the case of Austria-Hungary, Verdross
declares that the exception to the rule of continuity is formed not by the fact of revolution
alone, but by the fact that " *ausserdem* ...mehrere neue revolutionäre Verfassungen
nebeneinender gesetzt werden. Da nun das völkerrechtliche Gewohnheistrecht bei einer
revolutionären Verfassungsänderung die Staatsidentität nur gelten lässt, sofern sich die
neue Verfassung *grundsätzlich* für *denselben* Personenverband durchsetzt, der auch der
alten Verfassung unterstellt war, liegt *Untergang des Staates* vor, wenn der alte Menschen-
verband auf mehrere neue Verfassungen aufgeteilt wird. " *Verfassung*, p. 151.
2. See above, pp. 23-24.
3. See below, pp. 210-213.

c) *Fake Revolution.*

Another possible exception concerns what may be called the genuine character of the revolution. Since the customary rule under consideration provides for the continuity of the State *in case of revolution*, and not in case of anything else, it must be made abundantly clear that a given situation of fact is indeed a revolution.

It has been seen that revolution is by definition a State phenomenon. Only on this condition is it accepted by international law as a legal act, not affecting the continuity of the State concerned. The continuity of the State ceases to be protected the moment the revolution ceases to be a State occurence and, breaking the framework of the State, results in revolutionary dismemberment. But the revolutionary phenomenon must equally be denied, if, far from being the product of the State concerned, it is in fact the work of outside factors.

A different view seems to be adopted by Spiropoulos. According to him, the legality of a general *de facto* government is equally undisputed, whether that government has seized power by way of a violent revolution or whether it has been established by a foreign power [1].

It is submitted that such a view is incorrect and that it runs counter to all the basic principles of international law.

It would, indeed, be a serious confusion of ideas to suppose that international law mistakes intervention for revolution. The prohibition of intervention is, as has been seen, a well-established principle of international law, fully corresponding to its underlying conception of a community of separate and co-ordinated States. An intervention aiming at suppressing the revolution in a foreign State is just as contrary to international law [2], as is an intervention aiming at fomenting a revolution in a foreign State. This principle found a clear formulation in the judgment of the Civil Tribunal of the Seine *in re Flörsheim*, of July 2, 1932. The tribunal had to decide the validity of a contract made in France for the supply of arms and munitions for a *coup d'état* in Venezuela. Declaring such contract null and void, the Tribunal held :

" Any act, agreement or contract the execution of which may disturb the established order in the territory of a State, is contrary to international public order, and, therefore, illegal [3]. "

It is a well-known rule of customary international law that third States are under a clear duty of non-intervention and non-interference in civil strife within a State. Any such interference is an unlawful act, even if, far from taking the form of military assistance to one of the parties, it is merely confined to premature recognition of the rebel government [4].

---

1. " Für die Gültigkeit der Rechtshandlungen einer allgemeinen de facto-Regierung (Zwischenherrschaft) ist es völlig gleichgültig, ob die allgemeine de facto-Staatsgewalt infolge *gewaltsamen Umsturzes* zur Macht gelangt ist oder von einer *auswärtigen* Macht eingesetzt worden ist.". *Op. cit.*, p. 82, *f.-n.* 30.
2. See above, pp. 51-59.
3. *A.D.*, 1931-32, case no. 9.
4. Lauterpacht, *op. cit.*, pp. 11 and 95. This customary rule has also been embodied in conventional international law ; see e.g. the Habana Convention on Duties and Rights of States in the Event of Civil Strife, of February 20, 1928, Hudson, *International Legislation*, IV, p. 2416.

The rule has been given a clear and strict formulation by Commissar Litvinov in a speech in the League of Nations Assembly, on September 28, 1937, concerning the Spanish civil war :

" A handful of officers and generals in Spain revolted against the legally constituted Government. No one here will question the legality of the Spanish Government. What was the duty of other Governments in such circumstances ? Obviously, in accordance with international law, it was to give no help to the rebels against the lawful Government. Any help given to such rebels in the form of supplies of arms or, more particularly, of men, would be a flagrant breach of international law. Recognition of the head of the rebels as the head of a new Spanish Government would not improve the position. If that view is held, any revolt or rebellion could be legalized by simply stating that the rebels are henceforth the Government. Recognition of the rebels as a Government is in itself intervention [1]. "

If this is so, if third States are legally bound not to interfere in civil strife within another State, how much more so are they bound not to " make " a revolution in that State. Exactly the same principle of State independence which protects a genuine revolution within an independent State from intervention by third States, protects the legally existing state of affairs in that State from subversive action by third States. No such happenings in which the existing international delimitation of States has not been respected can ever be classified as revolution, but are always intervention [2].

Thus, there is intervention, and not revolution, if the revolutionary movement in one State is instigated and supported by a foreign State ; if the alleged revolution is conducted by citizens or, *a fortiori*, by organs of that foreign State ; if it takes place under foreign pressure, as for example military occupation.

The latter point requires some caution: for a genuine revolution under foreign occupation is not absolutely excluded. Yet, such occupation must necessarily raise a strong presumption against its genuine character. The presumption is further reinforced if the revolution fully conforms to the aims and policies of the occupying power ; if, for instance, it breaks out against an independent government which had previously resisted the demands made on the State by that foreign power, in order precisely to satisfy these demands. It has been said by an authority on plebiscites that no plebiscite can be taken seriously if it is held under the control of a State having an interest in the result ; it could only be considered valid in the unlikely event of a defeat of the controlling State [3].

Literally the same applies to the validity of a revolution under

---

1. *LNOJ*, 1937, Special Supplement, No. 175, p. 63.
2. " ...while subversive activities against foreign States on the part of private persons do not in principle engage the international responsability of a State, such activities when emanating directly from the Government itself or indirectly from organisations receiving from it financial or other assistance or closely associated with it by virtue of the constitution of the State concerned, amount to a breach of International Law ". Oppenheim-Lauterpacht, *op. cit.*, I, p. 261.
3. " It is certain that hereafter no plebiscite, even if held under an agreement between the two States, can command serious consideration if it is held under the control of one of them. Such plebiscite could be considered valid only should the party in control be defeated. This is a remote contigency. " Sarah Wambaugh, *Plebiscites since the World War*, Washington, Carnegie Endowment for International Peace, 1933, vol.I, p. 498.

foreign occupation. Should it develop on the lines desired by the occupying power, the presumption against its genuine character would be overwhelming. But such presumption might be excluded almost completely in case of the revolution running counter to the aims and policies of the occupying power, although this contingency is probably just as remote as the one of the defeat of the controlling State in a plebiscite. In any case, such presumption could be excluded only on the cessation of foreign occupation and pressure.

Generally speaking, every revolution taking place under foreign pressure or as a result of foreign engineering must be tested for its genuine character and evaluated according to the circumstances of the particular case.

The need for such individual evaluation is proved by historical experiences. Some of the revolutions which took place in countries occupied by France after the French Revolution were undoubtedly genuine, being expression of the same ideological trend of the period which had been responsible for the original revolution in France, whereas some were clearly engineered by direct and undisguised French intervention. It may be added that such fake revolutions resulted in most cases in the annexation by France of the allegedly revolutionary country and were thus clearly not revolutions, but conquests [1].

A striking example of a fake revolution in modern times is supplied by the Kuusinnen episode of the Russo-Finnish war of 1939-1940 [2]. On the refusal of Finland to accede to Soviet demands, the Soviet Union attacked Finland and, at the same time, a " Finnish People's Government " under Otto Kuusinnen suddenly sprang into existence in 'Terjoki, in Soviet-occupied territory. It was supposed to represent a Finnish revolution directed against the Helsinki government [3]. It not only acceded to Soviet demands on Finland [4] but actually requested Russian military assistance against the " Helsinki clique " [5]. The Soviet Union, which immediately recognized the allegedly revolutionary government and " established diplomatic relations with the Democratic

---

1. For interesting material on the subject see Wambaugh, *Monograph on Plebiscites*, pp. 33-57 and 173-369.
2. For details see Dallin, *Soviet Russia's Foreign Policy*, pp. 126-128 ; Makarov, *Der sowietrussisch-finnische Konflikt, Ztscht.f.a.öff.R.u.V.-r.*, 1940-41, p. 294.
3. For the true character of that allegedly revolutionary Finnish Government, see Dallin, *op. cit.*, p. 133. In his letter to the Secretary-General of the League of Nations of February 27, 1940, the Finnish Delegate said : " It is obvious, however, that such a puppet Government set up by a foreign and indeed a hostile Power, composed of Finnish Communists guilty of high treason and rebellion — a certain number of them had indeed been sentenced for those crimes — cannot have any authority in Finland or represent her. Finland cannot pay the least attention to it, and so far there has been no question of the recognition of this « Government » by any foreign Power. The only legitimate Government of Finland, as everyone knows, is still in the capital of the country, despite the Soviet allegations, and continues to direct the country's affairs. When, on the occasion of the examination by the League of Nations of the Soviet aggression in Finland — placed on the League's agenda at the request of the legitimate Government of Finland — the U.S.S.R. declared that she had nothing to do with that Government and pointed to the existence of the other « Government » mentioned above, the League of Nations paid no attention to these subterfuges, but proceeded with the study of the case and condemned the action of the U.S.S.R. " *LNOJ*, 1940, p. 22. Cf. the Finnish letter of December 7, 1939, *LNOJ*, 1939, p. 514.
4. See Molotov's telegram quoted below, p. 67.
5. Dallin, *loc. cit.*

Republic of Finland " [1] granted the request and claimed that she was thus merely extending help to a friendly government, and not making war on Finland [2]. On the strength of this fiction, stubbornly maintained in the midst of the raging war, the Soviet Government prevented Sweden from taking over the protection of Finnish interests in Russia [3] and rejected American offers of mediation for the purpose of re-establishing peace. The Soviet thesis found official expression in Comissar Molotov's telegram to the Secretary-General of the League of Nations, of December 5, 1939 :

" In accordance with instructions from the U.S.S.R. Government, I have the honour to inform you that that Government considers unjustified proposal to convene December 9th Council League of Nations and December 11th Assembly League of Nations on the initiative of M. Rodolphe Holsti and in virtue of Article 11, paragraph 1 of the League Covenant.

" The U.S.S.R. is not at war with Finland and does not threaten the Finnish nation with war. Consequently, reference to Article 11, paragraph 1, is unjustified. Soviet Union maintains peaceful relations with the Democratic Republic of Finland, whose Government signed with the U.S.S.R. on December 2nd Pact of Assistance and Friendship. *This Pact settled all the questions which the Soviet Government had fruitlessly discussed with delegates former Finnish Government now divested of its power.*

" By its declaration of December 1st, the Government of the Democratic Republic of Finland requested the Soviet Government to lend assistance to that Republic by armed forces with a view to the joint liquidation at the earliest possible moment of the very dangerous seat of war created in Finland by its former rulers. In these circumstances, appeal of M. Rodolphe Holsti to the League cannot justify convocation of the Council and the Assembly, especially as the persons on whose behalf M. Rodolphe Holsti has approached the League cannot be regarded as mandatories of the Finnish people.

" If, notwithstanding considerations set out above, Council and Assembly are convened to consider the appeal of M. Rodolphe Holsti, U.S.S.R. Government would be unable to take part in these meetings. This decision is also based on the fact that the communication from the Secretary-General of the League concerning convocation Council and Assembly reproduces the text of the letter from M. Rodolphe Holsti, which is full of insults and calumnies against the Soviet Government, this being incompatible with the respect due to the U.S.S.R. — Molotov [4]. "

1. Tass communiqué of December 1, 1939, quoted by Dallin, *op. cit.*, p. 134.
2. It will be observed that even, had the Kuusinnen Government been a genuine revolutionary body, its immediate recognition and, *a fortiori*, the military help granted it by the Soviet Union would in itself have constituted a violation of international law; for it would have been the classical case of premature recognition in a situation where the legal government is not only far from being displaced by the revolutionary one, but where, on the contrary, its troops have actually crossed the State frontiers in a victorious defensive. See the pertinent remarks by Mr. Litvinow, quoted above, p. 65.
3. Makarov, *op. cit.*, p. 307 ; Dallin, *op. cit.*, p. 133, *f.-n. LNOJ*, 1940, p. 22.
4. *It. mine, LNOJ*, Council, 1939, p. 512. However, for inconsistencies of the Soviet Government see Tass communiqué of November 29, 1939 : " For this reason, the Soviet Government was compelled yesterday to declare that it now considered itself released from the engagements which it had undertaken under the Treaty of Non-Aggression concluded between the U.S.S.R. and Finland and which has been irresponsibly violated by the Finnish Government. ... The Soviet Government has come to the conclusion that it could no longer maintain normal relations with the Finnish Government, and for this reason found it necessary to recall immediately its political and economic representatives from Finland. Simultaneously, the Government gave the order to the Supreme Command of the Red Army and Navy to be prepared for all eventualities and to take immediate steps to cope with any new attacks on the part of the Finnish military clique". *Ibid.*, p. 541. Whatever the accuracy of other statements included in the communiqué, there is — significantly enough — no mention of either the Kuusinnen Government or a People's Republic of Finland, while the communiqué deals with Russo-Finnish relations proper.

The Soviet claims did not achieve recognition. The fake Finnish revolution was qualified as such, and denied all validity by the League of Nations; moreover, it was seen by the League for what is was namely, an instrument of Soviet aggression against the Finnish State. In its Resolution of December 13, 1939, the League Assembly declared :

" ... and whereas it (the Soviet Union) has vainly attempted to justify its refusal on the ground of the relations which it has established with an alleged Government which is neither *de iure* nor *de facto* the Government recognized by the people of Finland in accordance with the free working of their institutions [1]... "

The final conclusion from this judgment was drawn on December 14, 1939, when the Council expelled the Soviet Union, as an aggressor, from the League of Nations [2]. Such was the verdict of international law on the fake revolution and the puppet government in Finland.

It is significant that the Soviet Union herself had to go back on the fiction she had so stubbornly maintained. Forgetting that officially she had never been at war with Finland, she re-opened negotiations and, on March 12, 1940, concluded a peace treaty with that country, represented by her legitimate Government. The allegedly revolutionary Kuusinnen Government vanished in the process just as promptly as it had appeared [3]. The case is not without precedent [4]: in 1920 an allegedly revolutionary Polish government was brought into Poland by the invading Red Army and installed in Soviet-occupied Polish territory. In the ensuing peace negotiations and the final Peace Treaty of Riga that government simply disappeared from the scene.

The principle on which the League of Nations acted in the case of Finland, namely the principle of denying all legality and validity to a fake revolution and qualifying it as a disguised act of aggression on the part of the " engineering " State fully conforms to general international law. Moreover, it has found repeated expression in conventional international law ; so, e.g. in Art. 5 of the Russo-Polish Treaty of Riga of March 18, 1921 [5] and in the Peace Treaties concluded by Soviet Russia with the three Baltic Republics [6].

Such fake revolution is not only declared illegal, but is also branded as aggression in a number of international instruments. Thus, Art. 1, para. 2 of the Finno-Soviet Non-Aggression Treaty of January 21, 1932, stipulates :

---

1. *Ibid.*, 1939, p. 540.
2. *Ibid.*, p. 506.
3. It may be observed that already in the course of the war Russia had been forced by events to behave as a belligerent and not as a State which is not engaged in war. Thus, on December 10, 1939, the Soviet Government notified foreign missions in Moscow the blockade of the Finnish coasts. Makarow, *op. cit.*, p. 322. The Finnish Government rightly drew the attention of the League to the fact that Russia could have " no justification for such measure, having previously declared that she was not in a state of war with Finland and still maintaining the same attitude. " *LNOJ*, 1940, p. 21.
4. See Dallin, *op. cit.*, p. 135.
5. Martens, *N.R.G.*, 3rd Series, XIII, p. 141 ; see below, pp.458-459.
6. With Estonia, Art. 7, 5, *ibid.*, XI, p. 869 ; with Lithuania, Art. 4, 1, *ibid.*, p. 880 ; with Latvia, Art. 4, 2, *ibid.*, p. 891. See also Art. 8 of the Russo-Turkish Treaty of 1921, *ibid.*, XVI, p. 39.

" Any act of violence attacking the integrity and inviolability of the territory or the political independence of the other High Contracting Party shall be regarded as an act of aggression, even if it is committed without declaration of war and avoids warlike manifestations [1]. "

The London Convention for the Definition of Aggression of July 3rd, 1933 declares :

" Accordingly, the aggressor in an international conflict shall be considered to be that State which is the first to commit any of the following actions : ... 5) Provision of support to armed bands formed in its territory which have invaded the territory of another State, or refusal, notwithstanding the request of the invaded State, to take, in its own territory, all the measures in its power to deprive those bands of all assistance or protection [2]. "

It is this particular form of aggression which is most probably envisaged in Art. 6 of the Inter-American Treaty of Reciprocal Assistance of Rio de Janeiro, of September 2, 1947 :

" If the inviolability of the integrity of the territory or the sovereignty or political independence of any American State should be affected by an aggression which is not an armed attack [3]... "

It is difficult to see what could be described as " an aggression which is not an armed attack " other than a fake revolution. The formula is repeated in Art. 25 of the Charter of the Organization of American States of Bogota, March 30 - May 2, 1948 ; moreover its Art. 15 states that :

" No State or group of States has the right to intervene directly or indirectly, for any reason whatever, in the internal or external affairs of any other State. The foregoing principle prohibits not only armed force but also any other form of interference or attempted threat against the personality of the State or against its political, economic and cultural elements [4]. "

The most elaborate outlawing of intervention under the cloak of revolution or, as it may be shortly called, fake revolution, is probably included in the well-known " Litvinov pledge ", i.e. in the Soviet Note of November 16, 1933 to the United States, on the occasion of the recognition of Soviet Russia by the latter. The text deserves to be reproduced in full :

" I have the honour to inform you that coincident wiht the establishment of diplomatic relations between our two Governments it will be the fixed policy of the Government of the Union of Soviet Socialist Republics :

1. To respect scrupulously the indisputable right of the United States to order its own life within its own jurisdiction in its own way and to refrain from interfering in any manner in the internal affairs of the United States, its territories or possessions.

2. To refrain, and to restrain all persons in government service and all organizations of the Government or under its direct or indirect control, including organizations in receipt of any financial assistance from it, from any act overt or covert liable in any way whatsoever to injure the tranquility, prosperity, order, or

---

1. *L.o.N.Tr.Ser.*, vol. 157, p. 397.
2. Hudson, *op. cit.*, VI, p. 412.
3. *U.N. Textbook*, p. 288.
4. *Ibid.*, pp. 294-295.

security of the whole or any part of the United States, its territories or possessions, and, in particular, from any act tending to incite or encourage armed intervention, or any agitation or propaganda having as an aim, the violation of the territorial integrity of the United States, its territories or possessions, or the bringing about by force of a change in the political or social order of the whole or any part of the United States, its territories or possessions.

3. Not to permit the formation or residence on its territory of any organization or group — and to prevent the activity on its territory of any organization or group — which makes claim to be the Government of, or makes attempt upon the territorial integrity of, the United States, its territories or possessions ; not to form, subsidize, support or permit on its territory military organizations or groups having the aim of armed struggle against the United States, its territories of possessions, and to prevent any recruiting on behalf of such organizations and groups.

4. Not to permit the formation or residence on its territory of any organization or group — and to prevent the activity on its territory of any organization or group, or of representatives or officials of any organization or group — which has as an aim the overthrow of, or the bringing about by force of a change in, the political or social order of the whole or any part of the United States, its territories or possessions [1]. "

It will be observed that none of the provisions quoted above has the slightest resemblance either to the principles of the Holy Alliance or to those of the American constitutionalism. None of them aims at the suppression of a genuine revolution in an independent State. They are directed against fake revolution, that is, foreign intervention disguised as revolution.

The notion of a fake, or puppet, government looms large in the provisions quoted. This is natural, since a fake revolution is intended to, and in case of success, bound to, produce a fake government. If this happens, will the identity and continuity of the State concerned still remain unaffected ?

The answer is supplied by the above analysis. It has been seen that international law safeguards the identity and continuity of a State in case of revolution, and not in any other case. A revolution is legal under international law ; a fake revolution, being a disguised form of aggression, is not. International law cannot accept and treat legal and illegal acts alike. It cannot attach identical legal consequences to two different situations. Moreover, it has been seen that the identity and continuity of the revolutionary State is safeguarded by the fact that its old basic norm is replaced by a new revolutionary basic norm produced from within the surviving territorial and personal delimitation [2] ; it is not replaced by the basic norm of any other State ; in other words, it is not produced from without the surviving delimitation. But in the case of a successful fake revolution resulting in a fake government, the new basic norm comes precisely from outside the State concerned, whatever the superficial appearances to the contrary. The State concerned can no longer be considered identical with the one existing prior to the fake revolution. Since its basic norm is in fact determined by a foreign State, it becomes a puppet State, and therefore non-identical with its predecessor ; its very character as State becomes doubtful.

---

1. *A.J.*, 1934, Supplement, pp. 3-4.
2. See above, p. 50.

This conclusion results forcefully from a judgment of the Mixed Tribunal of Cairo of 1923. The Tribunal had to decide upon the continuity or extinction of Armenia, following events which were alleged to be a revolutiln but which were found by the Tribunal to lack this character.

" It is universally admitted that the changes occurring in the institutions and form of the government of a people do not affect the identity of the State from the point of view either of its internal sovereignty or of its international relations. This principle, however, is only true with regard to changes which leave the State the power of preserving its character of an independent political body. "

Whereupon the Court held that Armenia had become extinct due to the fact that the actual organization of public power in the territory which, until 1920, formed the Armenian Republic, was now imposed by the armed forces of the Soviet Government of Russia [1].

There is thus no identity between a puppet State resulting from a fake revolution, and a previously existing independent State. Whether the displaced independent State can survive such fake revolution and disguised conquest — as it can survive belligerent occupation — or whether it becomes extinct, is, of course, an entirely different question.

8. REVOLUTION AND THE PRIMACY OF INTERNATIONAL LAW.

This analysis of revolution under international law cannot be brought to a close without some reference, however brief, to a subject of fundamental importance: namely, the relation between international and municipal law.

This study began with the theoretical assumption of the primacy of international law over municipal law [2]. It was stated that it could not have been undertaken on any other assumption ; for essential problems of the legal existence of States — their birth, death and transformation — can be made the subject of a juridical enquiry only from the point of view of primacy of international law.

The preceding investigation of the problem of revolution has supplied an emphatic empirical confirmation of this theoretical assumption. For it leads to the inescapable conclusion that the validity of international law is not dependent on State law.

While it is undoubtedly true that only the hypothesis of the primacy of international law can explain the identity and continuity of a State in spite of a revolution [3] it is equally true that such identity and continuity constitute in turn the incontrovertible proof of such primacy.

---

1. *Achikian v. Bank of Athens*, A.D., 1923/24, case no. 7.
2. See above, p. 2.
3. « Seule l'hypothèse de la primauté du droit des gens nous fait comprendre l'identité d'un Etat, au point de vue du droit international, en dépit du changement complet de la forme du gouvernement, elle seule garantit la continuité juridique en dépit d'une révolution, elle seule explique le phénomène de la révolution, parce que ce fait, qui se présente dans l'hypothèse du droit national, comme la rupture, la discontinuité du droit, incompréhensible juridiquement, comme un pur fait métajuridique, apparaît sous l'aspect de notre hypothèse comme état de cause juridique (« Rechtstabestand ») du droit des ns.ge.. » Kunz, *La Primauté du Droit des Gens*, RDILC, 1925, p. 596.

Verdross is therefore entirely justified in choosing the identity and continuity of the revolutionary State as the basis of his whole theory of the primacy of international law [1]. The internal legal order of a State may founder, but international law survives.

It further results from this relation between international and municipal law, that no municipal enactment can set aside an international rule. This is equally true with regard to State constitutions preceding a revolution and to *ex post* enactments of the restored post-revolutionary regimes. Unable to prevent a revolution on the internal level [2], constitutions are just as powerless to ward off the rule of international law providing for the international validity of revolutionary *de facto* governments [3]. With regard to *ex post* enactments seeking to declare the acts of a revolutionary government internationally invalid, they were always unfailingly dismissed by international tribunals. Thus, the Franco-Chilean Arbitral Tribunal, in the judgment quoted above, declared with respect to the Peruvian Congress' declaration of nullity of the acts of the revolutionary government :

« Attendu... que le Gouvernement conteste que cette loi ait été une loi d'occasion, et entreprend de la justifier par les principes du droit péruvien, en insistant sur l'idée « qu'elle n'a fait que proclamer une nullité qui frappait déjà les actes de la Dictature en vertu des dispositions de la Constitution » ; mais que ce point de vue trouve sa condamnation dans ce qui précède ; qu'en effet la Loi d'annulation, considérée en tant que promulguée en application de l'Article 10 de la Constitution péruvienne de 1860, qui déclare nuls les actes de ceux qui usurpent les fonctions publiques, ne peut naturellement déployer plus d'effet que le texte constitutionnel sur lequel elle se fonde [4]... »

Similarly, the Permanent Court of Arbitration in the case of *French Claims against Peru* declared :

" Whereas it is of slight importance [5] that a Peruvian law of October 25, 1886, declared " all the internal acts of the government performed by Nicolas de Pierola null ", since this law can not be applied to foreigners who treated in good faith [6]... "

---

1. " ...dass das auf die Staatsverfassungen aufgebaute Völkerrecht im Falle einer revolutionären Verfassungsänderung mit dem Zusammenbruch ihres Geltungsgrundes, der vorrevolutionären Staatsverfassung, auss er Geltung treten würde. ...Nun steht aber unbestrittenermassen ein Völkerrechtssatz in Geltung, der besagt, dass die unter der vorrevolutionären Staatsverfassung abgeschlossenen Verträge, wie überhaupt alle zur Zeit ihrer Geltung begründeten völkerrechtlichen Pflichten, weiter bestehen bleiben... Diese Weitergeltung der Verträge nach dem Untergang der Verfassung, auf Grund welcher sie abgeschlossen wurden, wäre aber... unmöglich, wenn die Staatsverträge letztlich von den Staatsverfassungen abhängig wären, da sie dann mit diesen Verfassungen zusammenstürzen müssten. Da sie aber von diesem Sturze nicht mitbetroffen werden, müssen sie einen Rechtsgrund aufweisen, der über den Staatsverfassungen steht. " *Verfassung*, pp. 16-17.
2. See above, pp. 29-30.
3. « En ce qui touche le droit international, il faut maintenir énergiquement... que ces dispositions restrictives sur la capacité des gouvernements de fait et sur la validité de leurs actes sont inopérantes et indifférentes. » Larnaude, *op. cit.*, p. 499. Gemma speaks in this connection of « absurdité logique », *op .cit.*, p. 361.
4. Descamps-Renault, *op. cit.*, p. 398.
5. Exception must be taken to the English translation. The original French text reads : « Attendu qu'il importe peu... » which conveys a far stronger meaning and which should properly be translated : " Whereas it is of *no* importance... ".
6. Scott, *The Hague Court Reports*, p. 33.

An identical attitude was adopted by the Arbitrator in the *Tinoco* case :

" It is obvious that the obligations of a restored government for the acts of the usurping *de facto* government it succeeds cannot, from the international standpoint, be prejudiced by a constitution which, though restored to life, is for purposes of this discussion exactly as if it were new legislation which was not in force when the obligations arose [1]... "
" In an international tribunal ... the unilateral repeal of a treaty by a statute would not affect the rights arising under it and its judgment would necessarily give effect to the treaty and hold the statute repealing it of no effect [2]. "

Finally, the U.S.-Mexican Claims Commission in the *Hopkins* case concluded

" that Hopkins contracts ... have not been nullified by any decree issued by Carranza, and that they have not been and cannot be nullified by any unilateral act of the Government of Mexico [3]. "

This being the clear position under international law, solemn proclamations by revolutionary governments of their willingness to honour the international obligations of their predecessors merely have the character of political reassurances. They are not acts of grace on the part of these governments ; nor do they involve the assumption of any new obligations. They are simply the fulfilment or an international duty, of which any other attitude would be a breach [4].

Thus, an investigation of positive international law shows that there can be no choice between the two working hypotheses, — that of the primacy of international law, and that of the primacy of municipal law [5]. Only one of them is correct, and it is the former. At the same time, the inability of States to undermine the validity of international law by means of municipal legislation supplies yet another argument against a voluntarist conception of international law.

III. THE RULE RELATING TO BELLIGERENT OCCUPATION.

1. SCOPE OF THE RULE.

The third customary rule lays down that a State's identity and continuity are not affected by belligerent occupation of its territory.

---

1. *A.J.*, 1924, p. 159.
2. *Ibid.*, p. 160.
3. *A.J.*, 1927, p. 166. " Einen groben Verstoss gegen allgemein anerkanntes Völkerrecht bedeutete es deshalb, wenn im Jahre 1886 der Peruanische Kongress alle Akte der Regierung Pierrola für null und nichtig erklärt hat. ... Landesrecht kann nie entgegenstehendes Völkerrecht brechen. " Spiropoulos, *op. cit.*, p. 96.
4. Art. VI of the United States Constitution declares that " All debts contracted and engagements entered into, before the adoption of this Constitution, shall be as valid against the United States under this Constitution, as under the Confederation. " Commenting on this Article, the Harvard Draft Convention in its comment to Art. 24 observes that a large number of such treaties and conventions " were still in force at the time the Constitution came into effect and under Art. VI continued to be binding upon the nation ". p. 1051. It is submitted that they continued to be binding upon the nation not under Art. VI of the Constitution, but under positive international law.
5. Kelsen, *Souveränität*, pp. 314-320, *Allg. Staatslehre*, pp. 128-132. See, however, *Reine Rechtslehre*, Leipzig und Wien, Franz Denticke, 1934, pp. 147-150.

Before analyzing it in detail, it is necessary to determine exactly what situation of fact is covered by the rule. For the very general term "belligerent occupation" is sufficiently wide to call for further subdivisions.

Thus, Prof. Guggenheim distinguishes between : *a)* belligerent occupation *sensu stricto*, i.e. during actual hostilities, *b)* occupation following an armistice, and *c)* belligerent occupation *sui generis* [1].

Which of these three types of belligerent occupation can give rise to the problem of State continuity?

a) Whatever opinion may be held as to the true nature of what Prof. Guggenheim calls "*occupatio sui generis*" [2], this problem need not be examined here at any length. For the only historical examples available, those of Germany and Japan after the Second World War, show that this sort of occupation did not break the continuity of the occupied State. The question never arose with regard to Japan, where the occupying Power allowed the Emperor and the Government to remain, and with whom a Peace Treaty was concluded on September 9th, 1951. On the other hand, the problem did indeed arise with regard to Germany who, for a certain period of time, was deprived of all the external characteristics of statehood. However, further historical developments seem to have confirmed the continuity of the German State, and the end of war between that State and the Western Allies was officially — although unilaterally — proclaimed by the latter in 1951 [3]. Thus, the positive solution of the German and the Japanese problem disposes of all doubt concerning the influence of the "occupation *sui generis*" on the continuity of the occupied State, and, failing other examples, it also, disposes of the question for the present [4].

b) Nor can occupation following an armistice give rise to the problem of State continuity. Such occupation does not, by definition, affect the continued existence of the occupied State, for the obvious reason that its legal basis is to be found in a convention between the occupying and the occupied State. It is hardly necessary to add that, in order to conclude the armistice convention, the occupied State (or, as will mostly be the case, the State whose territory is partly occupied) must needs continue to exist and that its continued existence cannot be open to doubt.

---

1. *Lehrbuch*, II, p. 926. For a diferent classification see Sauser-Hall, *L'occupation de l'Allemagne par les Puissances alliées*, Annuaire Suisse, 1946, p. 11. With regard to yet another classification undertaken by Cybichowski in his *Das völkerechtliche Okkupationsrecht*, *Ztsch.f. V-r.*, 1934, Prof. Guggenheim's view may be quoted according to which it is hardly necessary to create a special category of occupation for every historical event, *op. cit.*, II, *f.-n.* 472 on p. 927.

2. See below, p. 79.

3. The relevant dates were : July 9 for the United Kingdom, July 13 for France, and October 24 for the United States.

4. The writer is fully aware of the existence of the problem of State identity and continuity in the case of post-war Germany. If an analysis of this question has not been included in this work, this is not only because of the immensity of the problem (which would easily require a separate study), but, first and foremost, because such an analysis against the existing political background would seem to be premature.

c) The problem of State identity and continuity is thus limited
to belligerent occupation *sensu stricto* i.e. to occupation effected during
actual hostilities, on the strength of military seizure of territory, and
not on a conventional basis. It should also be mentioned that even
here the problem of State continuity can arise only if the occupation
covers the entire territory of the State in question. It is true that the
customary rule under consideration contains a general prohibition of
transfer of sovereignty over any occupied territory, whether it represents
a part of the whole of the territory of the State. But it is only the
second case which can give rise to the question of State continuity.

In order to evolve such a clear and unequivocal rule, it was first
necessary for international law to pass beyond the primitive stage in
which a bare situation of fact, however provisional and temporary,
could immediately and finally become the source of legal rights ; in
other words, to make a clear-cut distinction between occupation on the
one hand, and subjugation on the other. This achievement marked a
definite progress both in international relations and in the intrinsic
differentiation and development of the international legal order [1].

2. DEVELOPMENT OF THE RULE.

The development of the rule was a long one and finally crystallized
only well in the 19th century.

The problem was only touched upon, but not fully explored by
Grotius [2]. It was only a century later (1758) that the first modern notion
of belligerent occupation as distinct from the permanent transfer of
sovereignty was defined by Vattel. He considers occupation as a
temporary institution, conferring no title on the occupant, while
sovereignty over the occupied territory can be acquired either by a
treaty of peace or through a complete subjugation of the occupied
State [3].

It does not seem, however, that this distinction was immediately
adopted and further developed in the doctrine of international law,
nor indeed that it had any profound influence on State practice. It is

---

1. " In regard to occupation, International Law respecting warfare has progressed
more than in any other department. " Oppenheim-Lauterpacht, *op. cit.*, II, p. 432.
2. " At agri non statim capti intelliguntur simul atque insessi sunt. Nam quamquam
verum est eam agri partem quam cum magna vi ingressus est exercitus ab eo interim
possideri... tamen ad eum quem tractamus effectum non sufficit qualiscunque possessio sed
firma requiritur. Itaque Romani agrum extra portam quem Annibal castris insidebat
adeo non amissum indicabant, ut eo ipso tempore nihilo minoris venierit quam ante
venisset. Is ergo demum ager captus censebitur, qui mansuris munitionibus ita inclu-
ditur, ut nisi iis expugnatis parti alteri palam aditus non sit ". *Op. cit.*, II, VI, IV. Apart
from a certain touch of picturesque supplied by the " permanent fortifications ", it appears
that Grotius' reasoning was limited only to this : while denying the character of final
conquest to an obviously unstable possession of enemy territory, capable of being easily
retaken by the other warring party, he considered it a sufficient condition for a change
of sovereignty, when the possession was more stable and its re-capture more difficult.
It is thus a difference of degree, not the question of two autonomous notions.
3. « Les Immeubles, les Terres, les Villes, les Provinces, passent sous la puissance
de l'ennemi qui s'en empare, mais l'acquisition ne se consomme, la propriété ne devient
stable et parfaite, que par le Traité de Paix ou par l'entière soumission et l'extinction de
l'Etat auquel ces villes et provinces appartenaient ». *Op. cit.*, Livre III, chap. XIII, p. 174.

true that there were few, though unsuccessful, attempts to apply the principle prior to the 19th century [1]. However, as late as the 18th and the beginning of the 19th century, State practice was still to the contrary [2].

Another century had to elapse before the broken thread of Vattel's thought was taken up again by Heffter (1844). To him falls the merit of a clear-sighted and profound elaboration of the problem, which was to serve as a basis for the future development of customary and conventional international law on the subject.

Heffter emphatically denies that the mere taking possession of enemy territory enables the conqueror to assume full State authority over it, the common sense reason being that as long as war and resistance last, the fortunes of war may change. Only complete debellatio or " ultima victoria " can destroy the sovereignty of the conquered State, whose authority has so far only been suspended. Having made this fundamental distinction, Heffter is now able to lay down rules for belligerent occupation: the occupying power can lawfully take measures to consolidate its success, but it can never take over the full authority of the displaced sovereign. Should the latter re-conquer the territory, former legal relations will therefore be automatically restored, irrespective of whether the occupant had been content with mere occupation or had claimed sovereignty [3]. Heffter deplores practices which tend to perpetuate the confusion between occupation and a debellatio, such as forcing an oath of allegiance on the occupied population, confiscations, and so forth. He stigmatizes the fact that sometimes occupied lands have been dealt with as if they were truly the property of the occupant. Yet he seems to be confident that a change for the better is noticeable in the wars of his century [4].

With regard to the problem under discussion, Heffter's principles mean that belligerent occupation leaves the continuity of the occupied State intact ; its legal order is merely suspended for the duration of

---

1. Letter of the Spanish general de Villens to the Marshal de Noailles in 1694, following the French occupation of Olot in Catalonia : « Les peuples conquis par la force des armes ne doivent être considérés comme sujets du prince qui a la domination de leur pays, qu'au cas de véritable cession, à la suite de la conclusion de la paix. » Also the proclamation of the Council of Flanders of September 11, 1677, following French occupation : « Comme par la prise et l'occupation d'une ville, forteresse ou place durant la guerre, le souverain ne perd pas la propriété et la souveraineté du pays qui en dépend ou de ses appendances, notamment aussi longtemps que ceux-ci ne sont pas cédés par traité, Nous (Président et Conseillers du Roi) interdisons, de la part de sa Majesté, à tous ceux qui habitent dans ces places et pays, dans l'étendue de cette province de Flandre, de reconnaître un autre souverain que Sa Majesté prénommée, ou d'autres Conseils, tribunaux ou officiers de justice, que ceux établis par sa dite Majesté, sous peine de nullité de tout ce qui sera fait ou acquis, contrairement à la présente, et de confiscations des biens des contrevenants, et d'être appréhensibles et punissables, comme désobéissants et ennemis. » Both documents quoted by A. Jumeau, Le Refuge du Gouvernement National à l'Etranger, pp. 20-21.
2. See examples quoted by Martens, op. cit., III, p. 253 ; Oppenheim-Lauterpacht, op. cit., II, p. 432 and f.-n. 2. For the practice of the French Revolution see Cambon's decree of December 15, 1792 : « Dans les pays qui sont ou seront occupés par les armées de la République, les généraux proclameront sur-le-champ au nom de la nation française la suppression de toutes les autorités établies... » Quoted by Wambaugh, A Monograph on Plebiscites, p. 306.
3. Das europäische Völkerrecht der Gegenwart, pp. 287 and 407.
4. Ibid., pp. 289-290.

the occupation, and the liberation of its territory does not mean a creation of a new State, but the automatic restoration of the old.

These principles are already treated as obvious truths by Bluntschli in his main work on international law, the first edition of which appeared in 1867. He declares categorically that military authority in occupied territory is of an emergency and provisional nature. This character implies the limitation of such authority which is not entitled to effect any changes in the fundamental laws of the occupied State. In principle, the occupant has no legislative competence and is bound to leave the civil administration and the administration of justice in the occupied State intact, except in cases of military necessity. The authority of the occupied State is only suspended [1].

Thus, by the middle of the 19th century the principle of State continuity remaining unaffected by belligerent occupation was finally elaborated by writers and began to grow into a positive rule of international law through generally conforming State practice.

The great work of codifying these principles began with the publication of the first military code, namely the American instructions for the Government of the Armies in the Field, prepared by Dr. Francis Lieber in 1863 [2]. Although written for actual use in a civil, and not an international, war, the Lieber Code nevertheless emphasizes the provisional nature of military occupation by introducing the notion of a mere " suspension " of the " criminal and civil law, and of the domestic administration and government in the occupied place or territory and in the substitution of military rule of force for the same ". (Art. 3.) Yet Lieber admits the possibility of annexation prior to the conclusion of peace [3].

Such possibility is no longer admitted by the so-called Brussels Draft of 1874, which, however, remained unratified [4]. The Oxford Code, prepared by the Institute of International Law and adopted at its Oxford Session in 1880, already formulates the rule in quite an emphatic way :

" An invaded territory is not considered conquered before the end of the war ; until that moment, the occupant only exercises a factual power, which is essentially provisional. " (Art. 6.)

These principles were finally codified in 1899 and 1907 at The Hague. The following are the relevant Articles of the Regulations annexed to the 1907 Fourth Hague Convention (identical in the 1899 and 1907 texts), signed and ratified by 46 States.

Art. 42. Territory is considered occupied when it is actually placed under the authority of the hostile army. The occupation extends only to the territory where such authority has been established and can be exercised.

---

1. *Op. cit.*, pp. 303, 304, 306-307.
2. For the development of the law and doctrine of belligerent occupation see Graber D. A., *The Development of the Law of Belligerent Occupation*, 1863-1914 particularly chapter I.
3. " This Article which conflicts with modern standards ... may have been written by Lieber with the Civil War in mind. " Graber, *op. cit.*, p. 40.
4. Art. 2. The authority of the legitimate power being suspended and having in fact passed into the hands of the occupant...

Art. 43. The authority of the legitimate power having in fact passed into the hands of the occupant, the latter shall take all the measures in his power to restore and ensure, as far as possible, public order and safety, while respecting, unless absolutely prevented, the laws in force in the country.

3. THE HAGUE REGULATIONS.

In view of universally prevailing State practice at the time of the signature and coming into force of the Hague Conventions [1], it is true to say that they were no more than declaratory of existing international law. Thus, to invoke in a given case the so-called " general participation clause " (Art. 2) is practically meaningless, since the non-signature by any particular Power of the Hague Conventions cannot possibly have the effect of invalidating generally accepted rules of customary law [2]. This results clearly from the text of the Conventions whose Preamble states :

" Until a more complete code of the laws of war has been issued, the high contracting parties deem it expedient to declare that, in cases not included in the Regulations adopted by them, the inhabitants and the belligerents remain under the protection and the rule of the principles of the law of nations as they result from the usages established among civilized peoples, from the laws of humanity and from the dictates of the public conscience. "

This passage is of particular interest, as it throws additional and authoritative light on the problem of the relationship between the Hague Conventions and the existing customary law of the period. Accordingly, the Hague Conventions are an *incomplete* codification of existing customary law, which is supposed to supplement them and to remain binding in all cases not covered by the Conventions [3]. Thus, the Hague Conventions are not something different from existing customary law. Consequently, there is no foundation in the claim that the existing customary law and the Hague Regulations are two different things, providing for two different types of occupation, one under the Conventions where the continuity of the occupied State is safeguarded, and some other one, allowing every possible freedom to the occupant.

Yet, precisely such a claim was advanced by Cybichowski, according to whom it could hardly be maintained that a State, annexing occupied territory, commits a breach of international law. This is apparently so because the former law of war, which did not differentiate between occupation and annexation, has not been fully eliminated by the Hague codification [4]. This view, however, which seeks to put the clock two centuries back, is based on an obviously false assumption : the Hague Regulations did no " eliminating " whatever ; in particular, they did not

---

1. See below, pp. 107-109.

2. " Although Czechoslovakia was not a party to the Hague Convention of 1907, the rules of land walfare expressed in this convention are declaratory of existing international law and hence are applicable. " *Judgment,* p. 125.

3. Similarly Uhler, *Der völkerrechtliche Schutz der Bevölkerung eines besetzten Gebiets gegen Massnahmen der Okkupationsmacht,* p. 18. Prof. Guggenheim speaks of " die das geltende Völkergewohnheitsrecht *widerspiegelnde* Haager Landkriegsordnung... " *It. mine,* op. cit., II, p. 927.

4. *Op. cit.,* p. 298.

" eliminate " an older and different law of war. The latter had been eliminated not by any codification, but by the progressive development of the customary law on the subject in the course of the 19th century and this new customary law was, in turn, codified by the Hague Conventions. The idea of the Hague Conventions representing some sort of revolutionary break with the then existing international law and introducing an entirely new code, is not only the result of bad reading of the Hague texts, but moreover of a distortion of historical facts.

The view put forward by Prof. Guggenheim, according to whom customary law concerning belligerent occupation is not to be found exclusively in the Hague Conventions, is of an entirely different character. For, as regards belligerent occupation *sensu stricto*, Prof. Guggenheim does not admit the existence of any other rules than those contained in the Hague Regulations. Yet he seems to admit the possibility of a different type of occupation where a debellatio has in fact taken place, but the victorious Powers refuse to go to the length of annexation. This latter situation is described by Prof. Guggenheim as " *occupatio sui generis* " [1]. Since this new type of occupation only concerns Germany and Japan, it may perhaps be doubted 1) whether it still falls under the heading of belligerent occupation at all or whether it is not rather a case of debellatio, not followed by annexation [2], and 2) whether this isolated historical occurrence is sufficient to create a new customary rule. However that may be, Prof. Guggenheim nowhere suggests the existence of a different regime of occupation *sensu stricto*, i.e. during actual hostilities and nowhere admits the possibility of the customary law on the matter being something different from the Hague Regulations [3].

Thus, with regard to belligerent occupation *sensu stricto*, i.e. the only type of occupation relevant to the problem under discussion, the Hague Conventions and the customary law which supplements them, are exhaustive. They both safeguard the continuity of the occupied State. There is no other rule, either conventional, or customary [4].

---

1. See above, p. 74.
2. See Jennings, *R.V. Government in Commission, B.Y.*, 1946, p. 135 : " ...a final victory which results in the destruction of the Government of the occupied territory and the cessation of all hostilities is of itself sufficient to end the state of belligerent occupation whether or not it is accompanied by the ending of a purely technical state of war. "
3. " ...weil das Völkergewohnheitsrecht die kriegerische Besetzung nicht ausschliesslich in der Form der Haager L.K.O. regelt. Die Anwendung der besonderen Besatzungsformen setzt allerdings voraus, dass ein Stadium des Krieges vorliegt, in welchem keine militärischen Operationen gegen den besetzten Staat oder verbündete Staaten mehr im Gange sind, die zu einer Befreiung des besetzten Gebietes von der Herrschaft der Besetzungsmacht führen könnten. Bei einer solchen Sachlage vermöchte sie nämlich den räumlichen Geltungsbereich ihrer eigenen Rechtsordnung auf das besetzte Gebiet zu erstrecken. Daher darf sie sich im Rahmen des Besetzungsrechtes Befugnisse aneignen, die über ihre Zuständigkeit innerhalb der Besetzung während der Dauer militärischer Operationen herausgehen. Sie ist aber nicht verpflichtet, zum formellen Akt der Eingliederung des besetzten Gebietes in den eigenen Staat zu schreiten, insofern sie den provisorischen, vorübergehenden Charakter der Besetzung weiterhin anerkennt. " *Op. cit.* II, p. 927.
4. " Anche l'esame della pratica internazionale esclude pertanto la esistenza di alcuna deroga alla regola generale che l'occupazione bellica non fa acquistare alcuna nuova sovranità. " Balladore Pallieri, *La guerra*, p. 329.

4. NEGATIVE ASPECTS OF THE RULE.

It is only against the background of the continued existence of the occupied State that the true nature of belligerent occupation becomes intelligible. It is only this principle of continuity which explains all the restrictions which international law imposes on the occupying power. For the legal order of the occupant does not operate freely in the occupied territory, but finds its limits in the surviving legal order of the occupied State, as well as in international law [1]. The characteristic features, as well as the content, of the occupation regime have to be viewed in the light of this co-existence of legal orders.

a) *Temporary and Provisional Nature of Belligerent Occupation.*

Thus, while continuity of the occupied State remains the fundamental and permanent feature of belligerent occupation, the most significant characteristics of that occupation itself is that it is provisional and temporary [2]. This is why it is fundamentally restricted by the basic obligation, formulated in Art. 43 of the Hague Regulations, to respect the existing — and continuing — legal order of the occupied State. The particular restrictions, of which the Hague Regulations give a considerable list, are merely derived from this basic principle [3]. There is nothing the occupant can legally do to break the continuity of the occupied State. He cannot annul its laws ; he can only prevent their implementation. He cannot destitute judges and officials ; he can merely prevent them from exercising their functions. In other words, he can only interfere with the practical working of the legal order of the occupied State ; but whether that legal order is able to develop and operate, or whether it is technically prevented from doing so, it continues to be valid and to exist [4].

---

1. On the co-existence in occupied territory of the two legal orders of the occupying and the occupied State, see Balladore Pallieri, *op. cit.*, p. 334. As to the co-existence of these two orders with the international legal order intervening directly in the occupied territory, see Guggenheim, *Lehrbuch*, II, p. 924.

2. « ...*occupatio bellica transitoria*, parce qu'elle est essentiellement transitoire et provisoire. ... Tant que dure la guerre, l'occupation ne saurait être que provisoire, et cela lors même que l'Etat occupant serait d'ores et déjà résolu à ne jamais évacuer le territoire occupé. Car l'issue de la guerre est incertaine, et jusqu'à la dernière heure la fortune des armes peut changer. » Rivier, *op. cit.*, p. 300. See also Martens, *op. cit.*, III, p. 251 ; Verdross, *Völkerrecht*, p. 360. Prof. Guggenheim deals with belligerent occupation under the heading " Kriegerische Besatzung als provisorische Rechtsordnung " and declares that it has " stets provisorischen, vorübergehenden Charakter". *Op. cit.*, II, p. 922.

3. The unlimited power of the occupant was claimed by German writers during the last war. " Die tatsächliche Gewalt des Siegers im besetzten feindlichen Gebiet ist grundsätzlich schrankenlos. " " Seine Gewalt ist folglich allumfassend. " Waltzog, A, *Recht der Landkriegsführung*, Verlag Franz Vahlen, Berlin 1942, pp. 74-77. However, see German post-war literature, claiming not only the applicability to Germany of the Hague Regulations, but also their restricted interpretation. Thus, Stödter, R. *Deutschlands Rechtslage*, Hamburg, Rechts-und staatswissenschaftlicher Verlag, 1948 ; Kaufmann, E, *Deutschlands Rechtslage unter der Besatzung*, Stuttgart, K. F. Koehler, 1948.

4. " Si dice di solito che l'occupante abroga leggi preesistenti, o destituisce funzionari, ecc., ma tutte queste espressic ii sono assai improprie, perché ad una legge non può essere tolto valore se non dal suo ordinamento medesimo, e *l'occupante potrà intaccarne non il valore ma solo l'efficacia*, non già cioè abrogarla e renderla non più obbligatoria ma solo impedire che venga praticamente attuata e osservata. Del pari quanto agli organi dello Stato occupato si potrà loro impedire di esercitare le loro funzioni, ma non

Nor does the legal order of the occupying State extend to the occupied territory [1]. Exceptional legislative competence granted to the occupant by international law is limited not only by the overriding obligation to respect the legal order of the occupied country " unless absolutely prevented ", but also by basic object of the occupation : that of providing for the security of the occupant's armed forces. Even the overriding purpose of a continued prosecution of his war effort aimed at final victory, is severely hampered by a number of prohibitions, such as the prohibition to compel the population to take part in military operations or to give information. It follows that all these exceptional powers must be expressly granted by international law, and that, in the absence of such express authorisation, the competence of the occupied State continues to exist [2].

The restricted character of occupation is equally illustrated by rules relating to its termination, which had already been postulated by Heffter and Bluntschli [3]. The exceptional legal regime of the occupation does not survive the termination of the latter. As a rule, enactments of the occupied power will lose their validity immediately the occupation ends and the legal order of the liberated State will then automatically re-acquire its full scope [4]. These rules are not affected by the fact that the liberated State may wish to maintain those measures of the occupying power which had been enacted strictly within the limits of the latter's competences.

b) *The Requirement of Effectiveness.*

The power of the occupant is further restricted by the requirement of effectiveness, formulated not only with the utmost strictness, but also, in the narrowest sense of the term. According to Art. 42 of the Hague Regulations not only is effectiveness the *conditio sine qua non* of

---

si può impedire che essi continuino ad essere organi di quello Stato straniero, e che abbiano secondo questo competenza all' esercizio dello loro funzioni ". *It. mine*, Balladore Pallieri, *op. cit.*, p. 337. « Il est conforme à la nature juridique de l'occupation de guerre de ne pas tolérer l'abrogation du droit promulgué par le souverain légitime ; l'envahisseur ne peut qu'en paralyser, en fait, les conséquences dans les territoires ennemis qu'il a sous son contrôle. Il ne peut pas l'empêcher d'exister et d'être tenu pour du droit valable partout où il ne peut pas agir directement. » Sauser-Hall, *L'occupation de guerre et les droits privés*, *Annuaire Suisse*, 1944, p. 103.

1. "...the application of the laws of the occupying State do (sic !) not by the fact of the occupation extend automatically to the occupied territory. " Supreme Administrative Court of Czechoslovakia, on December 12, 1928. *A.D.* 1927/1928, case no. 378. " Dem besetzenden Staat gegenüber sind die besetzten Gebiete Ausland, in dem die Gesetze des besetzenden Staates keine Anwendung finden. " Liszt, *op. cit.*, p. 490.

2. Thus Balladore Pallieri : " ...onde per tutte quelle materie per cui non sussiste alcuna norma internazionale che le attribuisca alla competenza dell'occupante, continua la competenza dello Stato invaso ". *Op. cit.*, pp. 340-341.

3. See above, pp. 76-77.

4. « Les ordonnances de l'occupant, les dispositions organiques, politiques, militaires, prises par lui, ne survivent pas à l'occupation ; comme celle-ci, elles n'ont pu avoir qu'un caractère provisoire ; de plein droit donc, elles perdent leur force obligatoire, et les dispositions légales qu'elles ont abrogées recouvrent la leur. » Rivier, *op. cit.*, II, p. 315. « A la fin de l'occupation toutes les ordonnances promulguées par l'occupant sont abrogées de plein droit ; les lois de l'occupé y restent en vigueur et celles dont l'occupant a le droit de paralyser les effets en vertu du droit des gens reprennent de plein droit leur force. Toutes ces conséquences ne peuvent s'expliquer que par la persistance du pouvoir public de l'Etat envahi ; il n'est empêché de l'exercer que passagèrement. » Sauser-Hall, *op. cit.*, p. 68.

the very existence of belligerent occupation, but its scope is even then strictly territorial. In other words, even an effective occupation is not capable of producing legal effects outside the limits of actually occupied territory [1]. No such limitation has ever applied to a State normally functioning on its own territory, whose legal order radiates beyond its borders to the point of being normally enforced by courts of foreign States.

c) *Belligerent Occupation and De Facto Government.*

The principle of the continuity of the occupied State cannot be definitely asserted, unless a possible and dangerous confusion is first eliminated ; namely, the confusion between belligerent occupation and *de facto* government. However improbable, such a confusion did in fact occur when, for obviously political reasons, the British Government recognized the Italian Government as the *de facto* government of Ethiopia, at a time when, according to international law, that government should have been considered merely as an occupying power. This attitude of Great Britain, assimilating belligerent occupation to a *de facto* government, was confirmed in the well-known decision of an English court in the case *Bank of Ethiopia v. National Bank of Egypt and Liguori* [2]. This controversial decision [3] was criticised by Prof. Sauser-Hall, particularly with the view to a clarification of the notions involved. A *de facto* government, says Prof. Sauser-Hall, is a consequence of internal disturbances or civil wars, whereas belligerent occupation results from an international conflict. A *de facto* government can claim international recognition when it has firmly established itself, while belligerent occupation is by its very nature provisional. A *de facto* government aims at the definite overthrow and elimination of the regular government, while belligerent occupation is bound to end with the re-establishment of peace. Finally, a *de facto* government tends to substitute a new sovereignty for that of its political adversaries ; belligerent occupation, on the contrary, leaves the sovereignty of the occupied State intact [4].

This is the crux of the matter. For an assimilation of belligerent occupation and *de facto* government not only dangerously enlarges the powers of the occupant, but moreover, is bound to confuse and under-

---

1. « L'occupation s'étend à toutes les parties du territoire dont l'armée ennemie est réellement et matériellement maîtresse, mais pas au-delà. La possession doit toujours être effective ; une occupation fictive n'existe pas, n'est pas reconnue en droit des gens. » Rivier, *op. cit.*, II, p. 300. See also Balladore Pallieri, *op. cit.*, pp. 329-330 ; Sauser-Hall, *op. cit.*, pp. 88 and 110. An isolated judicial decision to the contrary by the Greek Aeropagos, of 1935, A.D. 1919/22, case no. 154, has been severely criticized by the Editor. — This is accurately reflected by a judgment of the Geneva Tribunal of 1917 : « Attendu que les mesures prises par un belligérant en pays occupés ne peuvent ressortir d'effets que dans les pays occupés et chez les belligérants ou leurs alliés... Attendu... qu'il s'agit là de mesures exceptionnelles de guerre qui ne peuvent trouver aucune application en Suisse... » *S.A. russe des Charbonnages, mines et usines de Sosnowice contre la Banque de dépôts et crédits, Erdmann et Flakenhausen ès qualité (intervenants)*, quoted by Sauser-Hall, *op. cit.*, 115-116.
2. A.D., 1935/37, case no. 38.
3. See below, pp. 265-267.
4. *Op. cit.*, pp. 70-71.

mine the clear notion of identity and continuity of the occupied State, which, as has been seen, is fully preserved by the international regime of occupation. A *de facto* government, it may be repeated, is an internal State phenomenon ; belligerent occupation is external to the occupied State. To mistake belligerent occupation for a *de facto* government would mean treating the occupied State as annexed, its continuity as interrupted, its identity as lost and its personality as merged with that of the occupant.

To sum up: belligerent occupation is certainly not merely " a fact ", as would appear from the rather unfortunate formulation of Art. 43 of the Hague Regulations which has been taken over by municipal enactments [1] and by a number of writers. It is a definite legal situation, envisaged and authorized by international law. As such, however, it remains exceptional and strictly limited. Its limitations are determined by the overriding principle of the continuity of the occupied State.

5. POSITIVE ASPECTS OF THE RULE.

This principle which, in its negative aspect, restricts the power of the occupant, provides, in its positive aspect, for the unchanged international status of the occupied State.

a) *Static Aspect.*

Thus, the territory of the occupied State remains exactly the same and no territorial changes, undertaken by the occupant, can have any validity. In other words, frontiers remain exactly as they were before the occupation. The same applies to the personal sphere of validity of the occupied State ; in other words, occupation does not affect the nationality of the population, who continues to owe allegiance to the occupied State [2]. There can hardly be a more serious breach of international law than forcing the occupant's nationality on citizens of the occupied State [3].

A fortiori, judges and officials continue to owe allegiance to the occupied State [4].

Further, while legal measures of the occupant are, as has been seen [5], strictly limited by the territorial extent of effective occupation, the legal order of the occupied State continues not only to be valid,

---

1. See below, p. 108, *f.-n.* 1.
2. This entails the possibility of a national being guilty of treason towards his State and being subsequently punished for it on the liberation of the territory. See McNair, *Legal Effects of War*, p. 333. The following passage from a decision by the Privy Council is particularly illuminating in this respect : " The protection of a State does not cease merely because the State forces, for strategical or other reasons, are temporarily withdrawn so that the enemy for the time being exercises the rights of an army in occupation. On the contrary, when such territory reverts to the control of its rightful Sovereign, wrongs done during the foreign occupation are cognizable by the ordinary Courts. The protection of the Sovereign has not ceased. It is continuous, though the actual redress of what has been done amiss may be necessarily postponed until the enemy forces have been expelled. " Quoted by McNair, *ibid.*
3. See Sauser-Hall, *op. cit.*, p. 78.
4. *Ibid.*, pp. 67-68 ; Martens, *op. cit.*, III, pp. 251-252 ; Rivier, *op. cit.*, II, pp. 304-306 ; Oppenheim-Lauterpacht, *op. cit.*, II, p. 342.
5. See above, pp. 81-82.

but to be actually enforced outside the occupied territory. Thus, United States courts took for granted the continued applicability and enforceability abroad of the laws of the occupied countries, whether enacted prior to the occupation on native soil, or in exile [1]. The same attitude was adopted by British courts [2].

b) *Dynamic Aspect.*

i) *Expansion of the Legal Order of the Occupied State.*

In addition to the above described static aspect of the continuity of the occupied State, there exists what may be called the dynamic aspect of the same principle. Namely, always in striking contrast to the territorial limitations of the occupant's measures, the legal order of the occupied State not only persists, but can continue to develop and even to expand from abroad into the occupied territory. This view was firmly upheld by Belgium ever since the First World War [3].

Examining the possibility of the effectiveness in the occupied territory of legislation of an exiled Government, Sir Arnold McNair says :

> It is at any rate arguable that, assuming the new law to fall within the category of that large portion of national law which persists during the occupation and which the enemy occupant cannot lawfully change or annul, it ought to operate in occupied territory in spite of the absence of power to make it effective during the occupation [4].

This view has the support of several municipal decisions. Thus in the case *De Nimal v. De Nimal*, in which a Royal Decree of October 28, 1914 was relied upon during the German occupation, the Brussels Court of Appeal held that laws enacted by the regular authority were binding and applicable in a country under military occupation as long as they did not prejudice the occupying Power [5]. This principle was generally upheld by Belgian courts [6]. Similarly, the Latvian Senate affirmed that :

---

1. See *Radovic v. The Prince Pavle*, A.D., 1941/42, case no. 45. *Anderson v. N. V. Transadine Handelmaatschappi, ibid.*, case no. 4.
2. See *Lorentzen v. Lydden*, A.D., 1941/42, case no. 34.
3. « Toutes les dispositions prises par le Gouvernement Belge sont, en principe, obligatoires, dans toute l'étendue du Royaume. Les règles qu'il édicte, les sanctions qu'il commine, s'étendent au territoire occupé aussi bien qu'au sol demeuré inviolé. Leur exécution seule a pu et peut être suspendue par la force ennemie. Aussi, dès la libération du territoire, ces arrêtés-lois, ces arrêtés et règlements devront-ils y être appliqués sans nouvelle publication. Tous les faits juridiques postérieurs aux arrêtés-lois, aux arrêtés et règlements du Gouvernement seront régis par eux. Les auteurs des infractions commises en territoire envahi aussi bien qu'en territoire libre auront à en répondre devant les juridictions nationales. » Quoted by Drucker, *The Legislation of the Allied Powers in the United Kingdom*, in Cz. Y., p. 57, *f.-n.*
4. *Op. cit.*, p. 382-383. Prof. Sauser-Hall is even more categorical : « S'il s'agit d'actes législatifs du souverain légal qui ne lèsent en rien les droits reconnus à l'occupant par les usages internationaux, mais au contraire, doivent permettre une certaine adaptation des habitants à la situation momentanée qui leur est faite, le vainqueur n'a pas le droit de s'opposer à leur publication ni à leur mise en vigueur. » The sovereign « a le droit de légiférer même pour les territoires occupés. » *Op. cit.*, p. 103-104. Prof. Sauser-Hall goes on to quote decrees of the French Government of National Defence of Bordeaux and the Delegation of Tours, during the Franco-Prussian war of 1870-71, which were promulgated for the whole of the French territory, whether occupied or not.
5. A.D., 1919/22, case no. 311.
6. See e.g. : *Auditeur militaire v. G. van Dieren, ibid.*, case no. 310.

" The fact of the occupation and evacuation does not in itself preclude the coming into force, within the occupied or evacuated parts of the State, of laws enacted by that State's central authorities, so long as these parts are not separated from the State by a public-law procedure [1]. "

A similar view was held by the Polish Supreme Court [2].
The same attitude was adopted by courts of the Allied countries after the Second World War. Thus the Belgian Court of Cassation *in re Hoogeveen et Al.*, November 6, 1944, confirmed the capacity of the exiled Government to legislate for occupied territory [3]. In the case *Public Prosecutor v. Reider Haaland* of 1945, the Norwegian Court of Appeal held that the Sovereign could issue decrees which were valid for the territories under enemy occupation [4]. In the case *Nederlands Beheerinstituut v. Robaver*, the District Court at The Hague held on December 17, 1947, that " the Netherlands Government in London could legislate for occupied Holland " and that " the temporary lack of sanctions did not exempt the citizens from their obligation of obedience to the law " [5]. This view was confirmed on appeal by the Court of Appeal at the Hague, on December 15, 1948 [6].
The principle is, however, not undisputed. Thus, the Belgian-German Mixed Arbitral Tribunal held in 1922 that a Belgian decree of December 10, 1916, forbidding trading between Belgian and German nationals, had no effect in occupied territory [7]. A similar attitude was adopted by the Court of Thrace, concerning the validity of Greek decrees in Bulgarian-occupied territory [8]. Similarly, the Greek Council of State in its Judgment no. 54 of 1945 stated that

" ... the enactment having been promulgated in Cairo by the Greek Government there established during the enemy occupation of Greece, cannot be regarded as having the force of law within Greece, as the said Government did not dispose of the physical force requisite to impose such laws and assure their application [9]. "

Whatever the divergence of practice, it is difficult to contest the logic of Sir Arnold McNair's contention. On condition of their conformity with the Hague Regulations, it is difficult to see why immediate validity of newly enacted laws of the occupied State should be refused in occupied territory, or why the non-cooperation of the occupant resulting in the material impossibility of their enforcement should render them invalid.
But even when the occupant refuses to admit the immediate applicability of the new law, it usually becomes immediately binding on the liberation of the territory and need not be re-enacted on native soil [10]. In other words, it is only their immediate enforceability, and not their validity which is affected by the occupation.

1. *Kulturas Balas Co-operative Society v. Latvian Ministry for Home Affairs, ibid.*, case no. 321.
2. *Stasiuk and Jagnycz v. Klewec*, A.D., 1927/28, case no. 380.
3. A.D., 1943/45, case no. 148.
4. *Ibid.*, case no. 154.
5. A.D., 1947, case no. 108.
6. *Rotterdamsche Bank Ltd. v. Nederlandsch Beheers-Institut*, A.D., 1948, case no. 174.
7. *Herwyn v. Muller, Rec. TAM*, II, p. 368.
8. *Ocupation of Cavalla case*, A.D., 1929/30, case no. 292.
9. *Re X. Y.*, A.D., 1943/45, case no. 147.
10. See below, pp. 100-101.

Thus, whether a law-abiding attitude of the occupying power makes it possible for the legal order of the occupied State to retain a certain amount of effectiveness in the occupied territory, or whether, in disregard of the Hague Conventions the occupant eliminates even the last traces of that effectiveness, the continuity of the occupied State is safeguarded, not by an act of will of the occupying power, but by a clear, objective rule of international law [1].

ii) *Sovereignty in Exile.*

Nothing illustrates this dynamic aspect of the continuity of the occupied State better than the existence and activity of exiled governments or, as is sometimes more radically said, States in exile.

It was during the first World War that this somewhat abstract conception was tangibly demonstrated by the physical existence on foreign soil of the governments and armies of the occupied States.

The case of Belgium, although best known, is of relatively less interest for the problem of State continuity under belligerent occupation. For not only was the total occupation of the Belgian territory by the German army never effected, but — which is even more important — the continued existence of the Belgian State was never seriously disputed by the occupant. Whatever German plans for the future of Belgium in case of a final German victory [2], they never openly proclaimed either the extinction of the Belgian State or its annexation [3].

During the whole period of German occupation the Belgian Government functioned on French territory, in Sainte-Adresse, Le Havre, the French Government having assured to its Belgian guest the full exercise of its sovereign independence [4]. The diplomatic corps followed the Government to Sainte-Adresse. The impossibility of convening the Belgian Parliament was met by legislation by Royal Decree. The Belgian army was maintained in the field. Belgian colonies were administered by the Government and a whole organisation of assistance to Belgian refugees was set up. The Government operated on French soil until the liberation of the country and its return home, when the Belgian State resumed its normal functioning on its own territory, with no break of continuity resulting from the period of occupation.

---

1. " ...e tutto ciò non in forza di un comando dell'occupante, di un riconoscimento da parte di questo dell'efficacia di quel ordinamento, ma unicamente per la persistenza di detto ordinamento, che continua rispetto a certe materie ad avere valore, e per la persistenza di quella organizzazione statale che l'occupante deve lasciare sussistere e non può cercare di sopprimere. " Bailadore Pallieri, *op. cit.,* p. 336.

2. See De Visscher, *La séparation administrative décrétée en Belgique par l'autorité allemande, RGDIP,* 1918, pp. 92-103.

3. This is particularly evident from the German reply of January 13, 1915, to the Belgian protest against the cancellation by the German authorities of the exequatur of neutral consuls in Belgium. In it, the German government never questioned the continued Belgian sovereignty, limiting itself to a different interpretation of the Hague Regulations. See Garner, J. W. *International Law and the World War,* London : Longmans, Green and Co., 1920, pp. 59-61.

4. For the position of the Belgian Government in France, see Jumeau A., *op. cit.,* pp. 69-83.

The position of the exiled Serbian government was much more significant [1] for the two following reasons : first, the enemy occupation extended to the whole of Serbian territory, and, secondly, the continued existence of the Serbian State was not uncontested, since the Bulgarian occupant (differing in this from the Austrian occupant) did not act within the prescribed framework of belligerent occupation ; on the contrary, far from respecting the continuity of the Serbian State, Bulgaria pronounced its extinction and generally treated the part of Serbia which she occupied, as annexed territory. Nevertheless, this unlawful attitude of Bulgaria had no effect on the legal status of occupied Serbia and its exiled government. Having established itself in Corfu, accompanied by the diplomatic corps, the Serbian Government continued its military and political activities, fully recognized and supported by the Allies. In November 1916, the re-organized Serbian army began the re-conquest of Serbian territory. The Serbian State survived not only the complete occupation of the country, but also the illegal action of Bulgaria. If, on the morrow of the First World War, it ceased to exist to be replaced by the new Kingdom of the Serbs, Croats and Slovenes, this fact had nothing whatever to do with war and occupation, but was the result of the free and spontaneous creation by the peoples concerned of a new and united State [2].

It is often forgotten that one more government survived the entire occupation of its territory, without, however, surviving the subsequent events. This was the government of Montenegro [3], which after the occupation of that country established itself at Neuilly. In this case too, it was not belligerent occupation which brought about the extinction of the Montenegrine State, but events taking place after the end of the occupation [4].

These precedents were to be repeated on a far greater scale during the Second World War. On the occupation of a great number of European countries, their governments availed themselves of the British invitation to settle down in London, to continue their activities and their war effort from there.

The unusually wide range of these activities represents a tangible illustration of the dynamic aspect of the continuity of these occupied States. This proposition is, of course, only true on the assumption of the unbroken organic link between the exiled governments and the States they represented ; in other words, on the assumption of their continued character of State organs. This statement may seem obvious ; it is, however, necessary in view of the fact that the organ character of the exiled governments has been unexpectedly denied by Prof. Guggenheim.

The reader of the first volume of Prof. Guggenheim's *Lehrbuch* is struck by the unusual role assigned by him to the governments in exile,

---

1. See Jumeau, *op. cit.*, pp. 84-104.
2. See below, pp. 237-262.
3. See Jumeau, *op. cit.*, pp. 147-150.
4. See below, pp. 240-241.

namely that of an independent subject of international law [1]. According to Prof. Guggenheim, exiled governments belong to the same category as sovereign States, the Holy See, belligerents and insurgents. This view drew the unavoidable critical comment from Prof. Verdross in his review of the *Lehrbuch* to the effect that exiled government are merely organs of a subject of international law, but not such a subject themselves [2].

It was in reply to this criticism that Prof. Guggenheim defended his view in the following manner :

" ... the exiled governments are not organs of a State, but particular subjects, not identical with those States whose territory is occupied by a third State. It is only individuals directly subordinated to the exiled governments who are responsible for their acts. The population of the occupied territory, however, is not subordinated to the exiled government, but to the surviving legal order of the State which continues to be valid in spite of the occupation and irrespective of the existence or non-existence of an exiled government, but whose effectiveness has been partly suspended [3]. "

It is earnestly submitted that Prof. Guggenheim's point of view does not find support either in theory or in the State practice.

From the theoretical point of view the argument is not easily understood. In particular, it is impossible to see why Prof. Guggenheim should split the unitary legal phenomenon of State into two artificial creations having nothing in common, and why he should introduce two subjects of international law where there is obviously only one.

If the reason for this splitting lies in the absence of effectiveness in the occupied territory, then the answer is that belligerent occupation is precisely the classical case, where the principle of effectiveness is relegated to the background and yields its place to contrary rules of international law. Prof. Guggenheim himself admits that the legal order of the occupied State continues to be valid in spite of the occupation and its effectiveness ; but if this is so, the government itself continues to preserve its status, as a part and an emanation of this surviving legal order. Why should the survival of a legal order stop abruptly at an artificially created limit, why should it embrace the whole of the legal structure of a State with the sudden exception of its central organ, the government ? Prof. Guggenheim does not answer this question. Why should the government of an existing State (and that Prof. Guggenheim does not question) be an integral part of its legal order as long as it remains in the territory and cease to be so when it acts outside the

---

1. *Op. cit.*, I, p. 199.
2. " Dazu ist jedoch zu bemerken, dass die Exilregierungen nur Organe eines Völkerrechtssubjektes, aber nicht selbst Völkerrechtssubjekte sind... " *Oesterreichische Zeitschrift für öffentliches Recht*, 1949, II, Heft 1.
3. *Transl. mine, op. cit.*, II, p. 787, f.-n. 62 : " ...handelt es sich bei den Exilregierungen nicht um Organe eines Staates, sondern um besondere Subjekte, die nicht mit jenen Staaten identisch sind, deren Gebiet von einem anderen Staat besetzt ist. Für Handlungen der Exilregierungen haften nur die ihnen unmittelbar unterworfenen Individuen. Das im besetzten Gebiet befindliche Volk ist jedoch nicht der Exilregierung unterstellt, sondern den nicht untergegangenen staatlichen Rechtsordnung, die trotz der Besetzung unobhängig vom Bestehen oder Nichtbestehen einer Exilregierung weiterhin gilt, deren Wirksamkeit aber zum Teil suspendiert ist. "

territory, is left unexplained. Why should an existing State be artificially considered as having no government when it in fact has one, and, on the other hand, why should an existing government be artificially cut off from its very basis, the continuing legal order whose survival is not subject to any doubt by Prof. Guggenheim? What basis, other than an existing legal order, can be found for a government which otherwise would be an artificial creation with no legal basis at all? It is submitted that there is no such thing as a " government " which is not a government of a given State.

A State, temporarily deprived of its organs, can be conceived [1]; but the idea of organs deprived of their State is simply inconceivable. According to Prof. Guggenheim, however, such organs would not only continue to exist in spite of losing their legal basis, but would, on the contrary, be elevated to the rank of an independent subject of international law.

A government of a State can lose this character only by the disappearance of the State itself [2]. But it is unthinkable that a State organ should lose this character merely because it temporarily transfers its activities abroad, while the State, of which it forms integral part, continues to exist. A State may function in foreign territory even under normal peace-time conditions and it is precisely this fact which has been used by Kelsen in order to disprove the traditional theory of the " impenetrability " of States [3]. Kelsen rightly distinguishes between the creation of norms (" faits-conditions ") and their enforcement (" faits conditionnés "), which includes the element of compulsion [4]. According to him, the former can be normally accomplished anywhere outside the State territory [5]; the latter cannot without the consent of the territorial State.

The same view is also held by Sir Arnold McNair :

" Unless the laws of the allied country limit the validity of governmental acts to those done upon the territory of that country... it is submitted that it is immaterial in an English Court where the official act is done... There is no principle of international law which says that a Government cannot act validly upon foreign territory with the consent of the local sovereign. Moreover, when a Head of State is visiting a foreign country either for the purpose of a holiday or in order to take a cure for gout, it is the regular practice for official decrees and other documents requiring his signature to be sent to him for that purpose. We suggest therefore that the validity of the decree of an allied Government made in London is no greater and no less than if it were made in its own capital, subject to any requirement of its own Constitution as to the locality of governmental acts [6]. "

---

1. Such would be the case of a State passing through a temporary period of anarchy; such would also be the case of post-war Germany, in the period following her military defeat, always on the assumption o˙ the continuity o˙ the pre-war German State. Cf. Guggenheim, *Validité*, p. 244, *f.-n.*
2. Apart from cases of dispossession of one government by another, which is an entirely different matter from the one discussed here.
3. *Les rapports de système entre le droit interne et le droit international public, Rec.* 1926, IV, p. 250.
4. *Théorie générale*, p. 194 et seq.
5. He quotes examples of ministers signing State documents when abroad, e.g. at a League of Nations session in Geneva, etc.
6. *Op. cit.*, pp. 357-358.

The two opinions quoted throw an additional light on the true nature of the exiled governments as organs of their respective States, i.e. as sovereign bodies, by emphasizing the difference between sovereignty, on the one hand, and the exercise of sovereignty, on the other. The territorial State does not invest exiled governments with rights which they hold exclusively on the strength of their own legal orders and of which they have never been deprived by belligerent occupation of their countries. It merely makes the exercise of these rights possible in its own territory [1]. The problem does not concern the existence or the source of the rights or exiled governments which do not become a delegation of the territorial State, but relates exclusively to the exercise of such rights on foreign soil.

Sir Arnold McNair makes this quite clear :

" The mere fact that a foreign Government has been deprived of the control of a part or the whole of its territory by an enemy in no way invalidates legislation passed or other acts of sovereignty done by it outside its normal territory, provided that its constitutional law contains no insuperable obstacle to the validity of such legislation or other sovereign acts and provided that His Majesty continues to recognize it as the *de iure* Government and recognizes no other Government as the *de facto* sovereign [2]. "

Stressing the irrelevance of the removal of the seat of the government, Oppenheimer states :

" It is not conceivable that sovereignties recognized by the English Crown should be prevented from doing in London what they could do if they were in their own countries [3]. "

Thus, *in re Amand* the King's Bench Division held :

" ... there is no flaw in the title of the Queen to do *here* what appertains to the Sovereign and the Government of the Netherlands [4]... "

Referring to the continued recognition by Great Britain of the Sovereign and the Government of the Netherlands, the Court rightly pointed out :

" That Government, however, did not thereby acquire any powers over Netherlands subjects not otherwise possessed by it according to Netherlands law [5]. "

The point was further elucidated by the Czechoslovak Military Court in London :

" What is the authority of the (British) Allied Forces Act in relation to a Czechoslovak military court established in Great Britain ? It must be emphasized that a Czechoslovak court cannot derive its power to exercise jurisdiction as a

---

1. " A State cannot exercise rights of sovereignty in the territory of another State without the latter's consent. " Oppenheimer, *Governments and Authorities in Exile*, p. 594.
2. *Op. cit.*, p. 357.
3. *Op. cit.*, pp. 582-583.
4. *It. mine*, quoted by Oppenheimer, *op. cit.*, p. 583.
5. *A.D.*, 1941/42, case no. 28.

Czechoslovak court from any source other than one of Czechoslovak law. ... This does not, however, mean that the Czechoslovak military courts may exercise their jurisdiction on the territory of Great Britain without limitation and in all cases ."

The Court then dealt with the question of the territorial sovereignty and the necessity for the Czechoslovak Army to respect the rules of British law which it examined and concluded :

" This does not mean that the Czechoslovak military courts in Great Britain cease to be Czechoslovak courts. They are and remain Czechoslovak courts in so far as they exercise their jurisdiction. A provision of British law as mentioned above means merely that in certain cases in which the Czechoslovak courts on Czechoslovak territory would have jurisdiction, they cannot exercise it while on British soil [1]. "

Clearly, it is always the legal order of the State which constitutes the legal basis for the existence of its government, whether such government continues to function in its own country or goes into exile ; but never the delegation of the territorial State nor any rule of international law other than the one safeguarding the continuity of an occupied State. The relation between the legal order of the territorial State and that of the occupied State, represented by its exiled government, is not one of delegation, but of co-existence [2].

It may perhaps also be added that, had exiled governments in fact been new subjects of international law, the problem of their recognition would inevitably have arisen. But no such problem was ever raised, either by the territorial State, by other Allied States, nor by any of the neutrals. No State proceeded to grant such recognition, which was quite unnecessary on the assumption that the occupied States and their organs abroad retained their identity, but which would have been necessary for the establishment of diplomatic relations with new subjects of international law [3].

On the strength of the above analysis it is submitted that it is theoretically impossible to regard exiled governments as legal entities detached from their respective States. On the contrary, they can only be conceived as organs of their States, acting on the basis of their own legal order whose continuity is unbroken by belligerent occupation.

This view is fully suported by State practice expressed in both international agreements and municipal legislation.

It might be convenient to begin with the latter. The British Parliament passed three important Acts dealing with the problem of foreign sovereignties in Britain. The first, the Allied Forces Act, 1940, provided that :

" Where any naval, military or air forces of any foreign power allied with His Majesty are for the time being present in the United Kingdom or on board any of His Majesty's ships or aircraft, the naval, military and air force courts and

---

1. *Allied Forces (Czechoslovakia) Case*, A.D., 1941/42, case no. 31.
2. Thus, Oppenheimer, *op. cit.*, pp. 594-595.
3. See below, pp. 438-439. See also the U.S. Note on Holland, of June 4, 1940, declaring that the U.S. Government " continues to recognize " the Royal Netherlands Government. Quoted by Flory, *Le statut international des gouvernments en exil et le cas de la France libre*, p. 36, f.-n. 1.

authorities of that Power may, subject to the provisions of this Act, exercise within the United Kingdom or on board any such ship or aircraft in relation to members of those forces, in matters concerning discipline and internal administration, all such powers as are conferred upon them by the law of that Power. " (S. 1 (1).)

It should be emphasized that the Act speaks of forces of a foreign Power, not of a foreign government. That the Act refers to a foreign State and not merely to some organisation or authority, is further shown by Subsection 2 of the same Section, which speaks not of a foreign allied power, but of a " foreign authority recognized by His Majesty as competent to maintain naval, military or air forces for service in association with His Majesty's Forces " and whose powers under the Act are far more limited than those of a " Power ". The underlying principle becomes clear when it is recalled that Subsection 1 was intended to refer to the exiled governments and Subsection 2 to General de Gaulle's Fighting French [1].

The Diplomatic Privileges (Extension) Act, 1941, was based on the same assumption :

" 1. Extension of diplomatic privileges to members of foreign governments. While any person is recognized by His Majesty to be

a) a member of the government of any foreign Power or of a provisional government, being a government for the time being allied with His Majesty and established in the United Kingdom ; or

b) a member of any national committee or other foreign authority for the time being established in the United Kingdom and recognized by His Majesty as competent to maintain armed forces for service in association with His Majesty's forces,

then, for the purpose of any enactment, rule of law or custom relating to the immunities and privileges of an envoy of a foreign Power accredited to His Majesty, and of the retinue of such an envoy, that person shall be treated, as if he were such an envoy and his official staff shall be treated as if they were his retinue...

2. Extension of diplomatic privileges to envoys accredited to allied foreign Powers. While any person is recognized by His Majesty to be

a) the envoy of a foreign Power accredited to any such foreign Power or provisional government as is mentioned in paragraph a) of subsection (1) of the foregoing section ; or

b) the representative of any such provisional government as aforesaid accredited to any such foreign Power as aforesaid ;

he shall be treated, for the purpose of any enactment, rule of law or custom relating to the immunities and privileges of an envoy of a foreign Power accredited to His Majesty and of the retinue of such an envoy, as if he were such an envoy [2]. "

Here, the special status of foreign " Powers " is even more clearly stressed by their being further distinguished not only from " any national committee or other foreign authority " but also from " a provisional government ".

Finally, the very title of the last Act, namely the Allied Powers (Maritime Courts) Act, 1941, speaks for itself.

---

1. Allied Forces Act, published in *The Public General Acts*, 1940, p. 479.
2. *Ibid.*, 1941, p. 2.

" During the continuance in force of this Act, it shall be lawful for any Power to which this Act applies to establish and maintain in the United Kingdom courts of justice, to be called Maritime Courts [1]... "

There can be no doubt that, for Britain, the exiled governments were identical with the States whom they represented and whose organs they were. The question is not merely one of words, but of substance. In an Act of Parliament, and one which laid down subtle distinction between the various bodies described, the terminology employed can hardly have been accidental. What sort of law were the courts of the " foreign Power ", represented by its exiled government, to apply, if not the law of their own State ? What nationals could form an army, if not the nationals of the State, since a " government in exile " cannot, as such, have any nationals of its own ?

A further proof that the exiled governments continued to be State organs is to be found in the numerous treaties and agreements to which they were parties. These treaties can be divided into two groups : those providing for the needs of the moment, and those concluded with a view to the future.

The first group dealt chiefly with current military problems, bearing on the organisation of the exiled armies in the territorial State, inter-allied military cooperation, and so forth [2]. If the diplomatic activity of the exiled governments had been limited to such agreements — as the activities of the Czechoslovak and Polish National Committees had been during the first World War — then Prof. Guggenheim's view that only individuals directly subordinated to those governments would be responsible for their acts might possibly be valid ; although it is difficult to see how an accidental group of people can become a subject of international responsibility.

But far from concluding only such agreements dealing with day to day problems arising in exile, the exiled governments were also parties to agreements directly affecting their States and giving rise to the latter's international responsibility in a normal manner. Only a few of the numerous agreements falling into this category may be quoted :

Agreements for Mutual Aid Pursuant to the Lend-Lease Act (concluded by the United States with Belgium on June 16, 1942, with Czechoslovakia on July 11, 1942, with Greece on July 10, 1942, with the Netherlands on July 8, 1942, with Norway on July 11, 1942, with Poland on July 1, 1942 and with Yugoslavia on July 24, 1942), especially

---

1. *Ibid.*, p. 147. For the unusual character of these courts, see Oppenheimer, *op. cit.*, pp. 593-594 ; cf. speeches at the opening ceremony of the Allied Maritime Courts by the Lord Chancellor, Viscount Simon and Dr. J. M. de Moor, reported in the *Law Quarterly Review* of 1942, vol. LVIII, no. 229, p. 41 et seq., as well as Viscount Simon's article on *Foreign Maritime Courts* in the *Journal of Comparative Legislation and International Law*, Third Series, vol. XXIV, Part. I, pp. 1-5. Here is a quotation from this article : " The interesting and important thing is that there are being set up within our own borders, under the authority of an Act of Parliament passed for the purpose, courts which are not the King's courts but are courts of another Power, staffed by judges who are not British judges and are not appointed by any British authority, and dealing with offences by foreigners which would not be triable in English courts at all. "

2. Oppenheimer, *op. cit.*, p. 577 ; Schwelb, *The Jurisdiction over the Members of the Allied Forces in Great Britain*, in Cz. Y.

in their final clauses relating to the future, — the Final Act of the United Nations Food and Agricultural Conference of June 3, 1943, the Agreement to set up the United Nations Relief and Rehabilitation Administration of November 9, 1943, — the Final Act of the Monetary and Financial Conference of July 22, 1944, — the International Agreement and the Final Act of the International Civil Aviation Conference of December 7, 1944.

It would hardly have occurred to anyone to conclude such agreements with mere " governments ", representing only themselves and having no link with their States which were thus to incur international responsibility and with whom alone such agreements could have been validly and reasonably concluded.

The Civil Affairs Agreements concluded by the United States and the United Kingdom with Belgium and the Netherlands and by the United States, the United Kingdom and U.S.S.R. with Norway on May 16, 1944, and concerning arrangements to be made for civil administration and jurisdiction in the Belgian, Dutch and Norwegian territories on their liberation by the Allied Forces fall into the same category [1].

A number of purely political agreements were also concluded with, or between, exiled governments, relating to the future policy of their States ; e.g. the United Nations Declaration of January 1, 1942, or the Polish-Soviet declaration of policy of December 4, 1941. The joint Allied declaration of January 5, 1943, concerning German acts of spoliation in the occupied countries, should also be mentioned in this connection.

Nor should it be forgotten that claims arising out of financial obligations incurred by the exiled governments were made against, and actually met by, the liberated countries and not by a group of individuals who happened to be abroad at the time those obligations were contracted. Moreover, even before the liberation, assets of the occupied States transferred abroad, and not the assets of individuals, were the subject of negotiations and were engaged by the respective exiled governments.

Prof. Guggenheim's final argument is that the population in the occupied territory was subject to the surviving legal order of the occupied State, but not to the exiled governments. It is again submitted that it is impossible to separate the government from the legal order, wherever the government may be. But, moreover, it has been seen [2] that it is possible for legislation, passed by an exiled government, to become operative in the occupied country. It is conceded that the problem has not been finally solved either in theory or in practice. Nevertheless, it took on a new aspect in the course of the Second World War, not so much as regards legislation, but the undoubted direction by exiled governments of the organized resistance movements in their countries, which often assumed the character of regular underground armies, recognized as such by the Allies as well as by the enemy [3]. As an

---

1. *Dept. of St. Bul.*, X, p. 479.
2. See above, pp. 84-86.
3. See below, pp. 443-444.

example of the effectiveness of a government in spite of the enemy control of the country itself, there could be nothing stronger, and the whole stormy history of the resistance movements during the last war bears witness to this. It is on the basis of this historical experience that organized resistance movements in an occupied country have been legalized and taken under the protection of international law by the 1949 Geneva Conventions [1].

The view that exiled governments were organs of the occupied States, acting on their behalf and on the basis of their own legal order, was forcefully and uniformly upheld by all judicial decisions on the subject.

In the case *Moraitis v. Delany* the United States Circuit Court of Appeals, Fourth District, held that :

" ... these international relationships the governments in exile are thoroughly competent to deal with. They are true governments set up and organized to protect the interests of their nationals, and their powers with regard thereto are recognized and respected by the friendly nations in whose territories they function. They exercise sovereign power, moreover, not only with respect to their nationals, but also with respect to the vessels of their countries [2]... "

The information supplied to the King's Bench Division in the first *Amand* case by the Attorney General was to the effect that

" H.M. Government recognize Her Majesty Queen Wilhelmina and her Government as the Sovereign and Government of the Netherlands and as exclusively competent to perform the legislative, administrative and other functions appertaining to the Sovereign and Government of the Netherlands [3]. "

In the case of *Anderson v. N.V. Transadine Handelmaatschappi*, heard by the Supreme Court of New York in May 1941, in which the plaintiffs questioned the validity of a Netherlands decree issued in exile, the Court stated :

" The Netherlands Decree is a valid act of the State of the Netherlands and has vested in the State of the Netherlands title and property sought to be attached. ... the acts of the Royal Netherlands Government must be deemed to be the acts of the State of the Netherlands. ... The circumstance that the Royal Netherlands Decree of May 24, 1940, was promulgated in London, England, rather than at The Hague, is immaterial, in view cf the fact that our government has officially recognized the Netherlands Government since its temporary residence in London. "

On appeal, the Court of Appeals held :

" There can be no doubt that the Decree of May 24, 1940, promulgated by the recognized Government of the State of Netherlands is part of the law of a friendly sovereign State [4]... "

The same attitude was adopted in 1948 by the District Court of the Southern District of New York in the case of the *State of the Netherlands v. Federal Reserve Bank of New York et Al* [5].

---

1. See below, p. 442.
2. *A.D.*, 1941/42, case no. 96.
3. *Ibid.*, case no. 28.
4. *Ibid.*, case no. 4.
5. *A.D.*, 1948, case no. 8.

The same view was adopted by the King's Bench Division, England, in the case of *Lorentzen v. Lydden* [1]. It is true that the facts in this case were slightly different, the Norwegian Decree in question having been issued during the Norwegian campaign, but still on Norwegian soil, in Trondhjem on May 18, 1944 ; thus, the Court had rather to examine its applicability and enforceability in Britain.

In a certificate submitted to the British Columbia Supreme Court *in re De Bruijn*, the Canadian Secretary of State for External Affairs stated :

" The Government of Canada recognizes the Government of the Queen of the Netherlands, as now constituted in the United Kingdom, as the *de iure* Government of the Netherlands, including the whole of the Netherlands Empire whether in enemy occupation or otherwise... "

Section 8 of the Foreign Forces Order of April 15, 1941, quoted in the judgment, recited :

" For the purpose of enabling the service courts and service authorities of a foreign Power [2]... "

not of a " foreign government ".

In *Haak and Others v. Minister of External Affairs*, heard before the Supreme Court of South Africa, Apellate Division, the Minister filed an affidavit, stating that

" ... the Netherlands Government in England was recognized by the Union Government ... as the properly constituted Government of the State known as Holland or the Netherlands (including its possessions in various parts of the world), a State which was actively associated with the Union in the present war, and that its representatives were recognized by the Union Government as acting on behalf of the said State or Government. "

The " Regulations to compel Conscripted non-Union Nationals to render war service ", quoted in the judgment, stated *inter alia* :

" Whenever any representative of *any State* which is associated with the Union in any war *a)* has informed the Minister of External Affairs ... that any national *of the said State* who is in the Union ... has been ordered by any person acting on behalf of the Government *of the said State* [3]... "

The Czechoslovak Military Court of Appeal in London stated in its judgment of July 15, 1942, that by the Allied Forces Act

" the military courts of any Allied Power, having for the time being armed forces in the United Kingdom were authorized to try on British territory members of those armed forces according to the law of that Power. One of these Powers is the Czechoslovak Republic [4] ".

There would thus seem to be no doubt that the exiled governments are not *sui generis* and a rather mysterious creation, deprived of a legal basis and conducting an independent activity of their own, involving at best a more or less limited number of their nationals abroad in

---

1. *A.D.*, 1941/42, case no. 34.
2. *Ibid.*, case no. 29.
3. *It. mine, ibid.*, case no. 30. See also : *Chemacid S.A. v. Ferrotar Corporation*, U.S. District Court, Southern District New York, September 15, 1943 ; *A.D.*, 1943/45, case no. 125.
4. *A.D.*, 1941/42, case no. 31.

responsibility, — but that they are regular surviving organs of regularly constituted surviving States, based organically on the surviving legal order of those States and conducting an activity bearing on those States and engaging their international responsibility. No other view is possible either in theory or in the light of the practice examined above. The exiled governments were not governments of the emigration, the emigration being by definition unable to produce a State organ. The notion of a national could not be upheld in any other case. Dutch, Norwegian, Belgian or Polish nationals in the course of the Second World War were not nationals of a " government " ; they were nationals of a State and as such subject, wherever this was materially possible, to the jurisdiction of the government of that State. It was on this basis that exiled armies were formed, accompanied by all the paraphernalia of normal conscription, compulsion and jurisdiction by the exiled governments. They were neither mercenaries nor foreign legions, but independent armies of sovereign States, whose legal basis was the law of their respective countries, to which they owed allegiance, and whose technical functioning on foreign territory alone was made possible by international agreements concluded for this purpose among sovereign States.

It clearly results from the whole foregoing analysis that the organ character of such governments in exile can only be affirmed in cases where they had been properly constituted in their own countries and simply transferred their activities abroad, following the total occupation of their territories, with no break in their legal and actual continuity. The legal title of such exiled governments is firmly anchored in their internal legality and in the uninterrupted transmission of power. They left their respective countries as regular State organs ; there was nothing to deprive them of that character. Only in such a case can it be safely claimed that the whole problem is merely one of the temporary dissociation of the State elements [1]. Only in such a case are third States bound to continue recognizing the exiled governments without enquiring into their internal standing, since such an enquiry would border on unlawful intervention.

It may perhaps be observed that the actual continuity of the exiled governments forms so strong an argument in favour of their continued character of State organs as to make up even for the often unavoidable flaws in their constitutional legality. The latter, whatever the initial basis and intention of the governments concerned, will rarely be fully achieved in exile [2]. Thus, Art. 21 of the Dutch Constitution expressly prohibited the transfer of the Government abroad [3]. Again, the internal legality of the re-creation of the Belgian Government in exile could

---

1. See Flory, *op. cit.*, p. 16.
2. Thus Flory : « Sur le plan interne, aucun gouvernement ne peut prétendre, dans son exil, respecter entièrement la lettre de sa constitution ; on pourra lui contester son départ, sa composition et l'ensemble de ses activités. Faudra-t-il alors, sous prétexte du respect de la constitution, lui enlever en droit la possibilité d'exister et le considérer comme un usurpateur ? » *Op. cit.*, p. 11. See, however, full constitutionality of the Polish Government in exile, below, p. 439.
3. *Ibid.*, p. 25.

have been strongly contested for various reasons [1]. Such flaws in the constitutionality of the exiled governments have been flatly ignored both by the State practice described above and by the relevant judicial decisions. Of these, the King's Bench Division held in *re Amand* :

" ... these are emergency circumstances and emergency circumstances render imperative the creation of emergency laws... when a state of emergency exists ... the constitution does not apply first and foremost, but the vital interests of State and people [2]. "

In *Hoogeven et Al.*, the Belgian Court of Cassation stated :

" There can be no doubt but that the legislative powers envisaged in Articles 79 and 82 of the Constitution ought, in principle, to be exercised by all the Ministers of the King, assembled in Council. But as the national sovereignty cannot be in suspense, its exercise cannot be impeded by the circumstance that certain Ministers are prevented from meeting with their colleagues [3]. "

It would therefore appear that, while the requirement of internal legality must in principle be fulfilled for an exiled government to possess the character of a State organ, minor flaws in such legality are easily cured by the overriding principle of its actual uninterrupted continuity [4].

It must therefore be concluded that, while the uninterrupted legal continuity of the exiled governments may not, in the last resort, be indispensable to the international continuity of the State, it is indeed indispensable to the organ character of such governments.

This submission is further confirmed by the entirely different position of those exiled governments which, far from merely transferring their activities abroad, are actually created on foreign soil, not only without any internal legal basis, but also following total break of governmental continuity. Failing any basis in the legal order of their States, failing an uninterrupted transmission of power, they can only claim a revolutionary basis for their legal existence. Yet, an alleged revolutionary creation on foreign soil by definition fails to satisfy the requirement of effectiveness [5]. Consequently, even if finally admitted, the organ character of such exiled governments will always necessarily rest on a presently unverifiable claim of such governments and on a more or less political and arbitrary decision of third States. The latter will have to decide upon the actual standing of such governments, a decision for which — as has just been seen — there is neither a necessity nor a justification in the case of continuing legal governments in exile. Consequently, even a recognized organ character of such newly formed governments in exile will be provisional, pending the confirmation of their claim on their return to their home countries.

---

1. *Ibid.*, p. 59, *f.-n.* 1.
2. Quoted by Taborsky, *The Czechoslovak Cause*, p. 107. The passage quoted is not reproduced in the report of the *Amand* case in *A.D.*, 1941/42, case no. 28.
3. *A.D.*, 1943/45, case no. 148.
4. It goes without saying that such continuity is not interrupted by a reshuffle in exile of the continuing governement within the framework of its legality.
5. As to the possibility of a " limited effectiveness " of a revolutionary governmental creation in exile, see below, p. 314.

The above difference between the continuing exiled governments which merely transferred their seat abroad, and the governments newly formed in exile after a period of complete break in governmental continuity, is clearly illustrated by the uncontested standing of the exiled constitutional governments of the Second World War, as contrasted with the precarious position of the Czechoslovak Government in exile and, to a much stronger degree, the French National Committee[1].

It is therefore submitted that Prof. Guggenheim's general denial of the organ character of exiled governments, could only be valid for the National Committees of the First World War, or for the governmental or pseudo-governmental bodies actually created in exile after a break in continuity, such as the Czechoslovak Government and the French National Committee during the Second World War. The former were indeed not State organs and merely represented themselves and a particular ideology; they were unrelated to any existing State and merely aimed at the creation of States in the future; there was no legal State order on which their existence was based and their international personality was seriously questioned [2]. The latter did indeed claim to have a legal connection with existing States. Yet, having been created on foreign soil with no legal continuity and with a presently unverifiable claim to revolutionary effectiveness, they could be denied the character of State organs. That character, whether ultimately recognized as in the case of the Czechoslovak Government, or consistently denied as in the case of the French National Committee, could be finally confirmed only on their return to their liberated countries.

But the constitutionally established and continuing exiled governments, far from sharing the status either of the National Committees or of the two above-mentioned bodies, continued to exist and to act as the legal governments of their countries whose legal continuity had not been affected by occupation [3]. As such, they constituted the living example of the application of the rule safeguarding the continuity of the occupied State [4]. As such, they were instrumental in carrying on, and giving tangible expression to, that continuity [5].

It was in this capacity that the exiled governments carried out acts of State sovereignty on foreign soil in every sphere, — legislative, administrative and judicial. Their main efforts were, of course, directed

---

1. See the respective chapters in Flory, *op. cit.*, and the British Parliamentary Acts quoted above, pp. 180-183; for the Czechoslovak case, see below, p. 311 et seq.

2. See Anzilotti, *op. cit.*, pp. 127-128; Udina, *Estinzione*, pp. 78-90; Blociszewski, *La restauration de la Pologne*, p. 65; see also Fauchille's controversial conception of a « reconnaissance comme nation », *op. cit.*, I, p. 311.

3. " ...such government is the only *de iure* sovereign power of the country the territory of which is under belligerent occupation. " Oppenheimer, *op. cit.*, p. 568, *f.-n.* « ...ils sont les uniques représentants de leur pays ; eux seuls peuvent l'engager et ont mission de diriger sa politique étrangère. » Flory, *op. cit.*, p. 187.

4. « L'existence des gouvernements en exil n'a, en effet, de raison d'être que dans la mesure où ils défendent leur pays, préparent la libération et assurent la continuité de l'Etat. » Flory, *op. cit.*, p. 185.

5. Since the above was written, Prof. Guggenheim, in his recently published *Traité de Droit International*, Librairie de l'Université, Georg & Cie S.A., Genève, 1955, abandoned his previous theory denying the organ character of the continuing governments in exile. « Conformément à l'opinion de Verdross, Oest.Z.f.ö.R. 1949, 144, le gouvernement en exil est toujours un organe de l'Etat occupé... » p. 209, *f.-n.* 1.

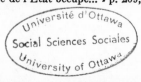

towards the further prosecution of the war alongside the Allies. Hence the creation on Allied soil of exiled armies, whose size, strength and the effective part played by them in the war is not to be underestimated. The creation and maintenance of these armies represented the highest expression of State sovereignty.

The exiled governments also engaged in intense legislative activity [1]. This legislation can be divided into two main groups : acts of an emergency nature, relating to current problems and affairs of the State in exile, and acts concerning the respective home countries.

The first group covered the organisation of the State and its organs on foreign soil (e.g. the creation of the Polish National Council, the Extraordinary Advisory Counctil of the Netherlands, the Czechoslovak State Council, the setting up of Maritime Courts on the basis of the Allied Powers (Maritime Courts) Act [2], conscription and military matters generally, economic problems, including the protection of State and private assets abroad, social welfare, education, and the like ; the second dealt with the legal effects in the occupied countries of measures enacted by the occupying Powers, the legal changes to be introduced on liberation, the organisation and status of the resistance movements, penal measures to be applied on liberation, and so forth.

It should be emphasized that both types of legislative were enforced. With regard to the first, Allied Courts invariably gave effect to the decrees of the exiled governments [3], whenever the need arose ; but more often than not such decrees were simply enforced without any dispute arising and consequently without the need for any assistance on the part of the Allied courts, e.g. conscription of nationals into exiled armies. When the size of these armies is recalled, it is surprising in how few cases the conscription measures of the exiled governments were challenged before local courts.

With regard to legislation of the second type passed in exile, this was either immediately implemented in the occupied countries [4] or at their liberation. Faced with a heritage of enemy legislation and judgments, the liberated countries proceeded to deal with the problem in accordance with decrees passed for this purpose by their governments in exile. These basic decrees, passed in the early stages of the occupation, declared null and void all acts of the occupying Powers transgressing the limits of the Hague Conventions. Of these, the most interesting are : the Polish Decree of November 11, 1939 [5] and the two Belgian decrees (" arrêtés-lois ") of January 1st, 1941.

---

1. See Oppenheimer, op. cit. ; Drucker, op. cit., as well as a series of articles in the Journal of Comparative Legislation and International Law, Third Series, namely : Lachs M., Polish Legislation in Exile, vol. XXIV, Part 1 ; Official of the Royal Norwegian Ministry of Justice and Police : Legislation in Exile — Norway, ibid., Part II ; Schwelb E., Legislation in Exile — Czechoslovakia, ibid., Part II ; Fayat H., Legislation in Exile — Belgium, vol. XXV, Parts III-IV ; Cohn E. J., Legislation in Exile — Luxembourg, ibid. ; Zeeman J. H. Legislation in Exile — The Netherlands, vol. XXVI, Parts III-IV.
2. See above, pp. 92-93.
3. See cases quoted above, pp. 95-96.
4. See Polish decree of September 1, 1942, concerning the organisation of the supreme authorities of the underground movement in Poland, below, p. 443.
5. See Drucker, op. cit., pp. 54-55.

In consequence of the latter Belgian Courts had relatively little to do after the liberation in order to clear away enemy legislation as this had been done for them by these two decrees passed in exile [1].

It may be added that the liquidation of the legislation of Belgian " Secrétaires Généraux " which very often exceeded the authorized limits (Law of May 10, 1940) with a view to placating the occupying power, went on equally on the basis of two Belgian decrees issued in London, on May 1 and May 5, 1944.

The position was exactly the same in Holland where two Royal Decrees passed in London on September 17, 1944, became the legal basis for dealing with enemy legislation and judgments [2]. Similarly in Czechoslovakia, the London Presidential Decree of August 3, 1944, on the re-establishment of the Czechoslovak legal order, became the basis of a legal reconstruction in that country [3].

The administrative activity of the exiled governments which is of less immediate interest here, wen on as a matter of routine, being obviously limited to the field of day to day problems in exile.

Their judicial activity again provides convincing proof of the continuity of the State, and not merely of the " government " abroad. The above-quoted passage of the judgment of the Czechoslovak Military Court in London [4] contains a searching analysis of the problem. Allied Courts in Britain delivered judgments in the name of their countries (or reigning Sovereign) and not in the name of their governments as separate entities.

Finally, the uninterrupted continuity of diplomatic and consular missions to Allied and neutral countries should be mentioned, as well as the functioning of the diplomatic corps accredited to the exiled governments.

There can thus be no splitting of the State into an occupied State on the one hand and an exiled government on the other. All that can be said is that during the Second World War the continuing legal order of the occupied State developed more fully abroad than in the occupied country itself where its effectiveness, but not its validity, was completely or partly suspended.

---

1. « ...dont le premier dispose que les ordonnances de l'occupant, prises dans les limites de son pouvoir de fait, sont abrogées de plein droit au fur et à mesure de la libé-ration du territoire, tandis que le second précise que les mesures prises par l'occupant en violation de la convention de La Haye, spécialement celles qui ont porté atteinte à la propriété privée, sont nulles et sont censées n'avoir jamais existé. » De Visscher P., *Enemy Legislation and Judgments in Liberated Countries : Belgium. Journal of Comparative Legislation and International Law, Third Series*, vol. XXIX, Parts III-IV.

2. Jansma K., *The Dutch Government's Treatment of the Decrees made by the German Authorities during the Occupation of the Netherlands, ibid.*

3. See Krob, *Aperçu des dispositions légales d'après guerre*, in *Bulletin de Droit Tchécoslovaque*, Année V, nos. 3-4. Examples could be easily multiplied. See, however, the enforcement by the Supreme Court of Norway on August 9, 1945, of the death penalty for treason in pursuance of a law enacted by the Norwegian Government in exile ; *Public Prosecutor v. Reider Haaland*, quoted above, p. 85.

4. See above, pp. 90-91.

6. Co-existence of Legal Orders in Occupied Territory.

A comparison of the scope of the two legal orders, of the occupied and the occupying State, co-existing in one and the same territory and limiting each other, throws an interesting light on one aspect of the principle of effectiveness in international law.

In the first place : of these two legal orders, that of the occupied State is regular and " normal ", while that of the occupying power is exceptional and limited. At the same time, the legal order of the occupant is, as has been seen [1] strictly subject to the principle of effectiveness, while the legal order of the occupied State continues to exist notwithstanding the absence of effectiveness. It can produce legal effects outside the occupied territory and may even develop and expand, not by reason of its effectiveness, but solely on the basis of the positive international rule safeguarding its continuity.

Thus, the relation between effectiveness and title seems to be one of inverse proportion : while a strong title can survive a period of non-effectiveness, a weak title must rely heavily, if not exclusively, on full and complete effectiveness. It is the latter which makes up for the weakness in title. Belligerent occupation presents an illuminating example of this relation of inverse proportion.

Belligerent occupation is thus the classical case in which the requirement of effectiveness as a condition of validity of a legal order is abandoned. The explanation of this unusual fact is to be found in the temporary nature of belligerent occupation. International law could not permanently relinquish the requirement of effectiveness, since this would mean reducing international law and relations to a pure fiction. But belligerent occupation is by definition not of a lasting character. Sooner or later it is bound to end, whether in favour of the occupied or the occupying State.

It follows that in an obviously temporary situation international law can dispense with the overriding principle of effectiveness and can admit a temporary divorce between effectiveness on the one hand and validity on the other. This disposes of any primitive notion of effectiveness ; the latter, instead of determining the law, is determined by it [2]. It would be absurd to claim that even a strong title can dispense with effectiveness altogether. But it can certainly emerge unscathed from a period in which its effectiveness has been suspended.

7. Transfer of Sovereignty and Premature Annexation.

The temporary institution of belligerent occupation can end either by the liberation of the occupied territory, with all the legal consequences

---

1. See above, pp. 81-82.
2. " ...da die Effektivität nur in dem Rahmen neues Recht begründen kann, den ihr die Völkerrechtsordnung anweist. Ausserhalb dieses Rahmens ist die blosse Herrschaft völkerrechtswidrige Gewalt, da eine schrankenlose Anerkennung der Effektivität jedes Unrecht legalisieren, damit aber das Völkorrecht überhaupt aufheben würde. " Verdross, Völkerrecht, 1. Ausgabe, Berlin 1937, p. 126.

involved, or by its annexation which, in the case of the occupation of its entire territory, will mean a final break of continuity and the extinction of the annexed State.

The two conditions for the transfer of sovereignty over occupied enemy territory have not changed since Vattel first formulated them : they are: either a peace treaty, or final subjugation, i.e. debellatio [1].

Hardly any comment is necessary with regard to a peace treaty, transferring sovereignty by way of a clear rule of conventional law and thus leaving no room for any doubt or speculation as to the validity of the title, the time at which the transfer is effected and so forth. The case is entirely different with regard to subjugation.

According to Oppenheim-Lauterpacht, it is " conquest followed by subjugation and not conquest alone " which

" is a mode of acquiring territory ... Conquered enemy territory ... remains legally under the sovereignty of the enemy until through annexation it comes under the sovereignty of the conqueror. Annexation turns the conquest into subjugation [2]."

Annexation is thus a legal, albeit a unilateral act. The fact of its being unilateral does not, however, mean that it can be effected whenever the occupant pleases. It does not have any legal effect, if undertaken *durante bello ;* its validity is conditioned upon a definitely victorious war, since

" so long as war continues conquest is not firmly established " [3].

Since annexation cannot be proclaimed before the actual end of the war, there is no room for a debellatio in a coalition war, in which the occupied State is only one of the Allies, even in the case of an occupation of the entire territory of that State. As long as the remaining Allies continue the struggle, the war has obviously not come to an end. The temporarily defeated State may find refuge in the territory of its Allies and continue the struggle together with them, thus giving positive and tangible proof of its continuity [4]. Recent history abounds in examples of this [5]. Even if the occupied State does not contribute to the common war effort, as long as the coalition war goes on, any attempted annexation is a clear breach of international law, creating no valid title whatsoever [6].

The criterion of the validity of an annexation is obviously less easy to define in a war between two States only, in which the entire territory of one of them has been occupied. At what stage can the annexation be legally effected in such a case? In practice indeed the criterion will be more difficult to establish, but the rule is no less emphatic : namely, the defeat of the occupied State must be so decisive and the enemy's victory so final, that the possibility of his expulsion can

---

1. See above, p. 75.
2. *Op. cit.,* I, pp. 518-519.
3. *Op. cit.,* I, p. 522. Cf. Heffter, *op. cit.,* p. 287 and Rivier, *op. cit.,* II, p. 300.
4. " Der Staat bliebe daher trotz Unterganges des Staatsgebietes erhalten, wenn seine Organe auf einem anderen, bisher nicht okkupierten oder von einem anderen Staate zedierten Gebiete ihre Tätigkeit fortsetzen. " Verdross, *Verfassung,* p. 149.
5. See above, pp. 86-101.
6. Cf. the case of Luxembourg in the last war.

reasonably be excluded [1]. The logic of this rule is compelling. If, as has been seen [2], a very considerable degree of effectiveness is necessary to render a mere occupation legal, how much greater and, indeed, final must this effectiveness be for the purpose of annexation.

This positive rule at the same time provides the negative notion of premature, and consequently, unlawful annexation. Such annexation, if eventually followed by actual subjugation, will necessarily result in the extinction of the conquered State and the extension of the conqueror's sovereignty over its territory. If, however, actual subjugation does not follow, if the fortunes of war change, the invader is expelled and the territory re-conquered, then the occupied State will re-assert its authority in its territory by virtue of its unbroken continuity.

History contains numerous examples of premature, and therefore illegal, annexations. However, most of them (as for instance the well-known case of the Italian annexation of Tripolitania and Cyrenaica in 1911) affected only a part of the enemy's territory. For this reason their illegal character was glaringly obvious (since there could be no question of a debellatio) ; but for this reason also they are not relevant to the problem of State continuity. What is relevant in this connection, is the premature annexation of the whole of a State's territory, naturally combined with a claim that the State concerned has become extinct. The classical example of this type of premature annexation is the British annexation of the two Boer Republics, which may therefore be examined in some detail.

In May and September 1900, i.e. two years before the actual end of the Boer war, Great Britain proclaimed the annexation not only of the occupied parts of the enemy's territory, but indeed, of the whole of the two Boer States, which she henceforth considered to be extinct ; she thus violated both the rule forbidding premature annexation and the rule requiring occupation to be fully effective [3]. The British proclamations gave rise to solemn protests by the Presidents of the Orange Free State and the Transvaal, who pointed out that their countries were far from being conquered, that their armies were still fighting, that the occupation of their respective capitals was but one of the many episodes of the war and that the proclamations were therefore null and void.

---

1. " ...annexation cannot be considered definitive and valid unless certain necessary conditions have been fulfilled e.g. the subjugation of the enemy effected so thoroughly and completely that his possible resistance may fairly and safely be regarded as a negligible potentiality. Consequently, if the invader issues a proclamation purporting to annex a given territory before this essential condition is fulfilled, the proclamation is invalid. " Phillipson, *Termination of Wars and Treaties of Peace*, pp. 21-22. « Il est nécessaire qu'un Etat soit définitivement conquis, au point que sur aucune de ses parties une résistance militaire quelconque puisse être organisée, pour qu'il y ait substitution de souveraineté. » Sauser-Hall, *op. cit.*, p. 61. " Eine solche « debellation » (affecting the entire territory) darf jedoch nicht leichthin vermutet werden. Sie setzt voraus, dass die im Zusammenhang mit der Besetzung erfolgten militärischen Akte beendet sind, sowie dass auch die Bundesgenossen des debellierten Staates darauf verzichtet haben, an der Aufhebung der Besetzung aktiv mitzuwirken. " Guggenheim, *op. cit.*, II, p. 819 ; Liszt, *op. cit.*, p. 150.

2. See above, pp. 81-82.

3. For the Boer War, see Despagnet, *Grande-Bretagne, République Sud-Africaine ou du Transvaal et Etat Libre d'Orange*, RGDIP, 1900, 1901 and 1902.

They were indeed glaringly so, and available data provide the proof of their illegality. According to a British writer, at the date of annexation

" the Boer forces had by no means been subjugated ; their organized resistance still remained and was, indeed, very vigorous and effective. Both in the Transvaal and in the Orange Free State the British subsequently met with considerable reverses ; and these reverses were inflicted by burghers who could not be considered other than the legitimate combatants of States whose independence was still in existence and whose Governments still issued orders which were obeyed. Indeed, from September 1, 1900, to September 1, 1901, the British losses amounted to 1.857 officers and 34.531 men ; so that it was manifestly impossible to claim that the armed contention was at an end [1] ".

There are additional figures concerning the territory actually conquered : as late as November 13, 1901, i.e. a year and a half after the annexation of the Orange Free State, and over a year after that of the Transvaal, the British Secretary of State for War announced the capture by British troops of 32.000 square miles of Boer territory ; this meant that 135.000 square miles, i.e. by far the greatest part, was still in Boer hands at the time of the purported annexation. Moreover, the above-quoted British " reverses " included not only the liberation of a part of Boer territory, but even a temporary invasion by the Boer forces of the Cap Colony (November-December 1900). On February 2, 1901, in his first speech from the throne, King Edward VII openly admitted that the war in South Africa was not at an end and expressed the hope of victory which had, in fact, not yet been achieved[2].

The British action met with universal condemnation, in which even prominent British statesmen joined [3]. In the House of Commons Great Britain's premature annexation was described as

" a monstrous proclamation, a proclamation absolutely opposed to the first principles of international law, a proclamation based upon a paper annexation made seven days before, which purported to treat the inhabitants of the two Republics as rebels — rebels, forsooth, on the basis of this paper annexation [4]. "

The British proclamations were not only absolutely ignored by the international community (even Portugal, in spite of very strong British influence, simply " accepted " the *fait accompli*, without any formal act of recognition), but on the contrary, the uninterrupted existence of the Boer Republics continued to be recognized. Thus, during his European journey in quest of aid and support for his country, President Krüger was everywhere received as a Head of State.

The final proof of the continuity of the two Republics, uninterrupted by the British proclamations, was, significantly enough, to be found in the attitude of Britain herself. For, notwithstanding their assertion that the two States had become extinct, the British authorities, faced with continuous Boer successes in the field, entered in March 1901 into peace negotiations with General Botha and, through him, with President

1. Phillipson, *op. cit.*, p. 23.
2. Despagnet, *op. cit.*
3. Graber, *op. cit.*, pp. 262-263.
4. Quoted by Phillipson, *op. cit.*, p. 24.

Krüger. Further proof of the continued existence of the allegedly extinct enemy States could hardly be required. It was, however, provided by the Peace Treaty, signed by all belligerents in Praetoria on May 31, 1902. It is true that the document was not described as a Peace Treaty. It was, however, signed by Lord Kitchener and Lord Milner, not simply in their capacity of military commanders, but expressly on behalf of the British Government, — and by Messrs. Steijn and Brebner, the generals de Wet and Olivier and Judge Hertzog on behalf of the Government of the Orange Free State, as well as by Messrs. Schalk-Burger and Reitz and the generals Botha, Delarey, Meyer and Krogh on behalf of the Government of the South African Republic [1]. By signing such a document, with such contracting parties, Britain herself went back on her previous attitude concerning the annexation and extinction of the Boer Republics. The Treaty of Praetoria only confirmed the invalidity of that annexation. The Orange Free State and the Transvaal did not cease to exist as a result of unlawful British action in May and September 1900 ; their extinction was not even consummated by an effective debellatio in the intervening period between the premature annexations and the Treaty of Praetoria. The existence of the two Republics came to an end as a result of a treaty concluded by the governments concerned ; it became a legal fact on the signature of the treaty, without having any retroactive effect and certainly without conferring ex post facto validity on the 1900 annexations. This too, is acknowledged in the instrument itself, in which Britain renounced her former claim to treat the Boer soldiers as mere rebels, liable to corresponding punishment [2].

It may be concluded that neither premature annexation, nor, a fortiori, occupation alone, played any part in the final extinction and loss of continuity by the two Boer Republics [3].

The conditions for a transfer of sovereignty and the invalidity of premature annexation have not undergone any change since the Boer War. An example of such premature annexation in recent times is provided by the Italian proclamation of the annexation of Ethiopia. Unlike the Boer case, the illegal action of Italy was never finally legalized either by a treaty of peace or a complete debellatio of the occupied country. It is believed that it was by reason of this illegality, combined with other unlawful acts committed by Italy that Ethiopia was able to re-assert her continued statehood at the end of the Italian occupation [4].

---

1. *British and Foreign State Papers*, vol. 95, p. 160.
2. A different opinion is voiced by Phillipson, for whom, notwithstanding the mention of the Boer Governments, the instrument represents an act of surrender and not a Treaty of Peace. *Op. cit.*, p. 17. Similarly, Oppenheim-Lauterpacht, *op. cit.*, II, p. 468, *f.-n.* 2.
3. Writers are almost unanimous in condeming the British action in South Africa : e.g. Liszt, *op. cit.*, p. 150 ; Balladore Pallieri, *op. cit.*, p. 328 ; even Oppenheim-Lauterpacht, who call it " somewhat premature ", *op. cit.*, II, p. 468, *f.-n.* 2. There are practically no " conflicting opinions " as is claimed by Cybichowski, whose defence of Britain's premature annexation, logically derived from his view that mere occupation is a title to acquisition of territory, fortunately represents an isolated case. *Op. cit.*, p. 298.
4. See below, pp. 263-282.

The above analysis shows that occupation alone can never be instrumental in breaking the continuity of the occupied State. Prior to a treaty of peace or a final and undoubted debellatio, it does not operate any change in the international status of the occupied State.

A final doubt should, however, be dealt with. What would happen if, in a war between two States only, one of them is permanently occupied by the other and no annexation is proclaimed? Would not the very permanence of such occupation, even without a formal act of annexation, result in the final extinction of the occupied State?

The question would seem to be purely theoretical. In the first place, always assuming that there is a clear case of debellatio, the actual annexation can be effected even without a formal proclamation. In the long run the conqueror will either have to disclaim annexation expressly [1], or he will be driven to perform certain acts which will fully make up for the absence of a proclamation. It seems almost inconceivable in practice that the conqueror should remain in the conquered territory for a very considerable period of time, merely as an occupant, i.e. voluntarily submitting to the numerous restrictions of the Hague Regulations. If, in the case of a final debellatio, he retains the conquered territory, he will be forced, sooner or later, to display the full panoply of sovereignty. It is simply unthinkable that a conqueror, having actually subjugated the enemy State, should do nothing about it, — i.e. neither conclude a treaty of peace providing for the restoration of the enemy State, nor overstep the tightly drawn limits of belligerent occupation, keeping an effective armed force in the territory, respecting its laws, allowing its tribunals to function, and generally submitting to all the limitations, workable only in a temporary situation. Thus, either the occupation will end by a conventional arrangement with the occupied State, or else, in the absence of a formal act, there will be *de facto* annexation.

8. STATE PRACTICE JUDICIAL DECISIONS AND DOCTRINE.

a) State Practice.

The principle that State continuity suffers no break as the result of belligerent occupation or, as is more frequently said, that belligerent occupation effects no transfer of sovereignty, has been generally adhered to in State practice. It is not intended, by this assertion, to gloss over the all too numerous violations of the rule. But it may still be submitted that, at least, until recently, the general practice of States conformed to the rule and that all violations were stigmatized as such and were thus prevented from eliminating the rule by way of *desuetudo* or contrary practice.

---

1. See the Allied declaration of June 5, 1945, on the assumption by the Allies of the supreme authority with respect to Germany which clearly states : " The assumption... of the said authority... does not effect the annexation of Germany. " Quoted by Stödter, *op. cit.*, p. 18.

In accordance with Art. 1 of the Fourth Hague Convention, the various manuals of military law of individual countries have duly adopted the Hague principles [1].

But even before the codification work of The Hague Peace Conferences, the rule in question appears to have been generally applied [2]. This may be illustrated by the events which occurred during the Franco-Prussian war of 1870-71 [3]. Even the mutual recriminations of the parties to the conflict confirm this view, based as they were on the very existence of this rule, both parties asserting emphatically that they had observed it, or attempting to find some justification for contraventions. Particularly striking in this respect is the study by Loening on the German occupation of Alsace [4]. Not only does Loening entirely subscribe to the rules formulated by Heffter and Bluntschli but he goes out of his way to eliminate any possible excuse for setting them aside. Thus he repudiates the theory according to which the occupation regime could be modified by the fact that the occupying power has already the definite intention *(animus)* to carry out an annexation [5]. It is not necessary for present purposes to enquire whether the German occupation authorities in Alsace did in fact fully adhere to the rules governing belligerent occupation, which, it appears, was by no means invariably the case [6]. What is relevant, is the fact

---

1. " The occupation of enemy territory during the war creates a condition entirely different from subjugation through annexation of the territory. During the occupation by the enemy, the sovereignty of the legitimate owner of the territory is only temporarily latent, but it still exists and in no way passes to the occupant. The latter's rights are merely transitory, and he should only exercise such power as is necessary for the purposes of the war, the maintenance of order and safety, and the proper administration of the country. ... The occupant, therefore, must not treat the country as part of his own territory, nor consider the inhabitants as his lawful subjects. " British *Manual of Military Law*, 1929 (Reprinted December, 1939), Published by H. M. Stationery Office, London, Amendments (No. 12), pp. 67-68. « L'occupation ne transfère aucun droit de souveraineté à l'occupant, mais seulement l'exercice de quelques-uns des droits de la souveraineté... » French Manual, quoted by Fauchille, *op. cit.*, II, p 216. " Military occupation is a question of fact. ... It does not transfer the sovereignty to the occupant... the sovereignty of the occupied territory is not vested in the occupying power. The occupation is essentially provisional. " U.S. *Basic Field Manual, Rules of Land Warfare*, U.S. Government Printing Office, Washington 1940, pp. 73-74. « L'occupation d'une partie du territoire ennemi n'est pas une appropriation de ce dernier. Le droit de l'Etat antérieurement souverain subsiste donc ; il est simplement suspendu, par un conflit avecc la puissance plus forte du conquérant, pendant la durée de son occupation et d'une manière provisoire. » Publication de la section historique du Grand Etat-Major allemand *(Kriegsbrauch im Landkriege)*, Les lois de la guerre continentale. Traduction et notes par Paul Carpentier, Paris, Librairie Payot, 1916, pp. 143-144. It is only the German Manual which includes the disquieting limitation of the rule to the occupation of a " part of enemy territory ".

2. « La règle orthodoxe fut... bien observée pendant les guerres du xixe siècle. » Sauser-Hall, *op. cit.*, p. 75. " Except for the Russo-Turk war in which the Russians reorganized the entire Bulgarian government during their occupation period belligerents generally adhered to the principle that the occupant should retain existing legislation as much as possible and only change it or pass new laws in case of urgency. " Graber, *op. cit.*, p. 268.

3. The case deserves to be quoted although, in view of the occupation of a part only, and rot of the whole of French territory, it has no immediate bearing on the problem of State continuity.

4. *Administration du Gouvernement Général de l'Alsace durant la guerre de 1870-71, RDILC*, 1872, p. 622 and 1873, p. 63.

5. « La simple intention d'une des parties ne peut produire d'effets en droit. » *Op. cit.*, 1872, p. 635.

6. See Graber, *op. cit.*, chapter VIII ; Fauchille, *op. cit.*, II, p. 216 ; Martens, *op. cit.*, III, p. 259.

that Loening takes the greatest pains to prove that these rules were observed, or, that apparent violations can be explained and are not of particular importance [1]. On the other hand, he is able to point to several instances of German respect for French sovereignty over Alsace, the most striking example of which is certainly the fact of holding free elections to the Bordeaux National Assembly in the whole of the occupied territory.

b) *Judicial Decisions.*

The rule has been fully confirmed by judicial decisions. As early as the beginning of the 19th century, the distinction between " hostile occupation and possession, clothed with a legal right by cession or conquest, or confirmed by length of time " was established by Lord Stowell in the *Boletta* case. Relying on his decision, the Privy Council held in *The Gerasimo* case in 1857 :

" ... the mere possession of a territory by an enemy's force does not of itself necessarily convert the territory so occupied into hostile territory, or its inhabitants into enemies [2]. "

In recent times it has been stated in an international arbitration that

" In no case does mere military occupation operate as a transfer of sovereignty [3]. "

The rule is confirmed by the highest national courts, such as the French Court of Cassation [4], the German Reichsgericht in Civil Matters [5], the Hungarian Supreme Court [6], the Polish Supreme Court [7], not to mention numerous decisions of lower courts.

Of the two decisions to the contrary, one can easily be explained : the Italian Court of Cassation in Rome upholding the view of the immediate extension of Italian sovereignty over Trieste in 1918, did not deny the rule, but relied on the disintegration of the Austro-Hungarian Empire [8]. In the second case, the French Conseil d'Etat took a similar stand with regard to Alsace-Lorraine, relying on the incompatibility between a German legal provision and

" the position in fact and in law created by the Armistice Convention of November 11, 1918, and the re-union of the territories of Alsace and Lorraine with France [9] ".

---

1. Thus, he criticizes the German proclamation to the population of Strasbourg, of October 8, 1870, — « ... la ville de Strasbourg, après avoir dû se rendre aux armes allemandes victorieuses, et avoir été soustraite à la domination française, est de nouveau réunie à l'Allemagne. » *Op. cit.*, vol. IV, p. 636.
2. Scott, *op. cit.*, p. 817.
3. Prof. Borel in the *Ottoman Debt Arbitration, A.D.*, 1925/26, case no. 360.
4. *A.D.*, 1919/22, *Naoum and Others v. The Government of the Colony of French West Africa*, case no. 312.
5. *A.D.*, 1923/24, *Army of Occupation (Jurisdiction) Case*, case no. 237.
6. *A.D.*, 1919/22, *Commune of Bacsborod Case, Czechoslovak Occupation (Hungary) Case*, cases no. 316 and 317.
7. *Republic v. Weisholc*, and *Republic v. Oficynski, ibid.* cases no. 337 and 338.
8. *Galatiolo v. Senes, ibid.*, case no. 319.
9. *A.D.*, 1931/32, *In re Ziwi*, case no. 231.

There is nothing in international law to support the French claim of " re-union " following a mere armistice, whatever the subsequent provisions of the Treaty of Versailles [1].

c) *Doctrine.*

In these circumstances it is clear that the rule safeguarding the continuity of the occupied State has been almost unanimously affirmed by writers [2].

9. PUPPET STATES AND GOVERNMENTS UNDER BELLIGERENT OCCUPATION.

Since the law relating to the continuity of the occupied State is clear and unequivocal, any acts of the occupying power which are not in accordance therewith are clear violations of international law. No difficulty either theoretical or practical can arise so long as such violations are the result of the occupant's own acts.

Recent experience has, however, shown that the occupant may well act *in fraudem legis* in such a way as to violate the rule in effect while at the same time seeking to avoid responsibility for such breach. This device consists in the creation by the occupying power of puppet governments or puppet States in the occupied territory [3]. Such agencies are supposed to commit, for the benefit of the occupying power, all unlawful acts which the latter does not want to commit openly and directly. Such acts may range from mere violations of the occupation regime in the occupied, but still surviving State to a disguised annexation of the occupied territory. The former may include the introduction by the alleged " national " government of compulsory labour for the benefit of the occupant, forcing an oath of allegiance on civil servants, or the taking of reprisals against citizens who lawfully assist in the war effort against the invader [4]. On the other hand, a disguised annexation aimed at destroying the independence of the occupied State, represents a clear violation of the rule preserving the continuity of the occupied State. This latter device was exposed by M. Litvinov :

---

1. See the pertinent criticism of the judgment by the Editor, *ibid.*
2. " Ein unabhängiger Staat besteht weiter, selbst wenn sein räumlicher Geltungsbereich entsprechend den Grundsätzen des Kriegsrechts provisorisch einem Feindstaat unterworfen ist. " Guggenheim, *op. cit.*, I, p. 199. See Rivier, *op. cit.*, II, p. 300 ; Martens, *op. cit.*, II, p. 251 ; Oppenheim-Lauterpacht, *op. cit.*, II, p. 433 ; Fauchille, *op. cit.*, II, p. 215 and 233 ; Liszt, *op. cit.*, pp. 150 and 489 ; McNair, *op. cit.*, p. 320 ; Balladore Pallieri, *op. cit.*, p. 326 ; Sauser-Hall, *op. cit.*, pp. 63-64, etc., etc. ; for the few exceptions, see below, pp. 120-122.
3. « Or, il y a un moyen très simple pour l'occupant de se soustraire à toutes les obligations mises à sa charge par le droit international, moyen qui consiste à instituer un gouvernement fantoche et de lui octroyer le pouvoir de légiférer sur toute matière échappant à sa compétence (à lui, occupant) et rentrant dans le domaine réservé au souverain légal. » Ténékidés, *La nature juridique des gouvernements institués par l'occupant en Grèce suivant la jurisprudence hellénique. RGDIP*, 1947, p. 127.
4. See Ténékidés, *op. cit.*, p. 127 : « Ainsi en Grèce, la plupart des ordres de l'occupant, qui, par leur nature, violaient les prescriptions du droit international, passaient par le canal pseudo-gouvernemental. » See similarly Uhler, *op. cit.*, p. 177.

" It must be made clear that the League of Nations has no intention of changing its attitude whether to the direct seizure and annexation of other people's territory, or to those cases where such annexations are camouflaged by the setting-up of puppet " National " governments, allegedly independent, but in reality serving merely as a screen for, and an agency of, the foreign invader [1]. "

In other words, the establishment of puppet governments and puppet States is a means of circumventing the limitations of belligerent occupation and of interfering with the continued existence of the occupied State, exactly in the same way as fake revolutions are a means of circumventing the international prohibition of intervention [2].

a) *Impossibility of Definition ; Presumption of Puppet Character.*

The question arises as to when it is legitimate to speak of puppet governments and States.

The following definition has been put forward :

" Puppet States are to be distinguished from puppet governments. A puppet State is an entirely new organism created by the occupant, whereas in a puppet government only the governmental functions are a creation of the occupant, the original State having been in existence before the occupation. Slovakia and Croatia are examples of puppet States [3]. "

Whether a pre-existing State, permanently endowed with a puppet government, would not *ipso facto* lose its State character and become a creation of the occupant in the same way as an originally created puppet State need not be considered at present [4] ; nor whether, the difference between a puppet government and a puppet State is not therefore merely one of degree and not of kind. *Prima facie*, the above definition seems correct as far it goes. However, as it is in the very nature of a puppet government of State to masquerade as an independent entity, — in other words, as there is no *formal* act of creation by the occupying power, the definition fails to give a precise answer to the question asked: namely, when does a government of a State qualify as a puppet? In speaking of " creation " by the occupant, the author seems to rely entirely on the the political aspect of a given situation and, in particular, the political relationship between the occupant and

---

1. *LNOJ*, 1938, p. 340.
2. See above, pp. 64-71.
3. Lemkin, *Axis Rule in Occupied Europe, Washington, Carregie Endowment for International Peace*, p. 11. Similarly Uhler : " Solche Schattenkabinette verdankten ihre Lebensfähigkeit allein der Anwesenheit einer fremden Besetzungsmacht, zu welcher sie in einem Verhältnis vollständiger Abhängigkeit standen. ...Dieser Weg der Einflussnahme auf die Verwaltung eines besetzten Landes durch die Okkupanten führt über die Staatsgewalt indem die oberste Verwaltung- und Regierungtätigkeit im besetzten Staat an Organträger übergeben wird, die vom Okkupanten designiert und kontrolliert werden. Tiefgreifender ist die Intervention des Okkupanten im besetzten Gebiet, wenn er sich nicht bloss auf eine personelle Aenderung in den administrativen Hauptfunktionszentren beschränkt, sondern an Stelle des bisherigen Staatswesens etwas ganz Neues schafft, einen staatlichen Organismus, der vor der Okkupation noch nicht existierte. Auch diese manu militari ins Leben gerufenen staatsförmigen Gebilde (« pupet States ») befinden sich zur Okkupationsmacht in einem maximalen Abhängigkeitsverhältnis, das Raum zur autonomen Willensbildung und -betätigung nicht lässt. Beispiele aus der Besetzungspraxis im letzten Krieg sind die in der Folge der Okkupation geschaffenen « souveränen Staaten » Kroatien und die Slowakei ". *Op. cit.*, pp. 199-200.
4. See below, pp. 172, 179, 187.

the entity in question. The political position may be so glaringly obvious as to eliminate all doubts as to the puppet character of a given government or State. It may, however, not be sufficiently obvious to be conclusive of the puppet character of such entities.

Two formal criteria seem to have been proposed. One would consist of the formally expressed consent of the occupant to the creation of the government in the occupied State [1]; the other of the incompatibility of the notion of a government in an occupied State with the notion of belligerent occupation [2].

The first criterion is, to some extent, relevant. However, it will happen only very rarely that the occupant, out to violate international law by means of " hidden devices ", will be imprudent enough to have his consent openly recorded.

The second criterion claims to be one of principle and, as such, is more important. Is there, however, any real incompatibility of principle between belligerent occupation and the continued existence *in* the occupied territory of the national government, and is such co-existence enough to prove conclusively the puppet character of the latter ? It is submitted that this is not necessarily the case. During the Second World War Denmark was certainly an occupied country. However, unlike the case of the other occupied countries, both the Head of the State and the Government remained and continued to function in the occupied territory without thereby becoming a puppet government in the slightest degree. The criterion certainly becomes more relevant in a case where there is not only a continuation but an actual change of government under the occupation, since it is difficult to imagine that such a change could take place without the acquiescence of the occupant. Even here, however, the criterion is not unfailing. There were changes of government in Italy during the Allied occupation in the Second World War, but these governments were nevertheless autonomous and not agencies of the occupying powers. The same can be said of the various Austrian Governments under Allied occupation.

It follows from the above that except in the case of an obvious imprudence committed by the occupant, it is practically impossible to lay down a formal criterion for the puppet character of a government or State set up under occupation. This impossibility results from the very function assigned by the law-breaking occupant to such entities: as has been seen, they are set up to commit violations of the occupation regime for the benefit of the occupant in such a way as not to involve him in responsibility ; in order to achieve this dual aim they must of necessity assume the character of bodies separate from, and independent of, the occupying power. Otherwise, they would serve no useful purpose.

It is then in the very nature of puppet governments and States, as law-breaking devices, to possess all the formal characteristics of genuine entities. Therefore they escape all definition. As in the case

---

1. Ténékidés, *op. cit.*, p. 123, *f.-n.* 4.
2. Ténékidés, *op. cit.*, p. 119 ; *In re G.*, Criminal Court of Heraklion, Judgment no. 107 of 1945, *A.D.*, 1943/45, case no. 151.

of a revolution under foreign occupation and pressure, however [1], it is both possible and necessary to introduce the *presumption* of such a character in the case of all governments and States which come into being under belligerent occupation [2]. The analogy with what has been said about revolution under foreign occupation is the more indicated, as such puppet governments and States under belligerent occupation may come into being precisely in an allegedly revolutionary way. Here again, the presumption would be weakened in the improbable event of the government, or State, being created *against* the aims and policies of the occupant [3]. Apart from this, however, the presumption would seem to be fully justified by the absence of freedom necessary for a spontaneous creation, as well as by the interests of the occupant. Here again, the presumption could only be rebutted after the liberation of the territory [4].

b) *Legal Nature of the Puppet Creations.*

Once it is clear that the puppet character of such governments and States cannot be determined by means of formal criteria but only with aid of the presumption suggested above, their legal nature is easy to define.

In the first place : they are, by definition, *not* what they pretend to be.

A puppet State is not a State at all according to international law [5]. It is the occupant's creation and his instrument, and to this extent the position is relatively clear, as the puppet State does not pretend to be related to, or act on behalf of, the occupied State.

With regard to puppet governments, their first and most prominent feature is that they are in no way related to the legal order of the occupied State ; in other words, they are neither its governments, nor its organs of any sort, and they do not carry on its continuity. It follows that any confusion between a puppet government and a *de facto* government of the occupied State is as inadmissible as a confusion between the occupying power itself and a *de facto* government [6].

---

1. See above, pp. 65-66.
2. Such a presumption seems to be implicitly adopted by Prof. Lauterpacht ; discussing the question of the alleged independence of Manchukuo, he says : " The answer which commended itself to impartial observers was that that province, *being under the military occupation and, generally, the controlling domination of Japan* in most aspects of its internal and external government, was not independent. " *It. mine, op. cit.*, p. 47.
3. See above, pp. 65-66.
4. "The military occupant cannot, under the guise of a spontaneous revolution, legally substitute a new government for the displaced *de iure* government. No revolt can change the sovereignty until the occupied area is either evacuated or reduced to small proportions. " Chen, *op. cit.*, p. 299.
5. " Ein Gemeinwesen, das auf der Grundlage eines Provisoriums — z.B. während eines Krieges — von den Besatzungsmächten oder mit deren Unterstützung in der Weise errichtet wird, dass seine Existenz von deren Willen abhängt, besitzt nicht die Voraussetzung eines unabhägigen, unmittelbar dem Völkerrecht unterworfenen Staates. " Guggenhem, *op. cit.*, I, p. 170.
6. See above, pp. 82-83. For the elimination of such confusion see Guggenheim, *op. cit.*, II, p. 937 ; Editor's Note to case no. 152, *A.D.*, 1943/45, and Ténékidés, *op. cit.*, pp. 120-121.

On the contrary, puppet governments are organs of the occupant and, as such, form part of his legal order [1]. The agreements concluded by them with the occupant are not genuine international agreements, however correct in form ; failing a genuine contracting party, such agreements are merely decrees of the occupant disguised as agreements which the occupant in fact concludes with himself. Their measures and laws are those of the occupant [2]. This determines the question of international responsibility for the acts of the puppet government. It is not the occupied State which is in any way responsible for the acts of the puppet government, or organs of a puppet State created in its territory ; it is solely the occupying power [3].

An interesting and comprehensive analysis of the legal nature of puppet governments under belligerent occupation is contained in Judgment No. 107 of the Greek Criminal Court of Heraklion in Crete, of 1945, from which extensive passages may usefully be quoted :

" ... it is clear that the Governments set up in Greece at the end of the military occupation of this country by the German and Italian armies are not based on the popular verdict or on nomination by the Head of State, who had fled with his Government out of the country. Nor are these Governments based on the power of the armed forces of the country ; these had been disarmed and dissolved by the invader. On the contrary, these Governments are based on the consent and the military power of the invader, from whose will they derive their power, which could be exercised only — an essential condition of such exercise — within the limits of the military interest and the political objects of the occupant. In consequence, these Governments cannot even be regarded as de facto Governments. Actually, they constitute mere organs of the occupant. ... Moreover, it is impossible to consider these Governments as being based on the tolerance of the Greek people, titular repository of all political power, seeing that that people, being under the yoke of the invader, was not able to express its opinion concerning the Governments which were imposed on it by the occupant. Moreover, the insubordinate attitude of a great part of the Greek people, and the distrust which the orders of these Governments inspired in them ; the nature of the legislative enactments of these Governments, reflecting this attitude of insubordination and distrust which showed itself in many ways and in many forms ; finally, the popular (pan-Hellenic) clamour which expelled these Governments at the moment of liberation ; all these prove that the hypothesis that these Governments were based on the will or the tolerance of the Greek people is without foundation.

It is clear, then, that the legislative or other measures taken by the said " Government " in the exercise of powers conceded to them by the occupant

---

1. " The so-called Governments are really no more than « organs » of the occupant. " Editor's Note to case no. 151, A.D., 1943/45. Guggenheim, loc. cit. ; Chen, loc. cit. ; Lemkin, loc. cit. ; Uhler, op. cit., p. 178, with his convincing description of the puppet government as " der verlängerte Arm der Okkupationsgewalt. "

2. Editor's Note to case no. 151, A.D., 1943/45 ; Lemkin, loc. cit. ; Chen, loc. cit.

3. " Das von einer solchen « Regierung » erzeugte völkerrechtliche Unrecht ist der Besetzungsmacht zuzurechnen. " Guggenheim, op. cit., II, pp. 937-938. " Da aber die Handlungen solcher Scheinregierungen dem Okkupanten zuzurechnen sind und materiell nichts anderes als Akte der Okkupationsgewalt sind... " Uhler, op. cit., p. 177. « Si les « gouvernements » institués par l'occupant étaient réellement des gouvernements de fait, ils auraient engagé soit par leurs accords avec des puissances étrangères, soit par des actes illicites internationaux qu'ils viendraient à commettre, la responsabilité internationale de l'Etat grec. Or, il y a là une conséquence que les gouvernements helléniques ayant pris et exercé le pouvoir après la Libération, refusent absolument d'admettre. » Ténékidés, op. cit., p. 125. With regard to the last mentioned view, it may be remarked that, although the attitude of the Greek Government was absolutely correct, the irresponsibility of the State for acts of a puppet government does not rest on the will of that State alone, but on the objective rule of international law. The attitude of the Greek Government merely conformed to the objective rule, it did not create it.

cannot in any way be regarded as laws emanating from a Greek Government and as such binding and to be applied by Greek courts after the withdrawal of the enemy forces. For it is on the will, with the consent, and by the power of these forces that the application of these enactments was based during the occupation. These measures cannot in any way be applied after the Courts have recovered their freedom to expound the law and to give judgment according to Greek law. The legislative measures enacted by the " Governments " set up by the occupant — measures which are essentially no more than laws promulgated by the occupant himself — will not be respected by the State when its authority is restored after the occupation unless they fall within the limits of the activities permitted by international law to the occupant. ... These laws, however, ... have no juridical force after the end of the occupation, and there is no obligation on the courts to apply them [1]... "

The judgment is also of interest in that it convincingly excludes any possibility of the puppet governments being organs of the occupied State : they are not constitutional governments, not being established in accordance with any constitutional procedure, and they are not *de facto* governments, failing any revolutionary basis, such as the support of the army or the people.

c) *Puppet Creations and the Hague Regulations.*

From the status of the puppet governments as organs of the occupying power the conclusion has been drawn that their acts should be subject to the limitations of the Hague Regulations. The suggestion, supported by writers as well as by decisions of municipal courts, seems at first both logical and convincing [2]. For it is true that puppet governments are organs of the occupying power, and it is equally true that the occupying power is subject to the limitations of the Hague Regulations. But the direct actions of the occupant himself are included in the inherent legality of belligerent occupation, whilst the very creation of a puppet government or State is itself an illegal act, creating an illegal situation. Were the occupant to remain within the strict limits laid down by international law, he would never have recourse to the formation of puppet governments or States. It is therefore not to be assumed that puppet governments will conform to the Hague Regulations ; this the occupant can do himself ; for this he does not need a puppet. The very aim of the latter, as has already been seen, is to enable the occupant to act *in fraudem legis*, to commit violations of the international regime of occupation in a disguised and indirect

---

1. *A.D.*, 1943/45, *In re G.*, case no. 151.
2. " Als Organ der Besetzungsmacht steht sie im Widerspruch mit der Haager Landkriegsordnung, insofern sie sich über das Okkupationsrecht herausgehende Zuständigkeit anmasst. " Guggneheim, *op. cit.*, II, 937. " ...a court seised of an action the judgment in which will depend on some enactment of a " Government " set up by the occupant, has the right and the duty to examine that enactment. It must satisfy itself that the enactment is in conformity with Art. 43 of the Hague Regulations, exactly as though the law had been enacted by the occupying authorities themselves... " Editor's Note on case no. 152, *A.D.* 1943/45. See also, Lemkin, *loc. cit.* ; Uhler, *op. cit.*, p. 178. In a letter to the Department of Justice of November 19, 1940 the Norwegian Supreme Court spoke of " the limits of the authority enjoyed by the Constituted State Councillor as representative of the power in occupation, according to the Hague Convention of 1907... " Quoted by Lemkin, *op. cit.*, p. 219. Similarly, the Norwegian District Court of Aker, in a judgment of August 25, 1943, assimilated decrees of Norwegian authorities installed by the Germans to measures of the occupant. *A.D.*, 1943/45, case no. 156.

form, in other words, to disregard the firmly established principle of the identity and continuity of the occupied State [1]. Herein lies the original illegality of puppet creations. By their very nature they are instruments of law-breaking. To place the acts of puppet governments or States on the same level as the acts of the normal organs of the occupant, would mean endowing them with a legality which is not contemplated by the Hague Regulations. Moreover, to endow them, even indirectly, with such legality, would mean destroying the very essence of the international regime of belligerent occupation by striking at its whole basis, namely the separate identity and the continued existence of the occupied State. It is suggested that puppet creations should not be measured by the Hague standards even in the improbable case of their acts conforming to these standards, — but that their mere creation should be considered an unlawful act for which responsibility rests with the occupying power.

d) *Outlawing of Puppet Creations by Positive International Law.*

Failing any express rule on the subject, the illegality of puppet States and governments could only have been deduced from other existing norms of international law.

But just as the occupant chose this particular method of law-breaking, owing to the absence of express rules bearing on the subject, — so, conversely, such express rules could not develop prior to the emergence of the phenomenon of puppet creations. In view of the growth and extent of this new method of law-breaking, international law had to lay down express rules regulating the matter. Clearly, since such rules do not represent a new departure, but are, on the contrary, a crystallization of existing rules and institutions, they had to conform to the basic principles of the international regime of occupation.

Such crystallization has been effected by the Geneva Convention relative to the Protection of Civilian Persons in Time of War, of August 12, 1949.

The Geneva Convention does not provide a new and autonomous notion of belligerent occupation. Supplementing 'the Hague Conventions, it is based on the definition of belligerent occupation contained in the latter. The Geneva Convention does not lay down basic rules for the regime of belligerent occupation ; that had already been done by the Hague Conventions to which the Geneva Convention expressly refers [2]. Thus, the foundation and the condition of application of the Geneva Convention is the clearly delimited separate identity and continued existence of the occupied State.

---

1. " Lag doch gerade der Hauptgrund zur Bildung einer Marionettenregierung und formellen Uebertragung der höchsten Regierungsbefugnisse im Bestreben, sich der völkerrechtlichen Pflichten zu entledigen, um in scheinbar legaler Weise im Rechtssystem des besetzten Landes nach Gutdünken Aenderungen vorzunehmen. " Uhler, *op. cit.*, p. 204. Cf. Ténékidés, *op. cit.*

2. Art. 154 : In the relations between the Powers who are bound by The Hague Convetions relative to the Laws and Customs of War on Land, whether that of July 29, 1899, or that of October 18, 1907, and who are parties to the present Convention, this last Convention shall be supplementary to Sections II and III of the Regulations annexed to the above-mentioned Conventions of The Hague.

It is against this fundamental background that the following key Article of the Geneva Convention has to be read and analyzed.

"Protected persons who are in occupied territory shall not be deprived, in any case or in any manner whatsoever, of the benefits of the present Convention by any change introduced as the result of the occupation of a territory, into the institutions or government of the said territory, nor by any agreement concluded between the authorities of the occupied territories and the Occupying Power, nor by any annexation by the latter of the whole or part of the occupied territory." (Årt. 47.)

Bearing the foregoing observations in mind, it is out of the question to suppose that Art. 47 of the Geneva Convention was intended to authorize any possible violations of the Hague occupation regime, — whether in form of illegal annexations, interference with the existing legal order of the occupied State, or agreements. On the contrary, Art. 47 provides that rights and duties resulting from the Convention are to be maintained even in case of open or disguised violations of the Hague Regulations. In other words, it outlaws in advance all possible measures of the occupant, which would attempt illegally to withdraw the occupied territory from the ambit of the Hague Regulations and thus to destroy the basis of the Convention's applicability [1].

The correctness of this interpretation follows with all the necessary clarity from an examination of the text of Art. 47, and from a comparison of the Geneva Convention with the Hague Regulations on the basis of Art. 154 of the former. But over and above this, it should not be forgotten that the 1949 Geneva Conventions were the direct result of the experiences of the Second World War, that their aim was precisely further codification and that they were intended to close the gaps of which the aggressors in that war took advantage in order to circumvent the law. The Diplomatic Conference which adopted the Conventions met in 1949 at Geneva with examples of law-breaking, and in particular disguised law-breaking, fresh in their minds. Throughout, all four Conventions establish clear-cut rules precisely on those matters in which international law proved to be particularly vulnerable during the late war. Thus, they expressly prohibit acts, whose illegal character might have been regarded as doubtful under the existing law, although offending against elementary notions of humanity [2]. But, moreover, they also prohibit all stratagems, standing on the borderline between

---

1. Thus Uhler : " Der Grundgedanke der *occupatio bellica* hat durch die neue Konvention keine Aenderung erfahren. Nach wie vor ist die grundlegende Norm für die Verwaltung eines besetzten Gebiets in dem die grundsätzliche Beachtung des Landesrechts und die Unantastbarkeit der Institutionen des okkupierten Landes statuierenden Art. 43 der LKO zu finden. Wenn nun in Art. 47 der Zivilkonvention von Aenderungen im staatsrechtlichen Gefüge des besetzten Staates die Rede ist, so darf daraus nicht der Schluss gezogen werden, dass der Begriff der *occupation bellica* dadurch ein anderer, von dem der LKO zugrunde liegenden verschiedener geworden ist. Die Funktion von Art. 47 der Zivilkonvention besteht lediglich darin, dort, wo ein Okkupant entgegen Art. 43 der LKO durch keinerlei militärische Notwendigkeit gerechtfertigte Aenderungen in der Staatsstruktur des besetzten Landes vornimmt, also die aus der Konzeption der kriegerischen Besetzung entspringende Forderung formalrechtlicher Art missachtet, doch wenigstens den materiell-rechtlichen Gehalt der *occupatio bellica* unter allen Umständen sicherzustellen." *Op. cit.*, pp. 207-208.
2. See problem of hostages, Art. 34, deportations, Art. 49, etc.

legality and illegality which are directed against the basic principles of international law, although not running counter to any express rule. It was precisely in order to prevent such stratagems that Art. 47 was included in the Convention relative to the Protection of Civilian Persons [1].

It is interesting to note the specific measures of the law-breaking occupant, which Art. 47 has in advance deprived of all validity, so as to prevent their undermining the continued binding force of the Convention within the occupied territory.

Art. 47 enumerates three measures of this kind. One is premature annexation, whose illegal character has already been established [2]. In other words, even in an illegally annexed occupied territory the Convention retains its validity, thereby not only continuing to protect the civilian population, but, it is submitted, further emphasizing the separate identity and continuity of the occupied State, without which such protection would not be possible.

The second is any interference by the occupant with the existing institutions or government, that is to say with the existing and continuing legal order of the occupied State. It is precisely here that the possibility of a puppet government is clearly included. Should *any* such changes result in the creation by the occupant of a puppet government or puppet State, this fact will be non-existent in the eyes of the Convention, which will continue to apply in the occupied territory. That territory will consequently retain the legal status it enjoyed before the occupation and prior to the changes in question.

The third measure declared invalid by Art. 47 is the conclusion of agreements between the occupying Power and the " authorities " of the occupied territory. In order fully to appreciate the meaning of this formulation, it is necessary to compare, or rather contrast, it with Art. 7 para. 1 and Art. 11 para. 5.

All these three provisions declare invalid certain agreements which may be concluded with a view to undermining or limiting the effect of the Convention. The relevant passage of Art. |7 para. 1 states :

" No special agreement shall adversely affect the situation of protected persons, as defined by the present Convention, nor restrict the rights which it confers upon them. "

This type of agreement is thus declared invalid solely by reason of its content, and not owing to any lack of capacity of the contracting parties.

Art. 11, para. 5 contains a prohibition of a different type. After having laid down rules concerning the Protecting Power and its substitutes, it says :

---

1. Thus Uhler, who sees the aim of Art. 47 in the will " die aus dem Besetzungsrecht fliessenden Rechte und Pflichten unbeschadet von solch politischen Manövern in jedem Falle sicherzustellen. Zu diesem Zwecke wurde in Genf eine Norm geschaffen, die die Rechtsfolgen der kriegerischen Okkupation auch dann zum Entstehen bringen lässt, wenn der Okkupant dies durch Umdeutung der *occupatio bellica* in irgend etwas anderes gerade zu verhindern sucht. " *Op. cit.*, p. 207.
2. See above, pp. 102-107.

" No derogation from the preceding provisions shall be made by special agreements between Powers one of which is restricted, even temporarily, in its freedom to negotiate with the other Power or its allies by reason of military events, more particularly where the whole, or a substantial part, of the territory of the said Power is occupied. "

The reason for invalidity in this case is not so much the content of such agreements, but the obviously unequal position of the parties. An agreement between the occupying Power and a State whose territory is entirely or to a great extent occupied by the former is obviously an agreement concluded under duress, in the absence of the necessary freedom of negotiation. In such a case, the Convention rightly assumes a reduced capacity on the part of the occupied State [1].

Both these provisions, however, expressly mention agreements, to which both parties are the original States (" High Contracting Parties " in Art. 7 and " Powers " in Art. 11). Under Art. 7, para. 1, the position of the would-be contracting parties is assumed to be normal, whereas under Art. 11, para. 5 it is not ; in both cases, however, the State character of the parties remains unaltered.

As against this, Art. 47 speaks of the original State only with regard to the occupying Power, whereas the other contracting party is no longer " a State " or even " a Government ", but merely an " authority of the occupied territory ". Moreover, this situation is listed among other cases of violations of international law, such as premature annexation and changes in the legal order of the occupied State. Theoretically, the somewhat vague description of the " authority of the occupied territory " could possibly include some legal authority, just as changes in the legal order of the occupied State could possibly be undertaken in conformity with the well-known reservation of Art. 43 of the Hague Regulations [2]. It is, however, submitted, that, despite this theoretical possibility, Art. 47 proceeds on the assumption that such changes are illegal and that such authorities are fake. It embodies the correct presumption of the puppet character of the authorities installed in the occupied territory. Thus, the invalidity of the agreement in this case does not result from its content, nor from the reduced capacity of one of the parties, but from the presumption that one of the would-be parties is not a genuine party at all. As such, it cannot conclude a valid agreement, and any agreements it enters into are for this reason null *ab initio*.

---

1. " Eine im Lichte der Erfahrungen des vergangenen Krieges besonders gewichtige Bedeutung ist dem fünften Absatz beizumessen. Er bestimmt, dass die die Schutzmacht und ihre Substitute betreffenden Normen nicht durch Spezialvereinbarung derogiert werden dürfen, die abgeschlossen werden zwischen Kriegführenden, von denen sich der eine gegenüber dem andern oder dessen Verbündeten in einem auch nur vorübergehenden Zustand von beschränkter Handlungsfägkeit befindet. Eine Beschränkung der Handlungsfähigkeit ist insbesondere infolge einer ganzen oder teilweisen Besetzung des Staatsgebietes des Kriegsgegners *ipso facto* anzunehmen. " Uhler, *op. cit.*, p. 266. In adopting this rule the Conference had in mind the conventions concluded between Germany and the Vichy Government, depriving French prisoners of war in Germany of their rights. This explains why the original proposal was submitted by the representative of France. See Uhler, *op. cit.*, p. 266, *f.-n.* 48.

2. " ...unless absolutely prevented... ".

This argument is reinforced by a further comparison of Art. 47 with Art. 7. It has been seen that the latter already prohibits any derogation to the Convention by means of a special agreement concluded, admittedly, between States. If Art. 47 were also intended to cover the same situation of an agreement between parties enjoying full legal capacity, it is submitted that it would be unnecessary, being a mere repetition of Art. 7. It is not to be assumed that there is such unnecessary repetition in the Convention. On the contrary, it must be assumed that Art. 47 covers a different situation from the one already covered by Art. 7. The same prohibition of restricting the application of the Convention which is embodied in Art. 7 on account of the content of such agreements, is included in Art. 47 on account of the absence of a properly constituted contracting party [1].

It can therefore be safely asserted that the Geneva Convention has positively outlawed the creation of puppets as a means of indirectly violating the international occupation regime. It has branded them as illegal. Whatever their claims, they are unable to break the continuity of the occupied State to which they are in no way related, whether they take the form of puppet States or puppet governments. In the event of the creation by the occupant of a puppet State or States on the territory of the occupied State, the latter survives, with its legal status unchanged. Although puppet governments may claim to be organs of the original State, this cannot affect the clear legal position according to which it is the dispossessed exiled governments, and not the puppets, which continue to act as the genuine legal organs of the occupied State and which carry on its legal continuity [2].

The Geneva Convention thus forms yet another safeguard of the identity and continuity of the occupied State, whose continued legal existence may not be tampered with by the occupying power either in an open or disguised manner.

10. Individual Attempts to Undermine the Rule.

The preceding investigation has shown the rule in question to be so firmly established that there are practically no exceptions to it. It is, however, necessary to consider certain attempts which have been made to undermine it.

Such attempts were made by writers on international law with an obvious view to justifying illegal action by their respective States. Thus Martens, no doubt with an eye on the Russian occupation of Bulgaria in 1878, claims for the occupying Power the freedom from

---

1. Thus Uhler : " Zudem sind solche Staatsverträge nichtig und geben dem Okkupanten keinen Rechtstitel für Deportationen, da auf der Gegenseite ein zum Vertragsabschluss berechtigtes, den okkupierten Staat verpflichtendes Organ nicht vorhanden, der Gegenkontrahent vielmehr nur der verlängerte Arm der Okkupationsgewalt ist. " Op. cit., p. 178.

2. " The principle that the de iure government, even if wholly dispossessed, is the government of the State is not affected by the new technique of foreign military occupants to govern through the instrumentality of a servile administration composed of local inhabitants. " Chen, op. cit., p. 299.

all restrictions, and in particular from the duty to respect the existing institutions of the occupied country, in cases where the war is being waged with the obvious purpose of annexing the occupied territory, or changing its structure [1].

A similar view was advanced by Anzilotti on the morrow of the unlawful Italian annexation of Tripolitania and Cyrenaica. His proposed modification of the rule is as follows : the principle that occupation is provisional and does not transfer sovereignty should be confined to cases where the conqueror himself considers his control of the occupied country or region as provisional ; in those cases, however, where he has decided to retain the occupied territory, occupation itself should be sufficient for the definite transfer of sovereignty [2].

It is hardly necessary to point out the dangerous and, indeed, mischievious character of such views. They tend to transform an objective rule of law into a subjective prerogative of the invading State, to be exercised at its absolute whim and discretion. They completely obliterate the fundamental distinction between occupation and subjugation, arrived at after decades of progressive development. They expose the population to untold hardships and uncertainties, forcing foreign allegiance upon it and possibly exposing it to reprisals from both sides in case the occupied territory should change hands [3]. They raise the victor of the day to the position of the lawful sovereign, contrary not only to established international law, but even to common sense. For the victor of to-day may not be the victor of to-morrow [4].

---

1. « L'occupation prend un autre aspect quand elle a lieu en vue d'une annexion, ou si le but même de la guerre est de changer ou d'améliorer l'organisation d'une province appartenant à l'ennemi. Dans ce cas, la puissance qui procède à une occupation a tout à fait le droit de tranformer complètement les institutions régnantes et l'ordre établi, afin de les mettre en harmonie avec ses intérêts politiques, ou afin de procurer quelque avantage aux habitants. » *Op. cit.*, p. 257.

2. *Formazione*, p. 11, *f.-n.* 2.

3. See Jumeau, *op. cit.*, p. 29.

4. " ...If adopted, it would inevitably involve the suppression of the entire doctrine of military occupation as embodied in modern international law. The purely temporary, provisional character of occupation would vanish ; and the first act of invasion might well signalize one of the two arbitrary and terrible alternatives — the total destruction of all on the invaded territory and the bringing of all under the yoke of the invader's sovereignty. That is, the moment the invaders arrived, with a view to taking possession of the country and permanently retaining it, they would consider the people their subjects, and would thus be in a position to regard resistance as high treason, and to compel all, non-combatants and armed forces alike, to take part in military operations ag inst their own country. Their refusal, due to their patriotism and devotion to their country, would be looked upon by the invader as a crime punishable with death ; their unswerving and self-sacrificing fidelity would be treated as the vilest offence that man is capable of ; their martyrdom would be regarded as the condign punishment of a traitor. Moreover, if a distinction is to be set up between invasion followed by subjugation and invasion followed merely by provisional military occupation, when is such distinction to become apparent in actual practice ? It is impossible to expect a definite announcement at the very commencement of a given war that it is to be a war of subjugation and annexation of territory. It is impossible for the invader to indicate and mark out the territory he intends to appropriate as soon as he has reached the enemy's country. Even if the war were announced as a war of conquest, would it follow that every portion of territory occupied was intended to be kept for good ? If only some of the territory occupied was intended to be so kept, how would the line of demarc tion be established between the region of military occupation proper and that of full annexation ? How would the practices and proceedings of the occupying army and of the annexing army be discriminated ? These and other questions of the same character in vain call for satisfactory answers. And even supposing for one moment that theoretically satisfactory

Yet another attempt to undermine the principle of uninterrupted State continuity under belligerent occupation was made by Cybichowski, by means of his theory that occupation is a title of territorial acquisition [1]. This theory seems to be based not only on the incorrect and unsubstantiated view of " another " regime of occupation existing apart from the Hague Regulations and customary law which they codify [2], but also on a truly unexpected confusion between belligerent occupation and the occupation *terræ nullius*. It is hardly necessary to point out that these are two entirely different things, *terra nullius* excluding by definition the notion of a State, and belligerent occupation being by definition based on this very notion. No analogy can possibly be drawn between the occupation *terræ nullius* which indeed may, but need not necessarily, become a title of acquisition precisely on account of the absence of a State to whom it could belong, — and the occupation of another State's territory which is not, and cannot, be such a title for the opposite reason. Moreover, Cybichowski's assertion being made *de lege lata*, is simply untrue. No attempt is made to prove it, unless the examples he adduces of the annexation of the Boer Republics or Tripolitania and Cyrenaica are to be regarded as " proof " ; but these are precisely the classical cases of unlawful annexation. In his tendency to remove all obstacles to such unlawful annexation, Cybichowski does not even hesitate to dispense with the requirement of full effectiveness [3]. Yet, such effectiveness, as has been seen [4], is not only absolutely necessary for a temporary belligerent occupation to be valid, but it is equally necessary for an occupation *terræ nullius* [5].

11. HOMOGENEITY OF THE SOCIAL SUBSTRATUM.

Until recently the practical and legal arguments against the above-mentioned views were far too weighty to allow them even a chance of success. However, a far more serious threat to the classical institution of belligerent occupation, based on the principle of the continuity of

---

answers to them might be furnished, the varying fortunes and vicissitudes of actual warfare would still be left out of account. It might happen that the invaders were eventually expelled from the territory they had originally occupied by way of annexation and had in turn gained a firm footing in another province, which they suddenly resolved, to annex in place of that from which they were ousted. Such changes would, of course carry with them all the dire consequences affecting the local populations. Indeed, the introduction of the more drastic species of military occupation would undoubtedly render warfare, still more than it is now, an unconscionable game of unrestrained licence and indiscriminate slaughter. " Phillipson, *op. cit.*, pp. 28-29. It is comforting to see the criticism which Anzilotti's suggestion encountered from Italian writers. Thus Balladore Pallieri : " Il puro desiderio di impossersarsi di un territorio non costituisce certo alcun titolo atto a farne acquisitare la sovranità. ...E una norma internazionale ammissiva di siffatta deroga non solo non avrebbe ragione di sussistere ma nemmeno sussiste... " *Op. cit.*, p. 328.
1. " Seit langem kann Gegenstand dieser Besetzung (Annexionsbesetzung), auch ein Territorium sein, das unter staatlicher Souveränität steht. " *Op. cit.*, p. 298.
2. See above, p. 78-79.
3. " Die Besetzung kann... weiter reichen, als die tatsächliche Macht des Heeres. ...Besetzung als Annexionstitel hat einen eigenartigen Charakter, da sie auch Gebiete umfassen kann, die sich tatsächlich nicht in der Gewalt der militärischen Streitkräfte befinden. " *Ibid.*, p. 298.
4. See above, pp. 81-82.
5. See Guggenheim, *op. cit.*, I, p. 400 and examples quoted.

the occupied State, seems to be developing. By reason of its historical and social background this threat is much more disturbing than the occasional opportunism of just a single State or writer.

It is a truism that the rules concerning belligerent occupation began to develop in the course of the 18th century, and that they finally crystallized in the 19th century, a period of European liberalism and relatively limited technical means of warfare [1]. Wars of this period, with the exception of Napoleonic wars, were still wars having a relatively limited objective and involving relatively limited risks ; they were not a matter of life or death to the belligerents. To quote a great Italian historian, they were " guerres limitées " not " guerres déchaînées " [2]. In such wars, it was both technically and politically feasible to " confine the players strictly within the white lines on the field " [3].

It would, however, be superficial or, at least inadequate, to explain the threat to the rules of belligerent occupation only by the technical progress or the constant increase of State control on the internal level [4]. The fundamental reason seems to be that international law can only exist and function on condition of a minimum of homogeneity of its social substratum [5]. This is particularly true in the case of belligerent occupation. For whatever superficial appearances of a common international law may be preserved in peace-time between totally different cultural and ideological communities, they are bound to break down once the dams are torn open and war is unleashed. Where there is not only a lack of homogeneity, but a complete gulf between the most elementary notions of the belligerents, it is not to be imagined that one of them, when occupying the other's territory, will respect and preserve his enemy's laws and institutions, — especially if their

---

1. " Ihr (meant : the *occupatio bellica*) Rechtsgehalt ist... das aus dem neuzeitlichen Gewohnheitsrecht... kristallisierte Produkt einer auf liberalen und rechtsstaatlichen Prinzipien beruhenden Gesellschaftsordnung ; ihre tragenden Ideen wurzeln in dem von der Rousseau-Portalis Doktrin ins Kriegsrecht übertragenen Gedankengut einer individualistischen, ein bestimmtes Mass von absoluten Freiheitsrechten fordernden politischen Weltanschauung. " Uhler, *op. cit.*, p. 17.

2. Ferrero, G. *La fin des aventures*, Paris ; Les Editions Rieder, 1931.

3. Smith, *The Government of Occupied Territory*, B. Y., 1944, p. 151.

4. Such a view seems to have been adopted by Smith in the article quoted above. For the reduction to its true proportions of the technical aspect of modern warfare and its inadequacy to justify retrograde changes in the law of war, see Moore, *International Law and Some Current Illusions*, New York, Macmillan Company, 1924, pp. 5-13. Against an impressive background of historical argument, the author concludes : " It is evident that, if we are now to abandon the distinction between combatants and non-combatants, and, reverting to primitive conceptions, to kill unarmed men and women as war workers and obliterate the youth of the land as war sproutage, the lapse into savagery cannot be justified on the ground that it was formerly imagined that war did not lay under contribution all national resources. " p. 13.

5. " Die Völkerrechtsgemeinschaft beruht in erster Linie auf dem Bewusstsein kultureller Zusammengehörigkeit bestimmter Völker ; dieses Bewusstsein hat dieselben Ursachen wie der Umstand, dass die rechtlichen Beziehungen unter diesen Staaten ähnliche oder identische, weil auf übereinstimmenden Rechtsvorstellungen beruhende sind. " Huber, *Soziologische Grundlagen*, p. 54. " Das Mass solchen gemeinsamen Rechts wird vor allem bedingt sein durch das Mass der Gemeinschaftlichkeit der Kultur. " *Ibid.*, p. 22. « Il ne suffit pas qu'il y ait un commerce international contractuel et régulier, il faut qu'il y ait un minimum d'homogénéité et un certain nombre de conceptions et de principes de droit étatique qui soient communs à tous. » Guggenheim, *Contribution au problème des bases sociologiques*, in *Rec. d'études en l'honneur d'Edouard Lambert*, Paris, 1933, p. 121. On "Uebereinstimmende Rechtsvorstellungen " see Verdross, *Völkerrecht*, pp. 12-13. Also Uhler, *op. cit.*, p. 298.

destruction has become a *conditio sine qua non* of his own survival. It was not so much the technical limitations of the 19th century which were mainly instrumental in bringing about a general respect for the law of belligerent occupation, but rather the generally prevailing legal, cultural and political homogeneity of the international community of that time.

This general homogeneity of the European community was for the first time undermined to a certain extent by the French Revolution ; this is the social background of the Cambon Decree [1] and the treatment by France of conquered countries [2]. That particular break was healed in the course of the 19th century, but a new gap opened in 1917 with the Soviet Revolution, resulting in a sharp division of the international community. It was in complete harmony with the inner logic of that Revolution, that, in the initial period and before embarking on an era of an apparently normalized international collaboration, Soviet Russia claimed her freedom from the limitations of the Hague Regulations. The wars of the Soviet Union lacked any common denominator between her and her opponents, such as may have existed between the France of Napoleon III and the Prussia of Bismarck. Where the Soviet armies would come, they would naturally enough not come to respect and even preserve the existing capitalist institutions of the occupied State or territory ; their purpose would be to change them [3]. The Soviet Union, like the Revolutionary France a century and a half before, claimed for herself the unilateral right of active intervention in the internal affairs of sovereign States which her armies might occupy, — intervention which was not to stop short of attempts against the identity and continuity of the occupied States.

It may also be said that it was probably in conformity with the inner logic of the totalitarian ideology and the character of National Socialist Germany to destroy institutions, forming a common European heritage, in countries which were occupied by the German armies. The extent of such destruction may have, and did indeed vary, but

---

1. See above, p. 76, *f.-n.* 2.
2. Thus correctly, Sauser-Hall : « Il est curieux que l'interdiction de modifier en quoi que ce soit la structure même de l'Etat occupé, a presque toujours été violée à des époques de violentes oppositions idéologiques entre les peuples. » *Op. cit.*, p. 74.
3. " Bei der Beachtung des spezifischen Klassencharakters aller Kriege des sozialistischen Staates entsteht die Frage, ob man, sich leiten lassend von den allgemeinen Grundlagen des modernen internationalen Rechtsbewusstseins, die Tatsache als unrechtmässig bewerten kann, dass auch die Sowietmacht sich nicht im mindesten verpflichtet fühlt, wenn sie als Okkupant hervortritt, die Unverletzlichkeit der Ausbeutung und die Unerschütterlichkeit der kapitalistischen Ordnung in den Grenzen des okkupierten Territoriums zu beschirmen, sonder.. dass sie im Gegenteil, kämpfend für ihr sozialistisches Sein, jede mögliche Hilfe (Finnland, Polen, Estland, Lettland) dem Streben der örtlichen arbeitenden Massen zur Organisierung der Gesellschaft auf sozialistischer Grundlage angedeihen lässt. Die revolutionären Comités, die Unterstützung des Entstehens nationaler Sowjetrepubliken und die sonstigen Elemente der sogennanten « Sowjetisierung » sind die Folgen davon. ...Der Haager Okkupationskodex, der die Beibehaltung der örtlichen Staatsordnung vorschreibt, und der auf der versteckten Voraussetzung der Gemeinsamkeit, zuweilen auch der Identität, der sozialen und rechtlichen Formen bei beiden Gegnern beruht, erscheint als untauglich, eine neue Norm — die Sicherstellung des für die der Wirksamkeit der Kriegsgesetze unterworfenen Bevölkerung möglichst grossen Maximums an sozialer Gerechtigkeit — setzt sich durch. " Korovin, *Das Völkerrecht der Uebergangszeit*, pp. 136-137.

the principle remained. Nor was it conceivable that Allied armies occupying Germany should respect and preserve National Socialist laws and institutions, including racial laws, concentration camps, the administration of justice, and the like [1]. For the Hague Regulations to apply, there was not the lowest common denominator ; the gulf was complete [2].

This gulf, whatever its nature may be, is vividly described by Prof. Korovin :

" ... can we demand observance of the Hague rules of military occupation (respect for the sovereignty of the local government and so on) in the event of the occupation of the territory of an aggressor State by troops of peace-loving nations ? Or can we permit the thought that in such a case the occupation army would provide armed protection for those same reactionary social forms and political institutions which led the country on the path of international crime ? And, conversely, can we confine a sacred people's war against an aggressor and enslaver, a heroic struggle of millions of people for their country's independence, for its national culture, for its right to exist, can we confine this war within the strict bounds of the Hague rules which were calculated for wars of a different type and for a totally different international situation [3] ? "

And Prof. Korovin does not shrink from the following general conclusion, in which he may be dangerously right :

" In the final analysis it must be admitted that there is not and cannot be such a code of international law as would be equally acceptable to the cannibal and his victim, to the aggressor and the lover of freedom, to the " master race " and its potential " slaves ", to the champions of the sanctity of treaties and to those who would treat pacts as " scraps of paper ", to the advocates of humanising and abolishing war and to the proponents of totalitarian war, to those who " value every tear of a child ", to quote Dostoyevski, and to those who try to build a third or any other empire on a foundation of " women's corpses and children's skulls [4]. "

This then is the source of danger to the rule discussed. A disintegrated social substratum will be unable to carry the full weight of international law, and the rules governing war and occupation may well be the first to founder. But however great the danger of their possible breakdown in the future, this danger alone should never be anticipated to the extent of regarding the existing rules as already broken. This proposition is advanced all the more freely, since the classical rules governing belligerent occupation and providing for the continuity of the occupied State have recently been solemnly confirmed by the international community in the 1949 Geneva Convention.

---

1. For Allied measures in occupied Germany, see Sauser-Hall, *L'occupation de l Allemagne, Annuaire Suisse*, 1946, p. 9.
2. That the institution of belligerent occupation depends far more on the existence or absence of such ideological homogeneity than on the technical means of warfare, may be seen from an entirely different treatment by the Allies, in the course of one and the same war, of Germany and Italy. There is little doubt that the Allied occupation of Italy proceeded by and large in accordance with the Hague principles. See documents quoted by Smith, *loc. cit.* In particular, compare the proclamation to the Italians of Field Marshal Alexander, *ibid.*, with the German proclamation of General Eisenhower. Quoted by Stödter, *Deutschlands Rechtslage*, p. 15.
3. *The Second World War and International Law*, A.J., 1946, p. 753.
4. *Ibid.*, pp. 742-743.

At the present moment therefore the rule still stands : the identity and continuity of the occupied State are, without any exception, preserved by international law.

IV. CONCLUSIONS.

It was stated at the beginning of this enquiry that the problem of the identity and continuity of a State can only arise in consequence of some grave event interfering with that State's normal existence. Three such events can now be finally excluded as possible causes of a break in State continuity : territorial changes, revolutionary changes, and belligerent occupation. In all these three cases the identity and continuity of the State concerned is fully safeguarded by clear and undoubted rules of international law.

The value of these rules, which have now been examined lies, in the first place, in their absolute certainty. There is no doubt as to their general validity. Consequently, any problem of State identity and continuity, falling under any of these three headings, can easily be solved by a correct application of the rules in question.

Furthermore, the value of these three rules lies in their objective character. Firmly anchored in general international law, they are binding on the international community and cannot be set aside by individual States. Nor can the State concerned disclaim its continuity, and the resulting obligations, because it has suffered territorial or revolutionary changes or has undergone a period of belligerent occupation. Nor can third States, either individually or collectively, deny such continuity in the three cases discussed.

The problem of State identity and continuity can, however, arise in other and more complicated circumstances than territorial or revolutionary changes or belligerent occupation. It is therefore necessary to enquire whether international law contains any other rules, or at least, admits of any other tests of the identity and continuity of States.

CHAPTER III.

TESTS OF STATE IDENTITY AND CONTINUITY.

I. *IRRELEVANT TESTS.*

The search for other possible tests of the identity and continuity of States may well begin with an immediate rejection of all such tests which are obviously irrelevant. This applies in the first place to certain external features of the State which have no bearing on its essence.

Among such irrelevant tests is that of the State's name. It is true that in some cases the name of a State may convey a certain meaning with regard to its legal structure. This would be so in the case of the United States of America, the Union of Soviet Socialist Republics or the Austro-Hungarian Empire. Similarly, the change of name of Czechoslovakia to " Czecho-Slovakia " after Munich was meant to reflect a change in the internal structure of that country. In international law, however, the name of the State is of no relevance. In principle, a State is free to adopt any name it pleases [1] as well as to change it at will, and no such changes can possibly affect its identity. In the discussion concerning the continuity or otherwise of the Kingdom of Sardinia within the new Kingdom of Italy, the change of name was emphatically dismissed by both sides as legally irrelevant [2]. Nor did the question of name play any part in the discussion concerning the identity or otherwise of Serbia with the Kingdom of Serbs, Croats and Slovenes [3], not to speak of the fact that the latter was soon to change its name again, to Yugoslavia. The irrelevance of a country's name with regard to the problem of its continuity was one of the arguments used by the Austrian Delegation at Saint-Germain-en-Laye in their struggle for the principle of non-identity of the new Republic with the Empire [4]. In the discussion concerning the identity or otherwise of the Soviet Union with Imperial Russia the point was not even raised. Whether a State calls itself Persia or Iran, Switzerland or Confoederatio Helvetica, is of no importance whatever.

The title of the sovereign is similarly irrelevant. It is true that here again such title may have a certain meaning either with regard to the State's structure or to the extension or otherwise of its territory. But although Queen Victoria adopted the title of Empress of India and King George VI abandoned it, in neither case was Great Britain's

1. For a very special exception see below, p. 230.
2. See below, p. 192.
3. See below, p. 252.
4. See below, p. 215.

identity in any way affected. The position was the same with regard to the King of Sardinia changing his style to that of the King of Italy [1]. If such a change of style is the result of legally relevant changes, such as considerable territorial expansion, particularly by way of conquest, it may indeed give rise to a diplomatic and juridical problem with regard to its recognition by other States. Such a problem arose when Victor-Emmanuel III assumed the title of Emperor of Ethiopia. The importance of the question does not, however, lie in the name, but in the facts of which the change of title is merely the expression, and in no case does it affect the identity of the original State.

Nor is any importance to be attached to the identity of the capital. The fact of Italy moving her capital from Turin to Florence and from Florence to Rome [2] was as irrelevant to the problem of Sardinian — or Italian — identity and continuity, as the moving of the Polish capital from Cracow to Warsaw in the 16th century was to that of Poland. Nor did the shifting of the Russian capital from Leningrad to Moscow play any part in the discussion concerning the identity of Soviet Russia with Imperial Russia. Conversely, the identity of the capital is by no means decisive for the identity of the State [3].

In view of what has already been said about the population [4], no changes in the human composition of the State can have any effect on its identity and continuity. It has been seen that population is by definition a changing element. More particularly its national composition is of no relevance. Whether a State acquires or loses minorities, its legal status is not affected. Transfers of population aimed at, and securing, the elimination of minorities, took place between Turkey and Greece, Turkey and Bulgaria, without affecting the identity and continuity of the countries concerned in any way. That the argument of the national composition of the State could have been seriously introduced into the discussion of Austria's legal status merely goes to prove the overwhelmingly political character of that discussion [5].

The irrelevance of all such purely fortuitous and legally meaningless characteristics of the State to the problem of its identity and continuity can therefore be taken for granted [6].

II. TESTS TO BE ELIMINATED.

The above tests have been mentioned and disposed of for the sake of completeness. They have never been seriously put forward by anyone. Certain other tests have, however, been actually suggested for determining the identity and continuity of States in doubtful cases, that is to say in cases where the three firm rules provide no answer to the problem. It is these tests which have now to be examined.

---

1. See below, p. 192.
2. *Ibid.*
3. See below, p. 215.
4. See above, pp. 4 and 48.
5. See below, pp. 214-215.
6. For irrelevant changes, see Oppenheim-Lauterpacht, *op. cit.*, I, p. 148.

1. UNILATERAL DECISION OF THE STATE CONCERNED.

It has been suggested that, in the absence of exact criteria, the will and the decision of the State concerned ought to be decisive in determining its identity and continuity [1].

Although this test has been proposed as a purely auxiliary one, that is to say, failing other, objective criteria, it is submitted that it is inadmissible. In the first place, it is wholly incompatible with the security of international relations [2]. If the proposal were accepted, a State could terminate its treaties, evade its obligations and escape the consequences of its illegal acts, by the simple means of declaring itself " new ". The test proposed is thus subversive of any notion of international responsibility. The point was clearly appreciated and emphatically repudiated by Clemenceau in his well-known Note to Germany on the morrow of the First World War [3].

In spite of the emphatic rejection of any such test, the State's own will and conviction may be admitted to a very limited extent as a controvertible piece of evidence of its identity and continuity. Such evidence will, of course, be stronger, if it is to be found not only in diplomatic correspondence, negotiations, and generally acts aimed at defending a preconceived thesis *pro foro externo*, but rather on the internal level, as representing a spontaneous conviction, and not being intended to produce effects in the outside world. Even so, it will at best be very weak evidence, which has to yield before more objective criteria. It does not, in itself, constitute a test.

2. CONVENTIONAL LAW.

In the hope of finding a test of State identity and continuity, certain writers have turned to conventional international law [4]. It is, however, submitted that such an attitude results from a misconception of the nature of the latter.

A treaty creates rights and obligations for the parties to it ; it can change or regulate a given situation. But it cannot call an existing situation something else, without changing it.

A treaty does not *create* the fact of identity or non-identity of a State. Being concluded *after* the events which have brought about the extinction, or preserved the continuity, of a State, all that a treaty can properly do is to state the correct position under general international law [5]. The value of a treaty provision on the subject is thus purely declaratory. For the actual situation to which the treaty refers already

---

1. " ...in mancanza di norme sicure di diritto internazionale generale or particolare che diversamente dispongano, si tenga massimamente conto della volontà dello Stato che afferma la novità della propria esistenza. " Udina, *op. cit.*, p. 291.
2. See above, pp. 24-25.
3. See above, p. 33.
4. See below, pp. 226-228.
5. « Il arrive parfois qu'un traité légitimant et confirmant la situation de droit... n'intervient qu'après que cette situation de droit a été établie conformément au principe d'effectivité. » Kelsen, *Théorie Générale*, p. 180 et seq.

exists and has already been classified under general international law. If the makers of the treaty draw correct conclusions from general international law as applied to the particular situation, then the treaty will do no more than confirm the existing legal position. If, on the other hand, they seek to embody in the treaty a view which is obviously contrary to general international law, then the treaty will to this extent be a mere fiction and will be effective only as regards concrete obligations and only as between the parties to it. Thus, not only the value of a treaty as a test of State identity and continuity, but also its actual effectiveness may be greatly reduced by its non-conformity with general international law [1].

Conventional law is thus by its very nature not the proper instrument to provide a solution of the problem [2]. Such a solution can only be given by general international law which conventional law can neither change nor override. It is not to be imagined that a treaty proclaiming the extinction of a State following internal revolution, territorial changes or belligerent occupation, could prevail against customary norms to the contrary. It could possibly be enforced, even if contrary to general international law, within the limits of what the parties could effectively do, but it is hardly to be expected that it should be recognized by an international tribunal.

The above proposition is by no means arbitrary. It was fully confirmed in the *Tinoco* case. Speaking of the Central American Convention of 1907 which outlawed revolutionary governments, the Arbitrator declared :

" Such a treaty could not ... amend or change the rules of international law in the matter of *de facto* governments [3]. "

Thus, a treaty cannot supply the test of State identity and continuity, except in so far as it conforms to general international law.

3. RECOGNITION.

A. NATURE OF RECOGNITION.

To fall back on recognition by third States as the criterion of State identity and continuity in doubtful cases appears at first sight to be an attractively simple solution. For, if adopted, it would render any further search for such criteria unnecessary. In doubtful cases, i.e. in cases not covered by any of the three rules previously discussed, international recognition would finally determine the issue.

---

1. See below, pp. 229-235.
2. « Tout d'abord, il faut affirmer que la question de l'identité d'un Etat avec un autre ne peut être réglée par traité. Cette question ne peut être résolue que d'après les dispositions du droit des gens commun. » Kelsen, *Naissance de l'Etat*, p. 633. Cf. Verdross, *Verfassung*, p. 151. The same idea of conventional law being incapable of providing the test sought is implicit in the writings of all those writers who affirm the element of fiction in an international treaty claiming to decide the question of the identity and continuity of a State, see below, p. 228.
3. *A.J.*, 1924, p. 155.

Such a solution has indeed been proposed by Raestad in an interesting article on the extinction of States [1]. Raestad asks whether it is possible for a State to survive a debellatio, and, adopting the constitutive view of recognition, answers that, just as recognition by third States is decisive for the birth of a State, so it is decisive as regards its extinction. Consequently, if a State survives a debellatio, this can only be by the will of third States [2]. It follows that a State can exist in either of the two ways : either " by its own means ", as long as its legal order is normally effective in its territory ; or by the will of other States not to recognize a debellatio [3]. Only when the third States finally withdraw their recognition from the conquered State, does the latter become definitely extinct. Thus, according to Raestad, the will of third States, as expressed in recognition, is the source of the continued existence of a State whose continuity has been gravely endangered.

Raestad's suggestion automatically raises the perennial problem of the constitutive or declaratory nature of recognition. For it is clear that, in order to be the source of the continued existence of a State, recognition must be constitutive, and not declaratory. Moreover, it must be a legal, not a political act. The problem is thus exactly the same as in the case of the original recognition of a new State. For the object of recognition is in both cases the *existence* of a State, and it makes little difference that in one case it is a new, and in the other a continued existence. In both cases the question reduces itself to this : can the existence of a State have its source in the will of third States ?

B. Declaratory and Political Nature of Recognition.

It is submitted that recognition is both declaratory and political. An adequate defence of this proposition would require a separate study, — a task which, apart from being impossible within the framework of this enquiry, has now become practically redundant, especially since the publication of the two exhaustive monographs on the subject : one by Prof. Lauterpacht supporting the constitutive, and one by Mr. Chen supporting the declaratory theory of recognition [4].

Nevertheless, as controversial a proposition as the one advanced above, should not be left entirely unsubstantiated, especially as it may be decisive for the problem of State identity and continuity. It is therefore necessary to examine at least those aspects of the problem of recognition which have an equal bearing on both the new and the continued existence of States.

---

1. *Op. cit.*
2. « Après qu'une debellatio a eu lieu, si l'Etat existe encore, c'est en vertu de la volonté d'autres Etats. » *Op. cit.*, p. 449.
3. « ...par ses propres moyens ou par la volonté des autres Etats de ne pas reconnaître une debellatio. » *Op. cit.*, p. 449. The idea [of a State existing under normal conditions « par ses propres moyens » seems hardly compatible with the constitutive view of recognition, such as seems to be adopted by Raestad throughout his study.
4. Lauterpacht, *Recognition in International Law;* Chen, *The International Law of Recognition.*

1. DECLARATORY.

a) *Relativity of State Existence under the Constitutive Theory.*

One of the strongest arguments against the constitutive theory of recognition is that it inevitably results in an assertion of the mere relativity of State existence.

With regard to new States, it means that since a State actually comes into being by way of recognition, it is clear that is exists only in relation to those States which have recognized it. Thus, not only is the actual beginning of a State's existence different in time in relation to every recognizing State, but, moreover, " States exist only in a relative sense " [1]. In other words, they exist and do not exist at the same time. This result which is impossible both in theory and in practice, has in fact been philosophically admitted by Prof. Kelsen in a well-known article which marked his abrupt conversion from the declaratory to the constitutive theory [2]. Such resignation has in turn been strongly attacked by Prof. Lauterpacht [3]. But his answer is somewhat disappointing. He does not attempt to prove that this is not the position, according to the constitutive doctrine, but merely states that it reflects the weakness of existing international organisation and that the situation should change under his proposed collectivisation of the process of recognition [4]. It is submitted that to answer an argument *de lege lata* with an argument *de lege ferenda*, is to leave it unanswered. The absurdity of a simultaneous existence and non-existence of one and the same State thus remains one of the weakest points in the constitutive doctrine ; it may be remarked that the constitutive theory is therefore destructive of the very notion of an international community [5].

Thus the constitutive theory of recognition is unable to provide a safe and reliable test of the existence of States. If this is so with regard to the birth of States, it applies even more strongly with regard to their continued existence ; for it has been seen that the continuity of States

---

1. Chen, *op. cit.*, p. 4 ; Brierly, *Règles générales*, p. 54.
2. " A State exists legally only in its relations to other States. There is no such thing as absolute existence. Since we have to acknowledge the relativity of time and space ...relativity of legal existence is no longer paradoxical. " *Recognition in International Law*, A.J., 1941, p. 609.
3. " The grotesque spectacle of a community being a State in relation to some but not to other States is a grave reflection upon international law. It cannot be explained away, amidst some complacency, by questionable analogies to private law or to philosophical relativism. " *Op. cit.*, p. 78.
4. *Op. cit.*, p. 58 : " ...this is a criticism not of the constitutive doctrine, but of the imperfection of international organisation.... " *Op. cit.*, p. 67.
5. « ... de cette théorie il résulterait qu'un Etat n'a d'existence juridique que vis-à-vis de ceux qui l'ont reconnu. On ne pourrait alors concevoir une existence juridique pure et simple, c'est-à-dire l'existence en un sens objectif des Etats. Et on ne pourrait affirmer l'existence d'une communauté internationale que dans la mesure où l'on pourrait démontrer que tous les Etats que l'on a l'habitude d'y faire rentrer auraient reconnu tous les autres. Une pareille preuve est évidemment tout à fait impossible. » Kelsen, *Théorie générale*, p. 271. " Since no State is a member of the international community in the absolute sense, there can be no real international community, because any State which has not recognized a particular State may deny that they belong to the same community. " Chen, *op. cit.*, p. 42.

is a polemical notion [1] and that the *continued* existence of a State is certainly a more controversial matter than its birth.

Yet, it is precisely for the doubtful cases of State identity and continuity, i.e. those not covered by any of the three rules previously discussed, that the test of recognition has been suggested by Raestad. This suggestion meets one the weightiest arguments of Prof. Lauterpacht in favour of the constitutive theory : namely, that it is sometimes so doubtful whether an entity is a State at all that only a constitutive act of recognition can finally dispel the doubt and " make " it a State [2].

In the first place, however, this argument is again on the border-line of the *lex ferenda*. Prof. Lauterpacht in fact seems to suggest that in doubtful cases constitutive recognition (which in the meantime, it appears, would have been collectivized and made a legal duty) *should* decide the issue ; he does not clearly suggest that it actually does so. Under present conditions, such a test of the existence or non-existence of a State would indeed be a poor solution to fall back on. For it happens precisely that one group of States recognizes such a " doubtful " entity as a State, whereas another group firmly refuses to do so. It may not be unnecessary to emphasize once again that, if this is the position with regard to the *beginning* of a State's existence, it is even more so with regard to the controversial problem of its *continued existence*. The controversial nature of this problem is bound to give rise to even more conflicting attitudes on the part of third States. What sort of evidence can possibly be found in such conflicting attitudes ? Which group of States is " right " in admitting or denying the new or the continued existence of a State ? Is it the larger group ? Or the group which includes the Great Powers, who may also be divided on the question ? Recognition by how many States would be sufficient to uphold the continuity of a State ? Would recognition by one State be enough ? If not, by how many ? Any attempt to distinguish between such two groups is as unscientific as it is absurd.

What is worse, the difficulty does not end with the problem of conflicting attitudes of various States. For one and the same State may well adopt a different attitude on the subject at different times, by recognizing the continued existence of a State, then withdrawing such recognition only in order to grant it again later. This makes recognition finally impossible as a test of the identity and continuity of States. For which attitude of one and the same State should be considered as decisive ? After all, it cannot be admitted that a State exists, then ceases to exist, but then exists once again, and, moreover, not as a new, but as *the* old State. Yet, this would in fact be the position if recognition were adopted as a test.

---

1. See above, p. 4.
2. *Op. cit.*, pp. 48-51. In reply to the theory of " doubtful " cases as a compelling reason for the adoption of the constitutive theory, Chen observes : " This objection is a formidable one. But, coming from Prof. Lauterpacht, it is less difficult to answer. For according to his own theory, recognition is a legal duty to be performed when conditions of fact so demand ; it is declaratory of facts, though constitutive of rights. There would be the same necessity of, and, therefore, the same difficulty in, ascertaining whether the fact of the fulfilment of statehood had taken place. " *Op. cit.*, pp. 74-75.

This objection is far from being a purely theoretical one. That the existence of conflicting attitudes on the part of third States *ipso facto* excludes any possibility of using recognition as a test, has been illustrated more than once in recent times. Was Manchukuo, or was is not, a State? According to Japan, El Salvador and a few other countries, it certainly was ; according to other States it was not. The case was even more disturbing with regard to Slovakia and Croatia. According to Germany, Italy and their satellites, and even to Poland, with regard to Slovakia, and to Switzerland, with regard to both, they were States ; according to all other States they were not. This immediately raises the problem of the *continued* existence of Czechoslovakia and Yugoslavia ; according to one part of the international community such continued existence was a fact ; according to another, their final extinction was no less a fact.

With regard to the adoption of inconsistent attitudes by a single State it may for instance be asked which of the varying attitudes of third States should be considered relevant to the problem of the continuity of Czechoslovakia, Austria or Ethiopia? For the continuity of these States, following their annexation, was recognized, de-recognized and recognized again, and, moreover, under identical circumstances of fact [1].

The value of such " test " hardly seems to require any further refutation. According to the natural meaning of words, a test is something to resolve a difficulty and to provide the answer to a possibly complicated question. But a " test " which does not, and cannot, serve this purpose, is no test at all.

b) *Incompatibility of the Constitutive Theory with the Objective Character of International Law.*

The above suggestion by Raestad, according to which recognition by third States should be the source of the legal continuity of a State, must be considered as an example of pure voluntarism. In this respect it stands on the same footing as the whole constitutive theory of recognition. For on closer analysis it becomes obvious that, while the declaratory theory deduces the existence — or the continued existence — of a State from an objective norm of international law, the constitutive theory deduces it from the will of third States. The age-long argument between supporters of the constitutive and the declaratory theory thus reveals itself as a dispute about the voluntarist or objective character of international law [2].

---

1. See below, Part II.
2. " In the last analysis the question of international recognition is but a reflection of the fundamental cleavage between those who regard the State as the ultimate source of international rights and duties and those who regard it as being under a system of law which determines its rights and duties under that law. " " For to argue that a State can become a subject of international law without the assent of the existing States, it is necessary to assume the existence of an objective system of law to which the new State owes its being. " Chen, *op. cit.*, p. 3 and pp. 18-19. « C'est une idéologie nettement

The fact that the declaratory theory destroys the voluntarist character of international law was clearly appreciated by Anzilotti. Basing his whole system on the will of States, as expressed in formal or tacit agreements, Anzilotti logically assumes that recognition is an agreement of a constitutive nature, and denies the existence of an objective norm which would itself determine the existence of a State. Should the existence of such an objective norm be proved, he adds, then his whole system would fatally founder [1]. But rather than sacrifice his whole system, the danger to which from the declaratory doctrine he clearly perceives, Anzilotti prefers to deny the existence of the norm in question.

Thus, the defence of the declaratory theory and the assertion of the existence of the objective norm in question becomes a defence of the objective character of international law [2].

Such a defence was in fact undertaken, in a masterly way, by Kelsen in his earlier writings. Kelsen starts from the assumption that international law, like any other legal system, itself determines the character of its subjects [3]. If this is so, such determination forms precisely the general norm, by which international law declares that a State has come into being. This is the only real " recognition ", which is granted to a new entity directly by the international legal order, when that entity has fulfilled the necessary conditions required by

---

subjectiviste qui se manifeste dans cette théorie de reconnaissance, acte constitutif de l'existence de l'Etat. ...il ne s'agit pas là d'une différence d'opinion sur les règles de droit positif, mais bien d'une opposition de politique juridique. » « C'est le dogme de la souveraineté qui s'efforce de nier la validité d'un ordre juridique superétatique, et de déduire le droit des gens uniquement de la volonté des Etats... » Kelsen, *Théorie générale*, pp. 268 and 270. According to Prof. Bourquin, the constitutive view « présente d'évidentes affinités avec la conception fondamentale du positivisme étatique. Elle en est, peut-on dire, le corollaire. » *Règles générales*, p. 109. Cf. Brierly, *Règles*, p. 53.

1. « Il n'est pas non plus inutile d'observer que, si l'existence de cette norme venait à être démontrée, la conception du droit international soutenue ici ne serait pas par ailleurs acceptable. Elle part, en effet, de la conception que les normes internationales sont le produit d'accords formels ou tacites ; mais cette norme, au contraire, ne serait pas le produit d'un accord ; elle s'imposerait au nouvel Etat en dehors de sa volonté et, par suite, elle ne serait pas couverte par la norme-base *pacta sunt servanda*, à laquelle doivent, par définition, se ramener toutes les autres normes de l'ordre international.|» *Op. cit.*, p. 166.

2. The point can — and should — be pressed even further. For what is at stake is the very existence of international law as a normative system, since no such system is possible on a voluntarist basis. While not denying the existence of international law *qua* law, Triepel is in this respect more logical than Anzilotti,for,starting from the voluntarist assumption, he denies the existence of general international law. " Da nun Völkerrecht *nur* aus Vereinbarung entstehen kann und eine Vereinbarung, bei der sich *sämtliche* existierenden Staaten betheiligt hätten, nicht nachzuweisen ist, so kann es ein *allgemeines* Völkerrecht im Sinne eines alle vorhandenen Staaten gleichmässig beherrschenden nicht geben. " *Völkerrecht und Landesrecht*, Verlag von J.C.B. Mohr, Tübingen, 1907, p. 83. The least harm that can be done to international law by the voluntarists is to truncate it .mercilessly in its fundamental part.

3. " Das Völkerrecht muss von sich aus bestimmen, was ein Staat ist. " " Ein Völkerrecht wäre nämlich schlechterdings unmöglich, ohne dass es selbst bestimmte, was ein Staat sei. " *Souveränität*, pp. 230-231. It is interesting to observe that this necessity, inherent in any legal system, to determine its own subjects is equally firmly upheld by Anzilotti who, however, refuses to draw the necessary logical conclusion: «... il est évident que tout ordre juridique détermine quels sont ses sujets...» *Op. cit.*, pp. 122. Cf. p. 160. Cf. the following compelling reason advanced by Prof. Bourquin : «...il est impossible de *concevoir l'Etat* en dehors de l'ordre juridique international, puisque toutes ses compétences en dérivent, y compris celle qu'il exerce sur son propre territoire et qui constitue, à ce point de vue, le minimum irréductible. » *Op. cit.*, p. 109.

international law for its subjects. Any other recognition is purely declaratory, i.e. legally irrelevant [1].

In his further criticism of the constitutive theory, Kelsen emphasizes, that according to the latter, recognition can be either an agreement or a unilateral act. The agreement theory, however, involves a *petitio principii*, for how can a treaty be concluded with an entity which is not a subject of law, i.e. not endowed with legal capacity. Thus there only remains the theory of the unilateral act. But in this case, the basis of validity of the new State lies in the will of others. And this, in Kelsen's view, is the negation of international law [2].

The alternative is inescapable : either the international legal system exists as an objective system of law and thus determines its own subjects, whose recognition by other States is then merely political and — as Kelsen drastically puts it — legally irrelevant ; or the international legal system, far from having an objective character and validity, rests solely upon the doubtful foundation of the will of States, and then recognition may indeed be constitutive, but what remains of international law *qua* law ?

Attempts to reconcile international law as an objective legal system with the constitutive view of recognition have recently been made. Such attempt is to be found in Prof. Lauterpacht's well-known book on recognition, in which he combines the constitutive theory with an

---

1. " Nur dass sie eben *generell*, nämlich durch einen *Rechtssatz* des Völkerrechts erfolgt, der bestimmt, unter welchen Bedingungen ein Staat als solcher Subjekt völkerrechtlicher Pflichten und Rechte ist. Ein solcher Rechtssatz muss als Bestandteil des Völkerrechts angenommen werden, da aus jedem Normensystem selbst beantwortet werden muss, welches die Subjekte seiner Pflichten und Rechte sind... " *Souveränität*, p. 230. Cf. *Allgemeine Staatslehre*, pp. 126-127. " Darin, dass das Völkerrecht von sich aus bestimmt, was ein Staat sei, oder wann ein Staat in die Sphäre des Völkerrechts, in die Ebene völkerrechtlicher Erkenntnis eintritt, liegt auch die generelle, ein für allemal erfolgende " Anerkennung " von Neustaaten. Liegt der von der Völkerrechtsnorm umschriebene Tatbestand vor, dann ist für die Völkerrechtsbetrachtung ein Staat in ihrem Sinne, ein Subjekt der Pflichten und Rechte des Völkerrechts existent. -...Eine weitere " Anerkennung " durch Willenserklärungen der Altstaaten hat demgegenüber nur deklaratorische, d.h. *juristisch gar keine* Bedeutung. " *Souveränität*, p. 231. Similarly Brierly : « Internationalement, la reconnaissance ne produit aucun résultat juridique. » *Op. cit.*, p. 61. Cf. Bourquin : « Dès l'instant où un groupement social réunit les caractères requis par le droit des gens pour constituer un Etat, il fait partie de l'ordre juridique international et sa reconnaissance par les autres Etats n'est, à cet égard, qu'un acte déclaratoire. » *Op. cit.*, p. 111. The denial of all legal relevance to recognition would, however, seem too categorical. In this sense, the following earlier view of Prof. Guggenheim : "Diese Anerkennungen haben indessen für die Begründung des Rechtsverhältnisses von Neustaat zur Staatengemeinschaft lediglich deklaratorische Bedeutung ; für die Begründung von besonderen völkerrechtlichen Beziehungen zwischen " anerkennendem " und " anerkannten " Staat können sie konstitutive Wirkung haben. " *Beiträge*, p. 13. Similarly Bourquin, *op cit.*, p. 111.

2. « Mais alors, l'existence juridique, la personnalité juridique de ce dernier, repose sur la volonté du premier, c'est-à-dire, ... que le principe ou la raison de validité (Geltungsgrund) de l'ordre juridique de l'Etat reconnu se trouve dans un autre ordre étatique. Mais alors on ne peut plus parler de cette coordination des Etats, qui est une hypothèse essentielle ou, d'une façon plus exacte, la fonction essentielle du droit international... Si on considère son Etat comme un ordre réellement suprême, alors il n'est que logique de fonder la validité d'un autre ordre, c'est-à-dire en employant une personnification, l'existence juridique d'un autre Etat, uniquement sur la volonté de son propre Etat. Mais cette théorie aboutit en fin de compte à la négation du droit international lui-même. » *Théorie générale*, pp. 270-271. It is obvious that the constitutive theory is as little compatible with the principle of State independence as it is with objective international law.

anti-voluntarist conception. According to this view, recognition, in spite of being constitutive, should not be an arbitrary act on the part of recognizing States ; on the contrary, since it is based on objective facts, it should be a legal duty. It is thus " declaratory of facts " and " constitutive of rights " [1].

The difficulty in following Prof. Lauterpacht's trend of thought results from the fact that the author constantly shifts his argument from the *lex lata* to the *lex ferenda*, while the reader is left somewhat uncertain as to which of the two he is referring to. It must be emphasized that *de lege lata* a legal duty to recognize does not exist, and that, moreover, it cannot exist together with the constitutive theory [2]. *De lege ferenda* it should be observed that a theory which makes recognition obligatory in conformity with the objective facts of a State's existence, defeats its own premise, since it ceases to be constitutive and in fact becomes declaratory however it may be described [3].

A similar attempt in the same sense has been made by Professors Kelsen and Guggenheim since their recent adoption of the constitutive theory.

The argument runs as follows : it is true, that international law, being an objective legal system, itself determines its subjects. But, as a matter of absolute procedural necessity, this determination must be established by someone, — failing a central organ, by existing States acting in their capacity of international organs [4].

This is a very much modified constitutive theory. Like that of Prof. Lauterpacht, it has the merit of avoiding the arbitrariness, otherwise implicit in the constitutive view, by requiring full conformity between international law's determination of its subjects and their actual recognition, undertaken by States as an act of procedure. It is, however, submitted that it is precisely this merit of the theory which constitutes its fundamental weakness : for by postulating such conformity, the doctrine falls back on general international law as the only truly decisive criterion of the existence of States. This is nothing but a return to the declaratory theory. For if it is true that it is international law which determines *in substance* its subjects, then recognizing States do no more than state the position under international law. What if they state it obviously incorrectly? What is the result of

---

1. *Op. cit.*, pp. 6 and 75.
2. See below, pp. 153-154.
3. See the judicious observations by Chen, quited above, p. 133, *f.-n.* 2.
4. " ...in the province of law there are no absolute, directly evident facts, facts " in themselves ", but only facts established by the competent authority in a procedure prescribed by the legal order. It is not theft as a fact in itself to which the legal order attaches a certain punishment. Only a layman formulates the rule of law in that way. The jurist knows that the legal order attaches a certain punishment only to a theft established by the competent court following a prescribed procedure. " Kelsen, *Recognition*, p. 606. " Wie jede rechtlich erhebliche Tatsache, kann aber die Feststellung der Existenz eines Staates nicht lediglich auf Grund der Anerkenung des Effektivitätsprinzipes, gleichsam entsprechend der Notorietät erfolgen. Eine *autoritative Konstatierung* dieses Zustandes ist notwendig. " Guggenheim, *Lehrbuch*, I, p. 181. Cf. Lauterpacht, *op. cit.*, p. 76. See Borchard's criticism of Prof. Kelsen's article : " Can you not establish the existence of a fact unless someone pronounces it to be a fact? " *Recognition and Non-Recognition*, A.J., 1942, p. 108.

their withholding recognition from a State fulfilling all conditions required by international law, or conversely, of their recognizing an obvious fiction ? Both these things have occurred sufficiently often for the question to be legitimately asked. Which, according to Professors Kelsen and Guggenheim, is then to prevail : international law which, on their own admission, decides the issue in substance, or the States which have disregarded this decision ? A precise answer to this crucial question has been supplied by Prof. Kelsen himself who clearly states that not only can recognition be premature, i.e. unlawful, but also that withdrawal of recognition (described by Kelsen as " *actus contrarius* ") is a violation of international law, in the case of a State " which in fact still exists " [1]. This decisive admission by Prof. Kelsen destroys his own constitutive view. For if recognition and withdrawal of recognition can be unlawful acts from the point of view of general international law, if they are powerless to create a State which " in fact " does not yet exist and to destroy a State which " in fact still exists ", then this " fact " of existence or non-existence of States, definitely prevailing over recognition or de-recognition, is not the result of such recognition or de-recognition, but of objective international law. This, by way of a long, complicated and, it is submitted, unnecessary *détour*, is nothing but an unqualified return to the declaratory theory, according to which objective norms of international law are decisive for the question of State existence, whatever the attitude of third States as expressed in recognition. Moreover, this theory again raises the whole problem of the relativity of the existence of States which has been dealt with above [2]. Recognition by how many States is necessary for an entity to become, or to continue to be, a State ? And what about a case of conflicting recognitions ?

Nor is the analogy with municipal procedure convincing. It is submitted that the following arguments of Chen are entirely correct :

" The forcible taking of property may or may not be robbery, upon which an ordinary citizen may, indeed, find it difficult to judge. But if the court decides that it is robbery, the court does not " create " the illegality of the act. The act is robbery not from the moment when the court pronounces its judgment, but from the moment the act was committed. Likewise, if a court pronounces that a person has reached majority, it merely says that a certain length of time has passed from the moment of his birth. It is the fact of a prescribed passage of time which produces legal consequences, and not the ascertainment of it. The pronouncement of the court might conceivably be made many years after the date of majority, but the legal consequences of majority do not date from the pronouncement. By analogy, a State exists as an international person as soon as it has fulfilled the requirements of statehood. The fact that States cannot have the same faculty for appreciating the fact of the fulfilment of these requirements is no reason for denying that there is an objective point of time at which such fulfilment takes place. Third States may be unable or unwilling to acknowledge this fact, but they certainly cannot alter it to suit their ignorance, caprice or self-interest [3]. "

---

1. *Op. cit.*, p. 611.
2. See above, pp. 132-134.
3. *Op. cit.*, pp. 48-49.

It may be added that it is certainly dangerous to compare present-day States, in the present-day condition of international organisation, to courts of law. Courts, whether municipal or international, have no other function than to administer law. States have several other functions, and recognition in particular is a clearly political act on their part [1]. It is therefore as incorrect as it is dangerous to ascribe to that political act the same meaning as to the strictly legal pronouncement of a court. Professors Kelsen and Guggenheim do not deny the political aspect of recognition, but, presumably in order to preserve the law-making function of States granting recognition, maintain that there are really two acts included in the apparently single act of recognition : a legal and a political one, the former being constitutive and the latter declaratory [2]. This view seems, however, to be an artificial one and is left unsupported by any evidence, especially from State practice [3]. But even, if the existence of two separate acts were admitted for the sake of argument, how can it be established that, at the time of granting recognition, States are sufficiently motivated by the " legal " aspect for such recognition to become the true and authoritative expression of international law ? Is it really to be supposed, contrary to all known practice of States [4], that at that moment they somehow divest themselves of their predominantly political interest in the question ? It seems that it is precisely this weakness of international organisation which lies at the root of Prof. Lauterpacht's proposal for a collectivisation of recognition. Only then would it indeed be possible to speak of a genuine act of procedure, determining a legally relevant fact. But to entrust this function to individual members of an unorganized society is really too grave, — especially as it affects nothing less than the question of life and death of States. It may finally be observed that it seems dangerous in the extreme to place the main emphasis on procedure in an underdeveloped legal system in which neither the procedure itself, nor the organs which are to apply it are unequivocally determined. In the absence of the most elementary requirements essential to a sound functioning of any procedure, such emphasis must inevitably lead to every single legal phenomenon becoming merely relative. This in turn is bound to undermine even the minimum of certainty and stability indispensable to the maintenance and conduct of legal relations.

It must therefore be concluded that attempts to reconcile the constitutive doctrine of recognition with the objective character of international law have not succeeded, — as indeed they cannot succeed in the present stage of international organisation. The two propositions remain mutually exclusive. It must therefore be repeated that it is general international law alone which, by means of an objective norm, decides the problem of the existence of States.

---

1. Even Prof. Lauterpacht admits " the dual position of the recognizing State as an organ administering international law and as a guardian of its own interest... " *Op. cit.*, p. 67.
2. Kelsen, *Recognition*, pp. 605-606 ; Guggenheim, *op. cit.*, I, p. 184, *f.-n.* 54.
3. Borchard questions " the existence of the distinction posited and its practical importance, if it did exist. " *Op. cit.*, p. 108.
4. See below, pp. 155-157.

c) *Determination of State Existence by Objective Norm.*

The existence of this objective norm has been claimed by Kelsen as a matter of logic. It is, however, submitted that its actual existence is also proved by consistent State practice. For it is on the basis of this objective norm that States have acted in matters of both recognition and non-recognition.

alfa) State Practice in Matters of Recognition.

The classical example of a new State becoming a subject of international law immediately on its birth and prior to any recognition, — that is to say, on the strength of objective international law alone — is to be found in one of the great European pronouncements on international law, namely, the famous Protocols of the London Conference of 1831, dealing with the birth of Belgium as an independent State. The Protocol of February 19, 1831, contains the following relevant passages :

« Chaque nation a ses droits particuliers ; mais l'Europe aussi a son droit : c'est l'ordre social qui le lui a donné.

Les Traités qui régissent l'Europe, la Belgique devenue indépendante les trouvait faits et en vigueur, elle devait donc les respecter, et ne pouvait pas les enfreindre...

... les événements qui font naître en Europe un Etat nouveau ne lui donnent pas ... le droit d'altérer le système général dans lequel il entre [1]... »

In order fully to appreciate the meaning of this statement, it is necessary to bear in mind the fact that the Protocol was signed *before* the recognition of Belgium by the very Powers who drafted it and consequently refers precisely to an *unrecognized* State [2].

It follows therefore that Belgium. was considered a State solely by reason of her having achieved independence, and independently of any act of recognition. As such, Belgium was immediately subject to, and bound by, the international law of Europe. This did not result either from the will of Belgium herself, or from the will of the third States, but solely and exclusively from the objective character of that law. It was thus in accordance with this objective law alone that Belgium became a State and was consequently bound by its provisions. The London Protocol is thus a clear confirmation of the existence of this objective norm determining the birth of a State, — and is also one of the most forceful affirmations of the objective character of international law. As such, it may be considered as yet another proof of the inescapable connection between this character of international law and the declaratory nature of recognition [3].

---

1. Martens, *N. R.*, vol. X, p. 199.
2. «...que l'indépendance de la Belgique ne sera reconnue par les cinq Puissances, qu'aux conditions et dans les limites qui résultent desdits arrangements du 20 janvier 1831. » *Ibid.*, p. 202.
3. Cf. the Report of the International Committee of Jurists on the Aaland Islands : " Finland, by declaring itself independent and claiming on this ground recognition as a legal person in international law, cannot escape from the obligations imposed upon it by such settlement of European interests. " *LNOJ*, Special Supplement, No. 3, p. 18.

It is submitted that the whole of State practice in matters of recognition is based precisely on such objective criteria. Nowhere in this practice is there a claim that new States or governments are " created " by means of recognition. In the above-quoted case of Belgium in 1831, such a claim was positively denied by what was at that time the Concert of Europe, and the existence of Belgium prior to recognition was expressly affirmed. Apart from the political reasons for the recognition [1], it may safely be said that far from regarding the latter as a creative act, States generally try to ascertain the objective facts relating to the existence or non-existence of a new State in order to decide whether to recognize it or not. With this object in view Canning sent special missions to the South American States, in order to determine whether they had in fact achieved full statehood [2]. Similarly, a Commission of Enquiry was sent to South America in 1817 by the United States [3], which also sent an observer to Albania after the First World War for the same purpose [4].

While deferring the recognition of Buenos Aires as premature in 1817, Secretary Adams admitted, that there is a stage at which such recognition can be claimed and granted.

" It is the stage when independence is established as a matter of fact [5]... "

Replying to the Spanish protest against the recognition by the United States of the insurgent governments in South America, Adams described recognition as a " mere acknowledgment of existing facts " [6]. In his report to the Senate Committee on Foreign Relations, of June 18, 1836, Secretary Clay stated:

" The policy which has hitherto guided the Government of the United States in respect to new powers has been to act on the fact of their existence [7]... "

Referring to the Cuban insurrection in his message of December 1, 1875, President Grant declared that " the creation of a State is a fact " and refused to grant recognition to the Cuban insurgents on the grounds that they had not achieved statehood.

" A recognition under such circumstances would be inconsistent with the facts [8]... "

With the exception of the Civil War period [9] and Wilsonian " constitutionalism ", it may be said that the practice of the United States has consistently borne out the declaratory principle. Only recently, on the occasion of the recognition by the United States of the new State of Israel, the American Delegate to the United Nations declared :

---

1. See below, pp. 155-157.
2. Smith, *Great Britain and the Law of Nations*, I, pp. 127-131.
3. Moore, *op. cit.*, I, p. 81.
4. Hackworth, *op. cit.*, I, p. 197.
5. Moore, *op. cit.*, I, p. 78.
6. *Ibid.*, p. 88.
7. *Ibid.*, p. 96.
8. *Ibid.*, p. 108.
9. See Chen, *op. cit.*, p. 83.

" When it (the right to grant recognition) was exercised by my Government, it was done as a practical step, in recognition of realities ; the existence of things and the recognition of a change that had actually taken place [1]. "

It can therefore be safely affirmed that it is not recognition which precedes and conditions the legal birth of a State, but on the contrary, it is this birth alone which precedes and conditions its recognition by third States. Hackworth is therefore fully justified in stating :

" The existence in fact of a new State or a new government is not dependent upon its recognition by other States [2]. "

bêta) State Practice in Matters of Non-Recognition.

That the existence of a State is determined by objective international law alone results with equal force from the State practice in matters of non-recognition. The existence of unrecognized States, and governments, is patently obvious and it could hardly be seriously maintained that, for example, the Soviet Government did not legally exist prior to its international recognition which, in the case of the United States took place sixteen years after its establishment. Could any amount of fiction to which the United States resorted [3] alter the fact that there existed, over one sixth of the globe's surface, an effective government, exacting obedience from 150 million inhabitants, engaging in normal international intercourse and enacting laws, which in course of time came to be recognized even by American courts [4] ? Did the continued presence of Ambassador Bakhmeteff and his successor in Washington make the Kerensky regime a legal reality long after it had actually ceased to exist or was it merely a fiction which was as incapable of resurrecting that regime as it was of destroying the legal existence of the Soviet Government [5] ?

The existence of unrecognized States and governments has time and again been confirmed by the practice of States which, notwithstanding their own non-recognition, have engaged in active intercourse with such allegedly non-existent entities. This acknowledgment by third States of the legal existence of entities which they themselves have not recognized has manifested itself in various ways.

i) Negotiations.

In the first place, actual negotiations have taken place on the basis of non-recognition. Such negotiations were conducted, and diplomatic notes exchanged between the new State of Belgium and the Great Powers in 1830 and 1831, and by the European Powers with the non-

---

1. Quoted by Chen, *op. cit.*, p. 84.
2. *Op. cit.*, I, p. 161.
3. See Amos Hershey, *op. cit.*, A.J., 1922 ; Borchard, *The unrecognized Governments in American Courts*, A.J., 1932, pp. 261-271.
4. See below, pp. 151-152.
5. " ...by legal fiction, for some purposes which appertain more particularly to the other, the " political " branches of the government than to the judiciary, we must continue to assume that the the old Imperial (sic !) government is the only sovereign government of Russia. " *Sokoloff v. National City Bank of New York*, A.D., 1923/24, case no. 19.

recognized Soviet Government almost from its very inception, beginning with the Prinkipo invitation. There followed attempts at mediation in the Soviet-Polish conflict of 1920 and the Genoa and Hague Conferences. At Genoa in particular, the non-recognizing European Powers (with the exception of Britain and Poland who had previously recognized the Soviet Union) sat for weeks at the conference table with the non-recognized government of Soviet Russia, discussing with the latter the very question of its recognition. Can negotiations, and particularly negotiations with a view to actual recognition, be conducted with a non-existent entity ?

ii) *Agreements.*

In addition, international agreements have been concluded on the basis of non-recognition.

The following repatriation agreements were concluded by the Soviet Government with States which did not recognize it: (The date of subsequent *de facto* recognition is given in brackets, whenever available).

With Great Britain on February 2, 1920 (16.3.1921) [1], with Hungary on July 28, 1921 [2], with Austria on July 5, 1920 (7.12.1921) [3], with Denmark on October 18, 1919 (23.4.1923) [4], with Belgium on April 20, 1920 [5], with France on April 20, 1920 *(de iure* recognition on October 28, 1924) [6].

The discrepancy between the dates of these agreements and the dates of recognition speaks for itself. It is, however, not without additional interest to quote the Foreign Office Certificate in the first *Luther v. Sagor* case, of November 27, 1920, i.e., nearly ten months after the conclusion of the above-mentioned repatriation agreement with the Soviet Government. The Foreign Office stated that " for a certain limited purpose, H.M. Government has assented to the claim that *that* which M. Krassin represents in this Country, is a State Government of Russia " and that " H.M. Government have never officially recognized the Soviet Government in any way " [7].

Can it be seriously maintained that international agreements can be concluded with an entity which does not legally exist [8] ?

iii) *International Responsibility.*

The absence of recognition has never prevented States from insisting upon the international responsibility of non-recognized governments or

---

1. Martens, N. R. G., 3rd series, XI, p. 840 ; Kleist, *Die völkerrechtliche Anerkennung Sowjetrusslands*, Ost-Europa Verlag, Koenigsberg-Berlin, 1935, p. 94.
2. Quoted by Korovin, *Das Völkerrecht der Uebergangszeit*, pp. 30 and 72.
3. *Ibid.*, p. 71 ; Kleist, *op. cit.*, p. 94.
4. Korovin, *op. cit.*, p. 71 ; Kleist, *op. cit.*, p. 94.
5. Korovin, *op. cit.*, p. 71.
6. Taracouzio, *op. cit.*, p. 255, *f.-n.* 66 ; Kleist, *op. cit.*, p. 98.
7. *It. mine, A.D.*, 1919/22, case no. 26.
8. " The suggestion that a State can sign a treaty with someone who does not exist is absurd and does not bear examination. " Chen, *op. cit.*, p. 209.

States [1]. In his famous Note of March 25, 1825, concerning the revolted Spanish colonies in Central and South America, Canning already spoke of " the total irresponsibility of unrecognized States " as " too absurd to be maintained " [2].

In the *Tinoco* case between Great Britain and Costa Rica, the former pressed against the latter claims arising out of obligations incurred by the non-recognized Tinoco Government. It was argued by Costa-Rica that Britain was estopped from pressing her claim by reason of such non-recognition. In opposing this view, Britain herself took her stand on the declaratory nature of recognition, since the British attitude amounted to an admission that the Tinoco Government had legally existed and its acts were internationally binding on Costa Rica notwithstanding the absence of British recognition. This was summed up by the Arbitrator in the following words :

" Here the executive of Great Britain takes the position that the Tinoco Government which it did not recognize, was nevertheless a *de facto* government that could create rights in British subjects which it now seeks to protect [3]. "

The case for estoppel was denied.

A similar situation arose between the United States and Mexico in the *George Hopkins Claim*, in which the United States pressed against Mexico claims arising out of acts of the non-recognized Huerta Government. Here again, Mexico was unable to invoke the non-recognition of that government as an estoppel ; and here again, the United States by no means considered the government, which it had not recognized, as legally non-existent [4].

As recently as January 1949, Great Britain claimed reparation for the shooting down of British aircraft, from the State of Israel which, at that time, she had not yet recognized [5].

Can it be argued that a legal nothing can be made subject of international responsibility ?

Thus the practice of States in matters of both recognition and non-recognition clearly proves that it is objective international law alone which determines the existence, or non-existence, of a State. A State

---

1. " ...it is clear that non-recognition does not involve irresponsibility. Protection is a duty which the Crown owes to its subjects in every part of the world, and this duty is not diminished by any refusal to recognize the local government. " Smith, *op. cit.*, p. 79.
2. *Ibid.*, p. 167.
3. *A.J.*, 1924, p. 155. The Arbitrator also observed : „ It may be urged that it would be in the interest of the stability of governments and the orderly adjustment of international relations, and so a proper rule of international law, that a government in recognizing or refusing to recognize a government claiming admission to the society of nations should thereafter be held to an attitude consistent with its deliberate conclusion on this issue. Arguments for and against such a rule occur to me ; but it suffices to say that I have not been cited to text writers of authority or to decisions of significance indicating a general acquiescence of nations in such a rule. Without this, it cannot be applied here as a principle of international law. " *Ibid.*, p. 157.
4. " Has the American Government forfeited its right to espouse Hopkins claim because in 1913 it warned its citizens against the " usurper " Huerta and never rec - gnized his administration ? The Commission holds that such warnings and such failure to recognize the Huerta administration cannot affect the vested rights of an American citizen or act as an estoppel of the right of the American Government to espouse the claim of such citizen before this Commission. " *A.J.*, 1927, p. 166.
5. Brierly, *Outlook for International Law*, Oxford, Clarendon Press, 1944.

exists in accordance with such objective norms alone and the denial of such existence must equally be based on objective norms. Thus, it follows that just as no amount of non-recognition can divest a State of its State character, so no amount of recognition can make what is not a State into a State. This view is borne out by the well-known advisory opinion of the Committee of Jurists on the Aaland Islands question. Examining the problem of the birth of Finland as a State, the Committee emphatically rejected the test of international recognition, as being incapable of making up for the lacking criteria of statehood, especially where a strong political element is involved. Here is what the Committee said with regard to the acts of recognition of Finland by third States :

" Nevertheless, these facts by themselves do not suffice to prove that Finland, from this time onwards, became a sovereign State. The experience of the last war shows that the same legal value cannot be attached to recognition of new States in war-time, especially to that accorded by belligerent powers, as in normal times ; further, neither were such recognitions given with the same object as in normal times [1]. "

This proposition is also supported by writers [2]. It is thus not only an objective norm which determines the existence of a State, but, moreover, it is such a norm *alone ;* in other words, nothing can replace it as a means of determining the existence of States.

But if this is so with regard to the *new* existence of a State, then the position could not possibly be different with regard to its *continued* existence. Just as there is an objective norm relating to the birth of States, so there must also be objective norms bearing on their identity and continuity. It is a sheer impossibility to admit an objective criterion of their birth but to fall back on pure voluntarism as the criterion of their further existence [3]. The three rules previously discussed, safeguarding the identity and continuity of States in concrete cases are precisely such objective norms. If the identity and continuity of a State is to be preserved in cases other than those covered by the three rules, this must also be on the strength of objective norms.

d) *Dangers of the Constitutive Theory.*

A further aspect of the theory of recognition, bearing directly on the question of State continuity, must now be examined. This is the question of the practical dangers inherent in the constitutive theory, in

---

1. *LNOJ*, Spec. Sup. no. 3, p. 8. Cf. the *Cuculla* and *McKenny* arbitrations, see below, pp. 150-151.
2. Thus Kunz, assuming effectiveness as the only valid test of State existence, concludes " a) dass, da die Anerkennung nicht den Staat schafft und daher nicht den Mangel der Effektivität ersetzen kann, eine Anerkennung, welche ohne Vorhandensein dieser Voraussetzung gewährt wird, rechtsunwirksam ist ; b) in einer solchen Anerkennung ein völkerrechtliches Delikt des anerkennenden Staates gelegen sein kann. " *Anerkennung*, pp. 55-56. The same assertion, as has been seen, has been made by Prof. Kelsen, however inconsistent with a constitutive theory of recognition. See above, pp. 137-138.
3. If anything, only the contrary could be imagined. Cf. Lauterpacht, *op. cit.*, p. 58, where he asserts that although States come legally into being by means of constitutive recognition, no stigma of dependence on third States attaches to their *further* existence.

particular, the outlawing of an unrecognized State, whether by an initial refusal to grant recognition or by a later withdrawal of such recognition. If the non-recognized State is really legally non-existent and if such a State and its inhabitants are really outside the protection of international law, nor bound by it, then, logically, everything is permissible with regard to them and everything is permitted to them. The unrecognized State could be freely invaded by other States or could itself invade them, without any illegal act being committed and without there being any legal remedy. The citizens of the new State could be treated as outlaws in the territory of third States and such treatment could be reciprocated. No laws of war could apply in any conflict between recognized and unrecognized States. The examples could easily be multiplied and the gravity of the position could hardly be overestimated [1].

It is such dangers which Prof. Lauterpacht seeks to minimize.

" It is probable that the prospects involved in this criticism of the constitutive view are not as terrifying as may appear at first sight. The territory of the unrecognized community is liable to invasion, but, under traditional international law, a State may invade the territory of a *recognized* State as soon as it has gone through the formality of declaring war or has otherwise manifested its *animus belligerendi*. Should an unrecognized community become engaged in war, then in

---

1. See Chen, *op. cit.*, p. 4 ; Bourquin, *Règles générales*, p. 110 ; Kelsen, *Théorie générale*, p. 276 and his conclusion : « Il est plus qu'improbable qu'il se trouve des internationalistes résolus à tirer, le cas échéant, de telles conséquences de la théorie de la reconnaissance. » The following forceful passage by Kunz deserves particular mention : " Die Wichtigkeit dieses Argumentes kann... gar nicht scharf genug unterstrichen werden. Nehmen wir den Fall : Die neue Republik Oesterreich ist am 30. Oktober 1918 entstanden, wurde von den Ententemächten aber erst am 29. Mai 1919 anerkannt. Wenn also in dieser Zwischenzeit Oesterreich die auf seinem Gebiete befindlichen Engländer oder Franzosen getötet oder ihr Eigentum konfisziert hätte, wenn es in das Gebiet eines Nachbarst??tes, der es noch nicht anerkannt hatte, eingedrungen wäre, so wäre dies alles, ebenso wenn England oder Frankreich ähnlich gegen Oesterreich oder seine Staatsangehörigen gehandelt hätte, nach Cavaglieri " ethisch bedauerlich, völkerrechtlich irrelevant " gewesen. Denn zwischen den alten Staaten und dem völkerrechtlichen Nichts, gennant de facto-Staat, gibt es ja gar keine Rechsbeziehungen. Ganz derselbe Einwand ist auch gegen die neue Lehre von Verdross zu erheben, da nach ihm die nichtanerkannten Staaten höchtens durch Verpflichtungen der alten Staaten *inter se* geschützt sind, aber keine Rechtsbeziehungen zwischen altem und nichtanerkannten Staat bestehen. Was hilft uns da auch Verdross' Behauptung, dass die nicht-anerkannten Staaten potentielle Völkerrechtssubjekte sind ? Also im Verkehr zwischen, sagen wir England und der Republik Oesterreich, zwischen 30. Oktober 1918 und und 29. Mai 1919 galten keine Rechtsnormen, die Beziehungen waren so wie zwischen Staaten der Völkerrechtsgemeinschaft und sogenannten " Wilden " ? Das soll positives Völkerrecht sein ? Man denke an andere Konsequenzen : Belgien wurde durch Holland, obwohl 1830 " entstanden ", erst 1839 anerkannt. Wenn Belgien etwa 1838 mit einer Armee in holländisches Gebiet eingefallen wäre, wäre dies juristisch irrelevant ? Wenn ein Staat, der die 1903 neuentstandene Republik Panama noch nicht anerkannt hatte, ihre Küsten mit seinen Kriegsschiffen bombardiert hätte, wäre dies völkerrechtlich irrelevant gewesen ? Und wie in dem Fall, wenn die Republik Panama ein Bündnis mit den Vereinigten Staaten geschlossen hätte, die sie anerkannt hatten, denen gegenüber sie daher auch nach der Lehre von der konstitutiven Wirkung der Anerkennung Völkerrechtssubjekt war und sie nun von den Kriegsschiffen einer Macht, die Panama noch nicht anerkannt hätte, bombardiert worden wäre und die Vereinigten Staaten auf Grund des Bündnisvertrages interveniert hätten ? Der bombardierende Staat hätte sagen können, du, Amerika, hast Panama anerkannt, und dein Bündnisvertrag ist daher gültig, — ich aber habe Panama nicht anerkannt, für mich ist es völkerrechtlich nicht vorhanden, mein Vorgehen ist daher gegen Panama völkerrechtlich irrelevant. Die Konsequenzen dieser Lehre sind gar nicht auszudenken. Und diese Lehre will " aus der Staatenpraxis genommen " sein ? Schon dies eine Argument, das die Lehre von der konstitutiven Wirkung nie widerlegen konnte, genügt, um sie... zu vernichten. " *Op. cit.*, pp. 89-90. Cf. Bierly, *Règles*, p. 54

all probability the mutual observance of most rules of warfare will naturally follow for reasons of humanity, of fear of retaliation, of military convenience and of conservation of military energy, and, generally, for considerations similar to those for which rules of warfare are observed in a civil war between the lawful government and the rebels declared to be traitors. For the same reason third States will, unless they decide to become belligerents, observe neutral conduct in any wars in which the unrecognized community may be involved. The subjects of the unrecognized community may, it is true, be maltreated in foreign States without international law offering any protection, but here again the legal position represents only inadequately the realities of the situation. If a community is determined to treat some aliens in defiance of the canons of civilisation or of generally recognized international law, and if the State affected is a weak State, unable or unwilling to protect its subjects by retaliation or otherwise, then recognition will seldom prevent that kind of conduct. On the other hand, if the unrecognized State is in a position effectively to show its displeasure, the absence of recognition will not be likely to cause serious injury to its interests or to those of its subjects. Moreover, absence of recognition does not necessarily render impossible regular intercourse in connection with the protection of nationals abroad and for other purposes ; neither does it prevent measures of accomodation calculated to meet the circumstances of the case [1]. "

Such arguments are hardly convincing. The point is not that a recognized State may, under traditional international law, be invaded just like an unrecognized one, but whether the resulting conflict will be subject to international rules of war, applied as legal rules and not " for reasons of humanity ". Nor is it an answer to say that, whether it is a recognized or an unrecognized State, its citizens may in any case be maltreated by a stronger State if it chooses to do so. This is just as true as it is irrelevant ; for the question is whether such ill-treatment will, or will not, be a violation of international law, for which the guilty State is internationally responsible. It is inadmissible to equate an act which is repugnant on purely ethical grounds, with a violation of positive law, whether or not such violation escapes the proper sanction.

It would thus appear that not only is the validity of the above argument against the constitutive theory of recognition not undermined, but is actually confirmed by the very attempts to disprove it. Of such attempts, the following reasoning of Prof. Lauterpacht would seem to be a further outstanding example and may therefore be quoted at some length.

" Full recognition is, as a rule, refused for the reason that the conditions of recognition of statehood or governmental capacity are not entirely fulfilled. But it does not follow that the unrecognized community must be ignored altogether — as is convincingly shown by the manifold forms of official and unofficial intercourse with unrecognized governments. The unrecognized community is taken notice of so far as this proves necessary. Thus, for instance, an unrecognized State or government or belligerent cannot, in reliance on the formal logic of its non-recognition, claim the right to commit acts which if done by a recognized authority would constitute a violation of international law. States cannot be compelled to choose between recognition, which they deem themselves rightfully entitled to refuse, and passive toleration of unlawful acts. They can have recourse to remonstrances, protests, retorsion, reprisals, or war. They need not be deterred by the argument that that State or government, not being recognized, does not exist as a subject of international rights and duties and that it cannot therefore be

1. *Op. cit.*, pp. 52-53.

saddled with effective responsibility. For there can be no objection to treating the unrecognized State as if it were bound by obligations of international law if these obligations are so compelling as to be universally admitted and if the non-recognizing State acknowledges itself to be bound by them. To that extent the nascent community, although not recognized generally, may be recognized for particular purposes on the not unreasonable ground that the rules in question are general and mutual in their operation. Finally, if the offending authority declines, because it has not been recognized, to act or to be dealt with on the basis of law, it must be dealt with — and suppressed — as a physical evil. There is in cases of this description a discrepancy — an unavoidable one — between law and fact. The seceding community possesses a measure of statehood ; it does not possess enough of it to justify full recognition. In such cases the flexible logic of law adapts itself to circumstances. It refuses to accept the easy dichotomy : either no rights and duties or all rights and duties which follow upon recognition. A situation is thus created in which the unrecognized community is treated *for some purposes* as if it were a subject of international law, namely, to the extent to which existing States elect to treat it as such in conformity with general rules of international law. In many cases substantial rights of statehood have been accorded, notwithstanding the absence of recognition as a State, through recognition of belligerency or insurgency [1]. ''

This writer finds it completely impossible to adopt a " flexible logic " as illustrated by the above quotation. A community either is, or is not, a State. If it is, it has all the resulting rights and duties. If it is not, it cannot be treated " as if ". In particular, the suggestion, that a community to which the *rights* of statehood are denied by the withholding of constitutive recognition, should yet be made to bear all the duties of a State under the threat of " physical suppression ", seems to offend against more than logic alone.

Thus, always according to the constitutive theory, an unrecognized State would become both, the source of danger and a victim of lawlessness. The position would, however, become even more serious in case of a withdrawal of recognition. For it is only logical to assume that third States which have the power to " make " another State, can just as well " unmake " it [2]. Thus, third States could at will admit it to, or exclude it from, the benefits of international law [3]. As Chen rightly points out, the potential aggressor could first withdraw recognition from its future victim and declare it legally non-existent and would thus be free to commit any act of aggression it pleased against it, without being subject to any restrictions of international law [4]. This is, unfortunately, not a mere theoretical argument. It has been abundantly seen in recent years that an act of aggression against a State can be preceded by a declaration of its non-existence by the aggressor who thus seeks to free himself from his existing obligations towards his victim. Thus Hitler declared Czechoslovakia non-existent on the eve of the German invasion of March 15, 1939 [5] ; thus the Soviet

---

1. *Op. cit.*, pp. 53-54.
2. " ...it may be supposed that it would be open to the recognizing State to withdraw its recognition and thereby to outlaw, excommunicate and to put to legal death a life which it has once created. " Chen, *op. cit.*, p. 259. Cf. Kelsen, *Théorie générale*, p. 273.
3. " Consequently, a State would be free to disregard international law in its relations with a body which it has not recognized as a State... " Chen, *op. cit.*, pp. 41-42.
4. *Op. cit.*, p. 273.
5. See below, p. 300.

Union proclaimed the extinction of Poland prior to the Soviet invasion of that country of September 17, 1939 [1]. The very idea of such freedom being granted is preposterous [2].

Yet, to argue that constitutive recognition is not subject to withdrawal, is to adopt a conclusion inconsistent with the premise. If the basis of a State's legal existence lies in the will of third States, it is illogical to say that this power of third States ends there, and that the new State which is their artificial creation has found, somewhere in the process, a different basis for its existence, — a basis which is not indicated. The view that recognition cannot be withdrawn could only be upheld if it were proved [3] that there is a legal duty to recognize. But such a legal duty of third States, which the new State can claim as its right, disposes of the constitutive theory by attributing legal personality to the State before its recognition. The argument has thus come full circle.

This particular aspect of the problem has a special bearing on the question of State identity and continuity.

It may be recalled once again that the problem of its continuity or extinction will arise only under violent conditions, that it will be a defensive notion, put forward on behalf of a State whose existence has been endangered. Is it to be assumed that in such a situation a State, fighting for its continuity, may not rely on objective norms of international law, but that, on the contrary, third States will be entitled to administer the *coup de grâce* to its continued existence? Is it to be admitted that such existence can be terminated at will by third States? Such an admission would be contrary to every principle of international law. It has been seen that Prof. Kelsen, even when recently adopting the constitutive view has refused to accept it, stigmatizing the passing of such a death sentence on a still existing State as a violation of international law [4]. It is therefore correct to say that just as the birth of a State does not depend upon the will of third States, so also its continued existence and extinction do not depend upon such will [5].

To sum up : recognition, as a test of State identity and continuity must be rejected, since : *a)* it fails to provide a reliable test on account of its inherent relativity, *b)* it withdraws the question of the continued existence of a State from the realm of objective norms and makes it dependent upon the will of third States, and *c)* for this reason may

---

1. See below, pp. 433-434.
2. « Qu'un Etat puisse, dans ses rapports avec un autre Etat, mettre le droit international général en vigueur jusqu'à révocation, et ceci en vertu du droit international lui-même, est une idée tellement insensée qu'il n'est pas besoin d'y opposer une réfutation particulière. » Kelsen, *Théorie générale*, p. 286.
3. Which it is not, see below, pp. 153-158.
4. See above, p. 138.
5. Thus, correctly, Reut-Nicolussi : " So wenig die Entstehung eines Staates von der Anerkennung seitens der älteren Staaten abhängig ist, so wenig ist für seinen Untergang als solchen die Anerkennung durch eine Gruppe anderer Staaten kausal. " *Um die Rechtskontinuität Oesterreichs*, p. 245.

place the very continuity of a State in jeopardy. This rejection is equivalent to a rejection of the constitutive in favour of the declaratory theory of recognition [1].

e) *Judicial Decisions.*

This view is advanced all the more freely as, apart from theoretical arguments and the practice of States, partly reviewed above, it is strongly supported by international and municipal judicial decisions.

In what may be considered the leading case on the subject, the *Deutsche Continental Gas Gesellschaft v. Poland*, the Polish-German Mixed Arbitral Tribunal held on August 1, 1929 :

" The State exists by itself and the recognition is nothing else than a declaration of this existence recognized by the States from which it emanates [2]. "

The declaratory nature of recognition clearly results from the already quoted cases of *Tinoco* and *George Hopkins*. It has been seen that the non-recognition by Great Britain and the United States of the Tinoco and Huerta Governments respectively did not, in the eyes of the respective tribunals, have the result of denying the effective legal existence of these governments.

" Such non-recognition " — said Chief Justice Taft in the Tinoco case — " ... cannot outweigh the evidence disclosed by this record before me as to the *de facto* character of Tinoco's government, according to the standard of international law [3]. "

The Arbitrator thus reaffirmed that it is not recognition or non-recognition, but an objective rule of international law which is decisive for the existence or non-existence of a government.

In the *Cuculla* arbitration of 1876 between the United States and Mexico, the Mixed Commission had to decide whether the rebel Zuloaga " government " in Mexico had indeed been a *de facto* government, especially in view of the fact that it had been accorded a certain measure of recognition by the United States. The Commission held that this recognition had been accorded by the American Minister to Mexico without the approval of his government. However, far from confining himself to this particular objection, the American Commissioner Wadsworth dealt with the question of principle :

" Where, then, is the evidence of a *de facto* government ? The possession of the capital will not be sufficient, nor recognition by the American Minister with or without the approval of his government. Recognition is based upon the preexisting fact ; it does not create the fact. If this does not exist, recognition is falsified [4]. "

In the *McKenny* case, arbitrated in the same year by the same Commission, it was found that there had in fact been no express

---

1. It is to be observed that only those arguments in favour of the declaratory theory have been examined here, which seem to have an immediate bearing on the problem of the continued existence of States. For other arguments in favour of the declaratory view, reference is made to the much - quoted work by Chen.
2. A.D., 1929/30, case no. 5. Cf. Rec. TAM, vol. IX, p. 344.
3. A.J., 1924, p. 154.
4. Moore, *International Arbitrations*, III, pp. 2876-2877.

disapproval by the American government of the recognition of Zuolaga by its minister and that in no case could recognition be invalid on that ground. This did not prevent Commissioner Wadsworth from clearly stating :

" ... it will be seen that it is attempted to show that Zuloaga possessed the sovereign power in Mexico, because the minister and Government of the United States recognized his pretentions, and the question of fact is neglected and ignored... ... But, take it for granted that the Government of the United States was fully committed to the recognition by its minister of the Zuloaga government made January 27th, 1858, it by no means follows that this fact is conclusive against the Government of Mexico. All that can be claimed for it is that it would bind the United States so long as diplomatic relations continued with the government thus recognized — it could not bind the government and people of Mexico unless Zuloaga was in fact in possession of the sovereign power [1]. "

In the *Georges Pinson* case, arbitrated in 1933 by the Franco-Mexican Claims Commission, it was held by President Verzijl that :

" ... the question whether a government is or is not a government *de facto* is a simple question of fact, which does not depend on the constitutional law of the State affected nor international law, and which is in no way affected by the attitude adopted towards it by later governments, nor by the recognition, or refusal of recognition, either *de facto* or *de iure* by third States [2]... "

The decisions of municipal courts are perhaps less conclusive, firstly, because they are strongly motivated by the general political attitude of their own country, as e.g. the courts of the newly created States after the First World War, and secondly, because they may not be free to act, under the doctrine of judicial auto-limitation, prevailing in the Anglo-Saxon countries. Since the courts of these countries seek the ruling of the executive in all matters concerning recognition, it is clear that they do not normally embark upon an independent examination of the question. Thus, for a considerable period, American courts treated non-recognized States or governments as absolutely non existent. This, however, did not reflect an independent constitutive view on their part, but simply the above-mentioned constitutional principle of auto-limitation. But even under this principle, the persistent claim that an effectively existing State or government did not, in fact, exist was becoming untenable [3].

Thus, already in 1923, in the case of *Wulfsohn v. R.S.F.S.R.*, the Court of Appeals of New York held :

" Whether or not a government exists, clothed with the power to enforce its authority within its own territory, obeyed by the people over whom it rules, capable of performing the duties and fulfilling the obligations of an independent Power, able to enforce its claims by military force, is a fact, not a theory. For its recognition does not create a State, although it may be desirable [4]. "

---

1. Moore, *op. cit.*, pp. 2882-2883.
2. Green, *International Law through Cases*, pp. 773-774. However, in denying even international law as decisive for the legal existence of governments, Mr. Verzijl seems to have gone too far.
3. See Borchard, *op. cit.* ; Kleist, *op. cit.*, pp. 51-57. For a review of municipal decisions upholding the declaratory view, see Chen, *op. cit.*, pp. 88-93.
4. Green, *op. cit.*, p. 120.

In *Sokoloff v. National City Bank of New York* (1924), the New York Court of Appeals held :

" Juridically, a government that is unrecognized may be viewed as no government at all, if the power withholding recognition chooses thus to view it. In practice, however, since juridical conceptions are seldom, if ever, carried to the limit of their logic, the equivalence is not absolute, but is subject to self-imposed limitations of common sense and fairness, as we learned in litigations following our Civil War. ... These analogies suggest the thought that, subject to like restrictions, effect may at times be due to the ordinances of foreign governments which, though formally unrecognized, have notoriously an existence as governments *de facto* [1]. "

In *Salimoff and Co. v. Standard Oil Co.* (1933) the same Court declared :

" As a juristic conception, what is Soviet Russia ? A band of robbers or a government ? We all know that it is a government. The State Department knows it, the courts, the nation and the man on the street. ... Recognition does not create the State. It simply gives to a *de facto* State international status. ... The courts may not recognize the Soviet Government as the *de iure* government until the State Department gives the word. They may, however, say that it is a government, maintaining internal peace and order, providing for national defence and the general welfare, carrying on relations with our own government and others. To refuse to recognize that Soviet Russia is a government regulating the internal affairs of the country, is to give fictions an air of reality which they do not deserve [2]. "

In the case of *Hausner*, the Swiss Federal Court held on December 10, 1924 :

" The non-recognition of the Soviet by Switzerland is operative in another sphere, but the Swiss judge will take cognisance of the Russian rules of law so long as they do not öffend against the canons of public policy [3]. "

In 1920, the German Reichsgericht, admitting the existence of the Czechoslovak Republic since January 1919, declared :

" The question of recognition was irrelevant [4]. "

Decisions of courts of the above-mentioned new States are certainly to a great extent inspired by considerations of national prestige. Moreover, in their polemical aspect, they are directed against the view that their States had been created by the Peace Treaties, rather than

---

1. *A.D.*, 1923/24, case no. 19.
2. *A.D.*, 1933/34, case no. 8. That the State Department in fact " knew it " is evident from the certificate submitted by the Secretary of State in the same case, which reads :
" 1) The Government of the United States accorded recognition to the Provisional Government of Russia as the successor of the Russian Imperial Government, and has not accorded recognition to any government in Russia since the overthrow of the Provisional Government of Russia.
2) The Department of State is cognizant of the fact that the Soviet regime is exercising control and power in territory of the former Russian Empire and the Department of State has no disposition to ignore that fact.
3) The refusal of the Government of the U.S. to accord recognition to the Soviet regime is not based on the ground that that regime does not exercise control and authority in territory of the former Russian Empire, but on other facts. "
3. *A.D.*, 1927, p. 63 ; see also *Russian Reinsurance Co. v. Stoddard*, *A.D.*, 1925/26, case no. 40.
4. *Counterfeiting of Stamps (Czechoslovakia) case*, *A.D.*, 1919/22, case no. 24.

against the constitutive doctrine of recognition. However that may be, they all unanimously affirm the beginning of their States' existence from the moment of their actual establishment, and not of their recognition [1].

On the basis of the above investigation it may be safely asserted that the constitutive doctrine is just as untenable in logic as it is untrue in fact [2].

2. POLITICAL.

If recognition as has been submitted [3] is indeed an act of policy, then this circumstance further deprives it of any value as a test of an existing legal situation.

a) *Non-Existence of a Duty to Recognize.*

Whether recognition is a legal act or an act of policy is not to be determined by considerations *de lege ferenda*, but solely by ascertaining the existence or absence of positive rules of international law on the subject. In the absence of such rules it remains an act of pure policy which, though it may have legal consequences, is not itself governed by international law.

There is only one aspect of recognition which is undoubtedly governed by international law, namely premature recognition [4]. There can be no argument as to the existence of a positive international norm, prohibiting the granting of premature recognition. It may be doubted whether, in spite of the name, the norm in question really represents an autonomous rule concerning recognition, or whether it is rather an aspect of the general prohibition of intervention [5]. There can, however, be no doubt as to its existence and its relevance to the problem of recognition.

This is the only rule of customary international law relating to recognition. In other words, intervention is prohibited in every form, including the form of premature recognition.

Thus, the only undoubted positive rule regarding recognition has a prohibitive character: it is unlawful for third States to undermine the international status, the sovereignty and integrity of another State by granting premature recognition to its revolted provinces or colonies

---

1. See e.g. decisions of the Czechoslovak Administrative Tribunal, *A.D.*, 1919/22, cases no. 5 and 6, *A.D.*, 1923/24, case no. 2, *A.D.*, 1925/26, cases no. 8 and 9; Polish Supreme Court, *A.D.*, 1923/24, case no. 1. For Austria, *A.D.*, 1927/28, case no. 11.

2. " The main difficulty with the constitutive theory is that it is mere theory. ...The declaratory theory is not so much a theory as a principle tested in the laboratory of experience and precedence. " Marshall Brown, *The Effects of Recognition, A.J.*, 1942, pp. 106-107. This may justify the harsh jugdment, passed on Prof. Lauterpacht's book by Kunz, who does not hesitate to call it " a falsification of positive law ", and to declare : " As far as this principal thesis goes, Lauterpacht has entirely failed to prove it, the law is exactly the contrary. " *Critical Remarks on Lauterpacht's " Recognition in International Law ", A.J.*, 1950, p. 715.

3. See above, p. 131.

4. " There is no doubt that at least one aspect of the matter is by general agreement governed by international law, namely, what may be called the tortious or delictual aspect of recognition. It is contrary to international law to grant premature recognition. " Lauterpacht, *op. cit.*, p. 7.

5. Thus, correctly, Moore, *op. cit.*, I, p. 73 ; Chen, *op. cit.*, pp. 85-86.

before the latter have finally established their independence from the Mother Country. Apart from this one uncontested rule however, is recognition, or is it not, governed by positive international law ?

Translated into the terms of a classical argument, the question reads : is there a right to recognition and a duty to recognize ?

It is submitted that no such right and no such duty exist, that States are therefore free to act as they please in this respect and that this deprives recognition of a legal character.

In the first place, it must be emphasized that the conception of a duty to recognize could only be seriously upheld on the basis of the declaratory theory of recognition, and that it is logically incompatible with the constitutive view. It would appear almost superflous to point out that a legal right can only be exercised by a subject of law, or that a legal duty can be owed only to a subject of law [1].

Consequently, the problem of the duty to recognize can be seriously discussed only on the assumption of the declaratory character of recognition. Does such a duty — and the corresponding right — exist ? Is there any positive norm to that effect ?

It is submitted that the existence of such a norm has never been proved. It has indeed been categorically denied by writers who have devoted considerable attention to the problem [2].

The assertion of a duty to recognize cannot be allowed to stand alone, without the inevitable conclusion being drawn from it. The existence of such a duty would plainly mean that its non-fulfilment is an illegal act, an international tort [3]. But if it is an international tort, then the non-recognized State, or government, would be entitled to have recourse to reprisals and to claim reparation. Not a shred of evidence for such a view can be found in the past, nor is there any basis on which such a claim could be entertained in future [4].

---

1. No amount of Prof. Lauterpacht's dislike of formal logic — *op. cit.*, pp. 40 and 56 — and his advocacy of a " flexible logic " of law — *ibid.*, p. 54 — can possibly dispose of this axiom. Prof. Kelsen is entirely consistent with his own new premise when, claiming the constitutive nature of recognition, he strongly denies the existence of any duty to recognize. *A.J.*, 1941, pp. 609-610. However, see Guggenheim, *op. cit.*, I, p. 182, *f.-n.* 49. Prof. Scelle is equally consistent, combining as he does the assertion of a duty to recognize with an assertion of the declaratory nature of recognition, *op. cit.*, pp. 163-164. For the criticism of Prof. Lauterpacht's suggestion that the duty to recognize is owed to the international community, see Chen, *op. cit.*, p. 53.

2. Kunz, *Anerkennung*, p. 37 ; Chen, *op. cit.*, pp.50-54 ; Smith, *op. cit.*, p. 77 ; Brierly, *op. cit.*, pp. 56 and 59.

3. See in particular Dr. Schwarzenberger's letter to *The Times* of January 8th, 1950, criticizing an article by Prof. Lauterpacht in the same paper, of January 6, 1950. " Presumably, then, any refusal to grant such recognition is supposed to amount to an international tort. It is difficult to see what evidence can be adduced for this proposition. "

4. Once again, Prof. Lauterpacht, aware of the inescapable conclusions of his own argument, takes refuge in a position *de lege ferenda*. " The refusal of recognition on such grounds (arbitrary discretion, own interests, etc.) would constitute a legal wrong. This means — and we must not shrink from this conclusion — that an international tribunal endowed with the requisite jurisdiction and confronted with a clearly arbitrary refusal of recognition would be acting in accordance with its judicial duty if it were to find that international law is not without remedy against a wrong of this nature. " *Op. cit.*, p. 161. Not only is the " remedy " not indicated, but the whole argument of what " would happen " represents yet another instance of the permanent shifting of the platform of discussion, so disconcerting throughout Prof. Lauterpacht's book. In any case, Prof. Lauterpacht does not adduce any proof of the existence of the duty claimed.

b) *State Practice.*

The political character of recognition is strongly reflected in State practice. Moreover, States themselves regard it as an act of policy.

A typical example of a highly political act of recognition is certainly the recognition by the United States of Panama in 1903, a recognition which in fact bordered on intervention in the internal affairs of Colombia, against which Panama had revolted with the assistance of American armed forces. The action of the United States is to be explained by its overriding political interest in the Panama Canal [1]. Wilson's policy of recognition was a purely political one [2]. After the First World War the United States withheld recognition from the newly formed Baltic Republics for a considerable time, not on account of their not having achieved full and effective statehood, but solely out of political considerations: it was still hoped that pre-Soviet Russia would be re-established and it was sought to preserve her territorial integrity (with the exception of Poland and Finland) [3]. " Recognition as a nation " of Poland and Czechoslovakia during the First World War represents a particularly drastic example of a purely political move, belonging to what would to-day be termed " political warfare ". It could not even be considered as the emergence of a new positive rule, since not only is a " nation " not a subject of international law, but the word conveys no legal meaning whatever [4]. The political motives of recognition are emphasized with unwonted clarity in the correspondence which passed between the U.S. State Department and Commissioner Blake with regard to the recognition of Albania in 1922. In its instruction to Commissioner Blake of April 27, 1922, the State Department declared :

" The principal consideration in favor of early recognition by this country is that such action might be helpful to the existing or potential economic and philanthropic interests in Albania of American citizens. "

The Commissioner's answer of June 28, 1922 recommended recognition

" although the Albanian State has not yet definitely emerged from the stages of hopeful experiment "

and went on :

" Material factors are equally worthy of consideration. The country has important commercial possibilities and possesses rich natural resources awaiting development. If the American Government without due cause continues officially to hold aloof, legitimate American enterprises are at a disadvantage and a policy of delay and overcaution might be detrimental to present American prestige [5]... "

Nor could it be claimed that the non-recognition by the United States of the Soviet Government for a full sixteen years was the reflection

---

1. See Kunz, *op. cit.*, p. 102, *f.-n.* 140 ; Lauterpacht, *op. cit.*, p. 22.
2. See Kunz, *op. cit.*, pp. 147-150.
3. Hackworth, *op. cit.*, I, pp. 199-200 ; Kleist, *op. cit.*, p. 103 ; Erich, *Naissance et reconnaissance des Etats*, p. 483.
4. See Anzilotti, *op. cit.*, pp. 127-128 ; Kunz, *op. cit.*, p. 210.
5. Hackworth, *op. cit.*, I, pp. 197-198.

of the actual legal position and not a pure act of policy. This was frankly admitted more than once, but nowhere more clearly than in the well-known letter of Secretary Hughes to Samuel Gompers of July 19, 1923, in which Hughes justified his refusal to grant recognition on strictly political grounds, such as American abhorrence of the Soviet régime, the question of debts and indemnities, and the like, without for a moment denying the actual and effective existence of the Soviet Government [1].

The recognition by Great Britain of the Italian conquest of Ethiopia at a time, when the latter was far from being finally subjugated, was as much an act of policy, as its de-recognition at a time, when the effectiveness of Italian control was, if anything, more firmly established, — and no defence of British action by Prof. Lauterpacht can make it anything else [2].

In recent times, both the immediate recognition of the new State of Israel by the United States (without even ascertaining the facts) and the delay in recognizing it by Great Britain represented definite political acts. Speaking of this recognition in the United Nations, the American delegate, Mr. Warren Austin, declared in no uncertain terms :

" I should regard it as highly improper for me to admit that any country on earth can question the sovereignty of the United States of America in the exercise of that highly political act of recognition of the *de facto* status of the State. Moreover, I would not admit here, by implication or by direct answer that there exists a tribunal of justice or of any other kind, anywhere, that can pass upon the legality or the validity of that act of my country [3]. "

Examples could easily be multiplied. It is sufficient to mention the British recognition, and the American non-recognition, of Communist China, the French recognition of Viet-Nam and the Emperor Bao-Dai, and the Soviet recognition of Viet-Minh, the recognition of the Federal German Republic by the Western Powers and of the Democratic German Republic by the Soviet Union.

Yet another proof of the political character of recognition is to be found in the Anglo-American doctrine of judicial auto-limitation. The constitutional principle prevailing in the United States and Great Britain lays down that recognition is a political function falling properly within the competence of the executive, in other words, the political branch of the government ; the courts, therefore, are not supposed to decide the question of recognition or non-recognition themselves, but have to seek guidance from the executive. This guidance is binding on them, notwithstanding the fact that certificates from the Foreign Office usually leave the judge more room for interpretation than do

---

1. " The effective jurisdiction of Moscow was recently extended to Vladivostok. " Hackworth, *op. cit.*, I, p. 179. Cf. Judge Cardozo's observation in *Sokoloff v. National City Bank of New York* regarding the practice, " now a growing one, of withholding recognition whenever it is thought that a government, functioning unhampered, is unworthy of a place in the society of nations. " Cf. Borchard : " Governments, by way of reprisal, have often, sometimes for years, declined to recognize foreign political facts, such as new governments they disliked... " *Unrecognized Governments*, A.J., 1932, p. 261.
2. See Lauterpacht, *op. cit.*, p. 356 and Chen's criticism, *op. cit.*, p. 262 et seq.
3. Quoted by Brierly, *Law of Nations*, p. 125, *f.-n.* 1.

certificates of the State Department [1]. It has been seen that even strict adherence, to this principle has not prevented American judges from upholding the declaratory view of recognition [2] ; this, however, in no way alters the fact that they consider recognition as political, seek the ruling from the executive and act on that ruling [3].

c) *Judicial Decisions.*

The political character of recognition is borne out by judicial decisions just as strongly as its declaratory nature [4].

Of the international decisions already quoted, the U.S.-Mexican Claims Commission in the *George Hopkins Claim* expressly confirmed the political character of recognition, — at least for that particular case.

" The position assumed by the American government ... was purely political [5]... "

The same opinion is implicit in the judgment in the *Tinoco* case :

" The merits of the policy of the United States in this non-recognition it is not for the arbitrator to discuss, for the reason that in his consideration of this case, he is necessarily controlled by principles of international law, and however justified as a national policy non-recognition on such a ground may be, it certainly has not been acquiesced in by all the nations of the world, which is a condition precedent to considering it as a postulate of international law [6]. "

In the *Georges Pinson* case, Prof. Verzijl denied the constitutive character of recognition :

" it being notorious that international practice has frequently abused the grant or refusal of recognition *de facto* for political end... [7] ".

That the American courts should again and again have emphasized the political character of recognition, follows logically from what has already been said on the subject of judicial auto-limitation. It may, however, be of interest to quote a few of their direct pronouncements on the subject :

" Who is the sovereign *de iure* or *de facto* of a territory is not a judicial but is a political question, the determination of which by the legislative and executive departments of any government conclusively binds the judges, as well as all other officers, citizens and subjects of that government. This principle has always been upheld by this Court and has been affirmed under a great variety of circumstances [8]. "

---

1. " The courts of the United States have uniformly adhered to the view that the recognition of foreign governments is a political matter not subject to judicial inquiry or decision. " Hackworth, *op. cit.*, I, p. 165.
2. See above, pp. 151-152.
3. For the doctrine and practice of judicial auto-limitation in Anglo-Saxon countries, see Chen, *op. cit.*, pp. 238-255.
4. See above, pp. 150-153.
5. *A.J.*, 1927, p. 166.
6. *A.J.*, 1924, p. 153.
7. Green, *op. cit.*, p. 774.
8. *Jones v. United States*, quoted by the Supreme Court in *Oetjen v. Central Leathers Co.* of March 11, 1918, *A.J.*, 1918, p. 424.

" ... the question when, if at all, such *de facto* government shall be recognized, is a political one [1]... "

" Which is a sovereign, *de iure* or *de facto*, of a territory is not a judicial, but a political question for determination [2]. "

If then, on the above analysis, recognition is an act of pure policy, can it be seriously suggested that it ought to be allowed to decide a legal issue of such a magnitude as the existence, whether new or continued, of a State? It should be repeated that a political conflict surrounding the question of continuity or extinction of a State will be, if anything, stronger than a political conflict accompanying the birth of a new State. Thus the danger of adopting the highly political act of recognition as a criterion of the continued existence of a State would, if anything, be even greater than in the case of the birth of a new State.

3. THE INSTITUT DE DROIT INTERNATIONAL ; THE MONTEVIDEO CONVENTION.

It may be added that the proposition advanced above concerning the declaratory and political nature of recognition has the support of the high authority of the Institute of International Law which, in Art. 1 of its Resolution on the recognition of new States and Governments, adopted at its session of 1935, stated :

« La reconnaissance d'un Etat nouveau est l'acte libre par lequel un ou plusieurs Etats constatent l'existence sur un territoire déterminé d'une société humaine politiquement organisée, indépendante de tout autre Etat existant, capable d'observer les prescriptions du droit international et manifestant en conséquence leur volonté de la considérer comme membre de la communauté internationale.

La reconnaissance a un effet déclaratif.

L'existence de l'Etat nouveau avec tous les effets juridiques qui s'attachent à cette existence n'est pas affectée par le refus de reconnaissance d'un ou plusieurs Etats [3]. »

The Institute thus expressly accepted the declaratory character of recognition and it is difficult to see how any other meaning can be read into a statement of such clarity [4]. Quite logically, the resolution combines the declaratory theory of recognition with the affirmation of the existence of a general norm of international law, laying down the legal pre-requisites of statehood objectively and independently of the will of States. Moreover, any legal duty to recognize is denied by the description of recognition as an " acte libre ", which *ipso facto* implies its political, not its legal character [5].

---

1. *The Rogdai*, U.S. District Court, N. D. California, May 25, 1920, *A.D.*, 1919/22, case no. 27.
2. *The Penza; The Tobolsk*, U.S. District Court, E.D. New York, September 26, 1921, *A.D.*, 1919/22, case no. 28.
3. *Annuaire*, vol. II, 1938, pp. 300-301.
4. See, however, Guggenheim, *op. cit.*, p. 189, *f.-n.* 49.
5. This conclusion is reinforced by the express statement of the Rapporteur, Mr. Philip Marshall Brown : « ...l'acte de reconnaissance est avant tout et essentiellement une fonction politique et diplomatique... ». «La reconnaissance des nouveaux Etats est une fonction politique et diplomatique. » *Ibid.*, p. 181 and 184.

Finally, it may be added that the question is no longer open to discussion on the American Continent, where it has been settled by means of an international convention. The Montevideo Convention on Rights and Duties of States, of December 26, 1933, contains the following provisions :

" Art. 3. The political existence of the State is independent of recognition by the other States. Even before recognition the State has the right to defend its integrity and independence, to provide for its conservation and prosperity, and consequently to organize itself as it sees fit, to legislate upon its interests, administer its services and to define the jurisdiction and competence of its courts...

Art. 6. The recognition of a State merely signifies that the State which recognizes it accepts the personality of the other with all the rights and duties determined by international law. Recognition is unconditional and irrevocable [1]. "

C. RECOGNITION AS EVIDENCE OF STATE IDENTITY AND CONTINUITY.

The problem of international recognition has been investigated at some length in order to discover whether it could be made to serve as a test in doubtful cases of the identity and continuity of States. It was clear from the very outset of this enquiry that this could only be so if recognition were endowed with a constitutive and legal character. To be precise, it would then no longer be a test but would actually create such identity and continuity.

No such creative value can be attached to an act which has been found to be declaratory in character and, moreover, to represent a free act of policy on the part of the recognizing, or non-recognizing, States. Does this mean that the value of recognition in solving the problem of State identity and continuity can be summarily dismissed ?

It is submitted that, although declaratory and political, recognition is still of considerable value as evidence [2]. Such evidence is, however, merely *prima facie* and has to be handled with the greatest care, a view which is confirmed by international judicial decisions [3].

In the *Tinoco* arbitration, Chief Justice Taft laid down the following principles :

" ... it is urged that many leading Powers refused to recognize the Tinoco government, and that recognition by other nations is the chief and best evidence of the birth, existence and continuity of succession of a government. Undoubtedly, recognition by other Powers is an important evidential factor in establishing proof of the existence of a government in the society of nations [4]. "

" The non-recognition by other nations of a government claiming to be a national personality, is usually appropriate evidence that it has not attained the independence and control entitling it by international law to be classed as such. But when recognition *vel* non of a government is by such nations determined by inquiry, not into its *de facto* sovereignty and complete governmental control, but into its illegitimacy or irregularity of origin, their non-recognition loses something of evidential weight [5]... "

---

1. Hudson, *International Legislation*, VI, p. 620.
2. " It is strong evidence of the existence of the State... " Chen, *op. cit.*, p. 78.
3. " The best evidence of the *de facto* existence of a government is, no doubt, provided by its recognition by other States. But even so, it may not be conclusive, at least for an international tribunal. " Chen, *op. cit.*, p. 147.
4. A.J., 1924, p. 152.
5. *Ibid.*, p. 154.

The point was put even more strongly by Commissioner Wadsworth in the *McKenny* case :

" In determining this fact (whether or not " Zuloaga was in fact in possession of the sovereign power "), the recognition of the United States and of other foreign States may be considered as some evidence of the fact, entitled to more or less weight according to circumstances. In my opinion the recognition extended to Zuloaga by the ministers of these foreign States, under the circumstances, is entitled to very little, if any, weight in determining the question of fact [1]. "

In other words recognition granted or withheld in accordance with the principles of international law, *is* conclusive evidence. But recognition granted or withheld for reasons which have nothing to do with these principles but are overwhelmingly political to the extent of disregarding them, is not conclusive evidence.

" The recognition of a new government made by foreign powers " — said Commissioner Palacio in the *Cuculla* case — " only shows that said powers *believe* that such a government is really a government. If this belief is not correct, it will not produce any result [2]. "

Once again therefore, it is not recognition as such, but its conformity with objective international law, in other words, international law itself, which determines the existence or non-existence, continuity or discontinuity of States and governments.

It will therefore be proper to use international recognition as *prima facie* evidence of the identity and continuity of States in doubtful cases subject to careful scrutiny and always testing its conformity or non-conformity with the objective norms of international law.

One last note of warning may be sounded. It is to be feared that precisely in doubtful and controversial cases, recognition, or non-recognition, will, to use the words of Chief Justice Taft, " lose something of evidential weight ". For it is precisely such controversial cases which may involve special, and conflicting, interests of States. The polemical nature of the notions of State identity and continuity has already been seen [3]; it has been seen that the problem will normally arise against the background of some violent historical commotion. In such circumstances it is likely that individual States, or groups of States, will act on strongly political motives when recognizing the continued existence or the extinction of the State concerned. The evidential value of such recognition will therefore be in inverse proportion to their political interest in the question.

Moreover, apart from its theoretical value as evidence, recognition of the continued existence of a State may be of immense practical value : for although it will not actually secure the survival of the State whose continuity has been endangered, it may facilitate the concrete manifestation of such survival. The strongest example of this is to be found in the granting of hospitality to the State concerned in the territory of a recognizing State [4]. Similarly, the assertion of the unbroken

1. Moore, *op. cit.*, p. 2883.
2. *It. mine*, Moore, *op. cit.*, p. 2880.
3. See above, p. 4.
4. See above, pp. 86-101.

continuity of the State concerned will obviously be easier in practice, if its continued existence throughout a critical period has been uninterruptedly borne out by the continued recognition by third States.

It must be said in conclusion that the value of recognition for the problem of the identity and continuity of States should not be underestimated, although such recognition cannot be the source of the continued existence of States.

III. *TESTS DERIVED FROM THE CONCEPT OF THE STATE.*

The time has now come to enquire whether any useful test of the identity and continuity of States can be derived from the very concept of State.

However controversial this concept may be, some criterion of statehood must exist. If it did not, it would be improper and illegitimate to speak of States at all. But if it does exist, then it should be able to supply not only the general characteristics of States as distinct from other legal entities, but also the test of identity of an individual State.

i. THE STATE ACCORDING TO INTERNATIONAL LAW.

It cannot be denied that the conception of the State is one of the most difficult and recalcitrant notions of law in general [1]. For the purpose of this study, however, it is legitimate to discard an abstract investigation into the essence of the State as such, and to limit the problem to the phenomenon of the State according to international law [2]. Such limitation need not conflict with a consistently monist point of view [3]. It need not for a moment be admitted that the State in the sence of internal and of international law are two different things. The State is simply seen from " above ", as defined by a positive norm of a higher legal order, as the contents of that positive norm.

Viewed in this way, the contents of this positive norm are not particularly difficult to establish as is borne out by the considerable degree of unanimity among writers. This *communis opinio* can be

---

1. « Existe-t-il un critère de l'Etat... ? Il est difficile de l'admettre et difficile aussi d'y renoncer. » Scelle, *op. cit.*, p. 94.
2. " Jedoch muss man weiter zur Erkenntnis kommen, dass alle diese Bemühungen einem abstrakten Staatsbegriff, dem *Wesens*begriff des Staates gelten, dass wir aber *hier* es, wo wir vom " Staat im Sinne des Völkerrechts" handeln, nicht mit diesem Wesensbegriff des Staates, sondern mit dem aus der positiven Völkerrechtsordnung sich ergebenden Staatsbegriff zu tun haben, der Staat im Sinne des Völkerrechts " völker- rechtlicher Rechtstatbestand " ist. " Kunz, *op. cit.*, p. 17. « Le juriste international s'occupe, non de l'Etat abstrait, à supposer que celui-ci existe, mais *des Etats*. Pour lui, la coexistence d'Etats nombreux forme la principale de ses données, et il se voit forcé d'exiger qu'une théorie sur la nature des États puisse expliquer ou, du moins, ne pas contredire les relations ou il constate qu'ils se trouvent les uns par rapport aux autres. » Brierly, *Règles*, p. 25.
3. Although it could admittedly be adopted by a dualist. In this sense Anzilotti : « Si l'on veut parler d'Etats dans le droit international... il doit être bien clair que ce sont les Etats du droit international, non pas ceux de la sociologie, de l'histoire, ni non plus ceux du droit public interne. L'Etat, pour le droit international, vaut en tant que destinataire des normes et en tant que sujet de l'ordre juridique, que cette conception coïncide ou ne coïncide pas avec celle qui est propre aux autres disciplines. » *Op. cit,* p. 125.

summarized as follows : there is a State in the international law sense, when there is an independent legal order, effectively valid throughout a defined territory with regard to a defined population.

It will be observed that writers, particularly modern writers, insist not only upon the three " elements " — territory, population, legal order — but more especially upon the independence of the latter. According to most of them, it is precisely this independence which forms the essential characteristic of the State, which indeed *makes* a State [1]. Prof. Lauterpacht goes even so far as to postulate " actual " independence. He says :

" ... the first condition of statehood is that there must exist a government actually independent of that of any other State [2]. "

This statement clearly implies that there exists not only a legal conception of independence, which may be legally defined and ascertained, but also an " actual " independence, i.e. independence not only in law, but in fact. In order to be a State, a community therefore must be independent in the widest sense of the term.

In view of this emphasis on independence as a condition of statehood, it is necessary to consider whether it is in fact an indispensable element in the notion of State under international law.

2.   INDEPENDENCE AS A CONDITION OF STATEHOOD.

The positive answer to this question lies in the very nature of international law. For international law is, above all, a legal order governing relations between independent States, that is to say, between separate and distinct entities [3]. No international law would be either

---

1. « ...un « Etat au sens du droit international » est donné quand un ordre de contrainte qui n'est soumis à aucun ordre étatique, mais seulement au droit des gens, existe, qui est devenu efficace pour un territoire déterminé, c'est-à-dire qui est obéi, dans l'ensemble, par les individus dont il règle la conduite, par le fait que les organes qui créent et exécutent cet ordre fontionnent conformément à ses régles. » Kelsen, *Théorie générale*, p. 265. « Un Etat est formé lorsqu'un ordre de contrainte relativement souverain, c'est-à-dire dépendant exclusivement du droit des gens, se crée et devient efficace sur un territoire donné et vis-à-vis d'une population donnée. » Kelsen, *Naissance de l'Etat*, p. 614. " The community thus constituted must be independent, i.e. it must not be under the legal control of another community, equally qualified as a State. ...The State, in an international law sense, is a legal community which is subject only to general or particular international law but not to the law of any other State. " Kelsen, *Recognition*, p. 608. Cf. *Allg. Staatslehre*, p. 127 ; Brierly, *op. cit.*, p. 50. " Charakteristisch für den souveränen Staat erscheint nämlich, dass er keiner anderen Rechtsordnung als derjenigen des Völkergewohnheitsrechts unterworfen ist. " Guggenheim, *op. cit.*, I, p. 163. " ...vor allem muss es sich um eine unabhängige Rechtsgemeinschaft handeln, eine solche die ihre Zuständigkeit nicht aus einer anderen Staatsordnung herleitet, sondern ausschliesslich der Völkerrechtsordnung untergeordnet und als solche mit Verfassungsautonomie ausgestattet ist. " Verdross, *Verfassung*, pp. 130-131. « Envisagé en sa qualité de personne du droit des gens, l'Etat peut être défini : une communauté indépendante, organisée d'une manière permanente sur un territoire. » Rivier, *Principes*, I, p. 45. Scelle, *op. cit.*, p. 104. Oppenheim-Lauterpacht, after having enumerated three conditions of statehood, namely, people, country and government, add the following fourth one : " There must, fourthly and lastly, be a *sovereign* Government.. " *Op. cit*, I, p. 114.

2. *Op. cit.*, p. 26. Cf. p. 45.

3. " International Law governs relations between independent States. " *P.C.I.J.*, Ser. A 10, p. 18 ; its aim is " to regulate the relations between these co-existing independent communities ". *Ibid.* Cf. Judge Loder : " The family of nations consists of a collection of different sovereign and independent States. " Ser. A 10, p. 34.

possible or necessary, without a clear delimitation of its subjects, which together form the international community [1]. Thus, the independence of States forms the necessary prerequisite of international law, a condition wihch the latter could not renounce, without at the same time renouncing its own *raison d'être*. Just as the existence of co-ordinated, independent States cannot be conceived without a higher, co-ordinating legal order [2], so also the existence of this higher order cannot be conceived without these co-ordinated subjects, endowed with separate personality.

International law is therefore merely fulfilling its primary function, when it undertakes the actual delimitation of States. In so doing, it performs for the States a task which they cannot perform themselves, and at the same time it lays the foundation of its own existence [3].

Most conspicuous, but not most important is the territorial delimitation of States by international law [4]. For the final delimitation of a State is not achieved with the delimitation of its territorial sphere of validity alone. Equally, its personal sphere of validity and, above all, its own legal order, must be clearly determined. It may even happen that, in special circumstances such as the process of State formation, international law will provisionally accept, as its subject, a community with only a rough delimitation of its territorial and personal spheres of validity, on condition that its legal order is strictly delimited. In other words, international law will consider as a State an entity, whose independent legal order is clearly established on a territory with no definitely fixed frontiers and, consequently, with no definitely fixed population. No such concession can be made in the case of the State's legal order, which is its very essence and without which there can be no State. This order of priority, in which independence takes pride of place, is clearly indicated by the well-known decision of the Polish-German Mixed Arbitral Tribunal in the case of *Deutsche Continental Gas Gesellschaft v. Poland* of 1921 :

---

1. " If States were not sovereign, no international law would be possible, since the purpose of this law precisely is to harmonize and reconcile the different sovereignties over which its exercises its sway." Dissenting Opinion of Judge Weiss, *P.C.I.J.*, Ser. A 10, p. 43. " ...Internationale Beziehungen sind nur möglich zwischen Verbänden, welche wenigstens in der international zu regelnden Materie unabhängig sind. " Huber, *op. cit.*, p. 30.

2. " Sicherlich ermöglicht dieses überstaatliche objektive Recht das Nebenein-anderbestehen der einzelnen Staatsrechtsordnungen. Hätte jenes überstaatliche objektive Recht auch keinen weiteren Inhalt, als den, dass es die Vorstellung des Neben-einanderbestehens der einzelnen staatlichen Rechtsordnungen dem juristischen Denken ermöglichte, so würde es dennoch eine begriffliche Notwendigkeit erfüllen. " Guggenheim, *Beiträge*, p. 3.

3. « La tendance originaire du droit international, sa fonction primaire pour ainsi dire, est de délimiter les domaines de validité territorial, personnel, temporel et matériel des ordres juridiques des Etats les uns d'avec les autres, et ainsi de les coordonner. C'est là, en effet, une fonction que peut seul remplir le droit international dans la mesure où il est un ordre juridique supérieur aux Etats. » Kelsen, *Théorie générale*, p. 180. " Da das Völkerrecht das Zusammenleben der Staaten regelt, muss es vor allem die staatli-chen Geltungsbereiche untereinander abgrenzen. ...Das Völkerrecht grenzt den zeitlichen, den räumlichen, den persönlichen und den sachlichen Geltungsbereich der Staaten unte-reinander ab. " Verdross, *Völkerrecht*, p. 153.

4. Bourquin, *op. cit.*, p. 107.

« Pour qu'un Etat existe et puisse être reconnu comme tel avec un territoire sans lequel il ne pourrait ni exister ni être reconnu, il suffit que ce territoire ait une consistance suffisamment certaine (alors même que les frontières n'en seraient pas encore exactement délimitées) et que sur ce territoire, il exerce en réalité la puissance publique nationale de façon indépendante [1]. »

This passage clearly expresses the requirement of independence as a condition of statehood under international law. This need was stressed more particularly with reference to the concrete question to be decided, viz. whether Poland was a State during the relevant period. In this connection the Tribunal stated :

« Il est admis ... qu'en novembre 1918 et en tout cas fin 1918, l'Etat polonais existait *de facto*. Il disposait d'un territoire comprenant, dans ses grandes lignes, la Pologne du Congrès et la Galicie occidentale. Il possédait un gouvernement *indépendant*, dont la puissance publique s'affirmait lentement, mais toujours davantage [2]. »

This decision does not stand alone in emphasizing the need for independence as a condition of statehood. In 1920, the Committee of Jurists, set up by the League of Nations in order to investigate the problem of the Aaland Islands, had to consider the question of Finland's statehood at the relevant period. The Committe came to the conclusion that,

" ... for a considerable time, the conditions required for the formation of a sovereign State did not exist. "

It went on to recall the conditions of revolution and anarchy which prevailed at the time, the disorganisation of social and political life, the non-effectiveness of authorities, civil war with the participation of foreign troops, and so on, and concluded :

" It is, therefore, difficult to say at what exact date the Finnish Republic in the legal sense of the term actually became a definitely constituted sovereign State. This certainly did not take place until a stable political organisation had been created, and *until public authorities had become strong enough to assert themselves throughout the territories of the State without the assistance of foreign troops* [3]. "

The notion of independence as a condition of statehood clearly emerges from the italicized passage.

The Permanent Court of International Justice speaks of

" a principle which is a fundamental principle of international law, namely, the principle of the independence of States [4] ".

Within the framework of conventional law, the notion of independence as being inherent in statehood seems to emerge from the Montevideo Convention on Rights and Duties of States. It is true that Article 1, which contains the basic definition of a State, does not expressly mention independence and limits itself to the following :

1. *Rec. TAM.*, vol. 9, p. 346. Cf. international recognition of Israel before the actual determination of its frontiers. Cf. Scelle, *op. cit.*, p. 86, and the examples quoted.
2. *It mine, ibid.*, p. 343.
3. *It. mine, LNOJ*, Special Supplement, no 3, pp. 8-9.
4. *P.C.I.J.*, Ser. B 5, p. 27. Cf. the ever recurring emphasis of the Court on the principle of State independence. " Restrictions upon the independence of States cannot ...be presumed. " Ser. A 10, p. 18.

" The State as a person of international law should possess the following qualifications : *a)* a permanent population ; *b)* a defined territory ; *c)* government ; and *d)* capacity to enter into relations with the other States. "

Article 3, however, which proclaims the declaratory character of recognition [1], states that :

" ... Even before recognition, the State has the right to defend its integrity and independence. "

thereby assuming that a State as such does possess independence which it has the right to defend [2].

State practice equally insists upon independence as a test of statehood.

Thus, President Grant, in his message of December 7, 1875, stated the following conditions for the existence of a State :

" ... there must be a people occupying a known territory, united under some known and defined form of government, acknowledged by those subject thereto, in which the functions of government are administered by usual methods, competent to mete out justice to citizens and strangers, to afford remedies for public and for private wrongs, and able to assume the correlative international obligations and capable of performing the corresponding international duties *resulting from its acquisition of the rights of sovereignty.* A power should exist complete in its organization, ready to take and able to maintain its place among the nations of the earth [3]. "

It thus appears that both judicial decisions and State practice bear out the theoretical assertion according to which the independence of States forms a necessary prerequisite of international law. It is now necessary to analyze the meaning of this notion.

3. LEGAL MEANING OF INDEPENDENCE.

Independence has been defined by Judge Anzilotti in a passage, which has by now become classical, of his Individual Opinion in the case of the *Customs Regime between Germany and Austria :*

" ... the independence of Austria within the meaning of Article 88 is nothing else but the existence of Austria, within the frontiers laid down by the Treaty of Saint-Germain, *as a separate State and not subject to the authority of any other State or group of States.* Independence as thus understood is really no more than the

---

1. See above, p. 159.
2. Hudson, *International Legislation*, VI, p. 620. It is not quite clear whether the International Law Commission of the United Nations also intended to treat independence as a necessary characteristic of the State, when it formulated Art. 1 of its Draft Declaration on Rights and Duties of States in the following way : " Every State has the right to independence and hence to exercise freely, without dictation by any other State, all its legal powers, including the choice of its own form of government. " Whatever was meant, the Article gave Kelsen an opportunity of forcefully re-stating his point of view. " The statement " — he says — " that " every State has the right to independence " is hardly correct. Independence is not a right, it is an essential characteristic of the State. " *The Draft Declaration on Rights and Duties of States*, A.J., 1950, p. 267. Cf. Oppenheim-Lauterpacht : " Independence and territorial as well as personal supremacy are not rights, but recognized and therefore protected qualities of States as International Persons. " *Op. cit.*, I, p. 255.
3. *It. mine*, Moore, *Digest*, I, pp. 107-108. For further examples, see above, p. 141.

normal condition of States according to international law ; it may also be described as sovereignty *(suprema potestas)*, or external sovereignty, by which is meant that the State has over it no other authority than that of international law [1]. "

It will be observed that Anzilotti's definition of independence contains two elements : the " separateness " of the State and its direct subordination to international law. The two cannot indeed be separated. For only a " separate " State can be directly subordinated to international law and, conversely, only a State directly subordinated to international law can be " separate ".

A State exists as a " separate State ", if it is clearly delimited from any other State.

It has already been seen that, however important the territorial delimitation of a State may be, it is only secondary to the delimitation of its legal order. For if the latter were not separate and distinc, from

---

1. *It. mine*, P.C.I.J., Ser. A/B 41, p. 57. Cf. the opinion of the Court : " ...the independence of Austria, according to Article 88 of the Treaty of Saint Germain, must be understood to mean the continued existence of Austria within her presents frontiers as *a separate State* with the sole right of decision in all matters economic, political, financial or other with the result that that independence is violated, as soon as there is any violation thereof, either in the economic, political, or any other field, these different aspects of independence being in practice one and indivisible. " *Ibid.*, p. 45. Cf. also the Dissenting Opinion of Judges Adatci, Kellog, Rolin-Jacquemyns, Sir Cecil Hurst, Schücking, van Eysinga, Wang : " « Independence» is a term well understood by all writers on international law, though the definitions which they employ are diversified. A State would not be independent in the legal sense if it was placed in a condition of dependence on another Power, if it ceased itself to exercise within its own territory the *summa potestas* or sovereignty, i.e. if it lost the right to exercise its own judgment in coming to the decisions which the government of its territory entails. " *Ibid.*, p. 77. To avoid misunderstanding it may readily be admitted that, independence and sovereignty are in fact synonymous. Apart from the above statement by Anzilotti, see Max Huber in the *Island of Palmas* arbitration : " Sovereignty in the relations between States signifies independence. " Scott, the Hague Court Reports, 2nd Series, p. 92. Also Kelsen : " ...da im Grunde die " Freiheit " oder " Unabhängigkeit " des States identisch ist mit seiner " Souveränität "..." *Souveränität*, p. 62. It is impossible, within the framework of this study, to investigate fully the notion of sovereignty ; but there can be no more doubt, especially since the publication of Kelsen's classical work on the subject, that in its original meaning, sovereignty is incompatible with international law. It would then follow that the same applies to independence. It should, however, be observed that, whatever its real meaning, the word has lately come to signify no more than immediate subordination to international law. This clearly results from the above-quoted passage of Anzilotti. Prof. Guggenheim in his " Lehrbuch " similarly retains the expression of " sovereignty" not in its absolute, but in its relative sense of " Völkerrechtsunmittelbarkeit". Even so, and in spite of the equivalence of the two terms — " sovereignty " and " independence " — it is suggested that it would be advisable to discard the term " sovereignty " in favour of " independence ". Not only is " sovereignty " a discredited and aggressive notion ; but, although both notions are polemical, " sovereignty " could be assumed to be directed against the rule of international law, whereas " independence " could be assumed to be directed against the domination of the State by a foreign State or group of States. In this sense Verdross : " Diese Unabhängigkeit ist jedoch keine Unabhängigkeit vom Völkerrecht, sondern eine Unabhängigkeit vom Willen anderer Staaten. " *Völkerrecht*, p. 80. This, of course, is merely a suggestion, not a statement *de lege lata*. In any case, it should be made clear beyond any doubt that " independence " as used in this study means precisely this relative independence," Völkerrechtsunmittelbarkeit", and nothing else. For a theory claiming a difference between the two notions and an attempt at defining an autonomous notion of independence, see Rousseau : *L'indépendance de l'Etat dans l'ordre international*, Rec. 1948, II. For suggestions similar to the ones put forward above, see Scelle : « ...la seule notion juridique qui puisse être substituée à celle de la souveraineté, c'est la notion d'indépendance. » *Précis de Droit des Gens*, Paris, Rec. Sirey, 1932, I, p. 82. « ...la notion de Souveraineté... à laquelle se substituera celle de l'indépendance, c'est-à-dire de la liberté dans la limite des obligations juridiques. » *Pacte des Nations*, Paris, Rec. Sirey, 1919, p. 372. Cf. Politis, *Le Problème des limitations de la souveraineté et la théorie de l'abus des droits*, Rec. 1925, I, p. 21.

the legal order of any other State, then the territorial delimitation would be reduced, in its legal aspect, to the level of any provincial or communal delimitation within a State.

Further analysis of the notion of independence must therefore concentrate on the delimitation of the State's legal order.

Such delimitation can be expressed in several ways. It may be said that no State can be " created " from outside, that its existence must be based on its own " will ", that the State " exists because it exists " [1]. It is true that a State cannot be created from outside [2] ; but insistence upon the State's own " will " as the basis of its existence, or the explanation of this existence by its " inner essence " hardly conveys a precise legal meaning ; unless it means that the legal source of its legal order cannot be situated outside the State.

A sociological approach might insist on the need for a conscious, creative effort on the part of the human group forming the substratum of the State [3].

Apart from the sociological character of such a theory, it may be doubted whether the condition postulated is accurate. At best, it would apply to the so-called national States. But there have been States based on conquest and oppression, or States comprising an overwhelming percentage of national minorities, who certainly did not approve either of the State as such or of their own inclusion in that State. Such States are nonetheless States, however negative the attitude of their populations [4].

---

1. " Der Staat ist Staatskraft seines inneren Wesens. " Jellinek, op. cit., p. 266. " ...kann das Dasein eines Staates rechtlich nur auf seinem eigenen Willen ruhen. Ein Staat kann nie von einem anderen rechtlich geschaffen werden, welchen Anteil auch immer ein Staat oder mearere an dem historischen Bildungsprozesse eines anderen Staates haben mögen. " Ibid., p. 267. It is, however, to be observed, that Jellinek's argument is directed not so mucn against the possibility of a State being created by another State, as against the possibility of a legal explanation of a State's birth. Such impossibility admittedly exists as long as the process of State creation is not considered from the point of view of a legal order higher than the legal order of the State, i.e. of international law. Cf. Anzilotti : « ...un pouvoir juridique des Etats de créer un nouvel Etat est aussi inconcevable qu'un pouvoir juridique des hommes de donner la vie à un autre homme. » Op. cit., p. 229.

2. See below, p. 168.

3. « Pour qu'un Etat, même un Etat non-souverain et soumis à un pouvoir supérieur, prenne naissance, il faut un acte originaire, primaire et spontané de la part de cette collectivité qui doit former l'Etat nouveau. Cet acte est soustrait peut-être, à l'observation, les formes dans lesquelles il s'accomplit sont souvent peu précises, mais, enfin, il faut qu'il y ait une volonté créatrice, une prise de possession. » Erich, op. cit., p. 443. « ...il faut, en tout cas, qu'un élément national ait saisi l'occasion donnée, qu'il ait donc lui-même fait des efforts pour constituer un Etat. De nos jours, le pouvoir public, propre à l'Etat, suppose une origine spontanée, une force créatrice, inhérente à l'Etat lui-même. Il ne peut pas lui être imposé du dehors, si importantes que puissent être les forces qui ont pu contribuer à sa formation et qui ont pu créer les conditions réelles, indispensables pour que le nouvel Etat pût se constituer. » Ibid., pp. 444-445. « ...la naissance d'un nouvel État suppose une volonté nationale, comme un facteur indispensable. Sans cela, l'Etat n'est qu'une chimère, un produit artificiel. » Ibid., pp. 450-451.

4. Uhler formulates the relation of the population to the State authority in a much more careful way : " Sieht man auch von der Erfordernis einer inneren Zustimmung zur Staatsgewalt seitens der Rechtsunteitanen ab, so muss doch wenigstens die Staatsgewalt in eine. gewissen Beziehung zu den Normadressaten stehen. Sie muss in irgendeiner Form die Emanation des Staatsvolkes sein, sei diese auch nur durch die Staatsangehörigkeit gegeben. So sind selbst bei einer autokratischen Regierung die Menschen, die regieren, Normadressaten dieses Staates ; sie sind nicht exterritorial, die Bildung des Gesamtwillens erfolgt autonom, nicht heteronom. " Op. cit., pp. 36-47. Here the problem ceases to be one of the psychological attitude of the population and becomes one of the delimitation of the legal order.

In view of the unsatisfactory nature of these two explanations, it becomes both necessary and possible to define the " separateness " of the State in strictly legal terms ; and in these terms it simply means that every State is determined by the basic norm of its legal order, which it does not share with any other State [1]. This basic norm is its own ; it is not, and cannot be, derived from any other State order. In other words, the legal source, the reason of validity of the legal order of a State cannot be found in the legal order of one or several other States. The legal order of a State cannot be delegated by any other State of group of States, for if it were, the entity in question would not be an independent State, but a component legal order of that State or group of States by whom it would be delegated. This reference to " a State " or " a group of States " is necessary in order to exclude the possibility of the formation of an independent State in two cases : a) the case of a delegation of a new order by internal legislation of one other State, — and b) the case of such delegation by an agreement of two or more States, i.e. by a conventional norm of international law. In both cases the new creation would be a delegation : in the first case, of one, — in the second, of several States. It would lack that final delimitation which is given by its " own " basic norm and which makes it a separate and independent State under international law [2].

Thus, the reason of validity of the legal order of a State can only lie in general international law. It has been seen that an independent State cannot, by definition, be a component order of another State or group of States. If, however, the existence of international law is admitted at all, then a State not only can, but must, be a component part of the international legal order. It is the latter which determines the conditions and moment of its birth and which delimits it in every respect from other States. It is this immediate link between the international and the State's legal order which alone determines the separate identity of the latter. This again confirms the inescapable connection between the " separate existence " of a State and its direct subordination to international law. Together they form the notion of independence [3].

The legal meaning of independence can, therefore, be defined as follows : a State is independent when it derives its reason of validity directly from international law, and not from the legal order of any other State, that is to say, when it possesses a basic norm of its own which is neither derived from, nor shared with, any other State.

---

1. " Der ganze Normenbestand einer... Teilordnung ist von jedweder anderen Teilordnung dadurch abgegrenzt, dass er in einer relativ höchsten Norm kulminiert, die er mit keiner anderen Teilordnung gemeinsam hat. " Merkl, *op. cit.*, p. 509.

2. The impossibility of " creating " an independent State is strikingly illustrated by the dependent character of all such creations : e.g. the Free City of Cracow, the Ionian Islands, Albania in 1913, Danzig, not to mention Eastern Rumelia.

3. See Guggenheim, *op. cit.*, I, p. 163. Similarly Verdross: "Souveränität ist also nur ein anderer Ausdruck für die ausschliessliche Völkerrechtsunmittelbarkeit." *Verfassung*, p. 118.

4. " ACTUAL " INDEPENDENCE.

As against the legal notion of independence examined above, a question may arise with regard to " actual " independence which has rightly been postulated by Prof. Lauterpacht as a condition of statehood on the same footing as legal independence [1]. Prof. Lauterpacht further develops the idea by stating :

" If a community ... were to become, *legally or actually*, a satellite of another State, it would not be fulfilling the primary condition of independence and would not accordingly be entitled to recognition as a State [2]. "

Such a view raises several important questions. Is " actual " independence, as opposed to " legal " independence, a legitimate concern of a lawyer ? How is it to be defined ? How is it to be delimited, — particularly in view of the following warning by Judge Anzilotti :

" It follows that the legal conception of independence has nothing to do with a State's subordination to international law or *with the numerous and constantly increasing states of de facto dependence which characterize* the relation of one country to other countries [3]. "

When will a certain degree of dependence represent such a normal relation in the growing interdependence of the modern world, and when will it involve a real loss of independence and a status of actual subjection, in other words that of a satellite or a puppet State ? Where is the line to be drawn ?

The answer is, in the first place, that the question of " actual " independence is indeed a legitimate concern of a lawyer, and Prof. Lauterpacht is fully justified in raising it. For if independence is a condition of statehood, it must be genuine and not a mere fiction. In other words, a State must be genuine and not a puppet. Prof. Lauterpacht's requirement of " actual " independence, coupled as it is with the examples he quotes — namely, Slovakia, Croatia, Manchukuo — clearly shows that he has the puppet State in mind [4].

The notion of the fake, or puppet creation, has already been met with in the course of this study, namely — in connection with revolution and belligerent occupation [5]. In both cases it was found to be an instrument of disguised law-breaking, the object of a fake revolution being to circumvent the international prohibition of intervention, and that of fake governments or States under belligerent occupation to circumvent the international rules applying to the latter. In every case a fake creation is, in the final analysis, aimed at evading the international duty to respect the sovereignty and integrity, the continued legal existence of States. Thus, in both cases, far from being a genuine

---

1. See above, p. 162.
2. *It. mine, op. cit.*, pp. 27-28.
3. *It. mine, P.C.I.J.*, Ser., A/B 41, p. 58.
4. « ...et l'on doit constater que certaines créations d'Etat ont eu un caractère fictif : celles, par exemple, de l'Etat Croate ou de la Slovaquie au cours de la dernière guerre, pour les besoins de la cause de l'Axe. » Scelle, *op. cit.*, p. 128.
5. See above, pp. 64-71 and 110-120.

product of an independent State, it was in fact a creation of a third State for aggressive purposes, a violation of international law [1].

It has also been seen that precisely on account of this intended character of an instrument of disguised law-breaking, puppet creations escape all legal definition, that is to say, definition based on purely formal criteria. For it is of the very essence of puppet creations that externally the formal features of genuine entities are carefully preserved. With regard more particularly to the puppet State, it is an entity which, while preserving all the external paraphernalia of independence, is in fact utterly lacking such independence ; in other words, it is in reality not a State at all, but a mere organ of the State which has set it up, whose puppet, or satellite, it is. But for such false appearances and the preservation of the formal aspect of a State, the problem of its " actual " independence would not arise. The entity in question would clearly and openly be a dependent one, — i.e. not a State at all and its true legal nature could easily be ascertained by the usual formal criteria.

In view of the uselessness of such criteria, and in view of the fact that the puppet State — or government — will by definition be created by an outside State, it was proposed to introduce the presumption of the puppet character of any government or State which comes into being under foreign occupation or any other form of obvious foreign pressure. This presumption which is believed to be absolutely justified and necessary is, however, of no help in ascertaining the inner nature of a puppet State. Yet, an enquiry into its nature becomes necessary now that the subject is being examined not so much in its dynamic aspect of the *actio in fraudem legis* of the aggressor, as in its static aspect of the puppet State already established. In view of what has already been said, such an enquiry cannot proceed on formal, but on purely descriptive lines, that is, by way of a searching examination of each individual case.

Although the " puppet State " has become a household word only in recent times, the phenomenon itself is not new in the history of international relations and international law.

After the fall of Napoleon prolonged negotiations took place between France and the United States concerning claims of the citizens of the latter, arising out of the acts of Napoleon. Under the convention of July 4, 1831, France finally paid a global indemnity and the United States appointed a commission to distribute this sum among the various claimants. To this commission

" claims were submitted for the seizure and the sequestration or confiscation of American vessels in Dutch ports in 1809 and 1810. When the United States pressed these claims against Holland in 1815, the Dutch Government denied its responsibility on the ground that when the seizures occurred the Netherlands were under the actual government of France. The discussion continued from time to time for five years. On May 28, 1820, Mr. John Quincey Adams, as Secretary of State, instructed the minister of the United States at The Hague to forbear for the time to press the subject further. This step was taken at the request of the Dutch

1. See Guggenheim, *op. cit.*, II, p. 938, *f.-r.* 496.

Government, made through its minister at Washington, that the claims be not further pressed. As demands against the Netherlands the claims were thus practically abandoned. The commissioners under the convention with France decided that they constituted valid claims upon the French nation [1]. "

Since all claims could not be satisfied, several complaints were made. In order to explain the position, Commissioner Kane published a pamphlet, setting forth the general principles which the Commission had applied. In particular, it explained why claims against Holland were allowed as claims against France to be met out of the French indemnity, while similar claims against Denmark were not. Here is the relevant passage :

" But apart from spoliations in which the agency of the French Government through its own officers was in question, there was a large class of cases in which it was alleged that France influenced or compelled other nations to commit wrongs. This allegation especially affected claims growing out of spoliations in Holland and Denmark. ...

Holland, after some ten years of political changes, during which, though nominally independent, she was tributary to all the projects of France, had received, in the month of June 1806, a king of the Napoleon family. But it was manifest, that in placing Louis upon the throne, his brother had not renounced his control over the affairs of that country. The form of distinct sovereignties was presented to the public eye ; but the energies of the Dutch people were directed more than ever to the advancement of the imperial policy. At last, in the concluding month of 1809, a new crisis approached. At a moment, when the finances of Holland were in a state of extreme embarrassment, she was required to destroy her commerce with foreign nations which formed the principal source of her revenues. Louis ventured to remonstrate, and delayed compliance with the mandate. He was reminded in reply, that the country of which he was sovereign was a French conquest, and that " his highest and imprescriptible duties were to the imperial crown " ; and it was announced to him, in terms which could not be mistaken, that the project of uniting Holland to the empire was already matured, and that its consummation could only be postponed by his unqualified obedience. Among the most decided, though not the first tests of his submission, as he has since declared to the world, "the pretended treaty of the 16th of March, 1810, which was in fact a capitulation, was presented to him to be ratified ". "It was imposed " — he adds — " by the emperor ", and a prisoner as Louis was at the time at Paris, he had no choice but to yield. The French armies had forcibly possessed themselves beforehand of several of Dutch fortresses ; French officers of the customs occupied all the ports and outlets of the Kingdom ; and Napoleon, confounding apparently his purposes with their execution, had already directed his decrees to the authorities of Holland as if it was one of the departments of France. The assent of the king, however, did not avail to prolong his reign. The troops of his brother continued to advance, they menaced Amsterdam, the popular feeling was inflamed, and in the vain hope of averting a new revolution, Louis abdicated on the 1st of July in favour of his son. It was unnecessary ; the emperor's arrangements were already made ; a decree of thirteen articles was issued on the 9th from the palace of Rambouillet, the first of which declared that Holland was united to the empire.

The tenth article of the treaty of 16th March, 1810, was as follows : " All merchandise which has arrived in American vessels in the ports of Holland since the 1st of January 1809, shall be placed under sequestration, and shall belong to France, to be disposed of according to circumstances and to the political relations with the United States. It was executed in the spirit which suggested it, rather than according to its terms : every American cargo, without reference to the date of its importation, was sequestered at once... Some were afterwards released under the decree of 9th July, 1810, or by special favour ; but the greater number, after more or less delay, were sold by the imperial order, and their proceeds passed into the *Caisse d'amortissement* at Paris.

1. Moore, *Digest.*, I, pp. 252-253.

It was for the value of these cargoes that reclamations were made before the commissioners. The brief account which has been given of the political condition of Holland from the year 1809 till it was formally merged in the French Empire sufficiently explains the reason for allowing them. Holland was already a dependent kingdom, and Louis a merely nominal sovereign. The treaty was a form, in substance it was an imperial decree [1]. "

Commissioner Kane then went on to enumerate the wrongs inflicted by Denmark on the United States, and concluded :

" But the question before the board regarded not Denmark, but France. One cannot be charged with the acts of the other ; for neither was dependent. It may be that the conduct of King Frederic was dictated by his anxiety to conciliate the favour of the French emperor ; or perhaps he was moved by the portion of the spoil which might fall into his hands ; we had nothing to do with his motives or his fears. The act was his own ; the kingdom of Denmark was then, as now, independent. ... This then is the broad distinction between the cases of Holland and Denmark. The former war a nominal, the latter an actual sovereignty. The intervention of one was merely formal and was exacted by force ; the other was the voluntary pander to French avidity [2]. "

Commissioner Kane's description of a puppet State may be regarded as classic: the fiction of a separate sovereignty, exploitation of the people's resources for the benefit of the dominant State, utter disregard of its needs, economic or otherwise, in other words — " colonial " treatment, a permanent threat of destruction even of the appearances of independence, treaties, which in spite of their external form are nothing but decrees of the dominant State — all these are factors which international law could disregard only at the expense of completely ignoring the living reality which it is supposed to regulate. The legal consequences drawn by Commissioner Kane and his colleagues on the Commission as well as by the United States Government were, under the circumstances, only logical and consistent: namely the freeing of the restored Dutch State from all international responsibility for unlawful acts, committeed in its name by another State, and the placing of such responsibility firmly where it in fact belonged. By deciding the question of international responsibility in this way, the puppet character of the Dutch State under Louis Bonaparte was definitely established, and, at the same time, the identity of independent Holland with the Dutch puppet State squarely denied. The latter was not identical with the former and it did not continue its legal existence. This conclusion fully confirms the submission which has been made with regard to fake revolutions [3] : there can be no identity as between a genuine and a fake entity.

It may also be added that Commissioner Kane's analysis supplies an answer to the question which has been raised concerning the difference between the normal interdependence of States and satellite status [4] : it has been seen that, according to him, Denmark had preserved its State character in spite of a considerable degree of French influence,

1. Moore, *International Arbitrations*, V, pp. 4473-4474.
2. *Ibid.*, pp. 4475-4476.
3. See above, pp. 70-71.
4. See above, p. 169.

whereas Holland had not. Commissioner Kane arrived at this conclusion by examining the facts of each individual case. There is indeed no other way [1].

It was not to be expected that, when faced with the recurring use of puppet States as a means of law-breaking, international law in the 20th century should prove weaker and less resolute than in the 19th century. It will be seen that, on the contrary, it did not lag behind either the analysis or the conclusions of Commissioner Kane.

In the case of Manchukuo, the international community was confronted with what may be considered a classical example of aggression by the creation of a puppet State. The historical background of the case is well-known. Following her attack on China in 1931, Japan refrained from a straightforward annexation of Manchuria, preferring to set up in that part of China a puppet State which served all the purposes of annexation in everything but name. As behoves a puppet State, the purely formal aspect of Manchukuo's alleged statehood was carefully preserved, — so carefully indeed that there were found certain international lawyers who were ready to defend the genuine character of Manchukuo precisely on the basis of such formal criteria. An analysis of the formal aspect of the case can therefore best be carried out by following the reasoning of a defender of Manchukuo's statehood.

In his article on the subject, Prof. Cavaré asserts that the fundamental laws of Manchukuo were its own, and had not been granted by Japan [2]. This is quite true and is entirely in keeping with the nature of a puppet State. Whatever Japan's effective influence may have been, the appearance of autonomy in Manchukuo's basic law had to be maintained.

Prof. Cavaré further relies heavily on the international character of the relations between Japan and Manchukuo. The basic instrument of these relations was the Protocol of September 15th, 1932, by which Japan recognized the new State and which included a reciprocal guarantee. According to Prof. Cavaré, such reciprocity was proof of the independence of both parties to the Protocol. Here again, it is in the very nature of a puppet State to receive its directives from the dominant State not in the formal shape of the latter's municipal enactments, but precisely in that of international agreements. However innocent such agreements may appear, they may yet include stipulations which are hardly compatible with the actual independence of one of the parties. Thus, the September Protocol granted Japan the right to maintain her troops in Manchukuo. Yet even this flaw is dismissed by Prof. Cavaré, who does not seem to regard it as being in any way incompatible with Manchukuo's legal independence [3].

---

1. Speaking of acts susceptible of endangering Austria's independence, Judge Anzilotti stated : " But it must be added at once that, from their very nature, acts of this kind are particular instances : an act which in certain circumstances presents no danger whatsoever to a State's independence may well be extremely dangerous in circumstances of another kind. " *P.C.I.J.*, Ser. A/B, 41, p. 63.
2. « Cette constitution n'a pas été octroyée au nouvel Etat par le Japon. C'est lui-même qui se l'est donnée en vertu de son pouvoir constituant. » *La reconnaissance de l'Etat et le Mandchoukouo, RGDIP*, 1935, p. 32.
3. *Op. cit.*, p. 33.

Prof. Cavaré also stresses Manchukuo's right to enter into international agreements. The pretence of such a " right " was again necessary to enable Japan to impose her will on Manchukuo precisely by way of international agreements. The exchange of diplomatic envoys between the two countries stands on exactly the same footing. As to the official visit of a Japanese prince to the " Emperor " of Manchukuo, the point is too pathetic to require refutation [1]. The only argument of Prof. Cavaré which might seem to have some legal justification is the one bearing on international responsibility of Manchukuo. Was Manchukuo really the subject of such responsibility? Here the writer confuses the lodging of protests against local grievances by foreign consuls with international responsibility in the real sense of the term. In this connection he is himself forced to admit the démarche of the Soviet Ambassador in Tokyo in 1933, holding Japan responsible for the acts of Manchukuo. That remains the fact notwithstanding a later statement by Litvinov, the Soviet Commissar for Foreign Affairs, to the effect that the Soviet Union would hold Japan *and* Manchukuo jointly responsible for the latter's international acts [2].

Prof. Cavaré concludes the legal part of his analysis of Manchukuo's statehood by stating that generally speaking, that country possessed full power of decision in international matters and that Japan did not intervene *officially* to substitute her own decisions for those of the Manchukuo authorities [3]. This statement, however, destroys the whole argument : for, of course, Japan did not intervene *officially*, this being the very essence of a satellite relationship.

There is, however, no doubt that the facts listed by Prof. Cavaré are correct and that all the appearances of Manchukuo's independence were preserved together with all the formalities necessary to create an impression of international legal relations between herself and Japan. Formally, Manchukuo's basic norm was not derived from the Japanese legal order ; there were formal international agreements between Manchukuo and Japan ; there was an exchange of diplomatic missions ; and there was no official, or legally founded, interference by Japan in Manchukuo's international relations or internal affairs.

Yet, the international community refused to accept this picture as a genuine one.

Undismayed by all this array of false pretences, the League of Nations sent out a Commission to investigate on the spot Sino-Japanese relations, including the question of Manchukuo. This body, which, after the name of its Chairman, came to be known as the Lytton Commission, published an extensive report on the Sino-Japanese conflict a chapter of which was devoted to the Manchukuo question.

The opinion of the Commission is clearly to be seen from the fact that the word " State " or " government " is invariably written in

---

1. *Ibid.*, p. 34.
2. *Ibid.*, pp. 35-36.
3. « D'une façon générale, le Mandchoukouo possède pleinement son pouvoir de décision internationale. Officiellement, le Japon n'intervient pas, au moins pour substituer sa décision à celles des autorités manchoues. » *Op. cit.*, p. 36.

inverted commas. This detail alone would suffice to make it quite clear that it never occurred to the Commission to take the alleged statehood of Manchukuo seriously.

After having described all the consecutive stages of organisation of the new State, the Report d.clares :

" It is clear that the Independence Movement, which had never been heard of in Manchuria before September 1931, was only made possible by the presence of the Japanese troops. ... The evidence received from all sources has satisfied the Commission that while there were a number of factors which contributed to the creation of " Manchukuo ", the two which, in combination, were most effective and without which, in our judgment, the new State could not have been formed were the presence of Japanese troops and the activities of Japanese officials, both civil and military [1]. "

The Report goes on to examine the already existing regime in Manchukuo and states :

" In the " Government of Manchukuo ", Japanese officials are prominent and Japanese advisers are attached to all important Departments. Although the Premier and his Ministers are all Chinese, the heads of the various Boards of General Affairs, which, in the organisation of the new State, exercise the greatest measure of actual power, are Japanese. At first they were designated as advisers, but recently those holding the most important posts have been made full Government officials on the same basis as the Chinese. In the Central Government alone, not including those in local governments, or in the War Office and the military forces or in Government enterprises, nearly 200 Japanese are " Manchukuo " officials [2]. "

The Report describes the economic subservience of " Manchukuo " to Japan, her exploitation by Japan and the part played by the Manchukuo " Government " as the instrument of such exploitation. Thus, with regard to public utilities, including the all-important problem of railways, agreements were entered into with Japan, which had been consistently refused by the Chinese government. Customs, tele-communications, the Salt Gabelle, and the like, came under Japanese control, the privileged position of Japan being safeguarded in every case.

" As regards the " Government " and the public services ", — the Report goes on — " although the titular heads of the Departments are Chinese residents in Manchuria, the main political and administrative power rests in the hands of Japanese officials and advisers. The political and administrative organisation of the " Government " is such as to give to these officials and advisers opportunities, not merely of giving technical advice, but also of actually controlling and directing the administration. They are doubtless not under the orders of the Tokyo Government, and their policy has not always coincided with the official policy either of the Japanese Government or of the Headquarters of the Kwantung Army. But in the case of all-important problems, these officials and advisers, some of whom were able to act more or less independently in the first days of the new organisation, have been constrained more and more to follow the direction of Japanese official authority. This authority, in fact, by reason of the occupation of the country by its troops, by the dependence of the " Manchukuo Government " on those troops for the maintenance of its authority both internally and externally, in consequence, too, of the more and more important role entrusted to the South Manchuria Railway Company in the management of the railways under the jurisdiction of the

1. *Report of the Commission of Enquiry,* LON Publications, VII, 1932, 12, p. 97.
2. *Ibid.,* p. 99.

" Manchukuo Government ", and finally by the presence of its consuls, as liaison agents, in the most important urban centres, possesses in every contingency the means of exercising an irresistible pressure [1]. "

After describing both the creation of the " State of Manchukuo " and its actual organisation, the Commission turned to the problem of the attitude of the population, — a particularly important problem in view of the claim that the new " State " was a spontaneous creation of its population. Here, the Commission stressed the difficulties it had encountered in establishing free contact with the population. In spite of these difficulties, however, the Commission was able to obtain the necessary information.

" Many delegations representing public bodies and associations were received and usually presented to us written statements. Most of the delegations were introduced by the Japanese or " Manchukuo " authorities, and we had strong grounds for believing that the statements left with us had previously obtained Japanese approval. In fact, in some cases persons who had presented them informed us afterwards, that they had been written or substantially revised by the Japanese and were not to be taken as the expression of their real feelings [2]. "

At the same time, however, the Commission received a great number of letters.

" All these 1.550 letters, except two, were bitterly hostile to the new " Manchukuo Government " and to the Japanese. They appeared to be sincere and spontaneous expressions of opinion [3]. "

With regard to genuine Chinese officials who continued in the Manchukuo administration, the police and the army, the Report had this to say :

" The higher Chinese officials of the " Manchukuo Government " are in office for various reasons. Many of them were previously in the former regime and have been retained either by inducements or by intimidation of one kind or another. Some of them conveyed messages to the Commission to the effect that they had been forced to remain in office under duress, that all power was in Japanese hands, that they were loyal to China, and that what they had said at their interview with the Commission in the presence of the Japanese was not necessarily to be believed. Some officials have remained in office to prevent their property from being confiscated, as has happened in the case of some of those who have fled into China. Others, men of good repute, joined in the hope that they would have power to improve the administration, and under promise of the Japanese that they would have a free hand. Some of these have been disappointed and complained that no real authority was conceded to them. Lastly, a few men are in office because they had personal grievances against the former regime or for reasons of profit. The minor and local officials have in the main retained their offices under the new regime, partly because of the necessity for earning a living and supporting their families and partly because they feel that if they go, worse men might be put in their place. Most of the local magistrates have also remained in office, partly from a sense of duty to the people under their charge and partly under pressure. While it was often difficult to fill the higher posts with reputable Chinese, it was an easy matter to get Chinese for service in minor posts and local offices, though the loyalty of the service rendered in such circumstances is at least questionable.

---

1. *Ibid.*, p. 106.
2. *Ibid.*, p. 107.
3. *Ibid.*, p. 107.

The " Manchukuo " police are partly composed of members of the former Chinese police, partly of new recruits. In the larger towns, there are actually Japanese officers in the police, and in many other places there are Japanese advisers. Some individual members of the police who spoke to us expressed their dislike of the new regime, but said they must continue to serve to make a living.

The " Manchukuo " Army also consists in the main of the former Manchurian soldiers re-organized under Japanese supervision. Such troops were at first content to take service under the new regime provided they were merely required to maintain local order. But, since they have on occasions been called upon to engage in serious warfare against Chinese forces and to fight under Japanese orders side by side with Japanese troops, the " Manchukuo " Army has become increasingly unreliable. Japanese sources report the frequent defection of " Manchukuo " forces to the Chinese side, while the Chinese claim that one of their most reliable and fruitful sources of warlike supplies is the " Manchukuo " Army [1]. "

Passing the various classes of population in review, the Report confirms the businessmen's and bankers' dislike and fear of Manchukuo, and the hostility of the professional classes, such as teachers, doctors, and the like :

" They allege that they are spied upon and intimidated. The interference with education, the closing of Universities and some schools, and the alterations in the school text-books, have added to their hostility, already great on patriotic grounds [2]. "

Evidence of the attitude of farmers and town workers was more difficult to obtain, but

" opinion among foreigners and educated Chinese was to the effect that they were either hostile or indifferent to " Manchukuo " [3]. "

In any case

" It was, we were told, impossible to stimulate in the towns a show of popular enthusiasm for the inauguration ceremonies of " Manchukuo ". Generally speaking, the attitude of the town population is a mixture of passive acquiescence and hostility [4]. "

" The Chinese allege that many executions have taken place, and also that prisoners have been threatened and tortured in Japanese gendarmerie stations [5]. "

While admitting a certain measure of support for " Manchukuo " on the part of minorities, such as Mongols, Manchus, Koreans, and White Russians, the Report declared :

" ... we have come to the conclusion that there is no general Chinese support for the " Manchukuo Government ", which is regarded by the local Chinese as an instrument of the Japanese [6]. "

The opinion of the Commission as to the genuineness of the State character of Manchukuo clearly emerges from the Report, although the technical terms " puppet " or " satellite " State are not used. This general opinion is confirmed by the Commission's final conclusions and proposals for a settlement. The Commission stated *inter alia* that

1. *Ibid.*, pp. 107-108.
2. *Ibid.*, p. 108.
3. *Ibid.*, p. 109.
4. *Ibid.*, pp. 109-110.
5. *Ibid.*, p. 109.
6. *Ibid.*, p. 111.

" ... the maintenance and recognition of the present regime in Manchukuo would be ... unsatisfactory [1]. "

It has been thought necessary to quote the Lytton Report at such length since it is probably the fullest and most exhaustive description of an allegedly independent, but " actually " dependent, i.e. puppet State, — based not on formal criteria, but on a searching investigation of all the facts of the case. As compared with Commissioner's Kane description of the puppet State of Holland, it is even more thorough and detailed, which may reflect the progress which has been made in the technique of organizing puppet States. Thus, apart, from those elements which were already examined by Commissioner Kane, the Lytton Report throws additional light on the part played by the officials and advisers of the aggressor Power, the terrorization of the population, the methods of forcing local citizens into the service of the puppet State, the true character of the allegedly national police and army, and so forth.

At the same time, the Report, like Commissioner's Kane opinion, not only gives a classical description of the puppet State, but also supplies the answer to the question which was asked at the beginning of this enquiry, namely, how far is the problem of " actual " independence relevant under international law ? Can it possibly be ascertained, and, if so, in what way ? Where is the line to be drawn between a normal relationship of interdependence between States and a satellite status ?

The Report supplies the answer precisely because it does not attempt to apply any rigid formula or criterion ; because it investigates the facts of a particular case and, on the basis of such facts, arrives at the conclusion that the status of Manchukuo had by far surpassed the limits of normal international interdependence. In fact, the alleged independence of a puppet State turns out to be the most direct denial of the very principle of State independence. The Report does not mistake the fake entity for a genuine State [2].

In spite of its overwhelming importance to the problem of puppet States, the Report is, however, of less value with regard to the main question of State identity and continuity, than the opinion of Commissioner Kane. For, owing to the particular circumstances, namely, the establishment of the puppet State of Manchukuo in a part only, and not on the whole of the original State's territory, the question of its identity with the original independent State did not arise. The Lytton Commission had therefore no immediate reason to draw any conclusions as to the non-identity of the puppet with the genuine State, as had been done by Commissioner Kane. It would however, seem that this omission was entirely due to the special circumstances of the case mentioned above, and that the rejection by the Lytton Commission of

---

1. *Ibid.*, p. 128.
2. Cf. Lauterpacht : " It could not be accurately maintained that, at any time, Manchukuo existed as an independent State i.e. as a State in international law, and not as a subservient province of Japan, endowed for the purpose of deception which was not even intended to deceive, with flimsy and transparent paraphernalia of spurious statehood. " *Op. cit.*, p. 47. Guggenheim, *Validité et Nullité*, speaks of the « conquête japonaise dissimulée par la création d'un Etat tampon. » p. 211.

the genuine State character of Manchukuo would necessarily have resulted in the denial of its identity with China, had its territorial sphere of validity extended to cover the whole of Chinese territory.

In any case, all the proper conclusions were drawn within the limits of the particular case, not only by the Lytton Commission, but by the League of Nations on the basis of the Commission's Report. On February 24, 1933, the League Assembly adopted the following resolution :

" The Assembly recommends as follows :
Whereas the sovereignty over Manchuria belongs to China...
... the recommendations ... exclude the maintenance and recognition of the existing regime in Manchukuo [1]. "

Whatever the vicissitudes of the policy of non-recognition as adopted by the League may have been [2], this refusal of the international organisation to admit the State character of a puppet State — stands. It was to be confirmed years later, in the Cairo Declaration of December 1st, 1943, in which the United States, Great Britain and China stated :

" It is their purpose ... that all the territories Japan has stolen from the Chinese, such as *Manchuria*, Formosa and the Pescadores, shall be restored to the Republic of China [3]. "

The legal conclusions drawn in the cases of Holland and Manchukuo fully bear out the assertion made previously in this study [4], namely, that international law cannot, and does not, mistake a fake for a genuine phenomenon. It cannot, and does not, attach the same legal consequences to both. Just as it does not mistake intervention for revolution, so it does not mistake disguised aggression and annexation for a genuine, legally permitted, secession and the establishment of a new, independent State. Even before evolving clear positive rules on the subject, such as have now been embodied in the Geneva Convention [5], international law took up the challenge of an *actio in fraudem legis* by refusing to recognize a fake as genuine, by fixing international responsibility where it belonged and, in cases involving State identity and continuity, by denying the identity of the puppet with the independent State.

In spite of this lengthy analysis the notion of the puppet State would not, however, be exhausted, if a final point were not dealt with. For a puppet State need not necessarily be the result of an original puppet creation. It is also possible for an originally independent State to be reduced to the status of a puppet, without any new creation, without any interference with its original, independent basic norm, but simply by actual and permanent interference by a foreign State with its normal functioning. Prof. Guggenheim is thus fully justified in laying down the free and unhampered functioning of the State's own

1. *LNOJ*, Spec. Sup. 112, pp. 75-76.
2. See Sharp, *op. cit.*, pp. 152-172 ; Langer, *Seizure of Territory*, pp. 70-72.
3. *It. mine*, quoted by Langer, *op. cit.*, p. 126.
4. See above, p. 70.
5. See above, pp. 116-120.

organs as a further condition of true independence [1]. This view is fully supported by the Award of the Permanent Court of Arbitration in the *North Atlantic Coast Fisheries* case (1910). The United States argued that if her treaty of 1918 with Great Britain, granting her inhabitants fishing rights in specified areas of British territorial waters, gave Britain the right of " reasonable " regulation of the liberties granted, then such right could not be exercised by Britain alone, without the accord and concurrence of the United States. The Tribunal rejected this submission, stating that :

" ... to hold that the United States, the grantee of the fishing right, has a voice in the preparation of fishery legislation, involves recognition of a right in that country to participate in the internal legislation of Great Britain and her Colonies and to that extent *would reduce these countries to a state of dependence* [2]. "

The above analysis of the notion of independence, both in its legal and its " actual " meaning, leads to the following conclusion : a State is independent in the widest meaning of the term *a)* when it is formally strictly delimited from all other States by an autonomous basic norm of its legal order and, consequently, directly subordinated to international law, and *b)* when it is in fact free from subjection to any other State or group of States.

5. " DEPENDENT STATES. "

If the above propositions are true without exception, then the notion of a State in international law is unequivocal and firm. If, however, independence is not really a condition of statehood, and if dependent entities which are nevertheless States do in fact exist, then the notion of a State becomes so confused as to make it impossible to distinguish a State from any other territorial entity and, moreover, fails to provide any useful criterion for the problem of State identity.

The question therefore arises whether entities, lacking independence are States according to international law ? In other words : is there such a thing as a dependent State [3] ?

---

1. " Die staatlichen Organe müssen, unabhängig vom Willen eines fremden Staates die Möglichkeit besitzen, das Landesrecht zu setzen und zu vollziehen, um als solche eines souveränen Staates angesehen werden zu können. " *Op. cit.*, I, p. 170.

2. *It. mine* ; J. B. Scott, *The Hague Court Reports*, p. 170. Cf. also : " Considering that the recognition of a concurrent right of consent in the United States would affect the independence of Great Britain, which would become dependent on the Government of the United States for the exercise of its sovereign right of regulation... " " Because the exercise of such a right of consent by the United States would predicate an abandonment of independence in this respect by Great Britain... " *Ibid.*, p. 167.

3. It is clear that the question does not concern an independent State which has delegated the whole or part of its international competences to another State by treaty, in which case there is no abdication of its independent status ; the treaty can be terminated just as it was entered into, and in no case does a conventional obligation, however burdensome, limit the sovereignty of a State. See *P.C.I.J.*, Ser. A I, p. 25, and the Dissenting Opinion of Judge Anzilotti, *P.C.I.J.*, Ser. A/B 41, p. 58. The question concerns solely an entity whose international limitations, far from being the result of a convention, result from another legal order, standing between the " State " in question and international law. Such limitations are not conventional obligations which may be terminated ; they are a permanent feature of the legal status of the dependent entity, imposed upon it by a superior legal order. It is only the latter which can either enlarge or completely eliminate the " restricted " international competences of the dependent entity.

a) *Judicial Decisions, State Practice and Doctrine.*

The notion of dependent States is generally admitted, although, with the immediate proviso that they are of an " abnormal " or " exceptional " character. Elaborating his conception of independence in his Individual Opinion referred to above [1] Judge Anzilotti stated :

" The conception of independence, regarded as the normal characteristic of States as subjects of international law, cannot be better defined than by comparing it with the exceptional and, to some extent, abnormal class of States, known as " dependent States ". These are States subject to the authority of one or more States. The idea of dependence therefore necessarily implies a relation between a superior State (suzerain, protector, etc.) and an inferior (vassal, protégé, etc.) ; the relation between the State which can legally impose its will and the State which is legally compelled to submit to that will. Where there is no such relation of superiority and subordination, it is impossible to speak of dependence within the meaning of international law [2]. "

Nor did the Permanent Court of International Justice hesitate to call dependent entities " States " and to treat them as such. Thus, with regard to Danzig, it held that :

" ... the fact that the legal status of Danzig is *sui generis* does not authorize it (the Court) to depart from the ordinary rules governing relations between States and to establish new rules for the relations between Poland and Danzig [3]. "

In particular, the Court admitted a Danzig *ad hoc* judge, giving the following reasons for its decision :

" The Court held that the question submitted to it for an advisory opinion related to an existing dispute between the Free City of Danzig and Poland, within the meaning of Article 71, paragraph 2, of the Rules of Court. As one only of these States, namely, Poland, had on the Bench a judge of its nationality, the Senate of the Free City of Danzig availed itself of its right, under Article 71 of the Rules of Court, to choose a judge *ad hoc* to sit in the case [4]. "

State practice would also appear to support the notion of a dependent State. Dependent entities, such as India at that time, were allowed to sign the Treaty of Versailles, alongside independent States. Dependent entities have been admitted as members of the United

---

1. See above, pp. 165-166.
2. *P.C.I.J.*, Ser. A/B, 41, p. 57.
3. *P.C.I.J.*, Ser. A/B, 44, p. 23.
4. *Loc. cit.*, p. 8. In placing Danzig in the category of States, the court was fully conscious of her dependent status ; see Ser. B. 18, p. 11 : "...so far as these rights (Poland's) involve a limitation on the independence of the Free City, they constitute organic limitations which are an'essential feature of its political structure. " The whole of this Advisory Opinion, denying the possibility of Danzig's becoming a member of the International Labour Office, is based on her status of dependence with regard to Poland. Cf. Individual Opinions of Judges Anzilotti and Huber. See also the Court's Annual Report for 1923 : " The States, neither Members of the League of Nations nor mentioned in the Annex to the Covenant which have been notified by the Court of the Resolution of the Council to the effect that they are entitled to appear before it, are now as follows : ...Danzig (through the intermediary of Poland)... " See, however, the very special formulation in the footnote to this passage : " When the Court had received the request for an advisory opinion concerning the jurisdiction of the Danzig Courts, it formally announced on Oct. 1, 1927, that the Free City, having been, since 1922, formally recognized by the Court as *a legal entity* entitled to appear before it, would, like Poland, be permitted to appoint a national judge to sit in the case..." It. mine, Ser. E, 4, p. 128.

Nations Organisation, although Articles 3 and 4 of the Charter limit membership to States only [1].

Finally, traditional doctrine firmly upheld the conception of dependent States, whatever the reservations as to their " exceptional " character. Thus Rivier calls the dependent State an " abnormal creation " and speaks of its " exceptional " character [2]. Fauchille, while rightly rejecting the absurd notion of " half-sovereign " States [3], admits the equally illogical notion of vassal States with a " reduced sovereignty"[4]. Liszt speaks of half-sovereign States [5] in spite of his own definition of a State as an independent territorial entity [6]. Speaking of " not-full sovereign States ", Oppenheim-Lauterpacht ask whether they " can be International Persons and subjects of the Law of Nations at all ", and admit, that they cannot be " full, perfect and normal subjects of International Law ". Yet they admit their State character.

" Such imperfect International Personality is, of course, an anomaly ; but the very existence of States without full sovereignty is an anomaly in itself [7]. "

This theory has met with some response even from Verdross, who distinguished between States which are immediately subordinated to international law fully, partly, or not at all [8]. The idea is truly puzzling, for it is obvious that an entity either is or is not directly subordinated to international law ; *tertium non datur*. A " partial " subordination to that law can only be the result of a limitation of the " State " in question by a legal order which stands between it and international law. Such " partial " subordination can therefore, never be an immediate one [9]. But Verdross goes on to classify vassal States and member States of a federal State which possess international competences as subordinated partly to State law and partly to international law. However, having proposed this classification, he himself concedes that the phenomenon could be much more accurately described as a unitary State with decentralized organs for foreign affairs, especially since it is always the superior State which is the subject of international responsibility [10]. Moreover, when considering the extinction of sovereign and non-sovereign States, he admits that, in the former case the occurence is of an international, but in the latter case of an internal character [11]. It is difficult to imagine a clearer admission that the so-called dependent States are not States at all in international law.

---

1. The League of Nations is not mentioned in this connection, since the Covenant expressly permitted the membership not only of States, but equally of Dominions and colonies, see Art. 1.
2. *Op. cit.*, I, p. 80.
3. *Op. cit.*, I, p. 296.
4. *Ibid.*, p. 285.
5. *Op. cit.*, p. 95 et seq.
6. " Selbstherrliche Gebietskörperschaft ", *ibid.*, p. 86.
7. *Op. cit.*, I, p. 115.
8. " ...völlig, teilweise oder überhaupt nicht völkerrechtsunmittelbare Staaten..." *Verfassung*, p. 125.
9. Cf. Kelsen : " Das wäre überhaupt eine Fehlvorstellung : eine Person, die zum Teil einer Ordnung unterworfen, durch diese verpflichtet, zum Teil aber von dieser Ordnung frei ist. " *Souveränität*, p. 65.
10. *Op. cit.*, pp. 122-123.
11. *Op. cit.*, pp. 144-145.

So far the reader is only faced with an unsubstantiated assertion of the existence of dependent States, without any attempt at a definition, nor, which is far more disturbing, without any attempt at re-defining the State as such. For the acceptance of the idea of a dependent *State* introduces a complete confusion into the very notion of a State to the point of undermining it altogether. If the existence of both dependent and independent States is admitted, how is the distinction to be drawn between a State and any other territorial entity, — a province, a district or a parish ? How is it to be determined what is, and what is not, a State [1] ? And what would then be the criterion of the State's identity ?

b) *The Question of the State Character of Dependent Entities.*

The best-known attempt to define the essence of the dependent, as opposed to the independent, State, was made by Jellinek (probably with the political object of vindicating the State character of the constituent lands of the German Reich).

Jellinek begins by asserting that the essential characteristic of a State is the existence of a State power. (Staatsgewalt). This power cannot be derived from any other source (nicht ableitbar), i.e. it is based on the State's own power and its own right. (aus eigener Macht und daher zu eigenem Recht). When a community exercises such original authority, backed by its own, original means of coercion (Zwangsmittel), then it is a State. Moreover, a State must have its constitution and its organs. The constitution must be its own ; it cannot be granted by another State. The same applies to the organs, in particular to the supreme organ which a State cannot share with any other State, for it is precisely the exclusiveness of this supreme organ which forms the criterion of the State's identity. Furthermore a State must exercise all the essential functions proper to a State : legislative, executive and judicial, even though such functions may be limited. Finally, the sovereign State can freely determine the scope of its jurisdiction (den Inhalt seiner Zuständigkeit regeln), while the non-sovereign State can do so only to the extent of its State character (soweit seine staatliche Sphäre reicht) [2].

---

1. " Es soll sonach souveräne und nicht souveräne Staaten geben. Allein wann ist ein Staat souverän und wann ein nicht-souveränes Gemeinwesen ein Staat ? " Kelsen, *Allg. Staatslehre*, p. 117.

2. *Allg. Staatslehre*, pp. 465-482. In France, Jellinek's doctrine was taken over, almost literally, by Carré de Malberg. Describing Jellinek's theory as the most complete which now exists on this point — « la plus complète qui existe actuellement sur ce point », *Théorie générale*, I, p. 156 —, Carré de Malberg repeats his opinion, according to which it is both necessary and sufficient, for a community to be a State, to possess and exercise on the basis of its own constitution, i.e. of its own authority of self-determination, all the functions of State power. «...pour qu'une collectivité territoriale soit un Etat, il faut et il suffit qu'elle possède et exerce en vertu de sa propre Constitution, c'est-à-dire de sa propre puissance de s'organiser, toutes les fonctions de puissance étatique. » p. 171. He also insists on the « *compétence de compétence* » being the common characteristic of both sovereign and non-sovereign States, the only difference being that in the case of the former this competence is unlimited, whereas in the case of the latter it is not. How the « *compétence de compétence* » can be limited at all, is not explained, p. 176. Carré de Malberg also explains that, for a community controlled by a sovereign State to be itself a State, it is not enough to possess guaranteed rights of authority (droits de puissance),

The attempt of Jellinek — and others — to vindicate the State character of a dependent entity, has been devastatingly refuted by Kelsen.

Kelsen firstly examines the meaning of a power which is not derived from any outside source and proves conclusively that it means sovereignty and nothing else. It is clear that any power which is " under " a sovereign State is precisely derived from that State's legal order and it is only the power of a sovereign State which is underived. Nor is the conception of a limited power of determining jurisdiction maintainable : for the idea of a limited freedom is a contradiction in terms. It is only the sovereign State which freely determines its own jurisdiction. The inferior legal order is in no way free or independent ; in those spheres (Materien) in which it exercises control, it is precisely unfree and dependent, because such control rests on a delegation by the superior order ; in those spheres in which it does not exercise control, it simply does not exist. (" *ist* sie überhaupt nicht "). It is not legitimate to speak of a dependent State's " own " organ ; there cannot be such an organ, since all organs of dependent entities are at the same time organs of the superior legal order which alone forms the last point of imputability. The difference between the right of coercion of a dependent State and that of a parish is purely arbitrary, the former being as much delegated as the latter. Nor is territorial sovereignty an attribute of the dependent State, but only of the independent one [1].

Having thus, destroyed the argument point by point, Kelsen concludes that all attempts to define the non-sovereign State inevitably end in a definition of a sovereign legal order [2].

As the result of this searching analysis, Kelsen definitely denies the possibility of any legal definition of the non-sovereign State, which would at the same time preserve the notion of State itself by distinguishing it in principle, and not only in degree, from other subordinate legal entities [3].

There can thus be no doubt that a State in the international law sense is, and can only be, an independent State, that is, one directly subordinated to international law. All other territorial entities are not States. The word " State ", as currently used, therefore covers two

but it is moreover necessary that such rights should have the character of State rights. « Pour qu'une communauté dominée par un Etat souverain soit un Etat, il ne suffit pas qu'elle possède des droits de puissance qui lui soient garantis, mais il faut encore et surtout que les droits garantis soient par eux-mêmes des droits d'Etat, de puissance étatique. » p. 177. It is difficult to conceive a more perfect tautology.

1. *Souveränität*, pp. 53-85.
2. " Alle Versuche den Staat unter Ausschaltung des Souveränitätsmomentes zu definieren, laufen schliesslich doch auf die Definition einer souveränen Zwangsordnung hinaus. " *Op. cit.*, p. 55.
3. " Schon die kritische Analyse dieser typischen Konstruktionsversuche des nichtsouveränen Staates beweist, dass es nicht gelingen kann, das Wesen der als " Staat " bezeichneten Ordnung ohne Zuhilfenahme des Souveränitätsmomentes zu bestimmen, wenn der Staat gegenüber den ihm eingegliederten Gemeinwesen *grundsätzlich* unterschieden werden, wenn zwischen der staatlichen Rechtsordnung als einer Gesamtordnung und den ihr subordinierten Teilordnungen eine *absolute* und keine bloss *relative* Differenz bestehen soll. " *Op. cit.*, p. 85. Cf. *Allg. Staatslehre;* " Die Theorie, die auf Souveränität als Wesensmerkmal des Staates verzichtet, dennoch aber nach einer Wesensdifferenz gegenüber der Gemeinde sucht, will den Staat auf der einer Seite relativieren, auf der anderen Seite aber wieder verabsolutieren. » p. 118.

entirely distinct legal phenomena, an independent State and a dependent territorial entity. If the latter is what Anzilotti meant by an " abnormal class ", if this " abnormal class " in reality signifies a completely different legal category, then, and only then, can his argument and his terminology be accepted. But however untidy the terminology not only of everyday life, but even of legal science may still be, it should not be allowed to mislead anyone into believing that the words used describe a reality which in fact they do not [1].

It is this untidy terminology which explains the affirmation by traditional doctrine of the existence of dependent States, coupled with the insistence on their " abnormal " or " exceptional " nature. With regard to State practice, the unreality of this terminology has nowhere been more clearly shown than in the United Nations Organisation. It has been seen that according to Articles 3 and 4 of the Charter, membership of the Organisation was to be limited to States only. In spite of this, dependent communities, i.e. communities lacking State character, were admitted as original members. (India, the Philippines, Lebanon, Syria, and the Ukrainian and Byelorussian Soviet Socialist Republics.)[2]. Did their admission mean that the Organisation recognized their State character? On the contrary, as shown by the San Francisco debates, it was expressly recognized that some signatories were not " States ". Nevertheless the term " State " was maintained and a proposal that the term " signatories " should be used instead of " States " was rejected. The relevant passage of a Report of the Rapporteur of Committee I/I stated with reference to the suggested text :

" ... the definition adopted would serve to calm the fears of certain nations participating in our deliberations which, properly speaking, are not *States* and which for this reason might be denied the right of membership in the Organisation [3]. "

The following comment of Goodrich and Hambro on Articles of the Charter concerning membership is thus entirely justified :

" It is quite clear in view of the attendant circumstances that *the word* " *State* " *is not to be understood in its usual legal sense*. ... The word " State " would therefore appear to be used ... to include any Member of the Organisation, and any political body which at any given time is considered eligible for membership [4]. "

This misuse of the word " State " to cover entities lacking State character is possibly to be explained by the old dualist prejudice

---

1. See Kelsen : " Allein vermag das faktische Vorkommen eines Wortes den von ihm ausgesagten Begriff zu bestimmen ? Wo doch umgekehrt der Gebrauch des Wortes seine Rechtfertigung durch den Begriff erhält ? Kann die Wissenschaft ihre Erkenntnis aus dem Sprachgebrauch holen, wenn *sie* es ist, die den Sprachgebrauch zu regulieren hat ? " *Souveränität*, p. 54.

2. " However, among the communities which signed and ratified the Charter were some whose character as " States " in the sense of international law was doubtful, since they had not the degree of independence from other States which is required by international law... " Kelsen, *The Law of The United Nations*, London, Stevens and Sons Limited, 1950, pp. 59-60.

3. Quoted by Kelsen, *op. cit.*, p. 61.

4. *It. mine, Charter of the United Nations*, Boston, 1946, pp. 79-80. It would have, been simpler to call a spade a spade and, following the example of the League Covenant expressly admit communities or bodies lacking State character, than to misuse the word. This, however, has nothing to do with the present analysis.

according to which only States are subject of international law. Since entities other than States have become subjects of international law, was it not perhaps intended to save an artificial theory by means of an inaccurate terminology, attributing to these entities a character they do not possess? It would have been far simpler to admit that the participation of non-States in international relations, far from being evidence of their State character, represents yet another proof that it is not only States which are subjects of international law.

In conclusion it can be safely asserted that the notion of a " dependent State " is a *contradictio in adiecto*, that it does not stand up to a critical analysis and that it may therefore be legitimately rejected. Its rejection finally confirms that independence is an essential and inescapable condition of statehood.

6. INDEPENDENCE AS A CRITERION OF STATE IDENTITY.

The whole of the foregoing analysis has been undertaken with a view to finding a criterion of State identity. It is believed that such a criterion is provided by the notion of independence. This independence, in law as well as in fact, this comprehensive international delimitation, this differentiation of a State from any other State constitutes its separate personality and determines its identity.

This independence is chiefly, but not exclusively, expressed in the delimitation of the legal order of the State, that is, in its basic norm. Without such delimitation, its territorial and personal delimitation would be reduced to that of a province within a State. This delimitation explains the survival of the independent, i.e. identical State, in the case of changes in its territorial and personal sphere of validity. In this sense Kelsen's statement must be accepted, according to which it is the basic norm which determines the identity of a State [1].

However, the interdependence of the so-called State elements results in the necessity of adding an important proviso to Kelsen's opinion. For just as the delimitation of its legal order, i.e. the surviving basic norm, safeguards the independence and identity of a State in the case of territorial, and personal, changes, so that independence and identity is preserved by the surviving territorial and personal delimitation, when the legal order crumbles. The independence and, consequently, the identity of the State is preserved because the new basic norm, however unrelated to the old one, is still fully delimited from the legal order of any other State, being produced from within the surviving territorial and personal delimitation and is therefore still derived directly from international law [2]. Independence, and identity, would therefore not be preserved when not only the legal order of the State, but also its territorial and personal delimitation were to disappear. This may occur in either of two ways : in the first place,

---

1. " In ...der Grundnorm ruht... die Identität des Staates. " *Allg. Staatslehre* p. 249.
2. See above, pp. 50-51.

the new basic norm may be produced from without the remaining
territorial and personal delimitation of the State concerned, in other
words, it may be the extension to that State of the legal order of another
State ; this would mean the loss of the State's independence, either
open, as in the case of a straightforward annexation, or disguised, as
in the case of a fake revolution. Secondly, the remaining territorial and
personal delimitation may break down from within, with no single new
basic norm being produced from within, and covering, the old
delimitation ; this would also mean the loss of independence, and
identity, by the original State, in favour of several entirely new States
formed on its original territory. It should also be observed that it is
this interdependence of the territorial and personal delimitation and the
delimitation of the legal order which explains the non-identity of the
State suffering a very extensive loss of territory.

To consider, as Kelsen does, the basic norm as providing *exclusively*
the criterion of State identity would postulate its unchangeability. It is
however, submitted that it is not unchangeability, but independence,
as expressed in a comprehensive delimitation under international law,
on the basis of interdependence and interplay of State elements, which
finally determines the identity of a State.

Two important conclusions follow from the above analysis :

In the first place, it fully confirms the submission which has already
been made to the effect that there can be no relation of identity and
continuity between an independent State and a " dependent " one, even
if the two have the same territorial and personal sphere of validity. *A
fortiori*, there can be no relation of identity and continuity between an
independent State and a puppet State which has come to replace it on
the same territory and with regard to the same population. This absence
of identity even results from purely logical considerations : for a State
cannot be identical with a non-State and a non-State cannot carry on
the legal continuity of a State.

Thus there could have been no relation of identity and continuity
between the Polish Republic of the 18th century and the Kingdom of
Poland, as created by the Treaty of Vienna and endowed with a basic
norm by the Russian Emperor [1]. Conversely, the identity between the
Duchy of Finland, forming part of the Russian Empire, and independent
Finland, was denied by the Committee of Jurists investigating the
problem of the Aaland Islands ; after questioning the " State " character
of Finland within the Russian Empire precisely on account of its lack
of independence, the Committee stated :

" It follows from all these facts that the formation of an independent State
of Finland in 1917 and 1918, must be considered, at any rate in several aspects,
as a new political phenomenon and not as a mere continuation of a previously
existing political entity [2]. "

Secondly, if independence provides the criterion of State identity,
then it automatically provides the criterion of State continuity. In

---

1. See Art. 1 of the *Acte Final* of the Treaty of Vienna.
2. *Report*, p. 9.

other words, as long as the independence of a State is preserved, there is no change in the identity, and therefore no break in the continuity of the State. Conversely, the loss of independence produces the extinction of a State, i.e. the final break of its continuity.

Independence is therefore as indispensable to the continued existence of a State, as it is to its birth. A State cannot be born without it. With its loss, it becomes extinct [1].

This leads back again to the problem of State extinction. When is independence presumed to be finally lost ?

There is no difficulty in answering the question when the loss of independence is the result of a clear conventional arrangement, providing for a federation or fusion of independent States [2]. As regards all other cases, it is now possible to give a more detailed answer than at the beginning of this enquiry [3].

Accordingly, the independence of a State is *not* lost when it loses territory, since its independent basic norm remains to carry on its continuity. Similarly, that independence is *not* lost in the case of a revolution, when the basic norm breaks down, on condition that the remaining, i.e. territorial and personal, delimitation of the State survives. On exactly the same basis a State can survive not only revolution, but even a period of anarchy and absence of government, provided that such period is temporary. For, always on the assumption that the State's territorial and personal delimitation survives, the problem is not essentially different from that of revolution : for, during a revolution the old basic norm is more or less immediately replaced by a new one valid for a more or less unchanged territorial and personal delimitation, while in the case of temporary anarchy and absence of government the critical period is merely longer. If, however, the new basic norm finally emerges out of the chaos, with no breaking down of the territorial and personal delimitation either through replacement by several different basic norms or by an extension into the original State of the legal order of another State, then the State's independence, identity and continuity remain unaffected.

The problem becomes quite different when *the entire* international delimitation of the State breaks down, that is to say, when its legal order becomes displaced and when, in addition, there is either an internal breakdown of the territorial and personal delimitation, or an extension into the original State territory of the legal order of another State. In

---

1. Thus Verdross, *Verfassung*, p. 145. Cf. Prof. Guggenheim who — after declaring that no convention, however restrictive can limit the sovereignty of a State — adds : " Sein Rechtsstatus verändert sich jedoch, wenn er freiwillig oder gezwungen seine *unmittelbare* Unterstellung unter das Völkerrecht einbüsst, indem er sich in die Abhängigkeit eines anderen souveränen Staates begibt. " *Lehrbuch*, I, p. 166. Incorrect but consequent with his premises, Jellinek : " Unverändert bleibt ein Staat in solcher Eigenschaft, wenn er vermöge einer *capitis deminutio* von einem souveränen sich in einen nicht-souveränen verwandelt. " *Op. cit.*, p. 275.

2. It is not true to say with Jellinek that this particular case of State extinction is " legal ", whereas any other is " meta-juridical " and incapable of legal valuation, *op. cit.*, pp. 276-279. Every case of extinction, as well as of the birth, of States is capable of a legal evaluation ; only the former is being directly regulated by a legal arrangement.

3. See above, pp. 7-9.

the first case there is undoubtedly State extinction by way of dismemberment. The same should be assumed in the second case. However, the analysis of belligerent occupation has shown that even in that case the immediate extinction of a State is not to be presumed, on condition that its displacement is merely temporary [1]. The extension of a foreign legal order into the State's territory must not only be effective, but also final. Whether, apart from belligerent occupation, any other case of a State surviving the temporary breakdown of all its international delimitation exists under positive international law, has yet to be examined on the basis of State practice [2].

7. INTERNATIONAL RESPONSIBILITY AS A CRITERION OF STATE IDENTITY.

The argument developed above would not be complete without an observation on an all-important consequence of independence : namely, international responsibility.

Independence is a juridical, not a meta-juridical notion. It follows that it cannot imply a *solutio legibus*, an absolute freedom. There is no absolute freedom in law.

Hence the necessary and unavoidable limitation, the price of independence, is international responsibility. The two are inescapably correlative [3].

This being so, international responsibility should furnish exactly the same criterion of State identity and continuity as independence. The continuing, independent State will, naturally enough, continue to be the subject of international responsibility for its own acts and omissions [4]. For, as has been seen, there is no succession to international responsibility, particularly in matters of delict [5]. Consequently, if, after the event which could have cast a doubt about its continued existence, a State will continue to bear, or be made to bear, the whole of its previous international responsibility, it will clearly be the same State, whose continuity has not been broken.

The situation will, however, change immediately independence is lost. It is only logical that international responsibility for the " dependent

---

1. See above, pp. 73-126.
2. See below, pp. 549-587.
3. " It is an admitted principle of international law that a nation possesses and exercises within its own territory an absolute and exclusive jurisdiction, and that any exception to this right must be traced to the consent of the nation, either express or implied. The benefit of this principle equally enures to all independent and sovereign States, and is attended with a corresponding responsibility for what takes place within the national territory. " Diss. Op. by Judge Moore, *P.C.I.J.*, Ser. A 10, p. 68. See also Rousseau : « Si le principe fondamental qui caractérise et résume la condition juridique de l'Etat dans l'ordre international est le principe d'indépendance, c'est avec ce correctif immédiat : *sous réserve de la mise en jeu de la responsabilité internationale de l'Etat.*» *Op. cit.*, p. 250. Prof. Rousseau quotes striking examples of the correlation between independence and responsibility from the most recent cases of dependent entities achieving independence. See Anglo-Iraqui Treaty of June 30, 1930, Art. 8 ; Anglo-Egyptian Treaty of August 26, 1936, Art. 12 ; and Anglo-Burmese Treaty of October 17, 1947, Art. 2, *ibid.*
4. The emphasis is on " its own ". It is hardly necessary to add that even a surviving State cannot be made responsible for acts accomplished in its territory *not* by itself, and over which it has no control ; thus, e.g. the acts of an occupying Power.
5. See above, p. 11.

State " should be borne by the suzerain State, i.e. by the only genuine subject of international law [1]. *A fortiori*, this must be true for a puppet State which is nothing but an instrument, or organ, of the State which has created it. It has been seen that this was the conclusion reached by international law as early as the beginning of the 19th century [2].

A note of warning should, however, be sounded. It is true that independence and international responsibility are inseparable. But the independence of a State need not be declared by anybody [3], while responsibility does. The problem is : by whom and by means of what procedure will this responsibility in a particular case be declared and imposed ?

In an imperfectly organized international community this is, unfortunately, not an exclusively legal function. Thus, international responsibility may be established either by an international tribunal by means of judicial procedure, or by third States by means of a political decision. While the former will supply the definite and positive test of a State's identity and continuity, the latter may not. It has been seen that the continued existence of revolutionary States has been confirmed by international tribunals by way of determining their continued international responsibility [4]. Such decisions are conclusive of the question of State identity and continuity. The same cannot be invariably said with regard to purely political decisions. For it may happen — and it has, in fact, happened [5] — that, out of political considerations and owing to the existing balance of forces, the question of international responsibility is not decided in accordance with general international law. A new State, although in no way identical with one which preceded it, may be effectively burdened with the whole international responsibility which attached to its predecessor. Thus, while a judicial decision will have to be accepted as a criterion of the continuity of the State concerned, the political decision can only be accepted as *prima facie* evidence, to be tested for its decisive character against the principles of general international law.

---

1. Thus Guggenheim : " Wer völkerrechtliches Haftungssubjekt ist, d.h. gegen wen sich die Unrechtsfolgen im Falle eines völkerrechtlichen Deliktes des neu errichteten Staates richten... hängt davon ab, wer mit der Führung der auswärtigen Politik betraut ist. " *Op. cit.*, I, p. 207. Cf. Verdross, *Verfassung*, p. 123.
2. See Kane's report, above, pp. 171-172.
3. See above, pp. 132-153.
4. See above, pp. 38-41.
5. See below, pp. 220, et seq.

PART II

Chapter I.

ITALY.

1. Sardinia's Identity with Italy.

The formation of the Kingdom of Italy was the first important event in modern times to give rise to a discussion of the problem of State identity and continuity.

The process of unification of Italy began with the fruitless attempt of Carlo Alberto of Sardinia, in 1849 ; it gathered irresistible momentum and achieved success after success in years that followed, culminating in the conquest of Rome in 1870. In the place of a multitude of small States — Kingdoms, Duchies, Papal States there finally emerged a single Italian State, extending over the whole of the Peninsula and Sicily, and having its capital in Rome.

There can be no doubt whatever that historically the unification of Italy took place under the *political* leadership of Sardinia. But whether the new Italy was *legally* identical with the old Kingdom of Sardinia, or represented an entirely new State creation, with no relation of continuity between the two is an entirely different matter.

In view of what has been said regarding the historical background of the problem of State identity and continuity [1], the question is a legitimate one. For the change of the Peninsula's political map was radical and violent enough for the question to be asked. As between Sardinia and the new Italy there was a difference of name, size, capital. Even on the assumption of Sardinia's identity with Italy, the former must needs have undergone so deep a transformation that such identity could not be maintained without thorough investigation.

It is therefore not altogether surprising that the problem gave rise to two conflicting theories : the one maintaining that the new Italy was simply the continuation of the old Kingdom of Sardinia, — the other asserting that all pre-existing Italian States, including Sardinia, had ceased to exist, giving place to an entirely new State, the Kingdom of Italy. These two views are contained in two articles by Santi Romano and Anzilotti respectively [2].

---

1. See above, p. 4.
2. *I caratteri giuridici della formazione del Regno d'Italia*, and *La formazione del Regno d'Italia nei riguardi del diritto internazionale*, Rivista di Diritto Internazionale, 1912.

It should be observed straight away that both writers start from an identical doctrinal premise. In the first place they are both equally emphatic in rejecting what have been called the irrelevant tests of State identity and continuity [1]. The formation of Italy involved a change in the State's name, a change in the Royal title, two transfers of the capital and a new State organisation. All these are dismissed by both Romano and Anzilotti, as having no relevance whatever to the problem [2].

What is more important, they both unreservedly accept the customary rule laying down that no territorial changes can affect the identity of a State [3]. Consequently, if, on the legal plane, the historical process of the Risorgimento represented a simple expansion of Sardinia's territorial sphere of validity, then there can be no doubt as to the answer : the Kingdom of Italy must be regarded as a continuation of Sardinia on an enlarged territory and under a new name [4]. Thus the problem of the continuity or disappearance of the Sardinian State involves no doctrinal difficulty. The answer depends entirely on a correct legal appraisal of the historical events leading to the creation of a united Italy : was it a case of Sardinia's expansion by way of annexation, or her union with the other Italian States ?

2. LEGAL NATURE OF THE RISORGIMENTO.

a) *Analysis of Relevant Documents.*

Among the relevant documents of the period there are, in the first place, the plebiscitary formulae of the various Italian provinces. These are far from being uniform :

Tuscany :

" Union with the Constitutional Monarchy of King Victor Emanuel or Separate Kingdom [5] " ;

Emilia :

" Annexation to the Constitutional Monarchy of King Victor Emanuel or Separate Kingdom [6] " ;

Naples and Sicily :

" The people wishes Italy One and Indivisible under Victor Emanuel, Constitutional King and his legitimate descendants [7] " ;

---

1. See above, pp. 127-128.
2. Anzilotti, *op. cit.*, pp. 7-8 ; Romano, *op. cit.*, p. 367. Similarly Huber, *Staaten-succession*, p. 37. Among the irrelevant tests Anzilotti also includes the " so-called natio- nal sentiment ", as incapable of furnishing an objective criterion.
3. Thus Anzilotti : " Il divenire più grande o più piccolo del gruppo organizzato non influisce sulla continuazione della potestà d'impero, perchè significa soltanto che questa potestà si esplica in uno spazio maggiore o minore, si rivolge ad un numero maggiore o minore di uomini ; e da ciò appunto il principio, universalmente ammesso, che non soltanto i mutamenti nella popolazione i quali sono continui, inafferàbili e pressochè irrelevanti, ma anchè i mutamenti territoriali non tolgono l'identità e quindi la continuità dello Stato. " *Op. cit.*, pp. 8-9, *f.-n.* 2.
4. " Una annessione o una serie indefinita di annessioni ad uno Stato non puo dare che un ingrandimento dello Stato annettente, ossia una modificazione di esso, non mai uno Stato nuovo, nel senso di un nuovo soggetto giuridico. " Anzilotti, *op. cit.*, p. 5.
5. Wambaugh, *op. cit.*, p. 514.
6. *Ibid.*, p. 520.
7. *Ibid.*, p. 631.

Umbria and the Marches :

" Do you wish to form a part of the Constitutional Monarchy of King Victor Emanuel II [1] " ;

Venetia :

" We declare our union with the Kingdom of Italy under the Constitutional Monarchical Government of King Victor Emanuel II and His Successors [2] " ;

Rome :

" We desire our union with the Kingdom of Italy under the Constitutional Monarchy of King Victor Emanuel II and His successors [3]. "

It is true that only the Emilian formula actually uses the word " annexation ". However, they all strongly convey the conception of the voting provinces joining the existing Sardinian State, and not the creating of an entirely new State entity by means of a union.

While a certain lack of precision in the plebiscitary formulae may perhaps be explained by the absence of proper coordination or by the ardour of the Italian population, which cared little for legal niceties, this cannot apply to the man who, of all people, must have had a clear view of events. On October 2nd, 1860, Cavour introduced a Bill into the Sardinian Parliament for the annexation of the Central and Southern provinces. The Bill consisted of a single Article :

" The King's Government is authorized to accept and establish by roy a decrees the annexation to the State of those provinces of Central and Southern Italy in which the will of inhabitants to form an integral part of our constitutional Monarchy shall be freely manifested through direct universal suffrage [4]. "

The Royal Sardinian incorporation decrees proceeded on exactly the same lines. Thus, the decrees of March 18, 1860, incorporating Tuscany and Emilia, stated that these provinces

" shall form an integral part of the State from the day of the date of the present decree [5] ".

There was no mention either of a union or of a new State. The provinces in question were simply being incorporated into the existing Sardinian State by the unilateral decrees of the latter. Nor was this fact altered when, begining with the Sicilian and Napolitan incorporation decrees, the formula was enlarged to read :

" shall form an integral part of the Italian State [6] ".

In accordance with the historical and emotional trend of the period, the already enlarged Sardinian State had come to be known as Italy.

The relevant documents thus bear witness to a series of annexations by the Sardinian State and not to a different process. Anzilotti, however,

---

1. *Ibid.*, p. 659.
2. *Ibid.*, p. 686.
3. *Ibid.*, p. 708.
4. *Ibid.*, p. 630. Cf. Cavour's speech on introducing the Bill, *ibid.*, pp. 623-630.
5. *Ibid.*, p. 537.
6. *Ibid.*, p. 654.

considers that the purely formal aspect of a legal act is not sufficient proof of its true nature which has rather to be determined by its content [1].

This objection is generally valid and in order to meet it, it is necessary to investigate the historical events themselves.

b) *Annexation or Union?*

While Romano treats the whole process of Risorgimento as a series of annexations by the Kingdom of Sardinia, whatever their particular form, Anzilotti distinguishes between cession by treaty in the case of Lombardy and Venetia, debellatio in the case of Rome, and a third title with regard to all the remaining provinces. (Tuscany and Emilia, Sicily and Naples, Umbria and the Marches.) On Anzilotti's own admission, clear-cut annexations like those of Lombardy, Venetia and Rome, could have had no effect whatever on the identity and continuity of the annexing State. The survival or disappearance of Sardinia is thus made to depend upon a legal evaluation of the manner in which that State had been joined by all those Italian provinces which it has not acquired either by cession or by debellatio. What, then, was this third title?

To Anzilotti the process, far from being a series of annexations by Sardinia, represents a clear case of union, resulting on the one hand from the will of Sardinia, and, on the other, from the will of the other provinces concerned. The latter was expressed in plebiscites, and Anzilotti argues that the respective plebiscitary formulae were far less important than the genuine desire for a union. He thus rightly considers union as the only possible alternative to annexation. But was there in fact a union between Sardinia and the remaining Italian provinces, with the admitted exception of Lombardy, Venetia and Rome?

i) *Legal Character of the Italian Provinces.*

The primary and indispensable condition of union under international law is that there must be two — or more — subjects of law, whose merger puts an end to their separate existence and creates a new entity, a new subject of international law. There can be no union between a State on the one hand, and a non-descript territory on the other. Such a merger is merely a territorial extension of the State concerned, but can never be a union, failing the other party.

Anzilotti is fully aware of this basic condition. This is why — although obviously impressed by the grandeur of historical events and the spontaneous will to unity of the Italian people, as expressed in the plebiscites — he attempts to relate that will to some existing States. According to him, it was not the will of a legally non-descript population, but the will of Italian States which, corresponding to the

---

1. " Ma non basta che un atto giuridico riceva una certa denominazione o assuma una certa forma per essere quel determinato atto, capace di quei determinati effetti; bisogna vedere se dell'atto in questione ricorrono i requisiti essenziali, o se, per avventura, la veste non copre un contenuto diverso. " *Op. cit.*, p. 6.

will of Sardinia, brought about a union. But owing to the abnormal
and revolutionary situation in those States, the voters, i.e. the population
at large, assumed the function of State organs and in this capacity
formulated and expressed a will imputable to the State and relevant
under international law [1].

The possibility of the population, or a part of the population,
assuming the character of State organs in a revolutionary situation and
thus producing legal effects which are relevant under international law,
is perfectly legitimate. Yet there still remains the question whether,
in the case of Italy, there were any States at all of which the population
could have become an organ, or whether this population expressed its
will outside any State framework, as an incoherent mass on what was
not State territory?

This question must be answered — in full agreement with
Romano — to the effect that there were no such States. The entities
which were joined to Sardinia were, in most cases, either not States
at all (like Umbria and the Marches), or, if they had been States before,
they did not join Sardinia as such. On the contrary, parts of these
States actually joined Sardinia separately, as in the case of the Kingdom
of the Two Sicilies where plebiscites were held, and the whole
incorporation procedure was applied, separately for Sicily and for the
mainland. On the other hand, in the case of Emilia, several previously
existing States (Modena, Romagna, Parma) were joined together for
the purpose of the plebiscite. It is certainly not accidental that Cavour's
bill [2] spoke of the annexation not of States, but of provinces of Central
and Southern Italy. Here the form of the document certainly fully
corresponded to its true content [3].

Thus, a union in the international law sense must be excluded if
only for the lack of a fully-fledged partner to such union.

ii) *The Plebiscites.*

The possibility of a union, of which the plebiscites would have
been the instrument, is further eliminated by the historical fact that
these plebiscites were everywhere held not before, but *after* the actual
annexation of the territories concerned by Sardinia [4]. It should be
remembered that such plebiscites took place in *all* the Italian provinces
which joined Sardinia, in whatever manner the process took place.
They took place in Lombardy, Venetia and Rome *after* the treaty of
cession and the debellatio respectively. The process was, however,
identical in all the other provinces. Thus the Sicilian plebiscite was
preceded not only by the proclamation of the Sardinian Constitution as
the fundamental law of Sicily, but also by Garibaldi's decree, expressly

---

1. " Il valore giuridico di quei plebisciti sta dunque nell' essere i medesimi la mani-
festazione di volontà dello Stato diretta alla fusione col regno di Sardegna ; il popolo, o
meglio i votanti, agirono come organi dello State, e la volontà loro ebbe, in forza della
costituzione o della legge, valore di volontà dello Stato. » *Op. cit.*, p. 18, *f.-n.* 1.
2. See above, p. 193.
3. See above, p. 194.
4. Romano, *op. cit.*, p. 361.

incorporating Sicily into Italy [1]. Prior to the plebiscites the official documents in the various provinces bore the heading " Italy and Victor Emanuel " or, even more clearly, were issued directly " In the name of H.M. Victor Emanuel, King of Italy ". In every case, the plebiscite was proclaimed either by local authorities appointed by Sardinia, or directly by Royal Sardinian Commissioners, and the proclamation was invariably made either in the name of the King, or, at least, bore the significant heading " *Regnando S.M. Vittorio Emanuele* " [2]. It should also be remembered that the Sardinian Parliament passed Cavour's annexation bill of October 2, 1860, *before* voting took place in the provinces to which it related. It is true that the Bill referred to a future annexation, subsequent to the vote, and that Cavour himself emphasized that the will of the people will be " religiously respected " [3]. But in view of the fact that the result of the plebiscite was a foregone conclusion and that the annexation had in fact already been accomplished, this could have been no more than a diplomatic move for the benefit of European cabinets.

Anzilotti attempts to explain away the above facts by placing them into the category of international relations between Sardinia and the other Italian provinces on the basis of the former's " protection " over the latter. But they would indeed be unusual international relations in which not only the authorities of one of the parties are appointed by the other, but in which the internal acts of the one are carried out either by the organs of the other, or in the other's name, or both, — not to speak of the fact that the already proved absence of State character on the part of those provinces militates against the very concept of international relations. The argument clearly fails. What preceded the plebiscites were not " international relations " but straightforward annexations of the plebiscitary territories by Sardinia. The plebiscites, far from being international, were an internal affair of the Italian State [4].

iii) *The Problem of Sardinia's Extinction.*

The creation of a new State of Italy is unthinkable without the extinction of Sardinia. But, far from becoming extinct, it was precisely Sardinia who effected the incorporation of the other Italian provinces by means of her unilateral decrees and laws. In addition, Romano rightly draws the attention to the impossibility of determining the moment of Sardinia's alleged extinction. Did she cease to exist with the publication of the Royal incorporation decrees, or perhaps only with the passing by Parliament of laws approving these decrees? Yet, were they not precisely decrees and laws of Sardinia [5]? And was not the incorporation consummated by these very internal acts of the Sardinian State?

---

1. " The Two Sicilies... constitute an integral part of Italy One and Indivisible, under its constitutional King Victor Emanuel and his descendants. " Wambaugh, *op. cit.*, 637.
2. *Ibid.*, pp. 513, 519, 631, 657, 686.
3. *Ibid.*, p. 627.
4. Romano, *op. cit.*, p. 358.
5. Romano, *op. cit.*, p. 354.

Anzilotti freely admits that this is the most serious objection. Indeed, to reconcile unilateral Sardinian incorporation laws and decrees with the conception of union is a sheer impossibility, and his attempt to do so is anything but convincing. The States, he argues, offered union, not incorporation ; in accepting the offer, Sardinia ceased to exist making room for the new State ; thus, the King, in issuing his decrees, no longer acted as the King of Sardinia, but as Head of the new State [1]. The argument may be ingenious, but in stretches reality to breaking point.

The same may be said with regard to the problem of the number of new States which, if Anzilotti's view is accepted, must have been born and become extinct after every new " union ", until the new Italy assumed her final shape. Admirably true to his original premise, Anzilotti does not hesitate to draw the logical conclusion and to affirm the requisite number of births and deaths or States [2]. The conclusion borders nonetheless on absurdity [3].

iv) *Sardinia's Constitution and Treaties.*

The final argument in favour of an annexation is to be found in the fact that the Sardinian Constitution remained the constitution of Italy and that, in conformity with the principle of variable treaty-limits, Sardinian treaties were extended to the whole of Italy. But even this argument is dismissed by Anzilotti. He admits that in a material sense both the Constitution and the treaties were indeed the same ; they had, however, acquired an entirely new legal basis [4].

In theory there could indeed have been a reception by the new State of the material legal order of the old one, just as there could have been a succession to treaty rights and obligations on a conventional basis. In the first case, however, a new basic norm providing for a reception would have been necessary, but no such new basic norm was ever established and no such reception ever took place. In the second case, an international convention would have been necessary providing for Italy's succession to the treaty rights and obligations of Sardinia, but no such convention was ever concluded. If, in spite of these omissions, both the Sardinian Constitution and the Sardinian treaty rights and obligations extended automatically to the whole of Italy, the only possible conclusion is that the relation between the two was one of identity and not of succession.

---

1. Anzilotti, *op. cit.*, pp. 21-22.
2. " Si hanno... tante successive formazioni statuali quante furono le fusioni degli ex Stati italiani col regno di Sardegna prima a con quello formatosi dalle precedenti fusioni poi. " *Op. cit.*, pp. 28-29.
3. " Ora ciò sembra contrario alla realtà delle cose : di questi Stati, che sarebbero venuti alla luce e che poi, in così tenera età, sarebbero stati colpiti da morte improvisa, nessun finora s'era mai accorto, donde il dubbio che essi vengano creati proprio adesso, per solo còmodo di... costruzione giuridica. ...Certo, non è possibile che si sia avuta l'idea di creare due Stati in un mese e tre in un anno per farne venir meno due, di cui uno dopo soli quattro giorni dalla sua nascità... " Romano, *op. cit.*, pp. 354-355.
4. " I trattati di cui parliamo vennero infatti a riposare sopra un fondamento giuridico nuovo ; materialmente furono vecchi trattati sardi, ma il motivo formale della loro obbligatorietà stava ormai nei nuovi accordi intervenuti fra il regno d'Italia e gli Stati esteri. " *Op. cit.*, pp. 25-26.

3. CONCLUSION.

Differences of opinion among writers concerning the Italian case were not, as has been seen, the result of any dispute as to the rules of international law which applied, but were due entirely to a different interpretation of the facts. Far from being denied, the rule that territorial changes do not affect the identity and continuity of a State, was firmly upheld by both Anzilotti and Romano.

Consequently, with the elimination of what is believed to be the wrong interpretation of the facts, the Italian problem can easily be solved in the light of this rule which is not only absolutely certain, but is also the only one applicable to the case. The answer therefore is that there was no union of the Kingdom of Sardinia with any other State, but only an extension of Sardinia's territorial sphere of validity. The legal order of Sardinia, as identified by its basic norm, continued to be valid within an enlarged territorial and personal sphere of validity. Since this extension could not affect the identity and continuity of the State, the Kingdom of Sardinia continued to exist under the name of Italy.

This conclusion, and the customary rule on which it is based, is borne out by judicial decisions. The Italian Court of Cassation declared on December 3, 1927 :

" ... An international treaty with a State takes effect also in regard to new territories added to the old State and forming with it the new national territory. The united Italian State arose by way of annexation, and that implied the automatic extension of the international treaties to the new territories. The international status of the contracting State does not undergo any change by reason of the growth of its territory [1]. "

The Court of Appeal of Genoa, in its judgment of April 4, 1939, dealt with the formation of Italy in greater detail :

" ... the Kingdom of Italy which arose not from a merger of various States previously existing, but through the incorporation of others by Sardinia, must be considered, for the reason of this formative process, to be a continuation pure and simple of the Kingdom of Sardinia and Piedmont, increased by subsequent annexations. ... It is sufficient to mention, in order to demonstrate the uninterrupted continuity of the original Sardinian State, that the constitution at present in force is still the Sardinian constitution ; that the provisional governments in the territories acted in the name of the King of Sardinia ; that, in due course, the treaties of the other former States fell into abeyance, but not those of the Sardinian State ; that the new kings and new legislatures retained their former denomination... Finally, there is the Sardinian law of March 17, 1861, no. 4671 which proclaims that " The King of Sardinia Victor Emanuel II, assumes for himself and for his successors the title of King of Italy ". It is evident that after the extinction of the other States, the Sardinian State survived. ... The State of Sardinia, which carried out the annexations thus constituted the fundamental nucleus of the Italian State [2]. "

---

1. *Gastaldi v. Lepage Hemery*, A.D., 1927/28, case no. 61.
2. *Costa v. Military Service Commission of Genoa*, A.D., 1938/40, case no. 13. See the judgment of the Court of St. Quentin, of October 30, 1885 : « Considérant qu'il importe peu qu'à la suite d'agrandissements territoriaux par voie de cessions, d'annexions, d'occupation, l'ancien royaume de Sardaigne soit devenu le royaume d'Italie... » Quoted by Huber, *op. cit.*, p. 195.

CHAPTER II.

AUSTRIA (I).

As compared with the problem of Italy's identity, discussed in the previous chapter, the emergence of the Austrian Republic in 1918 involved much more complicated issues which also possessed a highly practical aspect. For any solution of the problem of Austria's status must have produced far-reaching consequences not only for Austria herself, but also for a number of States which, in one way or another, came to be linked with Austria's fate.

The Austrian Republic had an overriding political and economic interest in upholding the thesis of her non-identity with the Austro-Hungarian Empire, as this would mean evading the political and economic obligations of the latter, arising chiefly out of responsibility for the war [1].

This Austrian interest was matched by an equally obvious interest of the Allies who sought to reap the fruits of military victory by insisting on the Republic's identity with the former Empire.

The problem was hardly less important for the new States born out of the ruins of the Austro-Hungarian Empire and also for those States which enlarged their territory at the latter's expense. With regard to the former, the question of Austria's continuity or extinction formed the preliminary question affecting the date of their birth and, consequently, the beginning of their legal jurisdiction in their territories, their personal spheres of validity, and so forth. With regard to the latter, the problem was whether their occupation of Austrian territory fell into the category of belligerent occupation, leaving the former sovereignty intact throughout the area, or whether it was an occupation *terræ nullius*. This, in turn, affected the validity of laws enacted in the territories in question, the problem of nationality of the inhabitants, and the like.

There were thus sufficient conflicting practical interests involved to obscure the picture and to render a solution difficult. None of these matters should, however, be allowed to interfere with a dispassionate and strictly legal examination of the problem.

---

1. This is freely admitted not only by Austrian writers — Kelsen, *Die Verfassung Deutsch-Oesterreichs*, p. 248 ; Verdross, *Der Friedensvertrag von St. Germain*, p. 476 — but also by the Austrian delegation to the peace negotiations at St. Germain-en-Laye, *Bericht über die Tätigkeit der deutsch-österreichischen Friedensdelegation in St. Germain-en-Laye*, vol. I, pp. 164-169 ; see also p. 42 and pp. 74-80.

1. HISTORICAL BACKGROUND.

The dismemberment of the Austro-Hungarian Empire forms a well-known chapter of modern history [1] and only those facts need be mentioned here which are of immediate relevance to the problem under discussion.

It is an undoubted fact that the final break-up of the Dual Monarchy was the result of military defeat. Yet long before this defeat actually took place, signs of the disintegration of the multi-national Empire were not lacking.

" The Hapsburg Monarchy was involved in a war against its own citizens and could only force its people to fight the external foe by employing the coercive agencies of war-time Absolutism [2]. "

" Hapsburg began the war against the Jugo-Slavs, and thereby antagonized the Czechs. In the course of the war it lost Poland without winning the Ukraine. All the subject races set their hopes on the victory of the Entente. Austria-Hungary was waging war not only against external enemies, but also against two-thirds of its own citizens [3]. "

The intense activity of Poles and Czechs in the Allied countries, culminating in the Allied recognition of their National Committees and armies, the drawing together of the South Slavs from both sides of the Serbian border, the Roman Congress of the oppressed nationalities of the Empire of April 1918, the Prague Congress and Resolution of May 1918, the formation of the respective National Councils in territory still formally belonging to Austria-Hungary — these were all milestones on the road to the downfall of the Dual Monarchy and to the creation of independent national States. It only needed final military defeat to seal the fate of the Monarchy.

It was against this background of progressive disintegration that Austria-Hungary officially sued for peace on October 4, 1918. While awaiting the Allied reply it took a last desperate step in order to save its existence : on October 16, the Emperor Charles issued his famous manifesto, proclaiming the transformation of the Monarchy into a federal State and inviting the various nationalities to form " National Councils " to co-operate in carrying it out [4]. It is impossible to disagree with Kelsen's view of this move [5] : a few years earlier such a manifesto could have been the beginning of a new development, which could have avoided the war altogether and consolidated the Monarchy ; in the prevailing circumstances, however, it was merely the signal for total disintegration, given from the highest quarter. (It is not insignificant that it should have come after the collapse of Bulgaria) It was the typical case of " too late " and " too little " at the same time. For,

1. For the history, see Udina, *L'estinzione dell'impero austro-ungarico;* Graham, *New Governments of Central Europe;* Bauer, *The Austrian Revolution;* Kelsen, *Die Verfassung Deutsch-Oesterreichs;* Kunz, *Die völkerrechtliche Option;* Trampler, *Deutsch-Oesterreich;* Heinrich Lammasch, *Seine Aufzeichnungen, sein Wirken und seine Politik;* Temperley, *A History of the Peace Conference in Paris,* vol IV.
2. Bauer, *op. cit.,* p. 27.
3. *Op. cit.,* p. 24.
4. Text quoted by Graham, *op. cit.,* pp. 501-502.
5. *Op. cit.,* p. 247.

in order to placate Hungary, the Manifesto contained an express reservation to the effect that the proposed transformation of the Monarchy would in no way affect the territorial integrity of Hungary. This meant a denial of future free development to the South Slavs, to the Slovaks, to the Rumanians and to the Italians of Fiume. Yet, while antagonizing them all, it did not even placate the Hungarians : on the publication of the Manifesto, the Hungarian Prime Minister Wekerle immediately declared that Hungary had now recovered her freedom of action with regard to the Dual Monarchy, — which was equivalent to proclaiming her separation and was in turn quickly followed by the assertion by Rumanians and Slovaks of their right to self-determination [1].

If the Manifesto sought to catch up with the oncoming revolution and to divert its forces into its own channels, the move miscarried as it was bound to. National Councils there were ; but their creation having preceded the Manifesto, they were already bent on creating national States and not on acting along the federal lines of the Manifesto. On October 16, Polish deputies had already left the Reichsrat ; on October 19, in Prague the Czechs proclaimed their separation from the Monarchy ; on the same day, the South Slavs in Zagreb declared that they had taken over authority over South Slav territory ; on October 25, Italian deputies in the Reichsrat proclaimed their secession from Austria-Hungary. The speed of events was now to become even more rapid : October 28 saw the proclamation of independence in Galicia and the assumption of power by the Polish Liquidation Commission ; on the same day the Czechoslovak State was born. The South Slavs proclaimed their independence on the 29th and the Hungarians on the 30th. It will be observed that the disintegration of the Monarchy proceeded on national lines.

Far from lagging behind, the German-speaking part of the Empire proceeded in exactly the same way. The fact needs stressing ; for it was not a question of certain revolted parts of the Empire seceding from it and leaving the original State intact, except for territorial losses. On the contrary, the action of the several parts of the Dual Monarchy covered the whole of its territory and population, and developed simultaneously on exactly the same lines and principles. The process was universal and not even the nucleus remained untouched. Vienna went the way of Prague, Budapest, Zagreb and Cracow.

On October 21, German-Austrian deputies in the Reichsrat formed a provisional National Assembly and, in their turn, proclaimed their secession from the Monarchy with the intention of forming a national State of their own. The resolution passed on that day declared :

" The German people in Austria has resolved to determine its future State organisation for itself, to form an independent German-Austrian State and to regulate its relations to the other nations by free agreements [2]. "

---

1. Graham, *op. cit.*, pp. 128-129.
2. Graham, *op. cit.*, pp. 502-503.

This sentence gives simultaneous expression to two things : the intention of forming a new State, and the acknowledgment of the dissolution of the Monarchy coupled with the recognition of the future statehood of the other national groups, relations with which were no longer to be an internal matter, but were to fall into the category of inter-State relations governed by international law.

Thus the National Assembly is not to be mistaken for a " National Council " proposed by the Imperial Manifesto. It was nothing of the sort either in fact or in intention. The fact that it was formed by deputies, elected to the former Reichsrat under the old Austrian law was no more than a technicality. This link with the old order was no more than accidental and was not intended to last. On the contrary, the resolution of October 21 stated clearly :

" The German nation in Austria will elect a Constituent National Assembly. ... Until the Constituent Assembly meets, the Reichsrat deputies of the German electoral circumscriptions have the duty of representing the German people in Austria [1]. "

At its first meeting of October 21, the Provisional Assembly elected an Executive Committe (Vollzugsausschuss), entrusting it with the immediate preparation of a State Constitution. The latter was duly drafted and adopted by the Assembly on October 30 [2]. On the same day the Assembly sent a Note to President Wilson, notifying him of the creation of the new State and requesting the opening of negotiations [3].

This date is generally accepted as the date of birth of the new State [4]. This is scrupulously correct. It may serve as an illustration of what is, and what is not, legally relevant to the creation of a State [5]. There was an independent act of creation, derived from no other State order, there was a basic norm, valid with regard to a certain territory and population, however loosely delimited, and, finally, the immediate effectiveness of this new order. On the other hand, there was no international recognition, no fixed nationality, and there were no defined frontiers ; beyond the basic norm, the legal order was not yet developed [6].

---

1. Graham, *op. cit.*, p. 503.
2. *Beschluss über die grundlegenden Einrichtungen der Staatsgewalt;* text quoted by Udina, *op. cit.*, pp. 116-120.
3. See below, p. 216.
4. " Mit dieser seiner ersten Verfassung entstand der neue Staat Deutschösterreich, nicht nur *de iure*, sondern auch *de facto*, denn diese Verfassung wurde sofort, ohne auf irgend einen Widerstand zu stossen, durchgeführt. " Kelsen, *op. cit.*, p. 247. Similarly Udina, *op. cit.*, p. 120. This is also confirmed by judicial decisions : e.g. Verwaltungsgerichtshof of Vienna on February 11, 1921, *A.D.*, 1919/20, case no. 7 ; the Czechoslovak Supreme Administrative Court, *ibid.*, case no. 4 ; the Austrian Administrative Court, *A.D.*, 1927/28, case no. 11.
5. See above, pp. 163-164.
6. " In welcher Lage waren wir da ? Wir waren ein Staat ohne festes, gesichertes, auch nur rechtlich festgestelltes Gebiet. Wir waren ein Staat, ohne abgegrenzte Staatsbürger. Wir sahen uns, um die rechtlichen Einrichtungen zu schaffen, genötigt, zuerst aus der unbestimmten Allgemeinheit des alten Oesterreichs das herauszulösen, was uns an Boden und an Menschen gehört. " Chancellor Renner in the National Assembly, on December 4, 1918 ; quoted by Trampler, *op. cit.*, p. 110.

The date of October 30, 1918, is therefore the date of the formation of the new State, — notwithstanding the later and different version given by the official Austrian delegation at Saint-Germain-en-Laye [1]. The fixing of this date has important consequences. The Dual Monarchy did not, in fact, cease to exist until several days later. The exact date is difficult to establish ; the most obvious one would seem to be November 11, the date of the qualified abdication of the Emperor. The inexactitude of this date is, however, readily recognized : for the abdication — such as it was — related exclusively to Austria and not to Hungary, for which a separate abdication act was issued on November 13. The last international act of the Monarchy was the signing of the armistice at Villa Giusti, on November 3, 1918, i.e. before the abdication, while several liquidation agencies still carried on after the abdication. The last Imperial Cabinet, under Professor Lammasch, took office as late as October 28 [2].

If then the new German-Austrian State was born on October 30, and the old Empire still lingered on at least until November 11, then it must logically be assumed that there was a period of co-existence of two different legal orders on one and the same territory [3]. This was no legal fiction, but a tangible reality. Bauer describes how, after the creation of the German-Austrian State and its first organs, imperial liquidation agencies were still functioning in the same premises as the newly created organs [4]. The same picture was presented by Chancellor Renner in his speech in the National Assembly of December 4, 1918 [5]. The Austrian case thus presents another illuminating example, — in addition to belligerent occupation, — of the possibility of a simultaneous co-existence of two different State legal orders in the same territory, however abnormal such co-existence may be.

In the meantime, the legal order of German-Austria was developing. While the Constitution of October 30 was still vague

---

1. See below, pp. 212-213.
2. It is interesting to note that the Reichstat met for the last time on November 12, after having previously met on October 30, i.e. on the very day of the meeting of the revolutionary National Assembly, members of the latter being at the same time members of the former. The Upper House met for the last time on October 30. The last " Reichsgesetzblatt " appeared on November 12. Udina, op. cit., p. 62.
3. The point is seen in all clarity by Udina, who speaks of a " compenetrazione, coesistenza di ordinamenti giuridici diversi nell'ambito dello stesso territorio, ma vigenti entro sfere personali diverse. " Op. cit., p. 61.
4. " In all the central offices, an Austrian State secretary appointed by the Political Council sat beside an Austrian Minister appointed by the Emperor. This duality of republican and monarchical adminis.ration in the same building was anomalous. " Op. cit., p. 60. Cf. Redlich, Heinrich Lammasch als Ministerpräsident, in Heinrich Lammasch, particularly, pp. 177-181.
5. " Wir haben bei der Uebernahme der Zentralgewalt einen Knäuel von Schwierigkeiten vorgefunden, der gelöst werden musste. Jedes Ministerium war ein Besitzstand des alten Oesterreichs, also ein internationaler Besitzstand. Dieser Besitzstand war herrenlos geworden. Innerhalb dieses Besitzstandes war der deutsche Besitzstand, der in unseren Staatsämtern sich ausdrückte, nur ein aliquoter Teil. Wir mussten nun kraft der Gebietshoheit des Staates die Verantwortung für das Ganze übernehmen, ohne die Absicht zu haben, über das Ganze zu verfügen. Es musste also in jedem Ministerium der Teil, der der Gesamtheit übrigbleibt, ausgeschieden und als sogenannte Liquidierungsmasse festgehalten werden, auf der anderen Seite musste der deutsch-österreichische Besitzstand fest in die Hand genommen und festgehalten werden. " Quoted by Trampler, op. cit., pp. 111-112.

about the final form of the State, the next law, passed on November 12 [1], definitely proclaimed the Republic [2]. There followed the law of November 22, fixing the territorial limits of the State pending the conclusion of international agreements, the law of December 5, concerning nationality, and the law of December 19, amending the constitution of October 30.

The State founded on October 30 was thus beginning to take shape. The problem to be examined is that of the relation of this State to its predecessor? In other words : was it a new State or a continuation of the old?

2. SCOPE OF THE PROBLEM.

a) *Legal Nature of the Austro-Hungarian Empire.*

Before the above question can be answered, it is necessary to determine which is the subject of international law with whom the identity, or non-identity, of the Austrian Republic is sought to be established. In other words : with precisely what State was the new Austria supposed to be identical or non-identical?

Any enquiry of this nature must necessarily start with an investigation into the legal character of the Austro-Hungarian Monarchy.

The Note of the Austrian Delegation to the peace negotiations in Saint-Germain-en-Laye, of June 16, 1919, makes the following point :

" Now, the draft which has just been submitted to us mentions an " Austria " with which the Powers were dragged into war (Preamble, para. 2) when *before* the collapse of the Austro-Hungarian Monarchy the idea of a war against the former " Austria " would have been inconceivable, considering that by virtue of the fundamental laws in force, only the Dual Monarchy of " Austria-Hungary " was invested with the juridical power to perform acts of international life [3]. "

The State whose legal nature is to be investigated, is the one based on the " Compromis " of 1867, the famous reform which, by means

---

1. *Gesetz über die Staats- und Regierungsform von Deutschösterreich.*
2. See Udina, *op. cit.*, p. 123.
3. Here, the Delegation adds the following foot-note : " ...The Commission should... recognize that a State by the name of Austria never existed *de iure*, and that consequently we could not be its successors nor represent it here. According to its original laws, voted in due form, the State in question never bore any other name than " The Kingdoms and countries represented in Parliament " (Reichsrat). These kingdoms and countries were, according to the text of the law, the kingdoms of Bohemia, Dalmatia, Galicia, etc. Therefore those are the countries that made the war, together with the Hungarian crown lands ; consequently, *de iure* and *de facto* : Bohemia, Galicia, Dalmatia, etc., all together. In the eye of constitutional law, Austria was only the designation of the ruling house, the " Domus Austriae ", but not of a special territory. The name " Austria " has been applied in current use, but can not be interpreted otherwise than as a general designation including equally the Bohemian, Polish, Jugoslav and Italian territories of the House of Austria. Neither the entire army nor that part of it belonging to Cisleithania has ever borne the name of the " Austrian Army ", it was, on the contrary, known only as the " Imperial and Royal Army ". The principle was even adopted that every army in the field should include in its formation troops of German, Czech, Magyar and Jugoslav nationality. These are the facts and this is the truth of the situation *de iure* ". English translation in Almond N. and Lutz R. H., *The Treaty of St. Germain*, p. 243. Original and French translation in : *Bericht*, vol. I, pp. 164-165.

of two internal laws (one Austrian and one Hungarian), changed the formerly unitary Monarchy into a composite State [1]. On the whole, there is a large measure of agreement as to the character of a " Real Union " which the Monarchy then assumed. No doubt, two distinct entities could from now on be discerned : the common monarch was Emperor of Austria and King of Hungary ; there were separate governments and parliaments, and a clear delimitation of frontiers ; the two parts of the realm were linked together in a customs union. On the other hand, all common affairs were in the hands of the so-called " Delegations " of the two Parliaments ; there was in Vienna a common Cabinet for the whole of the Monarchy, consisting of the Ministers for Foreign Affairs, War and Finance ; there was one foreign service, one army and navy, one supreme military court, one exchequer, one State Audit Office and one State bank. The State as a whole had a distinct name : while the Austrian " Reichshälfte " was called " Kingdoms and Countries represented in Parliament " (" die im Reichsrat vertretenen Königreiche und Länder "), and the Hungarian one " Lands of the Holy Hungarian Crown " (" Länder der heiligen ungarischen Krone "), the entire realm was, according to the imperial decree of November 14, 1868, called the " Austro-Hungarian Monarchy " (" Oesterreichisch-Ungarische Monarchie " or " Oesterreichisch-Ungarisches Reich "). What is most important : the passive and active right of legation was vested in the whole realm ; international negotiations were conducted, and treaties concluded, by Austria-Hungary as a whole [2]. Thus, whatever the internal position of the two " Reichshälften ", the one and only subject of international law was the Austro-Hungarian Monarchy [3].

---

1. Fo. details and analysis see Udina, *op. cit.*, pp. 15-37.
2. Cf. Klein, *Oesterreich-Ungarn* in *Wörterbuch des Völkerrechts*, vol. II, p. 205.
3. As a result of a searching analysis, Udina affirms " la unica soggettività giuridica internazionale dell'Austria-Ungheria. " *Op. cit.*, p. 36. Cf. Fauchille : « Au point de vue extérieur, les deux Etats apparaissent comme une souveraineté simple. Ils n'apparaissent jamais individuellement, représentés par des organes particuliers. » *Op. cit.*, I, p. 230. A contrary opinion was expressed by the Permanent Court of International Justice : " Although Austria and Hungary had common institutions based on analogous laws passed by their legislatures, they were none the less distinct international units. " Ser. B, 8, p. 43. This statement is subtantiated only by the fact that an arbitration had taken place between Austria and Hungary in 1903. But here two observations may be made : first, it is a fact that Austria and Hungary had frontiers between them and even entered into treaty relations with one another, — although this happened only after the 1907 modification of the « Compromis »; but their international character could be proved only by their international relations with the outside world, and not with one another. No one claims that the Swiss cantons possess international personality although they do have frontiers and conclude agreements with one another. Besides, here again, the possibility of arbitration between cantons is clearly admitted by Art. 102, p. 5 of the Swiss Constitution. Secondly, the whole exceptional interest of the arbitration in question consisted precisely in the fact that it took place between two entities which together constituted one subject of international law. Thus Blociszewski. *L'œil de la Mer, un conflit de frontière entre l'Autriche et la Hongrie réglé par jugement arbitral, RGDIP,* 1903, pp. 419-435. The separate international personality of the two " Reichshälften " was also asserted by the Court of Appeal of the Canton of Zurich, in a decision of July 5, 1920 : " ...each of the two States had international personality, and each of them was a contracting State in the international treaties concluded by the common organs". *A.D.,* 1919/20, case no. 45. To the contrary, the Tripartite Claims Commission of United States, Austria and Hungary, on May 25, 1927 : " The former Austrian Empire and the former Kingdom of Hungary, while existing as independent States, had no international status. " *A.D.,* 1927/28, case no. 54.

Nor did this character of the Dual Monarchy change as a result of the Austro-Hungarian agreement of 1907 which to a certain extent modified the " Compromis " of 1867. It is true that the latter replaced the existing customs union between Austria and Hungary by a treaty of commerce and introduced a new method of signing commercial treaties with foreign States : henceforth they were to be signed not by the Foreign Minister or a common representative alone, but also by one representative each of Austria and of Hungary. Nevertheless they were still the treaties of the Dual Monarchy [1].

Thus, whatever the internal organisation, there was only one subject of international law : the Austro-Hungarian Empire. It was this subject of international law which declared war on Serbia on July 28, 1914, thus starting the general conflagration of the First World War, and it was this same subject which sued for armistice and concluded one in Villa Giusti, on November 3, 1918.

The conclusion of the armistice was the last international act performed by the Dual Monarchy. A few days later it finally ceased to exist.

The fact of its extinction was too patently obvious to be contested from any quarter, either in theory or in practice [2]. It was freely admitted by the Allies [3]. It found its most official expression in the famous Preambles to the Treaties of Saint-Germain and Trianon, which read :

" Whereas the former Austro-Hungarian Monarchy has now ceased to exist..."

This being so, the question of new Austria's identity with the Austro-Hungarian Empire could not possibly arise ; it was automatically excluded, as indeed it could hardly nave been seriously maintained [4].

As Udina correctly points out, this situation was capable of only two interpretations : either the total break-up of the Monarchy resulting in the formation of a number of new States, or else the mere breaking of the union between its component parts [5]. Under the latter solution, the new Austria would have been identical with the " Kingdoms and Countries represented in Parliament ", while Hungary would have been identical with the " Lands of the Holy Hungarian Crown ". In fact, the question of new Austria's legal status, in the form in which it came

---

1. That the 1907 reform did not endow the component parts of the Empire with independent international personality is convincingly shown by Udina, op. cit., p. 24 et seq. Pro foro interno Udina points out the special position of Bosnia and Herzegowina which were not subordinaced to the sovereignty either of Austria or of Hungary, but to the common sovereignty of the Empire, op. cit., pp. 32-34.

2. See Guggenheim, Beiträge, p. 189.

3. « Appelées à consacrer la dissolution spontanée de l'ancienne monarchie austro-hongroise, les puissances alliées et associées... » La réponse des Puissances alliées et associées aux remarqves de la délégation autrichienne sur les conditions de paix, Bericht, II, p. 318.

4. " Non merita poi d'esser nemmeno presa in considerazione l'opinione, di carattero politico piuttosto che giuridico, per cui, basandosi su delle pure apparenze, si è voluto talvolta vedere nelle sola Austria odierna la continuatrice dell'antica Monarchia. " Udina, op. cit., pp. 13-14.

5. Op. cit., pp. 11-13.

up for discussion concerned its possible identity not with the Dual Monarchy, but only and exclusively with the old Austrian "Reichshälfte", i.e. with Cisleithania.

In view of what has been said concerning the legal nature of the Dual Monarchy, it may legitimately be asked whether the question, as so formulated, was admissible at all. It has been suggested by Prof. Guggenheim that, notwithstanding the extinction of the Dual Monarchy, the rights and obligations of its component parts remained [1]. But were there any such international rights and obligations which were specifically theirs, and not those of the Union as a whole? The preceding analysis has shown that this was not the case. Certainly, the obligations and responsibilities arising out of the war declared and conducted by the Union, under its common foreign policy, with its common army, after an armistice concluded by the Union as such, were not those of its component parts and can hardly fall under the heading of separate obligations mentioned by Prof. Guggenheim. In any case, could an undoubted subject of international law, such as the Austrian Republic, be at all identical with an entity which was *not* such a subject [2]?

The fact remains that it was precisely this relation of identity and continuity which formed the subject of discussion in the Austrian case. But it also remains a fact that, by being formulated in this way, the question was distorted and subjected to an initial doubt as to its very correctness and admissibility [3].

b) *Identity or Succession.*

Such a formulation of the problem was not the only initial sin committed during the Austrian discussion which was further obscured by the ever recurring confusion between the notions of identity and succession.

---

1. " Die Auflösung der Realunion bedingt somit keine Staatennachfolge, führt demnach dazu, dass diejenigen Rechte und Pflichten, die speziell Rechte und Pflichten der Union waren, untergegangen sind. Davon sind aber streng zu unterscheiden die völkerrechtlichen Rechte und Pflichten der Staaten, welche die Realunion vereinbart haben, die aus sich berechtigt und verpflichtet bleiben, soweit die Berechtigungen und Verpflichtungen gesondert ausgeübt werden können. " *Op. cit.*, p. 189.

2. See the opinion of the Committee of Jurists on a similar question concerning Finland, above, p. 187 : the opinion seems valid notwithstanding all the differences of historical and political background.

3. Before an enquiry into the problem thus limited, a similar question concerning Hungary may be briefly disposed of. Her identity with the former component part of the Dual Monarchy, asserted by the Allies, was not only not contested, but, on the contrary, emphatically confirmed by Hungary herself : « Nous voulons établir tout d'abord le fait que la Hongrie n'est pas un Etat nouveau-né après le démembrement de la Monarchie Austro-Hongroise, et ne peut être comparée, sous ce rapport, ni à l'Autriche allemande, ni à l'Etat tchéco-slovaque, ni à la Yougoslavie. Au point de vue du droit, la Hongrie d'aujourd'hui est restée telle qu'elle était dans son passé de plus de mille ans. Elle conserva sa situation d'Etat indépendant lors de son entrée dans l'union avec l'Autriche, et pendant toute l'existence de cette union appelée Monarchie Austro-Hongroise. » *Négociations de la paix hongroise*, publié par le Ministère hongrois des Affaires Etrangères, Budapest 1920, vol. I, p. 33. See also Notes of the Hungarian Delegation of January 14, 1920, as well as the oral statement of Apponyi of January 16, 1920. The discussion of the correctness or otherwise of the Hungarian thesis falls outside the scope of this study.

It must be clearly understood that the problem concerned *not* the Austrian Republic's succession to old Austria, but its identity with old Austria. There was a natural and unquestioned relation of succession between old Austria and all the new States, a relation which was freely accepted by the Austrian Republic herself. Consequently, if approached from the point of view of succession, the whole argument concerning new Austria's international status would have been completely meaningless.

In view of what has already been said regarding the two different and autonomous notions of succession on the one hand and State identity and continuity on the other [1], the above observations would seem so obvious as to be superfluous. Yet, they are called for by the above-mentioned confusion persistently introduced into the discussion by all sides, not excluding the Austrians themselves. In the documents of the period " succession " is sometimes used to signify " identity ", while sometimes the term is correctly employed to describe its opposite notion.

The correct view was expressed by the Austrian Delegation in its Note of August 6, 1919 :

" Its (the new Austria's) international personality could not, under any point of view, be identified with the former Austro-Hungarian Monarchy, nor with the former Austria ; on the contrary, as a successor of the acquired rights and of the obligations incurred or assumed, it is precisely in the same situation as all the other States formed out of the former Monarchy [2]. "

It was on this correct interpretation that the solution which the Austrian Delegation proposed to the Allies with regard to the obligations of the former Monarchy was based : namely, a proportional succession to these obligations by Austria and the other succeeding States. Only where there is no identity, can there be succession.

Yet, there was no consistency in the Austrian presentation of the case. Thus, in one and the same speech of June 2, 1919, at Saint-Germain, Chancellor Renner, while properly describing all the resulting States, including Austria as " all the succeeding States ", declared that

" she can no more than the former (i.e. the other new States) be considered the successor of the late Monarchy [3] ".

This confusion even penetrated into the Austrian Constitution, as modified to conform to the Saint-Germain Treaty [4] and was consistently upheld by Austrian courts. Thus, the Austrian Supreme Court stated on January 14, 1930

" that the Republic of Austria in no respect became a legal successor to the Imperial Reich, that it appeared rather as a State newly created by the Austrian people... [5] ".

1. See above, pp. 9-14.
2. Almond-Lutz, *op. cit.*, p. 239 ; *Bericht*, II, p. 93.
3. Almond-Lutz, *op. cit.*, p. 62 ; *Bericht*, I, p. 40.
4. See below, p. 230.
5. *Repertory of Decisions (Austria) Case*, A. D., 1929/30, case no. 10. See also A. D. 1919/22, case no. 39 ; A. D., 1931/32, case no. 32.

The same confusion can be seen on the Allied side : while assuming the Republic's identity with the Empire, the Allies did not hesitate to describe the former as " *the* successor " of the old Monarchy [1].

This fundamental error has been noticed, though not particular emphasized, by writers on the subject. Kelsen declares that the question to be answered is whether the Austrian Republic was identical with the old Empire *or* whether it was merely its successor alongside the other new States [2].

Similarly, Udina makes the necessary distinction [3]. Verdross also seems to be aware of it, although he does not formulate it clearly ; but his whole thesis of the continued validity of treaties concluded between the Dual Monarchy and Germany, coupled as it is with his emphasis on Austria's non-identity with the Empire, can only be explained by his differentiation between identity and succession [4].

The problem is not only one of correct terminology, which would itself be important enough. But, moreover, this confusion between identity and succession necessarily resulted in the wrong solution on the purely practical level. Basdevant, who has formulated the distinction most clearly [5], claims that all the errors made with regard to the true nature of the Austrian State can be traced back to the failure to draw this necessary distinction [6].

It would perhaps be optimistic to assume that, had the distinction been properly drawn, the solution of the Austrian problem would have been perfect. It might, however, have been more correct than it actually was. For no correct answer can be given to a badly formulated question.

---

1. See below, p. 222.
2. Exception must, however, be taken to Kelsen's manner of formulating the problem. Speaking of a revolutionary break of continuity between the old and the new Austria, he maintains that such a break can only be asserted from the point of view of the primacy of internal law, but that it disappears if considered from the point of view of the primacy of international law. This is an obvious truth and, if the case of post-war Austria had indeed been limited to an internal revolution, it is submitted that — as in the case of Germany — no problem would have arisen under international law. Since, however, there was far more than merely a revolution in Austria, Kelsen's emphasis on this particular aspect only distorts the picture. But what follows is even more surprising : " ...stellt man sich auf den Standpunkt eines Primates des VR, dann freilich ergibt sich als notwendige Konsequenz eine rechtliche *Kontinuität* zwischen Deutsch-Oesterreich und dem alten Oesterreich und es bleibt dann nunmehr die bereits oben angedeutete Frage zu entscheiden, ob Deutsch-Oesterreich mit dem alten Oesterreich *identisch* oder nur — gemeinsam mit den anderen auf seinem Gebiete entstandenen Nationalstaaten — als *Rechtsnachfolger* Oesterreichs anzusehen sei. " *It. mine, op. cit.*, p. 249. It is impossible to tell what Kelsen really means by " Kontinuität " in this context, especially as opposed to identity. For if there is continuity, then, automatically, there is identity, and there is no longer an alternative between identity and succession.
3. " ...problema più propriamente della successione da Stato a Stato e che puo essere risolto indipendemente da quello della « novità » o meno de¹ successore, presupponendo anzi questa, nel caso concreto, e in generale *la non identità* del successore col predecessore... " *It. mine, op. cit.*, p. 196. See also Kelsen, *Naissance de l'Etat*, p. 633.
4. *Gelten die... Staatsverträge... weiter...? Deutsche Juristenzeitung*, 1920.
5. « ...confusion entre deux problèmes qu'il faut soigneusement distinguer ; d'abord la question de savoir s'il y a eu extinction ou continuité de l'Etat autrichien ancien ; ensuite le problème désigné par le terme « succession d'Etats » qui se préoccupe des conséquences de l'extinction, du démembrement, de l'annexion des Etats et de la naissance ou des modifications corrélatives d'autres Etats. » *Condition internationale de l'Autriche*, p. 89.
6. « C'est faute d'avoir fait cette distinction que toutes les erreurs sur la véritable nature de l'Etat autrichien sont commises. » *Ibid., f.-n.*

3. The Austrian Problem in the Light of General International Law.

The solution of the problem of the Austrian Republic's legal status follows automatically once the question of old Austria's fate has been answered. In particular : did old Austria become extinct at the end of the First World War ? If it did, then, obviously, the new Republic could not have been identical with it and could not have continued its legal personality. The problem to be investigated therefore concerns the extinction or survival of the Austrian half of the Dual Monarchy (although such an enquiry is somewhat unusual with regard to an entity which has not been a fully-fledged subject of international law).

However complicated the facts and however conflicting the interests involved, it is believed that the solution of this problem can be arrived at relatively easily by a correct application of the customary rules, discussed above [1] to the historical facts.

a) *Revolutionary Dismemberment.*

It is uncontested that, towards the end of the war, simultaneous revolutions broke out over the entire Cisleithanian territory, including its German-speaking part. It is further uncontested that they were " anti-State " revolutions, centrifugal in character and aimed at a separation from the original State. It is also a fact that they all achieved their object.

With regard to the German-speaking nucleus of old Austria, the question must be asked whether the process was merely a secession or revolutionary dismemberment ? The first alternative would involve the survival of old Austria, the second its extinction.

It has been seen that, in principle, a State cannot survive the simultaneous impact of territorial loss and revolution, since its entire delimitation under international law is destroyed by such a combined process, there being no elements left to carry on its continuity. It has also been seen, however, that a State can survive such simultaneous blows on condition that the territorial loss involved is relatively small, — in other words, on condition that the new revolutionary basic norm is valid for what is *more or less* the previously existing territorial and personal delimitation. This quantitative element provides the decisive criterion for the distinction between a secession, which even a revolutionary State can survive, and revolutionary dismemberment which it cannot [2]. It is the facts of the case which must therefore decide the issue.

The old Austrian " *Reichshälfte* " (i.e. without Hungary) covered an area of over 300.004 square kilometers with a population of 28.572.360. When the new revolutionary basic norm of the Austrian Republic came into existence, its sphere of validity was a territory of 79.833 sq. kms. with a population of 6.357.962. In other words, Austria had lost nearly

---

1. See above, pp. 15-73.
2. See above, pp. 61-63.

three quarters of her pre-war territory and over three quarters of her pre-war population. A part of former Austrian territory consisting of 78.554 sq. kms. with a population of 10.026.488 became the territory and population of the new Czechoslovak Republic which alone thus had a larger population than new Austria. A further 79.562 sq. kms. with a population of 8.173.528 went to Poland, which thus also acquired from old Austria practically the same amount of territory and more population than the Austrian Republic. 28.447 sq. kms. with a population of 1.626.698 went to Yugoslavia ; 10.388 sq. kms. with a population of 795.226 to Rumania ; 23.164 sq. kms. with a population of 1.589.472 to Italy, and 6 sq. kms. with a population of 2.986 to Fiume [1].

In the light of these facts and figures can it be reasonably maintained that the simultaneous revolutionary processes in old Austria merely resulted in a secession of a few border territories, leaving the original State essentially untouched in its international delimitation?

The answer is not, and cannot be, in doubt. The former basic norm which had been valid for the old Austrian territory, was replaced by several new basic norms valid for several new territorial and personal delimitations, among which the new Austrian State was not even the largest. The factual situation did not even remotely resemble a secession ; it was dismemberment, pure and simple. Unable to survive such dismemberment, failing any such protective rule of international law, old Austria became extinct, the greater part of its former territory and population becoming territory and population of several other States, of which only two were born entirely within that territory and population : Austria and Czechoslovakia. They both came into existence in exactly the same way and they were both equally different from Cisleithania [2].

This then is the compelling, and only admissible, conclusion under international law. It has been firmly upheld by writers who have devoted special attention study to the subject [3].

---

1. Brockhausen K., Der Friedensvertrag von St. Germain, in Neu Oesterreich edited by Dr. E. Stepan, Amsterdam und Wien, 1923.
2. « ...la nouvelle Autriche est aussi différente de l'ancienne Monarchie que la Tchécoslovaquie, qui vient de se créer exactement comme la République autrichienne par voie de révolution sur le territoire de l'ancienne Autriche. » Kelsen, Naissance de l'Etat, p. 633.
3. Kelsen, loc. cit.; Verdross, Verfassung, p. 151. « En Autriche, il ne s'est pas produit un changement de constitution juridique du groupe social... Il y a eu création de plusieurs groupes sociaux soumis chacun à une constitution nouvelle. La formation de ces constitutions révolutionnaires a amené le démembrement du groupe social antérieur, le démembrement de l'ordre juridique organisant. » Basdevant, op. cit., p. 88. " The Austro-Hungarian Empire simply split up, all the component parts winning their independence from the old régime. The retention of the name " Austria " or " Hungary " is purely accidental and has no legal significance. One component part is just as much or just as little responsible for the obligations of the old Austro-Hungarian Empire as any other. To pick out the new Republic of Austria and new Hungary to alone bear this burden involves a legal error. " Borchard, Sequestrated Property and American Claims — the Treaties of Versailles and Berlin, A. J., 1925, pp. 355-359 ; Kunz, op. cit., II p. 120 ; " ... (the Austrian Empire)... si estingue totalmente, per smembramento, o, più precisamente, per cessazione della potestà d'impero e per disgregazione degli elementi materiali, popole e territorio. " Udina, op. cit., p. 12.

It is this true picture of revolutionary dismemberment, and not of secession, which is correctly reflected in the Austrian documents of the period. It is in the light of the above considerations — and not of new Austria's political interests which are of no relevance to this enquiry — that the Austrian thesis of the Republic's non-identity with the Empire must be seen and examined. This thesis was introduced at the very outset of the Saint-Germain Conference by Chancellor Renner, head of the Austrian Delegation, in his speech on receiving the first draft of the Treaty on June 2, 1919 :

" The Danube Monarchy against which the Allied and Associated Powers have waged war, and with which they have concluded an armistice, has ceased to exist. The 12th of November 1918 may be considered the day of its death. From this day on, there was no Monarch any more, nor a big Power over which he could hold his sway, there was no more the fatal dualism, neither an Austrian nor Hungarian Government, no army and none other recognized institution vested with public power. There only remained eight nationalities deprived of any public organisation and overnight they created their own parliaments, their own governments, and their own armies, in short, their own independent States. In the same way as the other national States our new Republic too has sprung into life, consequently she can no more than the former be considered the successor of the late Monarchy. From this very point arises the fundamental contradiction under which we are labouring the most and which is waiting to be cleared before this high Assembly [1]. "

It is to be regretted that, in trying to present the general outline of the problem in the simplest possible way, the Chancellor achieved simplicity at the cost of accuracy. The statement quoted calls for more than one correction : the Monarchy may have died on November 12, but the succeeding States, including the new Austria, had already previously come into existence ; November 12th did not find a collection of helpless and disorganized national groups, suddenly deprived of " their " State ; the latter did not create their new States " overnight ", after having patiently waited for the death of the Monarchy ; on the contrary, their action contributed to its death [2]. Above all, the Austrian Republic was not born *after* the collapse of the Monarchy, but, as has been seen, a good while *before* [3]. Why should the Austrian Chancellor who himself was among the creators of the new State, have given a false account of its birth ?

Udina considers this move as an " inaccurate concession " [4]. It may be added that it was a concession which was not only inaccurate but frankly opportunist. It was necessary to the Austrian thesis to prove that the new Republic had nothing whatever in common with the Monarchy, and the simplest way of arriving at this result was to allege that it was born after the Monarchy had become extinct. To develop the highly subtle argument of two legal orders which, while co-existing in time and space, were yet entirely foreign to one another [5], would have meant further complication of an already sufficiently

---

1. Almond-Lutz, *op. cit.*, p. 62 ; *Bericht*, I, p. 40.
2. " Der Untergang der Monarchie erfolgte von innen her... " Kunz, *op. cit.*, II, p. 113.
3. See above, p. 203.
4. *Op. cit.*, p. 125, *f.-n.* 1.
5. See above, p. 203.

complicated problem, and this before an audience which was none too willing to listen to legal subtleties. This would seem to be the only explanation of a plainly inaccurate date being given for the creation of the new State, a date which was, however, officially adopted by the Austrian Delegation.

The statement may be historically inaccurate ; yet it fulfilled the purpose it was obviously meant to fulfil namely, to give a general, and, as such, a true, picture of the complete break-up of the Dual Monarchy, that is to say, of dismemberment and not secession.

The synthesis of the Austrian point of view is expressed in what may be considered the leading Note on the subject, addressed to the Peace Conference on June 16, 1919.

" The undersigned Delegation can but represent the Republic, founded November 12, 1918, on those of the territories of the former Austro-Hungarian Monarchy, which are inhabited by the people of German nationality. The Delegation is not qualified to represent any other State.

"... the German Austrian Republic was not founded until after the cessation of hostilities. It could not, in fact, ever have been in a state of war with any nation whatever. Moreover, it is stated in the text (Preamble, Section 3) that the former monarchy was replaced, in Austria, by a republican government. This is inaccurate, for in Cisleithania six different governments have been created to administer respectively the State founded on the land inhabited by the members of the nationality. One of these new States is called, by virtue of its original laws, in force up to the present, " the Republic of German Austria " [1]. "

The gist of this view was contained in the following formula which the Austrian Delegation proposed as a substitute for the original text of the relevant paragraph of the Preamble to the Treaty :

" Considering that the former Austro-Hungarian Monarchy has to-day ceased to exist and that in Austria its territories have been divided between the following States, i.e. German Austria, Italy, Poland, Rumania, the Serb-Croat-Slovene State, Czechoslovakia and Ukraina [2]... "

The Austrian theory of revolutionary dismemberment, which was fully in accordance with international law, was confirmed even by the Allies : in his letter of September 2, 1919, to the Austrian Delegation, Clemenceau declared :

" The policy of supremacy has produced its inevitable result : the dismemberment [3]. "

b) *Irrelevant Tests.*

Thus, the clear evidence of general international law supports the theory of revolutionary dismemberment of old Austria. The only possible arguments in favour of a contrary view were precisely those which have been qualified as irrelevant tests of State identity and continuity [4] : name, capital, national composition, and the like. It is

1. Almond-Lutz, *op. cit.*, pp. 243-244 ; *Bericht*, I, pp. 164-165.
2. Austrian reply of July 10, 1919, to the first draft of the Treaty, Almond-Lutz, *op. cit.*, p. 237 ; *Bericht*, I, pp. 326-327.
3. Almond-Lutz, *op. cit.*, p. 227 ; *Bericht*, II, p. 313.
4. See above, pp. 127-128.

true that such external features, providing a superficial link between two States, may be instrumental in raising the question of their identity or otherwise [1]. It may even be admitted that without the existence of some such common features the question would probably not be asked at all [2]. It is, nevertheless, inadmissible to raise such purely irrelevant matters to the dignity of a legal criterion.

Yet, it was precisely such arguments which were employed by the Allies to oppose the Austrian theory of the Republic's non-identity with old Austria. In his letter of September 2, 1919, quoted above, Clemenceau stated :

" The observations reveal a fundamentally erroneous conception of the responsibilities of the Austrian people. ... The Austrian people share in a large measure with their neighbour the Hungarian people, responsibility for the ills which Europe has suffered in the course of the last five years. "

Here the letter listed the faults and responsibilities of the Empire which, it may be recalled, were freely admitted by the Austrian Delegation. But — said Clemenceau — the Delegation had wished to burden the dynasty alone with this responsibility and, according to them,

" the Austrian people ... might escape the responsibility for the acts committed by a Government which was its own and had its seat in its capital ".

The letter went on to say that the Austrian people had welcomed the war, that it never revolted and went on fighting,

" proof sufficient that conformably to the sacred rules of justice Austria should be held to assume its entire share of responsibility for the crime which has unchained upon the world such a calamity ".

Moreover, the Hapsburg policy of German and Hungarian hegemony over the majority of the inhabitants of the Empire

" maintained itself, thanks to the vigorous support of the inhabitants of Austria and Hungary, to whom it assured political and economic domination over their compatriots ".

It was on the basis of such arguments that the Allies found it compelling to reject the Austrian thesis according to which the people of Austria

" ought to escape the duty of reparation, to the extreme limit of its faculties, to those to whom, with the government it supported, it has brought such grave injury [3] ".

Whatever the sacred rules of justice invoked, Clemenceau's letter does not contain one single legal argument. This is all the more striking when it is compared with the Note adressed by the same Clemenceau

---

1. " Degli elementi puramente esteriori ed accidentali quali l'uguaglianza de nome, la coincidenza della capitale con quella dello Stato estinto, e qualche altro, hanno fatto pensare... ad una sopravvivenza dell'antico Impero austriaco nell'Austria attuale. " Udina, *op. cit.*, pp. 58-59.
2. See above, p. 1.
3. Almond-Lutz, *op. cit.*, pp. 225-231 ; *Bericht*, II, pp. 310-317.

to the German delegation on a similar subject [1] ; there a well-established rule of international law was invoked to justify German responsibility in spite of a revolutionary change or government, and it went to the heart of the problem.   In the case of Austria, however, only political arguments were advanced, the merits of which are not material to the present enquiry.   From the legal point of view it is entirely irrelevant to single out the political attitude of a particular group of nationals. It is equally irrelevant and, moreover, inaccurate, to describe the government of a State as the government of that particular group ; and to rely on the fact of that government having been established in the " capital " of that particular group can hardly be taken seriously.

The rejection of all such irrelevant tests by the Austrian Delegation must therefore be considered as perfectly correct.

" What are, in fact, the reasons alleged as a basis for the identification of the young German Austrian Republic, but not the other resulting States, with the former monarchy ?   By what chain of argument could one arrive at a different solution for German Austria on the one hand and the other new States on the other, in regard to the inheritance of the former Cisleithania ?

Can it be the name ?   The name of the German Austrian Republic was expressly chosen to mark the difference between the former polyglot State, composed of nine nationalities, and the new Republic, including only one of them.   In any case the name cannot be taken as prejudicial to the thing.

Obviously, it cannot be the territory or the population either, for in number of inhabitants and in area German Austria is the least important of all the resulting States.

In the same way the situation of the capital on the territory of German Austria can not be invoked as a pretext for a different treatment.   The wealth and importance of Vienna have been the result of the economic strength of the great empire.   They vanish with it.   It is principally this disproportionate city in a small country without resources that causes the greatest difficulties.

The German Austrian Delegation does not wish, moreover, to take seriously the argument of certain publicists, according to which German Austria should be punished for the courage shown during the war by the Austrian soldiers of the German race.   Without ignoring the courageous devotion shown during the war, it would at the same time be unjust to attribute the merit of it solely to the inhabitants of the present German Austria.   Not only the Germans of the countries of the Alps, of the Sudetes, of Bohemia and of other parts of the former monarchy, but the Latin races, the Magyars, the Slavs and especially the Poles, Croats and Slovenes lent their spontaneous aid to that sad and proud duty which was imposed on them by a grave fault of the governments, but the devoted accomplishment of which surrounds the heroic defeat of our former country with a halo of glory.

It is the same case with the argument drawn from the fact that many representatives of the present Republic had worked as publicists or statesmen for the welfare of the former monarchy.   On this subject more ample information will be furnished to the Conference.   For the moment, the German Austrian Delegation confines itself to stating in this connection that, never, during the existence of the Dual Monarchy, was the direction of Foreign Affairs entrusted to a statesman who was a native of the countries now belonging to German Austria.   When the war was declared, the portfolio in question was in the hands of Count Berchtold, a Hungarian subject, assisted by Count Forgach, a Hungarian also, and by Baron Musulin, a Croat.   Moreover, during the recent decades Austria-Hungary was represented almost exclusively by Hungarian or Bohemian diplomats ; thus in 1914 almost all the ambassadorial posts were occupied by Hungarians, notably those at Paris, at St. Petersburg, at Berlin, at Rome, at Constantinople and at Tokyo.

---

1. See above, p. 33.

Since 1907, the Germans in the Austrian Chamber of Deputies have been in a minority incapable of controlling votes without joining some other national party. Consequently, the Austrian governments have always been composed in part of Czechs, Poles and sometimes of Slovenes.

To plead the cause of a suffering nation and to give it justice, it is of greatest importance to learn on what arguments it has been thought possible to designate precisely the smallest, the poorest, the most pacific and the most democratic of the States created from the former monarchy as its successor, by rendering it responsible not only for all the obligations incurred, but also for the consequences of faults committed and measures taken by the former governments with the co-operation of Hungarian, Polish, Czech, and Slovene statesmen [1]. "

c) *The Austrian Conviction.*

The " will " of the State concerned has been rejected as a test of its identity and continuity, as subversive of the objective character of international law and calculated to undermine all security in international legal relations. At the same time it has been found to be admissible as additional, controvertible evidence, whose value must be tested by its conformity or otherwise with general international law [2].

Consequently, Austria's own will and conviction could not possibly prevail against a different ruling of general international law concerning her legal status. But it certainly may be used as evidence, especially when it is found to stand the test of conformity with general international law.

It should be stated at the very outset that the particular revolution which took place on the German-Austrian territory proper was as much centrifugal with regard to the original State, as much " anti-State", as were all the other simultaneous revolutions, whether Polish, Czech, or Yugoslav. Udina is correct in stating that this revolution was never intended to change the form of the existing old State, but to create a new State on part of its territory [3].

The facts and documents of the period all indicate that the intention was to form a new State, and not to reconstruct the existing one. Considering the simultaneous events occurring elsewhere, it would hardly be conceivable that the Austrians should have formed the one and only national group of the old Empire which felt and thought otherwise.

The relevant passages of the National Assembly's first Resolution of October 21, 1918, concerning the formation of a new national State, have already been quoted [4]. On October 30, the Assembly sent a Note to President Wilson, which contained the following passages :

" We have the honour to inform you that the German nation in Austria has decided to create an independent German-Austrian State. ... The Germans in Austria are a population of 9,7 millions ; until now they have been citizens of the Austrian State ; now that the other nations are about to form independent States of their own, the German nation in Austria also constitutes itself an independent national State [5]. "

---

1. Almond-Lutz, *op. cit.*, pp. 245-246 ; *Bericht*, I, pp. 167-169.
2. See above, p. 129.
3. *Op. cit.*, p. 59.
4. See above, p. 202.
5. *Transl. mine*, quoted by Trampler, *op. cit.*, pp. 53-54.

At the first meeting of the Assembly, its Chairman, Dr. Waldner, declared :

" We withdraw without gratitude from this State to employ our national energies for ourselves alone and ... to build up a new community which will serve our people alone. ... Thus will the new German Austria be born from the dephts of her liberated national soul... Thus will the moral and spiritual qualities of our people permeate the new State [1]... "

At the same meeting, Dr. Viktor Adler, speaking on behalf of the Austrian Social-Democratic Party, declared :

" The German People in Austria is to form its own democratic State, its German National State [2]. "

The message of the Vienna University to the National Assembly read :

" At this historic moment the Senatus Academicus of the Vienna University considers it its duty solemnly to proclaim its allegiance to the newly-founded State. "

The message of the National Assembly to the people spoke of the decision to give German Austria a republican form of government and stated that the

" middle classes, peasants and workers have rallied together to found the new German-Austria ".

Speaking in the National Assembly on December 4, 1918, Chancellor Renner said :

" Forty four days have passed since October 21, when the representatives of the German nation came together to declare themselves a nation and a State. In those forty four days we had to organize as best we could the State which we had created and which we had called German Austria [3]. "

The same conviction is reflected in the declarations of accession to the new State of the various Austrian provinces. The declaration of Carinthia may be quoted by way of example :

" The land of Carinthia joins the other lands, united within the State of German Austria, on the basis of identical rights and obligations ; it pledges itself to share their fate in unbreakable community and brotherly harmony and it expects their legal representatives to accept this pledge and to reciprocate it in the same spirit [4]. "

All these statements are certainly evidence of the Austrian attitude. It would hardly have occurred to anyone to " declare accession " or " proclaim allegiance " to an existing State of which they in any case already formed a part. The statements quoted are telling proof that the conviction of a new State being formed was there, and that it was not confined to the highest State organs or to the capital, but permeated the broad mass of the population both in the capital and in the provinces.

1. *Transl. mine*, quoted by Trampler, *op. cit.*, p. 51.
2. Quoted by Graham, *op. cit.*, p. 504.
3. *Transl. mine*, quotations from Trampler, *op. cit.*, pp. 58, 64, and 110.
4. *Transl. mine*, quoted by Kelsen, *op. cit.*, p. 260.

d) *The Austrian Argument.*

If the above argument is accepted, the correct conclusions follow automatically. As a new State, Austria could not have been considered an enemy State, any more than the other succeeding States, since she had never waged war. No peace treaty could be concluded with her and she could not cede territories she had never possessed ; nor could she renounce rights she had never had.

These conclusions were upheld by the Austrian Republic with the utmost consistency, from its very birth, throughout the negotiations of Saint-Germain till the conclusion of the Treaty, and even subsequently [1].

Consequently, unlike the Austro-Hungarian Empire, the Austrian Republic never sued for peace. What it asked for was direct negotiations between all the parties concerned with a view to bringing about a general European settlement [2].

Nevertheless, the negotiations which, after a long period of waiting, were opened at Saint-Germain-en-Laye in May 1919, turned out to be peace negotiations. Undeterred, the Austrian Delegation defended its fundamental thesis and the resulting conclusions. The Austrian Note of August 6, 1919, stated :

" The State with which the Allied and Associated Powers have evidently the intention of concluding the proposed Treaty is called, by virtue of its constitutional laws, in so far as they remain in force, " The Republic of German Austria ". ... Since its creation, the German-Austrian Republic has been in the state of war with no other power ; therefore it could not conclude a Treaty of Peace ; the instrument which has just been presented to it can, consequently, only be considered as the draft of an international Treaty which is to regulate the situation of a new State on which weights part of the inheritance of a State which has collapsed on account of the war [3]. "

The incompatibility of the proposed Treaty with Austria's legal status as one of the succeeding States, not identical with the Monarchy, was elaborated in detail :

" The Treaty imposes, according to the text of the resumé published by the Supreme Council, on " Austria " the duty of ceding a great number of territories. This duty, whether fulfilled or about to be fulfilled, can be incumbent only on a State whose frontiers comprise or have comprised the territories in question. We are not in this position, and we never have been. Our young Republic welcomed with warm sympathy the creation of independent and democratic States on these territories ; it accepts spontaneously all regulations conceding to each of these States its natural territory, the same as it claims for itself the territory inhabited by the German-Austrian people...

The Treaty further says ... that German Austria should maintain certain international engagements made by the former Austro-Hungarian monarchy. Obviously there can be no question of the *maintenance* of such obligations, seeing that the latter were never incurred by the State founded on November 12, 1918.

---

1. See below, pp. 229 et seq.
2. The already mentioned Austrian Note to President Wilson of October 30, 1918, formulated this Austrian request as follows : " Der unterzeichnete Vollzugsausschuss der provisorischen deutsch-österreichischen Nationalversammlung bittet Sie daher, Herr Präsident, ihm Gelegenheit zu bieten, unverzüglich in direkte Verhandlungen mit den Vertretern aller kriegführenden Mächte über einen allgemeinen Frieden einzutreten. " Quoted by Trampler, *op. cit.*, p. 154.
3. Almond-Lutz, *op. cit.*, p. 239 ; *Bericht*, II, p. 93.

It would be more in accord with the real situation to make German Austria consent to any convention that you wish to apply to her case, without considering whether the former monarchy had or had not been a contracting party to the agreement in question [1]. "

More particularly, the Austrian Delegation took its stand against the proposal to make the Austrian Republic alone responsible for the war :

" Finally, it cannot be supposed that it is the intention of the Allies and Associates, as would seem to be implied by the text (among others) of Article 32, paragraph *e*, Part X, Section IV, to make German Austria responsible for the indemnification of damages caused outside of its frontiers by the authorities or populations of other parts of former Austria. In the same way the last sentence of Article 13, paragraph 1, Part X, Section IV ; Article 35, Section V, as well as other analogous provisions, can be explained only by the error of considering Austria as a belligerent which during the war, occupied foreign territories or took belligerent measures. The war was, however, waged only by the Austro-Hungarian monarchy, by means of the Imperial and Royal army [2]. "

While consistently denying Austria's identity with the Empire and insisting upon the consequences of such non-identity, the Austrian Delegation did not fail to propose to the Allies a positive solution, namely Austria's succession with the other succeeding States to the obligations of the extinct Monarchy proportionately.

" The territory as well as the population and the whole ensemble of the assets of the former Monarchy have passed to the States concerned. It would, therefore, be arbitrary and irreconcilable with the most elementary principles of right and justice to charge only one of these States with all the liabilities. ... Since the belligerent that was the former Monarchy has collapsed under the blows of its adversaries and from internal troubles, there remains to the victor only one of two things : either to build, so to speak, a mass administration which would represent as receiver of the bankrupt the assets and liabilities of the " *hæreditas iacens* " and which, after having settled the claims presented by each of the victorious States and recognized as justified by all, shall decide and execute the liquidation of the remainder between the succeeding States. The other alternative would be to conclude a special Treaty with each one of the succeeding States imposing upon it its quota of obligations. In neither of the two cases mentioned should one speak — from the point of view of international law — of the state of war which *is about to come* to an end, since the war with the State that has disappeared ceased spontaneously at the time of the disappearance of the latter and the new succeeding States have not yet been at war. It would be all the more inconceivable to treat only one as a defeated belligerent and all the others as victors [3]. "

Such were the correct legal conclusions drawn by Austria from her fundamental thesis. The question was whether they had any chance of achieving success in the existing political reality.

---

1. From the Note of June 16, 1919 ; Almond-Lutz, *op. cit.*, p. 244 ; *Bericht*, I, pp. 165-166.

2. From the Note of June 16, 1919 ; Almond-Lutz, *op. cit.*, pp. 244-245 ; *Bericht*, I, p. 166.

3. Almond-Lutz, *op. cit.*, pp. 239-240 ; *Bericht*, II, pp. 93-94. Cf. the relevant passages in Renner's speeches, Almond-Lutz, *op. cit.*, pp. 61-64 ; *Bericht*, I, pp. 40-42.

4. THE ALLIED DECISION.

a) *The Political Character of the Allied Decision.*

Whatever the political motives behind it, the Austrian argument proceeded on legal lines. No similar attempt seems to have been made by the Allies to consider the problem from a legal standpoint. Whether in official documents addressed to the Austrian Delegation, or in the inner Allied councils, the argument was a purely political one. This political problem fell under two distinct headings : 1) whether, as regards the future, it was politically more advantageous to identify the Austrian Republic with the Empire or to deny such identity ; 2) what was to be done as regards Austria's responsibility and obligations, in particular, her responsibility for the war.

With regard to the first problem,

" ... the difficulties of identifying Old Austria with the new Republic were still greater. If this was so, the Austrian Republic could claim to speak for, say, the German population of Czecho-Slovakia, or for any Germans likely to be included within Yugoslavia. A more serious danger lay behind this, for the Emperor Charles had never abdicated. He might therefore return as ruler of Austria, if New Austria was identical with Old Austria. He obviously could not return to a State created *de novo* without an amendment in the constitution whose basis and principle were republican. Hence the *de novo* policy was the only one which offered complete security to the Allies, but there were great difficulties in adopting it [1]. "

It was precisely the fear of such difficulties arising in future that led the British Delegation in Paris to support the view that the Austrian Republic was a new State [2].

Such preoccupations on the part of the peace-makers were perfectly legitimate on the political level. On the legal plane, however, it is obvious that, if such considerations were allowed to determine an existing situation under international law, then such determination was vitiated from the outset.

It was, however, impossible to deny to the Republic the rights of the former Empire, while making it bear the obligations of the latter, including responsibility for the war. This was the second political consideration of the Allies. At the end of the war they had found themselves cheated of the fruits of victory by the disappearance of the vanquished enemy. Who was to bear responsibility for the war ? Or were the Allies to forego their victory altogether ? How were they to deal with a situation which was no less unusual for having been the fulfilment of their own desire to break up the Hapsburg Monarchy ? And which of the two alternatives was the less dangerous : to consider Austria a new State, eliminating at one stroke all possible rights and title of the former Empire and simultaneously renouncing the fruits of victory, — or to treat her as an old State and exact responsibility, while risking a possible revival of Imperial claims ?

---

1. Temperley, *op. cit.*, IV, p. 398.
2. " On May 26, this question was raised by Mr. Headlam-Morley... who considered it dangerous to treat Austria as possessing the rights formerly belonging to the Austro-Hungarian Empire... " Gray, *Commentary on the History of the Treaty with Austria*, quoted by Almond-Lutz, *op. cit.*, p. 241. See *ibid.*, p. 250.

" To cut the Gordian knot " — says Temperley — " and to call Austria a wholly new State made it difficult to establish her previous responsibility and obligations. The solution was to maintain the identity of the old State with the New Austria [1]. "

As Udina rightly says, the Allies had in fact three courses open to them : either to make a virtue out of necessity by accepting the facts and merely presiding over a general settlement which would have brought no reward for victory ; or to treat all the new States in exactly the same way, summoning them all to the same conference table and imposing on them a proportional share of responsibility in their capacity of *de iure* and *de facto* successors to the Monarchy ; or, finally, to discriminate in an opportunist manner between the " good " States and the " bad " ones and to treat some of them, by means of a legal fiction, as defeated enemies, while qualifying others as Allies [2]. The Allies would not, however, consent to the first course, in view of all the sacrifices they had borne in the course of the war ; nor would they agree to the second, having regard to the obligations assumed during the war towards the oppressed nationalities of the Austro-Hungarian Empire. Thus, there only remained the third possibility.

It has been seen that the Austrian Delegation repeatedly offered the second solution, i.e. the common responsibility of all the succeeding States. Udina is, however, correct in regarding such a course as politically impossible, involving as it did an equal responsibility for the war on the part of the new Austria and the other succeeding States, whose revolt against the Empire the Allies had actively supported [3]. This aspect of the problem does not fall within the scope of the present study. In any case, a decision proceeding from political motives could only be based on political criteria ; such criterion was found in the national question which occupies such a prominent place in the above-quoted letter of Clemenceau to the Austrian Delegation [4]. And yet, that same letter included — rather surprisingly in the context — the admission by the Allies of the dismemberment of the Dual Monarchy [5].

b) *The Contradictions of the Allied Thesis.*

In addition to being based on political motives, the Allied thesis seems to have suffered from a considerable degree of confusion and a number of contradictions which were apparently present from the moment the problem first arose in Paris [6].

---

1. *Op. cit.*, p. 400.
2. " ...distinguere cioè, con criterio di opportunità, tra Stato e Stato, facendo una specie di sceveramento dei buoni dai cattivi, e imporre a taluni di rappresentare, con una specie di finzione giuridica, la parte dello Stato vinto, chiamando invece altri al proprio fianco come alleati... " *Op. cit.*, p. 187.
3. This may be the reason for Temperley's calling the Austrian thesis " good in law " but " bad in sense ", *op. cit.*, p. 397.
4. See above, p. 214.
5. See above, p. 213.
6. " ...I got word from the Secretariat to go up to the meeting of the Council of Four at 4 o'clock. Hudson and I went up and the question of minorities was under discussion. The clauses proposed for the treaty with Austria were adopted and then discussion was raised by Headlam-Morley as to whether Austria was a new State or not

Discussions which then took place were hardly a model of clarity. The British Delegation which, as has been seen, had been inclined from the beginning to treat Austria as a new State, continued to favour such a solution,

"but the Council was already committed to the opposite opinion, which President Wilson strongly supported. Mr. Headlam-Morley, notably, argued that Austria was to be considered a new State, not an Enemy Power, and had quoted a paragraph in one proof of the Treaty which declared that "Austria is recognized as a new and independent State under the name of the "Republic of Austria". This paragraph was, it may be noted, quite in line with a paragraph proposed by the Austrian Delegation. ... Mr. Tittoni replied that this Paragraph of the Draft implies only that *Austria was a new State in so far as her old frontiers and status had been changed* while President Wilson was of the opinion *that Austria was both a new State and an Enemy Power*. This view prevailed. ... In the final Draft of the Treaty the Paragraph does not appear, having been suppressed at the instance of Mr. Polk... [1]".

Nor was the Allied conception made any clearer in the official Allied answer to the observations of the Austrian Delegation, of September 2, 1919 [2]. In one and the same document Austria is described once as "un des Etats successeurs de l'Autriche-Hongrie", — another time as "le successeur de l'ancienne Monarchie autrichienne", while the other succeeding States "comptent parmi les Alliés". Elsewhere in the same document she is described as "responsable de la politique et des actes de la Monarchie austro-hongroise"; and finally, the Note rejects her claim to be considered "comme un tout nouvel Etat" [3]; the notion of a "tout nouvel Etat", obviously presupposing that a State can be either quite new or half new, forms a worthy counterpart to the idea of Austria being at the same time a new State and an enemy Power [4].

Nor does the confusion end here. It was with the Dual Monarchy that the Allied and Associated Powers concluded an armistice at Villa Giusti, thereby bringing hostilities to an end. But it was with the new German-Austrian State that they entered into relations with a view to concluding peace [5]. Furthermore, on May 29, 1919, the Chairman of the Verification Committee, M. Cambon, on returning their Full Powers to the Austrian Delegation, stated the following, on the instruction of the Supreme Council :

"The Allied and Associated Powers have decided to recognize the new Republic under the designation of "Republic of Austria". They therefore declare

---

and there was some talk on this and it was decided to refer it to persons to be named by the Drafting Committee. Headlam-Morley's idea was that Austria was a new State. I spoke rather against this and Clemenceau and Orlando both doubted it, though I think the discussion was not clear as to Austria as a State being a part of Austria-Hungary and Austria as a State in the international sense... " From Miller's *My Diary*, quoted by Almond-Lutz, *op. cit.*, pp. 240-241.

1. *It. mine*, Gray, *op. cit.*, quoted by Almond-Lutz, *op. cit.*, p. 250.
2. *Bericht*, II, pp. 318 et seq; Udina, *op. cit.*, p. 190.
3. *Bericlt*, II, p. 352; Udina, *op. cit.*, p. 191.
4. See above.
5. Letter of invitation to the St. Germain Conference, sent on behalf of the Supreme Council by the French Embassy in Vienna, on May 2, 1919, *Bericht*, I, p. 17.

their willingness to recognize the full powers which were delivered on May 19, as authorizing the delegates named therein to negotiate in the name of the Republic of Austria [1]. "

It is on this document that Udina bases his contention that, in spite of all the evidence to the contrary, the Powers did recognize Austria as a new State [2]. It is however, impossible to accept this interpretation. In the first place, it should be noted that, on receiving the full powers made out in the name of the " German Austrian " Republic, the Allies concentrated chiefly on the problem whether it was opportune to admit the existence of a " German " Austria or merely of " Austria ". Following consultations with the Yugoslav and Czechoslovak Delegations, both of whom objected to the name of " German Austria " on account of its possible implications, the Supreme Council directed M. Cambon to acknowledge the full powers of the delegation of the " Republic of Austria " only [3]. It would appear that, at that particular stage, the entire attention of the Allies was so much directed to the problem of the Republic's name that this and this alone found expression in the operative part of Cambon's reply, — whereas the implications of the words " the new Republic " do not seem to have been even discussed [4].

Far more decisive, however, is the fact that, despite all the admitted confusion, the final decision of the Allies undoubtedly assumed the new Republic's identity with the Empire, in order to determine her international responsibility. This final decision results, beyond any possibility of doubt, from Clemenceau's above-quoted letter [5], from the Allied answer to the Austrian delegation [6], — and, above all, from the Peace Treaty of Saint-Germain.

5. THE TREATY OF SAINT-GERMAIN.

a) *Analysis of the Text.*

In view of the circumstances described above, it is hardly surprising that the Treaty of Saint-Germain did not become a model of clarity and consistency.

The difficulty already arises with regard to the famous paragraph of the Preamble which was to be decisive for Austria's legal status :

---

1. Almond-Lutz, *op. cit.*, p. 50 ; *Bericht*, I, p. 30.
2. " Esso è il vero e proprio atto di riconoscimento del nuovo Stato austriaco, e non semplicemente del nuovo Governo repubblicano d'Austria, quando si tenga presente che soltanto quattro giorni dopo le potenze alleate ed associate trasmettevano ai plenipotenziari austriaci il primo testo incompleto delle condizioni di pace, in cui esse ripetevano il riconoscimento con una formula per la quale non potevano sorgere equivoci : « L'Autriche est reconnue comme nouvel Etat indépendant sous le nom de République d'Autriche. » *Op. cit.*, pp. 202-203.
3. Gray, *op. cit.*, quoted by Almond-Lutz, *op. cit.*, pp. 241-242.
4. Almond-Lutz, *op. cit.*, pp. 241-242. Moreover, the formula quoted by Udina has been subsequently dropped, see above, p. 222.
5. « Les principes sur lesquels était fondé le projet de Traité doivent donc subsister. Le peuple d'Autriche est, et restera jusqu'à la signature de la paix, un peuple ennemi. » *Bericht*, II, p. 312.
6. « ...la République d'Autriche ne saurait être considérée que comme le noyau constitutif survivant à la dislocation de l'agrégat autrichien. » *Bericht*, II, p. 338.

" Whereas the former Austro-Hungarian Monarchy has now ceased to exist, and has been replaced in Austria by a republican government. "

Any interpretation can be placed upon this passage read alone, which is another way of saying that no definite interpretation can be placed upon it at all. The crucial paragraph of the Treaty, reflecting its fundamental assumption, is capable of widely differing interpretations. On the basis of the text alone, there is no way of knowing whether the Treaty assumes merely a revolutionary change of government within the Dual Monarchy [1], its total break-up, or a splitting of the Dual Monarchy into its two component parts, and, consequently, whether the Austrian Republic is identical with her predecessor, and, if so, with whom : the Dual Monarchy or the Austrian " Reichshälfte " ? Only by having recourse to the travaux préparatoires [2] and, above all, by reading the paragraph in question together with the corresponding paragraph of the Treaty of Trianon [3], is it possible to discover its true meaning : namely, the assertion of Austria's identity with Cisleithania [4]. Thus, quite contrary to Udina's view [5], the two Treaties assume not a general break-up of the Austro-Hungarian Empire, but precisely a break in the link between its two component parts which are considered identical with the two former " Reichshälften ".

Nor is the operative part of the Treaty any more consistent. Thus, Art. 208, dealing with the succeeding States other than Austria, speaks of " States to which territory of the former Austro-Hungarian Monarchy is transferred and States arising from the dismemberment of that Monarchy... ", while Articles 203, 205 and 206 speak of

" ... States to which territory of the former Austro-Hungarian Monarchy is transferred, and ... States arising from the dismemberment of that Monarchy including Austria... "

Austria is thus on one occasion placed in the same category as all the other succeeding States, as being born in the same manner as they

---

1. See below, p. 234, the decision of the Italo-Austrian Mixed Arbrital Tribunal.
2. See above, pp. 220-223.
3. " Whereas the former Austro-Hungarian Monarchy has now ceased to exist, and has been replaced in Hungary by a national government. "
4. Even the mysterious word " now " eludes any reasonable interpretation. Cf. Udina : " Cosi pure sembra tutt'altro che decisivo l'argomento contrario tratto dal preambolo del Trattato di pace, in cui, tra i vari « considerando » si pone l'enunciazione che « l'ancienne Monarchie austro-hongroise a aujourd'hui cessé d'exister et a fait place, en Autriche, à un Gouvernement républicain » formulata in modo da consentire ambedue le interpretazioni. A proposito di essa, noteremo qui, per incidenza, che da taluno si è attribuita anche molta importanza ɛll'avverbio « aujourd'hui » che vi è compreso. Ora, che con quel comma del preambolɔ i contraenti abbiano inteso di constatare la cessazione dell'antico ordinamento giuridico alla data del Trattato sembra non possa ragionevolmente ritenersi, specialmente se si consideri che l'identico passo fu inserito nel Trattato di Trianon quasi un anno dopo, dimodochè si sarebbe avuto un ordinamento giurid'co per metà scomparso e per metà esistente (e si noti che in ambedue i Trattati si parla dell' ordinamento austro-ungarico, non di quello dell'antico Stato austriaco o dell'antico Stato ungherese), con la consequenza che alcuni Stati sarebbero rimasti sovrani su motà del territorio già loro riconosciuto, mentre nell'altra lo sarebbero divenuti un anno dopo. Quell' « oggi » ha, naturalmente, il significato più lato che spesso gli viene attribuito. " Op. cit., pp. 203-204.
5. See below, p. 228.

were, out of the dismemberment of the Dual Monarchy, — while on another occasion she is clearly excluded from this category [1].

Such inconsistencies certainly tend to obscure the picture. They cannot, however, prevail against the fundamental fact that the whole Treaty is based on the assumption of new Austria's identity with Cisleithania. For the Saint-Germain Treaty is above all a Treaty of Peace, putting an end to the state of war with a defeated enemy [2]. Whatever else can be said of it, it cannot possibly be maintained that a Peace Treaty can be concluded with a new State, coming into existence *after* the war.

The consequences of this fact follow automatically. Art. 177 contains the famous " war-guilt clause ", formulated in exactly the same terms as the corresponding clause of the Treaty of Versailles [3]. Reparations were therefore imposed on Austria as they had been imposed on Germany [4].

Further, Austria was made to cede territories which had belonged to the Austrian Empire and which the Republic had never claimed, together with those which she did claim and in respect of which a cession would have been justified even on the assumption of the Republic's non-identity with the Empire [5]. Similarly, Austria was made to " renounce " all rights, titles or privileges which the former Monarchy may have had with regard to territories outside Europe (Art. 95), and, in particular, all rights arising out of specific agreements concluded by the former Monarchy and relating to its interests outside Europe [6]. Furthermore, Austria was made to recognize the annulment of the Treaties of Brest-Litovsk and all other treaties, agreements or conventions concluded by the former Austro-Hungarian Government with the " maximalist Government in Russia " (Art. 87).

Articles 234-245 deal with Austrian treaty obligations. The Republic was made to continue the multilateral treaties of an economic and

---

1. It should also be observed that, on the admitted exclusion of Austria from this category by Art. 208, the use of the plural becomes inaccurate, since there were only two States actually born out of the dismemberment of the Dual Monarchy : Czechoslovakia and — precisely — the Austrian Republic.

2. Preamble, Para, 2.

3. " The Allied and Associated Governments affirm and Austria accepts the responsibility of Austria and her allies for causing the loss and damage to which the Allied and Associated Governments have been subjected as a consequence of the war imposed upon them by the aggression of Austria-Hungary and her allies. "

4. See Part VIII of the Treaty.

5. Articles 36, 47, 54, 59, 91 ; the formula reads : " Austria renounces, so far as she is concerned, in favour of Italy(of the Serb-Croat-Slovene State, the Czecho-Slovak State, Rumania, the Principal Allied and Associated Powers) all rights and title over the territory of the former Austro-Hungarian Monarchy situated beyond the frontiers of Austria laid down in Article 27... " The formula is identical for Hungary in the Treaty of Trianon, and the words " so far as she is concerned " once again confirm the underlying assumption of the two Treaties : the break-up of the Real Union into its two component parts and the consequent identity of the new Hungary with the " lands of the holy Hungarian crown " and of Austria with Cisleithania. The formula proposed by the Austrian delegation and rejected by the Allies read : « L'Autriche allemande reconnaît qu'il ne lui revient aucun droit ou titre sur les territoires situés au-delà de ses frontières.... » *Bericht* I, p. 349.

6. Art. 96, 97, 102, 103, 110, 113 ; it may be observed that here too, the Allies rejected the Austrian proposals according to which the Republic was simply to recognize that it did not possess these rights. *Bericht*, I, p. 370.

technical character to which the former Monarchy had been a party (Art. 234). Art. 241 provides that each of the Allied or Associated Powers shall notify to Austria

" the bilateral agreements of all kinds which were in force between her and the former Austro-Hungarian Monarchy, and which she wishes should be in force as between her and Austria ".

Like Germany under the Versailles Treaty, Austria was to be disarmed and kept under Allied control. Like Germany, she was prohibited from having conscription and allowed only a strictly limited and controlled standing army (Part V). As in the case of Germany, the assets of Austrian citizens in Allied countries were to be subject to liquidation (Art. 249). Finally, the war debt was charged on Austria alone (Art. 205).

Thus, in spite of certain inconsistencies and a lack of clarity, there is no doubt that the Treaty of Saint-Germain is a Peace Treaty, concluded by victorious Powers with an enemy State. As such, it is based on the assumption of the Austrian Republic's identity with Cisleithania.

b) *Interpretations of the Treaty.*

It would seem that the widely differing interpretations which were placed upon the Treaty of Saint-Germain are to be explained not only by its above-mentioned inconsistencies, but also by the varying attitude of writers towards the basic issue of how far the provisions of conventional law can, by themselves and independently of general international law, be decisive for the question of State identity and continuity.

In the first Part of this study it was submitted that conventional law is unable to supply an authoritative answer to the question of State identity and continuity [1], and that it cannot prevail against general international law. The main reason for this assertion was found to be the fact that a treaty is concluded only *after* the events which have brought about the extinction, or preserved the continuity, of the State concerned, and that, consequently, it can do no more than state the correct position under general international law. The possibility of a treaty undoing an existing factual situation merely by calling it something else, cannot be seriously admitted.

It is clear, however, that such a view cannot be adopted by voluntarists for whom the will of States, as soon as it is expressed in the form of an international convention, can work any legal miracle. Consequently, it is precisely the treaty which, in their opinion, provides an answer to the problem.

Thus, the actual interpretation of the Treaty of Saint-Germain by the various commentators is influenced by their fundamental approach to the subject, namely, whether or not they consider it a test of State identity and continuity.

The view that the Treaty provides such a test seems to be fully

---

1. See above, pp. 129-130.

accepted by Kaufmann. According to him, the Treaty assumes new Austria's identity with the Empire ; therefore new Austria *is* identical with the Empire [1]. This is at least a correct interpretation of the Treaty.

In a similar spirit Udina expects the Treaty to provide a decisive answer to the problem of Austria's identity. This, however, does not prevent him from interpreting the Treaty rather freely so as to make it conform to the conclusions at which he has already arrived on the basis of general international law, — that is, to make it express what it does not in fact express, namely the non-identity of the Republic with the Empire. This, however, is hardly a consistent voluntarist approach.

Udina thus admits the element of fiction in the Treaty. In particular, he regards it as a fiction that it claims to be a treaty of peace whose conclusion is supposed to terminate a state of war [2]. Yet, instead of going further and admitting that this underlying fiction permeates the whole treaty, he struggles with its specific provisions — which are nothing but logical consequence of this fictitious assumption — in the hope of showing that they establish new Austria's non-identity with Cisleithania. Thus, he claims that in reality the Treaty considers all the succeeding States as mere successors of the Empire, and simply imposes greater burdens on some than on others [3]. With regard to the re-imposition on Austria of the treaty obligations of the Empire, he suggests that, in spite of their material identity with the old ones, they could now be considered as new obligations. This might possibly be a valid observation, if Udina had attempted to adduce any arguments in its support and to indicate clearly the new legal basis on which the old treaties had now come to rest. For it could indeed be argued that such a conventional arrangement could in fact imply the succession of one subject of international law to the treaty rights and obligations of another, thereby excluding their identity. It is, however, to be remembered that the Treaty of Saint-Germain, starting from the assumption of a state of war still continuing between the contracting parties, merely effects a revival of pre-war treaties in exactly the same way as did the Treaty of Versailles in the case of Germany, without casting any doubt on the identity of Republican with Imperial Germany. As it is, the argument is left as unsubstantiated as Udina's doubt whether the Austrian " renunciation " of territories possessed the

---

1. The Austrian Republic is... " international-rechtlich identisch mit dem öster-reichischen Staat... der einen Teil der österreichisch-ungarischen Realunion bildete. Nach der Prämbel des Friedensvertrages von St. Germain hat zwar « l'ancienne monar-chie austro-hongroise », also die alte Realunion aufgehört zu existieren ; aber zwischen der heutigen Republik Oesterreich und dem ehemaligen Kaiserstaat besteht trotz Wechsels der Staatsform und trotz aller anderen tiefgreifenden Veränderungen völkerrechtliche Identität ; die ehemalige österreichisch-ungarische Monarchie hat, wie es in der Prämbel weiter heisst « fait place en Autriche, à un gouvernement républicain ». Man hat absicht-lich die ursprüngliche Formel der Conditions de Paix : « l'Autriche est reconnue comme nouvel Etat indépendant sous le nom de République d'Autriche » fallen gelassen ; und man hat ebenso absichtlich den österreichischen Vorschlag für die Prämbel verworfen, nach dem alle Nachfolgestaaten einschliesslich des neuen Oesterreichs selbst, als Erben des alten Kaiserstaates angesehen werden sollten. " *Der serbisch-kroatisch-slovenische Staat — ein neuer Staat*, p. 226.
2. *Op. cit.*, p. 187, *f.-n.* 1.
3. *Op. cit.*, p. 188.

character of cession. Nor is he impressed by the fact that the Allies deliberately left out of the Preamble the formula which would have declared Austria to be a new State [1]. All these arguments are intended to bear out Udina's main thesis according to which not only general international law, but also the Treaty of Saint-Germain, assume not merely a splitting of the Real Union into its two component parts, but a complete break-up of the old State. Yet he has no hesitation in admitting that the crucial third paragraph of the Preamble is capable of both interpretations [2]. In spite of all his ingenious efforts at interpretation, Udina's final conclusion is a modest one : he no longer claims that the total break-up of the old State is actually confirmed by the Treaty, but merely that the Treaty does not contradict it [3].

Similarly, Basdevant attempts to interpret the Saint-Germain Treaty so as to make it conform to the theory of non-identity ; in this he closely follows Udina's reasoning without, however, admitting the element of fiction on which the Treaty is based [4].

Verdross' interpretation of the Treaty seems to have varied. He initially held that the Treaty did affirm the identity of the Republic with the Empire and rightly considered such an attitude as unjustified [5]. Yet, his later trend of thought resembles that of Udina : while admitting that the Treaty did not expressly recognize the Austrian thesis of non-identity, he claims that it did not reject it either. Taking his stand on the Cambon Note [6] he argues that the Allies never in fact pronounced the legal identity of the old with the new Austria, but that they merely established a political continuity between the two, in order to justify the special burdens imposed on Austria by the Treaty. This is meant to prove that not even the Allies took the theory of identity seriously [7]. Yet this interpretation is hardly convincing. The motives behind the Treaty were certainly political, but their embodiment in the Treaty was meant to give them precisely legal force. It would also appear that Verdross himself is not particularly satisfied with this argument, since he finally declares that it is not conventional, but general international law alone which can provide a valid test of State identity and continuity [8].

From this intermediate position only one further step is necessary to rely exclusively on general international law, and to recognize the underlying assumption of the Saint-Germain Treaty as pure fiction. This fiction, inherent in the Treaty, is freely admitted by anti-voluntarist writers [9]. It is most forcefully asserted by Kelsen, whose general

---

1. See above, p. 222.
2. See above, p. 224, *f.-n.* 4.
3. " E riteniamo anche d'avere trovata una riprova della nostra opinione... nelle norme internazionali poste dei trattati destinati a dare rilevanza giuridica internazionale al nuovo assetto, od almeno d'avere dimostrato che quelle norme e la volontà di chi le pose non contrastavano per nulla colla tesi da noi accolta. " *Op. cit.*, p. 289.
4. *Op. cit.*, p. 83.
5. " Obgleich also die Republik Oesterreich niemals Krieg geführt hat, betrachtet sie der F. V. als kriegsführende Macht, mit der Friede geschlossen wird. " *Der Friedensvertrag*, p. 476.
6. See above, pp. 222-223.
7. *Verfassung*, pp. 150-151.
8. *Ibid.*
9. Guggenheim, *Beiträge*, p. 194 ; Kunz, *op. cit.*, II, p. 150.

conclusion is that a treaty is incapable of providing a criterion of State identity and continuity [1].

Kelsen's view is brilliantly supported by the particular example he chooses to demonstrate the fictitious character, indeed, the absurdity of the Treaty of Saint-Germain, namely, the problem of the birth of Czechoslovakia. For, either the continued legal existence of old Austria was assumed, in which case Czechoslovakia, existing on a part of former Austrian territory must have been legally non-existent at least until the conclusion of the Treaty, and could not, therefore, have been a party to it. Or else, the legal existence of Czechoslovakia on such territories was admitted, in which case old Austria must have ceased to exist prior to the conclusion of the Treaty and no cession of territory could have taken place (except perhaps of areas actually claimed by the Austrian Republic). But to maintain that old Austria continued in existence and at the same time to recognize Czechoslovakia as a State existing on Austrian territory which is only about to be ceded, is not only legally impossible, but offends against simple common sense [2].

It seems quite impossible to invoke any valid argument against this devastating judgment on the Saint-Germain Treaty or to undermine Kelsen's general conclusion. Hardly any other example could more convincingly illustrate the inability of conventional law to provide a test of State identity and continuity. If the Saint-Germain Treaty had confined itself to what is the proper function of conventional law, namely, the laying down of rules, whether general or particular, such rules may have met with approval or disapproval but there could never have been any element of " fiction ". As it was, such an element was present because the Treaty wrongly defined a situation existing under general international law.

It is thus seen that writers have adopted different interpretations of the Treaty not only on account of the latter's lack of clarity and inconsistencies, but also according to their basic attitude towards the function of conventional law. It is the erronous acceptance of conventional law as a criterion which enables Kaufmann to proclaim the identity of Austria with Cisleithania on the basis of the Treaty. Udina's underlying, albeit inarticulate, assumption is that it is general international law which is decisive in the matter. It is this assumption which leads him to interpret the Treaty so as to make it conform to his findings already arrived at on the basis of general international law. Finally, it is Kelsen's clear appreciation of the uselessness of conventional law in the matter which causes him to reject it as a test altogether and to decide the problem of State identity and continuity on the basis of general international law alone.

c) *Effectiveness of the Treaty.*

If, according to general international law, the declaratory part of the Treaty of Saint-Germain was indeed a fiction, then it is interesting

1. See above, p. 130, *f.-n.* 2.
2. *Naissance de l'Etat*, pp. 631-635.

to see to what extent this fiction was able to assert itself in the existing reality, in other words, what degree of effectiveness it could achieve. The answer to this question is provided by an examination of events following the conclusion of the Treaty.

The Austrian Republic submitted to all the requirements of the Saint-Germain Treaty but, within these limits, firmly maintained her original view of her non-identity with Cisleithania [1]. As early as November 5, 1919, the Austrian representative notified the Allied and Associated Powers of the modifications in the Austrian Constitution, voted by the National Assembly, to make it conform to the terms of the Treaty. In particular, the name of the Republic was changed from " German Austria " (Deutsch-Oesterreich) to " Republic of Austria " (Republik Oesterreich), the Anschluss clause providing for a future union of Austria with Germany was removed, the seal of the Republic was changed, and so forth [2]. Yet, Article 1 of the Law of October 21, 1919, on the State Constitution, stated :

" German Austria, within its frontiers defined by the Treaty of Saint-Germain, is a democratic Republic under the denomination of " Republic of Austria ". However, save for the obligations imposed upon it by the Treaty of Saint-Germain, the Republic of Austria does not assume a succession to the rights and obligations of the former Austrian State, namely of the " Kingdoms and Countries represented in the Reichsrat " [3]. "

This constitutional re-assertion of the fundamental Austrian thesis is regarded by Kelsen as being of little more than moral significance [4]. Yet, within the limits of, and in conformity with, the Peace Treaty, the Austrian Republic thus reserved its freedom of action, both internally and in international relations.

Austrian courts, both before and after the coming into force of the Saint-Germain Treaty, consequently upheld the theory of non-identity and rejected all claims resulting from the obligations of the former Empire, other than those which the new Austria had expressly accepted. Thus the Constitutional Court declared on May 7, 1919 :

" According to the existing law the Republic of Austria can be sued in respect of claims which have arisen against the former Monarchy only in those cases in which it has expressly announced that it succeeds in the individual case as successor to the former legal relation [5]. "

This opinion was consequently adhered to by other courts [6]. The Austrian thesis of the break-up of the Empire and the formation of new States was expressed by the Administrative Court (Verwaltungsgerichtshof) on February 11, 1922 :

---

1. " Oesterreich ist... zur Anerkennung dieser Fiktion völkerrechtlich *nur soweit* verpflichtet, als sie reicht. " Kunz, *op. cit.*, II, p. 150.
2. Almond-Lutz, *op. cit.*, p. 251 ; Kelsen, *op. cit.*, pp. 286-290.
3. Almond-Lutz, *op. cit.*, p. 252. It is hardly necessary to point out once again the wrong use of the term " succession ".
4. " Mehr als eine formal-juristische Konstruktion von gewisser moralisch-politischer Bedeutung kann in diesen Bestimmungen ... nicht erblickt werden. " *Op. cit.* p. 287.
5. *Military Pensions (Austria) Case*, A. D., 1919/22, case no. 38.
6. *Ibid.*, case no. 39, case no. 47 ; A. D., 1923/24, case no. 34 ; A. D., 1925/26, case no. 58 ; A. D., 1929/30, case no. 10 ; A. D., 1931/32, case no. 32.

" It is a juridical error to believe that the Austro-Hungarian Monarchy legally existed up to the date of the coming into force of the Treaty of Saint-Germain ; it is, juridically speaking, an error to believe that the new States, created on parts of the territories of the former Monarchy had, up to that date, no significance except as a fact. From the moment of the dissolution of the old Monarchy, the new States alone possessed an organisation and exercised legislative, administrative and judicial capacity. Even the Peace Treaty presupposes that the new States already existed legally before it came into force, otherwise the new States could not have been parties. The legal existence of the new Republic of Austria began on 30 October 1918, the moment when she came into life by the fundamental law of the Provisional National Assembly. ... Articles 70 and 78 of the Treaty are based on the fiction of regulating the nationality of citizens of the old Austrian Empire [1]... "

The Austrian courts were so consistent in this respect, that they did not hesitate to give the Peace Treaty itself a most far-reaching interpretation to make it conform with the Austrian view. Thus, the Supreme Court of Austria stated on June 23, 1925 :

" ... the Austrian Republic was not the same State as the Austrian Empire. There was nothing in Article 177 of the Treaty of Saint-Germain which was opposed to that opinion. Article 177 should be interpreted to the effect that " the Allied and Associated Powers intended to burden only one part of the inhabitants of the former monarchy, namely the inhabitants of the Austrian Republic, with the responsibility for the war conducted by the monarchy as a whole ; this is all that was intended in the Peace Treaty, and not universal succession proper ". Also, Article 36 of that Treaty, which speaks of the " renunciation " by Austria of territories formerly belonging to the Austrian Empire, means only that after the collapse of the Austrian Empire different claims were put forward to the different parts of its territories and that in the peace treaties these claims were either recognized or repudiated. "Renunciation" is not identical with " cession " [2]... "

The reasoning of the Supreme Court thus proceeds on exactly the same line as that of Udina and the same comments apply to it [3].

However, the fact remains that the theory of non-identity was consistently applied by Austria on the internal level : thus, the Republic refused to take over the obligations of the former Empire, it reserved its freedom of action with regard to former Imperial officials, it refused to be bound by judicial decisions of former Courts, and so forth.

It was with equal consistency that the Republic upheld the thesis of non-identity in her relations with States who were not signatories of the Saint-Germain Treaty. Thus, an Austrian circular Note to States which had been neutral during the war declared that, without being identical with the Empire, Austria had so far applied the latter's bilateral treaties provisionally and voluntarily, and that she now proposed the conclusion of conventions which would clearly determine which of those bilateral treaties were to be considered binding between herself and the States concerned. With regard to multilateral treaties, she notified neutral States (parties to multilateral treaties covered by the relevant provisions of the Saint-Germain Treaty) of her intention to

---

1. *A. L. B. v. Federal Ministry for the Interior*, A. D., 1919/22, case no. 7.
2. *Austrian Pensions (State Succession) Case*, A. D., 1925/26, case no. 25.
3. See above, pp. 227-228.

apply them voluntarily in their mutual relations [1]. Unlike the mere
revival, effected by the Saint-Germain Treaty, this was indeed creating
a new legal basis for these treaties, and it is correct to say with Udina
that, by not expressing any objection to such procedure, the States
concerned either implicitly or even explicitly recognized the thesis of
non-identity [2]. A distinctly contrary attitude seems to have been taken
only by the Netherlands [3]. The Swiss attitude was formulated with
great caution. On May 25, 1925, the two countries concluded a treaty,
the object of which was stated in the Preamble to be

" rendre applicables entre la Suisse et la République d'Autriche les traités
conclus entre la Suisse et l'ancienne Monarchie austro-hongroise ".

The Treaty provided that

" les traités conclus entre la Suisse et l'ancienne Monarchie austro-hongroise ... seront appliqués par les Parties contractantes ".

This formulation clearly implied the non-identity of the Austrian
Republic with the Dual Monarchy, although it did not necessarily imply
a similar non-identity between the Republic and Cisleithania. Yet the
Swiss Federal Council, while not committing itself to any specific
attitude, did not reject or even contest the Austrian thesis which had
obviously formed the basis of the negotiations [4].

The Treaty of Vienna, concluded in 1921 between Austria and the
United States, after the latter had failed to ratify the Treaty of
Saint-Germain, appears to be based on the assumption that the Austrian
Republic was a new State. This results from the wording of the
Preamble :

" Being desirous of *establishing* securely friendly relations between the two
Nations [5]... "

---

1. Udina, *op. cit.*, pp. 194-195. He quotes the unpublished Austrian Note to the
Netherlands, of July 27, 1921, stating *inter alia* that : « ...la République d'Autriche...
reconnait, sans préjudice de son origine indépendante de l'ancienne Monarchie, être liée
par la Convention de la Haye du 17 juillet 1905, relative à la procédure civile... » *Ibid.*,
f.-n. 2.
2. *Ibid.*, p. 196.
3. " ...the Court at its request, had been informed by the Dutch Government that,
according to a diplomatic correspondence between the new Austrian Government and
itself, the two Governments were at variance as to the juridical identity between the
former Austrian Monarchy and the new Austrian Republic, the Dutch Government
having declared that it considered the latter as juridically identical with the former, but
the new Austrian Government having denied the correctness of this opinion... " District
Court of Amsterdam, October 29, 1926. A. D., 1927/28, case no. 20.
4. The Federal Council's message to the Federal Assembly of September 15, 1925,
explained that in reply to Swiss soundings « le gouvernement autrichien proclama le principe... que les traités antérieurs continuaient à être en vigueur en Autriche, en tant que
faisant partie de la législation interne, aussi longtemps que les anciennes lois conservaient
leur validité, mais que la République autrichienne, qui n'est pas le successeur juridique
de l'ancien Etat, mais bien un Etat entièrement nouveau, issu du démembrement de
l'Autriche-Hongrie, n'est pas liée vis-à-vis de l'étranger par les dits traités, sous réserve
des dispositions contraires contenues dans le Traité de St. Germain à l'égard des Puissances Alliées et Associées. » The Federal Council added the following statement and
comment on the newly concluded convention : « Du fait de la dissolution de l'ancienne
Monarchie austro-hongroise et du nouvel ordre constitutionnel en Autriche, une certaine
insécurité était née dans le domaine des relations juridiques entre la Suisse et son voisin
de l'Est... on ne peut que se féliciter que ces relations se trouvent de nouveau placées
sur une base juridique bien déterminée et solide. » Quoted by Udina, *op. cit.*, pp. 197-199.
5. *It. mine*, Martens N. R. G. 3rd series, XI, p. 910.

That this formulation was not accidental is borne out by the corresponding passage of the Preamble to the Treaty of Berlin between the United States and Germany, which speaks not of " establishing ", but of " restoring " the friendly relations which had existed between the two nations " prior to the outbreak of war " [1].

In a statement, of November 21, 1921, the Pope declared that the Concordat concluded in 1855 with Austria-Hungary was no longer in force by reason of the extinction of the other contracting party and the formation of new States [2].

Finally at the Rome Conference of April-June 1921, all the succeeding States met, including Austria. No distinction was made between them and they were all officially described as

« des Etats auxquels un territoire de l'ancienne Monarchie a été transféré ou qui sont nés du démembrement de cette Monarchie [3] ».

The municipal decisions of the States who were parties to the Saint-Germain Treaty, vary considerably. Thus, the Supreme Court of Poland stated on February 20, 1923, that

" the Treaty of Saint-Germain settled the problem ... in a way which determines that the Republic of Austria is the exclusive representative of the so-called Austrian half of the Austro-Hungarian Monarchy (Cisleithanien) [4] ".

This was not, however, the view of Italy who was anxious to affirm Italian sovereignty over her newly acquired provinces as from the moment of actual occupation, as sovereignty over *terra nullius*, and not derived from cession by an allegedly still existing sovereign [5]. Thus the Italian Court of Cassation held :

" With the complete dissolution of the enemy army and the simultaneous dismemberment of the Austro-Hungarian Empire, the national integration has been accomplished almost automatically and *pari passu* with the military occupation of the provinces. The Treaty of Saint-Germain and the law of annexation did not add anything to the rights of sovereignty over these provinces, irrevocably acquired by the Kingdom of Italy by reason of the victory of our arms... Treaty and statutes will bring the present situation into accord with the exigencies of international law. But it is absurd to think that in the interval between the armistice and the coming into force of the law of annexation, at a time when not only the sovereignty of Austro-Hungary over these provinces, but that very State, had disappeared, the two provinces, *disiecta membra* of a now destroyed organism have been able to live a separate political life outside the sovereignty of the Italian State which had become responsible for all its administration, justice, army or finance [6]. "

This was again confirmed by the same Court in 1927 :

---

1. *Ibid.*, XII, p. 917. Cf. the decision of the Tripartite Commission, below, p. 235.
2. Udina, *op. cit.*, p. 200.
3. *Ibid.*, p. 264, f.-n. 2.
4. *Niemiec and Niemiec v. Bialobrodziec and State Treasury*, A. D., 1923/24, case no. 33.
5. " ...la giurisprudenza nazionale si è pronunciata in gran parte e sempre più fermamente nel senso che su quei territori sin dall'inizio si sia instaurata la sovranità italiana, per lo sfacelo completo dell'antica Monarchia... " Udina, *op. cit.*, p. 169.
6. *Galatiolo v. Senes*, A. D., 1919/22, case no. 319.

" The Italian sovereignty having succeeded to the Austrian in the annexed territories *by force of arms*, it is to be assumed that the Italian State replaces the Austrian with regard to juridical relations of private law existing between the latter State and the private citizens [1]. "

Similarly, Czechoslovakia had an interest in denying the fiction of cession contained in the Saint-Germain Treaty, and, consequently, the fiction of continued survival of the Austrian Monarchy until the ratification of the Treaty. It was stated by the Czechoslovak Supreme Administrative Court :

" The plaintiffs contend that the new States established on the territory of the former Austro-Hungarian Monarchy acquired their territory together with their subjects only as the result of the cession of that territory by Austria. ... This contention starts form the fiction that the Austrian State in its former boundaries existed until the ratification of the Treaty of Peace of Saint-Germain... The Treaties of Peace did not found the existence of the Succession States. On the contrary, the latter participated in the conclusion of these Treaties in the quality of contracting parties as internationally recognized possessors in fact and in law of the power of a State in a certain territory [2]... "

International judicial decisions are even more inconsistent. One of these adopts a neutral attitude, while the other two go to two opposite extremes.

The Special Arbitral Tribunal *(Reparation Commission v. German Government)* stated on September 3, 1924

" that the treaties of Saint-Germain and Trianon are based on the theory that Austria and Hungary, parties thereto, represented the former Austro-Hungarian Monarchy [3] ".

This was no more than a statement of the underlying conception of the two Treaties, without indicating the Tribunal's own view on the matter.

As against this, the Italo-Austrian Mixed Arbitral Tribunal in the case of *Seppili v. Oesterreichische Hypothekenbank* went to the length of maintaining a view which no one else ever thought of maintaining : the Tribunal interpreted the famous third paragraph of the Preamble to the Saint-Germain Treaty as meaning the identity of the Austrian Republic with the Austro-Hungarian Monarchy as a whole [4]. According to the Tribunal the latter never ceased to exist, and the events which took place in Austria were nothing more than a mere change of government [5]. In view of everything that has already been said on the subject, this piece of interpretation hardly requires any further comment.

1. It. mine, *Czario v. Valentinis*, A. D., 1927/28, case no. 52.
2. *Rights of Citizenship (Establishment of Czechoslovak Nationality) Case*, A. D., 1919/1922, case no. 6.
3. *A. D.*, 1923/24, case no. 6.
4. See above, p. 224.
5. " Che questa premessa constata bensì che l'antica monarchia austro-ungarica, quale regime dinastico e governativo, era caduta, dando luogo ad una nuova forma di Governo in Austria ; non però che questa avesse cessato di esistere come aggregato politico e nella sua entità territoriale ; che questa rimase giuridicamente invariata sino all'entrata in vigore del Trattato di San Germano, poichè soltanto in virtù della cessione, che l'Austria ne effetuò espressamente con l'art. 36, i territori in base ad esso transferiti cessarono di appartenerle... " *Rec. TAM.*, vol. IX, p. 553. It may be wondered whether the learned judges ever took into account the existence of the Treaty of Trianon.

An exactly opposite view was expressed in the Administrative Decision No. 1 of the Tripartite Claims Commission (United States, Austria and Hungary) of May 25, 1927 :

" It was against the Imperial and Royal Austro-Hungarian Government that the United States waged war. ... Following the armistice that government ceased to exist. ... In pursuance of the terms of the several treaties entered into force between the opposing Powers after the armistice, not only was the Austro-Hungarian Dual Monarchy dismembered but substantial parts of the territories of the former Austrian Empire and of the former Kingdom of Hungary were ceded some to new and some to existing States. The Austria and the Hungary dealt with by the United States in entering into the Treaties of Vienna and of Budapest respectively not only bore little resemblance either to the government or the territory of the Dual Monarchy with which the United States had been at war but differend essentially from the former Austrian Empire and the former Kingdom of Hungary. Unlike the Treaty of Berlin " *restoring* friendly relations " between the United States and Germany, these treaties in terms " *establish* " for the first time such relations between Austria and the United States and between Hungary and the United States [1]. "

There could hardly be a more incongrous picture than the one outlined above. In other words, the fictitious basis of the Saint-Germain Treaty achieved only a limited degree of effectiveness. Its fundamental thesis had by no means been uniformly accepted in State practice. It may be argued that the Treaty could not bind States which were not parties to it. It has, however, been seen that even its signatories, like Italy and Czechoslovakia, did not consider themselves bound by its basic assumption.

It may therefore be concluded that the Treaty of Saint-Germain, proceeding on an assumption which was contrary to general international law, and calling an existing situation something which it was not, resulted in a fiction, whereby the actual effectiveness of the Treaty found itself considerably reduced. The Treaty was unable to prevail against the supremacy of general international law and the pressure of existing facts. Just as general international law can set limits to what a treaty can *do*, so an existing reality can set limits to what a treaty can *do effectively*. This conclusion may serve as yet another example of the inherent limitations of a voluntarist conception of international law [2].

6. CONCLUSION.

There can be no doubt that the problem of identity or non-identity of the Austrian Republic with the Empire finds a clear solution in general international law. The legal order of the Austrian Empire, identified by its basic norm, had been replaced by an entirely new legal order, valid for an entirely new territorial and personal sphere of validity. Of

---

1. A. D., 1927/28, case no. 54.
2. « ...les fictions n'ont aucune force obligatoire en droit. Elles ont objectivement soit une autre portée juridique que celle qu'elles affirment elles-mêmes, soit même une portée nulle. De même que le contenu d'une loi, peut n'avoir aucune valeur juridique le contenu d'un traité. » Kelsen, *Naissance de l'État*, p. 633.

the delimitation of the old State under international law, there remained nothing. The question of the Austrian Republic's identity with Cisleithania is therefore to be answered in the negative.

Such answer is gained by a correct ascertainment of the facts which, in turn, must be examined in the light of the existing rules of international law. An opposite view can only be based on a doubt whether there is a principle of international law which denies the continued existence of a State in case of a revolutionary dismemberment, — or whether such dismemberment did in fact take place. The former would be inconsistent with international law ; the latter would be inconsistent with the facts.

It has been seen, however, that, as far as the peace-makers were concerned, their view of the Austrian case was distorted not by an error of judgment as to facts or law, but by extra-legal, purely political considerations. The justice or otherwise of these considerations is a matter falling outside the scope of this study. It may be assumed that the Allies were politically free to impose greater burdens on Austria than on the other succeeding States ; they were not, however, legally free to call an existing situation something it was not. Had they avoided the confusion between the notions of succession and identity [1], they might perhaps have adopted the solution of imposing such greater burdens on Austria under the heading of State succession. Their political aims would then perhaps have been achieved without coming into collision with general international law.

According to the latter there can be no doubt that the Austrian Republic was not, and could not have been, identical with the Austrian Empire.

---

1. See above, pp. 207-209.

CHAPTER III.

YUGOSLAVIA.

As in the case of Austria, the problem of the identity of the Kingdom of Serbs, Croats and Slovenes with the Kingdom of Serbia is not free from political complications and prejudice. Thus, it has often been assumed that the theory of post-war Yugoslavia being an enlarged Serbia was mainly defended by Serb or — at all events — pro-Serb writers, with obvious political purpose. Similarly, the contrary view is supposed to have favoured Croat federalist or even separatist tendencies. The history of events leading up to the formation of the Kingdom of Serbs, Croats and Slovenes (the S.C.S.-State) abounds in Serbo-Croat, or — more exactly — Serbo-Yugoslav differences, which could not have failed to have an influence on these events. Nor can there be much doubt that the final formation of the S.C.S.-State was influenced by the pressure which Italy brought to bear on the short-lived Yugoslav State, established on former Austro-Hungarian territory.

All these matters are of as little relevance to a legal analysis, as the Austrian Republic's desire to escape responsibility for war-debts and reparations or the Allied interest in the opposite course, and may therefore be omitted even from historical narrative.

1. HISTORICAL BACKGROUND.

The formation of the Kingdom of Serbs, Croats and Slovenes — the S.C.S.-State — was, next to the disintegration of the Austro-Hungarian Monarchy, the second historical event after the First World War which gave rise to the problem of State identity and continuity [1].

The South Slavs, i.e. the Serbs, Croats and Slovenes, had before the war formed part of different States. Only a minority of them, i.e. 5 millions, had lived in the two independent Kingdoms of Serbia and Montenegro. Seven millions belonged to the Austro-Hungarian Monarchy, where their territories were subject to further administrative divisions [2]; of these, mention may be made of the Kingdom of Croatia, which formed part of Hungary and possessed a Diet of its own. In

1. For history see : Temperley, op. cit.; Graham, op. cit.; Udina, op. cit.; Foreign Office, Historical Section, The Jugo-Slav Movement; Kaufmann, op. cit.; Zolger, Die Verfassung Jugoslaviens; Schilling, Ist das Königreich Jugoslawien mit dem früheren Königreich Serbien völkerrechtlich identisch; Holzer, Die Entstehung des jugoslawischen Staates; Ministère des Affaires Etrangères du Monténégro, Le rôle de la France dans l'annexion forcée du Monténégro; Fedozzi, La situation juridique et internationale du Monténégro, in Journal du Droit International, 1922, p. 549.
2. See Temperley, op. cit., IV, p. 171, f.-n.

spite of a certain degree of inaccuracy, it is proposed, for the sake of simplicity, to call the South Slavs of the Dual Monarchy " Yugoslavs ", while reserving the name of " Serbs " for South-Slavs, belonging to the Kingdom of Serbia.

In spite of political barriers, the ideal of national unity developed among the South-Slavs everywhere. Before, and even during, the war, four distinct tendencies gave different expression to this aspiration : the Pan-Serb, the Croat, the Trialist and the Yugoslav idea. The latter which sought the formation of an entirely new national State, embracing the whole South-Slav population, must at one time have seemed the most unrealistic ; for its realization depended not only upon a break-up of the Dual Monarchy, but also upon the elimination of Russian influence, definitely favouring the Pan-Serb solution, and — last not least — upon the overcoming of considerable internal friction among the South-Slavs themselves. It was, however, precisely the Yugoslav idea which was to emerge victorious from the First World War.

The Austro-Hungarian war on Serbia drove the South-Slavs into two enemy camps. Throughout all their tribulations, the Serbs — soon to be joined by Montenegro — pursued their war of defence and liberation within the framework of their independent State, with a government and an army of their own. No such possibility existed for the Yugoslavs, nationals of the Dual Monarchy, who were called upon to serve in the Imperial and Royal Army and subjected to considerable pressure and even reprisals at the hands of the administration. Until the later period of the war there was hardly any possibility of Yugoslav political action inside Austria-Hungary.

It was for this reason that a Yugoslav National Committee with headquarters in London was founded in the early stages of the war, under the chairmanship of Dr. Trumbic. The task of the Committee was to represent the Yugoslavs abroad, particularly in the Allied countries, and to pursue the aim of their liberation from Austro-Hungarian domination.

One of the most important problems facing the Committee concerned its relations with the Serbian Government which, after the occupation of the whole of Serbia in 1916, also went into exile. It was only in 1917 that representatives of the two bodies met in Corfu where, on July 20, they issued a Manifesto, known as the Pact of Corfu and signed by Pasic, the Serbian Prime Minister and Trumbic on behalf of the National Yugoslav Committee. The Manifesto proclaimed the common will of the Serbs, Croats and Slovenes to unite in one free and independent Kingdom. The following year the Congress of the oppressed nationalities of the Austro-Hungarian Empire took place in Rome. On April 18, 1918, the Congress published a common declaration, the so-called Pact of Rome, proclaiming the right of every nationality represented to " constitute its own nationality and State unity or to complete it ". The Pact also included a special agreement between the " representatives of the Italian people and of the Yugoslav people " [1].

---

1. See below, p. 250.

The agreement was of special political importance in view of the fact that relations between Italy and the Yugoslavs promised to be strained in consequence of the London Pact of 1915 which had practically disposed of large sections of Yugoslav territory in favour of Italy. Thus, the Yugoslav National Committee was slowly gaining in political stature, particularly since the fall of Tsarism which was committed to the Pan-Serb conception ; but it never achieved the degree of recognition which had been afforded the Polish and Czechoslovak National Committees.

Political action by the Yugoslavs within the Dual Monarchy itself had to proceed much more cautiously. On May 30, 1917, the Yugoslav Club of the Austrian Reichsrat put forward for the first time a definite demand for the re-uniting of all lands inhabited by Slovenes, Croats and Serbs, into one independent and democratic State, free from all foreign domination, under the Hapsburg dynasty. This last condition seems to have been considered both by the Yugoslavs and the Austrians as a purely tactical move, called for by the existing circumstances.

In 1918, however, this Yugoslav claim had already been overtaken by events. The disintegration of Austria-Hungary was proceeding at an ever growing pace [1]. In the course of October local national councils sprang into existence in Lubljana, Split, Zagreb, Sarajevo and Nowysad ; all of them recognized the supreme authority of the National Council of Zagreb, composed of 85 members representing various Yugoslav provinces and of 5 members each from the Yugoslav Club and the Croatian and Bosnian Diets. On October 29, the Croatian Diet solemnly proclaimed separation from the Dual Monarchy and the union of all Yugoslavs who had formerly belonged to it. The Ban of Croatia, as the Government representative, submitted to events and surrendered his executive powers to the National Council in the name of the Government. The National Council immediately assumed supreme authority in the new State. The Yugoslav armed forces acknowledged its authority. Two days later, on October 31, the Austro-Hungarian Ministry of War, acting on orders of the Emperor, transferred to the National Council the entire Imperial and Royal Navy on the Adriatic. On the same day the National Council notified the Allies of the constitution of the new State and informed them of its intention to unite with Serbia.

The desire for union undoubtedly received a sense of urgency due to the action of Italy who, basing herself on the Pact of London, proceeded to occupy Yugoslav territory. Thereupon the National Council asked Serbia for military assistance which was immediately granted. Moreover, representatives of the National Council, the Serbian Government and the Yugoslav London Committee met in Geneva on November 6, 1918, to consider ways and means of achieving union. It was from Geneva, on November 8, that Pasic, the Serbian Prime Minister, accorded recognition to the new Yugoslav State. A plan was drafted, providing for the formation of a common Serbo-Yugoslav

---

1. See above, pp. 200-201.

Cabinet, which, without for the time being replacing the existing Serbian Government and the Yugoslav National Council, would have the task of convening a Constituent National Assembly, common for all the Serbs, Croats and Slovenes. It was also decided that Montenegro was to form part of the new Yugoslav State. The Serbian Prime Minister undertook to work for the recognition of the new State by the Allied Powers.

The Geneva resolutions were not, however, implemented and it was only on November 24, with Italian pressure still acting as a stimulant, that the National Council finally proclaimed the union of the Yugoslav State with the Kingdoms of Serbia and Montenegro. On December 1st, a deputation from the National Council submitted this resolution to the Prince Regent of Serbia, whereupon the latter accepted the offer and proclaimed the union of the two States into one Kingdom of Serbs, Croats and Slovenes, the name being chosen in conformity with the Corfu Manifesto. In turn, the new Kingdom was proclaimed on December 4 by the National Council, and the union was confirmed by an Act passed by the National Council and the Serbian Skupshtina in joint session on December 16. There followed the formation of a government for the unified State on December 20, the dissolution of the National Council and the Skupshtina on the 28 and 29 of December respectively, and the summoning of a joint Provisional National Assembly, composed of deputies of the former Parliaments and other delegates from new territories, on March 16, 1919. There is general agreement that December 1 was the date of birth of the new State.

Following a general election, the Constituent Assembly met on December 12, 1920. On June 28, 1921, the State was given a Constitution.

A few words must now be said about Montenegro. There too, a National Assembly (the Great National Skupshtina of Podgorica) proclaimed on November 26, 1918, the deposition of the King and union with Serbia. It is, however, difficult to see in these proceedings any analogy with Yugoslav developments. Although the facts relating to Montenegro are indeed " exceedingly obscure " [1], the process would seem to have been as follows : in September and October 1918 a rising took place against the Austrian occupants and a provisional government was set up. At the same time Serbian troops occupied the country. The Podgorica Assembly, whose origins are shrouded in mystery or, at best, subject to partisan comment, met under Serbian occupation. Moreover, serious disturbances, including even guerilla warfare against the new regime took place and seem to have lasted for some time. According to Temperley,

"It is probable that the Assembly at Podgorica was most irregularly elected, and contained only partisans of union."

And he concludes :

---

1. Temperley, *op. cit.*, IV, p. 202.

" There seems to be no doubt that the Montenegrins, as a whole, desire to form part of united Yugoslavia, but that they cannot in a moment forget their particularist tradition and resent being administered in a draconian fashion by men who have spent their lives in Serbia [1]. "

This observation would seem partly to confirm allegations by the Montenegrin Government in exile concerning Serbian terror in the country [2].

The attitude of the Allies was at first undecided. The British Government

" were reluctant to accept the decision of the Podgorica Assembly as definite and decided to await the result of the elections to the Constituent Assembly [3] ".

The French Government adopted a similar attitude. It was only after these elections had taken place that recognition was withdrawn from the exiled King and Government of Montenegro and the union with Yugoslavia recognized [4].

On November 18, 1920, the exiled Government of Montenegro applied for admission to the League of Nations. The application was refused. However, the report of M. Mantoux, Director of the Political Section, to the Fifth Commission, included the following passage :

« Une Assemblée monténégrine réunie en 1918 a proclamé ... l'union avec l'Etat yougoslave. Il est vrai que la validité de cette décision et du mandat même de l'Assemblée élue, disent ses adversaires, sous la pression des Serbes et entourée de baïonnettes serbes, est contestée. Il est vrai qu'une opposition indivisible s'est manifestée contre l'annexion pure et simple de l'Etat yougoslave [5]... »

There is general agreement among writers to qualify the proceedings relating to Montenegro as a simple annexation of that country by Serbia [6]. Even Zolger who clearly suggests union and not annexation (without, however, formulating it *expressis verbis*), practically ignores the problem and, in discussing the legal status of the S.C.S.-State, concentrates exclusively on the relations between Serbia and the Yugoslav State, formed on former Austro-Hungarian territory [7].

Thus, the available evidence points to a straightforward annexation of Montenegro by Serbia. Consequently, the question of the identity of the new S.C.S.-State with the Kingdom of Serbia must be examined only in the light of relations between Serbia and the Yugoslav State.

---

1. *Ibid.*, pp. 202-203.
2. Ministère des Affaires Etrangères du Monténégro, *Le rôle de la France dans l'annexion forcée du Monténégro.*
3. Official statement quoted by Temperley, *op. cit.*, p. 204.
4. Udina disputes the validity of the elections, maintaining that they only proved Serbia's determination to annex Montenegro, *op. cit.*, p. 139, *f.-n.* 1. A similar opinion is being vigorously asserted by Fedozzi, *op. cit.*
5. *Le rôle de la France*, p. 201.
6. Udina, *op. cit.*, pp. 139-140 ; Fauchille, *op. cit.*, I, p. 374 ; Liszt, *op. cit.*, p. 90 ; Schilling, *op. cit.*, p. 55. Kaufmann speaks of the " verworrene Einzelheiten " of the proceedings and does not investigate the matter any further, *op. cit.*, p. 223.
7. *Op. cit.*

2. THE YUGOSLAV PROBLEM IN THE LIGHT OF GENERAL INTER-
NATIONAL LAW.

A) *Conditions of Union under International Law.*

The problem to be investigated is not a new one. On the contrary,
it is exactly parallel to the Italian case, and the same well-established
rules of international law apply. If what in fact took place was merely
territorial annexation by Serbia, then there can be only one answer to
the question: the post-war S.C.S.-State was identical with the pre-war
Kingdom of Serbia. If, however, there was a union, then the old
Kingdom of Serbia had disappeared and an entirely new State came
into existence. Thus, once again the theoretical foundations of the
question are not in doubt, and the correct answer to the Yugoslav
problem depends upon a correct ascertainment of the facts and a correct
application of the relevant rules of international law.

However, before proceeding with this investigation, it is necessary
to define more precisely the conditions of union under international law.

The legal nature of a union has been defined with all clarity by
Pufendorf, whose opinion (quoted by Kaufmann at the beginning of
his essay on Yugoslavia) may be reproduced here :

" Ad eiusmodi mutationem, qua civitas aliqua eadem esse definit, referunt
quoque si duo populi uniantur, non per modum foederis, aut per communem regem,
sed ut revera ex duabus civitatibus una fiat. ... Est tamen accurate considerandum,
an duo pluresve populi ita se coniugant, ut pari deinceps omnes iure novam aliquam
civitatem constitutum eant [1]. "

This classical definition lays down three conditions of union :

1. The first condition, slightly obscured by Pufendorf's inaccurate
and inconsistent terminology *(populi — civitates)* is the existence of
two, or more, States, subjects of international law, between whom a
union may take place. There can be no union between a State on the
one hand and a non-descript territory or province on the other. It has
been seen that one of the strongest arguments in favour of Italy being
just an enlarged Sardinia was precisely the non-State character of
territories which came to be joined to the Sardinian Kingdom [2].

2. The second condition concerns the process of union. Not only
a territory or a province, but also a whole State can be annexed. Thus,
the State character of the " second partner " does not automatically
exclude the possibility of annexation. What is necessary for a union is
that the process should, in Pufendorf's words, take place " *pari iure* ".
In other words : there can be no extension of the legal order of one
State over the other State. On the contrary, a union must be the product
of a joint will of the uniting States, formulated and expressed by proper
organs whose will is imputable to the respective States. The formulation
and expression of such will must therefore, by definition, take place in

1. *Ius naturae et gentium*, VIII, 12, 6 ; quoted by Kaufmann, *op. cit.*, p. 212.
2. See above, pp. 194-195.

conditions of complete freedom of action and mutual non-interference. The analysis of the Italian case has shown that actual annexations by Sardinia had taken place prior to any manifestation of will on the part of the annexed populations, — whatever the legal value of such manifestation in the particular case [1].

3. The third and last condition is merely a consequence of the preceding two : it is of the very essence of a union that it must result in the extinction of the uniting States as separate subjects of international law and the creation of an entirely new State, a " *civitas nova* ", which is not identical with either of them. It has been seen that at no moment could the extinction of Sardinia have been assumed and that, on the contrary, the Sardinian State with its Constitution and its international rights and obligations continued to exist, — neither the Constitution nor the treaties having come to rest on a new formal basis [2].

The above conditions of a union under international law can hardly be seriously contested. If then the principle is admitted, it is necessary to examine the Yugoslav case with a view to finding out whether the facts correspond to the above scheme. According to whether they do or do not, they will have to be qualified either as union or annexation. This will in turn solve the problem of the identity or non-identity of the S.C.S.-State with the Kingdom of Serbia.

It is therefore necessary to consider *a)* whether the South Slav territories which detached themselves from the Dual Monarchy actually assumed the form of a State, — *b)* whether or not their merger with Serbia took place *pari iure*, — and finally, *c)* whether both Serbia and the Yugoslav State (if it did exist) became extinct and made room for a new State entity.

a) *Parties to Union.*

It has been seen that on October 29, 1918, the National Council of Zagreb assumed supreme power over all Yugoslav territories formerly belonging to the Dual Monarchy, proclaiming their separation from that State and their new and independent existence [3].

The new entity assumed the official name of " the State of Slovenes, Croats and Serbs ". It had its own territory, however badly delimited and its own population. It exercised supreme authority through the National Council. It had its own laws [4]. It had an army and a navy. It was effective on its territory. The fact that it existed for only a short period of time cannot possibly divest it of its State character for as long as it lasted. It is therefore submitted that it did fulfil all requirements of a State under international law. The new State even achieved some degree of international recognition (without which, it is submitted, it would still have been a State, fulfilling as it did all the conditions of statehood). The first act of recognition came, curiously

---

1. See above, pp. 195-196.
2. See above, pp. 196-197.
3. See above, p. 239.
4. See Udina, *op. cit.*, pp. 131 et seq.

enough, from Austria-Hungary herself, when on October 31, the Emperor ordered the transfer of the whole Navy on the Adriatic to the Yugoslav State. This act has all the characteristics of the so-called implied recognition [1]. It is impossible to imagine a State transferring its entire Navy to some non-descript entity. The second country to recognize the new State was Serbia, on November 8. Kaufmann even claims that the Allies themselves recognized the new State on November 16 [2]. This claim is, however, exaggerated. The Allies consistently refused recognition; on November 16 only some limited contact between the National Council and the Allied Naval Command in Corfu was established for purely practical reasons [3].

The existence of a Yugoslav State is generally accepted by writers [4]. This is only natural in the case of those of them who go on to defend the theory that the S.C.S.-State was a new State (Kaufmann, Udina, Zolger), for otherwise they could not have maintained a union between the two States. But it is somewhat surprising to find that the State character of the Yugoslav State is also asserted by those writers who, in their final conclusions, exclude the union in favour of a territorial agrandizement of Serbia [5]. It would have been logical if, after admitting its State character, they would have proceeded to deny the union by proving that, in the further course of events, this new State was annexed by Serbia. The writers in question, however, take refuge in a doubtful dualistic argument, according to which the new Yugoslav State was indeed a State, but only under municipal and not under international law [6].

The very idea of an entity being a State and a non-State at one and the same time is inadmissible. It is equally inadmissible to suggest that an entity can be a State " internally " and not be a State " internationally ". As has been seen, the State character of an entity can be determined only and exclusively by criteria provided by international law [7]. But how is international law to determine the character of an entity which apparently does not fall within its province? The only obvious conclusion of this doubtful argument is that even the last-named writers could not altogether ignore and deny the actual existence on former Austro-Hungarian territories of the new Yugoslav State.

It can therefore be safely asserted that this State did in fact exist. This fact can only be distorted, but not denied.

---

1. Temperley, *op. cit.*, IV, p. 199; Holzer, *op. cit.*, p. 38.
2. *Op. cit.*, p. 219.
3. " ...il riconoscimento del governo di fatto di Zagabri a certi limitati effetti... " Udina, *op. cit.*, p. 133, *f.-n.* 1, where he rightly warns against overestimating the importance of this fact.
4. See, however, a contrary though unsubstantiated opinion of the German-Yugoslav Mixed Arbitral Tribunal in the case of *Franz Peinitsch c.* 1) *Etat allemand*, 2) *Etat prussien*, 3) *Banque Bleichroeder*, of September 18, 1922. « Sans parler du fait qu'il est au moins douteux qu'un «Etat Sudslave» ait jamais existé au sens que Peinitsch donne à ce terme... » *Rec. TAM*, vol. II, p. 621.
5. Holzer, *op. cit.*, p. 37; Schilling, *op. cit.*, p. 112.
6. " Staatsrechtlich ", not " völkerrechtlich "; Holzer, *op. cit.*, p. 64; Jovanovic as quoted by Holzer, *op. cit.*, pp. 61-64.; Schilling, *op. cit.*, p. 113.
7. See above, pp. 2, 135-136, 168.

b) *The Will to Unite.*

The first condition of union — the existence of two separate States — was thus fulfilled. It must further be considered whether, in fact, the two States united by way of parallel proceedings of their respective organs, formulating and expressing the will to union in a manner clearly imputable to the respective States, — or whether the new Yugoslav State was simply annexed by unilateral action of Serbia.

As has already been seen [1], the immediate impulse to union came precisely from the Yugoslav side, in the following proclamation of the National Council of Zagreb, of November 24, 1918 :

" The National S.C.S.-Council, in accordance with its former decisions, and the statements of the Government of the Kingdom of Serbia, proclaims the union of the State of Slovenes, Croats and Serbs, in the whole compact district of the former Austro-Hungarian Monarchy, with the Kingdoms of Serbia and Montenegro, in a united State of Serbs, Croats and Slovenes, and chooses a committee of 28 people with complete authority to organize without delay, in agreement with the Government of the Kingdom of Serbia and with the representatives of all parties in Serbia and Montenegro, a united State according to given directions [2]... "

A resolution of the same date transferred the regency of the united State to the Serbian Prince Regent

" who will summon the State Council to Sarajevo and appoint the first Government ".

The State Council was to consist of

" 1) all members of the South Slav National Council at Zagreb, 2) of fifty representatives of the Kingdom of Serbia, and 3) of five representatives of Montenegro and the Voivodina ".

The Regent was to appoint a Government from members of the State Council and elections to a Constituent Assembly were to be held [3].

On December 1st, the exchange of declarations took place between the Delegation of the National Council on behalf of the Yugoslav State and the Serbian Prince Regent on behalf of Serbia. The address of the Delegation spoke of the desire of the Slovenes, Croats and Serbs, who had created their own independent State on the territory of the former Dual Monarchy, to be united with Serbia and Montenegro in a single (" in einem einzigen ") national State of the Serbs, Croats and Slovenes. Accepting the offer, the Regent proclaimed the union of Serbia with the independent State of Slovenes, Croats and Serbs in a single Kingdom of the Serbs, Croats and Slovenes [4].

Indeed, nothing could be more remote from annexation, which is a unilateral action on the part of the annexing State. Instead of such unilateral action, the proceedings described represent a classical example of a parallel formation, expression and final exchange of will on the

---

1. See above, p. 240.
2. Graham, *op. cit.*, p. 636.
3. *Ibid.*, pp. 636-637.
4. Quotations in Zolger, *op. cit.*, p. 184, and Udina, *op. cit.*, pp. 134-135.

part of two uniting States, acting on a footing of full equality [1]. Nothing else was possible, since all the information available goes to show that the Yugoslav State would never have allowed itself be annexed and that a *unio æquali iure* alone came into consideration [2]. This is further borne out not only by the fact that the immediate initiative to fusion came precisely from the Yugoslav State, but also by the fact that it was the Yugoslav side which provided organisational and technical plans for carrying the union into effect.

It is of interest to see the counter-arguments which have been advanced to contest that the above-described events resulted in a union. Thus Schilling adopts an argument by Jovanovic to the effect that the Yugoslav-Serb exchange of declarations was neither a union nor an international agreement of any sort, because it took place between sections of one and the same nation [3]. Although Schilling puts forward this argument with evident satisfaction, it has little to do with international law. Is it to be assumed that, had the " races " been different, the process would have resulted in union in any event?

Having once adopted such a handy suggestion, Schilling carries it to the bitter end : there was no union at all ; there was simply an application of the maxim " gleiches Blut in ein gleiches Reich ", in complete analogy with the Italian Risorgimento and with the annexation of Austria by Germany in 1938 [4]. At this point a legal discussion with Schilling must cease.

As for Holzer, he considers it possible to deny the union and, consequently, the non-identity of the S.C.S. State-with Serbia, without analyzing the events in question.

No serious argument has therefore been advanced against the view that the process of formation of the S.C.S.-State consisted not in the unilateral annexation by Serbia, but in parallel proceedings of two independent States. The second condition of a union, i.e. mutual consent, was therefore fulfilled [5].

---

1. " Paritätische Willensübereinstimmung" according to Zolger: he gives the clearest appraisal of the events, when he speaks of " feierliche Erklärungen, welche die zur völkerrechtlichen Vertretung legitimierten Organe der beiden Staaten, der Zagreber Nationalrat und der König von Serbien am 1.12.1918 in Belgrad austauschten. " *Op. cit.*, pp. 183-184. Similarly Udina who describes the exchange of declarations as " atto formale di fusione " and continues : " Qui siamo di fronte a delle vere e proprie dichiarazioni di volontà, emesse dagli organi costituzionalmente ed internazionalmente competenti a produrle, e tendenti alla formazione di un nuovo Stato. " *Op. cit.*, p. 135.

2. Kaufmann, *op. cit.*, p. 223.

3. " Weder die Erklärung von Korfu noch die Dezemberakte sind Verträge zwischen völkisch-verschiedenen Gruppen, die sich *aequali iure* vereinigt haben, sie sind vielmehr Proklamationen über die Vereinigung ein und desselben Volkes gewesen. " Quoted by Schilling, *op. cit.*, p. 75. And, always on the assumption that Schilling summarizes his argument correctly, Jovanovic explains Kaufmann's insistence on a *unio aequali iure* by the fact that, under the influence of Austrian propaganda, Kaufmann mistook Serbs, Croats and Slovenes for three different nations.

4. *Op. cit.*, p. 131.

5. According to Zolger, there was no subjection, but spontaneous union, no annexation or occupation " sondern das Resultat paritätischer Willenseinigung und Willens-übereinstimmung zweier rechtlich koordinierter Subjekte. ...nicht eine Inkorporation, ...sondern Fusion zu einem neuen Gemeinwesen. " *Op. cit.*, p. 185. Similarly Udina : " ...nessun atto d'annessione da parte della Serbia, nessuna recezione or prevalenza d'un ordinamento giuridico sull' altro, ma formazione di uno del tutto nuovo. " *Op. cit.*, p. 136.

c) *Birth of a New State.*

There only remains the question whether the two uniting States became extinct, giving place to a *" civitas nova "*, a new subject of international law, not identical with either of them.

The gradual liquidation of the organs of the two separate States has already been described [1]. The two separate parliaments and the two separate governments ceased to exist. The separate legal orders of the two States were put out of force.

New organs of the new State were duly created in their place, including a new Parliament and a new Government [2]. They were not the Parliament and the Government either of Serbia or of the Yugoslav State [3].

The old legal order, the Serbian Constitution was duly replaced by a new constitution for the unified Kingdom on July 28, 1921. A doubt may, however, be entertained as to the legal order, the basic norm, which was in force in the new State between December 1918 and June 1921.

The answer is clear : the basic norm was no longer the Serbian Constitution. It could not have been this Constitution, even if there had been an intention to retain it provisionally. For obviously, the Serbian Constitution could not, and did not, provide for the merger of its own Parliament with that of another State, nor for the liquidation of its government in favour of one composed of Serbian and non-Serbian nationals, nor for elections throughout Serbian and non-Serbian territory to a Constituent Assembly which was to give a new constitution to Serbia and non-Serbia, a constitution of which Serbia alone would have not been in need. The provisional basic norm of the new State is to be found in the December Act of Union [4].

This is far from being a purely theoretical view. It was the December Act which laid down the fundamental law of the unified country for the transition period, which provided for the creation of new organs — government and parliament — which, by way of reception, took over the dynasty and which even determined the date and mode of future elections for the Constituent Assembly [5]. The new State thus had its new organs as well as its new, albeit provisional, legal order.

---

1. See above, p. 240.
2. See above, p. 240.
3. In his proclamation of January 7, 1919, the Regent declared : " ...I have... proceeded to the formation of our *first* State government. " *It. mine,* quoted by Graham, *op. cit.,* pp. 639-641.
4. Thus Zolger, *op. cit.,* pp. 185-186.
5. " ...dass die Herrschergewalt auf dem ganzen Gebiete des Einen Staates der Serben, Kroaten und Slowenen von Seiner Majestät König Peter bzw. in seiner Vertretung von Eurer königlichen Hoheit als Regenten ausgeübt und dass zugleich im Einverständnisse mit der Regierung Eurer königlichen Hoheit und mit den Vertretern aller nationalen Parteien Serbiens und Montenegros für den ganzen südslawischen Staat eine parlamentarische Regierung und eine nationale Repräsentanz gebildet werden solle. ... dass diese provisorische nationale Repräsentanz im gemeinsamen Einvernehmen des Nationalrates und der Volksvertreter des Königreiches Serbien gebildet und dass in Gemässheit der parlamentarischen Prinzipien die Verantwortlichkeit der Staatsregierung gegenüber dieser nationalen Repräsentanz konstituiert werde. ...In der gegenwärtigen

The third and last condition of a union under international law was thus fulfilled : a *civitas nova* took the place of two former States which had both become extinct.

The following notification from the new State to foreign countries is therefore fully in accordance with international law :

« Nous vous informons qu'il s'est constitué le 1er décembre 1918 un Royaume serbe-croate-slovène, qui englobe la Serbie et tous les pays yougoslaves de l'ancien royaume austro-hongrois, qu'un nouveau gouvernement a été constitué le 21 décembre 1918 par le roi et que toutes les légations de l'ancien royaume de Serbie s'appelleront désormais des légations du royaume serbe-croate-slovène. Cette union qui a pour résultat la transformation du royaume a été proclamé à Belgrade le 1er décembre 1918 par les délégués croates et slovènes munis de pleins pouvoirs par une assemblée réunie à cet effet à Zagreb et par les délégués serbes [1]. »

B) *Additional Evidence of Union.*

a) *International Recognition.*

The new State did not achieve international recognition immediately. At the beginning of 1919 the Allied and Associated Powers still recognized only the Serbian and not the S.C.S. delegates to the Peace Conference. This attitude gave rise to an energetic protest on the part of the new State.

« La décision du Conseil supérieur *(sic!)* de n'admettre à la Conférence de la Paix que les délégués du Royaume de Serbie et non du Royaume des Serbes, Croates, Slovènes, formé par l'union de la Serbie avec les provinces yougoslaves de l'ancienne monarchie austro-hongroise, risque de provoquer un conflit qui peut avoir des conséquences sérieuses. En effet, à l'heure actuelle il n'existe aucun Gouvernement purement serbe, qui pourrait nommer une délégation pour représenter « l'ancien royaume de Serbie », le Gouvernement de Belgrade étant aujourd'hui le Gouvernement commun des Serbes, Croates et Slovènes [2]. »

This view eventually prevailed. The United States was the first Power to recognize the new State officially on February 5, 1919. On May 1st, on the occasion of the verification of credentials for the Peace Conference, the credentials of the S.C.S. delegates were accepted. Great Britain granted recognition on June 2, and France on June 6. Recognition by Italy and the other States parties to the Versailles Treaty must date from the signature of that Treaty [3]. The new State was also recognized by neutral countries, such as Norway, Switzerland and Spain [4].

Uebergangsperiode müssten nach unserer Meinung die Vorbedingungen für die endgültige Organisation unseres (neuen) Staates geschaffen werden. Zu diesem Behufe müsste unsere (gemeinsame) Regierung vor allem die Konstituante vorbereiten, die nach Vorschlag des Nationalrates auf Basis des allgemeinen, gleichen, direkten, geheimen und proportionellen Stimmrechtes zu wählen wäre und spätestens sechs Monate nach Friedensschluss zusammenzutreten hätte. " Quoted by Zolger, *op. cit.*, p. 184.

1. Quoted by Kaufmann, *op. cit.*, p. 224.
2. Quoted by Kaufmann, *op. cit.*, p. 224.
3. Temperley, *op. cit.*, V, p. 158.
4. See Döring : " *Ist Jugoslawien (SHS-Staat) im Sinne des Versailler Vertrages, insbesondere im Sinne des Art.* 297 h *letzter Abschnitt, ein* " *Neuer Staat* "? *Juristische Wochenschrift*, 1922, pp. 352-355. All the documents quoted therein emphasize the fact of recognition being given to a new State.

There would have been no reason whatever for a renewed recognition of the old Kingdom of Serbia on the part of the international community. Serbia had been recognized by most States as early as 1878, she had been an Allied Power in the late war, and the idea of her having been suddenly and unnecessarily recognized a second time is completely unconvincing [1]. Schilling maintains that it was not the new State, but territorial changes in the old one which were recognized [2]. If so, it is hard to see why neither Greece nor Rumania were made the subject of recognition. Relying on Fauchille, Holzer claims that the recognition related only to " the changes in the internal political organisation " of the State [3]. But such changes, leaving the personality of the State unaffected, do not call for recognition ; should, however, specific political conditions render such recognition necessary, it would be accorded to the new government, emerging out of an internal transformation, and not a new State.

The evidence of the new characetr of the S.C.S.-State, provided by the international recognition of the latter, acquires full weight by reason of its conformity with general international law.

b) *The Yugoslav Conviction.*

Within the limits already indicated [4], the intention and conviction of the Serbs, Croats and Slovenes themselves may be taken into account as additional evidence. Their intention to create a new State is clearly shown by the documents of the period [5].

The first of these documents is the Corfu Manifesto [6], dealing with the problems facing Serbs, Croats and Slovenes in " their joint future State ", — i.e., if words have any reasonable meaning at all, in a State which did not exist as yet, which was a thing of the future. The passages which follow confirm this interpretation.

" The State of the Serbs, Croats and Slovenes ... *will be* a free and independent kingdom, with indivisible territory and unity of allegiance. It *will be* a constitutional democratic and parliamentary monarchy under the Karageorgevitch Dynasty. ... This State *will be* named " The Kingdom of the Serbs, Croats and Slovenes "."

The style of the Sovereign

---

1. Thus Udina, *op. cit.*, p. 144.
2. *Op. cit.*, pp. 136-137.
3. *Op. cit.*, p. 14.
4. See above, p. 129.
5. It may perhaps be observed that these documents only supply evidence with regard to the *intention* of the Serbs, Croats and Slovenes, and not with regard to the question of *union* which — as has been seen — has to be proved by altogether different criteria. More particularly, no argument as to the fact of union can be drawn from the documents of the period *before* the formation of the Yugoslav State. The existence of that State formed one of the basic conditions of union which could not be discussed at all before its coming into existence. For this reason Kaufmann's indiscriminate use of those documents, preceding the formation of the Yugoslav State, as evidence of actual union is open to objection. Kaufmann's methodical error seems to have been shared by Joavanovic, Schilling and Holzer. Finally, the legal value of these documents is more than doubtful ; their significance lies rather on the political plane. Thus, correctly, Holzer, *op. cit.*, p. 25, and Schilling, *op. cit.*, pp. 104-105. This finally deprives them of all value as evidence of actual union. If such union had not in fact taken place, no political statement would have altered the position.
6. See above, p. 238.

" *will be* " King of Serbs, Croats and Slovenes ". The State *will have* a single coat-of-arms, a single flag and a single crown... ".

There follow numerous provisions concerning local emblems, equality of the two alphabets, freedom of religion, equality of citizens, the Constituent Assembly and the Constitution which

" *will be* the basis of the entire life of the State. ... The nation of the Serbs, Croats and Slovenes, thus unified, *will form* a State of about twelve million inhabitants. This State *will be* the guarantee for their independence and national development... [1] ".

It is indeed a real *tour de force* to interpret the document as speaking merely of the Yugoslavs' entry into Serbia which country is not even mentioned throughout the text. In this connection it is interesting to compare the Corfu Manifesto with the corresponding documents of the Italian Risorgimento [2], emanating from non-Sardinian territories, which speak either directly of annexation by Sardinia or, at least, of a union with this clearly specified, already existing State. But the Corfu Manifesto leaves Serbia entirely out of the picture and there is not the slightest indication that the use of the future tense refers to some transformation of the existing Serbian Kingdom. On the contrary, in conformity with its starting point — " a joint future State " — the whole document is devoted to laying down the general outlines of that State which is still to be created. In this connection it may also be interesting to note that, although the document is signed by the Serbian Prime Minister, nowhere in the text is he described as the representative of the Serbian State. On the contrary, all the parties are uniformly described as " representatives of the Serbs, Croats and Slovenes " and claim to speak on behalf of the " nation " [3].

Article 1 of the Rome Pact [4] reads :

" Each of these peoples proclaims its right to constitute its own nationality and State unity or to complete it. "

This formulation is made clear beyond all doubt by means of the following passage of the Italo-Yugoslav agreement, forming integral part of the Rome Pact :

" ... the representatives of the two peoples recognize that the unity and independence of the Yugoslav nation is a vital interest of Italy, just as the completion of Italian national unity is a vital interest of the Yugoslav nation [5]. "

It is thus clear that the Yugoslavs, unlike the Italians, fall under that category which is not to complete their national State unity, for

---

1. *It. mine*, quoted by Temperley, *op. cit.*, V, pp. 393-396.
2. See above, pp. 192-193.
3. " È chiara l'intenzione di costituire un nuovo Stato, commune ai tre popoli. " Udina, *op. cit.*, p. 130. Similarly Kaufmann, *op, cit.*, p. 216. Contrary to the clear wording of the text, Schilling's insistence on the fact that the word " new " was not expressly used to describe the future State, need not be taken seriously. *Op. cit.*, pp. 103-104.
4. See above, p. 238.
5. Text in *The Jugo-Slav Movement*, p. 39.

there is nothing to be completed, since there is as yet nothing in existence ; on the contrary, they are to establish their unity for the first time [1].

In October 1918, when frank speaking already prevailed in Vienna, the Austro-Hungarian Yugoslav leaders issued a proclamation, Point 4 of which read :

" No section of the Croato-Serbo-Slovene Nation can be subjected to foreign domination ; this people must be united within the Yugoslav State [2]. "

The passage undoubtedly speaks of the nation as a whole, and not only of that part of it which belonged to the Dual Monarchy. The entire nation was to be united, not in the existing Serbian State but in a Yugoslav State which was still a thing of the future.

At about the same time, on October 25, the Italian deputies to the Reichsrat proclaimed that the Italian regions of the Austro-Hungarian Monarchy were henceforth to form part of Italy [3]. Nothing could have prevented the Yugoslavs from doing the same. But what they proclaimed was not uniting with Serbia ; it was the creation of a new State.

Finally, the South-Slav representatives, assembled in Geneva on November 9, 1918, proclaimed

" solemnly and unanimously, to the entire world, their union in one State, formed of Serbs, Croats and Slovenes. ... the new State appears and stands from to-day as an indivisible State-unit. ... The former frontiers no longer exist [4] ".

It is hardly possible to find a clearer expression of the conviction that a new State was being created.

---

1. Jovanovic — as quoted by Schilling, *op. cit.*, p. 74. — argues that this formulation of the text is to be explained by the fact that it was the Yugoslavs and not the Serbs who were party to it. The Yugoslavs, he says, had indeed no State of their own ; for them it was therefore not a question of completing, but of establishing their State ; if the Serbs, and not the Yugoslavs had been party to the Pact, they would have fallen into the category of those who had only to complete their State unity. However, Jovanovic seems to overlook the basic character of the Rome statement : it was not a pact between States, but precisely between the " oppressed nationalities of the Austro-Hungarian Empire " ; consequently, it was not an accident that the Austro-Hungarian Yugoslavs, and not Serbia, were party to it. Serbia could not have been a party to it, since she was a fully-fledged State and not an " oppressed nationality of the Austro-Hungarian Empire. " The Italian party to the Pact was not the Italian State, but Italians of the Dual Monarchy ; consequently it was not the former, but the latter who, in the above-quoted Article 1, spoke of " completing their State unity ", by which was meant their entry into the Italian State. In this sense Art. 1 covers two distinct groups of " peoples ", as they are rightly described in the text : the ones who, like Italians or Rumanians, were to complete their unity by joining existing national States, and the others, like Poles or Czechs, who had still to establish it. If the Austro-Hungarian Yugoslavs had shared the feelings and aims of the Austro-Hungarian Italians, their partners in the Rome Pact, they would equally have spoken of a completion of their State unity, meaning their entry into the Serbian State, just as the Austro-Hungarian Italians meant entry into the Italian State. The different formulation for two national groups — and this is what Jovanovic overlooks — is not an accident, but corresponds to two different political conceptions.
2. *The Jugo-Slav Movement*, p. 40.
3. " I deputati italiani alla Camera di Vienna affermano — conforme ai principi di libertà delle Nazioni, universalmente accettati — che tutte le regioni italiane finora soggette alla Monarchia austro-ungarica sono da considerarsi ormai staccate dal nesso territoriale di questo Stato e virtualmente facenti parti dell'Italia. " Udina, *op. cit.*, p. 54.
4. *The Jugo-Slav Movement*, p. 41.

c) *Irrelevant Tests.*

For the sake of completeness, the irrelevant tests of State identity and continuity must be briefly disposed of.

The fact of a State assuming a new name is no proof of its new character. The assumption of a new name, Italy, by the enlarged Kingdom of Sardinia, was no argument in favour of the latter's extinction. It is submitted that even a retention by the State of the name of Serbia could not have prevailed against the fact of Serbia's extinction.

The retention of Belgrade as a capital is as little proof of Serbia's continuity, as the change of Italian capital is a proof of Sardinia's discontinuity.

The same applies to the choice of the reigning dynasty. It remained as a new, not as a Serbian dynasty, on the basis of the December agreement. Its retention is as little proof of Serbia's continuity, as a change of dynasty in old Serbia would have been proof of the break in the latter's continuity.

3. THE YUGOSLAV PROBLEM IN THE LIGHT OF CONVENTIONAL LAW.

An analysis of the Yugoslav case on the basis of general international law has resulted in an inescapable conclusion that the S.C.S.-State was an entirely new State, not identical with either Serbia or the Yugoslav State, which both had ceased to exist [1]. It is interesting to see how this conclusion was reflected in post-war treaties.

a) *The Basic Assumption of the Peace Treaties and the Yugoslav Minorities Treaty.*

It is submitted that, in spite of certain inconsistencies [2], both the Peace Treaties and the Yugoslav Minorities Treaty assume the new character of the S.C.S.-State and its non-identity with the Kingdom of Serbia, — in the same way as certain inconsistencies could not obscure the fact that the Treaty of Saint-Germain considered the Austrian Republic as identical with Cisleithania [3].

It should be emphasized at the beginning of this analysis that all four Peace Treaties were signed not by Serbia, but by the Kingdom of Serbs, Croats and Slovenes. That this did not represent merely an irrelevant change of name, can be seen from the fact that the use of this style was admitted by the originally reluctant Powers only after a protest by the new State and its recognition as such [4]. Thus, in admitting

---

1. Thus Kaufmann, for whom the Yugoslav case reprensents a " Schulbeispiel " of an international union, proved sufficiently and conclusively in the light of general international law alone. *Op. cit.*, p. 226. It may be wondered why Kaufmann did not apply the same reasoning to Austria, instead of deciding the question of Austria's identity with the Empire precisely on the basis of conventional law; see above, pp. 226-227.

2. Cf. the German-Yugoslav Mixed Arbitral Tribunal in the case *Katz and Klumpp v. the Serb-Croat-Slovene State:* « Non seulement, en effet, la terminologie du Traité de Versailles n'est, d'une manière générale, pas d'une rigueur absolue... » *Rec. TAM,* vol. V, p. 968.

3. See above, pp. 223-226.

4. See above, pp. 248-249.

the S.C.S. delegates to the Conference and to the signing of the Treaty, the Allied and Associated Powers could not plead ignorance of the problem involved and its implications. Hence the importance of the S.C.S. signature.

It is true that the Saint-Germain Treaty in particular contains the same " double fiction " with regard to the S.C.S.-State as it does with regard to Czechoslovakia [1]. Article 47 reads :

" Austria renounces, so far as she is concerned, in favour of the Serb-Croat-Slovene State all rights and title over the territories of the former Austro-Hungarian Monarchy situated outside the frontiers of Austria as laid down in Article 27, Part II (Frontiers of Austria) and recognized by the present Treaty, or by any Treaties concluded for the purpose of completing the present settlement, as forming part of the Serb-Croat-Slovene State. "

Thus the Treaty assumes on the one hand that the Austrian Republic is identical with Cisleithania and, on the other, that the S.C.S.-State received its non-Serbian territories by cession. But the Austrian Republic was not identical with Cisleithania and the S.C.S.-State could not have received non-Serbian territories under the Saint-Germain Treaty, — for if so, the S.C.S.-State could not have been a party to that Treaty.

However, the basic assumption of the Saint-Germain Treaty with regard to the S.C.S.-State which was party to that treaty, is to be found in its Preamble. These are the relevant passages :

" Whereas the Principal Allied and Associated Powers have already recognized that the Czecho-Slovak State, in which are incorporated certain portions of the said Monarchy, is a free, independent and Allied State, and
Whereas the said Powers have also recognized the union of certain portions of the said Monarchy with the territory of the Kingdom of Serbia as a free, independent and Allied State, under the name of the Serb-Croat-Slovene State, and
Whereas it is necessary, while restoring peace, to regulate the situation which has arisen from the dissolution of the said Monarchy and the formation of the said States and to establish the government of these countries on a firm foundation of justice and equity... "

There can be no doubt that this passage of the Preamble refers to new States only. None of the old States is included, while the exclusion of Poland is to be explained by the, otherwise extraordinary, fact that the Saint-Germain Treaty did not transfer any territories to that country. The S.C.S.-State figures in the Preamble alongside Czechoslovakia, and the Preamble speaks of the "formation" of these two States, — an expression which could not possibly be used with regard to existing States. If the Preamble in fact referred to the old Kingdom of Serbia, it is inconceivable that it should have been recognized as a free, independent and allied State in exactly the same way as Czechoslovakia. No such recognition of any of the other Allied countries was included in the Treaty, whether or not these countries achieved territorial gains. The Saint-Germain Treaty clearly recognizes a new State, under a new name, newly formed by means of an international union.

---

1. See Kelsen, *Naissance de l'Etat*, pp. 632-633.

It is precisely here that an objection to the above argument could be raised : it might namely be observed that the Preamble refers to a union not between two independent States, but between " portions " and " territories ". Here it should be recalled that the Allies had never recognized the Yugoslav State and could hardly be expected to go back on that refusal in the text of the Treaty. On the other hand, the idea of " portions " of the Dual Monarchy on the one hand, and " the Kingdom of Serbia " on the other, conveying a notion of a merger between a State and a non-State, could have strongly suggested annexation on the part of Serbia. By using instead the term " territory of the Kingdom of Serbia ", the Preamble restores the balance between the two parties and preserves the idea of union, — whatever exception may be taken to the description of subjects of international law as " portions " or " territories ". Thus, not only does the unusual wording not undermine, but actually reinforces the conception of union.

Further, Kaufmann righthy draws attention to two different formulae, used with complete consistency throughout the Peace Treaties with regard to 1) ordinary cessions of territory in favour of old States, and 2) recognition of new States, coupled with cession of territory [1]. In the first case, the formula invariably reads :

" Germany (Austria, Hungary, Bulgaria)... renounces in favour of Belgium (Italy, Rumania, etc.)... "

whereas in the second case the following formula is used :

" Germany (Austria, Hungary, Bulgaria)... recognizes the full indepen-dence of... "

It is the second formula which is invariably and exclusively used with regard to three States, namely Poland and Czechoslovakia, whose character as new States is taken for granted, and precisely the S.C.S.-State.

The validity of this argument is contested by Schilling in a manner which would seem to indicate either a careless reading of the Treaties or a conscious misinterpretation. For Schilling asserts that a similar recognition by ex-enemy States occurs with regard to other countries, whose prior existence is not in doubt ; in particular, to Belgium, Austria and Russia [2]. The relevant provisions must therefore be verified.

Art. 32 of the Versailles Treaty, dealing with Belgium, reads :

" Germany recognizes the full sovereignty of Belgium over the whole of the contested territory of Moresnet (called Moresnet neutre). "

It is clear that the Article does not speak of the recognition of the independence and sovereignty of Belgium as a State, but merely of Belgium's sovereignty over a given territory. The provision has therefore no connection with the formula mentioned by Kaufmann, nor with the problem of new States.

---

1. The " re-integration " of Alsace-Lorraine into France falls into an entirely different and special category.
2. Op. cit., p. 143.

Art. 80 of the Versailles Treaty provides :

" Germany acknowledges and will respect strictly the independence of Austria within the frontiers which may be fixed in a Treaty between that State and the Principal Allied and Associated Powers, and agrees that this independence shall be inalienable, except with the consent of the Council of the League of Nations. "

This provision has nothing whatever in common with the formula adopted in the case of Poland, Czechoslovakia and the S.C.S.-State. The Article corresponds to Art. 88 of the Saint-Germain Treaty, and the notion of " recognition " as used here has an entirely different meaning, aiming at the prohibition of Anschluss. Here again there is no analogy with the formula mentioned by Kaufmann.

Finally, with regard to Russia, Art. 116 of the Versailles Treaty states :

" Germany acknowledges and agrees to respect as permanent and inalienable the independence of all the territories which were part of the former Russian Empire on August 1, 1914... "

and Art. 117 adds the following :

" Germany undertakes to recognize the full force of all treaties or agreements which may be entered into by the Allied and Associated Powers with States now existing or coming into existence in future in the whole or part of the former Empire of Russia as it existed on August 1, 1914, and to recognize the frontiers of any such States as determined therein. "

Here indeed, the formula is nearly the same as the one used with regard to the three new countries, Poland, Czechoslovakia and the S.C.S.-State. In this case, however, it covers exactly the same ground, referring as it does precisely to the recognition of new States. Instead of undermining, it therefore only confirms Kaufmann's interpretation [1].

However, the decisive provisions are undoubtedly to be found in the Yugoslav Minorities Treaty. The relevant part of its Preamble reads :

" Whereas since the commencement of the year 1913 extensive territories have been added to the Kingdom of Serbia, and
Whereas the Serb, Croat and Slovene peoples of the former Austro-Hungarian Monarchy have of their own free will determined to unite with Serbia in a permanent union for the purpose of forming a single sovereign independent State under the title of the Kingdom of the Serbs, Croats and Slovenes, and
Whereas the Prince Regent of Serbia and the Serbian Government have agreed to this union, and in consequence the Kingdom of the Serbs, Croats and Slovenes has been constituted and has assumed sovereignty over the territories inhabited by these peoples, and
Whereas it is necessary to regulate certain matters of international concern arising out of the said additions of territory and of this union, and
Whereas it is desired to free Serbia from certain obligations which she undertook by the Treaty of Berlin of 1878 to certain Powers and to substitute for them obligations to the League of Nations... "

---

1. For a further analysis of the relevant Articles of the St. Germain and Trianon Treaties, see Kaufmann, op. cit., pp. 234-235, and Döring, op. cit. ; cf. also Clemenceau's covering letter to the Allied Final Note to Austria, placing the S.C.S.-State in the category of new States, Bericht, II, p. 310.

By means of a searching analysis of the above text, combined with a parallel analysis of the Preambles to all the other Minorities Treaties, Kaufmann arrives at the inevitable conclusion that the Preamble fully confirms the fact of the S.C.S.-State being a new State, created by way of an international union. Without wishing to repeat Kaufmann's argument [1], the following should be emphasized.

The Preamble clearly distinguishes between two subjects of international law : Serbia on the one hand, and the Kingdom of the Serbs, Croats and Slovenes, formed by way of union, on the other. Thus, it is obviously Serbia who had undertaken certain obligations in the Treaty of Berlin, and it is again Serbia who had secured considerable territorial gains in 1913, as a result of the Balkan Wars. After the World War, however, " Serbia " disappears. The Preamble nowhere suggests that the South-Slavs of the Dual Monarchy had joined an existing Serbian State ; on the contrary, it declares that

" they determined to unite with Serbia ... for the purpose of forming a single sovereign independent State ".

Had the Preamble assumed annexation by a surviving Serbia, it would have been sheer nonsense to speak of a new State being formed ; but it is precisely the idea of such a new formation which is stressed ; it is emphasized once again in the third paragraph which does not say that Serbia assumed sovereignty over the South-Slav territories of the former Monarchy, but that such sovereignty was assumed by this new State, " constituted " as a result of the Yugoslav decision and the Serbian acceptance of that decision, in other words, by an international agreement.

As against this, Holzer argues that the Preamble does not speak of the Yugoslav State, as party to the union, but only of the " Serb, Croat and Slovene peoples of the former Austro-Hungarian Monarchy "[2]. This would indeed weaken the conception of union. But it has already been seen, when examining the Preamble of the Saint-Germain Treaty, that the Allies could not have been expected to go back on their consistent refusal to recognize the short-lived Yugoslav State [3]. In the Preamble to the Saint-Germain Treaty the balance between the parties to the union was restored by calling the Kingdom of Serbia — " Serbian territories " ; it would appear that here, in the Minorities Treaty, it is the words " of their own free will " in the second paragraph which are supposed to reinforce the idea of union, as opposed to annexation, and thus make up for the Allied refusal to admit the State character of the Yugoslav territories [4].

---

1. For which reference is made to *op. cit.*, pp. 231 et seq.
2. *Op. cit.*, p. 67.
3. See above, p. 254.
4. It may also be remarked that the Peace Treaties do not consistently use the word " State " where it normally should be used, e.g. in the already mentioned case of Serbia in the St. Germain Preamble ; also in Art. 116 of the Versailles Treaty which speaks of the independence of " territories ", — hardly a correct expression. Here again, the emphasis on "peoples", designed to maintain the political attitude of the Powers, does not necessarily exclude the State character of the " territories " or " peoples " in question, and is, moreover, much in keeping with the terminology and ideology of the period, concerning the " rights of the peoples ".

A more cogent argument could be based on the fifth paragraph of the Preamble which, dealing with obligations under the Berlin Treaty and new obligations towards the League of Nations, speaks of Serbia only. It may, however, be observed that, while the paragraph in question speaks of freeing *Serbia* from the old obligations under the Treaty of Berlin, the subject of the new obligations towards the League is not specified. This gap is filled by the passage which follows the Preamble and which states :

"The Principal Allied and Associated Powers taking into consideration the obligations contracted under the present Treaty by the Serb-Croat-Slovene State, declare that the Serb-Croat-Slovene State is definitely discharged from the obligations undertaken in Article 35 of the Treaty of Berlin of July 13, 1878."

It is thus not Serbia, but the new S.C.S.-State which is made the subject of the new obligations to the League. As for the repeated cancelling of old obligations, relating once to Serbia (in the fifth paragraph of the Preamble), and once to the S.C.S.-State (in the above-quoted passage), the problem is easily explained : it is old Serbia who had incurred obligations under the Treaty of Berlin ; it is these Serbian obligations which are being annulled in the fifth paragraph. Since, however, the S.C.S.-State succeeded, under Art. 12 of the Minorities Treaty [1], to the rights and obligations of Serbia, it is the S.C.S.-State, as Serbia's successor, which is freed from these obligations by the passage quoted. The procedure may sin by caution, but not by contradiction.

Thus, the Preamble to the Minorities Treaty which is undoubtedly the key document on the Yugoslav question, clearly affirms the new character of the S.C.S.-State and, consequently, its non-identity with Serbia. Failing arguments to the contrary which could be drawn from the text of the Treaty, Schilling takes refuge in the *travaux préparatoires* and the history of the successive drafts of the Preamble. This part of his work is of considerable historical interest. It may, however, be doubted whether it contributes to a legal solution. The basic question could be asked, whether it is at all necessary to consider the *travaux préparatoires*, when the final text is perfectly clear [2]. Moreover, before the final text is adopted, various and sometimes contradictory ideas are put forward, and what is said during these various stages of discussion can hardly prevail against the clear formulation of the final text. But, above all, Schilling's interpretation even of the *travaux préparatoires* is not only arbitrary, but betrays a complete confusion between the notions of identity and succession. Thus, when during a discussion in the Commission on New States the view was expressed

"that a clause should be inserted making it clear that Yugoslavia was bound by the obligations of the *former* Kingdom of Serbia [3]",

---

1. See below, pp. 258-259.
2. The P.C.I.J. has consistently admitted the existence of texts of full clarity : see Ser. B 7, p. 20 ; Ser. A 24, p. 13 ; Ser. A/B 50, p. 383. See also Guggenheim, *Traité de Droit International Public*, vol. I, pp. 132-133.
3. *It. mine*, Schilling, *op. cit.*, p. 149.

or when the British delegation proposed

"that the Serb-Croat-Slovene State should be bound by all Treaties made by Serbia[1]",

Schilling manages to ignore the obvious fact that such observations could only be made on the assumption of the non-identity of Serbia with the S.C.S.-State ; on the assumption of an identity between the two, no such observations would have been called for.

With regard to the successive drafts of the Preamble, they obviously develop in the direction of an ever growing clarity concerning the character of the S.C.S.-State as a new State[2]. Without entering into details, it is of interest to quote the very first draft :

"Whereas by the Treaty of Bucarest of 1913 and by the Treaty with Austria... large accessions of territory have been made to the Kingdom of Serbia, and
Whereas the King of Serbia, in consequence of these accessions of territory, changed his style and title to that of the King of the Serb-Croat-Slovene State..."

A comparison of this first draft with the final wording of the Preamble speaks for itself, for the two formulations express fundamentally different conceptions. By what reasoning Schilling, after a lengthy analysis, arrives at the conclusion that the fundamental meaning of the Preamble never varied from the first to the final draft, is not for this writer to explain.

Apart from the Preamble itself, individual Articles of the Treaty confirm its basic assumption of the non-identity of the Kingdom of Serbia with the S.C.S.-State. Thus, Art. 9, para. 3 states :

"The provisions of the present Article apply only to territory transferred to Serbia or to the Kingdom of the Serbs, Croats and Slovenes since the 1st January, 1913."

Once again, the Treaty distinguishes between Serbia and the S.C.S.-State. If it did not, it would have simply spoken of territories transferred to Serbia[3].

Art. 12 of the Treaty is of particular interest and importance :

"Pending the conclusion of new treaties or conventions, all treaties, conventions, agreements and obligations between Serbia, on the one hand, and any of the Principal Allied and Associated Powers, on the other hand, which were in force on the 1st August 1914, or which have since been entered into, shall *ipso facto* be binding upon the Serb-Croat-Slovene State."

The fundamental distinction between identity on the one hand, and succession on the other, has been sufficiently emphasized[4]. Art. 12 of the Treaty, providing for the succession of one subject of international law to treaty rights and obligations of another subject, represents the first clear formulation of that distinction in conventional international

---

1. *Ibid.*
2. Successive drafts quoted by Schilling, *op. cit.*, pp. 150-158.
3. Jovanovic may be right when he says that the formula " transferred to Serbia since January 1, 1913 or to the Kingdom of Serbs, Croats and Slovenes " should have been still clearer in the sense of non-identity. Quoted by Schilling, *op. cit.*, p. 160. But he is wrong in suggesting that the formula actually used throws any doubt on that non-identity.
4. See above, pp. 9-14.

law, just as it shows the possibility of universal succession, non-existing in general international law, being effected by a conventional norm [1]. At the same time, Art. 12 is yet another proof of the S.C.S.-State's non-identity with Serbia. It is inconceivable that such a provision should have been introduced with regard to an old subject of international law, whatever its territorial modifications. Indeed, as Kaufmann points out, no such provision was incorporated either in the Greek or in the Rumanian Minorities Treaty, these two States being identical with pre-war Greece and pre-war Rumania, notwithstanding considerable territorial gains. The rule of general international law providing for the continued identity of a State in the case of territorial changes adequately covered the situation. On the assumption that the S.C.S.-State was an enlarged Serbia, Art. 12 would not only have been superflous, but simply nonsensical [2].

It is thus to be concluded that the post-war Treaties incorporate the fundamental assumption that the S.C.S.-State was a new State and was not identical with the Kingdom of Serbia. In so doing, they fully conform to general international law.

b) *Specific Treaty Provisions and Judicial Decisions.*

As stated above, the S.C.S.-State belonged to the group of new States alongside Poland and Czechoslovakia [3]. But — if the expression may be used — it became a new State in a different way ; it was not formed out of territories which had belonged to other States but it has absorbed two independent States, one of which had existed for decades and had been an Ally in the late war. This fact must necessarily have found expression in certain provisions of the Peace Treaties, of a distinctly technical character. While the existence of such provisions must be admitted, their importance must not be exaggerated ; nor must they be allowed to prevail against the underlying, basic assumption of the Treaties, as analyzed above [4].

---

1. See above, pp. 13-14.
2. It is truly difficult to understand, how Art. 12 can be made to support an exactly contrary conclusion. Thus Schilling : " Die richtige Auffassung in der völkerrechtlichen Literatur, dass bei einer Inkorporation grundsätzlich alle Verträge des inkorporierenden Staates weiterhin in Kraft bleiben, hat ihren deutlichen Ausdruck im Art. 12 des jugoslawischen Minderheitenschutzvertrags gefunden. Wäre die Ansicht richtig, dass Serbien als Völkerrechtssubjekt untergegangen sei, so hätten grundsätzlich auch alle völkerrechtlichen Verträge Serbiens erloschen sein müssen. In diesem Fall hätten sie aber nicht gleichzeitig auf Jugoslawien Anwendung finden können. " *Op. cit.*, p. 166. Art. 12 was incorporated in the Treaty precisely because without it the old Serbian treaties would have become extinct. Schilling's interpretation only goes to show that has he understood neither the rule of State identity remaining unaffected by territorial changes, nor the difference between identity and succession. The same idea of succession between two different subjects of international law clearly emerges from the Note to the U.S. Secretary of State of the Yugoslav Chargé d'Affaires in Washington of September 29, 1921 : " ...the Government of the Kingdom of the Serbs, Croats and Slovenes considers the treaties and conventions concluded between the Kingdom of Serbia and the United States as applicable to the whole territory of the Kingdom of the Serbs, Croats and Slovenes, as constituted at the present. " Hackworth, *op. cit.*, V, p. 375.
3. See above, pp. 253-255.
4. For, as Kaufmann points out, " ...was eine spezielle Vorschrift besagt, nur dann für den grundsätzlichen Sinn eines Begriffes herangezogen werden kann, wenn die Rechtsurkunde grundsätzliche Aeusserungen über diesen Begriff völlig vermissen lässt. " *Op. cit.*, p. 242.

Thus, the S.C.S.-State was not a " new " State for the purpose of the currency provisions of the Peace Treaties (Art. 296 of the Treaty of Versailles, Art. 248 of the Treaty of Saint-Germain) for the simple reason that it had absorbed Serbia which had a currency of her own before the war, unlike Poland or Czechoslovakia [1].

More controversial was the legal status of the S.C.S.-State within the meaning of Art. 297 h 2, last paragraph, of the Versailles Treaty, dealing with the liquidation of German property in the Allied countries. While the old Allied States were entitled to retain the proceeds of such liquidation, the new States — as well as those not participating in the reparations — were bound to hand over such proceeds to the original owners. The question arose whether or not the S.C.S.-State was entitled to the former, more favourable treatment, in other words, whether, in spite of being new in accordance with general international law and the basic assumption of the Treaties, it was nevertheless to be considered an " old " State within the meaning of Art. 297 h.

Defending the German point of view, Kaufmann emphatically denies the " old-State " character of the S.C.S.-State under the Article in question. On the other hand, the German-Yugoslav Mixed Arbitral Tribunal arrived at the opposite conclusion in all cases of this nature submitted to it [2]. It is interesting to examine both the scope of these decisions and the reasons on which they were based, — in other words, to see whether they in any way invalidate the general conclusion as to the S.C.S.-State's non-identity with Serbia.

The main reason of the Tribunal's decisions is the obvious fact of the S.C.S.-State having absorbed Serbia. Since the latter had fought alongside the Allies from the very beginning of the war, the Tribunal held that it was not to be supposed that the Peace Treaties imposed on the S.C.S.-State a relatively less favourable treatment in matters of liquidation than that accorded the other war-time Allies. Thus, the concessions granted to Germany by Art. 297 h with regard to new States like Poland and Czechoslovakia, were not to be applied to the S.C.S.-State. This was the opinion of the Tribunal in the case of *Schumacher v. the German State and the Serb-Croat-Slovene State*, decided on October 1, 1922 :

« ... si l'on peut comprendre que les auteurs du Traité aient admis l'adjonction de ce texte, à titre de cession faite à la délégation allemande pour les Etats tels que la Pologne et la Tchécoslovaquie, ou pour les Etats qui ne participent pas aux réparations à payer par l'Allemagne, il serait plus difficile de concevoir qu'ils aient voulu imposer à l'Etat S.H.S. le traitement relativement défavorable prévu à l'article 297 litt. *h* chiffre 2, alinéa 2, sans tenir compte des sacrifices imposés par la guerre, dès son début, à l'allié de la première heure, qu'a été le Royaume de Serbie [3]. »

---

1. This is freely admitted by Kaufmann, who moreover adds that these provisions were worked out by a special technical commission, " der die politisch-technische Terminologie nicht geläufig war. " *Op. cit.*, p. 240.
2. Except for the case *Venteuse*, see Kaufmann, *op. cit.*, p. 211, in which the Tribunal declared itself incompetent to decide the question.
3. *Rec. TAM*, vol. II, p. 609.

This opinion was repeated in the judgment in the case *Dame Scheuhs v. the Serb-Croat-Slovene State* [1].

It will be observed that the Tribunal speaks of two different subjects of international law : Serbia and the S.C.S.-State. It would thus appear that, without formulating it *expressis verbis*, the Tribunal proceeded on the assumption of a relation of succession between the two.

This reasoning of the Tribunal was again repeated in the case of *Katz and Klumpp v. the Serb-Croat-Slovene State*, decided on September 30, 1925 :

« Ainsi que le Tribunal l'a déjà relevé dans ses sentences Schumacher et Scheuhs, cette contradiction et cette situation relativement défavorable faite à l'Etat S.H.S. seraient d'autant plus difficiles à comprendre que, parmi les Alliés, le royaume de Serbie est un de ceux auxquels la guerre, dès son début, a causé les plus grands dommages, fait en considération duquel sans doute l'Etat S.H.S. a, comme la Belgique, obtenu le droit d'être représenté à la Commission des réparations [2]. »

This was the only problem with which the Mixed Arbitral Tribunal was concerned in these various cases. The Tribunal only had to interpret the special technical provisions of Art. 297 h, and it interpreted them correctly within this limited scope. The Tribunal did not have to decide the question of the legal status of the S.C.S.-State in relation to Serbia either in the light of general international law, or of the basic assumption of the Treaties. It seems, however, that the Tribunal would have tended to confirm the new character of the S.C.S.-State in both respects. Thus, in the case *Katz and Klumpp*, the Tribunal stated :

« Il n'est donc pas inconcevable *a priori* que, même dans l'hypothèse où, en général, le Traité de Versailles aurait considéré le royaume S.H.S. comme un « nouvel Etat », l'expression « les nouveaux Etats » ait pu être exceptionnellement employée, non seulement à l'art. 296 d, mais aussi à l'art. 297 h, dernier alinéa, pour désigner seulement d'autres Etats [3]... »

« Mais, dans ce système, on ne saurait admettre que l'art. 297 h, dernier alinéa, puisse être invoqué contre l'Etat S.H.S., même si, par ailleurs, on devait tenir pour vraisemblable que d'une façon générale — c'est-à-dire abstraction faite de l'art. 297 h, dernier alinéa — le Traité considère le Royaume S.H.S. comme un « nouvel Etat » [4]. »

In the *Schumacher* case, the Tribunal declared :

« Si donc la question dont il s'agit est discutable au point de vue purement doctrinal et même si, à ce point de vue, elle devait — point sur lequel le Tribunal n'a pas à se prononcer en l'espèce — être résolue dans le sens de la thèse soutenue par le réquérant, il ne resterait pas moins vrai qu'en présence des textes cités ci-dessus, il n'est pas possible d'admettre que l'Etat S.H.S. soit un « Etat nouvellement créé » au sens des Traités de Saint-Germain et de Trianon [5]... »

In this case, while affirming the " old " character of the S.C.S.-State for the purpose of Art. 297 h, the Tribunal clearly admitted the possibility of a different conclusion under general international law.

---

1. *Ibid.*, p. 681.
2. *Rec. TAM*, vol. V, p. 972.
3. *Ibid.*, p. 968.
4. *Ibid.*, pp. 976-977.
5. *Rec. TAM.*, vol. II, p. 608.

The existence of special provisions in the Peace Treaties is thus not only admitted, but also explained, by the fact of the new State having absorbed the Kingdom of Serbia. There is, however, nothing either in the special provisions or in the relevant judicial decisions which would undermine the view that the S.C.S.-State was not identical with the Kingdom of Serbia either under general international law or under the Peace Treaties.

4. CONCLUSION.

An examination of historical facts in the light of general international law has shown the absence of identity between the old Kingdom of Serbia and the new S.C.S.-State. Additional evidence, such as conventional law and international recognition, has been found conform to general international law.

No other conclusion is possible. The Serbian legal order, identified by its basic norm, has been replaced by a new legal order, identified by a new basic norm, and that new legal order became valid for an entirely different territorial and personal delimitation. Of the old international delimitation of Serbia nothing remained, — just as nothing remained in the new Austrian Republic of the old international delimitation of the Empire, and unlike the Kingdom of Italy, where the old legal order of Sardinia merely extended its territorial and personal sphere of validity. Both, Serbia and the short-lived Yugoslav State became extinct, making room for a new subject of international law, the S.C.S.-State. The relation of that State to Serbia was one of succession, and not of identity.

CHAPTER IV.

ETHIOPIA.

1. THE ITALIAN INVASION AND ANNEXATION OF ETHIOPIA.

a) *Illegality of Invasion.*

On October 5, 1935, Italian armed forces invaded Ethiopia [1]. It is necessary to consider this fact in the light of existing legal obligations between the two countries.

The Italo-Ethiopian war of 1896 ended with the Peace Treaty of October 26, 1896, by which Italy

« reconnaît l'indépendance absolue et sans réserve de l'empire éthiopien comme Etat souverain et indépendant [2] ».

On December 13, 1906, a convention was concluded between Italy, France and Great Britain on the subject of Ethiopia. The contracting parties affirmed their common interest

« de maintenir intacte l'intégrité de l'Ethiopie »

and declared themselves

« d'accord pour maintenir le *statu quo* politique et territorial en Ethiopie tel qu'il est déterminé par l'état des affaires actuellement existantes et les arrangements suivants... »

Such arrangements, however,

« ne portent aucune atteinte aux droits souverains de l'Empereur d'Abyssinie [3] ».

The exchange of notes between Great Britain and Italy of the 14 and 20 December 1925, concerning their interests in Ethiopia, resulted in a protest by the latter. In the course of the correspondence which ensued, the following passage of an Italian Note to Ethiopia is of interest :

« Au nom de mon Gouvernement, j'ai l'honneur de confirmer à Votre Altesse que l'accord susmentionné a un caractère exclusivement économique et que non seulement il ne vise pas à léser les droits souverains du Gouvernement éthiopien,

---

1. For the history of the Italo-Ethiopian conflict, see Rousseau, *Le conflit italo-éthiopien devant le droit international.*
2. Art. 3, Martens *N. R. G.* 2nd series, XXV, p. 60.
3. Martens, *N. R. G.* 2nd series, XXXV, p. 556. For an Italian interpretation, according to which the agreement would have meant exactly the opposite of what it says, and its refutation, see Rousseau, *op. cit.,* pp. 7-11.

mais qu'il constitue une nouvelle preuve des intentions amicales de l'Italie et de l'Angleterre à l'égard de l'Empire éthiopien, qui reste absolument libre de donner une réponse favorable ou défavorable aux requêtes de caractère économique qui lui seraient présentées par chacun des deux Gouvernements [1]. »

Similar assurances were given by the two governments to the Secretary-General of the League of Nations.

On August 2nd, 1928, Italy and Ethiopia concluded a Treaty of Friendship, Conciliation and Arbitration which included — *inter alia* — the following provisions :

" There shall be continual peace and perpetual friendship between the Kingdom of Italy and the Ethiopian Empire. " (Art. 1.) " The two Governments undertake to submit to a procedure of conciliation or of arbitration the questions which may arise between them, and which they may not be able to decide by the normal process of diplomacy, without having recourse to force of arms. Notes shall be exchanged between the two Governments relative to the method of selecting the arbitrators. " (Art. 5.) [2]

The Treaty was concluded for twenty years.

Moreover, Italy and Ethiopia were both Members of the League of Nations and were bound by the Covenant, with all its relevant provisions for the pacific settlement of international disputes and, in particular, Article 10. Further, the two countries were signatories of the Pact of Paris.

In the light of the above, the conclusion is inescapable that the Italian aggression against Ethiopia constituted a violation of her binding international obligations and was therefore an illegal act.

b) *Illegality of Annexation.*

On May 9, 1936, four days after the Italian capture of Addis Ababa, an Italian decree proclaimed the annexation of Ethiopia and placed her under the full and entire sovereignty of Italy, the Italian King assuming for himself and his successors the title of Emperor of Ethiopia [3].

According to a letter adressed to the Secretary-General of the League of Nations by the Ethiopian delegate on June 26, 1936, the greater part of Ethiopian territory was at that time still free from enemy occupation [4].

Yet, on May 11, 1936, the Italian representative in the League Council protested against the presence at the Council table of the Ethiopian delegate and, in conformity with the Italian decree of annexation, declared :

" Nothing resembling an organized Ethiopian State exists. The only sovereignty in Ethiopia is Italian sovereignty [5]. "

---

1. Quoted by Rousseau, *op. cit.*, p. 17.
2. *British and Foreign State Papers*, vol. CXXIX, pp. 1-2.
3. Quoted by Rousseau, *op. cit.*, p. 206.
4. *LNOJ*, 1936, p. 781. Cf. Rousseau : « Il n'est guère contestable que l'occupation militaire italienne, si elle s'étendait au début de mai 1936 à la plus grande partie du territoire éthiopien, ne couvrait pas l'intégralité de ce territoire, les régions méridionale et occidentale échappant à cette époque à l'emprise matérielle de l'occupant. » *Op. cit.*, p. 215.
5. *LNOJ*, 1936, p. 535.

The rules of international law with regard to the annexation of occupied territory have already been examined [1]. It is clear that the proclamation of annexation by Italy of the whole of Ethiopian territory, necessarily involving the assertion of the extinction of the Ethiopian State, was, under the circumstances, a clear case of premature annexation, undertaken *durante bello*, in a country far from being finally subjugated. The proclamation was not based on a definite overthrow of the enemy ; it was not even based on that degree of effectiveness which is necessary for a mere belligerent occupation to be legal. It is hardly necessary to stress again the irrelevance of the occupation of the enemy capital. Thus, the Italian proclamation of annexation and alleged extinction of Ethiopia constituted an illegal act [2].

2. LEGAL NATURE OF THE ITALIAN DOMINATION OF ETHIOPIA.

Even an illegal annexation may grow into a valid title either by a subsequent conventional arrangement with the defeated enemy [3] or by his eventual subjugation and the effective establishment of the conqueror's rule in the occupied country. In the case of Ethiopia the first possibility never materialized. With regard to the second, the evidence available must be examined with a view to discovering whether the undoubted Italian domination ever achieved the degree of effectiveness and finality necessary to convert mere occupation into final subjugation.

With regard to the initial period, a much-discussed decision of a British court gave writers opportunity of forcefully asserting that Italian rule in Ethiopia was nothing more than belligerent occupation. The case in question, *Bank of Ethiopia v. National Bank of Egypt and Liguori*, was decided at a moment when the British Government had already recognized the Italian conquest of Ethiopia *de facto*, while continuing to recognize the Ethiopian sovereignty *de iure* [4].

The case turned on the question whether an Italian decree issued on June 20, 1936, was capable of dissolving the plaintiff company and appointing a liquidator. In spite of the plaintiff's argument that the

---

1. See above, pp. 102-107.
2. Apart from the main and self-explanatory aim of this illegal annexation, it would seem that it was also meant to facilitate the end of hostilities and the pacification of the unsubdued country by enabling Italy to treat the resisting Ethiopians not as regular soldiers, but as rebels, — a device of which ample use seems to have been made ; e.g. execution of Ras Desta and other Ethiopian chiefs. Rousseau, *op. cit.*, pp. 226-227.
3. On the pattern of the Treaty of Praetoria, see above p. 106.
4. The Foreign Office certificate stated that : " *a)* H. M. Government in the United Kingdom have not recognized the Italian annexation of Ethiopia *de iure* but they now regard the Italian Government as the Government *de facto* of the parts of Ethiopia which they control ; *b)* while detailed information is hard to obtain, such information as H.M. Government possess tends to show that the Italian Government control the whole of Ethiopia with the exception of certain areas in the South and South West of the country. " Quoted by Lauterpacht, *op. cit.*, p. 432, *f.-n.* 2. The Foreign Office also stated that, although it was difficult to fix the exact date of the British *de facto* recognition, the latter could be assumed to have taken place in the second half of December 1936, and that the Ethiopian Minister at the Court of St. James continued to enjoy recognition. Rousseau, *op. cit.*, p. 247.

decree in question overstepped the limits of belligerent occupation and that the Ethiopian Emperor continued to enjoy *de iure* recognition, the Court (Clauson J.) held :

" The recognition of the fugitive Emperor as a *de iure* monarch, appears to me to mean nothing but this, that while the recognized *de facto* government must for all purposes, while continuing to occupy its *de facto* position, be treated as a duly recognized foreign sovereign State, H.M. Government recognizes that the *de iure* monarch has some right (not in fact at the moment enforceable) to reclaim the governmental control of which he has in fact been deprived. Where, however, H.M. Government has recognized a *de facto* government, there is, as it appears to me, no ground for suggesting, that the *de iure* monarch's theoretical rights... can be taken into account in any way in any of H.M. Courts [1]. "

This decision has been subject to outspoken criticism [2], particularly by Sir Arnold McNair. After recalling that Clauson J. declined to accept the suggestion that any limitation could be placed on the full sovereignty of the Italian Government in Ethiopia, either because it was merely in belligerent occupation of that country, or because Britain continued to recognize the Emperor *de iure*, Sir Arnold pointed out that

" Clauson J. in this judgment has invested a Government in belligerent occupation of the territory of another with a degree of power which it is difficult to reconcile with the rules of international law, as accepted by this country, and moreover puts a premium upon aggression by the recognition which it gives to the decrees of a successful invader. ... The value of rules governing belligerent occupation and defining the powers of the occupant is sensibly diminished if within

---

1. *A. D.*, 1935/37, case no. 38. A similar view appears to have been adopted by the Tribunal civil de la Seine ; in an action brought by the Emperor to recover shares of the Franco-Ethiopian Railway Company, belonging to the Ethiopian Government, the Tribunal, on November 2, 1937, declared itself incompetent on the ground that the matter concerned an act of sovereignty by Italy. Rousseau, *op. cit.*, p. 250. On the other hand, Mr. Justice Clauson's conception was not upheld in *Haile Selassie v. Cable and Wireless Co. Ltd.*, *A. D.*, 1938/40, case no. 37. The Ethiopian Emperor claimed a sum of money from the defendant company, which contended that by virtue of the *de facto* recognition by H. M. Government of the Italian conquest of Ethiopia, the claim was suspended or, alternatively, transferred to the King of Italy. The Foreign Office certificate stated that 1) H. M. Government continued to recognize the plaintiff as *de iure* Emperor of Ethiopia, and that 2) H. M. Government recognized the Italian government as the government *de facto* of virtually the whole of Ethiopia. Mr. Justice Bennett refused to consider the case covered by the authority of three precedents invoked by the defendants, *United States of America v. McRae*, *Luther v. Sagor* and *Bank Ethiopia v. National Bank of Egypt and Liguori*. More particularly, drawing a sharp dividing line between the scope and consequences of *de facto* and *de iure* recognition, Mr. Justice Bennett limited the consequences of *de facto* recognition (and thus of the authority of the two latter cases) to property and acts *within* the territory under the control of the *de facto* authority. " The present case is not concerned with the validity of acts in relation to persons or property in Ethiopia. It is concerned with the title to a chose in action — a debt, recoverable in England. " " I ask myself, why should the fact that the Italian army has conquered Ethiopia and that the Italian government now rules Ethiopia divest the plaintiff of the right to sue. The only reason can be, I suppose, that the money is not the plaintiff's own money, and that it is a sum which he is under some obligation to spend for the benefit of the people of Ethiopia, — an obligation which he cannot now fulfil. There is a clear answer to this suggestion. I think it undesirable that I should state it. " Consequently, the Emperor's claim succeeded. It failed, however, before the Court of Appeal on December 2, 1938, not because the latter disagreed with Bennett J. on the facts as they then were, but because in the meantime H. M. Government recognized the King of Italy as the *de iure* Emperor of Ethiopia.

2. Lauterpacht, *op. cit.*, p. 286 ; Quincy Wright, *The British Courts and Ethiopian Recognition*, *A. J.*, 1937, p. 683 ; cf. Prof. Sauser-Hall on the confusion between belligerent occupation and *de facto* government, above, p. 82, and the underlying assumption that Italian domination in the relevant period was no more than belligerent occupation.

six weeks of his arrival in the enemy capital and before he has brought the whole country under his control he is to be invested with the full panoply of sovereignty... From a political point of view this enlargement of the status of belligerent occupation is retrograde and much to be deplored. During the past century it was gradually made clear ... that belligerent occupation is a provisional state of affairs and that it does not transfer sovereignty. That must await either subjugation or cession by treaty of peace [1]. "

The value of this criticism — applying as it does to the British Government no less than to the learned judge — in solving the problem of the legal nature of the Italian domination of Ethiopia lies in its emphatic assertion that, at least in its initial stages, that domination still retained the legal character of a mere belligerent occupation. This view is in fact strongly supported by the Foreign Office certificate which admitted that " certain areas in the South and South West of the country " were at the relevant date still defying the Italians [2]. It must therefore be concluded that, as between the Italian annexation decree of May 9, 1936 and December 1936, nothing happened which would have changed the provisional Italian occupation into a valid title.

There is evidence to show that this state of affairs persisted [3]. Towards the end of 1938, the situation in Ethiopia was described in the following manner by a leading British newspaper :

" The war ... is still going on. ... There is no other word to describe what is happening in Abyssinia to-day than war. "

It was emphasized that it was not a question of unorganized bandits, but of organized armies fighting under proper command " not for gain but for the freedom and independence of their country ". To combat these armies, the Italians maintained in Ethiopia 200.000 troops, 300 aircraft and 10.000 lorries, although they could ill afford the cost.

" It can hardly be said that the Italians are winning this war. "

Many instances were given of the progress of the fighting, of the organisation, exploits and successes of the Ethiopian troops and this situation was contrasted with the statement by Lord Halifax, the Foreign Secretary, at the League Council meeting of May 12, 1938, when he said :

" The Italian Government has obtained control of virtually all the former territory of Ethiopia, and while resistance is still continuing in certains parts of the country, there is no organized region of Ethiopian authority and no central control of administration. "

In conclusion, doubts were expressed as to whether Italy would be able to cope with the situation either strategically or economically without 'outside help. Should such help not be forthcoming

---

1. *Legal Effects of War*, p. 341. Cf. again Sauser-Hall : « ...le juge a confondu le stade de l'occupation de guerre avec celui de l'annexion. Il en est résulté une diminution de la protection accordée par le droit des gens à l'occupé, lequel n'est pas soumis à la souveraineté absolue de l'occupant. » *Op. cit.*, p. 73.
2. See above, p. 265, f.-n. 4.
3. See the *New Times and Ethiopia News* for the period.

" Italy's tenure of a traditionally free country will be as short-lived as any attempted before [1]. "

It was only to be expected that such persistent Ethiopian resistance to the invader would gather new strength from Italy's entry into the Second World War and, above all, from the subsequent Italian military reverses in Africa. That this was in fact so, is borne out by official British evidence :

" They (the British Government) arranged for the Emperor to proceed to Cairo and eventually Khartoum, to afford such assistance as he might in raising his country against the Italians and in recruiting Ethiopian military units to participate in a campaign against the Italians in East Africa. In the winter of 1940-41 considerable progress was made in launching the campaign of the Ethiopian Patriot Forces from the western border of the country in close co-operation with the forthcoming campaign of Lieut.-Gen. Sir William Platt and Lieut.-Gen. Sir Alan Cunningham from the Sudan and Kenya against the northern and southern ends of the Italian East African possessions. In the middle of January 1941, the Emperor re-entered Ethiopia in person from the West and placed himself at the head of the patriot movement [2]... "

This passage clearly shows the continued struggle within Ethiopia against the Italian rule during the Second World War and prior to the actual entry of Allied troops into the country. The fact that Great Britain gave the Ethiopians outside assistance does not affect the position. The British Government stated officially that, on re-entering his country together with the British troops, the Emperor " placed himself at the head of the patriot movement " which was already in existence.

The question may, however, be asked as to what took place in Ethiopia between the end of 1938, when the evidence available apparently ends (apart from the *New Times and Ethiopia News* which, however, has a strong pro-Ethiopian bias), and the years 1940-1941, when it begins again. Here also, it is the same official British source which provides the answer. On entering the country the Emperor established contact

" with his chiefs and notables, *some of whom throughout the five years of Italian occupation have not ceased to fight the Italians* [3] ".

In this way, the whole period of Italian domination of Ethiopia is finally covered by evidence to the effect that the Italians never achieved the final subjugation of that country. Unless this evidence is disbelieved and failing any evidence to the contrary, it must be concluded that Italian rule in Ethiopia has never become anything else than belligerent occupation.

---

1. *Manchester Guardian* of September 8, 9, 10 and 12, 1938.
2. *British Military Administration of Occupied Territories in Africa during the Years* 1941-43. Cmd. 6589, p. 8.
3. *It. mine, ibid.*

3. International Recognition of the Italian Conquest and of Ethiopia's Extinction.

a) *Facts.*

On July 4, 1936, the League of Nations Assembly decided to discontinue the half-hearted sanctions against Italy. On April 9, 1938, the British Government, which had recognized the Italian conquest of Ethiopia *de facto* as far back as December 1936, took the initiative in setting aside further obligations under the Covenant [1]. The Council meetings, held in Geneva on the 9 and 10 of May, 1938, were devoted to a long debate in which the desire of most Members to regain their freedom of action with regard to the Ethiopian problem became evident. Although no vote was taken, the results of the debate were summed up by the President to the effect that

" the great majority of the Members of the Council feel, so far as the question we are now discussing is concerned, it is for the individual Members of the League to determine their attitude in the light of their own situation and their own obligations [2] ".

As a result of the Council's meeting several more States recognized the Italian conquest of Ethiopia. The whole process of gradually withdrawing recognition from Ethiopia (starting with the closing down of Legations in Addis-Ababa) and transferring it to Italy, first by *de facto* and then by *de iure* recognition has been described in the works of Prof. Rousseau and Mr. Langer. According to the list, submitted to the House of Commons on June 29, 1938, by Mr. Butler, Under-Secretary of State for Foreign Affairs, the following States, Members of the League, had recognized " in one form or another " the Italian conquest of Ethiopia.

---

1. The Foreign Secretary's letter to the Secretary-General of the League, quoted by Langer, *Seizure of Territory*, p. 140. This initiative is described by Prof. Lauterpacht as indicative of a " punctilious attitude " which, according to him, was " of greater significance than the further question whether, in view of the rule of unanimity, such release could be validly given except by a unanimous decision of the Assembly or of the Council. " *Op. cit.*, p. 418. Cf. the statement by Mr. Noel-Baker in the House of Commons of May 20, 1938 : " It is not for me to cite the terms of the resolutions which were adopted in February 1932 by twelve Members of the Council on the Manchurian question, and unanimously by the Assembly a few weeks later, on 11 March 1932. Those resolutions are well-known. They declare that it is incumbent upon Members of the League, as a result of the provisions of Article 10, not to recognize changes of territorial status or sovereignty brought about by Covenant-breaking war. That is precisely what we are intending now to do, and since we are intending to do it, the Government said : « Oh, well, we must cover ourselves in some way. We are setting aside a most important, indeed, a fundamental principle of international law, what President Wilson called the heart, of the Covenant, and therefore we must have the approval of the League.» What happened in Geneva about Abyssinia ? Before they went there, the Government were extremely reluctant to tell us what proposals they were going to put forward. But everybody knows that they wanted to have a resolution of the Council. In my view, if they had got a resolution of the Council, unanimously adopted, it would still not have been sufficient to set aside Article 10. It could not have wiped out the unanimous resolution of the Assembly of 1932. But when they got to Geneva, having wanted a resolution, they found that they could not get it, and so they fell back on the device of having a discussion, a series of isolated and detached declarations by different Members of the Council. " Quoted by Langer, *op. cit.*, pp. 149-150.
2. Quoted by Langer, *op. cit.*, p. 149.

Hungary	November 1936
Albania	November 1936
Switzerland	December 1936
Chile	December 1936
Great Britain	December 1936
France	December 1936
Honduras	March 1937
Poland	May 1937
Yugoslavia	November 1937
Ecuador	December 1937
Latvia	January 1938
Netherlands	March 1938
Bulgaria	March 1938
Belgium	March 1938
Rumania	April 1938
Greece	April 1938
Turkey	April 1938
Czechoslovakia	April 1938
Finland	April 1938
Lithuania	May 1938
Panama	May 1938
Eire	May 1938
Estonia	May 1938
Peru	May 1938
Sweden	May 1938
Norway	May 1938
Uruguay	May 1938
Denmark	May 1938
Argentina	June 1938 [1]

Moreover, Austria granted recognition in June 1936. Among the States outside the League, Germany granted *de iure* recognition in October 1936, and Japan in 1937. Furthermore, Italian sovereignty over Ethiopia was also recognized by the Vatican [2]. The United States, on the other hand, never recognized the conquest. It may also be added that Ethiopia's name was retained on the official list of States Members of the League [3] and of the International Labour Organisation [4].

The granting of *de iure* recognition proceeded at such a pace that on November 2, 1938, the British Prime Minister could state in the House of Commons :

" Of all the countries in Europe, there are only two, namely ourselves and the Government of Soviet Russia, which have restricted themselves to *de facto* recognition. The latest country to recognize formally Italian sovereignty in Ethiopia is France, and their new Ambassador is to be accredited to the King of Italy, Emperor of Ethiopia. We propose to follow the same course [5]... "

1. *Parl. Deb., Com.*, vol. CCCXXXVII, col. 1890.
2. Rousseau, *op. cit.*, p. 239 and pp. 244-245.
3. Langer, *op. cit.*, pp. 151-152.
4. *I.L.O. Yearbooks* for 1938-39 and 1939-40.
5. *Parl. Deb., Com.*, vol. CCCXL, col. 210.

De iure recognition by Great Britain was accordingly granted on November 16, 1938, — at about the same time when the Manchester Guardian described the situation in Ethiopia as one of war [1].

b) *Legal Evaluation.*

Thus, illegal invasion and annexation of Ethiopia by Italy has achieved international recognition, which automatically implied international recognition of the extinction of the Ethiopian State [2].

Prof. Lauterpacht considers international recognition a means of validating an originally illegal act by way of a " quasi-legislative " act of the international community [3]. The question must therefore be asked whether it is in fact possible for the international community to invest an unlawful act with legality [4] and hardly any case is better suited for this kind of enquiry than that of Ethiopia.

The key problem is whether the international recognition of the Italian conquest was itself in conformity with international law, both customary and conventional.

It is readily admitted that under traditional customary international law no illegality attaches to the recognition of an effective conquest, this being merely the logical consequence of the admissibility of war. It is, however, very doubtful whether recognition of a premature annexation would be legal, such annexation being itself an illegal act. It has been seen [5] that the only certain norm of international law with regard to recognition generally is the one prohibiting premature recognition of a revolted province as a State, this being a clear violation of the international prohibition of intervention. There would seem to be an analogy with the premature recognition of a State's extinction. It would appear that just as the grant of premature recognition to a revolted province violates the international prohibition of intervention, so the grant of recognition of a premature annexation violates the international law of neutrality. If this reasoning is correct, then the international recognition of the Italian conquest of Ethiopia must be regarded as being of doubtful legality even under general international law.

In the Ethiopian case, however, it is hardly necessary, except for States non-Members of the League, to have recourse to customary international law, since the case is fully covered by conventional law.

With regard to States Members of the League, their original obligations in the matter were fully covered by Art. 10 of the Covenant, whose operative passage declared :

---

1. See above, p. 267.
2. " So hat die Schweiz durch die Anerkennung der Souveränität Italiens über Aethiopien gleichzeitig die Existenz des äthiopischen Staates aberkannt. " Guggenheim, *Lehrbuch*, I, p. 185, *f.-n.* 59.
3. *Op. cit.*, p. 429.
4. This enquiry can be undertaken without again entering into a refutation of the constitutive view of recognition.
5. See above, p. 153.

" The Members of the League undertake to respect and preserve as against external aggression the territorial integrity and existing political independence of all Members of the League... "

The simplest interpretation *a maiori ad minus* is enough to prove that the Article implies a duty of non-recognition. If Members of the League were bound to take active steps against a wrong-doer, it is obvious that they were at the very least bound not to recognize the wrong done. This view is supported by the authority of Schücking and Wehberg in their commentary on the Covenant [1].

On March 11, 1932, with the Manchurian situation in view, the League Assembly passed its famous resolution that

" ... it is incumbent upon the Members of the League of Nations not to recognize any situation, treaty or agreement which may be brought about by means contrary to the Covenant of the League of Nations or to the Pact of Paris. "

Despite attempts to place divergent interpretations on the clear meaning of the Resolution, the opinion of Oppenheim-Lauterpacht must be accepted according to which its binding force is obvious, since it is merely " declaratory of the obligations of Article 10 ", constituting " the very minimum of the duties of a guarantor " [2].

Finally, as regards the signatories of the Kellogg Pact, whether or not they were Members of the League, it is reasonable to argue that they were similarly prohibited from recognizing the unlawful acts specified by the Pact [3].

It follows that the international recognition of the Italian conquest of Ethiopia constituted a clear and undoubted violation of positive international law and was thus itself an illegal act [4].

To claim that it could validate another illegal act is to heap illegality upon illegality in the hope that something legal will emerge from the process.

Being illegal, international recognition was unable to invest the unlawful acts of Italy with any degree of legality. It may be added that no amount of international recognition could set aside the firm rule of international law which preserves the continued existence of a State under belligerent occupation.

---

1. " Der Garant darf also gewaltsame Besitzänderungen nicht anerkennen und muss ihre Revision durch alle Mittel herbeizuführen suchen. " *Satzung*, comment on Art. 10, p. 458.

2. *Op. cit.*, I, p. 138. Cf. Guggenheim, *Validité et Nullité*, p. 228.

3. « On en pouvait déduire que tout résultat obtenu à la suite d'une guerre offensive et notamment toute modification territoriale devrait désormais être considérée comme nulle et non avenue. Ces déductions nécessaires se sont concrétisées dans la doctrine américaine dite de la non-reconnaissance... » Scelle, *op. cit.*, p. 178. Similarly Guggenheim, *Lehrbuch*, I, p. 19, and Sharp, *op. cit.*, pp. 125-129.

4. Such illegality is not to be set aside by Prof. Lauterpacht's explanation, according to which " the object of the recognition *de iure* as given in 1938 " was " the achievement of a general settlement aiming at the pacification of Europe and the world. " *Op. cit.*, p. 356. This is hardly a legal argumen+ as against the clear rules of international law examined above. Nor, it may be said, does it support the " legal " nature of recognition, emphasizing, as it does, its function as an instrument of policy.

4. ETHIOPIA'S RESTORATION.

a) *State Practice.*

On June 11, 1940, Italy declared war on the Allies. This fact did not, however, bring about an automatic reversal of the Allied attitude with regard to Ethiopia ; on the contrary, the change took some time to crystallize. Thus, in the case of Britain, the Government at first limited itself to the following statement of June 19, 1940 :

"In view of Italy's unprovoked entry into the war against this country, H.M. Government hold themselves entitled to reserve full liberty of action in respect to any undertaking given by them in the past to the Italian government concerning the Mediterranean, North and East African or Middle East areas [1]."

On July 3, 1940, it was further stated that H.M. Government no longer recognized the King of Italy as Emperor of Ethiopia [2].

In the House of Lords, Viscount Halifax stated on August 13, 1940 :

" H.M. Government have already declared that they no longer hold themselves bound by any undertakings given by them in the past to the Italian Government concerning the Mediterranean, North or East African or Middle Eastern areas. This of course includes any understanding given in respect of Italian sovereignty over Abyssinia [3]."

Only in September did the formulation become slightly clearer. On the 17th, Lord Davies asked whether the Government were now in a position to state

"that the restoration of the liberty of Ethiopia is included in our war aims and whether every assistance within our power will be given to the people of Abyssinia to regain their independence".

To which Lord Templemore answered :

" H.M. Government who naturally have no territorial or other ambitions in Ethiopia, are anxious to see that country liberate itself from Italian aggression. They will afford every assistance to those Ethiopians who have taken up or will take up arms against the invader [4]."

This was still far from being a clear and unequivocal withdrawal of recognition of the Italian conquest, and even more so from a renewed recognition of Ethiopia. The former found its express formulation only in connection with a case decided by the Palestine Supreme Court on December 11, 1940 [5]. In a letter of November 30, 1940, the High Commissioner for Palestine informed the Chief Justice as follows :

"I have been acquainted by the Secretary of State for the Colonies that the *de iure* recognition by H.M. Government of the Italian conquest of Ethiopia has been withdrawn."

---

1. *Parl. Deb., Com.,* vol. CCCLXII, col. 139.
2. *Ibid.,* col. 814.
3. *Parl. Deb., Lords,* vol. CXVII, no. 82.
4. *Ibid.,* col. 89.
5. *Azash Kebbeda Tesema and others v. Italian Government, A.D.,* 1938/40, case no. 36.

Even this withdrawal did not bring about an automatic recognition of the Ethiopian State and Emperor. As late as February 4, 1941, the British Foreign Secretary limited himself to the statement that

" H.M. Government would welcome the re-appearance of an independent Ethiopian State and recognize the claim of Emperor Haile Selassie to his throne [1]. "

On August 6, 1941, i.e. three months after the Emperor's return to Addis Ababa, Mr. Eden stated in the House that

" H.M. Government have made abundantly clear their intention to recognize an independent Ethiopia as soon as the military situation permits. Such recognition would be followed by the establishment of diplomatic relations [2]. "

It would be idle to speculate whether, at the dates quoted, the British Government still considered the Ethiopian State as extinct and whether terms like " re-appearance " and " claim to the throne " were intended to mean the birth of a new State or a restoration of the old. What is relevant, is the fact that, whatever the intermediate stages, the final British attitude was made unmistakably clear even while the war lasted.

The White Paper on the British Military Administration of Occupied Territories in Africa quoted above, had this to say with regard to Ethiopia :

" The circumstances surrounding Ethiopian affairs required a different approach to that which could be and was adopted in all the other territories. H.M. Government had recognized the Italian annexation of Ethiopia but the Emperor who had escaped from the country during the Italian invasion and had eventually received hospitality in England, had never renounced his claim to sovereignty. When Italy came into the war in June 1940, H.M. Government revoked their recognition of Italian annexation. ... The Emperor in returning to his country and thus resuming contact did so in his own view and in that of the world as the rightful sovereign of the country. It would, therefore, have been out of place for the Commander-in-Chief to have assumed, as common form demanded in those other parts of Italian East Africa, which had not been within the Emperor's domain, the full powers of a military conqueror overriding a latent Italian sovereignty which had been determined by British military occupation. Nevertheless military exigencies required ... that a British Military Administration be set up to translate the wishes of the Commander into practice in the administrative field. The decision of H.M. Government so to proceed led to the institution of a British Military Administration in Ethiopia based not on the usual No. 1 or empowering Proclamation issued by or under the authority of the Commander-in-Chief, but upon a proclamation.., of the Emperor Haile Selassie in which he enjoined all the inhabitants of Ethiopia to obey the orders of the Commander-in-Chief [3]... "

The legal implications of this document and of the facts it describes are quite clear. The Italian annexation of Ethiopia was completely disregarded and the country was therefore not treated as occupied enemy territory. Moreover, in spite of the still pending British recognition, it was not treated as some sort of *terra nullius* where the freedom of action of the British military authorities could have been unlimited. On the contrary, the British preferred to find the legal

---

1. *Parl. Deb., Com.*, vol. CCCLXVIII, col. 804.
2. *Ibid.*, vol. CCCLXXIII, col. 1920.
3. *British Military Administration*, pp. 8-9.

basis for their military administration in an act of the Emperor of Ethiopia, the Head and organ of the same State which had been declared extinct by Italy and de-recognized by Britain only a few years earlier. No new State creation, no formation of new organs had taken place in the meantime.

It may be observed that this British attitude meant repudiating not only the Italian annexation, but equally Britain's own recognition of that annexation.

The first treaty between the United Kingdom and Ethiopia, the Agreement and Military Convention of January 31, 1942, was also based on the assumption that Ethiopia's continuity had not been broken by years of foreign occupation :

" Whereas the Government of the United Kingdom recognize that Ethiopia is now a free and independent State and H.M. the Emperor Haile Selassie I is its lawful Ruler, and the re-conquest of Ethiopia being now complete, wish to help H.M. the Emperor to re-establish His Government...
Art. 1. Diplomatic relations between the United Kingdom and Ethiopia shall be re-established [1]... "

It is clear that the terms used — " re-establishment " of the Emperor's government and, even more, " re-establishment " of diplomatic relations between the two countries — would have made no sense with regard to a new State. The continued identity of the Ethiopian State was thus affirmed in an international instrument.

The re-establishment of diplomatic relations between Ethiopia and other countries followed in due course [2].

On October 9, 1942, the Foreign Office announced Ethiopia's formal adherence to the United Nations [3]. In this capacity she was invited to the United Nations Conference in San Francisco in April 1945, and became one of the original members of the U.N.O. She also took part in the Paris Peace Conference in 1946.

b) *The Italian Peace Treaty.*

Before examining the 1947 Peace Treaty with Italy, it may be of interest to mention the discussions of the Council of Foreign Ministers which preceded it. Ethiopia's name is not to be found under two headings, re-appearing again and again in these discussions, — namely " former Italian colonies " and " territorial changes ". Obviously, it was never assumed by the Council that Ethiopia had been an Italian colony or that she in any way formed part of Italian territory. This being the position, the view thus implied by the Council of Ministers is to be interpreted in one way only, i.e. as affirming the unbroken continuity of the Ethiopian State.

On February 10, 1947, the Allied and Associated Powers signed the Peace Treaty with Italy. Section VII, concerning Ethiopia, reads as follows :

1. Cmd. 6334. See the Swiss Federal Council: « Les relations officielles entre les deux pays sont ainsi *rétablies.* » *It. mine, Annuaire Suisse,* 1947, p. 142, *f.-n.* 5.
2. See the *New Times and Ethiopia News* for the period.
3. *New Times and Ethiopia News.*

Art. 33. Italy recognizes and undertakes to respect the sovereignty and independence of the State of Ethiopia.

Art. 34. Italy formally renounces in favour of Ethiopia all property (apart from normal diplomatic and consular premises), rights, interests and advantages of all kinds acquired at any time in Ethiopia by the Italian State, as well as all parastatal property as defined in paragraph 1 Annex XIV of the present Treaty.
Italy also renounces all claims to special interests or influence in Ethiopia.

Art. 35. Italy recognizes the legality of all measures which the Government of Ethiopia has taken or may hereafter take in order to annul Italian measures respecting Ethiopia taken after October 3, 1935 and the effects of such measures.

Art. 36. Italian nationals in Ethiopia will enjoy the same juridical status as other foreign nationals but Italy recognizes the legality of all measures of the Ethiopian Government annulling or modifying concessions or special rights granted to Italian nationals, provided such measures are taken within a year from the coming into force of the present Treaty.

Art. 37. Within eighteen months from the coming into force of the present Treaty, Italy shall restore all works of art, religious objects, archives and objects of historical value belonging to Ethiopia or its nationals and removed from Ethiopia to Italy since October 3, 1935.

Art. 38. The date from which the provisions of the present Treaty shall become applicable as regards all measures and acts of any kind whatsoever entailing the responsibility of Italy or of Italian nationals towards Ethiopia, shall be held to be October 3, 1935.

Moreover, Art. 74 B provides for the payment of reparations to Ethiopia to the value of 25.000.000 U.S. dollars.

A preliminary observation may be made : once again, as in the discussion of the Council of Foreign Ministers, the Ethiopian problem is not dealt with under the heading of " territorial changes " or " Italian colonies ". Ethiopia is thus not " created " out of Italian territory, nor is she a former colony about to receive its freedom. She is not a creation of the Peace Treaty, but a party to it. Her existence as a State is taken for granted by the Treaty. This by itself does not, however, answer the question whether the Treaty considers her a new State or the continuation of an old State, with which she is identical. An answer to this question must be sought in an analysis of the relevant Articles of this Section of the Treaty.

In the first place, a distinction must be drawn between those Articles which impose on Italy the duty to recognize and respect Ethiopian independence and sovereignty and which eliminate both the former privileged position and possible future claims to such a position by Italy in Ethiopia, on the one hand (Art. 33, 34, 36), and those which are of immediate concern to the problem of Ethiopia's continuity (Art. 35, 37, 38).

This latter term is not actually used in the text ; it is, however, implicit in the relevant Articles, none of which would have made sense with regard to a " new " State.

Although neither the word " nullity " nor the word " aggression " appear in the text (as they appear in the Albanian Section of the Treaty), the Articles in question represent a clear declaration of nullity of the Italian conquest. No other interpretation is possible of the " carte blanche " contained in Art. 35, and giving Ethiopia the unlimited right to annul all Italian measures taken with regard to Ethiopia as from October 3, 1935. No such international authorization is possible with regard to lawful acts, since it would undermine all security in international relations. The basic date from which Ethiopia is free to undertake any such acts of voidance is the date of the Italian invasion. This date is again given as the date for the Italian restitution of looted property (Art. 37) and as the date for fixing the responsibility both of Italy and her citizens (Art. 38). This is hardly accidental. The declaration of nullity of Italian unlawful acts is thus not a declaration *ex nunc*, operating from the signature of the Treaty, but *ex tunc*, going back not only as far as the proclamation of annexation on May 9, 1936, but even as far as the date of actual Italian aggression on October 3, 1935. What is being stigmatized as unlawful is not only premature annexation, but the original act of aggression itself, with all its consequences. This act of aggression and its consequences are thus both illegal and invalid ; as such, they did not bring about Ethiopia's extinction. On the contrary, her continued existence after October 3, 1935 is affirmed and she can take all the necessary steps to assert retroactively her undiminished sovereignty in her own territory throughout this period [1].

Finally, an affirmation of Ethiopia's unbroken continuity, is also to be found in the Article providing for Italian reparations to Ethiopia. It is only obvious that no reparations could possibly have been paid by Italy to a new State, recently created out of her former territory, but that they are to be paid by Italy as compensation for a wrong done to an old State.

The whole period of Italian domination in Ethiopia is thus given an entirely different legal evaluation from the one accepted by the international community prior to 1941 : instead of a valid annexation involving the extinction of the Ethiopian State, the Peace Treaty proclaims its unbroken continuity, that is, the identity of the pre-invasion with the post-invasion Ethiopia.

5. CONCLUSIONS.

a) *Ethiopia's Continuity in the Light of General International Law.*

The State practice with regard to Ethiopia's restoration, renewed international recognition, bilateral conventions, and finally, the Italian Peace Treaty, are all impressive evidence of Ethiopia's survival, — in other words, of its continued identity.

This evidence which has been qualified as controvertible [2] becomes conclusive when found to be in conformity with general international law. In the case of Ethiopia, this conformity is absolute.

An investigation of facts on the basis of all the evidence available,

---

1. It may also be remarked that measures of annulment carried out by Ethiopia for this purpose do not rest on a unilateral decision, as in the case of the decree of the Czechoslovak Government of July 27, 1945, quoted by Prof. Guggenheim, *Validité et Nullité*, p. 243, *f.-n.* 2, but on an express rule of international conventional law. This eliminates any possible doubt as to the internationally permitted limits of such measures of voidance on the part of the restored sovereign. Cf. Guggenheim, *op. cit.*, p. 244.
2. See above, pp. 159-161 and 129-130.

has yielded the conclusion that the Italian domination of Ethiopia had never become anything more than belligerent occupation with varying degrees of effectiveness. Belligerent occupation, as is known, can never bring about the extinction of the occupied State. On the contrary, its continuity is fully safeguarded by a clear rule of international law. This rule cannot be set aside by the fact that the occupant, without achieving full subjugation of the occupied country, chooses to call it annexation instead of occupation.

It is on the basis of this objective rule, and this rule alone, that Ethiopia survived *in extremis* the whole impact of facts, actions and circumstances which, on the face of it, could have brought about her extinction : foreign invasion, occupation, proclamation of premature annexation, withdrawal of recognition by the international community, and so forth. There remained not even a government in exile, or recognized legations which could have been instrumental in carrying on Ethiopia's continuity through the critical period. It is true that there remained the Emperor, as the exiled claimant to his throne and country, and as a defender *in partibus* of the rights of his people [1]. This, however, provides a very weak link between the pre-war and the post-war Ethiopia and it may be seriously doubted whether the continued claim of the Head of the State alone would have been able to safeguard Ethiopia's continued existence. Whatever value may be attached to the Emperor's claim, does not result from that claim as such, but from the fact that it was based on a sound legal principle, and thus — indirectly — from that principle itself. An assertion of that sort would have been deprived of even a semblance of legal relevance, if made in the face of a situation authorized by international law, as, for example, effective and genuine revolution. As it was, it could have acquired a certain limited importance only because it was itself a reflection of a rule of law.

It is to this rule of law that the above evidence of Ethiopia's continuity conformed.

A final doubt may, however, be dealt with. The view that Italian domination in Ethiopia was mere belligerent occupation is based on the available evidence on which there is no reason to cast any serious doubt. Thus, for instance, the British testimony of uninterrupted armed Ethiopian resistance to the invader did certainly not come from a biased source ; it would hardly have helped to justify the former British policy of the recognition of the Italian conquest subsequently to invent facts proving that this conquest had never been effective.

---

1. " ...I am at least entitled to ask that the rights of my people continue to be recognized. ...As Emperor of Ethiopia, backed by the loyal devotion of my chiefs and warriors and by the affection of my people, and concerned to put an end if possible to their sufferings, I renew the declaration which I made to the League of Nations. I am prepared, now as before, to discuss any proposal for a solution which, even at the cost of sacrifices, would guarantee my people the free development of their civilization and independence. Should this appeal, however, meet with no response, war against Italy will continue whatever happens, until the triumph of right and justice has been won. " *LNOJ*, 1938, pp. 337 and 339. It is interesting to note that the Emperor speaks of a " continuation " of the war against Italy, thus confirming that this war has never come to an end ; this, in turn, confirms the view of the Italian domination in Ethiopia being simple belligerent occupation.

It could, however, be argued that the evidence is not sufficient to qualify the Italian domination as mere belligerent occupation with absolute certainty. In such a case, which is the rule of general international law which will give such provisional and controvertible evidence absolute finality?

Ex superabundante cautela the argument may be taken up and answered : if indeed, in spite of all the evidence quoted, the case was not one of belligerent occupation, then the evidence of Ethiopia's unbroken continuity yet conforms, if not to a fully crystallized rule, then to a fundamental principle of any legal system : *ex iniura ius non oritur*. It would then be the first case of an effective application of this principle by the international community in face of an unlawful act. It is submitted that this principle forms an adequate test of the conformity of State practice, conventional law and so forth, with general international law.

b) *Irrelevance of International Recognition.*

It is believed that the Ethiopian case makes an instructive contribution to the problem and nature of international recognition discussed above [1].

In the first place it fully confirms that recognition, far from being a legal act, based on legal criteria, is an act of pure policy. On what legal principle was the granting and the withdrawal of recognition from the Italian conquest of Ethiopia based? It has been seen that this recognition, apart from being itself a violation of the positive obligations of the recognizing States, related to an illegal act. Was the illegality of the Italian invasion and annexation of Ethiopia any less illegal when recognized, than when de-recognized, by the international community?

Since legality or illegality of the recognized situation provides no criterion, it might be expected that the principle of effectiveness would provide the determining factor. Yet Italian rule in Ethiopia was just as effective at the time of the British withdrawal of its recognition in 1941, as it was at the time of its recognition in 1938 or even 1936 ; always on the assumption that it has never achieved full effectiveness, necessary to convert mere belligerent occupation into valid annexation, it is not unreasonable to suppose that it had become even more effective, owing to the consolidation of Italian power in the course of time [2].

---

1. See above, pp. 130-161.
2. Prof. Lauterpacht, while admitting that the withdrawal of British recognition of the Italian conquest was independent of any cessation of effective Italian rule in Ethiopia, argues that even in this case British action " cannot be regarded as arbitrary ". " The legal explanation of that measure was probably the fact that the object of the recognition *de iure* as given in 1938, namely, the achievement of a general settlement aiming at the pacification of Europe and of the world, was destroyed by the action of Italy in 1940 in declaring war upon Great Britain and France. " *Op. cit.*, p. 356. If this is intended to be a — " probably " — legal explanation, then it is indeed difficult to see in what a political explanation would consist. Translated into unpleasantly frank terms, the proposition simply means that a legal principle — and with it, Ethiopia's right to live — could be " legally " trampled underfoot as long as it was believed that such a procedure could secure some benefit ; but that it again became a binding legal principle the moment its disregard no longer had any purchasing power.

Moreover, the recognition of the Italian conquest does not seem to have been taken unduly seriously by the recognizing States themselves, who did not consider even themselves bound by this act. It has been seen that when the British army entered Ethiopia, it acted on the principle of the continued legal existence of that State even *before* British recognition of its survival. The British White Paper on the subject may be quoted once again ; explaining the correctness of British behaviour in Ethiopia, it says :

" H.M. Government had recognized the Italian annexation of Ethiopia, *but* the Emperor ... had never renounced his claim to sovereignty [1]. "

Thus, in explaining Ethiopia's survival and its acknowledgement by Britain in 1941, the latter herself repudiated her own recognition of that country's extinction as irrelevant to the fact of its legal continuity, in favour of some other, prevailing principle. It happens that this contrary and stronger principle was rather poorly chosen, the Emperor's own claim having heen hardly sufficient by itself to uphold Ethiopia's continuity. This, however, is less important than Britain's own repudiation of any constitutive value of her recognition of such continuity. The White Paper also says :

" The Emperor in returning to his country and thus resuming contact did so in his own view and in that of the world as the rightful sovereign of the country [2]. "

That the Emperor considered himself the rightful sovereign, is not subject to doubt. It is, however, asserted in an official British document that this view was equally shared by " the world ". It may be recalled that the Emperor's return to Ethiopia took place before his renewed recognition by the international community, including Britain. It is then to be assumed that this undefined " view of the world ", not expressed in an official act of recognition, must again have been something which prevailed against the inconsistencies and vagaries of the recognition policy. It is of no interest whether this unusual formulation refers to some moral considerations or a principle of natural law ; but it is of interest to note that it serves once again as a means of repudiating any constitutive, or even legal, value of the British recognition by Britain herself.

Finally, the Treaty of Peace, re-asserting Ethiopia's unbroken continuity throughout the critical period beginning with the Italian invasion, constitutes an overwhelming proof of the general repudiation by the international community of their policy of recognition of the Italian conquest. Such recognition is nullified by the Treaty together with the Italian annexation itself. Moreover, the Treaty stigmatizes that recognition as unlawful. It must be remembered that, by being retroactive, the relevant Articles on Ethiopia cover exactly the same period as was covered by the international recognition of Ethiopia's extinction. Thus, of the two attitudes of States with regard to Ethiopia during one and the same period, only one can be lawful : either the

---

1. *It. mine, British Military Administration*, p. 8.
2. *Ibid.*

one expressed by actual recognition of the conquest, or the one expressed retroactively in the Peace Treaty. In view of the foregoing analysis there is no difficulty in attributing legality to the latter, and to the latter alone.

At this stage, Prof. Lauterpacht's argument should again be taken up, according to which international recognition should be a means of validating an illegal act. It has already been thought necessary to reject this suggestion on the ground of the illegality of such recognition itself [1]. It is now possible to reject it in the light of State practice. For, in the case of Ethiopia, such practice expressly repudiated any validating character of recognition.

It may be added that, by repudiating their own recognition, States have *ipso facto* repudiated its constitutive nature. A constitutive argument, maintained *ad absurdum*, would lead to the conclusion that, by the eventual recognition of Ethiopia's continuity, State practice decided against any law-creating effect of international recognition. The adoption of the declaratory view spares one the necessity of such acrobatics.

c) *The Ethiopian Problem and the Objective Conception of International Law.*

The conclusions to be drawn from the Ethiopian case would not be complete without the observation that this case is utterly devastating for any voluntarist conception of international law.

The above submission would not be possible if, after the Italian defeat, Ethiopia had been re-created and acknowledged as a new State. It could then have been argued that there was full compatibility between the will of States, as expressed in their recognition policy, and the legal reality of both periods : the period of Italian domination during which — it could have been asserted — there was in fact no Ethiopia ; and the period after the cessation of that domination when — it could have been argued — a new Ethiopian State had come into existence. For both these periods the will of States could have been claimed as creating a legal situation which, in both cases, would have conformed to the final legal evaluation of the case. Besides, in the changing picture of the world, the extinction and re-birth of a State, involving its political and historical, but not its legal, identity, is not only possible, but has indeed taken place.

But Ethiopia was not a new State after the Italian defeat. It was the same State as before the invasion and was acknowledged as such.

Thus, contrary to Raestad's conception [2], it was not the will of third States which was the source of Ethiopia's continued existence while her territory was under enemy occupation. She did not survive owing to such will. On the contrary, she survived precisely against the will of the international community which, by recognizing the Italian conquest, joined in proclaiming her extinction. In spite of that

1. See above, pp. 271-272.
2. See above, p. 131.

will of the third States, of the invasion and occupation of her territory, and the absence of an organized government, Ethiopia survived only and exclusively on the strength of an objective principle of international law. The international community at first disregarded that principle only to submit to it eventually and to adopt it retroactively as their own. Objective international law thus fully prevailed against the temporary contrary will of the States.

This is the lasting value of an enquiry into the problem of identity and continuity of the Ethiopian State, to which no voluntarist conception of international law can give a logical and coherent explanation.

CHAPTER V.

CZECHOSLOVAKIA.

1. DISMEMBERMENT OF THE CZECHOSLOVAK REPUBLIC.

The history of the dismemberment of Czechoslovakia which preceded the Second World War need not be recounted in detail. Broadly speaking, it proceeded in two stages : the first was consummated at Munich in September 1938, the second consisted in the creation of the Protectorate of Bohemia and Moravia, the proclamation of independence of Slovakia and the annexation of Carpatho-Ruthenia by Hungary in March 1939.

a) *The Munich Agreement.*

The Munich Agreement, concluded on September 29, 1938, between Germany, Italy, Great Britain and France, provided for the cession of the Sudetenland by Czechoslovakia to Germany [1]. The events which preceded that agreement, the atmosphere which surrounded its conclusion and the consequences to which it gave rise are well known.

It is therefore hardly necessary to pass judgment on the Munich Agreement from the political or moral point of view. Its validity under international law has equally been contested [2]. It must, however, be admitted, with Prof. Guggenheim, that it was originally valid and was only later declared null and void as a result of subsequent events [3].

What definitely disposes of any doubts as to the original validity of the Agreement is its acceptance by Czechoslovakia, who could therefore not regard it as *res inter alios acta.* On September 30, 1938, the Czechoslovak Foreign Minister, Krofta, announced in the presence of the French, British and Italian Ministers that

" in the name of the President of the Republic and in the name of the Czechoslovak Government we accept the decisions taken at Munich without us and against us [4] ".

---

1. Text reproduced in *International Conciliation*, November 1938.
2. See Quincy Wright, *The Munich Settlement and International Law*, A. J., 1939, who considers that the Munich Agreement violated all existing treaty obligations of the contracting parties, and qualifies the action of the Powers not as " peaceful change ", but as intervention. The validity of the Munich Agreement is also contested by Taborsky, *Munich, the Vienna Arbitration and International Law*, in Cz. Y.
3. « La nullité de cet accord n'a été déclarée que longtemps après son entrée en vigueur, exécution effective et valable. ...La nullité n'existe donc pas *ab initio*. Les conditions de celle-ci n'ont été réalisées que postérieurement à l'établissement de l'acte, à une époque où ce dernier avait déjà déployé ses pleins effets d'acte valable. » *Validité*, p. 212.
4. Taborsky, *op. cit.*, p. 25.

That this acceptance was made under duress, is obvious. But under general international law, duress does not invalidate an agreement [1].

Having adhered to the Munich Agreement, Czechoslovakia subsequently acted on it by nominating a Czechoslovak member to the International Commission and to the German-Czechoslovak Commission, both formed in accordance with Part III of the Agreement. In further execution of the Agreement, on October 20, 1938, Czechoslovakia concluded a convention with Germany for the settlement of nationality questions.

It should be added that on November 2, 1938, the so-called Vienna Arbitration accorded to Hungary considerable portions of Czechoslovak territory in Slovakia and Carpatho-Ruthenia [2].

It is clear that the severe territorial losses in no way affected the legal personality and the continued existence of the Czechoslovak Republic. Her international status remained legally unchanged, and her internal developments proceeded within the limits of her own legal order. It was within these limits that Dr. Benes resigned the Presidency of the Republic on October 5, 1938 [3]. On November 30, a new President was duly elected in the person of Dr. Emil Hacha. On November 22, two Acts of the Czechoslovak Parliament effected the re-construction of the country on federal lines, granting far-reaching autonomy to Slovakia and Carpatho-Ruthenia [4]. The change was reflected in a slight alteration of the country's name which henceforth was hyphenated and became " Czecho-Slovakia ". It hardly needs pointing out that these internal changes affected the identity of the State just as little as its territorial losses.

b) *The Creation of Slovakia and the Protectorate of Bohemia and Moravia.*

In the beginning of March 1939, German-inspired separatist tendencies in Slovakia assumed unprecedented proportions [5]. The Prague Government was compelled to dismiss the Slovak Government and appoint a new one in its place. Thereupon, the dismissed Slovak Ministers appealed to Berlin, and the former Slovak Premier, Tiso, was immediately summoned to the German capital and received by Hitler. On his return to Bratislava, Slovakia's separation from Prague and her independence was proclaimed on March 14, 1939.

On March 15, 1939, the Czechoslovak President and Foreign Minister were in turn summoned to Berlin. There, following dramatic events, which have since become known [6], the following communiqué was issued :

1. See — e.g. — Oppenheim-Lauterpacht, *op. cit.*, I, pp. 802-803 ; Guggenheim, *Lehrbuch*, I, pp. 84 and 86 ; Rousseau, *op. cit.*, pp. 352-354 ; Fauchille, *op. cit.*, I, 3ᵉ Partie, pp. 297-299.
2. Taborsky, *op. cit.*, p. 36.
3. Letter of resignation in *International Conciliation*, November 1938, pp. 476-477 ; broadcast of resignation in Ripka, *Munich: Before and After*, pp. 237-239.
4. Langer, *op. cit.*, p. 216 ; Rabl. *Zur jüngsten Entwicklung der slowakischen Frage*, *Ztscht. f. a. öff. R. u. V.-r.* 1939/40, pp. 298-302 ; Ripka, *op. cit.*, pp. 241-245.
5. For the Czech account of these events, see Ripka, *op. cit.*, pp. 359-372.
6. Ministère des Affaires Etrangères, *Documents Diplomatiques*, 1938-1939, Paris : Imprimerie Nationale, 1939. Coulondre's despatch, no. 77.

" The Führer to-day, in the presence of the Reich Minister for Foreign Affairs, Herr von Ribbentrop, received the Czechoslovak President, Dr. Hacha, and the Czechoslovak Minister for Foreign Affairs, Dr. Chwalkowsky, at their request in Berlin. At the meeting the serious situation which had arisen as a result of the events of the past week on what was hitherto Czechoslovak territory was closely and frankly examined. Both sides gave expression to their mutual conviction that the aim of all efforts in this part of Central Europe should be the safeguarding of calm, order and peace. The Czechoslovak President declared that in order to serve this purpose, and in order to secure final pacification, he placed the destiny of the Czech people and country with confidence in the hands of the Führer of the German Reich. The Führer accepted this declaration and expressed his determination to take the Czech people under the protection of.the German Reich and to guarantee to it an autonomous development of its national life in accordance with its particular characteristics [1]. "

On March 16, 1939, the Bohemian and Moravian provinces of Czechoslovakia were occupied by German troops, and the German Führer issued the following decree :

" Art. 1. (1) The territories of the former Czecho-Slovak republic, occupied by the German troops in March, 1939, henceforth belong to the territory of the great German Reich and come under its protection as the " Protectorate of Bohemia and Moravia ".

(2) In so far as the defence of the Reich demands it, the Führer and Reichskanzler may take exceptional measures for individual portions of these territories.

Art. 2. (1) Inhabitants of the Protectorate of German race become German nationals and Reich citizens in accordance with the provisions of the Reich citizenship law of September 15, 1935. The regulations for the protection of German blood and German honour will therefore also apply to them. They will be subject to German jurisdiction.

(2) The remaining inhabitants of Bohemia and Moravia become nationals of the Protectorate of Bohemia and Moravia.

Art. 3. (1) The Protectorate of Bohemia and Moravia is autonomous and self-governing.

(2) It exercises the sovereign powers, allotted to it, within the framework of the Protectorate and in harmony with the political, military and economic affairs of the Reich.

(3) These sovereign powers will be exercised through its own organs and administrative authorities with its own officials.

Art. 4. The supreme head of the autonomous administration of the Protectorate of Bohemia and Moravia enjoys the protection and the dignity of the head of a state. The supreme head of the Protectorate must, for the performance of his duties, have the confidence of the Führer and Reichskanzler.

Art. 5. (1) As protector of the interests of the Reich, the Führer and Reichskanzler nominates a Reich protector in Bohemia and Moravia. His official residence is Prague.

(2) The Reich protector has, as representative of the Führer and Reichskanzler and as delegate of the Reich government, the task of ensuring the observance of the political principles of the Führer and Reichskanzler.

(3) The members of the government of the Protectorate will be approved by the Reich protector. This approval can be withdrawn.

(4) The Reich protector is empowered to acquaint himself with all measures of the government of the Protectorate and to give advice thereon. He can object to measures liable to prejudice the Reich and if there is danger in delay, can issue the instructions required by common interest.

---

1. *Cz. Y.*, p. 223. German original in *Ztscht. f. a. öff. R. u. V.-r.*, 1939/40, p. 506.

(5) The promulgation of laws, decrees and other regulations and the enforcement of administrative measures and of valid legal judgments is to be suspended if the Reich protector raises objection.

Art. 6. (1) The foreign affairs of the Protectorate, particularly the protection of its nationals abroad, will be transacted by the Reich. The Reich will direct foreign affairs in accordance with the common interest.

(2) The Protectorate will send a representative to the Reich government with the official title of " Envoy ".

Art. 7. (1) The Reich will afford military defence to the Protectorate.

(2) To carry out this protection the Reich will maintain garrisons and military establishments in the Protectorate.

(3) The Protectorate may set up its own organisation for the maintenance of internal security and order. Their organisation, effective strength, and armament will be decided by the Reich government.

Art. 8. The Reich has direct supervision over transport, including posts, telegraphs and telephones.

Art. 9. The Protectorate belongs to the customs-district of the German Reich and is subordinate to its tariff authority.

Art. 10. (1) Until further notice the crown, together with the Reichsmark, is legal tender.

(2) The relation between the two currencies will be decided by the Reich government.

Art. 11. (1) The Reich can issue decrees valid for the Protectorate as common interest requires.

(2) In so far as a common need exists the Reich administration can take over branches of the administration and set up the necessary Reich authorities therefor.

(3) The Reich Government can enforce the necessary measures for the maintenance of safety and order.

Art. 12. The legislation now in force in Bohemia and Moravia remains in force, in so far as it is not incompatible with the assumption of protection by the German Reich.

Art. 13. The Reich Minister of the Interior issues, in agreement with the Reich Ministers concerned, the legal and administrative orders necessary for the enforcement and amplification of this decree [1]. "

Thus, in the territory of the diminished Czechoslovak Republic an allegedly independent State of Slovakia was created and a German Protectorate was set up in Bohemia and Moravia, while the third part of Czechoslovak territory, Carpatho-Ruthenia, was annexed by Hungary.

Seen from the political point of view and in historical perspective, all these events, beginning with the Munich Agreement, form a logical whole and represent successive steps taken with a view to a final destruction of the Czechoslovak State.

Legally, however, they must be clearly distinguished. It goes without saying that, while the Munich Agreement and the subsequent annexation of the Sudetenland by Germany was originally valid, not a shadow of legality can be claimed for the events of March 1939. On the contrary, by her aggression against Czechoslovakia Germany violated the fundamental obligations to respect the sovereignty and territorial integrity of another State, the existing delimitation under international

---

1. *British and Foreign State Papers,* vol. CXXLIII, pp.485-488 ; German original in *Ztschl. f. a. öff. R. u. V.-r.* 1939/40, pp. 506-509.

law.   More particularly, Germany violated the Kellogg Pact, the German-Czechoslovak Arbitration Treaty of 1926, as well as the Munich Agreement itself.

Moreover, the Munich Agreement and the March events must be clearly distinguished from the point of view of the identity and continuity of the Czechoslovak State.   For, whereas the loss of the Sudetenland could not — and did not — in any way affect Czechoslovakia's legal continuity, it was the March events and they alone which raised the problem of her continued existence or survival.   It was then and only then that the problem of State continuity arose at all.

2. INTERNATIONAL RECOGNITION OF SLOVAKIA AND THE PROTECTORATE.

Faced with the German aggression against Czechoslovakia, the international community adopted at first a decidedly negative stand. Great Britain and France, who were both parties to the Munich Agreement, reacted with strong protests.

" We have lodged a formal protest with the German Government " — said the British Foreign Secretary in the House of Lords on March 20, 1939 — " in the sense of informing them, that we cannot but regard the events of the last few days as a complete repudiation of the Munich Agreement and a denial of the spirit in which the negotiators of that agreement bound themselves to co-operate for a peaceful settlement.   We have also taken occasion to protest against the changes effected in Czecho-Slovakia by German military action, and have said that, in our view, those changes are devoid of any basis of legality. "

Lord Halifax described the proceedings as an " arbitrary suppression of an independent sovereign State by force " and a " violation of what I must regard as the elementary rules of international conduct " [1].

On March 17, the French Government lodged a protest with the German Government.

" ... The Government of the Republic considers itself, through the action taken against Czechoslovakia by the German Government, confronted with a flagrant violation of both the letter and the spirit of the Agreement signed in Munich on September 29, 1938.   The circumstances in which the agreement of March 15 was imposed on the leaders of the Czechoslovak Republic could not, in the view of the Government of the French Republic, legalize the state of affairs registered in this agreement.   The French Ambassador has the honour to inform His Excellency the Reich Minister of Foreign Affairs that the Government of the Republic cannot in the circumstances recognize the legality of the new situation brought about in Czechoslovakia by the action of the Reich [2]. "

Of the States which were not signatories of the Munich Agreement, particular interest attaches to the Note addressed on March 18, 1939, by the Soviet Commissar for Foreign Affairs, M. Litvinov, to the German Ambassador in Moscow.   Far from confining itself to the creation of the Protectorate, the Note protested equally against the events in Slovakia and the Hungarian annexation, for which it held the German

---

1. *Documents*, p. 13.
2. *Cz. S. and Doc.*, 2, pp. 22-23.

Government responsible. Moreover, it included statements of a general character going far beyond the content of the particular case :

" The Soviet Government is not aware of any State constitution that entitles the Head of a State to abolish its independent existence as a State without the consent of his people. It is difficult to admit that any people would voluntarily agree to the destruction of their independence and to their inclusion in another State, still less a people that for hundreds of years fought for their independence and for twenty years maintained their independent existence. In signing in Berlin the Act of March 15, Dr. Hacha, President of Czechoslovakia had no authority from his people for doing so, and acted in manifest contradiction with Articles 64 and 65 of the Czecho-Slovak Constitution and the will of his people. Consequently, the aforesaid Act cannot be considered legally valid. "

The Soviet Note emphasized that the principle of self-determination, so often invoked by Germany, presupposes the free expression of popular will and went on :

" In the absence of any expression of the will of the Czech people, the occupation of the Czech provinces by German troops and the subsequent actions of the German Government cannot but be considered as arbitrary, violent and aggressive. The above remarks also refer in their entirety to the change in the status of Slovakia ... which was not justified by any expression of the will of the Slovak people. "

In consequence, the Soviet Government refused to recognize Czechoslovakia's incorporation into the Reich

" to be legitimate and in conformity with the generally accepted rules of international law and justice or the principle of self-determination of nations [1] ".

Unlike the French and British protests, the Soviet Note thus developed a more general point of view. In the first place, the Soviet Government stepped forward as a defender of legality under municipal law as a condition of the validity of international acts ; secondly, where fundamental changes in the condition or existence of States are concerned, it raised the freely expressed will of the people to the rank of yet another condition of validity ; thirdly, it did not hesitate to invoke international justice and the principle of self-determination as the basis of its refusal to recognize the German acts of violence.

On March 17, 1939, the United States Under-Secretary of State issued a statement, condemning German action in Czechoslovakia and declaring in particular :

" This Government ... cannot refrain from making known this country's condemnation of the acts which have resulted in the *temporary* extinguishment of a free and independent State and people [2]. "

Thus, German aggression against Czechoslovakia met with a decisive protest and a refusal of recognition on the part of the international community. This attitude was further reflected in the fact that the Czechoslovak Legations in these and other countries [3] were allowed to remain and to continue to exercise such functions as

1. *Ibid.*, pp. 23-25.
2. *It. mine, ibid.*, p. 20.
3. E. g. Poland, see *Four Fighting Years*, p. 172.

still remained to them. The closing of Legations in Prague was the result of German pressure and in no way affected the non-recognition of Czechoslovakia's destruction.

However, this non-recognition was not destined to last. One after another, members of the international community began to grant recognition in the first place to the " independent Slovak State ". On May 15, 1939, the Under-Secretary of State for Foreign Affairs declared in the House of Commons :

"In order to facilitate the conduct of normal business, H.M. Consul at Bratislava has on my noble Friend's instruction, sought and obtained from the Slovak Government recognition as H.M. Consul for Slovakia. The Slovak Government have been informed that H.M. Government regard this step as amounting to de facto recognition [1]. "

Notwithstanding her outspoken and reasoned protest, the Soviet Union recognized Slovakia on September 17, 1939, by accepting the first Slovak Minister to Moscow and closing down the Czechoslovak Legation [2]. Within a relatively short time from its foundation Slovakia was further recognized by the Vatican, Hungary, Spain, Switzerland, Poland, France, Japan and Manchukuo [3].

The recognition of Slovakia did not *ipso facto* imply the recognition of the Protectorate. But it certainly implied the recognition of Czechoslovakia's extinction, — particularly in cases where the *de facto* character of such recognition was not made clear beyond all doubt. This recognition of extinction of Czechoslovakia was further expressed in the closing down of Czechoslovak Legations in several countries [4].

As far as Great Britain was concerned, more was to come. On May 22, 24 and 26, 1939, the problem of recognition of the Protectorate itself came up for discussion in the House of Commons, several Members pressing the Government for a clear statement to the effect that the Protectorate would not be recognized under any circumstances. This assurance was refused [5]. On June 19, 1939, the Under-Secretary of State for Foreign Affairs informed the House that H.M. Ambassador in Berlin had been instructed to apply to the German Government for an *exequatur* for a Consul General in Prague. The *de facto* recognition of the Protectorate (" of the present position in Bohemia and Moravia "), implied in such a step, was admitted in the statement [6].

1. *Parl. Deb.*, *Com.*, vol. CCCXXXXVII, col. 961.
2. Langer, *op. cit.*, p. 233. « ...le retrait momentané par l'U.R.S.S. de son agrément à la représentation de la République Tchécoslovaque, dont le maintien avait donné lieu de la part du gouvernement soviétique à une note du 17 mars 1939 fortement motivée sur le droit de libre disposition des peuples... » Cassin R., *La position internationale de la Tchécoslovaquie*, in *Cz. Y.*, p. 64. In December 1939 Russia " ceased to recognize the Czechoslovak Legation in Moscow and entered into formal relations with the so-called Slovak State. " *Four Fighting Years*, p. 187.
3. Langer, *op. cit.*, p. 233.
4. E. g. the Soviet Union, see above, p. 588 ; Switzerland, see *Rapport de gestion du Conseil Fédéral*, 1939, p. 101.
5. The debate is summarized by Langer, *op. cit.*, pp. 224-229.
6. *Parl. Deb.*, *Com.*, vol. CCCXXXXVIII, col. 1786. Thus, of the non-Axis countries, only Great Britain went to the length of recognizing the Protectorate, — even if only *de facto*. It is interesting to note that the Germans refused the exequatur. Langer therefore comments that " in the end Germany had British recognition of, but H. M. Government no consuls in, the Protectorate. " *Op. cit.*, p. 230.

Of the great Powers, only the United States maintained its original attitude with complete consistency [1]. It never recognized any of the changes effected on Czechoslovak territory and it never ceased to recognize the Czechoslovak Republic *de iure*. Certain apparently contradictory steps, taken by the United States in view of the existing situation, bore a distinctly technical character [2].

Similarly, Czechoslovakia's name was retained on the list of States Members of the League of Nations [3] and the International Labour Organisation [4]. It disappeared, however, from the list of Members of the Universal Postal Union which now included Slovakia as a fully-fledged member, whereas the Protectorate was included with Germany [5].

Similarly, Slovakia appeared on the list of Members of the International Telecommunication Union, while the still retained name of Czechoslovakia carried a foot-note to the effect that, according to a German notification, Czechoslovakia was no longer Member of the Union [6].

It must therefore be concluded that, notwithstanding notable exceptions, the international community recognized Czechoslovakia's extinction either explicitly or or by implication.

3. LEGAL NATURE OF ENTITIES FORMED ON CZECHOSLOVAK TERRITORY.

It has been seen that — apart from straightforward annexation of certain provinces — two new entities came to be formed on the territory of the Czechoslovak Republic : the State of Slovakia and the Protectorate of Bohemia and Moravia. It is now necessary to determine the true legal nature of these entities and whether either of them was identical with the Czechoslovak Republic.

a) *Slovakia.*

Slovakia, as constituted on March 14, 1939, claimed to be an independent State. A purely formal analysis of the facts would confirm this claim. The formation of State by way of revolutionary secession of a province from the parent State is a very usual phenomenon in history and it is fully accepted by international law. Moreover, Slovakia's independence was proclaimed by genuine Slovaks who subsequently administered the country. The proclamation of independence took

---

1. See documents quoted by Langer, *op. cit.*, pp. 232-234.
2. Thus Mr. Welles' letter to the U.S. Secretary of Treasury of March 17, 1939 : " In view of the recent military occupation of the Provinces of Bohemia, Moravia and Slovakia of Czechoslovakia by German armed forces and the assumption of control over these areas by German authorities, the Department, while not recognizing any legal basis for the assumption of so-called « protection » over this territory, is constrained by force of the foregoing circumstances to regard the above-mentioned provinces as now being under the *de facto* administration of the German authorities. " *Cz. S. and Doc.*, 2, pp. 21-22.
3. Langer, *op. cit.*, p. 221.
4. I.L.O. Yearbooks, 1938-1940.
5. Bureau International de l'Union Postale Universelle, *Rapport de gestion*, 1939-1944.
6. *Rapport de gestion*, 1940-1944.

place in a country free from foreign military occupation. It took place against a background of certain genuine and long-standing separatist tendencies. Finally, as has been seen, the new entity achieved a considerable degree of international recognition.

Were this enquiry to stop here, the State character of Slovakia would have to be admitted. It has, however, been seen that it is of the very essence of a puppet State to preserve to the maximum all the formal characteristics of a genuine State. In all cases which are *prima facie* suspect, the question must therefore be much more critically examined from the point of view of " actual " independence [1].

In the case under consideration it is legitimate to state that the " revolutionary secession " was completely engineered by Germany. On the eve of the proclamation of independence, Slovak leaders went to Berlin to receive their orders. Immediately on the proclamation of independence, the new " State " abdicated that very same independence by appealing to Germany for protection. This was duly granted and a treaty to this effect was concluded on March 18, 1939 [2]. The new " State " was organized entirely on German National Socialist principles and made to serve the interests of the German Reich during the whole period of its existence, just as it served those interests by the very fact of its birth [3].

Lord Halifax was therefore fully justified in stating :

" ... there has always been a party in Slovakia which advocated autonomy. That autonomy was, in fact, achieved after Munich. ... The extremist elements in Slovakia, however, were not satisfied with these arrangements, but on all the evidence that is available to me I find it impossible to believe that the sudden decision of certain Slovak leaders to break off from Prague, which was followed so closely by their appeal for protection to the German Reich was reached independently of outside influence [4]. "

In the light of all the evidence available there is no doubt that the allegedly independent State of Slovakia was in reality a German puppet, created by Germany on a part of Czechoslovak territory [5]. No amount of recognition by third States could have invested it with a State character.

In such circumstances, any possibility of Slovakia's identity with the Czechoslovak Republic must be immediately excluded. It has to be admitted that such identity was indeed neither claimed by Slovakia nor asserted in any other quarter. On the other hand, in the case of the Protectorate of Bohemia and Moravia attempts were made to show that it possessed international personality and continued the legal existence of the Czechoslovak Republic.

---

1. See above, pp. 169-180.
2. Rabl., *op. cit.*, p. 320 ; text of the treaty — " Vertrag über das Schutzverhältnis zwischen dem Deutschen Reich und Slowakei " — in *Ztscht. f. a. öff. R. u. V.-r.*, 1939/40, pp. 510-511.
3. For details, see Rabl, *op. cit.* Of particular interest is the constitutional position of the German " Volksgruppe ".
4. Statement in the House of Lords, of March 20, 1939, *Documents*, p. 11.
5. See Guggenheim, *Lehrbuch*, I, p. 170, *f.-n.* 24 ; Scelle, *op. cit.*, p. 128 ; Lauterpacht, *op. cit.*, p. 28.

b) *The Protectorate.*

The possibility of the Protectorate continuing the legal personality of the Czechoslovak Republic could be summarily dismissed with the single argument that obviously there could have been no continuity of Czechoslovakia, — still less of the reformed Czecho-Slovakia — without Slovakia. The question was not merely one of a further loss of territory, the loss of Slovakia being in no way comparable to the loss of the Sudetenland. The participation of the Slovak lands within the common State of Czechs and Slovaks was the condition of the very existence of the Czechoslovak Republic as such. The loss of Slovakia, even if the Czech part of the Republic had preserved its independence, must necessarily have left an altogether different State in Czech territory. There would have been a split of the old Republic into two new and different State entities, none of which would have been identical with the former.

However, it would not be proper to ignore the discussion which took place with regard to the legal nature of the Protectorate and its relation to Czechoslovakia. It may be remarked that all those taking part in it [1] completely disregard the real meaning of the separation of Slovakia, as outlined above.

The discussion was initiated by Venturini in an article in which he sought to answer two basic questions : 1) whether the Protectorate possessed international personality and 2) whether, in case of an affirmative answer, it was identical with the Czechoslovak Republic ? [2]

Venturini found it possible to answer the first question in the affirmative on the basis of an analysis of the German decree of March 16, 1939, — unimpressed as he obviously was by the basic impossibility of deducing the State character of an entity from the internal law of another State. Thus he argues that the decree assured to the Protectorate all the necessary elements of statehood, such as a separate nationality (Art. 2), autonomy, sovereign powers (Art. 3), a Head of the State (Art. 4), retention of the old legal order (Art. 12), and even international relations between the protecting and the protected State, as expressed by the creation of the offices of the Reichsprotektor on the one hand and a Czech Envoy to the German Government on the other (Art. 5 and 6). The very fact of Germany taking over supreme State functions, as well as the inclusion of the Protectorate in the German customs system are further proof that there was no annexation, in which case no such provisions would have been necessary. Consequently, the Protectorate does possess international personality ; it is a genuine " international protectorate " which admittedly does not extinguish the personality of the protected State. Not even the absence of a regular treaty of protection would, in the eyes of Venturini, affect this conclusion, since several known protectorates, such as the Free City of Cracow, the Ionian Islands and Egypt, came into existence without a treaty of

---

1. With the exception of Klein, see below, p. 296.
2. *La nuova situazione giuridica dei territori della Cecoslovacchia*, in *Diritto Internazionale*, 1938.

protection. But Venturini even finds that there was such a treaty in the shape of the Hitler-Hacha communiqué of March 15, 1939.

With regard to the problem of Czechoslovakia's extinction, Venturini admits all the difficulties of establishing a conclusive criterion of State extinction in general ; yet he insists that nothing had occurred to bring about the end of the Czechoslovak State. Thus, the proclamation of Slovakia's independence, far from producing the extinction of the old Republic, had merely " modified " it. Nor could the creation of the Protectorate be instrumental in effecting such extinction. No new State had been created since, on the strength of Art. 12 of the German decree, the Czechoslovak laws remained in force, albeit only conditionally. Here Venturini admits that such laws as remained in force came to be based on a new formal source, namely on Art. 12, itself and that they were thus " formally new ", but he refuses to draw the only correct conclusion from this admission.

Thus, if Czechoslovakia did not cease to exist and if the Protectorate was endowed with genuine international personality, then, according to Venturini, the Protectorate was identical with Czechoslovakia and continued her international personality [1].

Venturini's argument was dealt with point by point by Raggi, in a penetrating essay on the legal nature of the Protectorate [2] ,which provides a negative answer to Venturini's two questions bearing on the international personality of the Protectorate and on its identity with the Czechoslovak Republic.

If an entity is to be a State — argues Raggi — it must be endowed with an underived juridical organisation [3]. In other words, its legal order cannot depend for its validity and existence on the will of another legal order [4]. Consequently, it was precisely the loss of this independent, underived legal order which produced the extinction of the Czechoslovak State ; an extinction which could not have been brought about either by the proclamation of Slovakia's independence, or by the Hungarian annexations or finally by revolutionary changes within the Czechoslovak State order, as expressed in the unconstitutional proceedings of Hacha and Chwalkowsky in Berlin. Moreover, under international law, a State must have a territory. According to Art. 1 of the German decree, however, the Protectorate has none, since its territory belongs to the Reich. Thus, Czechoslovakia ceased to exist if only for the simple reason that she had lost her entire territory. The new entity which has come to replace her is not a State, since it has none of the positive characteristics of a State, whereas all it does possess show its non-State character. Thus, the Protectorate has abdicated not only its external, but even its internal sovereignty, since it does not even possess supreme

1. " ...che tale personalità sia la stessa dello Stato cecoslovaco, in quanto il Protettorato di Boemia e di Moravia non è che lo stesso Stato che, pur notevolmente modificato nei suoi elementi costitutivi, territorio, popolazione e organizzazione giuridica, continua a sussistere. " *Op. cit.*, p. 76.
2. *Il Protettorato di Boemia e Moravia*, in *Rivista di Diritto Internazionale*, 1940.
3. " ...una organizzazione giuridica originaria ", *op. cit.*, p. 197.
4. " ...l'ordinamento non deve essere condizionato per la sua validità e per la sua esistenza dalla volontà di un altro ordinamento. " *Op. cit.*, p. 197.

power within its own territory : its legal order, far from being underived, draws its legal validity from the legal order of the Reich. This represents far more than a mere " modification ", and there is no analogy with a genuine international protectorate under which the protected entity preserves its international personality.

As for the maintenance in force of Czechoslovak laws, Raggi rightly points out that, far from proving the continuity of Czechoslovakia, it proves exactly the opposite. If the Protectorate were identical with Czechoslovakia, there would have been no need for an express stipulation to that effect and these laws would automatically have remained in force. Their very reception on the basis of a German decree means the end of the old State.

Venturini's argument, according to which it is not the German decree, but the Hitler-Hacha agreement which is the actual source of the Protectorate, is subjected by Raggi to a criticism which is as devastating as it is subtle : it is true — says Raggi — that that agreement could have embodied a Czechoslovak revolutionary norm which would have left Czechoslovakia's continuity unaffected, but only on condition that it left intact the underived character of the legal order of which such a norm would have formed part ; it is, however, impossible to maintain that the legal order in question has survived this revolutionary norm if, at the same time, the very same norm has deprived it of its independent, underived character. A revolutionary norm which, while forming part of the Czechoslovak legal order, yet relies on the legal order of another State which it designates as the competent source for determining future constitutional norms for Czechoslovakia, can only result in her immediate extinction [1].

Turning to the analysis of the German March decree, Raggi disproves all the conclusions which had been drawn from its text by Venturini. The decree does in fact provide for a certain degree of autonomy of the Protectorate, but this is not enough to make it a subject of international law. Thus, the expression " sovereign rights " used in Art. 3 is made meaningless by the actual content of the Articles which follow. The title of " Head of State " cannot prevail against the fact of that Head's subordination to the German Führer (Art. 4). There are no international relations between Germany and the Protectorate : the Reichsprotecktor is far more than a diplomatic agent, considering his enormously wide powers, as for instance the power to confirm the Ministers of the Protectorate, to veto its laws, to issue laws for it, and

---

1. " Una norma nuova sulla produzione giuridica, avente carattere rivoluzionario e tale da non interrompere la continuità dell'ordinamento preesistente, potrebbe infatti essere contenuta nell'accordo del 15 marzo, solamente a patto che non fosse leso il carattere originario dell'ordinamento a cui la norma appartiene. Non occorre insistere per dimostrare come sia assolutamente contradittorio l'ammettere la continuazione del precedente ordine giuridico malgrado la norma rivoluzionaria e il constatare nello stesso tempo che questa norma rivoluzionaria fa venir meno il carattere di originarietà dell' ordinamento di cui é parte. Una norma posta attraverso un procedimento rivoluzionario la quale, appartenendo all'ordinamento cecoslovacco si riferisce nello stesso tempo alla fonte dell'ordinamento di un altro Stato, designandola come fonte competente a porre nell'ordinamento ceco norme costituzionali relative al futuro assetto politico del popolo e del paese ceco, non conseque altro risultato che quello di produrre l'immediata estinzione dell'ordinamento cecoslovaco. " Op. cit., p. 207.

so forth (Art. 5). Nor is the Czech Minister to the German Government a diplomatic agent ; his title cannot make up for the lack of effective diplomatic functions. The expression " foreign affairs " used in Art. 6 is not sufficient to prove international personality.

There is thus no international protectorate which necessarily presupposes the international personality of the protected State. On the contrary, the relation is one of internal, not of international law [1]. Moreover, a protectorate must be based on an international agreement [2]. But the act of March 15, whatever else it may have been, was certainly not a convention establishing a protectorate, limiting itself to a vague mention of some undefined " protection ".

This leads Raggi to an examination of the Hitler-Hacha communiqué with a view to discovering whether it in fact constituted a bilateral agreement. He admits that there were parties to it and that they were endowed with full legal capacity since no doubts existed as to Czechoslovakia's statehood prior to March 15. The text would even indicate a common will. Yet this text is too vague to give rise to any specific mutual obligations. Moreover, there is no certainty that violence was not used. Finally, even if there was a convention, such convention could not possibly establish a protectorate and at the same time destroy the legal order of Czechoslovakia [3].

There is thus only one possible conclusion, which Raggi does not hesitate to draw : the relations between Bohemia and Moravia on the one hand and the Reich on the other, are not those of a protecting and a protected, but those of a suzerain and a vassal State. A vassal State, however, is in reality no State at all ; its organs are the organs of the suzerain because its legal order forms part of the legal order of the suzerain. All that the German decree of March 16, 1939, did, was to endow Bohemia and Moravia, which already formed part of the Greater German Reich, with a large measure of autonomy, thus giving rise to a relation of vassalage between the two entities [4].

It must be admitted that German writers are, on the whole, equally correct in denying any international personality to the Protectorate and in constructing its legal relation to the Reich as one of purely internal, and not international, law. This generally accepted German thesis suffers, however, from an insoluble contradiction : on the one hand it is obviously in the German political interest to deny the international personality of the Protectorate ; it is equally in their interest to present the extinction of Czechoslovakia as having taken place independently of any German action ; yet, on the other hand, they are anxious to provide some sort of internationally valid title for Germany's aggression

---

1. " ...vincolo di carattere interno e non internazionale ", *op. cit.*, p. 209.
2. Here Raggi disposes of Venturini's argument concerning protectorates not based on an agreement : with regard to the Free City of Cracow and the Ionian Islands, they were primarily new creations, not protectorates ; the Protectorate character of Egypt is equally doubtful, *op. cit.*, pp. 209-210.
3. " ...ci sembra assurdo e contraddittorio che con un medesimo atto si manifesti il consenso al sorgere di un eventuale futuro rapporto di protettorato e, contemporaneamente, anche il consenso alla cessazione dell'originarietà dell'ordinamento interno... " *Op. cit.*, p. 212.
4. *Op. cit.*, p. 222.

and find such title in the allegedly internationally valid Hitler-Hacha agreement. But how could an agreement be concluded with a country which allegedly had already ceased to exist?

A typical example of such pseudo-legal acrobatics is supplied by Megerle [1] who begins with the statement that Czechoslovakia had ceased to exist at midday on March 14, 1939, as a result of total dismemberment[2]. From that moment there was no longer " either internationally, or in fact, or conventionally " (?) any Czechoslovakia to which the Munich Agreement could still apply [3]. Consequently, Hacha was no longer President of Czechoslovakia, but could still speak and act for the Czech people of Bohemia and Moravia. As a result, he was able to conclude a voluntary agreement in the name of the Czech Government and nation, being invested with the necessary powers [4]. In consequence of all these miraculous proceedings, Hitler entered Prague

" with the authority of an unimpeachable international agreement and a historical justification [5]

Such a " legal " theory hardly requires any comment.

A vaguely similar — though slightly less nonsensical — explanation is supplied by Grewe [6], who sees the basis of the Protectorate in both, the Hitler-Hacha agreement and the decree of March 16, issued in execution of that agreement. The resulting relationship is for him not only international, but also internal [7] ; he thus attempts to combine the two. In the search of an internationally valid title, Hugelmann also accepts the Hitler-Hacha agreement as legal basis of the March decree [8], whereupon he nevertheless excludes any international element from the resulting relationship and insists upon the purely internal legal nature of the Protectorate. Consequently, it is in reality no international protectorate at all and, like Raggi, Hugelmann considers that the theory of a " Vassallenstaat " would be the most appropriate one. However, he does not insist upon this theory in order not to hurt the feelings of the Czechs — an attention truly touching under the circumstances.

Uninhibited by such scruples, and little caring for an " international title ", Klein gives a correct and straightforward interpretation of the Protectorate [9]. According to him, Czechoslovakia ceased to exist as a result of Slovakia's proclamation of independence and the creation of the Protectorate. The latter has nothing whatever in common with an international protectorate. It resulted in no international, but only in

---

1. *Deutschland und das Ende der Tschecho-Slowakei*, in *Monasthefte für auswärtige Politik*, 1939.
2. *Op. cit.*, p. 769.
3. *Ibid.*, p. 770.
4. *Ibid.*, p. 771.
5. *Ibid.*
6. *Protektorat und Schutzfreundschaft, ibid.*, 1939, p. 341.
7. "...nicht nur ein völkerrechtliches, sondern auch ein staatsrechtliches Verhältnis." *Op. cit.*, p. 344.
8. *Das Reichsprotektorat Böhmen und Mähren, ibid.*, p. 399.
9. *Die staats-und völkerrechtliche Stellung des Protektorats Böhmen und Mähren,* in *Archiv des öffentlichen Rechts, Neue Folge,* 31. Band, 3.Heft.

an internal relation of protection[1]. Therefore, in spite of certain characteristics of statehood, the Protectorate is not an independent State and not a subject of international law. It has no territory, and no State power of its own, neither in foreign affairs nor in military matters ; whatever autonomy it possesses, has been delegated to it by the Reich. Between the two there are no international relations : the Czech " Gesandter " is not a diplomatic agent, nor a member of the diplomatic corps, and is not accredited to the " Führer ". The Protectorate is

" an integral part of the Reich ... the legal status of which is determined exclusively by German State law [2] ".

There is therefore no need to seek analogies in the field of international law. The Protectorate is an unprecedented and unique creation of the National Socialist State philosophy [3].

An entirely different attitude was adopted by the Roman Court of Appeal in its judgment of February 27, 1941 [4]. Dismissing the claim of one of the parties that the bilateral Italo-Czechoslovak conventions had lost their validity following Czechoslovakia's extinction, the Court maintained that there could be no question of the extinction of an international personality in a case where a State had exchanged its absolute sovereignty for the restricted sovereignty of a protected State. No such change had taken place, since the State preserved its territory, its separate legal order and its nationals. The loss by the Protectorate of the active and passive right of legation did not involve the loss of its personality. To sum up : the subordination of a State to the protection of another State does not affect its international personality, and the treaties concluded by it prior to the creation of the Protectorate remain in force unless they should be incompatible with the Protectorate.

This judgment was rightly criticized by Biscontini [5]. In his view, the Court analyzed the institution of the Protectorate in abstracto, without caring to examine the terms of this particular Protectorate, which it directly ignored. This is borne out by the fact that the Court apparently did not ascertain from the relevant text to whom the territory of Bohemia-Moravia belonged. This initial error vitiated its entire reasoning. The Protectorate did not result from an international arrangement but from an annexation [6]. The Protectorate, like the

1. " ...kein völkerrechtliches, sondern nur ein staatsrechtliches Schutzverhältnis. " Op. cit., p. 260.
2. Transl. mine. " ...ein integrierender Bestandteil des Reiches... dessen Rechtsstellung ausschliesslich das deutsche Staatsrecht bestimmt. " Op. cit., p. 265.
3. " Das Protektorat Böhmen und Mähren ist eine vorbildlose, originäre, selbständige, eigengesetzliche und der völkischen Grundeinstellung des Nationalsozialismus vollauf entsprechende säkuläre Schöpfung nationalsozialistischen Staatsdenkens. " Op. cit., p. 258. The writer gives up any attempt to translate the above.
4. Basch c. Grassi, Rivista di Diritto Internazionale, 1941, pp. 376-379.
5. Sulla condizione giuridica del Protettorato di Boemia e Moravia, ibid., p. 379.
6. " Un accordo internazionale in base al quale uno Stato acquisti il potere di far riposare la disciplina dei propri rapporti con un altro Stato sopra sue norme interne, si qualifica come un trattato di annessione, e 'a norma interna che consideri come fatto di produzione di nuove norme illimitatamente le norme di un ordinamento straniero è una norma la quale legittima la estensione del potere di impero dello Stato straniero, e cioè l'estinzione dell'ordinamento giuridico cui essa appartiene. " Op. cit., pp. 381-382.

Government General in Poland, is an entirely new National-Socialist creation, a phenomenon of the new imperial organisation being built by Germany on racial principles. In conclusion Biscontini denies the international personality of the Protectorate and consequently, its capacity to continue the international personality of Czechoslovakia.

Obviously, Germany could not have approved of an interpretation of the legal position of the Protectorate such as was supplied by the Court of Appeal of Rome. This would explain the exchange of notes between Germany and Italy of May 22, 1941, according to which

" the provisions of the Convention between the Kingdom of Italy and the Reich (of February 19, 1937) shall exclusively apply in the territories of the Protectorate of Bohemia and Moravia, instead of the Convention concerning the Execution of Judgments in Civil and Commercial Matters which had been concluded on April 6, 1922, between the Kingdom of Italy and the extinct Czechoslovak Republic [1] ".

Thus, whatever the speculation of writers or even judges, Germany imposed on her ally her own official legal version [2].

Finally, it is of interest to examine the views of a Czechoslovak writer. In his work on Czechoslovakia, Taborsky rejects the protectorate theory and considers the situation as one of pure annexation [3]. It is to be regretted that, in order to arrive at this conclusion, he gets involved in arguments which are both weak and inconsistent. According to him, an international protectorate must be based on an international agreement. Whereupon he goes to all lengths to prove the invalidity of the Hitler-Hacha agreement, without first dealing with the preliminary question whether there was an agreement at all. Obviously, he considers that an agreement did take place, for he enumerates alleged reasons for its invalidity, such as 1) the lack of competence on the part of Hacha, 2) coercion, 3) the fact of the agreement being *contra bonos mores*, 4) incompatibility with former obligations, including the Munich Agreement, and 5) violation of the fundamental rights of States [4]. However, the lack of competence under Czechoslovak municipal law is far from being generally admitted as a vitiating factor in international law ; the arguments bearing on *bonos mores* or the fundamental rights of States belong to the arsenal of the least defensible theories of natural law ; the question of incompatibility with former treaty obligations could be a more convincing objection, however, it does not behove Taborsky, who questions the validity of the Munich Agreement *ab initio*, to make use of the very same agreement for the specific purpose of presenting it as a superior prohibitive norm with regard to the Berlin agreement. His only strong argument is thus that of coercion, which there undoubtedly was.

The Berlin agreement being invalid, Taborsky continues, all the consequent acts, including the decree of March 16, are similarly invalid. A Protectorate must be based on a treaty and here, there was no treaty. Thus, all said and done, it was only based on the German decree.

1. *Transl. mine, ibid.*, p. 240.
2. See below, p. 300.
3. *The Czechoslovak Cause*, pp. 40-41.
4. *Ibid.*, pp. 35-39.

It is impossible to accept Taborsky's reasoning. Either the March decree was invalid because it was based on an agreement which was itself invalid ; or, there was *no* agreement at all, — and not an *invalid* agreement, and the March decree was the only source of the Protectorate ; but then the reason of its invalidity cannot be sought in the invalidity of an agreement on which it was not based.

The above summary contains indeed a rich variety of opinions. Yet, it is submitted that there is only one correct view of the legal nature of the Protectorate and its relation to the Czechoslovak Republic. Although the possibility of a Bohemia and Moravia continuing without Slovakia the legal personality of Czechoslovakia has already been excluded [1], it is still necessary to consider the legal nature of the Protectorate as such. Such an enquiry must necessarily begin with the problem of its legal basis which could have been either a bilateral international agreement or a unilateral norm of the German State. It is submitted that Taborsky would have found his task much easier if, instead of attempting to deny the validity of the Berlin agreement by somewhat doubtful arguments, he would have adopted the method of Judge Anzilotti in his Dissenting Opinion in the *Eastern Greenland* case:

" Did the two Governments agree upon anything ? and upon what ?
If so, was the agreement valid ? [2] "

for obviously, the validity of an agreement can be discussed at all if such an agreement was in fact entered into.

Theoretically, there could indeed have been an agreement, even a verbal one, between two State organs competent to exercise treaty-making power [3]. Yet, even the most informal agreement requires genuine mutual consent bearing on a defined object. On the basis of the text of the Berlin communiqué, however, it is difficult to affirm that the two Heads of States agreed upon anything at all ; but it is sheer impossibility to say — on what. In law " placing the destinies of the Czech people and country in the hands of the Führer " and " accepting this declaration ", as well as " expressing the determination of taking the Czech people under the protection of the German Reich " — means precisely nothing. It is impossible to interpret such language, which may mean everything and nothing. On the basis of the text alone and without any knowledge of subsequent events, it cannot possibly be guessed, whether the " agreement " related to an alliance, a treaty of protection of the Slovak model, an entry into some federated State or a straigth incorporation. It is submitted that an agreement with no defined object is no agreement at all [4]. This disposes of Anzilotti's second question.

---

1. See above, p. 292.
2. *It. mine*, P.C.I.J., ser. A/B, no. 53, p. 88.
3. *Ibid.*, p. 91.
4. Cf. Verdross : " Ein gültiger Vertrag ist daher gar nicht zustande gekommen, wenn entweder überhaupt keine Willenseinigung über den Vertragsinhalt vorliegt, oder wenn der vereinbarte Inhalt zu unbestimmt ist, um daraus erkennen zu können, was die Vertragsteile gewollt haben. " *Völkerrecht*, p. 132.

It is therefore believed that the very text of the Berlin communiqué excludes the possibility of an international convention. Consequently, no effort is necessary to prove the invalidity of something which never existed. Nor is it necessary to consider what effect an agreement would have had on the legal nature of the Protectorate.

Nor do official German sources (as opposed to some of the writers mentioned above) contain the slightest suggestion that the Berlin communiqué was an international agreement providing the legal basis for subsequent German acts. On the contrary, German action with regard to the Protectorate bore an openly and unequivocally unilateral character. It should be recalled in this connection that the actual military occupation of Czech territory began not after, but before the Hitler-Hacha meeting, on March 14. It was on that date, preceding the Berlin communiqué by more than 24 hours that Moravska Ostrava, Mistek and Vitkovice were occupied by German troops [1].

On March 15, i.e. on the day of the signature of the Berlin communiqué, Hitler issued a proclamation to the German people of which the following passages are worth quoting :

" ... As a reaction against these renewed attacks on their freedom, national groups have separated from Prague. *Thereby Czecho-Slovakia ceased to exist.* ... In order definitely to eliminate this menace to peace and order, and to create the prerequisites for the necessary new regulations in this area, I have decided, as from to-day, to allow German troops to march into Bohemia and Moravia [2]. "

Not a word about an agreement of any sort ; the document represents a unilateral German act. It may also be observed that it includes the first official and authoritative German version of the situation, according to which Czechoslovakia ceased to exist as a result of internal disintegration. German troops were thus marching not into a State territory, but into a legal vacuum, a *terra nullius*, capable of being appropriated. Since the extinction of Czechoslovakia, according to the German version, preceded the German invasion, it is difficult to see with whom a treaty of protectorate or, for that matter, any other treaty could be concluded. The same view is expressed in Hitler's order to the German Wehrmacht [3].

Thus, the German creation of the Protectorate was not based on any agreement, whether valid or invalid. Its sole legal source was the German decree of March 16, 1939, which did not even pretend to invoke an international basis for its validity. It was a purely internal norm of the German legal order. There was neither a corresponding Czechoslovak norm, nor an international norm arrived at by agreement.

The conclusions of Raggi and Biscontini are therefore fully justified.

---

1. " It is to be observed — and the fact is surely not without significance — that the towns of Mährisch-Ostrau and Vitkovice were actually occupied by German S.S. detachments on the evening of the 14th March, while the President and the Foreign Minister of Czecho-Slovakia were still on their way to Berlin and before any discussion had taken place. " Lord Halifax in the British House of Lords, on March 20, 1939, *Documents*, p. 10. See also Ripka, *op. cit.*, p. 378.

2. *It.mine*, German original in *Monatshefte für auswärtige Politik*, 1939, pp. 357-358. English translation in Ripka, *op. cit.*, pp. 379-380.

3. "Die Tschecho-Slowakei befindet sich in Auflösung", *Monatshefte*, 1939, p. 358.

The basic norm of the Protectorate, far from being situated within the legal order of the Czechoslovak Republic, was entirely foreign to it. Whatever legal order was introduced, or maintained, in the Protectorate, came to rest upon an internal norm of a foreign State. The source of the new legal entity was rooted in the legal order of another State, being the outcome of that State's independent and decisive will and the concretisation, on a lower level, of the basic norm of that other State. Legally the Protectorate had nothing in common with Czechoslovakia ; it was a dependent entity created by a foreign Power in a part of Czechoslovak territory and with regard to a part of the Czechoslovak population. As such, it could not have been identical with Czechoslovakia and could not continue the latter's international personality.

In these circumstances it is incomprehensible why the Nurnberg Tribunal, sitting eight years later and having all the evidence available at its disposal, should have upheld a conception roughly similar to that of the Roman Court of Appeal of 1941 [1].

" Bohemia and Moravia were occupied by military forces. Hacha's consent, obtained as it was by duress, cannot be considered as justifying the occupation. Hitler's decree of 16th March, 1939, establishing the Protectorate, stated that this new territory should " belong henceforth to the territory of the German Reich ", an assumption that the Republic of Czechoslovakia no longer existed. But it also went on the theory that Bohemia and Moravia retained their sovereignty subject only to the interests of Germany as expressed by the Protectorate. Therefore even if the doctrine of subjugation should be considered to be applicable to territory occupied by aggressive action, the Tribunal does not believe that this Proclamation amounted to an incorporation which was sufficient to bring the doctrine into effect. The occupation of Bohemia and Moravia must therefore be considered a military occupation covered by the rules of warfare. Although Czechoslovakia was not a party to the Hague Convention of 1907, the rules of land warfare expressed in this Convention are declaratory of existing international law and hence are applicable [2]. "

It is hardly necessary to repeat all the arguments against the Rome judgment as well as any other theory that the Protectorate had an international personality. Yet, the interpretation of the Nurnberg Tribunal calls for a few further observations.

In the first place, it may well be asked, whether and how it is possible to draw conclusions of such magnitude, bearing on the continuity or extinction of a State, from an interpretation of a Hitlerite decree. To shift the *punctum saliens* of the problem from an objective legal assessment of facts to the interpretation of the invader's decree is to endow the invader with a law-making power which apparently prevails against objective law, to regard him, and not objective law, as the decisive factor in the case, and to make the solution depend upon his will. What would the position have been if the German decree had been formulated even more explicitly so as to exclude any possibility of the Tribunal's second interpretation ? Would such a text still be law for the Tribunal and would the Tribunal have felt compelled to pronounce Czechoslovakia's extinction in 1939 on the basis of a German decree ?

---

1. See above, p. 297.
2. *Judgment*, p. 125.

Moreover, even the admissibility of the Tribunal's second interpretation must be called into doubt. For when the Tribunal asserts that the proclamation was not sufficient to effect the incorporation of the Protectorate, then it may indeed be wondered what more can be required for such an incorporation. It must further be asked how it was possible for " Bohemia and Moravia " to " retain " a sovereignty it had never possessed, considering that there had not been in existence any such subject of international law [1].

Finally, it is not al all clear whether the Tribunal merely assimilates German-occupied Czechoslovakia to a territory under belligerent occupation *sensu stricto*, — or whether it considers that it actually was belligerent occupation. Whatever the implications of the first possibility [2], the second must be emphatically rejected. The situation in German-occupied Czechoslovakia was not belligerent occupation ; it did not result from a war and it did not therefore automatically fall under the regime of the Hague regulations [3].

If the above reasoning was adopted by the Tribunal in order to re-affirm Czechoslovakia's unbroken continuity, then it is submitted that such continuity could certainly not be based on possible gaps in the German decree, nor on the non-existent sovereignty of a " Bohemia and Moravia " ; nor could the Protectorate, being what it was, be in any way instrumental in carrying on and safeguarding that continuity.

The whole foregoing analysis has, it is believed, supplied the negative answer with regard to the legal status of the Protectorate, by clearly disclosing what it was not. It was not a State, being conditioned by internal norms of a foreign State, it did not possess territory, its supreme organs were delegated by that foreign State, and even its population was determined by that same State, although in a negative way, by the removal of certain categories of persons from its personal sphere of validity. The Protectorate had neither a foreign nor an internal policy of its own and was generally entirely subordinated to the German Reich. It may be added that, even the " autonomy " of the Protectorate, provided for by the March decree, could at any time be brought to an end by an arbitrary and final decision of the German Führer (Art. 1 (2)). The expression " sovereign rights " used in the decree is thus a typical example of legal fiction and it would offend against common sense to attach the slightest meaning to it, in face of overwhelming proof to the contrary. Exactly the same observation applies to the fact that certain decisions of the Reich did not assume

---

1. It may also be pointed out that the sentence concerning subjugation is far from being clear. It may be legitimately doubted whether the doctrine of subjugation still finds a place in international law after the Covenant of the League of Nations, the Kellogg-Pact, etc.: but the doubt expressed in the words "even if the doctrine of subjugation should be considered to be applicable to territory occupied by aggressive ac.ion " is simply incomprehensible : to what else could that doctrine be applied ? — Unless, of course, the Tribunal distinguished between Hitler's kind of occupation and " proper war ", which latter would then be " non-aggressive ", — an interpretation which the writer hardly dares ascribe to the Tribunal.

2. See below, pp. 584-586.

3. Similarly Prof. Guggenheim who suggests that the illegal occupation of Cze-choslovak territory bears an *analogy* with belligerent occupation, — thereby clearly implying that it was not in fact such an occupation. *Validité*, pp. 243-244.

the form of internal German norms but of bilateral agreements between Germany and the Protectorate [1]. These agreements were entirely fictitious since they were concluded by a State with an entity which, far from being a subject of international law, actually formed part of that same State, and since they merely incorporated what were glaringly unilateral decisions [2].

It is, however, not without interest to see what the Protectorate actually was on the positive side. For, while denying its State character, it is nevertheless impossible to speak of a straightforward annexation in the traditional sense of the term. Such an annexation would have required a wholesale incorporation of the annexed State or area into the legal system of the annexing State. While a certain degree of autonomy could be preserved for the annexed area, at least for a time [3], on the whole, the entirety of the laws of the annexing State would become valid in the newly acquired territory. Above all, its inhabitants would necessarily and automatically become nationals of the annexing State. This is exactly what did not happen in the case of the Protectorate. Proceeding on the racial principle, Germany would not grant German citizenship to alien races, who were moreover considered as inferior races. This explains why the non-German territorial acquisitions of the Third Reich assumed such unorthodox forms, as the Protectorate of Bohemia and Moravia and the Government General of Poland. Biscontini's observation quoted above is fully justified [4] : being engaged in building what may be termed a colonial Empire in Europe, Germany was in the process of elaborating entirely new legal forms to suit the purpose ; it would be vain to attempt to force these forms into the classical pattern of international law with which they had indeed nothing in common.

c) *Conclusion.*

It must therefore be concluded that neither of the entities set up on Czechoslovak territory possessed international personality. Slovakia was a puppet State of the German Reich. The Protectorate, without being " classically " annexed, was a province of that Reich, endowed with a colonial status. Neither of them could have been, and neither of them was, identical with the Czechoslovak Republic.

4. THE PROBLEM OF CZECHOSLOVAKIA'S EXTINCTION.

It has been seen that the writers who ascribe international personality to the Protectorate at the same time defend the thesis of

---

1. Accord concernant le domaine et la dette publique de l'ancienne République tchécoslovaque, signed in Berlin, on 4.10.1941 ; Martens, *N.R.G.* 3rd series, XXXIX, p. 646 ; Accord relatif à l'Arrangement concernant le règlement des dettes contractées en couronnes austro-hongroises, conclu le 18 juin 1924 entre l'Autriche et la Tchécoslovaquie ; signed in Prague on 23.12.1940 and in Berlin on 7.3.1941 ; *ibid.* XLI, p. 17 ; Convention concernant les assurances sociales, signed in Prague on 14.3.1940, *ibid.* p. 144.
2. See Commissioner Kane on fictitious treaties, above, p. 172 and Art. 31 of the Italian Peace Treaty, below, pp. 336-337.
3. Cf. the position of Alsace-Lorraine in the German Reich after 1871.
4. See above, pp. 297-298.

Czechoslovakia's survival and her continuity in the form of the Protectorate, — whereas those who deny the international personality of the Protectorate insist on Czechoslovakia's extinction [1]. Is there a necessary and automatic connection between these two views? Must it be admitted with Raggi, Klein and Biscontini that, if the Protectorate did not in fact continue Czechoslovakia's legal personality, that continuity was broken?

Before examining the question, it is necessary briefly to dispose of the German claim according to which such extinction had taken place *before* the German invasion [2]. Such claim was made, let it be repeated, in plain contradiction to another German claim, according to which there was an international — Hitler-Hacha — agreement at the basis of the German action. For it is clear that if Czechoslovakia ceased to exist before Hacha was summoned to Berlin, then Hacha was no longer the Head of a State and could not therefore conclude any international agreement.

Moreover, if the Czechoslovak Republic had indeed ceased to exist, this could only have happened as a result of German aggression, never before. Hitler's proclamation of her extinction, which was patently untrue, was therefore intended as a means of regaining all freedom of movement with regard to an " ex-State " to whom no international obligations (not even the Munich Agreement) could any longer apply, — and, at the same time, of impressing on the international community the fact that Germany had not actually destroyed the legal existence of Czechoslovakia, but had only protectively stepped in where such destruction had already taken place. The possibility of the aggressor freeing himself from all international obligations towards his victim by the simple means of declaring it extinct prior to the actual aggression, cannot for a moment be admitted ; although, as has been seen, it would be the logical consequence of the constitutive theory of recognition [3].

In spite of all such German claims, the reverse could alone have been true, i.e. Czechoslovakia could have ceased to exist only as a result of a premeditated destructive action on the part of Germany. Her extinction could only have been the result, never the cause, of such action. The question when correctly formulated therefore reads : did Czechoslovakia become extinct as a result of the German aggression, — especially in view of the admitted fact that neither Slovakia nor the Protectorate continued her international personality?

A *prima facie* examination would yield an affirmative answer. There was a loss of everything that went to make the Czechoslovak State. Its territory was totally dismembered in favour of Hungary, Slovakia and Germany. Its population became legally related to these three entities. No Czechoslovak legal order and no State organs, except a few legations, were left. No Government was immediately created

---

1. See above, pp. 292 et seq.
2. See Hitler's proclamations above, p. 300.
3. See above, pp. 148-149.

in exile to take up the broken thread of Czechoslovakia's continuity. The dismemberment became internationally recognized in one way or another. Moreover, whatever the contrary thesis of the Nurnberg Tribunal [1], all these events took place in what must technically be qualified as peace-time, thus rendering inapplicable the regime ɾof belligerent occupation which would have preserved Czechoslovakia's continuity.

And yet, a year later, a Czechoslovak Government in exile made its appearance alongside those governments which had been driven out of their countries in consequence of their belligerent occupation. Did this new Czechoslovak Government mark the inception of a new State, similar in this respect to the National Committees of the First World War and relying to the same extent on a more or less arbitrary political interest of one of the warring parties? Or, far from being merely the expression and the result of a political contingency, did it represent the legal continuity of the Czechoslovak Republic as it had existed prior to March 15, 1939?

So far the method adopted in this study has consisted in examining each case in the light of the existing norms of general international law on the subject. The evidence of conventional law, international recognition, the attitude of States, has been investigated only at a later stage, and its conclusiveness has been tested by its conformity or otherwise with general international law.

However, in the cases examined so far, general international law was clear and explicit on the subject, and the conclusion could be relatively easily established by the proper ascertainment of facts and the correct application of norms.

The position is different with regard to Czechoslovakia. None of the three rules protecting the continuity of States applies to her : neither the rule concerning territorial changes (which indeed does protect her continuity against Munich, but not beyond), nor the rule concerning revolutionary changes, nor that concerning belligerent occupation. From this the conclusion could be drawn that, failing any such protective rule, Czechoslovakia indeed ceased to exist in consequence of German action. Such a view, however, would assume a petrification of international law which is not to be lightly admitted and which is hardly compatible with the inherently dynamic nature of any legal order.

Thus, in order to find a definite answer as to the extinction or continuity of the Czechoslovak State, it seems indicated to reverse the method which has been employed so far. The evidence available must therefore be examined in the first place ; but the results of such examination will yet have to be tested for their conclusiveness by their conformity with general international law.

---

1. See above, p. 301.

5. The Czechoslovak Thesis.

Following the events of March 15, 1939, Czechoslovak circles abroad very naturally proclaimed the continued legal existence of their occupied country. Such a thesis was courageously adopted and upheld in face of truly overwhelming odds.

The first difficulty consisted in the fact that, apart from the few surviving Czechoslovak Legations, former high-ranking State officials and politicians found themselves abroad in their purely personal capacity. This applies in the first place to Dr. Benes who, following his resignation of October 5, 1938, became a private citizen. Thus, all acts undertaken by Czechoslovaks abroad were, in the initial stages, of no relevance under international law (and, for that matter, even under Czechoslovak law).

The second difficulty resulted from the fact that the Czechoslovak statesmen abroad set themselves a double aim : to preserve the legal continuity of the Republic and to recover the Sudeten territories. However understandable such a link may have been politically, from a legal point of view it tried to put two entirely different things under one and the same heading [1]. In the first place, the loss of the Sudeten territories was the result of a valid international agreement to which Czechoslovakia herself had given her consent, while the dismemberment of March 15, was a unilateral, illegal act on the part of Germany, which had met with a protest from third States ; secondly, the struggle for Czechoslovakia's continuity concerned the period after March 15 and could not possibly have covered any other period. The conception of the legal continuity of the " pre-Munich Republic ", put forward in official Czechoslovak publications [2] was legal nonsense [3]. The continuity of the " pre-Munich Republic " was exactly the same as the continuity of the " pre-March Republic ", since there had been no change in the identity and continuity of the State before and after Munich, and prior to March 1939. The cession of the Sudetenland had nothing whatever to do with the problem of State continuity, and the identification of the two could only confuse the issue. The acknowledgment of the legal continuity of Czechoslovakia could be achieved without an annulment of the Munich Agreement. Yet, a link did in fact exist between the two problems since, conversely, the annulment of the Munich Agreement could not take place without automatically implying the recognition of Czechoslovakia's continuity [4]. By connecting the two problems, the Czechoslovaks in exile set themselves an aim which was as ambitious as it was dangerous : for they risked losing the fight for the Republic's continuity if they lost the fight for the Sudetenland. As will be seen when examining the British attitude in particular, this Czechoslovak

1. See above, p. 286-287.
2. *Four Fighting Years*, p. 173.
3. The confusion of the two issues is general among Czechoslovak writers, e. g. Kucera, *La continuité de l'Etat tchécoslovaque*, in the *Bulletin de Droit tchécoslovaque*, Année 5, no. 3-4, p. 54 : « La lutte à propos de la continuité de la République tchécoslovaque visait à faire supprimer même au point de vue de la forme le " diktat " de Munich ».
4. See below, pp. 322-323.

stand made recognition of the Republic's continuity less easily acceptable to Britain, traditionally averse to committing herself beforehand to frontier decisions [1]. A separation of the frontier issue and the continuity problem might perhaps have made such recognition easier. But, acting apparently on the principle of "all or nothing" the Czechoslovak statesmen in exile took the inevitable risk, even if an attempt to cover the two distinct problems by one formula must have resulted in artificial conceptions. There seem to have been three main arguments on which the Czechoslovak thesis was based.

a) *Illegality of German Aggression.*

Notwithstanding his purely personal capacity, Dr. Benes, immediately after the events of March 15, registered a protest with President Roosevelt, Prime Minister Chamberlain, Premier Daladier and Commissar Litvinov, as well as with the Secretary-General of the League of Nations [2]. On March 19, in an appeal to the American people, Dr. Benes said :

"I declare that the independence of Czechoslovakia was not crushed ; it continues, it lives, it exists [3]."

While this was mainly an emotional statement, his speech of June 8, 1939, already contained a legal argument :

"We do not recognize and we shall not recognize any legal or political fait accompli. We do not recognize any occupation of Czechoslovakia and our State continues to exist in the eyes of the law. ... The violent occupation of Czechoslovakia on March 15, 1939 is not recognized to-day by any country except the closest allies of Germany. A series of obligations which had bound our country to other nations or which other States had toward Czechoslovakia continue to function legally. Czechoslovakia is still a member of the League of Nations. All this forms an important legal basis for our struggle for freedom from temporary foreign occupation. Our rights are not forfeited. ... Furthermore, all that happened before and after March 15 during the negotiations between Prague and Berlin and which had been used by the Nazi regime to explain the establishment of the Protectorate of the Czech and Slovak lands, has no foundation in law. All that was enforced by fraud and violence. According to our laws all this is unconstitutional, illegal and enforced upon us by barbaric threats. The rights of our independent nation and State can in no form be affected by these illegal acts [4]."

A lengthy communiqué, which appeared in the Paris *Temps* of November 19, 1939, in connection with the formation of the Czechoslovak National Committee, stated *inter alia :*

« ... le prétendu protectorat établi sur la Bohême et la Moravie et la création de la Slovaquie, comme Etat fictivement indépendant, n'est rien d'autre qu'une occupation illégale et arbitraire de la Tchécoslovaquie par les armées allemandes. De ce fait résultent des conséquences politiques très étendues. Du point de vue international, la Tchécoslovaquie continue d'exister. L'occupation militaire de la Tchécoslovaquie oppose un obstacle matériel pour l'Etat tchécoslovaque à l'exercice de ses droits de souveraineté sur son territoire ; mais ces droits de souveraineté existent toujours. Par l'occupation allemande, ils ont été violés, mais non anéantis."

---

1. See below, p. 314.
2. *Cz. S. and Doc.* 2, pp. 15-17.
3. *Ibid.*, p. 31.
4. *Ibid.*, pp. 40-41.

On December 20, 1939, the newly formed Czechoslovak National Committee in Paris issued its first Manifesto which included the following passage :

" These acts (of March 15) are devoid of all legal validity and will never be recognized by any free citizen of our Republic. Neither have they nor can they have international validity [1]. "

It would thus appear that, in defending the legal continuity of Czechoslovakia, Czechoslovak statesmen abroad took their stand on the principle *ex iniuria ius non oritur*, on the inability of illegal acts validly to change an existing legal situation. Accordingly, Czechoslovakia survived, because the illegal acts committed against her could not have brought about her extinction.

b) *Belligerent Occupation.*

On December 16, 1941, Dr. Benes — who in the meantime had again assumed the Presidency in exile — issued the following declaration of war :

" In accordance with Art. 3 par. 1 of section 64 of the Constitutional Charter I hereby proclaim that the Czechoslovak Republic is in a state of war with all countries which are in a state of war with Great Britain and the United States of America and that the state of war between the Czechoslovak Republic on one side and Germany and Hungary on the other, has been in existence since the moment when the Governments of these countries committed acts of violence against the security, independence and territorial integrity of the Republic [2]. "

Such a retroactive declaration of war is surely unique in the history of international relations. What makes it even more unusual is the mysterious vagueness of the date to which it was supposed to relate. Which were the actual " acts of violence " from which Dr. Benes dated the existence of a state of war between Germany, and Hungary, and Czechoslovakia ?
Whereas the now recognized President refrained from specifying a date, the answer to this question is to be found in a much earlier statement by Dr. Benes, of February 1, 1940, i.e. before his assumption of the Presidency in exile :

" Czechoslovakia has been at war with Germany since the summer of 1938. ... since March 1939, the Czechoslovak lands are a militarily occupied territory [3]... "

This is sheer fantasy. Neither in the summer of 1938, nor during the Munich period, nor in March 1939, was there a state of war between Czechoslovakia and Germany either in law or in fact. The legitimate governments of the time — under Benes and Hacha respectively — never declared war on Germany. Nor was there any actual fighting.
The declaration is such a challenge both to international law and ordinary common sense that it can only be explained by the determination

---

1. *Ibid.*, p. 47.
2. *Ibid.*, p. 84.
3. *Ibid.*, p. 88.

of the Czechoslovaks not only to reinforce the argument *ex iniuria* by that of belligerent occupation with regard to the problem of continuity, — but equally to include the Sudetenland within Czechoslovak territory under alleged belligerent occupation. It is submitted that neither object stood to gain by such an artificial theory. In particular, a Czechoslovak-German war at that period would have clearly resulted in a debellatio, there being no Czechoslovak resistance on the model of the Ethiopian guerillas, nor a continuing coalition war on behalf of Czechoslovakia.

While questioning the retroactive effect of Dr. Benes's declaration of war, it may readily be admitted that a state of war has indeed come to prevail between Germany and Czechoslovakia. It could be dated either from that declaration or from the moment the first Czechoslovak units went into action against the Germans (which — to the writer's knowledge — occurred only after Dr. Benes's declaration). The question is whether such a state of war between the two countries could retroactively invest the German domination of Czechoslovakia with the character of a regular belligerent occupation?

It is submitted that no such retroactive effect could be achieved. If the beginning of a state of war between Czechoslovakia and Germany could have any effect at all on German-occupied Czechoslovak territory (with the obvious exclusion of the previously ceded Sudetenland), then it could transform it into belligerent occupation only *ex nunc* and, moreover, only with regard to Czechoslovakia herself and other States adopting a similar attitude. The qualification of German domination of Czechoslovakia as belligerent occupation could therefore only have a meaning limited both in time and in legal effect. It could not have turned it into belligerent occupation *ab initio* and could thus not be instrumental in upholding the continuity of Czechoslovakia without the Sudetenland, — much less in asserting unbroken Czechoslovak sovereignty over the Sudetenland [1].

Thus, if Czechoslovakia had indeed survived the period of German domination, it was certainly not on the principle of belligerent occupation.

c) *Illegality under Czechoslovak Constitutional Law.*

The third Czechoslovak argument, again supposed to be equally valid for the problem of State continuity and for the recovery of the Sudetenland, seems hardly more fortunate. It contests the validity of both the Munich agreement and the March events on the basis of their incompatibility with Czechoslovak constitutional law [2].

---

1. By analogy the writer has adopted the reasoning of Prof. Guggenheim, who gives the same answer to a different question : namely, whether the voidance by the Allies of the Munich Agreement could have had a retroactive effect, and — if so — whether such effect was binding on anybody except the repudiating Powers. Prof. Guggenheim in the first place expresses doubts as to the possible retroactivity of such repudiation and, secondly, affirms that, as long as it could not be effectively implemented in the territory concerned, it had no general validity beyond the circle of the repudiating Powers. *Validité*, pp. 242-243.

2. Taborsky, *op. cit.*, pp. 9-14 and 35 : Kucera, *op. cit.*, p. 49 ; the *Temps* communiqué quoted above.

As far as the claim is made by Czechoslovakia, it is not even necessary to enter into the well-known controversy bearing on the constitutionality of proceedings being, or not being, a condition of validity of international agreements. For precisely in the Czechoslovak case the argument cannot be taken seriously.

With regard, in the first place, to the Munich Agreement, the argument of unconstitutionality, coming either from President Benes or from his supporters, sounds particularly unconvincing. For it was Benes himself and his government who accepted the Munich Agreement in an unconstitutional manner. If the argument was meant to be taken seriously at all, it ought inevitably to have been raised by somebody else, totally unconnected with the Benes regime, and at the same time Benes and his then government should have been arrayed before the Czechoslovak Senate for high treason and violation of the Constitution [1]. But it was inadmissible for Benes to make the claim and at the same time to remain President of the Czechoslovak Republic, just as it was inadmissible for his supporters to make the claim and to uphold his Presidency [2].

The argument is not much stronger with regard to the Hitler-Hacha " agreement ". It is true that under the 1920 Czechoslovak Constitution the President of the Republic had no right to alienate the State's independence, which would have required amending the Constitution which the President had no right to override. However, those who made that claim (quite unnecessarily, since — as has been seen — there was no agreement, and it is not in this non-existing agreement that the illegality of German action against Czechoslovakia need be sought) forget that

" the Czecho-Slovak Parliament, in December 1938, passed a new and very sweeping Enabling Act, valid for a period of two years, which granted the President of the Republic the right to change even the Constitution and constitutional laws by his personal decree [3] ".

The validity of that Act was as little challenged by Czechoslovaks themselves at the time, as the validity and legality of what took place during the so-called " Munich Intermezzo ", i.e. from Munich till March 15, 1939 [4].

Such seem to have been the arguments on which the Czechoslovak thesis of the Republic's continuity was based. Of these arguments,

---

1. See Art. 34, 67 and 79 of the Czechoslovak 1920 Constitution.
2. See e. g. Kucera, *op. cit.*
3. Ripka, *op. cit.*, p. 247.
4. Generally, the non-recognition by Czechoslovaks of the " Munich-Intermezzo " was alleged only *ex post*, and is no less fantastic than the theory of a German-Czechoslovak war dating back to the summer of 1938. In fact, its legality was at the time fully admitted by the Czechoslovaks. Dr. Benes himself was in the forefront, with his regular resignation and the letter of congratulations which he sent to Dr. Hacha on the latter's election to the Presidency. The argument that " informed Czech politicians ", including Dr. Benes himself, continued to consider Benes as their President in spite of his resignation, is hardly meant to be taken seriously. *Four Fighting Years*, p. 177. The same applies to the recurring thesis, acccrding to which Benes's resignation was an « abdication forcée » which still left him as the constitutional President. Kucera, *op. cit.*, p.53. There was no physical violence exerted upon Benes and certainly no one forced him to send his good wishes to Hacha from abroad.

those concerinng the unconstitutionality and belligerent occupation, bear all the traces of an artificial *ad hoc* theory. The first argument — *ex iniuria ius non oritur* — was certainly in conformity with the nature of international law as a normative system. It was raised by the Czechoslovaks against the effectiveness of German illegal domination of their country, — that is, against the antinomic principle of *ex factis ius oritur*.

6. CZECHOSLOVAKIA'S CONTINUITY AND STATE PRACTICE.

The Czechoslovak thesis of the Republic's unbroken continuity was not only a legal theory ; it was a political fighting programme. It had to be asserted in face of the greatest obstacles and opposition from friend and foe. The final aim was to be achieved by stages involving gradual changes in Czechoslovakia's international position. It is these developments which must now be investigated in some detail.

A) *The Period of Hostilities.*

a) *Initial Non-Recognition of Czechoslovakia's Continuity and the Resulting Status of the Czechoslovak Government in Exile.*

Between the German aggression of March 1939 and the outbreak of the Second World War there was no trace of any Czechoslovak State activity abroad, — with the sole exception of the survival of Czechoslovak Legations in some States. It was only the outbreak of the War which marked the beginning of a slow Czechoslovak return to international life. The formation of a Czechoslovak Legion in Poland, following German aggression against that country, may be considered the first, although inevitably short-lived, episode in this process [1].

The beginning of a legal revival took place in a way which is the more interesting for being completely unorthodox. On October 2, 1939, an unusual agreement was signed in Paris between the French Prime Minister and the Czechoslovak Minister to France. The agreement related to the constitution on French soil of an autonomous Czechoslovak Army. The competence of the French Prime Minister to sign an international convention is obviously not subject to doubt. More peculiar is the legal situation of the other contracting party, represented by a diplomatic agent who was not only not empowered by anybody to sign, but actually signed the agreement on behalf " of the Provisional Government of the Czechoslovak Republic ", that is, a body which simply did not exist [2]. It might therefore be wondered what it was that took place in Paris on October 2, 1939, between the French Prime Minister and M. Osusky. It is true that in the course of the First World War the Allied Governments concluded a number of agreements with the National Committees, i.e. bodies having no standing under traditional

---

1. *Four Fighting Years*, p. 175.
2. Taborsky, *op. cit.*, p. 68 ; *Cz. S. and Doc.*, 2, p. 64. It need hardly be pointed out that it was not the " Government " of the Protectorate which was meant.

international law, But here the case was far more astounding, since the convention was concluded on behalf of an actually non-existing authority.

This extraordinary situation was to be remedied only *ex post* and even then incompletely. Early in November 1939 a Czechoslovak National Committee was formed in Paris. On November 13, M. Osusky notified the French Government of this event, declaring that the Committee would be " qualified to represent the Czechoslovak peoples " and particularly " to execute the Agreement of 2nd October regarding the re-constitution of the Czechoslovak Army " [1]. Thus, a newly formed National Committee stepped in where a non-existing Provisional Government was supposed to operate.

Equally interesting is the legal standing of the Committee itself. It is certain that — with the possible exception of M. Osusky, the Minister in Paris — it was composed exclusively of private citizens. It had no legal basis whatever. From the point of view of both Czechoslovak constitutional law and international law, it was just a private body. Probably by reason of this fact, it came forward with very limited claims. It did not claim to be a State organ, nor to represent the State. It claimed to represent the " peoples " of Czechoslovakia, an expression which has no legal meaning. There is no means of knowing whether it refers to Czechs and Slovaks, or whether it covers all the minorities including the Sudeten Germans ; moreover, the " peoples " are not a subject of international law and can therefore hardly be legally represented.

The Czechoslovak National Committee thus had a standing which was no more solid than that of the National Committees of the First World War [2]. Its peculiar status was also reflected in the legal situation of the Czechoslovak Army in France which — unlike other Allied armies on foreign soil — was subjected to French jurisdiction and to the French military code [3].

But, whereas the National Committees of the First World War had no States whatever with which to link their own existence, the Czechoslovaks of 1939 had — at least according to their own conviction — a State of their own on which to base their legal existence. The fact that nevertheless the form of a mere National Committee was adopted, was explained from the Czechoslovak side by " Munich tendencies " still prevailing in Allied political circles and causing the French and British recognition to be " severely restricted " [4]. Thus, in spite of the actual outbreak of war against Germany, not only did the Allies not immediately repudiate the Munich Agreement, but did not even revert

---

1. *Ibid.*, p. 43.
2. Flory, *op. cit.*, p. 40.
3. " ...le titre de tribunal militaire tchèque était inexact. N'étaient tchèques dans cette organisation que la langue utilisée, les juges (et encore avec des pouvoirs limités puisqu'ils avaient des conseillers français et relevaient en appel, pour les conflits de juridiction et pour la grâce, de tribunaux français) et le délinquant. L'essentiel, c'est-à-dire la loi appliquée, était la loi française ; aucun doute n'était possible sur la nationalité de ces tribunaux ; ils étaient français. " *Ibid.*, p. 165.
4. *Four Fighting Years*, p. 178.

to their original attitude of non-recognition of the German aggression of March 15, and, consequently, to the continued recognition of the Czechoslovak Republic.

Probably aware of the weakness of its position, the Czechoslovak National Committee set itself initially only limited aims. As late as 1940, in a message to Czechoslovak representatives abroad, Dr. Benes spoke of the necessity

" to make preparations for the recognition, at a given suitable future moment, of a real Czechoslovak Provisional Government "

and declared :

" That would be the *final* step in our entire organisation [1]. "

Following the French defeat, the National Committee moved to London where, in 1940, it assumed the title of a Provisional Government. It was from this moment that the Czechoslovak representation in exile, no longer contented with the non-descript status of a National Committee made the implicit claim to be a normal, even if somewhat irregular, organ of the continuing Czechoslovak State : for it was then that it adopted the 1920 Czechoslovak Constitution as the legal basis of its existence and activity.

It may be seriously doubted whether even such an adoption was enough to invest the Provisional Government with genuine legality under Czechoslovak constitutional law [2]. For far from resulting from an uninterrupted legal transmission of power, that Government was a spontaneous creation of Czechoslovaks in exile ; from the point of view of the Czechoslovak legal order it represented a revolutionary act, notwithstanding the fact that the Constitution was invoked [3]. The problem arises, however, whether a revolution can be validly carried out anywhere else than in the State concerned. Within the State, the lack of legality involved in a revolution is made up by its effectiveness which thus marks the beginning of a new legality [4]. To this extent, the revolution is of no concern to international law and to the international community at large. But a revolution carried out abroad is an altogether different proposition. What would happen, if two revolutionary groups should arise in exile, each claiming to be the Government? Within the country, the final effectiveness of one of

---

1. *It. mine, Cz. S. and Doc.*, p. 60.
2. Cf. Flory, who speaks of a " faille constitutionnelle ", *op. cit.*, p. 38 et seq.
3. The latter — it may be observed — was not suited to provide a basis for a governmental activity abroad, and had therefore to be adapted to current needs by an act at least as revolutionary as the actual setting up of the Government. " ...a novel method of issuing the requisite emergency provisions has been adopted which, independently of positive pre-Munich law, seeks the solution in *original, creative, revolutionary legislation...* " *It. mine*, Schwelb, *Legislation in Exile : Czechoslovakia*, in *Journal of Comparative Legislation and International Law*, XXIV, Part II, p. 120. This revolutionary legislation consisted in the Constitutional Decree issued by the President on October 15, 1940 (Czechoslovak Official Gazette, 1940, no. 2) authorizing the President to legislate by decree " at the instance of the Government ", so long as Parliament cannot meet. These powers of the President extended even to amending the Constitution ; of such amendments the Constitutional Decree itself represents a clear instance.
4. See above, p. 58-59.

them provides the legal criterion. But any such criterion is lacking on foreign soil, and there is a considerable danger that the recognition or non-recognition of such a revolutionary body may depend — failing an objective principle — on the arbitrary judgment of third States [1].

It is nevertheless true that, in certain circumstances, a limited degree of effectiveness may be achieved by a revolutionary Government in exile. It may consist in the latter's ability to rally round itself all, or the great majority of, its nationals abroad, to organize armed forces and other State organs, and to contribute to the war effort of its Allies. A further proof of such limited effectiveness may be provided by the connection — if any — between such a government and the occupied territory and by its effective hold on the country, as reflected in the obedience to its directives, the existence of an underground movement, and so forth [2]. These factors would require careful and thorough ascertaining and appraisal.

The existence of any such substitute criteria would free the recognition of this type of government by third States from the stigma of complete arbitrariness. It is only logical to assume that the decision to grant recognition under such circumstances should be equivalent to an admission that the Government so recognized is in fact an organ of the State in question.

The newly formed Czechoslovak Government in exile had clearly achieved the limited degree of effectiveness as described above : it had in its favour a strong presumption of conformity with the wishes of Czechoslovaks at home ; it commanded the allegiance due to a legitimate Government from its nationals abroad ; it organized — or continued to organize — armed forces which owed it unquestioned allegiance ; it had the allegiance of the only remaining organs of the Czechoslovak State : the Legations and Consulates. Strengthened by these arguments, the Czechoslovak Provisional Government embarked on arduous negotiations with the British Government for its recognition as a regular and fully-fledged Government of the Republic, on equal footing with the other exiled, but constitutional, governments.

Yet, the British Government refused to admit the Czechoslovak thesis. In the course of the ensuing negotiations the Foreign Secretary stated that the British Government

" were prepared in principle to recognize the Czechoslovak Government *as representing the Czech and Slovak peoples* and to facilitate its activities. But Lord Halifax's letter contained three very important reserves : 1) the British Government had no intention of pledging itself in advance in frontier questions (in accordance with the general attitude of the British Government as far as Central Europe is concerned) ; 2) the British Government stated that *it did not necessarily share the Czechoslovak viewpoint concerning the legal continuity of the Czechoslovak Republic ;* 3) the British Government left for further negotiation in particular the question of the jurisdiction of the Czechoslovak Government over the Czechoslovak Armed Forces and non-military persons [3] ".

---

1. See above, p. 98.
2. Flory, *op. cit.*, p. 16, *f.-n.* 2, and p. 159.
3. *It mine, Four Fighting Years,* p. 181.

The position is clear : what was offered to the Czechoslovak exiles by the British Government, was the legal status of the National Committees of the First World War, with the courtesy title of " Government " (which title the Czechoslovak National Committee of that period equally achieved in 1918). But, as the italicized passages show, the British Government questioned the legal existence of the Czechoslovak Republic and, consequently, its limited recognition of the Provisional Government did not imply the acknowledgment of the latter as an organ of the State.

While it may be politically understandable that the British Government wanted to preserve its future freedom of action with regard to Czechoslovak frontiers, its denial of the continued existence of the Czechoslovak Republic in the very midst of a war against Germany taxes one's comprehension to the utmost limits. Without indulging in conjectures, the plain fact must be stated : as late as summer 1940 the British Government refused unequivocally to accept the legal continuity of the Czechoslovak State against whose dismemberment it had lodged a formal protest emphasizing its illegality.

It appears from Czechoslovak sources that Dr. Benes preferred rather to renounce for the moment the full recognition of his Government as a regular Government than to accept it on such disastrous conditions [1]. It was probably in order to avoid an express acceptance of such conditions that he merely applied for a recognition as Provisional Government [2]. This was granted on July 21, 1940 [3].

In conformity with the basic British thesis, the status of the Provisional Government was kept distinct from that of constitutional exiled governments functioning on British soil [4]. Between the British and the Provisional Czechoslovak Government there was no exchange of regular diplomatic agents, the former merely appointing a " British representative " [5]. The Provisional Government was both officially described and dealt with as a recognized authority *sui generis*, but not as an organ of an existing State. This clearly results from the formulation of the already quoted Diplomatic Privileges (Extension) Act of March 6, 1941 [6] :

---

1. *Four Fighting Years*, p. 181.
2. The applicaton bears out the revolutionary origin of the Government : " ...in view of the new situation resulting from the recent events in our country and in Europe in general, the National Committee, in agreement with our Army, with all our important political bodies abroad, and especially in agreement with the spirit of resistance — obvious and unbreakable — of the overwhelming majority of the entire population in our occupied country, has now decided to constitute a Provisional Czechoslovak Government with the whole State machinery — as far as would be possible to establish it on British territory." Quoted by Taborsky, *op. cit.*, p. 88.
3. The British Government — wrote the Foreign Secretary — " are happy to recognize and enter into relations with the provisional Czechoslovak Government established by the Czechoslovak National Committee to function in this country. " *Cz. S. and Doc.*, pp. 49-50.
4. This remains true notwithstanding a Sibylline statement by Mr. Churchill in the House of Commons on July 23, 1940 : " As far as the position of the Czechoslovak Government in relation to the Polish and other Governments established in this country is concerned, there may be certain differences of form but in principle there is no difference. " *Parl. Deb.*, *Com.*, vol. CCCLXIII, col. 615.
5. Taborsky, *op. cit.*, p. 89.
6. See above, p. 92.

" ... a member of the government of any foreign Power or of a provisional government, being a government for the time being allied with His Majesty and established in the United Kingdom... "

The difference between the two categories is striking not only on account of the word " provisional ", but also because of the absence of any link between the " provisional government " and a " foreign Power ", while such link is clearly present in the first category, i.e. the " government of any foreign Power ".

This is further borne out by the form and type of international agreements concluded with the Provisional Government (similar in this to those previously concluded with the Czechoslovak National Committee). With regard to their form, such agreements were *not* concluded in the name of the Czechoslovak Republic [1]. With regard to their content, they related only to current problems [2], such as military questions, finance, and the like. In this connection the following agreements may be quoted : the above-mentioned agreement of October 2, 1939, between the French Prime Minister and M. Osusky, the Anglo-Czechoslovak Military Agreement of October 25, 1940 [3], the Anglo-Czechoslovak Financial Agreement of December 10, 1940 [4]. No agreement directly affecting Czechoslovakia, involving her international responsibility and bearing on her future was concluded with either the Czechoslovak National Committee or the Provisional Government [5].

It must therefore be concluded that in the first stage of its existence the Czechoslovak Provisional Government in exile merely achieved the status of a subject of international law *sui generis*. It was unrelated to the Czechoslovak State, not having been recognized as an organ of an existing State. It is to this case, exceptional among the exiled governments of the Second World War, that Prof. Guggenheim's theory of an independent subject of international law does in fact apply [6]. But it must be observed that in the case of Czechoslovakia, this limitation of the status of her exiled government proceeded not from a different application of rules governing belligerent occupation, but from the denial by third States — at that stage — of the continuing existence of the Czechoslovak State.

b) *Implied Recognition of Czechoslovakia's Continuity and the Resulting Status of the Czechoslovak Government in Exile.*

Whatever their limited initial aspirations [7], the Czechoslovaks in exile were not to rest contented with such a solution, implying, as it did, not only a limitation of their Government's legal status but,

---

1. See below, p. 317.
2. See above, p. 93.
3. *Cz. S. and Doc.*, pp. 76-77.
4. *Cz. Y.*, p. 235.
5. An exception is constituted by the Polish-Czechoslovak Declaration on future collaboration of November 11, 1940, see *Cz. Y.*, p. 235; but the Polish Government in exile had already fully recognized the Czechoslovak Government.
6. See above, pp. 87 et seq.
7. See above, p. 313.

moreover, the non-existence of the Czechoslovak State. On April 18, 1941, Dr. Benes took the matter up again with the British Government. His memorandum of that date contained the following requests :

" 1) Full diplomatic and *de iure* recognition to be given to the Czechoslovak Government and *the question of the continuity of the Czechoslovak Republic to be settled.*

2) As a result of this recognition a British Plenipotentiary Minister to the Czechoslovak Government to be appointed, as well as a Czechoslovak Minister to the British Government.

3) From the international standpoint, the Czechoslovak Republic and its President and Government, to have the same legal and political position as the other fully recognized Allied Governments in London.

4) *The official terminology recognized and in use to be as follows : The Czechoslovak Republic, the President of the Czechoslovak Republic, the Government of the Czechoslovak Republic, the Legation of the Czechoslovak Republic. Future agreements signed with the Czechoslovak Republic will be concluded, as before September* 1938, *in the name of the Czechoslovak Republic.*

5) The provisional character of the Czechoslovak Government will be understood in the future as being only an internal concern of Czechoslovak democracy. This means that the present Czechoslovak Government will, after the war, at once submit to a democratic Czechoslovak constitution. From the international standpoint the provisional character of the Czechoslovak Government ceases to exist [1]. "

The document is of particular interest not only as representing yet another stage in the Czechoslovak fight for recognition of the legal continuity of the State, but also because it fully confirms the above conclusions with regard to the standing of the Provisional Government up to that date [2]. It confirms that the Provisional Government was not considered an organ of the Czechoslovak Republic, and the gist of Benes's Memorandum is precisely his attempt to have it recognized as such an organ, which, in turn, would automatically imply the recognition of Czechoslovakia's existence.

At this stage again Anglo-Czechoslovak negotiations dragged and it may be reasonably supposed that they were brought to a relatively satisfactory conclusion owing to extra-legal considerations. On June 22, 1941, Germany attacked the Soviet Union who was thus brought into the war on the side of the Allies. Czechoslovak negotiations with the Soviet Union were soon opened, notwithstanding the fact that, in December 1939, that country had ceased to recognize the Czechoslovak Legation in Moscow and had entered into formal relations with the so-called Slovak State [3]. As a result of these negotiations, a Soviet-Czechoslovak Treaty was concluded on July 18, 1941, with no implied limitations concerning either Czechoslovakia's existence or the status of her exiled government [4]. The Treaty was followed on September 28, 1941, by a military agreement between the two States, declaring expressly:

---

1. *It. mine, Four Fighting Years*, p. 186.
2. See above, pp. 315-316.
3. See above, p. 289.
4. *Cz. S. and Doc.*, p. 78.

" The Czechoslovak military unit in the U.S.S.R. is a part of the army of the sovereign Czechoslovak Republic, and is subject to Czechoslovak laws and decrees [1]. "

The recognition by the above text of the continued existence of Czechoslovakia cannot be subject to doubt. It was further reinforced by a declaration made to Benes by Molotov, to the effect that

" the Soviet Government had taken no part in the Munich discussions and never considered itself, and does not now consider itself, bound to any degree by what was agreed upon in Munich and by what took place in 1938 and 1939 in respect to Czechoslovakia [2] ".

The Czechoslovak point of view concerning the continuity of the Republic and, consequently, the standing of the exiled government as her organ, was thus fully accepted by the Soviet Union.

On the day of the conclusion of the Soviet-Czechoslovak Treaty the British Government granted full recognition to the Czechoslovak Government.

" At the same time Mr. Eden handed to Mr. Masaryk a Note stating that this decision implied that the British Government now regarded the legal position of the President and Government of the Czechoslovak Republic as identical with that of the other Heads of States and Governments now established in the United Kingdom, and that, in future official references in this country the terms employed would be in accordance with Dr. Benes's memorandum of April 18, 1941, and that the provisional character of the Czechoslovak Government would be understood in the future as being only an internal concern of Czechoslovak democracy. Nevertheless the British Government still insisted on its reservation concerning the legal continuity of the Czechoslovak Republic and that it took on no pledges in the matter of future frontiers in Central Europe [3]. "

The political motives for British insistence on her non-recognition of Czechoslovakia's continuity are probably to be sought in the frontier problem, artificially connected with the question of continuity [4]. But whatever the political motives, the British attitude suffers hopelessly from its own inherent contradictions. It is unusual, at the very least, to grant full recognition to a Government of a non-existent State. In 1917, when the State of Czechoslovakia had not yet come into existence, the Allied Government did indeed recognize a Czechoslovak Government, but as nothing more than a Provisional Government, the future organ of a State which was about to be created. The legal fiction involved in such proceedings was not, however, carried to the length of recognition of a regular and definite Government. It is hardly to be supposed that in 1941 the British Government went beyond that limit and agreed to do what it had refused to do in 1918 : namely to grant full recognition to the Government of a non-existing State.

---

1. *Ibid.*, p. 79.
2. Benes's statement to the Czechoslovak State Council of November 12, 1941 ; *ibid.*, p. 103.
3. *Four Fighting Years*, p. 188. The publication comments : " In this respect Britain's recognition of the Czechoslovak Republic and of its State institutions fell short of Russia's. " Flory incorrectly states that « cette fois le Gouvernement tchèque était parvenu à ses fins... » *Op. cit.*, p. 44.
4. See above, pp. 306-307.

Moreover, Mr. Eden's Note referred expressly to the Czechoslovak Republic and accepted Dr. Benes's request concerning the titles to be used and the form in which future agreements were to be concluded.

" Agreements which His Majesty's Government may in future conclude with the Czechoslovak Government will be made in the name of the Czechoslovak Republic, "

stated Mr. Eden [1]. Thus, at long last the British Government admitted the existence of the Czechoslovak State. But if that State did exist, then it must inevitably, have been the old pre-March Czechoslovakia, since no other Czechoslovak State had come into existence in the meantime.

It is therefore less important what the British Government intended to do than what it actually did ; and it results from the foregoing that it in fact did recognize the legal continuity of Czechoslovakia by granting full recognition to her Government and relating that Government expressly to the Czechoslovak Republic. No other legal interpretation seems possible. The same interpretation was adopted by the Czechoslovak Government. In a broadcast speech of July 25, 1941, the Czechoslovak Prime Minister, Mgr. Sramek, declared :

" ... she (Great Britain) has chosen this very moment to recognize the Czechoslovak Government *as the authorized Government of the free Allied Czechoslovak State*. As a consequence, the Czechoslovak State, its sovereignty and its external attributes, in conformity with the Czechoslovak Constitution of 1920, continue to exist in the territory of this country on the basis of the declaration made by the British Government in Parliament [2]. "

It is of interest to observe how this interpretation was reflected in the new status of the Czechoslovak Government, as compared with its status during the first period of non-recognition of the Czechoslovak State [3]. In the first place, an exchange of regular Envoys took place between Britain and Czechoslovakia [4]. Further, the international agreements to which the Czechoslovak Government was from now on a party, changed not only in form [5], being now clearly concluded on behalf of the Republic, but even in content : for it was only after the recognition of Czechoslovakia's existence that international agreements concluded by her representatives ceased to be confined to current problems of an administration in exile, and dealt with matters directly affecting the Czechoslovak State, its future and its international responsibility. Into this category fall the United Nations Declaration of January 1st, 1942, the Lend-Lease Agreement of July 11, 1942, and all the principal multilateral international conventions concluded during the war with a view to the future organisation of the post-war world [6]. The diplomatic correspondence relating to the annulment of the Munich

1. Quoted by Taborsky, *op. cit.*, p. 95.
2. *It. mine, Cz. S. and Doc.*, p. 51.
3. See above, pp. 315-316.
4. Taborsky, *loc. cit.*
5. See above.
6. See above, pp. 93-94.

Agreement must also be placed in this category [1]. It is also significant that internal legislation directly affecting the Republic, was only enacted by the Czechoslovak Government after its full recognition : e.g. the declaration of war against the Axis States by Dr. Benes on December 16, 1941, and a proclamation invalidating transfers of public or private proterty effected in the territory of the Republic since September 27, 1938.

The conclusion therefore is inescapable : whatever the verbal reservations on the part of Great Britain, the continued existence of the Czechoslovak Republic, represented abroad by a Government possessing the character of a State organ, seems to have been recognized in the actual State practice in this second phase of the development of the Czechoslovak case during the war.

c) *Annulment of the Munich Agreement and Final Recognition of Czechoslovakia's Continuity.*

In spite of this success, the Czechoslovak Government continued its struggle both for a clear and unequivocal recognition of its country's legal survival and for the recovery of the Sudetenland. On December 16, 1941 — the day of his declaration of war against the Axis countries — President Benes sent yet another Note to the British Government

" which consolidated the aims and basic assumptions of the Czechoslovak Republic : the non-recognition of Munich, of the Vienna arbitration of November 2, 1938, and of the acts of violence committed by Germany and Hungary against the Czechoslovak Republic in March, 1939. The Note stated that the Czechoslovak Government was the guardian of the legal continuity of the Czechoslovak Republic, that all illegal annexations must be restored ; ... and that from the point of view of international policy the separate Slovak State does not exist [2] ".

On August 5, 1942, i.e. over a year after the granting full recognition, the British Foreign Secretary addressed to the Czechoslovak Government a Note of particular importance. In the first place, the Note reiterated that the decision of July 18, 1941,

" implied that His Majesty's Government in the United Kingdom regarded the juridical position of the President and the Government of the Czechoslovak Republic as identical with that of other Allied Heads of States and governments established in this country [3] ".

The formulation is exactly the same as that of the Note of July 18, 1941 as quoted in the official Czechoslovak publication [4]. No documents are available to show whether in the meantime the British Government had undergone a change of mind with respect to Czechoslovakia's continuity. But now as then, the " identity " of the legal position of

---

1. See below, pp. 320-323.
2. *Four Fighting Years*, p. 189. " The Czechoslovak attitude " — adds the publication—" was that everything which had been done against Czechoslovakia from September 1938, and through 1939 had for the Czechoslovak people no political or international validity, as it took place only under German pressure and threats and involved the violation of Czechoslovakia's constitution and international obligations. " p. 190.
3. *Cz. S. and Doc.*, 2, p. 93.
4. See above, p. 318.

the President and Government of Czechoslovakia with that of the other Heads of States and Governments meant nothing if it did not mean Czechoslovakia's continuity and the connection between the Czechoslovak State and the exiled Government as its regular organ. Once again : it is of no importance what the British Government meant to do, but only what it actually did.

The British Note then went on to deal with the Munich problem in the following terms :

" I desire to declare on behalf of His Majesty's Government in the United Kingdom, that as Germany has deliberately destroyed the arrangements, concerning Czechoslovakia, reached in 1938, in which His Majesty's Government in the United Kingdom participated, His Majesty's Government regard themselves as free from any engagements in this respect. At the final settlement of Czechoslovak frontiers to be reached at the end of the war, they will not be influenced by any changes effected in and since 1938 [1]. "

This key passage of the British Note admittedly refers in the first place to the territorial problem of the Sudetenland. What is, however, of immediate interest here, is not the territorial problem as such, but the real significance of the · repudiation of the Munich Agreement for the problem of the continuity of the Czechoslovak Republic. It is chiefly from that point of view that the British Note, as well as all the other acts of repudiation of Munich, must be examined.

There is no doubt that the British Government did not declare the Munich Agreement null and void *ab initio* [2]. The British Government's avowed intention in not giving this repudiation retroactive effect was to leave the frontier question open and thus to safeguard its future freedom of action with regard to this problem. It may be doubted, however, whether such a thesis was at all possible, since it turned the Sudetenland into some sort of a legal no-man's land belonging neither to Germany, nor to Czechoslovakia, nor to any other State. It would rather appear that, whatever the date of the actual annulment, whether it took place *ex tunc* or *ex nunc*, the withdrawal of recognition of German sovereignty over the Sudetenland automatically meant the recognition of the Czechoslovak sovereignty ; the only difference would be that in case of a retroactive annulment the whole period of German domination of the Sudetenland would be considered illegal, whereas in case of an *ex nunc* annulment it would be considered that such domination, which had been legal for the period between the conclusion of the Munich Agreement and its repudiation, has lost its legality only at the date of repudiation. In both cases, if the annulment was to have any meaning at all, it had to consist in the recognition of the Czechoslovak sovereignty over the territory in question, and could not possibly create a legal vacuum [3]. If, therefore, the British reluctance to declare the Munich Agreement void *ad initio* was due to the desire to preserve for Britain

---

1. *Ibid.*, p. 94.
2. Guggenheim, *Validité*, p. 241.
3. It is quite a different problem whether a voidance *ex tunc* of an originally valid agreement is practically possible and what is the possible scope of its validity ; see Guggenheim, *op. cit.*, pp. 242-244.

the possibility of a new and entirely different solution of the Sudeten question in the future, then it must be said that it failed on the theoretical level just as it was to fail on the practical plane on Czechoslovakia's actual liberation [1].

However, if the British annulment was not *ex tunc*, it was not *ex nunc* either, if by *nunc* is meant the date of the British Note. For the reason for the repudiation was clearly stated, namely, the destruction by Germany of an originally valid agreement [2]. But this destruction, far from taking place on August 5, 1942, had taken place on March 15, 1939. It is then only logical to interpret the British declaration of nullity as having retroactive effect as from March 15, 1939. But in such a case it was also the declaration of nullity of Czechoslovakia's " extinction " by German action. The German act which was illegal enough to destroy the Munich Agreement must certainly have been illegal enough not to give Germany a legal title over Czechoslovakia, — in other words, not to effect the extinction of the Republic. It cannot possibly be assumed that the British Government considered the German aggression against Czechoslovakia both as an illegal act justifying British withdrawal from an international convention, and as a legal title for the German seizure of Czechoslovakia.

Moreover, if Czechoslovakia had not survived the German aggression of March 15, 1939, there would have been no point in voiding the Munich Agreement which — in this case — would have no longer had any object. If its purpose was to ensure Great Britain's freedom of movement with regard to frontiers of some future State which was only to be created, then it was utterly unnecessary, as the Munich Agreement never related to a different Czechoslovakia from the one which existed at the time of its concluslon.

Here it might be objected that the interpretation proposed above breaks down on the following argument : the British repudiation could possibly not imply Czechoslovakia's survival at all and could very well be made on the assumption on that State's extinction ; in such a case, far from implying Czechoslovakia's survival, it would be aimed directly and exclusively at Germany, whose sovereignty over the Sudetenland would thus be considered at an end, and this not in favour of an existing Czechoslovak State, but pending other future arrangement. The repudiation would then not have related to a non-existent Czechoslovakia, but to German sovereignty over the Sudetenland.

This objection does not however, stand up to a close analysis. For, of the parties to the Munich Agreement, the British declaration was not made to Germany but to Czechoslovakia. Moreover, it was included in the same document which, as has been seen, spoke of the President and Government of the Czechoslovak Republic and re-emphasized the identity of the legal position of these bodies with that of the

---

1. See below, p. 324 et seq.
2. See Guggenheim, *op. cit.*, p. 241. The main motive of the Note is in line with former British declarations on the subject : thus, immediately after the events of March 1939, Mr. Chanberlain called them " a complete repudiation of the Munich Agreement. " *Parl. Deb., Com.*, vol. CCCXLV, col. 887. Similarly, Mr. Churchill on Sept. 30, 1940 quoted by Guggenheim, *loc. cit.*

other Allied Heads of State and governments in Britain [1]. It is therefore impossible to construe the British repudiation as being addressed to Germany and as merely contesting German sovereignty over a given territory, with Czechoslovakia left entirely out of the picture. On the contrary, Czechoslovakia was in the very centre of the picture and it was she who was made the beneficiary of the British repudiation.

With the elimination of this, only possible, objection, the basic interpretation of the British repudiation of the Munich Agreement stands : namely that it implied the legal continuity of the Czechoslovak Republic [2].

This then is the only possible meaning of an annulment of the Munich Agreement. The continuity of Czechoslovakia was therefore also implicit in the declaration of General de Gaulle on behalf of the French National Committee, of September 29, 1942, which was, however, much more strongly worded than the British repudiation.

" ... the French National Committee, rejecting the agreements signed in Munich on September 29, 1938, solemnly declare that they consider these agreements as null and void as also all acts accomplished in the application or in consequence of these same agreements. Recognizing no territorial alterations affecting Czechoslovakia supervening in 1938 or since that time, they undertake to do everything in their power to ensure that the Czechoslovak Republic within frontiers prior to September 1938, obtains all effective guarantees for her military and economic security, her territorial integrity and her political unity [3]. "

This statement represents a clear and unequivocal declaration of nullity *ab initio* which is absolute and *ex tunc*, leaving no legal vacuum. The French National Committee thus reverted to the *status quo* of the pre-Munich period, recognizing both the unbroken legal continuity of Czechoslovakia and her sovereignty over the whole of its pre-Munich territory [4].

The final recognition of Czechoslovakia's legal survival by the non-Munich Powers was naturally easier and simpler and was, in any case, completely unequivocal. The position adopted by the Soviet Union has already been mentioned [5], although that country, without having to go back on the Munich Agreement, had yet to go back on her own attitude with regard to the de-recognition of Czechoslovakia. No such difficulties were encountered by the United States which had consistently

---

1. See above, p. 320.
2. Since, however, this *ad integrum restitutio* acknowledged only the legal personality, and not the territorial integrity of the Republic, the British Note was accepted with marked reserve by the Czechoslovak Government. " My Government " — wrote Masaryk — " accept your Excellency's Note as a practical solution of questions and difficulties of vital importance for Czechoslovakia which emerged between our two countries as a consequence of the Munich Agreement, maintaining, of course, our political and juridical position with regard to the Munich Agreement and events which followed it... Between our two countries the Munich Agreement can now be considered as dead. " *Cz. S. and Doc.*, p. 94.
3. *Ibid.*, p. 97 ; see also the joint declaration of the Czechoslovak and the Provisional French Government of August 22, 1944, quoted by Langer, *op. cit.*, p. 240.
4. It is not surprising that this declaration was welcomed by the Czechoslovak Government with considerably more enthusiasm than was the case for the British statement. See *Cz. S. and Doc.*, pp. 98-102.
5. See above, p. 317.

refused to regard Czechoslovakia as extinct. As early as July 30, 1941, the American Ambassador in London wrote to the Czechoslovak Foreign Minister :

" The American Government has not acknowledged that the *temporary extinguishment* of their liberties has taken from the people of Czechoslovakia their rights and privileges in international affairs, and it has continued to recognize the diplomatic and consular representatives of Czechoslovakia in the full exercise of their functions [1]. "

In consequence, it was now prepared to enter into formal relations with the Provisional Government and to have a Minister accredited to it. On October 28, 1942, the United States granted full recognition to the Czechoslovak Government, now no longer considered provisional [2].

The legal continuity of the Czechoslovak State finds yet another clear expression in the joint Czechoslovak-Mexican declaration of March 27, 1942, stating :

" The Czechoslovak and Mexican Governments... have decided to *renew* the diplomatic relations which were *interrupted* ... when in 1939 the German army, contrary to all tenets of justice, occupied Prague [3]. "

Particular interest attaches to the statement of the Mexican Foreign Minister of the same date which seems to be the only one to base the professed continuity of the Czechoslovak State on a firm foundation of principle :

" The resumption of relations with Czechoslovakia confirms a principle which Mexico has invariably upheld and which constitutes one of the traditions in the international attitude of our country. This principle consists in not recognizing, for any reasons whatever, territorial conquests made directly or indirectly by means of force [4]. "

It may thus safely be stated that whatever the initial vacillations and even inconsistencies, the legal continuity of the Czechoslovak Republic was already recognized by the Allied countries in the course of the war.

It should be added that Art. 19 of the armistice agreement with Hungary, concluded on behalf of the Soviet, U.S. and British Government by the Soviet Commander, declared null and void the Vienna Award of November 2, 1938 [5].

B) *After the Hostilities.*

Within a short time of the crossing of Czechoslovak frontiers by the Allied armies, Czechoslovak sovereignty was effectively restored

---

1. *It. mine; ibid.*, p. 55. Cf. the comment of the Czechoslovak Envoy in Washington : " Although the United States have never ceased to recognize the Czechoslovak Republic *de iure* ...nevertheless to-day's decision is of great importance because it means that the United States now renew normal contact with the legal Czechoslovak Government and the President. " *Ibid.*, pp. 54-55.
2. *Ibid.*, p. 58.
3. *It. mine; ibid.*, p. 56.
4. *Ibid.*, p. 57.
5. See above, p. 284. " This clause restored with retroactive force Czechoslovak sovereignty over the areas of Slovakia and Ruthenia, transferred under that award to Hungary. " Langer, *op. cit.*, p. 241.

over the whole of her pre-Munich territory [1]. This restoration involved the end of both the Protectorate and the puppet State of Slovakia which disappeared both as a physical fact and as alleged legal entities [2]. The annulment of the German seizure of Czechoslovakia as well as of the Munich Agreement was further confirmed by the Allied declaration of June 5, 1945, on the zones of occupation of Germany, declaring Germany's frontiers to be " as they were on 31st December 1937 " [3]. The clear implication of this declaration was that no part of Czechoslovakia formed part of German territory. That the declaration effected a *restitutio ad integrum* and not a transfer of German territory to Czechoslovakia is made quite clear by comparing it with later instruments providing for such transfers, especially those included in the Potsdam Declaration [4].

All international developments after the effective restoration of the Republic fully confirm her identity with the Czechoslovak State which had existed until March 15, 1939, — in other words, her continuity, unbroken by German aggression and seizure.

Paradoxically, as it may seem, the recognition of Czechoslovakia's continued sovereignty over her territory as it had been prior to her dismemberment, found expression in the very act of cession of Carpatho-Ruthenia to the Soviet Union [5]. For in order validly to cede that part of her territory, Czechoslovakia must have been considered the lawful sovereign and any notion of a no-man's land, of a *terra nullius*, with regard to Czechoslovak territory must have been excluded.

On February 10, 1947, Czechoslovakia signed the Peace Treaties with Italy, Rumania, Bulgaria and Hungary, alongside the other Allied and Associated Powers. Art. 44 of the Italian Treaty (Art. 10 of the Rumanian, Art. 8 of the Bulgarian and Art. 10 of the Hungarian) stipulated :

" 1. Each Allied or Associated Power will notify Italy, within a period of six months from the coming into force of the present Treaty which of its pre-war bilateral treaties with Italy it desires to keep in force or revive... "

In execution of this provision Czechoslovakia, by a Note Verbale of her Legation in Rome, of February 25, 1948, expressed the desire

" that the following bilateral conventions concluded before the war between Italy and Czechoslovakia should remain in force : 1. Consular Convention between the Czechoslovak Republic and the Kingdom of Italy, concluded at Rome on 1 March 1924 ; 2. Agreement between Czechoslovakia and Italy concerning the execution of

---

1. See Langer, *op. cit.*, pp. 239-244.
2. E. g. the *Rapport de gestion* of the Swiss Federal Council for 1945 : « Le 27 février 1945, nous avons reconnu le gouvernement de la République tchécoslovaque, le chargé d'affaires de Slovaquie ayant été informé en préalable que sa mission à Berne était considérée comme terminée... », p. 102.
3. *Doc.*, VII, p. 222.
4. " The conference has agreed in principle to the proposal of the Soviet Government concerning the ultimate transfer to the Soviet Union of the City of Koenisberg and the area adjacent to it... " *Doc.* VIII, p. 933. " ...the former German territories... shall be under the administration of the Polish State. " *Ibid.*, p. 934.
5. Treaty of June 29, 1945, Langer, *op. cit.*, p. 242. The treaty speaks of the respective " wish of the population " which was, however, never ascertained by any of the known methods.

judgments in civil and commercial matters, concluded at Rome on 6 April 1922 ;
3. Convention between Czechoslovakia and Italy concerning mutual protection of
the rights of their respective nationals, concluded at Rome on 6 April 1922 ;
4. Extradition Convention between Czechoslovakia and Italy, concluded at Rome
on 6 April 1922 ; 5. Convention between Czechoslovakia and the Kingdom of
Italy regarding the reciprocal delivery of documents, records, and papers concerning
members of the former Austro-Hungarian army, concluded at Rome on 23 May
1931 [1] ".

Similar Notes were presented to Rumania on March 1, 1948 [2],
Bulgaria on March 5, 1948 [3] and Hungary on February 27, 1949 [4].

In 1946 the Czechoslovak Government declared that the Czechoslo-
vak-Swiss Conventions of December 31, 1926, concerning Assistance in
Civil and Commercial Matters, had never lost their validity, to which
the Swiss Legation in Prague replied that Switzerland considered those
conventions as " valid and applicable " [5].

On this, Prof. Guggenheim comments that the Swiss answer left
open the question of the legal continuity of Czechoslovakia during the
period of German occupation [6]. This may be doubted. Whatever the
Swiss formulation, it includes a clear admission of the validity of the
conventions concerned. But how could they be valid if Czechoslovakia
was not the same subject of international law which had been a party
to them, considering that no new conventions having exactly the same
content had been negotiated and considering that there had been no
new norm, either internal or international, which would have taken
over those conventions on behalf of a new Czechoslovak State.

At the last session of the League of Nations Assembly in Geneva
in April 1946, Czechoslovakia — who, as has been seen, had not been
struck off the list of Member States — was present alongside all the
other Members of the League. If indeed Czechoslovakia was a new
State, then her attendance at the session should have been preceded by
an application for membership and an admission in the usual way.
Nothing of the sort took place. Nor did the Credentials Committee,
of which the Czechoslovak delegate was vice-chairman, raise any
objection to Czechoslovakia's presence. The Czechoslovak delegate
could indeed state that " ... Czechoslovakia up to the present day has
remained a member of the League " [7].

Nor had any new act of accession taken place with regard to the
International Labour Organisation which — like the League — had
never excluded Czechoslovakia from the list of its Members [8]. The
position was exactly the same with regard to the International
Telecommunication Union which, throughout all the years of the
German occupation, had retained Czechoslovakia on the list of Member
administrations, while simply including in a foot-note the German

---

1. *United Nations Treaty Series*, vol. XXVI, pp. 105-107.
2. *Ibid.*, pp. 111-113.
3. *Ibid.*, p. 117.
4. *Ibid.*, p. 123.
5. Guggenheim, *op. cit.*, p. 263, *f.-n.*
6. *Ibid.*
7. *LNOJ*, 1946, Special Supplement, no. 194, p. 42.
8. See above, p. 290.

notification claiming that Czechoslovakia's membership has ceased, and for obviously technical reasons, listed the Protectorate under Germany [1]. Finally, with regard to the Universal Postal Union, Czechoslovakia's name re-appeared on the list of Member States, the date of her entry into the Union being given as May 18, 1920 [2].

Similarly, without any new act of accession, Czechoslovakia continued to be a party to multilateral conventions which she had signed and ratified before 1939 [3].

This evidence of Czechoslovakia's continuity is not — to the writer's knowledge — challenged by any evidence to the contrary. It must therefore be concluded that Czechoslovakia's legal continuity throughout the period of her illegal seizure by Germany, in other words, the identity of the post-war with the pre-aggression Czechoslovakia, already recognized and acted upon during actual hostilities, was fully confirmed by subsequent State practice after hostilities and by Czechoslovakia's effective restoration.

7. CONCLUSION : LEGAL BASIS OF CZECHOSLOVAKIA'S CONTINUITY.

It may be recalled that Czechoslovakia's legal continuity during the period of German domination was not protected by the rules concerning territorial or revolutionary changes, nor — in spite of the artificial construction of Dr. Benes and the Nurnberg Tribunal — by the rule concerning belligerent occupation.

And yet, Czechoslovakia's continuity, the identity of the post-war with the pre-March 1939 Czechoslovakia was unanimously confirmed by uniform State practice. This practice, as described above, provides overwhelming evidence of Czechoslovakia's survival, without being called in question by contrary evidence from any quarter.

Yet, it is not this international recognition of Czechoslovakia's continuity which can provide the legal basis of her survival. It has been submitted that international recognition should be rejected as a test of State identity and continuity [4]. The concrete case of Czechoslovakia emphatically confirms the impossibility of such a test : for, if

---

1. Bureau de l'U.I.T., *Rapport de gestion*, 1939 and fol. The Report for 1945 includes the following Czechoslovak notification of June 9, 1945 : « La Tchécoslovaquie ayant signé la Convention internationale des Télécommunications (Madrid 1932) et les Règlements y annexés (Caire 1939) n'a jamais dénoncé cette convention et ces règlements ; elle restait et reste toujours membre de l'Union Internationale des Télécommunications. L'occupation de la Tchécoslovaquie par l'Allemagne et tous les événements politiques s'y rattachant ne pouvaient rien changer à ces faits ; ils ont seulement empêché l'Administration tchécoslovaque d'exercer les droits et de remplir les devoirs prévus par la Convention et les Règlements. En conséquence, toutes les communications de la part de l'Allemagne ou d'un autre Gouvernement ou d'une autre administration au sujet du service des télécommunications sur le territoire tchécoslovaque n'ont aucune légitimité et doivent être considérées comme non-existantes. » p. 4.
2. U.P.U., *Rapport de gestion*, 1945, p. 26.
3. E. g. the International Opium Convention of 1912, signed by Czechoslovakia in 1920, the Convention for the Suppression of the Traffic of Women and Children of 1921, the Convention for the Suppression of the Circulation and Traffic in Obscene Publications of 1923. See the Official UNO Publication : *Signatures, Ratifications, Acceptances Accessions, etc., concerning the Multilateral Conventions and Agreements in respect of which the Secretary-General acts as Depository*, 1949.
4. See above, pp. 130-161.

recognition — a highly political act — were to be decisive for the determination of a given legal situation, then it would follow that the Czechoslovak Republic passed through some very peculiar vicissitudes indeed as regards her international status : it existed for some time after March 15, 1939, then it ceased to exist, then it was in existence again and, what is supremely puzzling, not as a new State but precisely as the old one [1]. Moreover, even then it existed in relation to the Allied countries, while it did not exist in relation to the Axis and some of the neutrals (e.g. Switzerland). Over and above this, such recognition was upheld, then withdrawn, and then granted again in face of an unchanged situation of fact, i.e. the effective German domination of Czechoslovakia. It is therefore certainly not international recognition which can supply an answer to the question why Czechoslovakia survived her alleged extinction and what was the legal basis of this surprising fact.

Moreover, with the exception of a few Legations, there was a definite break in the functioning of all Czechoslovak State organs. The new organs which then came to be formed, were created in a revolutionary manner from the point of view of the Czechoslovak legal order, — with all the doubts attaching to a revolutionary creation in exile, i.e. without the effectiveness which could make up for the absence of legality.

Some legal basis has nevertheless to be found for what has been seen to consistute the uniform practice in favour of Czechoslovakia's continuity, as described above. In conformity with the basic assumption of this study, according to which it is general international law which is decisive for the question of State identity and continuity, such evidence has so far always been tested against existing positive rules. Failing a crystallised rule, applicable to the Czechoslovak case, against what principle is such evidence to be tested ?

It is submitted that if the verdict of the international community cannot be investigated for its conformity with a clear rule of general international law, it can still be investigated for such conformity with the very nature of international law as a normative system. No such system is possible without a sharp differentiation between legal and illegal acts.

This differentiation finds its expression in what Prof. Guggenheim has described as the fundamental rule of any legal system : *ex iniuria ius non oritur* [2]. It is this principle and this principle alone which can help to decide which of the two conflicting attitudes of third States with regard to Czechoslovakia was the lawful one : the one expressed in the recognition of Slovakia and the Protectorate, or the one expressed in the recognition of Czechoslovakia's continuity. Without such an objective principle there would be no criterion for assessing the legal merits of these conflicting attitudes, and Czechoslovakia's survival and extinction would both become equally probable and valid. Nor can the later attitude of the international community prevail against the

---

1. See above, pp. 316-324. As to the impossibility of a legal resurrection, i.e. the impossibility of identity without continuity, see above, p. 6.
2. *Op. cit.*, p. 226.

former, since it is by no means clear why the recognition of States should have more value at one date than at another, when the factual situation remains unchanged.

It is then this fundamental principle and this principle alone which can endow the evidence of Czechoslovakia's survival with any degree of legal finality and incontrovertibility. It is this principle alone which — throughout all changing attitudes of third States — can provide a legal explanation of that survival, which indeed *makes* it a legal survival and not an arbitrary political fiction.

It is this principle which formed the strongest argument of the Czechoslovaks in exile in favour of the legal continuity of their State. It has been seen, however, that it was invoked by them against the contrary principle : *ex factis ius oritur,* — in other words, against the overriding principle of effectiveness [1]. It may be asked why, of these two principles, that of *ex iniuria* so emphatically carried the day in the particular case.

Without for the present examining any possible new developments of modern international law, the following provisional answer is submitted : even under traditional international law the principle *ex factis ius oritur* has never been allowed to degenerate into what may be termed a primitive principle of effectiveness. In other words, a certain amount of finality, a consolidation of the new effective situation is required for the normative pressure of facts to prevail against the inherent legality of the system. Not even traditional international law lightly presumes the forcible extinction of one of its subjects, — as has been seen in connection with the strict conditions for the validity of an annexation [2]. The effectiveness of the illegal act must be final beyond doubt and every reasonable chance of a *restitutio ad integrum* must be excluded.

For the principle *ex factis ius oritur* to endow the German seizure of Czechoslovakia with finality and legality, conditions would have been necessary which certainly did not materialize between March 15 and September 1, 1939. A final and unopposed consolidation of the new situation, born of illegality, would have been necessary, and either the acquiescence of the victim State or the loss by it of every reasonable chance of restoration. But far from such last reasonable chance disappearing in a world settling down to a quiet period after a crisis, the German aggression against Czechoslovakia became one of the milestones on the road to a world war, in which Czechoslovak independence was to be taken up as one of the war aims of the coalition. The principle *ex iniuria ius non oritur* could under such circumstances never lose its validity, nor could the opposed principle have come into play.

On the strength of this principle, the Czechoslovak State survived for a certain time as a purely ideal notion, without any effectiveness in its territory and even without properly constituted State organs

---

1. See above, p. 308.
2. See above, pp. 102-107.

abroad which could have been instrumental in carrying on the continuity of the State throughout the critical period. It therefore appears that a State can survive for a reasonably limited period of time without a government. As for the legal validity of those organs of the Czechoslovak State which had been created abroad in a revolutionary manner, this revolution eventually proved to be effective.

It was therefore a fundamental rule of any normative system worthy of the name which — failing any other protective norm — stepped in to safeguard Czechoslovakia's continuity in a situation where everything seemed to militate against it : the effectiveness of German domination, international de-recognition, a break of continuity in the functioning of State organs, whether at home or abroad. If Czechoslovakia survived *in extremis*, this was only because the German aggression of March 15, 1939, was an illegal act.

It is thus an objective principle, and not a voluntarist argument, which provides the only possible legal explanation of the otherwise astounding phenomenon of Czechoslovakia's continuity. The evidence of such continuity, supplied by the State practice, can be considered as final and incontrovertible because it conforms, if not to an already fully crystallized positive rule, then to a fundamental principle, reflecting the very nature and spirit of international law [1].

---

1. For problems connected with the actual restoration of a temporarily suppressed State, see below, pp. 582-586.

CHAPTER VI.

ALBANIA.

1. THE ITALIAN INVASION.

On April 7, 1939, Albania, a Member of the League of Nations, was invaded by the Italian armed forces without a declaration of war and without warning. As a result of careful preparation and the crushing superiority of the Italians forces, the Albanian resistance was broken in the course of a few days, while the King fled the country.

Once in power, the Italian authorities convened on April 12, 1939, a body styled "the Constituent Assembly", which duly offered the Albanian Crown to the King of Italy. The offer was accepted on April 14, and a personal union between the two Kingdoms was proclaimed [1].

2. LEGAL NATURE OF ITALIAN-OCCUPIED ALBANIA.

a) *The Italian Thesis.*

The pattern of Italian action against Albania was thus fundamentally different from her action against Ethiopia, — just as it was different from German aggression against Czechoslovakia. Whereas in the two latter cases the extinction of the victim was proclaimed, a different technique was adopted with regard to Albania. Far from announcing her extinction, Italy emphasized her continued legal existence as a State, which claim alone could enable her to put forward the thesis of a union between the two States.

Certain appearances might indeed seem to bear out the Italian contention. Albania — unlike " Bohemia and Moravia " — had in fact been an independent State and could therefore become the partner to a union. The offer of the Albanian crown to the King of Italy was made by an assembly composed of Albanians. Following its acceptance by Italy, Albania was still left with a Prime Minister and Government of her own. Finally, it would appear that Albania retained her status of a subject of international law, concluding treaties not only with Italy, but even with third States [2].

---

1. *L'annexion de l'Albanie par l'Italie, RDI.*, 1939, p. 564. *Albania — Basic Handbook.*

2. Economic, Customs and Exchange Convention between Albania and Italy, April 20, 1939 ; *British and Foreign State Papers*, vol. CXLIII, p. 332 ; Convention between Albania and Italy on Civil and Political Rights, April 20, 1939, *ibid.*, p. 337 ; Agreement

b) *Puppet Character of Italian-Dominated Albania.*

None of these facts, however, prove the actual statehood of Italian-occupied Albania and, consequently, they disguise the true aim and nature of Italian action, which must be qualified as aggression and annexation.

The " Constituent Assembly " which offered the Albanian crown to Italy was indeed composed of Albanians. Moreover, even if illegal, it could theoretically have been a revolutionary authority. It has, however, been seen, that there is a strong presumption in favour of the puppet character of such an authority, if the alleged revolution takes place under foreign military occupation. How much stronger must such presumption be when that occupation is the immediate result of armed aggression by the occupying Power which has just ravaged the country, and when, moreover, it fully coincides with the designs of the aggressor [1]. It is indeed difficult to believe that the Albanians, whose country had just been invaded and bombed by the Italian forces, should have spontaneously reacted to this outrage by effecting a union with the aggressor. It is equally difficult to believe that, once physically overpowered, they have immediately and freely wished to do what they had refused to do previously, i.e. to become the tools of Italy's imperialistic designs.

This initial presumption is fully confirmed by the subsequent organisation of the Albanian " State ". This State was given its constitution in Rome, on June 6, 1939, and organised entirely on Italian Fascist lines. Notwithstanding the existence of an Albanian puppet government, the country was provided with an Italian " *Luogotenente* ", having his own Italian " shadow cabinet ". At the same time, Italy appointed Italian advisers to the Albanian Prime Minister and all other Ministers, Italian inspectors of the Albanian Fascist Party — whose Directorate anyway included Italian members — and Italian financial advisers even to the Prefects and sub-Prefects. Not content with this, Italy established her own, parallel and purely Italian administration, consisting of the *Luogotenente* with his military and political cabinet, the Command of the Armed Forces, the Carabinieri which superseded the Albanian gendarmerie, and the customs administration. At the request of the Albanian puppet government made in June 1939, the Albanian army was absorbed into the Italian army, the Albanian Foreign Office was abolished and Albania's foreign representation taken over by Italy [2]. The organisation of the Albanian puppet State seems to have proceeded on lines similar to that of Manchukuo [3].

---

between Albania and Italy regarding the Unification of the Diplomatic and Consular Services, June 6, 1939, *ibid.*, p. 337. Accord multilatéral (Albanie, Allemagne, Bulgarie, Croatie, Danemark, Finlande, Hongrie, Italie, Norvège, Pays-Bas, Roumanie, San Marino, Slovaquie) concernant l'Union postale et télégraphique européenne, October 19, 1942. Martens *N.R.G.* 3rd series, XL, p. 712.

1. See above, p. 65.
2. See the Italo-Albanian Treaty of June 3, 1939 : Art. 1. " La gestione di tutte le relazioni internazionali dell'Italia e dell'Albania é unificata ed é accentrata al Regio Ministerio degli affari esteri in Roma. " *Albania — Basic Handbook*, Part II.
3. See above, pp. 174-177.

The above brief description fully bears out the puppet character of the Italian-occupied Albanian State. It is submitted that such proof was in fact hardly necessary in view of the authoritative testimony which has since been offered to the world and which contradicts in every detail the Italian claim of a voluntary union : the Diaries of the Italian Foreign Minister, Count Ciano, describing with undisguised frankness and cynicism the Italian engineering of the Albanian case [1].

c) *The Albanian Puppet and Independent Albania.*

It follows that Italian-occupied Albania was not independent; it was not a State, but a puppet, a cloak to cover Italian aggression. Its basic norm was derived from the legal order of Italy ; it was controlled by Italy in law as well as in fact. For this reason it could not have been identical with the independent Albanian State which had preceded it [2].

3. THE ATTITUDE OF THE INTERNATIONAL COMMUNITY.

Immediately upon the Italian invasion of his country, King Zog protested to the Secretary-General of the League of Nations. Another Albanian protest from the Albanian Chargé d'Affaires in Paris followed [3]. However, the Secretary-General seems to have adopted an unco-operative attitude and the League never even considered the Albanian case [4].

The above " treaty " between Italy and Albania, whereby the latter abdicated in favour of the former the right to conduct its own foreign relations, became the signal for the winding up of foreign diplomatic missions in Tirana [5]. The British Government granted *de facto* recognition in November 1939 by applying to the Italian Government for an exequatur for the British consul in Durazzo [6], and after the French collapse in 1940 granted King Zog asylum on the express condition that he would not engage in any political activity [7].

On the other hand, the United States firmly refused to recognize the Italian conquest [8]. The Albanian Legation in Washington continued to exist until 1942, when the Albanian Minister died [9]. An identical attitude was adopted by Turkey and Egypt where the Albanian Legations were also allowed to remain [10]. Similarly, Albania's name was retained both on the League of Nations' and the International Labour Office list of Member States [11]. Yet, the Albanian problem did not give rise to any wide repercussions in international relations, in view of the progressive decline of the League of Nations and the approaching war.

---

1. Ciano, *Diaries*, edited by Hugh Gibson, Doubleday & Co. Inc., Garden City, New York, 1946, pp. 51-66.
2. See above, p. 187.
3. Langer, *op. cit.*, p. 245.
4. *Ibid.*
5. *Ibid.*, p. 247.
6. *Ibid.*, p. 248.
7. *Basic Handbook*, II, p. 61.
8. Langer, *op. cit.*, p. 248.
9. Wright, *Attitude of the United States towards Austria*, p. 100.
10. *Basic Handbook*, pp. 61-62.
11. Langer, *op. cit.*, p. 246; *I.L.O. Yearbooks*, 1938-39, 1939-40.

4. THE PROBLEM OF ALBANIA'S EXTINCTION.

The territory of the independent State of Albania had been completely occupied by the Italian-created puppet State, — in other words, by Italy herself. The alleged Albanian revolution was an Italian-engineered fake. Moreover, although it appears that there was some resistance to the Italian rule both before and after Italy's entry into the war, it does not seem to have been either continuous or sufficiently organized for Italian domination to be considered as mere belligerent occupation [1]. Thus, as in the case of Czechoslovakia, none of the three classical rules could have operated to uphold Albania's continuity.

It should be added that, with the exceptions mentioned above, the Italian conquest of Albania secured international recognition. No Albanian government in exile made its appearance either before or after the outbreak of the Second World War.

Thus, again as in the case of Czechoslovakia, a *prima facie* examination would lead to the conclusion that the independent Albanian State has become extinct. This was not, however, the solution of the problem of Albanian continuity adopted by subsequent State practice and treaty provisions which must now be examined.

5. THE RESTORATION OF ALBANIA.

Following Italy's entry into the war against the Allies on June 11, 1941, statements were made by the Allied Governments with regard to Albania. Thus, on December 17, 1942, the British Foreign Secretary declared in the House of Commons :

" H.M. Government ... wish to see Albania freed from Italian yoke and restored to her independence [2]. "

On December 12, 1942, the United States Department of State issued a statement that :

" ... Consistent with its well established policy not to recognize territorial conquest by force, the Government of the United States has never recognized the annexation of Albania by the Italian crown. The restoration of a free Albania is inherent in that statement of principle [3]. "

Already towards the end of the war Italy seems to have been losing whatever hold she had had on Albania. While reliable evidence concerning Albanian resistance is scarce, it would appear that in autumn 1944 the country was completely freed from Italian occupation [4]. Albanian authority was re-established and Albania made her re-entry on the international stage.

On November 10, 1945, i.e. long before the conclusion of the Italian Peace Treaty, the United States Government addressed to Albania a characteristic Note which stated *inter alia :*

---

1. *Basic Handbook*, II, pp. 53-58.
2. Quoted by Langer, *op. cit.*, p. 248.
3. Quoted by Langer, *loc. cit. ; Basic Handbook*, II, p. 60.
4. Langer, *op. cit.*, p. 250.

" ... The Government of the United States also desires that the Albanian authorities shall confirm that the treaties and agreements which were in force between the United States and Albania on April 7, 1939, remain valid [1]... "

In other words, true to its consistent attitude of non-recognition of Italian aggression and its consequences, the United States proclaimed the legal continuity of the Albanian State.

This continuity was equally emphatically affirmed by the key instrument on the subject, the Italian Peace Treaty of February 10, 1947, whose Section VI, concerning Albania, reads :

Art. 27. Italy recognizes and undertakes to respect the sovereignty and independence of the State of Albania.

. . . .

Art. 29. Italy renounces in favour of Albania all property (apart from normal diplomatic and consular premises), rights, concessions, interests and advantages of all kind in Albania, belonging to the Italian State or Italian para-statal institutions. Italy likewise renounces all claims to special interests or influence in Albania, acquired as a result of the aggression of April 7, 1939, or under treaties or agreements concluded before that date.

The economic clauses of the present Treaty, applicable to the Allied and Associated Powers, shall apply to other Italian property and other economic relations between Albania and Italy.

Art. 30. Italian nationals in Albania will enjoy the same juridical status as other foreign nationals, but Italy recognizes the legality of all Albanian measures annulling or modifying concessions or special rights granted to Italian nationals provided that such measures are taken within a year from the coming into force of the present Treaty.

Art. 31. Italy recognizes that all agreements and arrangements made between Italy and the authorities installed in Albania by Italy from April 7, 1939, to September 3, 1943, are null and void.

Art. 32. Italy recognizes the legality of any measures which Albania may consider necessary to take in order to confirm or give effect to the preceding provisions. "

Moreover, Art. 74 of the Treaty granted Albania reparations from Italy to the amount of 5.000.000 dollars.

The significance of these Treaty provisions for the problem of Albania's legal continuity is clear. In the first place, Art. 29 expressly stigmatizes the Italian action against Albania of April 7, 1939, as aggression. Italy is consequently made to renounce her special position in Albania, acquired as a result of that aggression. Moreover, the Treaty directly disposes of the Italian attempt made at the time to camouflage the seizure of Albania as union between two independent States, based on genuine bilateral treaties and arrangements : for it is precisely these treaties and arrangements, forming the alleged legal

---

1. Quoted by Prof. Guggenheim, *op. cit.*, p. 248 who adds : « Les Etats-Unis d'Amérique admettent la continuité de l'Etat albanais avant 1939 et après 1944... Cette déclaration admet la validité ininterrompue des conventions américano-albanaises conclues avant le 7 avril 1939. » Cf. the Soviet attitude : on December 22, 1942, the Soviet agency TASS wrote : « Les journaux de Moscou publièrent la déclaration du Commissariat du Peuple aux Affaires Etrangères de l'U.R.S.S., consacrée au problème de l'indépendance de l'Albanie. Le Commissariat du Peuple des Affaires Etrangères, dit cette déclaration, précise que l'Union Soviétique, qui sympathise entièrement avec la lutte courageuse pour la libération menée par les patriotes albanais contre les envahisseurs italiens, ne reconnaît aucune prétention de l'impérialisme italien au territoire de l'Albanie et désire voir l'Albanie libérée du joug des envahisseurs fascistes, et son indépendance restaurée. » *Basic Handbook*, II, p. 60.

basis of Italian domination of Albania which Italy is now made to recognize as null and void *ab initio*, i.e. retroactively, with the *ex tunc* date specified beyond any doubt. Simultaneously, Albania is given *carte blanche* to give whatever effect she wishes to that key provision, whereas Italy is made to recognize in advance the legality of any such measures which Albania may take [1].

Thus both the initial Italian aggression and its legal consequences are made subject of an annulment which is absolute, *ex tunc*, *ab initio*. Since the Italian action is thus deprived of any validity, the positive conclusion is that legally Albania never ceased to exist.

This is further borne out by the duty imposed on Italy to pay reparations to Albania. As in the case of Ethiopia [2] it is obvious that no reparations could have possibly been paid to a new State, but only to an old one, in respect of the unlawful acts of which it had been victim.

The analysis of the Albanian section of the Treaty would not be complete without a further analysis of its Art. 31, the significance of which goes far beyond the particular case of Albania. For the Article represents the first conventional provision bearing directly on the problem of puppet creations as a means of acting *in fraudem legis*.

Art. 31 clearly states that whatever local authorities existed in Albania after the Italian invasion were established by Italy. They were not *Albanian* authorities at all, which is made clear even by the omission of the word " Albanian " from the text. They had been " installed " by Italy. But since Italy was not competent to " install " in Albania Albanian governments or authorities, she could only install her own organs, by whatever name she chose to call them. This alone determines the puppet character of such authorities and of the State they were supposed to represent. For in no independent State are its authorities set up by a foreign Power.

However, the Treaty goes even further than laying down this vital principle. Being puppet authorities, that is, in fact organs of the Italian State, these authorities could not be party to valid international agreements, and they could not in any form engage Albania's international responsibility. Being concluded by fake authorities, these agreements were themselves fake. They were not international agreements at all, since Italy could not have concluded international agreements with her own organs, — i.e., with herself. They were unilateral decisions of the occupying Power, disguised as international conventions. The Treaty draws the only possible and correct conclusion by declaring them null and void *ab initio*. Albania is not bound by them ; her international responsibility is not engaged and they do not affect her in any way.

---

1. Prof. Guggenheim comments : « ...le traité... prévoit à l'article 31 que les conventions et arrangements conclus par les autorités établies par l'Italie en Albanie entre le 7 avril 1939 et le 3 septembre 1943 sont considérés nuls et non avenus. L'article 32 ajoute à la charge de l'Italie la reconnaissance de la force obligatoire des mesures prises par l'Albanie en vue de donner effet aux dispositions de l'article 31. Si l'Albanie le juge opportun elle peut donc annuler non seulement *ex nunc*, mais aussi *ex tunc*, les mesures prises par l'Italie en qualité de puissance occupante ou sous son influence entre le 7 avril 1939 et le 3 septembre 1943. » *Op. cit.*, p. 248.

2. See above, p. 277.

There is no other way in which international law can properly meet the challenge of an *actio in fraudem legis* by means of puppet creations. The same view was adopted and the same conclusion drawn over a century earlier by Commissioner Kane with regard to the French-engineered Dutch puppet State [1]. The same view was to be adopted and the same conclusions were again to be drawn two years later in a general norm embodied in the Geneva Convention, outlawing puppet governments created by an occupant [2]. Art. 31 of the Italian Treaty represents an individual norm on the subject, equally true to the nature of international law and equally pointing to the same evolution and crystallization of that law. In spite of its individual character, it thus assumes a far more general significance.

It can therefore be safely concluded that the Peace Treaty with Italy effected the full restoration of Albania on the basis of her continuity, that is, of the identity between the post-war and the pre-invasion Albanian State.

Moreover, as in the case of Ethiopia and Czechoslovakia, further evidence of Albania's continuity is to be found in the fact of her uninterrupted membership of international organisations, such as the International Labour Office, the Universal Postal Union and the International Telecommunication Union, without any new act of accession on her part. Similarly, Albania continued to be a party to multilateral conventions signed by her prior to April 7, 1939 [3].

6. Conclusion : Legal Basis of Albania's Continuity.

The conclusions to be drawn here are the same as in the case of Czechoslovakia.

All the available evidence, unchallenged from any quarter goes to prove Albania's survival and her effective restoration on the basis of her legal continuity. At the same time, there is no crystallized rule of general international law against which such evidence — derived from State practice and conventional law — could be tested. But as in the case of Czechoslovakia, there remains the fundamental principle *ex iniuria ius non oritur* to which this evidence fully conforms.

In the face of such evidence, and failing any other protective rule, the inevitable conclusion is that the Albanian State survived the Italian conquest, effective foreign domination, partial recognition of that conquest by third States, and even the absence of any continuing State organs either in the country or in exile, on the strength of this principle alone. The latter was thus affirmed in international practice for the second time within a short period [4].

---

1. See above, pp. 171-173.
2. See above, pp. 116-120.
3. *Signatures, Ratifications*, etc.
4. Perhaps even for the third time if Italian domination of Ethiopia had in fact passed the stage of mere belligerent occupation ; see above, p. 279. For problems connected with the actual restoration of a temporarily suppressed State, see below, pp. 582-586.

CHAPTER VII.

AUSTRIA (II).

1. AUSTRIA'S SPECIAL POSITION UNDER INTERNATIONAL LAW.

The birth of the Austrian Republic at the end of the first World War has been examined in Chapter II, Part II. As an independent State, Austria was entitled to the protection of that independence by general international law. As a Member of the League of Nations she was protected by the Covenant, in particular by Art. 10. But over and above this, Austrian independence had been singled out for special protection under conventional international law; it was in fact imposed as a legal duty on Austria herself as well as on the international community. With regard to Austria, Art. 88 of the Treaty of Saint-Germain stated :

" The independence of Austria is inalienable otherwise than with the consent of the Council of the League of Nations. Consequently Austria undertakes in the absence of the consent of the said Council to abstain from any act which might directly or indirectly or by any means whatever compromise her independence, particularly, and until her admission to membership of the League of Nations, by participation in the affairs of another Power. "

This obligation was re-affirmed in the Geneva Protocol of October 4, 1922, in which Great Britain, France, Italy and Czechoslovakia, as well as the acceding countries, Spain and Belgium, undertook to

" respect the political independence, the territorial integrity and the sovereignty of Austria ",

whereas Austria undertook

" in accordance with the terms of Art. 88 of the Treaty of Saint-Germain, not to alienate its independence; it will abstain from any negotiations or from any economic or financial engagement calculated directly or indirectly to compromise this independence. This undertaking shall not prevent Austria from maintaining, subject to the provisions of the Treaty of Saint-Germain, her freedom in the matter of customs tariffs and commercial or financial agreement, and, in general, in all matters relating to her economic regime or her commercial relations, provided always that she shall not violate her economic independence by granting to any State a special regime or exclusive advantages calculated to threaten this independence ".

These basic obligations were again re-affirmed in the Lausanne Protocol of July 15, 1932.

In the prevailing situation it was clear that Austrian independence had to be protected chiefly against Germany. For this reason a provision to a similar effect had been included in Art. 80 of the Treaty of Versailles, even prior to the signing of the Saint-Germain Treaty :

" Germany acknowledges and will respect strictly the independence of Austria within the frontiers which may be fixed in a Treaty between that State and the Principal Allied and Associated Powers ; she agrees that this independence shall be inalienable, except with the consent of the Council of the League of Nations. "

The corresponding duties of Austria and Germany with regard to the former's independence were thus clearly laid down in international instruments, equally binding on the international community as a whole ; their full impact was made clear beyond all doubt in the Advisory Opinion of the Permanent Court of International Justice concerning the *Austro-German Customs Regime* [1].

This special position of Austria calls for comment. It is entirely true to say with Judge Anzilotti that Art. 88 of the Saint-Germain Treaty represents a *lex specialis* as compared with general international law, in that, not content with recognizing Austria's independence, it makes it illegal for her to alienate it even of her own free will (but for the consent of the Council of the League), just as it makes it illegal for any other State to accept the renunciation of that independence in its favour [2]. There must indeed have been a forceful reason for such an unusual derogation from general international law, a reason which Judge Anzilotti stated with his usual clarity : the Article in question

" was not adopted in the interests of Austria, but in the interests of Europe as a whole [3] " — " in the higher interest of the European political system and with a view to the maintenance of peace [4] ".

Thus, Austria's independence was raised to the rank of a major general interest, embodied in the objective law of Europe and subjected to special international protection.

The importance of Austrian independence as a major European interest was again proclaimed by Great Britain, France and Italy in a communiqué of February 17, 1934, reciting that these Powers were

" convinced of the necessity to maintain the independence and integrity of Austria in agreement with the respective treaties ",

and re-affirmed on September 27 of the same year, as well as at the Stresa Conference of 1936 [5].

Finally, Germany's obligation to respect Austrian independence, imposed by Art. 80 of the Versailles Treaty, was repeated in the bilateral

---

1. *P.C.I.J.*, Ser. A/B, 41 ; reference is, however, made to Judge Anzilotti's Individual Opinion, according to which the proposed customs regime was incompatible not only — as the Court held — with the Geneva Protocol of 1922, but equally with Art. 88 of the Treaty of St. Germain.
2. *P.C.I.J.*, Ser. A/B, 41, Ind. Opinion, pp. 58-59.
3. *Ibid.*, p. 57.
4. *Ibid.*, p. 64.
5. *The Red-White-Red Book*, pp. 58-59.

Agreement on the Re-establishment of normal Austro-German Relations, of July 11, 1936, of which the two first Articles may be quoted :

" 1. In the sense of the statement of the Führer and Chancellor of the Reich of May 21, 1935, the German Government recognizes the full sovereignty of the Federal State of Austria.

2. Each of the two Governments considers the inner political condition in the other country, including the question of Austrian National Socialism, as a domestic affair of the other country which it will not influence either directly or indirectly [1]. "

2. THE ANSCHLUSS.

a) *Facts.*

The historical facts of the Anschluss are well-known and have only recently been authoritatively re-stated by the Nurnberg Tribunal [2]. The most important of these facts may be briefly recalled.

On February 12, 1938, under growing presure from Germany, the Austrian Federal Chancellor visited Hitler in Berchtesgaden. A subsequent communiqué, published in Berlin and Vienna, provided *inter alia* for a political amnesty for National Socialists in Austria, for their freedom of action " within the ranks of the Patriotic Front and all other Austrian organisations ", and, above all, for the inclusion of National Socialists into the Federal Government [3]. In consequence, Seyss-Inquart was appointed Austrian Minister of Public Security.

At the beginning of March, the Austrian Chancellor announced the holding of a plebiscite for the 13th of the month, in which the population of Austria would decide the question of the maintenance of Austrian independence. This brought about a quick chain of reactions from the German Government. On the 11th, a German ultimatum required the abandonment of the plebiscite. Under the threat of immediate German invasion the ultimatum was complied with. But another one followed immediately : this time Germany demanded the dismissal of the Austrian Chancellor and Government and the formation of a new government under Seyss-Inquart. Under the same threat of invasion, Austria submitted to the second ultimatum. However, before resigning, the Austrian Chancellor succeeded in informing in a broadcast speech the Austrian people and the world at large of what had occurred and declared that Austria was " yielding to force " [4]. Immediately afterwards, Seyss-Inquart assumed control. A telegram bearing his signature was published in which he requested the German Government to send troops into Austria " to prevent bloodshed ". On

---

1. *Ibid.*, p. 60. Statement referred to in point 1 read : " Germany has neither the intention nor the wish to interfere in the internal affairs of Austria, to annex it, or to realize the Anschluss. " Quoted by Wright, *The Legality of the Annexation of Austria by Germany*, A. J., 1944, p. 625.
2. *Judgment*, pp. 17-19 ; see also Wright, *op. cit.*, pp. 631-633 ; Langer, *op. cit.*, pp. 155-157 ; the relevant documents from the *Red-White-Red Book*.
3. Text quoted by Wright, *op. cit.*, p. 627.
4. " ...dass wir der Gewalt weichen. " Verosta, *Die internationale Stellung Oesterreichs*, p. 24.

the 12th, German troops were already well within the Austrian borders ; Hitler was welcomed in Linz by Seyss-Inquart who declared that Art. 88 of the Saint-Germain Treaty was no longer valid. On the 13th, a law was published by the Seyss-Inquart Government, providing for Austria's incorporation into Germany. It should be added that the Austrian President refused to sign the law and resigned his office, whereupon he was succeeded by Seyss-Inquart himself who signed it in the name of Austria [1]. A corresponding German law of the same date reproduced the Austrian law and in turn provided for Austria's absorption into Germany [2]. Third States and the League of Nations were notified by Germany that the Austrian State has ceased to exist [3].

On April 10, 1938, a plebiscite was arranged in which the Austrian population was to express its opinion on the incorporation into Germany. According to official figures, of 4.284.795 voters 4.273.884 approved of the incorporation [4].

The Austrian Government ceased to exist. None was formed in exile. No Austrian diplomatic mission abroad remained in function [5].

b) *Legal Evaluation.*

The above summary of events shows that Germany did not proceed against Austria either on the pattern of a straightforward aggression, as in the case of the Italian attack on Ethiopia, or on the Czechoslovak pattern. The proceedings were rather alleged to represent Austria's voluntary merger with Germany, admittedly achieved in a revolutionary manner. Such a claim appears to be supported by the fact of the German army supposedly marching into Austria at the invitation of an Austrian Chancellor, of the incorporation being effected by an Austrian — as well as a German — law and finally by the overwhelming result of the plebiscite. The possibility of a free, although revolutionary, merger of the Austrian Republic with the German Reich cannot therefore be dismissed without further analysis.

The Berchtesgaden agreement, providing for the nomination of German agents to the Austrian Government already bore the characteristics of a piece of drastic intervention by one country into the internal affairs of another, in spite of its acceptance by the Austrian Government. German intervention proceeded a step further with the ultimatum requiring the cancellation of the plebiscite. There followed the actual appointment by Germany of the last allegedly Austrian Government.

It need hardly be emphasized once again that no government of an independent State can be appointed and installed by a foreign State. Germany was not competent to install an Austrian Government in

---

1. *Judgment*, p. 19.
2. See Klinghoffer, *Les aspects juridiques de l'occupation de l'Autriche par l'Allemagne*, pp. 31-55.
3. Langer, *op. cit.*, p. 158 ; Verosta, *op. cit.*, pp. 29-31.
4. *Journal des Nations*, Geneva, of April 12, 1938, quoting Bürckel, the commissary for the plebiscite. — Figures given by Klinghoffer, *op. cit.*, p. 57, differ from the above, being 4.447.138 and 4.443.208, respectively.
5. Langer, *op. cit.*, p. 161.

Austria. She could only install there her own delegated authorities, her own organs, however described. In relation to Austria and her legal order, these authorities were a typical puppet government.

Being a mere tool, the puppet Austrian Chancellor had no competence to throw open Austrian territory to a foreign army. But even that invitation was a fake : Seyss-Inquart's alleged telegram was never signed or sent by him ; it had been dictated by Goering to the German Embassy in Vienna [1].

What is even more important, is the fact that a puppet government, that is, an organ of a foreign State, could not issue a valid Austrian law ; consequently, the allegedly Austrian law of incorporation was legally non-existent. It may also be observed that this law was issued *after* the actual invasion of Austria by the German army. With regard to the corresponding German law, it should be noted that not only did it also follow, and not precede, the German invasion, but that is was actually dated from Linz, that is, Austrian territory [2]. Consequently, any suggestion that the two corresponding laws amounted to an international agreement, must be categorically dismissed. In the first place, they could not have been the basis of Germany's annexation of Austria, since they were enacted after such annexation ; in the second place, there could have been no international agreement for the simple reason that one of the contracting parties was absent, since the allegedly Austrian incorporation law was passed by organs of the German State [3].

There remains the possibility of the plebiscite of April 10, 1938, being a revolutionary act by which the Austrian population, assuming the function of a State organ, effected a merger with the German Reich.

The presumption of the fake character of revolution under foreign occupation has already been adequately discussed. In the Austrian case this presumption is further reinforced by the fact, also discussed previously, that, once overpowered, the Austrians allegedly agreed to do what they had refused to do freely, that is, to submit to the incorporation designs of Germany [4]. If such an overwhelming percentage of the Austrian population had in fact been in favour of an incorporation, then it is difficult to see why Germany feared the result of a plebiscite on the same question in an independent Austria to the extent of demanding its cancellation by way of an ultimatum. Further, the plebiscite took place several weeks after the actual seizure of Austria by Germany ; thus, again, it could not have served as the basis of a fusion which had already been accomplished. Moreover, in the course of those weeks not only was the German military hold on the country tightened, but the German administration, including the Gestapo, had fully taken over. In such circumstances, the plebiscite

---

1. *Judgment*, p. 18.
2. Klinghoffer, *op. cit.*, p. 54 ; Verosta, *op. cit.*, pp. 29-31.
3. Cf. the Italian Peace Treaty on the alleged Italo-Albanian agreements above, pp. 336-337.
4. See above, pp. 65-66.

was a foregone conclusion [1]. To quote once again the convincing argument of an authority on the question : such a plebiscite could be taken seriously only in the improbable event of its results being in clear contradiction to the wishes of the occupant [2]. This, as has been seen, was not the case in Austria where, on the contrary, the customary 99, 73 % in favour of the occupant was duly achieved, thus defeating the very purpose of the occupant by its utter lack of moderation [3].

There was thus no free, revolutionary merger of Austria with the German Reich. There was a violent absorption of Austria into Germany, which constituted the first step on Germany's road to further conquests.

By proceeding with the Anschluss, Germany acted in clear violation of general international law protecting the integrity and independence, in other words, the internationally delimited separate personality of States. Furthermore, Germany violated her own conventional obligations concerning Austria, — in the first place, Art. 80 of the Treaty of Versailles, as well as Art. 434 of that same Treaty by which she had recognized in advance the treaties to be concluded by the Allied and Associated Powers with her ex-allies, and which thus covered the Saint-Germain Treaty. She further violated her freely accepted obligations under the bilateral German-Austrian agreement of July 11, 1936. There can also be no doubt that she violated the Briand-Kellogg Pact.

It must therefore be concluded that, far from representing a voluntary merger, the Anschluss constituted an unlawful act on the part of Germany. This unlawful act was directed against a specially protected major European interest.

3. INTERNATIONAL RECOGNITION OF THE ANSCHLUSS AND OF AUSTRIA'S EXTINCTION.

a) *Facts.*

As regards third States, only Great Britain and France lodged direct protests with the German Government [4]. Only one more formal protest seems to have been lodged, namely by Mexico, this time with the Secretary-General of the League of Nations [5]. Apart from this, the reaction of the international community did not go beyond expressions of general condemnation of the German action, however strongly worded [6]. Whereupon, Austria's extinction seems to have been taken for granted. Lord Halifax, for instance, declared in the House of Lords, on March 16 :

---

1. Thus the British Foreign Secretary in the House of Lords, on March 16, 1938; quoted by Langer, *op. cit.*, p. 161.
2. Wambaugh, quoted above, p. 65, *f.-n.* 3.
3. " The very result of the plebiscite as announced, namely, 99,73 % for to 0,27 % against (!), is sufficient to indicate its untrustworthiness as an index of the real attitude of the Austrians, for such unanimity in human affairs is almost morally impossible, even on innocuous questions. " Wright, *Attitude of the United States towards Austria*, p. 89.
4. Verosta, *op. cit.*, pp. 25-26.
5. Verosta, *op. cit.*, pp. 32-34.
6. See statements quoted by Verosta, *op. cit.*, pp. 26-41 and Langer, *op. cit.*, pp. 157-160.

" His Majesty's Government are therefore bound to recognize that the Austrian State has now been abolished as an international entity and is in process of being entirely absorbed into the German Reich [1]... "

Foreign missions in Vienna either closed down or were turned into consulates [2]. Austria's name disappeared from the League of Nations' roster [3], as well as from the list of States Members of the International Labour Office and the Universal Postal Union, while the corresponding list of the International Telecommunication Union carried a non-committal note stating that according to a communication from the German administration Austria has ceased to be a Member [4]. It must further be pointed out that the Munich Agreement on the Sudetenland implied a renewed and unmistakable recognition of Austria's extinction, since further extension of German frontiers could not be conceived without the assumption of German sovereignty over Austria [5].

The strongest reluctance to recognize the Anschluss is to be found in the attitude of the United States. Yet, even this initial attitude was made particularly difficult for the American Government in view of the fact that it was not only the German Embassy, but actually the Austrian Minister to Washington himself who officially notified the extinction of his country and the consequent taking over of his mission by the German Embassy [6]. Even so, in its first reaction the United States appears to have emphasized the purely practical character of the steps it was taking to conform to the new situation. Thus, the first of the two Notes addressed on April 6 to the German Foreign Minister declared:

" The Government of the United States finds itself under the necessity as a practical measure of closing its Legation at Vienna and of establishing a Consulate General ",

while the second included the following significant passage :

" In view of the announcement made to the Government of the United States by the Austrian Minister on March 17, 1938, my Government is under the necessity for all practical purposes of accepting what he says as a fact and accordingly consideration is being given to the adjustments in its own practices and procedure in various regards which will be necessitated by the change of status of Austria [7]. "

Yet, this same Note already expressed the American Government's expectation that the German Government would live up to its duties as Austria's successor. This was followed up by the Note of June 7, 1938, insisting on the principle of international law, according to which

" in case of absorption of a State, the substituted sovereignty assumes the debts and obligations of the absorbed State, and takes the burdens with the benefits [8] ".

---

1. Quoted by Langer, *op. cit.*, p. 161.
2. Reut-Nicolussi, *Um die Rechtskontinuität Oesterreichs*, p. 245 ; Langer, *op. cit.*, p. 161.
3. Langer, *op. cit.*, p. 164.
4. *I.L.O. Yearbooks* for 1938-39 and 1939-40 ; *Rapports de gestion* of the U.P.U. and I.T.U.
5. Reut-Nicolussi, *op. cit.*, p. 245.
6. Langer, *op. cit.*, pp. 161-162.
7. Langer, *op. cit.*, p. 162.
8. *Ibid.*, p. 166.

Thus, not only the clear admission by the United States of Austria's " absorption by Germany", but the very fact of insisting upon succession, meant recognition of Austria's extinction. This plain fact cannot be argued away by limiting its significance to purely practical steps which the United States found itself compelled to take [1]. Nor can any such reasoning be applied to the arrangement of November 11, 1939, by which the United States consented to consider as extinct her extradition treaty with Austria and to have the extradition treaty with Germany extended to cover Austrian territory [2].

The final proof of the recognition of Austria's extinction by the Anglo-Saxon countries is supplied by the treatment of Austrian nationals in Britain and the United States [3]. The existence of a separate Austrian nationality was denied, Austrians were considered German nationals and, at the outbreak of war, they were placed in the category of enemy aliens, while their property was considered enemy property [4].

There can therefore be no doubt that the German seizure of Austria and, consequently, the extinction of the latter, achieved international recognition.

---

1. Thus, incorrectly, Langer, *op. cit.*, p. 163.
2. The recognition of Austria's extinction, implied in this act, is admitted even by Langer, *op. cit.*, p. 167.
3. See the lengthy analysis by Langer, *op. cit.*, pp. 167-181.
4. This fact was strongly reflected in the attitude of American courts. While in May 1939, the Municipal Court of the City of New York, Borough of Manhattan, in the case of *Johnson v. Briggs Inc.* could still speak of the lack of evidence " of the recognition by this government of the alleged seizure of Austria by the German Government " and declare that " So far as this Court knows, the annexation of Austria by Germany has not received official recognition ", A. D., 1938/40, case no. 33, — all subsequent decisions accept the fact of annexation. Thus, in the case *Land Oberösterreich v. Gude*, the U.S. Circuit Court of Appeals for the Second Circuit, declared on February 13, 1940 : " This change has occurred in a manner acceptable to our notions of international law; the Anschluss has in no wise been disavowed by the Department of State. " *Ibid.*, no. 34. Similarly, in the case of *United States ex Rel. Zdunic v. Uhl, District Director of Immigration and Naturalization*, the District Court, Southern District of New York, held on August 11, 1942 : " ...the so-called " Anschluss " was consummated, and Austria became and since has been a state of the German Reich... " A. D., 1941/42, case no. 164. In *United States ex Rel. D'Esquiva v. Uhl*, the Circuit Court of Appeals, Second Circuit, described Austria on August 18, 1943, as " a place which has now been recognized by our government as a component part of a nation with which we are at war. " Even Secretary Hull's statement of July 27, 1942 (see below, p. 347) was not considered by the court as conclusive evidence to the contrary, since it was not clear to the court whether it meant definite non-recognition of Austria's annexation or just a condemnation of the proceedings. A. D., 1943/45, case no. 8. In *United States ex Rel. Schwarzkopf v. Uhl*, the same Court equally took its stand on a recognition, at least *de facto*, by the United States of Austria's annexation, although it considered that fact immaterial to its decision as to the nationality. *Ibid.*, no. 54. Finally as late as December 1, 1944, the Supreme Court, although this time asserting American non-recognition, re-affirmed the applicability of German law in Austria. *Eck v. N.V. Nederlandsch Amerikanische Stoomvaart Maatschappij*, A. D., 1946, case no. 13. It is therefore impossible to acquiesce in Wright's claim — *op. cit.*, — according to which the United States never recognized Austria's extinction, — even if such claim is made on the basis of the following opening passage of Secretary Hull's statement of July 27, 1942 : " It is probable that such confusion, if it exists, has arisen from administrative steps which may have been taken by this Government in pursuance of its own laws designed to afford adequate protection to this country's interests in dealing with the situation presented by the imposition of military control over Austria and residents of Austria by Germany. "

b) *Legal Evaluation.*

At this stage an analysis of the legal value of this recognition must be undertaken, in the same way in which it was undertaken in the case of Ethiopia [1].

It is submitted that — as in the Ethiopian case — the recognition of the German conquest by States Members of the League was in clear violation of their obligations under the Covenant and particularly Article 10, as well as of the Assembly Resolution of March 11, 1932. For the United States, the recognition ran directly counter to what had been proclaimed to the world as a fundamental principle in the Stimson Doctrine. It may also be argued that such recognition was contrary to the Briand-Kellogg Pact.

But, moreover, these acts of recognition dealt an illegal blow to that specially protected Austrian independence which had been erected by the Peace Treaties into a major European interest, — in other words, it ran counter to the objective law of Europe. This interest had not been subject to a revision ; it was simply violated by the signatories of the treaties in question. For it is true to say that in no case could recognition by individual Members of the Council of the League take the place of the consent of the Council as a body, as required by Art. 88 of the Saint-Germain Treaty [2] ; and it is equally true to say that no legal revision of that Treaty could have been brought about by individual acts of law-breaking on the part of its signatories.

The international recognition of Austria's extinction was thus itself tainted with illegality. As such, it could not have rendered the German aggression legal [3], even if it were to be assumed *per maxime inconcessum* that such miraculous constitutive powers can attach to an act of recognition.

4. The Problem of Austria's Extinction.

The position of Austria prior to the outbreak of the Second World War may be summarized as follows : *a)* there was an effective absorption of Austria into Germany ; *b)* that absorption had achieved international recognition ; *c)* no organ, however rudimentary, of the Austrian State was left to assert and carry on her legal continuity. The extinction of a State could hardly seem more complete [4].

And yet, within eighteen months of the Anschluss, the Second World War broke out, and already in the first years of the conflagration Austria was described by Allied statesmen as the first victim of Hitler's Germany on whose behalf also the Allied sword had now been drawn [5].

On September 9, 1942, the British Foreign Secretary declared :

---

1. See above, pp. 271-272.
2. Thus Klinghoffer, *op. cit.*, pp. 20-21.
3. Thus, Reut-Nicolussi, *op. cit.*, pp. 245-246.
4. " ...dadurch ist äusserlich ein Bild des Unterganges des Staates entstanden. " Reut-Nicolussi, *op. cit.*, p. 245.
5. Churchill in November 1940 and February 1942 ; see Verosta, *op. cit.*, pp. 42 and 46.

" The policy of H.M. Government towards Austria was stated by my Rt. Hon. Friend the Prime Minister at the Mansion House on 9th November 1940, when he said that Austria is one of the countries for whom we have drawn the sword and for whom our victory will supply liberation. While H.M. Government cannot of course commit themselves at this stage to recognize or support the establishment in the future of any particular frontiers in Central Europe, I must make it plain that H.M. Government equally do not regard themselves as being bound by any change effected in Austria since 1938 [1]. "

The statement of the United States Secretary of State of July 27, 1942, was even more emphatic :

" This Government very clearly made known its opinions as to the manner in which the seizure of Austria took place and the relation of that seizure to this Government's well-known policy toward the taking of territory by force. *This Government has never taken the position that Austria was legally absorbed into the German Reich* [2]. "

On November 1, 1943, the Moscow Conference of Great Britain, the United States and the Soviet Union declared the annexation of Austria null and void. In April 1945, following the Soviet capture of Vienna, the restoration of the Austrian Republic was proclaimed by representatives of the Austrian political parties. The re-born Austrian State is to-day a political and legal reality. Is it a new State creation on the territory of the old State which has become extinct in 1938, — or is it identical with the 1938 Austrian Republic which, far from being extinct, continued its legal existence throughout the years of annexation and de-recognition ?

It must at once be admitted that — as in the case of Czechoslovakia and Albania — Austria's continuity was not protected by any of the three existing rules on the subject. There was obviously no question of a territorial loss. Nor was there room for an application of the rule concerning revolutionary changes ; in the first place, the alleged revolution in Austria was a fake ; but, moreover, even if it had been genuine, a State cannot survive a revolution whose aim and achieved result is precisely the abolition of its State character. Finally, in the total absence of war there was no belligerent occupation, whatever the possibility of an *analogy* between illegal seizure of territory and belligerent occupation.

Yet again — as in the case of Czechoslovakia and Albania — any rash conclusion as to Austria's extinction would have to proceed on an inadmissible assumption of a final petrification of international law and on a denial of the possibility of its further development. Such a view would in turn be contradicted by the inherently dynamic nature of any legal system.

For this reason, in the absence of a clear ruling of general international law, it is again necessary to examine in the first place the actual international practice with regard to Austria. The results of this examination must in turn be tested for their legal relevance against the principles and nature of international law.

---

1. *Parl. Deb., Com.*, vol. CCCLXXXIII, col. 123-124.
2. *It. mine*, quoted by Langer, *op. cit.*, p. 171.

The fact that the long-expected Treaty with Austria has not yet materialized cannot form any obstacle to such an investigation. For time has not stood still in the eleven years which have elapsed from the Moscow Declaration and the nine years which have elapsed since the re-birth of the Austrian State, and sufficient evidence has accumulated during this period to permit conclusions as to the identity or otherwise of the present Austrian Republic with the one of 1938. Whatever the future Treaty may contain, it will not be able to prevail against the existing situation such as has in fact been established in the course of these years. This situation must now be analysed.

5. The Restoration of Austria.

a) *State Practice.*

The basic pronouncement on the legal status of Austria is to be found in the Moscow Declaration by the United Kingdom, the United States and the Soviet Union, of November 1, 1943, — i.e. during actual hostilities and in face of the continued effectiveness of German domination of Austria. The Declaration read :

" The Governments of the United Kingdom, the Soviet Union and the United States of America are agreed that Austria, the first free country to fall victim to Hitler's aggression, shall be liberated from German domination.

They regard the annexation imposed upon Austria by Germany on March 15, 1938, as null and void. They consider themselves in no way bound by any changes effected in Austria since that date. They declare that they wish to see re-established a free and independent Austria, and thereby to open the way for the Austrian people themselves, as well as those neighbouring States which will be faced with similar problems, to find that political and economic security which is the only basis for lasting peace.

Austria is reminded, however, that she has a responsibility which she cannot evade for participation in the war on the side of Hitlerite Germany and that in the final settlement account will inevitably be taken of her own contribution to her liberation [1]. "

The Declaration was endorsed by the French Committee of National Liberation in a statement issued at Algiers, on November 16, 1943 [2].

The Declaration represents a clear and unequivocal statement of nullity which is absolute and unqualified [3]. It is a voidance *ex tunc*, thus nullifying the German aggression itself, as well as all legal consequences resulting therefrom. Since the German annexation of Austria is null and void, i.e. incapable of producing any legal changes, it is only logical that the Powers concerned declare themselves in no way bound by such changes and proclaim it as their aim not to create an Austrian State, but to " re-establish " it. The Declaration represents a recognition of Austria's *status quo*, unchanged in any way by the

---

1. *Doc.*, vol. VI, p. 231.
2. Verosta, *op. cit.*, p. 54.
3. Thus, correctly, Verdross, *Die völkerrechtliche Identität von Staaten*, p. 20 ; similarly, Verosta, for whom this " Nichtigkeitserklärung " is " unbedingt und absolut. " *Op. cit.*, p. 7.

invalid Anschluss. No other interpretation is logically possible. For if the Anschluss was null and void from its inception, then it could have no legal consequences and Austria remained exactly as she had been [1].

The full significance of this declaration of nullity and its absolute character result with particular clarity from its comparison with the guarded Note by which the British Government repudiated the Munich Agreement [2]. There, the declaration of nullity was only implied, not stated *expressis verbis ;* moreover, it was not made *ex tunc*, with specific reference to a given date, and it was only by way of interpretation that it could be related back to the events of March 15, 1939, but not to the original act. Here, the actual formula of " null and void " is used ; the *ex tunc* date is specified and the text is clear enough to make any interpretation unnecessary. The underlying political reason for this difference is probably the fact that the Munich Agreement was an international engagement to which Great Britain herself was a party, while the annexation of Austria was a unilateral illegal act in which none of the Powers participated and against which they indeed protested. But, whatever the reason, the striking difference remains to emphasize the absolute character of the Moscow Declaration.

Nor is this conclusion affected by the third paragraph of the Declaration in which political tendencies were allowed to prevail against elementary logic [3]. If Austria was Hitler's " first victim " and a country to be liberated and not vanquished, if the Anschluss was null and void, then it is difficult to see how Austria — that is, the State, — could be made responsible for contributing to the war on Germany's side any more than, for instance, Czechoslovakia, whose whole industry worked full steam for the German war machine. If what was meant was the contribution not of the State, but of individual Austrians — however numerous — then the Declaration should have said so and should have threatened them with individual sanctions. It would have been the proper way of reconciling political necessity with legal logic. As it stands, the third paragraph of the Declaration is merely an example of bad drafting [4].

It is, however, necessary clearly to appreciate not only what the Moscow Declaration was, but equally what it was not. Thus, it is impossible to agree with an Austrian writer who claims that it proves that there never had been any recognition of the Anschluss by the

---

1. " The statement, therefore, can have no other meaning than that in the eyes of the Conference Powers the annexation of Austria by Germany had not the effect of establishing German sovereignty over the Austrian territory, nor, consequently, the effect of ending the legal existence of Austria, notwithstanding the fact that the German occupant had temporarily succeeded in imposing *de facto* control on that country and that no organs of Austrian sovereignty such as a government-in-exile or diplomatic representatives had remained in function abroad. " Langer, *op. cit.*, p. 182.

2. See above, pp. 321-323.

3. Thus, correctly, Langer, *op. cit.*, p. 183, and Klinghoffer, *The Coming Austria*, pp. 36-38.

4. It is not the only one. It is truly disturbing to see the statement of such magnitude misquoting historical dates : the Anschluss, as is well known, took place on March 13, 1938, and not March 15.

Powers [1]. The fact of such recognition cannot possibly be open to doubt [2]. The additional interest of the Moscow Declaration lies precisely in the fact that the Powers declared null not only an illegal act of a third State, but indeed, their own recognition of that illegal act, and that, moreover, they did it in unchanged conditions of fact, that is, during the continued effectiveness of the German rule in Austria. This was neither new nor unique, as can be seen from the examples of Ethiopia, Czechoslovakia or Albania.

The overall significance of the Moscow Declaration cannot be overestimated. It was the first international proclamation of Austria's continuity, in spite of her physical absorption by Germany, the international recognition of her extinction and a total absence of any State organs. As such, it formed the basis of Austria's legal restoration and set the course which later international events were to follow.

No immediate practical effect could be given to the Declaration prior to an effective liberation of Austrian territory. Nevertheless, it was followed — although perhaps not soon enough — by the recognition of the Austrian nationality of Austrians residing in the Allied countries, — a recognition long denied and now granted with all the resulting consequences [3].

The unchanged status of Austria found an emphatic confirmation in the Four Power Agreement of July 9, 1945 on the respective zones of occupation, in which Austrian territory is described as the one within Austrian frontiers as they were on December 31, 1937 [4]. If, following Germany's defeat, Austria had been created as a new State, it is difficult to see why her new frontiers should have been automatically those of the old State, without any discussion and any new, and possibly differing, delimitation. The Agreement quoted must be read in conjunction with the Four Power Statement on the occupation zones in Germany, of June 5, 1945, defining German territory as the one within German frontiers " as they were on 31st December, 1937 [5] ". The latter further reinforces the submission that post-war Austria was not a new State, created out of former German territory, since the Agreement not only does not convey the idea of a cession, but merely takes it for granted that the German territory did not include Austria. In this sense, the meaning of the Four Power Agreement on the occupation zones in Germany for the problem of Austria's continuity is comparable to its meaning for the same problem with regard to Czechoslovakia [6]. When read together, these two complementary

---

1. Klinghoffer, *op. cit.*, p. 14.
2. See above, pp. 343-345.
3. For details see Langer, *op. cit.*, pp. 185 and 205. Prof. H. Wright even concluded that Austrians should be entitled to the same rights and privileges as were extented to the Czechoslovaks, Poles, Danes, Dutch, Norwegians and nationals of other overrun countries and suggested the creation of an Austrian Government in exile. *The Legality of the Annexation*, pp. 634 and 635.
4. Verosta, *op. cit.*, p. 71.
5. *Doc.* VII, p. 222.
6. See above, p. 325.

agreements emphasize Austria's continuity even more strongly than in the case of Czechoslovakia, where only the Statement on Germany applied.

At the Potsdam Conference of July 17—August 2, 1945, the Powers agreed that " reparations should be not exacted from Austria [1] ". Should Austria have been an enemy State, or have formed part of an enemy State, it could not be explained why she should be the only one to be exempted from the duty to pay reparations. As it was, the above decision of the Powers fully conforms to the initial thesis of the Moscow Conference, according to which Austria had never legally formed part of the German Reich and was, on the contrary, a victim of German aggression to be liberated from German domination. Only on the assumption of Austria's liberation, and not of her defeat, does the Potsdam decision on reparations become understandable.

A further example of the acknowledged Austrian continuity is to be seen in the question of the so-called " German assets " in Austria. According to the principle of exacting no reparations from Austria, the U.S. State Department correctly defined such assets as those properties owned by Germany in Austria before 1938 or imported into Austria after that date. Whatever Germany acquired under the illegal and invalid Anschluss, could not be treated as German property, if the declaration of nullity was to be adhered to. Running counter to the Moscow Declaration, such a view would equally infringe on the United Nations declaration of nullity of forced transfer of property in German-occupied countries of 1943. Difference of opinion arose on the subject between the Western Powers and the Soviet Union, and President Truman informed the Austrian Chancellor on July 10, 1946, that the United States would not recognize any definition of German assets which did not conform to the United Nations Declaration of 1943 and to the Moscow Declaration on Austria. Finally, even the Soviet Union made a formal concession to this view : she abandoned former requirement to have all former German property in Austria, however acquired, surrendered to her and agreed that Austrian government or private property taken over by Germany after the Anschluss without compensation or by violence should be returned to its former owners, although the burden of the proof was placed on the Austrian Government [2].

It should further be pointed out that there had never been any recognition of Austria as a State on the part of the Allies ; what was recognized was the Austrian Government, i.e. a new Government of an existing State, the latter requiring no recognition [3].

Thus, ever since the Moscow Declaration, the Allied practice with regard to Austria has been consistently based on the assumption of her legal continuity. Practically all relevant Allied documents refer to her

---

1. *Doc.* VII, p. 933.
2. See *Doc.* vol. VIII, p. 286.
3. The recognition of the Austrian Government took place on January 7, 1948 ; see Langer, *op. cit.*, p. 201. Cf. Von besonderer Seite, *Gilt das Konkordat*, *Oest. Monatshefte*, p. 221.

" liberation ". Whatever else the future Treaty with Austria may bring, it has already been made abundantly clear that it will *not* be a Peace Treaty, since in the voluminous diplomatic correspondence, official declarations, and so forth, it is consistently and purposely referred to as the *State Treaty* [1]. It is thus taken for granted that the Allies had never been at war with Austria, that is, that she had never formed part of the German State, that her legal continuity was uninterrupted by the German aggression and domination, and, consequently, that present-day Austria is identical with the pre-Anschluss Republic.

The above conclusions are fully borne out by the following summary of Austria's legal position, contained in an official statement of the United States Government of October 28, 1946 :

" ... The United States has ... regarded Austria as a country liberated from forcible domination by Nazi Germany, and not as an ex-enemy State or a State at war with the United States during the Second World War. The Department of State believes that this view has received diplomatic recognition through the Moscow Declaration on Austria and the Declaration issued at Algiers on November 16, 1943, by the French Committee of National Liberation concerning the independence of Austria. In accordance with the objectives set forth in the Moscow Declaration to see re-established a free and independent Austria, an Austrian Government was formed after free elections were held on November 25, 1945. This Austrian Government was recognized by the four Powers represented on the Allied Council, as announced simultaneously on January 7, 1945, in Vienna and the capitals of these States. In its meeting of April 25, 1946, the Allied Council, moreover, considered a statement of the United States Government's policy in Austria made by General Mark Clark, and expressed its general agreement with section I, " Status of Austria ", in which the United States maintained that since Austria has been liberated from Nazi domination it should be treated as a liberated area. In the opinion of the Department of State, the judgment of the International Military Tribunal rendered at Nurnberg on September 30 — October 1, 1946, gave further international confirmation to this view of Austria's status by defining the invasion of that country as an aggressive act — " a premiditated aggressive step in furthering the plan to wage aggressive wars against other countries ". The Nurnberg judgment also states that " Austria was in fact seized by Germany in the month of March 1938 ".

In order to clarify the attitude of the United States Government in this matter, *the United States Government recognizes Austria for all purposes, including legal and administrative, as a liberated country comparable in status to other liberated areas and entitled to the same treatment*, subject only to the controls reserved to the occupying Powers in the new agreement on control machinery in Austria of June 28, 1946. *The United States Government believes that the international acts mentioned above are adequate reason for all Members of the United Nations to regard Austria as a liberated country* [2]. "

In its comment on the Soviet Note on Austria of August 14, 1952, the State Department declared on August 18, 1952 :

" The United States was never at war with the Republic of Austria [3]. "

The United States Note to the Soviet Government of September 5, 1952, stated :

---

1. See Press reports, particularly *The Times*, for the period.
2. *It. mine*, *Doc.* VIII, p. 285.
3. *Dep. of St. Bul.*, XXVII, p. 322.

" ... the right to maintain armed forces belongs inherently to a free and independent nation and should not have to be specifically granted to a nation never considered to have been an enemy [1]. "

Although the practice of the Allies with regard to Austria's continuity was consistently uniform, these were certain isolated deviations ; a case in point is Field Marshal Alexander's proclamation on the entry of British troops into Austria [2]. It is, however, hardly possible to set such isolated and not particularly authoritative statements against the established highest-level policy.

The assumption of Austria's legal continuity is by no means limited to the Allied countries alone. Thus, Switzerland considers her pre-Anschluss treaties with Austria as in force, without any new enactment [3]. Similarly, according to the Official Journal published by the Austrian Federal Ministry of Justice of November 10, 1949, the Austrian and Belgian Governments recognized the continued validity of three Austro-Belgian extradition treaties, concluded before 1938 [4]. It should be

---

1. *Ibid.*, p. 404.
2. Verosta, *op. cit.*, p. 63.
3. " Mit Note vom 4. August 1947 liess das eidgenössische politische Department die österreichische Gesandtschaft wissen, dass schweizerischerseits sämtliche Bestimmungen der internationalen Uebereinkunft, betreffend das Zivilprozessrecht vom 17. Ju.i 1905 im Verhältnis zu Oesterreich nach wie vor angewendet werden. ...mit Note vom 28. November 1947 gab die österreichische Gesandtschaft dem politischen Department bekannt, dass die österreichische Regierung der in der schweizerischen Note zum Ausdruck gebrachten Stellungnahme hinsichtlich Fortdauer der Geltung des Haager Zivilprozessabkommens vom 17. Juli 1905 vollkommen beipflichtet. " Sammlung der Eidgenössischen Gesetze, Nr. 9, Seite 236, vom 20. März 1948. Quoted by Von besonderer Seite, *Gilt das Konkordat? Oester. Monatshefte*, 1950, p. 431. Equally No. 3 of the same collection of 1950 lists 21 treaties and conventions between Switzerland and Austria which had al! been concluded prior to 1938, as continuing in force. *Ibid.* Prof. Guggenheim, who denies the continuity of Austria, comments : " Die " Mitteilung " entspricht allerdings nicht den formellen Rechtssätzen des schweiz. Bundesstaatsrechts über die Gültigkeitsvoraussetzungen völkerrechtlicher Verträge. Da sie verschiedene Auslegungsvorschriften bezüglich völkerrechtlicher Verträge enthält und da, wie oben erwähnt, die Republik Oesterreich nach Weltkrieg II nicht mit der früheren Republik Oesterreich identisch ist, hätte die " Uebereinkunft " im Wege der dem fakultativen Referendum unterstehenden Vertragserzeugung in Kraft gesetzt werden müssen. " *Lehrbuch*, II, p. 932, *f.-n.* 482. Prof. Guggenheim does not give any reasons for denying Austria's continuity in face of all the existing evidence to the contrary. His own comment, however, seems to defeat his thesis. For, if the proper Swiss procedure for the conclusion of new treaties had not been chosen by Switzerland, this would seem to be additional proof of their being old treaties rather than of a disregard of Swiss laws by the Swiss Government. This interpretation is reinforced by the consistent attitude of the Swiss Federal Council. Prof. Guggenheim's report on public international law in the *Annuaire Suisse* of 1951, includes the following item : « Continuité des traités conclus entre la Suisse et l'Autriche : Le Recueil officiel des lois et ordonnances de la Confédération, année 1950, p. 87, contient ce communiqué de la Chancellerie fédérale, daté du 5 janvier 1950 : « Le gouvernement suisse et le gouvernement autrichien sont tombés d'accord sur le fait que les traités suivants, conclus entre la Suisse et l'Autriche, continuent à être en vigueur. » Suit une liste de traités entre la Suisse et l'Autriche, conclus entre 1868 et 1936, p. 169. » — As before, Prof. Guggenheim maintains his criticism of the official Swiss position, adding that the communiqué « ne correspond pas à l'opinion officiellement exprimée par la Suisse lors de la reconnaissance de l'Autriche par la Suisse en 1945. » This latter observation may be contested : the *Rapport de gestion* relied on by Prof. Guggenheim not only does not deny Austria's continuity, but states that « la question de la *reprise* des relations diplomatiques avec l'Autriche n'a pas encore été résolue. » *It. mine, Rapport de gestion du Conseil Fédéral*, 1945, p. 100. It is to be assumed that the word « reprise » and not e.g. « établissement » was not chosen accidentally. This seems confirmed by the Federal Council's consistency in the matter. Thus, the *Rapport de gestion* of 1946 says : « ...après que le conseil allié pour l'Autriche eut consenti à ce que le gouvernement fédéral renouât des relations diplomatiques avec la Suisse. » p. 114.
4. Von besonderer Seite, *op. cit.*, p. 431.

added that of forty States which had expressed their recognition after 1945, only a few recognized the Austrian State, whereas the great majority, including — as has been seen — the Great Powers, simply granted recognition to a new Austrian Government [1].

The conclusion is inescapable that ever since the liberation of Austria, and even before, State practice proceeded consistently on the assumption of her legal continuity.

b) *Conventional Law.*

As has been seen, the Four Powers statements on the occupation zones in Austria and Germany implicitly affirmed Austria's legal continuity [2]. The same idea results from one of the important post-war international agreements, namely, the so-called "General Treaty", concluded on May 26, 1952, in Bonn, between the United Kingdom, the U.S.A. and France on the one hand, and the Federal German Republic on the other hand. In particular, Art. 1, point 1, of Chapter 5 of the Convention on the Settlement of Matters arising out of the War and Occupation, states :

" Upon the entry into force of the present Convention, the Federal Republic shall establish, staff and equip an administrative agency, which shall, as provided in this Chapter and the Annex thereto, search for, recover and restitute jewellery, silverware and antique furniture (where individual articles are of substantial value), and cultural property, if such articles or cultural property were, *during the occupation of any territory*, removed therefrom by the forces or authorities of Germany or its Allies or their individual members (whether or not pursuant to orders) after acquisition by duress (with or without violence), by larceny, by requisitioning or by other forms of dispossession by force. "

Art. 5, 1 thereupon lists the countries to which the above stipulation shall apply :

" The provisions of this Charter shall apply in respect of the following countries as of the respective dates set forth below :

Country	Date
Austria	12th March, 1938.

. . . . [3] "

There follow, in chronological order of German invasion, Czechoslovakia, Poland, Denmark, Norway, etc.

The meaning of these provisions could hardly be clearer. Austria is treated as a country which had been occupied by Germany ; she is listed among all the other countries which had suffered German aggression and domination ; the date of German aggression against Austria is specified ; Germany's obligation of restitution towards Austria are laid down in exactly the same way as towards all the other German-overrun countries. No such treatment and no such status of equality between Austria and the other invaded countries could be possible on the assumption that, during the relevant period, Austria

---

1. *Ibid.*, p. 221. Cf. Verdross, *op. cit.*, p. 21.
2. See above, pp. 350-351.
3. *It. mine*, Cmd. 8571.

had legally formed part of the German Reich. But if this was not the case, then the Republic of Austria automatically survived in law, with its separate existence unextinguished and its legal continuity unbroken by German aggression.

c) *Practice of International Organisations.*

Before examining the practice of the principal international organisations, the characteristic attitude of a temporary international agency may be noted. The United Nations Relief and Rehabilitation Administration (UNRRA) was created to bring post-war relief to liberated, but not to enemy countries. Relief action for the benefit of an ex-enemy country would have required a change in the organisation's statutes. Yet, UNRRA's help and assistance was accorded to Austria without any such amendment. Thereby, the organisation clearly excluded Austria from the category of enemy countries, placing her under the heading of liberated territories [1].

The League of Nations, it is true, adopted a guarded attitude, resulting in a half-way solution. In reply to the Austrian Note, claiming continued Austrian membership [2], the Assembly adopted on April 12, 1946, a resolution which, after expressing satisfaction at Austria's restoration, invited

" the representatives of the Austrian Government to be present as observers at the present Assembly of the League [3] ".

The League thus did not adopt a clear attitude on the matter ; nevertheless it may be said that, without expressly confirming Austria's continuity, the League did not deny it either.

The International Labour Organisation, on the other hand, adopted a straightforward and unequivocal course. Even before Austria's actual liberation the problem was introduced in the Organisation in the following resolution of May 12, 1944 :

" The International Labour Conference takes note with satisfaction of the Moscow Declaration expressing the wish of the signatories to see *re-established* a free and independent Austria, recalls the active participation of Austria in the International Labour Organisation from 1919 to 1938, and expresses the hope that a free, independent and democratic Austria will soon *resume* her participation in the International Labour Organisation [4]. "

A resolution on similar lines was adopted by the 26th Session of the I.L.O., on June 1, 1944 [5].

Finally, the decisive resolution adopted by the 30th Session of the Organisation on June 24, 1947, stated :

" The General Conference of the International Labour Organisation,
Having been seized of an application from the Government of Austria for the re-admission of Austria to the I.L.O. ; and

---

1. See Verosta, *op. cit.*, p. 94.
2. See below, p. 361.
3. Quoted by Langer, *op. cit.*, p. 203.
4. *It. mine*, quoted by Klinghoffer, *The Coming Austria*, pp. 11-12.
5. *I.L.O., Off. Bulletin*, vol. XXVI, no. 1.

Recalling that it has always been the firm conviction of the Organisation that its ends could be more effectively advanced, if the membership of the Organisation could be made universal,

Decides to *re-admit* Austria to the I.L.O. with the same rights and obligations as the other Members of the Organisation.

The Conference takes note that Austria recognizes the principle that the obligations resulting from Conventions ratified by her prior to 13 March 1938 continue to be binding and that the Austrian Federal Government will eliminate as soon as possible changes in its laws and regulations bearing upon the application of these Conventions which were made by the German authorities *during the occupation of Austria.*

The Conference authorizes the Governing Body to make the necessary arrangements with the Government of Austria in regard to its financial contribution.

The *re-admission* of Austria will take effect as soon as the Government of Austria has communicated to the Director-General of the I.L.O. its formal acceptance of the provisions of the Constitution of the I.L.O., of the Constitution of the I.L.O. Instrument of Amendment, 1946, and of the present Resolution [1]. "

Thus the I.L.O. did not admit Austria as a new Member. It *re-admitted* her, on the basis of her former membership. It may be observed that this step was taken at the express request of the Austrian Government, which — faithful to its basic assumption of Austria's continuity [2] — applied precisely for a re-admission, not for admission. In thus responding to the Austrian request, the I.L.O. must have acted in full knowledge of the implications. That it fully shared the Austrian point of view is sufficiently borne out by the qualification of German domination of Austria as an occupation, as well as by the acceptance of the Austrian view with regard to the continued validity of pre-Anschluss Conventions, without any new act of accession on Austria's part. Finally, it must be observed that the actual term " re-admission " was certainly not used lightly by a Conference which at the very same session " admitted " the new State of Iceland to the membership of the Organisation [3].

The Universal Postal Union proceeded on similar lines. In 1946 the name of Austria re-appeared on the list of States Members of the Union, the date of Austria's original accession to the Union being still given as July 1, 1875 [4]. The idea of Austria's continued membership, uninterrupted by German invasion, dispensing with the need for a new act of accession could hardly be more clearly expressed [5].

Similarly, the list of States Members of the International Telecommunication Union, again carries the name of Austria as from 1945 [6].

It is finally necessary to note the implied recognition of Austria's legal continuity by the United Nations Organisation. The official UNO publication of 1949 lists a number of multilateral conventions concluded

---

1. *It. mine, I.L.O., Off. Bull.* of July 31, 1948, vol. XXX, no. 1, pp. 70-71.
2. See below, pp. 359-362.
3. *Ibid.*, pp. 21-22.
4. *Rapport de gestion*, U.P.U., 1946, p. 34.
5. The U.P.U. thus assumes a relation of identity not only between the post-war and the pre-Anschluss Austria, but even between the Austrian Republic and the Empire. This is, however, of no relevance to the problem now discussed.
6. *Rapport de gestion*, 1945, p. 2.

before 1938, to which Austria continues to be a party [1]. Here again, no new act of accession on the part of Austria took place.

Thus, with the sole exception of the now extinct League of Nations, all international organisations recognized Austria's legal continuity.

d) *Judicial Decisions*.

The Nurnberg Tribunal did not have to decide the immediate question of Austria's legal continuity. It is, however, submitted that it did in fact do so by implication. For, after analysing the events of March 1938, the Tribunal came to the conclusion that the seizure of Austria by Germany, far from being the result of a spontaneous merger, constituted

" a premeditated aggressive step in furthering the plan to wage aggressive wars against other countries [2] ".

Had the above statement been made by any other international tribunal, it might in itself have been no criterion as to the legal continuity of a country which had fallen victim to foreign aggression. It should, however, be borne in mind that the Nurnberg Tribunal was no ordinary tribunal, and was sitting in judgment precisely over acts which had been qualified not merely as illegal acts, but as international crimes, — in this particular instance, as " crimes against peace ". With the merits of this new notion in international law this study is not concerned. The fact, however, remains that, within the framework of its Charter as well as of its subsequent judgment, the Tribunal qualified the Anschluss as an act of aggression, that is, a crime against peace. If therefore, in the eyes of the Tribunal, the German seizure of Austria was not simply an illegal act, but moreover a crime, then it is simply inconceivable that such a crime could have become the source of a legal right or could have created any legally valid situation. Consequently, it could not have brought about Austria's legal extinction, nor could it have endowed Germany with any legal title over Austria. It follows that, in the eyes of the Nurnberg Tribunal, the legal status of Austria remained unchanged by the illegal and criminal fact of German aggression, — in other words, that Austria continued to exist in law, and that the post-war Austria must therefore be legally identical with the pre-Anschluss Austria. This is the only possible interpretation of the Nurnberg Judgment as regards the legal status of Austria. It has been seen that it was precisely such interpretation which was adopted by the United States Government, which considered the Judgment as an " international confirmation " of Austria's legal status as a liberated, and not an ex-enemy State [3].

Thus, the only international judicial decision dealing with Austria confirms the uninterrupted legal continuity of the Austrian Republic.

---

1. *Signatures, Ratifications, Acceptances, etc.* ; a few examples may be mentioned : the Opium Convention of 1925, the Convention for Limiting the Manufacture and Regulating the Distribution of Narcotic Drugs of 1931, the Convention for the Suppression of the Traffic in Women and Children of 1921.
2. *Judgment*, p. 17.
3. See above, p. 352.

It is now necessary to turn to municipal decisions.

In 1949 the Swiss Federal Tribunal not only upheld the existence of Austria as a State, notwithstanding the absence of the State Treaty and the limitations on Austrian sovereignty resulting from continued Allied occupation, but, moreover, fully confirmed Austria's legal continuity. In particular, the Tribunal recognized the Austrian nationality of those persons who had possessed it on March 13, 1938 [1].

Similarly, the Court of Appeal of Turin, on July 28, 1948, in case *Bruni v. Pizzorno*, held that treaties, concluded by Austria prior to March 13, 1938, had automatically re-acquired their validity [2].

On the other hand, this view was not shared by Dutch courts. Thus, *in re Ten Amsterdam Oil Companies*, the Division for Judicial Settlement of the Council for the Restoration of Legal Rights, held on April 16, 1946, that a person claiming Austrian nationality

" could not be regarded as an " Austrian ", because " Austrians " had become German subjects as result of the annexation of Austria by Germany [3] ".

Similarly, the District Court of Amsterdam decided on May 20, 1947, that

" according to international law, the German Reich comprised on May 10, 1940, and subsequently, the territory of Austria [4] ".

Similarly, German decisions available assume — explicitly or implicitly — the extinction of the Austrian Republic as a result of the Anschluss and consequently consider that in the period 1938-1945 Austria had formed part of Germany [5].

Finally, the Austrian Courts have — naturally enough — been upholding the thesis of Austria's continuity ever since the country's liberation [6].

---

1. " Es unterliegt keinem Zweifel, dass der neue österreichische Staat — sei es direkt oder indirekt — je nachdem der künftige Staatsvertrag, der seine völkerrechtliche Stellung regeln wird, auf der Annahme einer Okkupation oder Annexion beruhen wird, eine Fortsetzung des früheren bildet. Es ist daher ohne weiteres gegeben, seine Staatsangehörigkeit an diejenige des früheren, im Zeitpunkt des Anschlusses anzuknüpfen, zumal die durch diesen bewirkte Zugehörigkeit zum Deutschen Reich zweifellos mit der 1945 eingetretenen Lostrennung Oesterreichs vom letzteren dahingefallen ist. Die Zuerkennung der österrichischen Staatsbürgerschaft an diejenigen Personen, die am 13.3.1938 österreichische Bundesbürger waren und seither keine andere Staatsangehörigkeit erworben haben, stellt offenbar keinen Rechtmissbrauch dar und verstösst weder gegen den guten Glauben noch gegen den Grundsatz der gegenseitigen Achtung der Souveränität ; sie beruht auf einem personalen Anknüpfungspunkt, der sie vollauf rechtfertigt. " Bundesgerichtliche Entscheidungen 1949, 75, I, 291. Quoted by Prof. Guggenheim in his report on International Law in *Annuaire Suisse*, 1950, pp. 145-146.

2. Quoted by Verdross, *op. cit.*, p. 21.

3. *A. D.*, 1946, case no. 20.

4. *Ibid.*, Editor's Note. The two decisions were subjected to implied criticism by the Editor : " These cases illustrate the fact that Dutch Courts continued to recognize the merger of Austria in the German Reich as a matter of law, notwithstanding the Declaration of Moscow of November 1, 1943... " *Ibid.* Cf. in the same spirit *Veenendaal v. Pommeranz*, A .D., 1948, case no. 55.

5. See Hahn, H. J., *Deutsche Rechtssprechung* 1945-1950, *Ztschft.f.a.öff.R.u. V.-r.*, Bd. XIV, No. 1/2, pp. 256-257. See also *A. D.*, 1948, cases no. 56 and 57.

6. See below, pp. 361-362.

6. THE AUSTRIAN THESIS.

It is finally necessary to examine the attitude of Austria herself, within the limits to which this attitude is relevant [1].

The basic document in this connection is the proclamation of Austria's independence by Austrian political parties, of April 27, 1945 [2]. This document consists of a long Preamble and five Articles. A superficial examination of these two parts reveals an apparent contradiction between them, in that the Preamble emphatically affirms an effective annexation of Austria by Germany, whereas the operative part equally emphatically takes its stand on the continuity of the Austrian Republic. Thus, the Preamble speaks of annexation no less than three times, and with the greatest emphasis on the third occasion :

" ... that the National Socialist Government of the Reich of Adolf Hitler by virtue of this entire (original : " völlig ") political, economic and cultural annexation of the country has driven the people of Austria, deprived of all its rights (original : " macht- und willenslosgemacht ") into a senseless and hopeless war of conquest which no Austrian ever wanted [3]... "

As against this the operative part of the proclamation states in the relevant Articles :

" Art. I. The democratic republic of Austria is *re-established* (original : " wiederhergestellt ") and shall be conducted in the spirit of the constitution of 1920.

Art. II. The Anschluss imposed on the Austrian people in the year 1938 is null and void.

. . . .

Art. IV. From the day of the publication of this declaration of independence all the military, official (original : " dienstliche ") or personal oaths taken by Austrians with regard to the German Reich and its Government are to be considered as null and void and not binding.

Art. V. From this day on all Austrians are *again* in loyalty bound as citizens to the Republic of Austria [4]. "

There can be no doubt that the Articles quoted express unequivocally the idea not of the birth of a new State, but of the continuity of the old Republic. Otherwise, the declaration of nullity of the Anschluss would have been meaningless. Moreover, according to the text, Austria is not " constituted ", she is merely re-established. Austrians *again* owe allegiance to their country whose citizens they are. Is it to be supposed even for a moment that the legislator, who took his stand so clearly and decisively on the conception of Austria's continuity, intended to contradict himself so fundamentally in one and the same instrument as to pronounce Austria's extinction in the Preamble ?

The only possible misunderstanding can result from the repeated use of the word " annexation ". Leaving aside for the moment an analysis of this far from unequivocal term [5], the following interpretation

---

1. See above, p. 129.
2. Verosta, *op. cit.*, pp. 59-62 ; the *Red-White-Red Book*, pp. 211-212.
3. *Red-White-Red Book*, p. 211.
4. *It. mine, ibid.*, p. 212.
5. See below, pp. 363-364.

of the proclamation may reasonably be submitted : while the proclamation in its operative and decisive part clearly affirms Austria's legal survival, it is just as emphatic in asserting the undoubted historical fact of Austria having been physically overpowered and prevented from exercising her rights as a State. Whatever Austria was forced to do during the critical period, was not her responsibility, since it was the result of the *de facto*, physical incorporation of the country into Germany. If Austria was to escape responsibility for Germany's acts, that physical fact could not be emphasized strongly enough. This is why the repeated insistence on annexation in the Preamble reaches its peak in the above-quoted passage, in which the *de facto* annexed country is said to have been forced into the German war. This would seem to be the only explanation of the apparent contradiction : the Anschluss — or annexation — was illegal and invalid ; as such, it was unable to effect Austria's legal extinction ; but it did in fact take place with the result of Austria being made to participate in Germany's misdeeds ; thus, Austria survived the Anschluss as the same legal entity, but declined to share in a responsibility which was not hers. This underlying conception of the proclamation seems to be in conformity with the trend of thought of the Nurnberg Tribunal which, while qualifying the Anschluss as a criminal aggression, merely stated the obvious when it said that " Austria was in fact seized by Germany in the month of March 1938 [1] ".

This interpretation is advanced all the more freely as it is fully confirmed by every Austrian pronouncement since the proclamation. Thus, in an important speech in the National Council, of April 12, 1946, the Austrian Chancellor declared :

" ... Austria was then occupied and deprived of her capacity to act, without any validation by a legal title, that is, in violation of international law. Consequently, Austria was prevented from exercising her sovereignty, without such sovereignty thereby becoming extinct and without the State as such ceasing to exist. With the elimination of the National Socialist rule of violence, the Austrian people regained its capacity to act and the Austrian State regained its freedom and independence [2]. "

The message of the Austrian Federal Government to the National Council, on the occasion of Austria's accession to the new constitution of the International Labour Organisation in 1946, read :

" In consequence of Austria's occupation by Germany, Austria's international capacity to act was suspended as from March 11, 1938. Because of the absence of an Austrian Government, Austria was since that date unable to fulfil her international obligations. The valid international treaties which Austria had concluded between 1918 and 1938, did not become extinct during the German occupation ; their operation was merely suspended [3]. "

---

1. *Judgment*, p. 17.
2. *Transl. mine*, quoted by Von besonderer Seite, *op. cit.*, pp. 226-227.
3. *Transl. mine*, *ibid.*, p. 429. See further examples quoted. This conception is shared by Austrian writers. Thus Ludwig, chairman of the Foreign Committee of the National Council : " Nach östereichischer Auffassung war Oesterreich von 1938 bis 1945 woh¹ rechtsfähig, aber nicht handlungsfähig... " quoted by Verosta, *op. cit.*, p. 121. Ranzenhofer : " ...dass der österreichische Staat während der Dauer seiner gewaltsamen Zugehörigkeit zum Deutschen Reiche *de iure* weiterbestanden hat und nur *de facto* seine Souveränität nicht ausüben konnte. " *Der künftige Staatsvertrag mit Oesterreich, Oester-reichische Monatshefte*, I, 1945/46, p. 364.

This Austrian thesis is further consistently borne out by every official declaration [1]. Besides, hardly any other thesis could be expected from a country which had undoubtedly fallen victim to foreign aggression, which could have no possible interest in legalizing that aggression *ex post*, and which, moreover, had an overriding interest in avoiding responsibility for the war. It is clear that a contrary thesis would spell disaster for Austria [2].

In consequence, all basic enactments of a constitutional character of the re-born Republic proceed on the assumption of Austria's continuity [3]. A few deviations from that principle in other laws of a non-constitutional character can as little prevail against the whole evidence available of the higher level as could an isolated declaration of a military commander prevail against the contrary and stronger evidence of State practice [4].

On the international level the thesis was definitely formulated in the Austrian Note of April 1, 1946, to the Secretary-General of the League of Nations, in connection with the summoning of the League Assembly.

" My Government is of the opinion " — the Note declared — " that Austria continues to be a Member of the League of Nations. "

It is true that after the Anschluss Germany notified the League to the contrary. However, the Anschluss itself had by now been definitely qualified as null and void by the various international acts which the Note listed.

" The Austrian Federal Government therefore considers that the afore-mentioned declaration of the German Reich of March 18th, 1938, concerning the situation of Austria in regard to the League of Nations must, for its part, be deemed to be null and void, and accordingly considers Austria to be a Member of the League of Nations [5]. "

In a Memorandum to all States Members of the United Nations, dated July 31, 1952, the Austrian Government stated :

" The Statute of the Republic of Austria is based upon the Treaty of Saint-Germain [6]. "

Finally, the Austrian courts consistently and emphatically uphold the thesis of Austria's continuity. Thus, in *re Veit*, the Austrian Supreme Court held on November 23, 1946 :

---

1. Von besonderer Seite, *op. cit.*, pp. 227 and 429-430.
2. See the declaration of the Chairman of the Foreign Affairs Committee, quoted by Verosta, *op. cit.*, pp. 118-126, more particularly pp. 123-125.
3. For an analysis of these basic laws, see Von besonderer Seite, *op. cit.*, pp. 223-226.
4. See above, p. 353. The existence of such laws is admitted and considered as " Entgleisungen " ; see Ludwig, quoted by Verosta, *op. cit.*, p. 123. They were, however, made use of by Dr. Schärf to contest the thesis of Austrian continuity. *Gilt das Konkordat? Zukunft*, 1950, Nos. 2 and 5. It seems rather correct to admit with Von besonderer Seite that no undue weight is to be attached to every particular simple law in face of the stronger evidence to the contrary in constitutional law, *op. cit.*, p. 223 and 426.
5. Quoted by Langer, *op. cit.*, pp. 202-203.
6. *Dep. of St. Bul.*, XXVII, p. 221.

" Austria, as a State, did not participate in the war [1]... "

In *Jordan v. Austrian Republic and Taubner*, decided on October 15, 1947, the same Court concurred in the decision of the Lower Court to the effect that Austria " was not the legal successor of the German Reich " and declared :

" In March 1938, the Republic of Austria lost its independence and sovereignty as the result of its occupation by the German Reich. On April 27, 1945, it was liberated from the National Socialist rule of force. That liberation did not create a new State. The Austrian Republic recovered its sovereign rights and was declared to be again an independent State. From March 13, 1938, to April 27, 1945, the sovereign prerogatives in the territory of the Austrian Republic were exercised by the Government of the German Reich. ... On April 27, 1945, the Austrian Republic did not take over power from the German Reich. It recovered, after the collapse of the National Socialist regime, that authority which it was prevented from exercising between March 13, 1938 and April 27, 1945 [2]. "

According to all the evidence available, this is the established view of Austrian courts [3].

7. CASES OF DENIAL OF AUSTRIAN CONTINUITY.

The available evidence concerning Austria's legal continuity has thus been examined. With a few exceptions, it has been found that it emphatically confirms such continuity. These exceptions — the undecided attitude of the League of Nations, the contrary view of the municipal courts of Holland and Germany, declarations of a military commander and a few isolated deviations from the established thesis by Austria herself — cannot prevail against the overwhelming evidence to the contrary. It may therefore be safely concluded that international practice recognized Austria's continuity.

It may, however, be asked whether this practically uniform confirmation does not represent a mere arbitrary fiction on the part of the international community. The answer to this question should be sought in the views of those writers who deny Austria's continuity.

Such continuity is denied by Prof. Guggenheim [4]. But Prof. Guggenheim limits himself to a straight denial, without giving any reasons, whereas his own comment on the Swiss attitude hardly supports his thesis.

With regard to the remaining arguments against Austria's continuity, it must be stated that they all suffer from so pronounced a political bias as to gravely impair whatever legal value they may contain.

A typical example is furnished by an article in the California Law Review in which the writer warns against the re-establishment of a free

---

1. *A. D.*, 1946, case no. 137.
2. *A. D.*, 1947, case no. 15.
3. See Seidl-Hohenveldern, *Oesterreichische Rechtsprechung*, 1945-1950, *Zt. für a. öff. R. u. V.-r.*, Oktober 1951, Bd. XIV, nr. 1/2, in particular : Z 32, 33, 55, 56, 80, 81, 82, 83, 85, 88, 89, 90, 91, 97. See also *A. D.*, 1948, case no. 18.
4. See above, p. 353, *f.-n.* 3.

Austria, since, according to him, this would imply the restoration of the Schuschnigg regime [1].

Writing in 1950, in a restored and yet non-Schuschnigg Austria, Dr. Schärf was no longer haunted by that particular fear. However, his main, and avowed, interest in denying Austria's continuity seems to be the desire to see Austria freed from the obligations resulting from the pre-Anschluss Concordat [2]. To strengthen his thesis, Dr. Schärf takes a stand on the question of Austria's annexation by Germany, as opposed to the notion of a mere occupation which is being advocated by his opponents [3]. This leads in both cases to a frantic grasping at words in existing documents, — words on which the whole solution is made to depend and which, moreover, are interpreted rather freely, so as to fit an obviously preconceived theory. The argument of annexation must nonetheless be examined on its merits.

It should be remarked in the first place that the term " annexation " does not convey any clear meaning in international law [4]. In particular, there is no agreement among writers as to whether it covers a unilateral act of the conqueror, accomplished against the will of the defeated State, i.e. an original title [5], or whether it means *any* extension of territory of a State, including cession, i.e. representing a derivative title [6]. The term can thus be used for both, law-abiding and law-breaking processes [7]. Furthermore, annexation, whatever its legal basis, may, in some cases, grow into an internationally valid title over

---

1. " In November of 1943 it was announced that the participants in the Moscow Conference had decided to re-establish a free and independent Austria. There are weighty reasons for doubting that this was a wise decision ; but since there is every indication that it will be adhered to, it is more realistic to call attention to one aspect of the revival of Austria that is causing concern to Austrians and their friends throughout the world. This can be best stated in the question : is there any intention on the part of the leaders of the United Nations of restoring, or giving their blessing to a restoration of, the legal and political situation that existed just prior to Hitler's occupation of Austria in March of 1938 ? The casual reader of newpapers, as well as some well-informed specialists, would answer : No, the matter will be left to the Austrians. On the other hand, responsible spokesmen for the governments of England and the United States have stated that they do not recognize the legality of anything that has happened in Austria from the minute Schuschnigg was forced to resign as Chancellor. The implication of these statements may be that there is the intention to revive, at least temporarily, the pre-Nazi situation... " Gulick, Charles A., *Administrative and Judicial Processes as Instruments of Clerical Fascism in Austria, California Law Review*, vol. XXXII, 1944, p. 161. " A primary purpose here is to offer one segment of evidence which proves that it would be disastrous to resuscitate Dolfuss-Schuschnigg Austria. " *Ibid.*, p. 162.
2. *Gilt das Konkordat?* Two articles under the same title in Nos. 2 and 5 of the *Zukunft* of 1950. It is submitted that there exist other possibilities of freeing Austria from such obligations than by denying her continuity, — a procedure which in the particular instance, recalls throwing the baby out with the bath water. Dr. Schärf's argument it not made any more convincing by the fact that he himself was Vice-Chancellor in the Austrian coalition cabinet which forcefully upheld the thesis of Austrian continuity, nor by the other fact, that his opponents are apparently motivated by the opposed political desire to see the concordat upheld.
3. See below, p. 367.
4. Thus, correctly, Reut-Nicolussi : " ...dass der Ausdruck « Annexion » überhaupt nicht eindeutig genannt werden kann. " *Op. cit.*, p. 245. Similarly, Verosta, *op. cit.*, p. 3.
5. Thus, Liszt, *op. cit.*, p. 150 ; Verdross, *Völkerrecht*, pp. 185-186.
6. Thus Fauchille who speaks of an « annexion de territoire procédant soit d'une cession pacifique, soit d'une cession imposée », *op. cit.*, I, p. 856.
7. It may perhaps be recalled that, far from denoting necessarily a violent action the term can legitimately be used to cover the inclusion into a State of certain territories proceeding in full conformity with the wishes of the annexed populations ; see chapter on Italy.

the annexed territory, whereas in others it will not. Premature annexation [1] is precisely such a case in which international law denies the legal validity of an annexation even if effectively accomplished.

Consequently, if the " annexation " of Austria by Germany is intended merely to refer to the fact of the former's physical absorption into the latter, this is as true as it is irrelevant to the main problem which is : did this physical absorption, did this " annexation " grow into a valid international title which would have effected Austria's extinction? This crucial question remains unanswered by the annexation argument.

Austria's identity with the pre-Anschluss Republic has also been forcefully denied by Prof. Kelsen himself. It must come as a surprise to the reader that Prof. Kelsen should equally have adopted a predominantly political approach to the problem.

That this is so, seems to be borne out by the very title of the essay in which he deals with the subject : " The International Legal Status of Germany *to be established* immediately upon Termination of the War [2]. " In it, Prof. Kelsen advises the Allied Governments as to the best course to be pursued with regard to Germany and Austria, in order to achieve certain political aims.

To propose a political programme is perfectly legitimate. It is, however, an entirely different proposition if such a programme is supported by incidental legal arguments which may not be very convincing when analyzed on their own merits. Nor — it may be added — is the programme made any more acceptable, when it is also based on political prophesies which do not eventually materialize.

Prof. Kelsen begins by declaring that

" The refusal by the Powers in the Moscow Declaration to recognize the annexation of Austria by Germany has hardly more than a *political* character [3]. "

The statement is particularly surprising, coming — as it does — after Prof. Kelsen's adoption of the constitutive and legal view of international recognition [4]. Since Prof. Kelsen now assumes that recognition has both a legal and a political meaning, it is difficult to see on what particular grounds he qualifies the Moscow Declaration as purely and exclusively political. Or, is it to be assumed that the constitutive character of recognition which Prof. Kelsen now proclaims is to attach to recognition only, but not to withdrawal of recognition, or the refusal to recognize?

It is submitted that the legal significance of an act cannot be dismissed by labelling it as political. With regard to recognition and de-recognition in particular, it is submitted that its legality must depend upon its conformity with objective international law [5]. In his essay Prof. Kelsen does not adduce any argument to show that it was the

---

1. See above, pp. 102-107.
2. *It. mine*, A. J., 1944, p. 689.
3. *It. mine, ibid.*
4. See above, pp. 137-138.
5. See above, p. 160.

Moscow refusal to recognize the legality of the Anschluss, and not the Anschluss itself, that was contrary to any principle of international law. Prof. Kelsen then goes on to say :

" That Austria never ceased to exist as an independent State is a political fiction which will be very difficult to maintain at the moment of Germany's surrender, since at this time no Austrian Government will probably exist [1]. "

Apart from the fact that the prophesy was not fulfilled (the first Austrian Government came into being on April 29, 1945, i.e. before Germany's surrender), exception must again be taken to the dismissing of Austria's continuity as " political fiction ". It could certainly be described as a " legal fiction " ; as such, it would be neither better nor worse than the corresponding " legal fiction " — if one chooses so to call it — of State continuity under belligerent occupation. Its undoubted political motive is not, however, in itself sufficient to deprive it of legal value.

But the political substance of Prof. Kelsen's thesis seems to emerge from the following passage :

" One of the consequences of the non-recognition doctrine is that with the abolition of Germany's domination over the former Austrian territory the constitutional status of Austria, which prevailed at the moment of annexation, must revive automatically. ... At that date Austria was a fascistic State. If the victorious Powers wish to re-establish a democratic Austria, they must not adhere too closely to the non-recognition doctrine [2]. "

The establishment of such an unexpected connection between the international continuity of a State and the continuity of its internal regime inevitably raises anew all the fundamental questions relevant to the problem, and which — it is firmly believed — have long ago found their definite answers in positive international law. For it has been seen — and it has been confirmed by Prof. Kelsen himself more than once — that one of the clearest rules of international law lays down that the continuity of a State is in no way dependent on, nor linked with, the continuity of its government or regime. It is precisely this rule which preserves State continuity in case of revolutions [3]. Why then should the restoration of Austria as an independent subject of international law on the basis of her uninterrupted international continuity mean an automatic restoration of her old regime also on the basis of such continuity ? If the ultimate conclusions were to be drawn from such a view, it would be necessary to say that, in order to get rid of a bad form of government, it is indispensable first to effect the extinction of the State concerned and then to create it afresh with a new regime. Why should a re-born Austria be unable to get rid of her Fascist regime in an — admittedly — revolutionary way at the very moment of her effective liberation, and why should such revolutionary change be incompatible with her international continuity ? Conversely,

---

1. *Op. cit.*, p. 690.
2. *Ibid.*
3. See above, pp. 24-27.

why should this international continuity be made to depend — of all things — on the continuation of the Dolfuss-Schuschnigg regime?

It is only on the assumption of a primacy of municipal over international law that Prof. Kelsen's view could be upheld and accepted. For only then could a revolutionary break with the former Austrian legal order be construed as a break in the continuity of the Austrian State. But such view cannot possibly be reconciled with the primacy of international law which has been proclaimed by Prof. Kelsen himself [1] and which has been found to be fully confirmed by positive international law [2].

. With a rejection of a primacy of municipal law in favour of a primacy of international law, any possible connection between the continuity of the Austrian State and the continuity of the pre-Anschluss regime is eliminated. This in turn disposes of the would-be danger of a restoration of that regime in consequence of the recognition of Austria's continuity. It is, however, submitted that in no circumstances should this particular factor have figured in a legal argument. For, either Austria survived the Anschluss or she did not, and, consequently, her continuity should either be affirmed or denied. The case must be argued and decided on its merits. But a suggestion can hardly be accepted according to which such an affirmation or denial should be based not on rules and criteria of international law, but on a political judgment concerning a State's internal regime. For it is submitted that identity and continuity of States under international law are objective legal notions; they are not marks for good behaviour.

It may finally be observed that the effective solution of the problem of Austria's continuity proceeded precisely on the lines suggested above : while the continuity of Austria under international law was re-affirmed, a new internal regime came into being in a revolutionary manner.

In conclusion it is submitted, that none of the arguments challenging Austria's continuity has succeeded in undermining the overwhelming evidence in favour of such continuity, which is provided by international practice. It remains to be seen whether there exists any positive basis for endowing such evidence with full conclusiveness and finality under international law.

8. CONCLUSION : LEGAL BASIS OF AUSTRIA'S CONTINUITY.

The search for such a basis by those writers who support the theory of Austria's continuity has yielded various results.

As has been seen, some of them deny that Austria's extinction had been recognized by the international community [3]. But it has also been seen that such a claim is not supported by the facts. Thus, the alleged non-recognition of the Anschluss would be as incapable of forming the basis of Austria's survival in actual practice as it would be

1. See *Reine Rechtslehre*, pp. 147-150.
2. See above, pp. 71-73.
3. Langer, *op. cit.*, p. 163 ; Klinghofer, *The Coming Austria*, p. 14 ; Wright, *Attitude of the United States*, p. 101.

in theory [1]. The same observation must apply to writers who admit the fact of recognition while attempting to qualify it either as mere *de facto* recognition or recognition granted for practical reasons only [2].

Nor is it possible to find the basis of Austria's continuity in the survival of her " State population ", as is proposed by Verdross [3]. The physical survival of a population is a natural phenomenon and adds nothing to a legal argument concerning State continuity, since one and the same population can form the human substratum of different States. If, however, the continuity of a State is explained by the continuity of the *State* population, then — once again — Verdross begs the question [4]. For the question is precisely : how did it come about that the population did not lose its character of a " State population ", — in other words, that the State survived, endowing this population with such a character ?

Yet another argument forcefully insists on the German domination of Austria being not an annexation but an occupation, and as such, unable to effect her extinction [5]. It is, however, submitted that just as the notion of " annexation " does not decide the problem in favour of Austria's extinction [6], so the notion of " occupation " is unable to provide the basis for her survival. For the plain fact remains that Germany's domination of Austria *was not* belligerent occupation [7]. Whether or not it should, in its consequences, be treated by analogy to belligerent occupation, is an altogether different question, for which Verdross' new notion of " *occupatio quasi-bellica* " is of interest [8]. But in no case does the rule safeguarding State continuity under belligerent occupation apply automatically to Austria.

It would therefore seem that all the above theories suffer from a considerable amount of artificiality. It is submitted that Austria's legal survival can only depend upon inherent legality or illegality of the events involved [9].

It has been fully proved that the Anschluss constituted an illegal act on the part of Germany [10]. It must therefore be concluded that, as in the case of Czechoslovakia, Albania, and — possibly — Ethiopia, it was the principle *ex iniuria ius non oritur* which, failing any crystallised rule of international law protecting State continuity in the particular circumstances, formed the legal basis of Austria's survival. It is this

---

1. See above, pp. 130-161.
2. Verdross, *Völkerrechtliche Identität*, p. 20 ; Verosta, *op. cit.*, pp. 6-7.
3. *Op. cit.*, p. 21.
4. See above, p. 48.
5. See mainly the two articles by Von besonderer Seite in *Oesterreischische Monatshefte*.
6. See above, pp. 363-364.
7. See above, p. 347.
8. *Op. cit.*, p. 20.
9. " Eine sachliche Untersuchung des Falles muss... von der *inneren Gesetzlichkeit des Problems* ausgehen und dabei kommt ein Gesichtspunkt in Betracht, der alle anderen an Gewicht übertrifft und unseres Erachtens eine klare Antwort auf die gegenständliche Frage ermöglicht. Wir meinen die *völkerrechtliche Unzulässigkeit* des Vorgehens der nazionalsozialistischen Regierung und ihre Konsequenzen. " Reut-Nicolussi, *op. cit.*, p. 247·
10. See above, p. 343.

principle which again serves as the criterion of the legal conclusiveness and finality of the evidence to be found in international practice. This evidence, which overwhelmingly confirms Austria's continuity, cannot be dismissed as an arbitrary fiction for the simple reason that it fully conforms to this fundamental principle of international law. Once again, in the case of Austria, this principle has prevailed over the opposed principle *ex factis ius oritur*. There is no possible reason for applying a different argument to Austria than to those countries whose similar problems have previously been investigated and whose solution, in favour of their unbroken continuity, had been found not in State practice alone, but in the conformity of such practice with an objective principle of international law [1].

---

1. For problems connected with the actual restoration of a temporarily suppressed State, see below, pp. 582-586.

CHAPTER VIII

THE BALTIC STATES.

1. LEGAL POSITION OF THE BALTIC STATES PRIOR TO 1939.

The three Baltic States : Estonia, Latvia and Lithuania, came into existence at the end of the First World War by establishing effective national governments in their respective territories and proclaiming their independence [1]. The recognition *de iure* by the European Great Powers took place for Latvia and Estonia on January 26, 1921 in a letter signed by Briand on behalf of the Supreme Council. Lithuania was recognized *de iure* on December 20, 1922. The United States extended *de iure* recognition to all three States on July 28, 1922 [2].

In the meantime, the state of war which had existed between the Baltic States and Soviet Russia was brought to an end by means of three separate Peace Treaties, concluded by the latter country with Estonia on February 2, 1920, with Latvia on August 11, 1920, and with Lithuania on July 12, 1920. The fundamental Articles of these Treaties, defining the legal situation of the three States with regard to the State of which they had formed part, are practically identical. Thus, Art. 2 of the Peace Treaty with Estonia reads :

" On the basis of the right of all peoples freely to decide their own destinies, and even to separate themselves completely from the State of which they form part, a right proclaimed by the Federal Socialist Republic of Soviet Russia, Russia unreservedly recognizes the independence and autonomy of the State of Estonia, and renounces voluntarily and for ever all rights of sovereignty formerly held by Russia over the Estonian people and territory by virtue of the former legal situation, and by virtue of international treaties, which, in respect of such rights, shall henceforth lose their force.

No obligation towards Russia devolves upon the Estonian people and territory from the fact that Estonia was formerly part of Russia [3]. "

Art. 2 of the Peace Treaty with Latvia reads :

" By virtue of the principle proclaimed by the Federal Socialist Republic of the Russian Soviets, which establishes the right of self-determination for all nations, even to the point of total separation from the States with which they have been incorporated, and in view of the desire expressed by the Latvian people to possess

---

1. Estonia : February 24, 1918; Latvia : November 18, 1917; Lithuania : February 16, 1918.
2. For history see : *The Baltic States*, by the Information Department of the Royal Institute of International Affairs, Oxford University Press, London, New York, Toronto, 1938 ; Graham, M. W. *The Diplomatic Recognition of the Border States; Latvian-Russian Relations*, Documents, Published by the Latvian Legation in Washington 1944.
3. *LoN. Tr. Ser.*, XI, p. 51.

an independent national existence, Russia unreservedly recognizes the independence and sovereignty of the Latvian State and voluntarily and irrevocably renounces all sovereign rights over the Latvian people and territory which formerly belonged to Russia under the then existing constitutional law as well as under international treaties, which, in the sense here indicated, shall in the future cease to be valid. The previous status of subjection of Latvia to Russia shall not entail any obligations towards Russia on the part of the Latvian people or territory [1]. "

Art. 1 of the Peace Treaty with Lithuania reads :

" Proceeding from the right proclaimed by the Russian Socialist Federated Soviet Republic of all nations to free self-determination up to their complete separation from the State into the composition of which they enter, Russia recognizes without reservation the sovereign rights and independence of the Lithuanian State with all the juridical consequences arising from such recognition and voluntarily and for all time abandons all the sovereign rights of Russia over the Lithuanian people and their territory. The fact of the past subjection of Lithuania to Russia does not impose on the Lithuanian nation and their territory any liabilities whatever towards Russia [2]. "

The full and unreserved recognition of the new statehood of the seceding Baltic countries by their former Mother Country thus took place even before such recognition by third States. Russia's renunciation of all her previous rights over the Baltic countries, proclaimed to be final and permanent, assumed a particularly solemn form. This is to be explained by the fact that this renunciation did not result from a mere political contingency, but from a superior principle, officially adopted by the Russian Revolution. This principle, forcefully emphasized in the treaties in question, had indeed been repeatedly proclaimed by the Soviets. Its best-known formulation is to be found in the Declaration of the Soviet Government of November 15, 1917, signed by Lenin in his capacity of Chairman of the Council of People's Commissars and Stalin in his capacity of People's Commissar for National Affairs ; the second of the four principles proclaimed therein was

" The right for Russia's peoples of free self-determination even unto separation and establishment of independent States [3]. "

Following the creation on July 6, 1923, of the Union of Soviet Socialist Republics, all States maintaining diplomatic relations with Russia were notified

" that the People's Commissar for Foreign Affairs of the Union of Soviet Socialist Republics is charged with the execution in the name of the Union of all its international relations, including the execution of all treaties and conventions entered into by the above-mentioned Republics (the Russian Soviet Federated Socialist Republic, the White Russian S.S.R., the Ukrainian S.S.R. and the Transcaucasian S.S.R.) with foreign States, which shall remain in force in the territories of the respective Republics [4] ".

With regard to the Baltic States this meant that the U.S.S.R. had fully taken over treaties and agreements signed by them prior to that

1. *Ibid.*, II, p. 213.
2. *Ibid.*, III, pp. 122-123.
3. *Nazi-Soviet Conspiracy and the Baltic States*, p. 21.
4. Quoted by Taracouzio, *The Soviet Union and International Law*, pp. 280-281.

date with any of the Soviet Republics (peace treaties with the R.S.F.S.R., agreement with Soviet Ukraine, etc.). This was fully confirmed by the subsequent practice of the U.S.S.R., which continued to consider the original peace treaties as the basis of her relations with the Baltic States.

The period between the two wars witnessed the conclusion of an ever increasing number of agreements between the U.S.S.R. and the Baltic States, both bilateral and multilateral. The full list is far too long to be quoted and it is sufficient to mention the most important of these agreements :

Estonia :

Protocol signed in Moscow on February 9, 1929, between Estonia, Latvia, Poland, Rumania and the U.S.S.R., for the immediate entry into force of the Treaty of Paris of August 27, 1928, regarding renunciation of war as an instrument of national policy ;
Treaty of Non-Aggression and peaceful settlement of disputes between Estonia and the U.S.S.R., signed in Moscow on May 4, 1932 (renewed by a Protocol of April 4, 1934) ;
Conciliation Convention between Estonia and the U.S.S.R., signed in Moscow on June 16, 1932, forming integral part of the Treaty of Non-Aggression ;
Convention for the Definition of Aggression, signed in London on July 3, 1933.

Latvia :

Agreement on settlement of frontier disputes, signed in Riga on July 19, 1926 ;
Protocol signed in Moscow on February 9, 1929, for the immediate entry into force of the Treaty of Paris of August 27, 1928, regarding renunciation of war as an instrument of national policy ;
Treaty of Non-Aggression, signed in Riga on February 5, 1932 (renewed by a Protocol of April 4, 1934) ;
Convention relating to Conciliation Procedure, signed in Riga on June 18, 1932, forming integral part of the Treaty of Non-Aggression ;
Convention for the Definition of Aggression, signed in London on July 3, 1933.

Lithuania :

Non-Aggression Pact, signed in Moscow on September 28, 1926 ;
Protocol for the Renunciation of war as instrument of national policy, signed in Moscow on April 1, 1929 ;
Convention for the Definition of Aggression, signed in London on July 5, 1933.

Moreover, all the four States were signatories of the original Pact of Paris. Finally, since Russia's entry into the League of Nations, they were mutually bound by the Covenant.

This network of agreements laid down clearly defined rights and obligations for the parties in their mutual relations. The obligations under the Covenant require no comment. The Pact of Paris, outlawing war and providing for pacific settlement of all disputes, bound them in a dual manner, i.e. the Pact itself and the Protocol of 1929. The Non-Aggression Treaties were based on the re-affirmation of what was stated to be the unchanging foundation for their mutual relations as originally stipulated in the Peace Treaties. Thus, the Preamble to the Non-Aggression Treaty between the U.S.S.R. and Estonia declared *inter alia* :

" Considering that the Peace Treaty of February 2, 1920, constitutes now as heretofore the unshakable foundation of their mutual relations and obligations... "

while the corresponding Preamble to the Latvian Non-Aggression Treaty read :

" Having in view the Peace Treaty concluded on August 11, 1920, between Latvia and the Russian Socialist Federative Soviet Republic, the effect of which extends to the entire territory of the Union of Soviet Socialist Republics, and all the provisions of which remain invariably and permanently the firm foundation of the relations between the High Contracting Parties... Being firmly resolved to respect mutually and unreservedly each other's sovereignty, political independence, territorial integrity and inviolability... [1] "

In the case of Lithuania, Art. 1 of the Non-Aggression Pact declared that the relations between the two countries were to continue to be based on the Treaty of Peace.

The essence of the Non-Aggression Treaties was contained in Articles 1 and 2 of the Estonian and Latvian Treaties, and in Articles 2 and 3 of the Lithuanian Pact. They read :

Estonia :

Art. 1. Each of the High Contracting Parties guarantees to the other Party the inviolability of the existing frontiers between them, as defined by the Peace Treaty signed on February 2, 1920, and undertakes to refrain from any act of aggression or any violent measures directed against the integrity and inviolability of the territory or against the political independence of the other Contracting Party, whether such acts of aggression or such violent measures are undertaken separately or in conjunction with other Powers, with or without a declaration of war.

Art. 2. Each of the High Contracting Parties undertakes not to take part in political agreements manifestly directed in an aggressive sense against the other Party, nor in coalitions of the same nature having as their object to subject the other Party to an economic or financial boycott [2].

Latvia :

Art. 1. Each of the High Contracting Parties undertakes to refrain from any act of aggression directed against the other, and also from any acts of violence directed against the territorial integrity and inviolability or the political independence of the other Contracting Party, regardless of whether such aggression or such acts are committed separately or together with other Powers, with or without a declaration of war.

Art. 2. Each of the High Contracting Parties undertakes not be to a party to any military or political treaties, conventions or agreements directed against the independence, territorial integrity or political security of the other Party, or to any treaties, conventions or agreements aiming at an economic or financial boycott of either of the Contracting Parties [3].

It may be mentioned that Art. 3 of both Treaties expressly maintained in force the validity of treaties concluded or obligations assumed by the Parties prior to the Treaties, insofar as such treaties and obligations did not contain elements of aggression within the

---

1. It is interesting to note this second confirmation of the taking over by the U.S.S.R. of the international obligations incurred before July 6, 1923, by the individual republics. See above, pp. 370-371
2. *LoN. Tr. Ser.*, CXXXI, p. 305.
3. *Ibid.*, CXLVIII, pp. 123-125.

meaning of the Treaties. Thus, previous international obligations of the parties were expressly recognized and safeguarded.

Lithuania :

" Art. 2. The Lithuanian Republic and the U.S.S.R. undertake to respect in all circumstances each other's sovereignty and territorial integrity and inviolability.

Art. 3. Each of the two Contracting Parties undertakes to refrain from any act of aggression whatsoever against the other Party [1]... "

The validity of all the three Treaties was prolonged on April 4, 1934, to last until December 31, 1945.

The wording of the Non-Aggression Treaties is characterized by extreme precision and seems to cover every conceivable form of aggression. They outlaw not only direct acts of aggression in the widest sense of the term (" any act of aggression ", " any act of aggression whatsoever "), but even " any violent measures " or " any acts of violence " in the Estonian and Latvian Treaties. These broad terms confer on the parties the greatest possible measure of security against any possible attempt at their territorial integrity and political independence which, moreover, are both safeguarded in the strictest manner. The Estonian Treaty even goes so far as to use the term " guarantee ". Thus, the text does not leave any loophole or escape from the obligations undertaken. Similarly, Art. 2 of the Estonian and Latvian Treaty exclude any possibility of hostile action in combination with third States in the broadest possible manner, outlawing conventions or agreements directed not only against the political but even against the economic or financial interests of the contracting parties.

Such an outlawing of all aggression which is both broad and at the same time precise, would hardly seem to call for a further elaboration. Yet, precisely such an elaboration is to be found in the famous Conventions for the Definition of Aggression of 1933 (the so-called Litvinov Conventions). These Conventions, concluded on the initiative of the Soviet Government, contain a definition of aggression which, in its categorical character and its precision, has never been surpassed in any other international instrument.

The Preamble lays down the general principle

" that all States have an equal right to independence, security, the defence of their territories, and the free development of their institutions ",

whereupon it expresses the desire of the parties

" in the interest of general security to define aggression as specifically as possible, in order to obviate any pretext whereby it might be justified, ... in the interest of the general peace to ensure to all peoples the inviolability of the territory of their countries, ... to bring into force, as between their countries, precise rules defining aggression, until such time as those rules shall become universal ".

The relevant Articles of the Convention read :

---

1. *Ibid.*, LX, p. 153.

"Art. 1. Each of the High Contracting Parties undertakes to accept in its relations with each of the other Parties, from the date of the entry into force of the present Convention, the definition of aggression as explained in the report dated May 24th, 1933, of the Committee on Security Questions (Politis report) to the Conference for the Reduction and Limitation of Armaments, which report was made in consequence of the proposal of the Soviet delegation.

Art. 2. Accordingly, the aggressor in an international conflict shall, subject to the agreements in force between the parties to the dispute, be considered to be that State which is the first to commit any of the following actions :

(1) Declaration of war upon another State,

(2) Invasion by its armed forces, with or without a declaration of war, of the territory of another State,

(3) Attack by its land, naval or air forces, with or without a declaration of war, on the territory, vessels or aircraft of another State,

(4) Naval blockade of the coasts or ports of another State,

(5) Provision of support to armed bands formed in its territory which have invaded the territory of another State, or refusal, notwithstanding the request of the invaded State, to take, in its own territory, all the measures in its power to deprive those bands of all assistance or protection.

Art. 3. No political, military, economic or other considerations may serve as an excuse or justification for the aggression referred to in Art. 2 (for examples see Annex).
. . . "

In the Annex, referred to in Art. 3, the contracting parties declared

" that no act of aggression within the meaning of Art. 2 of that Convention can be justified on either of the following grounds, among others :

A. The internal conditions of a State :

e.g., its political, economic or social structure ; alleged defects in its administration ; disturbances due to strikes, counter-revolutions or civil war.

B. The international conduct of a State :

e.g., the violation or threatened violation of the material or moral rights or interests of a foreign State or its nationals ; the rupture of diplomatic or economic relations ; economic or financial boycotts ; disputes relating to economic, financial or other obligations towards foreign States ; frontier incidents not forming any of the cases of aggression specified in Art. 2.

The High Contracting Parties further agree to recognize that the present Convention can never legitimate any violation of international law that may be implied in the circumstances comprised in the above list [1]. "

The outstanding clarity and the unequivocal character of the text speaks for itself. A few remarks may, however, be made. In the first place, non-aggression is not only a passive, but an active duty of the contracting parties, as is borne out by point (5) of Article 2. Secondly, even the very full and imaginative list of the possible pretexts of an aggression is specifically stated not to be exhaustive. Thus, on no conceivable ground can an act of aggression be proceded with. The Litvinov Conventions, which in the Preamble claim to express

---

1. Convention of July 3, 1933, between Afghanistan, Estonia, Latvia, Persia, Poland, Rumania, U.S.S.R. and Turkey. *LoN. Tr. Ser.*, CXLVII, p. 69. An identical convention between the U.S.S.R. and Lithuania was signed in London, on July 5, 1933. *LoN. Tr. Ser.*, CXLVIII, p. 81.

universally valid principles, and in their final passage profess an unreserved respect of international law, thus closed every possible avenue to violence and law-breaking.

As between the parties, the Litvinov Conventions may therefore be considered as the crowning work in defining their relations on the basis of mutual respect for their sovereignty and territorial integrity.

This then was the legal situation of the Baltic States in 1939, arising out of general international law protecting their separate statehood, and of specific international conventions.

2. INCORPORATION OF THE BALTIC STATES INTO THE SOVIET UNION.

A. *Facts.*

The summer of 1939 witnessed an intense diplomatic activity in Europe, which preceded the outbreak of the Second World War and decided the original alignment of forces in that war. Since the late spring negotiations had taken place between Great Britain and France on the one hand, and the Soviet Union on the other, with a view to achieving a common front against the anticipated German aggression. A major stumbling block in these negotiations proved to be the question of the so-called " indirect aggression " on which the Soviet Union insisted. This indirect aggression was to cover mainly the Baltic States and to give Russia the right of immediate intervention the moment she considered that such aggression had taken place. The Baltic States were not to be consulted as to whether they were inclined to accept a Soviet guarantee, — probably since it was officially known that they were reluctant to accept any guarantee whatsoever [1]. In spite of far-reaching Anglo-French concessions on this, as on many other points, the negotiations did not yield any result [2]. The reason of their failure was later explained by the British Foreign Secretary in a speech in the House of Lords after the Soviet attack on Finland :

" We have tried to improve our relations with Russia, but in doing so we had always maintained the position that rights of third parties must remain intact and be unaffected by our negotiations. Events have shown that the judgment and the instinct of H.M. Government in refusing agreement with the Soviet Government on the terms of formulae covering cases of indirect aggression on the Baltic States were right. For it is now plain that these formulae might have been a cloak of ulterior designs. I have little doubt that the people of this country would prefer to face difficulties and embarrassment rather than feel that we had compromised the honour of this country and the Commonwealth on such issues [3]. "

On September 23, 1939, with the British and French missions still in Moscow, the Soviet Union concluded with Germany the Non-Aggression Pact which has since become known as the Ribbentrop-Molotov Pact. This Pact was accompanied by an additional Secret Protocol, point 1 of which read :

1. Chambon, *La tragédie des Nations Baltiques*, pp. 23-25.
2. See Bonnet G., *Fin d'une Europe*, Constant Bourquin, Editeur, Genève, 1948, pp. 175-215 ; Namier, L. B. *Diplomatic Prelude*, London : Macmillan and Co. Ltd., 1948, pp. 143-210.
3. *Latvian-Russian Relations*, p. 200.

" In the event of a territorial and political re-arrangement in the areas belonging to the Baltic States (Finland, Estonia, Latvia, Lithuania), the northern boundary of Lithuania shall represent the boundary of the sphere of influence of Germany and the U.S.S.R... [1] "

This was changed on September 28, 1939, in a supplementary Secret Protocol to the German-Soviet Boundary and Friendship Treaty in the following manner :

" The Secret Supplementary Protocol signed on August 23, 1939, shall be amended in item 1 to the effect that the territory of the Lithuanian State falls to the sphere of influence of the U.S.S.R., while, on the other hand, the province of Lublin and parts of the province of Warsaw fall to the sphere of influence of Germany (cf. the map attached to the Boundary and Friendship Treaty signed to-day). As soon as the Government of the U.S.S.R. shall take special measures on Lithuanian territory to protect its interests, the present German-Lithuanian border, for the purpose of a natural and simple boundary delineation, shall be rectified in such a way that the Lithuanian territory situated to the southwest of the line marked on the attached map should fall to Germany [2]. "

On September 1, 1939, the three Baltic States issued declarations of neutrality in the war which had just broken out. This neutrality was not, however, to be respected for very long period.

Towards the end of September, Estonia was faced with a demand by the Soviet Union to conclude a Treaty of Mutual Assistance, giving the latter country the right to establish military garrisons on Estonian territory. In consequence of heavy pressure brought to bear on Estonia, clearly bordering on an ultimatum, the desired Treaty was signed in Moscow on September 28, 1939 [3].

---

1. *Nazi-Soviet Relations*, p. 78.
2. *Ibid.*, p. 107.
3. " Excerpts from the Minutes of the Meeting of the Estonian Republican Government on 26.9.1939 : At the meeting of the Republican Government held on September 26th, 1939. at 4 p.m., with the President of the Republic K. Päts in the chair, the Foreign Minister K. Selter reported on recent events : a) his invitation to Moscow in order to sign the Commercial Treaty, b) Molotov's proposal to conclude a Treaty of Mutual Assistance according to a project which the Foreign Minister read to the Government, c) Molotov's warning " that the security of the Soviet Union and the achievement of the aims mentioned in the project would be safeguarded by different methods if the Estonian Government should refuse to sign the Treaty ", and d) Molotov's notification that the Soviet Government considers the matter urgent. ...Questioned by the President of the Republic Minister A. Rei answered that no room for doubt was left by Molotov's proposal and by the warning, which he added orally, that the Soviet proposal, if not in its form then in its substance, was an ultimatum and that Molotov's words forced him to conclude that very grave steps would have to be feared of the Soviet Union in case Estonia should not agree to sign the Treaty. Molotov repeatedly used the expression " I beg you not to compel the Soviet Government to use other, more radical methods of safeguarding our security " and " if the Estonian Government fails to accept the Soviet proposal, then the U.S.S.R. will achieve the aims mentioned in the Security Pact by resorting to other means ". Especially in view of the situation which had been created before that conversation, it was impossible to interpret Molotov's expressions as anything but a threat to use military force in order to enforce the Soviet demands. " *Nazi-Soviet Conspiracy and the Baltic States*, p. 41. See also the telegram of the German Foreign Office to the German Embassy in Moscow, transmitting to Ribbentrop the following despatch from the German Minister in Tallin : " ...The Foreign Minister (of Estonia) conveyed a request to inform the Reich Foreign Minister of the following, if possible before his departure for Moscow : The Estonian Government, under the gravest threat of imminent attack, perforce is prepared to accept a military alliance with the Soviet Union. " *Nazi-Soviet Relations*, p. 104. For further details concerning the pressure on the Baltic States, see Dallin, *op. cit.*, pp. 80-92.

The Treaty which has since been described by an Estonian lawyer as " reciprocal in form but unilateral in contents [1] ", provided for mutual assistance

" of every kind, including military assistance, in the event of direct aggression or threat of aggression on the part of a European Great Power against the maritime frontiers of the Contracting Parties in the Baltic Sea or against their land frontiers across the territory of the Republic of Latvia, and also against the bases provided for in Article 3 ". (Art. 1.)

It also granted the Soviet Union the right to maintain naval and air bases on Estonian territory, together with a limited number of land and air forces, the maximum of which was to be determined by special agreement. (Art. 3.)

However, the Treaty still professed to adhere to the existing basis of the Soviet-Estonian relations, as defined by previous bilateral agreements [2]. Thus, the Preamble read :

" Desirous of developing the friendly relations established by the Treaty of Peace of February 2nd, 1920, based on the recognition of independent political existence and non-intervention by either Contracting Party in the internal affairs of the other Contracting Party,
Recognizing that the Peace Treaty of February 2nd, 1920, and the Treaty of Non-Aggression and Peaceful Settlement of Disputes of May 4th, 1932, are and remain the solid foundation of their reciprocal relations and obligations... "

Moreover, Article 5 of the new Treaty expressly stated :

" The enforcement of the present Pact may in no way impair the sovereign rights of the Contracting Parties. or, more especially, their economic system or political structure. "

The Treaty was concluded for a specified period of time, namely for ten years, at the end of which, failing denunciation by either Party, it was to be automatically prolonged for a further five years [3].

Next, Latvian Ministers were summoned to Moscow [4], where, on October 5, 1939, they signed a similar Treaty. That Treaty again included obligation to render every kind of assistance and the right of the Soviet Union to maintain military bases on Latvian territory, as well as provisions safeguarding sovereign rights of the parties. It also contained references to existing bilateral treaties between the parties, providing for the mutual recognition of their independence and non-interference in their internal affairs. The period of validity was to be the same as that of the Estonian Treaty [5].

Lithuania's turn came on October 10, 1939, when a Soviet-Lithuanian Treaty on the same lines was concluded in Moscow [6].

The assurance that these treaties in no way impaired the acknowledged sovereignty and separate political existence of the three

---

1. N. Kaasik, *L'ultimatum soviétique à l'Estonie*, in *Annexation of the Baltic States*, p. 14.
2. See above, pp. 369-373.
3. *Nazi-Soviet Conspiracy and the Baltic States*, pp. 39-41.
4. *Latvian-Russian Relations*, pp. 192-198.
5. *Ibid.*, pp. 198-199.
6. For details on the Lithuanian negotiations, see Chambon, *op. cit.*, p. 28 and p. 33.

Baltic States was given by the Soviet Commissar for Foreign Affairs, M. Molotov, in a speech to the Supreme Soviet of the U.S.S.R. of October 31, 1939 [1]. It was again repeated as late as March 29, 1940 [2].

Nevertheless, on June 14, and 16, 1940, the Soviet Union addressed ultimatums to the three Baltic States, requiring the immediate formation of governments corresponding to Soviet desires and free passage for Soviet troops, whose numbers were no longer to be limited or bilaterally determined.

The Soviet ultimatums to Latvia and Estonia of June 16, 1940, are practically identical. They read :

" On the basis of facts at the disposal of the Soviet Government, as a result of deliberations which recently took place in Moscow between Molotov, Chairman of the Council of People's Commissars, and Merkys, Prime Minister of Lithuania, the Soviet Government considers it proved that the Estonian Government has not only failed to liquidate her military alliance with Latvia, which was concluded before the signing of the Soviet-Estonian mutual assistance pact and directed against the Soviet Union, but has expanded this alliance, drawing Lithuania into it and attempting to attract Finland. Prior to the signing of the Soviet-Estonian mutual assistance pact in the autumn of 1939, the Soviet Government was still able to close its eyes to the existence of such a military alliance, although it was essentially inconsistent with the previously concluded Soviet-Estonian non-aggression pact. However, after the conclusion of the Soviet-Estonian mutual assistance pact, the Soviet Government considers a military alliance between Estonia, Latvia and Lithuania, which is directed against the Soviet Union, not inly insufferable and unbearable, but even extremely dangerous and menacing to the security of the frontiers of the Soviet Union.

The Soviet Government believed that Estonia would denounce her military alliance with the other Baltic countries after the conclusion of the Soviet-Estonian mutual assistance pact and that the aforesaid military alliance would thus be liquidated. Instead, Estonia, together with the other Baltic countries, began to revive and expand the aforesaid military alliance, which is testified by such facts as : the convocation of secret conferences of the three Baltic countries in December 1939 and March 1940 in order to organize the amplified military alliance made to include Latvia and Lithuania, the consolidation of the bonds between the Estonian, Latvian and Lithuanian general staffs secretly from the Soviet Union, the creation in February 1940 of a special press organ of the Baltic military entente, the " Revue Baltique ", which is appearing in Tallinn in English, French and German, etc. All these facts indicate that the Estonian Government has grossly violated the Soviet-Estonian mutual assistance pact which forbids both parties " to

---

1. " The Pacts with the Baltic States in no way imply the intrusion of the Soviet Union in the internal affairs of Estonia, Latvia and Lithuania, as some foreign interests are trying to make believe... These pacts are inspired by mutual respect for the Governmental, social and economic system of each of the contracting parties. We stand for an exact and honest fulfillment of agreements signed by us on a basis of reciprocity and declare that foolish talks of sovietization of the Baltic States is useful only to our common enemies and to all kind of anti-Soviet provocateurs... " *Nazi-Soviet Conspiracy and the Baltic States*, p. 45.

2. " ...After the experience of half a year which has passed since the conclusion of mutual assistance pacts with Estonia, Latvia and Lithuania, it is possible to draw fully definite positive conclusions on the treaties with the Baltic countries. It must be admitted that the pacts of the Soviet Union with Estonia, Latvia and Lithuania have furthered the consolidation of the international position of the Soviet Union as well as of Estonia, Latvia and Lithuania. Despite the intimidation practised by imperialistic circles, hostile to the Soviet Union, the national independence of Estonia, Latvia and Lithuania and their autonomous policies have in no way suffered, while the economic relations of these countries with the Soviet Union have undergone considerable expansion. The execution of the pacts with Estonia, Latvia and Lithuania is proceeding satisfactorily and creating prerequisites for a further improvement of relations between the Soviet Union and these States. " *Ibid.*, pp. 45-46.

conclude alliances and to take part in coalitions directed against either of the contracting parties " (Article 4 of the Pact). This gross violation of the mutual assistance pact is taking place at a time when the Soviet Government pursues and continues to pursue an extraordinarily amicable and definitely pro-Estonian policy, scrupulously observing all the requirements of the Soviet-Estonian mutual assistance pact.

The Soviet Government is of the opinion that such a state of affairs can no longer be tolerated. The Soviet Government considers it absolutely necessary and urgent that :

1) a government be established in Estonia that would be capable and willing to warrant the honest execution of the Soviet-Estonian mutual assistance pact ;

2) free passage be promptly ensured to Soviet troops which are to be stationed in sufficient numbers in the most important centers of Estonia in order to guarantee the realization of the Soviet-Estonian mutual assistance pact and to prevent possible acts of provocation against the Soviet garrisons in Estonia.

The Soviet Government considers compliance with these claims to be the elementary stipulations without which it is impossible to assure the honest and loyal execution of the Soviet-Estonian mutual assistance pact[1]. "

The text of the ultimatum is supplemented by the following statement, made by M. August Rei, Estonian Envoy in Moscow :

" In the written text of the above ultimatum its authors have omitted two most essential points which were made to me orally by M. Molotov for communication to the Government of the Estonian Republic. The substance of these points was as follows : 1) The ultimatum had to be answered by 23 o'clock of the same day, viz. June 16 (Moscow time) i.e. within 8 ½ hours, including the time I needed to get in touch by telephone with my Government and to communicate to it the text of the ultimatum, as well as the time required for communicating the answer to me and hand it on to M. Molotov. 2) A plain threat that in case no answer indicating submission to the ultimatum would be received by the stated time, the Red Army units concentrated at the frontier of the Estonian Republic would be ordered to march into Estonia, suppressing all resistance by armed force. ... The Latvian Minister F. Kocins told me on the following day that M. Molotov had made to him oral statements of exactly the same import as those referred to in paragraphs 1 and 2. ... I have made the present statement in order to put down in a written document the aforementioned facts. I confirm the correctness of this statement with my signature, and am always prepared to corroborate it on oath. Signed : A. Rei. Stockholm, September 28, 1940 [2]. "

The Soviet ultimatum to Lithuania of June 14, 1940, slightly differed from the above pattern. It had been preceded by a period of strained relations between the two countries, the Soviet Union accusing Lithuania of torturing Soviet soldiers and persecuting Lithuanian citizens who had come into contact with Soviet military personnel, as well as making her responsible for cases of disappearance of Soviet soldiers. Lithuania immediately offered to appoint a commission of enquiry and to investigate the matter thoroughly. Moreover, the Lithuanian Prime Minister went to Moscow on June 7, 1940, whereupon a Lithuanian communiqué was issued on June 12, indicating that all the difficulties were on their way to solution. Nevertheless, the Soviet ultimatum was presented two days later. While otherwise identical with those presented to Latvia and Estonia, it also dealt with the

---

1. *Nazi-Soviet Conspiracy*, pp. 46-47. For the Latvian ultimatum see *Latvian-Russian Relations*, pp. 202-203.
2. *Nazi-Soviet Conspiracy*, pp. 47-48.

above-mentioned incidents concerning Soviet garrisons in Lithuania. Consequently, the *petitum* included not only the two points of the Latvian and Estonian ultimatums [1], but also the demand that the Lithuanian Minister of the Interior and the Chief of the Police should be brought to judgment [2]. It may be mentioned that after the final occupation and incorporation of Lithuania into the Soviet Union, nothing more was heard of the incidents in question and no report of any commission of enquiry has ever become available.

It may be pointed out that the main argument of these ultimatums, to the effect that Estonia and Latvia had infringed the Mutual Assistance Treaties with the Soviet Union by failing to liquidate their alliance, was in contradiction with Art. 3 of the Non-Aggression Pacts [3], by which the former international obligations of the parties were expressly safeguarded. The Treaty of Defensive Alliance between Estonia and Latvia had been signed in 1923, that is, nine years before the Non-Aggression Pacts, and duly registered with the League of Nations. Neither on the conclusion of the Non-Aggression Pacts, nor on the conclusion of the Mutual Assistance Treaties, nor at any other time did the Soviet Union raise any objections to that particular Treaty, and no obligation was ever imposed on, or undertaken by, Estonia and Latvia to liquidate it. The allegation to the effect that Estonia and Latvia had tried to include Lithuania in their defensive alliance is denied by both Estonian and Latvian sources, and this denial is in turn confirmed by the confidential report of the German Foreign Office of June 17, 1940 [4]. This report also points out that since the conclusion of the Mutual Assistance Treaties there was no co-operation directed against Russia among the Baltic States, for

" in view of the occupation of their countries by Soviet Russian troops, the three Baltic Governments were aware of the danger of such a policy ".

The " secret conferences " referred to in the ultimatums were routine meetings of the Baltic Foreign Ministers which were normally held every six months, as provided for by the Treaty of Friendship and Collaboration of September 12, 1934 (Art. 2), registered with the League of Nations. The argument concerning the " Revue Baltique " does not seem to call for comment.

It is therefore submitted that nothing occurred between the signature of the Mutual Assistance Treaties and June 14 and 16, 1940, which would have justified the Soviet Union's departure from her previous attitude of avowed respect for the sovereignty and territorial integrity of the Baltic States.

There being no hope of resistance on the part of the Baltic States, the Soviet ultimatum was accepted within the prescribed time limit, whereupon the Red Army occupied Estonia, Latvia and Lithuania.

---

1. See above, p. 379.
2. Makarov, *Die Eingliederung der baltischen Staaten in die Sowjet-Union*, Zt.chft. *f.a.öff.R.u.V.-r.*, 1940/41, pp. 698-700 ; Pick, *The Baltic Nations*, p. 130.
3. See above, p. 372.
4. *Nazi Soviet Relations*, p. 152.

The military occupation was followed by the dismissal of the old and the appointment of new Governments, according to Soviet wishes. Soon afterwards the new Governments dissolved Parliaments and ordered new elections which took place in the three States on July 15 and 16, 1940. The newly elected Parliaments met on July 21, and passed identical resolutions asking to be admitted into the Soviet Union.

The request for incorporation was accepted by the Supreme Soviet early in August 1940 [1]. The incorporation of the Baltic States into the Soviet Union was thus completed. A minor detail, however, remained to be settled between the Soviet Union and Germany, namely, the question of the strip of Lithuanian territory which, according to the Secret Russo-German Protocol of September 28, 1939, [2] was to be ceded to the Reich. Following Russo-German negotiations, lasting from July 1940 to January 1941, and the Soviet offer of financial compensation, another Secret Protocol was signed in Moscow on January 10, 1941, in which the Reich renounced its claim to the Lithuanian territory in question against 7.500.000 gold dollars to be paid by the Soviet Government by way of compensation [3].

In August 1940, the Baltic States were endowed with constitutions modelled on those of the constituent Soviet Union Republics [4]. On September 7, 1940, a Soviet decree extended Soviet citizenship to Estonian, Latvian and Lithuanian nationals [5]. The structure of the three States was consequently adapted to the Soviet pattern. At the same time, large-scale reprisals were taken against the population [6]. The Latvian collection of documents includes the following item :

"The Latvian Permanent Delegate in Geneva (Switzerland), Mr. Juliijs Feldmans, has obtained from the Headquarters of the International Red Cross in Geneva and communicated to the Latvian Legation in Washington the following list of murdered, exiled and missing Latvian citizens for the period of Bolshevik reign of terror in Latvia, as from June 17, 1940, to July 1941..."

The total number of persons murdered, exiled, and missing for the period is given as 34.250 [7]. The corresponding figures for Estonia and Lithuania are 60.973 and 34.250 respectively [8]. The deportations, in particular, seem to have been conducted in an organized and systematic manner, as is borne out by the relevant instructions of the Soviet authorities [9]. Soviet Embassies abroad claimed Estonian, Latvian and

---

1. Makarov gives the following dates : August 3, 1940 for Lithuania, August 5 for Latvia and August 6, for Estonia., *op. cit.*, p. 703.
2. See above, p. 376.
3. *Nazi-Soviet Relations*, pp. 166, 174, 176, 188, 267-268.
4. *Latvian-Russian Relations*, pp. 211-226.
5. Makarov, *op. cit.*, p. 704.
6. For conditions in the Soviet occupied Baltic States, see Chambon, *op. cit.*, passim ; Pick, *op. cit.*, pp. 136-137 ; Hampden Jackson, *Estonia*, pp. 239-262.
7. *Latvian-Russian Relations*, p. 232.
8. *Baltic Refugees and Displaced Persons*, Foreword by the Duchess of Atholl, Published by Boreas Publishing Co. Ltd., 1947, p. 11.
9. *Lavian-Russian Relations*, pp. 227-231. For the confirmation of the mass deportations by an English Court, see The " Jaak " and other Estonian vessels, *Lloyds List Law Reports*, vol. LXXXIII, p. 51.

Lithuanian citizens as their subjects and called on them to register as such with the respective Consular Departments [1].

On June 22, 1941, German-Soviet war broke out. In all three Baltic States popular risings took place against the retreating Soviet armies. According to information available, Estonian partisans fought all over the country, with thousands of casualties on both sides. The same happened in Latvia, while in Lithuania, the number of partisans has been estimated at 125.000 [2]. Provisional Governments were proclaimed before the advent of the German troops.

Germany had recognized the absorption of the Baltic States into the Soviet Union. Having invaded them in 1941, she tolerated the Provisional Governments only for a short time, after which the Baltic States were proclaimed part of the German " Ostland " under a German Commissar with Headquarters in Riga [3]. While denying to the Baltic population the right to an independent State existence, the Germans yet tried to enlist its support in the war against the Soviet Union. Repeated attempts were made to mobilize Baltic citizens either directly into the fighting units or, at least, into Labour Battallions. It appears that these attempts met with strong resistance on the part of the population. At the same time, documents pointing to the existence of organized resistance movements, directed both against the Germans and the Russians, have become available in the West [4]. At the time of the German retreat risings again occurred in the three countries and for a while even an Estonian National Government was proclaimed in Tallin under Otto Tief, a former Minister of Justice. After the Soviet re-conquest of the Baltic States no more was heard of it [5]. Tens of thousands of Balts escaped from the country, taking refuge in Sweden, Germany, Austria, etc. The number of Baltic refugees to-day is estimated at 300.000, a very high percentage, compared with the total population of 6.000.000 for the three countries [6].

The second Soviet occupation, which began in 1944, still lasts. According to the information available, the Baltic countries are again subjected to both ʹsovietization and russification and deportations of thousands of Balts into the interior of Russia continue [7].

---

1. Pick, op. cit., pp. 135-136 ; Makarov, op. cit., p. 704.
2. Harrison, Lithuania's Fight for Freedom, p. 30.
3. For the German occupation of the Baltic States, see Chambon, op. cit., pp. 71-91, and Pick, op. cit., pp. 139-144.
4. Pick, op. cit., pp. 150-152 ; Harrison, op. cit., pp. 46-50 and 59-62 ; Latvian-Russian Relations, pp. 235-237 ; Hampden Jackson, op. cit., pp. 256-257 ; Chambon, op. cit., pp. 71-91.
5. Hampden Jackson, op. cit., p. 256.
6. Chambon, op. cit., p. 144.
7. See Chambon, op. cit., pp. 92-107 ; Kareda, East and West—Estonia in the Soviet Grip, London, Boreas Publishing Co. Ltd., pp. 86-96 ; Conseil National Letton, La Lettonie sous le joug bolchéviste, p. 6. Hampden Jackson, op. cit., pp. 257-262. — Cf. the joint Note by Baltic diplomatic representatives in Washington to the State Department accusing Russia of genocide : " Communist terror and annihilation of the population continues unabated ; people disappear in the streets or from their homes. Mass deportations are being carried out quite methodically.. Innocent victims find themselves in slave labour camps in remote parts of Russia where death is the only relief from their suffering. " New York Times, July 28, 1950. — Urging ratification by the United States of

B. *Legal Evaluation.*

The absorption of the three Baltic States into the U.S.S.R. could have been the result either of a voluntary merger or of a unilateral act on the part of the latter. A free merger, presupposing an act of will on the part of the Baltic States as well as of the U.S.S.R., could, in turn, have been the result either of a legal or of a revolutionary process in the Baltic Republics. For, as has already been pointed out [1], there is nothing in general international law to prevent fully independent States from alienating this independence, nor to prevent another independent State, from accepting the offer. In the absence of obligations to the contrary which can only arise out of specific conventional provisions, both constitute undoubted rights of States [2]. Failing such provisions, the Baltic States were free to renounce their independence in favour of the U.S.S.R. which, in turn, was free to accept such renunciation.

All these possibilities will now be examined with a view to arriving at a proper legal assessment of the events just described.

a) *Voluntary Merger of the Baltic States with the U.S.S.R.*

i) *Legal Process.*

The first possibility to be examined is whether what took place was a merger based on the will of the Baltic States legally arrived at, that is, formed and expressed according to the laws of these States by their proper organs. Such an examination is all the more necessary since all the evidence points to the conclusion that this must have been the official Soviet version ; otherwise it would be quite enigmatic why the procedure was adopted of having the new Governments nominated by the Presidents of the Republic [3], ordering elections formally on the basis of existing electoral laws, having the new Assemblies meet and proclaim their respective resolutions, and so forth.

As has been seen, the existing Baltic Governments were dismissed as a result of the Soviet ultimatum, and the new ones were formed in accordance with Soviet desires. This is how the process of their formation was initiated, according to the information given by M. Molotov to the German Ambassador in Moscow on June 17, 1940 :

" For the negotiations concerning the formation of the new Governments the Soviet Government had, in addition to the Soviet envoy accredited there, sent the following special emissaries : To Lithuania : Deputy Commissar of Foreign Affairs, Dekanozov ; to Latvia : Vyshinski, the representative of the Council of Ministers ; to Estonia : Regional Party Leader of Leningrad Zhdanov [4]. "

the Genocide Convention, Mr. Berle, former Assistant Secretary of State, declared : " There was evidence... that the Soviet Union was engaged in genocidal acts against the populations of the Baltic Republics, — Lithuania, Estonia and Latvia. " *Ibid.*, January 13, 1951.

1. See above, p. 339.
2. See the already quoted Individual Opinion of Judge Anzioltti, *P.C.I.J.*, Ser. A/B, 41, pp. 58-59.
3. With the exception of Lithuania, see below, p. 384.
4. *Nazi-Soviet Relations*, p. 154.

These emissaries presented lists of new Governments to the Presidents of Estonia and Latvia, as well as to the Prime Minister of Lithuania (the President of that last country having escaped abroad). Acting under duress, the two Presidents dismissed the existing Governments and nominated new ones in accordance with the Soviet lists [1]. In Lithuania, the dismissal and appointment was performed, in the absence of the Head of the State, by the actual Prime Minister, who had no such powers under the Lithuanian Constitution [2].

It is obvious that this procedure of effecting governmental changes was wholly at variance with the constitutional law of the countries concerned. None of the Baltic constitutions provided for the nomination of national governments according to lists drawn up by organs of a foreign State. From the point of view of international law, such nomination, actually undertaken by the government of a foreign State, resulted in the creation of mere puppet governments [3]. This basic fact disposes of any claim of legality of the subsequent events. Yet, these events shall now briefly be reviewed.

On July 6, 1940, the Soviet-installed Governments dissolved Parliaments in all the three Republics and ordered new elections to be held on the 14th and 15th of July.

These elections have since been described in detail. The following account is based chiefly on the testimony of M. August Rei, former President of Estonia and the last Estonian Minister in Moscow [4], whose evidence as a legal expert was fully accepted by Mr. Justice Atkinson in *A/S Tallinna Laevauhisus and Others v. Tallinna Shipping Co. and Another* and served as the basis of judgment in the case [5].

In Estonia, on July 6, 1940, the Government issued a decree fixing the date of the elections for July 14 and 15, and introducing a number of changes in the Estonian Electoral law. The Government was not, however, legally entitled to effect any changes in the said law which could have been changed only in the normal legislative way, i.e. by the vote of the two Chambers to be promulgated by the President of the Republic. The most important of these changes were the following : 1) the period allowed for the election campaign: according to paragraph 27 of the Estonian Electoral Law, a period of 35 days had to elapse between the announcement and the holding of the elections ; thus, elections announced on July 6 could not legally be held on July 15 ; 2) control of elections : according to the Electoral Law, the control was to be exercised by a Supreme Electoral Committee, which included the Chancellor of Justice, the Secretary of State, the President of a

1. The procedure with regard to Latvia is described in some detail by the then Latvian Minister for Public Affairs, Alfreds Berzinsh, *I saw Vishinsky bolshevize Latvia* pp. 23 et seq.
2. In some cases, persons appointed Ministers were not even citizens of the States concerned. *Latvian-Russian Relations*, p. 236.
3. " In June 1940, the territory of the Estonian Republic was occupied by the troops of the U.S.S.R., and on June 21, 1940 a new government was set up under the control of the government of the U.S.S.R. " " *The Jaak* " *and other Estonian vessels*, Shipping Claims Tribunal, *Lloyds List Law Reports*, vol. LXXXIII, p. 49.
4. Rei, *Have the Baltic Countries Voluntarily Renounced Their Freedom?*
5. *Lloyds List Law Reports*, vol. LXXIX, pp. 251-261.

division of the Tallinn District Court, the Lord Mayor of Tallin. " It is a body " — commented Mr. Justice Atkinson in the case quoted — " in whom everybody would have complete confidence [1] ". Even so, there was an appeal to the Supreme Court of Justice against the decisions of this Committee. The governmental decree of July 6, replaced this body by a new Supreme Electoral Committee, composed of a chairman and six members appointed by the Government, and abolished the right of appeal to an independent and impartial Court of Justice ; 3) several minor changes were introduced, as — for instance — the cancellation of Art. 40 of the Electoral Law, according to which every voter had to hand in his ballot paper personally. All these basic changes in the Electoral Law were followed, during the period July 6 — July 14, 15, by a number of arbitrary decisions and regulations. " Of course " — observed Mr. Justice Atkinson — " all those directions were wholly illegal according to the Constitution of Estonia [2] ".

All candidates were to be nominated by July 9, i.e. three days after the announcement of the elections. The Government-sponsored " Working People's League " nominated candidates for all the 80 Estonian constituencies. The opposition parties did the same. However, on the morning of July 10, the Government supplemented their original decree by a decision that every candidate had to announce his electoral programme by 2 p.m. of the same day. The Working People's League, having all the necessary propaganda machinery at its disposal, had already done so before, in a programme which was identical with that of its corresponding organisations in Latvia and Lithuania. In the few hours left to them for complying with the new condition, all but four of the independent candidates managed to write down and hand in their election programmes. Nevertheless, on the following day all of them were disqualified by the new Electoral Committee, with the exception of seventeen who were said to have withdrawn their candidatures voluntarily [3]. Thus, on polling day only approved candidates remained in the field.

The story was similar in Latvia where, according to the Constitution and the Electoral Law of 1922, any 100 electors had the right to submit a list of candidates. This right was, however, vitiated by an order from the Central Electoral Commission to the effect that groups presenting lists of candidates had to produce evidence that their political platform had previously received due publicity. No such evidence could be adduced, since not only had the entire Press and the wireless been taken over exclusively by the new authorities but, moreover, the Ministry of Public Affairs issued an order, directing all printing establishments to refuse to print any material dealing with the elections, unless such material had previously been approved by the Ministry [4]. The opposition parties' attempt to fight the election was

1. *Lloyds' List Law Reports*, vol. LXXIX, p. 254.
2. *Ibid.*, p. 255.
3. *Ibid.*, p. 255 ; Rei, *op. cit.*, pp. 25-26 ; for the manner of disqualifying candidates or making them withdraw their candidatures see *Annexation of the Baltic States*, pp. 31-36.
4. Berzinsh, *op. cit.*, pp. 36-37.

finally frustrated by the arrest of their leaders [1]. Consequently, in Latvia as in Estonia, only the official candidates were allowed to stand.

In Lithuania there was no need to disqualify the candidates in any of the above-mentioned ways, since from the very outset only the candidatures of the " Working People's League " were admitted [2].

It must therefore be concluded that the elections, ordered by illegal governments by means of illegal decrees, were, moreover, actually carried through by illegal methods. It should be added that a considerable amount of intimidation was used to compel the electorate to vote [3]. The almost unanimous vote calls for identical comment as the one made on the Austrian plebiscite under German occupation [4]. Moreover, even these official election results underwent strange variations. Thus, for instance, according to Estonian sources, the results from Estonia were released by the TASS agency in London twenty-four hours before the polling was completed [5].

The fruit of these elections were new Parliaments in the three Baltic States, whereby, in the case of Estonia, it was forgotten that her Constitution provided not for one, but for two Chambers, namely the Chamber of Deputies and the National Council. The following comment on the new Estonian Parliament, made by Mr. Justice Atkinson, would appear to be equally applicable to the other two Parliaments :

" Dr. Rei says that this new Chamber of Deputies was, of course, an unlawful body — it was just a cooked assembly, and to judge by the Constitution nothing it did could have any legal validity in Estonia — and that the Estonian Courts would have been bound to declare, if the matter had come before them, that this so-called legislation was null and void. But even apart from the illegality of the election of the Chamber of Deputies, they had no legislative power without the second Chamber, which was not re-elected and never again convened [6]. "

These Parliaments met in all three countries on July 21, 1940. On the same day the Latvian and Lithuanian Parliaments passed without debate a resolution asking for incorporation into the Soviet Union. The meeting of the Estonian Parliament was interrupted on the 21st, and resumed on the 22nd, when the same resolution was passed. Apparently the Estonian Government tried unsuccessfully at the last moment to obtain for their country some sort of autonomous status on the pattern of Outer Mongolia [7]. The text of the three resolutions was identical [8].

Apart from the illegal origin of the three Parliaments, the further question must be asked whether they had a right, according to the respective Constitutions, to dispose of their countries' independence. The answer is in the negative. The Estonian Constitution provided for legislation jointly by the two Houses of Parliament, to be promulgated

1. *Ibid.*, pp. 35-36.
2. Rei, *op. cit.*, p. 27.
3. *Ibid.*, pp. 29-31.
4. See above, pp. 342-343.
5. *Annexation of the Baltic States*, p. 33 ; see also Rei, *op. cit.*, pp. 33 et seq.
6. *Lloyd's List Law Reports*, *loc. cit.*
7. Rei, *op. cit.*, p. 41.
8. For more details concerning the Baltic elections, see Chambon, *op. cit.*, pp. 58-60 ; *Latvian-Russian Relations*, pp. 206-208 ; Kaasik, *op. cit.*, p. 19 ; Pick, *op. cit.*, pp. 132-134.

by the President. As has been seen, however, the Second Chamber was not convened, nor was the Constitution changed, which in itself implied the invalidity of all laws passed by the new Chamber of Deputies alone. Moreover, Article 1 of the Constitution provided that " Estonia is an independent and sovereign Republic ", and the alienation of that independence would have required compliance with the whole complicated procedure laid down for amending the Constitution, which was in fact never resorted to.

Article 77 of the Latvian Constitution reads :

" If the Saeima (Parliament) shall amend Articles one, two, three or six of the Constitution, then such amendments, in order to become valid, must be put to the plebiscite."

Article 1 in particular states :

" Latvia is an independent democratic republic."

Thus, the alienation of Latvian independence would have required a plebiscite which never took place.

Article 1 of the Lithuanian Constitution reads :

" The Lithuanian State is independent and sovereign."

No amendment of the Lithuanian Constitution was attempted either.

The foregoing analysis leads to the inescapable conclusion that the incorporation of the Baltic States into the Soviet Union was wholly illegal according to the laws of these States.

ii) *Revolution.*

Such illegality, however, would be completely irrelevant under international law, if it could be proved that what occurred in the Baltic States was in fact a revolution. Sweeping aside the old legal order, the victorious revolution could have established a new one, and the merger with the U.S.S.R. could have been achieved according to such new, revolutionary legality.

The possibility of such a revolution having taken place in the Baltic States must therefore be briefly examined, although — as has already been observed — no such claim was ever put forward by the Soviet Union [1].

After what has been said in general about the conditions of a genuine revolution as opposed to foreign intervention [2], and after an examination of the Albanian and Austrian cases [3], an evaluation of the events occuring in the Baltic States need not be unduly prolonged.

These events took place in heavily occupied countries, the occupation taking place as a result of an ultimatum which can hardly be considered a friendly act.

If it is true to say that there must be a strong presumption against

1. See above, p. 383.
2. See above, pp. 64-71.
3. See above, pp. 331-337 and pp. 338-368.

the genuine character of a revolution taking place under foreign occupation [1], then, indeed, such presumption is here strongly reinforced by all accompanying circumstances. Far from being a State phenomenon, that is, taking its course within the separate delimitation of the territorial, personal and legal sphere of validity of the three States, the alleged revolution was, on M. Molotov's own admission to the German Ambassador [2], directed from the beginning by high officials of the Soviet State. Soviet political officers and security services took a direct part in the proceedings, exerting every manner of pressure on the population. Furthermore, the presumption is not excluded by the alleged revolution running counter to the designs of the occupying Power [3]. On the contrary, it fully conformed to the Soviet intentions with regard to the Baltic States, as shown in the Anglo-French-Soviet negotiations [4] and as expressly embodied in the Soviet-German Secret Protocols [5].

It must further be borne in mind that a revolution is a spontaneous phenomenon ; in the Baltic case, however, it took place with an uncanny identity of timing and procedure in what were, after all, three entirely separate States. Yet, the dates of consecutive stages of that allegedly revolutionary development were nearly as identical as were the resolutions produced by the allegedly revolutionary bodies.

Moreover, the Parliaments whose completely illegal character has just been seen, lacked even a revolutionary mandate from the electorate to effect a merger with the U.S.S.R. It cannot be emphasized strongly enough that, even in the course of the illegal election campaign, the question of alienating the independence of the Baltic States had never been submitted to the electorate ; the elections — such as they were — were not a plebiscite for or against fusion with the U.S.S.R. ; they were merely elections to new parliaments. Not only was the intention of incorporating the countries into the Soviet Union never divulged but, on the contrary, the slogan of national independence was constantly employed throughout the election campaign [6]. The identical resolutions of the three Parliaments providing for the alienation of Baltic independence, fell like a blow on an electorate which, throughout all the preceding stages, has been given assurances to the contrary. Consequently, even if the elections were to be taken seriously as a revolutionary development, no allegation can possibly be made that the Baltic populations ever formulated or expressed their will to join the Soviet Union even in a revolutionary manner. Consequently, far from representing the triumph of a revolutionary electorate, the elections fully deserved the following comment by Mr. Justice Atkinson :

" I think one might think it was a glorious triumph for those who engineered the election [7]... "

1. See above, p. 65.
2. See above, p. 383.
3. See above, p. 65.
4. See above, p. 375.
5. See above, pp. 375-376.
6. Rei, *op cit.*, pp. 31-33 ; Kaasik, *op. cit.*, p. 20.
7. *Lloyds List Law Reports*, p. 255.

Neither the terror which was let loose in the Baltic States before and after their incorporation, nor the vast numbers of refugees from these countries, would in themselves constitute a proof that no genuine revolution had taken place. Both terror and flight are accompanying phenomena of practically any violent revolution (e.g. the French and the Russian Revolutions), without thereby casting a doubt on their genuine character. However, in the Baltic States reprisals were carried out by organs of a foreign State ; the tens of thousands of deportees, including Heads of State, high officials and prominent personalities, were rounded up by Soviet, not by Baltic security organs and they were carried off into the interior of the Soviet Union.

This fake character of the Baltic " revolution " was openly admitted. Thus, the resolution of the puppet Parliaments proclaiming merger with the U.S.S.R. stated explicitly :

" Now, the people, *helped by the mighty Red Army* have ... established in their own country the Soviet Government... If the people have been able to establish in their own country the only just order — Soviet order— *it is all due to the Soviet Union* [1]... "

It was even more openly admitted by M. Molotov in a conversation with the then Lithuanian Foreign Minister, Prof. Kreve-Mickevicius, of June 30, 1940, in which he informed his Lithuanian guest of the Soviet Union's decision to incorporate the Baltic States [2]. This conversation took place a fortnight before the Baltic elections.

The conclusion is obvious : no revolution took place in the Baltic States in the summer of 1940. The verdict, included in the already-quoted Soviet Note to Germany of March 18, 1939 [3], applies as fully to the Baltic States as it applied to Czechoslovakia :

" It is difficult to admit that any people would voluntarily agree to the destruction of their independence and to their inclusion in another State... "

b) *Seizure by the Soviet Union.*

The above analysis has resulted in the exclusion of the possibility of a voluntary fusion between the Baltic States and the U.S.S.R., failing the corresponding will on the part of the former, whether expressed in a legal or in a revolutionary manner. The only remaining alternative is a unilateral action on the part of the U.S.S.R.

This unilateral action consisted in forcible annexation of the three States. Such annexation, far from being effected only with the Supreme Soviet's acceptance of the resolutions of the three Parliaments, had in fact taken place through the military occupation of the Baltic States and the appointment of their governments which in turn — always under Soviet direction and with Soviet participation — provided for the creation of pseudo-parliamentary bodies. From the moment a foreign Power dictated the composition of the Baltic Governments, their independence was already lost. The subsequent events, which

---

1. *It. mine*, Harrison, *op. cit.*, p. 27.
2. Chambon, *op. cit.*, pp. 52-57.
3. See above, p. 288.

were probably intended to give the proceedings an appearance of legality for the benefit of the outside world, were thus in no way decisive for the loss of Baltic independence. If the elections had no more legal value than the Austrian plebiscite, the resolutions of the puppet parliaments had certainly no more value than the offer of the Albanian Crown to the King of Italy by the Albanian Assembly [1]. Once again, puppet creations proved to be the means of circumventing the law.

The forcible annexation of the Baltic States was thus an illegal act, both under customary and conventional international law. Under the former, the annexation constituted a violation of all its basic principles, such as the principle of State sovereignty and independence, the prohibition of violent seizure of territory and the prohibition of intervention. It has been seen that all these basic principles were expressly recognized and embodied in the agreements concluded by the Soviet Union with the Baltic States.

More particularly, the whole action of the Soviet Union with regard to the Baltic States represented a series of gross violations of practically every provision of every major convention between the countries concerned.

The Secret Protocols with Germany constituted a violation of Article 2 of the Estonian and Latvian Non-Aggression Treaties. Even failing a provision of corresponding clarity in the Lithuanian Non-Aggression Treaty, there can hardly be any doubt that these Protocols violated both its letter and its spirit.

The threat of force used in order to bring about the conclusion of the so-called Treaties of Mutual Assistance ran directly counter to the letter and the spirit of the Peace Treaties, the Non-Aggression Treaties, the Conciliation Conventions, the Kellogg Pact and the Protocol for the Renunciation of War. Nor was the use of an ultimatum compatible with the obligation to settle disputes by pacific means, as it resulted from the Non-Aggression Treaties, Conciliation Conventions, the Kellogg Pact and the Protocol for the Renunciation of War. Finally, military occupation, forcible intervention and ultimate annexation, constituted violations of every Soviet obligation towards the Baltic States, not excluding the obligations covered by the so-called Treaties of Mutual Assistance themselves [2]. The Soviet action constituted an act of aggression within the meaning of Article 2 (2) of the Conventions for the Definition of Aggression of 1933 ; according to the Article 3 as well as to the Annex of the same Conventions, there was no possible justification for this act.

The only conventional instrument to be excluded from the above list is perhaps the Covenant of the League of Nations ; in fact, in June 1940, the U.S.S.R. was no longer Member of the League and, consequently, no longer bound by the provisions of the Covenant, having been expelled from the League on December 14, 1939, following her aggression against Finland.

---

1. See above, p. 331.
2. See above, pp. 376-377.

It may be recalled that before her re-entry into, and re-annexation of, the Baltic States in 1944 and 1945, the Soviet Union had, in the course of the war, become party to agreements which are difficult to reconcile with the forcible seizure of these States. Thus, on January 1, 1942, the Soviet Union subscribed to the principles of the Atlantic Charter, as embodied in the United Nations' Declaration. On May 26, 1942, she had signed a Treaty with Great Britain, Art. 5 of which read :

" The High Contracting Parties, having regard to the interests of the security of each of them, agree to work together in close and friendly collaboration after the re-establishment of peace for the organisation of security and economic prosperity in Europe. They will take into account the interests of the United Nations in these objects, and they will act in accordance with the principles of not seeking territorial aggrandizement for themselves and of non-interference in the internal affairs of other States [1]. "

3. Legal Nature of the Baltic Soviet Socialist Republics.

Any attempt to treat an illegal act *per non est* can only lead to the most absurd fictions. Once performed, it is certainly not non-existent in actual fact. The illegal act of forcible absorption of the Baltic States by the U.S.S.R. has been carried out and brought about the creation of the three Baltic Soviet Socialist Republics [2].

Between the Baltic S.S.R.s and the independent Baltic States there is identity of territory, population and capitals ; there is, if not identity, then at least a similarity of name. There is therefore every incentive to an investigation of their legal nature with a view to discovering their legal relation to the independent Baltic States.

Such an enquiry is all the more necessary as the Soviet Union has already furnished her own interpretation of the situation. On the occasion of the signature of the International Telecommunication Convention of the Atlantic City, of 1947, the Soviet Union made the following reservation :

" ... the U.S.S.R. Delegation considers it unjustified that the following sovereign States, fully fledged participants of the Madrid Convention, were without any legal foundation not included in the list of Members of the Union set forth in Annex 1 : the Latvian Soviet Socialist Republic, the Lithuanian Soviet Socialist Republic, the Estonian Soviet Socialist Republic and the Peoples Republic of Mongolia [3]... "

The Soviet Union thus makes a twofold claim: 1) that her constituent Union Republics are sovereign States, and 2) that the Baltic S.S.R.s are identical with the independent Baltic States.

---

1. *British and Foreign State Papers*, vol. CXXXXIV, p. 1040.
2. The fact finds due acknowledgment in the numerous judicial decisions of American courts in Baltic cases. Thus, e.g. : " In the summer of 1940 the Russian armies occupied the Baltic coast and there was soon set up a puppet soviet republic of Latvia. " *In re Graud's Estate.* Surrogate Court, New York County, *A. D.*, 1943/45, case no. 10. " On June 17, 1940, the armies of the Union of Soviet Socialist Republics occupied Estonia and thereafter the Soviet Socialist Republic of Estonia was created. " *The Maret*, Circuit Court of Appeal, Third Circuit, *A. D.*, 1943/45, case no. 9.
3. *Final Acts of the International Telecommunication and Radio Conferences, Atlantic City*, 1947. International Telecommunication Union, Atlantic City, 1947, pp. 90-91 E.

The two claims form an inseparable whole. For indeed, if the Baltic S.S.R.s are just as independent, that is, immediately subordinated to international law, as the Baltic States had been, then — the territory and population remaining identical — there is no reason to question their identity with the Baltic States. It is therefore necessary to investigate the problem of their actual sovereignty within the larger framework of the sovereignty of the constituent Union Republics of the U.S.S.R.

The Baltic S.S.R.s were created in 1940 as constituent Republics of the Soviet Union under the 1936 Soviet Constitution, i.e. before the amendments of February 1, 1944, and they now continue in force under the same Constitution as amended on that date. Even before these amendments it was argued by M. Vyshinsky that all Union Republics were sovereign States within the Union. In his view

" The basic signs of the sovereignty of the Union Republics, are that : 1) each Union Republic has its own constitution, 2) the right to free withdrawal from the Union is preserved in behalf of each Union Republic, and 3) the territory of Union Republics cannot be changed without their consent [1]. "

It is hardly possible to accept M. Vyshinsky's claim. None of the " signs " listed by him has any relevance to the problem of sovereignty, if this term is taken to mean the immediate subordination to international law.

More particularly, it is undoubtedly true that each Union Republic has its own constitution. This is also the case with respect to the American States and the Swiss cantons, yet it does not make them into independent States. It may also be remarked that, according to Art. 16 of the Union Constitution, the constitutions of the Republics have to conform to the latter, and control over this conformity is vested in the Union under Article 14 (d). With regard to the right of free withdrawal from the Union, this would indeed be an argument in favour of the Republics' independence exactly to the same extent to which it would transform the U.S.S.R. from a Federal State into a Confederation of States. Neither proposition can, however, be seriously entertained. The U.S.S.R. is not a mere Confederation of States, whereas Article 17 of the Union Constitution, providing for the right of secession is a dead letter not only in fact, but actually in law. The commentators on the Soviet Constitution have this to say on the subject :

" ... there is to be noted in this connection the fact that many of those charged with treason and counter-revolution in the purges of 1937-38 were accused of working to dismember the Soviet Union [2]. "

---

1. *The Law of the Soviet State*, New York : The Macmillan Company, 1948, p. 284. At that period M. Vyshinsky did not yet consider the conduct of foreign relations a neccessary characteristic of the sovereignty of Union Republics ; on the contrary, he branded such ideas as Ukrainian bourgeois nationalist, Trotskyist and counter-revolutionary. *Ibid*, p. 227.
2. Harper-Thompson, *The Government of the Soviet Union*, D. Van Nostrand Co. Inc. Toronto, New York, London, 1949, pp. 52-53.

The effectiveness of Article 17 may thus be doubted. Finally, with regard to the right of the Union Republics not to have their territory changed without their consent, it does indeed seem that, according to the Constitution, their opposition to such a change could hardly be formally overruled. This, however, only affects their legal position under the municipal law of the Union and not under international law, and is of no significance from the point of view of their possible international status [1].

M. Vyshinsky's arguments are thus irrelevant to the question of the international legal position of the Union Republics. The answer to the problem must be sought in the actual text of the Soviet Constitution. Its Article 14 in particular, in its original 1936 version, defined the sphere of jurisdiction exclusively reserved to the Union as a whole in the following manner, automatically excluding the competence of the Union Republics :

" The jurisdiction of the Union of Soviet Socialist Republics, as represented by its highest organs of State power and organs of State administration, embraces :

a) Representation of the U.S.S.R. in international relations, conclusion and ratification of treaties with other States,

b) Questions of war and peace,

c) Admission of new Republics into the U.S.S.R.,

d) Control over the observance of the Constitution of the U.S.S.R. and ensuring conformity of the Constitutions of the Union Republics with the Constitution of the U.S.S.R.,

e) Confirmation of alterations of boundaries between Union Republics,

f) Confirmation of the formation of new Territories and Regions and also of new Autonomous Republics and Autonomous Regions within Union Republics,

g) Organisation of the defence of the U.S.S.R., direction of all the Armed Forces of the U.S.S.R.,

h) Foreign trade on the basis of State monopoly,

i) Safeguarding the security of the State,

j) Determination of the national economic plans of the U.S.S.R.,

k) Approval of the consolidated State budget of the U.S.S.R., determination of the taxes and revenues which go to the Union, the Republican and local budget,

l) Administration of the banks, industrial and agricultural institutions and enterprises and trading enterprises of all-Union importance,

m) Administration of transport and communications,

n) Direction of the monetary and credit system,

o) Organisation of State insurance,

p) Contracting and granting of loans,

q) Determination of the basic principles of land tenure and of the use of mineral wealth, forests and waters,

r) Determination of the basic principles in the spheres of education and public health,

s) Organisation of a uniform system of national economic statistics,

t) Determination of the principles of labour legislation,

u) Legislation concerning the judicial system and the judicial procedure, criminal and civil codes,

---

1. Moreover, evidence available with regard to the Autonomous Soviet Socialist Republics would permit a doubt as to the effectiveness of the above rights even of Union Republics : shortly after the war the Kalmuk, the Crimean, the Volga-German and the Chechen-Ingusch Autonomous Soviet Socialist Republics, as well as the Karachai Autonomous Region, had not only their frontiers changed, but were totally suppressed, and their population deported as a punishment for " treasonable activities " during the war. Harper-Thompson, *op. cit.*, pp. 55 and 333, *f.-n.* 4.

v) Legislation concerning Union citizenship ; legislation concerning rights of foreigners,

w) Issuing of all-Union Acts of amnesty.

Consequently, Art. 15, stating that

" the sovereignty of the Union Republics is limited only in the spheres defined in Art. 14 of the Constitution "

and that

" outside of these spheres each Union Republic exercises State authority independently "

can hardly be considered as securing the independence of the Union Republics. Moreover, the jurisdiction of the Union Republics is further limited by a number of provisions of the Constitution, e.g. Art. 20 (providing for the Union law to prevail over the law of Union Republics in case of divergence), Art. 68 (a), (providing for the direction of all-Union as well as of Union Republican Ministries by the Council of Ministers of the U.S.S.R.), Art. 69 (providing for the right of the Council of Ministers of the U.S.S.R. to suspend decisions and orders of the Councils of Ministers of the Union Republics), Art. 76 (providing for the direction by the Union-Republican Ministries of the corresponding Ministries of the Union Republics), Art. 81 (stating that the Council of Ministers of a Union Republic shall issue decisions and orders on the basis of the existing Union and Union-Republican laws, as well as of the decisions and orders of the Council of Ministers of the U.S.S.R.), Art. 85 (laying down similar rules for individual Ministers), Art. 87 (providing for the subordination of each Union-Republican Ministry to the Council of Ministers of the Union-Republic, as well as to the corresponding Union-Republican Ministry of the U.S.S.R.).

This then was the constitutional position of the Baltic S.S.R.s in the years 1940-1941. On February 1, 1944, the following amendments to the Soviet Constitution came into force :

Art. 18 *a*. Each Union Republic has the right to enter into direct relations with foreign States and to conclude agreements and exchange diplomatic and consular representatives with them.

Art. 18 *b*. Each Union Republic has it own Republican military formations.

Consequently, minor changes were introduced into some other Articles of the Union Constitution in order to bring them into harmony with these amendments. Thus, according to the new Art. 14 (a), the jurisdiction of the U.S.S.R. now embraces equally the

"establishment of general procedure governing the relations of Union Republics with foreign States ",

and, according to Art. 14 (g),

" determination of directing principles governing the organisation of the military formations of the Union Republics ".

The Ministries of the Armed Forces and of Foreign Affairs were transferred from all-Union to Union-Republican rank, all the limitations on such Ministries in the Union Republics being maintained [1].

Can it be assumed that the Union Republics became independent, sovereign States as a result of these amendments?

The answer must of necessity be in the negative. All previous limitations remain and the Federal State still stands between the Union Republics and international law. The new rights of the Union Republics mean no more than the authorization of the Swiss cantons to conclude agreements on minor matters with neighbouring States in exceptional cases [2]. They are granted by the Constitution of the Federal State, they have their source in municipal, not in international, law and are liable to revocation by that same Federal State which has granted them [3]. The reason of validity of the Union Republics continues to be found in municipal, not in international law. They are not directly subordinated to international law; they are therefore not independent and therefore not States [4].

Nor could it be argued that the admission of two of the Union Republics as Members of international organisations had endowed them with the character of independent States [5]. On the contrary, the unreality of such a theory to which attention has already been drawn, is particularly clearly borne out by the very example of the Ukrainian and Byelorussian S.S.R.s [6]. Moreover, it is difficult to see how, merely by reason of such admission, the two Union Republics would become States, whereas all the other Union Republics, with exactly the same legal status, would not.

In view of the foregoing analysis, as well as of the basic concept of State as adopted in this study [7], the Soviet view concerning the sovereign State character of the Union Republics cannot be accepted.

For this reason alone, the possibility of a legal identity between the Baltic S.S.R.s and the independent Baltic States must be eliminated. It has been seen that there can be no such relation of identity between an independent and a " dependent " State, even if the two have the same territorial and personal sphere of validity [8].

This conclusion is further reinforced by the particular circumstances which accompanied the creation of the Baltic S.S.R.s. It has been

---

1. See Art. 68 (a), Art. 76, Art. 85, Art. 87. Quotations from Harper-Thompson, *op. cit.*
2. Guggenheim, *Lehrbuch*, I, pp. 276-277.
3. *Ibid.*, *f.-n.* 323.
4. See above, pp. 180-186.
5. See above, p. 185.
6. " The admission of Byelorussia and Ukraine as separate members of the United Nations presents an anomalous situation, in that neither of the two States, if they can be called such, possessed any degree of international personality previous to their admission to the United Nations. Whether their activities as members of the organisation will be followed by their *de facto* independence of control by the central government of the U.S.S.R. and their assertion of the prerogatives of sovereign States, remains to be seen. Thus far they appear to represent indirectly the Soviet Union. " Fenwick, *op. cit.*, p. 139. Prof. Scelle speaks of « ...l'Ukraine ou la Biélorussie, fictivement « étatisées » par décision du gouvernement de Moscou... » *Op. cit.*, p. 128.
7. See above, pp. 161-186.
8. See above, p. 187.

seen that their creation was entirely illegal under the constitutional laws of the three States and that, insofar as they may be said to have come into existence as a result of revolution, this could only have been a fake revolution. Here the distinction between a genuine and a fake revolution, already referred to, comes fully into its own : for, as has been seen, whereas a genuine revolution in no way affects the identity and continuity of the revolutionary State, a fake revolution, that is to say, intervention, does. For this reason there can be no relation of identity and continuity between an independent State existing prior to a fake revolution, and an entity which has emerged out of such a revolution [1].

Finally, it must be recalled that a State is identified by its basic norm, whether such norm is produced in a legal or a revolutionary manner ; in the latter case, the autonomy of the basic norm is safeguarded by the surviving personal and territorial delimitation, from within which the new basic norm is being produced with no outside intervention [2]. In other words, for the continuity of a State, as for its birth, its reason of validity must be directly rooted in international law ; it cannot be situated within the legal order of another State. Its basic norm cannot be the concretisation on a lower level of a basic norm of that other State.

It was for this reason, — and not due to further loss of territory — that the identity of the Protectorate of Bohemia and Moravia with the Czechoslovak Republic has been denied [3]. If that reasoning was valid for Czechoslovakia, it must be equally valid for the Baltic States.

As compared with the independent Baltic States, the basic norm of the Baltic S.S.R.s is to be found outside their legal order. It is consequently not identical with the basic norm of the former, whether created in a legal or in a revolutionary manner. The original reason of validity of the Baltic S.S.R.s was the intervention of the U.S.S.R. ; their actual basic norm is the basic norm of the U.S.S.R. The territory of the Baltic States has come to carry a different legal structure. As in the case of Czechoslovakia, the new basic norm is to be found within a legal order of another State, being the outcome of that State's independent and decisive will and a concretisation on a lower level of the basic norm of that other State. There is then no relation of identity and continuity between the Baltic S.S.R.s and the independent Baltic States.

Insofar as the Soviet Union claims that they are not directly annexed territories but autonomous bodies with a legal will of their own, they must be considered puppet creations, exactly in the same way in which the Protectorate or Italian-dominated Albania have been classified as such. These puppet creations have been established on the territory of the independent Baltic States ; they cover the same territory and include the same population. The existence of these two sets of entities, — if the expression may be used — related to the same

---

1. See above, pp. 70-71.
2. See above, pp. 186-187.
3. See above, pp. 292-303.

territory and population and yet unrelated to, and non-identical with, each other, has been clearly appreciated by American courts when dealing with Baltic cases. Thus, in the case of *The Denny*, the District Court of the District of New Jersey, held :

" The sovereignty of the State, Lithuanian Soviet Socialist Republic, *created on the territory of the Republic of Lithuania*, and the newly established soviet government of that State, have not achieved recognition. The Republic of Lithuania is recognized as the sovereign State, and recognition is accorded its duly accredited representatives [1]. "

In *The Signe, renamed Florida*, the District Court of the Eastern District of Louisiana spoke of

" the government of the Estonian Soviet Socialist Republic, constituent governmental structure in the U.S.S.R., *whose absorption of the Republic of Estonia within itself (and the creation of the supplanting Estonian Soviet Socialist Republic to take its place)* is not recognized by the United States [2] ".

In *re Graud's Estate*, the Surrogate Court of the New York County held :

" In the summer of 1940 the Russian armies occupied the Baltic coast and there was soon set up a puppet Soviet Republic of Latvia which was duly welcome into the U.S.S.R. ... Our government as a national policy has refused recognition of any puppet government of any country which has been the victim of aggression and has refused recognition of *de facto* control set up by an aggressor. It has continued to recognize *the original Republic of Latvia*, with which it has treaty relations, *as the only legitimate* government of the territory known as Latvia [3]. "

As has been seen, the recent history of international relations has witnessed the setting-up not only of puppet governments, but also of puppet entities which have actually been claimed by the aggressor to be States, on territory lawfully belonging to the original State and recognized as such by the outside world. The first case was that of Manchukuo, set up as a " State " on Chinese territory. There followed the establishment of Slovakia on the territory of the Czechoslovak Republic, — not to speak of the Protectorate for which no claim to statehood was ever advanced by Germany. In the course of the Second World War a Kingdom of Croatia was created on the territory of occupied Yugoslavia. The difference between these creations and the puppet Baltic S.S.R.s seems to be one of degree : while the former were established on *a part* of the territory of the original State, the latter — like Italian-dominated Albania — were established *on the whole* of its territory. This difference of degree cannot be considered one of substance.

4. THE PROBLEM OF THE EXTINCTION OF THE BALTIC STATES.

The next question to be examined is that of the extinction of the independent Baltic States. An answer, whether in the affirmative or in the negative, automatically solves the problem of their continuity.

---

1. *It. mine, A. D.*, 1941/42, case no. 18.
2. *It. mine, A. D.* 1941/42, case no. 19.
3. *It. mine, A. D.*, 1943/45, case no. 10.

If indeed they became extinct, then there is no possible subject of such continuity, the Baltic S.S.R.s not being identical with their territorial predecessors. If the answer is in the negative, then the Baltic States continue to exist and to possess the same international personality as before the invasion and annexation of their countries.

This is not the first problem of possible State extinction following an illegal act of forcible annexation, to be examined in this study. In all the other cases, however, such examination took place against the background of an already effective solution ; the victim States had already been restored on the basis of their recognized continuity. This effective restoration having been achieved, it was possible to examine the international position of the restored State and to determine, from the evidence available, whether it continued the legal personality of the old one or whether, on the contrary, it represented a new State creation. It was such evidence of the old State character of the restored State, tested for its conformity with the principles and nature of international law, which yielded the final proof of its continued existence, uninterrupted by the illegal act to which it had fallen victim.

This method cannot be adopted in the case of the Baltic States where effective Soviet control still continues. The Baltic S.S.R.s remain an effective reality. No restoration of the independent Baltic States has taken place. What may, or may not, happen in future, does not fall into the scope of this enquiry.

In these circumstances there would seem to be a strong *prima facie* case in favour of the extinction of the Baltic States. They have suffered a total loss of territory. Their population has become related to another State order. Their own legal order is nowhere effective. Their countries have not been occupied as a result of a war and are therefore not under belligerent occupation. None of the three classical rules of international law safeguards their continued existence.

Yet, before finally accepting such a conclusion, it is necessary to examine actual State practice with regard to the continuity or extinction of the Baltic States.

5. THE BALTIC PROBLEM IN THE LIGHT OF STATE PRACTICE [1].

The Soviet claim of a voluntary merger of the Baltic States with the U.S.S.R. and of their legal identity with the Baltic S.S.R.s has found no acceptance in the outside world. The forcible annexation of the Baltic States has not been recognized *de iure* by the international community with the exception of Germany prior to 1941, and Sweden to-day. The attitude of the various States is, however, not uniform and will be examined in some detail. Since there has been no international judicial decision on the subject and since all the municipal decisions available come from countries professing the doctrine of

---

1. For several items of information included under this and the subsequent heading the writer is gratefully indebted to Their Excellencies, M. August Torma, M. Karl Zarins and M. Bronius Balutis, the Estonian, Latvian and Lithuanian Ministers in London.

judicial auto-limitation, it has been found possible to examine such decisions under the same heading as the practice of the State concerned.

a) *The United States.*

The attitude of the United States has, from the very beginning, been one of absolute and uncompromising non-recognition of the annexation of the Baltic Republics, with all the legal and practical consequences resulting therefrom. This attitude was made clear on July 23, 1940 in a statement by the Under-Secretary of State, Mr. Sumner Welles and has not undergone any changes since then.

" During these past few days the devious processes whereunder the political independence and territorial integrity of the three small Baltic Republics — Estonia, Latvia and Lithuania — were to be deliberately annihilated by one of their more powerful neighbours, have been rapidly drawing to their conclusion. From the day when the peoples of these Republics first gained their independence and democratic form of government the people of the United States have watched their admirable progress in self-government with deep and sympathetic interest. The policy of this Government is universally known. The people of the United States are opposed to predatory activities no matter whether they are carried on by the use of force or by the threat of force. They are likewise opposed to any form of intervention on the part of one State, however powerful, in the domestic concerns of any other sovereign State, however weak. These principles constitute the very foundations upon which the existing relationship between the twenty one sovereign republics of the New World rests. The United States will continue to stand by these principles, because of the conviction of the American people that unless the doctrine in which these principles are inherent once again governs the relations between nations, the rule of reason, of justice, and of law — in other words, the basis of modern civilization itself — cannot be preserved [1]. "

The statement is characterized by a correct evaluation of the events which led to the absorption of the Baltic States into the U.S.S.R. Far from admitting a voluntary merger, the United States qualifies these events as an attempt at deliberate annihilation, accomplished by devious processes. Far from admitting a revolution in the Baltic States, the statement correctly speaks of foreign intervention. Consequently, the American refusal to recognize such illegal act is being based on a principle of international law, which the United States had made its own. The principle involved is *ex iniuria ius non oritur* on which the United States has squarely taken its stand.

The automatic consequence of a refusal to recognize the illegal annexation was the continued, full and unquestioned recognition of the legal continuity of the Baltic States. This attitude found a particularly forceful expression in certificates of the State Department, submitted to American courts.

In the first Baltic case which came up before an American court in 1940

" there was offered in evidence a communication of our State Department as of October 24, 1940, reciting that this Government does not recognize the absorption of Estonia by the Union of Soviet Socialist Republics and indeed,

---

1. *Doc.* III, pp. 429-430.

continues to recognize Johannes Kaiv as Consul General of Estonia. ... Not only does our Government not recognize the validity of these decrees but also the executive order of the United States Government No. 6560 of April 10, 1940, supplemented by executive order of July 15, 1940, popularly known as "freezing orders" in effect prevents the transfer of property of nationals of invaded countries so that such property may not inure to the benefit of the aggressors [1]".

This position was maintained, perhaps even more clearly and forcefully, in later cases. Thus, the certificate of the Secretary of State of April 15, 1941, affirmed the non-recognition by the United States of the absorption of Estonia by the U.S.S.R. as well as the non-recognition of

"the legality of the so-called nationalization laws and decrees or of any of the acts of the regime now functioning in Estonia".

The letter of Mr. Loy Henderson, Assistant Chief, Division of European Affairs, to the counsel for the Estonian Consul in New York, of December 20, 1940, stated that the Government of the United States

"regards as still in force the Treaty of Friendship, Commerce and Consular Rights between the United States and Estonia signed on December 23, 1945,"

and

"also continues to recognize Mr. Johannes Kaiv as Acting Consul General of Estonia in New York [2]".

The same principle was upheld in *The Signe* [3] and in *The Signe (renamed Florida)* [4] where it was re-stated with extreme vigour :

"6. The United States Government does not recognize such absorption of Estonia by such Union of Soviet Socialist Republics, nor the present governmental regime functioning in such Republic, nor any of the acts of said regime.

7. The Treaty of Friendship, Commerce and Consular Rights between the United States and Estonia, dated December 25, 1925, is considered in effect by the United States Government.

8. Said Government continues to recognize Johannes Kaiv to be the duly accredited Acting Consul General of Estonia in the United States and in charge of Legation for the temporarily supplanted government of the Republic of Estonia."

With regard to Latvia, the Court summarized the Government's attitude as follows :

"Our government has pursued the consistent governmental policy of denying validity to the acquisition of territory or ostensible sovereignty acquired by forcible dispossession of the governments created by the people of invaded territories. Our government has continued to recognize and still recognizes as a valid subsisting government the Republic of Latvia and the diplomatic officers accredited to this country by that government. So long as that recognition continues and so long as it remains our governmental policy to deny recognition to forcible occupations of countries with which this country is at peace, the right of the original government of any seized territory to protect the interests of its nationals must be recognized by the courts [5]."

---

1. *The Kotkas*, A. D., 1941/42, case no. 15.
2. Both documents quoted in *The Maret*, A. D., 1943/45, case no. 9.
3. A. D., 1941/42, case no. 16.
4. *Ibid.*, case no. 19.
5. *In re Graud's Estate*, A. D., 1943/45, case no. 10.

In the case of *The Denny* the Court stated :

" The acceptance of the Republic of Lithuania into the Union of Socialist Soviet Republics is not recognized by the United States of America [1]. "

In the case *A/S Merilaid and Co. v. Chase National Bank of City of New York* the U.S. Supreme Court again re-asserted the fixed policy of the American Government :

" ... the Government of the United States does not recognize the incorporation of the Republic of Estonia into the U.S.S.R., and it has refused to recognize the Estonian Soviet Socialist Republic [2]. "

In conformity with the doctrine of judicial auto-limitation, prevailing in the United States, the American courts thus implemented the government's policy, acting on the assumption of the legal continuity of the Baltic States, unbroken by their illegal annexation. Thus, no effect was given to decrees issued by the Governments of the Baltic S.S.R.s, precisely on account of American non-recognition of these governments [3]. Acts of Baltic citizens residing in the occupied territory were considered as having been carried out under duress [4]. Application for letters rogatory to the Supreme Court of the R.S.F.S.R. was denied [5]. The standing of the Baltic consuls in court was upheld [6].

In harmony with this attitude of the U.S. Executive, the diplomatic and consular missions of the Baltic Republics in the United States continue their normal activities and enjoy all diplomatic privileges not only *de facto* but also *de iure*, on a footing of complete equality with all other foreign representatives. The Diplomatic List of the State Department includes the Baltic Legations with the names and full rank and titles of their personnel. Baltic passports are not only recognized, but actually required for travel and emigration purposes. Thus, an Estonian sailor is not permitted to land in the United States unless provided with a regular and valid Estonian passport.

Nor is it to be assumed that the continued legal existence and activities of the Baltic diplomatic missions are a mere result of courteous inertia. The following incident is certainly unique in diplomatic practice : following the death of the Latvian Envoy in Washington, the Latvian Minister in London, basing himself on his Emergency Powers and acting as " quasi-Foreign Minister " [7] appointed a new Envoy. The appointment was accepted by the United States Government

---

1. *A. D.*, 1941/42, case no. 18.
2. *A. D.*, 1947, case no. 6. In the latest reported case, the *Latvian State Cargo and Passenger S. S. Line v. Clark*, the District Court for the District of Columbia fully maintained the general attitude of U.S. courts in Baltic cases ; see *A. D.*, 1948, case no. 16.
3. *The Maret*, *A. D.*, 1943/45, case no. 9 ; *In re Graud's Estate*, *ibid.*, case no. 10 ; *A/S Merilaid*, *A. D.*, 1947, case no. 6.
4. *The Signe renamed Florida*, *A. D.*, 1941/42, case no, 19.
5. *The Kotkas*, *A. D.*, 1941/42, case no. 15 ; *The Signe*, *ibid.*, case no. 15 ; *The Regent*.
6. *The Signe renamed Florida*, *In re Graud's Estate*, *The Maret*, *Buxhoeveden v. Estonian State Bank*, *A. D.*, 1943/45 case no. 82. For an exhaustive survey see Briggs : *Non-Recognition in the Courts : the Ships of the Baltic Republics*, *A. J.*, 1943, p. 585.
7. See below, p. 410.

and the new Envoy, Mr. Feldmans, presented his credentials to the Secretary of State on June 28, 1949 [1].

Particular weight attaches to a re-statement of the attitude of the U.S. Government, which is to be found in the Second Semiannual Report of the Displaced Persons Commission to the President and the Congress, of October 24, 1949. In view of certain ambiguities of the Displaced Persons Act, the Commission found it necessary to

" secure from the Department of State an interpretation of what are considered to be *de facto* annexed countries and territories ".

The answer, as given in the document, was as follows :

" The *de facto* annexed countries and territories contained in the Department of State's definition are located in eastern Europe and include those whose transfer to other powers have not been recognized by the United States Government. In the main, the countries and territories comprised within the definition are those which are now under the rule of a power other than the one which exercised sovereignty in 1937, exclusive, of course, or areas transferred in accordance with the treaties of peace, signed 1947, between the Allied and Associated Powers and Bulgaria, Finland, Hungary, Italy and Rumania. Also excluded is an area in northern Finland transferred to the Soviet Union pursuant to a 1947 Finnish-Soviet agreement and, as well, the so-called Subcarpathian Ukraine (Ruthenia) transferred to the U.S.S.R. in accordance with the Czech-Soviet agreement of June 29, 1945. The countries and territories in question are eight in number and fall into three major categories, according to their status, as follows :

A. Formerly independent States, incorporated into the U.S.S.R. The United States Government has stated publicly that it does not recognize the incorporation of these States into the Soviet Union.

1. Estonia.
2. Latvia.
3. Lithuania [2]. "

In order to appreciate the full significance of the above, it is necessary to compare it, with the following paragraph of the Report :

" B. Territories placed under the administration of the U.S.S.R. or Poland as a result of decisions of the Potsdam Conference (1945). In the view of the United States Government, final determination of sovereignty over these areas will not be made until there is a peace treaty with Germany."

The difference between the two paragraphs may be noted. Thus, while the U.S. Government admits the possibility of determining the sovereignty of the areas specified in paragraph B in a future peace treaty with Germany, there is no similar provision for the Baltic States. It would thus appear that the United States does not envisage any

---

1. *Dep. of St. Bul.*, XXI, pp. 33-34. Since the Latvian Minister in London had acted in his capacity of Foreign Minister and not as Head of State, he could only appoint Mr. Feldmans as Chargé d'Affaires, and could not therefore have him accredited to the President, but only to the Secretary of State. Mr. Feldmans having already before his appointment held the rank of Minister Plenipotentiary, his name is listed in a rather unusual manner in the State Department's Diplomatic List, — namely, " Mr. Jules Feldmans, Minister Plenipotentiary, Chargé d'Affaires. "
2. *The Displaced Persons Commission, Second Semiannual Report to the President and the Congress*, August 1, 1949, U.S. Government Printing Office, Washington 1949, pp. 12-13.

future transfer of sovereignty over these territories or even any further discussion of the problem. There is a note of finality with regard to the non-recognition of the annexation of the Baltic States, which is lacking with regard to the territories enumerated in paragraph B.

This attitude of the United States is not confined to the internal American level. It has been upheld in dealings with third States and particularly with the Soviet Union herself.

Thus, on the occasion of the signature of the indictment of the major German war criminals, the U.S. prosecutor made the following reservation which was filed the same day with the Secretary of the Tribunal :

"In the indictment of German war criminals signed to-day reference is made to Estonia, Latvia, Lithuania and certain other territories as being within the area of the U.S.S.R. This language is proposed by Russia and is accepted to avoid delay which would have been occasioned by the insistence on an alteration in the text. The indictment is signed subject to this reservation and understanding.

I have no authority either to admit or to challenge, on behalf of the United States, the Soviet claims to sovereignty over such territories. Nothing, therefore, in this indictment is to be construed as a recognition by the United States of such sovereignty or as indicating any attitude, either on the part of the United States or on the part of the undersigned, toward any claim to redisposition of such sovereignty [1]."

In April 1950, a Soviet-U.S. incident took place in connection with the alleged flight of an American military aircraft over Baltic territory. The Soviet Government protested against " this gross violation of the Soviet frontier " [2]. Denying the allegation, the State Department stated in its answer that

" the United States Navy Aircraft in question ... did not fly over any Soviet or *Soviet-occupied territory* or territorial waters adjacent thereto [3] ",

thus again insisting on the fact that in its view the Baltic States were not Soviet, but merely Soviet-occupied, territory.

The foregoing survey of the United States attitude leads to the clear and inescapable conclusion that the non-recognition by the United States of the forcible absorption of the Baltic States into the Soviet Union is complete and absolute. At the same time, the United States recognizes the continued legal existence of these States, as shown by the maintenance of their diplomatic missions, by the *locus standi* of their consuls in the U.S. courts, by the continued validity of the U.S.-Baltic treaties, and so forth [4].

b) *Great Britain.*

The British attitude seems considerably less clear than that of the United States.

---

1. Quoted by Langer, *op. cit.*, p. 284.
2. *The Times*, April 12, 1950.
3. *It. mine; The Times*, April 19, 1950.
4. In view of the above, it is rather surprising to find an American writer express the view that " Lithuania, Latvia and Estonia lost their separate international personalities upon their annexation by the U.S.S.R. in 1940, the international community having made no protest or otherwise indicated its refusal to recognize the Soviet decrees ". Fenwick, *op. cit.*, p. 150.

It is true that, following the annexation, all funds belonging to the Baltic States were frozen, Baltic vessels were not permitted to leave port and were later requisitioned by the Government, Baltic seamen were detained in Britain, [1] and Baltic Legations in London continued to function. There was, however, no official reaction comparable to the statement of Mr. Sumner Welles [2], although only a year earlier the British Prime Minister had voiced his country's attitude on the subject in definite terms :

" It is the general policy of H.M. Government to maintain respect for the integrity of all sovereign States. In particular, they are aware of the desire of Finland and the Baltic States to preserve their independence and neutrality, and as this is also the objective of H.M. Government they will naturally take full account of these considerations in the present negotiations [3]. "

It does not appear that these principles were strictly adhered to in Anglo-Soviet negotiations subsequent to the absorption of the Baltic States. According to official statements, all British measures referred to above were the subject of negotiations between Britain and the U.S.S.R. [4]. No such conversations have ever taken place between the United States and Russia.

No official documents have yet been issued either concerning the Cripps mission to Moscow even before the outbreak of the German-Soviet war, or the negotiations which preceded the Anglo-Soviet Treaty of May 26, 1942 [5]. The text of the Treaty does not contain any mention of the Baltic States, nor, for that matter, of any other Soviet territorial acquisitions or claims. On the contrary, the text incorporates the principles which had already been proclaimed in the Atlantic Charter, i.e.

" of not seeking territorial aggrandizement for themselves (i.e. the parties) and of non-interference in the internal affairs of other States ". (Art. 5) [6].

However, it was precisely shortly after the conclusion of that Treaty that the names of the Baltic States disappeared from the *Diplomat's Annual* (Annual Edition of the Diplomatic Bulletin), while the names, titles and rank of the Baltic envoys — and counsellors — were relegated to an Annex, entitled " List of Persons no longer included in the Diplomatic List but still accepted by H.M. Government as Personally Enjoying Certain Diplomatic Courtesies ", — without any indication as to which country they represent. This unusual position has been maintained up to present day and the Diplomat's Annual still contains

---

1. Dallin, *op. cit.*, p. 245.
2. See above, p. 399.
3. *Par. Deb., Com.*, vol. CCCXXXXIX, col. 1784. July 10, 1939.
4. Mr. Butler's statement in the House of Commons on the Baltic gold reserves, of August 14, 1940, *Parl. Deb., Com.*, vol. CCCLXIV, col. 754 ; statements concerning the legal and political status of the Baltic countries being " under consideration ", especially following a communication from the Soviet Government, August 21 and 22, 1940, *ibid.*, col. 1276 and 1504 ; Mr. Butler's statement on Baltic ships, requisitioned by British authorities being " under discussion between H. M. Government and the Soviet Government ", November 6, 1940, *ibid.*, vol. CCCLXV, col. 1312.
5. For the Cripps mission, however, see Dallin *op. cit.*, pp. 321-325, based mainly on Press reports.
6. See above, p. 391.

an Annex, listing three Ministers Plenipotentiary of unnamed States. This extraordinary procedure was, however, not adopted by the Foreign Office List which continues to list the Baltic diplomatic missions in the normal manner.

Yet, on October 19, 1945, the Foreign Office stated that the British signature of the indictment of the German war criminals did not imply the recognition of the Baltic States as forming part of Soviet territory [1].

The position was to a certain extent clarified when the first Baltic case came up before a British court [2]. The Court having asked for the usual certificate of the Foreign Office, the answer was as follows :

" 1. H.M. Government recognize the Government of the Estonian Soviet Socialist Republic to be the *de facto* Government of Estonia, but do not recognize it as the *de iure* Government of Estonia.

2. H.M. Government recognize that Estonia has *de facto* entered the Union of Soviet Socialist Republics, but have not recognized this *de iure*.

3. H.M. Government recognize that the Republic of Estonia as constituted prior to June, 1940, has ceased *de facto* to have any effective existence. The effect of such recognition, and in particular the date to which it should be deemed to relate back, appear to me to be questions for the Court to decide in the light of the statements set out above and of the evidence before it.

4. H.M. Government recognized the Republic of Estonia as constituted prior to June, 1940, to be neutral and after the 22nd June, 1941, recognized the Government of the Union of Soviet Socialist Republics to be belligerent. The territory of Estonia came under German military occupation early in July, 1941, and terminated towards the end of September, 1945 [3]. "

It was only two years later that a statement to the same effect was made in the House of Commons by the Under-Secretary of State for Foreign Affairs, Mr. McNeil on behalf of the British Government. Asked by Prof. Savory, on February 10, 1947,

" whether H.M. Government have ever approved of the incorporation of Estonia, Latvia and Lithuania in the U.S.S.R. ",

Mr. McNeil replied :

" No, Sir, H.M. Government recognize that the Baltic States have *de facto* been absorbed into the Soviet Union, but have not recognized this *de iure* [4]. "

There was no reply to a further question by Professor Savory :

" Does not the right hon. Gentleman realize that this annexation of three independent States is a flagrant violation of clause 2 of the Atlantic Charter, in accordance with which no territory may be transferred without the free will and consent of the inhabitants concerned [5] ? "

In order to appreciate the true meaning of this *de facto*, but not *de iure* recognition, it must be borne in mind that the Baltic Legations in London continue to exist. In spite of the unusual manner of their

1. Langer, *op. cit.*, p. 284.
2. *A/C Tallinna Laevauhisus and Others v. Tallinna Shipping Co. and Another*, 1945.
3. *Lloyd's List Law Reports*, vol. LXXIX, pp. 251-252.
4. *Parl. Deb.*, *Com.*, vol. CCCCXXXIII, col. 5.
5. *Ibid.*

inclusion in the Diplomat's Annual [1], the personnel of these Legations still enjoy full diplomatic privileges. Moreover, they continue to transact normal business, such as the protection of their nationals and the issuing of passports. Official exchanges between the Baltic missions and the Foreign Office continue to take place [2]. More particularly, the Latvian Legation in London continues to appoint honorary consuls in Britain, duly notifying the Foreign Office of these appointments which are fully recognized.

It may thus be asked what exactly the *de facto* recognition by Britain of the annexation of the Baltic States really signifies. It may well be that the British Government has resorted to this particular form of recognition in order to acknowledge the existence of undoubted facts on the one hand, while registering its disapproval of these facts on the other [3]. In view of the continued recognition of, and dealings with, the Baltic Legations in London, it can hardly mean more than this. The recognition of facts which have taken place in the Baltic States on the one hand, and the refusal to recognize these facts *de iure* as well as the continued recognition of the London Legations, on the other, leads to the conclusion that Great Britain still recognizes the existence of the Baltic States, even though they have ceased to exercise *de facto* authority in their territories [4].

At all events, in the *Tallinna* case, referred to above, the Court did not follow previous decisions concerning *de facto* recognition [5] and refused to give effect to the nationalization decrees of the Soviet authorities in Estonia. Moreover, the Foreign Office certificate does not seem to have been particularly relied upon by the Court. Having held the decrees in question to be confiscatory and having expressed the principle that " it is well settled that our Courts will not give effect to legislation of that kind ", the Court decided 1) that the decrees in question did not have the effect attributed to them by the defendants, i.e. to dissolve the plaintiff Tallinna Shipping Co., 2) that none of these decrees or laws were legal under the Estonian Constitution and

---

1. See above, p. 404.
2. Thus, e.g. the Estonian Minister's in London correspondence with the British Prime Minister and Foreign Office, concerning compensation claims for British-requisitioned Estonian vessels ; see The " Jaak " and Other Estonian Vessels, Lloyd's List Law Reports, vol. LXXXIII, p. 49.
3. This interpretation is apparently supported by the authority of Prof. Lauterpacht : " ...there would seem to be full scope for *de facto* recognition in situations where conditions other than effectiveness of power are a legitimate consideration. This applies in particular to recognition of a new international title which has its origin in an international wrong, as was the case of the Italian annexation of Abyssinia in 1936. In such cases, *de facto* recognition, which takes into account the actuality of power while expressly refusing to admit its legality in the field of international law is a proper device for combining disapproval of illegal action with the requirement of international intercourse. " *Op. cit.*, p. 341. As to possible compatibility of *de facto* recognition with non-recognition, see Guggenheim, *Validité*, pp. 232-233.
4. For practical effects of British non-recognition of the annexation of the Baltic States in British-occupied Germany, see the *Lithuanian Nationals (Germany) Case*, A. D., 1948, case no. 17.
5. E.g. *Luther v. Sagor*, A. D., 1919/22, case no. 26 ; or *Bank of Ethiopia v. National Bank of Egypt and Liguori*, A. D., 1935/37, case no. 36.

3) that, apart from their illegality, they did not apply to choses in action situated outside the country [1].

British Courts have so far ignored the Soviet annexation of, and legislation in, the Baltic States. As late as August 1949, the Shipping Claims Tribunal passed judgment on compensation claims for six Estonian ships requisitioned by the Ministry of Transport, the notices of claim for compensation having been lodged by the Estonian Minister in London. The Tribunal took note of the fact that, as early as October 9, 1940, the Soviet Government, by means of a Note to the British Embassy in Moscow, had claimed property in all the six ships. In July 1947, the Soviet Ambassador in London had been notified by the Foreign Secretary of the commencement of the proceedings and invited to present the Soviet claims. The Soviet Embassy replied by reiterating the Soviet claim to the property concerned and by denying the jurisdiction of any British Court to deal with the matter. Consequently, the Soviet Government was not represented, and the Minister of Transport made no admission as to the validity of the Soviet claim.

After having recalled the Soviet occupation of Estonia and accepted Dr. Rei's evidence on points of Estonian law, the Tribunal concluded that there was no evidence whatsoever

" to show that the shipping associations have ever been abolished by Soviet or Soviet-sponsored legislation ".

The claimants wholly succeeded in four cases out of six ; two claims failed solely because the respective Estonian shipping associations were found not to be properly represented before the Tribunal according to Estonian law ; in both these cases, however, the Tribunal listed reasons for an *ex gratia* payment to be made by the Ministry of Transport to the individual part-owners [2].

c) *Canada.*

Canada seems to have adopted a similar attitude to Great Britain. While the annexation of the Baltic States has not been granted *de iure*

---

1. In his criticism of the judgment in the *British Yearbook* of 1946, J. F. Fawcett argues that it would have been sufficient for the Court to rely merely on the confiscatory nature of the Soviet decrees, instead of taking into consideration the illegality of the new *de facto* Estonian Government, considering that a revolution had taken place in Estonia, and that the certified *de facto* recognition of the British Government merely implied a certain political attitude of the Foreign Office towards this revolution. Mr. Fawcett's findings must be strongly opposed : no revolution had taken place in Estonia. It is submitted that if events in Estonia had constituted a revolution, Mr. Justice Atkinson would not have found it neccessary to insist, as he did, on the illegality of the decrees and laws of the new government. On appeal, the judgment was upheld by the Court of Appeal, in October, 1946, although the question of Estonia's forcible incorporation into the U.S.S.R. was no longer relied upon. *A. D.*, 1946, case no. 6.

2. The " *Jaak* " and Other Estonian Vessels ; Lloyd's List Law Reports, vol. LXXXIII, pp. 45-55. It is interesting to note the Tribunal's refusal to accept an alleged a revocation of the power of attorney by an Estonian subject in Soviet-occupied Estonia : " In any case, we are not satisfied that if the telegram was actually sent by Mr. Bergmann himself, it was freely or voluntarily sent. The proper inference, in our view, having regard to the context of this telegram in relation to others which passed at the time, and in the light of the state of affairs prevailing at the time, is that the telegram, if genuine, was sent as the result of some form of coercion or undue pressure. " *Ibid.*, p. 52.

recognition, and while Lithuanian Consulates are still allowed to pursue their activities, Canada has nevertheless accorded *de facto* recognition to the Soviet seizure of the Baltic States [1]. Canada's attitude calls for similar comments and conclusions as in the case of Great Britain.

d) *France.*

Following her military defeat in 1940, France did not adopt a policy of non-recognition of the Soviet seizure of the Baltic States. On August 8, 1940, the Soviet representative demanded that the Baltic Legations in Paris should be closed down within ten days. The keys of the buildings were then handed to the Soviet Embassy by the Prefect of the Police. Even in unoccupied France, the status of the Baltic missions was not respected. The official character of the Lithuanian consul at Marseilles was denied by the police. On June 22, 1941, the premises of the Baltic Legations were requisitioned by the Germans.

After the liberation of Paris, in September 1944, the diplomatic representatives of the Baltic States approached the French Government with the request for an authorization to resume their activities, including the consular service. The authorization was not granted [2].

Although no official pronouncement was made, it would thus appear that the recognition of the annexation of the Baltic States is implied in the French attitude.

e) *Switzerland.*

Already in 1946, the Report of the Federal Council spoke of the " former Baltic States ". The following year the Swiss position was clarified, when the Report included the following passage :

« Le Conseil Fédéral s'est vu amené à réexaminer la situation des anciennes représentations diplomatiques et consulaires d'Estonie, de Lithuanie et de Lettonie en Suisse et de leur personnel. Depuis le 1er janvier 1941 déjà ces représentations n'étaient plus reconnues comme telles par le Conseil Fédéral. Le 15 novembre 1946, il a pris une décision aux termes de laquelle les avoirs publics des ci-devant Etats baltes, ainsi que les archives de leurs anciennes représentations, se trouvant en Suisse, sont placés sous la gestion fiduciaire de la Confédération [3]. »

The Report was subjected to criticism by Prof. Guggenheim who declared that the statement concerning the Soviet sovereignty over the Baltic States was not in conformity with positive international law [4].

---

1. The certificate of the Department of External Affairs in the case *Estonian State Cargo and Passenger S. S. Line v. Laane and Baltser (The Elise)*, of January 1947, recited *inter alia* that the Government of Canada " does not recognize *de facto* the Republic of Estonia as constituted prior to June, 1940 " and that it " recognizes that Estonia has *de facto* entered the U.S.S.R., but has not recognized this *de iure*. " It also stated that the Government of Canada " recognizes the Government of the Estonian U.S.S.R. to be the *de facto* government of Estonia, but does not recognize it as the *de iure* government of Estonia. " A. D., 1948, case no. 50.
2. Chambon, *op. cit.*, pp. 198-199.
3. *Rapport de gestion*, 1947, p. 18.
4. " M. E. befinden sich die Feststellungen des Geschäftsberichts hinsichtlich der territorialen Souveränität Sowjetrusslands über Ostpreussen und die baltischen Staaten nicht in Uebereinstimmung mit dem geltenden Völkerrecht. " *Annuaire Suisse*, 1948, p. 165.

While this criticism is fully justified [1], it should, however, be pointed out that the Federal Council has adopted a half-way solution in the matter : while recognition was withdrawn from the Baltic missions, their property and archives were not handed over to the U.S.S.R. but taken over by the Confederation for " gestion fiduciaire ".

f) *Other State·.*

Of other States, Eire has had occasion to formulate her attitude in connection with cases of Estonian and Latvian ships before Irish courts [2]. The Eire High Court arrived at the following conclusions :

" 1. That the Government of Eire, having stated their opinion that the States of Latvia were not under the sovereign independent authority of the Union of Soviet Socialist Republics, the court must treat as nullities the various transactions and documents alleged to have culminated in the alleged sovereignty and purporting to pass property in those ships.

2. Inasmuch as the sovereignty of the U.S.S.R. over Latvia and Estonia had not been established the vessels were not the property of the U.S.S.R. and the orders given by radio telegram to the various masters must be treated as having been without legal authority and the certificates of delivery given upon such orders of no legal effect ."

Portugal refused to recognize the annexation. Treaties with the Baltic States were considered to be suspended [3].

No recognition was granted either by the South-American States or by the Vatican, where Baltic diplomatic and consular missions are still in existence [4].

The names of the Baltic States were never struck off the League of Nations' roster [5]. However, no Baltic representative attended the winding up session of the Assembly. The Baltic States are no longer listed by international organisations.

6. THE BALTIC THESIS.

The legality and validity of the Soviet annexation has been forcefully denied by the remaining organs of the Baltic States, the Baltic Legations.

The Baltic Envoys in the Western World entered solemn protests against both the invasion of their countries followed by the illegal appointment of new governments and illegal elections, and against the incorporation of their countries into the Soviet Union [6].

---

1. See below, pp. 412-416.
2. *Ramava, A. D.*, 1941/42, case no. 20 ; *A. J.* 1942, pp. 490-504.
3. Makarov, *op. cit.*, p. 705.
4. See below, p. 410.
5. Langer, *op. cit.*, p. 282.
6. E. g. statement of the Latvian Minister in Washington, after reciting facts pertaining to the invasion and elections, concludes : " In view of these facts the Latvian Minister, having been appointed by the constitutionally elected President of Latvia, Alberts Kviesis, and therefore speaking in the name of the Latvian nation, reserves the right not to recognize the results of the coming elections and the acts emanating therefrom." Note of protest of the Latvian Minister in London : "Taking into consideration all that is mentioned above, I as representative of the independent Latvian Government accredited in London in 1933 by appointment from President Kviesis, and since 1936 representing President Ulmanis, who has now, on July 19, 1940, been deposed from his

The last free governments of the Baltic Republics had no means of escaping abroad, nor have the Balts, up to the present time, formed governments in exile. Thus, according to the Baltic view, the continuity of the Baltic States is vested in, and carried on, by the existing Legations. Moreover, certain organisational precautionary measures had been taken in advance. Thus, for instance on May 18, 1940, the Latvian Minister in London had been granted, by the Latvian Government, emergency powers " in case it should no longer be possible to communicate (from Latvia) with Latvia's diplomatic and consular missions in Western Europe ". The emergency powers constituted the Minister the actual head of all Latvia's diplomatic and consular missions abroad, with the exception of those in Estonia, Lithuania, Finland, Sweden, Germany and the U.S.S.R., and generally conferred on him a status similar to that of an actual Foreign Minister [1]. In the case of Lithuania, the former Minister at the Vatican is acting as head of the Lithuanian diplomatic service. Both appointments have been recognized by the United States, as was strikingly illustrated by the Feldmans episode [2].

The Baltic representatives are availing themselves of the continued recognition which they enjoy and which renders their further activities possible. Thus, the Estonians maintain Legations in London and Washington, as well as a number of consulates in South America. The Latvians have Legations in London, Washington and Rio de Janeiro, as well as a number of consulates. The Lithuanians maintain their Legations in London, Washington, Montevideo, Rio de Janeiro and the Vatican, and consulates in several countries, including Canada [3]. It has already been seen that all these missions engage in normal diplomatic and consular activities, including dealings with the respective Foreign Ministries, protection of their many citizens abroad, legal protection of property, issuing and prolonging passports.

What has been said regarding the limited effectiveness of a government in exile [4], can be legitimately applied to the Baltic Legations, as the surviving organs of their States : they appear to enjoy the adherence of the whole Baltic community in exile which gives unreserved support to the view of invalidity of Soviet annexation [5]. Moreover, as can be judged from such evidence as has succeeded in finding its way out of the occupied countries, this attitude is equally strongly shared

office, have the honour to ask H. M. Government to regard the recent happenings in Latvia as enacted under duress, and venture to express the hope that H. M. Government will understand my position and will not recognize the incorporation of Latvia in the U.S.S.R. " Protest of the Latvian Minister in Washington : " The Supreme Soviet of the Union of Soviet Socialist Republics has proclaimed, on August 6, 1940, the incorporation of the Republic of Latvia into the Soviet Union. The Latvian Minister considers this act to be an outrageous infringement of international law, practice and morals and he solemnly protests against this violation of Latvia's integrity. " *Latvian-Russian Relations*, pp. 204, 210, 211.

1. *Latvian-Russian Relations*, pp. 201-202.
2. See above, pp. 401-402.
3. See the full list of Baltic consulates in the United Kingdom and the British Commonwealth, in the Foreign Office List 1952.
4. See above, p. 314.
5. See Chambon, *op. cit.*, pp. 156-188 and 214-217.

by the people at home. Thus an appeal by the underground National Committee of the Republic of Estonia, dated from Tallin, June 23, 1944, declared :

" *The Republic of Estonia*, created during the heroic War of Liberation, *continues to exist* despite the repeated occupation of its territory and the acts of violence to which it has been subjected contrary to the generally accepted rules of international law. The Estonian people has never renounced its political independence... The Estonian people does not recognize, nor has ever recognized, as its representative, either the so-called Soviet Estonian Government imposed on it by the forces of foreign arms and by terror, or the so-called Estonian Self-Government which consists of servile accomplices of the present forces of occupation and partly even of citizens of a foreign State. The Estonian nation is firmly determined *that the lawful organs of the independent democratic Republic of Estonia shall resume their activity*. ... the National Committee of the Republic of Estonia has been created by the unanimous will of the people. The National Committee assumes the exercise of power until the constitutional organs begin to function in Estonia. It consists of Delegates of all political and social organisations at home and abroad which uphold the cause of national independence. It is in touch with the Estonian Diplomatic Representatives abroad who are working in close collaboration with it. The National Committee of the Republic of Estonia holds that all those organs of the Republic whose activities have been interrupted by foreign occupation shall resume these activities as soon as possible [1]... "

A similar appeal was launched by the National Committee in 1948, that is, already under the second Soviet occupation [2].

The underground Central Council of Latvia proclaimed identical principles and an identical programme in 1944.

" According to international law the Latvian Republic has not lost its sovereignty nor the U.S.S.R. acquired this sovereignty by the fact of the occupation of Latvia by the U.S.S.R. No country has recognized *de iure* Latvia's incorporation in the U.S.S.R., except Germany. Latvia was occupied by armed forces and the occupying power could not have other rights than those stipulated in the Hague Convention of 1907 [3]. "

Thus, the official and unanimously accepted Baltic attitude is one of protest against the forcible incorporation of the Baltic States into the U.S.S.R. Such incorporation is not recognized and is denied all validity by the surviving Baltic organs which, as has been seen, continue to enjoy international recognition. Consequently, for the Baltic States, as represented by the respective Legations, the Soviet annexation is null and void [4]. As such it was unable to break the legal continuity of the annexed States. The future restoration of their States — in which the Balts believe — will therefore, according to their thesis, mean the restoration of the old States, and not creation of new ones.

One more observation may be permitted with regard to the Baltic thesis : the Baltic Legations do not claim to be the organs of the Baltic S.S.R.s opposed to the actual governments of these entities, — exactly as President Benes and his exiled government did not claim to be organs of the Protectorate. They claim to be organs of the original Baltic States, whose legal order has become ineffective in their own

1. *It. mine*, quoted by Pick, *op. cit.*, pp. 150-152.
2. *Nazi-Soviet Conspiracy*, pp. 56-57.
3. *Latvian-Russian Relations*, p. 237.
4. See below, pp. 558-561.

countries and on whose territory the Baltic S.S.R.s have been created, — exactly as President Benes and his exiled government claimed to be organs of an ineffective Czechoslovak Republic, continuing as an ideal notion in face of the occupation of its territory by foreign-created puppet entities.

7. CONCLUSION.

In the light of the above it is interesting to compare the present situation of the Baltic States on the one hand with that of Czechoslovakia, Albania and Austria during the period of the foreign domination of those countries on the other.

In both categories of cases there is a total absence of effectiveness of the States concerned in their territories. In both cases, this loss of effectiveness is the result of an illegal act by a third State. In none of them, with the exception of Czechoslovakia at a later stage, is there a surviving government in exile. There is, however, the continuity of the Baltic Legations, comparable to the continuity of the Czechoslovak and, in a far more limited degree, Albanian Legations. The foreign domination of the Baltic States, like the foreign domination of those States, continues against the general background of international instability [1].

However, the continuity of the Baltic Legations, as compared with those of Czechoslovakia and Albania, is far more than an act of courtesy. While hardly any legal significance can be attached to the continued existence of the latter in view of the simultaneous recognition of the actual conquest of their countries, the Baltic Legations continue as fully-fledged organs of existing States, against the background of continued international recognition.

For, whatever the variations in the attitude of individual States with regard to the Baltic States, it may safely be concluded that the greater part of the international community has so far refused to recognize the Soviet annexation of these States and has, expressly or impliedly, upheld their continued legal existence. Such continuity forcefully results from State practice as examined above [2].

Any other explanation would hardly seem possible. The diplomatic and consular missions do not exist as such ; they represent a State whose organs they are. There can be no citizens of an inexistent State. No passports or other documents issued by organs of a non-existing State can be internationally valid. No associations, formed and acting according to the laws of their States can be accorded a *locus standi* before the courts of other countries, if the legal basis of their existence has disappeared. No bilateral treaties can continue to be valid, if one of the contracting parties has ceased to exist.

---

1. The list of countries with which an analogy is sought should, of course, include Ethiopia, on the assumption that the Italian domination of that country was not belligerent occupation. See above, pp. 278-279.
2. See above, pp. 398-409.

Yet, such a conclusion would appear to be in direct contradiction to what has been said on the subject earlier in this study. It has been affirmed, in particular, that international recognition could not, in itself, be the source either of the birth or of the continued existence of States [1]. It has also been affirmed that both recognition and refusal to recognize are highly political acts, which in certain circumstances may give rise to obvious fictions. To recall one particular example : it has been said that the refusal of the United States to recognize the Soviet Government could in no way detract from the legal existence of the latter, just as the continued recognition of the Russian Ambassador of the Kerensky Government in Washington could not endow that Government with any amount of real existence and was nothing more than a piece of political fiction [2]. The question may therefore properly be asked : why should the continued recognition of the Baltic envoys carry any more weight than the continued recognition of Ambassador Bakhmeteff ? Or why should the continued recognition of the Baltic States be considered decisive for their legal existence, while a de-recognition, under similar circumstances, of Czechoslovakia or Albania has been dismissed as an element which could be decisive for their extinction ?

It is submitted that the contradiction is more apparent than real, and that such doubts would proceed from a fundamental misconception of both the true nature of international recognition and the spirit of international law. For although it has been found necessary to reject the constitutive view of recognition both for the birth and the continued existence of States, it has been found equally necessary to retain it as strong evidence of a legal situation. Whether or not it is conclusive, has to be determined in accordance with the objective principles of international law. It is thus not recognition alone but its conformity with objective international law which is decisive for the legality of a given situation [3].

One test of the conformity or otherwise of recognition with general international law is supplied by its actual object. It is clear that to recognize a *legal act or situation* is in fact to conform to general international law, whereas to recognize an *illegal act or situation* is not [4]. This is the answer to the apparent contradiction between the dismissal of the legal value of the continued recognition of the Kerensky Government on the one hand, and the affirmation of the legal value of the continued recognition of the Baltic States on the other.

What took place in Russia in 1917 was a genuine revolution, which was as effective as it was legal under international law [5]. The United States' refusal to recognize this revolution, motivated by purely political reasons, concerned a legal act and a legal situation. Under such circumstances, it bordered on intervention [6]. The standing of the Kerensky Ambassador in Washington was fictitious not only because

1. See above, pp. 130-161.
2. See above, p. 142.
3. See above, pp. 159-161.
4. Similarly Chen, *op. cit.*, pp. 411-412.
5. See above, pp. 51-59.
6. See Anzilotti, *op. cit.*, p. 179.

the regime which had appointed him was ineffective, — but, above all, because the legal basis of his mission was eliminated by the internationally legal process of revolution.

The refusal to recognize the annexation of the Baltic States concerns an act which is illegal under international law. The standing of the Baltic envoys may be impaired by the ineffectiveness of the legal orders of which they are organs, but the legal basis of their mission had not been eliminated by any legal means under international law.

Nowhere is the fundamental soundness of this view seen more strikingly than in the doctrines which are associated with the name of Secretary Stimson. It is frequently overlooked that the man who was responsible for the world-wide launching of the doctrine of non-recognition of illegal acts was the same Stimson who definitely abandoned the Wilsonian doctrine of " constitutionalism " [1] in favour of a policy of recognition of revolutionary governments. There is thus no contradiction between rejecting recognition as evidence in the Kerensky case and accepting it in the Baltic case, — just as there is no contradiction between the declaratory nature of recognition and the doctrine of non-recognition of illegal acts [2].

It is thus not international recognition alone which is decisive for the legal continuity of the Baltic States. Such continuity cannot be considered as a result of an arbitrary action on the part of the international community. On the contrary, it conforms to the basic principle of all law, according to which illegal acts should be debarred from producing legal results. In the last resort it is therefore once again the principle *ex iniuria ius non oritur* which, failing any other protective rule, constitutes the legal basis of the continuity of the Baltic States, just as it constituted the legal basis of the survival of Czechoslovakia, Albania, Austria and, possibly, Ethiopia. In the case of the Baltic States the international community continues to profess and to apply that principle which, in turn, endows the evidence gained from State practice with finality and conclusiveness.

It must, however, be asked, why the antinomic principle *ex factis ius oritur* has not yet been able to prevail, and how much longer can the international legal system withstand the anomaly of a " divorce between validity and effectiveness " [3] ?

Before attempting to draw any general conclusions as to possible new developments in international law [4], the case of the Baltic States can, for the present, be examined in the light of traditional international law alone. Not even the latter capitulates immediately before effective illegality, since it requires the complete finality of the illegal act. It has been seen that this is the case even with regard to war-time

---

1. See above, p. 55.
2. " In view of the differing character of the two types of case, it may be said that the doctrine of non-recognition of illegal acts or situations is not in any way a contradiction to the declaratory theory of recognition, as applied to new States or governments. " Chen, *op. cit.*, p. 415.
3. Guggenheim, *Validité*, p. 231.
4. See below, pp. 551-587.

annexation [1]. It may be recalled that the Institute of International Law has adopted an extremely cautions attitude regarding State extinction, requiring it to be definite and final [2]. Speaking of illegal seizure of territory, Prof. Guggenheim considers that such seizure does finally acquire validity if the restoration of the *status quo* does not take place within a reasonable time [3]. It must therefore be asked whether the Soviet annexation has not in fact acquired the necessary finality and what this " reasonable time-limit " really signifies.

The two questions are strictly interconnected and must be answered simultaneously, especially as in both cases there are no fixed criteria to be applied with mathematical precision ; on the contrary, once again a legal phenomenon escapes definition and is to be grasped not by means of definition, but by means of an assessment of every particular case on its own merits.

In the case of the Baltic States the finality of Soviet annexation cannot be admitted at the present time. The Soviet claim to the domination of the Baltic States continues to be rejected by the international community. No general post-war international instrument has confirmed the existing state of affairs in the Baltic. No general peace-making in Europe has taken place and no foundations of any new international delimitation have been laid. This does not mean that a constitutive and validating effect would attach to such settlements *per se*. It merely means that nothing even approximately final has taken place which would totally destroy any *reasonable chance* of an *ad integrum restitutio* of the Baltic States.

It is precisely the persistence of this reasonable chance of restitution which determines the time-limit up to which the international legal system can withstand a divorce between validity and effectiveness. This is formulated by M. Litvinov with all his accustomed lucidity :

" We have to reckon not only with the question whether any struggle between the aggressor and his victim has come to an end, but also — should that have occurred for the time being — whether there are any chances of the struggle being renewed, and likewise we have to reckon with other circumstances which may bring about a change in the situation created by aggressive acts of violence [4]. "

Far from the possibility of such changes being excluded, the Soviet domination of the Baltic States continues to be effective against a background of the gravest international instability. Just as the German seizure of Austria and Czechoslovakia, far from closing a period of territorial changes and introducing a new era of international stability, became — on the contrary — a milestone on the road to a general conflagration, so the Soviet territorial expansion has brought about an international insecurity and tension whose end is not yet in sight. The manner in which this state of affairs may end cannot be

---

1. See above, pp. 102-107.
2. See above, pp. 8-9.
3. " Die Einverleibung erlangt jedoch Rechtswirksamkeit, wenn die Wiederherstellung des früheren Zustandes *innert nützlicher Frist* nicht gelingt. " *It. mine, Lehrbuch*, I, p. 404.
4. *LNOJ*, 1938, p. 341.

foreseen, — nor does it fall within the framework of this study to indulge in such speculation. But it is necessary to investigate and present the facts as they are, particularly, if it is precisely the investigation of such facts which alone forms the basis of a legal evaluation.

It would be a bold thing to assert to-day that the possibility of a restoration of the three Baltic States has finally vanished beyond all hope. The State or States who would already affirm this to-day would run the risk of having to go back on their own attitude at some future time, as in the case of Czechoslovakia, Albania and Austria.

Any speculation as to whether, in the long run, the Baltic States will become legally extinct or whether there will be a *restitutio ad integrum* is entirely out of place. It may, however, be safely asserted that no such extinction has yet taken place, that they continue to exist legally, and that, should their effective restoration take place within a reasonable time, this would not mean the creation of new States ; on the contrary, it would mean the restoration of the old, pre-annexation States which would have survived the illegal acts committed against them, with their full international standing — rights and obligations — unimpaired.

CHAPTER IX

POLAND [1]

The problem of State continuity with regard to the Polish Republic has arisen twice since the outbreak of the Second World War, — the first time, following the German-Soviet partition of Poland in 1939, and the second, in consequence of the Yalta solution of the Polish problem. The two should therefore, for reasons of clarity, be examined under two separate headings, although they are in fact closely connected.

The problem concerned the Polish State which had been born in 1918, at the close of the First World War, and whose continued legal existence had never been contested prior to 1939. In order to be able to provide a correct legal assessment of later developments, it is therefore necessary to summarize the legal position of the Polish State on the eve of the Second World War.

I. LEGAL POSITION OF POLAND AT THE OUTBREAK OF THE SECOND WORLD WAR.

a) *The Delimitation of the Polish State following the First World War.*

The establishment of the Polish State took place in late autumn 1918 by way of a definite delimitation of its separate legal identity, i.e. of its legal order, valid on a given, though not finally delimited, territory [2], which had up till then formed part of the three partitioning States : Russia, Germany and Austro-Hungary. Within a short time, Poland achieved general international recognition, was invited to the Paris Peace Conference and became one of the signatories of the Treaty of Versailles and an original member of the League of Nations [3].

The final territorial and, consequently, personal, delimitation of the Polish State proceeded by stages and was achieved only much later. While the Polish-German frontier was laid down by the Versailles Treaty (either directly or indirectly, by way of plebiscites), the Polish-Czechoslovak frontier was fixed on July 28, 1920, by the Conference of Ambassadors and the Eastern frontier was laid down in the Peace Treaty of Riga of March 18, 1921, between Poland and Russia [4]. On March 15, 1923, in execution of Art. 87, para. 3 of the Versailles Treaty

---

1. Documents quoted in this chapter for which no reference is given were obtained from the archives of the exiled Polish Government in London.
2. See *Deutsche Continental Gas Gesellschaft v. Poland*, quoted above, pp. 163-164.
3. For particulars see Blociszewski, *La restauration de la Pologne et la diplomatie européenne*, and Roth, *Die Entstehung des polnischen Staates*.
4. See below, p. 419.

which had made it incumbent on the principal Allied and Associated Powers to fix the frontiers of Poland, which have not been specified by that Treaty, the Conference of Ambassadors decided to recognize the Polish-Russian and the Polish-Lithuanian frontiers [1] and to

" recognize to Poland, which accepts, all rights of sovereignty over the territories comprised between the frontiers above defined and the other frontiers of the Polish territory... [2] ".

On April 5, 1923, the United States of America joined in this recognition [3].

The final all-round delimitation of the Polish State under international law was thus completed. Further developments in Poland's relations with third States took place on the basis of this delimitation.

b) *Polish-Soviet Relations.*

The ideological basis of Polish-Soviet relations may be sought in the first acts and declarations of the new Bolshevik Government of Russia. Art. 3 of the Decree of the Council of People's Commissars of August 29, 1918, signed by Lenin, Karakhan and Bontch-Bruyevitch, read :

" All agreements and acts concluded by the Government of the former Russian Empire with the Governments of the Kingdom of Prussia and the Austro-Hungarian Empire in connection with the partitions of Poland, are annulled for ever by the present Resolution, in view of the fact that they are contrary to the principle of the self-determination of peoples and to the revolutionary, legal conception of the Russian nation, which recognized the inalienable right of the Polish nation to decide its own fate and to become united [4]. "

This decision was communicated to the German Government on September 3, 1918, in a Note Verbale citing thirteen international conventions relating to Poland as the object of Russian annulment [5].

Of the numerous Russian pronouncements in the same spirit, one more may be quoted : it is point 1 of the declaration of the Council of People's Commissars of January 28, 1920, signed by Lenin, Tchitcherin and Trotzky :

" The Council of People's Commissars declares that the policy of the U.S.S.R. [6] towards Poland is based not on any occasional, transient considerations of war or diplomacy but on the inviolable principle of self-determination of nations and it has recognized and recognizes unreservedly the independence and sovereignty of the Polish Republic and declares this recognition to be the basis of all its relations with Poland from the moment of the formation of an independent Polish State [7]. "

---

1. For the Lithuanian problem see Scelle, *La situation juridique de Vilna et de son territoire, RGDIP*, 1928, pp. 730-780.
2. *Pol.-Sov. Relations*, no. 4.
3. *Ibid.*, no. 5.
4. *Ibid.*, p. 71.
5. Quoted by Roth, *op. cit.*, pp. 18-19. The legal value of the Russian annulment was subjected to criticism; see Blociszewski, *op. cit.*, p. 154, Roth, *op. cit.*, p. 21 ; this does not, however, call for detailed discussion, particularly since the partition treaties in question were definitely set aside and superseded by later international instruments such as the Treaties of Versailles, St. Germain and Riga. But its value as an official expression of intention of the new Russia remains.
6. Obviously a mistake in the text, instead of the correct " R.F.S.S.R. ".
7. *Pol.-Sov. Relations*, p. 72.

The Polish-Russian war was terminated by the Peace Treaty of Riga, of March 18, 1921, between Poland on the one hand, and the Russian Federated Soviet Socialist Republic and the Ukrainian Soviet Socialist Republic on the other hand, the R.F.S.S.R. acting on its own behalf as well as on behalf of the White-Ruthenian Soviet Socialist Republic [1]. With the signature of this Treaty, Polish-Russian relations left the realm of unilateral declarations of a political rather than a legal value and became subject of legal regulation.

Art. 1 of the Treaty provided for the cessation of the state of war between the contracting parties. Art. 2 laid down the new Polish-Soviet frontier [2]. Art. 3 further confirmed the new territorial delimitation by stating :

" Russia and the Ukraine abandon all rights and claims to the territories situated to the west of the frontier laid down by Art. 2 of the present Treaty. Poland, on the other hand, abandons in favour of the Ukraine and of White Ruthenia all rights and claims to the territory situated to the east of this frontier. The two Contracting Parties agree that, in so far as the territory situated to the west of the frontier fixed in Art. 2 of the present Treaty includes districts, which form the subject of a dispute between Poland and Lithuania, the question of the attribution of these districts to one of those two States is a matter which exclusively concerns Poland and Lithuania [3]. "

Art. 5 contained the famous non-interference clause [4]. The remaining Articles settled the problems of option, repatriation, debts, amnesty, minorities, return to Poland of Polish art treasures, and so forth. Thus, the Treaty of Riga laid down the legal foundation for relations between the contracting parties [5].

---

1. In the documents quoted in this chapter, the terms " White Ruthenia ", " White Russia " and " Byelorussia " are used alternatively. This made it impossible for the writer to observe a uniform terminology.

2. It should be observed that the Riga frontier practically corresponds to the line of the second partition of Poland in 1793 ; for text and maps see Grabski, *The Polish-Soviet Frontier.*

3. The second part of this Article calls for an explanation. On July 12, 1920, in the course of the Russo-Polish war, Russia concluded a Peace Treaty with Lithuania by which she ceded to the latter the city and region of Wilno, at that moment occupied by the Red Army. See *LoN. Tr. Ser.*, vol. III, p. 106. In the Treaty of Riga, Russia went back on her previous action : acknowledging definitely the new Russo-Polish frontier as laid down in Art. 2, she expressly recognized the Polish-Lithuanian dispute as a matter of concern to these two States alone, and undertook to refrain from any interference in the matter. In 1926, on the occasion of the signature of the Russo-Lithuanian Non-Aggression Treaty, Russia in turn went back on her obligations under Art. 3 of the Riga Treaty. See, however, on the Wilno problem the Final Protocol of the Protocol prolonging the Polish-Russian Non-Agression Treaty, below, p. 421.

4. Quoted below, see pp. 458-459 ; it has to be borne in mind that the Article was inserted into the Treaty following the Soviet attempt to install in Poland a fake Polish-Soviet Government, see above, p. 68 ; cf. the Litvinov pledge, see above, pp. 69-70.

5. *LoN. Tr. Ser.*, vol. VI, p. 51-169. " ...we have concluded a peace treaty giving full satisfaction to the vital, legitimate and necessary interests of the Polish nation. ... None of the peace treaties concluded by Russia and Ukraine admits preparations for a new war, because none of these treaties leaves any problem unsolved, or solved merely on the basis of the relative strength of the contracting parties, as was formerly done at the expense of some of the nations concluding such treaties. ...By the conclusion of the Peace Treaty with Poland we have closed the circle of peaceful relations between all the nations which belonged to the former Russian Empire, liquidating the policy of violence of the Tsars. " From the final speech of the chairman of the Russian-Ukrainian Delegation, M. Joffe ; quoted by Weyers, *Poland and Russia*, pp. 50-51.

It has already been seen that, on the occasion of the formation of the Union of Soviet Socialist Republics (by way of a merger of the Russian Federated Socialist Soviet Republic, the White Russian S.S.R., the Ukrainian S.S.R. and the Transcaucasian S.S.R.) on July 6, 1923, the Union undertook to execute all treaties and conventions which had been entered into by the constituent Republics with foreign States [1]. Apart from the general notification of the above to foreign States, the Soviet Government addressed on December 14, 1923, a special Note to Poland, confirming once again its intention to abide by the terms of the Riga Treaty, signed by the R.F.S.S.R., the Ukrainian S.S.R. and the White-Russian S.S.R., as well as of all other treaties and conventions concluded by these States with Poland [2].

On October 4, 1928, the Soviet Union acceded to the Pact of Paris of August 27, of that year, of which Poland had been one of the original signatories. Since the ratification of the Paris Pact proceeded relatively slowly, a protocol was signed in Moscow on February 9, 1929, by Estonia, Latvia, Poland, Rumania and the U.S.S.R., for its immediate entry into force between the contracting parties [3]. The Pact of Paris was thus doubly binding on the U.S.S.R. and Poland, exactly as in the case of the U.S.S.R. and the Baltic States.

On July 25, 1932, the Polish-Soviet Non-Aggression Pact was signed in Moscow. The preamble took its stand on the Treaty of Riga as " the basis of the reciprocal relations and undertakings " of the parties, while Art. 1 impliedly invoked the Pact of Paris and the subsequent Protocol of 1929. By the same Article the parties undertook to

" refrain from taking any aggressive action against or invading the territory of the other Party, either alone or in conjunction with other Powers ".

Moreover, the Article outlawed as between the parties

" any act of violence attacking the integrity and inviolability of the territory or the political independence of the other Contracting Party ", " even if such acts are committed without declaration of war and avoid all possible warlike manifestations ".

Art. 2 provided that, in the case of one of the parties being attacked by a third State or a group of States, the other party would not give aid or assistance, either directly or indirectly, to the aggressor during the whole period of the conflict. An act of aggression by one party against a third State was to give the other party the right to withdraw from the Pact without prior denunciation. Under Art. 3 each Party undertook

" not to be a party to any agreement openly hostile to the other Party from the point of view of aggression ".

Art. 4 safeguarded the international rights and obligations of the parties under agreements concluded by them before the coming into force of

---

1. See above, p. 370.
2. See Dabski, J. Pokój Ryski (The Peace of Riga), Warszawa 1931, pp. 197-198.
3. See above, p. 371.

the Pact, so far as the said agreements contained no aggressive elements. Art. 5, repeating the conviction expressed in the Preamble, of the necessity for the peaceful settlement of international disputes, bound the parties to submit " any disputes and differences. of whatever nature or origin " to a procedure of conciliation, in accordance with a Convention which was to be concluded separately but was nevertheless to form an integral part of the Pact [1]. Art. 6 provided for the speediest possible ratification of the Treaty, while Art. 7 fixed its duration for a period of three years. Unless denounced six months before its expiry, the Pact was to be automatically renewed for a further two years. The protocol of signature No. 1, attached to the Pact, provided that neither the expiry nor a denunciation of the Treaty could limit or cancel the obligations of the parties under the Pact of Paris of 1928 [2].

On July 3, 1933, there was concluded in London the famous Convention for the Definition of Aggression (the Litvinov Convention), between Rumania, Estonia, Latvia, Poland, Turkey, the U.S.S.R., Persia and Afghanistan [3].

On May 5, 1934, the Non-Aggression Pact was extended by a Protocol, signed in Moscow, until December 31, 1945. Art. 1 of the Protocol gave each party the right to denounce the Treaty by giving notice to that effect six months before the expiry of the above-mentioned period. In the absence of such denunciation, the Treaty was to be automatically prolonged for a further two years ; similarly, it was to be prolonged for a further period of two years on each occasion when not denounced by either of the Parties in the manner provided by Art. 1. Release from the obligations incurred was thus regulated with extreme precision. The Final Protocol once again declared the Riga Treaty to constitute the basis of mutual relations between the parties, which were stated to have no obligations and not to be bound by any declarations inconsistent with the provisions of that Treaty and in particular with its Art. 3 [4].

In connection with the proposed entry of the Soviet Union to the League of Nations, an exchange of notes took place between Poland and Russia, on September 19, 1934. Here, the Soviet Government fully agreed with the Polish Government that

" after the eventual invitation to and entry of the U.S.S.R. into the League of Nations, the relations between the U.S.S.R. and the Republic of Poland will remain on the basis of the treaties existing between them, all of which, including the Pact of Non-Aggression and the Convention for the Definition of Aggression, will continue to preserve all their force [5] ".

---

1. The Conciliation Convention was in fact signed in Moscow on November 23, 1932.
2. For text see *Pol.-Sov. Relations*, pp. 85-88. *LoN. Tr. Ser.*, vol. CXXXVI, pp. 41-53.
3. See above, pp. 373-375.
4. See above, p. 419, *f.-n.* 3. " Consequently, the Government of the U.S.S.R. confirms that the Note from the People's Commissar, G. V. Tchitcherin, of September 28, 1926, to the Lithuanian Government cannot be interpreted to mean that the Note implied any intention on the part of the Soviet Government to interfere in the settlement of the territorial questions mentioned therein." *LoN. Tr. Ser.*, vol. CLVII, pp. 431-439.
5. *Pol.-Sov. Relations*, p. 94.

The Soviet-Polish relations were thus precisely and strictly defined, particularly with regard to problems of aggression and mutual respect of political independence and territorial integrity. Moreover, from 1934 onwards, the two countries were bound by obligations under the Covenant of the League of Nations.

The last instance of confirmation of the legal position between Poland and the Soviet Union occurred in a joint communiqué, issued by the two Governments on November 26, 1938 [1].

c) *Polish-German Relations.*

The legal basis of Polish-German relations was laid down in the Treaty of Versailles : in Art. 87 Germany recognized the complete independence of Poland.

On October 16, 1925, Poland and Germany signed in Locarno an Arbitration Treaty, providing for the submission of all disputes between the Parties to arbitraton or conciliation [2].

On August 27, 1928, the two States signed the Pact of Paris. On January 26, 1934, the Polish-German Declaration of Non-Aggression was signed in Berlin. It referred expressly to the Pact of Paris, stating that the contracting parties had decided to base their relations on the principles of the Pact. Any use of force in the settlement of disputes was unreservedly excluded. The Declaration was concluded for a period of ten years and did not contain any provisions for its earlier denunciation [3].

d) *Polish-British Relations.*

Relations between Great Britain and Poland became closer only in 1939, in face of the growing menace of German aggression. On March 31, 1939, Mr. Chamberlain informed the House of Commons of the British guarantee of Poland's independence. The terms of the guarantee were unusually wide, leaving to Poland the decision as to whether there was a threat to her independence, which would automatically have brought the British undertakings into operation [4].

The unilateral British guarantee, changed into a bilateral guarantee on April 6, 1939, [5] was to be superseded by a regular pact of mutual

1. " Relations between the Polish Republic and the U.S.S.R. are and will continue to be based to the fullest extent on all the existing Agreements, including the Polish-Soviet Pact of Non-Aggression, dated July 25, 1932. This Pact, concluded for five years and extended on May 5, 1934, for a further period ending December 31, 1945, has a basis wide enough to guarantee the inviolability of peaceful relations between the two States. " *Ibid.*, pp. 94-95.
2. *LoN. Tr. Ser.*, vol. LIV, p. 329.
3. *Off. Doc.*, no. 10.
4. " ...I now have to inform the House that during that period, in the event of any action which clearly threatened Polish independence, and which the Polish Government accordingly considered it vital to resist with their national forces, H. M. Government would feel themselves bound at once to lend the Polish Government all support in their power. " *Ibid.*, no. 69.
5. *Ibid.*, no. 71. " With the view of making European security truly collective the British Government attached importance to the need of securing from Poland an undertaking of mutual assistance. " Raczynski, *The British-Polish Alliance, Its origin and meaning*, p. 16.

assistance. Negotiations for this purpose were opened soon after the Prime Minister's statement.

In the meantime, on August 23, 1939, the German-Soviet Pact of Non-Aggression was signed in Moscow, in the midst of the parallel Anglo-Franco-Russian negotiations for strengthening the peace front against the possibility of German aggression. The conclusion of this Pact met with strong reaction on the part of the Western States. In particular, already on August 22, 1939, on receiving news of the impending signature of the German-Soviet Pact, the British Government issued a communiqué stating that this event would in no way affect British obligations to Poland which the British Government was determined to fulfil [1]. Speaking in the House of Commons on August 24, 1939, the Prime Minister declared :

" The House will recollect that the guarantee which we had given to Poland was given before any agreement with Russia was talked of, and that it was not in any way made dependent upon any such agreement being reached. How then could we, with honour, go back upon such an obligation, which we had so often and plainly repeated ? Therefore, our first act was to issue a statement that our obligations to Poland and to other countries remained unaffected [2]. "

In other words, the British Government was not to be deterred from fulfilling its obligations to Poland by the unexpected fact of Soviet Russia concluding a treaty with the very State whose act of aggression was considered imminent. That this was so is further proved by the fact that, prompted by this new development, negotiations for the conclusion of a British-Polish Alliance proceeded at an accelerated pace [3].

On August 25, 1939, Great Britain and Poland concluded the following Agreement of Mutual Assistance and Secret Protocol.

1. *The Agreement.*

Art. 1. Should one of the Contracting Parties become engaged in hostilities with a European Power in consequence of aggression by the latter against that Contracting Party, the other Contracting Party will at once give the Contracting Party engaged in hostilities all the support and assistance in its power.

Art. 2. (1) The provision of Article 1 will also apply in the event of any action by a European Power which clearly threatened, directly or indirectly, the independence of one of the Contracting Parties, and was of such a nature that the Party in question considered it vital to resist it with its armed forces.

---

1. See *RDI* 1939 on Poland, Section : Documents, p. 458.
2. *Documents*, p. 109. Cf. Mr. Chamberlain's message to Hitler of August 22 : " ...apparently the announcement of a German-Soviet agreement is taken in some quarters in Berlin to indicate that intervention by Great Britain on behalf of Poland is no longer a contingency that need to be reckoned with. No greater mistake could be made. Whatever may prove to be the nature of the German-Soviet agreement, it cannot alter Great Britain's obligations to Poland which H. M. Government have stated in public, and which they are determined to fulfil... " *Ibid.*, p. 97.
3. " On Friday (i.e. 25 August) I received an urgent message from the Foreign Office that the British Government had agreed to the immediate signing of the Treaty. In view of the altered situation, and not without effort, I made telephoned and ciphered representations to my Minister, and finally obtained his approval of all the clauses of the Agreement. Fifteen minutes later, in Lord Halifax's study, we were putting our signatures to the duplicate copies of the Agreement of Mutual Assistance and to the Secret Protocol, the provisions of which were from then on binding on both countries. " Raczynski, *op. cit.*, p. 21.

(2) Should one of the Contracting Parties become engaged in hostilities with a European Power in consequence of action by that Power which threatened the independence or neutrality of another European State in such a way as to constitute a clear menace to the security of that Contracting Party, the provisions of Article 1 will apply, without prejudice, however, to the rights of the other European State concerned.

Art. 3. Should a European Power attempt to undermine the independence of one of the Contracting Parties by processes of economic penetration or in any other way, the Contracting Parties will support each other in resistance to such attempts. Should the European Power concerned thereupon embark on hostilities against one of the Contracting Parties, the provisions of Article 1 will apply.

Art. 4. The methods of applying the undertakings of mutual assistance provided for by the present agreement are established between the competent naval, military, and air authorities of the Contracting Parties.

Art. 5. Without prejudice to the foregoing undertakings of the Contracting Parties to give each other mutual support and assistance immediately on the outbreak of hostilities, they will exchange complete and speedy information concerning any development which might threaten their independence and, in particular, concerning any development which threatened to call the said undertakings into operation.

Art. 6. (1) The Contracting Parties will communicate to each other the terms of any undertakings of assistance against aggression which they have already given or may in future give to other States.

(2) Should either of the Contracting Parties intend to give such an undertaking after the coming into force of the present agreement, the other Contracting Party shall, in order to ensure the proper functioning of the Agreement, be informed thereof.

(3) Any new undertaking which the Contracting Parties may enter into in future shall neither limit their obligations under the present Agreement nor indirectly create new obligations between the Contracting Party not participating in these undertakings and the third State concerned.

Art. 7. Should the Contracting Parties be engaged in hostilities in consequence of the application of the present Agreement, they will not conclude an armistice or treaty of peace except by mutual agreement.

Art. 8. (1) The present Agreement shall remain in force for a period of five years.

(2) Unless denounced six months before the expiry of this period it shall continue in force, each Contracting Party having thereafter the right to denounce it at any time by giving six months' notice to that effect.

(3) The present Agreement shall come into force on signature.

2. The Secret Protocol.

The Polish Government and the Government of the United Kingdom of Great Britain and Northern Ireland are agreed upon the following interpretation of the Agreement of mutual assistance signed this day as alone authentic and binding :

1. (a) By the expression " a European Power ", employed in the Agreement, is to be understood Germany.

(b) In the event of action within the meaning of Articles 1 or 2 of the Agreement by a European Power other than Germany, the Contracting Parties will consult together on the measures to be taken in common.

2. (a) The two Governments will from time to time determine by mutual agreement the hypothetical case of action by Germany coming within the ambit of Article 2 of the Agreement.

(b) Until such time as the two Governments have agreed to modify the following provisions of this paragraph they will consider that the case contemplated by paragraph (1) of Article 2 of the Agreement is that of the Free City of Danzig and that the cases contemplated by paragraph (2) of Article 2 are Belgium, Holland, Lithuania.

(c) Latvia and Estonia shall be regarded by the two Governments as included in the list of countries contemplated by paragraph (2) of Article 2 from the moment that an undertaking of mutual assistance between the United Kingdom and a third State covering those two countries enters into force.

(d) As regards Rumania, the Government of the United Kingdom refers to the guarantee which it has given to that country, and the Polish Government refers to the reciprocal undertakings of the Rumano-Polish alliance which Poland has never regarded as incompatible with her traditional friendship for Hungary.

3. The Undertakings mentioned in Article 6 of the Agreement, should they be entered into by one of the Contracting Parties with a third State, would of necessity be so framed that their execution should at no time prejudice either the sovereignty or territorial inviolability of the other Contracting Party.

4. The present protocol constitutes an integral part of the Agreement signed this day, the scope of which it does not exceed [1]."

The elaborate provisions of these instruments call for some comment.

The obligations of the parties in case of an act of aggression by " a European Power " were of a most categorical character. They involved immediate and full support and assistance to the other party, not only in the case of a direct aggression (Art. 1), but equally of a direct or indirect threat to its independence, which would be of such a nature that the party in question considered it vital to resist it with its armed forces (Art. 2, 1). As in the British guarantee of March 31, 1939, the decision as to the existence of such threat rested exclusively with the party attacked, and this decision was automatically to bring the obligations of the other party into operation. Moreover, even an action threatening the independence or neutrality of another European State and considered by one of the contracting parties as a clear threat to its own security, which would result in that contracting party being engaged in hostilities, was covered by the obligations of Art. 1 (Art. 2, 2). The Secret Protocol stated that the British guarantee contemplated in such cases covered Danzig and Lithuania, while the reciprocal Polish guarantee covered Holland and Belgium (para. 2 b). Latvia and Estonia were to be included in this list subject to an undertaking of mutual assistance between Great Britain and a third State covering these countries (para. 2 c). The obligations of Art. 1 were further extended to cover a case in which one of the contracting parties would find itself victim of attack as a result of resisting attempts to undermine its independence by economic penetration or in any other way, the contracting parties being in any case bound to support each other in such resistance (Art. 3). Methods of applying the obligations of mutual assistance were to be established by the competent military authorities of the parties (Art. 4). Exchange of speedy and complete information on developments likely to threaten the independence of the parties and to call their undertakings into operation was provided for (Art. 5). Past and future obligations of assistance against aggression of the

---

1. Cmd. 6616.

contracting parties towards third States were dealt with in a detailed manner : not only were the parties to be mutually informed of such obligations and their terms, but moreover, no new undertaking concluded in future could limit the obligations of the parties under the Agreement or create new obligations between the contracting party not participating in such undertakings and the third State concerned (Art. 6). Finally, in the event of hostilities, the parties were not to conclude either an armistice or a treaty of peace except by mutual agreement (Art. 7). The Agreement was concluded for five years, to continue in force, unless denounced by one of the parties six months before its expiry and was to come into force immediately on signature (Art. 8).

The Secret Protocol, constituting an integral part of the Agreement (para. 4 of the Protocol), supplied the authentic and binding interpretation of the latter (Preamble). According to its para. 1 a, the expression " European Power " employed in the Agreement signified Germany. However, the obligations of the parties were by no means limited to the case of a German aggression only. Para. 1 b of the Secret Protocol specified that in the event of aggressive action, as defined in Art. 1 and 2 of the Agreement by a European Power other than Germany, the parties would consult together on the measures to be taken in common. Thus, the obligations were not confined to the case of Germany. Moreover, the parties were to consult not on *whether* any measures were to be taken in common, but only on *what* measures were to be taken ; agreed common action was thus made mandatory on the parties. Since para. 1 b directly referred to Art. 1 and 2 of the Agreement and since the precise meaning of these two Articles was in turn supplied by para. 2 b and c of the Protocol, it follows that here again the reciprocal British-Polish guarantee covered Danzig and Lithuania, and Holland and Belgium respectively. With regard to Latvia and Estonia, similar observations apply as in the case of a German attack, — to the extent to which the obligations of the parties were different in case of a German attack (immediate support and assistance) and different in case of an attack by another Power (measures to be taken in common). Para. 2 d mentioned previous undertakings of the parties with regard to Rumania.

The text of what may be termed the key stipulation of the Secret Protocol, supplying the authentic interpretation of the problem of possible future undertakings of the parties towards third States, dealt with in Art. 6, 3 of the Agreement, may be repeated :

" 3. The Undertakings mentioned in Article 6 of the Agreement, should they be entered into by one of the Contracting Parties with a third State, would of necessity be so framed that their execution should at no time prejudice either the sovereignty or territorial inviolability of the other Contracting Party. "

That particular safeguard

" was inserted in the Protocol largely in view of Russian demands, raised during the Moscow talks between Britain, France and the U.S.S.R. — that in the event of war with Germany, Russian armies should be given the right of way and operational bases in the Wilno district and in south-east Poland [1] ".

---

1. Raczynski, *op. cit.*, p. 22.

Consequently, the political independence and territorial integrity of the contracting parties were safeguarded not only against Germany, but *erga omnes*. The question may be asked whether this safeguard amounted to an actual guarantee of existing frontiers. The Polish Ambassador in London who negotiated and signed the Agreement states that

" Frontier guarantees were not explicitly mentioned ",

but declares that

" The obligations under the Agreement were ... wider than those implied in a simple guarantee of frontiers. They were, of course, designed to safeguard the other Ally's independence — not in the abstract, which would be nonsensical, but within a given territory, i.e. that which was his at the date of the signature of the agreement [1]. "

It must therefore be concluded that the mutual Anglo-Polish obligations under the Agreement contained a guarantee of the parties' independence and territorial integrity, valid *erga omnes*, although the form and contents of such obligations were different in the case of German aggression than in any other case. In view of the date of signature — two days after the Ribbentrop-Molotov Pact —, of the general situation prevailing at the time, as well as of the specific consideration of possible Russian demands on Poland, it is clear that obligations regarding the sovereignty and territorial integrity of Poland were undertaken by Great Britain in full awareness of all their implications.

II. THE PROBLEM OF POLAND'S CONTINUITY :
FIRST PHASE.

1. THE GERMAN-SOVIET PARTITION OF POLAND.

a) *Facts.*

On August 23, 1939, Germany and Russia concluded a Pact of Non-Aggression. According to Art. 1, the contracting parties undertook to abstain in their mutual relations from any act of violence, any aggressive action and any attack, whether individually or in conjunction with other Powers. Art. 2 provided that in the case of one of the parties being the object of belligerent action by a third Power, the other party would in no way assist that third Power. The striking feature of this formulation was that friendly neutrality was promised not in the specific case of the other party falling victim to an aggression, but generally in case of the other party being involved in hostilities with a third State ; friendly neutrality was thus not excluded in case of an aggression

---

1. *Ibid.*, pp. 21-22. It is clear, moreover, that the recognition by the Agreement of Poland's interests in Lithuania, Latvia, Estonia and Rumania could only have made sense on the correct legal assumption of her existing territorial delimitation, such as had been finally achieved and internationally recognized in 1923, see above, p. 418. Thus, correctly, Komentator, *Jaltanski Rozbior Polski w swietle Prawa Narodow (The Yalta Partition of Poland in the light of International Law)*, in *Sprawy Miedzynarodowe (International Affairs)*, no. 4, pp. 24-25.

actually committed by one of the contracting parties [1]. Art. 3 provided
for constant future contact and consultation between the Parties bearing
on problems affecting their common interests. Art. 4 excluded the
participation of any of the parties in a grouping of Powers aimed directly
or indirectly at the other party. Finally, Art. 5 provided for the peaceful
settlement of all disputes between the Parties. The Pact was concluded
for ten years with a provision for its prolongation for a further five years
failing denunciation by one of the parties (Art. 6) and was to be ratified
as soon as possible (Art. 7) [2].

The Pact was accompanied by a Secret Protocol, the terms of which
did not become known until years later, and which provided for a
partition by the contracting parties of countries lying between them [3].
Para. 2 dealing with Poland, read :

" In the event of a territorial and political re-arrangement of the areas
belonging to the Polish State, the spheres of influence of Germany and the U.S.S.R.
shall be bounded approximately by the line of the Rivers Narew, Vistula and San.
The question of whether the interests of both parties make desirable the maintenance
of an independent Polish State and how such a State should be bounded can only
be definitely determined in the course of further political developments. In any
events both Governments will resolve this question by means of a friendly
agreement [4]. "

On September 1, 1939, at dawn, Germany attacked Poland, without
a declaration of war. The Second World War had begun. On
September 3, 1939, Great Britain and France declared war on Germany
in fulfilment of their treaty obligations to Poland. On September 17,
with the Polish-German campaign in full progress, the Soviet Union
invaded Poland from the East. Soviet action was accompanied by the
following Note which the Soviet Deputy People's Commissar for
Foreign Affairs, M. Potemkin read to the Polish Ambassador in Moscow
and which the latter refused to accept :

" The Polish-German war has revealed the internal bankruptcy of the Polish
State. During the course of ten days' hostilities Poland has lost all her industrial
areas and cultural centres. Warsaw no longer exists as the capital of Poland. The
Polish Government has disintegrated, and no longer shows any sign of life. This
means that the Polish State and its Government have, in fact, ceased to exist.
Therefore the Agreements concluded between the U.S.S.R. and Poland have ceased
to operate. Left to her own devices and bereft of leadership, Poland has become
a suitable field for all manner of hazards and surprises, which may constitute a
threat to the U.S.S.R. For these reasons the Soviet Government, which hitherto
has preserved neutrality, cannot any longer observe a neutral attitude towards
these facts.

The Soviet Government further cannot view with indifference the fact that
the kindred Ukrainian and White Ruthenian people, who live on Polish territory
and who are at the mercy of fate, are left defenceless.

In these circumstances, the Soviet Government has directed the High
Command of the Red Army to order the troops to cross the frontier and to take
under their protection the life and property of the population of Western Ukraine
and Western White Ruthenia.

---

1. Contrast with Art. 2 *in fine* of the Polish-Soviet Non-Aggression Pact.
2. *Nazi-Soviet Relations*, pp. 76-77. The pact has been called « véritable pacte de
non-agression mutuelle en vue d'une agression commune », even before the secret protocol became known. *RDI*, 1939, p. 117.
3. See above, pp. 375-376.
4. *Nazi-Soviet Relations*, p. 78.

At the same time the Soviet Government proposes to take all measures to extricate the Polish people from the unfortunate war into which they were dragged by their unwise leaders, and enable them to live a peaceful life [1]. ”

On September 18, while the fighting on Polish territory was still continuing, the Soviet thesis of the extinction of Poland was again taken up by Russia and Germany jointly, in the following communiqué :

“ In order to avoid all kinds of unfounded rumours concerning the respective aims of the Soviet and German armies operating in Poland, the Government of the U.S.S.R. and the German Government declare that the operations of these armies do not involve any aim contrary to the interests of Germany and of the U.S.S.R. or to the spirit and the letter of the German-Russian pact of non-aggression. On the contrary, the aim of these armies is to restore peace and order destroyed by the collapse of the Polish State and to help the Polish population to reconstruct the conditions of their political existence [2]. ”

There followed a second communiqué of September 22, establishing a demarcation line between the Soviet and German armies in Poland [3].

The final partition of Poland between Germany and the U.S.S.R. was effected by the German-Soviet Boundary and Friendship Treaty of September 28, 1939, confirming the thesis of Poland's extinction in a conventional arrangement. Moreover, the partition was undertaken on the express assumption of the fate of Poland being a concern of the partitioning Powers alone, to the exclusion of the international community at large and Poland's allies in particular. The Treaty read :

“ The Government of the U.S.S.R. and the German Government, following the collapse of the former Polish State, consider it as exclusively their own task to restore peace and order in these territories and to assure to the peoples inhabiting them a peaceful existence which will correspond to their national characteristics. With this object in view they have concluded the following Agreement.

Art. 1. The Government of the U.S.S.R. and the German Government establish, as the frontier between their respective State interests in the territory of the former Polish State, a line which is marked on the attached map and which will be given in more detail in a supplementary Protocol.

Art. 2. Both countries recognize as final the frontier between their respective State interests, as set out in Article 1, and will resist any interference with this decision on the part of other Powers.

Art. 3. The German Government will carry out the necessary State reconstruction on the territory west of the line indicated in Article 1, and the Soviet Government on the territory east of this line.

Art. 4. The Government of the U.S.S.R. and the German Government regard the above-mentioned reconstruction as a reliable foundation for the future development of friendly relations between their peoples.

Art. 5. This agreement is subject to ratification. The exchange of instruments of ratification is to take place as soon as possible in Berlin.

The agreement enters into force from the moment of its signature.

MOLOTOV.   RIBBENTROP [4]. ”

---

1. *Off. Doc.*, no. 175.
2. *Nazi-Soviet Relations*, p. 100.
3. *Pol.-Sov. Relations*, p. 99.
4. *Ibid.*, pp. 99-100 ; *Nazi-Soviet Relations*, pp. 105-106.

The published agreement was accompanied by two supplementary Secret Protocols. One of them introduced a change into the previously decided demarcation line ; as against the Secret Protocol of August 23 [1], the Soviet Union now conceded to Germany a larger part of Poland than had been originally envisaged in exchange for the inclusion of Lithuania, formerly attributed to Germany, into her own sphere of influence [2]. The second promised the mutual support of the partitioning Powers in suppressing any Polish national movement [3].

The new demarcation line, which came to be known as the Ribbentrop-Molotov Line, followed the River Bug, then turned sharply westwards to join the River San which it followed down to the Carpathians. As a result of this partition, out of 150.048 square miles of Polish territory with about 35.340.000 population, 72.866 square miles with 22.250.000 inhabitants went to Germany, while 77.620 square miles and 13.090.000 inhabitants went to Russia [4]. Thus, while in the Northern and Central part of Poland Russian gains corresponded almost exactly to the line of the third Polish partition of 1795, in the South the Soviet Union gained Eastern Galicia which, far from ever belonging to Russia, had been held during the partition period by Austria [5]. Of the most important Polish cities, Warsaw, Poznan and Cracow remained west, Lwów and Wilno east of the Ribbentrop-Molotov Line [6].

Of the German-occupied part, the Western Provinces, embracing 35.714 square miles with a population of 10.740.000, were directly incorporated into the German Reich [7]. The remaining part was formed into a " General Government " whose legal nature escapes all definition [8]. Without being directly annexed to the Reich, it was not considered a territory under belligerent occupation either [9]. As a *sui generis* creation it was reminiscent of the Protectorate of Bohemia and

---

1. See above, p. 428.
2. See above, p. 376.
3. " Both parties will tolerate in their territories no Polish agitation which affects the territories of the other party. They will suppress in their territories all beginnings of such agitation and inform each other concerning suitable measures for this purpose. " *Ibid.*, p. 107.
4. See Polish Ministry of Information, *The German New Order in Poland*, London, Hutchinson, 1943, pp. 9-10.
5. See map in Grabski, *op. cit.*, p. 9.
6. See M. Molotov on the two cities : " The Soviet Union agreed to transfer the city of Vilna to the Lithuanian Republic, not because Vilna has a predominantly Lithuanian population. No, the majority of the inhabitants of Vilna are non-Lithuanian. " *N. Y. Times*, Nov. 1, 1939. Speaking at the Four Power Conference in Paris on May 4, 1946, in support of the Yugoslav claim to Trieste, M. Molotov stated that " admittedly there was a majority of Italians in Trieste, but the ministers were faced with no more difficult a situation than was the Soviet Union when it claimed Lwów. The city had a majority of Poles, but as it was surrounded by a Ukrainian countryside, it was rightly and inevitably brought within the Soviet Ukraine. " *The Times*, May 6, 1946.
7. For particulars see *Dokumente der deutschen Politik*, Bd. 7, Teil 2, in particular pp. 599-603.
8. For a German view, see Klein, *Zur Stellung des General-gouvernements in der Verfassung des Grossdeutschen Reiches. Archiv des öff. Rechts, Neue Folge*, 32 Band, 3 Heft, p. 227.
9. See *Dokumente*, Bd. 7, Teil 2, pp. 668-684, in particular the " Erlass des Führers über die Verwaltung der besetzten polnischen Gebiete ", of October 12, 1939, *ibid.*, no. 127, and comment : " ...ein Gebiet deutscher Machthoheit, aber kein Bestandteil des (von ihm durch eine Zollgrenze getrennten) Grossdeutschen Reiches... " *Ibid.*, p. 669.

Moravia, without the appearances of autonomy. The German thesis of the extinction of Poland was upheld by German courts [1].

With regard to the Soviet-occupied Eastern Poland, it was divided into a Northern part, called Western White Ruthenia, with the "capital" first in Wilno and then in Bialystok, — and a Southern part, called Western Ukraine with the " capital " in Lwów. The Northern part was subsequently subdivided when on October 10, 1939, the Soviet Union transferred the city and region of Wilno to Lithuania [2]. On October 22, 1939, elections to the National Assemblies of Western White Ruthenia (now without the Wilno region) and Western Ukraine were held. The elected Assemblies met in Lwów and Bialystok respectively and produced identical resolutions asking for the incorporation of the regions concerned into the Soviet Union. The request was granted by the Supreme Soviet which, on November 1 and 2, 1939, issued the respective incorporation decrees [3]. A subsequent decree of November 29, 1939, imposed Soviet nationality on all Polish citizens in the incorporated regions, whether resident or refugees [4]. In the autumn of 1940 and the spring of 1941, the Soviet authorities conscripted certain classes of the Polish population into the Red Army [5]. Moreover, large-scale deportations of Polish citizens into the interior of Russia were carried out. It is estimated that over one million inhabitants were thus deported in the four main waves of deportation, viz. February 1940, April 1940, June 1940 and June 1941 [6].

b) *Legal Evaluation.*

While the German-Soviet Non-Aggression Pact — with the exception of its ominously sounding Art. 2 [7] — is hardly open to any legal objection, this does not apply to the Secret Protocol. There can be no reasonable doubt that a treaty for the destruction of an independent third State can claim neither legality nor validity under general international law, even in its most traditional form ; for it is in flagrant contradiction to the very assumption on which alone an international law can exist : that of the co-existence of separate, independent and internationally protected States. Whatever explanation can be found in traditional international law for the recognition of an effective debellatio, cannot possibly serve as a legal basis for an international convention aiming at a destruction of third States not yet attacked and overpowered, — in other words, States effectively continuing within their international delimitation. If an attempt against the continued

1. *K. v. K. (Polish Nationality Case)* A. D., 1941/42, case no. 170. Speaking of the principle of the continuity of an occupied State, Oppenheim-Lauterpacht state : " That principle was flagrantly violated by Germany during the Second World War, especially in relation to Poland. " *Op. cit.*, II, p. 448, *f.-n.* 2. As is shown, the same flagrant violation was committed by the Soviet Union.
2. See Polish protest of October 18, 1939, *Pol.-Sov. Relations*, p. 102.
3. *Ibid.*, pp. 102-104.
4. *Ibid.*, pp. 104-105.
5. *Ibid.*, p. 105.
6. *Ibid.*, pp. 17-21.
7. See above, pp. 427-428.

legal existence of an already overpowered and occupied State, in the form of premature annexation, is illegal and invalid [1], how much more so must be an attempt against its very existence even before an occupation. Independence being an inherent, protected and necessary quality of States [2], the liquidation of such independence cannot possibly form the proper object of an international convention [3]. It is not to be imagined that an international tribunal could uphold the validity of such a convention.

Over and above this, the Secret Protocol violated the existing conventional obligations of the parties. It was incompatible with Germany's recognition of Polish independence, as stipulated in the Versailles Treaty, nor with the spirit of the Pact of Paris, nor, finally, with the German-Polish Arbitration Treaty of 1926. As regards the Soviet Union, the Secret Protocol violated all her conventional obligations towards Poland, as described above [4] and in particular Art. 1 and 3 of the Soviet-Polish Non-Aggression Pact [5].

If the Secret Protocol alone represented a violation of international law, this is even more true of the actual invasion of Poland by the two States. By this act of aggression, Germany violated the above-mentioned Arbitration Treaty, the Pact of Paris, and probably even the Non-Aggression Declaration of 1933, since the repudiation of the latter by Hitler on April 28, 1939 was of doubtful legality [6].

The Soviet invasion of Poland was a clear violation of the Covenant, the Pact of Paris, the Protocol of 1929, the two Non-Aggression Treaties and the Litvinov Convention. More particularly, as an " act of violence " against " the integrity and inviolability of the territory or the political independence " of Poland, even if committed " without declaration of war " and avoiding " warlike manifestations ", it fell under the provisions of Art. 1 of the Non-Aggression Treaty of 1932. Inasmuch as it undoubtedly gave assistance to Germany in finally overcoming Polish armed resistance, it violated Art. 3 of that Treaty. As an act of aggression, it fitted exactly into the definition of aggression

---

1. See above, pp. 102-107.
2. See above, pp. 162-165.
3. " It is a unanimously recognized customary rule of International Law that obligations which are at variance with universally recognized principles of International Law cannot be the object of a treaty. " Oppenheim-Lauterpacht, *op. cit.*, I, p. 808 ; « ...il faut certainement admettre que la volonté ne peut tendre ni à une chose matérielle-ment impossible (impossibilité naturelle), ni à une chose interdite par le droit (illicité ou impossibilité juridique)... » Anzilotti, *op. cit.*, p. 340. " ...it is believed that a treaty between two States the execution of which contemplates the infliction upon a third State of what customary international law regards as wrong is illegal and invalid *ab initio.* " McNair, *The Law of Treaties*, p. 113. Illegality of object as a reason of nullity of a conventional norm need not, therefore, necessarily rest on any natural law assumption ; it may result from the very system of international law with which it cannot be reconciled.
4. See above, pp. 419-422.
5. See above, p. 420.
6. The Declaration had been concluded for a period of ten years and did not include a provision for its earlier denunciation. See above, p. 422. That the German aggression against Poland was a violation of the Pact of Paris, as well as of Germany's obligations to settle disputes with Poland by pacific means, was emphasized by the British and French notifications of the state of war with Germany to the League of Nations. See *LNOJ*, 1939, p. 397.

as laid down in, and proscribed by, the Litvinov Convention, particularly in point 2 of its Art. 2 [1], and Art. 3 specifying that

" no political, military, economic or other considerations may serve as an excuse or justification for the aggression referred to in Art. 2 ".

It equally fell within the provision of the Annex which declared that no act of aggression within the meaning of the Convention could be justified either by the internal condition or the international conduct of a State. All these conventional obligations were in force between the Soviet Union and Poland on September 17, 1939 and there was no way of reconciling them with Soviet action [2].

The Soviet reply to this dilemma is to be found in the key passage of the Potemkin Note, asserting that the Polish State and Government had ceased to exist and that

" therefore the Agreements concluded between the U.S.S.R. and Poland have ceased to operate [3] ".

According to the Soviet view there was thus no act of war on the part of the Soviet Union against Poland, no aggression and no violation of binding international agreements ; by the alleged extinction of the Polish State such agreements automatically lapsed and on September 17 the invading Soviet troops marched into a legal vacuum. It is therefore necessary to examine, whether, at the relevant date, the Polish State had or had not in fact become extinct.

The Soviet Note adduces three reasons for the extinction of Poland as a State : the loss by Poland of all her industrial areas and cultural centres, the fact that Warsaw " no longer existed as the capital of Poland", and the disintegration of the Polish Government, all of which are supposed to have taken place during the first ten days of hostilities.

Apart from the obvious untruthfulness of the facts quoted (at the relevant date, the Polish armies were still in possession of the whole of Eastern Poland, besieged Warsaw not only " existed " but fought back, and the Polish Government was sufficiently in existence for the Soviet Ambassador to continue to be accredited to it and to perform his functions together with the rest of the Diplomatic Corps) [4], none of them has the slightest relevance under international law to the continuity or extinction of a State. Had Poland, on the 17th of September, been totally overrun and occupied by the German army, the proclamation of her extinction would still have been contrary to the firm rule of international law, providing for the continuity of a State under belligerent occupation [5]. A fortiori, the allegation of

---

1. " Invasion by its armed forces, with or without a declaration of war, of the territory of another State. "
2. It must further be pointed out that the Soviet invasion of Poland had not been preceded either by a conflict or by a formulation of claims of any sort. " There can be no greater violation of the Law of Nations than for a State to begin hostilities or to declare war in time of peace without previous controversy, and without having endeavoured to settle the conflict by negotiation. " Oppenheim-Lauterpacht, op. cit., II, p. 291.
3. See above, p. 428.
4. See Off. Doc., no. 173.
5. See above, pp. 73-126.

extinction of a country in the midst of a defensive war cannot be seriously considered. Its very weakness is proof that Soviet action was as little to be reconciled with existing international obligations as was Germany's invasion of Czechoslovakia on March 15, 1939; in both cases, the extinction of the victim State was claimed by the aggressors in order to evade existing obligations and to present the alleged extinction as the reason for their action where — *per maxime inconcessum* — it could only be its result. [1] That such an alleged extinction could at best be the result, and not the cause, of aggressive action, was as plainly admitted by M. Molotov with regard to Poland as it had been admitted by Hitler with regard to Czechoslovakia. In his speech to the Supreme Soviet of October 31, 1939, M. Molotov declared in particular :

" ... one swift blow to Poland, first by the German Army and then by the Red Army, and nothing was left of this ugly offspring of the Versailles Treaty [2]... "

As in the case of Germany, so in the case of the Soviet Union, the right of an aggressor to free himself from his existing international obligations towards his victim by the simple device of declaring the latter extinct, cannot be taken seriously [3].

As has been seen, the Soviet thesis of Poland's extinction was adhered to by Germany, although no attempt was made to justify this thesis at the time. At the Nurnberg trial the German defence put forward the thesis of subjugation, on which the Tribunal, the Soviet judge concurring, had this to say :

" A further submission was made that Germany was no longer bound by the rules of land warfare in many of the territories occupied during the war, because Germany had completely subjugated those countries and incorporated them into the German Reich, a fact which gave Germany authority to deal with the occupied countries as though they were part of Germany. In the view of the Tribunal it is unnecessary in this case to decide whether this doctrine of subjugation, dependent as it is upon military conquest, has any application where the subjugation is the result of the crime of aggressive war. The doctrine was never considered to be applicable so long as there was an army in the field attempting to restore the occupied countries to their true owners, and in this case, therefore, *the doctrine could not apply to any territories occupied after the 1st September* 1939 [4]. "

---

1. See above, p. 300.
2. *New York Times*, November, 1 1939.
3. See above, p. 304. For detailed refutation of the Soviet thesis, see *RDI*, 1939, pp. 114-116. With regard to the — legally irrelevant — argument concerning the Soviet protection of Ukrainians and White-Ruthenians, the author observes « le principe de la parenté de sang des peuples de l'Union soviétique avec les populations ukrainiennes et blanc-russiennes résidant en Pologne, que l'U.R.S.S. invoque en faveur de son intervention et qui traduit sans doute une influence des principes identiques soutenus en Allemagne hitlérienne », p. 116. Cf. the rejection by the Nurnberg Tribunal of the German justification of the invasion of Austria by " many matters in common between the two peoples that made this union desirable... " " These matters " — the Tribunal held, the Soviet judge concurring — " even if true, are really immaterial, for the facts plainly prove that the methods employed to achieve the object were those of an aggressor ". *Judgment*, p. 19. Cf. Soviet comment on Hungary's occupation of part of Yugoslavia in 1941, under the alleged necessity of protecting nationals : " ...it could easily be understood in what a position Hungary might find itself if it, while in misfortune, should be subjected in its turn to an attack of this kind — since in Hungary there are also substantial national minorities. " *Doc.*, III, p. 331, *f.-n.* 2.
4. *It. mine, Judgment*, p. 65.

It is worth while quoting the following comment by a Polish writer :

" The Nurnberg Judgment confirms our view that in 1939 there could have been no subjugation of Poland since the Polish Army continued to participate in the war, — and, more particularly, it refuses to apply the doctrine of subjugation to territories occupied by Germany since September 1, 1939, i.e. since the German attack on Poland. In view of the fact, that consequences of that attack became the basis of the Soviet thesis concerning the end of the Polish State (Soviet Note of September 17, 1939) the refusal to recognize the legality of that basis automatically destroys the legality of conclusions resulting from it. ... Thus, the arguments of the Soviet Note of September 17, 1939, bearing on the end of the Polish State, were internationally dismissed with the participation of the Soviets [1]. "

If the thesis of the extinction of the Polish State ran counter to positive international law, so did the disposal of Polish territory by the partitioning Powers [2]. No more need be said with regard to the German occupation. Some attention must, however, be devoted to the developments under Soviet occupation which followed a different pattern. In spite of the untenable thesis of Poland's extinction, these developments did not take place in a vacuum but within the territorial sphere of validity of the Polish State. No such administrative division as was undertaken [3], with subsequent elections to the " National Assemblies " of these newly-created entities could have been legal according to Polish municipal law. Nor could this law possibly provide for a part of the country applying for incorporation into a foreign

---

1. *Trans. mine.* Komentator, *op. cit.*, pp. 14-15, and *f.-n.* 30. As a matter of principle, the thesis of Poland's extinction, as contained in the Soviet Note of September 17, has been analyzed on its merits. Such analysis was, however, hardly necessary in view of facts and documents which have since become available and which show the Soviet Union's own lack of conviction in her theory ; it appears that the problem of how to justify the Soviet invasion had been subject of prolonged negotiations between Molotov and the German Ambassador in Moscow as from September 3, 1939. On September 10, Molotov divulged the future thesis about Poland's extinction. In consequence, the German Ambassador sent the following wire to the German Foreign Office on September 14 : " ...For the political motivation of Soviet action (the collapse of Poland and the protection of Russian " minorities ") it was of the greatest importance not to take action until governmental center of Poland, the city of Warsaw, had fallen. Molotov therefore asked that he be informed as nearly as possible as to when the capture of Warsaw could be counted on. " *Nazi-Soviet Relations*, pp. 92-93. See also *ibid.*, pp. 86, 90, 91, 95 and 96. It must further be observed that not only the thesis of Poland's extinction but the actual initiative in physically suppressing even a rump Polish State originated on the Soviet side. See in particular the despatch of the German Ambassador in Moscow to his Foreign Office of September 20, 1939 : " Molotov stated to me to-day that the Soviet Government now considered the time ripe for it, jointly with the German Government to establish definitely the structure of the Polish area. In this regard, Molotov hinted that the original inclination entertained by the Soviet Government and Stalin personally to permit the existence of a residual Poland, had given way to the inclination to partition Poland along the Pissa-Narew-Vistula-San Line. " *Ibid.*, p. 101. On September 25, the same suggestion was repeated by Stalin to the German Ambassador : " Stalin stated the following : In the final settlement of the Polish question anything that in the future might create friction between Germany and the Soviet Union must be avoided. From this point of view, he considered it wrong to leave an independent Polish rump State. " *Ibid.* pp. 102-103.
2. « Les annexions prématurées sont nulles et sans valeur lorsqu'elles sont contemporaines des hostilités. L'époque contemporaine fournit plusieurs applications de cette pratique abusive : ...le partage de la Pologne par le traité germano-soviétique du 28 septembre 1939, fondé sur la prétendue dissolution de l'Etat polonais nous fournit encore un exemple d'annexion prématurée. » Rousseau, *Droit International Public*, Paris, Rec. Sirey, 1953, pp. 250-251.
3. See above, p. 431.

State. The claim that the above-described proceedings [1] were legal under Polish law can therefore be summarily dismissed, especially since — unlike in the Baltic States [2] — such a claim was never put forward from any quarter. Yet, failing any such legal basis, the events in question might possibly represent a revolutionary movement in these territories, aiming at, and achieving, an internationally valid secession from the Polish State.

Such a view must, however, be dismissed in the light of what has already been said about the conditions of a genuine revolution generally, and in the light of the analysis of similar events in the Baltic States in particular [3]. The presumption of the fake revolution under foreign occupation not only applies, but is additionally reinforced by the fact of such revolution being in full conformity with the designs of the occupying Power.

More particularly, in the case of Eastern Poland, the so-called elections to the new " National Assemblies " were actually organized and carried through by the organs and citizens of the occupying Power, by the exercise of pressure and intimidation of the electorate, and with no freedom of choice, there being only one approved list of candidates. In particular, the first announcement of the forthcoming elections took place in form of a decision of the Soviet Commander-in-Chief of the Ukrainian front, General Timoshenko, on October 6, 1939. It is true that the initiative was later ascribed to the " temporary administrations " of Lwów and Bialystok, but these too were Soviet-appointed bodies. For the organisation and conduct of the elections a committee was set up in each of the two areas. Among members of these committees there figured : Gretchuha, chairman of the Supreme Soviet of the Ukrainian S.S.R., Korneychuk, member of the Praesidium of the said Supreme Soviet (later Deputy Commissar for Foreign Affairs of the U.S.S.R.), Natalevitsch, chairman of the Praesidium of the Supreme Soviet of the White-Ruthenian S.S.R., Grekhova, chairman of the Supreme Council of the White-Ruthenian S.S.R., etc. Among the candidates to the Assemblies there figured : Molotov, Chairman of the Council of People's Commissars of the U.S.S.R., Marshal Voroshilov, General Kovalev, Commander-in-Chief of the White-Ruthenian front, Ponomarenko, member of the Military Council of the White-Ruthenian Front, etc. [4]. Pressure on the electorate by the whole military, police and administrative apparatus of the occupying Power was reinforced by a wave of arrests and deportations. Failure to vote or voting against the official candidate was made practically impossible.

According to Soviet sources, 96.71 % of the electors voted for the Assembly of Lwów, and 92.83 % for that of Bialystok [5]. This uncanny unanimity, as well as the identity of programmes and

---

1. See above, p. 431.
2. See above, p. 383.
3. See above, pp. 387-389.
4. *Pol.-Sov. Relations*, pp. 6-11.
5. *Ibid.*, p. 10.

resolutions voted by the two Assemblies call for the same comment as was made with regard to similar proceedings in the Baltic States [1].

The two Assemblies met on October 26 and 28, 1939, respectively. According to *Pravda* of October 27, and October 29, the following Soviet dignitaries were unanimously elected to the honorary Praesidia : Stalin, Molotov, Voroshilov, Kalinin, Kaganovich, Mikoian, Andreiev, Zhdanov, Chruszczev, Beria and Shvernik, with the addition of Timoshenko for Lwów, while Stalin was elected honorary President of both Assemblies.

In view of the above there can therefore be no question of a spontaneous, revolutionary, secessionist movement in the Eastern territories of Poland. On the contrary, the elections and incorporation were the work of the Soviet State, carried out in what had already become an illegally incorporated area of the Polish State.

This unilateral action by the Soviet Union was authoritatively confirmed by M. Molotov in his speech of October 31, 1939 (i.e. before the formal acceptance of the territories in question into the U.S.S.R. by the Supreme Soviet) :

" The territory that has passed to the U.S.S.R. is equal in area to a large European State [2]... "

M. Molotov's use of the past tense was perfectly correct. The actual incorporation of Eastern Poland into the Soviet Union was accomplished long before the elections, immediately on the entry of the Red Army and Soviet administrative authorities, including the NKVD. Not only was the occupied territory subjected to a new, Soviet-imposed administrative subdivision [3], but the existing Polish administration and local authorities were immediately suppressed. City mayors, parish heads and administrative officials of every grade were removed, many of them being arrested and deported into the interior of Russia. They were replaced by Soviet-appointed " temporary administrations ", set up with the participation of Red Army Commanders, NKVD officials and other Soviet citizens. All branches of life were adapted to the Soviet pattern at great speed, under the direction and with the participation not only of the Soviet army and police, but equally of the innumerable Soviet political leaders, official personalities, agitators, propagandists, etc. who had been sent into Eastern Poland from Russia [4].

Such unilateral action of the Soviet State bearing on territory and population of another independent State, continuing its legal existence under belligerent occupation, must be qualified as violating positive international law.

---

1. See above, p. 388.
2. *New York Times*, November 1, 1939.
3. See above, p. 431.
4. The Soviet Press of the period did not hesitate to describe Soviet-occupied Poland as part of the Soviet Union. Thus, *Izviestia* of September 26, 1939, qualified Soviet invasion as an event " changing the State allegiance " of the occupied territories ; on September 30, the same paper reported an appeal of the Soviet Commander of the Ukrainian front, General Timoshenko, to the local population for increased work for " its great Soviet fatherland ", etc.

2. ATTITUDE OF THE INTERNATIONAL COMMUNITY.

The German-Soviet thesis of the extinction of Poland met with an outright rejection by the international community.

The following statement was issued by the British Ministry of Information on September 18, 1939 :

" The British Government have considered the situation created by the attack upon Poland ordered by the Soviet Government. This attack made upon Great Britain's ally at a moment when she is prostrate in face of overwhelming forces brought against her by Germany cannot in the view of H.M. Government be justified by the arguments put forward by the Soviet Government. The full implication of these events is not yet apparent, but H.M. Government take the opportunity of stating that nothing that has occurred can make any difference to the determination of H.M. Government, with the full support of the country, to fulfil their obligations to Poland and to prosecute the war with all energy until their objectives have been achieved [1]. "

The attitude of the United States, which at that time was still neutral, was expressed in the following statement by the Secretary of State, of October 2, 1939 :

" More than twenty years ago the United States recognized and has since maintained diplomatic relations with the Polish Government. Poland is now the victim of force used as an instrument of national policy. Its territory has been taken over and its Government has had to seek refuge abroad. *Mere seizure of territory, however, does not extinguish the legal existence of government.* The United States therefore continues to regard the Government of Poland as in existence, in accordance with the provisions of the Constitution of Poland, and continues to recognize Count Jerzy Potocki as its Ambassador in Washington. For the present at least Mr. Biddle will remain near the Government to which he has been accredited [2]. "

A similar attitude was adopted by the whole international community, with the exception of the partitioning Powers and their satellites. Polish diplomatic missions continued to function in allied and neutral countries, and diplomatic representatives continued to be accredited to the Polish Government in exile [3].

The point requires stressing, for it is sometimes erroneously stated that the newly formed Polish Government in exile achieved recognition on the part of the international community. Nothing of the sort ever happened or, indeed, could have happened. There was no need for an act of recognition [4]. Neither was Poland after the partition a new State, nor was her government a " new " government, either under Polish constitutional or under international law [5]. What the international community did, was not to " recognize " either the Polish State or its Government, but to affirm its continuity in face of the proclamation of its extinction by the occupying Powers. It was on this basis that

---

1. *The Times,* September 19, 1939.
2. *It. mine; Dep. of. St. Bul.,* vol I, p. 342.
3. See *RDI,* 1939, pp. 127-128, and 500-502. The examples quoted do not exhaust the list. Cf. *A. J.,* 1940, p. 134.
4. See Guggenheim, *Lehrbuch,* p. 200 ; Scelle, *op. cit.,* p. 176 ; Lauterpacht, *op. cit.,* p. 91, *f.-n.* 1.
5. See below, p. 439.

France and later Great Britain, offered hospitality to the exiled Government and enabled it to function in their territory [1].

In view of its conformity to the rule of international law providing for the continuity of a State under belligerent occupation, this attitude of the international community is conclusive evidence of the continuity of the Polish State.

3. THE EFFECTIVE CONTINUITY OF THE POLISH STATE.

Unlike the case of Albania, Austria or — for a certain period — Czechoslovakia, the continuity of the Polish State was never reduced to a purely ideal notion. On the contrary, it achieved the maximum of effectiveness possible under existing conditions, both in exile and in occupied Poland.

a) *In Exile.*

The legal basis and character of the exercise of State sovereignty in exile has already been dealt with at some length [2]. Alongside other State organisations in exile, the Polish Government, firmly based on its constitutional and actual continuity within the legal order of Poland [3], displayed from the very outset most widespread activities in every field.

It was only natural that such activities were primarily concerned with the effective prosecution of the war. Following the total occupation of Poland, the Polish army was re-created in France and took an active

---

1. E. g. the French Prime Minister's communication to the Polish Ambassador in Paris of September 20, 1939, « que l'hospitalité de la France alliée est assurée au Président de la République et au gouvernement polonais et que le Gouvernement français est prêt à prendre toutes dispositions à l'effet d'assurer, en sauvegardant les droits souverains du Chef de l'Etat polonais, l'exercice extraterritorial de ses pouvoirs et de ceux de son Gouvernement. » Quoted by Fiedorowicz, *Continuité de l'Etat*, p. 167. Cf. the invitation adressed by Poincaré to the King of Belgians « pour assurer en France le séjour de Votre Majesté et de ses Ministres en pleine indépendance et souveraineté. » *Royaume de Belgique, Correspondance diplomatique relative à la guerre de 1914-1918*, no. 56.
2. See above, pp. 86-101.
3. Notwithstanding its entirely new composition, the Polish Government in exile represented the immediate continuation of the Government which had functioned in Poland itself prior to, and during, the invasion. The transmission of power to the exiled Government was effected in full conformity with the Polish Constitution ; there was no break in continuity. See the two communiqués of the Polish Embassy in Paris, of September 30, 1939, bearing on the appointment of a new President and Government respectively, *RDI*, 1939, pp. 496-497. Whatever the political implications of the reshuffle, legally the Polish Government in exile represented the old, constitutional and continuing Government of the Polish State, and not a new creation on foreign soil. Hence its status in exile of a fully-fledged organ of the State it represented. See above, pp. 97-99. On the constitutional status of the Polish Government in exile see Oppenheimer, *op. cit.*, p. 570. Similarly Fiedorowicz : « La prise de pouvoir par le nouveau gouvernement s'est faite sans interruption, conformément aux lois constitutionnelles polonaises. » *Op. cit.*, p. 162. Also Flory, *op. cit.*, pp. 250-251 and 278 ; see in particular : « ...la Constitution polonaise fut respectée autant qu'il était possible au cours de cette période troublée. Il y avait somme toute peu de différence entre la situation constitutionnelle du Gouvernement polonais de 1939 et celle de 1945. Cette continuité fut d'ailleurs largement reconnue puisqu'en dehors des Etats de l'Axe, le Gouvernement polonais en exil et ses représentants diplomatiques furent acceptés par tous les pays. » p. 250. The writer insists on the « continuité légale aussi parfaite que possible du Gouvernement polonais au cours de son exil. » *Ibid.*, pp. 250-251. For details and political meaning of the re-organisation of the Polish Government in exile in the sense of its far-reaching democratisation, see Fiedorowicz, *op. cit.*, pp. 165-167 ; *RDI*, 1939, pp. 126-127 and 496-499 ; Flory, *op. cit.*, p. 250.

part in the French campaign. After the French collapse, yet another reconstruction of the Polish armed forces took place in Britain, on the basis of several Anglo-Polish agreements to this effect [1]. As a result, Poland built up on foreign soil an army, navy and air force ; these forces were larger than any of the other armies in exile and made themselves effectivaly felt in the course of the hostilities [2].

Polish legislative activity in exile included acts passed to meet the immediate needs of the organized Polish community abroad, as well as acts dealing with the actual or future problems of the occupied country itself [3].

Administrative activity was not only concerned with the functioning of State organs abroad, but equally with social welfare and assistance, protection of refugees, setting up of Polish schools and university faculties, and so forth.

Judicial activity consisted in the functioning of Polish military courts, as well as of the Maritime Courts [4].

Particularly noteworthy was the diplomatic activity of the Polish Government, as expressed in numerous bilateral and multilateral agreements. Poland was party to all major international agreements, bearing either on the actual prosecution of war, as for example the Lend-Lease Agreement, or the United Nations Declaration, or on the future of post-war world as for example the F.A.O., the U.N.R.R.A., the Bretton Woods, and other agreements [5]. Bilateral agreements were not limited to current military problems [6], but also dealt with future political problems, e.g. the Polish-Czechoslovak agreement of November 11, 1942 on the subject of a future confederation of the two States. The Polish Government in exile continued to be accompanied by the Diplomatic Corps, and Polish diplomatic and consular missions in allied and neutral countries continued to function. It may therefore be stated that the Polish Government abroad had achieved the maximum effectiveness attainable by sovereignty in exile.

b) *The Underground State.*

No such open and official effectiveness could be achieved in occupied Poland. As has been seen, the occupying Powers — Germany and Russia, and, at a later stage Germany alone — proceeded on the assumption of the extinction of the Polish State which was equivalent to disregarding its legal order. *A fortiori,* they could not be expected to recognize any extension of that legal order from abroad into the

---

1. Thus, e. g., Agreement concerning the Formation of a Detachment of the Polish Navy in Great Britain, of November 18, 1939 ; Provisional Military Agreement of December 2, 1939 ; Agreement respecting Polish Land and Air Forces of August 5, 1940 ; Protocol concerning the Lending of British Warships to the Polish Navy of December 3, 1940 ; Protocol concerning the Organisation and Service of the Polish Air Force, of June 4, 1944, etc.
2. E. g. the Polish contribution to the winning of the Battle of Britain in 1940, the exploits of the Polish Navy, including participation in the African and Normandy landings, the capture of Monte Cassino by the Polish Second Corps in May 1944.
3. See above, p. 100 and below, p. 443.
4. See above, pp. 92-93 and 101.
5. See above, pp. 93-94.
6. See above, f.-n. 1.

occupied country [1]. In the face of such illegal conduct of the occupying Powers, the effectiveness of the Polish legal order in Poland was asserted in a new and unorthodox manner, by the creation of what has come to be known as the " Underground State ".

The Polish Underground State belongs to the same category of resistance movements in occupied countries which, starting as spontaneous, uncodified and revolutionary phenomena, came to be accepted by the international community as a new departure in international law. They had certainly not been provided for by the Hague Regulations ; on the contrary, it could be not unreasonably deduced from the contents of their relevant Articles that they were positively prohibited [2]. The possibility of their legitimate co-existence with the rights of the law-abiding occupant under the Hague Regulations may still be subject to doubt [3]. Yet, the fact remains that the European resistance movements came into being against a *law-breaking* occupant, which may go a long way towards explaining their recognition first in State practice and later by positive international law [4]. Claiming that members of such movements are entitled to be treated in accordance with the Hague Regulations [5], Oppenheim-Lauterpacht declare that such right

" applies, in particular, to cases in which the resistance movement against the enemy, while lacking military cohesion, is authorized by and acts in accordance with the orders of the lawful Government [6] ".

This was precisely the position of all European resistance movements during the Second World War [7]. Notwithstanding their sometimes spontaneous origin these movements were directly subordinated to the respective exiled governments and were, moreover, given a definite status within the legal order of the occupied States [8]. Such bodies were in turn recognized by the Allies as part of the regular armed forces of their respective States, and, consequently, of the Allied Forces, as in the case of the French Forces of the Interior [9].

---

1. See above, pp. 84-86.
2. See Fitzmaurice G. G., *The Juridical Clauses of the Peace Treaties*, Rec. 1948, II, pp. 274-275.
3. See Oppenheim-Lauterpacht, *op. cit.*, II, p. 215.
4. Writing before the Geneva Conventions, Fitzmaurice asserted that in certain conditions of modern warfare and occupation " the emergence of partisan or resistance movements is a certainty, and constitutes something for which International Law must make provision. " *Op. cit.*, p. 275.
5. " It must now be held that so long as these persons, though operating in occupied territory, fulfil the conditions which the Hague Regulations prescribe generally as qualifying irregular forces for the privileges and treatment enjoyed by the armed forces of the belligerents, they are entitled to the same treatment and privileges. " Oppenheim-Lauterpacht, *op. cit.*, II, p. 212.
6. *Op. cit.*, II, p. 213.
7. In the case of France, the control from abroad was assumed by General de Gaulle's France Libre.
8. Thus, the Dutch Royal Emergency Decree of September 1944, gave the Netherlands Forces of the Interior the status of a part of the Dutch Army. *Ibid.*, p. 213, *f.-n.*
9. In June 1944 the French Forces of the Interior, constituted as a combatant force under a French high officer, were recognized by the Supreme Commander of the Allied Expeditionary Force as integral part of that force. Formal announcements to that effect were made. Fitzmaurice, *op. cit.*, p. 276. Oppenheim-Lauterpacht, *op. cit.*, II, p. 214, *f.-n.* 2.

It was on the basis of such developments in State practice that the problem of resistance movements was dealt with by international conventions. In one particular instance, the legal phenomenon of a resistance movement was acknowledged in the Italian Peace Treaty [1]. In 1949, the Geneva Conventions laid down a general norm, recognizing the legal status of resistance movements and granting them the protection of international law alongside members of the regular forces [2].

The Polish Underground State represented a resistance movement *sensu largo*, consisting as it did not only of the actual guerilla forces, later to be known as the Home Army, but equally of the whole civilian State structure, headed by a Delegate of the Polish Government assisted by a shadow parliament and disposing of a complete network of administration, courts of justice, an educational system, official publications, etc. The foundations of this organisation were laid in Poland immediately after the military defeat of 1939, and regular contact with the Government in exile was established within the shortest possible time. Further stages involved a process of unification both on the political and military side. Politically, the structure rested on a coalition of the main political parties [3], whose representatives formed the so-called underground parliament, the Home Political Representation, later enlarged and re-named the Council of National Unity. An integration of the originally isolated military groupings led to the creation of the official Polish Home Army under a Commander-in-Chief, appointed by the Commander-in-Chief of the Polish armed forces abroad. The head of the whole movement, the Government's Delegate was nominated by the Polish Government in exile. The secret newspaper " The Polish Republic " was the official organ of the Delegate's office,

---

1. " Whereas after the said Armistice Italian armed forces, both of the Government and of the Resistance Movement, took an active part in the war against Germany... "
2. Convention relative to the Treatment of Prisoners of War: Art. 4. a) Prisoners of war, in the sense of the present Convention, are persons belonging to one of the following categories, who have fallen into the power of the enemy : ... 2) Members of other militias and members of other volunteer corps, including those of organized resistance movements, belonging to a Party to the conflict and operating in or outside their own territory, even if this territory is occupied, provided that these mi'itias or volunteer corps, including these organized resistance movements, fulfil the following conditions : a) that of being commanded by a person responsible for his subordinates, b) that of having a fixed distinctive sign recognizable at distance, c) that of carrying arms openly, d) that of conducting their operations in accordance with the laws and customs of war. " Cf. Art. 13 of the Convention for the Amelioration of the Condition of the Wounded and Sick in Armed Forces in the Field, and of the Convention for the Amelioration of the Condition of Wounded, Sick and Shipwrecked Members of Armed Forces at Sea. — «Une véritable reconnaissance des mouvements organisés de résistance comme éléments des forces armées dans la guerre moderne a été effective à Genève, en 1949, sous le couvert d'une application à leur profit des regles protectrices des Conventions. » La Pradelle, *La Conférence Diplomatique et les nouvelles Conventions de Genève du* 12 août 1949, Paris, Editions internationales, 1951. — Cf. the post-war municipal decisions on the subject : thus, in the case *Baffico v. Callieri*, the Court of Appeal of Turin, Italy, held on January 5, 1948 : " It is to-day an undisputed principle, affirmed by the courts and supported by the most authoritative writers, that the commands of the partisans had a lawful existence and had, consequently, the competence to carry out within the occupied territories activities supporting the lawful government. " *A. D.*, 1948, case no. 128. This appears to be the consistent attitude of Italian courts, see *ibid*. cases no. 129, 130, 151. Similarly Dutch courts, *ibid*. cases no. 131 and 132.
3. The Polish Socialist Party, the Polish Peasant Party, the National Party and the Christian Labour Party ; neither the extreme Right Wing nor the Communists were included.

containing official announcements, directives to the population, and so forth. Contact with the Polish Government was maintained by means of secret wireless stations as well as couriers circulating between Warsaw and London [1].

The activities of the underground organisation covered the armed struggle itself, sabotage and diversion against the German occupant, intelligence in collaboration with Allied intelligence services [2], as well as the current social, economic, relief and educational problems of the population.

In due course, the Polish Underground State acquired such a degree of control over the Polish people that it was found necessary to give it a formal legal standing. On September 1, 1942, a decree to that effect was signed by the Polish Government in London, finally establishing the legal foundations of the authority and powers of the underground organisation. In particular, the Government's Delegate in Poland was now included in the Polish Cabinet with the rank of Deputy Prime Minister. Later, three more underground leaders, drawn from the Polish Socialist Party, the Polish Peasant Party and the National Party respectively were included in the government with ministerial rank, with the result that, according to Polish law, a part of the Polish Government resided and functioned in England, whereas the other part resided and functioned in occupied Poland [3].

Formal international recognition of the Home Army was achieved during the Warsaw Rising, when, on August 30, 1944, the British and United States Governments issued practically identical statements on the subject. The British Declaration read :

" H.M. Government have consistently done all in their power to ensure that all members of the armed forces of the Powers at war with Germany should be treated by the German military authorities in accordance with the laws and customs of war. They are, however, receiving numerous reports which show that members of the Polish Home Army, which is engaged in active operations in the struggle against the common enemy are being treated by the German military authorities in a manner contrary to the laws and customs of war.

---

1. For the history and organisation of the Underground State, see e.g. Karski, *The Secret State*, Houghton Mifflin Co., Boston, The Riverside Press, Cambridge, Mass., 1944 ; Bor-Komorowski, *The Secret Army*.
2. See Churchill, *The Second World War*, vol. V, *Closing the Ring*, pp. 207-208.
3. The September decree was revealed to the world at large in a broadcast speech from London of the Polish Prime Minister, of January 5, 1944 : " In making public the existence of such a Decree, we desire to inform the Polish citizens in the home country about the legal foundations of the authority and competence of that Member of the Polish Cabinet who, as deputy Prime Minister, is charged with the duties of Delegate of the Polish Government in Poland. He has authority to carry out all the functions of the Government concerning home administration. The Delegate of the Government carries out his duties in accordance with the orders and instructions of the Government of the Republic, with the assistance of his office, acting in close co-operation with the Polish Political Representation and the Commander of the Polish Secret Army. Thus the hard State duty of securing the continuity of the legal Government in underground Poland is carried on. The Delegate of the Government in Poland, appointed by the President of Poland as a member of the Cabinet, carries out in Poland, until the return of the Prime Minister, the duties of Acting Prime Minister, just as the deputy Prime Minister does in London during the absence of the Prime Minister. The Minister Delegate of the Government in Poland will reveal his name and official residence at the appropriate moment... " Mikolajczyk, *The Rape of Poland*, pp. 271-272. About promulga'ion of decrees of the exiled governments by means of wireless, see Flory, *op. cit.*, p. 159 and p. 16, *f.-n.* 2.

H.M. Government therefore make this formal decision :

1) The Polish Home Army, which is now mobilized, constitutes a combatant force forming an integral part of the Polish Armed Forces,

2) Members of the Polish Home Army are instructed to conduct their military operations in accordance with the rules of war, and in so doing they bear their arms openly against the enemy. They operate in units under responsible commanders. They are provided with a distinctive emblem or with Polish uniforms.

3) In these circumstances reprisals against members of the Polish Home Army violate the rules of war, by which Germany is bound. H.M. Government therefore solemnly warn all Germans who take any part in or are in any way responsible for such violations that they do so at their peril and will be held answerable for their crimes [1]. "

It may therefore be concluded that the occupied Polish State continued to exist in fact as well as in law.

It was on behalf of this continuing Polish State that the Polish Government entered protest against the original Soviet aggression as well as against all the subsequent violations of international law by Germany and the Soviet Union, declaring such illegal acts null and void, and reserving the rights of Poland and her citizens [2].

4. RENEWED RECOGNITION OF POLAND'S CONTINUITY BY THE SOVIET UNION.

Of the two partners to the partition of Poland of 1939, the German thesis of Poland's extinction was never modified in the further course of the war. It fell to the ground with the German defeat and does not, therefore, call for further analysis. Entirely different, however, was the development with regard to the U.S.S.R., whose political situation underwent a radical change as a consequence of the German attack of June 22, 1941.

As has been seen [3], the Soviet incorporation of Eastern Poland lacked any valid legal title. The factual basis of such incorporation was to be found a) in the effectiveness of Soviet domination, and b) in the agreement with Germany. With the German attack, the Russo-German partition treaties fell to the ground and within a short time Russia lost all effective control over the Eastern Polish territories which were wholly occupied by Germany [4]. Moreover, the thesis of Poland's

---

1. For the U.S. text see *Doc.* VII, pp. 894-985.

2. *Pol.-Sov. Relations,* pp. 97, 98, 100-101, 102, 105-107. See, in particular, Polish Note to the Secretary-General of the League of Nations on the subject of the Soviet-German partition agreement, declaring that " it can have no legal effect whatever, being absolutely contrary to the fundamental principles of international law in force. The Agreement in fact contains stipulations disposing of the territory of a State Member of the League of Nations which has been the victim of unprovoked aggression. I am instructed by my Government to reiterate before the League of Nations a solemn protest against the Agreement in question and to declare that it will always be regarded by the Polish nation and by the Polish Government as null and void. " *LNOJ,* 1939, p. 386.

3. See above, pp. 433-437.

4. The much discussed question of the survival or otherwise of treaties between the warring parties need hardly be entered into here ; for it is obvious that, by their very nature, the Soviet-German partition treaties could not have survived the German attack and the radical change in the whole German political conception for Eastern Europe, in which a permanent demarcation line between Germany and Russia, running across Polish territory, has lost its whole *raison d'être.*

extinction could now no longer be entertained by the Soviet Union which, on entering the Allied camp, found the Polish State as a fully-fledged partner, continuing the war alongside the other Allies.

Under such circumstances, the Soviet-Polish Pact of July 30, 1941, became the instrument of settling the Soviet-Polish conflict.

" The Government of the Republic of Poland and the Government of the Union of Soviet Socialist Republics have concluded the present Agreement and decided as follows :

1. The Government of the Union of Soviet Socialist Republics recognizes that the Soviet-German treaties of 1939 relative to territorial changes in Poland have lost their validity. The Government of the Republic of Poland declares that Poland is not bound by any Agreement with any third State directed against the U.S.S.R.

2. Diplomatic relations will be restored between the two Governments upon the signature of this Agreement and an exchange of ambassadors will follow immediately.

3. The two Governments mutually undertake to render one another aid and support of all kinds in the present war against Hitlerite Germany.

4. The Government of the Union of Soviet Socialist Republics expresses its consent to the formation on the territory of the Union of Soviet Socialist Republics of a Polish Army under a commander appointed by the Government of the Republic of Poland, in agreement with the Government of the Union of Soviet Socialist Republics. The Polish Army on the territory of the Union of Soviet Socialist Republics will be subordinated in operational matters to the Supreme Command of the U.S.S.R. on which there will be a representative of the Polish Army. All details as to command, organisation and employment of this force will be settled in a subsequent Agreement.

5. This Agreement will come into force immediately upon its signature and without ratification. The present Agreement is drawn up in two copies, each of them in the Russian and Polish languages. Both texts have equal force. "

The Pact also included the following protocol :

" 1. As soon as diplomatic relations are re-established, the Government of the Union of Soviet Socialist Republics will grant amnesty to all Polish citizens who are at present deprived of their freedom on the territory of the U.S.S.R., either as prisoners of war or on other adequate grounds.

2. The present Protocol comes into force simultaneously with the Agreement of July 30, 1941 [1]. "

The outstanding significance of this document lies in the Soviet Union's wholesale repudiation of her previous theory of the extinction of the Polish State. The July Pact was concluded with Poland ; with that same Polish State whose legal existence had never been interrupted since its birth in 1918, and which continued the coalition war, having survived not only the occupation of its territory but also the whole series of illegal acts committed against it. It could not be concluded with anyone else, since there was no " other " Polish State ; there was no question of the creation of a new State, different from the one which had existed on September 1, as well as on September 17 and 28, 1939, and which continued to exist within the same international delimitation of its legal, territorial and personal spheres of validity. Diplomatic

1. *Pol.-Sov. Relations,* pp. 107-108.

relations between the two parties were not inaugurated ; they were " restored " and " re-established ". These expressions of the Pact accurately reflected the legal position under international law. A further admission of the uninterrupted continuity of the Polish State was to be found in the protocol to the Pact, speaking of Polish citizens in the territory of the U.S.S.R. It has been seen that, in accordance with the Soviet thesis of Poland's extinction there was — logically enough — no longer any " Polish nationality " in the eyes of Russia. Indeed, how could there be citizens of a non-existing State ? Moreover, as has been seen [1], the Soviet Union had by means of an internal decree imposed Soviet nationality on the population of Polish Eastern territories, including Polish refugees from Western Poland. Thus, according to the Soviet thesis up to that date, there were not — and could not be — any Polish nationals on Soviet territory, the imprisoned and deported Poles being considered as Soviet nationals. The acknowledgment of their unchanged Polish citizenship by the Soviet Union in the July Pact is to be explained only on the basis of a Soviet return to the only correct view of Poland's uninterrupted continuity.

Thus, by signing the July Pact, the Soviet Union unreservedly went back on the illegal and incorrect theory of State extinction which she had professed during the whole period between September 17, 1939, and July 30, 1941. The correct thesis of Poland's continuity to which she now reverted meant the continuity of international rights and obligations. In other words, by acknowledging Poland's uninterrupted continuity, the Soviet Union *ipso facto* acknowledged her as the subject of all international rights and obligations as they had existed before the proclamation of the now abandoned Soviet theory of extinction. Without such acknowledgment, the Soviet recognition of Poland's continuity would have made no sense ; more than that, it could technically not take place. In other words, the recognition of Polish continuity meant nothing else than the renewed recognition by the Soviet Union of all Poland's international rights and obligations, whether customary or conventional, — the latter including all the instruments, whether multilateral or bilateral, which had been binding on the two States from the Treaty of Riga to the Protocol of 1934, prolonging the Soviet Polish Non-Aggression Treaty.

It is against this basic assumption of the July Pact that the unilateral Soviet declaration incorporated in that Pact must be read, proclaiming the Soviet repudiation of the Soviet-German partition treaties. In spite of their original illegality and invalidity under general international law [2], it was only correct for the Soviet Union, as the contracting party, to declare this invalidity *expressis verbis*. But the statement had no more than declaratory value, both, under general international law and under the conventional stipulations of the July Pact itself (since, clearly, the partition treaties, entered into on the assumption of Poland's extinction, could not be reconciled with the principle of Polish continuity, as expressed in that Pact) and was not constitutive of such invalidity.

---

1. See above, p. 431.
2. See above, pp. 431-432.

The above interpretation of the July Pact could possibly be questioned on one assumption only : that of a state of war having prevailed between Poland and the Soviet Union between September 17, 1939 and July 30, 1941, and of the July Pact being in fact, if not in name, a Peace Treaty. If that had been the case, then it could be argued that the war between the parties had had an extinguishing effect on at least some of their previous bilateral treaties, and that the July Pact opened an entirely new era in their mutual relations. In discussing this problem it has to be borne in mind that the whole controversy concerning the survival or otherwise of treaties between belligerents refers exclusively to a genuine war, and not to any other war-like measures stopping short of war [1].

There are indeed serious arguments in favour of a state of war between Poland and the Soviet Union during the relevant period. The final solution of the problem depends on the admission or rejection of purely objective criteria which, failing a declaration of war or a qualification as war by at least one party to the conflict or by third States, would decide the issue of existence or non-existence of war independently of any constitutive statement to that effect [2]. If such objective criteria are applied, it can hardly be open to doubt that proceedings including armed invasion of the territory of another State, actual hostilities [3], taking prisoners-of-war and placing them in prisoner-of-war camps — can only mean war [4]. As regards the July Pact, it must equally be admitted that it actually confirmed the status of prisoners-of-war of captive Polish units in Russia and that it provided for the granting of an amnesty by one of the parties to the citizens of the other, — a procedure used in international law exclusively in the Treaties of Peace [5].

It must, however, be borne in mind that in the case of the Soviet-Polish conflict, the parties, and the international community, refrained from qualifying it as war [6]. Moreover, throughout the period of invasion of the Polish territory the Soviet Union acted not on the assumption of war (which requires an enemy), but on the express assumption of

---

1. « Si le principe est que la guerre rend caducs les traités bilatéraux antérieurement conclus entre les Etats belligérants, il importe de bien noter qu'il doit évidemment s'agir ici de guerre au sens formel. ...les mesures coercitives autres que la guerre (hostilités sans guerre, blocus pacifique, représailles, boycottage économique) restent sans influences sur les traités. » Rousseau, *Principes*, p. 556.

2. In favour of such objective criteria see the judgment of the King's Bench Division in *Kawasaki Kisen Kabushiki Kaisha of Kobe v. Banthan S. S. Co. Ltd.*, A. D. 1938/40, case no. 201. Similarly Scelle : « ...La volonté proclamée par des gouvernements de ne pas recourir à la guerre, alors que cependant ils déclenchent le recours à la force, ne saurait faire qu'il n'y ait pas guerre, car la *négation* de l'utilisation de la compétence ne peut prévaloir contre l'évidence de cette utilisation. » *Op. cit.*, p. 845, *f.-n.* 1.

3. See *Pol.-Sov. Relations*, p. 96.

4. The state of war between the Soviet Union and Poland is taken for granted by Prof. Guggenheim, *Lehrbuch*, II, p. 594, *f.-n.* 248 and p. 817, *f.-n.* 150.

5. E.g. Art. 7 of the Treaty of Villafranca of 1859 ; Art. 21 of the Treaty of Zurich, of 1859 ; Art. 10 of the Treaty of Prague of 1866 ; Art. 23 of the additional Treaty of Brest Litovsk of 1918 ; Art. 10 of the Treaty of Riga of 1921.

6. Even in its most strongly worded protests, the Polish Government never spoke of war. The most that was said was that " The Polish Government reserve the right to call upon their Allies in regard to the obligations devolving upon them by virtue of the treaties in force. " *Pol.-Sov. Relations*, p. 98.

the extinction of the Polish State (which excludes war), and at all stages of the Polish problem categorically denied the existence of war and occupation in the relations between the two States, even by implication [1]. Since, therefore, the awoved basis of Soviet action against Poland was not war but the alleged extinction of the Polish State, a Soviet return to the thesis of Polish continuity must have left existing treaties in force and the Soviet Union could not claim the extinction of such treaties by war, while denying the existence of war itself [2].

The conclusion of the July Pact was the occasion for a forcible re-statement of Poland's continuity within her existing international delimitation by Great Britain, in the following Note, handed to the Polish Prime Minister after the signature of the Pact by the British Foreign Secretary :

" On the occasion of the signature of the Polish Soviet Agreement of to-day, I desire to take this opportunity of informing you that in conformity with the provision of the agreement of mutual assistance between the United Kingdom and Poland of the 25th of August 1939, H.M. Government in the United Kingdom have entered into no undertakings towards the U.S.S.R. which affect the relations between that country and Poland. I also desire to assure you that H.M. Government do not recognize any territorial changes which have been effected in Poland since August 1939 [3]. "

---

1. See the Soviet Note of January 5, 1942, to the Polish Embassy in Kuibyshev, rejecting the notion of a Soviet occupation of Polish Eastern provinces, " because the entrance of the Soviet forces into Western Ukraine and Western White Ruthenia in the autumn of 1939 was not an occupation but an attachment of the districts mentioned to the U.S.S.R. as the result of the freely expressed will of the population of those districts. " *Pol.-Sov. Relations*, p. 168. Needless to say that the will of the population had not been freely expressed, and in any case, the elections — contrary to the implication of the Note — followed, and did not precede, the Soviet entry into Eastern Poland.

2. It should, however, be pointed out that even an avowed state of war between the two countries would have left probably quite a few of their bilateral agreements intact and most certainly the Peace Treaty of Riga. Among the treaties which survive war, Oppenheim-Lauterpacht enumerate those " concluded for the purpose of setting up a permanent condition of things. " *Op. cit.*, II, p. 303. Cf. McNair, *op. cit.*, pp. 538-540. Similarly, Guggenheim : " ...so die Verträge zur Abgrenzung des räumlichen Geltungsbereiches der Staaten, die zwischen den kriegfürenden und dritten Staaten bis zu einer neuen Regelung in Kraft bleiben. Diese erfolgt gewöhnlich in den den Krieg abschliessenden Friedensverträgen. Die Tatsache, dass die Friedensverträge solche Veränderungen des räumlichen Geltungsbereiches jeweils in konstitutiver Weise ordnen, beweist, dass die bisherige Regelung duch den Krieg weder suspendiert noch aufgehoben wurde. " *Op. cit.*, I, p. 121. Cf. the impressive reminder by Rousseau : « Ni la cession de la Lombardie et de la Vénétie par l'Autriche à l'Italie au traité de Villafranca du 11 juillet 1859, ni la cession de l'Alsace-Lorraine par la France à l'Allemagne aux termes du traité de Francfort du 10 mai 1871, ni celle de Héligoland par la Grande-Bretagne en vertu de l'accord du 1er juillet 1890, ni celle des territoires congolais par la France à l'Allemagne en vertu de l'accord du 4 novembre 1911 n'ont été atteintes par la guerre de 1914 : elles ne pouvaient prendre fin que par une abrogation conventionnelle. » *Op. cit.*, p. 571. Any other interpretation would, moreover, undermine the whole meaning of the international occupation regime which precisely maintains the unchanged, separate legal status of the occupied State ; see above, pp. 73-126. On the assumption of a break-down of the existing territorial delimitation as a result of war, the very notion of belligerent occupation would become senseless, because there would be no territory to which it could apply.

3. *Pol.-Sov. Relations*, pp. 108-109. A similar statement was issued on behalf of the U.S. by Under-Secretary of State Sumner Welles. " The United States' position towards Poland, he (Sumner Welles) pointed out, was made clear immediately after that country was invaded. It was one of not recognizing any change in her status as a free, sovereign, and independent nation. That position, he added, is maintained and continued. His understanding of the Russian-Polish agreement was that it was in line with the United States policy of non-recognition of territory taken by conquest. " *New York Times*, August 1, 1941.

On August 14, 1941, the Polish-Soviet Military Agreement was signed in Moscow, providing for the organisation of a Polish army in the U.S.S.R. The Agreement stipulated *inter alia :*

" 2. A Polish army will be organized in the shortest possible time on the territory of the U.S.S.R., wherefore :

a) it will form part of the armed forces of the sovereign Republic of Poland,

b) the soldiers of this army will take the oath of allegiance to the Republic of Poland.

. . .

6. ... Officers and other ranks will be called from among Polish citizens on the territory of the U.S.S.R...

8. All soldiers of the Polish Army on the territory of the U.S.S.R. will be subject to Polish military laws and decrees. Polish military courts will be established in the units for dealing with military offences and crimes against the establishment, the safety, the routine or the discipline of the Polish Army [1]... "

Following the Polish-Soviet agreement, diplomatic relations between the two countries were restored ; the liberation of Polish prisoners and deportees in Russia, as well as the formation of the Polish Army was begun ; a large network of Polish assistance and welfare organisations was set up in Soviet territory under the direction of the Polish Embassy. In December 1941 the Polish Prime Minister paid an official visit to Russia, in the course of which a Soviet-Polish Declaration of Friendship and Mutual Assistance was signed in Moscow on December 4. In it, the parties pledged themselves, *inter alia*, to base their mutual relations in peace-time " on good neighbourly collaboration, friendship and reciprocal honest fulfilment of the obligations they have taken upon themselves " and insisted on the " respect of international law " as " the decisive factor " in the creation of a new organisation of international relations [2]. The first phase of the problem of Poland's continuity was thus closed.

III. *THE PROBLEM OF POLAND'S CONTINUITY :* SECOND PHASE.

1. THE SOVIET-POLISH CONFLICT 1941-1945.

a) *Facts.*

As has been seen, the renewed recognition by the Soviet Union of Poland's continuity meant the return to the legal *status quo* between two parties, — as indeed it could have meant nothing else. It was, however, soon made clear that, notwithstanding the conclusion of the July Pact, the Soviet Union continued to lay claims to the Eastern territories of Poland and, consequently, to the population of these territories, although the full extent of the Soviet claims was only gradually revealed.

---

1. *Pol.-Sov. Relations*, pp. 126-128. **Cf.** the Soviet-Czechoslovak Military Agreement of September 28, 1941, above, pp. 317-318.
2. *Pol.-Sov.. Relations*, p. 109.

In a Note of December 1, 1941, to the Polish Embassy in Kuibyshev, the People's Commissariat for Foreign Affairs put forward a new thesis with regard to the nationality of Polish prisoners and deportees in the U.S.S.R. : while upholding the validity of the Soviet decree of November 29, 1939, imposing Soviet nationality on the population of Polish Eastern provinces [1], the Note stated that the present recognition of the Polish citizenship of persons of Polish origin was not a legal obligation, but an act of good will on the part of the Soviet Union ; therefore it could

" in no case serve as a basis for an analogous recognition of the Polish citizenship of persons of other origin, in particular those of Ukrainian, White Ruthenian or Jewish origin, since the question of the frontiers between the U.S.S.R. and Poland has not been settled and is subject to settlement in the future [2] ".

These assertions were answered by the Polish Embassy in a Note pointing out their incompatibility with both the July Pact and the Military Agreement which did not introduce any notion of origin or race and therefore applied to all Polish citizens without exception. The Note also recalled the fact of Polish legislation being based on the principle of equality of all citizens regardless of their origin or race and denied the applicability of Soviet decrees to Polish citizens on Polish territory. With regard to the frontier problem, the Embassy, while emphasizing Polish territorial integrity, pointed out the self-contradictory character of the Soviet formulation, since

" such a view would be tantamount to a unilateral settlement by the Soviet Union at the present time of a problem which, in accordance with this same statement of the People's Commissariat for Foreign Affairs, is subject to settlement in future [3] ".

In January 1942, an exchange of notes bearing directly on the territorial issue took place between the Polish Embassy and the People's Commissariat for Foreign Affairs. The Embassy's protest against the inclusion of the Polish city of Lwôw among Soviet towns in a Soviet Note concerning German atrocities on Soviet territory, was rejected by the Soviet reply which curtly stated that the city of Lwôw " or any other town on the territories of the Ukrainian S.S.R. and the White Ruthenian S.S.R. " belonged to the U.S.S.R. [4]

In other words, this time the Soviet Union expressly claimed sovereignty over Eastern Poland, and no longer implied the possibility of future frontier revision. Once officially adopted, it was from now on to remain the definite thesis of the Soviet Government. It must be clearly understood that what was expected of the Polish Government in the ensuing conflict was not an act of cession but straight acknowledgment of the unilateral Soviet decision.

Throughout the whole of 1942 and the beginning of 1943, Soviet pressure on the Polish Government progressively increased, proceeding

1. See above, p. 431.
2. *Pol.-Sov. Relations,* p. 165.
3. *Ibid.,* pp. 166-167.
4. *Ibid.,* pp. 205-207.

on the two above-mentioned and closely interconnected claims with regard to the half of Polish territory and one third of the Polish population. This pressure made itself felt in all Polish problems arising on Soviet territory, — whether they concerned the Polish Army in the U.S.S.R. the recruitment to which was stopped [1], the relief organisation for Polish deportees which was gradually liquidated [2], the release of Polish citizens from captivity which ceased [3] or the citizenship of the mass of Poles in the Soviet Union [4].

On January 16, 1943, the Soviet Government took yet another step with regard to Polish citizens. In a Note of that date, the Soviet Government reiterated its thesis of the Soviet nationality of all Polish citizens of Eastern Poland, and again qualified the previous Soviet recognition of the Polish nationality of such persons of Polish descent as an act of good-will, performed " by way of exception ", by the Soviet authorities. Since, however, the Polish Government had adopted " a negative attitude " to this Soviet interpretation of the July Pact, the Note now declared

" that the statement included in the Note of December 1, 1941, regarding the readiness to treat some categories of persons of Polish origin on an exceptional basis must be considered as without validity and that the question of the possible non-application to such persons of the laws governing citizenship of the U.S.S.R. has ceased to exist [5] ".

As compared with the previous Soviet attitude, this meant that henceforth all Polish citizens on the territory of the U.S.S.R., whether of Jewish, Ukrainian or Polish origin, would be considered as Soviet nationals, in other words, that the relevant provisions of the July Pact had become meaningless [6]. This new step resulted in a new wave of hardships for the Polish deportees in the Soviet Union who were from now on subjected to all means of pressure to make them accept Soviet passports [7].

1. *Ibid.*, pp. 32-33 and 145.
2. *Ibid.*, pp. 50-55 and 182-205.
3. *Ibid.*, pp. 24-25 and 115-116.
4. *Ibid.*, pp. 56-57 and 163-177.
5. *Ibid.*, p. 171.
6. " ...according to para. 1 of the Supplementary Protocol to the Polish-Soviet Agreement of July 30, 1941, the Soviet Government undertook to set free all Polish citizens detained on Soviet territory for whatsoever reason. On July 30, 1941, there were on Soviet territory no other categories of Polish citizens than those to whom this status is now denied by the Soviet Government. So it was precisely to these persons in their status of Polish citizens, that the amnesty applied. It must be emphasized that the point mentioned above which was the subject of laborious negotiations, constitutes one of the essential clauses of the Agreement of July 30, 1941. " From the Note of the Polish Foreign Minister of January 26, 1943, to the Soviet Ambassador, *ibid.*, p. 173.
7. " In the town of Syzran, district of Kuybyshev, officials of the People's Commissariat for Internal Affairs are threatening with imprisonment or confinement in labour camps all Polish citizens who refuse to accept Soviet passports. Endeavours are also being made to persuade those who resist by the argument that " Poland no longer exists ", which is flagrantly inconsistent with the obligations undertaken by the Government of the U.S.S.R. Those refusing to accept Soviet citizenship are as a rule kept in confinement without food or water until they sign a document agreeing to accept a Soviet passport. Similar reports are coming in from the Krasnoyarsky Kray, and the Kirov, Kuybyshev and Akmolinsk districts. In the town of Kuybyshev three inmates of the Embassy's Home for Invalids are affected by these arrests. " From the Polish Embassy's Note of March 8, 1943, *ibid.*, p. 175.

The growing crisis in Polish-Soviet relations reached early in 1943 — at about the Stalingrad period — a point in which the opposing points of view were put forward by both governments in public statements. The Polish declaration of February 25, 1943, stated *inter alia* :

" The Polish Government, representing Poland in the boundaries in which Poland, first among the Allied nations, took up the fight imposed on her, have from the moment of the conclusion of the Polish-Soviet Treaty of July 30, 1941, maintained the unchangeable attitude that so far as the question of frontiers between Poland and Soviet Russia is concerned, the *status quo* previous to September 1, 1939, is in force [1]... "

This was countered on March 1, 1943, by a Soviet statement accusing Poland of imperialism in denying the right of the " Ukrainian and Byelo-Russian peoples to reunion with their blood brethren [2] ".

On April 26, 1943, following the discovery by the Germans of mass-graves of Polish officers in the Katyn Wood near Smolensk, the Soviet Government broke off relations with the Polish Government [3]. This development marked yet another stage in the Soviet-Polish relations.

In the absence of official relations between the two Governments, the Soviet Government now entered into close relations with a body, formed in the Soviet Union in strong opposition to the Polish Government and described as the " Union of Polish Patriots [4] ". That body, although called into being before the rupture of diplomatic relations only then stepped prominently into the limelight. In particular, at the request of this body the Soviet Government agreed to the formation on Soviet territory of a Polish division " to be named after Tadeusz Kosciuszko for the purpose of the common struggle with the Red Army against the German invaders [5] ". Thus, after having just stopped recruitment into the Polish Army formed in the U.S.S.R. by the Polish Government in accordance with the July Pact and the Military Agreement [6], the Soviet Union now embarked on the creation of a new Polish army, under the auspices of a private body and composed — according to the official Soviet thesis — of Soviet citizens. Such creation was in fact undertaken in face of strong protests on the part of the Polish Government [7]. The Soviet-created Polish force was in due course sent to the front, while the Union of Polish Patriots assumed

1. *Ibid.*, pp. 207-208.
2. *Ibid.*, p. 209.
3. *Ibid.*, pp. 245-246.
4. See the Union's attack on the Polish Government published in the official *Izviestia* of April 24, 1943 ; quoted in *Doc.* V, p. 532.
5. Moscow-published *Free Poland* of May 8, 1943.
6. See above, p. 451.
7. « Cette décision du gouvernement soviétique doit être considérée par le Gouvernement polonais comme portant atteinte aux droits souverains de l'Etat polonais qui seul a le droit de disposer de la vie de ses citoyens dans les rangs de l'Armée nationale. ...Se basant sur les principes du droit international et les stipulations explicites des accords polono-soviétiques, le Gouvernement polonais a le devoir d'élever sa voix pour la défense des citoyens polonais si nombreux encore en territoire de l'U.R.S.S. et ainsi qu'ils le désirent ardemment eux-mêmes, réclamer leur incorporation dans l'armée polonaise. » From the Polish Note to the British Foreign Office, of May 13, 1943.

a quasi-official character and was raised to the status of a quasi-governmental agency and the Soviet Government's partner in international dealings [1].

Efforts undertaken throughout all this period by the Polish and the British Government to bring about a resumption of Polish-Soviet relations did not yield any result. The published communiqué of the Teheran Conference of December 1, 1943 did not make any mention of the Polish problem. Yet, it was precisely at Teheran that the Western Powers agreed to Soviet claim to Eastern Poland. This decision was withheld from the Polish Prime Minister by both Mr. Eden [2] and President Roosevelt [3], both of whom actually denied it. It was only revealed to him during the Moscow Conference of October 1944 [4] by Mr. Molotov in the presence of Mr. Churchill, Mr. Eden and the American Ambassador in Moscow [5].

On January 4, 1943, the Red Army, in its victorious counter-offensive against the Germans, crossed the Eastern frontier of Poland. On this occasion the Polish Government issued a statement in which, while invoking Poland's rights, the principles of the Atlantic Charter and binding international treaties, it expressed hope for an agreement with the Soviet Union [6]. The Soviet Government replied with a lengthy statement denying the capacity of the Polish Government to speak and act for Poland and contrasting it with the " Polish patriots " collaborating with the U.S.S.R. With regard to the territorial problem, the statement presented the matter as settled by pointing out that the

" Soviet Constitution established the Soviet-Polish border with the assent of the population of the western Ukraine and of western White Russia, as expressed in a plebiscite carried out in 1939 on a broad democratic basis ".

However, the Soviet Government expressed its willingness to effect " corrections in favour of Poland " so as to turn the Molotov-Ribbentrop Line into the Curzon Line " which was accepted in 1919 by the Supreme Council of Allied Powers [7] ".

In turn, the Polish Government issued on January 14, 1944, a statement in which, while declining to continue public discussions of Soviet allegations, they disclosed that they were

" approaching the British and United States Governments with a view to securing through their intermediary the discussion by the Polish and Soviet Governments, with the participation of the British and American Governments, of all outstanding questions, the settlement of which should lead to friendly and permanent co-operation between Poland and the Soviet Union [8] ".

---

1. See Stalin's message to the U.P.P. of June 17, 1943 ; *Doc.* V, p. 532.
2. Mikolajczyk, *op. cit.*, p. 48.
3. *Ibid.*, p. 59.
4. See below, p. 455.
5. Mikolajczyk, *op. cit.*, p. 96. Cf. Roosevelt's own statement in Yalta : " He (Roosevelt) had stated at Teheran, he recalled, that he believed the American people were inclined to accept the Curzon Line as the eastern frontier of Poland. " Stettinius, *Roosevelt and the Russians*, p. 143. See also Churchill, *The Second World War*, vol. V. *Closing the Ring*, pp. 319-320, 348-351, 356-357.
6. *The Times*, January 6, 1944.
7. *The Times*, January 11, 1944.
8. *The Times*, January, 15 1944.

The declaration which was handed to the Soviet Ambassador in London by the British Foreign Secretary, met with an outright rejection by the Soviet Government [1]. The Soviet refusal to enter into negotiations with the Polish Government was confirmed again in their reply to the offer of good offices by the United States [2].

One more development must be noted in connection with the Soviet entry into Poland. According to the Moscow radio, a " National Council of the Homeland " was created on January 1, 1944, in Warsaw. The National Council, claiming representation and leadership of the Polish nation in its resistance to the Germans, was formed in strong opposition to both the Polish Government and the existing Polish underground movement. Its formation was hailed by the Union of Polish Patriots in Moscow who in due course recognized it as the true representative of the Polish people [3].

On July 22, 1944, the Red Army crossed the Ribbentrop-Molotov Line. The following day, Moscow Radio announced the creation in Chelm, the first locality west of that line, of a Polish Committee of National Liberation. This body which was later to establish its headquarters in Lublin, came to be generally known as the Lublin Committee.

The Committee was composed of members of the underground National Council of the Homeland and the Moscow Union of Polish Patriots. Formally it was called into being by a decree of the former, " as a provisional executive authority to lead the nation's struggle for liberation... [4] ". The Committee issued a manifesto which declared the Polish Government in London to be " an illegal and self-styled authority ". With regard to the Eastern frontier of Poland, the manifesto declared that it should be

" a frontier of neighbourly friendship, not a barrier between ourselves and our friends. It should be settled in accordance with the principle of Polish territory for Poland, White Russian, Ukrainian and Lithuanian territory for Soviet White Russia, Ukraine and Lithuania [5] ".

Hopes were expressed in Allied circles that, despite the formation of the Lublin Committee, the Soviet Government would refrain from any steps which would further complicate the situation between the Allies. However, on July 26, 1944, representatives of the Committee were solemnly received in Moscow where, on the same day, they signed an agreement with the Soviet Government ; under the terms of that agreement the latter handed over to the former the administration of Polish territories west of the River Bug [6].

At the same time, the Polish Prime Minister undertook a journey to Moscow, — an unorthodox venture in view of the absence of relations between the two countries as well as the recognition by the Soviet

---

1. *The Times*, January 18, 1944.
2. *Dep. of St. Bul.*, January 29, 1944, vol. XII, no. 240, Publ. 2058, p. 116.
3. *Soviet Monitor*, July 1, 1944.
4. *The Times*, July 25, 1944.
5. *Ibid.*
6. *The Times*, July 28, 1944.

Government of the Lublin Committee. In fact, the Prime Minister was received in Moscow as if he were a private person, whereas the delegation of the Committee was granted all honours due to a recognized Government [1]. The journey yielded no results, since the Soviet Government demanded an unreserved acceptance of the Ribbentrop-Molotov Line as the Soviet-Polish frontier and a merger of the Polish Government with the Lublin Committee [2].

On August 1, 1944, with the Soviet armies virtually at the gates of Warsaw, the Warsaw garrison of the Home Army went into open action against the retreating Germans. Thereupon, the Soviet offensive suddenly stopped [3] and the Warsaw insurrection which was supposed to give only the *coup de grâce* to the routed Germans, turned into a desperate two months' struggle by an underequipped and undernourished underground army and local population against the organized German war machine, including heavy artillery, tanks and air force. Warsaw fell on September 3, 1944, after having exhausted all food and ammunition. The number of casualties was 250.000.

On September 9, 1944, the Lublin Committee signed repatriation agreements with the Ukrainian and Byelo-Russian S.S.R.s, providing for the evacuation of Polish citizens from the Ukraine and Byelorussia to Poland and of Ukrainian and Byelorussian citizens from Poland to Ukraine and Byelorussia. A similar agreement was signed on September 22, with the Lithuanian S.S.R. [4].

In October of the same year the British Government once again tried to break the deadlock over Poland, by arranging for a second visit to Moscow by the Polish Prime Minister, on the occasion of a simultaneous visit there by Mr. Churchill and Mr. Eden. Once again, the attempt failed, the Soviet demands being the same as in July, with the sole difference that the required merger of the Polish Government with the Lublin Committee was now to take place on terms even more destructive for the Polish Government [5].

On January 1, 1945, the Lublin Committee took the title of the " Provisional Government of Poland ". On this occasion it issued a decree announcing that it would not recognize any financial obligations incurred by the Polish Government in exile, and served notice to this effect on all Governments and bodies concerned [6].

On January 5, 1945, the Praesidium of the Supreme Soviet of the U.S.S.R. extended recognition to this Provisional Government, and immediately appointed a Soviet Ambassador [7]. In London it was

---

1. *Soviet Foreign Policy during the Patriotic War*, Hutchinson and Co. London, New York, Melbourne, Sydney, II, pp. 96-97, 98-100.
2. Mikolajczyk, *op. cit.*, pp. 75-87.
3. Churchill to Eden, on August 14, 1944 : " It certainly is very curious that at the moment when the Underground Army has revolted the Russian armies should have halted their offensive against Warsaw and withdrawn some distance. " Churchill, *The Second World War*, vol. VI, *Triumph and Tragedy*, p. 117.
4. *Soviet Foreign Policy*, II, pp. 121-122 and 138.
5. See below, p. 474, *f.-n.* 2.
6. *The Times*, January 1 and 2, 1945.
7. *The Times*, January 6, 1945.

" authoritatively stated that the Soviet announcement in no way affected the policy of H.M. Government to continue to recognize the Polish Government in London. Since the Lublin Committee took on the title of Provisional Government, both the British and American Governments have been in correspondence with Moscow in the hope that any unilateral action could be delayed until the three Governments had the chance to review the whole tragic Polish problem again. This correspondence, however, did not bring agreement and the Soviet Government informed the Western Powers of its decision [1] ".

At the same time, the American Secretary of State announced that the United States would continue to recognize the Polish Government in London [2].

Thus, the deadlock seemed complete not only between the Polish and the Soviet Governments, but equally between the Soviet Union and the Western Allies on the subject of Poland.

In Poland itself, the new state of things was taking shape and the general outlines of the new structure were established early in 1945.

b) *Legal Evaluation.*

i) *Incompatibility of Soviet Claims with the Continuity of the Polish State.*

In attempting a legal evaluation of the developments described above, it should not be forgotten that in September 1939 the Soviet Union had adopted the thesis of Poland's extinction which, in common with Germany, she upheld for nearly two years; nor that, in the July Pact, she had gone back on this thesis, again recognizing the uninterrupted continuity of the Polish State. Subsequent Soviet actions have therefore to be examined for their conformity with one of these two, mutually exclusive, attitudes.

The continued Soviet claim to the territory and population of Eastern Poland, as related above, was not only in direct contradiction with the letter of the July Pact in which the Soviet Union had repudiated the partition treaties with Germany and acknowledged the Polish nationality of Polish prisoners and deportees in Soviet territory; it went further than this, being incompatible with the very notion of Poland's unbroken continuity as expressed in the July Pact. What could have been legally conceivable and compatible with such continuity, would have been a political demand for a future frontier revision; that was not, however, the attitude of the Soviet Union who proclaimed her sovereignty over Eastern Poland as an established and existing legal fact. As has been seen, in the absence of any legal title, the factual basis of the Soviet claim with regard to Eastern Poland had consisted exclusively in the effectiveness of her domination and in the agreement with Germany. Since the German attack on Russia, the two elements disappeared; moreover, it would have been extremely awkward for the Soviet Union to base her claim on the partition treaties and to present

---

1. From the Diplomatic Correspondent, *The Times*, January 2, 1945.
2. *Ibid.*

them as a conventional international title [1]. There thus remained two arguments to be invoked : the " elections " of October 1939 and the Soviet Constitution.

The true character of the " elections " has already been analyzed and the conclusions of such analysis are in themselves sufficient to dismiss the Soviet claim [2]. But, moreover, the invokation of these elections by the Soviet Union now was in flagrant contradiction with her signature of the July Pact. By this Pact, it may be repeated, the Soviet Union herself repudiated the very basis of her invasion of Poland in 1939, which was not war, but the alleged extinction of the Polish State. But since, according to the Soviet Government's own admission in the July Pact, the Polish State had never become extinct, then the Soviet armies and authorities entered in September 1939 not a *terra nullius* but the territory of an existing State. If that was so, how could the Soviet Union legally conduct elections on a foreign State's territory ? Thus, the reliance of the Soviet Government on the " elections " as a title for Soviet acquisition of Eastern Poland, was a reliance on an act which, on the Soviet Government's own admission, must have been illegal at the time of its commission.

There remains the argument of the new Soviet frontier having been established by the Soviet Constitution [3]. The conception of a State frontier being laid down by the municipal law of the State concerned represents a truly unique assertion : it is a challenge to international law which can hardly be surpassed. For if a State were able to determine its territorial sphere of validity by municipal enactments, this would mean the end of international law which — whatever else it may or may not be competent to do — holds the exclusive monopoly of such delimitation [4]. The possibility of a State determining its own territorial sphere of validity by internal legislation might perhaps exist where the territory in question has previously been

---

1. This politically embarrassing circumstance was no doubt responsible for the use by the Soviet Government of the term " Curzon Line " instead of " Ribbentrop-Molotov Line ", although the same thing was meant in substance. It may be remarked that the Curzon Line is one the most equivocal terms, since it is hardly known whether it refers to the Supreme Council provisional administration line of December 8, 1919, which did not affect Eastern Galicia at all, — or to the proposed armistice line of July 10, 1920 ; whether its line A or B is meant in Eastern Galicia, etc., etc. In any case, it confuses the problem of the Polish-Russian border proper with the altogether different problem of the status of previously Austrian Eastern Galicia, as discussed in the period following the First World War. It should, moreover, be recalled that neither of these lines had ever been proposed as a frontier of Poland ; on the contrary, Poland's rights to the territories east of the Curzon Line were expressly reserved by the Supreme Council in its resolution of December 8, 1919 ; see Grabski, *op. cit.*, pp. 7-8. According to Temperley, the line was considered a " provisional minimum frontier ", *op. cit.*, vol. VI, p. 275. For a succinct presentation of the complicated problem see Smogorzewski, *About the Curzon Line and Other Lines.* For the contemporary Soviet rejection of the line as unfavourable to Poland, see Temperley, *op. cit.*, VI, p. 320, and Smogorzewski, *op. cit.*, p. 14. However, the very introduction of the term to replace the " Ribbentrop-Molotov Line " was a political and diplomatic achievement of the Soviet Union.
2. See above, pp. 436-437.
3. See above, p. 453.
4. « La délimitation de l'espace à l'intérieur duquel la compétence de l'Etat s'exercera régulièrement ne peut être l'œuvre de son droit interne. ...Le territoire étatique ne peut être circonscrit qu'en vertu de normes internationales. » Bourquin, *op. cit.*, p. 107 ; see above, p. 163.

terra nullius (and, moreover, not contiguous to the territory of any other State) ; it cannot, however, be seriously entertained as a means of laying down a frontier between two actually existing States.

Thus, both the Soviet claims and the arguments on which they were based cannot be reconciled with the admitted continuity of the Polish State. What was illogical- in the first stage of this renewed Polish-Soviet conflict, was the fact that they were pressed against the Polish Government, i.e. the organ of this existing Polish State, and within framework of resumed Polish-Soviet diplomatic relations.

It is submitted that the Polish Government in exile was in no case competent to effect the cession of half of Poland's territory, either on the basis of the existing Polish Constitution [1] or in view of the inherent limitations of a government in exile [2]. But, moreover, it could most certainly not accept the *fait accompli* of the loss of Eastern Poland thus joining in the theory of the extinction of the Polish State, on which alone such a view could be entertained. By doing so, the Polish Government would have admitted Poland's extinction in 1939, it would have undermined its own legal position as an organ of a continuing State on an equal footing with other exiled governments, thereby reducing itself to the level of a " National Committee ", and it would indirectly have validated all illegal acts committed in Poland by Germany in violation of the occupation regime and on the assumption of Poland's non-existence as a State.

It is in the light of this inherent contradiction between the Soviet claim to sovereignty over Eastern Poland and the unbroken continuity of the Polish State that subsequent events, including the rupture of Polish-Soviet relations in 1943, must be viewed. For the Soviet claims, whatever the illogicality of their having at first been pressed against the Polish Government, could only be entertained on the assumption of a Soviet return to the original, though incorrect, thesis of Poland's extinction.

ii) *Soviet Intervention.*

The events to be considered now are the formation of the Union of Polish Patriots and the Soviet-sponsored Polish Army in the U.S.S.R. As has been seen [3], the Union of Polish Patriots was formed in active opposition to the Polish Government and assumed, with the passage of time, the position of its rival. Art. 5 of the Soviet-Polish Treaty of Riga, containing the famous non-interference clause, stipulated :

"Each of the Contracting Parties mutually undertakes to respect in every way the political sovereignty of the other Party, to abstain from interference in its internal affairs, and particularly to refrain from all agitation, propaganda or interference of any kind, and not to encourage any such movement.

---

1. Art. 52, 1. Agreements with other ocuntries : commercial, customs tariff, permanently burdening the State Treasury, containing obligations to impose new burdens upon the citizens or evoking change in the frontiers of the State — require before ratification the agreement of the Legislative Chambers expressed in the form of a law. Cf. the analogous Art. 49 of the 1921 Constitution.
2. See Flory, *op. cit.*, pp. 33-34 and 116-117.
3. See above, pp. 452-453.

Each of the Contracting Parties undertakes not to create or protect organisations which are formed with the object of encouraging armed conflict against the other Contracting Party or of undermining its territorial integrity, or of subverting by force its political or social institutions, nor yet such organisations as claim to be the Government of the other Party. The Contracting Parties, therefore, undertake to prevent such organisations, their official representatives and other persons connected therewith, from establishing themselves on their territory, and to prohibit military recruiting and the entry into their territory and transport across it, of armed forces, arms, munitions and war material of any kind destined for such organisations. "

It is difficult to see how the Union of Polish Patriots could have come into being and embarked on large-scale activities without the knowledge of Soviet authorities. Yet, even on the assumption of its spontaneous creation, the Soviet Government was bound to suppress it according to the above-quoted stipulations. *A fortiori*, it was legally bound not to create or sponsor it. But, as has been seen, far from either preventing or suppressing it, the Soviet Government gave it its complete support [1] and acknowledged its powers to deal on Soviet territory with all matters pertaining to Poles which, up till then, had been within the competence of the Polish Government [2]. Being a violation of existing conventional stipulations, the creation and sponsoring of the Union by the Soviet Government at the same time represented a clear act of intervention under general international law.

Particularly interesting in this connection is the composition of the Union, since it included among its leading personnel persons who, notwithstanding their Polish origin, were not only undoubted Soviet citizens but also high dignitaries of the Soviet State. These were former Polish citizens, who voluntarily and individually renounced Polish nationality immediately on the Soviet entry into Eastern Poland and became increasingly active in the political and State life of the Soviet Union. Thus, the chairman of the Union was Mme. Wasilewska, member of the Supreme Soviet of the U.S.S.R., honorary colonel of the Red Army and wife of the Ukrainian People's Commissar for Foreign Affairs, Korneychuk ; the Praesidium included M. Jedrychowski, member of the Supreme Soviet of the Lithuanian S.S.R. Such persons having never resigned their functions within the organs of the Soviet State, it is to be assumed that they combined these functions with the leadership of the U.P.P. Moreover, according to the Soviet Government's own thesis as proclaimed on January 16, 1943, [3] there were no Polish citizens whatever in the Soviet Union, all Poles in Soviet territory having been claimed as Soviet citizens. Thus, according to the Soviet theory, the Union of Polish Patriots was composed exclusively of Soviet citizens. Yet, it claimed to be a rival political body to the Government of the Polish State and it was treated as such by the Soviet authorities.

The conclusion is therefore inescapable that the Soviet Government

---

1. See above, pp. 452-453.
2. Thus, the U.P.P. took over the premises of the Polish Embassy, the previously liquidated relief organisations for the Poles in the U.S.S.R., the supreme authority over a Polish Army, etc.
3. See above, p. 451.

actually delegated a group of its own citizens to perform quasi-governmental functions with regard to matters falling within the domestic jurisdiction of the Polish State [1].

The creation by the Soviet Union of Polish armed units in the U.S.S.R. in collaboration with the Union of Polish Patriots, — that is, in collaboration with its own organs — merely represented a further step in the same direction. While the rank and file of these units undoubtedly consisted of Polish prisoners and deportees, their officers' corps was mainly Soviet [2].

According to the Soviet Government's own view, however, not only the delegated officers, but the whole of this alleged Polish army was composed of Soviet citizens. Thus, if the Soviet view is accepted, the illegality of Soviet action would have to be considered even more striking ; for the allegedly Polish army in the U.S.S.R. was an organ of the Soviet State not only because of the manner of its creation, but equally by reason of its composition.

It must therefore be stated that the Soviet action in creating by its own acts an authority and an army of another State and thus assuming the exercise of the latter's sovereign rights, constituted a clear violation

---

1. " Russia's armies have penetrated into Eastern Poland, which she contends is Russian territory, just as she claims that the Baltic States are as much Russian as California is American. In this contention she has insisted on the so-called Curzon Line as the final boundary between Poland and Russia. Making no headway in this regard in negotiations with the Polish Government in exile, which insists on the pre-war boundary, Moscow has attacked the Polish Government as pro-Fascist and non-representative of the Poles at home and appears to have set up a " Polish National Council ", reportedly headed by the wife of the Vice Commissar of Foreign Affairs of Russia who was recently made Foreign Commissar of the Russian Ukraine, which Council, Stalin declares, is more representative of the Polish people. Russia at the same time has also, significan*ly, granted greater autonomy to the constituent republics of the U.S.S.R. which apparently would allow treaty arrangements between the Ukraine and a puppet government of Poland in regard to Polish independence and boundary question. Stalin is undoubtedly proceeding unilaterally in this matter, for he has rebuffed mediation by Mr. Hull and Mr. Churchill... " Woolsey, The Polish Boundary Question, A. J., 1944, p. 441. " ...it seems clear that Russia in 1939 set aside a territorial arrangement which she had made and repeatedly confirmed and which she had solemnly pledged to respect and carry out ; that, although Stalin repented in 1941 and reestablished the status quo ante, he is now brow-beating the Government of his conquered neighbour, which he had already recognized and treated with... into submitting to his unilateral demands on the pain of setting up a puppet government in Poland which will do his bidding. " Ibid., pp. 447-448.

2. On receiving information relating to the sending of the first Polish Division thus formed to the front, the Polish Government submitted on September 1, 1943, a further Aide-Mémoire on the subject to the British Foreign Office, stating inter alia : " The Polish Government take this opportunity to reiterate their words of warning contained in the Polish Note of May 13, 1943, against the organisation by the Soviet Government, without the knowledge and consent of the Polish Government, of military formations claiming to be Polish and composed in part of Polish citizens, such an action amounting to a violation of the sovereign rights of Poland and of the Polish-Soviet agreements of July 30, 1941, and August 14, 1941... These formations, which, according to Soviet declarations, are composed of volunteers, are officered mainly by Soviet citizens, while amongst the rank and file they number many Poles deported at one time to the interior of the U.S.S.R., as well as prisoners-of-war and Poles who escaped from German ranks into which they had been forcibly conscripted. It is beyond doubt that these Poles are incorporated into these formations under direct pressure resulting from the special conditions of Soviet life and system when not influenced by the spuriously Polish national character of these formations. In actual conditions of warfare on the Eastern European front the fighting strength of these formations will plainly be of little practical value to the U.S.S.R. It can therefore be said that their value will in the first instance be that of a political instrument, a role which the Soviet Governemnt intends presumably to reserve to these formations as also to the " Union of Polish Patriots " in the event of the Red Army entering Polish territory. "

of the fundamental principles of international law. Combined with the consistent Soviet refusal to enter into any contact with the Polish Government as the official organ of the existing Polish State, it meant a complete by-passing not only of that Government but actually of that State itself whose existence was once again ignored. This would strengthen the view of a Soviet return to the theory of extinction of the Polish State as adopted in September 1939 and as temporarily abandoned in July 1941 [1].

This conclusion is indeed reinforced by the unilateral Soviet action bearing on Polish nationality, although this action lacked consistency.

What needs stressing is in the first place the inadmissibility and the illegality under international law of one State determining the nationality of citizens of another State, whether such determination takes place in a positive or negative way (i.e. by conferring or by denying that nationality) [2]. It is a principle of international law that the problems of nationality fall within the domestic jusridiction of the State concerned [3]. This, however, does not mean that the State enjoys unlimited freedom in the matter [4]. In particular, no State is entitled to force its own nationality on the citizens of another State [5]. On the contrary, such imposition of citizenship is rightly considered to be one of the gravest breaches of international law ; it is a breach against which the Hague occupation regime protects the population of the occupied territory [6].

---

1. See above, pp. 456-458.
2. " Kein Staat kann bestimmen, wie eine fremde Staatsangehörigkeit erworben oder verloren wird. " Verdross, *Völkerrecht*, p. 210.
3. " ...in the present state of international law, questions of nationality are, in the opinion of the Court, in principle within this reserved domain. " *P.C.I.J.*, Ser. B 4, p. 24. Cf. Art. 1 of the Hague Convention of 1930 on Certain Questions Relating to the Conflict of Nationality Laws : " It is for each State to determine under its own law who are its nationals. This law shall be recognized by other States in so far as it is consistent with international conventions, international custom and the principles of law generally recognized with regard to nationality. " Hudson, *op. cit.*, V, p. 359.
4. " Der Staat besitzt keine unbeschränkte Freiheit in der Wahl der Anknüpfungspunkte für die Staatsangehörigkeit. " Guggenheim, *op. cit.*, I, p. 285. It is in particular limited by conventions as well as by customary international law. " Der Begrenzung der landesrechtlichen Anknüpfungsmöglichkeiten entspricht auch der Umstand, dass selbst der Staatsangehörigkeitsbegriff eine Mehrheit von Staaten voraussetzt, von denen ein jeder seine eigenen Staatsangehörigen besitzt, die er zu einer besonderen Rechtsgemeinschaft zusammenfasst. " *Ibid.*, p. 286. " Um die Staatsangehörigkeit auf ein Individuum zu erstrecken, muss der Staat eine nähere tatsächliche Beziehung zwischen sich und dem in Betracht kommenden Individuum geltend machen können. " *Ibid.*, p. 286. " Ist die nähere tatsächliche Beziehung nicht gegeben, so darf die Staatsangehörigkeit nicht verliehen werden. " *Ibid.*, p. 287.
5. " ...a State is not allowed to naturalise aliens residing on its territory without their consent... " Oppenheim-Lauterpacht, *op. cit.*, I, p. 257 ; « ...bien que le droit positif actuel laisse à chaque Etat le droit exclusif de déterminer ses nationaux — il est certain qu'un Etat ne pourrait englober dans sa compétence personnelle des ressortissants étrangers. » Rousseau, *L'indépendance de l'Etat dans l'ordre international*, Rec. 1948, II, p. 203 ; « Un législateur étatique peut librement réglementer l'acquisition ou l'octroi de sa nationalité, mais il ne peut pas normalement nationaliser en bloc une collectivité d'individus ressortissants d'un autre Etat... » Scelle, *op. cit.*, pp. 84-85 ; see also Verdross, *op. cit.*, p. 211. " Der Satz steht heute wohl allgemein fest, dass niemandem die Staatsangehörigkeit gegen seinen Willen aufgezwungen wird. " Kunz, *Die völkerrechtliche Option*, I, p. 10. For confirmation, see the decisions of the U.S. — Mexican Claims Commission, Moore, *International Arbitrations*, III, pp. 2468-2483.
6. See above, p. 83.

It goes without saying that a person can only be deprived of his nationality by his own State. Yet, the Soviet Union arrogated to itself the right of both granting and withdrawing Polish nationality. In this, the Soviet attitude passed through no less than six contradictory stages which may now be shortly summarized.

1) Following the Soviet-German partition of Poland, proceeding on the assumption of Poland's extinction, Soviet decrees imposed Soviet citizenship on all Polish nationals in the Soviet-occupied territories. The illegality of this action resulted from the illegality of its basis, i.e. the invasion and partition of Poland and the illegal proclamation of her extinction.

2) In the July Pact, the Soviet Union, repudiating her previous action against Poland in its entirety, acknowledged unreservedly the Polish nationality of the imprisoned and deported Poles in the U.S.S.R. to whom it undertook to grant an amnesty, without formulating any exceptions. Consequently, a Soviet decree of August 12, 1941, ordered such amnesty for " all Polish citizens on Soviet territory " [1], no suggestion being made of any kind of restrictive interpretation. The ensuing, although shortlived, Soviet practice of liberating some of these persons, of permitting Polish relief activity and, above all, of allowing the formation of a Polish Army in the U.S.S.R., fully confirmed the renewed recognition of Polish citizenship by the Soviet Union.

3) In its Note of December 1, 1941 [2], the Soviet Government adopted a fundamentally different attitude, denying altogether the obligations it had undertaken in the July Pact with regard to Polish nationality ; it now declared that the recognition of such citizenship of persons of Polish descent was merely an act of good will on its part, and insisted on the Soviet citizenship of Polish citizens belonging to national minorities. In this way, Polish citizens in the U.S.S.R. were divided into two groups on the basis of racial discrimination. No attempt was made to reconcile this attitude with the clear wording of the July Pact.

4) In its Note of January 16, 1943, the Soviet Government declared its decision henceforward to consider all Poles in the U.S.S.R., without exception, as Soviet nationals.

5) A slight modification of this sweeping attitude seems to have been made by Stalin and Molotov in their conversations with the Polish Ambassador in the period between February and April 1943. Still another view was put forward, according to which the Soviet Government, while continuing to claim all Polish citizens domiciled in Eastern Poland as its nationals, would be prepared to re-consider the nationality of such Polish citizens who had only a temporary residence in these territories [3].

---

1. *Pol.-Sov. Relations*, p. 110.
2. See above, p. 450.
3. *Pol.-Sov. Relations*, pp. 213-245.

6) The sixth and last Soviet decision on the matter deserves more detailed attention. On June 22, 1944, while the Soviet armies were well advanced in Poland and expected shortly to cross the Ribbentrop-Molotov Line, the Supreme Soviet issued the following decree [1] :

" 1. It shall be laid down as special exception from effect of Ukas [2] of Presidium of the Supreme Soviet of the U.S.S.R. concerning acquisition of Soviet citizenship by inhabitants of Western Oblast [3] of Ukrainian and White Russian Soviet Socialist Republics of 29th November 1939 and also as regards Soviet citizens of Polish nationality from other oblasts of U.S.S.R. that those of them who are serving personnel of Polish Army in U.S.S.R. or who have formerly served in its ranks and also persons who are actively collaborating with the Polish Army in its struggle for the liberation of Poland from the German Fascist invaders, have right to adopt Polish citizenship. The same rights are accorded to members of families of the serving personnel of the Polish Army in the U.S.S.R. and of above mentioned persons helping the Polish Army in the U.S.S.R.

2. Citizenship of children below the age of fourteen is determined by their parents' option of citizenship. All children from 14 to 18 years have the right to choose their citizenship themselves. If the parents opt for different citizenships, the citizenship of the children of less than 14 years of age is determined by agreement between the parents or, in absence of such an agreement, citizenship of minor children will be that of the one of the two States on the territory of which they will live.

3. Notifications of desire to opt for Polish citizenship must be submitted to the Commission of the Praesidium of the Supreme Soviet of the U.S.S.R. for consideration of questions concerning adoption, release and deprivation of citizenship of the U.S.S.R., either directly or through the command of the Polish Army in the U.S.S.R., and representatives of the Union of Polish Patriots in the U.S.S.R. shall be included in the Commission. "

It may be remarked, in passing, that the decree confirms the submission made above [4] to the effect that both the Union of Polish Patriots and the Polish units in the U.S.S.R. were — according to the Soviet view — composed of Soviet citizens. The further implications of the decree are, however, even more serious.

It is true that the decree was couched in such terms as to avoid a direct grant of Polish nationality by the Soviet authorities. This view seems to be supported by the resort to the notion of " option ". This notion, however, does not fit into the general context of the Decree. Option is a notion of conventional international law ; it cannot be conceived otherwise than as the result of an agreement between States and must therefore necessarily have its basis in an international treaty [5]. There can be no unilateral decision as to option. Yet, in the case under consideration, since the other contracting party was missing, it is far from clear in favour of which State the proposed " option " was to operate.

Moreover, although there was no express grant of Polish nationality, it should be emphasized that the matter was determined not by simply releasing the persons in question from Soviet citizenship but by actually

---

1. Published in the Gazette of the Supreme Soviet of the U.S.S.R. on June 30, 1944.
2. Decree.
3. District.
4. See above, pp. 459-460.
5. See Kunz, op. cit., I, pp. 88-91.

conferring on them the right to *Polish* nationality. On the assumption of the procedure taking place not on the basis of a Treaty to which there was another contracting party, but on the basis of an internal decree, this in practice could amount to nothing else than an actual grant of Polish nationality, which was hardly in the giving of the Soviet State.

The problem was thus put on an entirely different basis than had been the case under the July Pact and the subsequent Soviet action as described under 2) above. Then, there had been a bilateral agreement but this was unilateral action. There, going back on her previous thesis of Poland's extinction, the Soviet Union had equally gone back on her unilateral imposition of Soviet nationality on Polish citizens, and had reverted to the recognition of their Polish citizenship such as it had existed before the Soviet invasion of Poland. Here, there was no return to the *status quo ;* the imposition of Soviet citizenship on Polish citizens was not repudiated ; only " by way of exception ", right to acquire Polish citizenship was granted to certain categories of persons, and, as will be seen, these persons were by no means either *all* those who were Polish citizens on September 17, 1939, or such Polish citizens *only*.

This leads to an examination of the categories of persons affected by the decree. They fell into two distinct groups : *a)* those whom the decree called " inhabitants of Western Oblast of the Ukrainian and White Russian S.S.R.s ", i.e. Eastern Poland, — i.e., genuine Polish citizens on whom Soviet nationality had been illegally imposed ; *b)* those whom the decree called " Soviet citizens of Polish nationality from other Oblasts of the U.S.S.R. ", i.e., genuine Soviet citizens who before September 1939 were both nationals of, and resident in, the Soviet Union, and who had never held Polish nationality. These two categories of persons, and their families, were now declared eligible for Polish citizenship on condition of their former or actual service with the Soviet-created Polish Army in the U.S.S.R., or of " active collaboration " with that army, i.e. activities in connection with the Soviet-created Union of Polish Patriots. With regard to the first category, the decree denied even the right to Polish nationality to great numbers of Poles in the U.S.S.R., e.g. families of Poles serving with the Polish armed forces in the West. With regard to the second category, it practically conferred Polish citizenship on undoubted Soviet citizens who had been delegated to perform either civilian or military functions in the Soviet-created Polish organisations in Russia. In other words : the Soviet Government on the one hand continued to deny the Polish citizenship of Poles who had never legally lost it, while on the other hand it delegated its own citizens as the citizens — and organs — of the future Polish State. In the absence of a time-limit for the " notifications of the desire to opt for Polish citizenship ", the Soviet Government thus secured a practically unlimited power of delegating as Poles not only all those Soviet nationals who were already leading the allegedly Polish army and organisation in the U.S.S.R., but also of continuing such delegation in future.

It may also be observed that, while the decree refrained from specifying who would actually grant Polish citizenship to the persons concerned (to whom the Soviet Union granted merely the " right " to such citizenship), it did state that notifications were to be submitted to a Commission of the Praesidium of the Supreme Soviet which would include a representative of the Union of Polish Patriots. But it has already been seen that the Union itself was composed of Soviet citizens, — all of them Soviet according to the Soviet version, and some of them genuinely so. Thus, matters pertaining to Polish citizenship were to be the subject of decisions taken by a Soviet Commission with the collaboration of Soviet citizens from outside that Commission.

Such positive and negative determination by one State of the personal sphere of validity of another State finds no precedent in international relations. It will be remembered that Germany undertook a negative determination of the nationals of the Protectorate, by withdrawing from such category persons of German origin [1]. However, having subordinated the Protectorate openly to the German State, she did not find it necessary to endow either the Reichsprotektor or any other German official with the nationality of the Protectorate [2].

It must therefore be concluded that the Soviet Government took unilateral decisions not only concerning Polish territory, but also concerning Polish organs and Polish nationality. Under existing international law, both customary and conventional [3], these acts fall under the heading of intervention and are therefore illegal. Moreover, such acts were incompatible with the recognition by the Soviet Union of the continued legal existence of the Polish State, whose territory, State organs and population had already been determined and were legally still in existence.

iii) *The Problem of a Revolution in Poland.*

The interventionist character of Soviet action can thus be subject to no doubt. Yet, it must be recalled that, while all these acts took place on Soviet territory, in Poland itself an underground body — the National Council of the Homeland — had come into being in opposition to the Polish Government and the Polish Underground State, and it was this National Council, and not a Soviet agency, which had called the Lublin Committee into being. The legal nature of these developments must therefore be enquired into.

It need hardly be emphasized that the National Council — as opposed to both the civilian underground movement and the Home Army — had no standing in Polish law. It was not a State organ which could have validly issued laws and decrees. It was certainly not constitutionally empowered to set up an executive authority, i.e. a

---

1. See above, p. 285.
2. In its Notes to the British and U.S. Governments of July 19 and 20, 1944, respectively, the Polish Government reserved the right of Polish citizenship of all Polish citizens in the Soviet Union and declared that all action taken under the Soviet decree with regard to Soviet citizens who had never previously held Polish nationality, would not be binding on the Polish Government.
3. See above, pp. 458-459.

pseudo-government, of the Polish State [1]. However, failing such legality, the National Council could have been a genuine revolutionary body, and all the events in Poland subsequent to the nomination of the Lublin Committee could have constituted a genuine revolution against which the constitutional legality of the Polish Government would have been of no relevance whatever.

The first question to be answered is therefore how far the National Council of the Homeland was a spontaneous creation representing a truly revolutionary upsurge of the Polish population or, at least, of a considerable part of it.

With regard to its creation, it must be noted that the National Council was formed on January 1, 1944, i.e. five days before the crossing by the Red Army of the Polish Eastern frontier and four and a half years after the occupation of Poland, that is, at a time when practically the whole active resistance of the population had already been highly organized within the framework of the civilian underground movement and the Home Army. It is therefore hardly surprising that the Council was disowned and its claims rejected by the united Polish resistance movement [2]. Moreover, while it was equally strongly repudiated by the whole Polish community in exile, it very soon established close links with the Union of Polish Patriots in Moscow, whose character has already been ascertained. In particular, a few members of the Council succeeded in June 1944 in making their way to Moscow, there to establish direct contact both with the Union and the Soviet authorities [3]. In turn, the Union formally " recognized the National Council " as " the true representative " of the Polish people [4]. However, the practical non-existence of the revolutionary movement which the Council was supposed to lead was fully revealed during the Warsaw rising [5].

With the formation of the Lublin Committee the fusion of the National Council with the Union of Polish Patriots was finally accomplished. This is why further enquiry into possible revolutionary developments in Poland must be undertaken in relation to that new body.

The first observation to be made is that the Lublin Committee came into being under Soviet military occupation. This alone, as has been seen [6], gives rise to a strong presumption against its genuine character. It remains to be seen whether there are any other factors which either support or weaken this presumption.

Among the supporting factors there is, in the first place, the full and absolute conformity of the Lublin Committee and its policy with the set policy of the Soviet Government. Thus, it is significant that, while there was no sign of any activity of either the National Council or the Union of Polish Patriots in any of the Polish territories claimed

---

1. Both the National Council and the U.P.P. had expressly repudiated the Polish Constitution in force, adopting instead — in the words the Committee's first Manifesto — " the basic provisions " of the former Constitution of 1921. *The Times*, July 25, 1944.
2. Bór-Komorowski, *op. cit.*, p. 135.
3. *Ibid*.
4. *Soviet Monitor*, July 1, 1944.
5. See below, pp. 470-472.
6. See above, pp. 65-66.

by the Soviets, the alleged spontaneous creation of the Committee took place at the exact spot which, according to the unilateral Soviet decision, was the first locality outside its border, and at the exact moment when the Red Army reached that locality. There was thus not the slightest deviation from the official Soviet territorial theory.

This conformity was further reflected in the Committee's first Manifesto [1] and even more strongly, in the repatriation agreements which it concluded with the constituent Soviet Socialist Republics [2]. By signing these agreements, on the underlying assumption of an already existing territorial delimitation, the Lublin Committee implicitly accepted the unilateral Soviet decision on the subject without even a semblance of negotiation or discussion, not to speak of a treaty of cession or any other frontier agreement. The extent of Ukrainian, Byelorussian and Lithuanian territory on the one hand, and Polish territory on the other, was taken for granted. Actual transfer of the population, which was begun almost immediately, could only be undertaken on the assumption of a final delimitation of the respective State territories. These agreements were entered into long before anything like an international frontier settlement had taken place. Whatever the subsequent events, it was these agreements, together with the transfer of population following immediately afterwards, which must be considered as having determined the territorial issue as between the Lublin Committee and the Soviet Union.

Thus, in place of an actually existing international dispute between the Soviet Union and Poland, there appeared a perfect harmony between the former and the Lublin Committee, a harmony achieved exactly on the lines of Soviet demands. As in the Finnish case the actual Soviet-Finnish war was denied by the Soviet Union, so in the Polish case there was a denial of the Soviet-Polish conflict. Like the Kuusinnen Government in the Finnish case, the Lublin Committee stepped in to accept Soviet demands which had met with a rejection by the Polish Government [3]. The unreserved accession by the Lublin Committee to all Soviet demands which had been found unacceptable by the independent Polish Government, would alone be sufficient to support the presumption of its fake character [4]. For it is hardly to be supposed — as it was hardly to be supposed in the case of Albania, Austria, or the Baltic States — that, once under Soviet domination, the Poles spontaneously agreed to do what they had consistently refused to do previously, namely, to surrender half of their country and one third of their population to the Soviet Union. It must therefore be concluded that the Lublin Committee not only fully conformed to Soviet policy on Poland, but that, moreover, it was actually instrumental in carrying out that policy in the same way as had been done by the Kuusinnen Government in the case of Finland.

---

1. See above, p. 454.
2. See above, p. 455.
3. See above, pp. 66-68.
4. See above, p. 65.

If these facts alone reinforce the presumption of the Lublin Committee being a puppet, that is to say an organ of the Soviet State, this submission is further borne out by the actual composition of the Committee. Out of its fifteen members ten were drawn from the Union of Polish Patriots. These included the already-mentioned M. Jedrychowski of the Lithuanian Supreme Soviet and Mme. Wasilewska, member of the Supreme Soviet of the U.S.S.R. who now became no less than Vice-Chairman of the Committee [1]. With regard to some other members of the Committee, their previous links with Poland must be considered doubtful [2].

Far from there being any evidence of popular revolutionary support for the Lublin Committee, all the evidence indicates the negative attitude of the resistance movement, and the population over which it exercised overwhelming control, — an attitude easily understood in the light of the danger to Poland's integrity and independence. In the defence of this integrity and independence, the Polish community at home took a most definite stand. To quote only a few instances : a message of the Council of National Unity [3] of early in 1944 stated *inter alia :*

" We, Poles, in face of most terrible dangers have the right to ask for the assurance :

that our country will not be robbed of its territories,
that no one will have the right to interfere in our internal affairs and that the rights of our Government, which has full support of Polish public opinion, will be respected,
that the integrity and independence of the Polish State will be held sacred by the world, regardless of how many of us will still be alive after this war [4]... "

On February 15, 1944, another message, couched this time in quite concrete terms, was sent to the Polish Prime Minister in London by the Council of National Unity and the Government's Delegate in Poland. It included the following passages :

" 3. We favour entering into conversations, with the participation of the Allies, with a view to resumption of diplomatic relations with the Soviets, on condition of full respect of our sovereignty and of non-interference in our internal affairs.

4. We object firmly to any discussions with the Soviets with regard to the revision of the Eastern boundaries. We stand by the inviolability of the frontiers as settled by the Treaty of Riga, which was signed also by the representatives of

---

1. According to the *Neue Zürcher Zeitung* of March 28, 1950, (Mittagausgabe), Mme. Wasilewska was again returned to the Supreme Soviet in the Soviet elections of 1950. It would thus appear that, after having been delegated to perform, for a certain period of time, governmental functions in Poland, she again resumed exclusively her official functions in the supreme organs of the Soviet Union. While discussing the question of Polish citizenship with the Polish Ambassador in February 1943, Stalin expressly quoted her case : " Take, Mr. Ambassador, the example of Wanda Wasilewska, a Pole from Warsaw who considers herself a Soviet citizen. " *Pol.-Sov. Relations*, p. ‿20.
2. " With methodical purpose she (Russia) proceeded to support and deal with a puppet administrative authority in Poland called the " National Committee of Liberation ", which is reputed to contain a number of Soviet and communist agents, and which appears to be spreading and carrying out communistic policies in Poland. " Woolsey, *Poland at Yalta and Dumbarton Oaks, A. J.*, 1945, p. 296.
3. See above, p. 442.
4. Quoted by Mikolajczyk, *op. cit.*, p. 284.

the Ukraine, for the reasons that the Soviets de not want frontier readjustments, just as the Danzig Corridor was not the real aim of the Germans, but aim at the sovereignty and integrity of Poland.

5. No one in Poland would understand why Poland is to pay the Soviets the costs of war with her territories and her independence [1]... "

A special message to the same effect was sent by the underground Polish Socialist Party to the British Labour Party [2]. All these documents were submitted by the Polish Prime Minister to President Roosevelt [3]. Far from giving revolutionary support to the Lublin Committee, the attitude of the Polish population and its organisations formed a major stumbling block in the Soviet and Lublin policy.

The eventual elimination of this obstacle took place against the background of actual offers of collaboration which, on the instructions of the Polish authorities both at home and in exile, were made to the incoming Soviet armies. The aim of these instructions was twofold : a last hope of some sort of agreement with the Soviet Union on the basis of an actual fighting co-operation against the Germans, and the assertion of Poland's sovereignty over the whole of Polish territory. Home Army units as well as civilian authorities were to reveal themselves to the Soviet troops, to offer collaboration and to take over the administration of the territories which had been cleared of the Germans [4].

Whatever hopes were placed in such a policy were disappointed. The first alarming incident took place when the Polish Underground Army obtained possession of an order from Moscow to Soviet partisans operating in Eastern Poland, which read :

" In conformity with Comrade Nozenko's instruction all partisans are ordered to disarm Polish units. All who resist are to be shot on the spot. All organisation to be liquidated and their leaders shot. Signed Dubov [5]. "

This information was forwarded to the British Foreign Office by the Polish Government. For his part, M. Mikolajczyk, the Polish Prime Minister, sent it to the British Foreign Secretary and the U.S. Chargé d'Affaires with the following additional information :

" Following this order, one of the detachments of the Polish Underground Army has been surrounded by Soviet partisans on December 1, 1943. Nine officers and 135 men have been taken. Their Polish distinctions have been torn off. The men were forbidden to use their language and the commander of the detachment and 4 officers were shot. The fate of the remaining officers and men is unknown. During the disarming of this detachment 7 men were killed and 12 wounded. "

Such events became daily routine after the entry of regular Soviet troops into Poland, both east and west of the Ribbentrop-Molotov Line. At the same time, Poles were forcibly mobilized into the Soviet-sponsored Polish Army.

On March 28, 1944, the Polish Ambassador presented the following Note to the British Foreign Office :

1. *Op. cit.*, p. 284.
2. *Ibid.*, p. 57.
3. *Ibid.*, p. 56.
4. Bor-Komorowski, *op. cit.*, p. 177.
5. From the Polish Ambassador's Note to the Foreign Office, of January 16, 1944.

" ... the Polish Government have received from Poland information dating
from the current month. It has caused them grave and justified anxiety. It goes
out to show that the Soviet authorities are conscripting Poles from the parts of
Poland which have been recently occupied by Soviet forces. The information dated
March 15, shows that at least in two places, in Przebraze and Rozyszcze, Soviet
authorities have arrested Polish Underground soldiers and killed their Commanders.

" The Commander in charge of Polish Underground Forces in Volhynia has
issued instructions that should similar hostile acts be repeated by Soviet authorities
the Polish Underground troops would cease disclosing their identity.

" Polish detachments would also be forced to pass over to self-defence, a
measure fraught with grave consequences. The Commander of the Volhynia
district appeals with insistence for the appointment of inter-allied commission by
way of a safeguard against the repetition of similar grave incidents.

" The Polish Government appeal to H.M. Government for immediate
intervention with the Government of the U.S.S.R. with the view to preventing
occurences which would affect in a tragic manner the relations between Poland
and the U.S.S.R. "

The Note contained enclosures, bringing further facts from Poland
to the notice of the British Government.

On July 7, 1944 units of the Polish Home Army took Wilno
attacking from the South and from within, thus opening the city to the
Soviet forces. After having been congratulated and entertained by
Soviet commanders, the Polish units were rounded up, disarmed and
deported to Kaluga [1]. The same happened in Lwów [2].

Such incidents were of a frequency which makes their enumeration
impossible [3]. However, the following urgent message from the
Government's Delegate and the Commander-in-Chief of the Home
Army should be quoted ; it was transmitted by the Polish Ambassador
to the British Foreign Secretary on July 31, 1944 :

" It follows from the present events that directing units of the Home Army
are being arrested by the Soviet authorities after revealing themselves. We have
to expect that the same fate is reserved to the whole leading civil and military
personnel.

... The Polish Government has the right to demand assurance of safety of
people who are fighting to the end for the common cause, and who cannot be
treated other than Allies with full rights.

In connection with the above we request the immediate inducement of
recognition by the Allied Supreme Headquarters of the Polish Home Army as part
of the Allied Armies similar to the recognition given to the French Home Army,
and the Government taking up a decision, acknowledging civil administration as
the Polish section of the AMGOT for the duration of war activities. "

Such recognition, as has been seen, was in fact granted [4] without
the Soviet Government taking notice of it.

On August 1, 1944, the Home Army went into open action against
the Germans in Warsaw. During the two months of the rising, the
capital was virtually free, held by the Home Army and run by the
Polish administration. The Government's Delegate, the Home Council
of Ministers and the Council of National Unity acted in Warsaw
thoughout the rising in permanent wireless contact with the Polish

---

1. Bôr-Komorowski, *op. cit.*, pp. 194-195.
2. *Ibid.*, pp. 195-197.
3. Messages from Poland were constantly handed over to the Foreign Office by the
Polish Ambassador ; thus Notes of July 27, 1944, August 24, 1944, October 19, 1944.
4. See above, pp. 443-444.

Government in London. There was thus unmistakably revealed both the strength and the degree of organisation of the Polish underground movement, and the complete unity of the population in their allegiance to the Polish State [1]. At the same time, the coming into the open of all underground elements in Warsaw revealed the negligible extent of the influence of the National Council of the Homeland [2], thus definitely destroying its claim to be a revolutionary representation of the Polish people. While the National Council as such was non-existent throughout the rising, its military organisation, the so-called People's Army, could produce but a handful of soldiers as against the 35.000 regular Home Army troops. Consequently, while the Home Army became the object of international recognition [3], no notice whatever was taken of either the National Council or its meagre military units.

For several days the Soviet Government and the Lublin Committee denied the existence of any fighting in Warsaw [4]. When in the long run it became impossible to maintain that attitude in face of the facts, the Soviet Government — and the Committee — not only abstained from giving help to the fighting capital but actually prevented help from reaching it. Thus, Home Army units from the provinces, summoned on August 14, 1944, by the Commander-in-Chief to make for Warsaw in order to relieve the fighting garrison, were stopped on their way and disarmed [5]. Above all, the Soviet Government refused permission for Allied planes, making for Warsaw from Italian bases with supplies of ammunition, to land on the right bank of the Vistula, in Soviet-occupied Polish territory [6]. Thus, a regular shuttle service for the relief of the Polish capital could not be effected. Allied bombers, taking off from Bari without fighter escort and unable to land and refuel east of Warsaw, were massacred over Warsaw by German anti-aircraft artillery, and relief flights had to be discontinued. The matter became the subject of urgent correspondence between President Roosevelt, Prime Minister Churchill and Marshal Stalin [7], but the appeals to Stalin yielded no results. Only towards the end of the rising did

---

1. " That rising, whatever else anybody may think about it, was perhaps the most heroic episode of the war. The whole population rose. ...That is more convincing than a plebiscite. You could have a plebiscite that gave you 99.99999 " Yesses " and could not get so convincing a proof as that was, where the allegiance of the Poles went. The allegiance of the Poles went to the so-called « émigré » Government. " From the speech by Mr. Pickthorn, M. P., *Parl. Deb.*, *Com.* Dec. 15, 1944, vol. CCCCVI, col. 1508-1509. See Churchill's statement on the Warsaw rising, *ibid.*, vol. CCCCIII, col. 1139-40.

2. See above, p. 466.

3. See above, pp. 443-444.

4. See Stalin's reply to Churchill of August 5, 1944, Churchill, *op. cit.*, p. 115.

5. Bor-Komorowski, *op. cit.*, p. 294.

6. See Vyshinsky's statement to the U.S. Ambassador, of August 16, 1944 : " The Soviet Government cannot of course object to English or American aircraft dropping arms in the region of Warsaw, since this is an American and British affair. But they decidedly object to American or British aircraft, after dropping arms in the region of Warsaw, landing on Soviet territory, since the Soviet Government do not wish to associate themselves either directly or indirectly with the adventure in Warsaw. " Quoted by Churchill, *op. cit.*, p. 118. See also Eden's statements in the House of Commons on September 27, 1944, *Parl. Deb.*, *Com.*, vol. CCCCIII, col. 217-220.

7. See Churchill, *op. cit.*, pp. 115-126, in particular, joint appeal by Churchill and Roosevelt to Stalin of August 19, 1944, *ibid.*, pp. 119-120, and Stalin's reply, *ibid.*, p. 120. See also the British despatch to Moscow cf September 4, 1944 : " The War Cabinet wish the Soviet Government to know that public opinion in this country is deeply moved by the events in Warsaw and by the terrible sufferings of the Poles there. Whatever the

the Soviet planes drop some meagre supplies which could no longer redress the balance. On September 15, the Soviet army occupied the Warsaw suburb of Praga, but did not advance any farther [1]. The Soviet Government never joined in the Allied recognition of the Polish Home Army [2].

On the basis of the evidence available it is therefore legitimate to claim that, far from there being in Poland any revolutionary movement opposed to the Polish Government and in favour of the Lublin Committee, there was a definitive movement against the Committe and in favour of the Government. This fact was fully realized and confirmed in the highest Allied quarters. On October 27, 1944, Mr. Churchill (as he then was) declared in the House of Commons :

" If the Polish Government had taken the advice we tended them at the beginning of this year, the additional complication produced by the formation of this Polish National Committee of Liberation at Lublin would not have arisen [3]... "

He repeated the same idea in his speech of December 15 :

" Just as I said that if the Polish Government had agreed in the early part of this year, upon the frontier, there never would have been any Lublin Committee to which Soviet Russia had committed herself [4]... "

The implication was clear. The Lublin Committee, according to Mr. Churchill, had been created by the Soviet Union in order to accept her claims which a Polish Government could not accept.

Nor was there any doubt in Mr. Churchill's mind regarding an alleged revolutionary movement in Poland, which would have supported the Soviets and the Lublin Committee against the Polish Government, when he said in the same speech :

" ... when they (the Soviet armies) move forward, as move forward they surely will, and the Germans are expelled from large new tracts of Poland, the

---

rights and wrongs about the beginning of the Warsaw rising, the people of Warsaw themselves cannot be held responsible for the decision taken. Our people cannot understand why no material help has been sent from outside to the Poles in Warsaw. The fact that such help could not be sent on account of your Government's refusal to allow U.S. aircraft to land on aerodromes in Russian hands is now becoming publicly known. If on top of all this the Poles in Warsaw should now be overwhelmed by the Germans... the shock to public opinion here will be incalculable. The War Cabinet themselves find it hard to understand your Government's refusal to take account of the obligations of the British and American Governments to help the Poles in Warsaw. Your Government's action in preventing this help being sent seems to us at variance with the spirit of Allied co-operation to which you and we attach so much importance both for the present and the future. — Out of regard for Marshal Stalin and for the Soviet peoples, with whom it is our earnest desire to work in future years, the War Cabinet have asked me to make this further appeal to the Soviet Government to give whatever help may be in their power, and above all to provide facilities for U.S. aircraft to land on your airfields for this purpose. " Ibid., pp. 125-126. Cf. Bor-Komorowski, op. cit., pp. 295-296, and Miko-lajczyk, op. cit., p. 84.

1. See Churchill's comment : " They wished to have the non-Communist Poles destroyed, but also to keep alive the idea that they were going to their rescue. " Op. cit., p. 127. For Polish efforts to establish operational contact with the Soviet army under Marshal Rokossovski and the Soviet refusal, see Bor-Komorowski, op. cit., pp. 243-245, 339-340, 344-346, 359 and 362 ; cf. Churchill, op. cit., p. 127.

2. See Churchill's view of the Soviet attitude to the rising : " They (the men in the Kremlin) did not mean to let the spirit of Poland rise again at Warsaw. Their plans were based on the Lublin Committee. That was the only Poland they cared about. " Op. cit. p. 124.

3. Parl. Deb., Com., vol. CCCCIV, col. 494-495.

4. Ibid., vol. CCCCVI, col. 1481.

area administered by the Lublin Committee will grow, and its contacts with the Soviet Government will become more intimate and strong. I do not know what misfortunes will attend such a development. The absence of an agreement may well be grievious for Poland, and the relationship and misunderstandings between the advancing Russian armies and the Polish underground movement may take forms which will be most painful to all who have the permanent well-being of Poland and her relationship with Russia at heart. ... If, during those marches, fierce quarrels and fighting break out between large sections of the Polish population and the Russian troops, very great suffering — which can still be avoided — will infallibly occur, and new poisoned wounds will be inflicted upon those who must dwell side by side in peace, confidence and good neighbourliness [1]... ”

In the same debate, following Mr. Churchill's speech, the fake character of the Lublin Committee was taken for granted from all sides of the House and stigmatized as an attempt against Polish independence [2].

It was with this puppet body [3] that the Polish Government could have merged, according to Soviet proposals made to the Polish Prime

1. *Ibid.*, col. 1482.
2. “ The Lublin Committee have set themselves up in the occupied part of Poland and are apparently preparing to be the Polish Government. I want to be frank and say that I do not consider them to be fully representative. ” Price, Labour, *ibid.*, col. 1493. “ ...the Polish Government in London were to amalgamate with the Lublin Government. I think we might sweep away at any rate one subterfuge. Neither the British Government, nor the Polish Government regard Lublin as anything else but a fake.” Raikes, C., *ibid.*, col. 1496. “ I agree, respectfully, with the hon. Member who said that we need not waste time with the Lublin Committee, because everybody knows it is bogus.‘ Is there anybody who will dare to say that it is less bogus than the Vlasov Committee ? ” Pickthorn, C., *ibid.*, col. 1508. “ What does Russia demand of Poland ? She demands half her territory, and that she should be governed by the Lublin Committee, which, the world knows, is an utterly unrepresentative body of Poles, provided by Russia, and whose authority and power rest solely on the Russian NKVD, or political police, the child of the OGPU, and Russian bayonets. ” Graham, C., *ibid.*, col. 1514-1515. “ I agree with an earlier speaker that it would be idle to go into the personal lives of the members of the Lublin Committee, but I think I may say that, if ever it became a Government, it would be the most curious medley since the administration of Uncle Tom Cobleigh. It is a Government composed of one party and one party only ; nine out of the 14 members of it are avowed members of the Communist Party. It is true that the Union of Polish Patriots, out of which it has arisen, is said to be composed of a very large number of different parties, but we in the Labour Party at least are sufficiently familiar with that technique. We have learnt to recognize the Communist Party under many different names... ” Thomas, Lab., *ibid.*, col. 1523-1524. “ A country cannot have independence, if it cannot have an independent Government, unless its frontiers are assured, and in my opinion the Lublin Committee was never regarded seriously by the Russians and was merely put up as a stalking horse to give what they thought they wanted so far as boundaries were concerned. ...The Lublin Committee is utterly fictitious and the Russians, who are very sensible and wise people in these matters, know perfectly well, just the same as everybody else does, that the Lublin Committee is bogus and was utterly unnecessary except in order to achieve a certain ulterior purpose. ” Petherick, C., *ibid.*, col. 1545.
3. “ At ten o'clock the same evening we met the so-called Polish National Committee. It was soon plain that the Lublin Poles were mere pawns of Russia. They had learned and rehearsed their part so carefully that even their masters evidently felt they were overdoing it. For instance, M. Bierut, the leader, spoke in these terms : “ We are here to demand on behalf of Poland that Lvov shall belong to Russia. This is the will of the Polish people. ” When this had been translated from Polish into English and Russian I looked at Stalin and saw an understanding twinkle in his expressive eyes, as much as to say, “ What about that for our Soviet teaching ? ” The lengthy contribution of another Lublin leader, Osobka-Morawski, was equally depressing. Mr. Eden formed the worst opinion of the three Lublin Poles. ” Churchill, *op. cit.*, p. 205. “ I myself thought that difficulties would arise in a discussion for a merger of the Polish Government with the Lublin Poles, whose representatives continued to make the worst possible impression on us, and who, I told Stalin, were “ only an expression of the Soviet will. ” They had no doubt also the ambition to rule Poland, and were thus a kind of Quislings. ” *Ibid.*, p. 207, Cf. *ibid.*, p. 209.

Minister in Moscow in July and October 1944 [1]. " Merger " is hardly an adequate description of the suggested procedure, since in fact only a few members of the Polish Government could have joined the Lublin Committee, though not of course on the basis of Polish law but on the basis of the Committee's actual standing. Thus, while unable to change the basis and the essence of the puppet creation, the Polish Government could merely have gone out of existence of its own free will, thus accepting and actively upholding the Soviet solution, and, at the same time, eliminating the Polish problem from international relations. These considerations, clearly appreciated by the Polish Prime Minister and constituting the basis of his refusal, were formulated in his observations handed to the American Ambassador in Moscow [2].

---

1. See above, pp. 454-455.
2. " Observations of the Polish Prime Minister on the situation of Poland in connection with the Moscow Conference held in October 1944.

After the meeting held on October 13th I have given much thought to the problems discussed with the view to assess the situation in a most objective way. The results can be summed up as follows.

1) At the Teheran Conference decisions were taken as to the change of Poland's eastern frontier without the knowledge and consultation of the Polish Government.

In view of the fact, however, that there exist public pronouncements of the British and U.S. Governments, which are in force inasmuch as public opinion is concerned, namely that the British and U.S. Governments do not recognize any territorial changes which take place during the war, except changes arrived at with the consent of the parties concerned, it is now expected that the Polish Government or its Premier should — of their own volition — express consent to the decisions of the Teheran Conference.

2) The Soviet Government have brought into being — without consulting the Allied Governments — the Polish Committee of National Liberation which is a de facto rival Polish Government. The prerogatives of the Committee such as the conclusion of international agreements, the emission of banknotes, conscription to the army, the transfer of the population, the decreeing of laws changing the social and economic structure of the country, etc., etc., require some form of legalization.

It is expected that this would be achieved by the fusion of the legitimate Polish Government with the rival Polish Government created by the Soviets.

The Polish Government or its Premier would now have to :

a) legalize the Soviet Government's unilateral decision of investing Soviet agents with powers of a Polish Government,

b) approve before world public opinion the " faits accomplis, " created by the Soviet Government without consultation with the Allies,

c) ratify all activities of the Committee in Poland, including arrests and deportations.

3) By merging with the Committee of National Liberation the Polish Government would have to renounce its own legal basis of existence. Consequently, all possibilities of a return to the legal foundations of the Polish State would be wrecked. All ensuing acts would be imposed on the people of Poland in the presence of the Red Army and the NKVD. Thus the Polish Government is expected voluntarily to destroy — after the ratification of the truncation of Poland and the legislation of the Committee — the legal foundations of the Republic and her supreme authorities.

4) Poland would thus lose her eastern lands, and, in the remainder of her territory Poland's independence would be effaced by the rule of agents of the Comintern in Poland.

No effective guarantees to show that the aforesaid course of events will not take place, have been put forward.

On the other hand it is expected from the Polish Government :

a) to agree to the loss of Poland's eastern provinces,

b) to legalize the status of the Polish Committee of National Liberation by its merging with the Polish Government and to approve the Committee's unlawful acts,

c) after the legalization of the Committee to destroy the legal foundations of the Polish Republic,

d) to express consent to the effacement of independence in the remainder of Poland.

In other words, the Polish Government is expected to commit suicide of its own volition.

The present Polish Government and its Premier will not be persuaded to do this and are inept to play such a role.

Moscow, October 14th, 1944. "

The conclusion is clear : no revolution had taken place in Poland. The events described were not internal Polish revolutionary phenomena, taking place within the existing separate delimitation of the Polish State ; they were due entirely to Soviet decisions implemented by Soviet citizens and Soviet organs, — in the last stage in territory under Soviet military occupation. Failing any co-operation from the Polish population which might have endowed the process with a semblance of internal revolution, it was found necessary to proceed against this population. The revolution was a fake ; it was disguised intervention and aggression [1].

iv) *Creation of a Puppet State.*

The process has been examined in some detail for the reason that, it is submitted, it represents a classical example of the creation of a puppet entity.

As has been seen, the puppet nature of the Lublin Committee — later renamed Provisional Government — was universally admitted [2]. The problem, however, calls for further analysis in order to find out whether the new creation was in fact merely a puppet government or whether it did not in fact represent a puppet State. This is a fundamental question, of immediate relevance to the problem of the identity and continuity of the Polish State.

It has been sufficiently emphasized that international law cannot, and does not, attach the same consequences to different acts ; more particularly, that it cannot, and does not, treat in the same way a genuine revolution which is legal and a fake revolution which, being a disguised form of aggression, is not. It has been seen that the identity and continuity of a revolutionary State are safeguarded by international law because its old basic norm is produced from within the surviving territorial and personal delimitation. There is no extension into the revolutionary State of a legal order of another State, and the general delimitation under international law remains intact. But in the case of a fake revolution the new basic norm is produced from outside the State concerned, representing in fact a delegation by the intervening State. In such a case, the State concerned is no longer identified by a basic norm of its own, whether legal or revolutionary. Far from being its own, its basic norm is a concretisation on a lower level of a basic norm of a foreign State. In such a case, therefore, there is no more room for the application of the customary rule providing for the identity and continuity of the State concerned. Such identity and continuity must therefore be denied [3].

The general application of these principles has resulted in a denial of a relation of identity and continuity between the Protectorate of Bohemia and Moravia with the Czechoslovak Republic [4], the Italian-annexed Albania with the independent Albanian State [5] and the Baltic

---

1. See above, pp. 64-71.
2. See above, pp. 472-473, and below, p. 478.
3. See above, pp. 64-66.
4. See above, pp. 292-303.
5. See above, pp. 332-333.

S.S.R.s with the independent Baltic States [1]. Exactly the same reasoning must be applied to the case under consideration. The inevitable conclusion therefore is that what was created in Poland by the Soviet Union was not merely a puppet government, but a puppet State, non-identical with the Polish Republic and not continuing its international personality.

Far from having its reason of validity in general international law, that State was entirely determined, delimited and delegated by the Soviet Union. It was set up on a part of Polish territory, unilaterally determined by the Soviet Union which thus fixed its territorial sphere of validity. Its personal sphere of validity was equally laid down by the Soviet Union by firstly withdrawing from it about 13 million citizens from the annexed territories and then, regulating Polish citizenship in both a negative and a positive way, as already described [2]. Above all, the legal order determining the identity of the State was not derived either from the constitutional laws of Poland or from a revolutionary change taking place within a more or less unchanged territorial and personal delimitation ; on the contrary, it was derived from the legal order of the Soviet Union, by a delegation of the latter's organs, both civilian and military, to establish it. The Polish Republic and the Soviet-created Polish puppet State had not one single element in common, and the process of the puppet formation can, in this particular case be traced not only " actually " [3], but even on the purely formal level.

Viewed in this way, the Soviet-created puppet State can take its place as yet another typical example alongside Napoleonic Holland, as analyzed by Commissioner Kane, and Manchukuo, as analyzed by the Lytton Commission [4]. In Commissioner Kane's words, it could claim only a " nominal independence ", although " the form of distinct sovereignties was presented to the public eye ". It conformed almost entirely to the Lytton Commission's description of Manchukuo : thus, the whole process was only possible because of a military occupation ; officials of the delegating State occupied administrative key positions in the delegated State ; its army was subject to the control of the former ; popular opposition was suppressed, while desperate efforts were made by loyal citizens to achieve some improvement of the situation by accepting work within the puppet organisation. Here too, the preservation of external forms, such as recognition, exchange of diplomatic representatives, conclusion of agreements, was intended to conceal a reality which was the very opposite of what it claimed to be. The " recognition " of the puppet State was no international recognition. It was the final confirmation, chiefly for external use, of the recognizing

1. See above, pp. 391-397.
2. See above, pp. 461-465.
3. See above, pp. 169-180.
4. See above, pp. 171-173 and 174-178. As between the Lublin Poland and Manchukuo, the external conditions are admittedly different : whereas the latter was set up on a part of Chinese territory, the remainder of which continued to belong to the original Chinese State, the former was set up on the entirety of what remained of Polish territory after the Soviet annexation of Eastern Poland. This in no way affects the striking similarity in substance between the two puppet States.

State's own creation [1]. The exchange of diplomatic envoys was meaningless, since the dominant State was already well represented within the puppet State by its own organs functioning as organs of the latter. International agreements were unilateral decisions of the dominant State, clothed in a conventional form, just as were the agreements between the Protectorate and Germany or Albania and Italy ; they were thus — in Commissioner Kane's words — treaties in form ; in substance they were decrees.

An attempt to reduce a problem of this magnitude to a mere contest between two Governments — one genuine and the other admittedly fake — could therefore proceed solely from a very superficial analysis of the existing legal situation. Failing a genuine revolution or civil war there were no elements whatever on which such a view could be based. The Polish Government was the supreme executive organ of the Polish Republic as it had existed ever since 1918. The Lublin Committee was the supreme executive organ of a new and different entity which possessed neither the territorial and personal spheres of validity, nor the basic norm — whether legal or revolutionary — nor the sum total of international rights and obligations of the Polish Republic. An inaccurate assessment of the legal situation contained the seeds of the most serious confusion.

The Soviet action in Poland could therefore not have been, and was not, undertaken on the assumption of the continuity of the Polish State, — a correct assumption under general international law, shared by the whole international community with the exception of the Axis powers and their satellites, and temporarily adhered to by the Soviet Union herself in the July Pact and subsequent Polish-Soviet agreements [2]. On the contrary, this action had its roots in the events of 1939, including the theory of Poland's extinction and the German-Soviet partition of that country, with the Soviet Union now re-asserting her full share of that partition. This theory and practice, originally upheld by the Soviet Union in alliance with Germany, was now taken up by the Soviet Union within the framework of an anti-German coalition. Further, inasmuch as the Soviet Union laid claim to Polish territory in Northern and Central Poland up to the River Bug, i.e. the line of the third partition, she repudiated her own earlier repudiation of these very same partition treaties, proclaimed in the early years of the Soviet regime as a matter of revolutionary principle [3]. Inasmuch as she claimed Southern Polish territories in Eastern Galicia, she went beyond the partition treaties, extending to the former Austrian share in those partitions. In fact, the entire basis of the relations between Poland and the Soviet Union, as they had existed between the two wars, was now

---

1. In this particular respect the analogy with Manchukuo is less complete : for the official Japanese recognition of Manchukuo took place seven months after its establishment, and even this was considered a short period by such a defender of Manchukuo's genuine statehood as Prof. Cavaré, *op. cit.*, p. 40. But the period between the formation of the Lublin Committee and its recognition was four days.

2. See above, pp. 444-449.

3. See above, pp. 418-419.

for a second time set aside in favour of an entirely new departure from a *tabula rasa*, a departure, moreover, not between two States but between the delegating State and its delegated puppet.

2. THE YALTA DECISION ON POLAND.

a) *The Decision.*

It was under such circumstances that President Roosevelt, Prime Minister Churchill and Marshal Stalin met at Yalta in the Crimea on February 4, 1945, for a conference which was to last until February 11. Throughout the conference the Polish problem figured high on the agenda [1].

The problem of Poland's territorial integrity no longer divided the three Allies. For, in spite of the declarations by the Western Powers professing unchanged recognition of Poland's territorial status, and in spite of the denials made to the Polish Government [2], those Powers had agreed as far back as the Teheran Conference to accede to the Soviet territorial claims. With regard, however, to the question of the Polish Government, the position taken up by the Soviet Union and by the Western Powers respectively seemed to be poles apart. As has been seen, the Soviet Union had already completed the creation of a puppet State intended to replace the existing independent Polish State. The Western Powers did not seem to realize that it was in fact a puppet *State*. and not merely a puppet *government* which had been created; they did not, however, have any doubts as to its puppet character [3]. The conference therefore opened with the expression of their firm determination not to recognize it and to have it replaced by a new Polish Government; the elimination of the puppet was to safeguard Poland's independence on her reduced territory [4].

The Polish problem at Yalta was thus reduced to a thorny and prolonged argument about the future Polish Government, in which the

---

1. See Churchill, *op. cit.*, p. 319; Stettinius, *op. cit.*, passim.
2. See above, p. 453.
3. See above, pp. 472-473.
4. Roosevelt stated in a letter to Stalin : " ...we cannot recognize the Lublin Government. " Stettinius, *op. cit.*, p. 149. Churchill declared that " the British Government could not agree to recognize the Lublin group as the government of Poland. " *Ibid.*, p. 148. He insisted that according to British information the Lublin Government did not have the support of the overwhelming mass of the Polish people and frankly admitted his apprehension of an " angry outcry " in Britain, were the British Government to recognize it. Speaking of the Polish Army he further pointed out that " If the British Government transferred its support to the Lublin Government, it would be regarded by this army as an act of betrayal of Poland. " Britain, he argued, has already completely given way to the Soviet Union on the problem of Polish frontiers. " After that, to break altogether with the lawful government of Poland which had been recognized during all these years of war, would be an act that would bring the most severe criticism at home. " *Ibid.*, p. 192. Eden put it bluntly : " ...it was a fact that hardly anyone in Great Britain believed that the Lublin Government was representative of Poland. " *Ibid.*, p. 201. Churchill further added : " We knew... that there were bitter feelings among the Poles. He understood that the Lublin Government had declared its intention to try members of the Polish Home Army and the underground forces as traitors. These reports... caused great anxiety and perplexity in Great Britain. " *Ibid.*, p. 215. Churchill's account of the Yalta Conference, published two years later, tallies essentially with that of Stettinius ; see *op. cit.*, pp. 319-339.

Anglo-Saxons emphatically insisted on the need for an entirely new Government, while the Soviet delegation, equally emphatically, insisted on the maintenance of the Lublin Government which would possibly be merely " enlarged " or " added to ".

The following text was finally adopted :

" We came to the Crimea Conference resolved to settle our differences about Poland. We discussed fully all aspects of the question. We re-affirm our common desire to see established a strong, free, independent and democratic Poland. As a result of our discussions we have agreed on the conditions in which a new Polish Provisional Government of National Unity may be formed in such a manner as to command recognition by the three major Powers.

The agreement reached is as follows :

A new situation has been created in Poland as a result of her complete liberation by the Red Army. This calls for the establishment of a Polish Provisional Government which can be more broadly based than was possible before the recent liberation of Western Poland. The Provisional Government which is now functioning in Poland should therefore be re-organized on a broader democratic basis with the inclusion of democratic leaders from Poland itself and from Poles abroad. This new Government should then be called the Polish Provisional Government of National Unity.

M. Molotov, Mr. Harriman and Sir A. Clark Kerr are authorized as a Commission to consult in the first instance in Moscow with members of the present Provisional Government and with other Polish democratic leaders from within Poland and from abroad, with a view to the re-organisation of the present Government along the above lines. This Polish Provisional Government of National Unity shall be pledged to the holding of free and unfettered elections as soon as possible on the basis of universal suffrage and secret ballot. In these elections all democratic and anti-Nazi parties shall have the right to take part and to put forward candidates.

When a Polish Provisional Government of National Unity has been properly formed in conformity with the above, the Government of the Union of Soviet Socialist Republics, which now maintains diplomatic relations with the present Provisional Government of Poland, and the Government of the United Kingdom and the Government of the United States will establish diplomatic relations with the new Polish Government of National Unity, and will exchange Ambassadors by whose reports the respective Governments will be kept informed about the situation in Poland.

The three Heads of Government consider that the eastern frontier of Poland should follow the Curzon Line with digressions from it in some regions of five to eight kilometres in favour of Poland. They recognize that Poland must receive substantial accession of territory in the North and West. They feel that the opinion of the new Polish Provisional Government of National Unity should be sought in due course of the extent of these accessions and that the final delimitation of the western frontier of Poland should thereafter await the Peace Conference. "

i) *Territorial Clauses.*

It may be convenient to begin the analysis of this document by its territorial clauses. The Yalta decision took its stand squarely on the so-called Curzon Line, which in this version — unlike in the previous ones [1] — simply meant the Ribbentrop-Molotov Line of September 28, 1939 with slight modifications. It thus confirmed, in the midst of a war against Germany, the German-Soviet partition of Poland of that date, notwithstanding the express repudiation of that partition by the Soviet Union herself in the July Pact. In so doing,

---

1. See above, p. 457, *f.-n.* 1.

it adopted almost literally the formulation of the Soviet Note of January 11, 1944 [1] which had already introduced both the term " Curzon Line " and the suggestion of slight Soviet territorial concessions from that line. The Yalta Declaration did not make any attempt at justifying this decision. It was fairly clear that in the existing circumstances such a justification could hardly have been sought in the Ribbentrop-Molotov Agreement ; but the Soviet thesis concerning the alleged will of the population had not been taken over either. It is not known whether this omission was due to the Western Allies' reluctance to recognize *ex post* the validity of Soviet-conducted elections in Polish territory, or to the possible difficulty of explaining the retrocession to Poland of even a small part of an area whose entire population, regardless of the districts concerned, had allegedly voted almost unanimously for their inclusion into the Soviet Union [2].

At the same time, the document proclaimed the need to grant Poland substantial accession of territory in the North and the West, and, although the actual word " compensation " was not used, the connection between the two territorial operations seemed fairly obvious [3]. It is, however, to be observed that while Poland's territorial losses were definitely determined, the provisions concerning her territorial gains were more than vague. Similarly, while the future Polish Government was to be consulted with regard to the gains, no such consultation was provided for with regard to the losses. Finally, while the gains had to await the decision of the Peace Conference, no further procedure was envisaged with regard to the losses, which were final [4]. No provisions whatever were made concerning the fate of the population of the amputated territories.

ii) *Government and Elections.*

So much for the territorial and personal spheres of validity of the future Poland. Within such delimitation there was to be set up a Government which was to satisfy the requirements of the three Powers. (The problem of its satisfying the requirements of the Poles does not seem to have been taken into consideration.)

In providing for this future Government, the Yalta decision took as its starting point the existing Lublin Government as its basis and nucleus, notwithstanding the protestations to the contrary which had

---

1. See above, p. 453.
2. If, in fact, the alleged will of the population was to be taken into account according to the Soviet thesis, then it is difficult to see why violence was done to the population of the Bialystok region, eventually retroceded to Poland, since—according to the 1939 Soviet figures — this population too had produced over 90 % votes in favour of the inclusion into the U.S.S.R., and since no new vote was taken before the retrocession. " If the Curzon Line was considered just, why make concessions «in favour of Poland» ? " Wright, *Poland and the Crimea Conference*, A. J., 1945, pp. 306-307.
3. " Is it an admission of guilt to recognize that by way of compensation « Poland must receive substantial accessions of territory in the North and the West» ? " Wright, *op. cit.*, p. 307.
4. " Why be so definite in delimiting the eastern frontier and yet « feel... that the final delimitation of the western frontier of Poland should... await the peace conference » ? " *Ibid.*

been made during the Conference by the Western Allies [1]. It is true that the words " a new Government " appeared in the introductory paragraph of the document. But this general description which can be applied to any normal change of government, cannot prevail against the operative text itself. The Lublin Government was accepted and was merely to be re-organized. The " re-organisation " of that Government is mentioned twice in the text, and it is to be observed that it is described once as the provisional Government " now functioning in Poland ", and once as " the present Provisional Government ", its character of " government " thus being clearly acknowledged. The view that the future government of Poland was to be the Lublin Government is further reinforced by the description of the manner in which the proposed re-organisation was to proceed i.e. the " inclusion " into that Government of " democratic leaders from Poland itself and from Poles abroad ". It is truly impossible to see how a re-organisation of a Government can be conceived to mean the formation of an entirely different government, — nor how undefined individual members can be " included " into a body not yet in existence. With regard to the latter it must be observed that, while the expression " democratic leaders " conveyed no precise legal meaning whatever, the description of the existing governmental body was clear and unmistakable. In any case, whatever personal changes might have been envisaged, and even carried out, a " re-organisation " certainly meant a reshuffle on the existing legal basis [2].

This re-organisation of the Lublin Government was to take place under the authority of a commission, composed of the Soviet Foreign Minister and the British and American Ambassadors to the Soviet Union. The powers of this commission were left vague ; it was not said that it was actually to nominate a Polish Government. The problem of the constitutional authority which was to appoint it was left unsolved ; but, since the President of the Polish Republic was not mentioned [3] and the Lublin Government was taken as the starting point for the future changes, it was to be assumed that formally the new Government was to be nominated by the Lublin Head of State, which is what in fact happened. However, the Commission of three was not only given power

1. See above, pp. 478-479.
2. " Why should the « complete liberation » of Poland " call for the establishment of a Polish provisional government ", when the Soviet Government as late as August (obvious mistake : the date was April) 1943 was on amicable terms with the Polish Government in London ? What has the Polish Government in London done to warrant the recognition of a rival Provisional Government in its place by the Soviet Government ? If there was need of the government being " more broadly based than was possible before the recent liberation ", why could not the Polish Government in London " be re-organized on a broader democratic basis with the inclusion of democratic leaders from Poland itself " rather than a Provisional Government set up in Poland by the Soviet Government ? ...Why does the Yalta statement qualify the phrase " the Government of the Union of Soviet Socialist Republics ", with the phrase, " which now maintains diplomatic relations with the present provisional government of Poland ", and not qualify the phrase " the Government of the United Kingdom and the Government of the United States of America ", likewise with a phrase, " which now maintain diplomatic relations with the Polish Government in London " ? " Wright, *op. cit.*, pp. 305-306.
3. See below, pp. 483-484.

to initiate proceedings with regard to the future Government, but the final decision was obviously, to rest with them, especially since that government was to " command recognition by the three major Powers ", whose representatives they were. In this connection, the actual composition of the Commission has to be borne in mind : for it consisted of the Foreign Minister of a State which for the past two years had been engaged in an open conflict with the Polish State, and of two Ambassadors of third States, accredited precisely to his government. That body, moreover, was to meet and to " create " the Polish Government in the capital of the party to the conflict [1]. The organs of foreign States were thus to perform the highest constitutional functions of the Polish State.

It would appear that some doubt as to the true nature of a body set up in such a manner was entertained by the Western Powers, and that it found expression in the description of that government and, to a greater extent, in the imposition on it of obligations with regard to future elections. Significantly enough, it was to be called a " provisional " government, — a title which could hardly be reconciled with the existing Polish State and Government but which could be introduced on the assumption of the Lublin Government representing the starting point for the change. Within the existing Polish State, represented by a legal and fully-fledged Government, there was no need for a reduction of the latter's status to that of a " provisional " government. None of the exiled governments returning from London to their liberated countries had changed into a " provisional " one, whatever other changes took place.

With regard to elections, it would appear that they represented the last line of defence of the Western Powers regarding the independence of Poland, inasmuch as they were intended to replace the Commission-formed government by a genuine one and to endow the action taken in Yalta with some sort of validity [2].

It must, however, be observed that the electoral territory as well as the electorate itself had been defined in advance and that it had been so defined in accordance with the previous unilateral decision by the Soviet Union [3].

Moreover, the conduct and result of such elections was a foregone conclusion, if they were to be controlled by the Lublin Government,

---

1. " Why should the proposed « commission » of three " consult in the first instance in Moscow " ? Why should it not do its consultations in London or in Poland ? " Ibid. « On ne voit vraiment pas selon quelle compétence juridique ces personnages étrangers sont « autorisés » à réorganiser le gouvernment de Pologne ? » Flory, op. cit., p. 253.

2. In his speech to the Congress of March 1, 1945, Roosevelt spoke of " a... Polish nation with a government ultimately to be selected by the Polish people themselves. " It. mine. Dep. of St. Bul., vol. XII, p. 325, thus admitting by clear implication the real nature of the Commission-formed Government for Poland.

3. It should be remembered in this connection that during the German occupation of Alsace-Lorraine in 1871, the occupying power righthy permitted French elections to be held throughout the whole pre-war French territory, including the part occupied by German troops, despite the German intention to annex it.

even a re-organized one [1]. Therefore Churchill's initial idea was that not only should elections be held but that Great Britain should transfer recognition from the Polish Government only *after* they had taken place [2]. Yet, it was finally decided to grant recognition *beforehand*, and no safeguards whatever were provided for the conduct of the elections [3]. Finally, the very provision specifying the parties which were to be allowed to take part in the elections, had an ominous ring, owing to the divergent interpretation placed by the three Powers on such words, as e.g. " democratic ". Moreover, in view of the fact that Poland was well known to be the only German-occupied State which had never produced a Quisling Government, the suggestion that there might be " pro-Nazi " political parties in Poland was as insulting as it must have been suspect [4].

iii) *Yalta and the Polish State.*

On the basis of such a document it was asserted in high Allied quarters that the Yalta decision on Poland represented a success of the Western Powers and that, in particular, far from bowing to the Lublin Government, it had provided for an entirely new Government of Poland [5] and thus safeguarded her independence [6].

This claim cannot be admitted. For the Polish State itself was absent not only from the Yalta conference table but, moreover, from the actual text of the Yalta decision.

---

1. Mr. Eden declared at Yalta : " The British people would feel that if the elections were controlled by the Lublin Government they would not be free elections truly representing the will of the Polish people. " Stettinius, *op. cit.*, p. 202.

2. " Before H. M. Government would transfer recognition, Churchill warned, it would have to be convinced that a new government, representative of the Polish people, had been created and was pledged to an election based on a secret ballot and universal suffrage with all democratic parties having the right to nominate their candidates. When such elections were held, Great Britain would disregard the London Government and salute the new government. " *Ibid.*, p. 192. Cf. Churchill, *op. cit.*, p. 331.

3. " Will the " free and unfettered elections... on the basis of universal suffrage and secret ballot " be like the " free " plebiscites held in Estonia, Latvia and Lithuania ? Latvia, for example, signed a 10 year Pact of Mutual Assistance with the Soviet Government on October 5, 1939, yet parliamentary elections shortly afterwards resulted in 97,6 % Communist vote, although the population was 55 % Protestant and 24 ½ % Catholic. It is not strange that the new parliament asked to be incorporated in the U.S.S.R. or that the latter acceded to the request on August 5, 1940. " Wright, *op. cit.*, p.306. " ...it may be pertinent to ask under whose control, military or otherwise, are the " free and unfettered elections " to be held ? Are the political prisoners to be released and the deported Poles returned, and allowed to vote ? Is there to be freedom of press and assembly for campaigning purposes ? " Woolsey, *Poland at Yalta and Dumbarton Oaks*, A. J., 1945, p. 298.

4. " There are in part of the communiqué dealing with Poland some sinister references to the suggestion or the fact that only anti-Nazis will be allowed to vote and take part in these elections. What does that mean ? Does it mean that anybody who is declared by the Provisional Government — or it may be by the Lublin Government for all I know — to be a Nazi is not to be allowed to vote ? If this is the case, there can be no possible free elections in Poland, because it has only to be declared that a man is a Nazi — and he may be the leader of the Socialist Party for all we know — and he will not be entitled to vote. I would ask the Foreign Secretary when he replies to deal with that point, and to tell us why that peculiar expression «anti-Nazi» was put in that document. I suggest it is clearly dragged in for this reason. There are no Nazis in Poland and there never have been — they have no Lavals, no Darlans, no Quislings, no collaborationists. Why then was this expression introduced into that part of the document ? " Major Petherick in the House of Commons, *Parl. Deb.*, *Com.*, vol. CCCCVIII, col. 1427-1428.

5. Stettinius, *op. cit.*, pp. 267-268.

6. Churchill, see below, p. 499.

Far from in any way upholding the principle of the continued existence of the Polish State, the Western Powers at Yalta fully accepted the already implemented Soviet decisions on Poland, embarking on a solution of the Polish problem from a *tabula rasa* [1]. They accepted in particular : *a)* the territorial shape of Poland as determined by the Soviet Union, *b)* the population as determined by the Soviet Union, and finally *c)* the puppet government as created by the Soviet Union [2]. Such an operation could not be carried out on the assumption of the continued existence of the Polish State, with its own legal order and its full and separate delimitation under international law. It inevitably implied a complete by-passing of that State.

It is for this reason that, while the Lublin Government figured prominently in the document, there was not even a mention of the Polish Government, with which the Western Allies maintained diplomatic relations, whose armies were actually engaged in fighting under Allied command and whose Home Army had only recently become the object of Allied recognition. This was not the by-passing of a constitutional Government in favour of a revolutionary one ; it was a by-passing of an existing State, its organs, its legal order and its territorial and personal delimitation, in favour of an entirely new creation, and this by-passing had been effected in a manner which no invader in belligerent occupation of a country could legally have resorted to.

More particularly, according to the Yalta decision, the future Polish Government could have no legal source in the Polish State. It was not to be created in accordance with the constitutional laws of Poland ; nor could it be a revolutionary Polish Government, since the possibility of Foreign Ministers and Ambassadors producing a revolutionary government for a third State need not be seriously entertained.

This disappearance of the Polish State — and not only of its Government — in the Yalta decision was further borne out by the disappearance of the existing conflict between Poland and the Soviet Union. For the Yalta Conference did not effect a pacific settlement of that international dispute. At Yalta there was no longer any such dispute, since one of the parties had been eliminated. Instead of the existing Polish party to the dispute there appeared what was alleged to be a Polish ally of the Soviet Union, with no conflict between the two. In other words, the situation represented an exact replica of the Finnish case [3]. But, while in the Kuusinnen case, the Soviet *actio in fraudem legis* in producing a puppet government was denounced by the international community, it succeeded in the case of the Lublin Committee. The " disappearance " of an international dispute in this manner could not have occurred on the assumption of Poland's continuity, — just as no such " disappearance " could have occurred

---

1. " All that Mr. Churchill and Mr. Roosevelt seemed able to do was to try and give a democratic tinge to a Stalin dictate of possibly a year before. " Woolsey, *op. cit.* p. 297.

2. Prof. Lauterpacht is fully justified in speaking of " the decision taken at the Crimea Conference by Great Britain, the United States and Russia to recognize the Polish Provisional Government in Poland... " *Op. cit.*, p. 353, *f.-n.* 1.

3. See above, p. 467.

on the assumption of Finland's continuity where a genuine settlement of the Finno-Soviet conflict had to be effected by means of a bilateral Treaty between the two States.

Nor is the imposition on a State of obligations regarding its internal problems, such as elections or the rights of political parties, a usual phenomenon in the case of a continuing independent State ; on the other hand, it represents a time-honoured procedure with regard to new States, about to enter into the international community. This principle was expressed in the well-known Note, addressed by Clémenceau to Paderewski on June 24, 1919, prior to the signature of the Polish Minorities Treaty.

« Depuis longtemps il est d'usage, d'après le droit public européen, que lorsqu'un nouvel État est créé ou lorsqu'un ancien Etat s'incorpore des territoires importants, la reconnaissance formelle de la situation nouvelle par les grandes Puissances comporte en même temps la demande par ces Etats au Gouvernement ainsi reconnu, de s'engager à pratiquer certains principes de gouvernement déterminés et cela sous la forme d'un accord revêtant un caractère international. »

Whereupon Clémenceau quoted examples of undoubtedly new States, such as Serbia, Montenegro and Rumania at the Berlin Conference of 1878, the Kingdom of Holland in 1814 and the Kingdom of Greece.

At Yalta Poland was not acquiring territories ; on the contrary, she was losing them. While the loss was definite, the gain was only a promise. Consequently, conditions concerning Poland's internal government were certainly not imposed by reason of her territorial aggrandizement. They could only be explained on the assumption of the new character of the State which was to be created on the basis of the Yalta decision.

The above analysis is confirmed by the very wording of the Yalta declaration, as well as by comments made by its authors. Thus, the declaration spoke expressly of the " establishment " of a " strong, free, independent and democratic Poland ". Yet, on the correct assumption of the unbroken continuity of the Polish State, there was nothing to be " established ", since this State was already in existence [1]. Equally, in his speech to the Congress of March 1, 1945, Roosevelt declared that " Our objective was to help *create* a strong, independent and prosperous nation... [2] ". But, if the Polish State continued to exist, there was indeed nothing to be " created ". What could be " established " and " created " anew was only a new State. None of these terms alone can be taken as decisive ; but read in conjunction with the real meaning permeating the whole of the Yalta decision on Poland, they acquire their full significance.

It must therefore be concluded that — whether consciously or unconsciously — the Western Allies adhered to the Soviet thesis of a

---

1. Cf. the " re-establishment " of Austria in the Moscow declaration of 1943, see above, p. 348 ; similarly, the "re-establishment" of diplomatic relations with Ethiopia, see above, p. 275.

2. *It. mine* ; *Dept. of St. Bul.*, vol. XII, p. 325.

break in the continuity of the pre-war Polish State and the creation of a new entity in its stead. What they actually did at .Yalta is more important than what they thought they were doing.

The new State was to be endowed with a government which was not of its own choosing. The Soviet Union was just as little entitled to install a Polish Government in Poland, as Italy was entitled to install an Albanian Government in Albania [1]. Like Italy in the Albanian case, all that the Soviet Union could do was to install in Poland only her own delegated organs. Nor could a Soviet-British-American commission produce a Polish Government. In consequence, the government proposed at Yalta for Poland was to be delegated by foreign Powers, — in substance by the Soviet Union, in form by the three Yalta Powers jointly. Since, however, the possession by a State of an independent government of its own is the essential condition and prerequisite of statehood [2], it has to be concluded that the Yalta decision gave an international imprimatur to the destruction of Polish independence and to the establishment in Poland not merely of a puppet government, but of a puppet State.

b) *Legal Evaluation.*

i) *Legal Nature of the Yalta Decision.*

The Yalta decision was contained in a document bearing the official name of a " declaration ". In view of the irrelevance of the title to the legal nature of an international instrument [3] it has to be seen whether that declaration represented an international treaty, i.e. a valid contractual engagement between the parties [4].

It would indeed be difficult to answer this question in the affirmative on the basis of the text alone, and this not merely on account of the unusual form which the document assumed [5].

The first question is : who were the actual parties to the Yalta Declaration ? If the Declaration was a valid international engagement,

---

1. See above, p. 336.
2. See Lauterpacht, *op. cit.*, p. 26.
3. See *P.C.I.J.*, Ser. A/B 41, p. 47 ; Guggenheim, *op. cit.*, I, p. 54 ; Rousseau, *op. cit.*, p. 154 ; Oppenheim-Lauterpacht, *op. cit.*, I, p. 809.
4. Such seems to be the opinion of Oppenheim-Lauterpacht : " A mere general statement of policy and principles cannot be regarded as intended to give rise to a contractual obligation in the strict sense of the word. On the other hand, official statements in the form of Reports of Conferences signed by the Heads of States or Governments and embodying agreements reached therein may, in proportion as these agreements incorporate definite rules of conduct, be regarded as legally binding upon the States in question. The Reports of the Conferences of the Heads of Governments of Great Britain, the United States and Russia at Crimea in February 1945 and at Potsdam in August of that year may be mentioned as examples. " *Op. cit.*, I, p. 788.
5. Briggs speaks of the " careless informality and the execrable draftsmanship of this highly important instrument... " *The Leaders' Agreement of Yalta*, A. J., 1946, p. 377. It is true that his article refers to the Japanese part of the Yalta decisions which was released by the State Department only a year later, see *Dept. of St. Bul.*, vol. XIV, p. 282 ; it is believed, however, that his criticisms — as well as those of Pan, *Legal Aspects of the Yalta Agreement*, A. J., 1952 — equally apply to the whole of the Yalta decisions, not only on account of the close similarity of form and substance, but also because the Yalta decisions were subsequently considered by authoritative spokesmen as forming an indivisible whole ; see the statement by Mr. Foster Dulles, below, pp. 541-542.

then it must have bound the United States, Great Britain and Soviet Russia, and not Messrs. Roosevelt, Churchill and Stalin. Yet, far from indicating anywhere that the parties were the United States, Great Britain and the Soviet Union, the document merely mentions the three Heads of Government who speak in the first person plural [1]. Nowhere is it indicated that these three personalities were acting on behalf of their respective States, nor is there any mention of their authorization or full powers [2]. The declaration is signed by the three personalities named, without any reference to their official standing [3]. The whole document thus bears such a pronounced personal character as to justify the question upon whom it is legally binding [4].

The document does not specify any date for its entry into force, nor does it provide for either its termination, denunciation, or prolongation. While failing to provide for its ratification, it neither contains the usual clause which would dispense with the need for ratification. Nor was it in fact ever ratified by any of the three States, which in itself would go a long way towards denying its character as a treaty [5].

Thus, even on the correct assumption that a considerable degree of formlessness is permissible in international conventional law, the Yalta Declaration seems to run counter to all accepted notions of a valid international agreement.

In such circumstances it is necessary to turn to the interpretation supplied by the parties themselves. Such interpretation, however, is as unhelpful as is the Yalta text itself.

---

1. " We came... We discussed... We re-affirm... We have agreed... " — With regard to the Far Eastern section of the Yalta decision, cf. Briggs' criticism of the term " leaders ", particularly from the point of view of American constitutional law. " Op. cit., p. 377.

2. While the latter omission could be understood in the case of President Roosevelt, the only Head of State at the Conference, it can hardly be considered normal in the case of either Mr. Churchill or Mr. Stalin.

3. Cf. Pan, op. cit., p. 42.

4. " ...whether the United States, in contrast possibly to President Roosevelt, was ever legally bound upon signature of the agreement by the latter. " Briggs, op. cit., p. 380.

5. As to the necessity of ratification for the validity of a treaty which does not expressly provide for its non-ratification, see P.C.I.J. : " "...conventions, save in certain exceptional cases, are binding only by virtue of their ratification. " Ser. A 23, p. 20. Similarly, protocols of the Berlin Conference of 1878 : « Le Congrès considère... que ce sont les ratifications, et non pas seulement la signature, qui donnent aux traités leur valeur définitive. » Quoted by Rousseau, op. cit., p. 191. See also Guggenheim : " Die Ratifikation ist somit in der Regel eine notwendige Voraussetzung für die Gültigkeit eines völkerrechtlichen Vertrages. " Lehrbuch, I, p. 71, while quoting exceptions. Similarly, Oppenheim-Lauterpacht, op. cit., I, p. 815. « Aujourd'hui il est hors de doute que le traité n'est conclu que par l'échange des ratifications entre les parties contractantes, de sorte que la ratification est vraiment un élément de la validité du traité. » Rousseau, op. cit., p. 190. Similarly Scelle, op. cit., p. 619. The exceptions adduced — agreements concluded between Heads of State, agreements providing for their non-ratification — do not apply to the Yalta Declaration. As to the necessary presumption of the need for ratification in the case of a treaty's silence, see the Harvard Draft Convention on the Law of Treaties, Art. 7 and comment. With regard to the constitutional provisions of the United States where the Yalta Agreement, not being ratified, never obtained the necessary consent of the Senate, Briggs expresses doubts as to the President's competence to commit the United States in matters of such importance by way of a mere executive agreement, op. cit., p. 381.

In the first period following the Yalta Conference, its resolutions were invariably referred to as a " decision ", whatever that term may mean in international law. This interpretation was supplied by the signatories not only individually [1], but also jointly in the Potsdam Declaration which is the only existing authentic interpretation of the the Yalta resolution [2].

It was only at a later stage that the parties began to describe it as an international agreement proper, insisting on rights and obligations resulting out of that agreement not for the individual signatories, but indeed, for the countries concerned [3]. This finds support in the fact that the Yalta decisions had indeed been internationally acted upon by the three States concerned. Thus, after considerable initial doubt, the contractual nature of the Yalta decision must probably be admitted, in view of both, the eventual interpretation supplied and the action taken by the parties. However, the above analysis bears out the difficulty in arriving at a correct legal assessment of something which an American lawyer has called " a historical curiosity and a legal monstrosity [4] ".

ii) *Legality of the Yalta Decision.*

The next question concerns the legality or otherwise of the Yalta decision.

On the assumption that the decision represented a regular contractual engagement, it must be stated in the first place that such an engagement could only have bound the parties to it and no one else, according to the positive rule of international law which lays down that *pacta tertiis nec prosunt nec nocent* [5]. This rule, firmly upheld by

---

1. " The *decision* with respect to the boundaries of Poland..." Roosevelt in Congress on March 1, 1945 ; it. mine, *Dep. of St. Bul., loc. cit.*
2. " ...the formation in accordance with the decisions reached at the Crimea Conference, of the Polish Provisional Government of National Unity... " " ...the Polish Provisional Government of National Unity, in accordance with the decisions of the Crimea Conference, has agreed to the holding of free and unfettered elections... " *Doc.* VIII, pp. 933-934.
3. Thus, in particular, the British and American démarches undertaken in connection with the elections in Poland, see below, p. 506 ; the American Note to Russia of January 5, 1947, spoke of the " sanctity of international agreements " and of resulting " most solemn obligations ", *Doc.*, vol. IX, pp. 637-639 ; the State Department's Listing of Treaty Violations by the Soviet Union, released on May 29, 1948, included the Yalta and Potsdam decisions among the treaties violated, *ibid.*, vol. X, p. 613 ; in the House of Commons debate of October 10, 1946, Mr. Mayhew, speaking for the Government, rejected the suggestion that British concern with Polish elections meant any interference with Polish domestic affairs declaring : " ...this is an international bargain. " *Parl. Deb., Com.*, vol. CCCCXXVII, col. 1276. All the latest American declarations with regard to the Yalta decisions seem to be made on the assumption of an international agreement violated by the other party to it, which in turn would give the United States the usual freedom to withdraw from the convention ; see below, pp. 541-542.
4. Briggs, *op. cit.*, p. 383.
5. « Or, quelle est la valeur de la Conférence de Crimée ? Considérable sur le plan politique. Mais sur le plan juridique ? Il ne s'agissait aucunement d'une conférence constitutive, d'un directoire international. Ceux qui commençaient d'être appelés les « trois grands » n'avaient aucun mandat d'aucun pays et ne pouvaient donc engager qu'eux-mêmes. » Flory, *op. cit.*, p. 252. " Whatever may be the real nature of the agreement, if it has to to with the cession of territories of an ally, it must obtain the consent of that ally ; if it deals with an enemy State, it should certainly be embodied in the form of a peace treaty. " Pan, *op. cit.*, p. 50.

international judicial decisions [1], municipal decisions and State practice [2], as well as by writers [3], means that for third States treaties to which they are not parties are *res inter alios actae*. This rule represents a logical consequence of the principle of State equality and independence [4] and so long as the latter principle forms the very basis of international law it is impossible to admit that a State has to abide by conventional rules in the creation of which it had taken no part [5].

Consequently, failing a validation by Poland on the pattern of the Czechoslovak acceptance of the Munich Agreement, no obligations whatever could have resulted for Poland from the Yalta decision, nor could this decision have any binding force or validity for that country [6].

Moreover, apart from their invalidity for Poland, the legality and validity of the decision *inter partes* is open to grave doubt. For by entering into the Yalta compact, the contracting parties disposed of the rights of the Polish State without any legal authority, and — it may be recalled — of *all* such rights, to the extent of the actual destruction of that State. No such procedure can conceivably be legal under general international law. On the contrary, as Prof. Basdevant has stated :

« ... on constate l'existence d'une règle de droit international positif qu'aucune autorité humaine n'existe qui soit investie du pouvoir juridique d'enlever à un Etat les compétences appartenant à celui-ci. Un Etat ne peut être privé, par un moyen juridique, desdites compétences que de son consentement [7]. »

Prof. Guggenheim is no less categorical :

---

1. " ...it is certain that, in any case, Art. 435 of the Treaty of Versailles is not binding on Switzerland, who is not a party to that Treaty, except to the extent to which that country accepted it. " *P.C.I.J.* Ser. A/B, 46, p. 141. " It is evident that whatever may be the right construction of a treaty, it cannot be interpreted as disposing of the rights of independent third Powers. " Prof. Huber in the Island of Palmas arbitration, Scott, *The Hague Court Reports*, 2nd Series, p. 97.
2. See examples quoted by Rousseau, *op. cit.*, pp. 452-484.
3. " ...on peut dire qu'il est universellement reconnu qu'un traité ne peut pas donner existence à des obligations à la charge des tiers... " Anzilotti, *op. cit.*, pp. 420-421. Similarly, Fauchille, *op. cit.*, I, p. 357 ; Guggenheim, *op. cit.*, I, p. 89 ; Verdross, *op. cit.*, p. 145 ; Oppenheim-Lauterpacht, *op. cit.*, I, p. 831.
4. Especially as interpreted by Prof. Guggenheim to mean equal opportunity of taking part in the creation of rules of law, *op. cit.*, I, p. 164.
5. It should be emphasized that existing exceptions to that rule never create such obligations for third States as would directly affect their own rights and their own legal status ; thus, the obligation to respect a territorial settlement between two or more States, a settlement establishing a major general interest — e.g. the demilitarization of the Aaland Islands, see the Report of the Committee of Jurists, pp. 17-19 — settlements within the framework of the international law of communications, etc., etc. See Oppeheim-Lauterpacht, *op. cit.*, I, pp. 832-834 ; Guggenheim, *op. cit.*, I, pp. 90-93 ; Rousseau, *op. cit.*, pp. 477-484.
6. « Or, l'U.R.S.S., les Etats-Unis et la Grande-Bretagne étaient bien les seuls pays à prendre part à l'entretien de Yalta ; aucun représentant polonais n'y fut convié. On s'étonne dans ces conditions qu'une telle conférence ait pu disposer de l'avenir de la Pologne, organisant ses pouvoirs publics et modifiant ses frontières, sans même que le gouvernement existant et la population soient le moindrement consultés. » Flory, *op. cit.*, p. 252.
7. *Règles générales*, Reç. 1936, IV, p. 580.

" The personal, territorial and material spheres of validity which are granted to a sovereign, i.e. independent State by customary international law can neither be restricted nor extinguished without its consent [1]. "

Failing any possibility of a *legal* disposal by third States of the rights of another State, such rights can merely be suppressed in fact. But in view of the existence of the positive rule invoked by Prof.Basdevant, such facts constitute a clear instance of law-breaking and the suppression of existing rights constitutes an illegal act under general international law.

Being concluded in clear violation of general international law, the Yalta decision was further illegal under conventional international law in force between the Yalta States and Poland.

The Yalta Powers violated jointly and severally the principles of the Atlantic Charter which — whatever the doubt concerning the binding force of the original document — were formally adopted by the United Nations' Declaration of January 1, 1942, to which the United States, Great Britain, the U.S.S.R. and Poland were all parties, and which were thus raised to the status of legally binding conventional rules [2]. These principles should be recalled :

" First, Their countries seek no aggrandizement, territorial or other.
Second, They desire to see no territorial changes that do not accord with the freely expressed wishes of the peoples concerned.
Third, They respect the right of all peoples to choose the form of government under which they will live ; and they wish to see sovereign rights and self-government restored to those who have been forcibly deprived of them [3]. "

Further, Great Britain and the Soviet Union jointly violated Art. 5 of the British-Soviet Treaty of Alliance, by which the parties undertook to

" act in accordance with the principle of not seeking territorial aggrandizement for themselves and of non-interference in the internal affairs of other States [4] ".

---

1. *Transl. mine.* " Ohne Zustimmung des souveränen, bzw. unabhängigen Staates kann der vom Völkergewohnheitsrecht ihm zuerkannte persönliche, räumliche und sachliche Geltungsbereich nicht eingeschränkt oder aufgehoben werden. " *Lehrbuch*, I, p. 165.
2. *Doc.*, vol. IV, pp. 203-208.
3. Woolsey, after recalling that the principles of the Atlantic Charter had not only been incorporated in the United Nations' Declarations, but equally agreed to at the Inter-Allied Meeting in London on September 24, 1941, and embodied in the series of Mutual Aid Agreements of 1942 and in the British-Soviet Treaty of Alliance, asks : " Can it be said that Russia and the other powers are not solemnly bound to abide by the commitments of the Atlantic Charter and that Russia was not specifically obligated, as from September 24, 1941, to apply these principles in the solution of the Polish problem ? The question answers itself, if there is any virtue at all in these international engagements. " *Op. cit.*, p. 296. " Can this fifth partition of Poland be said to conform to the first three principles of the Atlantic Charter quoted above ? In my opinion it can not. ...It is submitted that whatever may be the proper boundary of eastern Poland in view of ethnic, strategic and other factors, and whatever may be the make-up of the improvised Polish Government, these things are being imposed on the Polish nation without its consent and under untoward circumstances (dating back to 1939) of military occupation, foreign administration, movement of populations, repression of sentiment, redistribution of lands and the like. It is but inflicting a festering sore of discontent and revolt on the body politic of a gallant and faithful ally. Can such a decision make for a stable new world ? Is it not contrary to the ideals and aims of a just peace which is to be maintained by the new world organisation ? " *Ibid.*, pp. 297-298.
4. See above, p. 391.

The action of the Soviet Union was a violation of all instruments concluded between that country and Poland, beginning with the Riga Treaty [1], the continued validity of which she had automatically acknowledged in the July Pact, by acknowledging the continued existence of the Polish State [2].

The United States, apart from the above-mentioned multilateral United Nations' Declaration, was not bound to Poland by any conventional agreement and, consequently, acted at Yalta merely in defiance of all her proclaimed principles in the field of international law [3] and of that Declaration itself. On the other hand, the British obligations to Poland had been clearly defined in bilateral conventional instruments and repeatedly reiterated by the British Government.

These obligations under the Anglo-Polish Treaty and its Secret Protocol of August 25, 1939, have already been fully analyzed [4]. It has been seen that they fully safeguarded both the sovereignty and the territorial integrity of the contracting parties and that they prevented the parties from entering into any agreements which might prejudice such sovereignty or integrity. It may also be recalled that these provisions had been included in the Treaty having regard to possible Russian claims on Poland [5], two days after the signature of the Ribbentrop-Molotov Pact and after clear statements to the effect that no reversal of Soviet policy could influence the British determination to fulfil her obligations to Poland [6].

These obligations had been consistently reiterated by the British Government. It was in accordance with these obligations that the Foreign Secretary officially affirmed the British non-recognition of any territorial changes in Poland on the occasion of the signature of the Polish-Soviet July Pact [7]. Even prior to that date, Mr. Churchill declared in the House of Commons on September 5, 1940 :

" We have not at any time adopted, since this war broke out, the line that nothing could be changed in the territorial structure of various countries. On the other hand, we do not propose to recognize any territorial changes which take place during the war unless they take place with the free consent and good will of the parties concerned [8]. "

On January 26, 1944, following the Soviet entry into Poland and Soviet declarations claiming territorial sovereignty over Eastern Poland [9],

---

1. See above, pp. 419-422.
2. See above, pp. 444-449.
3. E. g., the following statement by the U.S. Secretary of State of April 30, 1934, bearing on Japan's policy with regard to China : " In the opinion of the American people and the American Government, no nation can, without the assent of the other nations concerned, rightfully endeavour to make conclusive its will in situations where there are involved the rights, the obligations, and the legitimate interests of other sovereign States. " *Documents on International Affairs*, 1934, Edited by J. W. Wheel-Bennett and S. Heald. Oxford University Press, London : Humphrey Milford. Issued under the auspices of the Royal Institute of International Affairs, 1935, p. 477.
4. See above, pp. 423-427.
5. See above, p. 426.
6. See above, p. 423.
7. See above, p. 448.
8. *Parl. Deb.*, *Com.*, vol. CCCLXV, col. 40.
9. See above, pp. 453-454.

the Foreign Secretary referred to this particular statement, as well as to his own Note to Poland in connection with the July Pact, and declared :

" This remains the position. H.M. Government, of course, stand by the principles enunciated in the Atlantic Charter [1]. "

The problem was the subject of yet another exchange of views between the Polish and the British Government early in 1942, during the British-Soviet negotiations which had preceded the conclusion of the British-Soviet Treaty of May 26, 1942. The Polish Government drew the attention of the British Government to the fact that, should the rights of Poland not be safeguarded in the Soviet-British Pact, the British Government might find itself unable to discharge its obligations towards Poland. In reply, the Foreign Secretary stated the following in his Note of April 17, 1942 :

" ... I can assure you that any agreement which may now be concluded with the Soviet Government will 'not modify the intention of H.M. Government to regard their policy for the post-war settlement in Europe as based upon the principles of the Atlantic Charter, which have already been accepted by the Soviet Government. Secondly, until the war situation is clearer than it is at the present time, H.M. Government intend to abide by the principles set out in the Prime Minister's statement of the 5th September, 1940. ... The policy of H.M. Government towards Poland is governed by the Anglo-Polish Agreement of the 25th August, 1939. This policy has been confirmed and strengthened by the experience of the last two and a half years, during which Polish and British forces have fought side by side on land, on sea and in the air, and the Polish people have steadfastly refused, in spite of manifold sufferings, to collaborate in any way with the forces of the occupation. H.M. Government would not therefore be likely to contemplate entering into an agreement with a third party which would injure the interests of so loyal an Ally. ... In any case H.M. Government do not propose to conclude any agreement affecting or compromising the territorial status of the Polish Republic. "

The Note made it clear that the principle of Polish territorial integrity did not suffer any exceptions whatsoever, when it dealt more particularly with

" ... Vilna and any other territory within the frontiers of Poland on the 25th August, 1939. The Polish Government have already been assured that H.M. Government do not recognize any territorial changes effected in Poland since August 1939, and it is intended to safeguard this assurance in any agreement which may be concluded with the Soviet Government. "

On Mr. Churchill's testimony, the Soviet Government had in fact

" brought up specifically the question of agreeing to the Russian occupation of Eastern Poland. This was rejected as incompatible with the Anglo-Polish Agreement of August 1939 [2] ".

It was against the background of such positive and emphatically acknowledged obligations that the British Government gave its agreement to Soviet territorial claims at the Teheran conference [3], that

---

1. *Parl. Deb.*, *Com.*, vol. CCCXCVI, col. 664.
2. Churchill, *The Second World War*, vol. IV, *The Hinge of Fate*, p. 296.
3. See above, p. 453.

it embarked on official support of these claims in the Prime Minister's speeches of February 22, October 27 and December 15, 1944 [1], and that finally it became a party to the Yalta decision on Poland. According to the very terms of Point 3 of the Secret Protocol [2], that decision was precisely so framed as to prejudice both the sovereignty and the territorial inviolability of Poland. Consequently, by participating in the Yalta agreement, Great Britain assumed new obligations which — even on Britain's own admission — were in clear contradiction to her existing treaty obligations. These new obligations engaged Britain's international responsibility and, being entered into in violation of the Anglo-Polish Treaty, constituted an illegal act.

No attempt has ever been made to justify British action by reference to the Treaty [3]. On the contrary, according to Mr. Churchill, any British recognition of the Soviet claims against Poland was considered at the relevant period as " incompatible with the Anglo-Polish Agreement [4] ". It was not explained how such recognition, duly resisted in 1942, on account of its incompatibility with the Anglo-Polish Agreement, had become compatible with that Agreement in 1945, *caeteris paribus*. This being the case, the situation is covered by the following statement by Prof. Lauterpacht :

" It is unlawful for a State to act or to agree to act in violation of the international rights of another State. This rule necessarily applies to the conclusion of a treaty the performance of which would interfere adversely with the existing contractual rights of another State. A treaty which to the knowledge of both contracting parties is contrary to pre-existing treaty obligations binding upon one or both of them is, in general, illegal, invalid and unenforceable [5]. "

It may also be observed that, by procęeding with a violation of the fundamental clauses of the Anglo-Polish Agreement, Great Britain became prevented from fulfilling her further obligation to Poland under its Art. 7, not to conclude an armistice or treaty of peace except by mutual consent.

---

1. See *Parl. Deb., Com.*, vol. CCCXCVII, col. 697-698, vol. CCCCIV, col. 494-495 and vol. CCCCVI, col. 1478-1489.
2. See above, p. 426.
3. An attempt to deny the violation by Britain of the Anglo-Polish Treaty seems to have been made by the Foreign Secretary in the Yalta Deabte in the House of Commons on February 28, 1945. The argument was, however, abandoned never to be concluded, in view of the quotations made in the House from the as yet unpublished Secret Protocol. *Parl. Deb., Com.*, vol. CCCCVIII, col. 1508-1511.
4. See above, p. 492.
5. *Op.*, p. 426. Cf. Lauterpacht, *The Covenant as the " Higher Law "* : " International law cannot recognize and it must actively discourage a state of affairs in which the law-creating faculty of States is abused for violating existing law as laid down in international agreements. Governments cannot be permitted to discredit international law and to render it unreal by filling it with mutually exclusive obligations and by reducing treaties to conflicting makeshifts of political expediency. ...The rule postulating the invalidity of treaties conflicting with previous treaty obligations is a necessary deduction from the law-making effect of treaties in general and must be regarded as a beneficent principle calculated to enhance the authority of the law of nations and to safeguard its unity as a system of law. " *B. Y.*, 1936, pp. 64 and 65. Cf. the Harward Law School's *Draft Convention on the Law of Treaties*, Art. 22, *A. J.*, 1935, Sup. 4. In the absence of any divergence of opinion as to the illegality of such a treaty, the doctrine is yet divided on the subject of its invalidity. A contrary opinion to the one quoted above of Prof. Lauterpacht, is being upheld by Sir John Fischer Williams, *op. cit.*, p. 280. As to illegal and invalid acts, see below, pp. 558-561. The invalidity of the Yalta decision was declared by Poland, see below, pp. 495-496.

Finally, it must be remembered that in 1945 the Covenant of the League of Nations was still in force for both Great Britain and Poland, and that British action in Yalta was a violation of its Art. 10 [1].

While no official British claim has ever been put forward regarding the legality of British participation in the Yalta decision [2], an attempt at defending its legality has been made by Prof. Lauterpacht, who examined this decision from the point of view of its conformity with the " proper exercise of the function of recognition ". It may be observed that such a viewpoint necessarily leaves out of account the discussion of the legality of Yalta's territorial clauses. With regard to the remaining problem of government, Prof. Lauterpacht considers that

" Notwithstanding the political implications of the decision taken at the Crimea Conference by Great Britain, the United States and Russia to recognize the Polish Provisional Government in Poland and to withdraw recognition from the Polish Government in London, the decision — and its execution — cannot be deemed to be inconsistent with a proper exercise of the function of recognition. It was clear that, in the long run, the claim of the latter to continued recognition — a claim based not on the circumstance of effectiveness of power but on legal continuity in relation to the Polish Government and State as they existed in 1939 — was bound, in accordance with the legal principle of recognition of governments, to yield to the claim of the authority yielding effective power in Polish territory *provided that such power was exercised by a government independent of the control of any other State and supported by a freely expressed vote of the population.* The latter condition was stipulated by the Potsdam decision [3]. "

This conclusion would indeed be fully correct on the assumption of the correctness of its premise, i.e. of an internal conflict between a government which is merely legal and one which is effective, such as would arise in the case of revolution or civil war. If this had been the case, then not only would the transfer of recognition be correct and legal, but moreover, a refusal to recognize the revolutionary government could be considered as an unlawful act of intervention [4]. For this reason Prof. Lauterpacht, true to his own consistent views on the subject, himself added the all important dual proviso of the effective government's independence of any other State and the freely expressed vote of the population. It is with this proviso that his argument stands or falls. Yet, the puppet character of the Lublin Government has been sufficiently proved and Prof. Lauterpacht does not adduce any proof to the contrary. Moreover, the free elections in Poland never materialized [5]. Consequently, his argument serves to reinforce the conclusion advanced above : the transfer of recognition from a lawful to a puppet government must, on Prof. Lauterpacht's own view, have been an illegal act ; *a fortiori*, so was the actual participation in the

---

1. It is of interest to compare the above with the list of instruments which, according to Pan, were violated by the Far Eastern section of the Yalta decision : 1) the Washington Nine Power Treaty of 1922, in particular its Art. 2, 2) the Sino-Soviet Agreement of 1924, 3) the Atlantic Charter, and 4) the Cairo Declaration. *Op. cit.*, pp. 51-55.
2. As opposed to its much defended political expediency ; see the speeches of the Prime Minister and the Foreign Secretary in the Yalta Debate, *Parl. Deb., Com.*, vol. CCCCVIII, col. 1275-1284 and 1498-1516.
3. *It. mine, op. cit.*, p. 353, *f.-n.* 1.
4. See above, p. 413.
5. See below, pp. 506.

organisation of that puppet government. It may also be added that, in his repeated reliance on free elections in Poland as a justification for the British action [1], Prof. Lauterpacht is expecting the British Government to observe a higher standard than that required by positive international law. For as the law stands to-day, its recognition of a genuine revolutionary government in Poland would have been fully warranted even failing popular support [2].

There is therefore no possible explanation which would save the action of Great Britain — as well as that of the Soviet Union — at Yalta from the stigma of illegality under existing conventional obligations. In committing a breach of these obligations, these Powers violated the rule *pacta sunt servanda* which is a fundamental principle and the corner-stone of international law, without which no conventional international law is conceivable and whose embodiment in one of the great collective pronouncements may here be recalled :

« ... les Puissances reconnaissent que c'est un principe essentiel du droit des gens qu'aucune d'elles ne peut se délier des engagements d'un traité ni en modifier les stipulations, qu'à la suite de l'assentiment des parties contractantes au moyen d'une entente amicale [3]. »

The above analysis thus leads to the inescapable conclusion that the Yalta decision was illegal both under customary and conventional international law.

This illegal act was refused any validation by the existing and still recognized Polish Government, which, on February 13, 1945, issued the following statement :

" ... the decisions of the Three Power Conference were prepared and taken not only without the participation and authorisation of the Polish Government, but also without their knowledge.

The method adopted in the case of Poland is a contradiction of the elementary principles binding the Allies and constitutes a violation of the letter and spirit of the Atlantic Charter and the right of every nation to defend its own interests.

---

1. See *ibid.*, p. 173, *f.-n.* 2.
2. Yet another attempt to justify British action at Yalta should be noted. Following the release of the Secret Protocol, there appeared in *The Times* of April 6, 1945, a comment by the paper's Diplomatic Correspondent, generally held to express official views. Its relevant passage read : " As regards Article 3 of the Protocol, it has not been violated by any agreement entered into by the British and American Governments at Yalta. ...At Yalta the British and American Governments took no operative decision affecting the territorial integrity of Poland. What they did decide, in concert with the Soviet Government, was that a commission should be formed which would endeavour to secure the formation in Poland of a government which all three Powers could recognize. The British and American Governments undertook that they would then recommend that Government to agree to re-draw the Russo-Polish frontier and to accept the Curzon Line. " The statement does not correspond to the facts. Nowhere in the Yalta text was there a word about a recommendation by the Western Powers to the future Polish Government with regard to the Eastern frontier. The three heads of Governments took an authoritative decision on that subject, without any conditions or reservations, and without any reference to any Polish Government, present or future. This results particularly from the comparison of the relevant passages concerning the Eastern and the Western frontiers respectively : consultation with a Polish Government was contemplated for the case of the Western frontier only, see above, p. 480. Moreover, the Diplomatic Correspondent's denial as to the " operative decision " was disproved by the subsequent authentic interpretation by the Potsdam Declaration, as well, as by the individual statements of the Yalta signatories ; see above, p. 488.
3. London Protocol, 1871.

The Polish Government declares that the decisions of the Three Power Conference concerning Poland cannot be recognized by the Polish Government and cannot bind the Polish Nation.

The Polish Nation will consider the severance of the Eastern half of the territory of Poland through the imposition of a Polish-Soviet frontier following the so-called Curzon Line as a fifth partition of Poland now accomplished by her Allies. The intention of the Three Powers to create a " provisional Government of National Unity " by enlarging the foreign appointed Lublin Committee with persons vaguely described as " democratic leaders from Poland itself and from Poles abroad " can only legalize Soviet interference in Polish internal affairs. As long as the territory of Poland remains under the sole occupation of Soviet troops, a Government of that kind will not safeguard to the Polish nation even in the presence of British and American diplomats the unfettered rights of free expression.

The Polish Government who are the sole legal and generally recognized Government of Poland and who for five and a half years have directed the struggle of the Polish State and Nation against the Axis countries both through the Underground Movement in the Homeland and through the Polish armed forces in all the theatres of war, have expressed their readiness — in a memorandum presented to the Government of Great Britain and the United States — to co-operate in the creation of a Government in Poland truly representative of the will of the Polish Nation. The Polish Government maintains its offer. "

Moreover, the Polish Government addressed a Note of protest to the British Government, as signatory of the Anglo-Polish Treaty, which stated *inter alia :*

" ... 1. The Resolutions of the Conference concerning Poland have been made without the participation, knowledge and consent of the Polish Government, which is recognized by the British Government and the Government of the United States as also by all the United Nations except Soviet Russia, as the legal Government of the Polish Republic. From the very beginning of the war the British Government co-operated with the Polish Government, without ever questioning its authority, in all matters concerning the Polish State. Nevertheless, at a moment decisive for the independence of Poland, the British Government have not considered it necessary to consult with the Allied Polish Government on matters concerning Poland.

2. The Resolutions of the Crimean Conference entirely ignored the fact of the existence of the Polish State, represented by its lawful authorities : the President of the Republic and the Polish Government, under whose orders are fighting for five and a half years the Army, the Navy and the Air Force of Poland, and until recently fought the Home Army and functioned the Administration of the Underground Polish State, and who have the support of the overwhelming majority of the Polish Nation. "

The Note went on to enumerate the various British pledges to Poland and concluded that the Yalta decision constituted

" an infringement of both the Polish-British Alliance and the Atlantic Charter".

" In view of the above " — the Note stated — " the Polish Government, as the only legal and genuine representative of the will of the Polish Nation, cannot recognize the Resolutions of the Crimean Conference concerning Poland as legally valid and enters a solemn protest against these Resolutions. "

c) *The Implementation of the Yalta Decision and its Legal Significance.*

The above analysis of the Yalta decision [1] has been fully confirmed by its actual implementation. In spite of the agreed text this implementation proved a complicated and arduous task, and was

---

1. See above, pp. 479-486.

achieved only after a long controversy between the Western Powers on the one hand and the Soviet Union on the other. While the latter, relying on the letter of the Yalta decision, insisted on a mere reshuffle of the Lublin Government, the former reverted to the conception of an entirely new government for Poland [1], and it is impossible to tell whether this was due to a belated misreading of the text they had actually signed or to the pressure of public opinion, generally inflamed by the Yalta results.

In the British House of Commons in particular, the Yalta decision was subjected to severe criticism from all parts of the House. Thus, Mr. Arthur Greenwood, leader of the Parliamentary Labour Party, declared :

" ... it is foreign to the principles of British justice that the fate of a nation should be decided in its absence and behind its back. ... it really is a cardinal sin for three Great Powers — one of whom has an interest which we have not got — in the absence of the people whose lives are being bartered away, to determine the future of any country [2]. "

Capt. McEwen :

" ... the view taken by the Polish Government and shared by not a few in this country, is that it amounts to little more or less than a complete acceptance of the Russian point of view [3]. "

Capt. Graham :

" On 15th December practically every speaker in the House affirmed the utterly unrepresentative quality of the Lublin Committee, yet it seems that the opinion of this House has been flouted by the decisions of the Yalta Conference. ... this body, vaguely expanded, is to be the new Provisional Government of Poland [4]... "

Mr. Petherick :

" This is the fifth partition of Poland, although it is only the first in which this country has taken part [5]. "

The new Government

" is to be chosen, we understand, by three eminent men — a brace of Ambassadors and a Foreign Secretary. I wonder if we should like that very much and if we would show much confidence in a Government so chosen for us. Would

1. " After a fairly promising start Molotov was now refusing to accept any interpretation of the Crimea proposals except his own extremely rigid and narrow one. He was attempting to bar practically all our candidates for the consultations, was taking the line that he must support the views of Bierut and his gang, and had withdrawn his offer to let us send observers to Poland. He clearly wanted to make a farce of consulting the « non-Lublin » Poles — which meant that the new Government of Poland would be merely the existing one dressed up to look more respectable to the ignorant — and also wanted to stop us seeing the liquidations and deportations and all the manœuvres of setting up a totalitarian régime before elections were held and even before a new Government was installed. If we did not get things right the world would soon see that Mr. Roosevelt and I had underwritten a fraudulent prospectus when we put our signature to the Crimea settlement. " Churchill, *Triumph and Tragedy*, p. 370. See the extensive correspondence on the subject between Churchill and Roosevelt, *ibid.*, pp. 370-382.
2. *Parl. Deb., Com.*, vol. CCCCVIII, col. 1298 and 1299.
3. *Ibid.*, col. 1326.
4. *Ibid.*, col. 1334.
5. *Ibid.*, col. 1426.

any country in the whole wide world accept such a Government? Surely one of the principles of the Atlantic Charter is the right of every people to choose its own form of Government. But this Government is being chosen for the Poles [1] ".

Major Lloyd :

" I look upon the intentions of the Agreement as downright annexation of a large portion of Poland's territory, without the consent of her Government. I believe myself that it is a very definite breach of the Anglo-Russian Treaty. ... I believe it is a very definite moral breach of the Anglo-Polish Treaty, and I am quite certain that we have once and for all departed, with our eyes wide open, from even the guidance of the Atlantic Charter which has now been whittled down to a mere meaningless symbol [2]. " " Now I want to come to the question of the supersession — for it is supersession — of the legal Government of Poland which we have recognized all these long years, by a prefabricated Government to be hand-picked by three estimable gentlemen. It is in future to be recognized by all the three Great Powers concerned, and will supersede the legitimate Government of Poland which commands the Armed Forces of the Polish Republic. They have done spendidly throughout the war and, I firmly believe, still retain the over-whelming loyalty of the majority of the Polish people. This prefabricated Lublinised Government is to be the future Government of Poland. ... It is adding insult to injury not only to break our pledges to Poland but to compel the Polish people to accept a prefabricated Government of this type [3]. "

Mr. McGovern :

" The Prime Minister and the President of the United States would not admit that they were compelled to accept the decision because their pride would not let them do otherwise. The fact is, however, that they found an accomplished fact in Poland. Marshal Stalin had created the Lublin Committee, and he backs it every inch of the way, because it is his Committee and his Government. He created it and he is determined that it will operate. There will be further deportations and murders until he carried his way in the plebiscite [4]. "

Mr. Pickthorn :

" ... so far as I know it is the first time in history that one country has had both its regime and its boundaries altered in the course of a war by three other nations — all in alliance with it, or at least, two of them in alliance in every sense of the word, and the third is in alliance in one sense or another — without that country being present [5]. "

A particularly interesting point was made by Major Lord Willoughby de Eresby :

" When I say " Poland ", I do not mean, and we did not mean, Poland as decreed by Soviet Russia or underwritten to-day by the British Government or Poland as imagined by the late Lord Curzon, but a Poland with similar frontiers to those we guaranteed, and over which we went to war [6]... "

Particular anxiety was voiced with regard to the future elections in Poland. Thus, Lord Dunglass asked whether there were

" arrangements to end the shootings and deportations and the outlawing of the Polish Home Army [7] ".

---

1. *Ibid.*, col. 1427.
2. *Ibid.*, col. 1450.
3. *Ibid.*, col. 1451.
4. *Ibid.*, col. 1608.
5. *Ibid.*, col. 1635.
6. *Ibid.*, col. 1466.
7. *Ibid.*, col. 1306.

Major Lloyd reminded the House of

" a radio appeal ... put out by the Prime Minister of the Government of
Lublin the other day in which he said that it was necessary to extirpate the traitors,
bandits, incorrigible malefactors and brawlers of that Home Army, and also all
followers of the London Government. No doubt those who so heroically defended
Warsaw, and the followers of the London Government — and they number
hundreds of thousands, including more than 90 % of the Polish Armed Forces —
will be called malefactors and brawlers, and treated accordingly. Unfortunately,
there is all too good reason to believe that many of these unfortunate people have
already suffered greatly and gravely, and that some, indeed, have lost their lives [1] ".

Mr. Raikes quoted the Lublin decree of January 17, 1945,
outlawing the Home Army and asked why this decree had not been
rescinded [2].

The following amendment was moved by a group of members of
all parties :

" but, remembering that Great Britain took up arms in a war of which the
immediate cause was the defence of Poland against German aggression and in which
the overriding motive was the prevention of the domination by a strong nation
of its weaker neighbours, regrets the decision to transfer to another power the
territory of an ally contrary to treaty and to Article 2 of the Atlantic Charter and
furthermore regrets the failure to ensure to those nations which have been liberated
from German oppression the full right to choose their own government free from
the influence of any other power [3] ".

The amendment was heavily defeated in a debate in which the
coalition government had asked for a vote of confidence and had put
on the whips [4]. In consequence, some of the members who had voiced
strong criticism of the Government's action at Yalta, found themselves
voting for the Government.

Faced with such criticism, the Government's spokesmen, while
insisting on the fairness of the territorial settlement, concentrated on
the problem of Poland's independence, which they considered as
safeguarded by the Yalta decisions. Thus Mr. Churchill :

" But even more important than the frontiers of Poland within the limits
now disclosed is the freedom of Poland. The home of the Poles is settled. Are
they to be masters in their own house? Are they to be free, as we in Britain and
the United States or France, are free ? Are their sovereignty and their independence
to be untrammelled, or are they to become a mere projection of the Soviet State,
forced against their will by an armed minority to adopt a Communist or totalitarian
system [5] ? "

Mr. Churchill assured the House that this was not to be the
case. It was precisely the future representative Government which, in
his opinion, was to safeguard Poland from becoming a " mere projection
of the Soviet State ". He therefore went on to reassure the House :

---

1. *Ibid.*, col. 1452.
2. *Ibid.*, col. 1495.
3. *Ibid.*, col. 1421-22.
4. Twenty five members voted against the Government, eleven members of the
Government abstained from voting and the Parliamentary Secretary to the Ministry
of Town and Country Planning resigned from the Government. Churchill, *op. cit.*, p. 352.
5. *Parl. Deb.*, *Com.*, vol. CCCCVIII, col. 1279-1280.

" The agreement does not affect the continued recognition by H.M. Government of the Polish Government in London. This will be maintained until such time as H.M. Government consider that a new Provisional Government has been properly formed in Poland in accordance with the agreed provisions ; nor does it involve the previous or immediate recognition by H.M. Government of the present Provisional Government which is now functioning in Poland [1]. "

The Foreign Secretary took the same line of defending the territorial settlement, while admitting the Polish character of the cities of Lwów and Wilno [2], but assuring the House of the Government's determination not to recognize the Lublin Government :

" In examining that Government, if and when it is brought together, it will be for us and our Allies to decide whether that Government is really and truly, as far as we can judge, representative of the Polish people. Our recognition must depend on that. *We would not recognize a Government which we did not think representative. The addition of one or two Ministers would not meet our views.* It must be, as far as it can be made, representative of the Polish parties as they are known, and include representative national Polish figures. That is what we mean [3]. "

Since even after these statements members continued to express grave anxiety lest the Lublin Government should, after all, be recognized by Great Britain, Mr. Eden once again reverted to the subject on the last day of the debate, in even stronger terms :

" We have in no sense recognized the Lublin Committee, and, may I add, we have no intention of recognizing the Lublin Committee. We do not regard it as representative of Poland at all. When my right hon. Friend and I met the representatives of this Committee in Moscow, I must say that they did not make a favourable impression upon us [4]. *There is no question, and the House need not be anxious that there is any question, of our affording recognition to them — not at all.* ... we shall see whether a broadly representative Polish Government can be created. If it can be created and if we are satisfied that it is representative, then and only then will we and the United States Government recognize it. If it cannot be created, we shall stay as we are [5]. "

An identical assurance was included in an urgent cable which President Roosevelt sent to Stalin on April 1, 1945, saying that

" any such solution which would result in a thinly disguised continuation of the present government would be entirely unacceptable, and would cause our people to regard the Yalta agreement as a failure [6] ".

Thus, after having signed the Yalta decision, the Western Powers were now once again determined to prevent the final establishment in Poland of a puppet State. The Soviet Government, however, firmly upheld its original thesis. The Commission of Three, instituted by the Yalta conference, could not commence its activities because, as Ambassador Harriman informed the State Department

---

1. *Ibid.*, col. 1281.
2. *Ibid.*, col. 1500.
3. *It. mine, ibid.*, col. 1505.
4. See above, p. 473, *f.-n.* 3.
5. *It. mine, ibid.*, col. 1669.
6. Stettinius, *op. cit.*, p. 276. Cf. Churchill's letter to Stalin of the same date, Churchill, *op. cit.*, pp. 382-383.

"Molotov was insisting that only Polish leaders acceptable to the Lublin Government be invited to consult with the commission appointed at Yalta. ... Molotov also returned to his old thesis that the new government should be little more than an enlarged Lublin Government [1]".

The ensuing deadlock was not broken by urgent appeals which President Roosevelt and Mr. Churchill, acting in agreement, addressed to Marshal Stalin. In his reply to the President of April 7, 1945, the latter claimed that the deadlock had occurred

"because the British and American ambassadors had violated the Yalta agreement in insisting upon the complete liquidation of the Lublin Government and the formation of an entirely new government [2]".

While these negotiations were going on, the Polish Government in London announced the disappearance in Poland of the Deputy Prime Minister and three other Ministers of the Polish Government [3], still recognized by all the Allies with the exception of Russia, the chairman of the Council of National Unity, the last Commander-in-Chief of the now disbanded Home Army, as well as several members of Polish political parties, all of whom had been invited by the Soviet authorities to take part in Soviet-Polish negotiations under guarantee of personal safety [4].

On April 11th, Mr. Eden informed the House that he had instructed H.M. Ambassador in Moscow to make enquiries in the matter [5]. On May 2, anxiety had grown enough for the Secretary of State for Foreign Affairs to be subjected to a series of questions on the subject. The following reply was made on behalf of the Government by Mr. Law :

"H.M. Government have not ceased to press the Soviet Government as to the whereabouts of the prominent Poles referred to. No information has, however, been received by H.M. Embassy at Moscow in reply to their repeated enquiries [6]."

Mr. Law further assured the House that

"the Foreign Secretary has done, and is still doing, all he can to obtain information on this point [7]".

---

1. Stettinius, *op. cit.*, p. 275.
2. *Ibid.*, p. 276. Cf. Churchill, *op. cit.*, pp. 384-385. Roosevelt died while parallel replies to Stalin were being drafted by the Foreign Office and the State Department. Stettinius, *op. cit.*, p. 276. For further diplomatic correspondence on the subject see Churchill, *op. cit.*, pp. 425-439, in particular, Stalin's letter to Churchill of May 5, 1945 : " We insist, and shall insist, that there should be brought into consultation on the formation of the future Polish Government only those persons who have actively shown a friendly attitude towards the Soviet Union and who are honestly and sincerely prepared to co-operate with the Soviet State. ...It appears from your message that you are not prepared to regard the Polish Provisional Government as the foundation of the future Government of National Unity, and that you are not prepared to accord it its rightful position in that Government. I must say frankly that such an attitude excludes the possibility of an agreed solution of the Polish question. " *Ibid.*, pp. 436-437.
3. See above, p. 443.
4. See the communiqué of the Polish Government of April 6, 1945, *Poland and Great Britain before and after the Crimea Conference, Documents*, pp. 18-19. " The most valuable representatives of the Polish Underground had disappeared without a trace in spite of the formal Russian offer of safe-conduct. " Churchill, *op. cit.*, p. 434.
5. *Parl. Deb.*, Com., vol. CCCCIX, col. 1798.
6. *Ibid.*, col. 410, col. 1382-83.
7. *Ibid.*

It was on May 5, 1945, in San Francisco, during the United Nations Conference on International Organisation, that Mr. Molotov broke the silence which had been maintained by the Soviet Government for a month, in spite of the most pressing enquiries. A communiqué issued on that day by the British Delegation to the conference, stated :

" The British and United States Government have been making persistent enquiries of the Soviet Government about the group of prominent Polish democratic leaders, who were reported to have met the Soviet military authorities in Poland for discussions at the end of March. They have now been officially informed by M. Molotov, on behalf of his Government, that these leaders have been arrested on the charge of " diversionary activities against the Red Army ".

Mr. Eden and Mr. Stettinius immediately expressed their grave concern to M. Molotov at receiving this most disquieting information after so long a delay, and asked him to obtain a full explanation concerning the arrest of these Polish leaders, a complete list of their names and news of their present whereabouts.

The Foreign Secretary has reported this most serious development to H.M. Government, and has informed M. Molotov that meanwhile he cannot continue discussions on the Polish issue [1]. "

A similar statement was made by Secretary Stettinius at his Press conference in San Francisco on the same day [2].

At his Press Conference at San Francisco, Mr. Eden had this to say on the subject :

" Our information about events in Poland is incomplete to-day, but I must emphasize that the list of sixteen Poles reported as having disappeared and about whom we enquired of the Soviet Government more than a month ago included nearly all the leading figures of the Polish underground movement. These men maintained an excellent record of resistance against the Germans throughout the war... Most of these men were just the type who should, in our view, have been consulted about the new National Government of Poland [3]. "

For a while there seemed no possibility of breaking the deadlock between the Western Powers and the Soviet Union, which now seemed deeper than ever. At this stage President Truman sent Mr. Harry Hopkins on a special mission to Moscow. The result of that mission was that in return for the Soviet promise of imposing only a " light punishment " on the arrested Polish underground leaders and the Soviet agreement to the invitation to Moscow of the former Polish Prime Minister, M. Mikolajczyk, on whose invitation the Western Powers particularly insisted, the latter waived all their previous reservations and agreed to recognize a slightly enlarged Lublin Government [4]. The

---

1. *Poland and Great Britain*, p.22.
2. See *Doc.*, VII, p. 902.
3. *The Times*, May 12, 1945.
4. Mr. Hopkins' conversations on the subject with the Soviet leaders are particularly illuminating with regard to the puppet character of the Soviet-sponsored Polish State. With regard to the re-organized Polish Government, Stalin said that "there were eighteen or twenty ministries in the present Polish Government and that four or five of these portfolios could be given representatives of other Polish groups taken from the list submitted by Great Britain and the United States. " At this stage Molotov whispered something to Stalin who then said he meant four, not five, portfolios. Sherwood R. E., *The White House Papers of Harry L. Hopkins*, Eyre and Spottiswoode, London, 1949, p. 890. With regard to certain " fundamental rights " which Hopkins thought should be observed in Poland, such as freedom of speech, of assembly, right of public trial, *habeas corpus*, etc., Stalin declared that " in regard to the specific freedoms mentioned by Mr. Hopkins, they could only be applied in full in peacetime, and even then with certain limitations ", *ibid.*, p. 895.

invitations were now issued by the Commission of Three, and from June 18 to June 21, 1945, there took place in Moscow the trial of the arrested Polish leaders and the conference to enlarge the Lublin Government. As a result, the Polish leaders, with the exception of three of the party representatives and the interpreter, but including the Ministers, the former Commander-in-Chief of the Home Army and the Chairman of the Council of National Unity, were sentenced to terms of imprisonment varying from 4 months to 10 years [1], and the Lublin Government was enlarged by the inclusion of four new members. This reshuffle was found satisfactory by the Commission of Three, including the representatives of those same Powers who had assured Marshall Stalin, their parliaments and the world at large that no such solution would ever be acceptable to them. Following the Commission's approval, the enlarged Lublin Government was formally nominated by the Lublin Head of State. The Government thus formed was recognized by Great Britain and the United States on July 5, 1945 [2]. This act was equivalent to the withdrawal of recognition from the Polish Government in London.

The last diplomatic act of the Polish Government before its de-recognition by the Western Powers was to lodge solemn protests with the respective governments. It is submitted that the following Note of the Polish Ambassador to Mr. Eden correctly reflects the position under international law :

" In view of the recognition on July 6th, 1945, by the British Government of the so-called Polish Provisional Government of National Unity, I have the honour to declare that I was accredited as Ambassador Extraordinary and Plenipotentiary to the Court of St. James's by the constitutional President and Government of the Polish Republic, to whom I owe allegiance, and that consequently I am not in a position to delegate my functions, powers and office to anyone, without appropriate instructions from the President and Government of the Polish Republic, who continue to be the sole constitutional and independent representatives of Poland.

Acting on the instructions of my Government, I have the honour to bring to your knowledge that

1. The authority of the President and Government of Poland, to whom I owe allegiance, derives from the constitutional laws of the Polish Republic enacted by the nation through a freely elected Parliament which remain of unimpaired legal validity and which could not be changed in conditions of duress under which the nation exists to-day. Under this authority, the President and Government of Poland maintained normal diplomatic relations with the British Government, and concluded with that Government a number of agreements, including the Agreement

---

1. " This was in fact the judicial liquidation of the leadership of the Polish Underground which had fought so heroically against Hitler. The rank and file had already died in the ruins of Warsaw. " Churchill, *op. cit.*, p. 435.

2. See Churchill's comment : " It is difficult to see what more we could have done. For five months the Soviets had fought every inch of the road. They had gained their object by delay. During all this time the Lublin Administration, under Bierut, sustained by the might of the Russian armies, had given them a complete control of Poland, enforced by the usual deportations and liquidations. They had denied us all the access for our observers which they had promised. All the Polish parties, except their own Communist puppets, were in a hopeless minority in the new recognized Polish Provisional Government. We were as far as ever from any real and fair attempt to obtain the will of the Polish nation by free elections. There was still a hope — and it was the only hope — that the meeting of " the Three ", now impending, would enable a genuine and honourable settlement to be achieved. So far only dust and ashes had been gathered, and these are all that remain to us to-day of Polish national freedom. " *Op. cit.*, p. 507.

of Mutual Assistance of August 25th, 1939, which I had the honour to sign in London on behalf of the Polish Government, as well as agreements between Poland and other Powers, including all the bilateral undertakings entered into during the war and concerning military, naval, aviation, financial, economic and shipping matters, of which I would mention specifically :

a) The Polish-French Protocol, signed at Paris on September 4th, 1939, concerning the execution of the Polish-French Alliance.

b) The Agreement between Poland and the U.S.S.R. signed at London on July 30th, 1941.

c) The Agreement concluded at Washington between the Polish Government and the Government of the United States on July 1st, 1942, concerning Lease and Lend.

Furthermore, multilateral agreements to which the Polish Government is a party include :

1. Declaration of the United Nations, signed at Washington on January 1st, 1942, called the " Atlantic Charter ".

2. Inter-Allied Declaration against acts of dispossession committed in territory under enemy occupation or control, signed at London on January 5th, 1943.

3. The Final Act of the United Nations Food and Agricultural Conference, signed at Hot Springs on June 3rd, 1943.

4. Agreement to set up a United Nations Relief and Rehabilitation Administration, signed at Washington on November 9th, 1943.

5. Final Act of the Monetary and Financial Conference of the United Nations, signed at Bretton Woods on July 22nd, 1944.

6. Agreement on Principles having reference to the Continuance of Co-ordinate Control of Merchant Shipping, signed at Longo on August 5th, 1944.

7. International Sanitary Convention, signed at Washington on January 5th, 1945.

8. The International Agreement and the Final Act of the International Civil Aviation Conference, signed at Chicago on December 7th, 1944.

When all the said agreements were being concluded, not one constitutional State questioned the validity of the Polish Constitution or of the powers of the Polish President and the Government appointed by him. Neither was any doubt ever raised by such States as to the right of the Polish President and Government to lead the Polish Nation in the struggle against the German aggressor and to exercise supreme command over the Polish Armed Forces fighting at the side of the Allied Nations.

Throughout the war the Polish Nation made immense sacrifices for the common cause of the United Nations. The Resistance Movement in the Homeland as well as the Polish armed forces on all fronts — on land, on sea and in the air — never ceased, until the day of victory, to struggle against the enemy, under the leadership of the constitutional President and Government of the Republic, which they recognize as the sole constitutional authority of the Polish State.

2. The territories of the Polish Republic remain under a foreign military occupation and under the ruthless control of foreign military and police forces. The accomplished facts which have taken place in Poland since the outbreak of war are not the result of the will of the Polish people expressed either by constitutional or revolutionary means. The war which began in defence of the integrity and independence of Poland, ended in depriving her of that independence and in placing the country under the control of an alien Power.

3. In these circumstances, neither I myself, nor my Government are in a position to recognize the accomplished facts unilaterally enacted in Poland.

The persecutions, which thousands of Poles are enduring to-day, and which afflict with particular severity all those citizens of the Republic who have actively demonstrated their devotion to the cause of freedom and independence by their implacable struggle against the German invader, prove beyond any doubt that the so-called Polish Provisional Government of National Unity in no way represents the will of the Nation, but constitutes a subservient body imposed on Poland by force from without.

4. The first attribution of the independence of a State is its freedom to choose a Government. In the present circumstances, the source of the authority of the Government headed by Mr. Osóbka-Morawski is a decision made not by the Polish nation, but by three foreign Powers, one of which controls *de facto* the whole administration of Poland through its army and police forces. The legal basis of the authority of that Government can be compared with the legal basis of the so-called governments set up in occupied countries during the war by Germany. In both cases they are based on the will of a foreign Power.

5. In such circumstances, and acting on instructions from my Government, I most solemnly protest against the recognition by the British Government of a Government imposed on Poland by force by an alien power, which amounts to the recognition of the suppression of Poland's independence. Once more in history the Polish Nation is being deprived of its independence, though this time not as a result of events which took place in Eastern Europe alone, but after a war which the United Nations waged in defence of law and justice. Notwithstanding the recognition by other Powers of its present subjection, the Polish Nation will never give up its right to independent existence and will never cease to struggle for it.

6. As a protest against acts of violence inflicted on the Polish Nation, I am obliged to refuse to delegate my functions, without the approval of the constitutional Government of Poland, and to regard as an impostor any person pretending to be authorized to claim my office.

I have the honour to be, Sir, etc.

Edward Raczynski. "

Failing the validation of the Yalta decision and its implementation by a free organ of the independent Polish State, their illegality could not be healed by the subsequent validation by the enlarged Lublin Government [1]. In the first place, such validation had been made sure in advance, since a prior acceptance of the Yalta decision even by individuals had been made the condition of an invitation to the Moscow Conference. Secondly, not only was the enlarged Lublin Government no free agent, being merely a delegated body, but, moreover, this alleged validation of an illegal act was performed by a body which was actually itself the result of that illegality. The idea of a validation being given after the performance of the illegal act by an organ created for that purpose in the course of such performance, would deprive the notion of validation of all meaning. In the particular case it corresponded exactly to the validation of the Italian invasion and annexation of Albania by the Italian-convoked Albanian Assembly [2] or to the validation of the Anschluss by means of incorporation laws passed by Seyss-Inquart [3].

It has therefore to be concluded that the implementation of the Yalta decision on Poland conformed to that decision as closely as the latter conformed to the Soviet *faits accomplis* in Poland to which it gave international approval without changing them. Except for the addition

---

1. Its Prime Minister officially notified the Western Powers that " the Provisional Government of National Unity has recognized in their entirety the decisions of the Crimea Conference on the Polish question. " *Doc.*, VII, p. 904.
2. See above, p. 331.
3. See above, p. 342.

to the Lublin Government of four ministers — who were all soon to be eliminated — the Yalta solution did not effect any changes in the legal position.

Nor were any such changes effected *ex post* by the elections provided for by the Yalta decision. Instead of being held " as soon as possible ", they did not actually take place until January 19, 1947, and, as had been foreseen by Mr. Eden at Yalta [1], were neither " free " nor " unfettered ". In fact, not only were the opposition parties practically deprived of all means of fighting the elections, by devices such as the suppression of electoral lists, the removal of candidates' and voters' names from the register, exclusion from the count, — but moreover, the period preceding the elections was one of ever increasing political terror in Poland, including the arrest and murder of the opponents of the regime [2]. Yet the Soviet Government found ways and means of justifying these events and, consequently, refused the American and British requests to co-operate with them in making representations to the Warsaw Government [3]. The elections were consequently fake, and were officially stigmatized as such by the British and American Governments [4].

---

1. See above, p. 483, f.-n. 1.
2. See the House of Commons debates, vol. CCCCXVIII, col. 143 ; vol. CCCCXIX, col. 1243-4 ; vol. CCCCXXI, col. 2-3 ; vol. CCCCXXIII, col. 299 ; vol. CCCCXXV, col. 366-425 ; vol. CCCCXXVII, col. 1249-1282 ; vol. CCCCXXXI, col. 1932-34 ; vol. CCCCXXXIII, col. 1150-51, etc., etc. See also the American Note to M. Molotov of January 5, 1947 : " My Government is especially perturbed by the increasingly frequent reports of repressive measures which the Polish Provisional Government has seen fit to employ against those democratie elements in Poland which have not aligned themselves with the « bloc » parties. ...these repressive activities on the part of the Provisional Government have now increased in intensity to the point where, if they do not cease immediately, there is little likelihood that elections can be held in accordance with the terms of the Potsdam Agreement... " The Note goes on to quote cases of arrest, murder, dismissal of members of the opposition from employment, house-searches, attacks by secret police and members of the Communist party, etc., etc., *Doc.*, vol. IX, pp. 637-639.
3. See Molotov's answer to the above-quoted American Note, of January 13, 1947, *ibid.*, pp. 639-640 ; see also Mr. Mayhew's statement in the House of Commons, of February 3, 1947, vol. CCCCXXXII, col. 1376-77.
4. See the statement by Mr. Mayhew quoted in the previous foot-note, in particular : " H. M. Government cannot regard these elections as fulfilling the solemn contract which the Polish Provisional Government entered into with them and with the United States Government and Soviet Government that free and unfettered elections would be held. They cannot, therefore, regard the results as a true expression of the will of the Polish people. " See also the statement of the State Department, released on January 28, 1947, describing both the pre-election period and the elections themselves and concluding : " The United States Government considers that the Polish Provisional Government has failed to carry out its solemn pledge. " *Doc.*, IX, pp. 709-710. The *Listing of Treaty Violations by the Soviet Union*, submitted by the State Department to the Senate Committee on Foreign Relations on May 29, 1948, included the following statement : " On several occasions prior to the elections and following persistent reports of reprehensible methods employed by the Government against the democratic opposition, this Government reminded the Polish Provisional Government of its obligation under the Yalta and Potsdam agreements and was joined on these occasions by the British Government. On January 5, 1947, the British and Soviet Governments were asked to associate themselves with this Government in approaching the Poles on this subject, and the British made similar representations to the Soviet Government reiterating the request that the Soviet Government support the British and American Governments in calling for a strict fulfilment of Poland's obligations. The Soviet Government refused to participate in the proposed approach to the Polish Government. The British and American representations were summarily rejected by the Polish Government as " undue interference " in the internal affairs of Poland. " *Doc.*, vol. X, p. 613.

Far from divesting itself from its puppet character by means of free elections, Yalta-Poland developed in the direction of further vassalization [1].

To sum up, the Yalta solution left the state of affairs in Poland exactly where it had been before Yalta, except for international recognition.

3. LEGAL NATURE OF YALTA-POLAND AND ITS RELATION TO THE POLISH REPUBLIC.

a) *General International Law.*

The legal nature of the Poland which finally emerged from Soviet intervention and the Yalta decision follows automatically from the above analysis of *a)* the puppet entity set up by the Soviet Union in Poland prior to Yalta, and *b)* the Yalta decision and its implementation. Before drawing final conclusions, the irrelevant tests of the identity and continuity of States may briefly be disposed of.

It is true that both, Yalta-Poland and the Polish Republic [2] bore the same name [3]. They possessed the same capital in Warsaw. Yalta-Poland embraces the greater part of the Polish population and 53 % of Polish pre-war territory.

While it is precisely the existence of such common features which makes an investigation of the problem of identity and continuity possible at all [4], their irrelevance to the final solution of that problem has already been shown [5]. The case of the Baltic States has furnished the proof that not even a complete identity of territory and population is necessarily decisive for the identity of a State, since such territory and population may carry an altogether different legal structure [6]. An investigation into Yalta-Poland's legal nature cannot therefore be based on the existence of such irrelevant tests and must be directed to the substance of the matter.

It has been seen that the entity established in Poland by the Soviet Union prior to be Yalta Conference was a puppet State, entirely delegated by the Soviet Union by means of consistent intervention, partly disguised as revolution, and, as such, not identical with the Polish Republic [7]. However inconsistent with Polish-Soviet treaties of the

---

1. Thus, the consequent adaptation of political and economic life to the Soviet pattern, including suppression of political parties, land collectivization, etc., etc.; on the purely formal side, there is to be noted the formula of the oath of the Polish Army, swearing allegiance to the Soviet alliance ; the spectacular, though by no means isolated case of the nomination of the Soviet Marshal Rokossovski to the post of the C.-in-C. of the Polish Army ; direct references in the new 1952 Constitution to the Soviet Union, etc., etc.

2. It is proposed, for the sake of clarity, to use henceforth the terms " Yalta-Poland " and the " Polish Republic " respectively.

3. Although even this has recently undergone a slight modification, Yalta-Poland having adopted the official name of the "Polish People's Republic " under its 1952 Constitution.

4. See above, p. 1.

5. See above, pp. 127-128.

6. See above, p. 396.

7. See above, pp. 475-478.

inter-war period and with their re-confirmation by the Soviet Union in the July Pact and subsequent Soviet-Polish instruments, such action has been found to be fully consistent with the Soviet thesis of the extinction of the Polish State, as proclaimed jointly with Germany in 1939. This is further borne out by the retention by the Soviet Union of her extended territorial and personal sphere of validity as established at that period.

It has been seen that, notwithstanding temporary vacillations by the Western Powers, the Yalta decision on Poland and its implementation accepted and confirmed this situation. There is, consequently, little to be added to the above analysis of the Soviet-created Polish puppet State as it had existed prior to Yalta [1]. Now as then, the immediate subordination to international law of the independent Polish Republic was replaced by a delegation of the new State. Now as then, the basic norm identifying the Polish Republic was replaced by a basic norm derived from outside. Now as then, the delegated entity, for which a government was chosen and confirmed by the delegating Powers, was set up for an altogether different territorial and personal delimitation. Everything that went to delimit the separate, independent Polish State under international law, had been lost in the process : its legal order, its territory, its population. In particular, the total elimination of all organs of the Polish Republic must be borne in mind : its Government, its authorities in the Home country and, in due course, its army [2]. Now as then, all international delimitation of the State having broken down, there remained not one single element to support the identity and continuity of that State in face of all-round changes in its structure. There is thus not one single element on which to base a thesis of the identity of Yalta-Poland with the Polish Republic [3].

Similarly, the puppet character of the new State and its complete delimitation by the Soviet Union was maintained together with the Soviet regulation of Polish nationality and the participation of Soviet citizens in the supreme organs and functions of the new State. Lublin-Soviet agreements, embodying unilateral Soviet decisions remained in force [4], such agreements being of the same fictitious character as those which had been concluded in the past between France and Holland [5], or, in more recent times, between Germany and the Protectorate or Italy and Albania [6]. Now as then, the new State entirely fitted the description of a puppet as supplied by Commissioner Kane in 1831 and by the Lytton Commission in 1931.

---

1. See above, pp. 475-478.
2. See below, pp. 517-526.
3. See above, pp. 168 and 186-187. As to the continued application between Yalta-Poland and some third States of some of the conventions to which the Polish Republic had been a party, see below, pp. 529-531.
4. See below, p. 512.
5. See below, p. 172.
6. See above, pp. 303 and 336. It is interesting in this connection to note the positive attitude of the Yalta-Government towards the frontier settlement depriving Poland of 47 % of her territory : " The Council of Ministers underlines the historical importance of the final settling of the frontier between Poland and the Soviet Union, answering to the most vital interests of the two neighbouring Slav nations and which from now on will constitute an unshakable corner-stone for their everlasting friendship... " *Informa-*

Thus, Yalta did not effect any change in the substance of the case. What has changed, however, was its legal basis. For the basic norm of Yalta-Poland, while always remaining foreign to either the legal or the revolutionary order of the Polish Republic, henceforth came formally to rest on a delegation not by one but by three foreign States. However complete the acceptance by the Western Powers of the Soviet set-up in Poland, Yalta-Poland's reason of validity — while still not being derived from general international law — had now formally become rooted not in unilateral Soviet action, but in a conventional delegation. It is clear that this fact could not create an identity between Yalta-Poland and the Polish Republic [1], just as the non-identity of the Protectorate of Bohemia and Moravia with the Czechoslovak Republic could in no way have been affected, if two other Powers had later joined in the original German delegation. Nor could it, under existing circumstances, either eliminate or even weaken the preponderant Soviet position, as seen in the decisive part played by the Soviet Union in the formation of the new Government. Yet the fact remains that the only legal basis of Yalta-Poland, which has been found to be a) a new creation, b) a puppet State, c) as such, non-identical with the Polish Republic, is a joint delegation by the three Yalta Powers.

This is the only possible conclusion under general international law which, as has been seen, is supremely competent to decide the issue of State identity and continuity [2].

Yet, a different interpretation could nevertheless be advanced : that of a Soviet occupation of Poland. It is, however, submitted that this would represent a gross simplification of a complex problem and a misreading of the actual position.

For the present state of affairs in Poland is the result of the Soviet creation of a puppet State *following upon* actual military occupation, but it is not itself such occupation. The presence in Poland of the Soviet armies was an instrument and a *conditio sine qua non* of such creation ; it was this and nothing else. More particularly, neither in its early stages, nor subsequently, did it become occupation in the technical, well-defined meaning of the term.

It may be useful to recall that, whatever doubts may have been entertained as to the legal relations prevailing between Poland and the Soviet Union in the years 1939-1941 [3], there can be no doubt that no state of war existed between them in 1944. The Soviet armies at that period did not enter Polish territory in the course of a war against Poland. The resulting situation was, consequently, not belligerent occupation [4].

---

tion on Poland, Ministry of Foreign Affairs, Press and Information Department, Dx 13. Cf. the Tass interview with the Prime Minister of the Provisional Government on the morrow of the signature of the frontier agreement, *Soviet-Polish Relations, A Collection of Official Documents and Press Extracts*, 1944-1946. Published by *Soviet News*, London, 1946, pp. 44-45.

1. See above, p. 168.
2. See above, pp. 129-130.
3. See above, pp. 447-448.
4. Cf. the similar view of the situation in Czechoslovakia and Austria, following German action against those countries, above, pp. 308-309 and 367.

What is more important : there is no doubt as to the actual Soviet military occupation of Poland both at the time of the creation of the puppet State and since, whatever the effective degree of intensity of such occupation. But if the problem were reduced merely to this, i.e. if the position were one of open, admitted occupation, then the relations between the occupying and the occupied States would fall within the framework of the international occupation regime, on the unavoidable basis of the continuing existence of the Polish legal order and of the temporariness of the occupation. Such a state of things, which is basically and admittedly temporary, could not have brought about in the international field those consequences which were actually brought about by the creation of a puppet State.

On the basis of a mere occupation, i.e. of a legal status of an admittedly temporary nature, there would have been no possibility of a Yalta solution, which — as been seen — confirmed the very situation created in Poland by means of a Soviet occupation, but not that occupation itself. On the basis of a mere occupation there would have been no possibility of imposing the puppet creation on the international community to the extent of having it recognized, admitted to international intercourse, seated and voting in international organisations, and so forth, in other words, of having a fake State accepted for a genuine one. On the basis of a mere occupation there would have been nothing to accept, since that occupation would have been bound to cease. In other words, a mere occupation would have offered no possibility of the international community recognizing the Soviet set-up in Poland [1].

This precisely is the very essence of the problem : it is not a question of a mere occupation which sooner or later is bound to come to an end ; it is a question of new techniques in law-breaking, which avoid both the stigma of an open annexation and the inconvenience of a merely temporary advantage. It is the action *in fraudem legis*, which has already been examined in connection with puppet creations [2] and which consists in committing illegal acts and securing illegal gains, while preserving, or trying to preserve, the appearances of formal legality. As such, it confronts the international community with a new problem, far more complicated than either open annexation or mere occupation. The former would nowadays be very difficult for third States to

---

1. It could, of course, be argued that creation of puppet States may, and has, in fact, taken place under what is technically belligerent occupation as well as under non-belligerent occupation, and that, moreover, it can take place without any occupation at all. Croatia, Manchukuo and Slovakia are the relevant examples for each of these possibilities. Consequently, the position and the results in all these cases would be exactly the same, and it would be purely pedantic to argue that in case of an admitted belligerent occupation the puppet is created in violation of the Hague Regulations, whereas in case of a non-belligerent occupation its creation is a violation of general international law. — This is true. But the actual chances of success in imposing the puppet creations on the international community — and this is what matters here — are incomparably greater when such creation is undertaken without war and belligerent occupation. In the absence of clear obligations such as result for third States from a belligerent occupation, there is bound to be far less resistance to an acceptance of the fake for the genuine. Thus Slovakia stood far more chance of international recognition than Croatia.

2. See above, pp. 70-71, 110-120, 169-180.

condone ; the latter could be disregarded pending its termination ; but the *actio in fraudem legis* here analyzed creates a unique opportunity for the law-breaker to obtain international recognition of his illegal gains, whether this recognition is the result of the international community being unaware of the true position, or its unwillingness to do more than pay lip-service to the principles of international law. It is this *actio in fraudem legis* — and not a mere occupation — and its acceptance by the international community which is the crux of the matter and a new departure in the international relations of recent times. Such techniques must not be forced under an artificial heading, but analyzed on their own merits and called by their proper name, if international law itself is not to be reduced to a sham.

The creation of a puppet State in Poland, far from representing a mere occupation, belongs legally to the same category and historically to the same period as Manchukuo, Slovakia, Albania or Croatia. To regard Yalta-Poland as a merely occupied State is to overlook completely the real significance of these new techniques and processes, and the fundamental danger they present to international law. For, contrary to what would be the case under mere occupation, Yalta-Poland is not the old, continuing, occupied State, but a new puppet State. It is submitted that, in view of the recurrent use of such means of disguised law-breaking, the correct analysis of the Polish case may be of a value far transcending the limits of that case alone.

b) *State Practice.*

It is of interest to see whether, and to what extent, the above conclusions under general international law as to the non-identity of Yalta-Poland with the Polish Republic, are borne out by the actual State practice. To this end the practice of the Yalta Powers with regard to Poland will be briefly surveyed, with particular interest attaching to the practice of the Soviet Union which indeed may be considered authoritative on the question.

i) *The Soviet Union.*

It has been seen that even before the Yalta Conference the Soviet Union — or her constituent republics — entered into a number of agreements with the Lublin Committee both before and after its assumption of the title of Provisional Government : thus, the agreement concerning the administration by the Committee of Polish territory West of the River Bug of July 26, 1944 [1] and the repatriation agreements with the constituent Soviet Republics [2]. It has also been seen that these agreements proceeded on the assumption of an already existing territorial delimitation between the two States. The same significant feature attaches to the Treaty of Friendship, Mutual Assistance and Post-War Collaboration, concluded between the Soviet Government

---

1. See above, p. 454.
2. See above, p. 455.

and the Provisional Government in Moscow, on April 21, 1945 [1].
Art. 5 of that Treaty laid down the principle of the territorial integrity
of the contracting parties. Once again, since the Treaty had not been
preceded by any territorial arrangement, it must be concluded that,
like the previous agreements, it took the existing territorial delimitation
for granted.

The agreements concluded between the two States after the Yalta
decisions and their implementation are of even greater interest. On
July 6, 1945, there was concluded in Moscow an agreement concerning
option and the transfer of Poles from the U.S.S.R. Once again, without
any bilateral determination of the respective State frontiers, the existing
territorial delimitation was taken for granted and subsequent provisions
concerning citizenship, option and repatriation proceeded on the
assumption of the finality of this delimitation [2]. Moreover, the agreement
adopted and confirmed the Soviet thesis of the Soviet nationality of
the deported and imprisoned Poles in the U.S.S.R. and it effected a
wholesale reception of Soviet decrees on Polish nationality, including
the delegation by the Soviet Government of genuine Soviet citizens as
Polish nationals [3] ; Art. 1 of the agreement reads :

" The Government of the U.S.S.R. agrees to grant to persons of Polish and
Jewish origin who until September 17, 1939, had possessed Polish citizenship and
who a e resident on the territory of the U.S.S.R., the right to change their Soviet
citizenship according to their expressed wish, and to allow them to remove into
Polish territory. On the strength of the decisions of the Praesidium of the Supreme
Soviet of the U.S.S.R. of June 22 and July 14, 1944, an analogous right is being
granted to persons of Polish origin, enumerated in these decisions. "

In other words, the agreement served to provide an international
form for the previous Soviet positive and negative determination of the
personal sphere of validity of the new Polish State. In particular, it
should be noted that the thesis of the Soviet nationality of those persons
who had held Polish citizenship on September 17, 1939, i.e. on the
date of the Soviet invasion of Poland — a thesis necessarily abandoned
by the Soviet Union in the July Pact — could be only upheld on the
assumption that the Polish Republic had actually become extinct on
that date and that, consequently, the Polish party to the agreement was
a new State. The 1939 Soviet thesis of the discontinuity of the Polish
Republic was thus embodied in a bilateral instrument and fully accepted
by the other contracting party.

On August 16, 1945, the Soviet Government and the new Polish
Provisional Government concluded in Moscow a Treaty on the Soviet-
Polish State frontier. The Preamble to the Treaty stated :

" The Praesidium of the Supreme Council of the U.S.S.R. and the President
of the National Council of the Polish Republic, desiring to settle the problem of
the State frontier between the U.S.S.R. and Poland in a spirit of friendship and
accord... ",

---

1. *Doc.*, vol. VII, pp. 856-858.
2. See Art. 3 : " The High Contracting Parties undertake to begin the repatriation
from the territory of the U.S.S.R. to Poland, and from the territory of Poland to the
U.S.S.R., of all persons indicated in Art. 1 and 2 of the agreement. "
3. See above, pp. 463-465.

while Art. 1 read :

" In accordance with the decision of the Crimea Conference to establish the State frontier between the U.S.S.R. and the Polish Republic along the " Curzon Line " deviating from that line in Poland's favour in some districts from 5 to 8 kilometers according to the map in scale 1:500.000 annexed hereto, conceding additionally to Poland : a) the territory east of the " Curzon Line " up to the Western Bug River and Solokia River (south of the town of Kryłów) with a deviation in Poland's favour of up to 30 kilometers at the maximum ; b) part of the territory of the Bialowieza Forest in the sector Niemirów-Jałówka, situated to the east of the " Curzon Line ", including Niemirów, Hajnówka, Bialowieza and Jałówka, with a deviation in Poland's favour up to 17 kilometers at the maximum [1]. "

It is submitted that this Article represents a key provision for the question whether Yalta-Poland continues the legal personality of the Polish Republic, and that it answers this question in the negative. On the assumption of such continuity, the frontier agreement would necessarily have represented a cession by Poland of her Eastern territories to the Soviet Union ; for the territorial sphere of validity of the Polish Republic was bounded in the East by the frontier laid down in the Riga Treaty, and there was no means of transferring the area between that frontier and the " Curzon Line " otherwise than by way of a regular cession by Poland in favour of the U.S.S.R. However, far from effecting any such cession, it is on the contrary the Soviet Union which " concedes " to the new Poland strips of " her " territory. The full implications of this settlement become particularly obvious, when compared with the regular cessions as effected in favour of the Soviet Union by other States on the basis of their continuity. Thus, the Soviet-Czechoslovak agreement for the cession of the Carpatho-Ukraine, of June 29, 1945, read :

" The Carpatho-Ukraine, which according to the Czechoslovak Constitution bears the name of Sub-Carpathian Russia, and which on the basis of a pact of September 10, 1919, concluded at Saint-Germain-en-Laye, entered the Czechoslovak Republic with the rank of an autonomous republic, will according to the wish manifested by the population of the Carpatho-Ukraine and on the basis of the friendly agreement of both contracting parties, unite with its longstanding motherland, the Ukraine, and is included in the Ukrainian S.S.R.
" The frontier between Slovakia and the Carpatho-Ukraine, existing since September 29, 1938, will, with modifications described, become the frontier between the U.S.S.R. and the Czechoslovak Republic in agreement with the map attached [2]. "

The relevant Articles of the Peace Treaty with Finland of 1947 read :

" Art. 1. The frontiers of Finland ... shall be those which existed on January 1, 1941, except as provided in the following Article.
Art. 2. In accordance with the Armistice Agreement of September 19, 1944, Finland confirms the return to the Soviet Union of the province of Petsamo (Pechenga) voluntarily ceded to Finland by the Soviet State under the Peace Treaties of October 14, 1920 and March 12, 1940... "

---

1. *Dep. of St. Bul.*, vol. XIV, pp. 341-343.
2. *Doc.*, VII, p. 864.

The Czechoslovak and Finnish provisions represent regular cessions in favour of the Soviet Union by two States, whose territorial delimitation until the coming into force of such treaties was uncontested and was altered only as a result of such cession. Moreover, the previous legal position of the ceded territories is fully described by reference to existing treaties — the Czechoslovak agreement quoting even the relevant provisions of Czechoslovak municipal law. There is nothing similar in the Polish-Soviet frontier treaty : neither an act of cession, nor any reference to the Treaty of Riga or any other previous international instruments between the two countries. There is no continuity of mutual rights and obligations, no continuity of legally determined international relations, no continuity of the Polish partner which emerges as a completely new subject in its dealings with the Soviet Union from which it even receives strips of territory which had formerly formed part not of the Soviet Union but of the Polish Republic [1].

The post-Yalta treaties concluded by the Soviet Union with Yalta-Poland clearly indicate that Yalta-Poland was a continuation of that same Soviet-delegated State whose origin and growth have been analyzed above [2]. They take their stand either on unilateral Soviet decisions and decrees of that period or on the agreements concerning population and territory which had been concluded by the Lublin Committee with the Soviet Union or the constituent Soviet Republics. There is not a single reference to any agreement concluded between the pre-war Polish Republic and the U.S.S.R., a significant omission in view of the recurrent Soviet practice of referring to previous instruments in any new agreement. While the old Polish-Soviet agreements have suffered a total eclipse, the Lublin-Soviet agreements have survived and have formed the basis of further relations between the two parties [3]. Thus, according to Soviet practice, Yalta-Poland represents a continuity

---

1. " The Soviet Union went further than the Crimea decisions, and magnanimously conceded to Poland additional territory east of the Curzon Line in the area of the Rivers Western Bug and Solokia, and part of the Bialowieza Forest in the sector of Niemirow and Jalowka. In this area the deviation from the Curzon Line, determined by the Crimea decision at 5 to 8 kilometers, reaches 17 to 30 kilometers in Poland's favour. " *Izviestia* of August 18, 1945 ; quoted in *Soviet-Polish Relations*, p. 43. The above analysis fully disproves the inaccurate and — it may be added — superficial comment by Langer : " The wording of the preamble, which speaks of the border in terms of a problem yet to be settled, and of Article 1, which refers to the decision of the Crimea Conference "to establish " that border, would appear to indicate the willingness of the Soviet Government to base its claim to the frontiers of western Byelorussia and the western Ukraine no longer on the unilateral annexation of 1939 but on multilateral agreements concluded with other Great Powers and, following this, the assent of the Power directly concerned. " *Op. cit.*, p. 280. Both in Yalta and in the frontier treaty, the Soviet Union's thesis of her territorial sphere of validity already established on the basis of her unilateral decision, fully carried the day ; the Yalta decisions did not represent a new and different decision but the assent of the Western Powers to the Soviet, point of view ; with regard to the " following assent of the Power concerned ", it has just been shown that it has not been given by the " Power concerned " but by a new and different body.

2. See above, pp. 449-478.

3. Thus Fisher, commenting on the option and repatriation treaty of July 6, 1945 : " The agreement did not alter the provisions of the agreements of September 9 and 22, 1944, between the Polish Committee of National Liberation and the Ukrainian, Byelorussian and Lithuanian Soviet Socialist Republics concerning the mutual exchange of population. " *Agreements and Treaties concluded by the U.S.S.R. in 1945*, in *Dep. of State Bul.*, vol. XV, pp. 395-396.

of Lublin, not of the Polish Republic ; and the Lublin agreements in turn start from a *tabula rasa*, initiating entirely new relations with an entirely new subject of international law. This is the only possible interpretation of the Soviet practice with regard to Yalta-Poland and this practice, considering the preponderant role of the Soviet Union in bringing about the new state of affairs, must needs be considered as particularly relevant and weighty. This practice appears finally to confirm the Soviet return to the 1939 thesis of the extinction of the Polish Republic, as expressed in Molotov's statement of October 31, 1939 :

" Everybody realizes that there can be no question of restoring the old Poland [1]. "

ii) *Great Britain.*

Unlike the clear and unequivocal Soviet practice, the British thesis with regard to the legal status of Yalta-Poland is much more difficult to define.

On the face of it, it would appear that the British Government considered the events in Poland as a mere change of government and that, consequently, the question of Yalta-Poland's identity with the Polish Republic did not arise in the British practice. This attitude implies the view that events in Poland could be reduced to an internal contest between two rival governments, one of them legitimate and the other revolutionary. Yet, precisely such a view is not to be reconciled with the firm opinion previously held by Great Britain as to the puppet character of the Lublin Government, and with the consequent British refusal to recognize it [2]. It has been seen that Britain eventually recognized the Lublin Government precisely on those terms on which she had pledged herself not to do so, but this fact alone was not sufficient to endow that government with the character of the revolutionary organ of the existing Polish State. Yet, despite such inconsistencies, several British acts with regard to Yalta-Poland would imply British recognition of that State as continuing the legal personality of the Polish Republic.

In this connection, it is necessary to mention the following Anglo-American statement, incorporated in the Three Power Declaration of Potsdam, of August 2, 1945 :

" The British and United States Governments have taken measures to protect the interest of the Polish Provisional Government of National Unity as the recognized Government of the Polish State in the property belonging to the Polish State located in their territories and under their control, whatever the form of this property may be. They have further taken measures to prevent alienation to third parties of such property. All proper facilities will be given to the Polish Provisional Government of National Unity for the exercise of the ordinary legal remedies for the recovery of any property belonging to the Polish State which may have been wrongfully alienated [3]. "

---

1. *New York Times*, November 1, 1939.
2. See above, pp. 472-473, 478, 500.
3. *Doc.* VIII, p. 933. It is significant that this declaration was made by the two Anglo-Saxon Powers without the Soviet Union joining in, although there was Polish State property in Soviet territory as well.

Further, according to an official statement in the House of Commons in 1945, the British Government recognized the continued validity of the 1939 Anglo-Polish Treaty between Britain and Yalta-Poland [1]. On November 17, 1948, the Under-Secretary of State for Foreign Affairs, Mr. Mayhew declared :

" If the Treaty is carefully read, it will be seen to be highly inappropriate to the present situation in Europe [2]. "

Whatever the precise meaning of this statement, it would nevertheless appear that for a certain time the British Government continued to consider the Treaty as valid between Yalta-Poland and Great Britain, and that any change in that position occurred only under the *clausula rebus sic stantibus*, and not by reason of the non-identity of the other party.

Equally, the British Government insisted on the financial liability of the new Polish Government for the obligations of the Polish Government in London [3]. In fact, financial problems were settled between the two governments by means of an agreement concluded on June 24, 1946 [4].

While the above facts point to a complete absence, on the part of Britain, of any doubt as to Yalta-Poland's identity with the Polish Republic, other British acts are not lacking which would seem to undermine such a conclusion.

In this respect, attention should be drawn to the manner of liquidating the numerous Polish assets in Great Britain. In the case of an ordinary change of government it would have been normal for the new government automatically to take such assets over, whether for the purpose of continuing or liquidating the existing Polish administrative machinery in London. In fact, no British intervention had taken place on the occasion of the two changes of Polish Government which had taken place on British soil in July 1943 and November 1944. It would also have been normal for a liquidation to proceed in collaboration between the British and the Yalta-Government. This is not what happened [5]. Instead of handing over the Polish assets directly to the new Government, the British Government called a special body into being, the Interim Treasury Committee for Polish Questions, for

---

1. " Art. 8 of the Agreement provides that the Agreement shall remain automatically in force for five years, that is to say till August 1944. Thereafter the Agreement was to continue in force subject to denunciation by either party at six month's notice. Neither party to the Agreement having given notice of denunciation, the Agreement continues in force. " Mr. Noel-Baker on November 21, 1945, *Parl. Deb., Com.*, vol. CCCCXVI, col. 547.

2. *Ibid.*, vol. CCCCLVIII, col. 357.

3. " H. M. Government have made it clear to the Polish Government that no settlement would be satisfactory that did not cover the question of the liability of the Polish Provisional Government for outstanding Polish indebtedness to H. M. Government... " *Ibid.*, vol. CCCCXIV, col. 664. Mr. McNeil's statement in the House of October 15, 1945.

4. *Information an Poland*, Dx 32-33.

5. « Si le Gouvernement de Varsovie n'avait fait que succéder au Gouvernement polonais de Londres, il n'y aurait eu aucune difficulté. Ce ne fut pas le cas. De la coexistence de deux gouvernments polonais devaient naître plusieurs questions délicates. » Flory, *op. cit.*, p. 255.

the purpose of " supervising the orderly liquidation of the machinery in this country of the London Polish Government [1] ". Far from working in collaboration or consultation with the Yalta-Government [2], the Interim Treasury Committee on the contrary relied to the fullest extent on the assistance of senior officials of the Polish Ministries in London [3]. Consequently, although the Interim Treasury Committee was formally a British body, the liquidation of Polish administrative machinery in Britain, and in some cases its continuance, was effected in co-operation between the British and the Poles of London [4].

It may, of course, be argued that the British Government, by means of the Interim Treasury Committee, took over the control of Polish assets in Britain as a measure of security in negotiating an all-round financial settlement with the Provisional Government [5].   Moreover, most of these assets have in fact become subject of a subsequent agreement between the two Governments under Article 5 of the above-mentioned financial agreement [6]. Yet, the procedure was hardly normal on the assumption of a mere change of government in Poland, especially if it is realized that the British Government had acquired the right to dispose of the assets in question on the basis of a deed of assignment entered into on July 4, 1945, between the Polish Ambassador in London, acting on behalf of his government, and the Solicitor for the Affairs of H.M. Treasury ; in other words, the Treasury became party to the negotiations with the Yalta-Government and acted throughout with regard to Polish assets, as an assignee and agent of the Polish Government in London.

Much more striking was the British solution of the problem of the Polish Army in Britain or in other theatres of war under British command. This problem, which gave rise to numerous repercussions to the point of being raised in the United Nations Organisation [7] must now be analyzed, in spite of the considerable difficulty in giving a clear and coherent account of developments which were bedevilled by attempts to dress them in a legal cloak which did not fit them.

Anglo-Polish military collaboration and, indeed, the existence of the Polish Army under British command, had been the result of bilateral international agreements, in particular, of the Agreement concerning the Polish Navy of November 18, 1939, and the Agreement concerning the Land Forces of August 5, 1940. It need hardly be observed that

---

1. The Foreign Office communiqué of July 5, 1945, *The Times*, July 6, 1945.
2. See the statement to this effect of the Chancellor of the Exchequer in the House of Commons on February 2, 1947, *Parl. Deb.*, *Com.*, vol. CCCCXXXIII, col. 188.
3. See Flory, *op. cit.*, p. 256.
4. « Cet organe, le premier de ce genre qui ait fonctionné, est tout à fait remarquable. C'est ce que les Anglais appellent un Buffer-Body, c'est-à-dire un organisme-tampon, dirigé par des Anglais mais avec une importante participation polonaise. Grâce à' cette institution très souple, la liquidation put se faire entre Anglais et Polonais de Londres sans que ces derniers aient de contact avec le Gouvernement de Varsovie. » Flory, *loc. cit.*
5. Thus, Mr. McNeil in the House of Commons on October 15, 1945 : " These activities and the other affairs and assets of the former Polish Government in London must necessarily remain under the control of the Interim Treasury Committee until a general settlement of all these matters has been reached with the Polish Provisional Government in Warsaw. " *Parl. Deb.*, *Com.*, vol. CCCCXIV, col. 663-664.
6. See above, p. 516.
7. See *Yearbook of the United Nations*, 1946-1947, pp. 407-408.

the Polish Armed Forces were neither a private army, nor an army of the Polish Government. They were an army of the Polish State and, as such, its organ [1]. In the case of identity between Yalta-Poland and the Polish Republic which had entered into these military agreements, no change whatever should have occurred with regard to the legal status of these Forces : they should have remained organs of Yalta-Poland which would have remained party to the agreements in question. There would have been neither the possibility nor the necessity for Britain to proceed unilaterally in a matter clearly falling within the scope of international relations. The situation, however, developed in a different manner.

It is true that following the de-recognition of the Polish Government in London, the British Government engaged in negotiations with the Provisional Government in Warsaw on the subject of the Polish Forces in the West. However, in the course of these negotiations, a Note from the Warsaw Government of February 15, 1946, declared that the British Government had rejected its demand to allow its officers to take command over the whole of the Polish armed forces, complained about " the previous state of things being maintained " and " the old reactionary command and officers' corps " being still in existence and, moreover " in touch " with the London Polish Government, and concluded :

" ... the Polish Government has the honour to inform H.M. Government that from to-day the Polish land, sea and air troops abroad can no longer be considered as Polish army units. Therefore the Government of National Unity demands the instantaneous disbanding of those troops and demands that they should be deprived of the right to wear the colours of the Polish State and the insignia used by the Polish Army [2]. "

In other words, the Government in Warsaw refused to recognize the Polish Armed Forces as the army of the State whose Government they were [3].

Thus, with the British de-recognition of the Polish Government in London, and with the Warsaw Government's de-recognition of the Polish Armed Forces, the British Government found itself without the other party to those international agreements which formed the legal basis of the existence of a Polish army under British command. Since neither of these diplomatic moves could actually dispose of the continued physical existence of that Polish army, the British Government was faced with the necessity of a) unilateral liquidation of an international problem, and b) demobilization of an army which they had not mobilized

---

1. This, the only possible view, is fully confirmed by the Allied Forces Act, 1940, Section 1, subsection 1. Cf. Oppenheim-Lauterpacht : " Armed forces are organs of the State which maintains them... " Op. cit., I, p. 758. " Whenever armed forces are on foreign territory in the service of their home State, they are considered exterritorial and remain, therefore, under its jurisdiction. " Ibid., p. 759.

2. Daily Digest of World Broadcasts and Radiotelegraph Services, Part I, No. 2406, of February 17, 1946.

3. " ...the Polish Provisional Government addressed to H. M. Government, and published, a Note in which they declared that they could no longer regard the units of the Polish Armed Forces under British command, as forming part of the Armed Forces of Poland. " Mr. Bevin in the House of Commons, on March 20, 1946, Parl. Deb., Com., vol. CCCCXX, col. 1876.

and which was not their own [1]. In this difficult situation the British Government decided to deal with the problem not by way of an international *actus contrarius*, but by way of internal legislation, and to demobilize Polish soldiers not from the Polish Army, but from a British organisation. Such was the origin of the Polish Resettlement Act, 1947, [2] and the Polish Resettlement Corps.

The Resettlement Corps was to be an unarmed British military formation which Polish soldiers were invited to join and which was to train and prepare them for civilian life outside Poland. The Resettlement Act dealt with the application to these soldiers of British laws, such as the Royal Warrant as to pensions, allowances from the Assistance Board, application of health and educational services, and so forth. However, since the transition of Polish soldiers from the Polish Army into the Resettlement Corps could be effected only gradually, it was foreseen that the Polish Forces as such would necessarily continue in existence for at least the transition period ; for this reason the Act applied to those Forces as well as to the actual Resettlement Corps at the same time.

Thus, from the British point of view, the continued existence of the Polish Army under British command after the de-recognition of the Polish Government in London, passed through three different stages : *a)* from such de-recognition to the de-recognition of that Army by the Warsaw Government, *b)* the period after the passing of the Polish Resettlement Act and *c)* the period between the two. It is of interest to analyze, in the light of the British thesis, the legal position of the Polish Army in each of these stages from the point of view of the legal status of Yalta-Poland in relation to the Polish Republic.

a) The negotiations conducted by the British Government with the Government in Warsaw during the first period would indicate that, true to their thesis of identity between Yalta-Poland and the Polish Republic, the British Government now considered these Forces as Armed Forces of Yalta-Poland. This is difficult to reconcile with the actual situation in which the Polish Forces as a body remained in an unchanged position, bound by their oath of allegiance to the Polish Republic as represented by the President and subordinated to the Polish Commander-in-Chief, appointed by the President, and to the Chief of Staff in London. They continued to act as an Allied army, fulfilling their duties in the occupation of Italy and Germany, on the basis of existing British-Polish agreements, and subject to the Polish military code. Not until the end of August 1945 did the British withdraw recognition from the Polish Commander-in-Chief. As was pointed out by the Warsaw Government, they consistently refused the latter's demand to have the Polish Army subordinated to its own command. In view of the British recognition of that Government, the situation was certainly unusual, yet, it could after all be claimed that a provisional state of affairs was being maintained pending an agreed outcome of the negotiations.

---

1. « Le pouvoir de démobiliser une armée appartient normalement au gouvernement dont elle dépend. » Flory, *op. cit.*, p. 257.
2. *Public General Acts*, X, 1947, I, p. 92.

b) The theory that the Polish Army was an organ of Yalta-Poland could by no stretch of imagination be upheld after the repudiation of these Forces by the Yalta-Government. Since, as has been seen, these Polish forces could not technically be turned into a British Resettlement Corps overnight and had to continue for a transition period, the British Government substituted for the international agreements an internal Act of Parliament as a basis of their future limited existence in Britain. This was the meaning of Section 9 of the Resettlement Act.

The Section contained " provisions as to discipline and internal administration of certain Polish Forces ", as they had existed in Britain under the two Polish-British military agreements of November 18, 1939 and August 5, 1940, which were specifically referred to in the Act. The Act thus took its stand on these two agreements, even if only for the purpose of definition. The Polish Forces, which were to be under command of a British Administrator (Subsection 1) were to observe

" in matters concerning their discipline and internal administration, the rules in force as to those matters under the law of Poland on first day of January, nineteen hundred and forty-five, and a member of the said forces who contravenes or fails to observe any of the said rules in relation to which a punishment is thereby prescribed shall be guilty of an offence against this section and shall, on conviction thereof in accordance with the provisions of this section, be liable, subject to the provisions of this section, to the punishment prescribed by those rules ".

In other words, for the duration in Britain of the Polish Army, existing in consequence of the Polish-British agreements, and before their absorption into the Resettlement Corps, the British legislator effected a wholesale reception into the body of British legislation of the relevant Polish law, as it had existed on January 1, 1945, i.e. the law of the Polish Republic [1]. But even such reception proved far from being simple, and its compatibility with the British recognition of the Government in Warsaw was vigorously questioned in Parliament by members favourable to that Government. Thus, Mr. Bing, referring to the " treaty mentioned in the first Clause of the Bill " quoted Articles 1 and 4 of the latter. The former read :

"Polish Armed Forces ... shall be organized and employed under British Command, in its character as the Allied High Command, as the Armed Forces of the Republic of Poland allied to the United Kingdom. "

The latter stipulated :

" The soldiers of the Polish Land Forces will take an oath of allegiance to the Polish Republic [2]. "

Having quoted these articles, Mr. Bing asked :

" Can the Attorney General tell us, how this rule, which was in force on 1st January 1945, is to be enforced, and perhaps he will tell us to whom these people owe allegiance? Quite clearly, it is not the British Crown, because the rules in force on 1st January, 1945, expressly exclude that. They cannot owe allegiance

---

1. " What we have done in relation to these people is that we have, as it were, incorporated for the time being into British law the Polish law. " Lord Chancellor, *Parl. Deb., Lords*, vol. CXXXXVI, col. 268.
2. *Parl. Deb., Com.*, vol. CCCCXXXIV, col. 397.

to the London Polish Government, because that Government has ceased to exist. If the Attorney General's interpretation of the law is correct, they cannot owe allegiance to the present Polish Government, because on that date, according to his argument, it had not come into being [1]. "

Major Bramall, enquiring into the problem of whose Polish law was to be applied, said :

" The Polish Government regard the passage in a British Bill which proposes to enact as the law of this country Polish law at a time when that Government was not even in existence, with great disapproval. Furthermore, *it proposes that we shall say that Forces which have been declared by a Polish Government not to be the Forces of the Republic of Poland, are in fact Forces of that Republic.* We say that we disregard the action of the Republic of Poland in disavowing these Forces, and furthermore, *we say that we recognize law which is not the law of the Government of Poland at the present time. We recognize law of the Government of Poland which preceded this Government and which has been disavowed by this Government* [2]. "

All these difficulties were, no doubt, very real, and the perpetuating in Britain of the legal order of the Polish Republic in face of the British recognition of Yalta-Poland must have been considered unusual. Yet, it could be argued that the British legislator was free to enact whatever law he chose, such law automatically becoming British law. It could also be argued that the continued existence of the Polish Forces, which in any case was supposed to be only temporary, had now come to rest on the legal foundation of British law and that the position was now more or less legalized for the future, however unorthodox the procedure[3]. Yet, there always remained the problem of the legal position of the Polish Forces in the period between their repudiation by the Warsaw Government and the passing of the Polish Resettlement Act.

c) During that period, the Polish Armed Forces could no longer have been even theoretically considered as the Armed Forces of Yalta-Poland, nor had their existence as yet come to rest on a British Act of Parliament. On the contrary, such existence continued to be based on the relevant Anglo-Polish agreements and, partly, on the Allied Forces Act acccording to which they must have been Forces of a State. But, according to the Yalta-Government they were not the Forces of Yalta-Poland, while according to the British they were apparently not the Forces of the Polish Republic either. Yet, in the period now under consideration, as in the preceding one, the Polish Armed Forces continued not only in existence, but in service, as a fully-fledged Allied force, under the same allegiance, the same command and the same law as hitherto. The Polish military code continued to apply, Polish military courts continued to pass sentences " In the name of the Polish

---

1. *Ibid.*, col. 398.
2. *It. mine, ibid.*, col. 402.
3. " They (the Polish Forces) will be bound in matters of administration and disicipline by the law of Poland as sustained by the Polish Government recognized by H. M. Government on 1st January 1945. ...Here is a Polish force which exists — we cannot shut eyes to that — a force which, so long as it continues to exist... must continue to be administered and disciplined. It has hitherto been administered and disciplined under the law of Poland, substantially as it was in 1945. " The Attorney General, *ibid.*, col. 403.

Republic " and these judgments continued to be enforced by the British authorities in accordance with the Allied Forces Act and the relevant sections of the Visiting Forces Act which it incorporated [1]. Faced with the political and diplomatic impossibility of negotiating the subsequent fate of these Forces with the Polish Government in London[2], the British Government found itself compelled to negotiate with Polish commanders, in full awareness of the fact that these commanders had been nominated by the Polish Government and continued to regard it as their supreme authority. In fact, on March 15, 1946, i.e. one month after the repudiation of the Polish Army by the Government in Warsaw, the British Government summoned Polish Commanders from Italy, Germany, Scotland and the Middle East for negotiations concerning the proposed Resettlement Corps. The Polish Command promised its collaboration while at the same time requesting a postponement of the decision until the promised elections in Poland had taken place and until the Peace Conference. It must be concluded that in these negotiations the Polish High Command performed the functions of an organ of the Polish State, a party to the Anglo-Polish military agreement, thus fulfilling, in unusual circumstances, the functions normally fulfilled by the State Government, — and that the British Government continued to recognize one organ of the Polish State while having withdrawn recognition from another.

The question necessarily arises : whose armed forces was the Polish Army at that period ? Whose legal order were they applying in British territory, under British control and with British assistance in matters of enforcement ? What was the reason for the continued validity of international agreements which formed the legal basis of their existence ? It has been seen that the Government in Warsaw which had repudiated this army was not a party to these agreements which nevertheless continued to retain their full validity ; nor were the Polish Forces an organ of Yalta-Poland, nor did they apply the latter's law. It would be no answer to say that they continued as the Armed Forces of the Polish Government in London, that they were applying the legal order of that Government and that that Government itself, despite its de-recognition, continued as the contracting party to the Anglo-Polish military agreements. For a Government as such does not possess an army, it is not an independent subject of international law, it is not a party to agreements but a mere organ of the State whose international legal business it transacts, it " has " no legal order, it is only an expression of the legal order of the State.

This would therefore seem to lead to the following, truly astounding conclusion : not only was the continued unchanged legal position of the Polish Forces in this period incompatible with the thesis of identity between Yalta-Poland and the Polish Republic, — but, moreover, a

---

1. See *Public General Acts*, 1940, p. 479.
2. Which, for its part, refused, to proceed with a demobilisation and instead issued on June 28, 1945, a decree granting unlimited leave to all soldiers of the Polish army. See Flory, *op. cit.*, p. 258.

fragmentary continuity of the latter was not only acknowledged, but actually enforced by Great Britain for a considerable period of time.

Doubts of that nature were indeed forcibly expressed in the Parliamentary Debates, where it was sought to find a legal interpretation to cover an unusual and recalcitant situation. Thus, already at the Second Reading of the Resettlement Act, Mr. Wyatt said :

" ... the whole question of the legality of Polish Forces at present here has not been settled. Yesterday, in reply to a question asking what statutory authority entitled the Polish Forces to try and detain members of those Forces, my right hon. Friend, the Secretary of State for War said that the authority was the Allied Forces Act, 1940. That is not the case. That Act was applied to the Polish Forces by an agreement with the Polish Government in London, on 6th August 1940. ... As from 6th July 1945, Statutory Order 1819 of the Allied Forces Act 1940, ceased to apply to the Polish Forces in England, because recognition had been withdrawn from the Polish Government in England. Therefore, the Polish Forces in England were no longer the Forces of an Allied Power, as the Polish Government in Warsaw, to whom the agreement had been transferred on that date, declared that they did not recognize them as being a part of the Polish Army. In view of that, the Polish Forces in England have been an illegal army for the past 18 months [1]. "

It was to meet an extraordinary situation that an extraordinary provision was introduced into the Act, namely, Section 9 (8) :

" As respects any period between the first day of January, nineteen hundred and forty-five, and the passing of this Act, the powers conferred by subsection (1) of section one of the Allied Forces Act, 1940, shall be deemed to have been exercisable in relation to the said forces by reference to the law of Poland in force on that day and as if the said forces had not ceased to be recognized by the Government of Poland, and any Order in Council made under or by virtue of that Act shall be deemed to have had effect accordingly. "

This subsection was to be the unilateral, retroactive British solution of the problem of the Polish Army's legal existence under British command during the period under discussion. It was intended to put a legal interpretation on a situation which, in the light of the British thesis of a mere change of government in Poland, escaped all definition. The unique difficulty in explaining the continued existence of the Polish Armed Forces after the de-recognition of the Polish Government, with their unchanged legal status based on international agreements, with their legal code and military courts whose sentences were enforced by the British authorities, can best be expressed in the words of the sponsors of the Act themselves. In introducing the subsection, the Home Secretary, Mr. Ede, said :

" I believe this proposed new Clause is unprecedented in the history of this House, because we have to deal with a situation which is unprecedented in English history. ... We had an ally for whom we went to war ; the invasion of whose territory was the cause which brought us into the war. There have been changes in the Government of that particular State. Certain nationals of that State, some of whom enlisted direct into the Polish Army while it was still on Polish territory, and other of whom joined the Polish Forces at subsequent stages, have, in the end, been left, in conjunction with our Forces, in various parts of the world after the

---

1. *Parl. Deb., Com.*, vol. CCCCXXXIII, col. 446-447. Febr. 12, 1947. Cf. Mr. Silverman, vol. CCCCXXXIV, col. 425 and 427.

Government of Poland to which they first owed allegiance had passed away. ... There was a complicated stage at which there were two Polish Governments, one in Warsaw and one in London, with both of which as I understand it, at one stage we were, at any rate, in connection. Then a stage arrived at which this country decided no longer to recognize the Polish Government in London ; and the only Polish Government which we recognized was the Polish Government in Warsaw. Some of the Poles who were then serving with our Forces did not find it possible to give their allegiance to the Government in Warsaw, and they had no desire to return to Poland [1]... " " It has been in the interest of this country that a semblance of military authority has been established over these men, and, by some means or other, they have been reasonably kept together, and under a state of discipline. Therefore, subsection 8 frankly puts the position that it can no longer be contended that these forces have in fact been a legal military force, and, that certain actions may have been taken in those circumstances, which might entail unfortunate consequences for people, who, at the request of successive British Governments, have maintained discipline over these men. We, therefore, frankly bring before the House a Subsection which is an indemnity for these people, if, in fact, they have been placed in any jeopardy as a result of their actions [2]. "

In turn, the Attorney General defended the subsection in the following manner :

" We are seeking to deal with a temporary situation in regard to the Polish forces — I use that term in a neutral sense [3]... The position here is at once simple and ... unique. Certainly it is simple in this sense, that what it is intended to do is to put beyond legal doubt the continued validity of action which until recently at all events was admittedly legal. Until the unilateral action taken by the present Polish Government it was admittedly legal, and even now, although its legality may be in doubt, it has been done in good faith and in circumstances which really left no practical alternative in the hands of those responsible for the continued administration of the Polish Forces in which discipline has still to be maintained, despite the fact that the present Government no longer continue to recognize this force as part of the existing Polish Army [4]. " " ... but it does not follow ... that the unilateral action of the Polish Government in withdrawing their recognition of the Polish Forces resulted in the Allied Forces Act of 1940 being no longer legally applicable [5]. " " I am not saying now, and I do not want to suggest to the House for a moment, that the Allied Forces Act of 1940 continues to apply. I am saying that there are two views upon this matter... As far as I am aware, ... no member of the Polish Forces has made any claim that he has been illegally detained, or has sought to exercise any kind of remedy [6]. " " ... the body of law which will be applied under this new Clause is not the body of law which may be recognized by the existing Polish Government, but is that which was recognized by the Government of Poland, which itself was recognized by H.M. Government [7]. "

In winding up the debate, the Home Secretary once again insisted on the need for retroactive legalization :

" There are certain people, all of them Poles, who are not acquainted with the civil law of this country and the rights that those people had from July 5th in this country, but who went on exercising, with the knowledge of the British Government, the powers they had previously been exercising. I do not think the Government could do other than ask the House to indemnify people who had so acted in this matter [8]. "

---

1. *Ibid.*, vol. CCCCXXXIV, col. 353-354.
2. *Ibid.*, col. 362.
3. *Ibid.*, col. 382.
4. *Ibid.*, col. 384.
5. *It. mine, ibid.*, col. 385.
6. *It. mine, ibid.*, col. 385-386.
7. *It. mine, ibid.*, col. 388-389.
8. *It. mine, ibid.*, col. 435.

The introduction and justification of the subsection by the Lord Chancellor in the House of Lords was similar :

" There is not a shadow of doubt but that the legal position of these Poles is obscure. It may well be that the administration which has taken place since we withdrew our recognition of the London Government is irregular and invalid. It may even be that those who have been dealt with under the law would have rights of action in respect of illegal imprisonment and the like. It is not for me here and now to express a definite opinion one way or the other, and I merely say that the matter is one of ambiguity and of doubt. It is an ambiguity and doubt which we must regularize and put straight. ... we have no option but to regularize retrospectively that which has been done since January 1, 1945, by enacting that Section 1 of the Allied Forces Act, 1940, shall be deemed to have been in force as though the Polish Forces had still been recognized by the Government of Poland. The difficulty which justifies this wholly exceptional and indeed unprecedented procedure is that the existing Government of Poland have refused to recognize these Forces and on the other hand it is at least doubtful whether the bulk of these Forces are willing to go back to their own country. Now those are wholly unprecedented circumstances. None of us can conceivably like a provision such as this, but in view of those circumstances I ask your Lordships to say that we are taking the only practical course which is open to us [1]. "

It is clear, from the foregoing quotations, that the British Government, including the holder of the highest judicial office in Britain, not only considered their own Bill as something of a legal earthquake, but that they found themselves moreover in the greatest difficulty in providing a clear and definite legal explanation either for what they were doing or for the continued existence of the Polish Army in Britain during the period after the de-recognition of the Polish Government and before the passing of the Act.

It is submitted that this was so, because no clear and definite legal explanation could possibly be supplied on the assumption of a mere change of Polish Government within one and the same Polish State. On this assumption indeed, the retroactive legalisation of the legal status of the Polish Forces in Britain, especially after the declaration of the Warsaw Government to the effect that they were not the Forces of the State of which that Government was the supreme executive organ, was incompatible with the recognition of that Government by Britain. This point was correctly made in the House of Commons by sympathizers with the Warsaw Government.

The only assumption possible, and the only one which would have enabled British spokesmen to put forward a clear and logical explanation, instead of the doubt and ambiguity which they themselves freely admitted, was the assumption of a change not of Government, but of State, and, consequently, of the existence of two different States : one created in Poland, of which the Polish army in Britain was, by common admission, not an organ ; and one which had been de-recognized and displaced, but whose legal order had survived its de-recognition to the point of securing effectiveness in Great Britain herself. The legal reality proved to be stronger than any artificial legal construction. It was this legal reality which forced the British Government and Parliament to adopt the solution contained in Section 9 (8), of the

1. *Parl. Deb., Lords*, vol. CXXXXVI, col. 269-270.

Resettlement Act, and which, at the same time, made it impossible for them to give their action a legal interpretation compatible with their foreign policy.

But it could be argued — with the Lord Chancellor — that, whatever unprecedented steps the British Government had taken, were based on purely practical considerations, simply because something had to be done and there was no practical alternative. It is beyond the scope of this study to indulge in speculations as to what Great Britain could, or should, have done in order to make her action consistent with the thesis of a legal identity between Yalta-Poland and the Polish Republic which had been a party to the relevant military agreements with Britain. It may even be admitted that she could not in the circumstances have done anything else. But if this is correct, then the British thesis of a legal identity between Yalta-Poland and the Polish Republic was limited as regards its effectiveness just as a treaty, inconsistent with general international law, finds its effectiveness reduced [1]. For the fact remains that for a considerable period of time Great Britain not only admitted, but actually enforced a continuation on her territory of the legal order and the organs of a Polish State which was not the legal order nor the organs of Yalta-Poland, but those of the Polish Republic.

iii) *The United States.*

It would appear that the United States, like Britain, acted with regard to Poland on the assumption of a mere change of government within one and the same State, — although, in view of the determined American view of the puppet character of the Lublin Government, the same observations would apply to the inconsistency of the United States, as have been made with regard to Britain [2]. Nevertheless, the fact remains that the United States, together with Britain, signed the Potsdam Declaration with regard to the Polish State property [3]. It also appears that the United States continued to consider Polish-American conventions as valid between herself and Yalta-Poland [4].

As against this attitude, a certain doubt is introduced by the continuing American refusal to recognize Soviet sovereignty over Eastern Poland. As has been seen, in October 1949 the State Department supplied the Congressional Displaced Persons Commission with a list of areas located in eastern Europe

" whose transfer to other Powers have not been recognized by the United States Government [5] ".

Point C on the list read :

" Territories incorporated into the U.S.S.R. as a result of agreements to which the United States has not acceded :

8. Former Polish territory east of the 1945 Polish-U.S.S.R. boundary. "

---

1. *See above*, p. 235.
2. See above, p. 515.
3. See above, p. 515.
4. Thus, the Polish-American treaty of friendship, commerce and consular rights ; see *Dept. of St. Bul.*, vol. XXV, p. 913.
5. See above, p. 402.

If the above is not simply a meaningless statement, which can hardly be assumed, then it raises a number of problems transcending by far the territorial issue alone. For the question arises as to the reason for an American refusal to recognize a territorial arrangement concluded by a government recognized by America, — particularly in view of her express recognition in the same document of the Finnish and Czechoslovak territorial settlements [1].

Without indulging in undue speculation, it may yet be recalled that the United States has traditionally refused to recognize illegal acts. The submission in this particular case is reinforced by the marked parallelism in the document quoted between American non-recognition of Soviet sovereignty over the Baltic States and over Eastern Poland, the former being clearly and repeatedly stigmatized as illegal by the United States [2]. But if this is indeed the basis of American non-recognition, then, failing any specific conventional limitations, the illegality of a bilateral frontier agreement can only and exclusively result from a lack of competence on the part of one of the contracting parties. While a contracting party, endowed with the necessary competence, can validly enter into any territorial agreement it chooses, no such territorial, or indeed any other agreement can be validly concluded by an incompetent party such as e.g. a puppet government or State. It has been seen that this rule was fully confirmed by the Albanian Section of the Italian Peace Treaty [3]. On no other conceivable ground can a bilateral territorial settlement be contested by third States. Thus, the American non-recognition appears to be directly related to the legal nature of the Polish entity which was instrumental in effecting the transfer. While there can be no doubt as to the capacity of the Polish Republic validly to dispose of Polish territory, such doubt does indeed arise in relation to a puppet entity. But since this puppet entity had been set up with American participation (not to speak of the previous American approval of the merits of the territorial settlement at Yalta), then the present American non-recognition seems to cast a doubt even on the legality of the previous action of the United States in the matter. It is not submitted that this *is* in fact the American interpretation but that it is the only possible explanation of this, otherwise inexplicable, attitude.

There is also another aspect to the problem : since the United States contests the validity of the transfer of Eastern Poland to the Soviet Union, it follows that she continues to recognize the territory in question as forming part of the Polish State, — in other words, that she reserves Poland's rights to this territory. However, such a continued recognition of the *status quo* can only have a meaning with regard to a State which was a party to that *status quo*. But it has been seen that Yalta-Poland, set up from the very beginning West of the Ribbentrop-

---

1. American " non-accession " to the agreement in question can hardly be taken seriously as a reason for non-recognition. A bilateral frontier treaty needs no accession on the part of third States in order to be binding on them ; see above, p. 489, *f.-n.* 5.
2. See above, pp. 399-403.
3. See above, p. 336.

Molotov Line, never possessed — nor even claimed — these territories ; on the assumption that it possessed them in the past, it must have ceded them to the Soviet Union, and this, as had been seen, was precisely not the case [1]. The idea of a third State reserving the right to territories of a State which has neither possessed nor claimed them [2] seems incomprehensible. Such a reservation can only make sense with regard to a State which itself possessed the territories in question, which did not recognize their loss and which continues to press its legal claim with regard to them. Consequently, such reservation cannot logically refer to Yalta-Poland. It could make sense only with regard to the Polish Republic — on the assumption that it has survived — which has never acquiesced in the loss of Eastern Poland and never renounced its legal claim to that part of its territory.

To sum up : 1) A territorial cession by the independent Polish Republic cannot be challenged by a third State. Failing a conventional limitation on a State's freedom to dispose at will of its territory, such a challenge can only result from doubts as to the competence of one of the parties to the territorial agreement. 2) There is no possibility of a continued recognition of a territory as part of a State which has never possessed it.

Consequently, the American non-recognition of the territorial changes in Poland cannot be logically explained on the assumption of Yalta-Poland being identical with the Polish Republic. Viewed in this way, the American attitude with regard to Eastern Poland has a direct bearing on the problem of the identity and continuity of the Polish State, and it would seem that it presupposes not only the non-identity of the two, but also a fragmentary continuity of the Polish Republic on whose behalf alone such a territorial reservation could be made.

The foregoing analysis of the practice of the three Powers which had been parties to the Yalta decision on Poland, has yielded the following results :

a) According to consistent Soviet theory and practice, Yalta-Poland is a new State whose creation followed the extinction of the Polish Republic in 1939, following the German-Soviet invasion. The extension of the Soviet territorial and personal sphere of validity, achieved at that period in a *terra nullius*, was fully maintained and was confirmed by the cession by the Soviet Union to Yalta-Poland of strips of that territory, acquired in 1939, as well as by the release from Soviet citizenship of certain classes of Polish nationals, acquired by her at the same time. Far from continuing the legal personality of the Polish Republic, with its international status and delimitation, Yalta-Poland represents the continuation of that new State whose foundations were laid in Russia with the formation of the Union of Polish Patriots and the Polish Army in the U.S.S.R., and whose first organ on Polish territory was the Lublin Committee. As against this consistency in

---

1. See above, pp. 512-514.
2. In fact, authorized spokesmen of Yalta-Poland actualy disclaimed them, see above, p. 508, *f.-n.* 6.

Soviet theory and practice in both periods discussed, the abandonment of that thesis in favour of a recognition of Poland's continuity in the July Pact appears as a matter of mere political expediency. The new State has, for its part, fully adhered to the Soviet view, by agreeing to the confirmation of every single Soviet decision in form of bilateral agreements.

b) No similar consistency is to be found in the practice of the two remaining signatories of the Yalta decisions. In principle both Great Britain and the United States seem to have acted on the assumption of an identity between Yalta-Poland and the Polish Republic. Yet both took steps which were not only incompatible with such an assumption but which, moreover, strongly suggest the continuance of the Polish Republic.

In conclusion it must be stated that both, according to general international law and to the practice of the Soviet Union which in this case is of particular evidential value, Yalta-Poland is a new State, non-identical with the Polish Republic. According to the practice of Great Britain and the United States the position is not clear. In these circumstances, not only more weight must be attached to general international law and to Soviet practice but, moreover, the recurring confusion of States as to the actual object of their recognition must be borne in mind : it is true that in July 1945 the Western Powers claimed to recognize a new Government in Poland and not a new State. The possibility cannot, however, be excluded that, by granting recognition to a new government, they in fact recognized a new State [1] and that their subsequent practice merely indicates a relation not of identity, but of succession, between Yalta-Poland and the Polish Republic.

It is this relationship of succession which alone can explain the survival of certain treaties of the Polish Republic as between Yalta-Poland and third States [2]. As against the overwhelming evidence to the contrary, examined above, such limited survival cannot be interpreted to mean the identity of Yalta-Poland with the Polish Republic ; it merely means the taking over by the successor State of certain treaty obligations of its predecessor.

This view could be countered by the argument that there is, in principle, no succession to conventional rights and obligations ; on the contrary, according to the principle of variable treaty limits [3], the

---

1. " Since the continuity of States is not interrupted by a change of government, the recognition of governments must be considered as entirely different matter from the recognition of States. Cases often arise, however, in which the distinction is not altogether self-evident. It is sometimes difficult to say whether a given case belongs to the category of a change in the personality of the State or a change of Government... " Chen, *op. cit.*, p. 99. " The practice of States in the matter of recognition often contributes to the confusion created by the obscure nature of the change. Evidently they make little effort to keep the recognition of States and the recognition of governments in watertight compartments. The recognition of a new State is often accomplished by the recognition of its government. " *Ibid.*, p. 101. It is interesting to note the list of cases in which new States were actually recognized by way of recognition of their governments : thus Armenia, Israel, Korea, Poland in 1919. *Ibid.*, pp. 101-102.

2. See above, pp. 516 and 526 ; such limited survival seems to extend to some other States besides the two Anglo-Saxon Yalta Powers, e. g. Switzerland.

3. See above, p. 15 et seq.

successor's own treaties normally extend to his newly acquired territory [1]. In a very general way the rule can certainly be accepted as valid, notwithstanding either admitted exceptions [2] or the considerable amount of uncertainty both in doctrine and in State practice [3].

Yet, such an argument would completely overlook the fundamental distinction which has to be drawn between the case of succession by an old State and by a new one. For it is perfectly clear that the principle of variable treaty limits, which takes the place of succession to conventional rights and obligations, can apply only to a successor which is an old State and which possesses pre-existing treaties to be extended into its newly acquired territory. But a *new* succeeding State has by definition no pre-existing treaties of its own, which could be extended into its new territory. Consequently, such territory would not be covered by any existing conventional norms whatever. Yet, an immediate conventional regulation of certain problems may be necessary and of interest either to the successor State itself, or to third States, or to both. This explains why, contrary to the above-mentioned general principle, a new State may be made to adhere to conventional obligations of its predecessor to which it had not itself been a party. There are innumerable examples of such settlements. Thus in 1831, Belgium was made to adhere to the 1814-1815 treaties to which the Kingdom of Holland had been a party [4]. In 1878, Rumania, Serbia and Bulgaria were made to succeed to the treaties of commerce and navigation, as well as to the capitulations, concluded by the European Powers with Turkey [5]. Similarly in 1919, Poland and Czechoslovakia were made to adhere to a number of specified conventions to which Austria-Hungary had been a party [6], while Yugoslavia was made to succeed to the entire body of Serb conventions [7].

Such succession by new States to conventional rights and obligations of their predecessor can apply to bilateral as well as multilateral treaties, with or without any new treaty expressly providing for such succession [8]. Thus Ecuador and Panama considered themselves bound by treaties of commerce concluded between France and Colombia prior to their secession from the latter [9]. Similarly, Yugoslavia considered herself bound by Serbian treaties of commerce, and, again, the Serbo-Swiss

1. See Guggenheim, *Beiträge*, pp. 137-140; *Lehrbuch*, I, pp. 425-426; Schönborn, *Staatensukzessionen*, pp. 42-43; Verdross, *Völkerrecht*, p. 193.

2. See — e.g. — Guggenheim, *op. cit.*, pp. 426-428; Verdross, *loc. cit.*; Udina, *La succession des Etats*, pp. 704-751.

3. See in particular, Rousseau, *Cours*, pp. 282-286.

4. « Unie à la Hollande, et faisant partie intégrante du Royaume des Pays-Bas, la Belgique avait à remplir sa part des devoirs européens de ce Royaume et des obligations que les Traités lui avaient fait contracter envers les autres Puissances. Sa séparation d'avec la Hollande ne saurait la libérer de cette part de ces devoirs et de ces obligations. » 7th Protocol of London, December 20, 1830; Martens, *N.R.*, X, p. 125.

5. Articles 8, 37 and 49 of the Treaty of Berlin; Martens, *N.R.G.* 2nd series, III, p. 449.

6. Art. 19 of the Polish Minorities Treaty : « La Pologne s'engage à adhérer, dans un délai de 12 mois à dater de la conclusion du présent Traité, aux Conventions internationales énumérées à l'Annexe I. » Cf. Art. 20 of the Czechoslovak Minorities Treaty.

7. See above, p. 258.

8. " Vor allem zeigt uns die Staatenpraxis, dass Staatsverträge vom Gebietsnachfolger häufig stillschweigend erneuert werden. " Verdross, *op. cit.*, p. 193.

9. Rousseau, *op. cit.*, p. 284.

treaty of commerce of February 28, 1907, continued to be applied by Yugoslavia until September 27, 1948, on which date a new treaty was concluded between the two countries [1]. Article 8 of the commercial treaty between the German Reich and Austria-Hungary continued to be applied between the German Reich and Czechoslovakia [2]; similarly, Switzerland and Czechoslovakia continued to apply the Hague Convention on civil procedure of 1905 [3].

Thus it appears that, failing any pre-existing conventions, a new State and third States may, in their common interest and by common agreement, continue to apply treaties of the predecessor in order to avoid a complete conventional vacuum in their initial relations.

Yalta-Poland completely displaced the Polish Republic on that part of its territory which was not made the subject of Soviet annexation. As a new State, it was not a party to any pre-existing treaties which it could have extended into the territory in question. While the complete conventional vacuum with regard to the Soviet Union and the Eastern European States was filled relatively quickly by the conclusion of new treaties, the same vacuum with regard to other third States was in some cases and for some time avoided by the continued application of some of the old Polish treaties by common agreement between Yalta-Poland and such third States.

IV. THE PROBLEM OF CONTINUITY OR EXTINCTION OF THE POLISH REPUBLIC.

1. THE REAL ISSUE.

An analysis of the problem of the extinction or continuity of the Polish Republic has to contend against the persistent and, with the exception of the Soviet Union, general confusion as to the real issues involved, — a confusion which, as has been seen, has bedevilled the Polish problem ever since the Yalta Conference and even earlier [4]. Consequently, before such an analysis is undertaken, an attempt should be made first, to put that confusion on record, and secondly, to disentangle the relevant from the misleading elements in the case.

With regard to the Western Powers, the confusion and inconsistency began at Yalta itself, with their expressed conviction that, in adopting the Yalta decision, they agreed to something other than what that decision in fact provided for. There followed assurances that they would not carry out what they had actually signed and, finally, the implementation of what they said they would not implement. While emphasizing the puppet character of the Lublin Government, i.e. denying the fact of a revolution or civil war between two factions within the Polish State, they yet found it possible to reduce the problem to one of a contest between two Governments, notwithstanding the

---

1. *Ibid.*, pp. 283-284.
2. Verdross, *op. cit.*, p. 193.
3. *Ibid.*
4. See above, p. 477.

admitted absence of all elements on which alone such a theory could be built. While in principle considering the overall change in Poland's international status — including a bodily shift of a whole country on the map, a withdrawal of millions of people from its personal sphere of validity and the imposition of a Three-Power-formed Government — as a mere change of government and not of State, they took measures incompatible with their view of the identity of the Polish Republic with Yalta-Poland. While Great Britain continued to recognize in its territory organs of the Polish Republic, and to enforce a Polish legal order which was not the legal order of Yalta-Poland, the United States refused its recognition to a territorial settlement which it had helped to make.

The confusion seems to extend even to those States which, having refused recognition to the Yalta settlement, continue to recognize the Polish Government in London, without ever having stated clearly whether they relate that Government to the Polish Republic or to Yalta-Poland. Nor was the problem stated with an absolute clarity even by the London Polish Government itself, except for an appeal to the Nation of a political rather than legal value [1]. The confusion is finally brought to its peak by reliance on the irrelevant tests of State identity and continuity : for Yalta-Poland is called " Poland " [2], there are " Polish " diplomatic missions all over the world, whether they emanate from the Yalta or the London Government, and this also applies to " Polish " delegations to international conferences.

While it is neither the object nor the intention of this analysis to argue away the existence of such confusion, yet some definite legal conclusion must be arrived at in spite of the prevailing chaos.

Of the two contradictory theories with regard to the identity or otherwise of Yalta-Poland with the Polish Republic, obviously, only one can be correct. It is submitted that the choice can safely be made by relying on the conclusions gained from an analysis of the case in the light of general international law and Soviet practice [3]. Not only are these two of the greatest evidential value but moreover their consistency is additionally reinforced by the presence of conflicting elements in the opposite thesis [4]. According to general international law and Soviet practice Yalta-Poland is a new State, entirely different from the Polish Republic, and — as in the Baltic case — the conflict is one between two State entities (one of them admittedly a puppet), and not between two governments, — particularly in the absence of any premise for the second possibility, such as would be provided by a revolution or civil war. Consequently, there has been a change not of government, but of State, and the two " Polish Governments ", occupying an unduly exaggerated place in the argument, are no more than organs of two different States which they respectively represent. Consequently, the recognition of one or the other of these two governments must necessarily mean the recognition of one or the other State, — exactly

1. See below, p. 536.
2. Whatever its newly adopted official name, see above, p. 507.
3. See above, pp. 507-511 and 511-515.
4. See above, pp. 515-528.

as a recognition of Hacha must necessarily have meant the recognition of the Protectorate, whereas a recognition of Benes must have meant the recognition of the Czechoslovak Republic ; — or as a recognition of Pavelic must have meant the recognition of Croatia, whereas a recognition of King Peter must have meant the recognition of Yugoslovia. Of these two States, one is fully effective, as in the case of Manchukuo, Slovakia or Croatia ; the other — if it still exists — is deprived of all effectiveness and can therefore only exist as a temporary ideal notion as in the case of Czechoslovakia or Austria in the period of their displacement.

This is the only real issue at stake. A political confusion, a legal analysis stopping half-way instead of being carried to its logical conclusion, a chaotic and untidy interpretation can obscure this issue ; it cannot change it.

It is in the light of the above analysis that the problem of the extinction or continuity of the Polish Republic must now be investigated.

2. THE PROBLEM OF THE EXTINCTION OF THE POLISH REPUBLIC.

The State which, for the sake of clarity, has been here called Yalta-Poland, has been found as little identical with the independent Polish Republic, as was the Protectorate of Bohemia and Moravia with the Czechoslovak State, or the Baltic S.S.R.s with the independent Baltic States.

Yet, that State whose puppet nature cannot be subject to doubt in the light of the preceding analysis, to-day constitutes an effective reality on the map of Europe, again like the Protectorate, Slovakia or the Baltic S.S.R.s. Moreover, it has achieved international recognition to a degree never attained by any of those entities. In fact, it is recognized by the great majority of the international community and it is a fully-fledged member of the United Nations Organisation. It has thus effectively superseded the Polish Republic. In these circumstances, there seems to be a strong case for concluding that the latter has become extinct.

Such extinction has indeed been declared, although — in view of the fundamental confusion referred to above — the verdict referred not to the Polish Republic but to its Government. Thus, the Report of the Potsdam Conference stated :

" The establishment by the British and United States Governments of diplomatic relations with the Polish Provisional Government has resulted in the withdrawal of their recognition from the former Polish Government in London which no longer exists. "

The causality between the withdrawal of recognition and extinction was claimed even more strongly by a spokesman of the British Government :

" Upon the recognition by H.M. Government of the Polish Provisional Government in Warsaw, the Polish Government in London ceased to exist [1]. "

---

1. Mr. McNeil, on October 15, 1945, *Parl. Deb., Com.*, vol. CCCCXIV, col. 663-4.

This is a very radical claim, even for the orthodox constitutive school of thought [1]. Yet, it does not dispense with the need for an investigation of the problem on its own merits.

The Polish Republic has to-day lost its effectiveness on the whole of its territory, part of which has been annexed by, and incorporated into, the Soviet Union, and part of which forms the territorial sphere of validity of Yalta-Poland. The continued existence of the Polish Republic is therefore not protected by the customary rule preserving State continuity in case of territorial changes.

Nor is such continuity protected by the second of the customary rules examined which lays down that the personality of the State is not affected by revolutionary changes. For what took place in Poland was not a revolution which would have taken place within the separate territorial and personal delimitation of that State, producing a new basic norm from within such remaining delimitation. On the contrary, a new puppet entity was imposed from outside.

Nor can the situation prevailing to-day throughout pre-war Polish territory possibly be brought under the heading of belligerent occupation [2]. The legal status of Eastern Poland is not one of belligerent occupation, but of annexation ; nor is the Western part of the country under belligerent occupation, notwithstanding the presence of Soviet troops, but it has become the territory of Yalta-Poland. Consequently, none of the three protective rules, examined in the first part of this study, can apply to the Polish Republic.

There thus seems to be every reason to conclude that the Polish Republic has been extinguished in favour of Yalta-Poland. Yet, any such final judgment should be preceded by a short analysis of the Polish thesis, admittedly of a very limited evidential value [3], of the divergent practice of a part of the international community, of a comparison of the Polish case with analogous cases discussed previously and, finally, of the reasonable chances, if any, of Poland's restoration.

3. THE POLISH THESIS.

The absolute Polish refusal to recognize the validity of the Yalta solution is clearly expressed in the formal international acts of the Polish Government. Unlike the Czechoslovak case, such resistance to the destruction of the State did not come from a group of private citizens abroad [4], but from a fully-fledged Government, represented by regular diplomatic missions and performing valid international acts in normal diplomatic intercourse with the international community under conditions of continuing recognition. This fact is in no way impaired by such recognition being withdrawn soon after ; for the protests were validly formulated and validly accepted by third States and they remain formally on record.

---

1. « Les pouvoirs anglais n'ont, en effet, aucune autorité pour supprimer un gouvernement étranger. » Flory, op. cit., p. 261.
2. See above, pp. 509-511.
3. See above, p. 129.
4. See above, p. 306.

Following its de-recognition, the Polish Government did not go into liquidation and has, on the contrary, remained in existence in London, although such existence is of necessity precarious, failing recognition by the territorial State [1]. Is it to be supposed that, in the face of all objective evidence, it has thus remained in existence as an emigré Government forced out of its country by internal strife and as a body claiming to be the Government of Yalta-Poland in competition with the Yalta-Government?

Failing a clear pronouncement in any of the international documents quoted [2], the Polish thesis must be reconstructed from all the elements available and in the light of the above attempt at eliminating the general confusion prevailing in the Polish problem [3].

It must be observed in the first place that the Polish Government correctly denied the character of a revolution to the events in Poland. It therefore eliminated those elements on which alone a view of two competitive governments within one and the same State can be based. Moreover, by declaring that those events were not " the result of the will of the Polish people expressed either by constitutional or revolutionary means [4] ", it implicity admitted the internationally legal and internally law-creating character of a genuine revolution against which its own legal title would have had to yield. Thus, contrary to widespread opinion [5], the Polish Government's claim to unimpaired legal standing was not based on its own legality under Polish constitutional law alone, nor on the illegality of the events in Poland under that law, but on their illegality under international law. The recurrent emphasis of the Polish Government on its own legality, combined with its implicit acknowledgment of the right to revolution, was therefore obviously made not in opposition to a revolutionary movement in Poland, but to the internationally illegal acts of intervention.

More particularly, the complete by-passing in the Yalta decision and in its implementation of the existing Polish State was stressed. Even prior to Yalta, in the Polish Prime Minister's Memorandum to the American Ambassador in Moscow of October 1944, the possible acceptance of the then Soviet demands had been qualified as the " destruction of the legal foundations of the Polish Republic [6] ". Following the Yalta Conference, the fact of the Polish State having been ignored by its decision was made the subject of a protest to the British Government [7]. The Polish Ambassador's Note to the British Foreign Secretary following the formation of the Yalta-Government qualified the proceedings as the suppression of Polish independence [8].

---

1. See Flory, *op. cit.*, pp. 262-264. It may be observed that that existence did make itself effectively felt in Britain at the occasion of the liquidation of the Polish Army, see above, p. 522.
2. See above, pp. 495-496 and 503-505.
3. See above, pp. 531-533.
4. See above, p. 504.
5. Cf. Lauterpacht, above, p. 494.
6. See above, p. 474, *f.-n.* 2.
7. See above, p. 496.
8. See above, pp. 504-505.

Finally, in its appeal to the Nation of June 26, 1945, on the eve of its de-recognition by the Western Powers, the Polish Government declared :

" To-day, over the charred remains of the Polish Republic an entirely new body is to be constituted, without the frontiers which are due to Poland, without legal and constitutional continuity, deprived of the traditions in which Poland lived and thrived for a thousand years... "

It must therefore be concluded that the Polish thesis too, takes its stand on a change not of government, but of State. It must further be concluded that the Polish Government in London has remained in existence not as an independent subject of international law with no relation to any State whatever, nor as a competitive organ of Yalta-Poland, but as the continuing organ of the continuing Polish Republic. Consequently, the Polish thesis of continuity cannot mean a continuity of government since, failing any internal strife, such a problem cannot even arise by any standards, internal or international. It can only mean the continuation of the old, physically displaced Polish Republic, of which the Government in London is no more than an organ. It is on behalf of that Polish Republic, which had gone to war against Germany in 1939, that the Polish Government acted throughout the period, and it is the continued legal existence of that Republic which is being claimed from the Polish side.

The question must now be asked : on what basis is this claim advanced ?

As has just been seen, unlike the Czechoslovak thesis after 1939 the constitutional law of Poland has hardly been relied on. Moreover, again unlike the Czechoslovak thesis, it was never asserted from the Polish side that the Polish territories were under belligerent occupation by the Soviet Union.

There thus only remains the principle *ex iniuria ius non oritur* as the basis of the Polish claim. It has been seen that the Polish Government in London — at that time the uncontested and generally recognized organ of the Polish Republic — had formulated the strongest protest against the Yalta decision and its actual implementation, refusing to recognize their validity. Consequently, to the Polish Republic, as represented by its Government acting through the diplomatic missions, the illegal acts committed against Poland and their consequences are null and void [1], and therefore unable to extinguish the legal existence of the Republic.

This Polish thesis is maintained by the Polish Government in exile and its still existing and recognized diplomatic missions [2], both claiming the character of continuing organs of the Polish Republic, by the entire large and highly organized Polish community in exile which, like the Balts, refuses to accept the *faits accomplis* in Poland, and is shared by the six million Americans of Polish descent represented in Congress. It has been upheld throughout all the post-Yalta years with the utmost

1. See below, pp. 558-561.
2. See below, p. 537.

consistency, but against truly overwhelming odds : withdrawal of recognition by the great majority of States, ineffectiveness in the home country, and the destructive influence of the time factor. It may therefore be legitimately asked whether this Polish thesis still has a place in international law, or whether it merely belongs to the category of legally irrelevant acts of faith.

4. CONTINUITY OF THE POLISH REPUBLIC.

a) *Continued International Recognition.*

Notwithstanding the formation of the Yalta-Government, the Polish Government in London continued to enjoy international recognition by a number of States for a certain period of time, and it continues to be recognized even to-day, although the number of recognizing States has become much more limited.

Within the British Commonwealth of Nations, only Canada recognized the Yalta-Government practically simultaneously with Great Britain, on July 6, 1945. Australia continued to recognize the Polish Government in London until November 1, 1945, while the corresponding date for New Zealand was December 17, 1945. South Africa continued recognition until May 9, 1946, i.e. nearly a year longer than Great Britain. The same slow process took place in South America. The Argentine Government continued recognition until June 20, 1946, and Uruguay, Paraguay and Bolivia were still recognizing the Polish Government in June 1948.

By reason of such continued recognition the Polish Government was able to continue validly to perform acts on behalf of the Polish Republic, e.g. protests against the frontier agreement between the Soviet Union and the Yalta-Government of August 16, 1945, against the sending of Soviet troops into Poland in October 1945, and against the omission from the Nurnberg indictment of German crimes in Poland. To-day, the Polish Government continues to be recognized by Cuba, Eire, the Lebanon, Spain and the Vatican. Polish diplomatic and consular missions continue to function in those countries and, what is somewhat curious, they have official dealings with the missions of those States who have themselves recognized the Yalta-Government. In the Vatican, in particular, it is the Polish Ambassador who is the Doyen of the Diplomatic Corps, performing on behalf of that Corps all the functions connected with his office. Passports issued or prolonged by Polish consular missions in those countries enjoy full recognition, although such passports are not recognized by States recognizing the Yalta-Government.

This recognition by a limited number of States of the continued existence of the Polish Republic (it has been seen that the recognition of the Government cannot, under existing circumstances, mean anything else) is based on their non-recognition of the illegal acts which had been committed against Poland. The object of this recognition is a

State whose legal order is no longer effective, but whose effectiveness was not displaced by any legal process under international law [1]. It is therefore conform to the basic principles of the latter [2].

b) *Recent Developments.*

Notwithstanding the above instances of continued international recognition, the assertion of a continued legal existence of the Polish Republic, based solely on the illegal nature of the acts which had displaced it and which had been effectively implemented ten years ago, would seem to border on unreality in view of existing facts. However illegal the original acts, setting up Yalta-Poland, it could be asserted that the principle *ex factis ius oritur* has had ample time to prevail over the principle *ex iniuria ius non oritur*, which is the one and only possible basis for such an assertion.

However, seen against the background of recent State practice with regard to the question of State extinction or continuity following illegal acts, the problem loses a considerable amount of its *prima facie* unreality. For the assertion of the legal continuity of Austria or Czechoslovakia during the period of their effective physical displacement must have seemed neither more nor less unreal, and yet that principle fully carried the day in the final solution.

For this reason the investigation of the extinction or continuity of the Polish Republic must take place not in an artificial isolation, presupposing that international law has come to a standstill in its development, but against the background of the recent State practice in analogous cases.

Of these cases, the continuity of Czechoslovakia, Albania and Austria was finally re-asserted in the ultimate State practice despite the fact of their previous physical displacement and general de-recognition.

It will be recalled that in the case of Czechoslovakia, such final re-assertion took place after a period of effective physical displacement, general international de-recognition, and a complete break in the continuity of her supreme State organs. The physical displacement of Czechoslovakia was not even met by an internationally valid act of protest emanating from internationally competent organs which would have had the capacity of qualifying the illegal acts committed against her as null and void, and of reserving her rights [3]. The re-creation of the Czechoslovak State organs in exile took place in a completely unorthodox manner. Yet, the Czechoslovak Government was finally recognized and, what is more, recognized precisely as the organ of the displaced Czechoslovak State (and not of the Protectorate). It should be added that this recognition took place under the same conditions of Czechoslovak non-effectiveness on Czechoslovak territory as had apparently warranted the de-recognition of that State. The subsequent effective restoration of the Czechoslovak Republic was effected on the basis of her continuity.

---

1. See above, p. 414.
2. See above, pp. 413-414.
3. See above, p. 306.

Albanian continuity was re-asserted following her total disappearance from the international scene for a number of years.

Similarly, Austria's eclipse following the Anschluss was complete. This did not prevent a de-recognition of the Anschluss by the same Powers who had recognized it, under conditions of unchanged effectiveness of German domination, nor the final assertion of Austrian continuity following Germany's defeat.

On the assumption of the Italian domination of Ethiopia having passed the stage of mere belligerent occupation, the latter country would equally have to be included in the list.

All these States have thus survived *in extremis*, in face of their effective physical suppression, general de-recognition and a break in the continuity of their State organs. Deprived not only of effectiveness, but moreover of any outward manifestations of survival (the latter situation lasting only for a limited time in the case of Czechoslovakia), they have continued their legal existence as purely ideal notions, unprotected by any of the three customary rules bearing on the subject, on the only possible basis of the principle *ex iniuria ius non oritur*, belatedly adopted by the international community.

With regard to the still unsolved question of the Baltic States, their continued legal existence has been asserted on the basis of the lack of finality of the Soviet conquest, the persistance of a reasonable chance of restitution, and their continued recognition by a large number of States, such recognition being in conformity with the principle of legality.

Seen in such a perspective and against such a background, the Polish case assumes a legal reality which it could have far less easily claimed before these new developments in international law.

In the first place, the Yalta decision which forms the international basis of the physical displacement of the Polish Republic by Yalta-Poland has never received any validation on the part of Poland, either by an act of her Government or by a quasi-revolutionary act of her population which could have found expression in genuine elections of an internationally validating character [1]. Nor was it allowed to pass unchallenged. On the contrary, both the Yalta decision and its implementation were denied any validity by what was still the internationally recognized competent organ of the Polish State, acting within the framework of normal international procedure. The de-recognition of that State has never become complete, as it is still accepted by a part, however small, of the international community. Nor was there any break in the continuity of the State organs, since both the Government and its recognized diplomatic missions continued in existence and carried on the legal continuity of the State. The importance of these surviving organs should not, however, be overestimated : their existence can never be a source, nor even a *conditio sine qua non* of Poland's continuity ; it can merely be an outward manifestation of that continuity which — failing the

1. For the validation of the creation of a puppet State by that same puppet State, see above, p. 505.

applicability of any of the three customary rules — can only proceed from the same principle which had been instrumental in preserving the continuity of Czechoslovakia, Albania, Austria and — possibly — Ethiopia : the principle of the inability of illegal acts to produce legal effects.

The legal position of the Polish Republic is therefore not weaker, and in some respects even stronger, than had been the position of the above-mentioned States during the period of what has been termed their existence as ideal notions. Nor is it weakened by the fact that, instead of being directly annexed by the Soviet Union, the Polish Republic was displaced by Yalta-Poland. Indeed, such direct annexation on the Austrian pattern would perhaps make for a simpler picture, by avoiding a considerable amount of confusion. But it has been seen that neither the existence nor the international recognition of the Protectorate or Slovakia on the territory of the Czechoslovak Republic, of Croatia on Yugoslav territory, of an Italian-engineered Albanian puppet on Albanian territory, had prevented the restoration of the original States on the basis of their continuity. The Protectorate, Slovakia and Croatia disappeared from the international scene without leaving a trace, even in the practice of those countries which had recognized them and had relations with them. The disappearance of the Albanian puppet, on the other hand, was declared *expressis verbis* in the Italian Peace Treaty and provided the occasion for the formulation of the first international norm outlawing puppet entities [1].

Thus, the actual situation of the Polish Republic is certainly not *per se* a proof of its extinction. Yet, the fact remains that, unlike the States mentioned above and like the Baltic States, no restoration of the Polish Republic has so far taken place and, consequently, the question of its continuity cannot be discussed against the background of an effective solution. In the meantime, the divorce between legality and effectiveness in Poland's case has already lasted for ten years. The question must therefore be asked whether, as in the Baltic case, there still exists any such reasonable chance of restitution as would make possible the denial of an extinction of the Polish Republic and the assertion of the possibility of its restoration on the basis of its continuity.

c) *Chance of Restitution.*

As in the case of the Baltic States, the Soviet domination of Poland through the instrumentality of a puppet State, is being maintained against the background of the gravest international instability. But here the analogy ends : for, whereas the Soviet domination of the Baltic States has its source in unilateral illegal Soviet acts and is being met by a strong opposition on the part of the international community, a similar domination of Poland finds its basis in an international agreement to which the United States of America and the United Kingdom were parties, and has been generally admitted by the international community, by means of the recognition of Yalta-Poland.

---

1. See above, pp. 336-337.

Despite the undoubted illegality of the Yalta decision, its implementation could have become so consolidated as finally to prevail over the ineffective legal rights of the Polish Republic. However, far from such consolidation taking place, the Yalta agreement, constituting the formal basis of Yalta-Poland's existence, is in the very process of being undermined.

The first intimation of a possible American retreat from the Yalta agreements occurred on the occasion of the signature of the Japanese Peace Treaty. Contrary to the stipulations of the section of the Yalta decisions dealing with the Far East and providing unconditionally for a transfer to the Soviet Union of the Southern Sakhalin and the Kurile Islands, the Japanese Peace Treaty did not effect any such transfer, confining itself to a mere renunciation by Japan of her sovereignty over those territories. In defending that solution at the San Francisco Conference of September 1951, Mr. Foster Dulles declared :

" Some Allied Powers suggested that Article 2 should not merely delimit Japanese sovereignty according to Potsdam, but specify precisely the ultimate disposition of each of the ex-Japanese territories. This, admittedly, would have been neater. But it would have raised questions as to which there are now no agreed answers. We had either to give Japan peace on the Potsdam surrender terms or deny peace to Japan while the Allies quarrel about what shall be done with what Japan is prepared, and required, to give up [1]. "

Already at that time it was thus made clear that the United States did not consider itself bound by the Yalta provisions. This point was made even clearer in a subsequent statement by Mr. Foster Dulles in which he answered Soviet charges against the Japanese Treaty :

" As regards South Sakhalin and the Kurile Islands, the treaty carries out the provisions of the Potsdam surrender terms, the only agreement by which Japan and the Allied Powers as a whole are bound. So long as other Governments have rights under the Yalta Agreement which the Soviet Union has not fulfilled, there is at least question as to whether the Soviet Union can, with " clean hands " demand fulfilment of the parts of that agreement it likes [2]. "

According to this statement, which is of the greatest importance for the problem under discussion, the reason for the American attitude is to be found in the non-fulfilment by the Soviet Union of her part of obligations under the Yalta agreement. It is therefore on the principle *inadimplenti non est adimplendum* that the United States, without so far expressly retreating from the agreement, proclaimed her freedom of movement with regard to it. But even more important is the second conclusion of the statement : namely, the part of the Yalta agreement which, according to Mr. Foster Dulles, the Soviet Union has failed to carry out, has nothing to do with its Japanese section, but, according to official declarations of the United States, it is precisely the Polish section and, in particular, as regards the Polish elections [3]. It is therefore of particular interest to note that the United States consider the Yalta decisions as one inseparable whole, so that a violation by one contracting

---

1. *Dept. of St. Bul.*, vol. XXV, pp. 454-455.
2. *Ibid.*, p. 462.
3. See above, p. 506, *f.-n.* 4.

party of a single provision of these decisions gives the other party the right to apply the sanction of a non-application of, or even withdrawal from, the agreement. Consequently, any action undertaken by any contracting party with regard to this agreement must be understood as affecting the whole of it.

It is in the light of this American interpretation that the Resolution of the United States Senate, of March 20, 1952, consenting to the ratification of the Peace Treaty with Japan must be read :

" As part of such advice and consent the Senate states that nothing the treaty contains is deemed to diminish or prejudice, in favor of the Soviet Union, the right, title, and interest of Japan, or the Allied Powers as defined in said treaty, in and to the South Sakhalin and its adjacent islands, the Kurile Islands, the Habomai Islands, the island of Shikotan, or any other territory, rights, or interests possessed by Japan on December 7, 1941, or to confer any right, title, or benefit therein or thereto on the Soviet Union ; and also that nothing in the said treaty, or the advice and consent of the Senate to the ratification thereof, implies recognition on the part of the United States of the provisions in favor of the Soviet Union contained in the so-called " Yalta agreement " regarding Japan of February 11 1945 [1]. "

In other words, the United States Senate has repudiated one part of the Yalta agreement which, according to the declared American opinion, forms one indivisible whole.

Whatever the implications of the above Resolution, the problem of a direct and clear repudiation, of the Yalta agreement, particularly its European part, was taken up again during the American electoral campaign in 1952. The relevant passages of the Republican Party's campaign platform criticized the foreign policy of the previous American administration and stated :

" ... They abandoned friendly nations such as Latvia, Lithuania, Estonia, Poland and Czechoslovakia to fend for themselves against the Communist aggression which soon swallowed them. ... they flouted our peace-assuring pledges such as the Atlantic Charter, and did so in favour of despots, who, it was well known, consider that murder, terror, slavery, concentration camps and the ruthless and brutal denial of human rights are legitimate means to their desired ends.

Teheran, Yalta, and Potsdam were the scenes of those tragic blunders with others to follow. The leaders of the Administration in power acted without the knowledge or consent of Congress or of the American people. They traded our overwhelming victory for a new enemy and for new oppressions and new wars which were quick to come.

... *The Government of the United States, under Republican leadership, will repudiate all commitments contained in secret understandings such as those of Yalta which aid Communist enslavements.* It will be made clear, on the highest authority of the President and the Congress, that United States policy, as one of its peaceful purposes, looks happily forward to the genuine independence of those captive peoples [2]. "

In the course of the electoral campaign, on October 11, 1952, General Eisenhower gave a specific pledge to Americans of Polish descent to repudiate the Yalta agreement [3].

---

1. *Dept. of St. Bul.*, vol. XXVI, p. 688.
2. *It. mine, New York Times*, July 11, 1952.
3. *New York Times*, October 12, 1952.

While the above statements were no more than electoral promises and could, as such, in no way bind the United States in the international field, no such limitations apply any longer to official statements of the highest American authority now in power. On February 2, 1953, President Eisenhower delivered his first message on the State of the Union in which he said :

" We shall never acquiesce in the enslavement of any people in order to purchase fancied gain for ourselves. I shall ask the Congress at a later date to join in an appropriate resolution making clear that this Government recognizes no kind of commitment contained in secret undertakings of the past with foreign Governments which permit this kind of enslavement [1]. "

While the Yalta decisions were not expressly mentioned, there is no doubt whatever that it was precisely these decisions which were envisaged [2].

At the time of writing no formal American repudiation has yet taken place, and it is not the task of this study to speculate whether, when and in what form it will be effected. There can, however, be no doubt that the present American administration has officially committed itself to an anti-Yalta policy within the wider framework of what has been called a " liberation policy " with regard to the Soviet-dominated countries of Central and Eastern Europe. In such a policy, indeed, the Yalta agreement, confirming precisely " the enslavement of a people " can logically have no place.

This view seems to be further reinforced by the recent pronouncements of those responsible for American foreign policy. In his by now famous speech of April 16, 1953, President Eisenhower included the following principles among the " few clear precepts " which govern United States conduct in world affairs :

" Third : Any nation's right to a form of government and an economic system of its own choosing is inalienable.
Fourth : Any nation's attempt to dictate to other nations their form of government is indefensible [3]. "

Speaking of the issues now dividing the world, the President declared :

" None of these issues, great or small, is insoluble — given only the will to respect the rights of all nations [4]. "

Finally, when speaking of a " broader European community ", President Eisenhower stated in quite concrete terms :

" This community and the full independence of the East European nations could mean the end of the present unnatural division of Europe. Is it (the new leadership of the Soviet Union) prepared to allow other nations, including those in Eastern Europe, the free choice of their own form of government [5]? "

---

1. *The Times*, February, 3 1953.
2. See e.g. the comment from the Washington Correspondent of *The Times*. " This was the " repudiation of Yalta " promised in the Republican platform. " *Ibid.*
3. *New York Times*, April 17, 1953.
4. *Ibid.*
5. *Ibid.*

Developing this theme, Secretary Dulles stated on the following day :

" ... one of the illusions against which we must be most on our guard is *the illusion of a settlement based upon the status quo.* The present status involves the captivity of hundreds of millions of persons of distinct nationalities, race, religions and culture. The hardest task that the Soviet rulers have is to beat this disunity into Communist conformity. If that could be done, then the menace of Soviet communism would immeasurably increase, for such successes are never accepted as satisfying, but they merely whet the appetite for more.

It was of the utmost importance that we should make clear to the captive people that *we do not accept their captivity as a permanent fact of history.* If they thought otherwise and became hopeless, we would unwittingly have become partners to the forging of a hostile power which could encompass our destruction.

President Eisenhower, anticipating some of the events that have occurred, acted immediately after his inauguration to propose that our national position should be made clear through a solemn resolution concurred in by the Congress and the President. The Congress has yet to act. However, I am persuaded, and I trust that the captive peoples are also persuaded that Congress in fact fully shares the view that President Eisenhower has expressed. In any event, the Chief Executive has formulated his position on this important matter, and by doing so has foreclosed another of the hopes which Soviet rulers may have optimistically entertained [1]. "

There is thus a considerable chance of an American withdrawal from, and repudiation of, the Yalta agreement. It has been seen that, whatever the original unilateral acts of the Soviet Union, Yalta-Poland has its reason of validity in an agreed delegation of the three Yalta-Powers. With the disappearance of the Yalta agreement, this reason of validity itself disappears. Apart from destroying such existing reason of validity, an American repudiation of Yalta would, failing a legal vacuum, mean an American return to her pre-Yalta position with regard to the Polish problem.

Should the destruction of Yalta-Poland's reason of validity, automatically combined with the re-assertion of the *status quo* by the United States in fact take place, it would certainly not work wonders by itself, failing an effective restoration of that *status quo*. Nor is there any certainty that, even if such repudiation were to materialize, an effective change of the actual situation in Poland would necessarily follow at all. But it is submitted that, in eliminating the international foundation of that situation, it would make the chance of a Polish *ad integrum restitutio* stronger than it has ever been since the Yalta decision and that it would thereby weaken the impact of the time factor on Polish continuity.

These things may, or may not, happen. Yet, whatever happens, it can already now be stated that the Polish problem has been internationally re-opened after a period of merely apparent finality. The international consensus on the present status of Poland which is the basis of the actual situation, in fact, no longer exists. It is submitted that already at the present stage the destructive influence of the time factor on the Polish Republic's continuity has been seriously weakened by the general reversal of that historical and political trend which had formed the background of the Yalta decision.

---

1. *It. mine, ibid.*, April 19, 1953.

In the light of the preceding analysis, the assertion of the continued legal existence of the Polish Republic appears to carry far more weight than might have been assumed at first. There is certainly no more, but also no less, to be said with regard to Poland than was said with regard to the Baltic States. In spite of the effective establishment of puppet entities in their respective territories, none of these States has yet become extinct, although they continue as purely ideal legal notions. As in the Baltic case, the existing continuity of the Polish Republic which is claimed from the Polish side and recognized by certain members of the international community and which the United States would no longer appear to be so reluctant to admit in principle, can be no more than a temporary phenomenon in the prevailing conditions of divorce between legal title and effectiveness. As such, it may well finally give way and become extinct, if every reasonable chance of a *restitutio ad integrum* disappears, or if such restitution does not effectively take place within some reasonable time. If that happens, then Yalta-Poland, arising historically and legally out of the German-Soviet partition of Poland of 1939, taken up as the basis of Soviet acts of intervention in the years 1943-1945 and internationally confirmed at Yalta, will have survived and finally asserted itself as a political, historical and legal reality. If, however, far from disappearing, a chance of restitution grows and finally materializes, then the still persisting Polish continuity will have served to safeguard the rights and obligations of the Polish Republic under international law, and a restoration of Polish independence will mean not the creation of yet another new Polish State to follow the present puppet entity, but a recovery by Poland of her international status which she will never have lost.

PART III.

CHAPTER I.

RE-STATEMENT OF THE PROBLEM AND CLASSIFICATION OF THE CASES EXAMINED.

The present enquiry into the problem of the identity and continuity of States, defined as identity and continuity of their international rights and obligations, is now drawing to its close. At this stage a summary of the results obtained is called for.

It may be recalled that the importance of the problem lies in the fact that it affects the very existence of States, being only another aspect of the problem of State extinction [1]. Bearing on the life and death of States it cannot, and does not, arise in normal and settled conditions, but only as a result of an event or a combination of events which interfere with a State's normal existence so gravely as to justify an initial doubt as to its survival [2]. The problem can therefore be discussed only on the assumption that States share the mortality of all things human [3]. The aim of this study has been to discover precisely which of such events finally break their continuity and spell their extinction, and out of which the States affected emerge intact in their international status [4].

A survey of the existing norms on the subject has shown that international law fully protects the continued existence of States in three well-defined cases : namely, territorial changes, revolution and belligerent occupation. In all these cases, the identity and continuity of States is protected by fully crystallized positive rules.

The very fact that international law affirms the identity and continuity of States in these three cases, combined with the denial of the immortality of States, shows that international law does not protect the continued existence of States always and in every case. For neither international law itself, nor the international reality which it regulates, are static phenomena. While safeguarding State existence in certain, well-defined cases, international law admits and recognizes State extinction, and, moreover, not only as a result of a legal settlement, e.g. union, but also as a result of such events which destroy the entire existing international delimitation of the State affected.

1. See above, p. 1.
2. See above, p. 4.
3. See above, p. 6.
4. See above, p. 14.

However, in spite of this realistic and necessary admission, it would appear that international law is basically reluctant lightly to admit the extinction of a State [1]. This reluctance, while relatively easily explained in case of territorial or revolutionary changes, assumes a striking character in the case of belligerent occupation, where the refusal to admit such extinction is upheld to the point of dispensing with the otherwise preponderant principle of effectiveness, — that is, where international law maintains the legal existence of a totally occupied State as a purely ideal notion.

Such reluctance is easily understood in the light of the very nature of international law, based as it is on the co-existence of separate independent States, and inconceivable without such basis [2]. It is additionally explained by its natural tendency to provide for a maximum amount of security in international legal relations. This latter principle, which has been seen to be at the root of the first two customary rules investigated [3] postulates a reasonable stability of existing international rights and obligations. The abrupt discontinuity of such rights and obligations by State extinction is, failing universal succession, only partly remedied by such partial succession as may exist. Seen from this angle, the protection afforded to States by international law is not only in their own interest, but in that of the international community as a whole [4].

It would thus appear that, although States cannot claim immortality under international law, their extinction is neither easily presumed nor lightly accepted.

It is in the light of these observations that the concrete cases, examined in Part II of this study, should now be considered.

While it is true that practically every one of these cases arose under different circumstances of fact, yet they all fall naturally into two groups : cases which are covered by the existing norms of international law, and those which are not. In the first group, the proper ascertainment of facts and the correct application of rules provided the answer to the question of the continuity or extinction of the States concerned. In the second group, no such rules were available.

This being the position, two courses were theoretically open to the writer : the first consisted in stating the absence of any protective rules and, consequently, in affirming the extinction of the States concerned, the emphasis being placed on their admitted mortality ; such a course would have been possible only on the clearly admitted assumption of a final petrification of international law. The second course consisted in an effort to analyze the relevant State practice — while admitting the absence of any protective rule — in order to discover

---

1. The extreme caution with which the Institut de Droit International has formulated the question will be recalled, see above, pp. 8-9.
2. See above, pp. 162-163.
3. See above, pp. 15 and 24-25.
4. " Das Völkerrecht ist eine Rechtsordnung, welche nicht den momentanen Verhältnissen zwischen zwei einzelnen Staaten, sondern dem durchschnittlichen und dauernden Wesen der Beziehungen aller Staaten zueinander entsprechen soll und auch entspricht. " Huber, Grundlagen, p. 10.

whether it contributed to any new development in international law, the emphasis being placed on the basic protection which that law affords to States ; such course must have proceeded on the assumption of international law's inherently dynamic nature. Of these two courses, this writer has adopted the second, in full awareness of its implications, and in the firm conviction that a static view of international law is contrary not only to all legal experience but also to the inherent nature of any legal system.

Moreover, on closer analysis it will be seen that the above classification of the cases examined into two groups is additionally justified by yet another criterion ; the latter is to be found in the nature of that event which had cast an initial doubt on the continued existence of the States concerned and which had thus constituted the *fons et origo* of the problem. For, in clear contradistinction to the first group, in the second group that event was invariably an illegal act. The problem therefore naturally arose whether international law which has been found to be basically reluctant to admit State extinction and which, moreover, has been found to protect State existence against such possible dangers as are not illegal *per se* — territorial changes, revolutions and belligerent occupation — whether that same international law withdraws such protection in face of an illegal act ? In other words : was it to be lightly admitted that international law does not protect the legal continuity of States against illegal acts striking at their very existence, while affording them such protection by means of fully developed rules in case of territorial changes, revolutions and belligerent occupation ? The question is all the more legitimate as the fundamental reluctance of international law lightly to admit State extinction is here reinforced by the natural resistance to illegal acts, inherent in international law as in any legal system. No such system, worthy of the name, which would abdicate its own legality is conceivable, and the principle of legality, expressed in the maxim *ex iniuria ius non oritur*, is a fundamental principle of international, as of any, law [1].

This then is the main division of the cases examined in Part II of this study, as it now emerges from the above considerations.

With regard to the first group, it is submitted that the problem can now be considered closed. For the cases of that group merely illustrate, confirm and complete what had already been subject of an extensive investigation in Part I of this study.

On the other hand, the cases of the second group call for further analysis. It has been seen that, failing any existing protective rule on the subject, it was precisely the principle of legality, *ex iniuria ius non oritur*, which was heavily relied upon in reaching a solution. Yet, whatever the weight and authority of this principle, the limitations to which it is subject precisely in international law cannot be denied, such limitations being expressed by the opposite maxim *ex factis ius oritur*. The legal continuity of the illegally overpowered States gravitates between these two antinomic principles.

---

1. See e.g. *P.C.I.J.* Ser. A 24, p. 16 ; Ser. B 15, pp. 26-27 ; Ser. A/B 48, p. 285 ; Ser. A/B 53, p. 93.

Therefore, the solution arrived at in each particular case must seem not only controversial, but clearly provisional, pending a general assessment of the State practice on which it was based, especially in the light of the above antinomy. Without such assessment this study would not be complete. It must therefore be attempted in the following concluding pages.

Chapter II.

GENERAL ASSESSMENT OF STATE PRACTICE IN CASES NOT COVERED BY EXISTING RULES.

1. The State Practice Examined.

Before any assessment of the relevant State practice can be undertaken, it must be made clear precisely which State practice is being examined. It will be remembered that in those cases in which the continued legal existence of States had become problematic as a result of illegal acts on the part of third States, the international community, generally speaking, adopted two different attitudes in the matter : it first recognized the results of the illegal acts and, consequently, the extinction of the victim States ; it then withdrew recognition from the results of the illegal act and recognized the uninterrupted continuity of the victim States.

These two attitudes are contradictory and mutually exclusive ; this is not only because the recognition of extinction and the recognition of continuity both took place in an unchanged situation of fact, i.e. effective physical suppression of the victim State in favour of the fully consolidated domination of the aggressor, — but also, because the object of eventual international recognition was not a newly created State, but a continuing State, which obviously presupposes that it had never become extinct. Consequently, the two acts of recognition, bearing on one and the same object, under identical circumstances of fact, cannot both be correct : one of them is wrong.

This contradiction cannot be solved on the basis of the constitutive theory of recognition which — contrary to all logic and even common sense — would have to accept the two acts as equally valid and equally creative of a legal situation, — that is, achieving the legal miracle of one and the same State having, and having not, become extinct. But when recognition is reduced from a miracle-working instrument to its true proportions, the choice is no longer difficult : the wrong act was obviously the earlier one. The correctness of the later attitude was fully borne out not only by the subsequent, uniform and definite State practice, often embodied in international conventions (e.g. the Italian Peace Treaty), but also by its essential conformity with the principle of legality of international law as expressed in the maxim *ex iniuria ius non oritur.* It is therefore this definite attitude which must be considered as *the* relevant State practice on the subject, and it is this attitude alone which forms the subject of the present concluding investigation.

This State practice — let it be repeated — bore on the legal continuity of States whose existence had become endangered by illegal acts to the point of their actual physical suppression for a certain period of time.

The essence of the matter thus lies in the affirmation of the legal existence of a State as a purely ideal notion. This point cannot be emphasized strongly enough. For the question does not concern a miraculous resurrection of a State which had once become extinct and has subsequently been restored, in which case the problem would not be one of State continuity, but one of a new State creation. On the contrary, the *punctum saliens* is the actual legal existence of the State *during* the actual period of its physical suppression which view alone allows the affirmation of continuity.

Such ideal existence of States had indeed more than once been maintained by judicial decisions. Thus, in the well known decision of the Roman Court of Appeal *in re Savini* it was held :

" ... a State may exist outside its natural boundaries and still preserve the character of a person in public international law in its relations with other States and particularly in its relations with the State whose hospitality it enjoys [1]. "

In the already quoted case of. *Moraitis v. Delany*, concerning a Greek sailor liable to deportation, the District Court of Maryland had to interpret a provision of the statute providing for the deportation of aliens to " the country whence they came ". In view of the occupation of Greece, the Court was faced with the question whether he could be deported to England where the exiled Greek Government was in residence. Interpreting the statute " territorially " rather than " governmentally ", the District Court decided against such deportation. This decision was overruled by the Circuit Court of Appeals which held :

" It is true, of course, that the term " country " as used in the statute must be construed, ordinarily, to refer to the territory... But a man's " country " is more than the territory in which its people live. The term is used, generally, to indicate the State, the organisation of social life which exercises sovereign power in behalf of the people. ... Ordinarily the State exercises sovereignty only within the territory occupied by its people ; but a different situation is presented when the territory is overrun by its enemies and its government is in exile in the territory of a friendly nation exercising power in international matters in behalf of its nationals. In such cases, the government in exile has taken over the only exercise of sovereign power left to the people of the country and is the only agency representing the country with which a foreign government can deal [2]. "

Consequently, by ordering the deportation of the Greek sailor concerned not to occupied Greece but to the United Kingdom, the Court implicitly upheld the existence of a State outside its borders, which had been explicitly affirmed in the *Savini* case [3].

Seen in this light, the problem raises a number of most difficult and controversial questions : in the first place, the question of the law-

---

1. A. D., 1927/28, case no. 106.
2. A. D., 1941/42, case no. 96.
3. Cf. decisions quoted above, pp. 90-91 and 95-96. Cf. Scelle : « Il peut donc... y avoir Etat et gouvernement étatique, au moins exceptionnellement, sans disposition effective d'un territoire. » *Op. cit.*, p. 87.

creating faculty of illegal acts, secondly, the question of defences — if any — which a weak legal system and a decentralized legal community can raise against them, and finally, the crucial question of effectiveness.

The relevant State practice, described above, was strongly in favour of the legal continuity of such States and, consequently, in favour of a relation of identity between the finally restored and the formerly suppressed States [1]. In so doing, it denied the law-creating faculty of illegal acts, it actively opposed them and, finally, it squarely overruled the principle of effectiveness in favour of that of validity under conditions of glaring divorce between the two. It thus ran directly counter to a number of unfortunate but real limitations of international law. This being the position, it must be asked whether such practice was unrealistic and arbitrary, or, on the contrary, realistic and law-abiding, whether it was merely incidental to a given set of political and military circumstances or whether, on the contrary, it represented a natural trend and, consequently, a lasting development in international law.

To answer this question it is necessary to review the problems thus raised.

2. The Problem of Illegal Acts.

The first problem to be examined in this connection is that of illegal acts.

a) *Illegal Acts Generally.*

Illegal acts are not something foreign and external to law. They belong to its very essence. The proper classification of illegal acts *within* the framework of a legal system constitutes the lasting achievement of the Kelsenian pure school of law.

In order to form part of a legal system — and, for that matter, of any normative system — a rule must be capable of being violated. A legal rule is subject to the category of normativity, not of causality. Normative rules do not correspond to the existing reality of fact which they do not cover with mathematical precision and certainty. If that were the case, they would cease to be normative, and become natural, laws. It is only due to the existing tension between the norms and their actual observance, to the necessary margin of their violation, that a legal system preserves its normative character. Within this necessary margin of violation, the illegal act thus turns from a " negation " of law into its integral part, representing no more and no less than the condition of putting into operation the legal mechanism of sanction [2].

---

1. « Il résulte... de la pratique récente, en relation avec la conquête de l'Ethiopie par l'Italie, avec la création des protectorats de la Bohême et de la Moravie, ainsi qu'avec la constitution des Etats fantoches de Slovaquie et de Croatie, que le droit international moderne n'est pas disposé à admettre à la légère la validation d'actes nuls et illicites. La prescription acquisitive ne peut être facilement présumée. » Guggenheim, *Validité*, p. 232.

2. Kelsen, *Reine Rechtslehre*, pp. 26-28; *Allg. Staatslehre*, pp. 51-52; *General Theory*, pp. 51-53; Guggenheim, *Lehrbuch*, I, p. 3.

To the obvious question concerning the actual extent of that necessary margin of law-breaking, Kelsen replies with the theory of the " superior " and " inferior " limit [1]. Should a legal system not be observed at all, or be observed only to an insignificant degree, then the " inferior limit " of effectiveness would be passed : there would in fact be no more law. But it would meet with exactly the same fate in case of its total and absolute observance ; should legal norms entirely correspond to existing reality to the extent of excluding the possibility of their violation, then the " superior limit " would be passed : the normative character of law would disappear in favour of causality, and law itself with it [2].

Therefore, on condition of their not assuming undue proportions, the existence and recurrence of illegal acts do not, in themselves, present any danger to international law, or, for that matter, to any legal system [3]. What does present such danger — always on the assumption of illegal acts not overstepping the admitted margin — is the absence of sanction, particularly as expressed in the law-creating capacity of such acts. It is not the existence of illegal acts which forms the supreme challenge to international law, but the possibility of their giving rise to legal titles on equal footing with lawful acts.

Consequently, in order to survive as a normative system, international law should not only lay down a theoretical distinction between a legal and an illegal act — such distinction representing the irreducible minimum of any legal order — but it should *act* on that distinction, in refusing to accept the illegal act as a legal title.

b) *Illegal Attempts against State Independence.*

It is against the background of such general considerations that the particular illegal act under discussion must be more closely examined.

This act represents a supreme attempt against the highest of the internationally protected interests of a State : its existence. It therefore represents the most drastic illegality that can be committed. At the same time, when effectively executed, it creates an effective, new repartition of territorial competences which it is nearly impossible for international law to ignore [4]. It thus appears that the illegal act in question combines in itself supreme illegality with supreme law-creating force, thus exposing the basic problem of international law in all its vulnerability.

It must be borne in mind that, as regards its contents, the illegal act under discussion does not stand alone in international law and

---

1. *Allg. Staatslehre*, pp. 18-19 ; *General Theory*, p. 120.
2. Thus, on the assumption of the possibility of a perfect human society, the " withering away " of State and law in the Marxist system is just as correct a proposition as Ovid's Golden Age which " *sine lege fidem rectumque colebat* ".
3. With this proviso, the following opinion of Prof. Lauterpacht correctly reflects the position : " ...the validity of the law is not dependent upon its actual observance in any given set of circumstances, just as the validity of grammar is not dependent upon our compliance with its rules in any given case. " *Op. cit.*, p. 427.
4. See below, p. 565.

relations. On the contrary, it takes its place alongside a war of conquest and debellatio from which it cannot in substance be distinguished. Both these attempts against the existence of a State confront international law with the same problem : that of their admissibility. Is it to be assumed that the same international law which is fundamentally inclined to protect the existence of its subjects, admits of their violent destruction, or that it tolerates no minor frontier violation but allows a total suppression of a State [1] ?

The classical recognition of an effective debellatio undoubtedly proceeded from an open or tacit admission of the legality of war itself, this in turn proceeding from the practical impossibility of its prohibition[2]. But, whatever views may be held on the highly controversial question of the legality or otherwise of " official " war, no shadow of legality can be claimed for that attempt against the existence of a State which is now being examined. For it has been seen that in every single case investigated such attempt was made by the aggressor State in clear violation of his conventional obligations.

Ever since the Covenant of the League of Nations, the general tendency of international law has been to eliminate or, at least, to limit the traditional " legal " phenomenon of war. It is a somewhat unexpected tribute to the strength and consistency of this tendency to find that, since to wage an open war has become something at least bordering on clear illegality, the aggressors of the period resorted to acts of violence against other States while denying the existence of war, — in other words, that they substituted for an official war a " war in disguise [3] ". This being the position, it is hardly to be supposed that the same international law which sought to outlaw the traditionally " legal " war would passively submit to an undoubtedly illegal " war in disguise ", or that — the essence of the two being the same — such phenomena, essentially disruptive and subversive of the international legal order, were to be checked in one of their forms and left entirely unchecked in the other.

---

1. " No State would be entitled to a limited interference in the sphere of interests of another State, but every State would be fully justified in committing an unlimited interference in such a sphere. ...This is similar to a social order according to which petty thievery is punished while armed robbery goes free. " Kelsen, *General Theory*, p. 340. It is on the basis of this fundamental doubt bearing on the alleged unlimited freedom of States to resort to war that Professors Kelsen and Guggenheim have put forward a new and, in relation to the old theological concept, secularized theory of *bellum iustum*. See Kelsen, *op. cit.*, pp. 328-331 and 340, and Guggenheim, *Lehrbuch*, I, p. 591. This immense and crucial problem cannot possibly be discussed here, although the writer's doubts as to the possibility of such construction and its practical workability should be recorded. Cf. Prof. Kelsen himself, *op. cit.*, pp. 336-338 and 341. See also the criticism by Kunz, *Bellum Iustum and Bellum Legale*, A. J., 1951, pp. 528-534.

2. " Some writers deny that international law recognizes conquest as a mode of acquiring territory, and other propose that it should not do so in future. But though it is a mark of the law's weakness that it recognizes title by conquest, it is inevitable that it should do so, as long as it is unable to prohibit the war altogether. " Brierly, *Law of Nations*, p. 94. For the theory of the legality of war, see Liszt, *op. cit.*, p. 445, Fauchille, *op. cit.*, II, pp. 7-8, Scelle, *op. cit.*, p. 846, Rivier, *op. cit.*, II, p. 201 ; for the theory of war as " legally indifferent ", see Oppenheim-Lauterpacht, *op. cit.*, II, pp. 201-202. See also Prof. Guggenheim's pertinent criticisms of the " *Indifferenztheorie* ", *op. cit.*, II, pp. 591-592.

3. Kunz, *op. cit.*, p. 333.

Faced with this new challenge, international law responded with the policy of non-recognition.

3. NON-RECOGNITION.

a) *Historical Development.*

The policy of non-recognition of territorial conquest can apply to the seizure of a part or of the whole of a State's territory. It is clear that the problem of State continuity or extinction is involved only in the latter case.

The beginning of this movement is usually associated with the Stimson doctrine [1], although it would be more accurate to trace it back to Art. 10 of the Covenant [2]. Yet, the conception of such non-recognition had not been absent from international law previously ; for it was the duty of third States not to recognize premature annexation. The modern policy of non-recognition would therefore seem to be well rooted in traditional international law ; moreover, it serves to confirm the natural analogy between war and the illegal seizure of a State territory without war mentioned above. This analogy is now seen to extend equally to the consequences of the two acts : for just as the illegal attempt against the existence of States is in substance equivalent to war, so the non-recognition of its results is modelled on the non-recognition of premature annexation.

Nevertheless, it is true to say that the movement received its greatest impetus from the famous statement of the United States Secretary of State. It was in the Notes of January 7, 1932, addressed to the governments of China and Japan that Mr. Stimson declared :

" The American Government ... cannot admit the legality of any situation *de facto* nor does it intend to recognize any treaty or agreement entered into between those Governments, or agents thereof, which may impair the treaty rights of the United States or its citizens in China, including those which relate to the sovereignty, the independence or the territorial or administrative integrity of the Republic of China, or to the international policy relative to China, commonly known as the open-door policy ; and that it does not intend to recognize any situation, treaty or agreement which may be brought about by means contrary to the covenants and obligations of the Pact of Paris of August 27th, 1928, to which Treaty both China and Japan, as well as the United States are parties ."

There can be little doubt that the famous resolution of the League of Nations' Assembly of March 11, 1932, bearing on non-recognition [3] was directly inspired by the Stimson declaration.

It is, however, chiefly on the American continent that the doctrine gained particular strength and momentum. From the consistency of that development, from the number and weight of successive conventional provisions as well as from the consistent American practice, it can be legitimately deduced that the non-recognition of

---

1. For non-recognition generally see Sharp, *Non-Recognition as a Legal Obligation ;* also Lauterpacht, *op. cit.,* pp. 409-435 ; Chen, *op. cit.,* pp. 411-443, and Langer, *op. cit.,* pp. 34-39 and 95-117.
2. See above, pp. 271-272 and Guggenheim, *Validité,* p. 228.
3. See above, p. 272.

illegal acts of territorial conquest and their consequences has grown
into a regional customary law which would henceforth survive even the
absence of its original conventional basis.

This consistent development, dating back to 1826,[1] has again and
again been embodied in recent American conventions. Thus, the
Anti-War (Saavedra Lamas) Treaty, signed in Rio de Janeiro on
on October 10, 1933, stipulates :

" They declare that as between the High Contracting Parties territorial
questions must not be settled by violence, and that they will not recognize any
territorial arrangement which is not obtained by pacific means, nor the validity
of an occupation or acquisition of territory that may be brought about by force [2]. "
(Art. 2.)

The Montevideo Convention on the Rights and Duties of States,
of December 26, 1933, declares :

" The Contracting States definitely establish as the norm of their conduct
the precise obligation not to recognize territorial acquisitions or special advantages
which have been obtained by force, whether this consists in the employment of
arms, in threatening diplomatic representations, or in any other coercive
measure [3]. " (Art. 11.)

The Act of Chapultepec of March 8, 1945, declares :

" 5. The American States have been incorporating in their international
law, since 1890, by means of conventions, resolutions and declarations, the following
principles :

a) The prescription of territorial conquest and the non-recognition of all
acquisitions made by force [4]... "

This was re-affirmed in the Treaty of Petropolis (Rio de Janeiro)
of September 2, 1947 :

" ... the High Contracting Parties re-affirm their adherence to the principles
of Inter-American solidarity and co-operation, and especially to those set forth in
the preamble and declarations of the Act of Chapultepec, all of which should be
understood to be accepted as standards of their mutual relations and as the juridical
basis of the Inter-American System...[5]. "

Finally, the Charter of the Organisation of American States of
Bogota, of March 30 — May 2, 1948, declared :

" The territory of a State is inviolable ; it may not be the object, even
temporarily, of military occupation or of other measures of force taken by another
State, directly or indirectly, on any grounds whatever. No territorial acquisitions
or special advantages obtained either by force or by other means of coercion shall
be recognized [6]. " (Art. 17.)

These American conventional provisions go much further in
establishing the principle than did the original Stimson doctrine. For,

---

1. For history, see Sharp, *op. cit.*, pp. 75-90.
2. Hudson, *International Legislation*, VI, p. 448.
3. *Ibid.*, p. 623.
4. *U. N. Textbook*, p. 283.
5. *Ibid.*, pp. 286-287.
6. *Ibid.*, pp. 294-295.

while the latter proclaimed non-recognition of acts contrary to certain well-determined conventional obligations, the former cover any illegal act of violence affecting an independent State generally.

In spite of the failure of the policy of collective non-recognition in the unfortunate case of Manchukuo, it was precisely non-recognition with which third States again opposed — though at different stages — the forcible suppression of States in Europe. It would therefore seem that non-recognition has become the established policy of law-abiding States in face of an illegal attempt against the territorial integrity and independence of another State. It must therefore be asked what is the true legal meaning and function of non-recognition — whether it be a unilateral declaration of policy or a legal obligation resulting from a convention, — and what are its possibilities of offering effective resistance to illegal acts.

b) *Legal Significance of Non-Recognition.*

Non-recognition was conceived as a sanction of an illegal act. Since this by itself does not contain a sufficient indication of its content, the question arises : how exactly does it penalize the wrongdoer?

Before answering this question, it is necessary to point out that whatever legal force there is in non-recognition, does not result from its constitutive powers, — non-recognition being just as little miracle-working as recognition. Such legal force attaches to non-recognition because, far from being aimed at a *legal* act or situation, i.e. being itself an unlawful intervention, it is aimed at an *illegal* act or situation and is therefore expressive of the very nature of international law [1].

It is because of this conformity with international law that non-recognition is capable of performing its true legal function which is : to qualify the illegal act as null and void, thus destroying its law-creating faculty, and thereby to uphold and preserve those rights which have been violated [2].

In order fully to appreciate this function of non-recognition, it is necessary to bear in mind the traditional classification of irregular acts which consists in distinguishing between an illegal act *sensu stricto* and an act which is null and void.

According to traditional doctrine, illegal acts *sensu stricto* consist in actual violation of a superior norm, whereas acts which are null and void are characterized by the absence of certain elements necessary for their validity, such as a competent party, a proper object, true consent and valid form [3]. In the case of illegal acts the sanction consists in the international responsibility of the law-breaker, expressed in the duty

---

1. See above, pp. 413-414.
2. Thus Lauterpacht : " This construction of non-recognition is based on the view that acts contrary to international law are invalid and cannot become a source of legal rights for the wrongdoer. That view applies to international law one the " general principles of law recognized by civilized nations. " The principle *ex iniuria ius non oritur* is one of the fundamental maxims of jurisprudence. An illegality cannot, as a rule, become a source of legal right to the wrongdoer. " *Op. cit.*, p. 420.
3. Anzilotti, *op. cit.*, p. 339. For an exposition of the traditional theory see Guggenheim, *Validité*, pp. 198-199.

to make reparation, while the result of the illegal act is — as a rule — allowed to stand, its law-creating capacity thus being acknowledged [1]. Only in the case of acts null and void the sanction consists in the refusal to admit the validity of the situation brought about by the irregular act.

The classical formulation of this view is to be found in Judge Anzilotti's Dissenting Opinion in the *Eastern Greenland* case :

" ... the Court could not have declared the occupation invalid, if the term " invalid " signifies " null and void ". A legal act is only non-existent if it lacks certain elements which are essential to its existence. Such would be the occupation of territory belonging to another State, because the status of a *terra nullius* is an essential factor to enable the occupation to serve as a means of acquiring territorial sovereignty. But this does not hold good in the case of the occupation of a *terra nullius* by a sovereign State in conformity with international law, merely because the occupying State had undertaken not to occupy it. Accordingly, it would have been for the Norwegian Government to revoke the occupation unlawfully carried out, without prejudice to the Danish Government's right to apply to the Court, as reparation for the unlawful act, to place this obligation on record [2]. "

There is indeed no doubt that " to prohibit and to annull are two different things [3] ". Yet it may be asked whether this distinction, which may be justified and useful in the field of private law — particularly the law of marriage — can, in international law, withstand the pressure of actual facts (not to mention the question whether a recognition in principle of the law-creating faculty of the illegal act under the mere sanction of international responsibility, can in any degree enhance the very legality of that law).

A negative answer to this question results from Prof. Guggenheim's exhaustive study of the subject, in which the actual overlapping of illegal and invalid acts has been convincingly shown [4]. On the basis of a searching analysis, Prof. Guggenheim reaches the conclusion that the difference between the two categories is essentially relative and that international law treats as null not only acts lacking certain " elements " but equally acts traditionally qualified as merely illegal [5]. There is for instance no possibility of distinguishing in practice between an invalid

---

1. « La conséquence n'est pas la non-validité, la nullité de l'acte, mais un acte illicite qui, tout en étant contraire à la règle hiérarchiquement superposée déploie — selon la doctrine dominante — les effets d'une règle valable. » Guggenheim, *op. cit.*, p. 198.

2. *P.C.I.J.*, Ser. A/B, 53, p. 95. It would appear that the Court did accept Judge Anzilotti's distinction ; the different conclusion which it reached seems to be based not on a different notion of illegal and invalid acts, but on a different evaluation of the facts of the case, in particular, the existence at the relevant period of an effective Danish sovereignty over Eastern Greenland. For another instance of judicial distinction between illegality and invalidity of an act, see the decision of the Central American Court in the case between Nicaragua and Costa-Rica, *A. J.*, 1917, pp. 181-229 and comment by Prof. Guggenheim, *op. cit.*, p. 225.

3. Grotius, *op. cit.*, II, Chap. V, XVI, 1.

4. *Op. cit.*, pp. 256-258. In spite of the above-mentioned rigid division, the possibility of such overlapping has been admitted even by the traditional doctrine. Thus Anzilotti : « L'acte accompli contrairement à ces obligations est un fait illicite : il reste ensuite à voir, dans chaque cas, si l'ordre juridique se limite à refuser à l'acte toute valeur (nullité de l'acte), ou en fait dériver une responsabilité sans annuler l'acte, *ou si l'ordre juridique établit l'une et l'autre chose ensemble.* » It. mine, *op. cit.*, p. 340.

5. « La différence entre l'acte nul et l'acte illicite est, en conséquence, de nature essentiellement relative. En effet, la nullité n'est pas seulement attribuée aux actes auxquels certains « éléments essentiels » font défaut ; elle existe également dans le domaine intrinsèque de l'acte qualifié traiditionnellement d'illicite. » *Op. cit.*, p. 256.

act which has been executed and an illegal act, nor between an invalid act and an illegal act which has not been executed [1].

Prof. Guggenheim's examination of positive international law leads him to conclude that, contrary to the rigid notions of the traditional doctrine, international law recognizes that nullity can arise in cases other than those in which one or more of the " four elements " are lacking [2]. Thus, in particular :

« La nullité de certains actes illicites, le droit de leur refuser la reconnaissance, reposent sur l'idée que la violation de la règle de droit international peut, indépendamment de la sanction qu'elle comporte en vertu des principes relatifs à la responsabilité internationale, avoir la conséquence de ne pas pouvoir créer une situation juridique valable. L'acte illicite est — du moins dans une certaine mesure — assimilé à l'acte nul, conformément à l'adage déjà mentionné : *ex iniuria ius non oritur* [3]. "

A case in point is precisely the illegal attempt against the continued existence of a State [4]. It is obvious that neither the victim of such an attempt nor third States are under any sort of obligation to recognize it [5]. On the contrary, it is by exercising their right of non-recognition that they render the illegal act invalid, deny it any law-creating faculty and thus create a new category of acts null and void [6]. Non-recognition thus becomes the instrument of depriving an illegal act of any possible validity.

This view fully conforms to State practice. It has been sufficiently seen that States which are the victims of aggression react against it not only by mere protests and by invoking its illegality, but equally by an emphatic denial of its validity, i.e. of its faculty to create a legal situation or title [7].

This, then, is the legal significance of non-recognition. As a sanction of the illegal act, it penalizes the law-breaker by denying to him the intended result of his law-breaking, namely, the validity of the situation brought about by him in an unlawful manner. This is its aspect of sanction *sensu stricto*, i.e. an act directed against, and affecting, the illegal

---

1. *Op. cit.*, p. 258.
2. «...la non-validité de l'acte... ne découle pas de l'absence d'éléments essentiels qui selon la doctrine dominante constituent la validité de l'acte en droit international. » *Ibid.*, p. 210.
3. *Ibid.*, p. 226.
4. « L'exemple le plus frappant... de cette forme de nullité est fourni par le postulat qui déclare non valables les conquêtes survenues sans le consentement du sujet qui en est victime, ainsi que certains autres actes de violence. » *Ibid.*, p. 226.
5. *Ibid.*, pp. 226, 237 and 256 ; cf. Lauterpacht, *op. cit.*, p. 410.
6. « Leur nullité n'a pas son fondement dans l'absence de certains éléments essentiels, mais dans la volonté des destinataires des normes du droit international qui refusent de reconnaître certains actes illicites, et les considèrent comme absolument nuls. ...les sujets qui ont invoqué cette espèce de nullité sont parvenus à créer une nouvelle et importante catégorie d'actes nuls.. » *Ibid.*, p. 36.
7. See above, pp. 307-308, 359, 409, *f.-n.* 6, 444, *f.-n.* 2, 496. As a further exemple see also the Yugoslav Ambassador's protest to the State Department against the creation of the puppet State of Croatia : " The Royal Yugoslav Government desires to register its most emphatic protest against this unlawful action of the German Reich and considers null and void all acts relating to the creation of the so-called " Independent State of Croatia. " *Doc.*, III, p. 332. See also Secretary Hull's reply to the Polish Ambassador's protest of Oct. 27, 1939, against the annexation by Germany of Polish Western Provinces, to the effect that the United States Government " has taken note of the Polish Government's declaration that it considers this act as illegal and *therefore* null and void. " *It. mine*, Doc., II, p. 363.

act and its author. But the act of non-recognition also has another aspect, concerning the victim of the illegal act, whose full and unimpaired rights are reserved. Failing a legal vacuum it follows logically that to deprive the illegal act of any possibility of creating a legal situation is equivalent to upholding the legal *status quo ante*. Non-recognition thus fulfils both a negative and a positive function ; the two are inseparably included in one and the same act, yet, this dual function of non-recognition should be clearly appreciated.

c) *Limits of Non-Recognition.*

The policy of non-recognition has been the subject of conflicting comment.

It has been generally admitted that the refusal to recognize an illegal act or its consequences constitutes a minimum obligation of both law and decency [1].

While there is undoubted force in this argument, it has been found equally necessary to point out the largely unreal character of such a limited sanction. For it is true to say that non-recognition by itself achieves nothing : it does not effect a *restitutio ad integrum ;* it in no way modifies the existing effective situation ; apart from possibly annoying the successful aggressor, it cannot displace him [2]. Consequently, while rendering the illegal act absolutely invalid, it is not capable of making such invalidity fully effective [3]. Finally, it may well serve as a hypocrital conscience-clearing device for the non-recognizing States in case they do nothing further in the matter, whatever their positive and more concrete obligations [4].

---

1. " In a society in which the enforcement of law is precarious, there is a natural tendency to regard successful breaches of the law as a source of legal right. Non-recognition obviates that danger to a great extent. It is the minimum of resistance which an insufficiently organized but law-abiding community offers to illegality ; it is a continuous challenge to a legal wrong. In a sense, the effectiveness of non-recognition grows with the passage of years. For it brings into relief the contrast between the consolidating power of the successful defiance of the law and its status as a mere nullity. As such it adds susbtantial emphasis to the legal character of international law. It shows the vital difference between a law worthy of the name and a law concealing behind its misleading designation the unfettered rule of violence. " Lauterpacht, *op. cit.*, pp. 430-431. Sharp calls non-recognition the expression of the " disapproval of the world community towards States or governments which seek to gain territory or other advantages in violation of existing peace instruments. " *Op. cit.*, p. 217. McNair, who compares non-recognition to a protest, admits that in cases of grave wrongdoing, non-recognition "of the consequences of wrongdoing is the minimum which considerations of international decency require. " *The Stimson Doctrine of Non-Recognition, B. Y.*, 1933, p. 74. Scelle recognizes « que le refus, au moins provisoire, de reconnaissance, peut constituer un moyen de pression, une sanction éventuelle, de la violation du Droit. » *Op. cit.*, p. 179.

2. " Non-recognition as a sanction exists only in legal concept. " Chen, *op. cit.*, p. 441.

3. Thus Guggenheim, *op. cit.* See in particular : « Sans pouvoir imposer leur manière de voir à tous les destinataires des normes du droit international, et en particulier à tous les Etats souverains, les sujets qui ont invoqué cette espèce de nullité sont parvenus à créer une nouvelle et importante catégorie d'actes nuls, strictement limités dans leur application au domaine de leur propre compétence territoriale et personnelle. » *Ibid.*, p. 226.

4. " ...it is idle to think that mere non-recognition will solve the problem and operate as an adequate sanction. ... there is a danger of its becoming a slogan which will serve as an excuse for thinking that an effective method of preventing breaches of international order has been discovered and that no further action is required beyond a declaration of non-recognition. " McNair, *op. cit.*, p. 74.

Once again, it fell to M. Litvinov to summarize the merits and drawbacks of the non-recognition policy with all his usual lucidity :

" Among the means for combatting aggression and defending its Members which the League of Nations has at its disposal, non-recognition does not by any means play a conspicuous part. It is improbable that anyone would assert that the mere threat of non-recognition might avert aggression, or that non-recognition itself might free the victim of aggression from the grip of the conqueror. It was also my view that non-recognition should be accompanied by other more effective methods of combatting the aggressor, provided by Article 16 of the Covenant. Unfortunately, we have to recognize that the League of Nations has in some cases adopted resolutions on non-recognition without at the same time applying other means, more capable of arresting or repelling aggression. One might go so far as to say that resolutions on non-recognition were adopted when it became obvious that Members of the League were unwilling to inflict more telling blows on the aggressor, or when other action undertaken against him was being brought to an end. There must even be reasonable ground for the impression that resolutions on non-recognition were intended, as it were, to make up for failure to fulfil the other obligations imposed by the Covenant on League Members, in regard to the victims of aggression and, so to speak, thereby to clear their conscience. — It would be quite wrong, however, to assert that resolutions on non-recognition are in themselves devoid of any particular value. While such resolutions have in every case a certain moral significance, and give satisfaction to public opinion, they also cause the aggressor some preoccupations and inconveniences, as is evidenced by the efforts which aggressors usually make to obtain recognition of their conquests, if only in an indirect way. — But, according to circumstances, non-recognition may be of vast importance, not only morally but also politically — particularly when the victim of aggression itself continues to fight for its independence and for the integrity of its territory. In such cases, the recognition of the results of acts of violent aggression, or the abandonment of the policy of non-recognition, would be equivalent to abetting the aggressor directly, and to stabbing his victim in the back by discouraging and demoralizing it [1]. "

But, above all, in view of the unrelenting pressure of facts, non-recognition can be no more than temporary. At the risk of creating a " *paralysie juridique* [2] " it cannot be upheld *ad infinitum*. This truth has nowhere been more strikingly illustrated than in the example of the resigned abandonment of the non-recognition policy with regard to Manchukuo. As an inherently temporary expedient, non-recognition could therefore only make sense if it were no more than a warning to the aggressor, signifying that action will follow, if he does not yield to that act of pressure alone. In other words, it would make sense in an organized international community which would be both able and willing to let deeds follow words [3]. It would thus seem that the real meaning of the duty of non-recognition implied in the Covenant emerged clearly not only from Art. 10, — but also from Art. 16 ; whatever the League's practice, the duty of non-recognition under the Covenant cannot be torn out of its general context. Adopted by a community lacking the will and the means to translate the passive

---

1. *LNOJ*, 1938, pp. 340-341.
2. Scelle, *op. cit.*, p. 179.
3. Chen, who considers that non-recognition alone does not constitute a sanction, admits that " it is indispensable for the application of any other form of sanction. " *Op. cit.*, p. 442.

attitude of non-recognition into action, it becomes a policy of frustration, to be abandoned sooner or later, with more or less embarrassment [1].

Thus, whatever its merits, non-recognition is severely limited : it does not effect a change in the existing situation ; it gives rise to a nullity which is merely relative, being limited to those who refuse recognition [2] ; it cannot last. But the refusal to admit the validity of an existing situation can make sense only if that situation is, sooner or later, to be brought effectively to an end ; the reservation of violated rights can make sense only if such rights can again be effectively implemented in future. Being a basically temporary expedient, non-recognition is therefore bound to give way to a new adaptation either of fact to law, or vice-versa [3].

It must therefore be concluded that, while representing a significant development in the direction of greater legality in international law, the policy of non-recognition of the illegal seizure of a part or the whole of a State's territory finds its limits exactly where non-recognition of premature annexation had found them before : in the overriding principle of final effectiveness.

4. THE PRINCIPLE OF EFFECTIVENESS.

The problem of effectiveness arises out of the crucial issue of the relation between norms and facts, between the world of ideas and the world of reality. Whatever the methodical attempts at purity in separating the world of " is " (Sein) from the world of " ought " (Sollen), their mutual interdependence is not to be eliminated. As facts are dependent on law in that they are given their legal evaluation by norms, so legal norms are conditioned by facts. For the validity, and indeed, the very existence, of legal norms depends upon their effectiveness in the material world. As has been seen, the optimum conditions for the existence of a legal system are those in which its norms find a very high — though not absolute — degree of effectiveness in the realm of facts [4].

---

1. « ...devançant l'évolution organique de la société internationale, l'on a préconisé le refus de la reconnaissance à tout gouvernement de fait ayant occupé le pouvoir en violation d'une norme de droit international, et surtout en recourant à la violence. ...on pourrait efficacement pratiquer le refus de reconnaissance des situations gouvernementales illégalement occupées, si la société internationale était institutionnellement outillée, non seulement pour prononcer la nullité juridique des investitures irrégulières et leur refuser la reconnaissance, mais pour les annuler en fait, par l'utilisation de voies d'exécution effectives, permettant de rétablir le statu quo ante. » Scelle, op. cit., pp. 178 and 179. « On aboutit, en effet, à demander à la communauté internationale de statuer comme un juge sur la conduite de personnes jusqu'ici regardées comme pleinement souveraines. Mais pour lui permettre de remplir ce rôle d'une façon effective, il faut fournir à la communauté internationale les organes nécessaires. » Williams, op. cit., p. 291.
2. The term " relative " used here refers to the number of non-recognizing subjects, not to the category of nullity.
3. « ...si la non-reconnaissance d'un acte nul n'est pas suivie de son abrogation, son application répétée, ininterrompue et constante, entraîne fatalement sa validation ; car la réalité sociale n'admet pas un divorce permanent entre validité et effectivité. La validité d'une norme doit correspondre à son effectivité, son ineffectivité à sa nullité. » Guggenheim, op. cit., p. 231. Cf. Chen : " The function of non-recognition is to hold the legal situation in suspense, pending a definitive settlement which may result either in the restoration in fact of the status quo ante, or in the adjustment of law to the changed situation of fact. " Op. cit., p. 441.
4. See above, p. 554.

This then is the normal and healthy meaning of the requirement of effectiveness for a normative system. Yet, the same notion is sometimes used in what may be termed a pathological meaning : not in the sense of the effectiveness of law, but of the effectiveness of law-creating illegal facts as against the norm. This is precisely the current meaning of the principle *ex factis ius oritur*.

A norm, once enacted, may *depend* for its validity on the world of facts, or, more precisely, on its own reflection in the world of facts. But it should *arise* out of another norm only. The fact that, in actual reality, a norm can, and does, arise equally out of a fact, is a challenge to the given social organisation and to the requirements of logic alike, and it becomes particularly acute if the fact in question is the result of illegality. Yet, again and again in the field of law bare facts invade the realm of norms with law-creating force [1].

The principle of effectiveness in this pathological sense applies in an inverse proportion to the degree of development of a given legal system. The more primitive the system, the greater the discrepancy between validity and effectiveness and, consequently, the greater the law-creating force of illegal acts. In a highly developed legal State order, equipped with courts and police, possession of stolen property by the thief, however effective, will produce no legal title. In the decentralized and weak system of international law, unlawful annexation may grow into such a title.

This comparison shows that the preponderance of pathological effectiveness is not an inherent weakness of law ; it is a defect which may be remedied by a creative effort of man. Neither a primitive nor a highly developed legal system can dispense with the requirement of effectiveness as such ; but what a developed system can do, and in fact does, is to eliminate it in its pathological sense of an illegal effectiveness prevailing against law and becoming itself the source of law, — and even here it stops short of the case of successful revolution which is a supreme attempt not against one or the other of the binding norms but against the entire existing legal order as such.

International law has not reached that stage of development. Therefore, any discussion of illegal acts and the defences which international law may put up against them, must take into account the deep antinomy to which this law is subject at the present stage of its development.

On the one hand, a strict differentiation between legal and illegal acts is the *conditio sine qua non* of the existence of international law as a normative system [2]. Whatever the other weaknesses which a normative system may survive, it cannot survive an obliteration of that distinction. It represents its irreducible minimum beyond which it would cease to be such a system, in other words, it would cease to be law.

This is succinctly expressed by Prof. Lauterpacht :

---

1. No amount of purely intellectual operations can alter this fact ; thus Kelsen's description of such facts not as " law-creating ", but as losing their " factual " nature in favour of a " normative " one : " ...Metamorphose des Faktischen zum Normativen... " *Souveränität*, p. 241.

2. See above, p. 554.

" ... to admit that, apart from well-defined exceptions, an unlawful act, or its immediate consequences, may become *suo vigore* a source of legal right for the wrongdoer, is to introduce into the legal system a contradiction which cannot be solved except by denial of its legal character. International law does not and cannot form an exception to that imperative alternative [1]. "

If this is true — and it is submitted that it certainly is — then a rule protecting the continued legal existence of States against illegal acts becomes necessary to the survival of international law itself and grows into a condition of its very existence *qua* law. If this is true then, in further consequence, the recent practice of States as examined above and as expressed in the upholding of the principle of the legal continuity of an illegally suppressed State even as a mere ideal notion, acquires the wider meaning of action not only in defence of an individual State, but indeed, of international law itself.

Yet, any attempt to reduce international law to " ideal notions " endangers its existence as an effective normative system to exactly the same extent. For the object of international law is not to supply abstract theories but to regulate the living reality of international relations and to promote a genuine and working intercourse between its subjects on the unavoidable basis of delimited, effective territorial competences. In the long run, the admission of " ideal notions " in place of effective State existence on the basis of a concrete territorial delimitation is therefore equivalent to putting international law squarely out of existence.

" International law " — says Max Huber — " ... cannot be presumed to reduce a right such as territorial sovereignty, with which almost all international relations are bound up, to the category of an abstract right without concrete manifestations [2]. "

An international legal order which would sacrifice the principle of territorial effectiveness to abstract legal purity, would be as respectable as it would be non-existent. Yet, the upholding of a merely ideal existence of an effectively displaced State would precisely be such a case.

" Law " — says Prof. Lauterpacht — " must be based on facts — in so far as such facts are not in themselves contrary to law [3]. "

Yet, such facts may persist, a weak law being unable to eliminate them. Deprived of its natural basis in facts, can law take refuge in fictions without thereby ceasing to be law?

Thus, in order to remain a legal system worthy of the name, international law must draw at the same time on effectiveness and validity. It cannot exist without either. Faced with a divorce between the two, it is exposed to an antinomy endangering its very existence, — either by making it renounce the fundamental difference between

---

1. *Op. cit.*, p. 421.
2. Island of Palmas Arbitration, Scott, *Hague Court Reports*, 2nd Series, p. 93. Cf. Anzilotti : « La délimitation des sphères de liberté des sujets a pour base la délimitation territoriale des Etats, qui est véritablement la prémisse sur laquelle reposent leurs relations et le point de départ du développement de ces relations. » *Cours*, Préface, p. X.
3. *Op. cit.*, pp. 5-6.

legality and illegality, or by making it unreal. Consequently, in the prevailing stage of international integration, there seems to be the catastrophic alternative between either denying the normative character of international law, or creating a fiction, incapable of serving even the minimum needs of international intercourse.

This antinomy, expressed in the two contradictory maxims — *ex iniuria ius non oritur* and *ex factis ius oritur* — cannot be glossed over. Yet, to admit this antinomy is not to admit the primitive notion of effectiveness [1]. The latter would destroy a normative system, even a primitive one, just as completely as would the absence of effectiveness. International legal relations would be turned into a jungle and the legal system would find its unglorious end under the impact of sheer violence [2].

It has been seen that even traditional international law can, and does, to a certain extent regulate the scope and impact of effectiveness, refusing it a law-creating force under conditions in which — rightly or wrongly — such effectiveness is assumed to be only temporary. In particular, international law does not admit a premature annexation, not even where the conqueror's domination is effective. While such effectiveness is required for the mere stage of belligerent occupation, it is not considered sufficient for a full debellatio for which a further element is required : that of finality [3]. For this reason, notwithstanding the unlawful proclamation of annexation by the invader, international law and a law-abiding international community react by arresting the process at the stage of mere belligerent occupation [4]. A legal right, temporarily deprived of effectiveness is upheld undiminished, whereas the strictest requirement of effectiveness is applied to a weak title [5].

This attitude is not based on a *certainty* that the occupation will come to an end and that the restoration of the occupied State will necessarily follow. There is no such certainty, since the occupation may well finally turn into a full-scale debellatio. Consequently, in upholding the continued legal existence of an occupied State whose premature annexation has been pronounced by the occupying power, international law does not act on a *certainty* of its restoration but on an *uncertainty* of its extinction. There can be no more telling proof of the international law's inherent tendency to postpone — even at a risk — the passing of a death sentence on a State until the moment of absolute and incontrovertible finality.

It is then within such limits and such limits alone that international law is able to dispense with the principle of effectiveness, whether in its normal or in its pathological meaning. These limits are set by the reasonable doubt as to the finality of the effective situation illegally brought about. The resulting predominance of validity over effectiveness

1. Such as would result from the acceptance of Kaufmann's destructive formula : " Nur wer kann — darf ". *Das Wesen des Völkerrechts und die Clausula Rebus sic stantibus,* Tübingen, J.C.B. Mohr (Siebeck), 1911, p. 231.
2. See Verdross, quoted above, p. 102, *f.-n.* 2.
3. See above, pp. 103-104.
4. See above, pp. 102-107.
5. See above, p. 102.

has the merit of enhancing the legality of international law by postponing the verdict of State extinction and prolonging the chances of restoration. It does this and no more. In other words, it postpones the antinomy in time. It does not solve it.

5. RESULTING ASSESSMENT OF THE RELEVANT STATE PRACTICE.

It is against the background of the foregoing analysis that the State practice now being examined has to be assessed.

The starting point of this practice was the correct qualification of the attempt against the existence of a State as illegal. This illegal act was in turn refused recognition, i.e. qualified as null and void, incapable of creating a new legal title. Thereby the unimpaired legal status of the overpowered State was fully upheld. The requirement of territorial effectiveness has been dispensed with, on the assumption of the temporary character of the existing illegal situation. Where any organs of the overpowered State have survived or been re-created, recognition has been granted to them. Where the suppression of a State has been accompanied by the creation of puppet entities, their identity with the independent original States has been denied, and all their claims to validity rejected, either implicitly, by disregarding such entities as in the case of the Protectorate of Bohemia and Moravia or Slovakia, or expressly, as in the case of Albania. No international responsibility was consequently imposed on the restored States for the acts of puppets. Finally, the restoration of the victim States took place on the acknowledged basis of their continuity.

In the light of the foregoing analysis it now appears that there in nothing either revolutionary or unreal in this practice. On the contrary, it seems to be solidly rooted in traditional international law, and, moreover, to correspond to its more recent tendencies. This submission is further reinforced when the essential analogy of the illegal act here discussed with a war of conquest is borne in mind. It then becomes clear that what the State practice examined has done was neither more nor less than to adapt the old and traditional principles governing war, premature annexation and belligerent occupation to the illegal seizure of a State. For it is consistent with the inner logic of the problem that, just as the illegal act in question is in substance equivalent to a war of conquest, so its consequences are equivalent, and have in fact been assimilated, to mere belligerent occupation. This result has been secured notwithstanding the contrary claim of the aggressor, this claim in turn being analogous to a proclamation of premature annexation. In the whole process described above, there is at every step a complete analogy with belligerent occupation in its classical form [1].

---

1. On the assimilation of the illegal seizure of a State to belligerent occupation see Guggenheim, *Validité*, pp. 243, 244, 259 and 280; *Lehrbuch*, II, p. 936; see also Verdross on " *occupatio quasi-bellica* ", quoted above, p. 367. Langer's tentative suggestion to the effect that this type of occupation should to a certain extent be assimilated also to a " *de facto* government " — *op. cit.*, pp. 103-105 — is inadmissible and betrays a confusion of notions. For the basic difference between an occupying authority and a *de facto* government, see above, pp. 82-83.

The analogy is particularly striking in what may be considered the most vulnerable point of this practice : the upholding of the legal existence of a State as an ideal notion as against the effective domination of the aggressor. Seen in its proper perspective, it no longer seems vulnerable. For not only is such a divorce between validity and effectiveness *the* typical feature of belligerent occupation, but, moreover, it has just been seen that the reason for this is to be found not in the certainty of the occupied State's restoration but in the uncertainty of its final extinction, — that is, in the safeguarding of the legal existence of the occupied State even at a risk. There is the same element of uncertainty and risk in the situation here examined, although such risk may be greater in a non-belligerent than in a belligerent occupation, in the absence of immediate hostilities taking place on behalf of the overpowered State. The difference between the two is thus merely one of degree, not of substance ; for in both cases third States uphold the principle of the continuity of the occupied State on the underlying assumption of the lack of finality of the existing situation [1]. But if this is so and if the analogy is consistently upheld, then not even final success is necessary to justify *ex post* the validity of such policy while it lasted, just as even the final turning of a belligerent occupation into a debellatio cannot *ex post* undermine the validity of continued recognition of a merely occupied State while it was in fact merely occupied.

This evaluation of the State practice discussed makes it now possible to answer the question, which had been asked at the beginning of this analysis, as to its reality or, on the contrary, its unreality [2]. The answer now is that far from representing an entirely new and revolutionary departure in international law, it simply constitutes a further development of its old and time-honoured institutions which are both real and workable even in a weakly organized and decentralized community. This conclusion in turn makes it possible to give a tentative answer to a further question : namely, whether the practice examined was merely incidental to a given set of political and military circumstances or whether, on the contrary, it can be considered a permanent and lasting development in international law. While a refusal to indulge in any speculations or prophecies must be firmly maintained, the following submission may nevertheless be made : there is no reason to doubt the full applicability of the rules governing the conduct of States in matters of war, premature annexation and belligerent occupation, to what is in substance an identical situation ; there is, consequently, every reason to believe in the existence of conditions for the permanency of such practice. This submission is made all the more freely in face of the consistent tendency of international law to oppose measures of violence directed against the existence of States, by attempting to eliminate or,

---

1. " ...the conquest of a territory which is unconfirmed is precisely equivalent to a case of belligerent occupation extended into the time of peace. The occupant does not acquire the title, not because the control is ineffective, but because the ultimate decision has not been reached. " Chen, *op. cit.*, p. 432.

2. See above, p. 553.

at least, to restrict " official " war and to confront other acts of State suppression with non-recognition [1]. In the light of this tendency it is difficult to believe that modern international law will show itself weak and helpless where traditional international law reacted with all the strength at its disposal under then existing conditions, — and that it will not equally postpone for as long as possible the verdict of a State's extinction, while prolonging for as long as possible its ideal validity at the expense of effectiveness.

6. THE PROBLEM OF A NEW RULE.

This latter submission forcibly suggests another question : has not international law recently developed a fourth rule, — customary or conventional — protecting the legal continuity of States, which would take its place alongside the already existing three rules on the subject?

a) *Customary.*

The question of the formation of a new customary rule is highly delicate and dangerous. While it is certainly not for an individual writer to presume to know the answer, an analysis of the problem should nevertheless be attempted.

While the general process of the formation of customary rules may be described [2], it is infinitely more difficult, failing a determination by an international tribunal, to establish with any degree of certainty whether any particular rule exists [3]. Under such circumstances it is only natural to rely heavily on the recent formulation by the International Court of Justice of the conditions for the creation of a customary rule. In the *Colombian-Peruvian Asylum Case*, the Court rejected the Colombian submission as to the alleged existence of the customary rule claimed, declaring :

" But it (the Colombian Government) has not shown that the alleged rule... was invoked or — if in some cases it was in fact invoked — that it was, apart from

---

1. See above, pp. 556-563.
2. « Dans l'ordre logique, il y a donc, antérieurement au précédent et, par suite, à la coutume établie, l'idée que la règle s'est formée sous l'empire des nécessités de la vie internationale. La société internationale postule l'existence de certaines règles : *ubi societas ibi ius*. Les nécessités de la vie sociale internationale ne suffisent pas pour donner à cette règle la force d'application qui est la caractéristique des règles de droit, qui seule permet à ces règles de remplir la fonction sociale du droit : assurer l'ordre selon la justice, dans une société donnée, en protégeant et limitant les activités en présence. Du moins, la règle s'est formée sous l'empire de ces nécessités de l'ordre international. Elle s'affirme dans le précédent : celui-ci l'extériorise, la proclame, il la fait passer du domaine de la raison pure dans l'ordre positif. Le précédent gagne ensuite de l'autorité quand il est l'objet d'une réaction favorable de la part de ceux qui comptent suffisamment dans la vie internationale ; ici, la réaction de la doctrine est à prendre en considération à côté de celle des gouvernements et des juges internationaux ; la doctrine bénéficie de cet avantage qu'elle peut ici intervenir plus rapidement. Les précédents s'affermissant, la coutume s'établit, la règle devient règle de droit international positif. Ainsi, la coutume se rattache à la vie sociale internationale, elle en est le produit ; elle comporte des éléments positifs, les précédents, et c'est par ceux-ci que la règle entre dans le droit international positif. » Basdevant, *op. cit.*, pp. 513-514.
3. " Allem Gewohnheitsrecht ist eine gewisse Unsicherheit in bezug auf Existenz und Umfang eigentümlich, soweit es nicht von einer einheitlichen Rechtssprechung tatsächlich formalisiert worden ist. " Huber, *Grundlagen*, p. 43.

conventional stipulations, exercised by the States granting asylum as a right appertaining to them and respected by the territorial States as a duty incumbent on them and not merely for reasons of political expediency. The facts brought to the knowledge of the Court disclose so much uncertainty and contradiction, so much fluctuation and discrepancy in the exercise of diplomatic asylum and in the official views expressed on various occasions, there has been so much inconsistency in the rapid succession of conventions on asylum, ratified by some States and rejected by others, and the practice has been so much influenced by considerations of political expediency in the various cases, that it is not possible to discern in all this any constant and uniform usage, accepted as law, with regard to the alleged rule [1]... "

It has thus been made clear *a contrario* what the highest international judicial organ considers as the conditions of the formation of a positive rule of customary international law [2].

With regard to the problem discussed it must therefore in the first place be seen whether there has indeed been " a constant and uniform usage ". Such usage must include consistent repetition, [3] a sufficient degree of generality, [4] and a certain lapse of time [5].

Repetition in this case there has certainly been ; the principle has been acted upon in every single case in which the occasion for its application arose. The condition of generality has equally been fulfilled. As to time, the application of the principle has already extended over several years. In view of the full consistency of its application and of the absence of any " contradiction or fluctuation " it can reasonably be claimed that the principle discussed passes the Court's test satisfactorily and that it conforms to the requirements of a constant and uniform usage. The existence of the material element of the custom could therefore be asserted.

With regard to the second element of custom, namely the *opinio iuris sive necessitatis*, the Court clearly affirms its necessity for the formation of a positive customary rule [6]. In acting in a certain manner

---

1. *Judgment of November 20*, 1950 ; *I.C.J. Reports*, 1950, p. 277.
2. The fact that the Court's opinion bears on a *regional* customary rule only, cannot detract from its general validity.
3. " Ein Gewohnheitsrechtssatz erlangt Geltung durch dauernde Uebung. " Guggenheim, *Lehrbuch*, I, p. 48. « Pour qu'une disposition coutumière acquière valeur obligatoire, il faut donc qu'elle ait été constamment acceptée par les Etats qui se sont trouvés dans la situation d'avoir à l'appliquer. » Rousseau, Principes, p. 837.
4. Art. 38, b, of the Statute of the Court speaks of a " general ", not a " universal " practice. " Einstimmigkeit wird nicht gefordert. " Guggenheim, *op. cit.*, I, p. 47 ; similarly Rousseau, *op. cit.*, p. 838, and Basdevant, *op. cit.*, p. 509.
5. " Ihre zeitliche Dauer kann sehr verschieden sein. Unter Umständen genügen wenige Jahre. " Guggenheim, *op. cit.*, I, p. 48. « Mais il est difficile de déterminer avec précision le degré de durée que doit présenter la coutume internationale... » Rousseau, *op. cit.*, p. 837. However, Prof. Rousseau admits that even one precedent can create custom. « ...la longue durée n'est pas un élément indispensable. » Basdevant, *op. cit.*, p. 513.
6. This is the second time that the highest judicial organ of the international order has proclaimed, and even more clearly, the necessity of the psychological element of custom ; cf. *Lotus, P.C.I.J.*, Ser. A 10, p. 28. Such necessity is strongly denied by the pure school of law ; see in particular Guggenheim, *Lehrbuch*, I, pp. 45-51, and *Les deux éléments de la coutume en Droit International*, in *La Technique et les Principes du Droit Public, Etudes en l'honneur de Georges Scelle*, Paris 1950. A discussion of this problem is hardly possible within the framework of this study. The writer merely wishes to put on record her own conviction — in conformity with the Court and traditional doctrine — of the necessity of the psychological element, if only on account of the impossibility of distinguishing otherwise between mere usage and a positive rule of law.

States must consider it a legal duty. This requirement is further reinforced by the repeated repudiation by the Court of " political expediency " as the underlying motive of a given practice.

While the extremely complex problem of the possibility of adducing proof of such a conviction cannot be analysed here [1], the repeated reliance by the Court on " political expediency " as disqualifying a precedent from becoming a customary rule may be particularly helpful in the present connection. For, while it can hardly be contested that the former practice of States, involving the de-recognition of States which were the victims of illegal acts and the recognition of their annexation and extinction, had been overwhelmingly dictated by political expediency, the same cannot be said with regard to their subsequent constant practice of recognizing the continuity of such States. The political interest of States in placating the aggressors during the period immediately preceding the Second World War can hardly be subject to doubt ; but it is difficult to see what immediate political interest these same States had in the restoration of the victim countries on the basis of their unbroken continuity, and not on the basis of a new creation. On the contrary, it could be asserted that this latter form of restoration would rather have suited the interests of third States, leaving them completely free from any conventional obligations they may have had towards the restored States.

Thus, measured by the Court's standards, the recent State practice, backed by the generally conforming practice of international organisations [2], expressed in conventional law [3], and supported by a considerable volume of municipal decisions [4], would form a strong case for asserting the existence of a new customary rule on the subject. The case seems to be reinforced by the general trend against the illegal seizure of a State, particularly as expressed in the principle and growing policy of non-recognition [5]. Such a rule — if it were found to exist — would in its content correspond exactly to the rules governing the attitude of third States in connection with a war of conquest, premature annexation and belligerent occupation.

The existence of such a rule, however, has not yet been confirmed by an international judicial decision. But, should a case of this kind ever come before an international tribunal, it is not improbable that it would adopt as its own the opinion of Judge Altamira :

" ... the conditions particular to the general process of the development of a customary rule must be borne in mind. Often in this process there are moments in time in which the rule, implicitly discernible, has not as yet taken shape in the eyes of the world, but is so forcibly suggested by precedents that it would be

---

1. See Sorensen M., *Les sources du droit international*, Einar Munksgaard, Copenhague 1946, pp. 108-109.
2. See above, pp. 270, 290, 326-327, 333, 337, 355-357.
3. See above, pp. 275-277, 335-337, 354-355.
4. See above, pp. 358, 361-362, 399-401, 406-407, 409. For the significance of uniform municipal decisions for the development of international law, see Lauterpacht, *Decisions of Municipal Courts as a Source of International Law*, B. Y., 1929, p. 65.
5. See above, pp. 556-563.

rendering good service to the cause of justice and law to assist its appearance in a form in which it will have all the force rightly belonging to rules of positive law appertaining to that category [1]. "

b) *Conventional.*

Whatever the difficulties of an investigation into the possible birth of a new customary rule, it should, in principle, be an easy matter to tell whether such a new rule has been embodied in an international convention. Yet, even here, the answer may not be either easy or certain, owing to the difficulties in interpreting the relevant provisions.

The relevant conventional text in this connection is the common Article 2 of the 1949 Geneva Conventions. Its first two paragraphs read :

" In addition to the provisions which shall be implemented in peace-time, the present Convention shall apply to all cases of declared war or of any other armed conflict which may arise between two or more of the High Contracting Parties, even if the state of war is not recognized by one of them.

The Convention shall also apply to all cases of partial or total occupation of the territory of a High Contracting Party, even if the said occupation meets with no armed resistance. "

The basic problem is to what situation of fact the second paragraph of this Article applies. *Prima facie* there seem to be two alternatives : either the second paragraph covers classical belligerent occupation in time of war, in which case it is irrelevant to the problem here discussed ; or it extends the protection afforded to an occupied State into what is technically peace-time, thus assimilating the illegal seizure of a State to belligerent occupation and affirming the principle of the legal continuity of the State thus seized.

The interpretation of the text must start from the generally agreed assumption that the Geneva Conventions show a clear tendency to enlarge the field of their own applicability, thus enlarging the very notion of war [2]. In fact, Article 2 para. 1 includes in this notion two situations of fact : *a)* a declared war, and *b)* any other armed conflict, which is not only undeclared, but which, moreover, is not recognized as war by one of the parties.

The first case thus seems to cover the traditional concept of war, as being declared *and* as involving armed contest, the latter resulting from the words " *any other* armed conflict " used in the second case. It would thus appear that the Conventions do not cover the case of a war which has been declared without such declaration being followed by actual hostilities. Since, however, the aim of the Conventions is to

---

1. Dissenting Opinion, *P.C.I.J.*, Ser. A, 10, pp. 106-107.   Prof. Basdevant, analysing the *Lotus* case speaks of « sinon peut-être une coutume tout à fait établie, du moins une coutume en voie d'établissement » — and describes the Court's refusal to confirm it as follows : « ...elle a établi un barrage contre le développement du droit coutumier. » *Op. cit.*, p. 517. Speaking of « des indications très intéressantes sur le processus de développement du droit coutumier et le rôle du juge à cet égard » in the dissenting opinion of Judge Altamira, he adds : « La formation historique de M. Altamira donne à ces indications une autorité particulière. » *Ibid.*, pp. 517-518, *f.-n.* 2.

2. See Pictet, *La Convention de Genève pour l'Amélioration du sort des malades et blessés des armées en campagne*, p. 29 ; Pictet, *La Croix-Rouge et les Conventions de Genève, Rec.* 1950, I, p. 41.

provide a practical regulation precisely for the case of hostilities, — whether declared or undeclared — and not to lay down theoretical definitions, it may well be understood that this particular situation has been left out, as the question of the Conventions' applicability in such a case simply does not arise in practice.

The second case is that of " any other armed conflict ", that is, of a situation which, while involving actual hostilities, has either not been preceded by a declaration of war or which, apart from being undeclared is not recognized as war by one of the parties [1].

As against these two situations, clearly defined in para. 1 of the Article, para. 2 extends the applicability of the Conventions to *all* cases of partial or *total* occupation of the territory of a party, even if such occupation encounters no armed resistance. The question therefore arises : does para. 2 introduce a new, i.e. a third situation of fact which is to be covered by the provisions of the Conventions, or does it merely further amplify one of the two situations included in para. 1, — and, if the former is true, what exactly is this third situation of fact?

A purely grammatical interpretation would seem to confirm the first alternative, in reliance on two words which appear to be decisive : the word " also " (in the French text : " également "), and the word " all ".

The word "also " seems forcefully to indicate the introduction of a new, additional situation, not yet covered by para. 1, and not merely an enlargement or amplification of the two situations already so covered. If the situation included in para. 2 were only an illustration or a further subdivision of the two preceding ones, it might be expected that it would not be introduced by the word " also ", conveying to the highest possible degree the idea of an addition and not of an amplification, but by the word " for example " or " thus " or " in consequence ", or finally, by leaving the connecting word out altogether. As it is, the existing connection, as expressed by the word " also " instead of any other, conveys most strongly the idea of an addition. Similarly, the word " all " has a categorical sound by far transcending the two situations enumerated in para. 1. If the interpretation is to proceed on the reasonable and usual meaning of words, then " all cases of ... occupation " mean all cases of occupation, and not cases of occupation resulting merely out of two definite situations of fact.

It may also be observed that this impression that the two paragraphs deal with two different problems or groups of problems, and not with one, is further reinforced precisely by the two sentences being placed in two different paragraphs, instead of being included in one single paragraph.

But even if the important words " also " and " all " were disregarded, and even on the assumption of para. 2 being an amplification

---

1. It is somewhat surprising that the Conventions did not provide for their applicability in a situation when, apart from the absence of a declaration of war, the actual state of war is not recognized by any party to the conflict, as was the case between Japan and China ; in such a case, unlike the case of a war, declared but not followed by hostilities, there is room, and indeed the necessity, for the Conventions' applicability.

and a further subdivision of, and not an addition to, para. 1, the question necessarily arises : to which of the two situations of fact covered by para. 1 could such subdivision refer ? The second of the two can be immediately eliminated : for it envisages an armed conflict which is precisely absent from the situation covered by para. 2. There thus remains only the first case : that of the " declared war " ; but it has just been seen that — on the correct interpretation of the words " any other armed conflict " — this declared war too involves an armed contest. But the situation envisaged by para. 2 is characterised precisely by the absence of any such armed contest. — It would therefore follow that — even apart from considerations bearing on the words " also " and " all " — the situation covered by para. 2 stands by itself, is not a subdivision or amplification of the two former ones, and, far from being related to them, represents something entirely different and new.

If this were in fact the case, then it must be determined what exactly this new and additional situation is. If the *argumentum a contrario* in relation to the first paragraph is logically and consistently maintained then it follows that it is neither a declared war involving actual hostilities, nor any other form of armed conflict. Obviously, it cannot be a declared war without any subsequent warlike acts, for in such a case an occupation of territory could not materialize at all. Such an elimination points forcefully to precisely that situation of fact which is the subject of this investigation : the illegal and violent attempt at the existence of an independent State, which is not war in the traditional sense of the term.

If this were indeed the case, then, by assimilating the illegal act here discussed to war, the Conventions would assimilate the ensuing period of foreign domination to belligerent occupation, and thereby uphold the unbroken continuity of the thus occupied State. This would mean raising the relevant State practice to the rank of a positive conventional rule, binding on those members of the international community who have signed the Geneva Conventions.

This conclusion finds authoritative support in the Report of the Third Commission to the Plenary Assembly by the Rapporteur Colonel Du Pasquier on what was then Art. 4 and has since become Art. 6 of the Convention on the Protection of Civilian Persons, dealing with the beginning and the end of the Convention's applicability.

« ... l'application commence avec le conflit *ou* avec l'occupation... *Il est bien entendu que le mot « occupation » ne vise pas l'occupation au cours d'une guerre, mais l'occupation brusquée, sans guerre, telle que la prévoit le deuxième alinéa de l'Article 2* [1]. »

This statement finds further support in such comments on the Conventions as have become available since their signature. Thus, Pictet says :

---

1. *It. mine. Actes de la Conférence Diplomatique de Genève*, vol. II, Section A, p. 799. The above statement, however authoritative and uncontradicted, is unfortunately the only comment on the Article in question to be found in the *travaux préparatoires*. See Pictet : « Ce projet ne donna lieu à aucun débat... » *La Convention de Genève*, p. 29.

« ... D'autre part, on a vu dans l'histoire des Puissances procéder à l'occupation d'un territoire étranger en affichant des intentions pacifiques, mais en réalité pour y établir leur domination ou obtenir des avantages qui sont normalement le fruit d'une victoire des armes. *Il fallait donc aussi que les occupations, quels que soient leur caractère ou leurs apparences, n'échappent pas au droit de Genève.* Ce double objectif est atteint par l'Article 2, qui instaure l'application des Conventions « en cas de guerre déclârée ou de tout autre conflit armé surgissant entre deux ou plusieurs Hautes Parties Contractantes, même si l'état de guerre n'est pas reconnu par l'une d'elles » et dans tous les cas d'occupation « même si cette occupation ne rencontre aucune résistance militaire » [1]. »

Similarly, according to de La Pradelle, the Conventions cover :

« 1. La guerre, au sens traditionnel, ainsi confirmé, de guerre déclarée ; 2. tout conflit armé entre deux ou plusieurs Parties Contractantes, même sans déclaration de belligérance ; 3. l'occupation partielle ou totale d'un territoire, avec ou sans résistance militaire ; 4. l'annexion pure et simple d'un territoire [2]. »

Thus, the interpretation of the text alone and such comment as there is, seem forcefully to confirm that recent State practice upholding the legal existence of an effectively overpowered State in what is technically peace-time has now been finally embodied in a positive conventional rule. This rule would then apply to such cases as the forcible seizure of Austria, Czechoslovakia, the Baltic States, and so forth.

Yet, in spite of this favourable evidence, a doubt must remain. For, whatever the Conventions' tendency to enlarge the notion of war, they nevertheless apply in principle to what is technically war-time, not peace-time ; the maintenance of this technical distinction results from the very wording of Article 2 which distinguished between its own provisions and such provisions which are to be " implemented in peace-time ". It could therefore be concluded that the situation covered by para. 2, although not representing traditional war and occupation, must at least take place against the background of some existing war. If this were so, then, — to speak in concrete terms — para. 2 would possibly apply to a case like the German occupation of Denmark *during* the last war, but not to cases like the German occupation of Austria or Czechoslovakia *before* that war. Yet, even this argument could be countered : for it would appear that the cases of conflict enumerated in Article 2, of whatever nature they may be, must refer to the conflict between the States concerned, and not between one of these States and third States. In other words, on the assumption of the " Danish "

---

1. *It. mine, La Croix-Rouge et les Conventions de Genève*, p. 41. See also Pictet in *La Convention de Genève*, on the need to enlarge the Conventions' applicability ; since former conventions on the subject applied only to war *sensu stricto* « il suffisait donc théoriquement, qu'une guerre ne fut pas légalement déclarée ou que, pour une raison ou pour une autre — telle par exemple la non-reconnaissance par l'une des parties du Gouvernement de la partie adverse — l'état de guerre ne fût pas reconnu d'un des côtés, pour que l'applicabilité de la Convention put être niée. On voit le danger qui devait en résulter. Trop de contestations de la légitimité du Gouvernement adverse, *de disparitions momentanées d'Etats souverains par annexion* ou par suite de capitulation, ont été invoquées comme prétextes à ne pas observer l'une ou l'autre des Conventions, pour qu'il ne devint pas urgent d'y remédier. » *It. mine*, p. 30.
2. *La Conférence Diplomatique et les nouvelles Conventions de Genève du 12 août 1949*, p. 209. Unfortunately, no reasons whatever are given for such a conclusion. Nor it is to be seen why the author includes Norway in the list of illegally seized States alongside Austria and Czechoslovakia, *ibid.*, pp. 208-209.

interpretation, the actual conflict between two States would have to be qualified as taking place in war-time or in peace-time not according to the nature of that conflict itself, but according to whether a party to such conflict is at the same time at peace or at war with third States.

The question therefore finally reads : does Article 2 para. 2 provide for the applicability of the Conventions exclusively in war-time, or equally in peace-time? In other words : does it merely re-state the principle of the legal continuity of a State under belligerent occupation, or does it outlaw any annexation, safeguarding the legal continuity of a State overpowered in time of peace?

The interpretation of the text, forcefully supported by the Rapporteur's opinion, as well as the comment available, would confirm the second alternative. The fact of the Conventions applying in principle to war-time, would confirm the first. The Article clearly calls for an authentic interpretation which no individual writer can supply. Yet, the possibility — even if it be no more than that — of the conventional embodiment of a rule, safeguarding the legal continuity of an illegally overpowered State, could not have been allowed to pass unnoticed in this study.

7. THE LIMITS OF THE RELEVANT STATE PRACTICE.

Whether or not the State practice discussed has achieved the rank of a positive rule of international law, its investigation would not be complete without an analysis of its outer limits and possibilities. The affirmation of the ideal existence of a suppressed State has been found realistic and workable even by traditional standards ; it has been found realistic and workable to dispense with the principle of effectiveness in favour of that of validity. Yet, it is not to be imagined that the principle of effectiveness can be flouted altogether. On the contrary, it will always preserve its impact on purely ideal notions and the resulting policy, and it will thus determine its limits. That impact will make itself felt in each of the two possible alternatives : that of the non-restoration in due time of the suppressed State and even, though to a lesser degree, that of its restoration. The two cases must therefore now be examined.

a) *Non-Restoration of the State Affected.*

The State practice discussed is determined by the nature of international law and of the international community such as they exist at the present stage, and not such as they may, or should, become in the future. This basic consideration, together with the consistent analogy between this practice and the traditional practice bearing on war, premature annexation and belligerent occupation, points unavoidably to its weak point : its dependence upon the time factor. For, as in matters of war, premature annexation or belligerent occupation, the operative factor in the practice of States upholding the principle of the ideal continuity of occupied States as against effectively existing new territorial delimitation is that of temporariness. It has been seen that international law cannot withstand a permanent divorce between validity and effectiveness under the threat of becoming a fiction to the point of disappearance, and that, consequently, such a permanent divorce must end by a new adaptation of fact to law or vice-versa.

The possibility must therefore be squarely faced that, in a decentralized community which does not use compulsion in order to vindicate violated rights, an existing illegal situation may not be brought to an end. Up to what time limit can the anomaly of a divorce between validity and effectiveness be maintained, what is the solution if the temporary illegal situation turns into a permanent one, and is there any *legal* way of healing the breach?

In search of such a solution Prof. Lauterpacht lists three possibilities of validating the illegal act, namely, prescription, validation by the injured party, and recognition by the international community, the latter representing a " quasi-legislative act [1] ". The very notion of validation forcefully suggests that Prof. Lauterpacht proposes the above means as a *legal* process and a *legal* remedy.

a) The controversy prevailing among writers with regard to prescription indicates that it is not an undoubted institution of international law. It is denied by several writers [2]. Others, while admitting it, attach several conditions to its effectiveness. Thus, according to Oppenheim-Lauterpacht prescription is the

" acquisition of sovereignty over a territory through *continuous and undisturbed* exercise of sovereignty over it during such a period as is necessary to create under the influence of historical development the general conviction that the present condition of things is in conformity with international order [3] ".

But such exercise may be disturbed by claims and protests of other Powers and Chen is therefore quite justified in doubting whether the conditions for prescription would ever be fulfilled

" if protests and claims are being kept up by the conquered State (if it still exists) or other States [4] ".

---

1. *Op. cit.*, pp. 427-430.
2. « Le droit international ne connaît pas l'institution de la prescription, tant acqui- sitive qu'extinctive, même sous la forme de ce qu'on appelle la prescription « immémo- riale » ; en règle, l'écoulement du temps ne suffit pas pour déterminer l'acquisition ou la perte des droits. » Anzilotti, *op. cit.*, p. 336-337, « ...en droit international il n'existe pas de principe général en vertu duquel le seul écoulement du temps détermine l'acquisition ou l'extinction de droits. » *Ibid.*, pp. 347-348. " Zu den natürlichen Tatsachen gehört im Gebiete des nationalen Rechts auch der Ablauf der Zeit. Auf dem Gebiete des Völker- rechts aber muss der rechtbegründende oder rechtvernichtende Einfluss der Zeit in Abrede gestellt werden. Die Verjährung hat völkerrechtlich weder als acquisitive (als Ersitzung) noch als extinctive die Kraft einer rechtserheblichen Tatsache. " Liszt, *op. cit.*, p. 241.
3. *Op. cit.*, I, p. 527.
4. *Op. cit.*, p. 431. Equally Fauchille admits prescription under several conditions, including that of its undisturbed and uninterrupted character. *Op. cit.*, I, 2, pp. 760-762. Similarly, Prof. Scelle — who also admits the interrupting effect of protests — adding a rather surprising proposal, according to which « le délai de la prescription est d'autant plus court que l'ordre juridique est plus primitif » ; in consequence, it should be parti- cularly short in international law. *Op. cit.*, p. 160. There is no attempt to justify this suggestion, the contrary of which would seem to be true : it would seem that — admit- ting for the sake of argument the existence of prescription in international law — it is

Thus there seems to be no solid ground on which to accept prescription as a valid institution of international law. This being the case, it must be discarded as a possible means of validation.

b) Validation by the injured party seems by far the most convincing way out of the illegal situation. It is not only the most natural one, but most in keeping with the nature and spirit of international law, since such validation would in fact amount to a convention between the parties. It is only *ex superabundante cautela* that the obvious condition of its genuineness must be added. It is clear that no legally relevant validation can result from a fake, as e.g. a validation undertaken by a puppet government created for that purpose, or by a fake plebiscite.

c) There remains — still according to Prof. Lauterpacht — the third possibility of validation by way of a " quasi-legislative act " : recognition on the part of the international community.

If Prof. Lauterpacht had put forward this proposal within the framework of an existing fully organized international community, functioning on a strictly legal basis and endowed with proper organs, and if such validation were to be performed by these organs, then the suggestion would be tempting ; although, on reflection, it may be wondered whether such a fully integrated community would not find other, and better, means of dealing with illegal acts than by giving them a collective blessing. But so long as such a " quasi-legislative " act lacks any legal basis, in other words, so long as it is an arbitrary act of the third States, it has little to commend it as a legal solution.

Moreover, any such conception runs counter to all the basic principles of international law. There is no positive rule of that law which would invest the Powers of the day with such semi-legislative and semi-judicial authority over other States. On the contrary, there are positive rules whereby such authority is excluded [1]. Such " validation " therefore would be quite incompatible either with the principle of State independence or that of State equality. Failing a legal basis, it would have as little binding force for the State of whose rights it would dispose without its consent, as treaties to the same effect [2].

In the light of the cases examined in this study, there is yet more to be said on the subject. Not only would such a verdict of third States lack any legal basis, but, moreover, there is no guarantee whatever that it would actually correspond to any principle of international law. The cases examined in Part II of this study have provided an unedifying spectacle of recognition being granted, withdrawn, granted again, with no regard not only for legal obligations, not only for the legality or

---

precisely in a more developed legal system that one could afford a shorter delay for prescription, in view of the fact that organized and effective remedies are open to the victim of an illegality, while they are seriously lacking in a primitive system. With regard to judicial decisions, see Guggenheim : " Keine völkerrechtliche oder Schiedsgerichtsentscheidung spricht sich positiv aus. " *Lehrbuch*, I, p. 146, *f.-n.* 296. The controversial nature of acquisitive prescription in international law is admitted by Prof. Lauterpacht himself, *op. cit.*, p. 428.

1. See Basdevant and Guggenheim, quoted above, pp. 489-490.
2. See above, pp. 488-489.

illegality of the given situation, but even for the existing facts. It has been seen that not even the principle of effectiveness was decisive for the recognition or de-recognition of the illegal conquest of Ethiopia, Czechoslovakia or Austria. The de-recognition of those acts of conquest took place in complete disregard of the principle of effectiveness which was supposed to have been decisive at the moment of their recognition. It is submitted that such experiences are reason enough for not entrusting an unorganized international community with the power and function of giving a legal validation to illegal acts.

Thus, in the present stage of international organisation, the only truly legal validation of an illegal act on Prof. Lauterpacht's list remains a genuine validation by the injured party. Such validation could be achieved, for instance, either by means of an agreement with the surviving competent organs of the seized State — e.g. with a legal Government in exile — or, failing such organs, by means of a freely expressed will of the population.

Since, however, such validation is not likely to be often-forthcoming, the whole list does not, in fact, contain any legal remedy capable of providing a way out of the deadlock.

The conclusion is inescapable : there is no *legal* remedy. The outer limits of applicability of the State practice discussed are the same as those which faced traditional international law in its resistance to premature annexation ; they are perhaps only reached at a later stage. Under existing international law and the existing degree of organisation of the international community, the final transformation of a temporary illegal situation into a permanent one *will* give rise to a new legality. In the absence of an effective international organisation, international law will have to capitulate before the overwhelming normative pressure of facts. That stage may be postponed, it cannot be avoided. This tendency of, and necessity for, international law to capitulate before overwhelmingly strong facts, this " wahre Schwäche des Völkerrechts [1] " is the only true and straightforward explanation of, and the only reason for, the new legality. Torn between validity and effectiveness international law will finally have to choose effectiveness in order not to become unreal [2]. The position is neither altered nor remedied by the suggestion of actually non-existing legal means of validation, nor by ingenious proposals to sever the illegal act from its consequences and not to recognize the former while recognizing the latter [3].

---

1. Kelsen, *Souveränität*, p. 241.
2. See above, pp. 565-566.
3. " There is no question here of legalizing the illegal act ; the question is one of disregarding the effects of the illegality. The results of an illegal act are a legal nullity ; they are legally non-existent. The wrongdoer acquires no right under it. But there is no logical objection to the community acquiescing, through collective or individual acts of its members acting in the general interest, in the assertion of a right which did not previously exist. To rule out that possibility altogether would mean to postulate for the law a degree of rigidity which may not be compatible with international peace and progress. Occasions may arise when the continuation of the policy or the obligation of non-recognition may not be conducive to the general good. When that happens, non-recognition may be adjusted to the requirements of peace and stability..." Lauterpacht, *op. cit.*, pp. 429-430.

If an illegal situation has maintained itself for such a long time as not to be temporary any longer, it is not prescription ; it is facts and facts alone which have prevailed over ineffective law. If a general peace conference definitely approves the illegal annexation of independent States, it is not a quasi-legislative act ; it is simply the loss of a reasonable chance of restitution which has finally sealed their destruction. There is no " validation " and no " legal " remedy under the law that has been violated. The basis of the new legality will not be in law but — as in the case of an internal revolution — in law-breaking [1].

This fundamental weakness of international law, imposing an utmost strain on its very existence as a normative system, is a necessary and unavoidable correlative of the weakness of international organisation. It must be admitted and accepted as long as there is no effective, centralized international organisation. But it must not, and it need not, be presumed, it must not, and it need not, be admitted except in the very last resort, when the normative pressure of facts has reached its summit and all reasonable chance of a *restitutio ad integrum* has disappeared for as long a period of time as can reasonably be assessed.

This fundamental proviso leads to the following observations : it must be concluded from the above analysis that a law-abiding attitude of the international community in face of illegal acts aimed against the existence of a State will depend on an assessment of the temporary or lasting character of such acts. Under existing conditions of decentralization, this assessment will necessarily be undertaken by every State individually. It is only obvious that — even apart from political considerations — such an assessment may be incorrect. What appeared to be a final consolidation of illegality may yet turn out to have been merely temporary, the final proof of this being the eventual restoration of the victim State within a reasonable period of time. Is then the restored State to be treated as a new State creation ? Is its international status, resulting from its unbroken continuity, to be denied to it only because third States have committed an error of judgment ?

The unavoidable necessity of international law's capitulation before overwhelming facts has been admitted ; it has been said that it represented a vital necessity which could be postponed but not avoided. But to admit such a capitulation when there is no need, after the disappearance of the compelling and wrongly assessed facts, is to ask international law to commit a purely gratuitous act of abdication. It means asking international law to legalize *ex post* illegal acts which have ceased to be effective, with not the slightest legal or factual necessity for such legalization. It is a capitulation which is the more objectionable since it is utterly pointless and unnecessary.

For this reason it is here claimed that the restoration of Ethiopia, Czechoslovakia, Albania and Austria on the basis of their continuity was essentially legal. If on the cessation of illegal effectiveness the

---

1. « Le « fait accompli » de la conquête et de l'annexion contraires à la volonté de l'Etat ayant subi l'acte nul et l'acte illicite se transforme — comme toute révolution réussie en droit interne — en un titre juridique déployant les effets d'un acte valable. » Guggenheim, *op. cit.*, p. 231.

continuity of these States would yet have been contested, this would have meant that the contesting States had volunteered to endow *ex post* the original illegal acts which legality for no conceivable reason. To require international law to perform such gratuitous acts of self-destruction is to undermine, for the sole sake of undermining, a legal system which is already sufficiently liable to capitulate in cases of supreme necessity [1].

While insisting on the need to preserve international law from suicidal moves, it is yet necessary firmly to eliminate a possible misunderstanding : the above reasoning can apply only to an illegal situation which was in fact temporary but was at a given moment wrongly assessed as permanent and which only later gave place to a different situation. What is being advocated here is not a *postliminium*, nor the theory of a miraculous resurrection of a State which had in fact become extinct [2].

It is therefore only logical to enquire into the *differentia specifica* between a mere liberation of a State which had never become extinct and a *postliminium*. Once again, as in so many cases, there are no ready-made criteria. In their absence, such a distinction will be the fruit of a searching analysis of all the relevant circumstances of the case, including the time factor. This analysis will also have to take due account of the international law's inherent reluctance lightly to admit the extinction of a State. It may generally be submitted that if the illegal domination of one State by another has persisted for a relatively short time, and if that time has been marked by international tension and instability and by the consistent opposition of third States to the existing situation, then its end will mean the full restoration of the temporarily suppressed State on the basis of its uninterrupted legal continuity. If, however, the illegal domination has persisted for a considerable period of time, unchallenged from any quarter, and if that period has been marked by stability and relative finality in existing international relations, then its end, accompanied by the new rise of the once suppressed State will mark the birth of a new State. There can be no relation of identity and continuity between ancient Greece and the new Kingdom of Greece making its appearance on the international scene in 1829 ; nor between the old Jewish State and the Israel of 1947 ; nor between the old Polish Republic and the Poland of 1918 [3]. But there can be, and there is, a relation of identity and continuity between the Czechoslovakia of 1939 and 1945, between the Albania of 1939 and 1945, between the Austria of 1938 and 1945. There can still be a relation of identity and continuity between the independent Baltic States of 1940 and such Baltic States as will recover their effective

---

1. Cf. Lauterpacht : " Law is not necessarily disintegrated by impotence ; but it is destroyed by unqualified submission to the lawlessness of force. " *Op. cit.*, p. 435.
2. See above, p. 6.
3. This view is put forward in direct opposition to some Polish writers and to the consistent jurisprudence of the Polish courts in the period between the two wars. See in particular : *A. D.*, 1919/22, cases no. 16, 17, 18. For doctrinal exposition see Hubert, S., *Rozbiory i odrodzenie Rzeczypospolitej (The Partitions and the Restoration of the Republic)*, Lwow, 1937.

freedom before an overwhelming normative pressure of facts will have brought about their final extinction ; and there can still be a relation of identity between the independent Polish Republic of 1939 and a Polish Republic which will have re-established herself on Polish territory in time to forestall her final extinction by those same overwhelming, law-creating illegal facts.

b) *Restoration of the State Affected.*

It has been seen that the principle of the legal continuity of an illegally suppressed State necessarily and logically involves its restoration on the full and acknowledged basis of its continuity. Such a mode of restoration would appear to be in full conformity with the time-honoured and judicially confirmed principle of a *restitutio ad integrum*, that is, with the obligation to re-establish the state of affairs which had existed before the commission of the illegal act [1].

Yet, it must be open to the gravest doubt whether in practice the principle of a truly integral restitution stands any chance of implementation or whether, in fact, it does not merely represent a maximum postulate from which important concessions will have to be made. For it is submitted that the actual effectiveness of illegal foreign domination cannot be disregarded and that it will leave its lasting traces even in the most favourable case of its elimination [2].

This argument starts from the plain impossibility of treating an executed illegal act as non-existent. It would be a sheer fiction to pretend that an executed illegal annexation has not in fact taken place, that an illegal occupation is not in fact occurring, or that a puppet government or State does not in fact exist. These things do exist, once they have been effectively established. Life goes on in the annexed or occupied territory, or under a puppet authority, some sort of a legal order is maintained and acts take place which are not illegal in themselves.

Even if acts of the occupying power or its puppets in the international field — such as the issuing of passports or the regulation of transport and communication — could be effectively disregarded [3],

---

1. " The essential principle contained in the actual notion of an illegal act — a principle which seems to be established by international practice and in particular by the decisions of arbitral tribunals, is that reparation must, as far as possible, wipe out all the consequences of the illegal act and re-establish the situation which would, in all probability, have existed if that act had not been committed." *P.C.I.J.*, Ser. A 17, p. 47. Similarly, the arbitral award in the *Martini* case between Italy and Venezuela of 1930 : " These obligations must be annulled under the heading of reparations. In pronouncing their annulment, the Arbitral Tribunal emphasizes that an illegal act has been committed and applies the principle that the consequences of the illegal act must be effaced. " *A. D.*, 1929/30, case no. 93. Cf. Guggenheim, *Lehrbuch*, II, p. 572 ; Anzilotti, *op. cit.*, p. 525. The principle of the *restitutio ad integrum* was embodied in Art. 10 of the Covenant — see Scelle, *op. cit.*, p. 853 and p. 144 — and in paragraph 3 of the Atlantic Charter.
2. Cf. Guggenheim, *Validité*, p. 259 ; also : « Si la mesure réparatrice affirme cependant que l'acte annulé n'a jamais sorti d'effets dans le cadre des ordres juridiques internes et international, il s'agit d'une pure fiction qui ne correspond aucunement à la réalité. Seules les *conséquences* des actes nuls et illicites peuvent être supprimées. En vue d'*effacer* un acte exécuté dans le passé, on ne peut procéder qu'à des mesures de compensation pécuniaires ou morales. » *Ibid.*, p. 263.
3. Which was not the the case with regard to Manchukuo, see Sharp, *op. cit.*, p. 152 et seq. and Guggenheim, *op. cit.*, pp. 38-39.

no such treatment can be meted out to purely internal acts bearing on routine administration or on the legal status of individuals. To pretend that everything in an illegally occupied territory or under a puppet government is non-existent, is not only to press legal fiction beyond all reasonable limits, but to create a situation never to be disentangled in future [1]. Apart from the sheer practical impossibility of enforcing such an extreme point of view, it would hardly be in the interest of the restored State itself to plunge the liberated country into endless chaos and anarchy.

Before proceeding with the argument, it may be of interest to recall a great precedent, whose value for the problem discussed is undiminished by the fact that it arose not out of an inter-State contest but out of a civil war : the liquidation by the United States of the legal heritage of the secessionist government following the Civil War.

It is obvious that under the Federal Constitution of the United States, the secession of the Southern States and the setting up of a secessionist government constituted an illegal and invalid act. This is how it was qualified by the United States Supreme Court :

" Considered ... as transactions under the Constitution, the ordinance of secession, adopted by the convention and ratified by a majority of the citizens of Texas, and all the acts of her legislature intended to give effect to that ordinance, were absolutely null. They were utterly without operation in law. The obligations of the State, as a member of the Union, and of every citizen of the State, as a citizen of the United States, remained perfect and unimpaired. It certainly follows that the State did not cease to be a State, nor her citizens to be citizens of the Union. If this were otherwise, the State must have become foreign, and her citizens foreigners. The war must have ceased to be a war for the suppression of rebellion, and must have become a war for conquest and subjugation [2]. "

Yet, notwithstanding this categorical and absolute declaration of nullity, the Supreme Court proceeded :

" It is not necessary to attempt any exact definitions, within which the acts of such a State government must be treated as valid, or invalid. It may be said, perhaps with sufficient accuracy, that acts necessary to peace and good order among citizens, such for example, as acts sanctioning and protecting marriage and the domestic relations, governing the course of descents, regulating the conveyance and transfer of property, real and personal, and providing remedies for injuries to person and estate, and other similar acts, which would be valid if emanating from a lawful government, must be regarded in general as valid when proceeding from an actual though unlawful government ; and that acts in furtherance or support of rebellion against the United States, or intended to defeat the just rights of citizens, and other acts of like nature, must, in general, be regarded as invalid and void [3]. "

---

1. « L'application de la règle de la rétroactivité intégrale conduit cependant dans beaucoup de situations à des résultats difficilement acceptables. Si l'on cherchait par exemple — contrairement aux dispositions formelles de la quatrième convention de La Haye de 1907 — à tirer les conséquences extrêmes d'une occupation « illégale » à la suite d'une guerre d'aggression, contraire aux règles coutumières et conventionnelles du droit international, on arriverait à des résultats presque absurdes. C'est ainsi que les mariages, les concessions administratives, les décisions judiciaires civiles et pénales survenues sous le régime de l'occupation « illicite » seraient entachés de nullité absolue. » Guggenheim, *op. cit.*, p. 260.

2. *Texas v. White*, December 1868. Wallace J. W., *Cases Argued and Adjudged in the Supreme Court of the United States*, vol. VII, p. 726.

3. *Ibid.*, p. 733.

The Supreme Court repeated, and enlarged upon, this view in a subsequent case :

" We admit that the acts of several States in their individual capacities, and of their different departments of government, executive, judicial and legislative, during the war, so far as they did not impair or tend to impair the supremacy of the National authority, or the just rights of citizens under the Constitution, are, in general, to be treated as valid and binding. The existence of a state of insurrection and war did not loosen the bonds of society, or do away with civil government, or the regular administration of the laws. Order was to be preserved, police regulations maintained, crime prosecuted, property protected, contracts enforced, marriages celebrated, estates settled, and the transfer and descent of property regulated precisely as in time of peace. No one that we are aware of seriously questions the validity of judicial or legislative acts in the insurrectionary States touching these and kindred subjects, where they were not hostile in their purpose or mode of enforcement to the authority of the National Government, and did not impair the rights of the citizens under the Constitution [1]."

Not a word of comment need be added to these American decisions, admirable as they are in law and common sense. Notwithstanding their civil war background, when transferred into the field of international law their reasoning forcefully points to the application to the process of restoration of the only possible analogy : that of belligerent occupation.

This solution is in fact convincingly advocated by Prof. Guggenheim [2]. It is necessary to see what exactly such solution implies.

In the first place, as in the case of war and premature annexation, it is imperative to distinguish between the original illegal act and the subsequent acts performed in the occupied territory [3]. This is precisely what was done by the United States Supreme Court. Moreover, not all the subsequent acts can claim legal immunity ; their legality or illegality will have to be considered on their own merits, but it is only reasonable and natural to assume that they will have to be tested by the criteria of what is allowed to a belligerent occupant under the Hague regime [4]. This criterion fully and absolutely excludes any alteration of the international status of the victim State which — if the principle of its unbroken continuity is to have any meaning at all — must precisely emerge from the period of foreign domination with all its international rights and duties unimpaired, and with the continuing international delimitation of all its spheres of validity under international law. This

---

1. *Horn v. Lockhart, op. cit.,* vol. XVII, 1873, p. 580.
2. *Op. cit.,* pp. 243, 244, 259 and 260 ; see also Chen, *op. cit.,* p. 432.
3. « ...on doit se demander si le rétablissement de la situation antérieure comporte aussi l'annulation des actes consécutifs à l'occupation effectivement intervenue, ou plutôt si l'annulation ne se rapporte qu'à l'acte même de l'occupation, la validité juridique étant reconnue aux actes consécutifs. » Guggenheim, *op. cit.,* p. 259.
4. " Der okkupiertes Gebiet annektierende Staat kann daher auf dem von ihm einverleibten Gebiet nur jene Rechte beanspruchen, welche das Besetzungsrecht der Okkupationsmacht gewährt. Nach Wiedereinsetzung der zentralen Organe des okkupierten und widerrechtlich annektierten Staates dürfen daher jene Massnahmen der Besetzungsmacht vernichtet werden, die dem Okkupationsrecht nicht entsprechen. " Guggeheim, *Lehrbuch,* II, p. 936. « Quels sont ces actes ? Il n'y a pas de doute qu'il s'agit de ceux qui dépassent le cadre d'une occupation militaire, comme par exemple l'octroi de la nationalité de l'Etat occupant, contraire à l'Article 45 du règlement annexé à la quatrième convention de La Haye de 1907. » Guggenheim, *Validité,* p. 243.

is why neither changes in the nationality of the population, nor territorial changes, can be accorded even a provisional validity by the restored State or by third States.

This leads logically to a second distinction to be made : that between purely internal acts of the occupant and acts intended to produce international effects. If — as under belligerent occupation — the whole meaning of the continuity of the illegally suppressed State is not to be dissipated in the very process of restoration, then such a State cannot possibly be made to bear responsibility for whatever international acts the occupant — or its puppets — have performed. This is precisely the difference between the illegal seizure of a State and internal revolution, which would be completely obliterated if the restored State — like a restored or, on the contrary, a revolutionary government — were made to succeed to the international obligations of either the occupant or its puppets. It has been seen that, owing to the strictest requirement of effectiveness with regard even to a law-abiding occupant, his legal measures are limited to the occupied territory and cannot produce any legal results outside it [1]. In further consistent analogy, it cannot be seen why a different standard should be applied to the case under discussion. Should the repudiation of such acts by the restored State affect the interests of third States, which can only happen where the latter had recognized the illegal act, then the crude but proper answer is that they should not have done so, and that they alone, and not the victim State, must bear the consequences of a premature recognition. Yet, it is submitted that even in such a case the proper application of the principles governing restoration involves the acquiescence of third States in the voidance of such acts, undertaken by the restored State. This is precisely what took place with regard to Albania which, in Art. 32 of the Italian Peace Treaty, was given a formal international authorization to proceed with such measures of voidance as she thought necessary [2].

A third and final distinction must be made : that between an act which has been illegal from its inception, and one which has been legal and whose illegality has only been declared later. For it is obvious that the treatment of such acts — and their consequences — must be different and that, in particular, the legitimate interests of the third States which recognized the act during the period of its legality must be safeguarded. To speak in concrete terms : the Munich Agreement, validated by Czechoslovakia's accession, was not only initially legal in itself but also produced legal results until the time of its repudiation ; on the other hand, the unilateral Soviet seizure of the Baltic States was illegal *ab initio*, and so was the establishment in Poland of a Soviet puppet State, failing a validation by Poland and having taken place in violation of both customary and conventional law by the parties to the Yalta Agreement. Prof. Guggenheim is therefore perfectly justified in claiming that, whatever the policy and interests of the repudiating

---

1. See above, pp. 81-82.
2. See above, pp. 335-336.

Powers, acts performed during the period of the validity of the Munich Agreement cannot be considered null and void [1]. In the case of a Sudeten German serving in the German army following the incorporation of the Sudetenland into Germany, no question of nullity can arise, — not only because practically no " restoration " of any sort is conceivable, but, above all, because that Sudeten German had *legally* become German citizen and was *legally* conscripted into the Reichswehr. But neither the citizens of the Baltic States, nor the Polish deportees in the Soviet Union have ever legally become Soviet citizens ; nor have Soviet citizens, " delegated " by the Soviet Union as Poles, ever legally acquired Polish nationality. These acts are invalid *ab initio* and they are not binding either on the States affected or on third States.

Thus, the restoration of an illegally suppressed State combines the basic principle of its continuity with necessary and unavoidable limitations, in exactly the same way as a restoration of a State after belligerant occupation. In neither case does it — or can it — mean a legal earthquake [2]. But it is submitted that whatever limitations attach to it, they interfere with the principle of the uninterrupted legal continuity of the restored State just as little as in the case of similar limitations inherent in a restoration following belligerent occupation. In both cases — to quote the United States Supreme Court once again — the original act is " utterly without operation in law ", the rights and obligations of the overpowered State remain in both cases " perfect and unimpaired ".

8. CONCLUSION.

These then are both the possibilities and the limits of a law-abiding State practice in face of an illegal attempt against the continued existence of a State, seen within the framework of existing international law and the present day international community. While the possibilities, based on the principle *ex iniuria ius non oritur*, are far from negligible, the limits, determined by the principle *ex factis ius oritur*, are firmly set.

Thus, while modern international law — like traditional international law — has not been found wanting either in the protection it affords to independent States or in the defences it puts up against illegality, this is as much as can be said on the subject in a system and a community where pathological effectiveness is preponderant, where

1. *Op. cit.*, p. 242.
2. This can be seen on any concrete example. Thus, in Czechoslovakia, where the restoration proceeded on the basis of a Presidential decree on the re-establishment of the Czechoslovak legal order, issued in London on August 3, 1944 — see above, p. 101 — and ratified by a law in liberated Czechoslovakia on December 19, 1946, the whole legislation of the period of German domination was in principle to be considered null and void. Since, however, such a sweeping decision hardly stood a serious chance of implementation it was considerably limited by Art. 2 of the Presidential decree, laying down that, during the transition period, enactments of the period of occupation could be considered valid if they were not contrary either to the letter or to the democratic principles of the Constitution and if, moreover, they did not affect either penal law and procedure, or family law. This provision was subject to a detailed regulation by the law of October 2, 1946. Krob, *Aperçu des dispositions légales d'après guerre*, in *Bulletin de Droit Tchécoslovaque*, Année V, no. 3-4. See also Guggenheim, *op. cit.*, p. 243, *f.-n.* 2.

voluntarism is rampant and where the fundamental maxim *ex iniuria ius non oritur* still remains a " principle " without becoming a rule, for lack of force to support it.

The analysis of the existing defences against illegality has, it must be admitted, contributed nothing to the solution of the most crucial problem : that of the antinomy endangering the very existence of international law *qua* law [1]. In the existing reality it is at this point that a juridical exegesis must close.

For the solution of this antinomy does not lie on the intellectual and speculative, but on the organisational plane. What can contribute to such a solution, in other words : to a growing reality of international law, is not an intellectual construction but an organisational effort.

On whether this effort will be undertaken, with a singleness of mind and a sincerity of purpose, depends the fully effective protection not only of State existence, but of every legal interest — and every human value — against illegal suppression. Here lies the way to the *Civitas Maxima*. The other way leads not to the imperfect, yet bearable world such as existed in the 19th century, but to disaster. It is for man to make his choice.

---

1. See above, p. 566.

CHAPTER III.

GENERAL CONCLUSIONS.

It need hardly be repeated that this study has been undertaken as a juridical, not a historical, political or sociological analysis [1]. Law is a formal notion. So is the State. However indispensable the reliance on its material elements : territory and population, — however inseparable the organic interdependence of these material elements and the legal order which binds them together into a legal entity [2], the State is not a tangible phenomenon of the physical world, but a construction of the human mind which has joined all these elements into a single and separate whole.

This is why an enquiry into the material aspect of the identity and continuity of States had to be rejected from the start [3]. The question asked did not concern the " walls of the city [4] ". It did not concern its human substratum, nor its history or culture, nor its mountains, or rivers. It concerned only and exclusively the legal notion of identity and continuity of the legal entity called State, however relative and limited such a notion must necessarily be [5].

It follows that the criterion of such notions could not have been a material, but a formal one [6]. Neither territory alone, nor population alone could have supplied it. The identity of territory and population can vouchsafe the historical identity and continuity of a nation ; it discloses nothing about the identity and continuity of a State. This theoretical point of view has been found fully confirmed by the analysis of positive international law [7].

Nor was it possible to find the criterion of State identity and continuity in the one, unchangeable legal order of the State, expressed in its basic norm, however tempting such a solution [8]. For not only would such identification of the State with only one of its elements run counter to the principle of their organic interdependence, but, moreover, such a solution could not be upheld in face of existing positive international law [9].

---

1. See above, p. 3.
2. See above, pp. 50-51.
3. See above, p. 4.
4. Aristotle, *op. cit.*, p. 1276a, see above, p, 27.
5. See above, p. 5.
6. See above, p. 5.
7. See above, pp. 21-22 and 48-49.
8. See above, pp. 186-187.
9. See above, pp. 47-48.

After the elimination of such criteria, the real test of the identity and continuity of States was found in its independence, as expressed in an effective overall international delimitation, in a differentiation of a State from all other States [1]; such independence was found to be the essential condition of statehood [2] without which a State can neither begin, nor continue, to exist [3].

At the end of this study this criterion which is formal — though necessarily reflected in the world of reality — can now be fully vindicated. For it has stood the test in each of the four cases investigated, providing at the same time the common link between them and safeguarding the unity of the problem analyzed. It alone explained the identity and continuity of State in face of territorial changes, since their independence was not affected thereby. It alone explained such identity and continuity in case of revolutions, since the new basic norm of the revolutionary State was produced freely from inside its remaining delimitation, and its independence, its " separateness " from any other State was preserved in the process. It explained the identity and continuity of States under belligerent occupation, the latter being *ex definitione* a temporary institution, unable by itself to destroy the independent legal existence of the occupied State. It finally explained the survival of these States whose physical suppression, although not assuming the orthodox form of belligerent occupation, proved equally temporary and transient.

At the same time, the final loss of independence, either by way of a legal settlement or by way of a total obliteration of the entire international delimitation of a State, signified its extinction.

It was in reliance on this purely formal nature of the problem examined, of the notions discussed and of the criteria used, that it was possible in individual cases to reach conclusions which would have been inadmissible in an enquiry into the material aspect of the problem : thus it was found both possible and necessary to affirm the relation of identity and continuity between Sardinia and Italy, in spite of the overwhelming changes in her territorial and personal delimitation. For Sardinia — re-named Italy — had preserved her independence while enlarging her territorial and personal sphere of validity by way of a series of annexations. On the same basis it was found both possible and necessary to deny the identity of the Baltic States with the Baltic S.S.R.s in spite of the identity of their territory and population, since the latter do not possess that independence, that separate legal existence which had made the former what they legally were.

Like State identity and continuity, so State independence which is their criterion is a polemical notion [4]. However, the two possible aspects of such polemical character may be recalled : for independence is a defensive notion when directed against attempts on the part of third States, but it is an aggressive notion, when directed against

---

1. See above, p. 186.
2. See above, pp. 162-165.
3. See above, p. 188.
4. See above, p. 166, *f.-n.* 1.

international law. It is in the former sense, in the sense of freedom from foreign oppression but subordination to international law that is has been conceived and analyzed throughout this study. It is such ever growing subordination to international law which alone can ensure its survival, as the highest interest of a State, worthy of international protection.

POST SCRIPT

> ... jede wissenschaftliche "Erfüllung"
> bedeutet neue "Fragen" und will "über-
> boten" werden und veralten. Damit hat
> sich jeder abzufinden, der der Wissen-
> schaft dienen will. ... Wissenschaftlich
> überholt zu werden, ist — es sei wieder-
> holt — nicht nur unser aller Schicksal,
> sondern unser aller Zweck.
>
> Max Weber. [1]

To re-edit a book after fourteen years represents a venture which is as pleasing as it is dangerous. This is particularly true of a legal enquiry which—whatever the author's quest for objectivity—is inextricably involved with the changes in the political substratum.

This observation seems particularly relevant in an unstable world, torn by many contradictions, among which the one between the acceleration of history on the one hand and the perpetuation of provisional and unsettled situations on the other, is not the least conspicuous. To give one example: after the First World War, the Peace Treaty with Germany was concluded within nine months from the Armistice. Twenty-two years after the Second World War no such treaty is even remotely in sight. No formal general peace settlement has been effected and whatever peaceful situation exists in Europe, rests on provisional and haphazard foundations, often of a disconcertingly paradoxical character. Suffice it to mention again the case of Germany, formally an ex-enemy State, owing to the absence of a peace treaty,—and probably also according to Article 107 of the U.N. Charter—and, at the same time, a formal Ally of some of her former enemies within the framework of the NATO. No legal analysis can ignore these facts at the risk of getting divorced from reality, just as it cannot ignore the speed at which other events are moving and at which new situations are developing.

---

[1] *Wissenschaft als Beruf. Gesammelte Aufsätze zur Wissenschaftslehre.* Tübingen, Mohr (Siebeck), 1922, p. 534. Translation: "... all scientific 'achievement' means new 'questions' and requires to be 'surpassed' and to become outdated. Whoever wishes to serve science has to accept this. ... To be surpassed scientifically is — let it be repeated — not only our fate, but even more our aim."

Such a situation calls for some heart-searching on the part of the author at a moment of writing what can merely be a postscript to the 1954 edition and not its second volume.

At the risk of seeming immodest, the author does not feel any need of detracting from either the statements of fact or the conclusions of law made fourteen years ago. — It may be briefly recalled that the analysis then undertaken bore on both the theoretical foundations of the problem of the identity and continuity of States and the relevant State practice. Within the latter, two groups of cases were examined: those which, at a given stage of historical development, were given a definitive legal solution, and those which were not. The examination of the former group led the author to claim—however tentatively—that a "fourth norm" protecting State identity and continuity in face of a grave threat to its continued existence has developed, in addition to the three existing norms protecting such identity and continuity in case of territorial changes, revolutions and belligerent occupation: to wit, a norm arising out of the principle *"ex iniuria ius non oritur"*, and safeguarding the identity and continuity of an illegally overpowered State, on condition of its effective restoration within a reasonable time-limit. No other view could have accounted for the effective acknowledgement of the identity and continuity of such States as Ethiopia, Czechoslovakia and Albania. Cases of the latter group were not, at the time of writing, given a definitive legal solution and were therefore left open. The book was concerned with legal analysis, not with fortune-telling.

It may perhaps also be recalled that the general conclusions of the book oscillated between an emphasis on legality which must be inherent in international law as in any legal order worthy of the name, and a declared scepticism bearing on the outer limits of such legality when faced with the influence—healing or destroying—of the time factor as well as the inescapable principle of effectiveness. Neither of these are particular to international law though—for obvious reasons—they may be more predominant there than in municipal law. But even in the latter, they belong to the *constants* of law as such, whether seen in the law-creating force of revolutionary law-breaking or in the time-honoured institution of prescription. The interplay of fact and norm, the clash between the world of *Sein* and the world of *Sollen,* the antinomy of the two basic principles: *"ex iniuria ius non oritur"* and *"ex factis ius oritur"*, belong to the reality of the world around us and are not to be charmed away by any intellectual construction. By the very nature of things these assertions seem generally and unavoidably valid; they are certainly as valid to-day as they were fourteen years ago.

It is therefore only within certain definite limits that legality—whether in municipal or international law—can carry the day in the face of an overwhelming pressure of facts and time. It is with the deepest satisfaction that the author records the vindication of such legality in the case of the restored Austrian Republic. In fact, the Austrian State Treaty of May 15th, 1955, has set a seal of identity and continuity on the pre-Anschluss and post-war Austria [1]. No such vindication has occurred in the case of either the Baltic States or Poland.

These cases then would seem to require a re-appraisal which would burst the framework of a mere postscript. However, the major difficulty in undertaking such a re-appraisal by far transcends the purely technical limitation on space; the essential condition for any new serious enquiry of that sort is the selection of what may be called the "critical date".

The analysis of the legal situation of the Baltic States and Poland, contained in the first edition of this book, bore on the situation which existed at a fairly clear critical date: the end of the Second World War. Its outcome fixed the shape of things for some years to come, before the provisionally achieved rigidity turned into a flux. That flux nowadays appears to continue. No clear new historical parting line has emerged out of it which could serve either as criterion or as justification of a new enquiry. Indeed, it is not to be seen what, for instance, should be taken into account: the obvious acquiescence of the international community to the 1945 solution, or the evolutionary processes in the Soviet bloc, the end of which is not yet in sight? How far—if at all—could an evolution of what were originally puppet entities be assumed? [2] Should a new appraisal be undertaken in the light of the acceleration of history or, on the contrary, in the light of the persistence of provisional solutions? [3]

It is therefore submitted that any such study would, at this particular stage, be either belated—with respect to the immediate post-war solution, or premature—with respect to a new stabilization in fact and law which has not yet taken place. These problems seem to be just as open to-day as they were fourteen years ago when they were qualified as such in the first edition,—though much has appened to make them "open" in a different way.

The author can only hope that not only this particular question but the whole problem of State identity and continuity will one day be taken up again, with more cases examined, more facts available and within a broader historical perspective. For she believes, with Max Weber, that it is the aim of any scientific achievement to be ever surpassed in man's striving for truth.

Geneva, February 1968.   K. M.

---

[1] See comment by Kunz, *The State Treaty with Austria, A.J.*, 1955, pp. 534-542; more particularly: "The treaty ... recognizes Austria's extinction in fact between March 13, 1938 and May 8, 1945, and yet recognizes her identity and continuity. It is therefore a treaty proving Marek's proposed "fourth rule" as to the identity of states: complete but illegal suppression of a state in time of peace, but continuance of a mere "ideal legal notion" of the state in question; identity and continuity, provided this state is re-established in fact within a reasonable time". (p. 541).
[2] See Bernhardt, *Kontinuität*, W.V.B., Bd. II, 1961, pp. 296-297.
[3] See above, p. 591.

SELECTED BIBLIOGRAPHY.

PART I.

GENERAL.

SOURCE BOOKS.

THE AALAND ISLANDS QUESTION. — Report of the Committee of Jurists. League of Nations Official Journal, Special Supplement N° 3.

ANNUAIRE de l'Institut de Droit International, 1936.

ANNUAL DIGEST AND REPORTS OF PUBLIC INTERNATIONAL LAW CASES, edited by Lauterpacht H., and others. 1919 —

DEPARTMENT OF STATE BULLETIN.

DESCAMPS-RENAULT. — Recueil international des traités du XX° siècle. Année 1901. Paris : Arthur Rousseau, éditeur.

DOCUMENTS DIPLOMATIQUES, Conférence économique internationale de Gênes. Ministère des Affaires Etrangères, Paris 1922.

DOCUMENTS CONCERNING GERMAN-POLISH RELATIONS and the outbreak of hostilities between Great Britain and Germany on September 3, 1939. London: H.M. Stationery Office, 1939. Cmd. 6106.

DOCUMENTS ON AMERICAN FOREIGN RELATIONS, World Peace Foundation, Boston, 1939 —

FONTES JURIS GENTIUM, Edidit Viktor Bruns, Berlin : Carl Heymanns Verlag, 1932.

GREEN, L.C. — International Law through the Cases. London: Stevens & Sons Limited, 1951.

HACKWORTH, G.H. — Digest of International Law. United States Government Printing Office, Washington, 1940-1944.

HARVARD DRAFT CONVENTION ON THE LAW OF TREATIES. A.J., vol. 29, Sup. no. 4.

INTERNATIONAL LEGISLATION, edited by Manley O. Hudson, Washington: Carnegie Endowment for International Peace, 1931-1941.

JUDGMENT of the International Military Tribunal for the Trial of German Major War Criminals. Nuremberg, 30th September and 1st October 1946. London: H.M. Stationery Office. Cmd. 6964.

LEAGUE OF NATIONS OFFICIAL JOURNAL.

LEAGUE OF NATIONS TREATY SERIES.

MARTENS, G.F. de. — Nouveau recueil de traités, 1817-1842.

MARTENS, G. F. de. — Nouveau recueil général de traités, 1843-1875 ; 2° série : 1876-1908 ; 3° série : 1909-1944.

MOORE, J.B. — A Digest of International Law. Washington: Government Printing Office, 1906.

MOORE, J.B. — History and Digest of the International Arbitrations to which the United States has been a party. Vol. III. Washington: Government Printing Office, 1898.

PARLIAMENTARY DEBATES. — Official Report. Published by H.M. Stationery Office, London.

THE PUBLIC GENERAL ACTS, etc. London, H.M. Stationery Office.

RECUEIL des Décisions des Tribunaux Arbitraux Mixtes.

REPORT OF THE COMMISSION OF ENQUIRY (Appeal by the Chinese Government). Series of League of Nations Publications, VII, Political. 1932. VII. 12.

SCOTT, J.B. and JAEGER, W.H.E. — Cases of International Law. St. Paul, Minn. West Publishing Co. 1937.

SCOTT, J.B. — The Hague Court Reports. New York: Oxford University Press, 1916, 1932.

UNITED NATIONS TEXTBOOK. — Universitaire Pers Leiden, Leiden 1950.

BOOKS AND MONOGRAPHS.

ANZILOTTI, D. — Cours de Droit International, trad. Gidel, Recueil Sirey, Paris 1929.

BALLADORE-PALLIERI, C. — La guerra. CEDAM, Casa Editrice Dott. Antonio Milani Già Litotipo, Padova, 1935.

BASDEVANT, J. — Règles générales du droit de la paix. Rec. 1936, IV.

BLUNTSCHLI, J.C. — Das moderne Völkerrecht der civilisirten Staaten als Rechtsbuch dargestellt. Dritte Auflage, Nördlingen : C.H. Beck, 1878.

BOURQUIN, M. — Règles générales du droit de la paix. Rec. 1931, I.

BRIERLY, J.L. — Règles générales du droit de la paix. Rec. 1936, IV.

BRIERLY, J.L. — The Law of Nations. Oxford : Clarendon Press, 1949.

CARRE DE MALBERG, R. — Contribution à la Théorie générale de l'Etat. Paris : L. Tenin, 1920-1922.

CHEN, Ti-Chiang. — The International Law of Recognition. Edited bv L.C. Green. London: Stevens and Sons Limited, 1951.

DALLIN, J. — Soviet Russia's Foreign Policy 1939-1942. New Haven, Yale University Press. Third edition, 1944.

ERICH, R. — La naissance et la reconnaissance des Etats. Rec. 1926, III.

FAUCHILLE, P. — Traité de Droit International Public. Paris : Librairie Arthur Rousseau, 1922.

FENWICK, C.G. — International Law. New York and London : Appleton-Century-Crofts, Inc. 1948.

GEMMA, S. — Les gouvernements de fait. Rec. 1924, III.

GRABER, D.A. — The Development of the Law of Belligerent Occupation, 1863-1914 — A Historical Survey. New York, Columbia University Press, 1949.

GROTIUS, H. — De Iure Belli ac Pacis Libri Tres. The Classics of International Law, edited by James Brown Scott. Carnegie Institution of Washington, 1913.

GUGGENHEIM, P. — Beiträge zur völkerrechtlichen Lehre vom Staatenwechsel. Berlin : F. Vahlen, 1925.

GUGGENHEIM, P. — La validité et la nullité des actes juridiques internationaux. Rec. 1949, I.

GUGGENHEIM, P. — Lehrbuch des Völkerrechts. Verlag für Recht und Gesellschaft A.G. Basel, vol. I, 1948 ; vol. II, 1951.

HEFFTER, A.W. — Das europäische Völkerrecht der Gegenwart. Achte Ausgabe, bearbeitet von F.H. Geffcken, Berlin, Verlag von H.W. Müller, 1888.

HUBER, M. — Die soziologischen Grundlagen des Völkerrechts. Verlag Dr. Walther Rothschild Berlin-Grunewald, 1928.

HUBER, M. — Die Staatensuccession. Leipzig : Verlag von Duncker & Humblot, 1898.

JELLINEK, G. — Allgemeine Staatslehre. Zweite, durchgesehene und vermehrte Auflage. Berlin : Verlag von O. Häzing, 1905.

JUMEAU, A. — Le refuge du gouvernement national à l'étranger (thèse de doctorat). Aix-en-Provence, 1941.

KELSEN, H. — Allgemeine Staatslehre. Berlin : Verlag von Julius Springer, 1925.

KELSEN, H. — Das Problem der Souveränität und die Theorie des Völkerrechts. Tübingen : Verlag von J.C.B. Mohr. (Paul Siebeck), 1920.

KELSEN, H. — General Theory of Law and State. Cambridge, Mass.: Harvard University Press, 1945.

KELSEN, H. — Théorie générale du droit international public. Rec. 1932, IV.

KOROVIN, E.A. — Das Völkerrecht der Uebergangszeit. Internationalrechtliche Abhandlungen, Verlag Dr. Walther Rothschild, Berlin-Grunewald, 1929.

KUNZ, J. — Die Anerkennung der Staaten und Regierungen im Völkerrecht. Handbuch des Völkerrechts, herausgegeben von Stier-Somlo. Zweiter Band, dritte Abteilung. Verlag von W. Kohlkammer, Stuttgart 1928.

LAGARDE, E. — La reconnaissance du gouvernement des Soviets. Paris : Payot, 1924.

LAUTERPACHT, H. — Recognition in International Law. Cambridge: At the University Press, 1947.

LISZT, F. — Das Völkerrecht. Zwölfte Auflage, bearbeitet von Dr. Max Fleischmann. Berlin : Verlag von Julius Springer, 1925.

MARTENS, F.F. — Traité de droit international, traduit du russe par A. Léo. Paris : Chevalier-Marescq, 1883-87.

McNAIR, Sir Arnold D. — Legal Effects of War. Third Edition, Cambridge: At the University Press, 1948.

McNAIR, A. D. — The Law of Treaties. Oxford: At the Clarendon Press, 1938.

OPPENHEIM-LAUTERPACHT. — International Law. Seventh Edition. London, New York, Toronto: Longmans, Green and Co. Vol. I, 1948, vol. II, 1952.

PHILLIMORE, Sir Robert. — Commentaries upon International Law. Third Edition. London, 1879-1889.

PHILLIPSON, C. — Termination of War and Treaties of Peace. London : T.F. Unwin, 1916.

RIVIER, A. — Principes du Droit des Gens. Paris : Librairie Nouvelle de Droit et de Jurisprudence, Arthur Rousseau, éditeur, 1896.

ROUSSEAU, Ch. — Principes généraux du droit international public. Tome I. Introduction - Sources. Paris : Editions A. Pédone, 1944.

SCELLE, G. — Manuel de Droit International Public. Paris : Editions Domat-Montchrestien, 1948.

SCHOENBORN, W. — La nature juridique du territoire. Rec. 1929, V.

SCHOENBORN, W. — Staatensukzessionen. Handbuch des Völkerrechts, herausgegeben von Stier-Somlo, zweiter Band, fünfte Abteilung. Berlin - Stuttgart - Leipzig : Verlag von W. Kohlhammer in Stuttgart, 1913.

SCHUECKING und WEHBERG. — Die Satzung des Völkerbundes. Zweite Auflage, Berlin 1924 : Verlag von Franz Vahlen.

SHARP, R.H. — Non-Recognition as a Legal Obligation. Thèse Genève, Liège (Belgique) : Imprimerie Georges Thone, 1934.

SMITH, H.A. — Great Britain and the Law of Nations, vol. I. London: P.S. King & Son, Ltd. 1932.

SPIROPOULOS, J. — Die de-facto Regierung im Völkerrecht. Verlag des Instituts für internationales Recht an der Universität Kiel, 1926.

UDINA, M. — La succession des Etats quant aux obligations internationales autres que les dettes publiques. Rec. 1933, II.

UHLER, O.M. — Der völkerrechtliche Schutz der Bevölkerung eines besetzten Gebiets gegen Massnahmen der Okkupationsmacht. Polygraphischer Verlag A.G., Zürich 1950.

VATTEL, E. — Le Droit des Gens ou Principes de la Loi Naturelle. The Classics of International Law, edited by James Brown Scott. Published by the Carnegie Institution of Washington, Washington, 1916.

VERDROSS, A. — Die Verfassung der Völkerrechtsgemeinschaft. Wien und Berlin : Verlag von Julius Springer, 1926.

VERDROSS, A. — Völkerrecht. Zweite Auflage. Wien : Springer-Verlag, 1950.

WILLIAMS, Sir John Fischer. — La doctrine de la reconnaissance en droit international et ses développements récents. Rec. 1933, II.

ARTICLES.

CAVARE, L. — La reconnaissance de l'Etat et le Manchukuo. RGDIP, 1935, p. 5.

CYBICHOWSKI, Z. — Das völkerrechtliche Okkupationsrecht. Ztscht. f. V.-r., 1934, p. 295.

DESPAGNET, F. — Grande Bretagne, République Sud-Africaine ou du Transvaal et Etat Libre d'Orange. RGDIP, 1900, pp. 84, 276, 655, 764 ; 1901, pp. 157, 603 ; 1902, pp. 129, 629.

DRUCKER, A. —The Legislation of the Allied Powers in the United Kingdom. Cz. Y.

HERSHEY, A. — The Status of Mr. Bakhmeteff, the Russian Ambassador at Washington. A.J., 1922, p. 426.

HERZ, H. — Beiträge zum Problem der Identität des Staates. Ztscht. f. öff. R., Bd. XV, 1935, p. 241.

KELSEN, H. — La naissance de l'Etat et la formation de sa nationalité. RDI, 1929, p. 613.

KELSEN, H. — Recognition in International Law. A.J., 1941, p. 605.

KOROVIN, E.A. — The Second World War and International Law. A.J., 1946, p. 742.

KUNZ, J. — Bellum Iustum and Bellum Legale. A.J., 1951, p. 528.

LARNAUDE, F. — Les gouvernements de fait. RGDIP, 1921, p. 457.

LOENING, E. — L'administration du gouvernement général de l'Alsace durant la guerre de 1870-1871. RDILC, 1872, p. 622 and 1873, p. 69.

MAKAROV. — Der sowjetrussisch-finnische Konflikt. Ztscht. f. a. öff. R. u. V.-r., 1940-1941, p. 294.

McNAIR, Sir Arnold. — Aspects of State Sovereignty. B.Y., 1949, p. 6.

McNAIR, A.D. — The Stimson Doctrine of Non-Recognition. B.Y., 1933, p. 65.

MERKL, A. — Das Problem der Rechtskontinuität und die Forderung des einheitlichen rechtlichen Weltbildes. Ztscht. f. öff. R., Bd. V, Heft 4, 1926, p. 497.

OPPENHEIMER, F.W. — Governments and Authorities in Exile. A.J., 1942, p. 568.

RAESTAD, A. — La cessation des Etats d'après le droit des gens. RDILC, 1939, p. 441.

SANDER, F. — Das Faktum der Revolution und die Kontinuität der Rechts-ordnung. Ztscht. f. öff. R., Bd. I, 1919, p. 132.

SAUSER-HALL, G. — L'occupation de guerre et les droits privés. Annuaire Suisse, 1944, p. 58.

SAUSER-HALL, G. — L'occupation de l'Allemagne par les Puissances Alliées. Annuaire Suisse, 1946, p. 9.

SCHEWELB, E. — The Jurisdiction over the members of the Allied Forces in Great Britain. Cz. Y., p. 147.

TENEKIDES, G. — La nature juridique des gouvernements institués par l'occupant en Grèce suivant la jurisprudence hellénique. RGDIP, 1947, p. 113.

PART II.

ACCORDING TO COUNTRIES.

ITALY.

ANZILOTTI, D. — La formazione del Regno d'Italia nei riguardi del diritto internazionale. Rivista di Diritto Internazionale, 1912, p. 1.

ROMANO, S. — I caratteri giuridici della formazione del Regno d'Italia. Rivista di Diritto Internazionale, 1912, p. 345.

WAMBAUGH, S. — A Monograph on Plebiscites — With a Collection of Official Documents. New York - Oxford University Press, 1920.

AUSTRIA. (I)

ALMOND, N. and LUTZ, R.H. — The Treaty of St. Germain. A Document-ary History of its Territorial and Political Clauses. 1935, Stanford University Press, Stanford University, California. London: Hum-phrey Milford, Oxford University Press.

BASDEVANT, Jean. — La condition internationale de l'Autriche. Paris : Librairie du Recueil Sirey, 1935.

BAUER, O. — The Austrian Revolution. London: L. Parsons, 1925.

BERICHT über die Tätigkeit der deutsch-österreichischen Friedensdelegation in St. Germain-en-Laye. Wien 1919. Deutschösterreichische Staats-druckerei.

GRAHAM, M.W. — New Governments of Central Europe. New York: Henry Holt and Company, 1926.

KELSEN, H. — Die Verfassung Deutschösterreichs. Jahrbuch des öffentli-chen Rechts der Gegenwart, 1920, Bd. IX, p. 245.

KLEIN, F. — Oesterreich-Ungarn. Wörterbuch des Völkerrechts und der Diplomatie, herausgegeben von Dr. Karl Strupp, Bd. 2. Walter de Gruyter & Co. Berlin und Leipzig 1925.

KUNZ, J. — Die völkerrechtliche Option. Ferdinand Hirt in Breslau, 1925-1928.

LAMMASCH, H. — Seine Aufzeichnungen, sein Wirken und seine Politik. Herausgegeben von Marga Lammasch und Hans Sperl. Wien und Leipzig : Franz Deticke 1922.

TEMPERLEY, H.W.V. — A History of the Peace Conference of Paris. Vol. IV. London: Henry Frowde and Hodder & Stoughton, 1921.

TRAMPLER, K. — Deutschösterreich, 1918/19 — Ein Kampf um Selbst-bestimmung. Carl Heymanns Verlag, Berlin, 1935.

UDINA, M. — L'estinzione dell'Impero austro-ungarico nel diritto internazionale. Seconda Edizione. CEDAM, Casa Editrice Dott. Antonio Milani Già Litotipo. Padova 1933 - XII.

VERDROSS, A. — Der Friedensvertrag von St. Germain-en-Laye. Jahrbuch des öffentlichen Rechts der Gegenwart. Bd. X, 1921, p. 474.

VERDROSS, A. — Gelten die zwischen Oesterreich-Ungarn und dem Deutschen Reiche abgeschlossenen Staatsverträge weiter im Verhältnis zwischen Deutschland und der Republik Oesterreich? Deutsche Juristen-Zeitung, 1920.

YUGOSLAVIA.

DOERING. — Ist Jugoslawien (S.H.S.-Staat) im Sinne des Versailler Vertrages, insbesondere im Sinne des Art. 297 h letzter Absatz, ein " Neuer Staat " ? Juristische Wochenschrift, 1922, p. 352.

FEDOZZI, P. — La situation juridique et internationale du Monténégro. Journal du Droit International (Clunet), 1922, p. 549.

FOREIGN OFFICE. Historical Section. — The Jugo-Slav Movement. London: Published by H.M. Stationery Office, 1920.

GRAHAM, M.W. — New Governments in Central Europe. New York: Henry Holt and Company, 1926.

HOLZER, E. — Die Entstehung des jugoslawischen Staates. Diss. Berlin, 1929.

KAUFMANN, E. — Der serbisch-kroatisch-slowenische Staat - ein neuer Staat. Niemeyers Zeitschrift für internationales Recht. Bd. XXXI, p. 211.

Ministère des Affaires Etrangères du Monténégro. Le rôle de la France dans l'annexion forcée du Monténégro. Rome : Imprimerie A. Manuce, 1921.

SCHILLING, K. — Ist das Königreich Jugoslawien mit dem früheren Königreich Serbien völkerrechtlich identisch ? Diss. Berlin, 1939.

TEMPERLEY, H.W.V. — A History of the Peace Conference of Paris. Vol. IV and V. London: Henry Frowde and Hodder & Stoughton, 1921.

UDINA, M. — L'estinzione dell'Impero austro-ungarico nel diritto internazionale. Seconda Edizione. CEDAM, Casa Editrice Dott. Antonio Milani Già Litotipo. Padova 1933 - XII.

ZOLGER, I. — Die Verfassung Jugoslaviens. Jahrbuch des öffentlichen Rechts der Gegenwart. Bd. XI, 1922, p. 182.

ETHIOPIA.

LANGER, R. — Seizure of Territory. Princeton, New Jersey: Princeton University Press, 1947.

ROUSSEAU, Ch. — Le conflit italo-éthiopien devant le droit international. Paris : Editions A. Pédone, 1938.

WAR OFFICE. — British Military Administration of Occupied Territories in Africa during the Years 1941-43. London: H.M. Stationery Office. 1945. Cmd. 6589.

CZECHOSLOVAKIA.

BISCONTINI, G. — Sulla condizione giuridica del Protettorato di Boemia e Moravia. Rivista di Diritto Internazionale, 1941, p. 379.

THE CZECHOSLOVAK INFORMATION SERVICE. Czechoslovak Sources and Documents. No. 1-4. New York, 1942-1943.

CZECHOSLOVAK Ministry of Foreign Affairs (Department of Information). Four Fighting Years. Hutchinson & Co. (Publishers) Ltd. London - New York - Melbourne, 1943.

CZECHOSLOVAK YEARBOOK OF INTERNATIONAL LAW. London, March 1942.

FLORY, M. — Le statut international des gouvernements réfugiés et le cas de la France Libre, 1939-1945. Paris : Editions A. Pédone, 1952.

GREWE, W.G. — Protektorat und Schutzfreundschaft. Monatshefte, 1939, p. 341.

HUGELMAN, K.G. — Das Reichsprotektorat Böhmen und Mähren. Monatshefte, 1939, p. 399.

KLEIN, F. — Die staats- und völkerrechtliche Stellung des Protektorats Böhmen und Mähren. Archiv des öffentlichen Rechts, Neue Folge, 31. Band, 3. Heft, p. 255.

KROB, O. — Aperçu des dispositions légales d'après-guerre. Bulletin de Droit Tchécoslovaque, Année V. No. 3-4. 1 mars 1947.

LANGER, R. — Seizure of Territory. Princeton, New Jersey: Princeton University Press, 1947.

MEGERLE, K. — Deutchland und das Ende der Tchecho-Slowakei. Monatshefte, 1939, p. 763.

RABL, K.O. — Zur jüngsten Entwicklung der slowakischen Frage. Ztscht. f. a. öff. R. u. V.-r., 1939-40, p. 284.

RAGGI, C.G. — Il Protettorato di Boemia e Moravia. Rivista di Diritto Internazionale, 1940, p. 194.

RIPKA, H. — Munich: Before and After. London: Victor Gollancz, 1939.

TABORSKY, E. — " Munich ", the Vienna Arbitration and International Law. Cz. Y., London, 1942, p. 21.

TABORSKY, E. — The Czechoslovak Cause. An account of the problems of International Law in relation to Czechoslovakia. London: H.F. & S. Witherby Ltd. 1944.

VENTURINI, G.C. — La nuova situazione giuridica dei territori della Cecoslovacchia. Diritto Internazionale, 1938, p. 74.

ALBANIA.

ALBANIA—BASIC HANDBOOK. Western Central District Office, 1943.

L'annexion de l'Albanie par l'Italie. RDI, 1939, p. 564.

LANGER, R. — Seizure of Territory. Princeton, New Jersey: Princeton University Press, 1947.

AUSTRIA. (II)

JUDGMENT of the International Military Tribunal for the Trial of German Major War Criminals. Nuremberg, 30th September and 1st October 1946. London: H.M. Stationery Office. Cmd. 6964.

KELSEN, H. — The International Legal Status of Germany to be established immediately upon Termination of the War. A.J., 1944, p. 689.

KLINGHOFFER, H. — Les aspects juridiques de l'occupation de l'Autriche par l'Allemagne. Rio de Janeiro, 1943.

KLINGHOFFER, H. — The Coming Austria. Rio de Janeiro, 1945.

LANGER, R. — Seizure of Territory. Princeton, New Jersey. Princeton University Press, 1947.

RED-WHITE-RED BOOK. — Justice for Austria. Descriptions, Documents and Proofs to the Antecedents and History of the Occupation of Austria. (from official sources). Printed and published by the Austrian State Printing House. Vienna 1947.

REUT-NICOLUSSI, E. — Um die Rechtskontinuität Oesterreichs. Wissenschaft und Weltbild, 3. Jahrgang, Juni 1950, Heft 6, p. 241.

SCHAERF, A. — Gilt das Konkordat? War der Anschluss Annexion oder Okkupation? Die Zukunft, Februar 1950, no. 2, p. 34.

SCHAERF, A. — Gilt das Konkordat? Ein Nachwort zur Debatte. Die Zukunft, Mai 1950, no. 5, p. 117.

VERDROSS, A. — Die völkerrechtliche Identität von Staaten. Festschrift Heinrich Klang. Springer Verlag in Wien.

VEROSTA, S. — Die internationale Stellung Oesterreichs. Eine Sammlung von Erklärungen und Verträgen aus den Jahren 1938 bis 1947. Wien 1947. Manzsche Verlagsbuchhandlung.

VON BESONDERER SEITE. Gilt das Konkordat? War der " Anschluss " Annexion oder Okkupation? Oesterreichische Monatshefte, 6. Jahrgang, April 1950, No. 4, p. 195.

VON BESONDERER SEITE. Gilt das Konkordat? War der "Anschluss" Annexion oder Okkupation? Noch ein Nachwort zur Debatte. Oesterreichische Monatshefte, 6. Jahrgang, Juli-August 1950, No. 78, p. 418.

WRIGHT, H. — Attitude of the United States towards Austria. Reprinted from House Doc. No. 477, 78th Congr., 2nd Ses. in Austria, Gunther Publications, 1775 Broadway, New York 19, N.Y. 1944.

WRIGHT, H. — The Legality of the Annexation of Austria by Germany. A.J., 1944, p. 621.

THE BALTIC STATES.

ANNEXATION OF THE BALTIC STATES. Facts and Documents not to be forgotten by UNO and the Peace Conferences. Dr. Hugo Vitols, Prof. U. Kaasik, J. Kajeckas, Prof. M.W. Graham. Stockholm 1946.

BERZINSH, A. — I saw Vishinsky Bolshevize Latvia. Published by the Latvian Legation, Washington D.C. 1948.

BRIGGS H.W. — Non-Recognition in the Courts; the Ships of the Baltic Republics. A.J., 1943, p. 585.

CHAMBON, H. de. — La tragédie des nations baltiques. Editions de la Revue Parlementaire, Paris 1946.

DALLIN, J. — Soviet Russia's Foreign Policy. 1939-1942. New Haven, Yale University Press. Third edition, 1944.

GRAHAM, M.W. — The Diplomatic Recognition of the Border States. Berkeley, Ca. University of California Press, 1935.

HAMPDEN JACKSON, J. — Estonia. London: George Allen & Unwin Ltd., 1948.

HARRISON, E.J. — Lithuania's Fight for Freedom. Published by the Federation of the Lithuanian Societies in Great Britain. London.

LATVIAN-RUSSIAN RELATIONS. Documents. Published by the Latvian Legation, Washington, D.C., 1944.

LLOYD'S LIST LAW REPORTS vol. 79 and 83.

MAKAROV. — Die Eingliederung der baltischen Staaten in die Sowjet-Union. Ztscht f. a. öff. R. u. V.-r., 1940/41, p. 682.

NAZI-SOVIET CONSPIRACY AND THE BALTIC STATES. Diplomatic Documents and other Evidence, compiled by August Rei. London: Boreas Publishing Co. Ltd., 1948.

NAZI-SOVIET RELATIONS 1931-1941. Documents from the Archives of the German Foreign Office. Edited by R.J. Sontag and J.S. Beddie. Department of State, 1948.

PICK, F.W. — The Baltic Nations. London: Boreas Publishing Co., Ltd, 1945.

REI, A. — Have the Baltic Countries voluntarily renounced their Freedom? New York, 1944.

POLAND.

BLOCISZEWSKI, J. — La restauration de la Pologne et la diplomatie européenne. Paris : A. Pédone, éditeur, 1927.

BOR-KOMOROWSKI, T. — The Secret Army. London: Victor Gollancz, Ltd.,
1950.

BRIGGS, H.W. — The Leaders' Agreement of Yalta. A.J., 1946, p. 376.

CHURCHILL, W.S. — The Second World War, vol. VI: Triumph and Tragedy.
London, Cassel, 1954.

DOKUMENTE DER DEUTSCHE POLITIK. Band 7. Das Werden des Reiches.
Junker und Dünnhaupt Verlag, Berlin 1940.

FIEDOROWICZ, G. — Continuité de l'Etat. RDI, 1939, p. 129.

FLORY, M. — Le statut international des gouvernements réfugiés et le cas
de la France Libre, 1939-1945. Paris : Editions A. Pédone, 1952.

GRABSKI, S. — The Polish-Soviet Frontier. London 1943.

KOMENTATOR. — Jaltanski rozbior Polski w swietle prawa narodow. (The
Yalta Partition of Poland in the light of International Law). Sprawy
Miedzynarodowe (International Affairs), No. 4/8. London, 1949.

MIKOLAJCZYK, S. — The Rape of Poland — Pattern of Soviet Aggression.
Wittlesey House, McGraw - Hill Book Company, Inc. New York and
Toronto, 1948.

NAZI-SOVIET RELATIONS 1931-1941. — Documents from the Archives of
the German Foreign Office. Edited by R.J. Sontag and J.S. Beddie.
Department of State, 1948.

PAN, S.C.Y. — Legal Aspects of the Yalta Agreement. A.J., 1952, p. 40.

POLAND AND GREAT BRITAIN BEFORE AND AFTER THE CRIMEA CON-
FERENCE. Documents. London, 1945.

POLISH-SOVIET RELATIONS 1918-1943. Official Documents. Issued by
the Polish Embassy in Washington by Authority of the Government
of the Republic of Poland.

RACZYNSKI, Count E. — The British-Polish Alliance — Its Origin and
Meaning. With a foreword by Lord Halifax. London: The Melville
Press Ltd. 1948.

REPUBLIC OF POLAND - MINISTRY OF FOREIGN AFFAIRS. Official Documents concerning Polish-German and Polish-Soviet Relations 1938-
1939. Published by Authority of the Polish Government by Hutchinson & Co. (Publishers) Ltd. London and Melbourne.

Revue de Droit International, 1939, tome XXIV.

ROTH, P. — Die Entstehung des polnischen Staates. Berlin: O. Liebmann,
1926.

SCELLE, G. — La situation juridique de Vilna et de son territoire. RGDIP,
1928, p. 730.

SMOGORZEWSKI, C. — About the Curzon Line and Other Lines. Free
Europe Pamphlet, London, 1945.

STETTINIUS, E.A. — Roosevelt and the Russians — The Yalta Conference.
London: Jonathan Cape, 1950.

WEYERS, J. — Poland and Russia. London, 1943.

WOOLSEY, L.H. — Poland at Yalta and Dumbarton Oaks. A.J., 1945, p. 295.

WOOLSEY, L.H. — The Polish Boundary Question. A.J., 1944, p. 441.

WRIGHT, H. — Poland and the Crimea Conference. A.J. 1945, p. 300.

ADDITIONAL BIBLIOGRAPHY

(For abbreviations see p. 606)

BAADE, H. — Baltische Staaten. Strupp-Schlochauer, Wörterbuch des Völkerrechts, (hereinafter quoted: W.V.R.), Verlag Walter de Gruyter & Co., Berlin, Bd. I, 1960, pp. 143-150.

BERNHARDT, R. — Kontinuität. W.V.R., Bd. II, 1961, pp. 295-297.

BLIX, H. — Treaty-Making Power. London, Stevens & Son, Ltd. and New York, Frederick A. Praeger, Publishers, 1960. (Chapter XI. The Treaty-Making Competence of Governments in Exile, pp. 147-194).

BRANDWEINER, H. — Zur Lehre von den Exilregierungen. Oesterreichische Zeitschrift für öffentliches Recht (hereinafter quoted: Oest. Zt. f. öff. R.), 1950-1951, Bd. III, pp. 497-519.

CAFLISCH, L. — Die Gründung Italiens in schweizerischer Sicht. Annuaire suisse, vol. XIX, 1962, pp. 103-120.

CAFLISCH, L. — The Law of State Succession — Theoretical Observations. Netherlands International Law Review, vol. 10, 1963, pp. 337-366.

CANSACCHI, G. — Realtà e finzione nell'identità degli Stati. Comunicazioni e Studi, vol. IV, 1952, pp. 23-97.

CLUTE, R.E. — The International Legal Status of Austria, 1938-1955. The Hague, Nijhoff, 1962.

GINSBURG, G. — A Case Study in the Soviet Use of International Law: Eastern Poland in 1939. A.J., vol. 52, 1958, pp. 67-84.

GINTHER, K. — War die Slowakei ein souveräner Staat? Oest. Zt. f. öff. R., Bd. XVII, 1967, pp. 142-172.

GRAYSON, C.T. — Austria's International Position 1938-1953. Genève, Droz, 1953.

KAFKA, G.E. — Oesterreich, die Besatzung und die Grundlagen der Völkerrechtsgemeinschaft. Oest. Zt. f. öff. R., Bd. VI, 1954, pp. 348-377.

KLINGHOFFER, H. — Die Moskauer Erklärung über Oesterreich. Oest. Zt. f. öff. R., Bd. VI, 1955, pp. 461-489.

KUNZ, J.L. — Identity of States under International Law. A.J., vol. 49, 1955, pp. 68-76.

KUNZ, J.L. — Oesterreichischer Staatsvertrag vom 15.5.1955. W.V.R., Bd. II, 1961, pp. 699-701.

KUNZ, J.L. — The State Treaty with Austria. A.J., vol. 49, 1955, pp. 535-542.

MATTERN, K.-H. — Die Exilregierung. Tübingen, Mohr (Siebeck), 1953.

MEISSNER, B. — Die Sowjetunion, die baltischen Staaten und das Völkerrecht. Köln, Verlag für Politik und Wirtschaft, 1956.

O'CONNELL, D.P. — State Succession in Municipal Law and International Law. Cambridge, At the University Press, 1967, 2 vols.

PFEIFER, H. — Der österreichische Staatsvertrag. Archiv des Völkerrechts, 5. Bd., 3. Heft, 1955, pp. 296-307.

SEIDL-HOHENVELDERN, I. — Die österreichische Staatsbürgerschaft von 1938 bis heute. Oest. Zt. f. öff. R., Bd. VI, 1953, pp. 21-39.

WEHBERG, H. — Die Stimson-Doktrin. Festschrift Spiropoulos, Bonn, Schimmelbusch, 1957, pp. 433-443.

ABBREVIATIONS.

A.J.	American Journal of International Law.
A.D.	Annual Digest and Reports of Public International Law Cases.
Annuaire Suisse .	Annuaire Suisse de Droit International.
B.Y.	British Yearbook of International Law.
Cmd.	Command Papers.
Cz. S. and Doc. ...	Czechoslovak Sources and Documents.
Cz. Y.	Czechoslovak Yearbook of International Law.
Dep. of St. Bul. ..	Department of State Bulletin.
Documents	Documents concerning German-Polish Relations and the Outbreak of Hostilities between Great Britain and Germany on Sept. 3, 1939.
Doc. dipl.	Documents diplomatiques, Conférence économique internationale de Gênes.
Doc.	Documents on American Foreign Relations.
Dokumente	Dokumente der deutschen Politik.
ICJ	International Court of Justice.
Judgment	Judgment of the International Military Tribunal for the Trial of German Major War Criminals.
LNOJ	League of Nations Official Journal.
LoN. Tr. Ser.	League of Nations Treaty Series.
Martens, N.R. ...	Martens, Nouveau recueil de traités.
Martens, N.R.G. ..	Martens, Nouveau recueil général de traités.
Monatshefte	Monatshefte für auswärtige Politik.
Off. Doc.	Official Documents concerning Polish-German and Polish-Soviet Relations 1933-1939.
Parl. Deb., Com. ..	Parliamentary Debates, House of Commons, Official Report.
Parl. Deb., Lords .	Parliamentary Debates, House of Lords, Official Report.
PCIJ	Permanent Court of International Justice.
Rec.	Recueil des Cours de l'Académie de droit international de La Haye.
Rec. TAM	Recueil des décisions des Tribunaux arbitraux mixtes.
RDI	Revue de Droit International.
RDILC	Revue de droit international et de législation comparée.
RGDIP	Revue générale de droit international public.
Ztscht. f.a.öff.R. u. V-r.	Zeitschrift für ausländisches öffentliches Recht und Völkerrecht.
Ztscht. f.öff.R.	Zeitschrift für öffentliches Recht.
Ztscht. f.V-r.	Zeitschrift für Völkerrecht.

TABLE OF CASES

(References are to pages)

TABLE OF CONTENTS

PART. I

CHAPTER I.

THE PROBLEM DEFINED.

CHAPTER II.

EXISTING RULES CONCERNING STATE IDENTITY AND CONTINUITY.

PART. II.
—

CHAPTER I.
ITALY. 191

CHAPTER II.
AUSTRIA (I) 199

CHAPTER VI.
ALBANIA. 331

CHAPTER VII.
AUSTRIA (II). 338

Chapter VIII.

THE BALTIC STATES. 369

Chapter IX.

POLAND. 417

PART III.
—

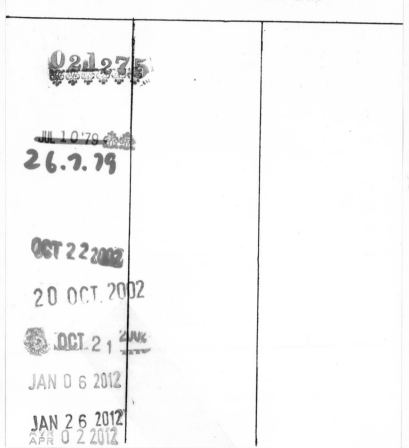